NEW ZEALAND
CRICKET

2003 NEW CRICKET ALMANACK

56th Edition

Edited by
Francis Payne
&
Ian Smith

Hodder Moa Beckett

in association with

The Editors welcome contributions from readers for inclusion in the *2004 Almanack*

Please correspond directly with the editors:

Francis Payne,
97 Bond Crescent,
Forrest Hill,
AUCKLAND.
Phone/Fax: (09) 410-5259
E-mail: francisp@xtra.co.nz

Ian Smith,
91 Kamahi Street,
Stokes Valley,
WELLINGTON.
Phone: (04) 563-7764
E-mail: ianelizabeth@paradise.net.nz

Front cover: Stephen Fleming reaches his double century against Sri Lanka   Fotopress

Back cover: The New Zealand team after winning the one-day tournament in Sri Lanka
Fotopress

ISBN 1-86958-963-7

© 2003 F. Payne & I. Smith
Published in 2003 by Hodder Moa Beckett Publishers Limited (a member of the Hodder Headline Group),
4 Whetu Place, Mairangi Bay, Auckland 9, New Zealand
Printed by PrintLink, Wellington, New Zealand

CONTENTS

NEW ZEALAND
CRICKET

Office Bearers
2002/03

Patron
Her Excellency The Hon. Dame Silvia Cartwright P.C.N.Z.M., D.B.E.
Governor-General of New Zealand

President
D.C. Hoskin

Vice-Presidents
The Presidents of Major Associations

Board
Sir John Anderson, K.B.E. *(chairman),* D.S. Currie Q.S.O, S.L. Boock,
A. Urlwin, A.R. Isaac, T.W. Jarvis, P.A. Sharp, D. Radford

Chief Executive
M.C. Snedden

Auditors
Ernst and Young, Chartered Accountants

Solicitor
L.M.C. Robinson, Saunders Robinson

Bankers
The National Bank of New Zealand

Life Members
M. Brito, C.F. Collins, O.B.E., W.A. Hadlee, C.B.E.,
J.H. Heslop C.B.E., J.L. Kerr, O.B.E., J. Lamason, T. Macdonald, Q.S.M.,
P. McKelvey, M.B.E., D.O. Neely, M.B.E.,
Hon. Justice B.J. Paterson, O.B.E. Q.C.,
K.L. Sandford, C.M.G.,Y. Taylor, Sir Allan Wright, K.B.E.

Honorary Cricket Members
J.C. Alabaster, F.J. Cameron, M.B.E., R.O. Collinge, B.E. Congdon, O.B.E.,
R.S. Cunis, A.E. Dick, G.T. Dowling, O.B.E., J.W. Guy, D.R. Hadlee,
B.F. Hastings, J.A. Hayes, H.J. Howarth, A.R. MacGibbon,
F.L.H. Mooney, R.C. Motz, V. Pollard, G.O. Rabone, J.R. Reid, O.B.E.,
B.W. Sinclair, J.T. Sparling, E.W.T. Tindill, O.B.E.,
W.M. Wallace, G.L. Weir.

Honorary Members
I.A. Colquhoun, H.H. Whiting.

National Selectors
Senior: Sir Richard Hadlee *(convenor),* B.J. McKechnie, R.A. Dykes, D.C. Aberhart.
Age Group: D.R. Hadlee *(convenor),* J.H. Howell, B.D. Morrison.
Women: L.J. Murdoch M.B.E. *(convenor),* E.A. Badham, K.E. Flavell, M.J.F. Shrimpton.

Honorary Medical Advisors
Dr R.M. Edmond, Dr H. Fuard, Dr P. Borrie, Dr R. Campbell,
Mr G. Nuttridge, Dr M. Chitgopeker, Dr D. Thomson, Dr D.S. Velvin.

National Code of Conduct Commissioner
N.R.W. Davidson Q.C.

Statistician
F. Payne.

FROM THE EDITORS

The 56th edition of the *New Zealand Cricket Almanack* covers all the highs and lows of another long season which began in August and ran through until May. With the World Cup taking centre stage, however, the TelstraClear Black Caps played fewer games than the previous season with four tests and 23 one-day internationals compared to the previous season's eleven tests and 27 one-day games.

New Zealand Cricket organised a four-team one-day competition, the World Series of Women's Cricket, with the top sides from the previous World Cup taking part. Australia went through the series unbeaten and won the final against New Zealand.

With the World Series also incorporating the annual Rose Bowl competition, it was a double triumph for the Australian side. The TelstraClear White Ferns continued their rebuilding phase with some more encouraging perfromances from inexperienced bowlers. Rebecca Steele, who only changed from medium-pace bowling during the winter, emerged as a left-arm spinner of high quality. The women's team are to go to India late in 2003, the tour which was originally scheduled for 2001 but cancelled after terrorist attacks. The men's team will also be in India from late September, so by the time the new *Almanack* appears we will be underway again. As we said last year, so it goes on.

Apart from all the international and domestic cricket we have coverage of New Zealanders taking part in Power Cricket in Wales, winning a double wicket tournament in St Lucia, playing for a World XI in Holland, the New Zealand Defence Force team in Queensland, a Wellington girls' team in South Africa and the women's Air Force team in Victoria. Then there is the mystery of the New Zealand team photo of 1900. Read on.

The Players' Strike

The start of the domestic season was delayed while New Zealand Cricket worked through player contract issues with the New Zealand Cricket Players' Association. The contract negotiation became a public issue following an announcement by the Players' Association that players would withhold services until a new contract was in place.

Among the key issues was a Players' Association demand for a greater share of New Zealand Cricket revenue for players. New Zealand Cricket maintained that players were already well paid and any increase in player payments would have to come from money budgeted for grass roots cricket. The contract dispute was resolved in November and New Zealand Cricket now looks forward to an improved relationship with the Players' Association.

In Sri Lanka (Part One)

The ICC tournament had four groups of three teams with only the group winners going through to the semi-finals. An unusual draw saw the top two teams play each other in the opening matches of three of the four groups, leaving limited interest in the remaining games.

New Zealand lost to Australia and then had to wait eight days to play Bangladesh in a match which had no bearing on the tournament. Sri Lanka and India had two attempts to reach a result in the final but the insistence to stage the match as a day/night fixture, at a time when afternoon downpours are frequent in Colombo, meant the title had to be shared.

At Home

The Indian side, coached by former New Zealand captain John Wright, visited New Zealand in December and January for The National Bank Series. After both Wellington and Hamilton had received almost a month's quota of rain in the week preceding the tests, the wickets heavily favoured the seam bowlers and the games were low scoring affairs. New Zealand won both tosses and both matches. The one-day series drew good crowds with New Zealand winning the series 5-2, after taking a 4-0 lead. Apart from two one-day hundreds by Sehwag, the Indian batting rarely flourished.

In the test matches India's four innings lasted 58.4 overs, 38.1 overs, 38.2 overs and 43.5 overs. Despite this, it could hardly have been envisaged that the mighty Indian batting lineup would not once bat through their complete fifty overs in the course of a seven match series. Batting first India were bowled out in 32.5 overs, 41.1 overs, 43.4 overs and 44.5 overs. Batting second they were dismissed in 43.4 overs and twice won (although with eight and nine wickets down) inside the fifty overs.

The World Cup

The World Cup was staged in South Africa, Zimbabwe and Kenya in February and March. There was controversy early on when England and New Zealand forfeited games against Zimbabwe and Kenya. The tournament appeared to lose its momentum along the way and many of the games were very one sided.

With their game in Kenya almost certain to be forfeited, New Zealand went into the World Cup knowing they had to win at least two of their matches against Sri Lanka, West Indies and South Africa. As if that was not enough, they were scheduled to meet those three teams in the first week of the tournament. Two losses in the first seven days would have meant that New Zealand's Cup campaign was all but over before it had hardly started.

A loss to Sri Lanka in the opening match left New Zealand with no margin for error. A sound win over West Indies followed but then South Africa ran up 306-6 in the next match. Stephen Fleming, however, responded with one of New Zealand's great one-day knocks and, although Duckworth-Lewis intervened, New Zealand's victory was well deserved.

Even so, after all that hard work New Zealand still needed Sri Lanka to beat South Africa. In the event, confusion in the South African camp over the Duckworth-Lewis target saw the game end in a sensational tie and New Zealand were in to the next stage. South Africa, meanwhile, were out of the World Cup, continuing the poor record of host nations at the event.

New Zealand defeated Zimbabwe in their first Super Six game and had Australia 88-7 in the next. Australia recovered, however, and New Zealand collapsed. Another disappointing effort against India followed. Australia comfortably defeated India in the final to become the first side to win the World Cup three times.

In Sri Lanka (Part Two)

New Zealand made a two test tour of Sri Lanka and played a tri-series with the hosts and Pakistan. The test series was drawn 0-0 with the highlight being Stephen Fleming's unbeaten innings of 274 and 69, the most runs by a New Zealand batsman in one test.

The one-day series was one of the more bizarre on record. The first three games were scheduled for Dambulla, basically a custom built cricket venue in a drier part of Sri Lanka, although somewhat off the beaten track. After monsoon rains flooded Colombo (where the remainder of the tournament was to take place) it was decided to play the other games at Dambulla. Unfortunately the wickets were very bowler friendly making for more low scores.

The original programme had a four day break between the third and fourth matches (when the series was supposed to move from Dambulla to Colombo) with New Zealand having a five day wait before they played again. When the decison was made to play all the remaining games at Dambulla, the second round games were set back a day (although the date of the final stayed the same). This meant a five day gap in the competition and six days between games for New Zealand. In addition, practice facilities at Dambulla were virtually non-existent.

New Zealand eventually went on to win the final, only their second success in any one-day tournament and their first in a triangular series. Given the circumstances, this was a top effort.

The Verdict

A 2-0 test series win at home followed by a 5-2 thumping of the same opposition in the one-day games, a drawn test series in Sri Lanka and victory in a one-day tournament on the sub-continent represents a handy season's work in anyone's book. Overall it was a good season for the Black Caps with two wins and two draws in four tests and two-one day series wins. New Zealand also maintained its number three ranking on the ICC test championship table.

However, this was World Cup year and the main focus had been on preparing the team for that role. Since the World Cup's inception in 1975 New Zealand had, more often than not, reached the semi-final stage. Having overcome all sorts of odds to reach the second stage of the 2003 competition, New Zealand succumbed when it mattered most and were eliminated.

During their tour of New Zealand, India's batting lineup was rendered almost runless. One writer claimed that the Indian batsmen were reduced to nervous wrecks. When it came to the showdown, however, it was the New Zealand lineup which surrendered.

The unusual conditions which prevailed for both the tour by India and in the one-day series in Dambulla make it difficult to provide accurate assessments of the New Zealand players' performances. What we can say, whatever the verdict, is that overall New Zealand did handle difficult conditions better than their opponents.

NEW ZEALAND
CRICKET

The Domestic Scene

The 2002/03 season saw Auckland retain their State Championship title (for the second season in a row the winner was not found until the very last day of competition) while Northern Districts won the State Shield in the tightest one-day competiton New Zealand has seen. Auckland continued its dominance of women's cricket by winning the State League final – their fourth title in a row.

There was again extensive live coverage of the State Shield by Sky Television and also a live telecast of the inaugural State of Origin match. This was an interesting concept and generally well received. The match consisted of four innings of 25 overs each and players were chosen based on which major association they had first represented.

The format of two 25 over innings is a sound one as it allows, in theory, most of the batting to be done by players who are actually in the team for their batting skills. It also lessens the chance of the tedious situation which often arises in fifty over matches, whereby tailenders have to scrape away in an effort to see out their full complement of overs.

Come in Spinner

In New Zealand's two tests against India, one of the world's leading spin bowlers, Daniel Vettori, batted and fielded but did not get to bowl a single delivery. Quite simply he was not needed on the seam bowlers' paradises on which the games were played.

It could be argued that New Zealand won the tests anyway but the issue goes a little deeper than that. In the 2002/03 season the figures of the leading spin bowlers in first-class cricket were not a pretty sight. They read:

	wkts	ave		wkts	ave
M.R. Jefferson	6	34.00	P.J. Wiseman	25	47.52
A.J. Redmond	13	36.92	J.S. Patel	5	48.00
G.P. Sulzberger	22	38.68	L.J. Woodcock	4	58.25
D.L. Vettori	6	41.83	T.R. Anderson	1	68.00
B.P. Martin	13	43.07	G.R. Loveridge	1	108.00
B.G.K. Walker	12	45.58	M.N. Hart	1	136.00
N.D. Morland	14	46.07			

In an effort to assist the development of the country's slow bowling, New Zealand Cricket took the unprecedented step of sending two spinners, Jeetan Patel and Bruce Martin, with the New Zealand team to Sri Lanka to act purely as net bowlers – not members of the official touring party. Apart from being able to develop their own bowling, Patel and Martin gave the New Zealand batsmen the opportunity to bat against spin bowling. The dearth of spinners in New Zealand, and their frequent lack of bowling opportunity in seaming conditions, also means that New Zealand batsmen are getting less and less practice at playing slow bowling, thus creating a twofold problem.

At an end of season debriefing it was acknowledged that in the quest for pace and bounce, (with early season wet weather added to the mix) some New Zealand pitches had been overprepared in that direction. The task remains to find the right balance to encourage both fast and slow bowlers as well as batsmen.

While there was a certain amount of despondency over the low scoring international series, later in the season runs flowed from all quarters in the State Championship. Teams scored over 500 (and still lost), there were many big individual hundreds, including a double and even a triple century. As we have said on previous occasions, it is most unfortunate that the New Zealand season ends at a time when the pitches and outfields are at their driest, hardest and fastest – great conditions for batting but also tailor-made for spin bowlers.

Acknowledgments

We wish to again thank the associations, scorers and officials throughout the country who supplied information to us. In particular we would like to acknowledge the help of Catherine Campbell *(Women's Cricket)* and the rest of the staff at New Zealand Cricket. We also need to thank Warwick Larkins, Warren Shirley and Iain Gallaway for their invaluable contributions to the *Obituaries* section and Chris McQuaid for his help with women's cricket.

Francis Payne & Ian Smith
July 2003

DIARY OF THE SEASON

September

1 Maia Lewis is appointed community cricket coordinator for Cricket Wellington. Her role will be to assist in the development of women's and secondary schools' cricket.

9 New Zealand Cricket announces a $3,088,236 turnaround from the previous year, recording a surplus of $1,347,265, after grants and distributions to associations had been completed. Its net operating surplus is $6,987,873. Total operating revenue is up $3,599,446 to $22,777,215. Significant areas of cost to NZC were in its administration and marketing which was up by $1,103,918 and in coaching and development which increased by $120,633 to $2,104,760. These were offset by costs involving international teams being down by $2,187,427 from $8,597,185. Grants and distributions to associations were up by $851,119 to $5,190,608 while special grants to ssociations were $1,347,265.

New Zealand Cricket's Annual report also notes the growth of junior playing numbers which are up 7092 to 69,748. Adult playing numbers increased by 4172 to 24,819 while male adult numbers increased by 3893 to 23,250.

Also highlighted were the increased attendances at international fixtures. Attendances during The National Bank one-day international series were up 18% on expectation and nearly 100,000 watched the five-match series against England, the highest average attendance for six years. A total of 62,000 attended the three tests.

11 Central Districts announces a $67,991 surplus for the year, a turnaround of $143,209. The New Zealand Cricket grant to the association, the one-day international against England and sponsorships, donations and grants worth $1,173,767 were the main reasons for the profit. Coaching and development, administration, women's cricket and junior cricket were all areas of increased costs.

New Zealand Cricket makes a change to the Provincial A competition for major associations' second elevens with the New Zealand Under 19 team to take part for the first time. The majority of the tournament will be played at the New Zealand High Performance Centre at Lincoln University, reducing the travel and accommodation expenses while also providing high quality playing surfaces.

New Zealand Cricket also changes the format of the national under-19 tournament by reducing three-day games to two days in an effort to produce more hard-fought one innings games while also having a separate one-day competition.

13 Otago announces the signing of former Pakistan test player Mohammad Wasim for the 2002/03 season. Wasim, who scored a century as a 19-year-old on test debut against New Zealand, played 18 tests between 1996/97 and 1999/00, scoring 783 runs at an average of 30.11.

Former Auckland batsman Alan Hunt is appointed coach of Northern Districts A for the 2002/03 season. Hunt, 42, played 67 first-class games between 1980/81 and 1992/93 and is a New Zealand Level Three coach. In recent seasons he coached the Auckland A side.

Cricket Wellington announce they have exceeded their budgetary expectations for the 2001/02 year, achieving a surplus of $59,000, to finish with a turnaround of $123,000. Revenues from New Zealand Cricket-funded programmes increased by $150,000, indoor training centre revenues increased by $50,000 and Pub Charities revenues increased by $100,000, although these were partly offset by a decrease in membership income of $56,000.

16 The Otago Association also enjoys financial improvement by recording a small surplus of $3400, representing a vast improvement and a turnaround of $186,948 within 12 months. Included in the final figures is an increase of $186,395 in New Zealand Cricket grants, and distributions, of $862,049, up from the previous year's $675,654. Total expenses had been reduced from the previous year while income had increased by $170,000. The association had also benefited from a capital advance of $300,000 in funds from NZC.

18 Former New Zealand left-arm spinner Stephen Boock and business consultant and company director Anne Urlwin are the nominations for two positions on the board of New Zealand Cricket, replacing Barry Dineen and Brigit Hearn. They are duly elected at the Annual General Meeting.

New Zealand fast bowler Shane Bond is offered a contract to play for Warwickshire in 2003. Bond spent a short stint with the county as a replacement for Shaun Pollock in 2002, taking 12 wickets in three first-class games.

Grant Bradburn, the longest serving player remaining in first-class cricket New Zealand, announces his retirement. Bradburn, who made his debut in 1985/86, played in 127 first-class games (including a record 115 for Northern Districts), scoring 4978 runs at 27.81 and taking 250 wickets. He also played seven test matches and 11 one-day internationals and was recalled to the New Zealand team in 2000/01 after an absence of ten years.

20 The Canterbury Association announces a loss of $54,231 for the past year, an increase of $21,077. Total operating revenue declined to $1,947,621, down $143,751 from the previous year. Administration costs were up by $20,368 to $379,044 and coaching and development costs were up by $41,376 to $230,468.

24 Former Otago and New Zealand wicketkeeper and coach Warren Lees is appointed coach of the Central Otago team. Lees' most recent coaching position was with the Metropolitan Development side in the Dunedin senior club competition in 2001/02.

October

1 Pre-season matches between the six first-class associations and New Zealand Academy are cancelled after the New Zealand Cricket Players' Association informs New Zealand Cricket that players are not prepared to attend until new contracts have been signed. The players contracts with NZC had expired on 30 September.

4 Former first-class umpire Bryan Malin dies in Wellington aged 55. Malin stood in 13 first-class games between 1990/91 and 1997/98.

9 New Zealand Cricket offers players at international and domestic levels a payment pool worth $4.7 million, an increase in monetary terms of $140,000. $2.7m would go to the international players' pool, $1.92m to the domestic players and $80,000 to a contingency fund. There would be 20 contracted players in the international pool with the top three on retainers of $120,000, the next three on $100,000, the next four on $70,000, 11-15 on $50,000 and from 16-20 on $40,000. In addition, all players, contracted or otherwise, would receive $4500 per test (up from $3000 for a home test and $1750 for an overseas test) and $2000 per one-day international (up from $1500 per home game and $1250 overseas). Non-contracted players would also receive an overseas tour allowance of $1000 per week.

New Zealand Cricket also says that each of the major associations would be allocated $320,000 and would be required to contract no fewer than nine players while also having two rookie contracts. The three highest-ranked players in each association would be offered a two-season contract. These would be worth $22,500 for the first year with the second year depending on the players' worth to the side. An additional $5000 would be paid each year if players in this category played eight State Championship matches in a year. If they also played eight or more State Shield games they would receive another $5000. That package would be worth $32,500. There would be two lower-ranked groups on retainers of $15,000 and $7500 respectively for total packages that could yield them $25,000 and $23,000 respectively. The rookie contracts would have a maximum value of $18,000. Non-contracted players would receive $1000 for a State Championship match, $500 for the State Shield and $250 for the State Max.

11 Michelle Lynch is appointed captain of the Auckland State League team. She takes over from Kathryn Ramel who has decided to take an indefinite break from cricket at all levels.

16 Haidee Tiffen is confirmed as captain of the Canterbury women's side taking over from Paula Flannery who is overseas.

Several England players confirm their participation in the 2002/03 State League. Leading batsman Claire Taylor will appear for Canterbury while wicketkeeper Mandie Godliman will play for Wellington. Fast bowler Clare Taylor will return to Otago and Charlotte Edwards will play another season for Northern Districts.

19 The New Zealand Cricket Players' Association accuses New Zealand Cricket chief executive Martin Snedden of breaching the bargaining protocol after he made details of a proposed remuneration settlement public. The NZCPA is now seeking a 60 per cent pay increase which would lift player payments to $7.3 million, compared to the $4.7m offered by NZC. Snedden agrees to a NZCPA request for mediation, although he understands that it will be specifically on the confidentiality of information issue, rather than remuneration. Snedden responds by saying that the NZCPA seems to be adopting a diversionary tactic to take people's focus away from the key issue, which is the affordability of player-payment demands. He says he had every right to make public any information belonging to NZC (a claim later backed up at mediation) and to comment if he believed the reputation of cricket in New Zealand was at risk of being harmed.

23 Former England batsman Graham Barlow, who is now the coaching and development manager for the Marlborough Cricket Association, is appointed coach of the Central Districts Under 19 team for the national tournament at Lincoln University in December.

24 New Zealand all-rounder Haidee Tiffen is appointed as the Women's Development Officer for Canterbury Cricket. She will be based at the CCA offices, while also spending time in the CCA District Associations and coaching at clubs and schools around Christchurch.

New Zealand women's team coach Mike Shrimpton donates a memento from the successful 2000 World Cup campaign for competition among women in the Central Districts region. Shrimpton, who played most of his cricket for Central Districts, and who is a life member of the association, donated the presentation bat he received as the World Cup winning coach for competition in the inter-district women's competition in Central Districts.

30 Pay talks between New Zealand Cricket and the Players' Association collapse with the two parties agreeing to reconvene with a mediator in Wellington in a last attempt to find a resolution. Talks lasted just over two hours before the negotiating teams called for a mediator to break the deadlock.

November

1 New Zealand Cricket tables a final settlement offer to the New Zealand Cricket Players' Association. The updated offer increases the size of the player payment pool by $300,000 to $5m. In the updated offer the domestic player payment pool increases to $2m (up 18%), each major association is able to contract 10 players, the top three ranked players will be able to earn $37,500 per season, players ranked four to six will be able to earn up to $29,500, players ranked seven to ten will be able to earn up to $23,500 and a captaincy allowance is introduced.

For international players the payment pool increases to $3m (up 11%), New Zealand Cricket will contract 20 players, the annual retainers are increased by more than 100% and match fees are increased significantly from the previous year.

NZC indicates that if the offer is accepted, the remuneration benefits payable under the NZC contracts will be backdated to 1 May 2002 and the domestic contracts backdated to 1 October 2002 without players being penalised for industrial action taken in October.

5 The New Zealand Cricket Players' Association rejects New Zealand Cricket's final offer two hours before the deadline for the offer expires. As a result, NZC is forced to cancel the State Max and the Provincial A competitions. The bargaining teams from NZC and the major associations formally disengaged from negotiations with the Players' Association, enabling them to approach players individually.

7 Major associations begin to successfully sign players from second tier ranks. Wellington announce that New Zealand Academy wicketkeeper Stu Mills, fringe first-class player Sam Fairley and Wellington B players Ben Jansen and Mark Tulloch had signed. Central Districts pick up Craig Spearman who is now classified as an overseas player.

8 Canterbury wicket-keeper Ben Yock becomes the first member of the New Zealand Cricket Players' Association' 128 members to break ranks and sign for the 2002/03 season. Meanwhile, the Indian board confirms that their tour of New Zealand will not be affected by the industrial dispute.

11 The New Zealand Cricket and major association bargaining teams reached agreement with the New Zealand Cricket Players' Association and put in place a player contract system for a four-year period from 2002 to 2006. Under the terms of the agreement the player payment pool is increased by $100,000 from that in the 1 November offer, and there is also some adjustment within the player payment pool including changes to the structure of player retainers. The number of players to be contracted by each major association is increased to eleven. The agreement does not include the funding of the Players' Association which had also been requested.

14 New Zealand Cricket announces that the Provincial A competition, which was cancelled during the player strike, will go ahead as originally planned. There is also clarification that although the State Max competition was cancelled, the Super Max game between New Zealand and India will go ahead as planned.

26 The names of the 20 players who have been offered New Zealand Cricket contracts are released. The criteria used include past performance, with particular emphasis placed on performance during the preceding twelve months and an assessment of a player's likely value to NZC or to that player's major association during the following twelve months. NZC agrees to a Players' Association request that player rankings be kept confidential. The players are: Andre Adams, Nathan Astle, Shane Bond, Ian Butler, Chris Cairns, Stephen Fleming, Chris Harris, Robbie Hart, Paul Hitchcock, Matt Horne, Craig McMillan, Chris Martin, Chris Nevin, Jacob Oram, Mark Richardson, Mathew Sinclair, Scott Styris, Daryl Tuffey, Daniel Vettori, Lou Vincent.

Andre Adams is suspended by the Auckland Cricket Association after an incident in a one-day semi-final match between Howick-Pakuranga and Adams' club, Grafton. Adams had words with an opposition batsman, and later pushed him. As a consequence Adams misses Auckland's first State Championship match.

28 Derbyshire announce they have signed Nathan Astle for the 2003 season. Astle had previously played in the county championship for Nottinghamshire in 1997.

29 New Zealand Cricket names the four women who will be part of the 2003 Academy intake. They are Katey Martin *(Otago)*, Sarah Tsukigawa *(Otago)*, Rosamond Kember *(Auckland)* and Vicky Brown *(Northern Districts)*.

30 Chris Cairns rules himself out of the first test against India saying he was targeting the first one-day international on Boxing Day as his comeback match. However, he subsequently says that he hopes to be available for selection for the second test.

December

2 Two members of the Indian team, Harbhajan Singh and Virender Sehwag, are fined $200 each by customs officials after dirty cricket boots were found in their luggage.

3 Pakistan files for compensation with the International Cricket Council against New Zealand for refusing to play a triangular series in September. New Zealand refused to play in Pakistan's Golden Jubilee triangular contest, also involving Australia, in September, saying they had never given final confirmation of their participation. Pakistan claim that New Zealand agreed to play the tournament as a result of their decision to play two tests instead of three during their rescheduled tour of Pakistan in April and May. Pakistan eventually moved the tournament to Nairobi after Australia expressed safety concerns about playing in Pakistan. After New Zealand's withdrawal, Kenya agreed to play in the tournament.

13 Police arrest two men caught pouring petrol on the field at the Basin Reserve prior to the second day's play in the first test between New Zealand and India. The men were trying to spell the words "No War" in two-metre high letters on the bowlers' run-up. Play was not affected.

14 Plans to play a one-day international between New Zealand and India at the Basin Reserve on Sunday, after the early finish of the first test, are dropped. It is understood India were not prepared to play even though the match would have been televised by Sky Television and had the support of tour sponsors The National Bank.

January

1 Jeff Wilson, who has made a comeback to cricket in 2002/03, features in the New Year's Honours List. He is awarded the MNZM for services to rugby.

3 New Zealand Cricket asks the International Cricket Council to pass on a request from the New Zealand government that the ICC transfer World Cup matches from Zimbabwe. The Minister of Foreign Affairs and Trade, Phil Goff, says that the government is seeking support from the international cricket community to move fixtures from Zimbabwe in order to make it clear to President Robert Mugabe that the whole international community views his actions as completely unacceptable.

7 Jacob Oram breaks the little finger on his left hand during catching practice the day before the fifth one-day international and misses the remainder of the series.

9 Nathan Astle returns to Christchurch with a recurrence of patella tendinosis in his left knee, the same injury he suffered during the tour to Pakistan. Lou Vincent takes his place in the squad for the sixth and seventh one-day internationals. It is later confirmed that Astle will require surgery after the World Cup and he misses the tour to Sri Lanka and is unable to take up his contract with Derbyshire.

16 New Zealand Cricket announces the inaugural State of Origin match, to be played the day after the State Shield final, with selection determined by the major association for which a player first played either first-class or senior representative one-day cricket. Each team will play two, non-consecutive, 25-over innings and the match will be covered live on Sky Television and TV3.

25 Maia Lewis is recalled to the New Zealand women's team. Lewis, 32, who had suffered major knee problems and had taken some time away from cricket, had not played for New Zealand since the World Cup in India in December 1997.

28 New Zealand Cricket outlines serious concerns about the safety of playing a World Cup match in Kenya, saying that they had received information which strongly suggested it would not be safe for the New Zealand team to travel to Nairobi for the scheduled match on 21 February. The information includes the report of the ICC delegation security team to Kenya and advice from independent security adviser Reg Dickason who, along with New Zealand team manager Jeff Crowe, represented New Zealand Cricket on the delegation. NZC are hopeful that the match may be shifted to another venue. The New Zealand government also advises the New Zealand team not to travel to Kenya.

February

2 Former international umpire and the driving force behind the National Cricket Museum Stan Cowman dies in Upper Hutt at the age of 79.

20 The International Cricket Council Board decides that New Zealand's World Cup match against Kenya will not be rescheduled and the points will be awarded to Kenya.

Chris Cairns is felled after being assaulted outside a Durban night club in the early hours of the morning. Cairns was with a group of players, support staff and New Zealand Press Association journalist Mark Geenty. New Zealand team manager Jeff Crowe says that Cairns had been asked to leave the nightclub by bar staff after reported loud behaviour by several members of the team.

27 New Zealand Cricket announces its review of the incident at the Durban night club saying that the behaviour of some of the players was unacceptable and should not be allowed either by the players or team management to recur. The eleven players who were at the nightclub (Andre Adams, Chris Cairns, Stephen Fleming, Craig McMillan, Brendon McCullum, Kyle Mills, Jacob Oram, Scott Styris, Daryl Tuffey, Daniel Vettori and Lou Vincent) are reprimanded and the players as a whole are reminded of their responsibilities

to act professionally off the field. Nathan Astle, Chris Harris, Mathew Sinclair and Shane Bond were not present at the nightclub. The conduct of two players, Chris Cairns and Brendon McCullum, is deemed to constitute misconduct and subsequently the pair are fined $500 each.

28 Lou Vincent (dislocated left thumb) and Kyle Mills (hamstring) are injured during practice at Benoni. Vincent misses the next two games and then plays against Australia while Mills does not play again during the World Cup.

March

5 New Zealand's Brent "Billy" Bowden, who is not on the elite panel of umpires, is named in the group of twelve to officiate in the Super Six portion of the World Cup. Bowden is later appointed as third umpire in the semi-final between Australia and Sri Lanka and is named fourth umpire for the final.

17 The Otago Association confirms that Glenn Turner will be continuing as coach of the Otago team in 2003/04. Turner has coached the side for the past two seasons.

22 The International Cricket Council announces that it is freezing 3.5 million dollars owed to England and $2.5 million owed to New Zealand after they forfeited World Cup matches. They have held back the money in case, as expected, sponsors and broadcasters demand compensation. Legal means are likely to be required to decide who should be held responsible.

27 The International Cricket Council Disputes Committee rejects Pakistan's claim for compensation from New Zealand Cricket following the cancellation of New Zealand's tour to Pakistan after September 11 and the abandonment of the re-scheduled tour after the Karachi bombing. New Zealand Cricket chief executive Martin Snedden said he was now working with the Pakistan Cricket Board to reschedule the cricket that was not played because of the terrorist disruptions.

28 Shayne O'Connor announces his retirement from first-class cricket. O'Connor, 29, had made a successful return from injury, capturing 42 wickets at 18.71 in the State Championship, but decided the time was right to move into a business venture in Alexandra. In 19 tests he took 53 wickets at 32.52 and in 38 one-day internationals took 46 wickets at 30.36. In 73 first-class matches from 1994/95 he captured 278 wickets at 23.66.

New Zealand Cricket names eight players in the New Zealand Cricket Academy draft for 2003. They are: Simon Allen *(Wellington)*, Neil Broom *(Canterbury)*, Peter Fulton *(Canterbury)*, Bevan Griggs *(Central Districts)*, James Hill *(Wellington)*, Mark Orchard *(Northern Districts)*, Richard Sherlock *(Central Districts)*, Ross Taylor *(Central Districts)*.

April

3 Shane Bond is named The National Bank New Zealand Player of the Year at New Zealand Cricket's awards night. Bond is also awarded the Winsor Cup and Walter Hadlee Trophy for bowling while Mark Richardson won the Redpath Cup and Stephen Fleming the Walter Hadlee Trophy for batting. Maia Lewis and Rebecca Steele won the Ruth Martin Cup and Phyl Blackler Cup, awarded for outstanding batting and bowling, while the State Medal and State Plate, awarded for outstanding performances in domestic cricket, went to Matthew Walker and Aimee Mason. Frank Cameron is awarded the Sutcliffe Medal for outstanding services to cricket.

John Bracewell, former New Zealand off-spinner and coach of Gloucestershire, indicates he would be interested in the position of Sri Lanka coach, which became vacant after the World Cup. Bracewell says that coaching New Zealand would be his main ambition.

4 Brent Bowden is named on the elite panel of international umpires. He is one of three added to the existing group of eight along with Darrell Hair and Simon Taufel from Australia.

8 Nicola Payne announces her retirement from international cricket. Payne, 33, who was born in Canada, played in 37 one-day internationals for the Netherlands and 28 for New Zealand.

In an effort to boost New Zealand's spin bowling resources, New Zealand Cricket take the unprecedented step of adding two unofficial players to the test squad to Sri Lanka. Wellington off-spinner Jeetan Patel and Northern Districts' left-armer Bruce Martin are included to bowl in the nets, also assisting the New Zealand batsmen's preparation, and obtain exposure to overseas conditions.

22 Nathan Astle begins a rehabilitation programme following an operation for a long-standing knee problem and a more recent hernia. He expects to be available for selection for New Zealand's tour to India later in the year.

May

4 Vaughn Johnson is reappointed as coach of Wellington. Johnson has been Wellington's coach since taking over part way through the 1998/99 season.

7 Gloucestershire sign fast bowler Ian Butler as a temporary replacement for their all rounder, Ian Harvey, while he is in West Indies for Australia's one-day series.

11 Shane Bond is forced to leave the field with a back injury during New Zealand's one-day match against Pakistan. The problem is later diagnosed as a stress fracture, forcing Bond to relinquish his county contract with Warwickshire for 2003.

16 Nottinghamshire sign Daniel Vettori as a temporary replacement for Stuart MacGill. While the Australian leg-spinner is playing against Bangladesh, Vettori will be available for three four-day games and four one-day matches.

23 New Zealand wins the Bank AlFalah Cup in Sri Lanka. This is their first win in a three-team tournament and only their second one-day title ever.

29 New Zealand Cricket accepts the Pakistan board's proposal to play five one-day internationals in Pakistan in November to compensate for the aborted Karachi test in May 2002. New Zealand will go to Pakistan immediately after their tour of India.

30 Michael Sharpe is reappointed as Canterbury coach for the 2003/04 season. It will be his third season in charge.

June

5 New Zealand Cricket releases the names of the 20 players who are offered contracts for the following twelve months. The individual player rankings are again kept confidential. The new players to be contracted are Paul Wiseman, Brendon McCullum and Kyle Mills while players missing from the previous year's list are Chris Nevin, Chris Martin and Paul Hitchcock.

8 The dates for New Zealand's visit to India are announced. The tour will run from 26 September to 18 November and will consist of two first-class games, two tests and a three-round triangular series with Australia. Venues for all games are to be confirmed.

9 Chris Cairns breaks a bone in his left hand while playing for Nottinghamshire and is expected to be out of action for six weeks. It is the first broken bone Cairns has suffered in his 15-year career.

11 Stephen Fleming agrees to a short-term contract with Yorkshire. Fleming, who played for Middlesex in 2001, will be with the county for eleven weeks.

12 New Zealand Cricket asks the Pakistan Cricket Board not to schedule any of their games at Karachi when they tour in November. On their last visit, in May 2002, a bomb exploded in Karachi near the hotel where the New Zealand team was staying and the remainder of the tour was called off.

Canterbury Cricket announces that Gary Stead, captain for the previous five seasons, will not be reappointed for the forthcoming season. Stead will still be considered as a player.

Canterbury also confirms the appointment of Kirsty Flavell as coach of the Canterbury women's team, taking over from Vicki Burtt who did not reapply. Flavell will resign from her position as New Zealand selector to concentrate on her new role. Flavell was the first woman to score a double century in a test match.

17 Auckland Cricket's chief executive, Lindsay Crocker, announces his resignation. Crocker, who played 54 first-class matches for Northern Districts, had held the position for seven years.

Former New Zealand Under 23 captain Sarah Beaman is named as coach of the Auckland women's team. She replaces Wally Stamp, who stood down after Auckland's win in the 2002/03 State League final. Beaman is the daughter of Jim Kelly *(Wellington)* and sister of Paul Kelly *(Auckland)*.

Otago and New Zealand wicketkeeper Brendon McCullum announces he is moving to Christchurch and will be available for Canterbury in 2003/04.

18 Former New Zealand one-day international Paul Hitchcock is reported to have quit Wellington and is set to return to Auckland after his current stint in English league cricket.

21 The International Cricket Council announces that $500,000 of the World Cup payment which was witheld from New Zealand for forfeiting its match against Kenya will be paid. The ICC says claims would be unlikely to exceed the amount withheld. A further $2 million remains frozen.

23 Northern Districts reports a significant improvement in its financial performance reducing its deficit for the year by $64,855 to just $8136. Sponsorship, donations and grants increased by $279,949 to $1,669,510 although playing costs went up to $901,967, an increase of $261,177. Coaching and development costs also increased, reaching $367,596, up by $132,272.

27 Canterbury wicketkeeper Gareth Hopkins announces he is moving to Otago following Brendon McCullum's arrival in Christchurch. Hopkins, who did not receive a contract from Canterbury in 2002/03, first played for the province in 1998/99 after moving from Northern Districts.

July

1 Denis Aberhart rules himself out of contention as New Zealand coach by taking up the position of head of St Andrew's College new English language unit. Aberhart was previously headmaster of St Paul's school in Christchurch before taking over as national coach in August 2001.

3 The venues for New Zealand's tour to India are announced. The test matches will be played at Mohali and Kanpur (although the order is still to be confirmed) and New Zealand's matches in the triangular series, which also involves Australia, will take place at Chennai, Faridabad, Pune, Cuttack, Guwahati and Hyderabad. The final of the one-day tournament will be played in Calcutta.

4 New Zealand Cricket names John Bracewell as New Zealand coach for a three-year term beginning on 1 November. Former Auckland Cricket Association chief executive Lindsay Crocker is named general manager. Technical adviser Ashley Ross will coach the team on their tour of India and Pakistan while Bracewell completes his obligations with Gloucestershire.

A new management structure is also outlined for the New Zealand team. Key changes include the creation of a TelstraClear Black Caps Unit which includes team management, administration and support staff as well as the team. The coach will have the ultimate decision making authority for cricket issues while the general manager will be responsible for the overall performance of the TelstraClear Black Caps Unit, including the coach, who will be responsible for the cricketing performance of the team. The changes are aimed at improving the team's overall performance, particularly in the one-day game.

PLAYERS OF THE YEAR

Stephen Fleming enjoyed one of the most successful seasons New Zealand has had for some time. The only setback was the failure to reach the World Cup semi-final. Fleming's status as captain has never been higher and he is regarded by many as the best captain in international cricket at present.

The season began with the ICC Champions Trophy where he had innings of 12 and 31. Returning to New Zealand, Fleming played for Wellington, scoring 55 against Central Districts before getting a pair against Auckland. In the low scoring test series against India, he was the only batsman who reached twenty in every innings with 25 at Wellington and 21 and 32 at Hamilton. In the one-day games he continued to open the innings and after a shaky start to the series finished with 47 at Queenstown and 60 not out at Hamilton. He became the second New Zealand player to score 5000 runs in one-day internationals.

At the World Cup he was New Zealand's most consistent and best batsman in the tournament. He got 1 against Sri Lanka and 25 versus West Indies. Against South Africa he played the innings of a lifetime, getting an unbeaten 134 to give New Zealand a vital win. He followed this with 32 against Bangladesh and 5 against Canada. In the Super Sixes he led from the front with 46 against Zimbabwe and when New Zealand collapsed against Australia and India he had scores of 48 and 30. In all he scored 321 at 45.85.

Fleming again showed his liking for Sri Lankan wickets. On the last tour in 1997/98 he hit his highest score of 174 not out and this time he surpassed that with a brilliant 274 not out in the first test. In the second innings he got an unbeaten 69 to record the most runs by a New Zealander in a test match. New Zealand drew the two-test series, something that many sides have found hard to achieve in Sri Lanka. In the one day tri-series, that New Zealand were victorious was due in no small way to Fleming's captaincy. He became the second New Zealand player to play 200 one-day internationals and his 65 in the final ensured New Zealand won its first tri-series title. Fleming was awarded the Walter Hadlee Trophy for one-day batting.

Jacob Oram's career did a complete u-turn over the last season. After suffering injuries in the previous season and missing a big part of the summer, Oram is now established in the test side as the third medium-pacer and all-rounder. He is also an integral part of the one-day side.

He started the season getting 96 and 52 not out against Otago and had bowling figures of 2-22 and 1-24. He had 1-7 off 15 overs against Wellington before being named in the test side against India. He got a duck in his first test innings but had figures of 2-31 and 3-36 with the ball. At Hamilton, he took 2-22 and 4-41 and got 26 not out to secure the second test win.

In the one-day series the only setback was a broken finger which kept him out of the last three games. In the first match of the series he took 5-26 and scored an unbeaten 27.

Back to full fitness he returned for the World Cup. In eight games he had only three innings but was New Zealand's second highest wicket taker (14) behind Shane Bond (17). His best returns were against West Indies (2-26), Zimbabwe (1-28 with four maidens) and 4-52 against Canada. Oram was also very proficient in the field and one of the best catches taken in the World Cup was his diving effort to dismiss Ridley Jacobs which all but ensured a New Zealand victory against West Indies.

On the test section of the tour to Sri Lanka, Oram was appointed joint vice-captain with Daniel Vettori. In the two tests he had scores of 33, 19, 74 and 16 and took four wickets at 29.00. He missed two one-day games with a stiff back but in the other three took eight wickets at just 8.25, including 3 for 12 off nine overs against Sri Lanka.

Over the entire international season, which included four tests and 22 one-day internationals for the New Zealand team, Oram was the leading wicket taker with 49 victims.

PROMISING PLAYERS

Tim McIntosh scored fifty in his first innings of the season setting him on the way to becoming the leading run scorer in New Zealand during the summer and ending with the second highest total ever in a season for Auckland. He scored only 8 in the first innings tie with Wellington but then was the sheet anchor in the second innings, scoring 70 not out, when Auckland succeeded in getting 223 to win.

There were two rare failures in the next game but in round four McIntosh hit top form getting 157 against Otago out of a first innings total of 289. Only one other player got 20 in this innings. In round seven he scored 80 against Central Districts and in the return against Otago he scored 44 and 5.

McIntosh passed 500 runs in the next game. He scored 64 against Canterbury in the first innings and then got 45 as Auckland won the game after declaring 230 behind on the first innings. During the game against Wellington he scored 27 and then in the final game against Northern Districts made 146 not out and 64. During the season he scored 820 runs at 58.57.

In his career of 35 games McIntosh has scored six centuries, showing great temperament at the crease and the ability to get big hundreds. Although missing out on selection for the Sri Lanka tour, his time may come soon if he continues scoring the way he has been.

Iain O'Brien had an important mission this past season. Because of injury, he had played only two games the previous summer following his impressive debut season in 2000/01, and wanted to show that he was not just a one season wonder.

In the first game against Central Districts he took 2-12 and 5-42. He took 1-35 and 1-47 against Auckland and at Rangiora he had a six wicket haul getting 6-103 off 45.3 overs. This was followed by 4-68 against Northern Districts.

O'Brien missed the fifth round game due to a heel injury but on his return he took 4-27 and 2-56 in the return match against Canterbury and then 1-33 and 3-63 at Napier. His injury returned causing him to miss the game against Northern Districts but he then got 3-50 against Auckland and in his final outing he took 2-77 and 0-18 against Otago.

In the eight matches O'Brien took 34 wickets at 18.55. He has now taken 84 wickets in just 20 matches which gives him one of the best wickets per match ratio in New Zealand. One of New Zealand's unheralded bowlers he doesn't get the headlines but just gets on with his bowling and the results have been impressive.

Jesse Ryder came into this season's cricket with a big reputation following his performances with the New Zealand Under 19 team. He was not selected for Central Districts in the early rounds of the State Championship but was called into the side for the State Shield. He got 5 in his first game but then got successive fifties against Wellington and Otago and finished the Shield with 219 runs at 24.33 from nine games with a strike rate of 83.

He was picked for the Championship game in round six getting 18 and 39 against Northern. This was followed by 45 against Auckland and a good double of 37 and 66 against Wellington. In the last game against Canterbury he made his maiden first-class century scoring an unbeaten 114.

Ryder ended the first-class season with 365 runs at 60.83. In his limited time he has shown that he oozes talent and looks like he has the potential to go to the next rung up.

Since this section was introduced in 1983, the following have been chosen as Promising Players of the Year: **1983**, P.S. Briasco, M.D. Crowe, T.J. Franklin, **1984**, K.R. Rutherford, D.A. Stirling, P.J. Visser, **1985**, T.E. Blain, T.D. Ritchie, W. Watson, **1986**, S.W. Duff, D.G. Scott, C.J.P. Smith, **1987**, M.J. Greatbatch, D.K. Morrison, B.A. Young, **1988**, J.P. Millmow, M.R. Pringle, S.A. Thomson, **1989**, F. Beyeler, C.L. Cairns, M.W. Douglas, **1990**, C.Z. Harris, C. Pringle, K.A. Wealleans, **1991**, P.W. Dobbs, P.W. O'Rourke, A.C. Parore, **1992**, M.N. Hart, L.G. Howell, J.W. Wilson, **1993**, S.P. Fleming, D.J. Nash, M.B. Owens, **1994**, R.L. Hayes, B.A. Pocock, A.T. Reinholds, **1995**, M.D. Bell, G.R. Jonas, C.D. McMillan, **1996**, C.J. Nevin, M.H. Richardson, P.J. Wiseman, **1997**, M.J. Horne, M.S. Sinclair, D.L. Vettori, **1998**, C.E. Bulfin, C.D. Cumming, S.B. O'Connor, **1999**, J.I. Englefield, C.S. Martin, L. Vincent, **2000**, T.K. Canning, B.P. Martin, J.D.P. Oram, **2001**, J.E.C. Franklin, K.D. Mills, D.R. Tuffey, **2002**, I.G. Butler, W.A. Cornelius, R.J. Nicol.

HAPPENINGS

Otago's oldest surviving first-class cricketer, Bernie Clark, died during the past year and his obituary appears in this issue of the *Almanack.*

Lindsay Weir remains New Zealand's oldest living test cricketer and the oldest test cricketer from any country. As far as is known, the oldest New Zealand first-class cricketers are:

		Born
G.L. Weir	*Auckland*	2/ 6/1908
J. Jacobs	*Canterbury*	16/ 4/1909
W.H. Dustin	*Wellington*	30/ 8/1909
D.N. Stokes	*Canterbury*	16/11/1909
L.V. Browne	*Wellington*	14/12/1909
D.C. Cleverley	*Auckland/Central Districts*	23/12/1909
H.T. Pearson	*Auckland*	5/ 8/1910
E.W.T. Tindill	*Wellington*	18/12/1910
J.L. Kerr	*Canterbury*	28/12/1910

• • •

Lindsay Weir, Don Cleverley, Eric Tindill and Jack Kerr are New Zealand's oldest surviving test cricketers. Cleverley and Jack Jacobs now both reside in Australia.

• • •

The oldest surviving Northern Districts players are J.L. Wyatt (born 7/3/1919), M.R.H. Barbour (born 10/7/1922) and B.N. Graham (born 27/10/1922).

The oldest surviving Otago cricketers are now C.P. Howden (born 21/10/1911), J.C. Scandrett (born 22/2/1915) and W.A. Hadlee (born 4/6/1915).

Hadlee is also the oldest surviving New Zealand captain. He is followed by W.A. Wallace (born 19/12/1916) who was vice-captain of the 1949 team to England and captain in two tests at home against South Africa in 1952/53.

• • •

Brendon Donkers became just the fourth player born in Hokitika to play first-class cricket when he made his debut for Canterbury against Otago at Carisbrook.

The only others from Hokitika are Robin Schofield, who played for Central Districts from 1959/60 to 1974/75, initially as a left-arm pace bowler then as wicketkeeper, Canterbury batsman George Weston, who played in 1903/04 and 1904/05, and left-arm bowler Arthur Rees, who appeared for Auckland in 1889/90 and Hawke's Bay in 1896/97.

• • •

Jesse Ryder, who made his debut for Central Districts against Northern at Napier, is one of just ten players born in Masterton who have played first-class cricket.

Amongst the others are Ernest Beechey, who played for Wellington from 1906/07 to 1918/19 and scored 180 (his maiden century) in his last match, Keith Smith, (Wellington and Central batsman from 1953/54 to 1960/61) and Bruce Donaldson, Auckland pace bowler in 1949/50, who also represented his province at rugby and rugby league. He also played for the New Zealand Maori rugby league team against Great Britain.

The O'Rourke brothers, Patrick and Matt, pace bowlers for Wellington and Auckland, were also born in Masterton, as were Central Districts players batsman Ross Glover, medium-pacer Mike Pawson, fast bowler Bruce Stewart and current team member Greg Todd.

Having staged their first first-class match in 2001/02 and hosted their inaugural one-day international this past season, Queenstown also now have their first locally born first-class cricketer.

Medium-pacer Daryll Reddington became the first Queenstown-born player to appear in a first-class match when he made his debut for Otago against Central Districts at Wanganui

• • •

New Zealand recorded their two lowest World Cup scores in successive matches in the tournament in South Africa. They were dismissed for 112 by Australia at Port Elizabeth and then 146 by India at Centurion.

Previously New Zealand's two lowest totals had both been against West Indies – 156 at Southampton in 1999 and 158 at The Oval in 1975.

• • •

In past *Almanacks*, we have noted that teams having two or even more captains during the season is no longer unusual.

The trend was reversed this past season with Auckland, Canterbury, Otago and Wellington using just one captain each throughout the State Championship and State Shield competitions, while Robbie Hart led Northern Districts in every game but one (when his brother Matthew took over). Central Districts, who had four different leaders in 2001/02, were the only side to use more than two captains.

The sides were led by:

	Official captain	*Replacement*
Auckland	Brooke Walker	–
Canterbury	Gary Stead	–
Central Districts	Jacob Oram	Craig Spearman, Glen Sulzberger
Northern Districts	Robbie Hart	Matthew Hart
Otago	Craig Cumming	–
Wellington	Matthew Bell	–

Stephen Fleming has now led New Zealand in 51 tests and 142 one-day internationals without ever having captained a provincial side.

• • •

At the end of the Bank AlFalah Cup tournament in Sri Lanka, Stephen Fleming had led New Zealand in 142 one-day internationals. Only eleven players have captained their side in as many as 100 one-day internationals and they are:

	P	W	L	T	NR	Win%
A. Ranatunga *(SL)*	193	89	95	1	8	46
A.R. Border *(A)*	178	107	67	1	3	62
M. Azharuddin *(I)*	173	89	76	2	6	51
S.P. Fleming *(NZ)*	142	58	75	1	8	40
Imran Khan *(P)*	139	75	59	1	4	53
W.J. Cronje *(SA)*	138	99	35	1	3	71
S.T. Jayasuriya *(SL)*	118	66	47	2	3	55
Wasim Akram *(P)*	109	66	41	2	–	60
S.R. Waugh *(A)*	106	67	35	3	1	63
I.V.A. Richards *(WI)*	105	67	36	–	2	63
S.C. Ganguly *(I)*	104	56	44	–	4	53

Fleming and Ganguly are the only currently active captains on the list. New Zealand's next highest is Geoff Howarth who had 60 games as captain (31 wins).

In the first test against Sri Lanka, Fleming became the first New Zealand captain to lead his side in 50 tests (J.R. Reid was captain in 34, G.P. Howarth in 30) and just the eighth player from any country to do so.

The players who have led their side in most tests are:

	P	W	L	D	Win%
A.R. Border *(A)*	93	32	22	39*	34
C.H. Lloyd *(WI)*	74	36	12	26	48
A. Ranatunga *(SL)*	56	12	19	25	21
M.A. Atherton *(E)*	54	13	21	20	24
W.J. Cronje *(SA)*	53	27	11	15	50
S.P. Fleming *(NZ)*	51	19	15	17	37
M.A. Taylor *(A)*	50	26	13	11	52
I.V.A. Richards *(WI)*	50	27	8	15	54
S.R. Waugh *(A)*	49	36	8	5	73

includes a tie

• • •

New Zealand played just four test matches during the past twelve months, winning two and drawing two. Stephen Fleming (454) scored the most runs while Shane Bond (17) captured the most wickets. Apart from Fleming's double century, there were eight scores of fifty or more, four to Mark Richardson.

In 22 one-day internationals over the same period (14 wins, eight losses) Fleming was again the leading scorer with 642 runs while Jacob Oram (34) took the most wickets.

• • •

A total of 18 players appeared in the 22 one-day internationals for New Zealand with only Stephen Fleming appearing in every match. Daniel Vettori played in 20 games. No players made their debuts this past season.

In the four test matches, 14 players were involved with eight players playing in every game. Jacob Oram was the only player new to test cricket.

• • •

The highest run scorer in first-class cricket over the past twelve months was, for the fourth year in a row, Mark Richardson who totalled 839. He was followed by Tim McIntosh (820), Craig Cumming (751) and Matthew Horne (745). The most first-class wickets were taken by Tama Canning with 46. Matthew Walker captured 45 wickets while Shayne O'Connor had 40 and Michael Mason 40.

• • •

New Zealand's most economical bowler in their 22 one-day internationals over the past twelve months was Daniel Vettori, who played in all but two of the games. Jacob Oram (150.2) bowled the most overs, just edging out Vettori, and took the most wickets (34).

The most economical bowlers were:

	M	O	M	R	W	Ave	Best	R/O
D.L. Vettori	20	148.3	13	494	18	27.44	4-14	3.32
C.Z. Harris	16	80	5	302	5	60.40	1-6	3.78
D.R. Tuffey	15	131.5	19	500	23	21.73	3-32	3.79
J.D.P. Oram	17	150.2	22	579	34	17.02	5-26	3.85
K.D. Mills	13	108.4	9	419	15	27.93	3-45	3.85

During the season, the Northern Districts pair of Hamish Marshall and Robbie Hart entered the list of batsmen who have scored 1000 runs in domestic one-day cricket without ever having scored a century.

Of the 26 players, seven appeared in 2002/03. The full list reads:

	M	I	NO	HS	Runs	Ave	100	50
M.D. Bailey	103	101	14	76*	2159	24.81	-	11
G.E. Bradburn	121	110	15	80*	2048	21.55	-	5
R.A. Lawson	80	78	7	83*	1989	28.01	-	14
M.J. Greatbatch	67	66	6	84	1922	32.03	-	18
A.H. Jones	64	62	4	95	1757	30.29	-	9
R.G. Petrie	100	87	13	85	1726	23.32	-	9
C.B. Gaffaney	67	66	1	79*	1455	22.38	-	6
M.J. Horne	54	53	1	96	1335	25.67	-	12
G.P. Sulzberger	62	56	6	71	1331	26.62	-	8
J.T.C. Vaughan	56	53	6	94	1299	27.63	-	7
R.A. Jones	62	61	5	78*	1288	23.00	-	3
D.N. Patel	60	58	1	94	1291	22.64	-	5
R.N. Hoskin	61	59	1	70	1251	21.56	-	5
M.H. Austen	51	51	1	95*	1222	24.44	-	8
I.S. Billcliff	51	49	0	67	1199	24.46	-	10
T.E. Blain	64	59	11	70	1181	24.60	-	6
A.C. Parore	48	45	5	79*	1161	29.02	-	8
S.R. Mather	66	60	5	74	1146	20.83	-	5
B.R. Blair	49	49	3	91	1128	24.52	-	8
M.J. Lamont	40	40	4	88	1092	30.33	-	10
H.J.H. Marshall	53	51	5	93	1084	23.56	-	7
R.G. Hart	113	87	30	56	1082	18.98	-	2
G.R. Larsen	87	73	18	66	1053	19.14	-	1
E.B. McSweeney	78	68	11	69	1028	18.03	-	3
R.B. Reid	35	35	2	95	1026	31.09	-	9
D.J. Nash	44	40	6	88	1025	30.14	-	5

Jones, Greatbatch and Horne appeared in a combined total of 221 one-day internationals.

•   •   •

The most economical bowler in the State Shield in 2002/03 was Auckland's Kyle Mills who conceded just 3.18 runs per over. The four most economical bowlers in the competition came from the finalists Auckland and Northern Districts. The most economical were:

		O	M	R	W	Ave	Best	R/O
K.D. Mills	(A)	37.2	2	119	8	14.87	3-21	3.18
T.K. Canning	(A)	90	10	292	12	24.33	3-20	3.24
S.B. Styris	(ND)	64	10	208	9	23.11	3-20	3.25
B.P. Martin	(ND)	61	6	201	9	22.33	2-22	3.30
C.Z. Harris	(C)	70	5	234	10	23.40	4-28	3.34

•   •   •

On the other hand, the most expensive bowlers in the State Shield were all from Auckland or Northern Districts. They were:

		O	M	R	W	Ave	Best	R/O
C.R. Pryor	(A)	44	1	254	8	31.75	3-37	5.77
G.L. West	(ND)	36	5	196	1	196.00	1-39	5.44
J.A.F. Yovich	(ND)	84.4	3	434	23	18.86	4-50	5.12
I.G. Butler	(ND)	53.1	6	262	9	29.11	3-15	4.92
A.R. Adams	(A)	46	3	222	7	31.71	4-37	4.83

Duuring his innings of 34 in Northern Districts' State Shield game against Canterbury at Taupo, Robbie Hart became just the third player to register 1000 runs and 100 dismissals in domestic one-day cricket. He was following in the footsteps of two Wellington keepers, Erv McSweeney and Chris Nevin, in accomplishing the feat.

Four matches later, when he caught Central Districts' Jamie How at Hamilton, Hart also went past McSweeney's record number of dismissals in domestic one-day matches. By the end of the season Nevin had also passed McSweeney.

The records of the three keepers are:

	Runs	*Ave*	*ct*	*st*	*total*
R.G. Hart	1082	18.98	104	28	132
C.J. Nevin	1821	27.59	112	12	124
E.B. McSweeney	1028	18.03	97	26	123

• • •

In the 30 State Championship matches played in 2002/03, the six teams used a total of 22 different combinations of opening batsmen. They were:

	Team	*I*	*NO*	*Highest*	*Agg*	*Ave*	*100*	*50*
R.A. Lawson & Mohammad Wasim	O	2	0	260	318	159.00	1	1
C.B. Gaffaney & C.D. Cumming	O	1	0	147	147	147.00	1	–
C.M. Spearman & G.R. Loveridge	CD	1	0	68	68	68.00	–	1
C.D. Cumming & Mohammad Wasim	O	10	1	191	593	65.88	3	1
P.J. Ingram & J.M. How	CD	8	0	178	492	61.50	2	2
M.H. Richardson & T.G. McIntosh	A	14	1	118	671	51.61	2	3
S.L. Stewart & R.M. Frew	C	2	0	76	102	51.00	–	1
M.D. Bell & R.A. Jones	W	19	2	124	771	45.35	1	5
C.M. Spearman & J.M. How	CD	4	0	103	157	39.75	1	–
M.H. Richardson & M.J. Horne	A	1	0	39	39	39.00	–	–
J.A.H. Marshall & N.K.W. Horsley	ND	15	0	83	411	27.40	–	2
C.B. Gaffaney & Mohammad Wasim	O	4	0	43	82	20.50	–	–
M.H.W. Papps & R.M. Miller	C	2	0	25	41	20.50	–	–
G.R. Stead & M.H.W. Papps	C	3	0	51	56	18.60	–	1
C.M. Spearman & P.J. Ingram	CD	7	0	42	120	17.14	–	–
R.M. Frew & G.R. Stead	C	4	0	35	64	16.00	–	–
J.A.H. Marshall & G.H. Robinson	ND	1	0	16	16	16.00	–	–
R.A. Jones & L.J. Woodcock	W	1	0	16	16	16.00	–	–
R.M. Frew & M.H.W. Papps	C	4	0	36	55	13.75	–	–
M.J. Horne & T.G. McIntosh	A	1	0	10	10	10.00	–	–
T.G. McIntosh & R.K. Lynch	A	1	0	7	7	7.00	–	–
C.D. Cumming & N.D. Morland	O	1	0	0	0	0.00	–	–

• • •

Despite twice losing their first wicket without a run on the board, Otago had the best average opening partnership in 2001/02 with 67.50. There were eleven century opening stands compared to just four in 2001/02. Each side's record was:

Team	*Pairs*	*I*	*NO*	*Highest*	*Agg*	*Ave*	*100*	*50*
Auckland	4	17	1	118	727	45.43	2	3
Canterbury	5	15	0	76	318	21.20	–	2
Central Districts	4	20	0	178	837	41.85	3	3
Northern Districts	2	16	0	83	427	26.68	–	2
Otago	5	18	1	260	1140	67.05	5	2
Wellington	2	20	2	124	787	43.72	1	5
TOTAL	**22**	**106**	**4**	**260**	**4236**	**41.52**	**11**	**17**

The average opening partnership in 2001/02 was 29.15.

A aron Barnes, in his last season before moving to Wales, narrowly missed becoming the sixth player to appear in 100 domestic one-day games. Three of the five who have done so are from Northern Districts and they are the only ones to have played 100 games for one team. The most games in domestic one-day cricket have now been played by:

matches		matches	
121	G.E. Bradburn *ND*	98	A.C. Barnes *A*
113	R.G Hart *ND*	95	R.G. Twose *ND, CD, W*
103	M.D. Bailey *ND*	94	C.Z. Harris *C*
101	M.W. Douglas *CD, W*	93	L.G. Howell *CD, C, A*
100	R.G. Petrie *C, W*	93	M.E. Parlane *ND*

A total of 68 players have made 50 or more appearances.

• • •

N ew Zealand took part in three one-day tournaments during the past twelve months. A summary of the 38 tournaments which New Zealand has now played in is:

	Series	Seasons
World Cup	8	1975-2002/03
World Series/Carlton & United/VB Series	8	1980/81-2001/02
World Championship of Cricket	1	1984/85
Sri Lankan Tournaments	3	1985/86-2002/03
Sharjah Tournaments	8	1987/88-2001/02
Rothmans Cup	1	1989/90
Wills World Series	1	1994/95
Mandela Trophy	1	1994/95
Bank of New Zealand Centenary Series	1	1994/95
Independence Cup Tournaments	2	1996/97-1997/98
ICC Tournaments	3	1998/99-2002/03
Singapore Tournament	1	2000/01

• • •

O tago registered nine centuries in first-class cricket during the summer, their most ever in one season. Craig Cumming made three, Mohammad Wasim two, Chris Gaffaney, Robbie Lawson, Marcel McKenzie and Brendon McCullum one each.
Otago's previous best effort was in 1987/88 when they totalled eight. Century makers that season were Richard Hoskin with three, Kevin Burns had two, while Ken Rutherford, Warren Lees and Kassem Ibadulla made one each.

• • •

Y arrow Stadium in New Plymouth, formerly Rugby Park, was the only non-first-class venue to host a State Shield game during the season. The details of the nine grounds where domestic one-day matches have taken place but where no first-class games have been played are:

Venue	Matches	Seasons
Ashburton Domain	4	1980/81-1988/89
Knottingley Park, Waimate	1	1984/85
Blake Park, Mt Maunganui	24	1987/88-2001/02
Memorial Park, Motueka	1	1987/88
Mandeville Sports Ground, Ohoka	1	1990/91
Dannevirke Domain	1	1992/93
Waikanae Park	4	1993/94-2001/02
Yarrow Stadium, New Plymouth	3	1998/99-2002/03
WestpacTrust Stadium, Wellington	2	1999/00-2000/01

The Cornwall Cricket Club in Auckland again organised the limited-overs national club competition which was played from 8 to 13 April 2003. Teams involved were East Christchurch-Shirley *(Canterbury)*, Green Island *(Otago)*, Otumoetai Cadets *(Northern Districts)*, Napier Technical Old Boys *(Central Districts)*, Eastern Suburbs *(Wellington)* and Cornwall *(Auckland)*.

Players with first-class experience who took part were Scott Golder, Paul Hitchcock, Tim Boyer and Lance Dry *(Eastern Suburbs)*, Aaron Barnes, Richard Morgan, Ian Billcliff, Robert Lynch, Rob Nicol and Heath Davis *(Cornwall, Auckland)*, Scott Pawson, Ryan Burson, Michael Papps, Andrew Ellis, Neil Broom and Carl Anderson *(East Christchurch-Shirley)*, Carl Findlay, Mike Pawson, Jesse Ryder and Paul Whitaker *(Napier Technical Old Boys)* and Bradley Scott *(Green Island)*.

In the final **East Christchurch-Shirley** 137 (Extras 32, S. Findlay 4-17) **lost to Napier Technical Old Boys** 138-8 (K. Turner 57, J.D. Pawson 3-12, R.D. Burson 3-35) by two wickets. Cornwall defeated Eastern Suburbs in the play-off for third and fourth while Otumoetai Cadets beat Green Island in the play-off for fifth and sixth .

Tournament awards were: Batting – Daniel Flynn *(Otumoetai Cadets)*, Bowling – Ryan Burson *(East Christchurch-Shirley)*, Player of the Tournament – Jesse Ryder *(Napier Technical Old Boys)*.

•   •   •

Craig Pryor was the most expensive bowler in the 2002/03 State Shield competition, maintaining his unenviable position as the most expensive bowler in domestic one-day history (minimum 100 overs). The most expensive bowlers in domestic one-day cricket have been:

		Overs	Mdns	Runs	Wkts	Ave	RPO
C.R. Pryor	*(A, O)*	153.4	3	851	22	38.68	5.53
C.D. McMillan	*(C)*	105.3	4	555	22	25.22	5.26
J.A.F. Yovich	*(ND)*	258	14	1279	59	21.67	4.96
M.D. Bailey	*(ND)*	192.5	7	924	25	36.96	4.80
R.L. Hayes	*(ND)*	243.5	17	1158	37	31.29	4.76
D.J. Reekers	*(C, O)*	163.3	8	769	22	34.95	4.71
A.J. Penn	*(CD, W)*	365.5	23	1723	72	23.93	4.70
D.G. Sewell	*(O)*	126	7	591	22	26.86	4.69
S.E. Bond	*(C)*	154.5	13	715	23	31.08	4.61
M.Y. Pasupati	*(W)*	211.3	14	974	31	31.41	4.60

•   •   •

A number of New Zealand players have a high ratio of catches per match over their first-class careers. Stephen Fleming has taken 206 catches in 157 first-class games while James Marshall, who has taken 67 in 55 matches, and Campbell Furlong, with 51 in 42, also average more than one per game.

Other players high on the list are Craig Spearman 107 in 112, Matthew Hart 103 in 122, Chris Gaffaney 61 in 66 and Richard Jones 55 in 64.

•   •   •

The first instance of penalty runs in a test match involving New Zealand occurred in the first test against India at the Basin Reserve. In New Zealand's first innings, Mark Richardson edged a delivery from Harbhajan Singh to Rahul Dravid who deflected the ball onto the helmet behind the wicketkeeper, resulting in five penalty runs being added to extras. Before the Laws were changed in 2000, five runs would have been credited to the batsman.

The only other penalty runs in New Zealand first-class cricket occurred in the State Championship match between Central Districts and Auckland at Palmerston North in 2001/02 when Jacob Oram edged a ball which hit the helmet behind wicketkeeper Reece Young.

The thirteenth Gillette Cup limited-overs competition for secondary schoolboys was decided from 6 to 8 December, 2002. After the qualifying rounds, Kelston Boys' High School *(Auckland)*, Hamilton Boys' High School, Wanganui Collegiate and Southland Boys' High School played off for the title in Palmerston North. A total of of 172 schools were entered in the eight zones. Results were:

Round 1
Wanganui Collegiate 239-7 defeated **Kelston Boys' High School** 125 by 114 runs
Southland Boys' High School 163-5 lost to **Hamilton Boys' High School** 165-5 by 5 wickets

Round 2
Wanganui Collegiate 187 played **Southland Boys' High School** (match abandoned).
Kelston Boys' High School 207-8 played **Hamilton Boys' High School** (match abandoned)

Round 3 *(games reduced to 45 overs)*
Hamilton Boys' High School 221-5 defeated **Wanganui Collegiate** 178 by 43 runs
Kelston Boys' High School 198 defeated **Southland Boys' High School** 99 by 99 runs

Final placings: Hamilton Boys' High School 1st, Wanganui Collegiate 2nd, Kelston Boys' High School 3rd, Southland Boys' High School 4th.

• • •

The ninth national secondary schools girls competition was also decided in Palmerston North from 8 to 10 December. Epsom Girls' Grammar School *(Auckland)*, New Plymouth Girls' High School, Napier Girls' High School and Burnside High School *(Christchurch)* were again the four finalists. A total of 117 schools were entered in eight zones. Results were:

Round 1
Epsom Girls' Grammar School 201-5 defeated **Napier Girls' High School** 158-7 by 43 runs
New Plymouth Girls' High School 149-8 defeated **Burnside High School** 133 by 16 runs

Round 2
Epsom Girls' Grammar School 202-4 defeated **New Plymouth Girls' High School** 115 by 87 runs
Burnside High School 155-7 lost to **Napier Girls' High School** 158-4 by 6 wickets

Round 3
New Plymouth Girls' High School 142-8 lost to **Napier Girls' High School** 144-5 by 5 wkts
Burnside High School 113 defeated **Epsom Girls' Grammar School** 79 by 34 runs

Final placings: Epsom Girls' Grammar School 1st, Napier Girls' High School 2nd, New Plymouth Girls' High School 3rd, Burnside High School 4th.

• • •

New Zealand fielded the same team in the two tests against India and after making three changes had the same lineup for each of the two tests in Sri Lanka. This was the third time in three seasons that New Zealand had played successive tests with the same eleven players, having also done so in the third test against Australia and then the first against Bangladesh in 2001/02.
Not startling, perhaps, until it is remembered that prior to the test against Bangladesh, New Zealand had not fielded an unchanged lineup since the second test against Sri Lanka at Hamilton in 1996/97. In that time New Zealand had played 39 test matches without ever having the same eleven players in successive games.

The unthinkable finally happened! Lou Vincent was run out – and then not just once but twice in three games. In the second round match against Sri Lanka at Dambulla on 19 May, Vincent was run out at the bowler's end, attempting to regain his ground after backing up a long way. Four days later, in the final against Pakistan, Vincent was again found short of his ground, this time at the batsman's end as he tried to complete a single. Vincent's partner on both occasions was Stephen Fleming.

Vincent had played in 40 first-class games (including 11 tests), 53 one-day internationals, 41 one-day games for Auckland plus 13 other one-day matches for New Zealand, North Island and New Zealand A – a total of 147 matches and 170 innings – before finally being run out.

In his relatively short one-day international career, Vincent has already batted in every position from opener to number eight (completing the set when he batted at number four in the ICC Champions Trophy). His most regular batting position has been at number five where he has batted 19 times. Otherwise his record is opening (6 matches), number three (10), number four (2), number six (14), number seven (3) and number eight (1).

• • •

During the season both Canterbury and Central Districts had the misfortune to lose outright after posting totals of over 500 in their first innings, something quite unique in New Zealand first-class cricket.

The highest scores posted in the first innings by teams which lost the match are:

Wellington (**608-9d** & 35-1)	Northern Districts (323-5d & 322-7)	1998/99
Somerset (**554** & 146)	New Zealand (420 & 282-4)	1999
Central Districts (**542-4d** & 109-3d)	Canterbury (290-8d & 362-8)	2002/03
Canterbury (**514-6d** & 129-7d)	Auckland (284-7d & 361-6)	2002/03
Canterbury (**496** & 476-2d)	Wellington (498-2d & 475-4)	1994/95
Central Districts (**460-4d** & forfeit)	Wellington (143-0d & 318-3)	1997/98
Wellington (**443** & 75)	Auckland (346 & 143-7)	1924/25
Canterbury (**435-8d** & 235-7d)	Central Districts (297-6d & 375-5)	1986/87
Wellington* (**426** & 197)	Auckland (522 & 159)	1918/19
Canterbury* (**423** & 248)	Auckland (416 & 287)	1925/26
Auckland (**411-9d** & 162-9d)	Canterbury (324 & 253-8)	1989/90

* batted second

• • •

When Matt Horne made 187 in Auckland's win against Canterbury at Hagley Park, it was only the second occasion in New Zealand first-class cricket that a batsman had made that score. The score was first achieved only as recently as 1998/99 by Craig Cumming for Canterbury against Wellington.

In addition, Horne is the only player in the history of New Zealand first-class cricket to be dismissed for 178, making that score for Auckland against Bangladesh in 2001/02. Furthermore, there is only one instance of an unbeaten 178 and that was made as far back as 1914/15 by the famous England all rounder Jack Crawford while playing for Otago against Wellington.

• • •

The lowest individual score which has never been achieved in New Zealand first-class cricket is 199 although no batsman has ever been dismissed for 193. David Stead, Canterbury v Central Districts at New Plymouth in 1980/81, and Martin Crowe, Wellington v Canterbury at Christchurch in 1994/95, both recorded scores of 193 not out.

The scores most recently obtained for the first time (out or not out) are:

162	B.A. Edgar	Wellington v Otago	Invercargill	1989/90
169	Saeed Anwar	Pakistan v New Zealand	Wellington	1993/94
189	M.S. Sinclair	Central Districts v Wellington	Masterton	1996/97
187	C.D. Cumming	Canterbury v Wellington	Wellington	1998/99

W hen India won the sixth one-day international at Eden Park by one wicket it was just the seventh time a match involving New Zealand had been decided by that margin. New Zealand have won twice by one wicket (both times at Christchurch), being on the losing end on the other five occasions. The details are:

West Indies 203-7	New Zealand 207-9	Christchurch	1979/80
New Zealand 213-8	Pakistan 214-9	Multan	1984/85
New Zealand 196-8	Australia 197-9	Christchurch	1992/93
Pakistan 232-9	New Zealand 236-9	Christchurch	1995/96
New Zealand 243	West Indies 247-9	Kingston	1995/96
New Zealand 273-9	Zimbabwe 274-9	Auckland	2000/01
New Zealand 199-9	India 200-9	Auckland	2002/03

• • •

I n the State Championship match at Colin Maiden Park, Gareth Hopkins became the first New Zealand wicketkeeper to score a century in each innings of a first-class match. Hopkins, who was not on the list of contracted players for Canterbury, also became just the second player to perform the feat for Canterbury, after Keith Thomson in 1966/67.

In Canterbury's first innings Hopkins and Andrew Ellis (who was making his first-class debut) put on 115 for the ninth wicket, breaking a Canterbury record against Auckland which had stood since 1897/98.

In addition, Hopkins' second innings score of 175 not out was just one short of the highest score by a Canterbury batsman against Auckland. The record (which was to be obliterated by Peter Fulton just three weeks later) had been held by Len Cuff since 1893/94 when he made 176 and shared in a famous first wicket stand of 306 with Jimmy Lawrence. This is still Canterbury's highest opening partnership in first-class cricket.

• • •

H opkins also put himself well up on the list of highest scores by wicketkeepers in New Zealand first-class cricket. The table reads:

205*	E.B. McSweeney	Wellington v Central Districts	Levin	1987/88
197	S.C. Guillen	Canterbury v Fiji	Christchurch	1953/54
180	F.L.H. Mooney	Wellington v Auckland	Wellington	1943/44
175*	G.J. Hopkins	Canterbury v Auckland	Auckland	2002/03
173	I.D.S. Smith	New Zealand v India	Auckland	1989/90
173	A.J. Stewart	England v New Zealand	Auckland	1996/97
163	A.B. Williams	Wellington v Canterbury	Christchurch	1896/97
160*	L.K. Germon	Canterbury v Wellington	Christchurch	1989/90
155*	A.C. Parore	Auckland v Otago	Dunedin	1991/92
153*	A.J. Stewart	England v New Zealand XI	Palmerston North	1996/97
152	W.K. Lees	New Zealand v Pakistan	Karachi	1976/77
151	E.C. Petrie	Auckland v Wellington	Auckland	1953/54

Hopkins' total of 288 runs in the match was a record for a wicketkeeper in New Zealand first-class cricket.

• • •

S achin Tendulkar managed just two runs (0, 1, 1) in his three one-day internationals in New Zealand – his worst return from one series during his illustrious career (314 matches to the end of the World Cup).

Tendulkar, whose first two one-day international innings were actually both ducks (one in Pakistan and one in New Zealand, both in 1989/90) did have a sequence of three successive ducks in 1994 but they were spread over two different series.

P eter Fulton rewrote several portions of the record books with his innings of 301 not out against Auckland at Hagley Park during the first week of March.

Fulton came in to the match with 506 runs in first-class cricket at 31.62 with a highest score of 84, also against Auckland, twelve months earlier. He was 188 not out by the end of the first day having recorded the highest score by a Canterbury batsman against Auckland, surpassing Len Cuff's 176 made as far back as 1893/94.

The next day he became just the seventh player to score a double century for Canterbury after Arthur Cox, Curly Page, Graham Dowling, Brian Hastings, Rod Latham and Chris Harris (who did so twice). At lunch Fulton was on 241 and when he took a two to go to 253 it became the highest innings in the long history of Canterbury first-class cricket, going past Harris' 251 not out against Central Districts in 1996/97.

After 570 minutes batting, and from the 445th ball he had faced, Fulton despatched a no-ball from Brooke Walker for four to go to 301 and the innings was declared closed. Fulton became just the sixth New Zealand batsman to score a triple century in first-class cricket and the first non-Otago player to do so. Bert Sutcliffe (twice), Roger Blunt, Glenn Turner, Ken Rutherford and Mark Richardson are the others.

• • •

F ulton's score was also the highest maiden century by a New Zealand batsman, surpassing Bill Carson's famous 290 for Auckland against Otago in 1936/37. The highest maiden centuries in New Zealand first-class cricket are now:

301*	P.G. Fulton	Canterbury v Auckland	Christchurch	2002/03
290	W.N. Carson	Auckland v Otago	Dunedin	1936/37
209	D.J. White	Northern Districts v Central Districts	Hamilton	1985/86
204	A. Cox	Canterbury v Otago	Christchurch	1925/26
203*	G.P. Burnett	Wellington v Northern Districts	Hamilton	1991/92

(Full details in New Zealand First-class Records)

• • •

D uring his innings Fulton hit 45 fours and three sixes, a total of 48 boundaries. Only three innings in New Zealand first-class cricket have included more boundaries and only one innings has contained more fours. The leaders in these records are:

Total *6s* *4s*

53	8	45	K.R. Rutherford (317)	New Zealand v D.B. Close's XI	Scarborough 1986
50	15	35	J.R. Reid (296)	Wellington v Northern Districts	Wellington 1962/63
49	3	46	B. Sutcliffe (385)	Otago v Canterbury	Christchurch 1952/53
48	3	45	P.G. Fulton (301*)	Canterbury v Auckland	Christchurch 2002/03
47	3	44	V.T. Trumper (293)	Sims' Australian XI v Canterbury	Christchurch 1913/14

(Full details in New Zealand First-class Records)

• • •

F ulton became just the fifth player in the history of first-class cricket to score a triple century but end up on the losing side. Two New Zealanders feature in the list which reads:

343*	P.A. Perrin	Essex v Derbyshire	Chesterfield	1904
338*	R.C. Blunt	Otago v Canterbury	Christchurch	1931/32
312	J.E.R. Gallian	Lancashire v Derbyshire	Manchester	1996
309	V.S. Hazare	The Rest v Hindus	Bombay	1943/44
301*	P.G. Fulton	Canterbury v Auckland	Christchurch	2002/03

(The highest score by a batsman on the losing side in a test match is 222 by N.J. Astle for New Zealand against England at Christchurch, 2001/02).

F ulton's score was the highest ever in a first-class match at Hagley Park where 30 games have been staged since the first back in 1866/67. The previous record was held by George Watson who made 175 against Otago on 24 February, 1881. This was the first century scored in New Zealand first-class cricket. It was Watson's first game in first-class cricket and his innings remains the highest by any New Zealand player on debut.

Watson's total, a phenomenal score for the time, was almost twice the previous highest in New Zealand first-class cricket up to that time – 88 by Charlie Corfe, also for Canterbury against Otago, in 1874/75.

The left-handed Watson opened the innings and hit the first ball of the game to the boundary. He ended with 17 fours, 13 threes, 17 twos and 34 singles. Canterbury made 381 and dismssed Otago for 77 and 72 to win by an innings.

With the match finishing early on the third day, a fill-in game was played between mixed sides from the two teams. Reports stated that after the match "champagne was provided and a bat presented to Watson for his great ininngs".

Canterbury's win was their eighth successive victory in first-class cricket. This remains the record for any New Zealand provincial side.

• • •

A mongst other interesting happenings in this historic match, Watson and Arthur Redmayne, a former pupil of Rugby School, put on 156 for the third wicket, the highest partnership in New Zealand first-class cricket up to that time. Remarkably, it remained the Canterbury third wicket record until 1947/48 when it was broken by Peter O'Malley and Brun Smith. It was Redmayne's only first-class appearance.

Earlier, Canterbury batsman Dave Ashby hit a delivery from Otago's Oscar Haskell "clean over the flags" the ball falling 127 yards fom the wicket. A report stated that such a hit had never before been seen on the ground.

• • •

W atson was born in the Bombay Presidency in India in 1855 where his father was the senior chaplain. He was sent to England and gained his education at the High Wycombe Royal Grammar School in Buckinghamshire. In 1868 he joined his father, who had settled in Tasmania, and in 1875 he came to New Zealand. He took up teaching and by early 1883 he was assistant master at Christ's College.

He played his last innings on 15 November, 1884, for the Midland club against the Addington XV in a Senior Cup match. Batting at number three, he was 4 not out at the end of the day. A week later, however, he was reported as being dangerously ill, suffering from an "internal disorder" (it was actually peritonitis) which had "seized him very suddenly". It was alleged that this was the result of having been hit by a cricket ball. He died the following day, 23 November, leaving his wife and three-year-old son Thomas.

Watson played four other first-class matches, scoring 367 runs in all at 40.78. In 1882/83 he made 36 and 52 against Auckland (the first half-century in a first-class game at Lancaster Park) and the following season scored 82 against the visiting Tasmanian team.

• • •

R eece Young achieved several notable landmarks during the season. During the match against Canterbury at Hagley Park he became just the second keeper after Paul Kelly to make 100 dismissals for Auckland. By the end of the season he had taken 110 catches and made two stumpings in 34 first-class matches (all for Auckland).

He also equalled his own Auckland record of 35 dismissals in a season and became the first Auckland keeper to make six dismissals in an innings when took six catches against Wellington at the Basin Reserve.

He had earlier equalled the Auckland record with five catches in Central Districts' first innings at Colin Maiden Park.

Gareth Hopkins also reached some wicketkeeping centuries during the season. First he completed one hundred dismissals in first-class cricket to end the season with 103 catches and 11 stumpings from his 51 matches.

He also became just the fourth keeper to make one hundred dismissals for Canterbury, ending the season with 101, behind Lee Germon, John Ward and Charlie Boxshall.

• • •

Stephen Fleming's unbeaten 274 in the first test at Colombo was the second highest ever made in a test against Sri Lanka. The three highest are all by New Zealand batsmen as the following list reveals:

299	M.D. Crowe	New Zealand	Wellington	1990/91
274*	S.P. Fleming	New Zealand	Colombo	2002/03
267*	B.A. Young	New Zealand	Dunedin	1996/97
266	D.L. Houghton	Zimbabwe	Bulawayo	1994/95
221	B.C. Lara	West Indies	Colombo	2001/02
219	M.J. Slater	Australia	Perth	1995/96
211	Ijaz Ahmed	Pakistan	Dhaka	1998/99
206	Qasim Omar	Pakistan	Faisalabad	1985/86
203*	Javed Miandad	Pakistan	Faisalabad	1985/86
200*	Inzamam-ul-Haq	Pakistan	Dhaka	1998/99

A.H. Jones (186), J.F. Reid (180), S.P. Fleming (174*) and R.J. Hadlee (151*) have also scored more than 150 for New Zealand against Sri Lanka.

• • •

The highest scores by captains in test cricket are now:

334*	M.A. Taylor	Australia v Pakistan	Peshawar	1998/99
333	G.A. Gooch	England v India	Lord's	1990
311	R.B. Simpson	Australia v England	Manchester	1964
299	M.D. Crowe	New Zealand v Sri Lanka	Wellington	1990/91
285*	P.B.H. May	England v West Indies	Birmingham	1957
274*	S.P. Fleming	New Zealand v Sri Lanka	Colombo	2002/03
270	D.G. Bradman	Australia v England	Melbourne	1936/37
257*	Wasim Akram	Pakistan v Zimbabwe	Sheikhupura	1996/97
242*	C.H. Lloyd	West Indies v India	Bombay	1974/75
240	W.R. Hammond	England v Australia	Lord's	1938
239	G.T. Dowling	New Zealand v India	Christchurch	1967/68

Dowling holds the record for the highest score by a player in his first match as captain.

• • •

Fleming's innings was also one of the highest ever played for New Zealand in any first-class match overseas. This table reads:

317	K.R. Rutherford	New Zealand v D.B. Close's XI	Scarborough	1986
306	M.H. Richardson	New Zealand v Zimbabwe A	Kwekwe	2000/01
274*	S.P. Fleming	New Zealand v Sri Lanka	Colombo	2002/03
259	G.M. Turner	New Zealand v Guyana	Georgetown	1971/72
259	G.M. Turner	New Zealand v West Indies	Georgetown	1971/72
243	B. Sutcliffe	New Zealand v Essex	Southend	1949
242*	M.D. Crowe	New Zealand v South Australia	Adelaide	1985/86
230*	B. Sutcliffe	New Zealand v India	New Delhi	1955/56

NEW ZEALAND v INDIA — 2nd Test at Hamilton, 2002/03
Back row: R.G. Hart, S.E. Bond, M.J. Mason *(12th man)*, J.D.P. Oram, D.R. Tuffey, S.B. Styris.
Front row: L. Vincent, M.H. Richardson, C.D. McMillan, S.P. Fleming *(captain)*, N.J. Astle,
D.L. Vettori.

NEW ZEALAND WOMEN — 2002/03
Back row: L.E. Milliken, F.S. King, M.A.M. Lewis, S.J. McGlashan, M.L. Lynch.
Second row: N.J. Browne, S.K. Helmore *(fitness trainer)*, M.J.F. Shrimpton *(coach)*, J. Reynolds
(manager), A. Peterson *(physioptherapist)*, R.J. Rolls.
Front row: K.L. Pulford, A.L. Mason, H.M. Tiffen *(vice-captain)*, E.C. Drumm *(captain)*,
N. Payne, R.J. Steele, A.J. Green.
Inset: S.K. Burke

Stephen Goodenough

NEW ZEALAND A WOMEN — 2002/03
Back row: K.J. Martin, M.J. Kane, B.H. McNeill, M.L. Lynch.
Second row: A.J. Green, R.J. Steele, L.J. Murdoch *(manager)*, C.W. Dickeson *(coach)*, H. Sligo *(physioptherapist)*, A.J. Lenssen, S.K. Burke.
Front row: D.J. Ramsay, M.J. Hannay, R.C. Milburn, M.A.M. Lewis, S.J. McGlashan, M.F. Fahey.

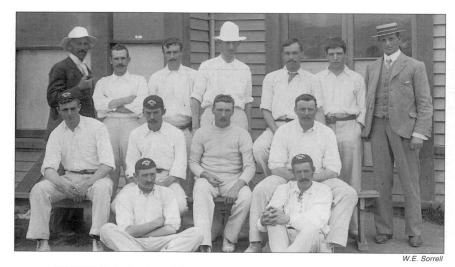

W.E. Sorrell

NEW ZEALAND v MELBOURNE CRICKET CLUB — 15-17 March, 1900
Back row: R. Spencer *(umpire)*, C.A. Richardson, E.F. Upham, H.B. Lusk, K.H. Tucker, D. Reese, F.C. Raphael *(manager)*
Second row: F.S. Frankish, L.T. Cobcroft *(captain)*, W.I. Stemson, J.C. Baker
Front row: W. Robertson, J.N. Fowke
(A previously unpublished picture? See story on page 38)

CANTERBURY — 2002/03

Back row: M.F. Sharpe *(coach)*, S.L. Stewart, B.P. Donkers, C.S. Martin, P.G. Fulton, H.J. Shaw, P.J. Wiseman, C.J. Anderson, G. McWhirter *(manager)*.
Front row: N.J. Astle, C.L. Cairns, C.D. McMillan, G.R. Stead *(captain)*, C.Z. Harris, S.E. Bond, S.J. Cunis.

CANTERBURY WOMEN — 2002/03

Back row: V. Burtt *(coach)*, K.A. Craig, S.K. Burke, R.J. Steele, R.C. Milburn, H.R. Daly, K.L. Gilray *(manager)*,
Front row: M.F. Fahey, S.E. Charteris, N. Payne, H.M. Tiffen *(captain)*, B.H. McNeill, R. Kelly, T. Gould.
Inset: H.J. Rae

CENTRAL DISTRICTS — 2002/03
Back row: M.J. Greatbatch *(coach)*, P.J. Ingram, L.J. Hamilton, M.J. Mason, B.E. Hefford, J.M. How, J.W.M. Haywood *(physiotherapist)*.
Front row: B.B.J. Griggs, G.P. Sulzberger, C.M. Spearman, J.D.P. Oram *(captain)*, M.A. Sigley, A.M. Schwasss, M.S. Sinclair.

NORTHLAND — 2002/03
Back row: C.A. Bray, W. Garnett, D.F. Potter.
Second row: G. Jones, J. Child, J.B. Lee, R.W. Anderson *(selector)*, D.R. Goodwin, D.R.T. Pinny.
Front row: M.W. Pinny, B.L. Hood *(captain)*, B.J. Chard.

NDCA

NORTHERN DISTRICTS — 2002/03

Back row: B.R. Blair *(coach)*, G.G. Robinson, G.W. Aldridge, I.G. Butler, D.R. Tuffey, J.A.F. Yovich, M.G. Orchard, B.P. Martin, S. Derry *(manager)*, P.J. Malcon *(selector)*.
Front row: N.M. Daley, N.K.W. Horsley, H.J.H. Marshall, M.N. Hart, R.G. Hart *(captain)*, S.B. Styris, J.A.H. Marshall, G.D. Irwin.

Barry Flewellen

NORTHERN DISTRICTS WOMEN — 2002/03

Back row: C.W. Dickeson *(coach,* B.L. Roderick, C.F. Garrood, N.J. Browne, A.J. Lenssen, A.J. Wilkins, L.E. Milliken, S. Moriarty *(manager),*
Front row: N.H. Carruthers, J.A. Simpson, J.M. Stafford, J.M. Fraser *(captain)*, V.J. Brown, K.M. Goodson, M.J. Hannay.

Lindsay McLeod

OTAGO — 2002/03

Back row: J.W. Wilson, Mohammad Wasim, P.D. McGlashan, R.A. Lawson
Second row: G.M. Turner *(coach)*, B.B. McCullum, M.N. McKenzie, J.W. Sheed,
W.C. McSkimming, J.M. McMillan, A. Stiven *(physiotherapist)*.
Front row: S.B. O'Connor, N.D. Morland, C.B. Gaffaney, C.D. Cumming *(captain)*, A.J. Hore,
K.P. Walmsley.

McRobie Photographics

OTAGO WOMEN — 2002/03

Back row: C.M. Thompson, S.W. Bates, R.J. Pullar, A.S.M. Hipkiss, S.J. Tsukigawa
Second row: S. Martin *(manager)*, K.J. Martin, E.J. Scurr, T.J. Morrison, C.E. Taylor,
G. Rodden *(coach)*.
Front row: A.E. Crawley, A.L. Kane, S.K. Helmore *(captain)*, K.M. Spence, M.J. Kane.

WELLINGTON — 2002/03

Back row: D. Painter *(assistant manger)*, R.A. Jones, G.T. Donaldson, A.J. Penn, J.E.C. Franklin, I.E. O'Brien, M.D.J. Walker, A.D. Turner, E. Cooper *(manager)*, V.F. Johnson *(coach)*.
Front row: N.R. Parlane, J.S. Patel, C.J. Nevin, M.D. Bell *(captain)*, M.R. Gillespie, L.J. Woodcock, L.J. Morgan, M.R. Jefferson.

Scoresheet of Peter Fulton's 301 not out
Canterbury v Auckland at Hagley Park

NATIONAL UNDER 19 TEAM — 2002/03

Back row: M.P. Goldstein, B.J. Wilson, A.S.T. Chambers, G.J. Hegglun, M.D. Bates, C.M. Smith, N.T. Broom, E.L. Standfield.

Front row: K. Patel *(coach)*, J.R. Hill, G.R. Hay, S.R. Allen *(captain)*, D.R. Flynn, B.J. Chard, D.R. Hadlee *(manager)*.

NATIONAL UNDER 17 TOURNAMENT TEAM — 2002/03

Back row: K. Noema-Barnett, C. Frauenstein, K. Forde, K. Read, C. Small

Front row: D. de Boorder, S. McLeod, B. Findlay, H. Templeton, M. Ellison, A. Devcich, T. Te Moni.

Fleming scored 162 runs on the second day of the first test. The most runs scored by a New Zealand batsman in a single day's test cricket are:

						Day
222	(0-222)	N.J. Astle	v England	Christchurch	2001/02	4
173	(126*-299)	M.D. Crowe	v Sri Lanka	Wellington	1990/91	5
169	(0-169*)	I.D.S. Smith	v India	Auckland	1989/90	1
162	(112*-274*)	S.P. Fleming	v Sri Lanka	Colombo	2002/03	2

• • •

Fleming batted for 655 minutes for his 274, the same time as Mark Greatbatch in his epic innings at Perth in 1989/90. The longest innings by New Zealand batsmen in first-class cricket are:

Mins	Runs				
741	306	M.H. Richardson	New Zealand v Zimbabwe A	Kwekwe	2000/01
704	259	G.M. Turner	New Zealand v West Indies	Georgetown	1971/72
685	180	J.F. Reid	New Zealand v Sri Lanka	Colombo	1983/84
671	212*	M.H. Richardson	New Zealand A v Sussex	Hove	2000
655	146*	M.J. Greatbatch	New Zealand v Australia	Perth	1989/90
655	274*	S.P. Fleming	New Zealand v Sri Lanka	Colombo	2002/03

(Full details in New Zealand First-class Records)

• • •

Fleming batted for 954 minutes in the match (six minutes short of 16 hours). This is by far the longest time that a New Zealand batsman has spent at the crease in a single first-class game. This list reads:

Mins	Scores				
954	274* & 69*	S.P. Fleming	New Zealand v Sri Lanka	Colombo	2002/03
876	76 & 146*	M.J. Greatbatch	New Zealand v Australia	Perth	1989/90
835	122 & 102	G.P. Howarth	New Zealand v England	Auckland	1977/78
828	75 & 138	J.G. Wright	New Zealand v West Indies	Wellington	1986/87
770	166* & 82	B.E. Congdon	New Zealand v West Indies	Port-of-Spain	1971/72

• • •

Only Hanif Mohammad, who batted for more than 970 minutes for Pakistan against West Indies at Bridgetown in 1957/58, has spent more time at the crease during a test match. Hanif scored 17 (time for innings not known) and 337.

Fleming spent all but 42 minutes of the match on the field of play – a total of 1599 minutes (26 hours and 39 minutes).

• • •

New Zealand's bowlers came in for some punishment in the last three overs of Zimbabwe's innings in the World Cup Super Six match at Bloemfontein. After 47 overs Zimbabwe had reached 190-7 but by the end of the innings Heath Streak and Sean Ervine had managed to extend the total by a further 62 runs.

Chris Harris conceded 23 runs in the 48th over and Daniel Vettori went for 13 in the 49th. Andre Adams, brought on for the last over, was no more successful as his over went (Streak facing): 4 (no-ball), 4, 2, 1, 6, 4, 4. With 26 off the final over, Adams finished with figures of 5-0-54-1.

Zimbabwe ended with 252-7 but New Zealand were able to pass their total with six wickets and 14 deliveries in hand.

Stephen Fleming is now one of just 10 players to score 300 or more runs in a New Zealand first-class match. Bert Sutcliffe achieved the feat on four occasions, twice requiring just a single innings to do so. Seven New Zealanders feature on the list which reads:

Runs				
385	B. Sutcliffe (385)	Otago v Canterbury	Christchurch	1952/53
380	G.S. Chappell (247* & 133)	Australia v New Zealand	Wellington	1973/74
370	R.C. Blunt (32 & 338*)	Otago v Canterbury	Christchurch	1931/32
355	B. Sutcliffe (355)	Otago v Auckland	Dunedin	1949/50
343	B. Sutcliffe (243 & 100*)	New Zealand v Essex	Southend	1949
343	S.P. Fleming (274* & 69*)	New Zealand v Sri Lanka	Colombo	2002/03
336	W.R. Hammond (336*)	England v New Zealand	Auckland	1932/33
329	M.D. Crowe (30 & 299)	New Zealand v Sri Lanka	Wellington	1990/91
325	B. Sutcliffe (197 & 128)	Otago v MCC	Dunedin	1946/47
323	R.H. Vance (69 & 254*)	Wellington v Northern Districts	Wellington	1988/89
318	P.G. Fulton (301* & 17)	Canterbury v Auckland	Christchurch	2002/03
306	M.H. Richardson (306)	New Zealand v Zimbabwe A	Kwekwe	2000/01
305	M.P. Maynard (195 & 110)	Northern Districts v Auckland	Auckland	1991/92

• • •

When New Zealand defeated India in the low scoring test at Hamilton, they scored 160-6 to win by four wickets. This was the highest total of the game and it was only the second time that New Zealand had won a test by making the highest innings total of the match.
The details are:

Pakistan (274 & 223) lost to New Zealand (220 & 278-8)	Dunedin	1984/85
India (99 & 154) lost to New Zealand (94 & 160-6)	Hamilton	2002/03

The match at Dunedin was the memorable occasion when Jeremy Coney and number eleven Ewen Chatfield added an unbeaten fifty runs to take New Zealand to victory after Lance Cairns had retired hurt after being hit on the head.

• • •

During the season two matches were tied on the first innings, the first occasion that this had happened in New Zealand first-class cricket. Even more remarkable was the fact that the ties took place on successive days in the same round of the State Championship.
On 6 December Auckland equalled Wellington's total of 113 (after being 106-9). The following day Canterbury, 230-9 overnight, after being 212-9, were bowled out for 236 to equal Northern Districts' score.
There have been only seven matches in New Zealand first-class cricket where the first innings have been tied, the last occasion being in 1975/76. They are: (team batting first listed first)

Score			
100	Wellington v Hawke's Bay	Wellington	1883/84
101	Canterbury v Otago	Christchurch	1890/91
171	Otago v Canterbury	Christchurch	1917/18
402	Pakistan v New Zealand	Auckland	1972/73
276	Otago v Auckland	Dunedin	1975/76
113	Wellington v Auckland	Auckland	2002/03
236	Northern Districts v Canterbury	Rangiora	2002/03

Otago were 93-4 in reply to Auckland's 93 at Dunedin in 1977/78 when rain prevented any further play.

In the match between Auckland and Wellington, Auckland scored 223-8 to win the game after Wellington had been bowled out for 219 in their second innings, thus producing similarity of scores in both the first and second innings.

Notable instances of closeness of scores in New Zealand first-class cricket are:

Otago (77 & 41)	Auckland (78 & 41-6)	Dunedin	1873/74
Canterbury (101 & 120)	Otago (101 & 121-9)	Christchurch	1890/91
Canterbury (146 & 133)	Wellington (145 & 135-7)	Christchurch	1900/01
South Island (364 & 371-8d)	North Island (365 & 374-8)	Dunedin	1947/48
Canterbury (319 & 264)	Auckland (320 & 264-9)	Auckland	1950/51
CD (277-9d & 228-9d)	Auckland (278-3d & 228-6)	Auckland	1985/86
Otago (102 & 180)	ND (103 & 182-2)	Hamilton	1985/86
ND (172 & 238-6d)	CD (173-6d & 238-6)	Masterton	1991/92
Canterbury (496 & 476-2d)	Wellington (498-2d & 475-4)	Christchurch	1994/95
ND (254 & 178)	Canterbury (256-8d & 178-9)	Christchurch	1994/95
Otago (175 & 334)	Canterbury (176 & 335-5)	Christchurch	1995/96
Wellington (113 & 219)	Auckland (113 & 223-8)	Auckland	2002/03

• • •

During the past season Stephen Fleming created a new landmark for most one-day international innings without ever being dismissed first ball. Fleming, who was the only player to appear in every one of New Zealand's 22 one-day internationals in 2002/03, went past David Boon's record in the third one-dayer against India at Jade Stadium on 1 January.

Only eight players have have had one hundred or more one-day international innings without suffering the dreaded first-baller. They are:

Inns		*Inns*	
195	S.P. Fleming *(NZ)*	133	D.J. Cullinan *(SA)*
177	D.C. Boon *(A)*	127	C.G. Greenidge *(WI)*
161	D.M. Jones *(A)*	110	M.A. Taylor *(A)*
141	M.D. Crowe *(NZ)*	105	K.C. Wessels *(A/SA)*

Only Chris Harris (198) has played more innings for New Zealand. He has been dismissed first ball twice – against Australia at Christchurch, 1992/93 and Pakistan at Nairobi, 2000/01.

• • •

In the two tests which India played in New Zealand they lost 40 wickets while their batsmen scored just 497 runs.

The average of 12.43 per wicket in a series (minimum two matches) was the lowest since 1958 (New Zealand in England) while six of the ten lowest averages for a series were made prior to 1900.

The top ten reads:

Ave	*Matches*	*Runs*	*Wkts*		
7.00	2	280	40	South Africa v England	1888/89
8.17	3	490	60	Australia v England	1888
10.25	3	615	60	South Africa v England	1895/96
10.43	2	417	40	Australia v England	1886/87
10.98	2	439	40	New Zealand v England	1954/55
11.30	3	678	60	South Africa v England	1912
12.15	2	486	40	England v Australia	1886/87
12.23	2	489	40	Australia v England	1890
12.24	5	1114	91	New Zealand v England	1958
12.43	2	497	40	India v New Zealand	2002/03

Northland Cricket farewelled Cobham Oval in April 2002, relinquishing the lease of the ground after 47 years to enable the Whangarei District Council to proceed with its sale to The Warehouse who wished to expand their facilities at the adjacent Okara shopping complex.

A new ground, of first-class standard, is currently being constructed within the Okara Park Reserve adjacent to the rugby ground. It is scheduled to be opened in 2004.

Cobham Oval staged eleven first-class matches between 1966/67 and 2000/01 and hosted international sides including West Indies, Zimbabwe, Pakistan and MCC. As a farewell to the ground, a Past versus Present match was arranged followed by a dinner and a nostalgic evening of entertaining speeches. This made for an enjoyable but very wet day – as has often been the case throughout Northland's history, the weather had the last word.

(Thanks to Bruce Scott for his assistance)

• • •

There were some extraordinary happenings in the State Shield match between Canterbury and Northern Districts at Timaru on 22 January.

Shortly before play began, a gale force northwesterly sprang up, so fierce that it threatened to delay the start of play or even force the abandonment of the game altogether. A large marquee was ripped from its moorings and ended up on the field of play, the metal stays twisted beyond repair. One man was injured when he was trapped beneath the marquee and struck by the metal supports. He was taken to hospital in an ambulance.

One of the sight screens was ripped to shreds, leaving only the framework, and the game went ahead with just one sight screen. Television cameramen were forced to abandon their elevated positions and the entire match was covered from ground level as the wind continued unabated throughout the day. The temperature remained around 30 degrees for the duration of the match.

The game was covered by Sky Television and was the first ever live telecast of cricket from Timaru.

• • •

Chris Cairns found conditions to his liking, however, recording the fastest fifty in domestic one-day cricket. He reached fifty off just 20 balls and was finally dismissed for 63 off 41 deliveries.

Ian Butler was the main victim of Cairns' assault, conceding 29 off one over (28 to Cairns plus a no-ball) and finishing with figures of 7-0-71-1. His fifth over read 644nb464. Cairns reached his fifty as follows: 04404404010016440464.

• • •

Cairns had come to the wicket with the score at 19-2 after Michael Papps was hit on the helmet by a ball from Butler and forced to retire hurt with a broken nose after the ball squeezed through between grille and visor. Papps returned at the fall of the eighth wicket with six runs required to win.

With Chris Harris controlling the strike, the only ball that Papps was required to face after resuming his innings turned out to be the last ball of the match, a wide bowled by Joseph Yovich to provide the winning run.

• • •

Michael Parlane's century in this match was one of only three scored in the State Shield in 2002/03. By a coincidence, all three were made in games covered live by Sky Television. Three days earlier Chris Nevin and Craig McMillan had both scored hundreds in the televised game between Wellington and Canterbury at the Basin Reserve, although Matthew Hart had a near miss being run out for 98 in a non-televised game on the same day.

The match at Timaru also provided a rare instance of a team not conceding any wides or no-balls in their 50 overs. This has been achieved only 10 times in 589 one-day domestic games, six times in the first two seasons of competition and only three times since 1985/86. The full list is:

	Bowling side		
Wellington (195-9)	Otago	Wellington	1980/81
Canterbury (265-9)	Wellington	Timaru	1980/81
Central Districts (207)	Auckland *	Napier	1980/81
Wellington (215-9)	Central Districts	Masterton	1981/82
Central Districts (244-8)	Canterbury †	Wanganui	1981/82
Wellington (204-8)	Auckland	Wellington	1981/82
Northern Districts (191)	Otago	Alexandra	1985/86
Otago (254-9)	Wellington	Alexandra	1993/94
Auckland (218-7)	Otago	Auckland	1999/00
Northern Districts (267-6)	Canterbury	Timaru	2002/03

* Auckland replied with 147 all out in 43.4 overs with no no-balls or wides
† Canterbury replied with 247-4 in 47 overs with no no-balls or wides

• • •

On the other hand there were extras aplenty in the State Shield match between Northern Districts and Wellington at Hamilton. Northern's innings of 271-8 included a New Zealand one-day record 55 extras, made up of five byes, 15 leg-byes, 31 wides and four no-balls. Ash Turner bowled 12 wides which cost 20 extra runs in total.

Wellington, in their turn, gave up 33 extras (including 22 wides) with the match total of 88 extras also being a New Zealand one-day record.

• • •

India's captain, Sourav Ganguly, had a forgettable one-day series in New Zealand scoring just 58 runs in seven innings. As it happened, however, his was by no means the worst effort by a specialist batsman during the past twelve months. Notable instances of a low return in a one-day series include:

	M	I	Runs	Ave	Series	
D.P.M. Jayawardene *(SL)*	9	7	21	3.00	World Cup	2002/03
Inzamam-ul-Haq *(P)*	6	6	19	3.17	World Cup	2002/03
I.V.A. Richards *(WI)*	5	5	28	5.60	Wills Series	1986/87
S.T. Jayasuriya *(SL)*	5	5	34	6.80	Wills Series	1991/92
R.B. Richardson *(WI)*	7	5	30	7.50	TIS	1992/93
Salim Malik *(P)*	5	5	38	7.60	TIS	1992/93
H.H. Gibbs *(SA)*	5	5	39	7.80	C & U Series	1997/98
S.C. Ganguly *(I)*	7	7	58	8.29	NZ v I	2002/03
S.P. Fleming *(NZ)*	6	6	51	8.50	Mandela Trophy	1994/95
A.R. Border *(A)*	8	7	68	8.57	World Cup	1991/92
N.J. Astle *(NZ)*	9	9	79	8.78	World Cup	1999

• • •

With Grant Bradburn, Mark Bailey, Simon Doull, Lee Germon and Adam Parore not reappearing in 2002/03, only three players remained in New Zealand first-class cricket with any connection to the 1980s.

Chris Cairns is now New Zealand's longest serving first-class player having made his debut in England in 1988 and in New Zealand the following summer. Chris Harris made his debut in 1989/90 as did Mark Richardson, although Richardson's debut, as left-arm spinner and tail-end batsman, did not actually take place until the latter part of the season in 1990.

A total of 22 wickets fell during the third day's play in the second test between New Zealand and India at Hamilton. Only three times in the entire history of test cricket had more wickets fallen in a single day's play, the last occasion being as far back as 1901/02, and only once in the last 50 years had as many as 22 batsmen been dismissed in one day.

There are eleven occasions when more than 20 wickets have fallen in one day's play:

Wkts	Day				
27	2	E (18-3 to 53 & 62)	A (60)	Lord's	1888
25	1	A (112 & 48-5)	E (61)	Melbourne	1901/02
24	2	E (69-1 to 145 & 60-5)	A (119)	The Oval	1896
22	1	A (92 & 502)	E (100)	The Oval	1890
22	1	A (82 & 20-2)	WI (102)	Adelaide	1951/52
22	3	E (292-7 to 347-9d)	I (58 & 82)	Manchester	1952
22	3	E (175-4 to 249 & 74-6)	SL (81)	Colombo	2001/02
22	3	I (92-8 to 99 & 154)	NZ (94 & 24-0)	Hamilton	2002/03
21	1	E (185 & 0-1)	SA (93)	Port Elizabeth	1895/96
21	2	E (126 & 3-1)	NZ (107)	Birmingham	1999
21	2	WI (267-9 to 267 & 54)	E (134 & 0-0)	Lord's	2000
also note :					
20	3	A (323-4 to 369)	WI (107* & 67-5)	Sydney	1930/31

* *one man absent*

• • •

The 22 wickets which fell on the third day at Hamiton was easily a record for one day's play in a test in New Zealand. This list reads:

Wkts	Day				
22	3	I (92-8 to 99 & 154)	NZ (94 & 24-0)	Hamilton	2002/03
18	4	NZ (12-0 to 123)	E (53-8)	Wellington	1977/78
18	1	A (221)	NZ (85-8)	Auckland	1973/74
18	4	NZ (306-5 to 365-9d)	B (205 & 90-4)	Hamilton	2001/02

• • •

The match at Hamilton is one of just 25 test matches where a team has won despite none of its players scoring a half-century, the last occasion being when England defeated West Indies at Lord's in 2000.

Rarer still, it was just the thirteenth test to produce a result without any player in the match reaching fifty, only the second in almost 70 years and just the fifth since 1896. These matches are *(winning team listed first)*:

England	Australia	Sydney	1886/87
England	Australia	Sydney	1886/87
England	Australia	Sydney	1887/88
Australia	England	Lord's	1888
England	Australia	Manchester	1888
England	South Africa	Port Elizabeth	1888/89
England	Australia	The Oval	1890
England	Australia	The Oval	1896
England	New Zealand	Christchurch	1929/30
Australia	South Africa	Melbourne	1931/32
England	West Indies	Bridgetown	1934/35
England	Australia	Birmingham	1981
New Zealand	India	Hamilton	2002/03

Remarkably, the only other test in New Zealand to produce a result without any player scoring a fifty was the first ever played in this country, against England, in 1929/30.

The only other time that New Zealand had won a test without any batsman reaching fifty was against Sri Lanka at Wellington in 1982/83. On that occasion New Zealand's highest scorer was Bruce Edgar with 47 not out in the second innings. Sri Lanka's Ranjan Madugalle (79) and D.S. de Silva (61) registered the only two fifties of the game.

The lowest highest score for a winning team in a test match is 22 by Percy McDonnell and Jack Blackham when Australia (116 & 60) defeated England (53 & 62) by 61 runs at Lord's in 1888.

•   •   •

New Zealand also achieved the rare feat of winning a test match without registering a fifty partnership during the test at Hamilton. New Zealand's best partnership was just 37 for the third wicket between Stephen Fleming and Craig McMillan in the second innings. India's best partnership was 49.

The only times when a team has won without a fifty partnership are *(winning team listed first with its highest partnership at the end of the line)*:

England	Australia	Sydney	1887/88	31
Australia	England	Lord's	1888	33
England	Australia	Sydney	1886/87	49
England	West Indies	Bridgetown	1934/35	27*
West Indies	Pakistan	Lahore	1986/87	49
New Zealand	India	Hamilton	2002/03	37

•   •   •

In the test at Hamilton, New Zealand found India's first innings of 99 an insurmountable hurdle, being bowled out for just 94. This was the first time in the long history of test cricket that both sides had been dismissed for less than 100 in their first innings.

The lowest totals made in the first innings of a test which proved too much for the opposition are:

99	India v New Zealand (94)	Hamilton	2002/03
112	Australia v England (61)	Melbourne	1901/02
113	England v Australia (42)	Sydney	1887/88
116	Australia v England (53)	Lord's	1888
116	Australia v West Indies (78)	Sydney	1951/52
133	Pakistan v England (130)	The Oval	1954
138	Australia v England (95)	Melbourne	1976/77

All the teams in the above list, apart from India, went on to win the game. By coincidence, the previous lowest first innings total to gain a lead in a match which was eventually lost by that team also belongs to India who made 147 and 93 against England's 136 and 108-1 at Lord's, 1936.

The lowest combined first innings total in a test is 155 by England (113) and Australia (42) at Sydney, 1887/88.

•   •   •

On the third day of the test at Hamilton, India went from 92-8 to 99 all out, New Zealand were then bowled out for 94, India batted again and were dismissed for 154 and New Zealand still had time to reach 24-0 by the close. A total of 22 wickets had fallen and part of all four innings had occurred on the same day.

The only other time in the entire history of test cricket when some part of all four innings took place on the same day was at Lord's in 2000. On the 2nd day of the match West Indies went from 267-9 to 267 all out, England were bowled out for 134, West Indies were then routed for just 54 and England faced seven balls to be 0-0 at the close.

This edition of the *Almanack* includes the obituary of Bernie Clark, who had been Otago's oldest living first-class cricketer. Clark was the son of the famous Otago and New Zealand batsman Jim Baker who played 37 games for the province between 1889/90 and 1906/07. (Baker was born Clark but his mother remarried and for a while he took the surname Baker, then Clark-Baker, but when son Bernie was born the surname Clark was preferred.)

Apart from his own belongings, Clark had kept a large amount of his father's cricket and rugby memorabilia (Baker also represented Otago at rugby). Amongst the items there were many team photos dating from the 1890s. One was a rare picture of the 1899/00 New Zealand team which played just once that season, against the Melbourne Cricket Club (who won by an innings). The photo is possibly the only one in existence or may even be the only one ever produced. It shows the New Zealand eleven in their playing gear, probably just before they took the field. A picture of the two teams combined appeared in the *Weekly News* but the "official" New Zealand team photo does not appear to have surfaced before.

The names of the players are not listed (although, of course, they are known). The only inscription on the photo reads "New Zealand Team 1900 – Selected by J. Baker". This is a significant find as it was not previously known who selected the team that season. Baker was sole selector from 1904 to 1906 (while he was still playing for Otago) but former New Zealand wicketkeeper Johnny Fowke (a team mate of Baker's) was the selector in 1902/03 when Lord Hawke's team undertook a groundbreaking and gruelling tour of New Zealand.

By profession Baker was a signwriter and may well have been responsible for the inscription which is clearly worded with his own role in mind. Did the players receive a similarly inscribed photograph or was this the only one ever made?

• • •

Baker selected himself for the game against the Melbourne Club in what was to be his last appearance for New Zealand. In the first of his two volumes of *New Zealand Cricket*, T.W. Reese picks Baker in his all-time New Zealand lineup.

Baker died in 1939 and amongst the memorabilia which Bernie Clark had lovingly looked after for all those years was his father's cap from that game. The hat is of the small skull-cap variety with a tiny peak. It features the silver fern and the date 1900. One assumes that it is one of only eleven (or possibly twelve) that were ever made.

Baker was also a member of the 1898/99 team which toured Australia. A picture of this side is on the back cover of *Men in White*. The touring party are shown resplendent in their straw boaters complete with a ribbon bearing the silver fern and the NZCC logo. While the hat may have long since disintegrated, the ribbon from Baker's boater remains in mint condition thanks to his son's meticulous care.

• • •

Another fascinating item from this treasure trove is a menu signed by the Wellington and Otago Plunket Shield teams at Christmas Dinner, 1934 (the match was played at the Basin Reserve on 24, 25, 26 December). The old Grand Hotel was the venue for the festivities which included musical numbers rendered by Frank Crowther's Novelty Orchestra.

Clark did not sign the menu himself but the other signatures make most interesting reading. All are easy to decipher, being carefully written with a fountain pen. Otago's team reads Vic Cavanagh and Charlie Saxton (future rugby legends), Vern Leader (also a noted mountaineer), Sonny Moloney (New Zealand representative killed at El Alamein during World War II), Ken Uttley (who later played for Canterbury and Wellington), Tommy Chettleburgh (who died while only in his 40s), twelfth man Lankford Smith and three more New Zealand representatives in Ced Elmes, George Dickinson and Jack Dunning.

Smith, just turned 20, made his first-class debut in Otago's next game and his career did not end until the 1956/57 season. A future Otago captain, he also had a long stint as a radio commentator, most notably in association with Iain Gallaway.

The Wellington players who signed were Denis Blundell (a future Governor-General), his opening bowling partner Jumbo Symes, Jimmy Ell (revealing a hitherto unknown second initial "A") and Stewie Wilson, Wellington's twelfth man.

Shane Bond's figures of 6-23 against Australia in the World Cup were the best in New Zealand's one-day history *(see New Zealand One-day International Records)*. It was also the second best analysis ever recorded against Australia with Bond featuring twice in the top ten which reads:

7-51	W.W. Davis	West Indies	Leeds	1983
6-23	S.E. Bond	New Zealand	Port Elizabeth	2002/03
6-50	A.H. Gray	West Indies	Port of Spain	1990/91
6-59	Waqar Younis	Pakistan	Nottingham	2001
5-15	R.J. Shastri	India	Perth	1991/92
5-17	C.E.L. Ambrose	West Indies	Melbourne	1988/89
5-21	Wasim Akram	Pakistan	Melbourne	1984/85
5-21	N. Boje	South Africa	Cape Town	2001/02
5-24	L. Klusener	South Africa	Melbourne	1997/98
5-25	S.E. Bond	New Zealand	Adelaide	2001/02
5-25	Shoaib Akhtar	Pakistan	Brisbane	2002/03

• • •

Bond's figures are also amongst the best in World Cup competitions. There are only eight occasions where a bowler has taken six or more wickets in a World Cup match with five of those instances occurring in the 2003 tournament in South Africa.

7-15	G.D. McGrath	Australia v Namibia	Potchefstroom	2002/03
7-20	A.J. Bichel	Australia v England	Port Elizabeth	2002/03
7-51	W.W. Davis	West Indies v Australia	Leeds	1983
6-14	G.J. Gilmour	Australia v England	Leeds	1975
6-23	A. Nehra	India v England	Durban	2002/03
6-23	S.E. Bond	New Zealand v Australia	Port Elizabeth	2002/03
6-25	W.P.U.J.C. Vaas	Sri Lanka v Bangladesh	Pietermaritzburg	2002/03
6-39	K.H. Macleay	Australia v India	Nottingham	1983

• • •

Bond has an outstanding record in one-day internationals against Australia having captured 22 wickets at just 10.45 runs apiece. The best averages against Australia by players taking ten or more wickets are:

	Wkts	Ave		Wkts	Ave
S.E. Bond *(NZ)*	22	10.45	Sikander Bakht *(P)*	13	18.84
S.T. Clarke *(WI)*	11	14.90	M. Hendrick *(E)*	15	19.80
C.R. Matthews *(SA)*	24	15.20	J. Garner *(WI)*	54	19.92
J.K. Lever *(E)*	13	16.07	E.J. Chatfield *(NZ)*	51	20.56

• • •

Even more impressive has been Bond's strike rate of 15 balls per wicket. This is by far the best by any bowler who has taken twenty or more wickets against Australia. The details are as follows:

	O	M	R	W	Ave	Balls/Wkt
S.E. Bond *(NZ)*	56.5	8	230	22	10.45	15.50
C.R. Matthews *(SA)*	99.5	12	365	24	15.20	24.95
Shoaib Akhtar *(P)*	124.4	8	687	25	27.48	29.92
Saqlain Mushtaq *(P)*	148.2	7	630	27	23.33	32.96
N. Boje *(SA)*	114.3	1	516	20	25.80	34.35
J. Garner *(WI)*	310.4	42	1076	54	19.92	34.51

Despite recording record figures in the match against Australia, Bond still finished on the losing side. The best figures for the losing team in a one-day international are:

6-14	Imran Khan	Pakistan v India	Sharjah	1984/85
6-23	S.E. Bond	New Zealand v Australia	Port Elizabeth	2002/03
6-35	S.M. Pollock	South Africa v West Indies	East London	1998/99
6-50	A.H. Gray	West Indies v Australia	Port-of-Spain	1990/91
5-9	M. Muralitharan	Sri Lanka v New Zealand	Sharjah	2001/02
5-18	G.J. Cosier	Australia v England	Birmingham	1977
5-20	G.S. Chappell	Australia v England	Birmingham	1977

Waqar Younis took 6-30 in a tie with New Zealand at Auckland in 1993/94

• • •

On a similar note, during the World Cup there were also some high scores made by batsmen who finished on the losing side, including Scott Styris whose 141 against Sri Lanka was the second highest innings ever played for New Zealand in a one-day international. The highest innings played by batsmen from the losing team are:

167*	R.A. Smith	England v Australia	Birmingham	1993
146	S.R. Tendulkar	India v Zimbabwe	Jodhpur	2000/01
145	A. Flower	Zimbabwe v India	Colombo	2002/03
143	S.R. Tendulkar	India v Australia	Sharjah	1997/98
143	H.H. Gibbs	South Africa v New Zealand	Johannesburg	2002/03
142*	A. Flower	Zimbabwe v England	Harare	2001/02
142	D.L. Houghton	Zimbabwe v New Zealand	Hyderabad	1987/88
141	S.B. Styris	New Zealand v Sri Lanka	Bloemfontein	2002/03
140	Saeed Anwar	Pakistan v India	Dhaka	1997/98
140	C.H. Gayle	West Indies v India	Ahmedabad	2002/03

Styris' score was the highest in a fifty-over game for New Zealand. Glenn Turner's record score of 171 not out against East Africa in 1975 was made in a sixty-over match.

• • •

A total of seven players were dismissed without scoring in Central Districts' innings of 67 in their State Shield match against Canterbury at Hagley Park on 7 January. Ian Sandbrook was run out without facing, Michael Mason went first ball, Bevan Griggs lasted two balls, Jamie How three and Brent Hefford and Lance Hamilton four. Greg Loveridge faced 13 balls for his duck. Remarkably, top scorer Craig Spearman hit 26 off 22 balls.

The previous record for most ducks in an innings in one-day domestic cricket was held by Otago with five when they were dismissed for 230 by Auckland at Alexandra in 1989/90. There are ten further instances of four ducks in one innings.

• • •

Stan Cowman, who died on 2 February aged 79, was the driving force behind the National Cricket Museum at the Basin Reserve. During the Second World War Cowman, while still a teenager, flew over the Atlantic in anti-submarine and convoy escort patrols and in 1964 brought his family to New Zealand where he set up a dental practice. He later became the senior dental surgeon at Hutt Hospital.

Yorkshire-born Cowman was a first-class umpire from 1973/74 to 1984/85 and stood in two one-day internationals. He was also an international hockey umpire and went on to become national president of both associations. During the test against Australia in 1985/86, Cowman laid out a collection of memorabilia which became the basis for the Cricket Museum which was opened in 1987. Cowman was honorary curator for the next 15 years until his death.

U nlike the 1999 tournament, when Daniel Vettori and Simon Doull did not get to play in a single game, New Zealand used every player in their squad during the World Cup in South Africa. There were, however, a total of 13 players who were in South Africa at some stage and for various reasons did not get to play. They were:
Australia: Nathan Bracken, Nathan Hauritz, Shane Warne, **England:** Steve Harmison, Matthew Hoggard, **India:** Ajit Agarkar, Sanjay Bangar, Parthiv Patel, **Kenya;** Alpesh Vader, **Namibia:** Marius van der Merwe, **Netherlands:** Ruud Nijman, **Sri Lanka:** Buddhika Fernando, **West Indies:** Ryan Hinds.
Zimbabwe used a total of 17 players, a record for one team at any World Cup tournament.

•   •   •

A number of personal landmarks were reached during the World Series of Women's Cricket held at Lincoln during January and February.
Australia's Cathryn Fitzpatrick became the first player to capture 100 wickets in women's one-day internationals when she dismissed India's Nooshin Al Khader on 1 February. The leading wicket takers are:

	Matches	Wkts	Ave
C.L. Fitzpatrick *(A)*	67	110	15.71
C.E. Taylor *(E)*	91	88	23.35
C.L. Mason *(A)*	46	83	13.85
C.A. Campbell *(NZ)*	85	78	25.87
L.A. Fullston *(A)*	41	73	13.26
K.M. Keenan *(NZ)*	55	70	17.90

•   •   •

A ustralian captain Belinda Clark became the greatest run scorer in women's one-day international cricket when she overtook Debbie Hockley's aggregate during her innings of 80 in the final of the World Series.
The leading run scorers are:

	Matches	Runs	Ave
B.J. Clark *(A)*	89	4077	54.36
D.A. Hockley *(NZ)*	118	4064	41.89
E.C. Drumm *(NZ)*	89	2424	34.14
K.L. Rolton *(A)*	67	2281	51.84
J.A. Brittin *(E)*	63	2121	42.42

•   •   •

W hen Rebecca Rolls caught Melanie Jones in the final she equalled Jane Cassar's record for most wicketkeeping dismissals in one-day internationals. The leaders in the keepers' list are:

	M	Total	ct	st
J. Cassar *(E)*	70	80	44	36
R.J. Rolls *(NZ)*	64	80	48	32
J.C. Price *(A)*	67	79*	54	25
C. Matthews *(A)*	47	49	35	14
S.L. Illingworth *(NZ)*	37	47	26	21 ·
A. Jain *(I)*	37	41	13	28

* Price also has one catch as a fielder

New Zealand's Debbie Hockley has the most catches by a fielder with 41 in 118 games, ahead of Australia's Belinda Clark who has 37 in 89 matches.

During the period covered by this edition of the *Almanack*, Daryl Tuffey captured a wicket in his first over in tests and one-day internationals on as many as eight occasions. He has now performed this feat a staggering 18 times in international matches, ten times in the first over of the game. He has twice taken two wickets in the first over of a match.

Tuffey took a wicket in his first over in three of India's four innings during the test series, including his first over in each innings of the second test at Hamilton, and twice dismissed Pakistan opener Mohammad Hafeez with the fourth ball of the match during the Bank AlFalah Cup. On the second occasion, which was the final, just for good measure Tuffey also produced a double wicket maiden to end the Pakistan innings.

• • •

Tuffey's first over successes in test cricket are:

					Inns	*Over*	*Ball*
M.E. Trescothick	lbw 0	v England	Auckland	2001/02	1	1	2
M.A. Butcher	c Richardson 0	v England	Auckland	2001/02	1	1	5
Shahid Afridi	c Hart 0	v Pakistan	Lahore	2001/02	1	1	3
V. Sehwag	bowled 2	v India	Wellington	2002/03	1	2	6
S.B. Bangar	c Oram 1	v India	Hamilton	2002/03	1	2	3
P.A. Patel	bowled 0	v India	Hamilton	2002/03	3	2	6
M.S. Atapattu	lbw 0	v Sri Lanka	Colombo	2002/03	2	1	4

Innings denotes innings of the match   *Over denotes over of the innings*

• • •

Tuffey's first over victims in one-day internationals are:

					Inns	*Over*	*Ball*
Saeed Anwar	bowled 0	v Pakistan	Napier	2000/01	1	1	1
Saeed Anwar	c Astle 2	v Pakistan	Christchurch	2000/01	2	1	6
M.S. Atapattu	lbw 0	v Sri Lanka	Sharjah	2000/01	1	1	2
K.C. Sangakkara	c Nevin 0	v Sri Lanka	Sharjah	2000/01	1	1	3
M.E. Trescothick	c Cairns 0	v England	Auckland	2001/02	1	1	3
S.T. Jayasuriya	lbw 0	v Sri Lanka	Sharjah	2001/02	1	1	3
Imran Nazir	lbw 0	v Pakistan	Rawalpindi	2001/02	2	1	1
S.C. Ganguly	bowled 0	v India	Napier	2002/03	2	1	3
S.C. Ganguly	c McCullum 0	v India	Wellington	2002/03	2	1	1
Mohammad Hafeez	c Styris 0	v Pakistan	Dambulla	2002/03	1	1	4
Mohammad Hafeez	c McCullum 0	v Pakistan	Dambulla	2002/03	1	1	4

Innings denotes innings of the match   *Over denotes over of the innings*

• • •

Former Pakistan test batsman Mohammad Wasim (who scored a century against New Zealand in his test debut in 1996/97) had a successful season for Otago, scoring 651 runs at 40.68 in the State Championship.

Wasim is not the first Pakistan test cricketer to play for Otago as Khalid "Billy" Ibadulla represented the province for three seasons from 1964/65. Ibadulla had been a regular member of the Warwickshire team since 1954 and scored 166 against Australia in his test debut in October 1964. Ibadulla was called into the Pakistan side for the third test of the series against New Zealand that summer and also toured England with the 1967 Pakistan team.

Ibadulla has been prominent in cricket coaching in Otago for many years. His son Kassem played for Otago from 1982/83 to 1990/91.

A number of other interesting overseas players have appeared for Otago over the years. Australian test batsman Harry Graham (century on test debut at Lord's in 1893) moved to Dunedin and played for Otago from 1903/04 to 1906/07. He also represented New Zealand against Australia.

Another Australian batsman, the legendary Charlie Macartney, had one season in 1909/10 while Bertie Tuckwell, who had played three times for Victoria in 1902/03, crossed the Tasman and ended up as a member of the New Zealand team which toured Australia in 1913/14.

Yet another Australian batsman to become domiciled in Dunedin was Ray Robinson who had played in the first test against England in 1936/37 (c Hammond b Voce in both innings without reaching double figures). Robinson played for Otago from 1946/47 to 1948/49.

In the mid-1960s Otago had the services of two players studying at the University's medical school, Samoan medium-pace bowler Ata Matatumua and West Indian Rudi Webster. Otago's league-of-nations side included all three of Ibadulla, Webster and Matatumua in two Plunket Shield games during the 1966/67 season. Webster, a fast bowler who played 60 matches for Warwickshire and is now a sports psychologist, has been part of the West Indies team management in recent seasons.

Neil Mallender spent ten seasons as Otago's overseas player from 1983/84 to 1992/93, capturing 268 wickets in first-class cricket. He is currently an international umpire and officiated in the World Cup in South Africa. Another player with a medical connection is Michael Austen, a doctor who arrived in New Zealand from South Africa in 1989 having previously represented Western Province.

England batsman Matthew Maynard spent two seasons with Otago in the late 1990s. In 1997/98 he reached a half century against Auckland off 22 balls, the fastest fifty in New Zealand domestic one-day cricket at the time.

• • •

Jesse Ryder became the youngest player to score a century in a first-class match for Central Districts when he made an unbeaten 114 against Canterbury at McLean Park. The only other player to register a hundred for Central while still a teenager was former New Zealand batsman John Guy, who was 19 years and 139 days when he made 115 against Otago in 1953/54.

Auckland's Rob Nicol scored his third century as a teenager when he made 147 not out against Northern Districts at Gisborne, having made two as an 18-year-old in his debut season. Only Giff Vivian, who made four centuries before his twentieth birthday (including three for New Zealand), has more first-class hundreds while still in his teens. Ian Rutherford made three centuries for Otago before he turned 20.

The youngest century makers in New Zealand first-class cricket are:

Age (year/days)			
16/277	F.A. Midlane	Wellington v Otago	1899/00
* 17/66 †	W.J. Mitchell	Northern Districts v Pakistan	1964/65
17/285	F.A. Midlane	Wellington v Auckland	1900/01
18/138	C.D. McMillan	Canterbury v Auckland	1994/95
18/190	I.A. Rutherford	Otago v Central Districts	1975/76
18/204	H.G. Vivian	New Zealand v Oxford University	1931
* 18/224	J.D. Ryder	Central Districts v Canterbury	2002/03
18/238	C.L. Cairns	Northern Districts v Auckland	1988/89
18/246	H.G. Vivian	New Zealand v Yorkshire	1931
18/274	R.J. Nicol	Auckland v Otago	2001/02
* 18/285	D.J. Hartshorn	Canterbury v Central Districts	1984/85
18/295	R.J. Nicol	Auckland v Canterbury	2001/02

† *first-class debut*
* *only first-class century*

W hen New Zealand met Australia in the ICC Champions Trophy in Colombo, the last wicket stand between Kyle Mills and Shane Bond ended up being the highest of the innings. This was only the fourth time that this had happened in a New Zealand innings, each time in a losing cause.

Stand	Total				
65	181	M.C. Snedden & E.J. Chatfield	v Sri Lanka	Derby	1983
46*	171-9	D.J. Nash & C. Pringle	v West Indies	Gauhati	1994/95
46	202	S.B. Styris & C.J. Drum	v India	Hyderabad	1999/00
50	132	K.D. Mills & S.E. Bond	v Australia	Colombo	2002/03

• • •

N ot only was the last wicket stand the best of the innings but Bond was also New Zealand's top-scorer. The list of players who have top-scored for their side while batting at number eleven in a one-day international is a very short one. Not surprisingly, perhaps, the team whose number eleven was top scorer lost the match on each occasion. The list reads:

Total				
171-9	S.B. Doull (34*)	New Zealand v West Indies	Gauhati	1994/95
192	P.J. Ongondo (36)	Kenya v West Indies	Nairobi	2001/02
132	S.E. Bond (26)	New Zealand v Australia	Colombo	2002/03
134	Shoaib Akhtar (43)	Pakistan v England	Cape Town	2002/03

Number eleven J. Garner scored 37 in West Indies' 228 against India at Manchester in 1983 being equal top score with A.M.E. Roberts who made 37 not out.

• • •

T he Marshall twins, James and Hamish, kept commentators and scorers on their toes when they shared in a hundred partnership in the State Shield final at North Harbour Stadium. This was the second time the brothers had recorded a century stand for Northern Districts. Their best partnerships together are (all for Northern):

First-class:

	wkt			
80	1st	v Wellington	Hamilton	1998/99
73	4th	v Canterbury	Christchurch	2001/02
67	1st	v Central Districts	Wanganui	1998/99
60	1st	v Wellington	Hamilton	1998/99
52	2nd	v Otago	Hamilton	2002/03

One-day:

	wkt			
112	4th	v Otago	Hamilton	2001/02
107	2nd	v Auckland	Auckland	2002/03
62	4th	v Otago	Alexandra	2001/02

• • •

I n New Zealand's opening match of the Bank AlFalah Cup in Sri Lanka, Pakistan lost their first three wickets before a run had been scored off the bat. Mohammad Hafeez, Faisal Iqbal and Yousuf Youhana had all been dismissed without scoring with the only runs being three wides, one leg-bye and one no-ball. After six overs the New Zealand bowling figures were Daryl Tuffey 3-1-3-1 (2 wides, 1 no-ball) and Shane Bond 3-2-1-2 (1 wide).
    The first runs off the bat came from the third ball of the seventh over when Taufeeq Umar took three off Tuffey.

During the Bank AlFalah Cup in Sri Lanka, New Zealand successfully defended their total of 156-8, bowling out the home team for just 147. The lowest one-day international totals that New Zealand has successfully defended are:

138-8*	v Australia (124)	Sydney	1982/83
153*	v England (144)	Auckland	1996/97
156-8	v Sri Lanka (147)	Dambulla	2002/03
158	v West Indies (154)	Georgetown	1995/96
183-8	v Sri Lanka (118-9)	Dunedin	1982/83
186-6	v Australia (156)	Dunedin	1985/86
187	v Pakistan (165)	Christchurch	1972/73
187-9*	v Pakistan (153-8)	Sialkot	1984/85

* overs had been reduced in these matches

• • •

New Zealand umpire Brent "Billy" Bowden had an eventful World Cup and beyond. The only official from New Zealand, Bowden was initially scheduled to stand in four matches during the group stages.

He received an unexpected bonus replacing England's Peter Willey who withdrew from the match between Zimbabwe and Australia at Bulawayo following the cancellation of England's game in Harare.

When the appointments were made for the Super Six matches Bowden was amongst the umpires named, being appointed ahead of some members of ICC's Elite Panel, and received further recognition by being named as fourth umpire for the final.

At the conclusion of the World Cup, Bowden was included on an enlarged ICC Panel and named to stand in one test (at the new venue of St Lucia) and three one-day internationals during Sri Lanka's tour to West Indies in June. He was also appointed to officiate in four matches of England's triangular series with Zimbabwe and South Africa and in the fourth test between England and South Africa at Leeds in August.

• • •

As if that wasn't enough, Bowden was also involved in some of the World Cup's more dramatic moments.

Bowden's first appointment was the match between Bangladesh and Sri Lanka at a new one-day international venue, City Oval, Pietermaritzburg. Just to get proceedings underway, Sri Lanka's Chaminda Vaas claimed a hat trick with the first three balls of the game and finished with four wickets in the first over.

Bowden then stood in the match between South Africa and Bangladesh at Bloemfontein, then went to Bulawayo for Zimbabwe against Australia, stood in Australia's match against Namibia at Potchefstroom and returned to Bulawayo for the game between Zimbabwe and Pakistan.

For the Super Six stage Bowden was appointed to Australia's match against Sri Lanka at Centurion and his final stint in middle was at Durban where surprise packet Kenya took on Australia. In this game, Brett Lee recorded the second hat trick of the tournament reducing his opponents to 3-3. As had been the case at Pietermaritzburg, Bowden watched from square leg as the drama unfolded.

• • •

New Zealand opening bowler Nicola Browne displayed her batting skills during the season when she became the first player to carry her bat through a completed innings in the State League.

In the match at Rangiora on 16 February, Browne opened the batting and was unbeaten on 50 from 93 balls when the Northern Districts innings ended at 94 after 40 overs. Canterbury scored 95-4 to win by six wickets.

Mayu Pasupati stole the show during Onslow's Pearce Cup senior club match against North City in March. The Onslow captain scored 30 in his first innings and then took 7-39 off 16 overs. On the second day Pasupati scored 50 off 25 balls followed by figures of 8.1-1-31-10. This was the best analysis recorded in Wellington club cricket in 127 years.

Pasupati became only the seventh player to take an all-ten in Wellington senior club cricket and his 17 wickets in the match have been bettered only once, when New Zealand all-rounder Ken Tucker took 9-46 in each innings for Wellington College Old Boys in 1915/16. The players who have taken ten wickets in one innings are:

10-120	L.F. Keys	Institute OB v Petone	1916/17
10-37	J.H. Hutchings	East v Thorndon	1919/20
10-32	W.A. Aldersley	Hutt v WCOB	1919/20
10-80	R.J. Duffy	Institute OB v Hutt	1934/35
10-59	G.F. Gillespie	Onslow v Karori	1976/77
10-72	A.G. Wharf	Johnsonville v Hutt	1996/97
10-31	M.Y. Pasupati	Onslow v North City	2002/03

• • •

During the past season Scott Styris and Mathew Sinclair both had the unusual, not to say bizarre, experience of being stumped without scoring in a test match. Nine New Zealand batsmen have perished in this fashion as the following table reveals:

M.L. Page	st Cameron b McMillan	South Africa	Christchurch	1931/32
J. Cowie	st Ames b Brown	England	Manchester	1937
J.W. Guy	st Binns b Smith	West Indies	Dunedin	1955/56
K.J. Wadsworth	st Bari b Pervez	Pakistan	Karachi	1969/70
V. Pollard	st Bari b Nazir	Pakistan	Lahore	1969/70
H.J. Howarth	st Taylor b Underwood	England	Christchurch	1970/71
S.P. Fleming *	st Healy b Warne	Australia	Hobart	1997/98
S.B. Styris	st Patel b Harbhajan	India	Wellington	2002/03
M.S. Sinclair	st Kaluwitharana b Muralitharan	Sri Lanka	Kandy	2002/03

* to complete a pair

• • •

Nathan Astle had a somewhat bizarre World Cup. He made 46 against West Indies, 54 against South Africa, 11 versus Canada and an unbeaten 102 against Zimbabwe – 213 for twice out. However, there were also three ducks, against Sri Lanka, Australia and India. In 22 World Cup matches Astle has been dismissed without scoring on five occasions.

Only Pakistan's Ijaz Ahmed, who played in 29 matches, has as many World Cup ducks. At the other end of the scale, Steve Waugh played in 33 World Cup games without ever being out for nought. Next best is none other than Chris Harris, who has played in 28 World Cup matches without registering the dreaded zero.

• • •

After being dismissed for nought against Sri Lanka in New Zealand's opening match of the World Cup, Astle dropped down to number three for the remainder of the tournament. This was the first time in five years and 113 one-day internationals that Astle had not opened the batting, the last occasion being on 16 January, 1998, when he batted at number five against South Africa in the Carlton & United Series (Bryan Young and Craig Spearman opened).

Over his entire career Astle has opened 154 times (taking the first ball just twice), has come in at number three on eight occasions (six times in the 2003 World Cup), batted at number four twice, number five once, number six four times (including his first two matches) and number seven on two occasions.

New Zealand took the unusual step of omitting left-arm spinner Daniel Vettori from their side for the sixth one-day international against India at Eden Park. As it happened, India also went into the game without a specialist slow bowler, the first time in 21 years (and only the third time ever) that neither side had taken a spinner into a one-dayer at Eden Park.

In 1980/81 New Zealand's attack consisted of Hadlee, Troup, Chatfield, Snedden, Coney and Cairns while India had Kapil Dev, Ghavri, Binny, Yograj Singh and Patil. The following season Australia used Thomson, Alderman, Pascoe, Chappell and Lillee with New Zealand's attack made up of Cairns, Hadlee, Snedden, Coney, Troup and Crowe.

In the most recent instance New Zealand's attack was Tuffey, Bond, Adams, Mills, Styris and Harris while India had Srinath, Zaheer Khan, Nehra, Agarkar, Bangar and Ganguly. By coincidence, although he was not used, India did have one part-time slow bowler in Yuvraj Singh, who is the son of Yograj Singh who played in the 1980/81 match.

●　　●　　●

Daniel Vettori had an unusual season. With the pace bowlers dominating during the test series against India, Vettori was not required to bowl a single over. In his last test in New Zealand, against England at Auckland, Vettori had bowled just two overs.

In the first one-day international which followed, the faster bowlers were again in total control but, with the score at 107-8, Vettori finally got to catch his captain's eye, sending down the 32nd over of the innings and dismissing Zaheer Khan. The Indian innings ended in the next over without Vettori being required again. Vettori played in five of the six remaining one-dayers contributing 21 overs (8, 0, 2, 5, 6).

By the time New Zealand went to Sri Lanka for the test series in April, Vettori had not bowled more than ten overs in an innings at all during 2003. His last significant bowling spell had been the 27 overs sent down in one innings for Northern Districts against Canterbury in early December.

Vettori finally got to the bowling crease in a test match sending down 33 overs in Sri Lanka's only innings at Colombo. More bowling beckoned in the second test at Kandy but as luck (or bad luck) would have it, Vettori was injured while batting and could not bowl at all during Sri Lanka's first innings of 97.3 overs. A token six overs in the second innings gave him a return of just 39 overs in four tests in 2002/03.

●　　●　　●

Despite his lack of opportunity, Vettori came close to achieving what would have been just the second hat trick for New Zealand in test cricket.

Vettori began the 152nd over of the Sri Lankan innings with figures of 32-7-94-0 and the score 483-7. With his second ball he trapped Kumar Dharmasena lbw and next ball Prabath Nissanka went the same way. Muttiah Muralitharan survived two extremely close lbw appeals before succumbing to a third.

Vettori's spell bears a remarkable resemblance to that of Peter Petherick, who took New Zealand's only hat trick, in his test debut at Lahore in 1976/77. Petherick had sent down 15.2 (eight-ball) overs and had figures of 0-97 before he dismissed Javed Miandad (163 on debut), Wasim Raja and Intikhab Alam with successive balls. Petherick finished with 3-103 off 18 overs. Intikhab, the third victim of the hat trick, was caught by his Surrey team mate, Geoff Howarth, at silly mid off.

●　　●　　●

Vettori was also made to wait for his World Cup debut. With conditions suiting the faster bowlers in England in 1999, Vettori did not get to play a single game. In the opening match of the 2003 tournament in South Africa, New Zealand opted for an all-pace attack and Vettori once more found himself on the sidelines – a total of ten World Cup games as a spectator.

He returned to the team for the next match against West Indies, however, and went on to bowl his full complement of ten overs in six of the remaining games.

Promising Auckland pace bowler Gareth Shaw had an interesting time in the State Shield match against Otago at Eden Park Outer Oval on 7 January. At first glance, Shaw's figures of 9-2-24-3 in Otago's total of 121 all out appear very creditable but they do not tell the full story.

Shaw's figures include 12 wides (half the runs he conceded) and overall there were 21 runs from wides in Otago's total. In his third over, bowling both sides of the wicket, Shaw sent down seven wides for a thirteen-ball over. The sequence was wide, wide, wicket, dot, wide, wide, 1 run, dot, wide, wide, wide, dot, dot. Otago opener Mohammad Wasim, possibly taken by surprise, missed a straight ball and was given out lbw.

• • •

Jacob Oram and Daniel Vettori won the Double Wicket World Championship held in St Lucia in April. The New Zealand pair went through the entire competition without losing a game.

In the early rounds they defeated Sri Lanka (Mahela Jaywardene and Aravinda de Silva), South Africa (Allan Donald and Steve Elworthy) and Australia (Greg Blewett and John Davison). England (Adam Hollioake and Andy Flintoff) were seen off in the semi-final and the Sri Lankan pair were beaten for a second time in the final.

Scores in the final were: **Sri Lanka** 70 (de Silva 47, Jayawardene 22, Vettori 2-49, Oram 1-50) **lost to New Zealand** 149 (Oram 106, Vettori 37, de Silva 0-82, Jayawardene 2-84) by 79 runs.

Oram hit 13 sixes in his innings of 106, and was the only century maker of the tournament. His 50 came up off 17 balls, and his century from 40 balls.

• • •

The World Indoor Cricket Championships were held in Wellington during September and October with Australia defeating New Zealand in both the men's and women's finals. Sri Lanka and India entered a team in each section while the men's group also included a team from England.

Players with first-class or domestic one-day experience in the New Zealand men's team were Leigh Kelly, Brendon Donkers, Guy Coleman, Gareth Irwin, Iain O'Brien and Mark Orchard. In the women's team were New Zealand representatives Maia Lewis, Helen Watson and Donna Trow.

• • •

North Harbour Stadium in Albany became the 60th first-class venue in New Zealand when Auckland hosted Otago from 9-12 January. It was the seventh ground used by Auckland who, since 1877/78, have also played at the Domain, Victoria Park, Eden Park, Cornwall Park, Eden Park Outer Oval and Colin Maiden Park.

The number of grounds used by each major association for first-class cricket is:

Grounds		Seasons
10	Otago	1863/64-2002/03
10	Northern Districts	1956/57-2002/03
9	Central Districts	1950/51-2002/03
7	Auckland	1877/78-2002/03
7	Canterbury	1864/65-2002/03
5	Wellington	1873/74-2002/03
4	Hawke's Bay	1884/85-1920/21
2	Taranaki	1891/92-1897/98
2	Nelson	1874/75-1887/88
1	Southland	1914/15-1920/21

Three other Canterbury first-class venues, Temuka Oval, Lincoln Green and Bert Sutcliffe Oval, have not been used by the provincial side.

When India took the field at Westpac Stadium in Wellington on 8 January, they became the first overseas team to play at nine different one-day international venues in New Zealand. Curiously, New Zealand has also only played at nine home grounds with the previous match in the series, when Queenstown hosted its first game, being New Zealand's ninth. Queenstown became the 144th venue to host a one-day international.

New Zealand has ten grounds which have been used for one-day internationals but Pukekura Park in New Plymouth has hosted only one game – Sri Lanka against Zimbabwe in the 1992 World Cup. India has played the first match at four of the venues. New Zealand's one-day international grounds are:

	Ground	First Match	Season
1.	Jade Stadium, Christchurch	NZ v P	1972/73
2.	Carisbrook, Dunedin	NZ v A	1973/74
3.	Basin Reserve, Wellington	NZ v E	1974/75
4.	Eden Park, Auckland	NZ v I	1975/76
5.	Westpac Park, Hamilton	NZ v I	1980/81
6.	McLean Park, Napier	NZ v SL	1982/83
7.	Pukekura Park, New Plymouth	SL v Z	1991/92
8.	Owen Delany Park, Taupo	NZ v I	1998/99
9.	Westpac Stadium, Wellington	NZ v WI	1999/00
10.	Queenstown Events Centre	NZ v I	2002/03

India has used 36 venues for one-day internationals

. . .

New Zealand ran up a total of 241-7 against West Indies in their World Cup clash at Port Elizabeth without any of their batsmen reaching fifty. Top scorer was Nathan Astle with 46. New Zealand's highest totals without an individual half-century are:

				Top Scorer
257-8	v South Africa	Napier	1998/99	A.C. Parore (44)
244-8	v Pakistan	Auckland	1995/96	C.M. Spearman (48)
242-9	v India	Brisbane	1980/81	J.V. Coney (49)
241-7	v Pakistan	Manchester	1999	R.G. Twose (46)
241-7	v West Indies	Port Elizabeth	2002/03	N.J. Astle (46)
238-9	v Pakistan	Birmingham	1983	B.A. Edgar (44)
235-9	v Pakistan	Lahore	1995/96	S.P. Fleming (42)
235-9	v Australia	Sydney	2001/02	C.Z. Harris (42*)

The highest total by any team in a one-day international without an individual fifty is 265-6 by England against Zimbabwe at Harare, 2001/02 (M.R. Ramprakash 47).

. . .

The 2002/03 State Max competition was cancelled because of the players' strike. For the record, the intended schedule was:

	Northern Zone	**Southern Zone**
16 Nov	Auckland v Northern Districts	Canterbury v Wellington
16 Nov	Central Districts v Northern Districts	Canterbury v Otago
17 Nov	Auckland v Central Districts	Otago v Wellington

	Final
17 Nov	Winner Northern Zone v Winner Southern Zone

All matches were set down for Lloyd Elsmore Park in Howick, Auckland, with live coverage by Sky Television scheduled for both days.

B rendon McCullum played an unusual innings in the State Shield match between Otago and Central Distrcts at Carisbrook. McCullum scored 50 from 59 balls (his maiden one-day half-century) hitting five sixes but no fours.

The most sixes in a domestic one-day innings are:

Sixes

9	C.L. Cairns (143)	Canterbury v Auckland	Christchurch	1994/95
7	R.T. Latham (83)	Canterbury v Central Districts	Rangiora	1980/81
7	R.G. Petrie (85)	Wellington v Northern Districts	Mt Maunganui	1994/95
7	L.G. Howell (88)	Canterbury v Wellington	Christchurch	1998/99
6	B.G. Cooper (97*)	Northern Districts v Auckland	Gisborne	1982/83
6	C.M. Spearman (126)	Central Districts v Canterbury	Nelson	1997/98
6	C.D. McMillan (109*)	Canterbury v Central Districts	New Plymouth	2001/02
6	C.M. Spearman	Central Districts v Otago	New Plymouth	2002/03

• • •

T here was also some extraordinary batting in the earlier State Shield encounter between the two teams at Pukekura Park.

After Otago had reached 243, thanks to a 93 run partnership for the eighth wicket between Warren McSkimming and Nathan Morland, Central were coasting at 100-0 after 11 overs, 141-0 after 15 overs and 154-0 after 17.1 overs.

A remarkable collapse then saw Central lose all ten wickets for the addition of just 79 runs in 25.1 overs. Most amazingly, Central, who finished only 11 runs short of victory, still had 7.3 overs of their innings remaining when the last man was out. Craig Spearman reached his fifty from only 28 deliveries and was dismissed for 97 from 59 balls, having threatened to break Aravinda de Silva's record of 65 balls for the fastest domestic one-day century.

• • •

I n their previous game Central had suffered a similar collapse against Wellington. Spearman and Ryder had put on 110 before the first wicket fell in the fifteenth over and although Central went on to win with 16.2 overs remaining they had only three wickets in hand.

In the game that followed the match against Otago at New Plymouth, Central were 14-4 against Auckland when rain put an end to proceedings and in their next game they were bowled out for 67 by Canterbury. This sequence represented the loss of 24 wickets for just 160 runs – all after being 154-0.

• • •

N ew Zealand bowled India out for 99 in the second test at Hamilton after winning the toss and sending their opponents in to bat. It may be something of a surprise to find that, in the entire history of test cricket, a team deciding to bowl first has dismissed the other side for under 100 on just twelve occasions.

New Zealand has managed this twice, both times against India, home and away. The full list, with results from the perspective of the side which won the toss, reads:

				Toss won by	Result
45	England v Australia	Sydney	1886/87	P.S. McDonnell	*Lost*
71	Sri Lanka v Pakistan	Kandy	1994/95	Salim Malik	*Won*
75	England v Australia	Melbourne	1894/95	G. Giffen	*Lost*
77	England v Australia	Lord's	1997	M.A. Taylor	*Drawn*
82	West Indies v Australia	Brisbane	2000/01	S.R. Waugh	*Won*
83	India v New Zealand	Chandigarh	1999/00	S.P. Fleming	*Drawn*
83	Zimbabwe v England	Lord's	2000	N. Hussain	*Won*
87	Pakistan v England	Lord's	1954	L. Hutton	*Drawn*
90	Australia v West Indies	Port-of-Spain	1977/78	C.H. Lloyd	*Won*
90	Bangladesh v Sri Lanka	Colombo	2001/02	S.T. Jayasuriya	*Won*
94	New Zealand v West Indies	Bridgetown	1984/85	I.V.A. Richards	*Won*
99	India v New Zealand	Hamilton	2002/03	S.P. Fleming	*Won*

The New Zealand Defence Force men's cricket team visited Australia in November playing six matches in Brisbane. Details were:

NZDF 235 (G. Whitley 51) **defeated Enoggera** 147-8 by 88 runs
NZDF 206-8 (G. Whitley 55, N. Hodges 54) **defeated Australian Army** 157 by 49 runs
Royal Australian Air Force 254-8 **defeated NZDF** 241(G. Whitley 69) by 13 runs
Royal Australian Navy 210 **lost to NZDF** 211-8 (D. Hamilton 83*, D. Robinson 50) by 2 wkts
Queensland Cricket Academy U19 268-6 **defeated NZDF** 171 (G. Whitley 53) by 97 runs
NZDF 153 **lost to Australian Defence Force** 157-6 by 4 wickets

. . .

The Royal New Zealand Air Force's women's team took part in the Victorian Women's Cricket Association Country Carnival in March. Details were:

RNZAF 127-7 (R. Blucher 35) **defeated East Gippsland** 125-5 by 2 runs
Hamilton/Gisborne 142-9 **lost to RNZAF** 146-1 (A. Walding 51, R. Blucher 50*) by 9 wkts
Albury v RNZAF abandoned
RNZAF 165-5 (R. Blucher 50) **defeated Shepparton** 89-8 by 76 runs

. . .

The Air Force team won the New Zealand Defence Force Cricket Tournament, held at Blenheim in February, for the third year in a row. Corporal Dallas Hamilton was named player of the tournament. In the RNZAF Inter Base Tournament, Ohakea won the men's title for the fourth time in five years and the women's title for the first time. Scores were:

Men: **Ohakea** 257-5 (M. Beaven 111, P. Roe 69) **defeated Wellington** 183 (M. Williams 67)
Women: **Woodbourne** 92 (K. Middlemiss 46) **lost to Ohakea** 93-4

. . .

Wellington won the inaugural Samsung Cricket Masters tournament which was held at Taupo in March, defeating Auckland by four runs in the final. **Wellington** made 196-9 (Andrew Jones 48, Erv McSweeney 39, Tim Ritchie 34) and **Auckland** 192 (Lindsay Crocker 45, Phil Horne 31, Bill Fowler 31). In the play-off for third and fourth **Central Districts** made 207 (Roger Pierce 38, Paul Gibbs 36, Barry Cooper 3-34) defeating **Northern Districts** 109 (Pierce 6-30) by 98 runs.

. . .

Former Otago, Wellington and Auckland batsman Ian Billcliff played for Canada during the World Cup in South Africa. Billcliff, who was born in Canada to New Zealand parents, scored 147 runs at 24.50 during the tournament with a highest score of 71 against Kenya at Cape Town.

. . .

During the Provincial A match between Wellington and Central Districts at the Basin Reserve, Central batsman Ross Taylor lofted a delivery from off-spinner Ben Jansen on to the roof of the R.A. Vance Stand.

The hit, which was in the vicinity of 120 metres, is believed to be the first to reach the upper arches of the distinctive stand. Taylor is a former New Zealand Under 19 captain who made his first-class debut during the 2002/03 season.

Shane Bond captured his 50th wicket in one-day internationals when he bowled Faisal Iqbal in New Zealand's first game in the Bank AlFalah Cup tournament in Sri Lanka. Bond was playing his 27th match, the least number required by any New Zealander to reach the landmark.

Geoff Allott held the previous New Zealand record, taking 28 matches, while the record for all countries is:

	Matches		*Matches*
A.B. Agarkar *(I)*	23	B.P. Patterson *(WI)*	26
D.K. Lillee *(A)*	24	C.E.L. Ambrose *(WI)*	26
S.K. Warne *(A)*	25	Waqar Younis *(P)*	27
L.S. Pascoe *(A)*	26	S.E. Bond *(NZ)*	27

• • •

New Zealand batsmen registered three centuries in one World Cup for the first time during the tournament in South Africa. In eight World Cups New Zealand has just eight centuries to its credit (scored by six batsmen), these being accumulated in four different years. None were scored in the 1979, 1983, 1987 or 1999 tournaments.

New Zealand's World Cup hundreds are:

171*	G.M. Turner	v East Africa	Birmingham	1975
114*	G.M. Turner	v India	Manchester	1975
100*	M.D. Crowe	v Australia	Auckland	1991/92
101	N.J. Astle	v England	Ahmedabad	1995/96
130	C.Z. Harris	v Australia	Madras	1995/96
141	S.B. Styris	v Sri Lanka	Bloemfontein	2002/03
134*	S.P. Fleming	v South Africa	Johannesburg	2002/03
102*	N.J. Astle	v Zimbabwe	Bloemfontein	2002/03

• • •

The first test between New Zealand and India began on 12 December, the earliest date that a test match has ever been staged at the Basin Reserve. Only one of the 146 tests staged in New Zealand, since the first in 1929/30, has ever been played earlier in the season.

Only nine tests have been played in New Zealand in December, all but one at either Hamilton or Wellington (who have hosted four Boxing Day tests). They are:

Dec				Dec			
8	v Pakistan	Christchurch	1995	26	v India	Wellington	1998
12	v India	Wellington	2002	26	v West Indies	Wellington	1999
16	v West Indies	Hamilton	1999	26	v Zimbabwe	Wellington	2000
18	v Bangladesh	Hamilton	2001	26	v Bangladesh	Wellington	2001
19	v India	Hamilton	2002				

• • •

Brendon McCullum had a productive time in his first season behind the stumps for New Zealand. In 19 one-day internationals he effected 39 dismissals, already placing himself third on the all-time New Zealand list behind Adam Parore (136) and Ian Smith (85).

In the second one-dayer at Napier he made four catches and a stumping, equalling Parore's New Zealand record of five dismissals and in the next match at Christchurch he became the first New Zealand keeper to take five catches in an innings, thus becoming the first wicketkeeper from any country to complete ten dismissals in successive games.

Previously South Africa's Dave Richardson had made nine dismissals in successive matches against Zimbabwe in 1995/96 while West Indies' Ridley Jacobs did the same during the World Cup in England in 1999.

For the first time in a New Zealand first-class season, there were two instances of teams registering a hundred partnership for the first wicket in each innings of a match. This is a rare feat having previously happened on just eleven occasions, nine times by the same pair in each innings and twice with a change in the batting order.

Mark Richardson and Tim McIntosh put on 104 and 118 for Auckland against Northern Districts at Eden Park's Outer Oval, becoming only the second Auckland pair to achieve the feat. The only other instance was the famous occasion against Canterbury in 1948/49 when Bert Sutcliffe and Don Taylor became the first pair in the history of first-class cricket to have double century opening partnerships in each innings of a match.

Otago's Craig Cumming and Mohammad Wasim put on 141 against Wellington at the Basin Reserve and in the second innings Cumming and Chris Gaffaney opened with 147. Gaffaney had been involved in an earlier instance with Robbie Lawson, also against Wellington, in 1996/97. Jim Shepherd and Rupert Worker (1923/24) and Glenn Turner and Wayne Blair (1972/73) also achieved the feat for Otago. *(Full details in New Zealand First-class Records)*

•   •   •

New Zealand reduced Pakistan to 17-5 in their opening match of the Bank AlFalah Cup, the second time during the season that they had captured five wickets in a one-day international before their opponent's score had reached 20.

Prior to the World Cup in South Africa, there had been only eight instances of this happening in all one-day internationals but there have been four cases since, including three during the World Cup. Details are:

Five for	Total			
12/5	71	Pakistan v West Indies (72-1)	Brisbane	1992/93
12/5	36	Canada v Sri Lanka (37-1)	Paarl	2002/03
14/5	81	Pakistan v West Indies (214-9)	Sydney	1992/93
14/5	43	Pakistan v West Indies (45-3)	Cape Town	1992/93
17/5	266-8	India v Zimbabwe (235)	Tunbridge Wells	1983
17/5	84	Kenya v Australia (85-2)	Nairobi	2002/03
17/5	84	Namibia v Pakistan (255-9)	Kimberley	2002/03
17/5	116	Pakistan v New Zealand (117-3)	Dambulla	2002/03
18/5	153	Pakistan v South Africa (156-3)	Colombo	2000/01
18/5	115-9	New Zealand v Sri Lanka (221-6)	Colombo	2000/01
19/5	167	Scotland v Pakistan (261-6)	Chester-le-Street	1999
19/5	77	Bangladesh v New Zealand (244-9)	Colombo	2002/03

•   •   •

There was some very fast scoring on the last afternoon of the State Championship match between Central Districts and Auckland at Horton Park in Blenheim. Auckland had squandered their first innings lead of 82 to be 122-9 on the last day before Heath Davis (who was injured and would not bowl) joined Kyle Mills to add 47 for the last wicket in 104 minutes to seemingly put the game out of Central's reach.

Central needed 252 from 32 overs at 7.87 per over when the overall scoring rate of the other three innings had only just exceeded two. Undaunted, Craig Spearman and Greg Loveridge began with 68 in 33 minutes. Fifty came in just 23 minutes and the hundred 30 minutes later. Central reached 150 in 88 minutes, as Spearman and Glen Sulzberger added 83 in 57 minutes, and 200 arrived after just 115 minutes. Andrew Schwass helped Spearman add 44 in 23 minutes and the 250 came up after 147 minutes as the home team raced to victory. Spearman reached fifty from 40 balls in 55 minutes and his century took only 77 balls and 121 minutes.

Mills conceded 73 runs from ten overs, Craig Pryor 57 from 8.2 and Auckland's captain, Brooke Walker, had 99 runs taken off 12 overs. In a final twist, with only medium-pacers and his own leg-spin to call on, Walker saw Auckland get through more overs than they actually needed to with the winning runs coming in the 33rd over.

A Wellington Under 16 girls development team visited South Africa in April, coached by former New Zealand opening batsman Bruce Edgar.

The team was: Olivia Dean, Hannah Bedford, Christina Boonen, Ella Brocklesby, Lucy Doolan, Paige Edgar, Holly Edgar, Philippa Gueorgieff, Rachel Harris, Amy Hensman, Emily Leslie, Priya Patel, Gina Ropiana and Alana Smith. The first two matches were played in Port Elizabeth, the others in Cape Town. Scores were:

Eastern Province 91 (P. Gueorgieff 2-12) **lost to Wellington** 94-2 (L. Doolan 41*) by 8 wkts
Wellington 121 (H. Bedford 19) **defeated Eastern Province** 89 (L. Doolan 6-17, P. Edgar 3-15) by 32 runs
Western Province 243-6 (P. Patel 3-18, P. Edgar 2-32) **defeated Wellington** 79 by 164 runs
Wellington 130-4 (H. Edgar 25*) **defeated Northern Suburbs** 119 (P. Edgar 2-16, P. Gueorgieff 2-22) by 11 runs
Wellington 206 (L. Doolan 117*) **defeated Southern Suburbs** 70 (P. Gueorgieff 2-6, A. Smith 2-7, C. Boonen 2-9) by 136 runs
Wellington 84 **defeated Pinelands High School** 57 (L. Doolan 3-6, G. Ropiana 3-10, P. Edgar 3-12) by 27 runs

• • •

D uring their 5-2 one-day series win against India, New Zealand won three games with more than 20 overs to spare. New Zealand's one-day wins with most overs remaining are:

Batting first:

Overs			
30.5	New Zealand (244-9) v Bangladesh (77)	Colombo	2002/03
23.3	New Zealand (276-7) v Australia (76)	Adelaide	1985/86

Batting second:

Overs			
32.1	Scotland (121) v New Zealand (123-4)	Edinburgh	1999
27	Canada (196) v New Zealand (197-5)	Benoni	2002/03
24.2	India (122) v New Zealand (123-3)	Queenstown	2002/03
23.1	India (108) v New Zealand (109-5)	Christchurch	2002/03
22.3	Pakistan (116) v New Zealand (117-3)	Dambulla	2002/03
21.4	Zimbabwe (138) v New Zealand (139-2)	Wellington	1997/98
21.2	India (122) v New Zealand (125-4)	Hamilton	2002/03
20.4*	Sri Lanka (206) v New Zealand (209-5)	Bristol	1983

* *60 overs per innings*

• • •

N athan Astle, Shane Bond and Stephen Fleming, who captained the side, were members of a Rest of the World XI which met The Brits in the inaugural Power Cricket series played at Cardiff's Millennium Stadium on 4 and 5 October.

The matches consisted of four innings of 15 overs each with bonuses for big hitting. Eight runs were scored for reaching the middle tier of seats, ten for a shot into the upper tier and twelve for hitting the closed roof. The World XI won both matches with Astle's 76 not out off 35 balls in the first game the highest score over the two days.

• • •

C hris Harris and Andre Adams played for a World XI in a match against the Netherlands to celebrate Hague CC's 125th jubilee in June. Harris scored 49 not out for the World XI, who made 225 for nine, and then took five for 41 as the home team were all out for 172.

Adams was one of five New Zealand player-coaches in the Dutch ten-team premier league in 2003 along with Darron Reekers, Tama Canning, David Kelly and Greg Todd, as well as Otago's Pakistan import Mohammad Wasim.

OBITUARIES

James Bernard CLARK

Born: Dunedin, 25 September, 1910

Died: Auckland, 21 January, 2003

Left-hand batsman, wicketkeeper

Bernie Clark, who at 92 had been Otago's oldest living first-class cricketer, played three games as wicketkeeper in the 1930s. His team mates included New Zealand representatives Sonny Moloney, Ced Elmes, George Dickinson, Jack Dunning and Ted Badcock as well as future rugby greats Vic Cavanagh and Charlie Saxton.

Clark, who played for the High School Old Boys and Albion clubs in Dunedin, came into the Otago side for the final Plunket Shield match of the 1933/34 season, taking over from Bill Hawksworth, who, two years earlier, had helped Roger Blunt put on 184 for the last wicket against Canterbury. This remains the highest last wicket partnership in New Zealand first-class cricket.

Clark made his debut against Wellington at Carisbrook on 16 February, 1934, in a match which Otago won by 199 runs. He made a very useful 25 batting at number ten, putting on 60 for the last wicket with Jack Dunning, before being bowled by future Governor-General Denis Blundell. Clark was also a member, and selector, of the High School Old Boys team which won the Dunedin senior club championship that season.

The following season Clark played in Otago's first two matches, against Wellington and Auckland. scoring 21 batting at number eleven in the latter game. However, by the time Otago's third and final Plunket Shield match took place, over seven weeks later, Frank Toomey had taken over as keeper and Clark was not to be called upon again.

Clark spent most of his working life with Whitcombe & Tombs (now Whitcoulls). He moved from Dunedin to Invercargill then to Auckland and from 1940 to 1958 was the accountant at head office in Christchurch. In 1947 he was one of the volunteers who helped fight the fire at Ballantyne's drapery store where 41 people died in New Zealand's worst fire disaster. In 1958 Clark was transferred to the London office and while in England took the opportunity to watch New Zealand play at Lord's.

Clark was the son of the famous Otago and New Zealand batsman Jim Baker who played a remarkable (for that period) 37 games for the province between 1889/90 and 1906/07, and was sole New Zealand selector from 1900 to 1906. Baker was born Clark but his mother remarried and for a while he took the surname Baker, then Clark-Baker, but when son Bernie was born the surname Clark was preferred.

A second member of the family represented New Zealand when Clark's granddaughter, Jessica Chapman, took part in the women's world snooker championships in England in April, 2003.

Clark's record in first-class cricket is:

M	I	NO	HS	Runs	Ave	ct
3	5	1	25	63	15.75	5

Donald Barry CLARKE

Born: *Pihama, 10 November, 1933*
Died: *Johannesburg, 29 December, 2002*
Right-hand batsman, right-arm fast-medium bowler

Legendary All Black fullback and goalkicker Don Clarke also had a successful cricket career as a fast-medium bowler for Auckland and Northern Districts.

Waikato-based Clarke made his debut for Auckland against Central Districts (in the days before the formation of the Northern Districts association) in the final Plunket Shield match of the 1950/51 season aged just 17. His figures of 4-31 in his first outing prompted the *Almanack* to say "He gives promise of developing into one of Auckland's main bowlers of the future. He is also a very promising representative Rugby footballer for Waikato in the full-back position. Stands 6 feet 2 inches and scales over 15 stone."

Earlier in the season Clarke had taken 5-30 for Waikato against Bay of Plenty in a Hawke Cup elimination match and 4-73 for Country against Town in the annual trial match. After Christmas he had success for Auckland Colts taking 7-28 against Bay of Plenty and 5-30 versus Hawke's Bay and at the end of the season he routed Wairarapa, returning figures of 8-41 off 15.4 overs in Waikato's successful challenge for the Hawke Cup.

After a football injury casued him to miss the 1951/52 season, Clarke reappeared for Auckland the following summer, capturing 12 wickets in four games, including match figures of 8-86 against Otago. He was very successful in 1953/54, capturing 24 wickets at 17.41 including two bags of five wickets – 5-64 against Canterbury and 5-47 against Otago – both second innings efforts. The *Almanack* said "... Don Clarke, whose fast-medium deliveries were sometimes quite hostile."

The following season Clarke repeated his haul of 24 wickets and at the end of the summer gained selection for North Island against the South in the trial match to help choose the New Zealand side to play England. He also appeared for the newly formed Northern Districts side, who, in an effort to gain first-class status, played three-day matches against Auckland, Canterbury and Central Districts. Clarke took 26 wickets in these three games, including a match return of 15-167 against Auckland. He also top scored in both innings against Canterbury making 68 not out and 68.

Football commitments and injuries meant Clarke played just once in the next two seasons (for the newly formed Northern Districts side) but he was back as a regular in 1957/58. He captured 24 wickets at 18.41 (including 5-82 against Auckland) and was by far and away Northern's most successful bowler. He was chosen for the Rest which played a New Zealand XI in a trial for the 1958 tour to England but bowled only a handful of overs.

After an absence of five years, Clarke reappeared 1962/63 for one final season, capturing 20 wickets as Northern won the Plunket Shield for the first time. In the match against Central Districts, played on what the *Almanack* described as "an inferior Wanganui wicket", he was almost unplayable. Bowling unchanged through Central's second innings of 71, his figures read 22.3-13-37-8 (the last four wickets taken at no cost) and Northern recovered from a first innings deficit to win by five wickets. As well as recording his best first-class figures in this match, and capturing ten wickets in a match for the only time, Clarke also hit his highest score of 47, coming in when Northern were 90-7 and being last out at 172.

Northern won three matches outright that season and gained first innings points in another to finish at the top of the table. Their only reversal came against Wellington when John Reid played his famous innings of 296, including the then world record total of 15 sixes. Reid scored his runs in just 220 minutes with 230 of them coming in boundaries. The *Almanack* noted that "Reid had been quite impartial in hitting his 6's, four being off Shaw, three each off Barton, Clarke and Alabaster, and two off Puna." Even so, in the total of 422 Clarke's final figures of 3-82 off 27 overs were quite respectable and it was only a final onslaught by Reid which saw 31 runs taken off his last five overs.

Former New Zealand wicketkeeper Eric Petrie played alongside Clarke for both Auckland and Northern Districts and thought that Clarke was unlucky to miss selection for the 1958 tour to England. He said that Clarke got a lot of late movement, was able to get a bit of lift from a normal wicket and got the ball up quite substantially at times as well as being able to bowl long spells if required. He also remembered Clarke as "a darned big hitter of the ball."

Clarke's prolific goalkicking, with the old-fashioned front-on style, dominated the world rugby scene during his international career which began in 1956 and was ended by a recurring knee injury in 1964. In 89 matches for New Zealand, including 31 tests, he scored 781 points (207 in tests). In all first-class rugby he totalled 1851 points in 226 matches.

In 1951, in his first season with Waikato, as a 17-year-old, he kicked two fine penalty goals on a heavy ground to help take the Ranfurly Shield from North Auckland. In the first test against the British Lions in 1959, his six penalty goals (the last two minutes from time) gave the All Blacks an 18-17 win over the visitors, who had scored four tries to nil. From his debut against South Africa in 1956 he was the first choice as All Black fullback until his retirement, missing just one test through injury. Apart from his kicking prowess he was a fine fullback with good positional sense, safe hands and a very difficult man to beat.

Clarke's brother Doug, a wicketkeeper batsman, played in six matches fror Northern with the brothers playing together against Auckland in 1957/58. Don, Doug and their three brothers, Brian and Graeme and All Black Ian, grew up on the family farm near Morrinsville. They all played rugby for Waikato during the 1950s and on one occasion, against Thames Valley in 1961, all five played together in the same game.

Clarke and his family moved to South Africa in 1977 where he worked for a manufacturing company and then as a sales manager for South African Breweries before setting up his own tree-felling business.

Clarke's record in first-class cricket is:

Season	M	I	NO	HS	Runs	Ave	50	ct	Wkts	Runs	Ave	5W	10W	Best
1950/51	2	4	2	6 *	8	4.00	–	– `	5	138	27.60	–	–	4-31
1952/53	4	8	4	25 *	84	21.00	–	2	14	389	27.78	–	–	4-38
1953/54	4	7	1	8	20	3.66	–	2	24	418	17.41	2	–	5-47
1954/55	5	9	2	23	40	5.71	–	–	24	549	22.87	–	–	4-45
1956/57	1	2	1	34 *	35	35.00	–	1	5	125	25.00	–	–	4-108
1957/58	6	11	3	29 *	107	13.37	–	2	25	472	18.88	1	–	5-82
1962/63	5	7	0	47	75	10.71	–	2	20	383	19.15	1	1	8-37
TOTAL	**27**	**48**	**13**	**47**	**369**	**10.54**	**–**	**9**	**117**	**2474**	**21.15**	**4**	**1**	**8-37**

For	M	I	NO	HS	Runs	Ave	50	ct	Wkts	Runs	Ave	5W	10W	Best
Auckland	14	27	9	25 *	152	8.44	–	4	66	1452	22.00	2	–	5-47
ND	11	19	3	47	212	13.25	–	5	49	950	19.38	2	1	8-37
North Island	1	1	0	0	0	0.00	–	–	1	42	42.00	–	–	1-42
Rest	1	1	1	5 *	5	–	–	–	1	30	30.00	–	–	1-14
TOTAL	**27**	**48**	**13**	**47**	**369**	**10.54**	**–**	**9**	**117**	**2474**	**21.15**	**4**	**1**	**8-37**

John HILL

Born: Gore, 22 September, 1930

Died: Invercargill, 26 August, 2002

Right-hand batsman, left-arm medium-pace bowler

Left-arm seamer John Hill played in eight first-class games in the early 1960s and represented Southland for over a decade. He first appeared for Southland in the 1953/54 season and hit the headlines two years later playing against the touring West Indies team.

During their two month tour, the West Indies played matches against minor associations Northland, Hawke's Bay, Nelson, North Otago, Waikato and Southland. The match at Invercargill was played early in the tour with Southland being bundled out for 139 on the first day after they had been 107-3 at lunch. The tourists, whose batting lineup included Gary Sobers, Collie Smith and Everton Weekes, were expected to pile on the runs but with New Zealand representatives Guy Overton and Jack Alabaster keeping one end under control, Hill ran through the visitors' batting and by stumps had taken 7-43 off 18.4 overs.

He added another victim the next morning to finish with 8-55 from 21.1 overs as West Indies were dismissed for 153. Southland made only 67 in their second innings but West Indies still lost five wickets chasing the target of just 54. Hill dismissed Sobers for a second time having also claimed the wickets of Smith and Weekes in the first innings.

Hill also had a successful time against the a major associations that season taking 6-42 against Canterbury, 4-60 against Auckland and capturing seven wickets in the match with Wellington. In March, Hill was selected for the New Zealand Colts team which met West Indies at Palmerston North in the final match of their tour but went wicketless as the tourists found some batting form. Rumour had it that Hill had come close to making the New Zealand team for the fourth test in Auckland, which, as it turned out, provided New Zealand with its historic first test win.

Despite his good showing in 1955/56 and consistent performances for Southland in subsequent years, Hill had to wait until the 1961/62 season, when he was 31 years old, to get the call up to the Otago team. Hill made his first-class debut at the Basin Reserve on Christmas Day, 1961, one of six players in the Otago team new to first-class cricket. The powerful Wellington eleven included five players who had represented New Zealand and their win by an innings and 95 runs was not totally unexpected. Hill, however, had a good first up game taking 4-76 off 24 overs. His victims were Bruce Murray, Barry Sinclair, John Beck and Les Butler all of whom had either played or would play for New Zealand.

Hill played only once more that summer but was a regular in the Otago lineup the following season, capturing 14 wickets in six games. He took 3-70 against Auckland and 3-42 against Northern Districts but saved his best performance for what turned out to be his final appearance in first-class cricket. Otago, who had been given permission to bolster their side with Bevan Congdon, Bruce Pairaudeau, Bert Sutcliffe and John Ward, met MCC just prior to the final test of the short tour. Hill finished with 4-61 off 25 overs, capturing the wickets of Peter Parfitt, Colin Cowdrey, Barry Knight and Fred Trueman and at one stage taking three wickets for two runs in 11 balls.

Hill also excelled at rugby and hockey. At Gore High School he played halfback alongside future All Blacks Robin Archer and Tuppy Diack and went on to represent Eastern Southland. After a broken wrist ended his rugby career he took up hockey and played for Eastern for several years at centre foward.

Hill's son Robbie also gave great service to Southland, appearing in over one hundred representative matches and playing for Otago from 1976/77 to 1989/90.

Hill's record in first-class cricket is:

M	I	NO	HS	Runs	Ave		ct		Wkts	Runs	Ave	Best
8	15	9	10	31	5.20		3		19	483	25.42	4-76

Stanley Neville JAMES

Born: *Wanganui, 3 January, 1932*

Died: *Wanganui, 12 October, 2002*

Right-hand batsman, right-arm medium-pace bowler

Medium-pace bowler Stan James appeared in one first-class match for Otago in the 1953/54 season. A member of the Albion-YMCA club, at a time when the two were amalgamated, James was one of nine players Otago introduced to first-class cricket that season.

James' representative career had begun the season before when he turned out for Wanganui. He took part in the Hawke Cup challenge when Wanganui lifted the trophy from Nelson, winning by just 13 runs

Moving to Dunedin, James appeared in an early season match against North Otago the next summer, taking 3-34 and 2-54, and was one of five players new to first-class cricket brought into the side to play against the touring Fijian side in February after the conclusion of the Plunket Shield. The Fijians played 17 matches with the games against Otago, Canterbury, Wellington and Auckland being ranked as first-class.

In the match at Carisbrook, Fiji scored 206 with James, who opened the bowling with future test bowler Frank Cameron, having 0-23 from six overs. Otago declared at 251-8 and then bowled Fiji out for 240. James captured his only wicket taking 1-50 from 14 overs. He dismissed Nat Uluiviti who went on to play Plunket Shield cricket for Auckland the following season while at University and who, coincidentally, had also earlier played for Wanganui, while attending the Technical College. Otago hit off the required 196 in even time. Cameron and Lankford Smith shared an unbroken ninth wicket stand of 35 to win the game, James padded up but again was not required to bat.

James returned to play for Wanganui, who still held the Hawke Cup, and opened the bowling for them for several more seasons. His best efforts in that time were 6-41 v Hawke's Bay in March 1957 and 5-70 v Manawatu and 5-63 and 6-67 v Waikato in a Hawke Cup challenge match in December the same year.

James initially worked for New Zealand Railways as a fitter and turner in Wanganui and then at Hillside Workshops in Dunedin. He was appointed assistant superintendent at the Manapouri Dam during its commissioning in the late 1960s. He spent 30 years at Manapouri and four at Monowai where he was involved with the installation of the television translator.

Despite suffering from multiple sclerosis from his late thirties, he was very active in the community and pursued such diverse interests as pig hunting, rugby union, ballroom dancing and involvement with the Te Anau Rotary Club.

John Logan JOLLY

Born: *Cromwell, 27 July, 1912*

Died: *Sydney, 9 July, 1995*

Left-hand batsman, right-arm medium-pace bowler

Jack Jolly played in one first-class match for Otago in 1933/34. Although he died in Sydney as long ago as 1995, details of his death have only recently come to light.

He was a member of the Otago University team when it entered senior ranks in the 1931/32 season and was one of five players in the side who appeared in first-class cricket, Norm Henderson, Bill Hawksworth, Alec Priest and Jim McHaffie being the others. In April 1933 Jolly scored an unbeaten 183 for Otago against Canterbury in the annual intercollege match played at Christ's College in Christchurch. Peter Howden, who is now Otago's oldest living first-class cricketer, scored 135 in the same innings. In four years Jolly also took 19 wickets in these games.

Jolly also had some notable performances in the Dunedin club competition where he captured 167 wickets at 14.77 in 48 matches for University. He took 8-45 against Old Boys and 7-18 against Albion early in 1933/34, form which earned him a place in the Otago side for an early season game against Southland. His only appearance in first-class cricket came in Otago's second Plunket Shield match of the summer which began at Eden Park on 30 December, 1933.

As many as eleven of the players who appeared in this match would represent New Zealand at some stage of their careers. Otago had Sonny Moloney, Ced Elmes, Jack Dunning and Ted Badcock while Auckland's lineup included Paul Whitelaw, Jack Mills, Lindsay Weir, Giff Vivian, Merv Wallace, Raoul Garrard and Mal Matheson. In addition, Auckland had All Black Ron Bush and in the Otago side Vic Cavanagh (who had been twelfth man against England the previous season) became an outstanding coach of the Otago rugby team.

Badcock, Dunning and Elmes (aided by three run outs) restricted the strong Auckland batting lineup to 263. Jolly, who opened the bowling, finished with 0-45 off 17 overs. Otago replied with 213 (Jolly caught and bowled by Bush for 10) and then Auckland ran up a lead of 380. Jolly had almost identical figures to his first effort taking 0-46 from 17 overs. Otago were then bowled out for 211 with Jolly out for 2, again a victim of Bush.

Jolly played against Hawke's Bay on the journey back home but Otago's third and final Plunket Shield match of the season did not take place for another six weeks. By the time the game took place, four of the players who played against Auckland had been replaced, Jolly being one of them. In 1936 Jolly was one of the recipients of the first cricket Blues awarded by New Zealand Universities.

Mark Moreton PARKER

Born: *Timaru, 2 October, 1975*
Died: *Kuta, Bali, 12 October, 2002*
Right-hand batsman

Mark Parker, who lost his life in the terrorist attack in Bali, played in three first-class matches for Otago in the 1996/97 season. He was holidaying on the island while returning from a successful summer playing for St Cross Symondians in the Southern Electric Premier Cricket League in England.

Parker appeared for Canterbury in the National Under 18 Tournament in 1992/93, hitting 89 against Central Districts, and the following season returned with scores of 71 against Otago and 77 versus Auckland. He was also in the Canterbury Under 20 side that summer and gained promotion to the second eleven side in the national competition.

He was also a member of the South Canterbury team which challenged Manawatu for the U-Bix Cup and gained a valuable early cricket lesson when he had to field for almost two full days watching the holders run up 650-9 before declaring and was then dismissed for a duck in the few overs remaining before stumps. Former Canterbury batsman and current Otago captain Craig Cumming was Parker's opening partner on that occasion.

Moving to Dunedin, Parker represented Otago in the National Second Eleven and Under 20 Tournaments in 1994/95 and 1995/96, being named Under 20 Tournament team captain in his second year alongside players such as Jacob Oram, Joseph Yovich, Gareth Hopkins, David Sewell and Grant Donaldson.

In 1996/97 Parker hit 57 against Canterbury in an early season second eleven game and in February he was called up into the Otago Shell Trophy side to replace Matt Horne who had been chosen to make his test debut against England. Batting in Horne's number three spot, Parker made 11 and 14 (dismissed by Scott Styris on both occasions) as Otago beat Northern Districts by five wickets at Molyneux Park. He also snapped up three catches.

Otago repeated their five wicket win when they met Central Districts at Invercargill, Parker making 7 and 13, and then made 311-7 in the fourth innings to defeat Wellington at the Basin Reserve. Parker made just 1 and 4 in this match and was not in the eleven for the final match of the round robin. Although Otago lost this game, they still finished in second place and met Canterbury in the final only to be on the receiving end of the New Zealand record score of 777 all out.

Transferring to Wellington, Parker linked up with the Onslow club for two seasons and had been intending to return to New Zealand to make one final effort to establish himself on the first-class scene. He had had three successful seasons in Hampshire, and led his Winchester-based club to second place and promotion from the Southern Premier League Division Three in 2002 with 757 runs (including two centuries) at an average of 84.11 – the best in any of the three divisions. A popular figure with his team-mates at St Cross, he was due to return for another season in 2003.

Parker was the son of former Otago, Canterbury and New Zealand batsman Murray Parker and nephew of John Parker (Northern Districts and New Zealand) and Ken Parker (Auckland).
Parker's record in first-class cricket is:

M	I	NO	HS	Runs	Ave	ct
3	6	0	14	50	8.33	5

Edward Richard TOVEY

Born: Sydney, 25 December, 1930

Died: Sydney, 31 May, 2002

Right-hand batsman, wicketkeeper

Dick Tovey was an outstanding wicketkeeper and a more than useful batsman who played a major part in Auckland winning the Plunket Shield in 1963/64 and he may well have come close to gaining New Zealand selection that season.

Born at King's Cross on Christmas Day, 1930, Tovey was educated at Newington College in Sydney, representing the school at cricket, rugby union and athletics. In his final year he was chosen to keep wickets for the GPS First XI before joining the Paddington club, where his consistent form behind the stumps gained him selection for the state Colts' side against Queensland Colts in successive seasons from 1953/54. In the first of these matches, he hit 69, dominating a fifth-wicket partnership of 99 in only 56 minutes with Bill Watson.

In 1956 the firm of James North, for whom he worked as a sales representative, transferred Tovey to Brisbane, where he played for the South Brisbane club. He gained selection for Queensland against his old state in the opening Sheffield Shield match of the 1957/58 season but was dropped after an uncharacteristically poor match with the gloves. In 1959 he was again transferred, this time to Auckland, where he played with the Papatoetoe club and represented Auckland over three seasons.

His debut for Auckland was actually against Dennis Silk's visiting MCC side in the opening match of their tour in December 1960. In his first Plunket Shield match Tovey claimed six catches in the match against Northern Districts and finished the season with 17 dismissals in six games.

Unavailable for away matches, Tovey appeared just once over the next two seasons but was a regular and important member of the side which won the Plunket Shield in 1963/64. Not only did he excel with his keeping but he played a vital role with the bat. When Tovey first came in to the Auckland side he had batted as high as number seven but by the start of the 1963/64 season he was batting at number eleven and had just 60 runs to show from 14 innings.

In the second match of the season, he came in as nightwatchman against Otago, signalling a change in his batting fortunes by making 41 and sharing a 77 run partnership for the third wicket with Ross Morgan in an otherwise low scoring game. He also took seven catches in the match, equalling the Auckland record which was not broken until 1988/89 when Ian Smith took eight catches against Central Districts.

In their penultimate match, Auckland were dismissed for just 69 by Northern Districts and at 135-6 in their second innings, following on, looked to have lost all chance of winning the Shield. Tovey joined John Behrent, however, and the pair proceeded to add 129, still Auckland's seventh wicket record against Northern. The partnership took only 100 minutes with Behrent making 74 in 118 minutes and Tovey 62 in 109 minutes. Bob Sutton and Bob Cunis managed a valuable 24 for the last wicket, leaving Northern 149 to win in 140 minutes (there were no over rate conditions in force at the time). Fine bowling by Hedley Howarth, who finished with 5-32, saw Auckland win a thrilling game by eight runs with four balls left in the match. This remains one of only four occasions in New Zealand first-class cricket when a side has won after following on.

In their final match, Auckland not only had to beat Wellington outright to win the title but they also had to prevent Wellington from gaining a first innings lead. In their first innings, Wellington were bowled out for just 157 with Tovey taking four catches and a stumping to equal the Auckland record of five dismissals in an innings. (This record was only beaten this past season when Reece Young took six catches against Wellington.) Auckland, however, crashed to 95-7 at the hands of Bob Blair and John Reid and it seemed the battle for the Plunket Shield was over.

At that stage Tovey and Behrent joined forces again and took the score to 131 by stumps. Next morning they overhauled Wellington's total, finally putting on 90 for the eighth wicket in just 71 minutes. Tovey was first to go for 48 and Behrent followed for 42. Auckland, with a lead of 44, bowled Wellington out for 193 with Tovey finishing with seven dismissals for the match. After early problems, Auckland went on to win by five wickets and claim the title.

The *Almanack* later noted that "Tovey enjoyed a most successful season, and could well have gained highest honours." Tall for a keeper (five foot eleven/180 cm), Tovey's sure sense of anticipation removed the need for him to dive and sprawl. He was also one of the last keepers to stand up to the quicker bowlers.

After returning to Sydney, he rose to be general manager of his firm, retiring in 1978 and spending two decades offering his sales expertise and experience as a consultant.

Tovey's record in first-class cricket is:

Season	M	I	NO	HS	Runs	Ave	ct/st
1957/58	1	1	0	18	18	18.00	-/1
1960/61	6	10	1	22	55	6.11	12/5
1961/62	1	2	1	3	5	5.00	3/-
1963/64	5	8	2	62	160	26.66	20/1
TOTAL	**13**	**21**	**4**	**62**	**238**	**14.00**	**35/7**

Geoffrey Thomas WRIGHT

Born: Darfield, 25 March, 1929

Died: Christchurch, 2 April, 2003

Right-hand batsman

Geoff Wright, who played one first-class game for Canterbury in the 1955/56 season, was the father of one of New Zealand's most successful and respected cricketers, John Wright.

Wright had the difficult task of trying to break into first-class cricket from the Malvern sub-association. The North Canterbury Association (now Canterbury Country) was not formed until 1962 so Wright and other cricketers from the area did not even have the chance to impress selectors with performances in minor association cricket. In November 1955 he was chosen to play for a Canterbury XI v South Canterbury and two weeks later scored a half-century for Combined Minor Associations against Canterbury in a Plunket Shield trial.

As a result of this, Wright was one of three players (who along with Brian Haworth made up the top four in the batting order) who made their first-class debut in Canterbury's opening Plunket Shield match of the 1955/56 season, which began at Carisbrook on 24 December. Interestingly, the other two debutants, Jack D'Arcy and Bruce Bolton, the opening batsmen for Canterbury in this match, both went on to open the batting for New Zealand.

After Canterbury's captain, Ray Dowker, won the toss and batted, the visitors scored at a good rate but lost wickets regularly and by lunch, with the score 125-4, the match was already well advanced. By this time Wright had come and gone, scoring the only runs of his brief first-class career, stumped by Jim Gill, giving Arthur Berry, another player making his debut, his first wicket in first-class cricket.

Canterbury made 296 but Otago could only come up with 178 in reply. Canterbury were then bowled out for 171 in their second innings, at one stage being 4-3. Wright was one of these early wickets, lbw to the lion-hearted Guy Overton for a duck. Overton, who had taken a hat trick in his first Plunket Shield match back in 1946/47, had toured South Africa with the New Zealand team in 1953/54. He was to play just one more first-class game, retiring after Otago's two home matches that season. He finished with 169 wickets in his 51 first-class games yet scored just 137 runs. Chief destroyer in the Canterbury innings was Bill Frame, yet another player making his debut in first-class cricket, who took ten wickets in his first match. Several years later Frame was to make the headlines again, for very different reasons, taking his own life in a tragic and unfortunate incident.

Otago required 290 runs to win the game but could manage only 173. Canterbury went on to win the Plunket Shield that season, winning all four games outright but Wright was not called upon again (although he played against Southland in a two-day game at Invercargill which began the day after the Plunket Shield match finished).

Shortly after, however, he captained a Canterbury Minor and Sub-Association team against the touring Riverina side from New South Wales. The Riverina side, made up of players from New South Wales country areas, was strong enough to defeat an Otago XI (containing several Plunket Shield players) in a three-day game at the beginning of the tour. He also played for a Canterbury XI against North Otago in 1957/58.

Wright continued to appear in games for the Minor Associations team and then the newly formed North Canterbury association until 1966/67. In his last season he was a member of the North Canterbury side which won the Hawke Cup for the first time. In the 1968/69 season Wright and 14-year-old John opened the batting for West Melton, combining in century partnerships against Greendale and Hororata.

Wright also played rugby for Canterbury Country from 1948 to 1950 and in later years was prominent in Canterbury bowling circles. In 1974 he was elected to the Paparua County Council and in the same year was made a Justice of the Peace.

Wright's twin brother Allan (who was later knighted) was one of the driving forces behind the formation of the North Canterbury Association and played a major role in the administration of cricket in the area. Allan Wright, ironically, had a far more extensive career than his brother at both minor association level and for Canterbury in representative games but never received a chance at first-class level. He was the manager of the New Zealand team in England in 1983 and was President of New Zealand Cricket in 1993/94. He was made a life member in the same season. A third brother, Ness, also represented North Canterbury.

NEW ZEALAND ACADEMY IN AUSTRALIA

The New Zealand Academy team took part in a triangular series with their Australian and South African counterparts in Townsville in August. New Zealand drew both their three-day games and won one of their one-day matches. The team was: J.M. How *(captain, Central Districts)*, M.R. Gillespie *(Wellington)*, J.M. McMillan *(Otago)*, K.D. Mills *(Auckland)*, S.M. Mills *(Wellington)*, R.J. Nicol *(Auckland)*, J.S. Patel *(Wellington)*, I.A. Robertson *(Canterbury)*, J.D. Ryder *(Central Districts)*, I.P. Sandbrook *(Central Districts)*, G.S. Shaw *(Auckland)*, J.W. Sheed*(Otago)*, S.L. Stewart*(Canterbury)*, J.A.F. Yovich*(Northern Districts)*. Coach, A. Ross; Manager, D.R. Hadlee.

AUSTRALIAN ACADEMY v NEW ZEALAND ACADEMY
At Endeavour Park, Townsville   3, 4, 5 August, 2002

Australian Academy 325-8d (L.G. Buchanan 109, W. Robinson 58, D.G. Dawson 41*, M.J. Cosgrove 32, J.M. McMillan 3-74) and 281 (W. Robinson 87*, L.G. Buchanan 60, C.J. Simmons 45, J.S. Patel 4-74) **drew with New Zealand Academy** 385 (J.D. Ryder 181, R.J. Nicol 78, I.A. Robertson 43*, B. Geeves 4-66, A.C. Bird 3-31).

SOUTH AFRICAN ACADEMY v AUSTRALIAN ACADEMY
At Endeavour Park No.2, Townsville   6, 7, 8 August, 2002

South African Academy 185 (A. Pieterson 39, M.A. Aronstam 33, W. Robinson 3-10, C.P. Simpson 3-40, B. Geeves 3-47) and 254 (R. McLaren 90, F. de Wet 54*, J.G. Strydom 37, A. Pieterson 34, B. Geeves 3-34, B. Casson 3-68) **lost to Australian Academy** 379-7d (L.G. Buchanan 165, C.J. Simpson 113, C.J. Simmons 37, A.K. Kruger 4-86) and 63-3 (C.J. Simmons 32*) by 7 wickets

SOUTH AFRICAN ACADEMY v NEW ZEALAND ACADEMY
At Endeavour Park, Townsville   9, 10, 11 August, 2002

New Zealand Academy 385-8d (J.M. How 89, S.M. Mills 82*, G.S. Shaw 54*, S.L. Stewart 41, A.K. Kruger 3-91) and 154-3d (J.M. How 52, J.D. Ryder 43) **drew with South African Academy** 243-5d (I. Khan 86, D.J. Jacobs 51*, J.R. Schorn 44) and 255-6 (A. Pieterson 85, D.J. Jacobs 52, I. Khan 47*, T.A. Bula 40*, K.D. Mills 4-44)

AUSTRALIAN ACADEMY v NEW ZEALAND ACADEMY
At Endeavour Park No.2, Townsville   12 August, 2002

Australian Academy 273 (C.J. Simmons 74, D.S. Wotherspoon 49, L.G. Buchanan 36, G.S. Shaw 3-59) **defeated New Zealand Academy** 193 (R.J. Nicol 73*, J.S. Patel 41, J.N. Burke 5-63) by 80 runs

AUSTRALIAN ACADEMY v SOUTH AFRICAN ACADEMY
At Endeavour Park No.2, Townsville   13 August, 2002

South African Academy 253-7 (M.A. Aronstam 84, J.G. Strydom 49, D.N. Jacobs 33) **defeated Australian Academy** 227 (C.J. Simmons 37, D.G. Dawson 35*, D.S. Wotherspoon 33, B.B. Kops 3-52) by 26 runs

SOUTH AFRICAN ACADEMY v NEW ZEALAND ACADEMY
At Endeavour Park No.2, Townsville   14 August, 2002

New Zealand Academy 249-6 (J.A.F. Yovich 83*, J.W. Sheed 77) **defeated South African Academy** 185 (J.G. Strydom 48, D.J. Jacobs 36, J.A.F. Yovich 3-22, M.R. Gillespie 3-39) by 64 runs

AUSTRALIAN ACADEMY v NEW ZEALAND ACADEMY
At Endeavour Park No.2, Townsville   15 August, 2002
Australian Academy 332-8 (D.S. Wotherspoon 126, C.P. Simpson 87, G.J. Bailey 43, M.R. Gillespie 3-57) **defeated New Zealand Academy** 165 (R.J. Nicol 58) by 167 runs

SOUTH AFRICAN ACADEMY v NEW ZEALAND ACADEMY
At Endeavour Park, Townsville   16 August, 2002
New Zealand Academy 197 (J.M. How 45, R.J. Nicol 42, F de Wet 3-23) **lost to South African Academy** 198-5 (D.J. Jacobs 100*, J.G. Strydom 36, R. McLaren 33*) by 5 wickets

AUSTRALIAN ACADEMY v SOUTH AFRICAN ACADEMY
At Endeavour Park, Townsville   17 August, 2002
Australian Academy 288-7 (D.S. Wotherspoon 91, L.G. Buchanan 53, C.J. Simmons 45, C.J. Ferguson 42*) **defeated South African Academy** 206 (H.M. Amla 39, M. van Vuuren 33, A.L. Fleming 4-44, B. Geeves 3-29) by 82 runs

ICC CHAMPIONS TROPHY

New Zealand travelled to Sri Lanka in September to defend the ICC title which they had won in Kenya two years earlier. While the tournament in the past had been a straight knockout competition, this time there were four groups of three with the winners going to the semi-final.

The Black Caps were drawn in the same group as Australia and Bangladesh and with the trans-Tasman game being the first match to be played in Group 1 it was inevitable that the winner would go through to the semi-final. Australia won in comprehensive fashion by 164 runs.

India and Sri Lanka were declared joint winners after the final was twice rained off. Ironically, Sri Lanka managed to bat 100 overs in total without any result being reached.

The New Zealand team was: S.P. Fleming *(captain, Wellington)*, N.J. Astle *(Canterbury)*, S.E. Bond *(Canterbury)*, C.Z. Harris *(Canterbury)*, P.A. Hitchcock *(Wellington)*, K.D. Mills *(Auckland)*, C.J. Nevin *(Wellington)*, J.D.P. Oram *(Central Districts)*, M.S. Sinclair *(Central Districts)*, S.B. Styris *(Northern Districts)*, G.P. Sulzberger *(Central Districts)*, D.R. Tuffey *(Northern Districts)*, D.L. Vettori *(Northern Districts)*, L. Vincent *(Auckland)*. Coach, D.C. Aberhart; Manager, J.J. Crowe; Physiotherapist, D.F. Shackel; Video Analyst, Z. Hitchcock.

C.D. McMillan *(Canterbury)* and B.G.K. Walker *(Auckland)* had made themselves unavailable because of concerns over security but were included in an extended party which played four matches in Australia prior to the main squad going to Sri Lanka. I.G. Butler *(Northern Districts)*, M.N. Hart*(Northern Districts)*, M.J. Horne*(Auckland)* and J.A.F. Yovich *(Northern Districts)* were the other players.

New Zealand Averages

BATTING	M	I	NO	HS	Agg	Ave	100s	50s	Ct	St	SR
M.S. Sinclair	2	2	0	70	88	44.00	-	1	1	-	56
C.Z. Harris	2	2	0	26	45	22.50	-	-	2	-	68
S.P. Fleming	2	2	0	31	43	21.50	-	-	3	-	82
S.B. Styris	2	2	0	26	42	21.00	-	-	1	-	102
S.E. Bond	2	2	0	26	34	17.00	-	-	1	-	125
J.D.P. Oram	2	2	0	30	31	15.50	-	-	-	-	88
D.L. Vettori	2	2	0	16	22	11.00	-	-	1	-	129
N.J. Astle	2	2	0	5	5	2.50	-	-	2	-	41
L. Vincent	2	2	0	1	1	0.50	-	-	2	-	16
D.R. Tuffey	1	1	0	0	0	0.00	-	-	-	-	0
K.D. Mills	2	2	2	23*	26	-	-	-	-	-	59
P.A. Hitchcock	1	1	1	2*	2	-	-	-	-	-	200

BOWLING	O	M	R	W	Ave	Best	R/O
D.L. Vettori	13.3	2	35	3	11.66	2-10	2.59
S.E. Bond	15	0	84	6	14.00	4-21	5.60
K.D. Mills	14	0	62	3	20.66	2-13	4.43
J.D.P. Oram	16	1	92	4	23.00	2-32	5.75
D.R. Tuffey	6	1	55	1	55.00	1-55	9.17
C.Z. Harris	5	0	38	0	-	-	7.60

NEW SOUTH WALES v NEW ZEALAND

At North Dalton Park, Wollongong   3 September 2002
New South Wales 207-7 (M.J. Slater 42, P. Maraziotis 41, D.J. Thornely 30, S.E. Bond
3-34) **lost to New Zealand** 208-4 (S.P. Fleming 48, S.B. Styris 46, L. Vincent 39*) by 6
wickets

TASMANIA v NEW ZEALAND

At Alan Davidson Oval, Sydney   4 September 2002
New Zealand 186 (M.S. Sinclair 37, G.P. Sulzberger 37*, S.J. Jurgensen 4-20) **defeated
Tasmania** 182 (L. Williams 32, J.D.P. Oram 4-23, D.R. Tuffey 4-47) by 4 runs

TASMANIA v NEW ZEALAND

At Alan Davidson Oval, Sydney   5 September 2002
Tasmania 248 (M.G. Dighton 110, S.B. Tubb 64*, D.J. Marsh 35) **lost to New Zealand**
253-4 (C.Z. Harris 114* – 104 balls, 5 fours, 8 sixes, C.D. McMillan 56) by 6 wickets

NEW SOUTH WALES v NEW ZEALAND

At Caringbah Oval, Sydney   6 September 2002
New Zealand 199 (S.P. Fleming 59, M.S. Sinclair 43, S.B. Styris 35, D.A. Nash 3-34)
defeated New South Wales 169 (D.J. Thornely 48, P.A. Jaques 43, S.E. Bond 5-32) by 30
runs

SOUTH AFRICA v NEW ZEALAND

At Nondescripts Cricket Club Ground, Colombo   11 September 2002
New Zealand 226 (N.J. Astle 64, C.Z. Harris 48) **lost to South Africa** 229-4 (H.H. Gibbs
102 retd, H.H. Dippenaar 57) by 6 wickets

ZIMBABWE v NEW ZEALAND

At Nondescripts Cricket Club Ground, Colombo   12 September 2002
New Zealand 262 (M.S. Sinclair 108, S.B. Styris 49, G.P. Sulzberger 30*, S.M. Ervine
3-44) **defeated Zimbabwe** 254 (G.J. Whitall 66, D.D. Ebrahim 62, D.A. Marillier 37,
D.R. Tuffey 3-51) by 8 runs

NEW ZEALAND v AUSTRALIA

Champions Trophy

at Sinhalese Sports Club Ground, Colombo on 15 September, 2002
Toss : Australia. Umpires : D.L. Orchard & R.B. Tiffin
Australia won by 164 runs

The top six Australian batsmen all reached twenty in a good team effort although Martyn was the only one to make fifty. The New Zealand bowling was disappointing and only Vettori was able concede less than five runs per over.

New Zealand lost Astle in the second over and never recovered, slumping to 82-9 in 19 overs. Only a 50 run stand for the last wicket got the total to 100. McGrath and Lee did all the damage as New Zealand were dismissed in the 27th over

AUSTRALIA	Runs	Mins	Balls	6s	4s
A.C.Gilchrist† c Sinclair b Tuffey	44	42	30	1	7
M.L.Hayden b Vettori	43	108	68	1	4
R.T.Ponting* c Fleming b Bond	37	46	31	-	8
D.R.Martyn c Harris b Bond	73	122	87	-	8
D.S.Lehmann c Vettori b Mills	35	64	52	-	3
M.G.Bevan b Oram	21	33	24	-	2
S.R.Watson not out	19	14	9	1	1
S.K.Warne c Bond b Oram	0	4	1	-	-
B.Lee not out	4	4	3	-	-
J.N.Gillespie					
G.D.McGrath					
Extras (lb 6, w 7, nb 7)	20				
TOTAL (50 overs) (7 wkts)	**296**	222			

NEW ZEALAND	Runs	Mins	Balls	6s	4s
S.P.Fleming* lbw b McGrath	12	13	11	-	3
N.J.Astle lbw b Gillespie	0	6	2	-	-
M.S.Sinclair c Gilchrist b McGrath	18	36	30	-	3
L.Vincent† c Martyn b McGrath	0	2	1	-	-
S.B.Styris c Gilchrist b McGrath	16	25	14	-	3
C.Z.Harris b Lee	19	43	18	-	4
J.D.P.Oram b McGrath	1	10	8	-	-
D.L.Vettori lbw b Lee	6	14	10	-	1
K.D.Mills not out	23	56	39	1	1
D.R.Tuffey c Warne b Lee	0	11	6	-	-
S.E.Bond st Gilchrist b Warne	26	30	21	-	5
Extras (b 4, lb 3, w 2, nb 2)	11				
TOTAL (26.2 overs)	**132**	132			

Bowling NEW ZEALAND	O	M	R	W
Bond	10	0	63	2
Mills	9	0	49	1
Tuffey	6	1	55	1
Oram	10	0	60	2
Vettori	10	1	25	1
Harris	5	0	38	0
AUSTRALIA				
McGrath	7	1	37	5
Gillespie	7	1	29	1
Lee	6	0	38	3
Watson	6	1	19	0
Warne	0.2	0	2	1

Fall of Wickets	A	NZ
1st	68	9
2nd	129	17
3rd	143	17
4th	217	44
5th	272	49
6th	276	51
7th	290	71
8th	-	78
9th	-	82
10th	-	132

NEW ZEALAND v BANGLADESH   Champions Trophy

at Sinhalese Sports Club Ground, Colombo on 23 September, 2002
Toss : Bangladesh. Umpires : E.A.R. de Silva & D.R. Shepherd
New Zealand won by 167 runs

Astle again went early but then New Zealand had record stands against Bangladesh for the 2nd, 5th, 6th, 7th, 8th and 9th wickets although Sinclair was the only player to get fifty. Ashraful got three late wickets.

Bangladesh had a dreadful start losing wickets in each of the first three overs. Only Tushar was able to reach 20 as Bond created havoc amongst the batsmen. New Zealand had a comfortable 167 run win but were eliminated from the tournament.

NEW ZEALAND

	Runs	Mins	Balls	6s	4s
S.P.Fleming* c Jubair					
b Mahmud	31	63	40	-	5
N.J.Astle c Kapali b Monjurul	5	13	10	-	1
M.S.Sinclair c Rafique					
b Ashraful	70	167	123	-	5
L.Vincent† c Masud b Mahmud	1	9	5	-	-
S.B.Styris run out	26	34	26	-	3
C.Z.Harris c Masud b Ashraful	26	50	48	-	2
J.D.P.Oram c Imran b Ashraful	30	29	26	1	1
D.L.Vettori c Muntasir					
b Manjurul	16	17	13	-	1
K.D.Mills not out	3	19	5	-	-
S.E.Bond st Masud b Rafique	5	8	7	5	-
P.A.Hitchcock not out	2	2	1	-	-
Extras (b 1, lb 9, w 14, nb 2)	26				
TOTAL (50 overs) (9 wkts)	**244**	209			

BANGLADESH

	Runs	Mins	Balls	6s	4s
Javed Omer c Astle b Oram	1	12	7	-	-
Al Sahariar lbw b Bond	0	1	1	-	-
Mohammad Ashraful c Styris					
b Bond	1	12	8	-	-
Tushar Imran c Astle b Oram	20	27	16	-	4
Alok Kapali c Fleming b Bond	2	8	6	-	-
Khaled Masud*† c Vincent					
b Bond	1	5	3	-	-
Khaled Mahmud c Fleming					
b Mills	11	25	12	-	2
Mohammad Rafique c Harris					
b Vettori	17	46	32	-	3
Fahim Muntasir c Vincent b Mills	5	12	12	-	-
Monjurul Islam b Vettori	10	27	20	-	2
Talha Jubair not out	1	8	3	-	-
Extras (lb 1, w 4, nb 3)	8				
TOTAL (19.3 overs)	**77**	96			

Bowling	O	M	R	W
BANGLADESH				
Monjurul	8	1	30	2
Jubair	5	0	46	0
Mahmud	10	0	41	2
Rafique	10	0	39	1
Muntasir	10	0	40	0
Kapali	2	0	12	0
Ashraful	5	1	26	3
NEW ZEALAND				
Bond	5	0	21	4
Oram	6	1	32	2
Mills	5	0	13	2
Vettori	3.3	1	10	2

Fall of Wickets		
	NZ	*B*
1st	11	2
2nd	77	8
3rd	79	8
4th	119	16
5th	167	19
6th	198	37
7th	216	46
8th	232	56
9th	242	70
10th	-	77

12 September, 2002
Colombo: **Sri Lanka beat Pakistan by 8 wickets**
Pakistan 200 (49.4 overs) (Saeed Anwar 52, Misbah-ul-Haq 47, Younis Khan 35, M.Muralitharan 3-29, C.R.D.Fernando 3-30);
Sri Lanka 201 for 2 (36.1 overs) (S.T.Jayasuriya 102*, P.A.de Silva 66*)

13 September, 2002
Colombo: **South Africa beat West Indies by 2 wickets**
West Indies 238 for 8 (50 overs) (C.H.Gayle 49, S.Chanderpaul 45, R.R.Sarwan 36);
South Africa 242 for 8 (49 overs) (J.N.Rhodes 61, H.H.Dippenaar 53, G.C.Smith 33, M.Dillon 4-60, C.L.Hooper 3-42)

14 September, 2002
Colombo: **India beat Zimbabwe by 14 runs**
India 288 for 6 (50 overs) (M.Kaif 111*, R.S.Dravid 71, V.Sehwag 48, D.T.Hondo 4-62);
Zimbabwe 274 for 8 (50 overs) (A.Flower 145, G.W.Flower 33, Z.Khan 4-45)

16 September, 2002
Colombo: **Sri Lanka beat Netherlands by 206 runs**
Sri Lanka 292 for 6 (50 overs) (M.S.Atapattu 101, K.C.Sangakkara 41, S.T.Jayasuriya 36);
Netherlands 86 (29.3 overs) (T.B.M.De Leede 31, M.Muralitharan 4-15)

17 September, 2002
Colombo: West Indies beat Kenya by 29 runs
West Indies 261 for 6 (50 overs) (B.C.Lara 111, S.Chanderpaul 43, C.H.Gayle 33);
Kenya 232 (49.1 overs) (S.O.Tikolo 93, B.J.Patel 35, P.T.Collins 3-18)

18 September, 2002
Colombo: England beat Zimbabwe by 108 runs
England 298 for 8 (50 overs) (M.E.Trescothick 119, N.Hussain 75, D.T.Hondo 4-45);
Zimbabwe 190 for 9 (48 overs) (H.H.Streak 50*, A.Flower 44, R.C.Irani 4-37, M.J.Hoggard 3-25)

19 September, 2002
Colombo: Australia beat Bangladesh by 9 wickets
Bangladesh 129 (45.2 overs) (Alok Kapali 45, J.N.Gillespie 3-20);
Australia 133 for 1 (20.4 overs) (M.L.Hayden 67*, A.C.Gilchrist 54)

20 September, 2002
Colombo: South Africa beat Kenya by 176 runs
South Africa 316 for 5 (50 overs) (H.H.Gibbs 116, G.C.Smith 69, J.H.Kallis 60, H.H.Dippenaar 31);
Kenya 140 (46.5 overs) (S.O.Tikolo 69, D.M.Benkenstein 3-5, J.L.Ontong 3-30)

21 September, 2002
Colombo: Pakistan beat Netherlands by 9 wickets
Netherlands 136 (50 overs) (R.P.Lefebvre 32*, Shahid Afridi 3-18);
Pakistan 142 for 1 (16.2 overs) (Imran Nazir 59, Shahid Afridi 55*)

22 September, 2002
Colombo: India beat England by 8 wickets
England 269 for 7 (50 overs) (I.D.Blackwell 82, N.V.Knight 50, R.C.Irani 37, A.J.Stewart 35, O.A.Shah 34);
India 271 for 2 (39.3 overs) (V.Sehwag 126, S.C.Ganguly 117*)

Points
Group 1 – Australia 8, New Zealand 4, Bangladesh 0.
Group 2 – India 8, England 4, Zimbabwe 0.
Group 3 – South Africa 8, West Indies 4, Kenya 0.
Group 4 – Sri Lanka 8, Pakistan 4, Netherlands 0.

25 September, 2002 (semi-final)
Colombo: India beat South Africa by 10 runs
India 261 for 9 (50 overs) (Yuvraj Singh 62, V.Sehwag 59, R.S.Dravid 49, S.M.Pollock 3-43);
South Africa 251 for 6 (50 overs) (H.H.Gibbs 116*, J.H.Kallis 97, V.Sehwag 3-25)

27 September, 2002 (semi-final)
Colombo: Sri Lanka beat Australia by 7 wickets
Australia 162 (48.4 overs) (S.K.Warne 36, A.C.Gilchrist 31, M.Muralitharan 3-26);
Sri Lanka 163 for 3 (40 overs) (M.S.Atapattu 51, K.C.Sangakkara 48, S.T.Jayasuriya 42)

29 September, 2002 (final)
Colombo: No result
Sri Lanka 244 for 5 (50 overs) (S.T.Jayasuriya 74, K.C.Sangakkara 54, M.S.Atapattu 34, Harbhajan Singh 3-27);
India 14 for 0 (2 overs)

30 September, 2002 (final replay)
Colombo: No result
Sri Lanka 222 for 7 (50 overs) (D.P.M.D.Jayawardene 77, R.P.Arnold 56*, Z.Khan 3-44);
India 38 for 1 (8.4 overs)

INDIA IN
NEW ZEALAND

The eagerly awaited tour of New Zealand by India turned out to be a disappointment for spectators. With the tourists having Tendulkar, Dravid, Ganguly and Sehwag in their line up high scores were expected but with the majority of wickets favouring the bowlers runs were at a premium.

There were valid reasons for the test wickets assisting the bowlers as there was substantial rainfall at both Wellington and Hamilton in the days prior to the tests but the one day wickets were generally too bowler friendly. In the two tests a total of 200 runs was achieved once when New Zealand did so in the first test. There were three individual fifties at Wellington but none at Hamilton. Zaheer Khan, Nehra, Bond, Tuffey and Oram all had excellent returns with the ball. New Zealand won the test series and maintained their third placing on the test table.

New Zealand also were victorious in the one-day series, winning 5-2. The runs were scarce again. At Napier New Zealand scored 254 and India replied with 219, this being the only time both sides reached 200. India also scored 200-9 when winning at Auckland. Sehwag scored two centuries, 108 at Napier and 112 in the second Auckland fixture, while the highest score by a New Zealander was 78 by Sinclair at Napier. For the one day series the Indian attack was bolstered by the return of Srinath which gave them a three-pronged pace attack that proved difficult for the New Zealand batsmen.

The series was the last before the World Cup. New Zealand, the victors, were eliminated in the Super Six stage while India went on to the final. The Indian side was again popular on and off the field. There were good attendances at the matches and interest in their fortunes was heightened due to the fact that former New Zealand captain John Wright was coach.

The touring party was: S.C. Ganguly *(captain)*, A.B. Agarkar, S.B. Bangar, S.S. Das, R.S. Dravid, Harbhajan Singh, M. Kaif, M. Kartik, V.V.S Laxman, A. Nehra, P.A. Patel, A. Ratra, V. Sehwag, S.R. Tendulkar, T. Yohannan, Z. Khan. Manager N.R. Chowdhary Coach J.G. Wright. A.R. Kumble, R.B. Patel, J. Srinath and Yuvraj Singh came for the one-day series replacing Das, Kartik, Ratra and Yohannan. D. Mongia arrived during the one-day series to replace Laxman who had not been selected for the World Cup.

India First-class Averages

BATTING	M	I	NO	HS	Agg	Ave	100s	50s	Ct	St
S.R. Tendulkar	3	6	1	52*	196	39.20	-	2	1	-
R.S. Dravid	3	6	0	76	132	22.00	-	1	2	-
V. Sehwag	3	6	0	61	113	18.83	-	1	1	-
S.B. Bangar	3	6	0	70	112	18.66	-	1	-	-
S.C. Ganguly	3	5	0	48	77	15.40	-	-	-	-
A. Nehra	3	5	2	14	41	13.66	-	-	-	-
Harbhajan Singh	3	5	0	29	68	13.60	-	-	3	-
V.V.S. Laxman	3	6	1	23	37	7.40	-	-	2	-
A.B. Agarkar	2	3	0	12	21	7.00	-	-	-	-
Z. Khan	2	4	0	19	28	7.00	-	-	2	-
P.A. Patel	3	5	0	10	33	6.60	-	-	8	1
T. Yohannan	2	3	3	8*	12	-	-	-	2	-

BOWLING	O	M	R	W	Ave	Best	5w	10w
Z. Khan	54.2	12	151	11	13.72	5-29	2	-
A.B. Agarkar	29.3	7	104	5	20.80	4-50	-	-
S.B. Bangar	27	7	63	3	21.00	2-23	-	-
Harbhajan Singh	56	5	167	7	23.85	2-20	-	-
A. Nehra	65.5	14	194	6	32.33	3-34	-	-
T. Yohannan	43	11	105	2	52.50	1-27	-	-
S.C. Ganguly	2	0	11	0	-	-	-	-

New Zealand Test Averages

BATTING	M	I	NO	HS	Agg	Ave	100s	50s	Ct	St
M.H. Richardson	2	4	1	89	144	48.00	-	1	1	-
S.P. Fleming	2	3	0	32	78	26.00	-	-	4	-
D.R. Tuffey	2	2	1	13	22	22.00	-	-	2	-
N.J. Astle	2	3	0	41	55	18.33	-	-	2	-
L. Vincent	2	4	1	21*	45	15.00	-	-	2	-
J.D.P. Oram	2	3	1	26*	29	14.50	-	-	2	-
D.L. Vettori	2	2	0	21	27	13.50	-	-	-	-
C.D. McMillan	2	3	0	18	31	10.33	-	-	2	-
R.G. Hart	2	3	1	11*	20	10.00	-	-	7	-
S.B. Styris	2	3	0	17	30	10.00	-	-	4	-
S.E. Bond	2	2	1	2	2	2.00	-	-	-	-

BOWLING	O	M	R	W	Ave	Best	5w	10w
D.R. Tuffey	50	19	113	13	8.69	4-12	-	-
J.D.P. Oram	49.5	10	130	11	11.81	4-41	-	-
S.E. Bond	56.1	16	196	12	16.33	4-33	-	-
S.B. Styris	12	0	54	3	18.00	3-28	-	-
N.J. Astle	11	4	27	1	27.00	1-13	-	-

India Test Averages

BATTING	M	I	NO	HS	Agg	Ave	100s	50s	Ct	St
R.S. Dravid	2	4	0	76	131	32.75	-	1	2	-
S.R. Tendulkar	2	4	0	51	100	25.00	-	1	1	-
A. Nehra	2	4	2	10*	27	13.50	-	-	-	-
A.B. Agarkar	1	2	0	12	21	10.50	-	-	-	-
V. Sehwag	2	4	0	25	40	10.00	-	-	-	-
Harbhajan Singh	2	4	0	20	39	9.75	-	-	2	-
S.C. Ganguly	2	4	0	17	29	7.25	-	-	-	-
Z. Khan	2	4	0	19	28	7.00	-	-	2	-
V.V.S. Laxman	2	4	0	23	27	6.75	-	-	1	-
P.A. Patel	2	4	0	10	26	6.50	-	-	6	1
S.B. Bangar	2	4	0	12	21	5.25	-	-	-	-
T. Yohannan	1	2	2	8*	8	-	-	-	-	-

BOWLING	O	M	R	W	Ave	Best	5w	10w
S.B. Bangar	17	5	27	2	13.50	2-23	-	-
Z. Khan	54.2	12	151	11	13.72	5-29	2	-
Harbhajan Singh	36	5	94	5	18.80	2-20	-	-
A. Nehra	47.5	11	125	5	25.00	3-34	-	-
T. Yohannan	25	9	43	1	43.00	1-27	-	-
A.B. Agarkar	13.1	1	54	1	54.00	1-54	-	-
S.C. Ganguly	2	0	11	0	-	-	-	-

New Zealand One-day International Averages

BATTING	M	I	NO	HS	Agg	Ave	100s	50s	Ct	St	SR
J.D.P. Oram	4	3	2	27*	41	41.00	-	-	1	-	58
L. Vincent	5	5	2	53*	120	40.00	-	1	2	-	62
S.E. Bond	3	2	1	31*	31	31.00	-	-	-	-	140
S.B. Styris	4	4	1	42	92	30.66	-	-	1	-	59
S.P. Fleming	7	7	1	60*	157	26.16	-	1	10	-	53
N.J. Astle	5	5	0	76	123	24.60	-	1	2	-	84
M.S. Sinclair	7	7	1	78	146	24.33	-	1	1	-	51
A.R. Adams	4	2	0	35	37	18.50	-	-	-	-	105
C.L. Cairns	3	3	0	25	49	16.33	-	-	-	-	74
B.B. McCullum	7	6	1	35	60	12.00	-	-	18	1	53
K.D. Mills	6	3	0	21	26	8.66	-	-	2	-	47
C.D. McMillan	4	4	0	22	31	7.75	-	-	2	-	42
D.R. Tuffey	7	3	0	5	10	3.33	-	-	1	-	50
C.Z. Harris	3	2	0	1	1	0.50	-	-	1	-	8
D.L. Vettori	6	3	3	16*	30	-	-	-	3	-	50
P.A. Hitchcock	2	1	1	2*	2	-	-	-	1	-	200

BOWLING	O	M	R	W	Ave	Best	R/O
C.Z. Harris	3	0	6	1	6.00	1-6	2.00
A.R. Adams	36.4	4	131	14	9.35	5-22	3.57
N.J. Astle	5	1	11	1	11.00	1-11	2.20
J.D.P. Oram	36.1	6	126	8	15.75	5-26	3.48
S.B. Styris	32	7	97	6	16.16	2-23	3.03
P.A. Hitchcock	16	0	68	4	17.00	3-30	4.25
D.R. Tuffey	66.5	8	217	12	18.08	2-11	3.24
K.D. Mills	57.4	7	191	9	21.22	3-45	3.31
D.L. Vettori	22	0	83	3	27.66	1-1	3.77
S.E. Bond	23	1	86	3	28.66	2-34	3.74

India One-day International Averages

BATTING	M	I	NO	HS	Agg	Ave	100s	50s	Ct	St	SR
V. Sehwag	7	7	0	112	299	42.71	2	-	1	-	78
S.S. Das	1	1	0	30	30	30.00	-	-	-	-	50
Yuvraj Singh	7	7	0	54	134	19.14	-	1	1	-	48
R.S. Dravid	7	7	0	21	116	16.57	-	-	8	-	37
Z. Khan	7	7	2	34*	74	14.80	-	-	1	-	63
V.V.S. Laxman	3	3	0	20	39	13.00	-	-	1	-	40
P.A. Patel	1	1	0	13	13	13.00	-	-	-	-	41
S.C. Ganguly	7	7	0	23	58	8.28	-	-	2	-	42
M. Kaif	7	7	0	24	55	7.85	-	-	4	-	46
A.R. Kumble	3	3	0	21	23	7.66	-	-	-	-	27
J. Srinath	7	7	3	15	30	7.50	-	-	-	-	36
Harbhajan Singh	2	2	0	14	14	7.00	-	-	-	-	77
D. Mongia	3	3	0	12	14	4.66	-	-	-	-	45
A. Nehra	6	5	4	2*	3	3.00	-	-	-	-	15
A.B. Agarkar	3	3	0	6	6	2.00	-	-	1	-	37
S.B. Bangar	3	3	0	4	6	2.00	-	-	1	-	37
S.R. Tendulkar	3	3	0	1	2	0.66	-	-	-	-	6

BOWLING	O	M	R	W	Ave	Best	R/O
J. Srinath	66.2	10	201	18	11.16	4-23	3.03
A.B. Agarkar	20.5	1	86	4	21.50	3-26	4.12
A.R. Kumble	20.4	1	69	3	23.00	2-38	3.33
Z. Khan	57	5	258	10	25.80	3-30	4.53
S.C. Ganguly	22.4	2	100	3	33.33	1-23	4.41
A. Nehra	52	6	192	5	38.40	2-16	3.69
Harbhajan Singh	10	0	56	1	56.00	1-56	5.60
S.B. Bangar	12	0	63	0	-	-	5.25

NEW ZEALAND v INDIA

Super Max International

at Jade Stadium, Christchurch on 4 December, 2004
Toss : New Zealand. Umpires : D.M. Quested & E.A. Watkin
New Zealand won by 21 runs

NEW ZEALAND

FIRST INNINGS	Runs	Balls	4	6	8	12
C.J.Nevin† c Yohannan b Khan	18	10	2	1	-	-
N.J.Astle b Yohannan	42	23	6	-	-	1
C.D.McMillan b Tendulkar	34	18	2	2	-	-
C.L.Cairns* c Sehwag b Tendulkar	7	3	-	1	-	-
S.B.Styris not out	1	1	-	-	-	-
J.D.P.Oram c Laxman b Sehwag	5	4	-	-	-	-
A.R.Adams not out	3	2	-	-	-	-
B.B.McCullum						
T.K.Canning						
S.E.Bond						
P.A.Hitchcock						
C.Z.Harris						
Extras (b 1, lb 6, w 6)	13					
TOTAL (10 overs) (5 wkts)	**123**					

SECOND INNINGS	Runs	Balls	4	6	8	12
c Bangar b Agarkar	12	7	1	1	-	-
b Khan	2	4	-	-	-	-
c Kaif b Tendulkar	7	7	1	-	-	-
c Bangar b Yohannan	6	5	1	-	-	-
st Ratra b Tendulkar	0	2	-	-	-	-
run out	3	2	-	-	-	-
(1) c Agarkar b Tendulkar	60	28	3	3	-	1
(8) not out	15	5	-	2	-	-
(lb 1, w 12)	13					
(10 overs) (7 wkts)	**118**					

INDIA

	Runs	Balls	4	6	8	12
V.Sehwag c Adams b Bond	9	7	2	-	-	-
S.R.Tendulkar c Nevin b Hitchcock	72	27	10	-	2	1
S.S.Das b Adams	25	13	5	-	-	-
V.V.S.Laxman* b Adams	9	4	2	-	-	-
M.Kaif c McCullum b Hitchcock	2	5	-	-	-	-
S.B.Bangar not out	6	4	1	-	-	-
A.B.Agarkar not out	0	1	-	-	-	-
A.Ratra†						
Z.Khan						
M.Kartik						
T.Yohannan						
P.A.Patel						
Extras (lb 4, w 6)	10					
TOTAL (10 overs) (5 wkts)	**133**					

	Runs	Balls	4	6	8	12
c Styris b Canning	23	18	-	1	1	-
c Styris b Oram	5	6	1	-	-	-
c Styris b Adams	28	19	3	1	-	-
(7) not out	7	5	1	-	-	-
c Harris b Adams	2	4	-	-	-	-
c Harris b Hitchcock	6	4	1	-	-	-
(4) b Adams	6	4	1	-	-	-
not out	0	0	-	-	-	-
(lb 2, w 8)	10					
(10 overs) (6 wkts)	**87**					

Bowling	O	M	R	W	O	M	R	W
INDIA								
Khan	2	0	21	1	2	0	10	1
Agarkar	2	0	26	0	2	0	26	1
Bangar	1	0	13	0				
Yohannan	2	0	10	1	2	0	10	1
Kartik	1	0	23	0				
Tendulkar	1	0	15	2	3	0	40	3
Sehwag	1	0	8	1	1	0	31	0
NEW ZEALAND								
Bond	2	0	20	1	2	0	14	0
Oram	2	0	33	0	2	0	25	1
Canning	2	0	34	0	1	0	9	1
Adams	2	0	18	2	2	0	15	3
Hitchcock	2	0	24	2	2	0	16	1
Astle					1	0	6	0

Fall of Wickets	NZ	I	NZ	I
	1st	1st	2nd	2nd
1st	26	30	20	14
2nd	98	108	22	39
3rd	105	121	43	63
4th	113	122	63	63
5th	120	128	65	74
6th	-	-	90	83
7th	-	-	118	-
8th	-	-	-	-
9th	-	-	-	-
10th	-	-	-	-

McCullum kept wicket in India's second innings

NEW ZEALAND
CRICKET

CENTRAL DISTRICTS v INDIA   First-class

at McLean Park, Napier on 6, 7, 8 December, 2002
Toss : Central Districts. Umpires : B.F. Bowden & D.B. Cowie
Close of play: 1st day: CD 69-1, Spearman 40, Sinclair 17; 2nd day: CD 295-9, Griggs 100, Hamilton 9
Match drawn

For the only first-class game before the first test, India chose its strongest side available. Zaheer Khan was injured and Yohannan took his place. The Indian batting failed for the first of many times on tour. Only Tendulkar and Ganguly were able to pass thirty as India were dismissed for 209. The Central bowlers shared the wickets with Mason and Schwass getting three each.

After Ingram went early, Spearman and Sinclair added 92 with both players getting fifties. Spearman needed 59 balls and Sinclair 79, but the rest of the innings belonged to Griggs. Playing as a batsman in this match, he went to fifty from 101 balls and reached his maiden century after a further 49.

Central declared overnight and the third day was used to give the tourists batting practice. Bangar, Sehwag and Tendulkar all got fifties in different types of innings. Sehwag got his from just 51 deliveries, while Tendulkar needed 92 and Bangar was more circumspect requiring 145. The game was called off at tea with there being no chance of a result

INDIA

FIRST INNINGS	Runs	Mins	Balls	6s	4s
S.B.Bangar c Sigley b Schwass	21	105	77	-	2
V.Sehwag c Sinclair b Mason	12	24	16	-	2
R.S.Dravid c Sigley b Mason	0	2	2	-	-
S.R.Tendulkar b Hamilton	44	88	63	-	6
V.V.S.Laxman c Sigley b Hamilton	9	63	50	-	-
S.C.Ganguly* c Sigley b Mason	48	104	81	-	5
P.A.Patel† c & b Schwass	7	6	8	-	1
A.B.Agarkar lbw b Schwass	0	16	2	-	-
Harbhajan Singh c Hefford b Sulzberger	29	84	48	1	2
A.Nehra c How b Sulzberger	14	71	55	1	-
T.Yohannan not out	4	14	16	-	-
Extras (b 2, lb 11, w 1, nb 7)	21				
TOTAL (68.3 overs)	**209**	296			

SECOND INNINGS	Runs	Mins	Balls	6s	4s
c Hefford b Sulzberger	70	215	162	1	7
c Sigley b Schwass	61	103	55	-	11
b Schwass	1	14	13	-	-
not out	52	104	94	-	7
not out	1	7	5	-	-
(nb 6)	6				
(53.4 overs) (3 wkts)	**191**	223			

CENTRAL DISTRICTS

	Runs	Mins	Balls	6s	4s
P.J.Ingram c Sehwag b Nehra	10	33	28	-	2
C.M.Spearman* c & b Yohannan	58	123	70	-	9
M.S.Sinclair c Harbhajan b Agarkar	52	121	84	-	9
G.P.Sulzberger c Laxman b Bangar	8	37	16	-	1
J.M.How lbw b Harbhajan	10	31	17	-	2
B.B.J.Griggs not out	100	215	150	1	11
M.A.Sigley† lbw b Agarkar	1	6	7	-	-
A.M.Schwass c Patel b Agarkar	0	1	2	-	-
M.J.Mason c Yohannan b Harbhajan	21	52	36	1	2
B.E.Hefford c Patel b Agarkar	9	62	53	-	-
L.J.Hamilton not out	9	60	41	-	1
Extras (b 3, lb 2, w 1, nb 11)	17				
TOTAL (82.2 overs) (9 wkts dec)	**295**	370			

Bowling	O	M	R	W	O	M	R	W
CENTRAL DISTRICTS								
Mason	17	3	46	3	11.4	4	21	0
Hamilton	22	8	52	2	11	0	71	0
Hefford	10	2	34	0	11	2	42	0
Schwass	13	2	46	3	14	4	28	2
Sulzberger	6.3	3	18	2	6	1	29	1
INDIA								
Agarkar	16.2	6	50	4				
Nehra	18	3	69	1				
Yohannan	18	2	62	1				
Bangar	10	2	36	1				
Harbhajan	20	0	73	2				

Fall of Wickets			
	I	CD	I
	1st	1st	2nd
1st	20	16	91
2nd	20	108	99
3rd	70	133	186
4th	84	135	-
5th	137	152	-
6th	144	153	-
7th	159	153	-
8th	161	200	-
9th	198	237	-
10th	209	-	-

NEW ZEALAND v INDIA

First Test

at Basin Reserve, Wellington on 12, 13, 14 December, 2002
Toss : New Zealand. Umpires : E.A.R. de Silva & D.J. Harper
Close of play: 1st day: NZ 53-1, Richardson 27, Fleming 11; 2nd day: NZ 201-7, Richardson 88, Vettori 0
New Zealand won by 10 wickets

Oram made his test debut for New Zealand. After winning the toss and sending India in to bat the home side struck twice in the first six overs with both openers back in the pavilion. Dravid remained resolute but no other player was able to get to twenty. Dravid got his fifty from 174 balls in 178 minutes in a fine hand. The four pace bowlers shared the wickets with Styris having career-best figures.

New Zealand lost Vincent early but were in a comfortable position at 181-3 before they lost their last seven wickets for just 66. Richardson played a great sheet anchor role with his fifty needing 177 minutes and 107 balls. He was eighth out at 228 and had played a match winning innings. Khan took five wickets in a test innings for the first time.

Trailing by 86, India capitulated against the New Zealand attack. Only Tendulkar was able to get past 12 in India's disappointing batting display. His fifty came in 114 minutes and 77 balls. Bond was the most successful bowler with 4-33.

New Zealand were left requiring 36 for victory and this was accomplished without losing a wicket in 9.3 overs. The match finished after tea on the third day.

INDIA

FIRST INNINGS	Runs	Mins	Balls	6s	4s	SECOND INNINGS	Runs	Mins	Balls	6s	4s
S.B.Bangar c Styris b Tuffey	1	26	18	-	-	lbw b Oram	12	51	45	-	1
V.Sehwag b Tuffey	2	9	6	-	-	lbw b Bond	12	30	15	-	2
R.S.Dravid b Styris	76	247	173	-	13	b Bond	7	23	14	-	1
S.R.Tendulkar lbw b Oram	8	47	26	-	2	b Bond	51	120	74	-	7
S.C.Ganguly* c Vincent b Bond	17	44	34	-	2	c Hart b Bond	2	2	3	-	-
V.V.S.Laxman c Hart b Bond	0	7	2	-	-	c Fleming b Oram	0	12	11	-	-
P.A.Patel† c Vincent b Oram	8	57	39	-	1	c Fleming b Tuffey	10	47	37	-	-
A.B.Agarkar c Astle b Styris	12	36	26	1	1	c McMillan b Tuffey	9	19	14	-	2
Harbhajan Singh c McMillan b Styris	0	2	1	-	-	c Styris b Tuffey	1	9	5	-	-
Z.Khan c Oram b Bond	19	39	29	-	3	c Styris b Oram	9	18	9	-	1
A.Nehra not out	10	6	5	-	2	not out	0	3	5	-	-
Extras (lb 1, w 1, nb 6)	8					(lb 1, nb 7)	8				
TOTAL (58.4 overs)	**161**	264				(38.1 overs)	**121**	172			

NEW ZEALAND

	Runs	Mins	Balls	6s	4s		Runs	Mins	Balls	6s	4s
M.H.Richardson lbw b Khan	89	403	244	-	10	not out	14	43	27	-	1
L.Vincent c Patel b Bangar	12	67	41	-	1	not out	21	43	30	-	3
S.P.Fleming* b Khan	25	111	71	-	3						
C.D.McMillan lbw b Bangar	9	17	13	-	1						
N.J.Astle c Harbhajan b Khan	41	97	66	-	6						
S.B.Styris st Patel b Harbhajan	0	7	5	-	-						
J.D.P.Oram lbw b Harbhajan	0	9	5	-	-						
R.G.Hart† lbw b Khan	6	50	42	-	-						
D.L.Vettori c Patel b Khan	21	60	34	-	2						
D.R.Tuffey not out	9	33	27	-	1						
S.E.Bond b Agarkar	2	11	8	-	-						
Extras (b 6, lb 12, w 2, nb 8, pen 5)	33					(w 1)	1				
TOTAL (91.1 overs)	**247**	437				(9.3 overs) (0 wkts)	**36**	43			

Bowling	O	M	R	W	O	M	R	W		Fall of Wickets				
NEW ZEALAND											I	NZ	I	NZ
											1st	1st	2nd	2nd
Bond	18.4	4	66	3	13.1	5	33	4		1st	2	30	23	-
Tuffey	16	7	25	2	9	3	35	3		2nd	9	96	31	-
Oram	15	4	31	2	12	3	36	3		3rd	29	111	31	-
Styris	6	0	28	3	4	0	16	0		4th	51	181	33	-
Astle	3	1	10	0						5th	55	182	36	-
INDIA										6th	92	186	76	-
Khan	25	8	53	5	3	0	13	0		7th	118	201	88	-
Nehra	19	4	50	0	4.3	0	21	0		8th	118	228	96	-
Agarkar	13.1	1	54	1						9th	147	237	121	-
Bangar	15	4	23	2						10th	161	247	121	-
Harbhajan	17	4	33	2	2	1	2	0						
Ganguly	2	0	11	0										

NEW ZEALAND v INDIA   Second Test

at Westpac Park, Hamilton on 19, 20, 21, 22 December, 2002
Toss : New Zealand. Umpires : E.A.R. de Silva & D.J. Harper
Close of play: 1st day: no play; 2nd day: India 92-8, Patel 8; 3rd day: NZ 24-0, Richardson 18, Vincent 6
New Zealand won by 4 wickets

Hamilton had its entire average December rainfall in the five days leading up to the test and consequently there was no play on the first day and only 37.1 overs played on the second day. New Zealand were unchanged but India omitted Agarkar and replaced him with Yohannan.

New Zealand again won a vital toss and India went on to be dismissed for their second lowest total in New Zealand. Only Laxman and Harbhajan (who slogged 20 off nine balls) were able to reach double figures as Bond and Tuffey tore through the Indian batting.

New Zealand were to fare worse than India with Khan getting career best figures as the home side was bowled out for its lowest score against India, giving the tourists an unlikely five run first innings lead. This was the first time in test cricket that both sides had been dismissed for under 100 in their first innings.

The third day saw 22 wickets fall as India were then bowled out for 154. Dravid and Tendulkar both reached thirty but Tuffey and Oram (best test bowling) took four wickets each.

New Zealand needed 160 to win and by close of play on day three were 24-0. Wickets fell regularly and, although only Vincent failed to reach double figures, when batsmen looked set a wicket fell. Hart, playing his first test on his home ground, hit the winning runs to give New Zealand the series win.

INDIA

FIRST INNINGS	Runs	Mins	Balls	6s	4s
S.B.Bangar c Oram b Tuffey	1	7	4	-	-
V.Sehwag c Richardson b Bond	1	31	21	-	-
R.S.Dravid c Hart b Tuffey	9	86	56	-	-
S.R.Tendulkar c Styris b Tuffey	9	40	31	-	1
S.C.Ganguly* c Fleming b Tuffey	5	10	9	-	1
V.V.S.Laxman b Bond	23	56	46	-	4
P.A.Patel† c Hart b Oram	8	69	45	-	1
Harbhajan Singh b Bond	20	10	9	-	5
Z.Khan b Oram	0	8	7	-	-
A.Nehra c Fleming b Bond	7	6	4	1	-
T.Yohannan not out	0	3	2	-	-
Extras (lb 12, nb 4)	16				
TOTAL (38.2 overs)	**99**	167			

SECOND INNINGS	Runs	Mins	Balls	6s	4s
c & b Tuffey	7	23	17	-	1
(7) c Tuffey b Bond	25	17	18	-	4
c sub (M.J.Mason) b Oram	39	154	100	-	6
b Tuffey	32	55	48	-	5
c Hart b Oram	5	11	6	-	1
b Astle	4	26	13	-	-
(2) b Tuffey	0	7	4	-	-
c Hart b Tuffey	18	41	37	-	2
c Astle b Oram	0	6	3	-	-
c Hart b Oram	10	20	12	-	2
not out	8	13	7	-	1
(lb 1, w 2, nb 3)	6				
TOTAL (43.5 overs)	**154**	192			

NEW ZEALAND

	Runs	Mins	Balls	6s	4s
M.H.Richardson lbw b Khan	13	66	37	-	2
L.Vincent c Dravid b Khan	3	30	22	-	-
S.P.Fleming* c & b Khan	21	108	66	-	3
C.D.McMillan c Dravid b Nehra	4	27	19	-	1
N.J.Astle c Harbhajan b Nehra	0	2	2	-	-
S.B.Styris lbw b Harbhajan	13	58	38	-	2
J.D.P.Oram c Tendulkar b Harbhajan	3	13	11	-	-
R.G.Hart† lbw b Khan	3	16	16	-	-
D.L.Vettori c Laxman b Khan	6	31	11	-	1
D.R.Tuffey run out	13	16	14	1	-
S.E.Bond not out	0	1	0	-	-
Extras (b 1, lb 4, nb 10)	15				
TOTAL (38.2 overs)	**94**	189			

	Runs	Mins	Balls	6s	4s
c Patel b Nehra	28	116	71	-	3
c Patel b Yohannan	9	79	52	-	1
c Khan b Nehra	32	88	58	-	5
lbw b Nehra	18	66	32	1	2
c Patel b Khan	14	41	28	-	1
c Patel b Harbhajan	17	61	37	-	2
not out	26	62	40	-	3
not out	11	28	21	-	1
(lb 4, nb 1)	5				
TOTAL (56.2 overs) (6 wkts)	**160**	273			

Bowling	O	M	R	W	O	M	R	W
NEW ZEALAND								
Bond	14.2	7	39	4	10	0	58	1
Tuffey	9	6	12	4	16	3	41	4
Oram	10	1	22	2	12.5	2	41	4
Styris	2	0	10	0				
Astle	3	2	4	0	5	1	13	1
INDIA								
Khan	13.2	4	29	5	13	0	56	1
Yohannan	9	4	16	0	16	5	27	1
Nehra	8	3	20	2	16.2	4	34	3
Bangar	2	1	4	0				
Harbhajan	6	0	20	2	11	0	39	1

Fall of Wickets	I	NZ	I	NZ
	1st	*1st*	*2nd*	*2nd*
1st	1	7	2	30
2nd	11	39	8	52
3rd	26	47	57	89
4th	34	48	64	90
5th	40	60	85	105
6th	70	64	110	136
7th	91	69	130	-
8th	92	79	131	-
9th	93	94	136	-
10th	99	94	154	-

NEW ZEALAND v INDIA First One-day International

at Eden Park, Auckland (d/n) on 26 December, 2002
Toss : New Zealand. Umpires : B.F. Bowden & E.A.R. de Silva
New Zealand won by 3 wickets

After Sehwag was dismissed in the second over, India recovered to be 63-2 in the 16th over but the dismissal of Das signalled a collapse with eight wickets falling for 45 and India being bowled out in the 33rd over. Oram continued his good form with the ball taking his first five wicket bag.

New Zealand also struggled being 52-6 before Oram steadied the innings and saw the home side winning by three wickets. Srinath immediately found conditions to his liking in his first game since joining the side for the one-day games, taking 4-23 off ten overs.

INDIA

	Runs	Mins	Balls	6s	4s
S.S.Das c Fleming b Mills	30	70	60	1	2
V.Sehwag b Bond	0	8	5	-	-
V.V.S.Laxman c Mills b Tuffey	9	28	21	-	1
S.C.Ganguly* b Oram	14	36	14	-	2
R.S.Dravid† c Vettori b Tuffey	20	79	51	-	2
Yuvraj Singh c Astle b Oram	2	2	3	-	-
M.Kaif c Fleming b Oram	6	17	13	-	1
A.R.Kumble lbw b Oram	0	2	3	-	-
J.Srinath c Sinclair b Oram	0	8	7	-	-
Z.Khan lbw b Vettori	14	37	20	-	2
A.Nehra not out	0	4	2	-	-
Extras (lb 6, w 5, nb 2)	13				
TOTAL (32.5 overs)	**108**	150			

NEW ZEALAND

	Runs	Mins	Balls	6s	4s
S.P.Fleming* lbw b Nehra	12	54	37	-	-
N.J.Astle c Laxman b Srinath	0	5	4	-	-
M.S.Sinclair c Ganguly b Khan	15	53	29	-	1
C.D.McMillan c Dravid b Srinath	4	33	19	-	1
L.Vincent lbw b Nehra	13	35	17	-	2
B.B.McCullum† c Dravid b Srinath	4	4	5	-	-
J.D.P.Oram not out	27	99	54	-	2
K.D.Mills c Dravid b Srinath	21	58	42	-	3
D.L.Vettori not out	5	37	22	-	-
D.R.Tuffey					
S.E.Bond					
Extras (lb 2, w 3, nb 3)	8				
TOTAL (37.4 overs) (7 wkts)	**109**	193			

Bowling	O	M	R	W
NEW ZEALAND				
Tuffey	6.5	1	23	2
Bond	7	0	32	1
Mills	8	2	20	1
Oram	10	4	26	5
Vettori	1	0	1	1
INDIA				
Srinath	10	3	23	4
Khan	9	1	43	1
Nehra	10	3	16	2
Kumble	7	1	15	0
Ganguly	1.4	0	10	0

Fall of Wickets	I	NZ
1st	5	1
2nd	28	29
3rd	63	29
4th	63	48
5th	65	52
6th	74	52
7th	74	86
8th	74	-
9th	108	-
10th	108	-

NEW ZEALAND v INDIA   Second One-day International

at McLean Park, Napier on 29 December, 2002
Toss : India. Umpires : D.B. Cowie & E.A.R. de Silva
New Zealand won by 35 runs

Hitchcock played his first one-day international in New Zealand when he replaced Bond while Harbhajan and Bangar replaced Kumble and Das for India.

Fleming went in the third over and then Astle and Sinclair added 136 for the second wicket, which turned out to be the only century stand of the series. Astle got his fifty off 71 balls, 19 fewer than Sinclair. Vincent was the only other batsman to reach double figures. India had two overs deducted due to a slow over rate.

Ganguly went to the third ball of the innings and then Sehwag took control. He got his fifty from 74 balls and reached his century from a further 37 deliveries. He was seventh out as India were dismissed 35 runs short to give New Zealand a 2-0 lead.

NEW ZEALAND

	Runs	Mins	Balls	6s	4s
S.P.Fleming* c Kaif b Srinath	1	14	6	-	-
N.J.Astle c Khan b Ganguly	76	148	95	1	5
M.S.Sinclair c David b Harbhajan	78	174	126	1	4
C.D.McMillan lbw b Srinath	5	10	7	-	-
L.Vincent b Srinath	34	46	32	-	2
J.D.P.Oram run out	4	7	7	-	-
B.B.McCullum† c Yuvraj b Khan	7	15	12	-	-
K.D.Mills b Khan	5	9	6	-	-
D.L.Vettori not out	5	13	6	-	1
D.R.Tuffey b Khan	5	8	6	-	-
P.A.Hitchcock not out	2	1	1	-	-

Extras (b 9, lb 9, w 6, nb 4) 28
TOTAL (50 overs) (9 wkts) .. **254** 227

INDIA

	Runs	Mins	Balls	6s	4s
S.C.Ganguly* b Tuffey	0	2	3	-	-
V.Sehwag run out	108	166	119	2	9
V.V.S.Laxman c McCullum b Mills	20	60	39	-	3
R.S.Dravid† run out	18	36	27	-	1
Yuvraj Singh st McCullum b Vettori	0	2	2	-	-
M.Kaif c McCullum b Tuffey	24	44	38	-	1
S.B.Bangar c McCullum b Oram	4	3	5	-	1
Harbhajan Singh c McCullum b Hitchcock	14	17	17	1	1
Z.Khan c McMillan b Mills	11	16	13	-	1
J.Srinath c Oram b Mills	3	10	6	-	-
A.Nehra not out	0	3	0	-	-

Extras (lb 3, w 7, nb 7) 17
TOTAL (43.4 overs) **219** 183

Bowling	O	M	R	W
INDIA				
Srinath	10	0	34	3
Khan	10	0	47	3
Nehra	8	0	42	0
Harbhajan Singh	10	0	56	1
Bangar	7	0	34	0
Ganguly	5	0	23	1
NEW ZEALAND				
Tuffey	10	2	35	2
Mills	9.4	0	45	3
Oram	8	0	50	1
Vettori	8	0	48	1
Hitchcock	8	0	38	1

Fall of Wickets		
	NZ	I
1st	10	0
2nd	146	57
3rd	157	104
4th	199	104
5th	204	182
6th	224	187
7th	233	204
8th	237	206
9th	252	217
10th	-	219

NEW ZEALAND v INDIA   **Third One-day International**

at Jade Stadium, Christchurch (d/n) on 1 January, 2003
Toss : India. Umpires : D.B. Cowie & E.A.R. de Silva
New Zealand won by 5 wickets

India decided to bat first but for the second time in the series were dismissed for just 108, this time off 41.1 overs. Only Dravid reached 20 as McCullum equalled the New Zealand record for dismissals in a one-day innings while Hitchcock had his best figures for New Zealand.

Despite losing two early wickets and then being 92-5, New Zealand were never in danger of losing and won with 23.1 overs to spare to take a 3-0 lead in the series.

INDIA

	Runs	Mins	Balls	6s	4s
V.Sehwag c McCullum b Mills	7	17	20	-	1
S.C.Ganguly* c McCullum b Tuffey	4	36	24	-	-
V.V.S.Laxman c McCullum b Hitchcock	10	59	36	-	1
R.S.Dravid† c Vettori b Hitchcock	20	69	59	-	2
M.Kaif c McCullum b Oram	17	42	26	-	3
Yuvraj Singh run out	12	60	44	-	1
S.B.Bangar c McCullum b Tuffey	1	10	9	-	-
A.B.Agarkar c Hitchcock b Astle .	6	16	11	-	1
Z.Khan not out	8	29	19	-	1
Harbhajan Singh c Vincent b Hitchcock	0	3	1	-	-
J.Srinath c Fleming b Oram	1	6	3	-	-
Extras (lb 8, w 9, nb 5)	22				
TOTAL (41.1 overs)	**108**	178			

NEW ZEALAND

	Runs	Mins	Balls	6s	4s
S.P.Fleming* c Kaif b Khan	4	34	28	-	-
N.J.Astle c Ganguly b Srinath ...	32	60	30	-	6
M.S.Sinclair c & b Agarkar	0	5	4	-	-
C.D.McMillan c Kaif b Agarkar ..	22	76	45	-	3
L.Vincent lbw b Agarkar	15	37	30	-	1
B.B.McCullum† not out	10	30	16	-	-
J.D.P.Oram not out	10	12	9	-	2
K.D.Mills					
D.L.Vettori					
D.R.Tuffey					
P.A.Hitchcock					
Extras (lb 6, w 9, nb 1)	16				
TOTAL (26.5 overs) (5 wkts)	**109**	130			

Bowling	O	M	R	W
NEW ZEALAND				
Tuffey	10	2	11	2
Mills	10	2	26	1
Oram	8.1	1	22	2
Hitchcock	8	0	30	3
Astle	5	1	11	1
INDIA				
Srinath	8	0	44	1
Khan	9	2	26	1
Agarkar	8.5	1	26	3
Bangar	1	0	7	0

Fall of Wickets	I	NZ
1st	10	37
2nd	15	39
3rd	38	50
4th	67	83
5th	82	92
6th	83	-
7th	90	-
8th	100	-
9th	102	-
10th	108	-

NEW ZEALAND v INDIA   Fourth One-day International

at Queenstown Events Centre on 4 January, 2003
Toss : New Zealand. Umpires : D.B. Cowie & E.A.R. de Silva
New Zealand won by 7 wickets

Queenstown hosted its first one-day international while India included Mongia who had come to New Zealand as a replacement for Laxman who had missed out on the World Cup squad.

The low scores continued as Adams scythed through the Indian line up. His 5-22 were his best one-day figures. Only Sehwag and Yuvraj reached 20.

Fleming had his best innings of the series and saw his side take an unbeatable 4-0 lead, winning the match with 24.2 overs left.

INDIA

	Runs	Mins	Balls	6s	4s
V.Sehwag c Astle b Adams	23	45	39	-	4
R.S.Dravid b Adams	18	65	52	-	1
D.Mongia c Vettori b Adams	12	38	20	-	1
M.Kaif c McMillan b Adams	0	9	4	-	-
S.C.Ganguly* c Mills b Tuffey	2	15	13	-	-
Yuvraj Singh c Tuffey b Styris	25	86	61	-	3
P.A.Patel† b Mills	13	35	31	-	1
A.B.Agarkar run out	0	8	3	-	-
Z.Khan c McCullum b Tuffey	1	12	6	-	-
J.Srinath not out	10	36	29	1	-
A.Nehra c McCullum b Adams	0	14	10	-	-

Extras (lb 1, w 11, nb 6) 18
TOTAL (43.4 overs) **122** 186

NEW ZEALAND

	Runs	Mins	Balls	6s	4s
S.P.Fleming* c Sehwag b Srinath	47	92	59	1	5
N.J.Astle c Dravid b Srinath	15	21	15	-	1
M.S.Sinclair not out	32	98	63	-	4
C.D.McMillan b Srinath	0	6	2	-	-
S.B.Styris not out	8	20	17	-	1
B.B.McCullum†					
J.D.P.Oram					
A.R.Adams					
K.D.Mills					
D.L.Vettori					
D.R.Tuffey					

Extras (b 1, lb 3, w 14, nb 3) .. 21
TOTAL (25.4 overs) (3 wkts) **123** 120

Bowling	O	M	R	W
NEW ZEALAND				
Tuffey	10	0	36	2
Mills	10	2	28	1
Oram	10	1	28	0
Adams	8.4	1	22	5
Styris	3	1	5	1
Vettori	2	0	2	0
INDIA				
Srinath	9.4	1	35	3
Khan	2	0	21	0
Nehra	10	1	37	0
Agarkar	4	0	26	0

Fall of Wickets	I	NZ
1st	38	28
2nd	55	101
3rd	57	103
4th	67	-
5th	69	-
6th	94	-
7th	100	-
8th	107	-
9th	118	-
10th	122	-

New Zealand Cricket Almanack

NEW ZEALAND v INDIA **Fifth One-day International**

at Westpac Stadium, Wellington (d/n) on 8 January, 2003
Toss : New Zealand. Umpires : D.J. Harper & B.F. Bowden
India won by 2 wickets

Fleming decided to bat first having earlier said he wanted to put his players under pressure now that the series had been decided. His decision certainly put the middle order under plenty of pressure as New Zealand collapsed to be 3-3 after 3.4 overs. Fleming reached 5000 one-day runs when he reached 12 and McCullum and Adams played useful knocks as New Zealand reached 168.

India also struggled and were 25-3 after 6 overs but Sehwag and Yuvraj played elegant innings. Yuvraj, whose fifty took 79 balls, steered his side toward victory and a cameo from Khan gave India its first win on tour with 6.4 overs to spare.

NEW ZEALAND

	Runs	Mins	Balls	6s	4s
S.P.Fleming* c Dravid b Nehra	19	74	41	-	2
N.J.Astle lbw b Khan	0	7	2	-	-
M.S.Sinclair b Khan	0	1	1	-	-
C.Z.Harris lbw b Khan	1	10	6	-	-
C.L.Cairns b Srinath	25	45	32	-	4
S.B.Styris b Nehra	13	50	33	-	1
B.B.McCullum† b Kumble	35	102	73	-	3
A.R.Adams c Kaif b Ganguly	35	34	27	3	3
D.L.Vettori not out	16	38	31	-	-
D.R.Tuffey b Srinath	4	8	9	-	-
S.E.Bond lbw b Kumble	0	4	7	-	-

Extras (b 4, lb 7, w 3, nb 6) 20
TOTAL (42.4 overs) **168** 193

Bowling	O	M	R	W
INDIA				
Srinath	10	2	24	2
Khan	8	0	30	3
Nehra	9	1	38	2
Ganguly	6	0	27	1
Kumble	9.4	0	38	2
NEW ZEALAND				
Tuffey	10	2	40	1
Bond	10	0	34	2
Adams	9.2	0	47	2
Styris	9	1	29	2
Vettori	5	0	14	1

INDIA

	Runs	Mins	Balls	6s	4s
S.C.Ganguly* c McCullum b Tuffey	0	1	1	-	-
V.Sehwag c Fleming b Styris	45	60	40	-	9
D.Mongia b Bond	2	18	10	-	-
S.R.Tendulkar lbw b Bond	0	9	10	-	-
R.S.Dravid† c McCullum b Styris	7	72	41	-	-
Yuvraj Singh c Harris b Vettori	54	124	85	-	8
M.Kaif c Fleming b Adams	1	20	13	-	-
A.R.Kumble hit wicket b Adams	2	9	10	-	-
Z.Khan not out	34	65	42	1	3
J.Srinath not out	1	14	10	-	-
A.Nehra					

Extras (lb 5, w 16, nb 2) 23
TOTAL (43.2 overs) (8 wkts) **169** 200

Fall of Wickets

	NZ	I
1st	0	0
2nd	0	19
3rd	3	25
4th	48	66
5th	51	91
6th	92	114
7th	140	116
8th	158	160
9th	167	-
10th	168	-

84

NEW ZEALAND v INDIA

Sixth One-day International

at Eden Park, Auckland (d/n) on 11 January, 2003
Toss : India. Umpires : B.F. Bowden & D.J. Harper
India won by 1 wicket

The New Zealand innings was based on an 80 run stand for the fifth wicket between Styris and Vincent off 119 balls. Styris went for 42 but Vincent reached fifty off 106 balls. After being 130-4, New Zealand collapsed to 147-9 before Bond played a cameo innings. His 31 not out came from just 15 balls and included three sixes. The last wicket added 52 off just 20 balls.

Sehwag then plundered the New Zealand attack getting 50 off 80 balls and then his second century of the series after 129 deliveries to put India on course for a comfortable victory. However, a late collapse, including two runs outs, saw India only just get home by one wicket with seven balls left.

NEW ZEALAND

	Runs	Mins	Balls	6s	4s
S.P.Fleming* c Dravid b Nehra	14	42	32	-	1
M.S.Sinclair b Srinath	18	75	54	-	1
C.Z.Harris lbw b Agarkar	0	6	6	-	-
C.L.Cairns b Srinath	13	33	22	-	2
S.B.Styris c Bangar b Ganguly	42	93	52	-	7
L.Vincent not out	53	137	107	1	3
B.B.McCullum† run out	0	4	0	-	-
K.D.Mills c Dravid b Srinath	0	10	7	-	-
A.R.Adams b Khan	2	14	8	-	-
D.R.Tuffey run out	1	5	5	-	-
S.E.Bond not out	31	15	15	3	2

Extras (b 4, lb 11, w 2, nb 8) .. 25
TOTAL (50 overs) (9 wkts) .. **199** 222

INDIA

	Runs	Mins	Balls	6s	4s
S.C.Ganguly* c McCullum b Adams	23	63	44	-	4
V.Sehwag c Fleming b Mills	112	175	139	3	11
R.S.Dravid† lbw b Styris	21	71	50	-	2
S.R.Tendulkar c McCullum b Tuffey	1	21	13	-	-
Yuvraj Singh c Fleming b Harris	8	30	25	-	-
M.Kaif b Adams	7	31	19	-	1
S.B.Bangar lbw b Adams	1	5	2	-	-
A.B.Agarkar run out	0	4	2	-	-
Z.Khan run out	1	4	2	-	-
J.Srinath not out	0	6	1	-	-
A.Nehra not out	1	4	1	-	-

Extras (lb 4, w 12, nb 9) 25
TOTAL (48.5 overs) (9 wkts) **200** 214

Bowling	O	M	R	W
INDIA				
Srinath	10	2	13	3
Khan	10	0	53	1
Nehra	10	1	31	1
Agarkar	8	0	34	1
Bangar	4	0	22	0
Ganguly	8	2	31	1
NEW ZEALAND				
Tuffey	10	0	46	1
Bond	6	1	20	0
Adams	9.5	0	41	3
Mills	10	0	43	1
Styris	10	1	40	1
Harris	3	0	6	1

Fall of Wickets

	NZ	I
1st	26	70
2nd	28	142
3rd	47	159
4th	50	182
5th	130	187
6th	131	194
7th	134	194
8th	144	197
9th	147	198
10th	-	-

NEW ZEALAND v INDIA   Seventh One-day International

at Westpac Park, Hamilton (d/n) on 14 January, 2003
Toss : New Zealand. Umpires : D.B. Cowie & D.J. Harper
New Zealand won by 6 wickets

India again started disastrously being 44-6 after 16.4 overs. The tail wagged and they ended with another score of 122 in another disappointing effort. Adams finished with 4-21 to give him 14 wickets in four games.

New Zealand were 32-3 after 6.4 overs before Fleming (50 off 85 balls) and Styris added 84 off 125 balls. This enabled the home side to win with 21.2 overs to spare and gave them a 5-2 series win. Srinath was again the pick of the Indian bowling lineup.

INDIA	Runs	Mins	Balls	6s	4s
S.C.Ganguly* b Adams	15	67	39	-	1
V.Sehwag c McCullum b Mills	4	23	19	-	-
S.R.Tendulkar c Fleming b Tuffey	1	7	6	-	-
D.Mongia c Fleming b Tuffey	0	1	1	-	-
R.S.Dravid† c Styris b Mills	12	30	26	-	2
Yuvraj Singh c Vincent b Styris	33	82	58	-	4
M.Kaif c McCullum b Adams	0	8	6	-	-
A.R.Kumble c Fleming b Adams	21	106	70	-	4
Z.Khan c McCullum b Styris	5	15	15	-	1
J.Srinath lbw b Adams	15	28	26	-	3
A.Nehra not out	2	7	6	-	-
Extras (lb 5, w 6, nb 3)	14				
TOTAL (44.5 overs)	**122**	192			

NEW ZEALAND	Runs	Mins	Balls	6s	4s
S.P.Fleming* not out	60	139	92	-	8
M.S.Sinclair b Srinath	3	11	4	-	-
B.B.McCullum† lbw b Khan	4	6	6	-	1
C.L.Cairns b Srinath	11	17	12	-	1
S.B.Styris b Kumble	29	95	53	-	4
L.Vincent not out	5	6	6	-	1
C.Z.Harris					
K.D.Mills					
A.R.Adams					
D.L.Vettori					
D.R.Tuffey					
Extras (lb 6, w 6, nb 1)	13				
TOTAL (28.4 overs) (4 wkts)	**125**	139			

Bowling NEW ZEALAND	O	M	R	W
Tuffey	10	1	26	2
Mills	10	1	29	2
Adams	8.5	3	21	4
Styris	10	4	23	2
Vettori	6	0	18	0
INDIA				
Srinath	8.4	2	28	2
Khan	9	2	38	1
Nehra	5	0	28	0
Kumble	4	0	16	1
Ganguly	2	0	9	0

Fall of Wickets	I	NZ
1st	14	5
2nd	17	12
3rd	17	32
4th	44	116
5th	44	-
6th	44	-
7th	93	-
8th	99	-
9th	117	-
10th	122	-

WORLD CUP

Australia became the first side to win the World Cup on three occcasions and the first since 1979 to successfully defend the title when they decisively defeated India in the final.

The New Zealand campaign suffered an early setback against Sri Lanka but then victories were obtained over West Indies and South Africa. Due to security concerns New Zealand did not go to Kenya so the game was forfeited. They beat Bangladesh and Canada and went into the Super Sixes after the game between South Africa and Sri Lanka ended in a tie.

After beating Zimbabwe, New Zealand needed to beat either Australia or India to ensure a semi-final. Australia were 84-7 but reached 208 and dismissed New Zealand for a mere 112. New Zealand were then dismissed for just 146 against India who won by three wickets.

On the individual side Fleming led from the front and was the only player to get 300 runs. His 134 not out against South Africa was the best innings of his 197 match career. Styris was the only other batsman to get 250 runs, including a brilliant 141 in the first game. Astle, who had three ducks, was disappointing despite getting a century against Zimbabwe. McMillan and Vincent had poor returns while Cairns averaged 37 but reached fifty only once. Bond was the leading bowler, getting 17 wickets, and Oram was consistent, getting 14 wickets. Adams took 10 wickets but was expensive while Vettori found wickets hard to come by, although he was economical. McCullum kept wickets well but dropped a crucial catch against India.

The New Zealand team was: S.P. Fleming *(captain, Wellington)*, C.L. Cairns *(vice-captain, Canterbury)*, A.R. Adams *(Auckland)*, N.J. Astle *(Canterbury)*, B.B. McCullum *(Otago)*, C.D. McMillan *(Canterbury)*, K.D. Mills *(Auckland)*, J.D.P. Oram *(Central Districts)*, M.S. Sinclair *(Central Districts)*, S.B. Styris *(Northern Districts)*, D.R. Tuffey *(Northern Districts)*, D.L. Vettori *(Northern Districts)*, L. Vincent *(Auckland)*. Coach, D.C. Aberhart; Assistant coach, A. Ross; Manager, J.J. Crowe.

New Zealand Averages

BATTING	M	I	NO	HS	Agg	Ave	100s	50s	Ct	St	SR
S.B. Styris	8	7	2	141	268	53.60	1	1	5	-	101
S.P. Fleming	8	8	1	134*	321	45.85	1	-	4	-	85
N.J. Astle	7	7	2	102*	213	42.60	1	1	1	-	80
C.Z. Harris	6	6	3	38*	116	38.66	-	-	1	-	68
C.L. Cairns	8	7	1	54	223	37.16	-	1	4	-	81
A.R. Adams	7	5	1	36	90	22.50	-	-	1	-	118
C.D. McMillan	6	6	0	75	125	20.83	-	1	1	-	79
B.B. McCullum	7	3	1	36*	41	20.50	-	-	9	-	53
D.L. Vettori	7	3	0	13	36	12.00	-	-	-	-	48
J.D.P. Oram	8	3	0	23	35	11.66	-	-	3	-	46
D.R. Tuffey	2	2	0	11	15	7.50	-	-	-	-	93
L. Vincent	4	3	0	9	17	5.66	-	-	2	-	48
S.E. Bond	8	3	2	3	5	5.00	-	-	3	-	23
M.S. Sinclair	1	-	-	-	-	-	-	-	-	-	-
K.D. Mills	1	-	-	-	-	-	-	-	-	-	-

BOWLING	O	M	R	W	Ave	Best	R/O
S.E. Bond	78	12	305	17	17.94	6-23	3.91
J.D.P. Oram	70	8	295	14	21.07	4-52	4.21
C.L. Cairns	8	0	54	2	27.00	2-16	6.75
N.J. Astle	16	0	83	3	27.66	3-34	5.19
A.R. Adams	57.4	3	347	10	34.70	4-44	6.01
S.B. Styris	34.4	0	183	4	45.75	2-23	5.27
C.Z. Harris	35	3	129	2	64.50	1-19	3.69
D.R. Tuffey	15	1	77	1	77.00	1-41	5.13
D.L. Vettori	65	1	259	2	129.50	1-38	3.98
C.D. McMillan	2	1	4	0	-	-	2.00
K.D. Mills	6	0	32	0	-	-	5.33

POOL A

10 February, 2003
Harare: *Zimbabwe beat Namibia by 86 runs (D/L method)*
Zimbabwe 340 for 2 (50 overs) (C.B.Wishart 172*, G.W.Flower 78*, M.A.Vermeulen 39, A.Flower 39);
Namibia 104 for 5 (25.1 overs)

11 February, 2003
Johannesburg: *Australia beat Pakistan by 82 runs*
Australia 310 for 8 (50 overs) (A.Symonds 143*, R.T.Ponting 53, Wasim Akram 3-64);
Pakistan 228 (44.3 overs) (Rashid Latif 33, Wasim Akram 33, Salim Elahi 30, I.J.Harvey 4-58, G.B.Hogg 3-54)

12 February, 2003
Paarl: *India beat Netherlands by 68 runs*
India 204 (48.5 overs) (S.R.Tendulkar 52, D.Mongia 42, Yuvraj Singh 37, T.B.M.De Leede 4-35);
Netherlands 136 (48.1 overs) (D.L.S.van Bunge 62, J.Srinath 4-30, A.R.Kumble 4-32)

13 February, 2003
Harare: *England forfeited the match*
Zimbabwe
England

15 February, 2003
Centurion: *Australia beat India by 9 wickets*
India 125 (41.4 overs) (S.R.Tendulkar 36, J.N.Gillespie 3-13, B.Lee 3-36);
Australia 128 for 1 (22.2 overs) (A.C.Gilchrist 48, M.L.Hayden 45*)

16 February, 2003
East London: *England beat Netherlands by 6 wickets*
Netherlands 142 for 9 (50 overs) (T.B.M.De Leede 58*, J.M.Anderson 4-25);
England 144 for 4 (23.2 overs) (N.V.Knight 51, M.P.Vaughan 51, D.L.S.van Bunge 3-16)

16 February, 2003
Kimberley: *Namibia lost to Pakistan by 171 runs*
Pakistan 255 for 9 (50 overs) (Salim Elahi 63, Yousuf Youhana 43, Rashid Latif 36);
Namibia 84 (17.4 overs) (Wasim Akram 5-28, Shoaib Akhtar 4-46)

19 February, 2003
Harare: *India beat Zimbabwe by 83 runs*
India 255 for 7 (50 overs) (S.R.Tendulkar 81, R.S.Dravid 43*, V.Sehwag 36);
Zimbabwe 172 (44.4 overs) (S.C.Ganguly 3-22)

19 February, 2003
Port Elizabeth: *England beat Namibia by 55 runs*
England 272 (50 overs) (A.J.Stewart 60, M.E.Trescothick 58, P.D.Collingwood 38, C.White 35, R.J.van Vuuren 5-43, G.Snyman 3-69);
Namibia 217 for 9 (50 overs) (A.J.Burger 85, D.Keulder 46, R.C.Irani 3-30)

20 February, 2003
Potchefstroom: *Australia beat Netherlands by 75 runs (D/L method)*
Australia 170 for 2 (36 overs) (D.R.Martyn 67*, M.L.Hayden 33);
Netherlands 122 (30.2 overs) (A.J.Bichel 3-13, I.J.Harvey 3-25)

22 February, 2003
Cape Town: *England beat Pakistan by 112 runs*
England 246 for 8 (50 overs) (P.D.Collingwood 66*, M.P.Vaughan 52, A.J.Stewart 30);
Pakistan 134 (31 overs) (Shoaib Akhtar 43, J.M.Anderson 4-29, C.White 3-33)

23 February, 2003
Pietermaritzburg: *India beat Namibia by 181 runs*
India 311 for 2 (50 overs) (S.R.Tendulkar 152, S.C.Ganguly 112*);
Namibia 130 (42.3 overs) (Yuvraj Singh 4-6)

24 February, 2003
Bulawayo: *Australia beat Zimbabwe by 7 wickets*
Zimbabwe 246 for 9 (50 overs) (A.Flower 62, A.M.Blignaut 54, G.W.Flower 37, G.B.Hogg 3-46);
Australia 248 for 3 (47.3 overs) (A.C.Gilchrist 61, D.S.Lehmann 56*, D.R.Martyn 50*, R.T.Ponting 38, M.L.Hayden 34)

25 February, 2003
Paarl: *Pakistan beat Netherlands by 97 runs*
Pakistan 253 for 9 (50 overs) (Yousuf Youhana 58, Taufeeq Umar 48, Abdur Razzaq 47);
Netherlands 156 (39.3 overs) (D.L.S.van Bunge 31, Wasim Akram 3-24, Shoaib Akhtar 3-26)

26 February, 2003
Durban: *India beat England by 82 runs*
India 250 for 9 (50 overs) (R.S.Dravid 62, S.R.Tendulkar 50, Yuvraj Singh 42, D.Mongia 32, A.R.Caddick 3-69);
England 168 (45.3 overs) (A.Flintoff 64, A.Nehra 6-23)

27 February, 2003
Potchefstroom: *Australia beat Namibia by 256 runs*
Australia 301 for 6 (50 overs) (M.L.Hayden 88, A.Symonds 59, D.S.Lehmann 50*, D.R.Martyn 35, L.J.Burger 3-39);
Namibia 45 (14 overs) (G.D.McGrath 7-15)

28 February, 2003
Bulawayo: *Zimbabwe beat Netherlands by 99 runs*
Zimbabwe 301 for 8 (50 overs) (A.Flower 71, A.M.Blignaut 58, H.H.Streak 44, D.D.Ebrahim 32, G.J.Whittall 30);
Netherlands 202 for 9 (50 overs) (D.L.S.van Bunge 37, R.P.Lefebvre 30, B.A.Murphy 3-44)

1 March, 2003
Centurion: *India beat Pakistan by 6 wickets*
Pakistan 273 for 7 (50 overs) (Saeed Anwar 101, Younis Khan 32);
India 276 for 4 (45.4 overs) (S.R.Tendulkar 98, Yuvraj Singh 50*, R.S.Dravid 44*, M.Kaif 35)

2 March, 2003
Port Elizabeth: *Australia beat England by 2 wickets*
England 204 for 8 (50 overs) (A.J.Stewart 46, A.Flintoff 45, M.E.Trescothick 37, N.V.Knight 30, A.J.Bichel 7-20);
Australia 208 for 8 (49.4 overs) (M.G.Bevan 74*, D.S.Lehmann 37, A.J.Bichel 34*, A.R.Caddick 4-35)

3 March, 2003
Bloemfontein: *Netherlands beat Namibia by 64 runs*
Netherlands 314 for 4 (50 overs) (K.J.J.Van Noortwijk 134*, J.F.Kloppenburg 121);
Namibia 250 (46.5 overs) (D.Keulder 52, B.G.Murgatroyd 52, A.J.Burger 41, M.Karg 41, J.F.Kloppenburg 4-42, Adeel Raja 4-42)

4 March, 2003
Bulawayo: No result
Pakistan 73 for 3 (14 overs) (Saeed Anwar 40*);
Zimbabwe

Final Pool Placings

POOL A	W	L	NR	T	Pts	PCF
Australia	6	–	–	–	24	16.0
India	5	1	–	–	20	12.0
Zimbabwe	3	2	1	–	14	3.5
England	3	3	–	–	12	–
Pakistan	2	3	1	–	10	–
Netherlands	1	5	–	–	4	–
Namibia	–	6	–	–	0	–

POOL B	W	L	NR	T	Pts	PCF
Sri Lanka	4	1	–	1	18	7.5
Kenya	4	2	–	–	16	10.0
New Zealand	4	2	–	–	16	4.0
West Indies	3	2	1	–	14	–
South Africa	3	2	–	1	14	–
Canada	1	5	–	–	4	–
Bangladesh	–	5	1	–	2	–

*Points carried forward (PCF) based on results against other
teams in the pool – 4 for a win or 2 for a tie against other
Super Six qualifiers and 1 for a win or 0.5 for a tie against
non-qualifiers.*
*The final positions of Kenya and New Zealand and West
Indies and South Africa were based on the result of the match
between the two teams.*

Final Super Six Placings

	W	L	NR	T	Pts
Australia	5	–	–	–	24.0
India	4	1	–	–	20.0
Kenya	3	2	–	–	14.0
Sri Lanka	2	3	–	–	11.5
New Zealand	1	4	–	–	8.0
Zimbabwe	–	5	–	–	3.5

NEW ZEALAND CRICKET

NEW ZEALAND v SRI LANKA
World Cup – Pool B

at Goodyear Park, Bloemfontein on 10 February, 2003
Toss : New Zealand. Umpires : S.A. Bucknor & N.A. Mallender
Sri Lanka won by 47 runs.

After Atapattu went in the sixth over, Jayasuriya (whose century came off 111 balls) and Tillakaratne added 170 off 178 balls for the second wicket. Sri Lanka were restricted to just 79 in the last 15 overs as the New Zealand bowlers came back well.

The batsmen, however, were in trouble with wickets lost in each of the first two overs and then another in the sixth. Styris played a masterful innings, scoring the second highest total by a New Zealand batsman in one-day internationals. His hundred came off 104 deliveries. Of the other batsmen, only Cairns got to twenty as New Zealand fell 47 runs short.

SRI LANKA

	Runs	Mins	Balls	6s	4s
M.S.Atapattu c Styris b Bond	6	24	17	-	-
S.T.Jayasuriya* lbw b Astle	120	147	125	-	14
H.P.Tillekeratne not out	81	190	106	-	5
D.P.M.D.Jayawardene lbw b Adams ...	1	5	3	-	-
P.A.de Silva c Styris b Astle	12	11	11	-	2
K.C.Sangakkara† c Adams b Astle ...	13	22	18	-	-
R.P.Arnold b Bond	12	10	14	-	-
W.P.U.J.C.Vaas b Adams ...	5	6	4	-	-
M.Muralitharan not out ...	4	7	6	-	-
C.R.D.Fernando					
P.W.Gunaratne					

Extras (b 3, lb 6, w 4, nb 5) 18
TOTAL (50 overs) (7 wkts) .. 272 215

NEW ZEALAND

	Runs	Mins	Balls	6s	4s
S.P.Fleming* c Sangakkara b Gunaratne	1	9	4	-	-
N.J.Astle run out	0	4	5	-	-
C.D.McMillan c Sangakkara b Gunaratne	3	20	12	-	-
S.B.Styris c Vaas b Arnold	141	177	125	3	6
C.L.Cairns c & b de Silva	32	71	56	-	2
L.Vincent† c Muralitharan b Jayasuriya	1	3	4	-	-
C.Z.Harris b Muralitharan	13	40	35	-	-
J.D.P.Oram st Sangakkara b Muralitharan	12	20	20	-	-
A.R.Adams c sub (T.C.B.Fernando) b Arnold	1	5	4	-	-
D.R.Tuffey c Sangakkara b Arnold	4	6	3	-	-
S.E.Bond not out	2	8	5	-	-

Extras (lb 10, w 5) 15
TOTAL (45.3 overs) 225 186

Bowling NEW ZEALAND	O	M	R	W
Tuffey	5	0	36	0
Bond	10	1	44	2
Oram	10	0	37	0
Adams	9	0	58	2
Harris	4	0	26	0
Styris	5	0	28	0
Astle	7	0	34	3
SRI LANKA				
Vaas	7	0	22	0
Gunaratne	5	0	24	2
Fernando	3	1	19	0
Muralitharan	9	1	42	2
Jayasuriya	8	0	32	1
de Silva	5	0	29	1
Arnold	8.3	0	47	3

Fall of Wickets	SL	NZ
1st	23	1
2nd	193	2
3rd	196	15
4th	213	93
5th	240	94
6th	256	150
7th	263	179
8th	-	182
9th	-	200
10th	-	225

EASTERNS v NEW ZEALAND

At Willowmoore Park, Benoni   4 February 2003

New Zealand 208-7 (C.Z Harris 51*, N.J. Astle 42, S.B. Styris 40) **defeated Easterns** 130 (D.N. Crookes 51*, J.D.P. Oram 5-35) by 78 runs

GAUTENG v NEW ZEALAND

At Soweto Oval   6 February 2003

New Zealand 306-5 (S.P. Fleming 122 retd, C.L. Cairns 70, C.D. McMillan 38, L. Vincent 31*) **defeated Gauteng** 190 (S. Burger 42*, W.A. Dugmore 33) by 116 runs

NEW ZEALAND v WEST INDIES World Cup – Pool B

at St.George's Park, Port Elizabeth on 13 February, 2003
Toss : West Indies. Umpires : D.B. Hair & R.E. Koertzen
New Zealand won by 20 runs.

The New Zealand batsmen all got starts in this game with only two failing to reach double figures but no one was able to get to fifty. Vincent reached 1000 one-day runs but the highlight was the eighth wicket stand of 53 off 37 balls by McCullum and Adams.

The West Indies innings began with a 34 run opening stand but when Lara was run out four balls later they collapsed to be 80-6. Sarwan and Jacobs then added 98 before Sarwan went and then a magnificent catch by Oram to get rid of Jacobs put the issue beyond doubt.

NEW ZEALAND

	Runs	Mins	Balls	6s	4s
S.P.Fleming* c & b Dillon	25	29	25	1	4
D.L.Vettori b Drakes	13	53	25	-	2
N.J.Astle c Jacobs b Hinds	46	86	70	-	6
S.B.Styris c Powell b Drakes	5	20	15	-	1
C.L.Cairns c Dillon b Hinds	37	51	44	1	2
L.Vincent c Hooper b Hinds	9	15	11	-	1
C.Z.Harris b Gayle	19	49	35	-	1
B.B.McCullum† not out	36	69	53	-	1
A.R.Adams not out	35	25	24	2	1
J.D.P.Oram					
S.E.Bond					
Extras (lb 10, w 4, nb 2)	16				
TOTAL (50 overs) (7 wkts) ..	**241**	202			

WEST INDIES

	Runs	Mins	Balls	6s	4s
C.H.Gayle c Fleming b Adams ..	22	35	29	-	5
W.W.Hinds c Styris b Adams	14	48	31	-	2
B.C.Lara run out	2	4	4	-	-
S.Chanderpaul lbw b Oram	2	21	7	-	-
C.L.Hooper* c Bond b Adams	3	8	11	-	-
R.R.Sarwan b Vettori	75	122	99	-	7
R.L.Powell b Oram	14	27	14	-	1
R.D.Jacobs† c Oram b Styris	50	96	73	1	3
V.C.Drakes not out	16	28	18	-	1
N.A.M.McLean run out	5	9	7	-	-
M.Dillon b Adams	8	11	6	-	-
Extras (b 1, lb 3, w 5, nb 1)	10				
TOTAL (49.4 overs)	**221**	209			

Bowling	O	M	R	W
WEST INDIES				
Dillon	10	1	30	1
McLean	6	0	38	0
Drakes	10	1	49	2
Hinds	10	0	35	3
Hooper	9	0	42	0
Gayle	5	0	37	1
NEW ZEALAND				
Bond	10	2	43	0
Adams	9.4	1	44	4
Oram	10	2	26	2
Cairns	1	0	21	0
Vettori	10	0	38	1
Astle	4	0	14	0
Styris	5	0	31	1

Fall of Wickets	NZ	WI
1st	42	34
2nd	58	36
3rd	66	42
4th	130	46
5th	141	46
6th	147	80
7th	188	178
8th	-	191
9th	-	200
10th	-	221

NEW ZEALAND v SOUTH AFRICA   World Cup – Pool B

at The Wanderers, Johannesburg on 16 February, 2003
Toss : South Africa. Umpires : S.A. Bucknor & P. Willey
New Zealand won by 9 wickets (D/L method)

A blistering innings by Gibbs enabled South Africa to score 306 against a New Zealand attack that struggled to contain. His first fifty came from 51 balls and he reached his hundred off 121 deliveries. All the other batsmen got starts while only Styris was able to concede fewer than five runs per over.

New Zealand were undaunted by the large total. After 12 overs they were 76-0 when a power cut caused a stoppage for 15 minutes. Rain caused an 11 minute interruption at 97-1 after 15 overs and when the third break came New Zealand were 182-1 after 30.2 overs. When they returned the target was 226 off 39 overs which was achieved with ease.

Fleming was brilliant as he struck the ball to all corners of the field. His fifty came from 51 balls and his fourth hundred needed 109. It was his highest one-day score.

SOUTH AFRICA	Runs	Mins	Balls	6s	4s
G.C.Smith c McCullum b Bond ..	23	43	28	-	5
H.H.Gibbs c McMillan b Oram .	143	195	141	3	19
N.Boje b Styris	29	59	37	-	4
J.H.Kallis c Vincent b Vettori	33	55	48	1	1
M.V.Boucher† c Cairns b Oram	10	21	14	-	1
L.Klusener not out	33	36	21	1	4
S.M.Pollock* c Oram b Adams ..	10	14	10	-	-
G.Kirsten not out	5	7	4	-	-
H.H.Dippenaar					
M.Ntini					
A.A.Donald					
Extras (lb 6, w 11, nb 3)	20				
TOTAL (50 overs) (6 wkts) ..	**306**	218			

NEW ZEALAND	Runs	Mins	Balls	6s	4s
C.D.McMillan c Boucher b Donald	25	60	32	1	1
S.P.Fleming* not out	134	159	132	-	21
N.J.Astle not out	54	98	57	-	4
S.B.Styris					
C.L.Cairns					
L.Vincent					
B.B.McCullum†					
J.D.P.Oram					
A.R.Adams					
D.L.Vettori					
S.E.Bond					
Extras (lb 8, w 8)	16				
TOTAL (36.5 overs) (1 wkt) .	**229**	159			

Bowling	O	M	R	W
NEW ZEALAND				
Bond	10	0	73	1
Adams	9	0	57	1
Oram	8	0	52	2
Styris	10	0	44	1
Vettori	10	0	58	1
Astle	3	0	16	0
SOUTH AFRICA				
Pollock	8	0	36	0
Ntini	8	1	33	0
Donald	5.5	0	52	1
Kallis	8	0	47	0
Boje	2	0	16	0
Klusener	5	0	37	0

Fall of Wickets	SA	NZ
1st	60	89
2nd	126	-
3rd	193	-
4th	243	-
5th	260	-
6th	287	-
7th	-	-
8th	-	-
9th	-	-
10th	-	-

NEW ZEALAND v KENYA   World Cup – Pool B

at Gymkhana Club Ground, Nairobi on 21 February, 2003
New Zealand forfeited the match

NEW ZEALAND v BANGLADESH   World Cup – Pool B

at De Beers Diamond Oval, Kimberley on 26 February, 2003
Toss : Bangladesh. Umpires : D.B. Hair & D.R. Shepherd
New Zealand won by 7 wickets.

Bangladesh decided to bat and they frustrated the New Zealand bowlers as they reached their highest score of the tournament. Ashraful got their first fifty of the series. New Zealand had Bangladesh 128-7 but were unable to finish off the innings as the captain Masud and Rafique put on an unbeaten 70, a record for Bangladesh for the eighth wicket in one-day internationals.

New Zealand had to score quickly to improve their run rate and this was achieved. McMillan passed 3000 runs as he raced to fifty from 65 balls. The win was achieved with 99 balls to spare

BANGLADESH

	Runs	Mins	Balls	6s	4s
Hannan Sarkar c McCullum					
b Bond	9	28	24	-	2
Mohammad Ashraful c & b Bond	56	129	82	1	6
Sanuar Hossain b Oram	5	18	11	-	-
Habibul Bashar c McCullum					
b Oram	0	1	1	-	-
Alok Kapali c Bond b Adams	9	35	22	-	-
Akram Khan c Fleming b Bond	13	34	38	-	-
Khaled Masud*† not out	35	92	54	-	5
Khaled Mahmud c McCullum					
b Oram	12	31	29	-	1
Mohammad Rafique not out	41	50	42	2	3
Monjurul Islam					
Tapash Baisya					
Extras (b 1, lb 4, w 10, nb 3)	18				
TOTAL (50 overs) (7 wkts)	**198**	212			

NEW ZEALAND

	Runs	Mins	Balls	6s	4s
C.D.McMillan b Mahmud	75	108	83	2	9
S.P.Fleming* c & b Mahmud	32	58	40	1	4
A.R.Adams c Ashraful b Mahmud	18	25	22	1	2
S.B.Styris not out	37	52	36	1	2
C.L.Cairns not out	33	28	21	1	3
M.S.Sinclair					
B.B.McCullum†					
J.D.P.Oram					
K.D.Mills					
D.L.Vettori					
S.E.Bond					
Extras (w 3, nb 1)	4				
TOTAL (33.3 overs) (3 wkts)	**199**	137			

Bowling	O	M	R	W
NEW ZEALAND				
Bond	10	1	33	3
Mills	6	0	32	0
Adams	10	0	50	1
Oram	10	1	32	3
Cairns	3	0	17	0
Vettori	10	0	19	0
Styris	1	0	10	0
BANGLADESH				
Monjurul	7	1	37	0
Baisya	8	0	56	0
Khaled Mahmud	10	0	46	3
Kapali	6	0	38	0
Sanuar Hossain	2	0	19	0
Ashraful	0.3	0	3	0

Fall of Wickets		
	B	NZ
1st	19	71
2nd	37	99
3rd	37	138
4th	71	-
5th	105	-
6th	107	-
7th	128	-
8th	-	-
9th	-	-
10th	-	-

NEW ZEALAND v CANADA

World Cup – Pool B

at Willowmoore Park, Benoni on 3 March, 2003
Toss : New Zealand. Umpires : A.V. Jayaprakash & B.G. Jerling
New Zealand won by 5 wickets.

After being sent in, the Canadian batsmen also proved stubborn. Australian Davidson, who had earlier scored the fastest century of the World Cup, blasted the Kiwi bowlers. His fifty came from just 25 balls in 41 minutes. When he was dismissed the innings lost momentum as Canada was dismissed for 196.

In another quest for quick runs, wickets were sacrificed and New Zealand were 32-3 after 4 overs but then good innings from Adams, Styris (fifty off 37 balls) and Harris saw New Zealand to a win with 27 overs left.

New Zealand qualified for the Super Six stage when South Africa tied with Sri Lanka later in the day.

CANADA

	Runs	Mins	Balls	6s	4s
I.Maraj lbw b Bond	0	16	14	-	-
J.M.Davison c Cairns b Harris	75	93	62	4	9
N.Ifill c McCullum b Oram	7	16	15	-	1
I.S.Billcliff c Fleming b Styris	8	31	24	-	-
N.A.de Groot lbw b Oram	17	56	49	-	3
J.V.Harris* c McCullum b Bond	26	62	39	-	3
A.Bagai† b Oram	1	6	2	-	-
A.M.Samad lbw b Bond	12	21	20	-	2
A.Codrington b Oram	7	30	17	-	1
A.Patel b Styris	25	43	29	-	3
B.B.Seebaran not out	4	20	12	-	-
Extras (lb 1, w 12, nb 1)	14				
TOTAL (47 overs)	**196**	197			

NEW ZEALAND

	Runs	Mins	Balls	6s	4s
C.D.McMillan c Bagai b Davison	14	18	13	-	3
S.P.Fleming* run out	5	7	2	-	1
N.J.Astle st Bagai b Davison	11	8	8	-	2
C.L.Cairns c Maraj b Davison	31	40	28	1	2
A.R.Adams c sub (S.Thuraisingam) b Seebaran	36	28	20	3	3
S.B.Styris not out	54	48	38	2	4
C.Z.Harris not out	38	38	29	-	4
J.D.P.Oram					
D.L.Vettori					
B.B.McCullum†					
S.E.Bond					
Extras (lb 3, w 5)	8				
TOTAL (23 overs) (5 wkts)	**197**	94			

Bowling	O	M	R	W
NEW ZEALAND				
Bond	10	3	29	3
Adams	6	0	38	0
Oram	10	1	52	4
Vettori	10	0	34	0
Styris	4	0	23	2
Harris	7	1	19	1
CANADA				
Patel	3	0	32	0
Davison	10	0	61	3
Codrington	2	0	33	0
Seebaran	7	0	61	1
Ifill	1	0	7	0

Fall of Wickets	C	NZ
1st	21	19
2nd	43	31
3rd	80	32
4th	98	97
5th	123	114
6th	129	-
7th	152	-
8th	153	-
9th	173	-
10th	196	-

POOL B

9 February, 2003
*Cape Town: **West Indies beat South Africa by 3 runs***
West Indies 278 for 5 (50 overs) (B.C.Lara 116, C.L.Hooper 40, R.L.Powell 40*,
S.Chanderpaul 34, R.R.Sarwan 32*);
South Africa 275 for 9 (49 overs) (G.Kirsten 69, L.Klusener 57, M.V.Boucher 49)

11 February, 2003
*Durban: **Canada beat Bangladesh by 60 runs***
Canada 180 (49.1 overs) (I.S.Billcliff 42);
Bangladesh 120 (28 overs) (A.Codrington 5-27)

12 February, 2003
*Potchefstroom: **South Africa beat Kenya by 10 wickets***
Kenya 140 (38 overs) (R.D.Shah 60, L.Klusener 4-16);
South Africa 142 for 0 (21.2 overs) (H.H.Gibbs 87*, G.Kirsten 52*)

14 February, 2003
*Pietermaritzburg: **Sri Lanka beat Bangladesh by 10 wickets***
Bangladesh 124 (31.1 overs) (Alok Kapali 32, W.P.U.J.C.Vaas 6-25, M.Muralitharan 3-25);
Sri Lanka 126 for 0 (21.1 overs) (M.S.Atapattu 69*, S.T.Jayasuriya 55*)

15 February, 2003
*Cape Town: **Kenya beat Canada by 4 wickets***
Canada 197 (49 overs) (I.S.Billcliff 71, J.M.Davison 31, J.V.Harris 31, T.M.Odoyo 4-28);
Kenya 198 for 6 (48.3 overs) (R.D.Shah 61, S.O.Tikolo 42, J.M.Davison 3-15)

18 February, 2003
*Benoni: **No result***
West Indies 244 for 9 (50 overs) (R.L.Powell 50, B.C.Lara 46, C.L.Hooper 45, Monjurul
Islam 3-62);
Bangladesh 32 for 2 (8.1 overs)

19 February, 2003
*Paarl: **Sri Lanka beat Canada by 9 wickets***
Canada 36 (18.4 overs) (R.A.P.Nissanka 4-12, W.P.U.J.C.Vaas 3-15);
Sri Lanka 37 for 1 (4.4 overs)

22 February, 2003
*Bloemfontein: **South Africa beat Bangladesh by 10 wickets***
Bangladesh 108 (35.1 overs) (M.Ntini 4-24);
South Africa 109 for 0 (12 overs) (G.Kirsten 52*, H.H.Gibbs 49*)

23 February, 2003
*Centurion: **West Indies defeated Canada by 7 wickets***
Canada 202 (42.5 overs) (J.M.Davison 111, V.C.Drakes 5-44);
West Indies 206 for 3 (20.3 overs) (B.C.Lara 73, W.W.Hinds 64, R.R.Sarwan 42*)

24 February, 2003
*Nairobi: **Kenya beat Sri Lanka by 53 runs***
Kenya 210 for 9 (50 overs) (K.O.Otieno 60, M.Muralitharan 4-28, W.P.U.J.C.Vaas 3-41);
Sri Lanka 157 (45 overs) (P.A.de Silva 41, C.O.Obuya 5-24)

27 February, 2003
*East London: **South Africa beat Canada by 118 runs***
South Africa 254 for 8 (50 overs) (H.H.Dippenaar 80, G.C.Smith 63, S.M.Pollock 32, A.Patel 3-41);
Canada 136 for 5 (50 overs) (I.Maraj 53*)

28 February, 2003
*Cape Town: **Sri Lanka beat West Indies by 6 runs***
Sri Lanka 228 for 6 (50 overs) (S.T.Jayasuriya 66, H.P.Tillekeratne 36, R.P.Arnold 34*);
West Indies 222 for 9 (50 overs) (S.Chanderpaul 65, C.H.Gayle 55, R.R.Sarwan 47*, W.P.U.J.C.Vaas 4-22)

1 March, 2003
*Johannesburg: **Kenya beat Bangladesh by 32 runs***
Kenya 217 for 7 (50 overs) (M.O.Odumbe 52*, R.D.Shah 37, Brijal Patel 32, Sanuar Hossain 3-49);
Bangladesh 185 (47.2 overs) (Tushar Imran 48, Akram Khan 44, M.O.Odumbe 4-38, S.O.Tikolo 3-14)

3 March, 2003
*Durban: **South Africa tied with Sri Lanka (D/L method)***
Sri Lanka 268 for 9 (50 overs) (M.S.Atapattu 124, P.A.de Silva 73, J.H.Kallis 3-41);
South Africa 229 for 6 (45 overs) (H.H.Gibbs 73, M.V.Boucher 45*, G.C.Smith 35)

4 March, 2003
*Kimberley: **West Indies beat Kenya by 142 runs***
West Indies 246 for 7 (50 overs) (C.H.Gayle 119, S.Chanderpaul 66);
Kenya 104 (35.5 overs) (V.C.Drakes 5-33)

NEW ZEALAND v ZIMBABWE   World Cup – Super Six

at Goodyear Park, Bloemfontein on 8 March, 2003
Toss : Zimbabwe. Umpires : D.B. Hair & R.E. Koertzen
New Zealand won by 6 wickets.

Adams took a wicket with his first delivery but then Zimbabwe reached 59 before losing three wickets for six runs. They were in trouble at 106-6 but then only lost one further wicket while adding 146 runs. The last three overs cost 62 runs. Taibu's fifty took 73 balls while Streak required 76.

Zimbabwe lost Murphy, who was injured practising during the lunch break, and Whittall so were two bowlers short. After early setbacks, Astle and Cairns added 121 off 148 balls to set up victory. Astle got fifty from 71 balls and then reached his 13th hundred after 122 balls. Cairns was dismissed immediately after getting his fifty with a six. The Black Caps won with 16 balls to spare.

ZIMBABWE

	Runs	Mins	Balls	6s	4s
C.B.Wishart c Styris b Cairns	30	64	50	-	4
D.D.Ebrahim b Adams	0	6	1	-	-
A.Flower run out	37	98	61	-	5
G.W.Flower c Cairns b Oram	1	7	6	-	-
G.J.Whittall c McCullum b Cairns	0	7	2	-	-
T.Taibu† lbw b Harris	53	102	79	1	3
A.M.Blignaut run out	4	10	5	-	-
H.H.Streak* not out	72	90	84	2	6
S.M.Ervine not out	31	22	14	1	4
B.A.Murphy					
D.T.Hondo					

Extras (lb 9, w 13, nb 2) 24
TOTAL (50 overs) (7 wkts) .. **252** 204

NEW ZEALAND

	Runs	Mins	Balls	6s	4s
C.D.McMillan c Taibu b Hondo	8	25	16	-	1
S.P.Fleming* lbw b Blignaut	46	65	42	-	10
N.J.Astle not out	102	187	122	-	11
S.B.Styris c sub (T.J.Friend) b Blignaut	13	29	22	-	1
C.L.Cairns b Ervine	54	99	73	2	3
C.Z.Harris not out	14	19	10	-	3
B.B.McCullum†					
J.D.P.Oram					
A.R.Adams					
D.L.Vettori					
S.E.Bond					

Extras (lb 5, w 10, nb 1) 16
TOTAL (47.2 overs) (4 wkts) **253** 213

Bowling	O	M	R	W
NEW ZEALAND				
Bond	10	1	37	0
Adams	5	0	54	1
Oram	10	4	28	1
Cairns	4	0	16	2
Vettori	10	0	52	0
Harris	10	0	45	1
Astle	1	0	11	0
ZIMBABWE				
Streak	10	0	59	0
Hondo	8.2	0	52	1
Blignaut	10	0	41	2
Flower G.W.	10	0	33	0
Whittall	3	0	19	0
Ervine	6	0	44	1

Fall of Wickets	Z	NZ
1st	5	27
2nd	59	72
3rd	63	97
4th	65	218
5th	98	-
6th	106	-
7th	174	-
8th	-	-
9th	-	-
10th	-	-

7 March, 2003
*Centurion: **Australia beat Sri Lanka by 96 runs***
Australia 319 for 5 (50 overs) (R.T.Ponting 114, A.C.Gilchrist 99, D.R.Martyn 52, C.R.D.Fernando 3-47);
Sri Lanka 223 (47.4 overs) (P.A.de Silva 92, B.Lee 3-52)

7 March, 2003
*Cape Town: **India beat Kenya by 6 wickets***
Kenya 225 for 6 (50 overs) (K.O.Otieno 79, R.D.Shah 34, M.O.Odumbe 34*, T.M.Odoyo 32);
India 226 for 4 (47.5 overs) (S.C.Ganguly 107*, Yuvraj Singh 58*, R.S.Dravid 32)

10 March, 2003
*Johannesburg: **India beat Sri Lanka by 183 runs***
India 292 for 6 (50 overs) (S.R.Tendulkar 97, V.Sehwag 66, S.C.Ganguly 48, M.Muralitharan 3-46);
Sri Lanka 109 (23 overs) (K.C.Sangakkara 30, A.Nehra 4-35, J.Srinath 4-35)

NEW ZEALAND v AUSTRALIA

World Cup – Super Six

at St.George's Park, Port Elizabeth on 11 March, 2003
Toss : New Zealand. Umpires : S.A. Bucknor & E.A.R. de Silva
Australia won by 96 runs.

Fleming's decision to put Australia in to bat looked to have paid dividends thanks to a magnificent performance from Bond. His 6-23 was the best bowling by a New Zealander in one-day internationals and was responsible for having Australia 84-7 after 26.3 overs. Bichel then got his first fifty from 70 balls as he and Bevan created an Australian record eighth wicket stand against New Zealand.

The New Zealand reply to the target of 209 was very disappointing. Only Fleming got past 16 and only three other players got to double figures. The last five wickets fell for 10 in 32 balls as New Zealand lost by 96 runs.

AUSTRALIA

	Runs	Mins	Balls	6s	4s
A.C.Gilchrist† lbw b Bond	18	24	20	-	2
M.L.Hayden c McCullum b Bond	1	11	4	-	-
R.T.Ponting* c Fleming b Bond	6	28	20	-	-
D.R.Martyn c McCullum b Bond	31	83	53	-	3
D.S.Lehmann c Astle b Adams	4	18	9	-	1
M.G.Bevan c Vincent b Oram	56	141	94	1	4
G.B.Hogg lbw b Bond	0	2	1	-	-
I.J.Harvey b Bond	2	9	11	-	-
A.J.Bichel c Cairns b Oram	64	86	83	1	7
B.Lee not out	15	11	6	2	-
G.D.McGrath not out	3	4	2	-	-
Extras (lb 1, w 4, nb 3)	8				
TOTAL (50 overs) (9 wkts)	208	212			

NEW ZEALAND

	Runs	Mins	Balls	6s	4s
D.L.Vettori c Gilchrist b McGrath	10	10	9	-	1
S.P.Fleming* c Gilchrist b Lee	48	116	70	-	7
N.J.Astle c Ponting b McGrath	0	3	3	-	-
S.B.Styris lbw b McGrath	3	15	6	-	-
C.L.Cairns c Lee b Bichel	16	35	25	1	2
L.Vincent c Martyn b Harvey	7	26	20	-	1
C.Z.Harris not out	15	53	24	-	-
B.B.McCullum† lbw b Lee	1	10	7	-	-
J.D.P.Oram b Lee	0	2	1	-	-
A.R.Adams b Lee	0	6	6	-	-
S.E.Bond c & b Lee	3	10	10	-	-
Extras (lb 4, w 5)	9				
TOTAL (30.1 overs)	112	147			

Bowling	O	M	R	W
NEW ZEALAND				
Bond	10	2	23	6
Adams	9	2	46	1
Vettori	10	1	40	0
Oram	7	0	48	2
Harris	10	1	24	0
Styris	3	0	18	0
Astle	1	0	8	0
AUSTRALIA				
McGrath	6	1	29	3
Lee	9.1	2	42	5
Harvey	6	3	11	1
Bichel	5	0	15	1
Hogg	4	0	11	0

Fall of Wickets	A	NZ
1st	17	14
2nd	24	14
3rd	31	33
4th	47	66
5th	80	84
6th	80	102
7th	84	104
8th	181	104
9th	192	108
10th	-	112

12 March, 2003
Bloemfontein: **Kenya beat Zimbabwe by 7 wickets**
Zimbabwe 133 (44.1 overs) (A.Flower 63, M.A.Suji 3-19, C.O.Obuya 3-32);
Kenya 135 for 3 (26 overs) (T.M.Odoyo 43*, M.O.Odumbe 38*)

NEW ZEALAND v INDIA

World Cup – Super Six

at SuperSport Park, Centurion on 14 March, 2003
Toss : India. Umpires : D.J. Harper & P. Willey
India won by 7 wickets.

New Zealand were put in to bat and lost wickets to the second and third balls of the innings. They never recovered, making just 146 thanks to some tail end resistance. Khan reached 100 one-day wickets.

Despite losing three early wickets India cruised to victory with Kaif and Dravid (who was dropped by McCullum when the score was 22-3) adding 129. Kaif reached fifty from 98 balls while Dravid took 83. New Zealand were eliminated when Sri Lanka beat Zimbabwe the following day.

NEW ZEALAND

	Runs	Mins	Balls	6s	4s
C.D.McMillan c Harbhajan b Khan	0	1	2	-	-
S.P.Fleming* c Tendulkar b Srinath	30	85	59	-	4
N.J.Astle lbw b Khan	0	2	1	-	-
S.B.Styris c Dravid b Nehra	15	37	21	-	1
B.B.McCullum† b Khan	4	24	16	-	-
C.L.Cairns c Khan b Harbhajan	20	50	26	-	1
C.Z.Harris lbw b Khan	17	45	37	-	2
J.D.P.Oram b Sehwag	23	62	54	-	1
D.L.Vettori c Ganguly b Harbhajan	13	39	40	-	2
D.R.Tuffey c & b Mongia	11	18	13	-	2
S.E.Bond not out	0	7	6	-	-
Extras (lb 5, w 4, nb 4)	13				
TOTAL (45.1 overs)	**146**	187			

INDIA

	Runs	Mins	Balls	6s	4s
V.Sehwag c Styris b Bond	1	9	6	-	-
S.R.Tendulkar c Oram b Tuffey	15	25	16	-	3
S.C.Ganguly* b Bond	3	10	6	-	-
M.Kaif not out	68	149	129	-	8
R.S.Dravid† not out	53	143	89	-	7
Yuvraj Singh					
D.Mongia					
Harbhajan Singh					
A.Nehra					
Z.Khan					
J.Srinath					
Extras (w 8, nb 2)	10				
TOTAL (40.4 overs) (3 wkts)	**150**	168			

Bowling	O	M	R	W
INDIA				
Khan	8	0	42	4
Srinath	8	0	20	1
Nehra	10	3	24	1
Harbhajan	10	2	28	2
Ganguly	2	0	4	0
Tendulkar	5	0	20	0
Sehwag	2	1	3	1
Mongia	0.1	0	0	1
NEW ZEALAND				
Tuffey	10	1	41	1
Bond	8	2	23	2
Oram	5	0	20	0
Vettori	5	0	18	0
McMillan	2	1	4	0
Styris	6.4	0	29	0
Harris	4	1	15	0

Fall of Wickets		
	NZ	**I**
1st	0	4
2nd	0	9
3rd	38	21
4th	47	-
5th	60	-
6th	88	-
7th	96	-
8th	129	-
9th	144	-
10th	146	-

15 March, 2003
*East London: **Sri Lanka beat Zimbabwe by 74 runs***
Sri Lanka 256 for 5 (50 overs) (M.S.Atapattu 103*, D.A.Gunawardene 41, K.C.Sangakkara 35);
Zimbabwe 182 (41.5 overs) (C.B.Wishart 43, A.Flower 38, G.W.Flower 31, S.T.Jayasuriya 3-30)

15 March, 2003
*Durban: **Australia beat Kenya by 5 wickets***
Kenya 174 for 8 (50 overs) (S.O.Tikolo 51, R.D.Shah 46, H.S.Modi 39*, B.Lee 3-14);
Australia 178 for 5 (31.2 overs) (A.C.Gilchrist 67, A.Symonds 33*, A.Y.Karim 3-7)

18 March, 2003 (semi-final)
*Port Elizabeth: **Australia beat Sri Lanka by 48 runs (D/L method)***
Australia 212 for 7 (50 overs) (A.Symonds 91*, D.S.Lehmann 36, W.P.U.J.C.Vaas 3-34);
Sri Lanka 123 for 7 (38.1 overs) (K.C.Sangakkara 39*, B.Lee 3-35)

20 March, 2003 (semi-final)
*Durban: **India beat Kenya by 91 runs***
India 270 for 4 (50 overs) (S.C.Ganguly 111*, S.R.Tendulkar 83, V.Sehwag 33);
Kenya 179 (46.2 overs) (S.O.Tikolo 56, Z.Khan 3-14)

AUSTRALIA v INDIA

World Cup – Final

at The Wanderers, Johannesburg on 23 March, 2003
Toss : India. Umpires : S.A. Bucknor & D.R. Shepherd
Australia won by 125 runs.

After sending Australia in, Ganguly saw Khan's first over cost 15 runs and from there on the Australian batting hardly faltered. Gilchrist, whose fifty came off 40 balls, was out to the last ball of the 14th over and Hayden went in the 20th but that was the last success that India's bowlers were to have.

Ponting reached fifty off 74 balls and went to his century just 29 deliveries later while Martyn reached his half-century off 46 balls. Their unbroken 234 run partnership was an Australian record for any wicket.

Tendulkar was out in the first over of India's reply and although Sehwag (fifty of 50 balls) was in good form he had little support and the result was never in doubt. Australia became the first team to win the World Cup on three occasions.

AUSTRALIA

	Runs	Mins	Balls	6s	4s
A.C.Gilchrist† c Sehwag b Harbhajan	57	66	48	1	8
M.L.Hayden c Dravid b Harbhajan	37	93	54	-	5
R.T.Ponting* not out	140	138	121	8	4
D.R.Martyn not out	88	112	84	1	7
D.S.Lehmann					
M.G.Bevan					
G.B.Hogg					
A.J.Bichel					
B.Lee					
G.D.McGrath					
Extras (b 2, lb 12, w 16, nb 7)	37				
TOTAL (50 overs) (2 wkts)	**359**	205			

INDIA

	Runs	Mins	Balls	6s	4s
S.R.Tendulkar c & b McGrath	4	2	5	-	1
V.Sehwag run out	82	107	81	3	10
S.C.Ganguly* c Lehmann b Lee	24	44	25	1	3
M.Kaif c Gilchrist b McGrath	0	4	3	-	-
R.S.Dravid† b Bichel	47	87	57	-	2
Yuvraj Singh c Lee b Hogg	24	48	34	-	1
D.Mongia c Martyn b Symonds	12	18	11	-	2
Harbhajan Singh c McGrath b Symonds	7	12	8	-	-
Z.Khan c Lehmann b McGrath	4	20	8	-	-
J.Srinath b Lee	1	6	4	-	-
A.Nehra not out	8	7	4	-	2
Extras (b 4, lb 4, w 9, nb 4)	21				
TOTAL (39.2 overs)	**234**	180			

Bowling	O	M	R	W
INDIA				
Khan	7	0	67	0
Srinath	10	0	87	0
Nehra	10	0	57	0
Harbhajan	8	0	49	2
Sehwag	3	0	14	0
Tendulkar	3	0	20	0
Mongia	7	0	39	0
Yuvraj	2	0	12	0
AUSTRALIA				
McGrath	8.2	0	52	3
Lee	7	1	31	2
Hogg	10	0	61	1
Lehmann	2	0	18	0
Bichel	10	0	57	1
Symonds	2	0	7	2

Fall of Wickets	A	I
1st	105	4
2nd	125	58
3rd	-	59
4th	-	147
5th	-	187
6th	-	208
7th	-	209
8th	-	223
9th	-	226
10th	-	234

NEW ZEALAND IN SRI LANKA

New Zealand enjoyed its most successful tour of the sub-continent, playing a two-test series against Sri Lanka and also a tri-series one-day competition with Sri Lanka and Pakistan. New Zealand came out with a drawn test series and won the one-day tournament.

The side was without Nathan Astle (injured), Craig McMillan (dropped) and Chris Cairns for the test series. They took first innings leads in both games and surprised many critics with their spirited display. Stephen Fleming led from the front, breaking the New Zealand test record for most runs in a game and could have become the first New Zealander to get a test triple century had he not unselfishly declared when on 274. Mark Richardson got three fifties in four innings (in the other he batted at seven) at an average of 67. Scott Styris and Jacob Oram had good innings when required. Shane Bond troubled the batsmen and he along with Oram and Paul Wiseman were the best of the bowlers.

In the one-day series runs were hard to come by. After extremely heavy rain in Colombo, the entire tournament was played at Dambulla. Originally, only the first three games were scheduled for that venue with games four to six set down for the SSC Ground at Colombo and the final was supposed to be a day/night match at the R. Premadasa Stadium. Following the rescheduling, the second round games were set back a day although the final was played on the planned date.

Fleming scored the only fifty for New Zealand but all the batsmen played their part on difficult pitches. Bond broke down during the first game and went back to New Zealand for a scan which showed a stress fracture. Oram, Daryl Tuffey and Vettori all bowled well. The tour marked the end of Jeff Crowe's tenure as manager while Denis Aberhart's contract as coach was up for renewal. The success was a fitting farewell as the side has made progress under their stewardship.

The touring party was: S.P. Fleming *(Wellington, captain)*, A.R. Adams *(Auckland)*, S.E. Bond*(Canterbury)*, I.G. Butler*(Northern Districts)*, C.L. Cairns*(Canterbury)*, C.Z. Harris *(Canterbury)*, R.G. Hart*(Northern Districts)*, M.J. Horne*(Auckland)*, R.A. Jones*(Wellington)*, B.B. McCullum *(Otago)*, K.D. Mills *(Auckland)*, C.J. Nevin *(Wellington)*, J.D.P. Oram *(Central Districts)*, M.H. Richardson*(Auckland)*, M.S. Sinclair*(Central Districts)*, S.B. Styris *(Northern Districts)*, D.R. Tuffey *(Northern Districts)*, D.L. Vettori *(Northern Districts)*, L. Vincent *(Auckland)*, P.J. Wiseman *(Canterbury)*. Manager; J.J. Crowe, Coach; D.C. Aberhart, Physiotherapist; D.F. Shackel, Video Analyst; Z. Hitchcock.

In the original selection, Adams, Cairns, Harris, McCullum, Mills and Nevin were selected for the one-day series only with one player to be added after the test series. Vincent was selected, ironically after not playing a game on the first part of the tour. The players who returned after the test series were Butler, Hart, Jones, Richardson and Sinclair. Wiseman, not originally in the one-day squad, remained with the party after Vettori's injury.

J.S. Patel*(Wellington)*and B.P.Martin*(Northern Districts)* went on the first part of the tour as unofficial members of the team in order to assist the development of spin bowlers in New Zealand and to give the New Zealand batsmen practice against spin bowling in the nets.

New Zealand Test Averages

BATTING	M	I	NO	HS	Agg	Ave	100s	50s	Ct	St
S.P. Fleming	2	4	2	274*	376	188.00	1	1	3	-
M.H. Richardson	2	4	1	85	201	67.00	-	3	1	-
J.D.P. Oram	2	4	0	74	142	35.50	-	1	1	-
S.B. Styris	2	4	0	63	112	28.00	-	1	-	-
P.J. Wiseman	2	3	1	29	52	26.00	-	-	-	-
D.L. Vettori	2	3	0	55	62	20.66	-	1	-	-
M.J. Horne	2	4	0	42	74	18.50	-	-	-	-
R.G. Hart	2	4	0	31	52	13.00	-	-	3	-
D.R. Tuffey	2	2	0	15	16	8.00	-	-	2	-
M.S. Sinclair	2	4	0	17	21	5.25	-	-	1	-
S.E. Bond	2	2	2	10*	11	-	-	-	-	-

BOWLING	O	M	R	W	Ave	Best	5w	10w
J.D.P. Oram	50	15	116	4	29.00	3-54	-	-
D.L. Vettori	39	9	105	3	35.00	3-94	-	-
S.E. Bond	59	13	194	5	38.80	3-97	-	-
P.J. Wiseman	82.3	21	251	6	41.83	4-104	-	-
D.R. Tuffey	46	14	117	2	58.50	1-45	-	-
S.B. Styris	3	0	28	0	-	-	-	-

Sri Lanka Test Averages

BATTING	M	I	NO	HS	Agg	Ave	100s	50s	Ct	St
H.P. Tillakaratne	2	2	0	144	237	118.50	1	1	3	-
D.P.M.D. Jayawardene	2	3	1	58	105	52.50	-	1	2	-
K.C. Sangakkara	2	3	1	67	104	52.00	-	1	3	-
R.S. Kaluwitharana	2	2	0	76	96	48.00	-	1	6	1
K.S. Lokuarachchi	2	2	1	28*	48	48.00	-	-	1	-
S.T. Jayasuriya	2	3	0	82	141	47.00	-	2	1	-
H.D.P.K. Dharmasena	2	2	0	31	36	18.00	-	-	1	-
W.P.J.U.C. Vaas	2	2	0	22	26	13.00	-	-	1	-
R.A.P. Nissanka	2	2	0	6	6	3.00	-	-	-	-
M. Muralitharan	2	2	1	2*	2	2.00	-	-	1	-
M.S. Atapattu	2	2	1	2*	2	2.00	-	-	-	-

BOWLING	O	M	R	W	Ave	Best	5w	10w
M. Muralitharan	161.5	59	320	13	24.61	5-49	1	-
W.P.J.U.C. Vaas	73.3	24	179	6	29.83	3-31	-	-
R.A.P. Nissanka	55.5	19	130	4	32.50	2-41	-	-
K.S. Lokuarachchi	67	12	208	4	52.00	2-47	-	-
H.D.P.K. Dharmasena	83	21	225	4	56.25	3-132	-	-
S.T. Jayasuriya	21	0	73	0	-	-	-	-

New Zealand One-day Averages

BATTING	M	I	NO	HS	Agg	Ave	100s	50s	Ct	St	SR
C.Z. Harris	5	4	2	24	53	26.50	-	-	2	-	47
B.B. McCullum	5	4	2	47*	51	25.50	-	-	11	-	62
S.P. Fleming	5	5	0	65	121	24.20	-	1	1	-	49
C.L. Cairns	5	5	1	28	87	21.75	-	-	1	-	75
L. Vincent	5	5	1	32	84	21.00	-	-	2	-	38
S.B. Styris	5	5	0	46	103	20.60	-	-	4	-	51
C.J. Nevin	5	5	0	28	93	18.60	-	-	1	-	54
J.D.P. Oram	3	2	0	20	32	16.00	-	-	-	-	50
K.D. Mills	4	3	0	17	34	11.33	-	-	2	-	47
D.L. Vettori	5	2	0	5	9	4.50	-	-	2	-	75
D.R. Tuffey	5	2	1	2*	4	4.00	-	-	1	-	100
P.J. Wiseman	1	1	0	2	2	2.00	-	-	-	-	66
A.R. Adams	1	1	0	1	1	1.00	-	-	-	-	50
S.E. Bond	1	-	-	-	-	-	-	-	-	-	-

BOWLING	O	M	R	W	Ave	Best	R/O
S.E. Bond	5	2	7	2	3.50	2-7	1.40
J.D.P. Oram	28.1	7	66	8	8.25	3-12	2.34
D.L. Vettori	48	10	117	10	11.70	4-14	2.44
A.R. Adams	3	0	14	1	14.00	1-14	4.67
D.R. Tuffey	44	9	151	9	16.77	3-32	3.43
S.B. Styris	33.5	4	130	6	21.66	2-30	3.84
P.J. Wiseman	6	0	27	1	27.00	1-27	4.50
K.D. Mills	31	2	134	3	44.66	1-30	4.32
C.Z. Harris	37	2	129	2	64.50	1-32	3.49

BOARD PRESIDENT'S XI v NEW ZEALAND   Two-day

at Nondescripts Cricket Club Ground, Colombo on 19, 20 April, 2003
Toss : Board President's XI. Umpires : L.V. Jayasundara & C.B.C. Rodrigo
Close of play: 1st day: NZ 74-0, Richardson 27, Horne 38
Match drawn

After losing three quick wickets the President's XI had a 131 run stand between Jayawardene and
Kaluwitharana before the keeper was dismissed for 55. Three further wickets fell quickly and then
Jayawardene, who had had a wretched World Cup, went for 108. Tuffey and Bond bowled well, Tuffey
getting 5-54 and Bond 3-52.

The New Zealand openers had an 88 run stand and this was followed by 99 runs for the second wicket.
Fleming went for 69 and then Richardson retired for 106. Styris also reached fifty with 64 off 81 balls.
All the batsmen had useful time at the crease. The match finished at the conclusion of the New Zealand
innings.

PRESIDENT'S XI

FIRST INNINGS	Runs	Mins	Balls	6s	4s
R.P.Arnold c Sinclair b Tuffey	4	18	18	-	1
M.G.Vandort c Fleming b Tuffey	25	37	23	-	3
T.M.Dilshan c Fleming b Bond	4	15	11	-	1
D.P.M.D.Jayawardene c Horne					
b Bond	108	204	136	2	15
R.S.Kaluwitharana*† lbw b Tuffey	55	125	98	1	9
L.P.C.Silva c Fleming b Tuffey	4	9	8	-	1
M.Pushpakumara st Hart b Vettori	2	14	5	-	-
M.S.R.Wijeratne c Sinclair b Oram	0	5	6	-	-
K.H.R.K.Fernando c Horne b Bond	20	50	38	-	4
M.F.Maharoof hit wicket b Tuffey	22	40	40	-	4
K.A.D.M.Fernando not out	1	32	17	-	-
H.G.D.Nayanakantha					
Extras (lb 5, nb 8)	13				
TOTAL (64.5 overs)	**258**	279			

NEW ZEALAND

	Runs	Mins	Balls	6s	4s
M.H.Richardson retired	106	283	220	-	18
M.J.Horne lbw b Nayanakantha	48	122	77	-	8
S.P.Fleming* c Silva b Maharoof	69	111	89	1	13
M.S.Sinclair c & b Arnold	29	99	59	-	3
R.A.Jones st Kaluwitharana					
b Jayawardene	14	85	52	-	-
S.B.Styris c Wijeratne b Maharoof	64	121	83	2	7
J.D.P.Oram b Fernando K.A.D.M.	14	39	37	-	1
R.G.Hart† b Nayanakantha	2	26	15	-	-
D.L.Vettori lbw b Fernando K.A.D.M.	6	8	8	-	1
P.J.Wiseman lbw b Fernando K.A.D.M.	5	13	7	-	1
D.R.Tuffey not out	21	14	10	-	5
S.E.Bond					
Extras (b 2, lb 6, nb 10)	18				
TOTAL (107.5 overs)	**396**	469			

Bowling	O	M	R	W
NEW ZEALAND				
Tuffey	14.5	1	54	5
Bond	15	3	52	3
Oram	9	1	48	1
Styris	2	2	0	0
Wiseman	10	1	49	0
Vettori	14	2	50	1
PRESIDENT'S XI				
Nayanakantha	20	3	57	2
Fernando K.A.D.M.	20	3	66	3
Maharoof	13.5	4	56	2
Fernando K.H.R.K.	12	1	68	0
Pushpakumara	20	4	84	0
Arnold	12	2	33	1
Dilshan	3	0	13	0
Silva	1	0	2	0
Jayawardene	6	2	9	1

Fall of Wickets		
	PXI	NZ
	1st	1st
1st	19	88
2nd	31	187
3rd	35	249
4th	166	275
5th	174	291
6th	181	331
7th	181	345
8th	230	352
9th	235	362
10th	258	396

SRI LANKA A v NEW ZEALAND   Two-day

at Nondescripts Cricket Club Ground, Colombo on 21, 22 April, 2003
Toss : Sri Lanka A. Umpires : S. Amarasinghe & J.W.K. Boteju
Close of play: 1st day: NZ 27-0, Richardson 19, Horne 4
Match drawn

Butler replaced Styris in the New Zealand side. The Sri Lankan batsmen all reached double figures with the exception of number eleven Lakshitha. However, only Chandana was able to reach fifty. The attack was steady with Tuffey and Bond again economical while Wiseman and Vettori had good workouts.

Richardson was again the shining light in the New Zealand reply with 93 but as was the case on the first day no one else was able to carry on once started. Chandana was the best of the Sri Lankan bowlers getting 5-98 off 33 overs. Once again the match finished at the conclusion of two innings.

SRI LANKA A

FIRST INNINGS	Runs	Mins	Balls	6s	4s
M.G.Vandort c Vettori b Tuffey	19	48	33	-	3
G.I.Daniel c Wiseman b Bond	15	30	21	-	3
T.M.Dilshan c Butler b Vettori	39	138	88	-	4
M.N.Nawaz c Oram b Bond	25	94	79	-	3
R.P.Arnold* b Butler	14	56	31	-	1
A.S.Polonowita c Wiseman b Vettori	20	37	34	-	4
H.A.P.W.Jayawardene† c Jones b Oram	22	41	33	-	3
M.S.R.Wijeratne not out	38	138	85	-	3
U.D.U.Chandana c Wiseman b Vettori	55	81	63	-	9
M.T.T.Mirando c Butler b Wiseman	23	18	19	-	4
A.B.T.Lakshitha c Hart b Wiseman	0	2	2	-	-
P.N.Ranjith					
Extras (lb 9, nb 5)	14				
TOTAL (80.3 overs)	**284**	351			

NEW ZEALAND

	Runs	Mins	Balls	6s	4s
M.H.Richardson c Nawaz b Chandana	93	242	171	-	13
M.J.Horne b Ranjith	4	32	26	-	-
S.P.Fleming* b Mirando	15	32	26	-	3
M.S.Sinclair lbw b Chandana	22	78	61	-	4
R.A.Jones c Polonowita b Chandana	1	5	3	-	-
J.D.P.Oram b Ranjith	26	58	50	-	5
R.G.Hart† not out	34	134	98	-	1
D.L.Vettori c Wijeratne b Mirando	10	14	13	-	2
P.J.Wiseman c Dilshan b Chandana	17	46	38	1	2
D.R.Tuffey b Chandana	17	25	29	-	3
S.E.Bond b Arnold	6	12	9	-	1
I.G.Butler					
Extras (b 11, lb 12, nb 15)	38				
TOTAL (84.5 overs)	**283**	348			

Bowling	O	M	R	W
NEW ZEALAND				
Tuffey	10	3	26	1
Bond	13	5	35	2
Butler	13	2	57	1
Oram	9	2	22	1
Vettori	19	1	72	3
Wiseman	16.3	3	63	2
SRI LANKA A				
Lakshitha	14	3	51	0
Ranjith	16	3	44	2
Chandana	33	9	98	5
Mirando	12	3	44	2
Arnold	9.5	1	23	1

Fall of Wickets		
	SLA	NZ
	1st	1st
1st	24	28
2nd	42	60
3rd	105	129
4th	120	131
5th	140	175
6th	158	196
7th	179	211
8th	259	250
9th	284	270
10th	284	283

SRI LANKA v NEW ZEALAND   First Test

at P. Saravanamuttu Stadium, Colombo on 25, 26, 27, 28, 29 April, 2003
Toss : New Zealand. Umpires : D.J. Harper & S.J.A. Taufel
Close of play: 1st day: NZ 207-2, Fleming 112, Sinclair 14; 2nd day: Sri Lanka 4-1, Jayasuriya 2, Vaas 2
3rd day: SL 267-4, Jayawardene 58, Tillakaratne 71; 4th day: SL 424-6, Tillakaratne 126, Dharmasena 19
Match drawn

Lokuarachchi and Nissanka made their debuts for Sri Lanka. On a pitch that was predicted to give considerable help to the spinners Fleming won a valuable toss. It was his 50th test as New Zealand captain. Horne went early but then Richardson and Fleming proceeded to set a new New Zealand second wicket record against Sri Lanka, adding 172 off 459 balls. Fleming and Styris added 157 before Styris (who was playing as a batsman only after injuring his shoulder) went for 63.

This was to be Fleming's game as he reached his highest score and then his first double century. His hundred took 270 minutes and 222 balls and the two hundred came from 382 balls in 503 minutes. With the New Zealand record in sight he declared to bowl at Sri lanka late on the second day. Atapattu went in the first over and nightwatchman Vaas early next day. Jayasuriya and Sangakkara put on 103 in 184 balls and then there were two century stands of 133 between Jayawardene and new captain Tillakaratne (century from 213 balls in 313 minutes) and 107 by Kaluwitharana and his skipper. Vettori claimed the last three wickets in five balls and was unlucky not to have claimed a hat trick.

With a 32 run lead New Zealand played out time. Horne and Fleming (opening in place of Richardson who had a muscle injury) put on 71 for the first wicket. The Sri Lankan spinners had useful spells as the match petered out to a draw.

NEW ZEALAND

FIRST INNINGS	Runs	Mins	Balls	6s	4s
M.H.Richardson b Vaas	85	325	260	1	7
M.J.Horne c Dharmasena b Nissanka .	4	41	32	-	-
S.P.Fleming* not out	274	655	476	1	28
M.S.Sinclair c Sangakkara b Dharmasena	17	81	57	-	1
S.B.Styris c Vaas b Dharmasena	63	172	140	2	5
J.D.P.Oram c Lokuarachchi b Muralitharan	33	76	56	-	2
R.G.Hart† c Jayawardene b Muralitharan	9	13	14	-	1
D.L.Vettori lbw b Dharmasena	7	13	8	-	1
P.J.Wiseman not out	16	9	7	1	2
D.R.Tuffey					
S.E.Bond					
Extras (b 2, lb 3, w 1, nb 1)	7				
TOTAL (174.5 overs) (7 wkts dec)	**515**	697			

SECOND INNINGS	Runs	Mins	Balls	6s	4s
(7) not out	6	68	44	-	-
(1) lbw b Lokuarachchi	42	120	95	1	3
(2) not out	69	299	234	-	5
(3) c sub (T.M.Dilshan) b Muralitharan	1	10	11	-	-
(4) lbw b Lokuarachchi	16	53	49	-	1
(5) c Kaluwitharana b Muralitharan	19	37	33	-	4
(6) c Sangakkara b Muralitharan	0	6	3	-	-
(b 2, lb 5, nb 1)	8				
TOTAL (78 overs) (5 wkts dec)	**161**	299			

SRI LANKA

	Runs	Mins	Balls	6s	4s
M.S.Atapattu lbw b Tuffey	0	3	5	-	-
S.T.Jayasuriya b Bond	50	158	111	-	8
W.P.J.U.C.Vaas c Fleming b Bond	4	22	15	-	-
K.C.Sangakkara c Oram b Wiseman ..	67	147	97	-	14
D.P.M.D.Jayawardene c Hart b Oram	58	205	148	-	8
H.P.Tillakaratne* b Bond	144	429	314	-	24
R.S.Kaluwitharana† c Sinclair b Wiseman	76	117	90	-	14
H.D.P.K.Dharmasena lbw b Vettori	31	156	102	-	3
K.S.Lokuarachchi not out	28	40	29	1	3
R.A.P.Nissanka lbw b Vettori	0	1	1	-	-
M.Muralitharan lbw b Vettori	0	3	3	-	-
Extras (lb 21, w 1, nb 3)	25				
TOTAL (152 overs)	**483**	645			

Bowling	O	M	R	W	O	M	R	W
NEW ZEALAND								
Vaas	29	8	73	1	7	2	27	0
Nissanka	23	9	53	1	6	1	18	0
Dharmasena	40	7	132	3	16	7	21	0
Muralitharan	58.5	16	140	2	30	15	41	3
Lokuarachchi	18	2	83	0	19	2	47	2
Jayasuriya	6	0	29	0				
NEW ZEALAND								
Tuffey	17	5	54	1				
Bond	28	6	97	3				
Oram	30	13	62	1				
Vettori	33	8	94	3				
Wiseman	41	13	127	2				
Styris	3	0	28	0				

Fall of Wickets	NZ	SL	NZ
	1st	1st	2nd
1st	20	0	71
2nd	192	11	76
3rd	235	108	108
4th	392	134	133
5th	471	267	133
6th	486	374	-
7th	499	444	-
8th	-	483	-
9th	-	483	-
10th	-	483	-

SRI LANKA v NEW ZEALAND   Second Test

at Asgiriya Stadium, Kandy on 3, 4, 5, 6, 7 May, 2003
Toss : New Zealand. Umpires : D.J. Harper & S.J.A. Taufel
Close of play: 1st day: no play; 2nd day: NZ 75-4, Richardson 32, Oram 0
3rd day: SL 94-2, Jayasuriya 53, Tillakaratne 10; 4th day: NZ 92-1, Richardson 51, Fleming 10
Match drawn

Both teams were unchanged. A wet outfield prevented any play on the first day and only 34 overs were possible on the second. New Zealand batted after winning the toss but were soon in trouble, losing three wickets before seven overs had been completed. From then on only Wiseman failed to reach double figures as New Zealand were able to get to 305. Oram hit his maiden test fifty, top scoring with 74, and Vettori reached his fifth first fifty before he was run out after a collision with Atapattu. Vettori was unable to bowl in the first innings and Atapattu had to retire hurt with a headache in his innings.

Jayasuriya and Tillakaratne were the mainstay of Sri Lanka's innings while Wiseman had a good spell in Vettori's absence and, with Oram bowling steadily, New Zealand again had a first innings lead.

The New Zealand innings stuttered on the last day. Resuming at 92-1, New Zealand lost nine wickets for 91 off 66.4 overs. Hart and Wiseman added 40 valuable runs for the eighth wicket off 28.1 overs. Muralitharan took his 450th test wicket and his 5-49 was the 37th occasion he had taken five wickets in a test innings surpassing, Sir Richard Hadlee's 36.

Sri Lanka were set 191 off 38 overs but once Jayasuriya went in the fourth over they made no attempt to win and the series ended in a 0-0 draw.

NEW ZEALAND

FIRST INNINGS	Runs	Mins	Balls	6s	4s	SECOND INNINGS	Runs	Mins	Balls	6s	4s
M.H.Richardson c Sangakkara b Lokuarachchi	55	219	185	-	9	c Kaluwitharana b Nissanka	55	145	101	1	6
M.J.Horne c Kaluwitharana b Vaas	1	10	4	-	-	c Tillakaratne b Muralitharan	27	88	73	-	5
S.P.Fleming* lbw b Nissanka	0	5	6	-	-	c Kaluwitharana b Dharmasena	33	147	110	-	3
M.S.Sinclair lbw b Vaas	3	15	11	-	-	st Kaluwitharana b Muralitharan	0	6	6	-	-
S.B.Styris c Tillakaratne b Muralitharan	32	95	62	-	5	c Muralitharan b Vaas	1	44	29	-	-
J.D.P.Oram c Kaluwitharana b Lokuarachchi	74	217	179	-	15	lbw b Muralitharan	16	52	48	-	2
R.G.Hart† lbw b Muralitharan	31	94	90	-	5	c Kaluwitharana b Vaas	12	115	88	-	1
D.L.Vettori run out	55	113	75	-	10	b Muralitharan	0	2	3	-	-
P.J.Wiseman b Muralitharan	7	24	27	-	1	c Tillakaratne b Vaas	29	121	111	-	3
D.R.Tuffey c Jayawardene b Nissanka	15	28	18	-	3	c Jayasuriya b Muralitharan	1	18	16	-	-
S.E.Bond not out	10	27	21	-	2	not out	1	5	1	-	-
Extras (b 3, lb 7, w 5, nb 7)	22					(b 1, lb 6, nb 1)	8				
TOTAL (111.5 overs)	**305**	435				(97.3 overs)	**183**	376			

SRI LANKA

	Runs	Mins	Balls	6s	4s		Runs	Mins	Balls	6s	4s
K.C.Sangakkara c Hart b Tuffey	10	28	19	-	2	not out	27	121	92	-	5
S.T.Jayasuriya c Fleming b Wiseman	82	170	109	-	14	c Richardson b Bond	9	17	10	-	2
D.P.M.D.Jayawardene c Hart b Oram	15	57	42	-	2	not out	32	103	78	-	5
H.P.Tillakaratne* b Wiseman	93	336	232	-	12						
R.S.Kaluwitharana† c Tuffey b Bond	20	60	46	-	2						
H.D.P.K.Dharmasena c Fleming b Wiseman	5	29	23	-	-						
K.S.Lokurachchi c Tuffey b Oram	20	77	57	-	2						
W.P.J.U.C.Vaas b Oram	22	45	34	-	4						
M.S.Atapattu retired hurt	2	10	9	-	-						
R.A.P.Nissanka b Wiseman	6	18	17	-	1						
M.Muralitharan not out	2	7	1	-	-						
Extras (b 6, lb 11, nb 4)	21					(lb 4)	4				
TOTAL (97.3 overs)	**298**	423				(30 overs) (1 wkt)	**72**	131			

Bowling	O	M	R	W	O	M	R	W
SRI LANKA								
Vaas	22	8	48	2	15.3	6	31	3
Nissanka	16.5	5	41	2	10	4	18	1
Muralitharan	34	10	90	3	39	18	49	5
Jayasuriya	8	0	24	0	7	0	20	0
Dharmasena	15	5	40	0	12	2	32	1
Lokuarachchi	16	5	52	2	14	3	26	0
NEW ZEALAND								
Tuffey	20	6	45	1	9	3	18	0
Bond	25	6	78	1	6	1	19	1
Oram	20	2	54	3				
Wiseman	32.3	4	104	4	9	4	20	0
Vettori					6	1	11	0

Fall of Wickets	NZ	SL	NZ	SL
	1st	1st	2nd	2nd
1st	6	30	65	14
2nd	7	69	109	-
3rd	11	126	110	-
4th	71	169	115	-
5th	109	189	136	-
6th	189	234	139	-
7th	222	264	139	-
8th	237	285	179	-
9th	271	298	182	-
10th	305	-	183	-

Atapattu retired hurt at 267-7

NEW ZEALAND v PAKISTAN

Bank AlFalah Cup

at Rangiri Dambulla International Stadium on 11 May, 2003
Toss : New Zealand. Umpires : E.A.R de Silva & D.J. Harper
New Zealand won by 7 wickets. Points: New Zealand 6, Pakistan 0

Tuffey struck in the first over and Pakistan never recovered. In the 12th over they were 17-5 and only some lusty hitting from Akhtar got the total past the 100 mark. Tuffey bowled well but Bond, who took 2-7 off five overs, suffered a back injury that was to keep him out of the rest of the tour and the English season.

New Zealand started quickly with the first wicket falling in the 10th over. The win was never in doubt and a bonus point was obtained with a win with 22.3 overs left.

PAKISTAN

	Runs	Mins	Balls	6s	4s
Mohammad Hafeez c Styris b Tuffey	0	3	4	-	-
Taufeeq Umar c Nevin b Styris	21	91	54	-	2
Faisal Iqbal b Bond	0	16	11	-	-
Yousuf Youhana b Bond	0	8	2	-	-
Younis Khan lbw b Tuffey	3	13	16	-	-
Abdur Razzaq c Styris b Oram	0	12	8	-	-
Shoaib Malik b Styris	9	53	33	-	1
Rashid Latif*† c Styris b Vettori	26	60	49	-	2
Shoaib Akhtar b Vettori	27	50	38	2	2
Mohammad Sami not out	11	30	27	-	1
Umar Gul c Vettori b Oram	2	20	18	-	-
Extras (lb 6, w 8, nb 3)	17				
TOTAL (43.1 overs)	**116**	182			

NEW ZEALAND

	Runs	Mins	Balls	6s	4s
C.J.Nevin c Umar b Gul	28	42	29	-	4
S.P.Fleming* c Hafeez b Razzaq	21	71	40	1	-
L.Vincent not out	25	90	58	1	2
S.B.Styris c Malik b Razzaq	6	30	23	-	-
C.L.Cairns not out	18	30	17	-	3
J.D.P.Oram					
C.Z.Harris					
B.B.McCullum†					
D.L.Vettori					
D.R.Tuffey					
S.E.Bond					
Extras (lb 5, w 11, nb 3)	19				
TOTAL (27.3 overs) (3 wkts)	**117**	132			

Bowling NEW ZEALAND	O	M	R	W
Tuffey	10	2	28	2
Bond	5	2	7	2
Oram	9.1	2	16	2
Styris	6	0	32	2
Vettori	9	3	18	2
Harris	4	0	9	0
PAKISTAN				
Shoaib	10	0	41	0
Sami	7	1	23	0
Gul	4.3	0	29	1
Razzaq	6	0	19	2

Fall of Wickets	P	NZ
1st	0	42
2nd	2	65
3rd	5	82
4th	12	-
5th	17	-
6th	42	-
7th	51	-
8th	96	-
9th	103	-
10th	116	-

10 May, 2003
*Dambulla: **Pakistan beat Sri Lanka by 79 runs***
Pakistan 199 for 8 (50 overs) (Mohammad Hafeez 53, M.Muralitharan 3-38);
Sri Lanka 120 (43.1 overs)

NEW ZEALAND v SRI LANKA   Bank AlFalah Cup

at Rangiri Dambulla International Stadium on 13 May, 2003
Toss : Sri Lanka. Umpires : S.J.A. Taufel & T.H. Wijewardene
New Zealand won by 5 wickets. *Points: Sri Lanka 5, New Zealand 1*

All remaining matches in the tournament had now been transferred to Dambulla due to heavy rain in Colombo. The wicket gave the bowlers plenty of assistance as New Zealand batted first in a 46 over match. All the batsmen found runs hard to obtain against a tight Sri Lankan attack but two run outs did not help.

Once Jayasuriya was out the Sri Lankan batsmen also found the going hard and the bowlers got New Zealand back into the game but finally Dilshan hit four successive fours to give Sri Lanka a win. New Zealand got a bonus point as Sri Lanka never attempted to get the bonus point themselves. Oram had an outstanding spell of 3-12 from 9 overs.

NEW ZEALAND

	Runs	Mins	Balls	6s	4s
C.J.Nevin run out	12	24	14	-	1
S.P.Fleming* c Sangakkara b Nissanka	2	7	4	-	-
L.Vincent lbw b Jayasuriya	32	109	72	-	2
S.B.Styris c Sangakkara b Nissanka	0	2	2	-	-
C.L.Cairns c & b Nayanakantha	14	21	17	-	2
J.D.P.Oram c & b Muralitharan	20	53	47	-	1
C.Z.Harris not out	20	73	62	-	1
B.B.McCullum† lbw b Muralitharan	0	19	10	-	-
K.D.Mills b Dharmasena	6	21	21	-	-
D.L.Vettori run out	5	10	8	-	-
D.R.Tuffey lbw b Muralitharan	2	5	3	-	-
Extras (b 4, lb 12, w 9, nb 1)	26				
TOTAL (43.1 overs)	**139**	175			

SRI LANKA

	Runs	Mins	Balls	6s	4s
S.T.Jayasuriya c Vettori b Oram	33	78	52	-	4
R.S.Kaluwitharana† c McCullum b Oram	48	146	118	-	4
K.C.Sangakkara hit wicket b Oram	1	8	7	-	-
M.S.Atapattu* c Vincent b Styris	18	65	54	-	1
D.P.M.D.Jayawardene c McCullum b Tuffey	2	19	11	-	-
T.M.Dilshan not out	18	27	17	-	4
W.P.U.J.C.Vaas not out	2	14	8	-	-
H.G.D.Nayanakantha					
H.D.P.K.Dharmasena					
R.A.P.Nissanka					
M.Muralitharan					
Extras (b 2, lb 8, w 2, nb 6)	8				
TOTAL (43.4 overs) (5 wkts)	**140**	180			

Bowling	O	M	R	W
SRI LANKA				
Vaas	9	2	23	0
Nissanka	5	0	11	2
Nayanakantha	5	1	26	1
Dharmasena	8	0	28	1
Muralitharan	8.1	1	16	3
Jayasuriya	8	1	19	1
NEW ZEALAND				
Tuffey	7	0	37	1
Mills	5	0	32	0
Oram	9	4	12	3
Vettori	9	1	19	0
Harris	10	0	27	0
Styris	3.4	2	3	1

Fall of Wickets		
	NZ	SL
1st	6	68
2nd	18	69
3rd	18	116
4th	46	116
5th	94	120
6th	102	-
7th	108	-
8th	127	-
9th	135	-
10th	139	-

18 May, 2003
*Dambulla: **Sri Lanka beat Pakistan by 12 runs***
Sri Lanka 172 (49.5 overs) (T.M.Dilshan 46);
Pakistan 160 (47.4 overs) (Shoaib Malik 33, M.Muralitharan 5-23)

NEW ZEALAND v SRI LANKA   Bank AlFalah Cup

at Rangiri Dambulla International Stadium on 19 May, 2003
Toss : Sri Lanka. Umpires : P.T. Manuel & S.J.A. Taufel
New Zealand won by 9 runs. *Points: New Zealand 5, Sri Lanka 1*

Sri Lanka again put New Zealand in to bat on a wicket which once more proved difficult to score quickly on. Wickets fell steadily but the run rate was slow. After 40 overs the score was 100-6 and only 46 runs in the last four overs got New Zealand to 156-8. McCullum hit his highest one-day score in a good cameo innings. Jayasuriya got his 250th wicket. The seventh wicket stand between McCullum and Mills was only the second fifty partnership of the tournament.

When Kaluwitharana went at 28-1 the innings had only been going 5.2 overs but then the bowlers clawed their way back into the game as the run rate slowed and wickets fell regularly. Vettori had his best figures in one-day internationals and his 4-14 were the most economical bowling figures by a New Zealander in Sri Lanka. Mills, who conceded 17 off his first two overs, came back well and bowled a maiden in the 49th over. Jayawardene tried to reverse sweep Styris with the first ball of the last over and was caught to give New Zealand a nine run win and a place in the final.

This was Fleming's 200th one-day international.

NEW ZEALAND	Runs	Mins	Balls	6s	4s
C.J.Nevin c Sangakkara					
b Nissanka	8	23	19	-	1
S.P.Fleming* lbw b Muralitharan	16	91	58	1	-
L.Vincent run out	12	51	42	-	-
S.B.Styris c Kaluwitharana					
b Muralitharan	29	69	53	-	2
C.L.Cairns c Dilshan					
b Jayasuriya	9	23	19	-	-
C.Z.Harris run out	4	11	7	-	-
B.B.McCullum† not out	47	65	63	3	2
K.D.Mills c Jayawardene					
b Jayasuriya	17	42	39	-	1
A.R.Adams run out	1	6	2	-	-
D.L.Vettori					
D.R.Tuffey					
Extras (b 1, lb 5, w 5, nb 2) 13					
TOTAL (50 overs) (8 wkts) .. **156**	222				

SRI LANKA	Runs	Mins	Balls	6s	4s
S.T.Jayasuriya c McCullum					
b Tuffey	9	47	28	-	2
R.S.Kaluwitharana† c McCullum					
b Adams	18	25	16	-	4
M.S.Atapattu* c sub (M.J.Horne)					
b Vettori	13	61	35	-	2
K.C.Sangakkara b Vettori	11	28	25	-	2
D.P.M.D.Jayawardene c Harris					
b Styris	38	137	103	-	1
T.M.Dilshan c Fleming b Vettori	7	23	18	-	-
W.P.U.J.C.Vaas c McCullum					
b Mills	4	15	10	-	-
H.D.P.K.Dharmasena c McCullum					
b Harris	11	7	8	-	1
K.S.Lokuarachchi lbw b Styris	8	35	25	-	-
M.Muralitharan c Mills b Vettori	4	21	18	-	-
R.A.P.Nissanka not out	6	20	13	-	-
Extras (b 3, lb 2, w 9, nb 4) 18					
TOTAL (49.1 overs) **147**	213				

Bowling	O	M	R	W
SRI LANKA				
Vaas	8	2	11	0
Nissanka	8	1	19	1
Dharmasena	10	2	19	0
Muralitharan	10	2	41	2
Lokuarachchi	5	1	25	0
Jayasuriya	9	0	35	2
NEW ZEALAND				
Tuffey	9	4	22	1
Mills	8	2	30	1
Adams	3	0	14	1
Styris	9.1	0	30	2
Vettori	10	4	14	4
Harris	10	2	32	1

Fall of Wickets	NZ	SL
1st	17	28
2nd	40	43
3rd	42	60
4th	69	63
5th	76	79
6th	88	87
7th	138	101
8th	156	121
9th	-	136
10th	-	147

NEW ZEALAND v PAKISTAN Bank AlFalah Cup

at Rangiri Dambulla International Stadium on 20 May, 2003
Toss : New Zealand. Umpires : D.J. Harper & P.T. Manuel
Pakistan won by 22 runs. *Points: Pakistan 5, New Zealand 1*

Wiseman played his first one-day international for more than two years, replacing the injured Adams. Yasir Hameed made his debut.

Fleming's decision to bowl first looked justified when two wickets fell in the first four overs but then Hameed and Youhana added 47. The seventh wicket stand of 71 between Malik and Razzaq was the highest of the tournament. Malik reached his fifty off just 59 balls and ended with the highest score of the competition so far. His innings was the main reason that 200 was needed just 29 balls. Vettori bowled well as did Mills, whose first seven overs cost 18.

New Zealand started steadily but lost wickets at regular intervals. Five of the top six batsmen got starts but after spending time at the crease got out when set. At 160-4 another 44 runs were needed off 38 balls but the last six wickets went for 21 as Pakistan booked a final place with a 22 run win. Akhtar and Sami bowled well in the final spell. Akhtar was later charged with ball tampering during the New Zealand innings and suspended for two games.

PAKISTAN

	Runs	Mins	Balls	6s	4s
Mohammad Hafeez b Mills	3	16	11	-	-
Taufeeq Umar b Tuffey	2	12	9	-	-
Yasir Hameed c Styris b Harris	25	71	57	-	2
Yousuf Youhana lbw b Vettori	17	75	52	-	1
Younis Khan c sub (M.J.Horne) b Vettori	26	50	44	-	2
Shoaib Malik c McCullum b Vettori	74	88	71	1	8
Rashid Latif*† c Cairns b Wiseman	2	11	15	-	-
Abdur Razzaq c Mills b Tuffey	23	43	27	-	1
Shoaib Akhtar not out	18	17	13	1	1
Mohammad Sami c Vincent b Styris	0	4	2	-	-
Danish Kaneria not out	0	2	0	-	-
Extras (lb 2, w 9, nb 2)	13				
TOTAL (50 overs) (9 wkts)	**203**	200			

NEW ZEALAND

	Runs	Mins	Balls	6s	4s
C.J.Nevin c Sami b Kaneria	28	87	72	-	2
S.P.Fleming* c Latif b Sami	17	44	33	1	1
L.Vincent lbw b Hafeez	2	7	5	-	-
S.B.Styris c Malik b Kaneria	46	132	95	1	1
C.L.Cairns b Kaneria	28	42	38	1	2
C.Z.Harris lbw b Sami	24	42	26	-	2
B.B.McCullum† c Younis b Shoaib	0	4	3	-	-
K.D.Mills c Umar b Shoaib	11	22	12	-	1
D.L.Vettori c Latif b Shoaib	4	6	4	-	-
P.J.Wiseman b Sami	2	5	3	-	-
D.R.Tuffey not out	2	2	1	-	-
Extras (lb 3, w 11, nb 3)	17				
TOTAL (48.1 overs)	**181**	203			

Bowling	O	M	R	W
NEW ZEALAND				
Tuffey	9	1	32	2
Mills	10	0	36	1
Styris	5	0	31	1
Vettori	10	1	34	3
Harris	10	0	41	1
Wiseman	6	0	27	1
PAKISTAN				
Shoaib	9.1	0	36	3
Sami	9	0	34	3
Hafeez	10	1	33	1
Kaneria	10	1	31	3
Malik	9	0	39	0
Razzaq	1	0	5	0

Fall of Wickets	P	NZ
1st	8	36
2nd	10	40
3rd	57	71
4th	61	113
5th	102	160
6th	108	161
7th	179	163
8th	191	172
9th	201	179
10th	-	181

NEW ZEALAND v PAKISTAN

Bank AlFalah Cup Final

at Rangiri Dambulla International Stadium on 23 May, 2003
Toss : Pakistan. Umpires : E.A.R. de Silva & D.J. Harper
New Zealand won by 4 wickets

Oram was fit after a back problem and replaced Wiseman while Athar made his debut and Shabbir replaced the suspended Akhtar.

After winning the toss and batting Pakistan lost Hafeez in Tuffey's first over. It was the eleventh time in 51 one-day internationals that the New Zealand bowler had taken a wicket in his first over. Hameed went in the fourth over and Pakistan were 11-2. They were 56-4 before Younis and Malik added 57 for the fifth wicket. These two were the only batsmen to get to thirty. Oram and Tuffey (who bowled a double wicket maiden to end the innings) both took three wickets, while Vettori and Styris bowled economically.

The top six batsmen in the New Zealand order all reached double figures as they chased 199. Only Fleming got past 23 but the contributions from the others all helped. Fleming got New Zealand's first fifty of the tournament. Sami caused some flutters when he dismissed Fleming and Styris in three deliveries (the second ball being a wide). New Zealand were assisted by some undisciplined bowling with 25 wides and six no-balls. The Black Caps finally won with 28 balls to spare.

It was New Zealand's first win in a tri-series and only its second win in a one-day tournament. It was also the last match for Jeff Crowe as manager while Denis Aberhart's coaching contract was due for review. It was, however, a fitting end to their association.

PAKISTAN

	Runs	Mins	Balls	6s	4s
Mohammad Hafeez c McCullum b Tuffey	0	2	4	-	-
Faisal Athar c McCullum b Oram	9	59	37	-	1
Yasir Hameed lbw b Mills	6	15	12	-	1
Yousuf Youhana run out	25	68	54	-	3
Younis Khan not out	70	148	83	-	7
Shoaib Malik b Vettori	34	41	45	-	6
Abdur Razzaq run out	10	27	21	-	-
Rashid Latif*† c Tuffey b Oram	20	31	31	-	2
Mohammad Sami c Harris b Oram	7	8	6	-	-
Shabbir Ahmed c McCullum b Tuffey	2	3	3	-	-
Danish Kaneria c McCullum b Tuffey	0	3	5	-	-
Extras (lb 6, w 3, nb 6)	15				
TOTAL (50 overs)	**198**	208			

NEW ZEALAND

	Runs	Mins	Balls	6s	4s
C.J.Nevin c Malik b Sami	17	51	39	-	2
S.P.Fleming* c Younis b Sami	65	140	107	3	5
L.Vincent run out	13	62	48	-	1
S.B.Styris b Sami	22	28	23	1	2
C.L.Cairns c Razzaq b Shabbir	18	48	27	-	3
J.D.P.Oram c Younis b Razzaq	12	20	17	-	3
C.Z.Harris not out	5	30	20	-	-
B.B.McCullum† not out	4	5	2	-	1
K.D.Mills					
D.L.Vettori					
D.R.Tuffey					
Extras (lb 13, w 25, nb 6)	44				
TOTAL (45.2 overs) (6 wkts)	**200**	195			

Bowling NEW ZEALAND	O	M	R	W
Tuffey	9	2	32	3
Mills	8	0	36	1
Styris	10	2	34	0
Oram	10	1	38	3
Vettori	10	1	32	1
Harris	3	0	20	0
PAKISTAN				
Sami	10	0	42	3
Shabbir	8.2	0	36	1
Razzaq	3	0	20	1
Hafeez	7	1	20	0
Kaneria	10	2	35	0
Malik	7	0	34	0

Fall of Wickets	P	NZ
1st	0	54
2nd	11	113
3rd	39	151
4th	56	152
5th	113	170
6th	136	194
7th	179	-
8th	194	-
9th	198	-
10th	198	-

INTERNATIONAL SUMMARY

2002/03

Test Matches

	Played	Won	Lost	Drawn
India	2	2	–	–
Sri Lanka	2	–	–	2
TOTAL	4	2	–	2

New Zealand Test Averages

BATTING	M	I	NO	HS	Agg	Ave	100s	50s	Ct	St
S.P. Fleming	4	7	2	274*	454	90.80	1	1	7	-
M.H. Richardson	4	8	2	89	345	57.50	-	4	2	-
J.D.P. Oram	4	7	1	74	171	28.50	-	1	3	-
P.J. Wiseman	2	3	1	29	52	26.00	-	-	-	-
S.B. Styris	4	7	0	63	142	20.28	-	1	4	-
M.J. Horne	2	4	0	42	74	18.50	-	-	-	-
N.J. Astle	2	3	0	41	55	18.33	-	-	2	-
D.L. Vettori	4	5	0	55	89	17.80	-	1	-	-
L. Vincent	2	4	1	21*	45	15.00	-	-	2	-
S.E. Bond	4	4	3	10*	13	13.00	-	-	-	-
D.R. Tuffey	4	4	1	15	38	12.66	-	-	4	-
R.G. Hart	4	7	1	31	72	12.00	-	-	10	-
C.D. McMillan	2	3	0	18	31	10.33	-	-	2	-
M.S. Sinclair	2	4	0	17	21	5.25	-	-	1	-

BOWLING	O	M	R	W	Ave	Best	5w	10w
D.R. Tuffey	96	33	230	15	15.33	4-12	-	-
J.D.P. Oram	99.5	25	246	15	16.40	4-41	-	-
S.E. Bond	115.1	29	390	17	22.94	4-33	-	-
N.J. Astle	11	4	27	1	27.00	1-13	-	-
S.B. Styris	15	0	82	3	27.33	3-28	-	-
D.L. Vettori	39	9	105	3	35.00	3-94	-	-
P.J. Wiseman	82.3	21	251	6·	41.83	4-104	-	-

One-day Internationals

	Played	Won	Lost	Tied	NR
India	8	5	3	–	–
Pakistan	3	2	1	–	–
Sri Lanka	3	1	2	–	–
Australia	2	–	2	–	–
Bangladesh	2	2	–	–	–
West Indies	1	1	–	–	–
South Africa	1	1	–	–	–
Kenya	1	–	1	–	–
Canada	1	1	–	–	–
Zimbabwe	1	1	–	–	–
TOTAL	**23**	**14**	**9**	**–**	**–**

New Zealand One-day International Averages

BATTING	M	I	NO	HS	Agg	Ave	100s	50s	Ct	St	SR
S.B. Styris	19	18	3	141	505	33.66	1	1	11	-	76
S.P. Fleming	22	22	2	134*	642	32.10	1	2	18	-	66
M.S. Sinclair	10	9	1	78	234	29.25	-	2	2	-	53
N.J. Astle	14	14	2	102*	341	28.41	1	2	5	-	80
C.L. Cairns	16	15	2	54	359	27.61	-	1	5	-	79
C.Z. Harris	16	14	5	38*	215	23.88	-	-	5	-	59
C.J. Nevin	5	5	0	28	93	18.60	-	-	1	-	54
L. Vincent	16	15	3	53*	222	18.50	-	1	8	-	49
A.R. Adams	12	8	1	36	128	18.28	-	-	1	-	113
S.E. Bond	14	7	3	31*	70	17.50	-	-	4	-	100
J.D.P. Oram	17	10	2	30	139	17.37	-	-	4	-	56
B.B. McCullum	19	13	4	47*	152	16.88	-	-	38	1	56
C.D. McMillan	10	10	0	75	156	15.60	-	1	3	-	67
K.D. Mills	13	8	2	23*	86	14.33	-	-	4	-	50
D.L. Vettori	20	10	3	16*	97	13.85	-	-	6	-	59
D.R. Tuffey	15	8	1	11	29	4.14	-	-	2	-	63
P.J. Wiseman	1	1	0	2	2	2.00	-	-	-	-	66
P.A. Hitchcock	3	2	2	2*	4	-	-	-	1	-	200

BOWLING	O	M	R	W	Ave	Best	R/O
P.A. Hitchcock	16	0	68	4	17.00	3-30	4.25
J.D.P. Oram	150.2	22	579	34	17.02	5-26	3.85
S.E. Bond	121	15	482	28	17.21	6-23	3.98
A.R. Adams	97.2	7	492	25	19.68	5-22	5.05
D.R. Tuffey	131.5	19	500	23	21.73	3-32	3.79
N.J. Astle	21	1	94	4	23.50	3-34	4.48
S.B. Styris	100.3	11	410	16	25.62	2-23	4.07
C.L. Cairns	8	0	54	2	27.00	2-16	6.75
P.J. Wiseman	6	0	27	1	27.00	1-27	4.50
D.L. Vettori	148.3	13	494	18	27.44	4-14	3.32
K.D. Mills	108.4	9	419	15	27.93	3-45	3.85
C.Z. Harris	80	5	302	5	60.40	1-6	3.78
C.D. McMillan	2	1	4	0	-	-	2.00

PROVINCIAL SUMMARIES

AUCKLAND CRICKET ASSOCIATION

Formed 1883, affiliated 1894/95.

Selectors: R.J.R. Irving, R.M.J. Armour and M.R. O'Donnell

Auckland retained the State Championship and showed improvement in the one-day game, being top qualifier in the State Shield but losing to Northern Districts in the final.

In the Championship Auckland's style of play was to bat once and get a good score and then bowl the opposition out twice. At times their scoring rate was slow but it was effective. Tim McIntosh was the leading run scorer in domestic cricket getting 820 runs at 58.57. Matt Horne scored 671 at 47.92, Rob Nicol 664 at 47.42 and Mark Richardson scored 494 at 35.28.

The attack in Championship games was based almost completely around Tama Canning, who took 46 wickets at 21.97, and Craig Pryor, who had returned from Otago, with 31 wickets at 33. No other bowler took more than 12 wickets. Keeper Reece Young had 35 catches.

In the State Shield their leading run scorers were Llorne Howell (345) and Aaron Barnes (289). Leading wicket takers were Canning (12), Heath Davis (10) and Kyle Mills (10). Mark O'Donnell was Auckland coach. The contracted players were: Canning, Howell, McIntosh, Mills, Richard Morgan, Nicol, Brad Nielsen, Pryor, Gareth Shaw, Brooke Walker and Young.

CANTERBURY CRICKET ASSOCIATION

Formed 1877, affiliated 1894/95.

Selectors: C.H. Thiele, M.F. Sharpe and G.L. Kench

Canterbury had a poor season compared to past achievements. They finished last in the Championship and failed to reach the semi-finals of the Shield.

There were two individual highlights during the season in the State Championship. Peter Fulton became the first non-Otago player to score a triple century when he got 301 not out against Auckland. while in the earlier clash with the eventual champions, Gareth Hopkins became the first wicket-keeper to score a century in each innings. Fulton was the leading run getter scoring 628 at 52.53. Gary Stead 472 at 31.46 and Michael Papps 469 at 31.26 were the next best. Warren Wisneski, Chris Martin and Paul Wiseman all took 19 wickets.

The highlight of the one-day season was Chris Cairns blasting the fastest fifty in New Zealand cricket taking just 20 balls to reach his half century. Evergreen Chris Harris (236), Papps (228) and Shanan Stewart (214) all scored 200 runs. Stephen Cunis and Martin were the leading wicket takers. Canterbury were again coached by Michael Sharpe. The contracted players were: Carl Anderson, Wade Cornelius, Andrew Ellis, Robbie Frew, Fulton, Papps, Aaron Redmond, Stead, Stewart, Wiseman and Wisneski.

CENTRAL DISTRICTS CRICKET ASSOCIATION

Formed 1950, affiliated 1954/55.

Selectors: B. Netten, P.S. Briasco and M.J. Greatbatch

Central Districts had a disappointing season, failing to qualify for the State Shield semi-finals and being out of the running for the Championship. However, they did have some individual highlights which augured well for the future.

After a slow start Jamie How ended with 694 runs at 46.26 with two big hundreds. Craig Spearman returned as an overseas player and led the side in Oram's absence, getting 564 runs at 37.60. Glen Sulzberger scored 532 at 48.36 and newcomer Jesse Ryder played the last six games making 365 at 60.83. Michael Mason was the leading wicket taker with 37 at 19.45. Brent Hefford got 25 wickets at 24.32 while Sulzberger took 19.

In the State Shield Spearman (350) and Ryder (219) were the only players to get 200 runs in a season when the team only reached 200 on three occasions. Mason (16) Campbell Furlong (12) and Andrew Schwass (11) were the leading wicket takers. The team was coached by Mark Greatbatch. The contracted players were: Furlong, Bevan Griggs, Lance Hamilton, Hefford, Peter Ingram, Greg Loveridge, Mason, Schwass, Martyn Sigley, Spearman and Sulzberger.

NORTHERN DISTRICTS CRICKET ASSOCIATION

Formed 1953, granted Plunket Shield status 1956/57

Selectors: P.J. Malcon and B.R. Blair

Northern Districts won the State Shield after finishing third in the round robin but were disappointing in the State Championship where they never threatened the leaders even though they beat champions Auckland in the last game.

Nick Horsley was the leading run scorer getting 582 at 36.37. Long serving Matthew Hart got 546 at 54.60, including his first double century. The Marshall twins were the only other players to pass 300. James scored 395 while Hamish got 376. Ian Butler missed three of the first four games but still finished as the leading wicket taker getting 25 at 23.88. Joseph Yovich took 24 at 34.00.

Northern's batting was their strength in the State Shield. Matthew Hart (301), Scott Styris (293), Michael Parlane (281), James Marshall (278) and Yovich (265) led the scoring. Yovich was the leading wicket-taker with 23 and Graeme Aldridge took 15. Bruce Blair was again the coach. The contracted players were: Aldridge, Simon Andrews, Matthew Hart, Horsley, David Kelly, Hamish Marshall, James Marshall, Bruce Martin, Parlane, Gareth West and Yovich.

OTAGO CRICKET ASSOCIATION

Formed 1876, affiliated 1894/95.

Selectors: G.M. Turner, C. Taylor and M.H. Austen

Otago had one of its better seasons finishing third in the State Championship. After four games they were leading the Shield table but losses and rain affected games ended their chances. In the four-day game they beat runners-up Wellington twice.

New captain Craig Cumming scored 751 runs at 46.93 and he was well assisted by import Mohammad Wasim 651 at 40.68 and Chris Gaffaney 436 at 33.53. Shayne O'Connor took 42 wickets at 18.75 but later announced his retirement. He had good support from Kerry Walmsley 37 at 21.00 and Warren McSkimming 26 at 24.61. Brendon McCullum kept wicket in the first three games but when he was called into the New Zealand one-day side Peter McGlashan, formerly of Central Districts, took over.

Cumming was also the leading one-day scorer with 230 runs while Wasim (230) and Marcel McKenzie (219) were the other batsmen to reach 200. O'Connor (16) was the leading wicket taker followed by Walmsley 12 and McSkimming 11. Otago were again coached by Glenn Turner. The contracted players were: Cumming, Gaffaney, McCullum, James McMillan, Mohammad Wasim, Nathan Morland, O'Connor, Jordan Sheed, David Sewell, Walmsley and Jeff Wilson.

WELLINGTON CRICKET ASSOCIATION

Formed 1875, affiliated 1894/95.

Selectors: V.F. Johnson and G.M. Hooper

Wellington had a frustrating season as they finished runners-up in the State Championship and were beaten semi-finalists in the State Shield. Even though they equalled the previous season's runners-up berth they played much better cricket than the summer before.

Richard Jones (726 at 45.50) was the leading run scorer and earned a place in the New Zealand side to Sri Lanka. Chris Nevin 532 at 35.47 and Matthew Bell 499 at 27.16 followed. Matthew Walker took 45 wickets at 18 followed by Iain O'Brien 34 at 18.55 and Andrew Penn 29 at 17.00. Nevin kept wickets well, getting 32 victims.

Nevin was also the leading run scorer in the State Shield with 312 at 28.36. Jones (278), Walker (241) and Bell (231) all reached 200 runs. Walker was again the leading wicket taker getting 18 at 19.33. Ash Turner 16 at 15.63 and Mark Gillespie 13 at 18.15 followed. Wellington were again coached by Vaughn Johnson. The contracted players were: Bell, Grant Donaldson, James Franklin, Gillespie, Mark Jefferson, Jones, O'Brien, Jeetan Patel, Penn, Turner and Walker.

STATE CHAMPIONSHIP REVIEW 2002/03

The format for the State Championship remained unchanged with each side playing ten four-day matches, meeting each of the other teams home and away with no final.

The competition once again began in late November. Three rounds were completed prior to Christmas before the State Shield began with one round of games taking place at the half-way stage of the one-day competition. The remaining six rounds were completed once the State Shield had concluded.

A total of 19 games ended in an outright decision (compared to 23 the season before) with Auckland, the eventual winners, Wellington and Otago registering four wins apiece. Northern Districts won three and Central Districts and Canterbury two each. There was also the unusual occurrence of two first innings ties, both in the same round of matches.

As had been the case the previous season, the outcome of the competition was not decided until the final day. Until they learnt that Wellington had lost in Alexandra, Auckland had still needed to beat Northern Districts outright to ensure that they retained their title.

While Auckland and Wellington remained at the top of the table, Otago moved up to third position after having finished last in 2001/02, when they lost nine matches outright. Northern Districts went up to fourth from fifth the season before. Central Districts dropped two places from third to fifth as did Canterbury who went from fourth to last.

Playing time was again six and a half hours per day, although this was extended if the number of overs to be bowled in the day had not been completed. Teams were required to bowl 100 overs a day with no reduction for change of innings. The only penalties for slow over rates were financial and these were calculated round by round instead of over the whole season.

Points were awarded as follows:

    a)   six points for an outright win
    b)   two points for a first innings win only if team did not win outright or match drawn (i.e. maximum for one team was six points)
    c)   three points for a tie
    d)   one point each for a first innings tie (providing the team did not win outright)
    e)   one point each for a no result on the first innings

Final points and placings were:

	P	OW	OL	1st Inns W	1st Inns L	NR	Total
Auckland	10	4	2	4	—	—	34
Wellington	10	4	3	2	1	—	31
Otago	10	4	3	—	3	—	26
Northern Districts	10	3	3	—	2	1	22
Central Districts	10	2	4	3	1	—	22
Canterbury	10	2	4	—	2	1	16

NB: Auckland gained first innings points in the match which Central Districts won outright, Northern Districts gained first innings points in the match which Central Districts won outright, Canterbury gained first innings points in the match which Auckland won outright, Otago gained first innings points in the match which Auckland won outright, Wellington gained first innings points in the match which Otago won outright and Central Districts gained first innings points in matches which Northern Districts and Canterbury won outright.

Wellington had a first innings tie in the match which Auckland won outright and Canterbury and Northern Districts had a first innings tie in a drawn game.

CENTRAL DISTRICTS v OTAGO   State Championship

at Victoria Park, Wanganui on 23, 24, 25, 26 November, 2002
Toss : Otago. Umpires : R.D. Anderson & E.A. Watkin
Close of play: 1st day: Otago 19-1, Gaffaney 9, Cumming 2; 2nd day: Otago 102-3 Cumming 42, McCullum 2
        3rd day: CD 132-2, Sinclair 73, Sulzberger 24
First innings win to Central Districts. Points: Central Districts 2, Otago 0

In the Otago side Wilkinson and Reddington made their first-class debuts while McKenzie (formerly Canterbury) and Mohammad Wasim made their Otago debuts.

Central recovered from 24-4 thanks to Oram who just missed his second first-class hundred. He put on 104 for the fifth wicket with How while Walmsley and McMillan shared eight of the wickets which fell. Apart from a five hour innings from Cumming, which extended across three days due to weather interruptions, the Otago batsmen struggled and Central gained a lead of 71.

Half-centuries from Sinclair, Sulzberger and Oram allowed Central to declare and set Otago a target of 306 to win. The challenge was never seriously accepted and both sides ended well short of victory. McCullum had time for a forceful unbeaten 78.

CENTRAL DISTRICTS

FIRST INNINGS	Runs	Mins	Balls	6s	4s	SECOND INNINGS	Runs	Mins	Balls	6s	4s
C.M.Spearman b Walmsley	6	24	20	-	-	(2) c Gaffaney b Walmsley .	23	36	22	-	2
P.J.Ingram b Walmsley	7	35	29	-	-	(1) c McCullum b Walmsley ..	1	17	13	-	-
M.S.Sinclair c McCullum b Reddington	1	13	10	-	-	b Walmsley	79	179	132	1	8
G.P.Sulzberger c Cumming b McMillan	3	25	16	-	-	not out	62	193	146	-	6
J.D.P.Oram* b Walmsley	96	307	242	1	9	not out	52	42	36	3	3
J.M.How c Cumming b Walmsley	47	140	96	-	7						
G.R.Loveridge b McMillan	34	81	64	1	6						
M.A.Sigley† b McMillan	0	6	3	-	-						
M.J.Mason c McCullum b Wasim	5	22	24	-	1						
B.E.Hefford not out	9	33	24	-	1						
L.J.Hamilton b McMillan	0	3	1	-	-						
Extras (b 1, lb 7, w 3, nb 15)	26					(b 1, lb 3, w 2, nb 11)	17				
TOTAL (85.4 overs)	**234**	343				(56.5 overs) (3 wkts dec) ..	**234**	240			

OTAGO

	Runs	Mins	Balls	6s	4s		Runs	Mins	Balls	6s	4s
C.B.Gaffaney c Sulzberger b Hamilton	11	82	68	-	1	lbw b Hefford	8	30	27	-	1
Mohammad Wasim lbw b Mason	5	27	17	-	1	b Loveridge	49	189	127	-	7
C.D.Cumming* c Sigley b Oram	68	301	212	1	5	c Sigley b Oram	22	79	54	-	2
M.N.McKenzie c Sinclair b Sulzberger	33	129	96	-	3	run out	18	126	98	-	-
B.B.McCullum† lbw b Hefford	2	24	18	-	-	not out	78	101	111	1	13
J.W.Sheed c Sinclair b Hamilton	0	27	18	-	-	not out	20	66	37	-	1
A.M.Wilkinson lbw b Hamilton	0	3	3	-	-						
N.D.Morland c Sigley b Oram	11	50	34	-	-						
K.P.Walmsley b Hefford	16	47	31	-	2						
J.M.McMillan c Spearman b Hamilton ..	3	46	38	-	-						
D.J.Reddington not out	0	6	5	-	-						
Extras (lb 5, w 2, nb 7)	14					(b 1, w 1, nb 5)	7				
TOTAL (88.5 overs)	**163**	356				(76 overs) (4 wkts)	**202**	301			

Bowling	O	M	R	W	O	M	R	W
OTAGO								
Walmsley	18	3	53	4	13	2	48	3
McMillan	23.4	5	56	4	16.5	4	70	0
Reddington	18	7	27	1	11	3	55	0
Wilkinson	10	1	38	0	2	0	15	0
Morland	13	3	50	0	7	0	27	0
Wasim	3	1	2	1	7	2	15	0
CENTRAL DISTRICTS								
Mason	11	7	11	1				
Hamilton	26.5	7	58	4	16	6	44	0
Hefford	19	8	24	2	13	6	15	1
Oram	17	7	22	2	15	6	24	1
Sulzberger	14	3	39	1	21	6	66	0
Loveridge	1	0	4	0	11	0	52	1

Fall of Wickets	CD	O	CD	O
	1st	1st	2nd	2nd
1st	9	14	16	11
2nd	16	24	40	65
3rd	16	92	161	95
4th	24	102	-	136
5th	128	110	-	-
6th	186	110	-	-
7th	196	141	-	-
8th	206	142	-	-
9th	233	163	-	-
10th	234	163	-	-

NORTHERN DISTRICTS v AUCKLAND   State Championship

at Harry Barker Reserve, Gisborne on 29, 30 November, 1, 2 December, 2002
Toss : Northern Districts. Umpires : B.F. Bowden & A.L. Hill
Close of play: 1st day: ND 271-6, H.J.H. Marshall 44, Yovich 6; 2nd day: Auckland 41-1, Richardson 17, Vincent 0
3rd day: Auckland 167-3, McIntosh 48, Nicol 50
First innings win to Auckland. *Points: Auckland 2, Northern Districts 0*

Horsley, former Northern age group player, returned to his home province having made his debut in first-class cricket for Auckland. Pryor also returned to his original province from Otago while Davis played his first first-class game for Auckland having last played a first-class match (for Wellington) in 1998/99.

Northern batted throughout the first day with James Marshall top scoring. The next day his twin brother dominated proceedings and when the innings ended he was left unbeaten twelve short of an elusive maiden hundred. It was his 33rd first-class match. Davis made a satisfactory comeback to first-class cricket with 4-93.

After a shaky start, and with time lost on days two and three, Auckland proceeded to grind their way to a first innings lead. Nicol was the star, reaching his highest score and his third century in just eleven first-class games. His century came from 294 balls in 368 minutes and he shared century partnerships with McIntosh and Pryor.

NORTHERN DISTRICTS

FIRST INNINGS	Runs	Mins	Balls	6s	4s
J.A.H.Marshall lbw b Canning	74	194	148	-	12
N.K.W.Horsley c Young b Davis	27	87	62	-	4
M.E.Parlane c Young b Davis	32	154	139	-	5
S.B.Styris c Canning b Pryor	33	95	62	-	2
H.J.H.Marshall not out	88	305	218	-	8
M.N.Hart b Horne	2	14	15	-	-
R.G.Hart*† lbw b Mills	20	86	50	-	2
J.A.F.Yovich c McIntosh b Davis	6	24	23	-	1
D.L.Vettori c Canning b Davis	15	42	31	-	2
D.R.Tuffey c Young b Canning	8	27	19	-	1
G.W.Aldridge c Canning b Pryor	12	59	43	-	-
Extras (lb 16, w 2, nb 23)	41				
TOTAL (131.1 overs)	**358**	548			

AUCKLAND

	Runs	Mins	Balls	6s	4s
M.H.Richardson c Hart R.G. b Aldridge	26	106	75	-	4
M.J.Horne b Aldridge	17	61	45	-	2
L.Vincent c Hart M.N. b Yovich	7	40	27	-	-
T.G.McIntosh c Marshall J.A.H. b Styris	50	201	150	-	-
R.J.Nicol not out	147	464	378	3	6
K.D.Mills lbw b Tuffey	13	48	37	-	1
T.K.Canning lbw b Vettori	10	78	53	-	-
C.R.Pryor not out	55	134	96	1	6
B.G.K.Walker*					
R.A.Young†					
H.T.Davis					
Extras (b 4, lb 9, w 2, nb 21)	36				
TOTAL (141 overs) (6 wkts)	**361**	572			

Bowling	O	M	R	W	O	M	R	W
AUCKLAND								
Mills	35	11	92	1				
Canning	23	6	58	2				
Davis	32	10	93	4				
Pryor	20.1	4	68	2				
Walker	4	2	7	0				
Horne	17	8	24	1				
NORTHERN DISTRICTS								
Tuffey	30	10	61	1				
Yovich	30	3	86	1				
Aldridge	18	6	31	2				
Styris	18	3	40	1				
Vettori	36	7	90	1				
Marshall J.A.H.	2	0	4	0				
Hart M.N.	7	0	36	0				

Fall of Wickets		
	ND	A
	1st	1st
1st	66	39
2nd	138	59
3rd	167	59
4th	202	169
5th	207	196
6th	264	241
7th	273	-
8th	304	-
9th	320	-
10th	358	-

OTAGO v CANTERBURY   State Championship

at Carisbrook, Dunedin on 29, 30 November, 1 December, 2002
Toss : Canterbury. Umpires : G.A. Baxter & D.M. Quested
Close of play: 1st day: Canterbury 105-4, Papps 33, Wiseman 6; 2nd day: Canterbury 393 all out
Canterbury won by an innings and 4 runs. *Points: Canterbury 6, Otago 0*

Otago had Cumming, McCullum and McSkimming to thank for any sort of total in their first innings with the other eight batsmen contributing just 40 runs. Canterbury had the luxury of nightwatchman Wiseman hitting 91, his highest score, and sharing a stand of 159 with Papps.

With Canterbury 272-8, Otago may have been reasonably satisfied but Cairns and Bond put on 103 for the ninth wicket in two hours to take the game right away from the home team.

Despite Wasim's first fifty for Otago, there was little resistance from the other batsmen as Astle took the bowling honours with 4-35 from 20 overs. Three of his victims were trapped in front and the other was bowled. Canterbury wrapped up the innings win inside three days. Donkers made his first-class debut in this match.

OTAGO

FIRST INNINGS	Runs	Mins	Balls	6s	4s	SECOND INNINGS	Runs	Mins	Balls	6s	4s
C.B.Gaffaney c Bond b Martin	13	59	50	-	2	b Astle	28	54	47	-	4
Mohammad Wasim b Bond	2	36	18	-	-	c Bond b Cairns	62	218	182	-	7
C.D.Cumming* c Papps b Astle	45	102	79	-	6	lbw b Astle	0	6	2	-	-
M.N.McKenzie c Bond b Donkers	3	49	34	-	-	c Hopkins b Donkers	4	19	15	-	-
B.B.McCullum† c Hopkins b Donkers	53	123	111	2	4	lbw b Harris	35	39	33	-	7
J.W.Sheed lbw b Astle	7	22	22	-	-	lbw b Astle	1	13	8	-	-
W.C.McSkimming not out	47	123	85	-	8	lbw b Astle	15	30	26	-	3
N.D.Morland b McMillan	6	19	20	-	1	run out	15	63	57	-	1
S.B.O'Connor c Hopkins b Astle	2	11	11	-	-	b Bond	6	34	33	-	-
J.M.McMillan c Hopkins b McMillan	0	6	6	-	-	b Cairns	2	3	5	-	-
D.G.Sewell b Bond	7	12	17	-	-	not out	3	18	20	-	-
Extras (lb 6, nb 15)	21					(b 1, lb 5, w 1, nb 5)	12				
TOTAL (73 overs)	**206**	285				(70.3 overs)	**183**	253			

CANTERBURY

	Runs	Mins	Balls	6s	4s
G.R.Stead* lbw b O'Connor	2	3	5	-	-
M.H.W.Papps c Sheed b McMillan	88	312	260	-	7
C.D.McMillan b McMillan	8	22	12	-	2
N.J.Astle c Morland b McSkimming	42	40	33	1	5
C.Z.Harris c Wasim b McSkimming	8	17	12	-	-
P.J.Wiseman c McKenzie b O'Connor	91	211	178	-	14
C.L.Cairns not out	76	196	106	1	4
G.J.Hopkins† c Sewell b McMillan	1	17	13	-	-
B.P.Donkers c McCullum b McMillan	0	18	15	-	-
S.E.Bond c O'Connor b Morland	52	120	120	-	9
C.S.Martin c Gaffaney b Morland	4	23	20	-	-
Extras (b 1, lb 9, w 1, nb 10)	21				
TOTAL (127.2 overs)	**393**	494			

Bowling	O	M	R	W	O	M	R	W
CANTERBURY								
Bond	17	5	54	2	12.3	1	45	1
Martin	15	3	45	1	5	1	11	0
Astle	13	5	34	3	20	5	35	4
Donkers	11	3	29	2	8	2	33	1
Cairns	5	0	15	0	5	2	10	2
McMillan	12	5	23	2				
Wiseman					12	3	30	0
Harris					8	1	13	1
OTAGO								
O'Connor	20	3	68	2				
McMillan	27	6	86	4				
Sewell	26	5	57	0				
McSkimming	18	1	69	2				
Morland	29.2	8	71	2				
Wasim	7	1	32	0				

Fall of Wickets	O	C	O
	1st	1st	2nd
1st	14	2	43
2nd	35	21	43
3rd	60	75	53
4th	85	91	103
5th	99	250	112
6th	163	254	135
7th	174	262	169
8th	185	272	174
9th	190	375	176
10th	206	393	183

WELLINGTON v CENTRAL DISTRICTS   State Championship

at Basin Reserve, Wellington on 29, 30 November, 1 December, 2002
Toss : Wellington. Umpires : M.P. George & E.A. Watkin
Close of play: 1st day: CD 20-1, Ingram 3, Sinclair 6; 2nd day: Wellington 191-6, Nevin 49, Walker 38
Wellington won by 10 wickets. *Points: Wellington 6, Central Districts 0*

Only 17 overs were possible on the first day as Central crawled to 20-1. The next day Franklin recorded career best figures as the visitors were routed for just 91 from 56.5 overs. Wellington had a lead of exactly 100 by the close and on the third morning Nevin and Walker completed a century partnership to give Wellington a 154 run advantage.

Central fared only slightly better in their second innings and even then had to thank Sigley and Mason for a 54 run stand for the eighth wicket. Penn and O'Brien captured nine of the wickets to take Wellington to a ten wicket victory on the third afternoon. Parlane (previously Northern Districts) made his debut for Wellington in this game.

CENTRAL DISTRICTS

FIRST INNINGS	Runs	Mins	Balls	6s	4s	SECOND INNINGS	Runs	Mins	Balls	6s	4s
P.J.Ingram b Penn	4	82	52	-	-	(2) lbw b Penn	0	19	13	-	-
C.M.Spearman c Walker b Franklin	7	30	19	-	1	(1) c Nevin b O'Brien	29	97	71	-	4
M.S.Sinclair c Walker b Franklin	10	68	56	-	2	c Parlane b Penn	18	38	26	-	3
G.P.Sulzberger c Bell b Franklin	29	156	91	-	1	c Nevin b Penn	3	10	8	-	-
J.D.P.Oram* c Walker b Franklin	6	23	21	-	1	c Nevin b Walker	19	79	58	-	3
J.M.How lbw b Franklin	0	2	2	-	-	c Parlane b O'Brien	11	29	22	-	1
B.B.J.Griggs lbw b Franklin	1	9	9	-	-	c Walker b Penn	14	68	52	-	1
M.A.Sigley† c Fleming b Jefferson	13	76	68	-	1	c Jones b O'Brien	33	97	63	-	5
M.J.Mason c Nevin b O'Brien	3	30	27	-	-	c Donaldson b O'Brien	34	47	42	1	5
B.E.Hefford not out	0	6	3	-	-	c Walker b O'Brien	7	20	21	-	1
L.J.Hamilton b O'Brien	0	1	2	-	-	not out	7	17	13	-	1
Extras (b 1, lb 7, w 1, nb 9)	18					(b 2, lb 6, w 2, nb 7)	17				
TOTAL (56.5 overs)	**91**	246				**TOTAL** (63.4 overs)	**192**	265			

WELLINGTON

	Runs	Mins	Balls	6s	4s		Runs	Mins	Balls	6s	4s
M.D.Bell* lbw b Hefford	7	32	32	-	-	not out	21	33	25	-	3
R.A.Jones lbw b Mason	23	99	57	-	3	not out	15	33	26	-	1
N.R.Parlane lbw b Hefford	0	1	2	-	-						
S.P.Fleming c Oram b Mason	55	106	83	-	10						
G.T.Donaldson b Oram	1	12	13	-	-						
J.E.C.Franklin lbw b Mason	0	10	6	-	-						
C.J.Nevin† b Hamilton	70	193	146	-	8						
M.D.J.Walker b Sulzberger	58	155	140	3	6						
M.R.Jefferson not out	7	33	12	-	1						
A.J.Penn c Hefford b Hamilton	0	4	6	-	-						
I.E.O'Brien c Sinclair b Hamilton	0	8	10	-	-						
Extras (lb 14, w 0, nb 10)	24					(w 2, nb 1)	3				
TOTAL (83 overs)	**245**	331				(8.2 overs) (0 wkts)	**39**	33			

Bowling WELLINGTON	O	M	R	W	O	M	R	W
Penn	17	9	18	1	20	3	62	4
Franklin	18	3	40	6	14	4	24	0
Walker	9	5	8	0	9	3	23	1
O'Brien	11.5	6	12	2	13.4	4	42	5
Jefferson	1	0	5	1	7	1	33	0
CENTRAL DISTRICTS								
Hamilton	19	2	95	3	4.2	0	20	0
Mason	24	6	73	3	4	0	19	0
Hefford	11	3	24	2				
Oram	15	12	7	1				
Sulzberger	14	3	32	1				

Fall of Wickets	CD 1st	W 1st	CD 2nd	W 2nd
1st	8	16	5	-
2nd	23	16	44	-
3rd	32	88	48	-
4th	45	89	64	-
5th	45	94	85	-
6th	47	105	96	-
7th	83	222	120	-
8th	91	241	174	-
9th	91	242	178	-
10th	91	245	192	-

CANTERBURY v NORTHERN DISTRICTS State Championship

at Dudley Park, Rangiora on 5, 6, 7, 8 December, 2002
Toss : Canterbury. Umpires : G.A. Baxter & D.M. Quested
Close of play: 1st day: ND 233-9, Vettori 78, Butler 10; 2nd day: Canterbury 230-9, Bond 23, Martin 2
3rd day: ND 163-6, R.G. Hart 33, Yovich 8
First innings tie. *Points: Canterbury 1, Northern Districts 1*

Northern lost James Marshall to the first ball of the game and were 131-7 when Vettori came to the wicket and then 140-8 shortly after. Vettori, who went on to make his highest score since his only first-class century in 1999, added 35 with Tuffey (who made 3) and then 61 for the last wicket with Butler (who scored 10).

Canterbury lost wickets at regular intervals with no batsman reaching 40. By stumps they were six runs short of Northern's total with just one wicket left. Next morning Bond and Martin levelled the scores before a run out ended the innings.

Northern battled to 163-6 in their second innings before rain ended play on the third afternoon and further wet weather prevented any play on the last day.

NORTHERN DISTRICTS

FIRST INNINGS	Runs	Mins	Balls	6s	4s
J.A.H.Marshall lbw b Bond	0	1	1	-	-
N.K.W.Horsley b Donkers	22	70	48	-	2
M.E.Parlane lbw b Donkers	19	122	98	-	2
S.B.Styris c McMillan b Donkers	1	11	12	-	-
H.J.H.Marshall run out	19	114	99	-	2
M.N.Hart c Hopkins b Martin	9	59	40	-	-
R.G.Hart*† lbw b Astle	19	106	88	-	2
J.A.F.Yovich b Astle	24	76	71	-	1
D.L.Vettori c Cairns b Astle	81	119	95	-	11
D.R.Tuffey c Papps b Bond	3	39	38	-	-
I.G.Butler not out	10	62	36	-	-
Extras (b 4, lb 6, w 2, nb 17)	29				
TOTAL (101.2 overs)	**236**	394			

SECOND INNINGS	Runs	Mins	Balls	6s	4s
c Astle b Bond	3	50	40	-	-
st Hopkins b Wiseman	57	161	124	-	9
run out	7	25	20	-	1
c Papps b Martin	11	29	21	-	1
b Martin	3	31	33	-	-
c Hopkins b McMillan	22	101	78	-	2
not out	33	103	92	-	1
not out	8	24	15	-	1
(b 6, lb 4, nb 9)	19				
(69 overs) (6 wkts)	**163**	265			

CANTERBURY

	Runs	Mins	Balls	6s	4s
G.R.Stead* c Hart R.G. b Styris	23	84	65	-	3
M.H.W.Papps lbw b Vettori	39	203	137	-	2
C.D.McMillan c Hart M.N. b Vettori	4	26	16	-	1
N.J.Astle lbw b Tuffey	11	29	29	-	1
C.L.Cairns c Horsley b Styris	22	44	31	1	2
G.J.Hopkins† c Hart M.N. b Marshall J.A.H.	10	80	66	-	-
P.J.Wiseman c Tuffey b Yovich	4	23	15	-	-
B.P.Donkers c Horsley b Tuffey	38	138	124	-	4
C.Z.Harris c Hart R.G. b Tuffey	28	78	55	-	2
S.E.Bond not out	27	69	56	-	2
C.S.Martin run out	3	49	24	-	-
Extras (lb 9, w 3, nb 15)	27				
TOTAL (100.3 overs)	**236**	416			

Bowling	O	M	R	W	O	M	R	W
CANTERBURY								
Bond	21	3	56	2	14	4	33	1
Martin	23	7	51	1	12	3	41	2
Astle	17.2	6	26	3	8	5	15	0
Donkers	18	6	37	3	5	2	7	0
Cairns	10	0	35	0	4	0	18	0
McMillan	4	2	6	0	4	0	15	1
Wiseman	8	4	15	0	22	10	24	1
NORTHERN DISTRICTS								
Tuffey	26.3	5	66	3				
Yovich	22	5	51	1				
Styris	21	5	49	2				
Vettori	27	7	56	2				
Marshall J.A.H.	4	2	5	1				

Fall of Wickets			
	ND	C	ND
	1st	1st	2nd
1st	0	51	28
2nd	41	62	44
3rd	43	80	69
4th	58	114	75
5th	82	117	95
6th	88	123	148
7th	131	148	-
8th	140	203	-
9th	175	212	-
10th	236	236	-

AUCKLAND v WELLINGTON   State Championship

at Eden Park Outer Oval, Auckland on 5, 6, 7, 8 December, 2002
Toss : Auckland. Umpires : B.G. Frost & A.L. Hill
Close of play: 1st day: Auckland 46-2, Richardson 17, Canning 13; 2nd day: Wellington 30-3, Parlane 8, Donaldson 5
3rd day: Wellington 124-6, Nevin 24, Walker 7
Auckland won by 2 wickets. *Points: Auckland 6, Wellington 1*

Wellington reached 12-0 after ten overs and then lost four wickets without addition in the space of eight deliveries. Mills dismissed Jones, Bell was run out for a 44 minute duck and Adams dismissed both Fleming and Donaldson for first ball ducks. Nevin survived the hat trick. Parlane helped get the score to 113 with Mills, Shaw, Adams and Canning sharing the wickets.

Auckland were 58-2 but Walker produced an inspired spell and reduced Auckland to 106-9. Pryor and Shaw levelled the scores before the last wicket fell producing the second first innings tie of the round.

A number of interruptions meant Wellington's second innings covered three separate days. Nevin hit an aggressive 73 to leave Auckland to score 220 to win on the last afternoon. Richardson went early but a dedicated innings from McIntosh held the Auckland innings together allowing Vincent and Canning to go for their shots. More good bowling by Walker kept Wellington in the game before Auckland got home by two wickets.

WELLINGTON

FIRST INNINGS	Runs	Mins	Balls	6s	4s	SECOND INNINGS	Runs	Mins	Balls	6s	4s
M.D.Bell* run out	0	44	32	-	-	run out	4	9	9	-	-
R.A.Jones c Young b Mills	9	40	29	-	-	c Shaw b Mills	11	33	24	-	1
N.R.Parlane c Young b Shaw	42	164	116	-	5	c McIntosh b Pryor	29	141	114	-	2
S.P.Fleming lbw b Adams	0	1	1	-	-	c Young b Adams	0	10	4	-	-
G.T.Donaldson b Adams	0	2	1	-	-	c Young b Mills	31	112	97	-	2
C.J.Nevin† lbw b Mills	6	11	15	-	-	c Walker b Shaw	73	124	103	1	10
J.E.C.Franklin lbw b Canning	23	116	100	-	1	c Vincent b Pryor	9	34	29	-	1
M.D.J.Walker lbw b Canning	1	12	15	-	-	lbw b Mills	15	42	32	-	2
M.R.Jefferson c Walker b Shaw	11	28	22	-	2	c Walker b Pryor	19	77	62	-	1
A.J.Penn not out	1	20	11	-	-	c Pryor b Shaw	5	9	7	-	-
I.E.O'Brien c Mills b Canning	3	5	5	-	-	not out	6	24	10	-	1
Extras (b 1, lb 8, w 4, nb 4)	17					(b 1, lb 6, w 5, nb 5)	17				
TOTAL (57.1 overs)	**113**	226				(81 overs)	**219**	313			

AUCKLAND

	Runs	Mins	Balls	6s	4s		Runs	Mins	Balls	6s	4s
M.H.Richardson b Penn	21	112	73	-	1	b Penn	4	10	10	-	1
T.G.McIntosh lbw b Walker	8	36	35	-	1	not out	70	301	197	1	5
L.Vincent c Parlane b Penn	0	6	7	-	-	c Penn b O'Brien	40	50	43	1	5
T.K.Canning c Parlane b Penn	15	64	49	-	2	(9) c & b Walker	41	80	64	2	2
R.J.Nicol b Walker	5	15	10	-	1	c Walker b Penn	27	45	38	-	4
K.D.Mills b Walker	7	26	18	-	1	lbw b Penn	0	7	4	-	-
C.R.Pryor not out	16	66	45	-	2	(8) c Fleming b Walker	14	51	33	-	3
B.G.K.Walker* lbw b Walker	0	2	3	-	-	(10) not out	9	32	12	-	1
A.R.Adams b O'Brien	21	21	12	1	3	(7) c Jones b Walker	6	15	12	-	1
R.A.Young† c Nevin b Walker	1	10	6	-	-	(4) c Parlane b Walker	1	3	3	-	-
G.S.Shaw lbw b Penn	1	14	11	-	-						
Extras (b 5, lb 8, w 1, nb 4)	18					(b 1, lb 7, w 1, nb 2)	11				
TOTAL (44.1 overs)	**113**	191				(69 overs) (8 wkts)	**223**	301			

Bowling AUCKLAND	O	M	R	W	O	M	R	W
Mills	18	8	24	2	27	8	55	3
Shaw	14	4	29	2	11	1	45	2
Adams	10	2	28	2	19	8	33	1
Canning	10.1	4	13	3	6	1	15	0
Pryor	5	2	10	0	18	0	64	3
WELLINGTON								
Penn	13.1	4	30	4	23	3	71	3
Franklin	4	1	4	0	2	0	13	0
O'Brien	12	2	35	1	16	6	47	1
Walker	15	5	31	5	28	6	84	4

Fall of Wickets	W	A	W	A
	1st	1st	2nd	2nd
1st	12	21	10	4
2nd	12	22	21	55
3rd	12	58	25	57
4th	12	59	82	100
5th	23	67	88	100
6th	94	72	111	108
7th	96	73	161	140
8th	102	99	190	206
9th	110	106	199	-
10th	113	113	219	-

OTAGO v NORTHERN DISTRICTS   State Championship

at Carisbrook, Dunedin on 10, 11, 12, 13 December, 2002
Toss : Northern Districts. Umpires : R.D. Anderson & M.P. George
Close of play: 1st day: Otago 153-0, Lawson 75, Wasim 68; 2nd day: Otago 453-8, O'Connor 7, Walmsley 7
3rd day: ND 133-5, Hart 20, Yovich 12
Otago won by 70 runs. Points: Otago 6, Northern Districts 0

Jeff Wison, who had been injured, made his long awaited return to first-class cricket in this game, having last played in 1996/97. Kelly (formerly Central Districts) played his first match for Northern while Daley made his first-class debut in place of Robbie Hart whose test commitments kept him out of the Northern first-class side for the first time since his debut in 1992/93.

After a late start, Matthew Hart, in his first game as captain, put Otago in only to see Lawson and Wasim put together a record for Otago's first wicket against Northern. Three Otago batsmen reached centuries on the second day as Otago prospered to the tune of 453-8. Lawson took 270 minutes and 223 balls, Wasim took 322 minutes and 264 balls while McCullum needed only 144 balls in 191 minutes.

After rain had disrupted much of the third day, Northern declared at their overnight score. Otago then batted for four overs setting a target of 329. Northern lost wickets regularly to be 93-5. Hart and Yovich added 84 in 95 minutes and Martin helped Hart add 61 in 55 minutes before Walmsley and O'Connor wrapped up the innings.

OTAGO

FIRST INNINGS	Runs	Mins	Balls	6s	4s	SECOND INNINGS	Runs	Mins	Balls	6s	4s
R.A.Lawson c Horsley b Aldridge	146	340	262	2	10						
Mohammad Wasim c Daley b Yovich	104	346	278	-	11						
B.B.McCullum† c Kelly b Aldridge	105	198	151	1	13						
C.D.Cumming* c Martin b Andrews	23	70	51	-	3	(1) b Aldridge	0	1	4	-	-
M.N.McKenzie st Daley b Martin	15	53	36	-	2	(3) lbw b Andrews	1	2	2	-	-
J.W.Wilson c Andrews b Martin	3	15	16	-	-						
J.W.Sheed c Daley b Aldridge	21	47	33	-	3	(4) not out	2	8	10	-	-
N.D.Morland lbw b Martin	3	12	9	-	-	(2) not out	2	17	10	-	-
S.B.O'Connor not out	7	16	16	-	1						
K.P.Walmsley not out	7	7	5	-	1						
J.M.McMillan											
Extras (lb 6, w 2, nb 11)	19					(b 1, nb 2)	3				
TOTAL (141 overs) (8 wkts dec)	**453**	556				(4 overs) (2 wkts dec)	**8**	17			

NORTHERN DISTRICTS

	Runs	Mins	Balls	6s	4s		Runs	Mins	Balls	6s	4s
J.A.H.Marshall c McKenzie b McMillan	34	107	74	-	2	c Morland b McMillan	7	42	25	-	1
N.K.W.Horsley run out	10	30	27	-	1	c McCullum b McMillan	30	83	58	-	6
D.P.Kelly lbw b O'Connor	26	97	69	-	5	b Walmsley	5	23	18	-	1
M.E.Parlane c McCullum b Wilson	25	109	85	-	4	c O'Connor b Morland	32	86	72	-	3
H.J.H.Marshall c McCullum b O'Connor	8	8	8	-	-	lbw b Walmsley	11	51	40	-	-
M.N.Hart* not out	20	115	97	-	1	c McCullum b Walmsley	66	183	156	-	9
J.A.F.Yovich not out	12	35	37	-	2	run out	52	95	68	2	6
B.P.Martin						c Sheed b Morland	34	55	44	2	2
G.W.Aldridge						lbw b O'Connor	6	44	26	-	1
N.M.Daley†						c Wasim b Walmsley	4	26	13	-	-
S.L.Andrews						not out	0	3	4	-	-
Extras (lb 5, nb 1)	6					(lb 10, nb 1)	11				
TOTAL (66 overs) (5 wkts dec)	**133**	253				(87.1 overs)	**258**	350			

Bowling	O	M	R	W	O	M	R	W		Fall of Wickets				
NORTHERN DISTRICTS											O	ND	O	ND
											1st	1st	2nd	2nd
Yovich	29	5	102	1						1st	260	18	0	29
Andrews	36	13	91	1	2	0	4	1		2nd	264	67	1	42
Aldridge	40	11	126	3	2	0	3	1		3rd	317	79	-	48
Martin	30	6	106	3						4th	364	79	-	83
Marshall J.A.H.	3	0	9	0						5th	380	114	-	93
Hart	3	0	13	0						6th	431	-	-	177
OTAGO										7th	435	-	-	238
O'Connor	17	4	28	2	18.1	6	34	1		8th	439	-	-	248
Walmsley	15	6	27	0	19	5	48	4		9th	-	-	-	258
McMillan	14	0	38	1	19	5	45	2		10th	-	-	-	258
Wilson	14	4	32	1	9	1	49	0						
Morland	6	4	3	0	22	6	72	2						

CANTERBURY v WELLINGTON **State Championship**

at Dudley Park, Rangiora on 10, 11, 12, 13 December, 2002
Toss : Canterbury. Umpires : B.G. Frost & A.L. Hill
Close of play: 1st day: Wellington 299-6, Parlane 71, Jefferson 9; 2nd day: Canterbury 145-3, Papps 59, Wiseman 3
3rd day: Canterbury 338-9, Harris 73, Martin 0
First innings win to Wellington. *Points: Wellington 2, Canterbury 0*

Wellington batted throughout the first day after Bell and Jones had opened with a 124 run partnership. The Wellington captain went on to reach his century in 231 minutes from 180 balls before being second out at 217. Fifties from Parlane and Jefferson allowed Wellington to reach 399.

Apart from Frew, all the Canterbury top order reached 30 but no one reached three fugures, Papps made 87 and Harris was left unbeaten on 78 after Canterbury's last wickets fell quickly. O'Brien took 6-103 from 45.3 overs.

With no chance of a decision, Wellington batted until tea when the game was called off.

WELLINGTON

FIRST INNINGS	Runs	Mins	Balls	6s	4s		SECOND INNINGS	Runs	Mins	Balls	6s	4s
M.D.Bell* c Frew b Martin	114	254	201	-	16		c Harris b Wiseman	43	118	105	-	8
R.A.Jones run out	55	141	112	-	6		c Frew b Wiseman	14	74	39	-	2
N.R.Parlane lbw b Wisneski	75	304	228	-	11		(5) not out	42	139	119	1	4
L.J.Morgan b Wisneski	24	86	75	-	-		lbw b Wiseman	12	38	40	-	1
G.T.Donaldson lbw b Wisneski	0	1	1	-	-		(3) c & b Stead	2	9	9	-	-
C.J.Nevin† b Martin	1	12	8	-	-		c Martin b Donkers	25	42	46	-	4
M.D.J.Walker c Hopkins b Wisneski	0	11	7	-	-		c Stead b Stewart	19	66	65	-	3
M.R.Jefferson b Martin	53	154	121	-	5		not out	7	24	20	-	-
A.J.Penn c Wisneski b Fulton	19	41	32	-	4							
J.S.Patel c Fulton b Wiseman	8	11	7	-	-							
I.E.O'Brien not out	14	22	12	-	3							
Extras (b 5, lb 14, nb 17)	36						(b 3, lb 7, w 6, nb 5)	21				
TOTAL (131.1 overs)	**399**	523					(73 overs) (6 wkts)	**185**	258			

CANTERBURY

	Runs	Mins	Balls	6s	4s
R.M.Frew lbw b Walker	7	65	46	-	1
G.R.Stead* c Parlane b Penn	47	138	116	-	8
M.H.W.Papps c Parlane b O'Brien	87	301	239	-	10
S.L.Stewart lbw b Penn	31	109	79	1	3
P.J.Wiseman c Nevin b O'Brien	38	142	104	1	4
C.Z.Harris not out	73	298	214	1	7
P.G.Fulton b O'Brien	0	5	3	-	-
G.J.Hopkins† lbw b Walker	30	153	135	-	1
B.P.Donkers c Nevin b O'Brien	14	82	59	-	2
W.A.Wisneski c Nevin b O'Brien	1	21	14	-	-
C.S.Martin c Jones b O'Brien	0	9	6	-	-
Extras (lb 7, nb 3)	10				
TOTAL (168.3 overs)	**338**	666			

Bowling	O	M	R	W	O	M	R	W
CANTERBURY								
Wisneski	34	4	126	4	6	0	24	0
Martin	35.1	11	82	3	10	2	32	0
Donkers	29	11	80	0	9	5	16	1
Stewart	3	0	18	0	6	1	12	1
Wiseman	28	7	69	1	25	11	47	3
Fulton	2	1	5	1	4	0	12	0
Stead					13	2	32	1
WELLINGTON								
Penn	33	15	53	2				
O'Brien	45.3	13	103	6				
Walker	39	11	62	2				
Jefferson	39	9	72	0				
Patel	12	2	41	0				

Fall of Wickets	W	C	W
	1st	1st	2nd
1st	124	35	56
2nd	217	69	60
3rd	271	142	76
4th	271	205	77
5th	275	216	114
6th	283	217	159
7th	311	301	-
8th	363	332	-
9th	395	338	-
10th	399	338	-

CENTRAL DISTRICTS v AUCKLAND State Championship

at Horton Park, Blenheim on 10, 11, 12, 13 December, 2002
Toss : Central Districts. Umpires : D.B. Cowie & I.W. Shine
Close of play: 1st day: Auckland 217-8, Walker 8, Nielsen 0; 2nd day: CD 86-1, Ingram 29, Sinclair 21
3rd day: Auckland 38-3, King 12, Nicol 1
Central Districts won by 4 wickets. *Points: Central Districts 6, Auckland 2*

Auckland batted slowly through the first day after early problems when they were 35-4. Nicol and Mills added 130 in 203 minutes and on the second morning Walker and Davis took part in a record last wicket stand for Auckland against Central.

The home team were hardly any more enterprising. Ingram hit his maiden fifty, reached after 242 minutes, but Central fell 82 runs short. The Central bowlers struck back, however, having Auckland 38-3 by stumps and next day dismissed them for 169, Mills and Davis (who was injured and did not bowl) adding 47 for the last wicket.

Central needed 252 to win and Spearman and Loveridge began with 68 in 33 minutes. Fifty had come up in just 23 minutes and the hundred came 30 minutes later. Central reached 150 in 88 minutes as Spearman and Sulzberger added 83 in 57 minutes and 200 arrived after just 115 minutes. Schwass helped Spearman add 44 in 23 minutes and the 250 came up after 147 minutes as the home team raced to victory. Spearman reached fifty from 40 balls in 55 minutes and his century took only 77 balls and 121 minutes.

AUCKLAND

FIRST INNINGS	Runs	Mins	Balls	6s	4s
M.J.Horne c Sigley b Schwass	22	86	64	-	4
T.G.McIntosh c Loveridge b Hefford	4	55	40	-	-
R.K.Lynch c Sigley b Todd	2	37	23	-	-
R.T.King c Sinclair b Hamilton	0	11	8	-	-
R.J.Nicol c Loveridge b Hefford	87	269	219	1	13
K.D.Mills run out	55	203	168	-	7
C.R.Pryor c Spearman b Schwass	11	42	30	-	2
B.G.K.Walker* not out	67	270	229	-	9
R.A.Young† c Spearman b Hefford	5	22	18	-	1
B.J.Nielsen run out	15	110	97	-	2
H.T.Davis b Hamilton	29	119	81	-	4
Extras (b 1, lb 14, w 4, nb 12)	31				
TOTAL (160.4 overs)	**328**	612			

SECOND INNINGS	Runs	Mins	Balls	6s	4s
(6) b Hefford	21	60	41	-	4
(1) lbw b Hamilton	4	11	9	-	-
(2) c & b Schwass	5	32	28	-	-
(3) lbw b Sulzberger	47	179	124	-	7
b Schwass	2	44	35	-	-
(7) not out	40	178	144	2	4
(8) lbw b Hefford	0	8	8	-	-
(4) c Sigley b Schwass	10	36	27	-	-
c Todd b Sulzberger	2	18	11	-	-
c Sigley b Schwass	24	104	91	-	1
(lb 5, w 3, nb 5)	13				
(89.3 overs)	**169**	350			

CENTRAL DISTRICTS

	Runs	Mins	Balls	6s	4s
P.J.Ingram lbw b Pryor	66	348	277	-	10
C.M.Spearman* c Young b Nielsen	31	51	44	-	6
M.S.Sinclair c McIntosh b Pryor	60	220	182	-	8
G.P.Sulzberger c Young b Pryor	0	7	2	-	-
G.R.Todd c Davis b Nicol	35	133	104	-	5
B.B.J.Griggs lbw b Nielsen	0	12	7	-	-
G.R.Loveridge c McIntosh b Mills	34	83	63	-	6
M.A.Sigley† lbw b Davis	0	5	2	-	-
A.M.Schwass run out	2	14	16	-	-
B.E.Hefford b Mills	5	23	17	-	1
L.J.Hamilton not out	0	6	2	-	-
Extras (b 1, lb 4, w 1, nb 7)	13				
TOTAL (118.1 overs)	**246**	453			

	Runs	Mins	Balls	6s	4s
(8) not out	6	3	2	-	1
(1) not out	117	148	89	6	2
run out	18	23	19	1	1
c Lynch b Walker	48	57	40	2	2
run out	4	6	5	-	-
(7) run out	0	3	1	-	-
(2) c King b Mills	27	33	26	1	2
(6) c King b Mills	20	23	14	-	3
(b 5, lb 6, w 1, nb 2)	14				
(32.2 overs) (6 wkts)	**254**	148			

Bowling	O	M	R	W	O	M	R	W
CENTRAL DISTRICTS								
Hamilton	40.4	18	69	2	15	8	25	1
Hefford	32	14	43	3	19	10	33	2
Schwass	33	13	55	2	20.3	5	44	4
Todd	7	1	37	1				
Sulzberger	44	17	89	0	30	16	51	3
Loveridge	4	1	20	0	5	1	11	0
AUCKLAND								
Mills	17.1	5	46	2	10	0	73	2
Davis	16	5	42	1				
Walker	13	5	16	0	12	0	99	1
Nielsen	41	15	88	2	2	0	14	0
Pryor	29	13	45	3	8.2	0	57	0
Nicol	2	1	4	1				

Fall of Wickets	A	CD	A	CD
	1st	1st	2nd	2nd
1st	10	42	7	68
2nd	35	152	13	102
3rd	35	152	33	185
4th	35	185	46	203
5th	165	188	84	247
6th	196	228	114	248
7th	202	229	115	-
8th	217	233	118	-
9th	252	245	122	-
10th	328	246	169	-

AUCKLAND v OTAGO

State Championship

at North Harbour Stadium, Auckland on 9, 10, 11, 12 January, 2003
Toss : Otago. Umpires : M.P. George & I.W. Shine
Close of play: 1st day: Auckland 128-4, McIntosh 78, Barnes 4; 2nd day: no play
3rd day: Otago 89-1, Lawson 49, Cumming 9
First innings win to Auckland. *Points: Auckland 2, Otago 0*

North Harbour Stadium became the 60th first-class venue in New Zealand when it staged this match. Rain interrupted the first day's play as Auckland batted 58 overs to be 128-4. No play at all was possible the next day but when play did resume McIntosh completed his hundred after facing 286 balls in 334 minutes. Barnes was the only other player to reach 20.

Otago made a good reply by stumps but lost three quick wickets on the last morning. All the Auckland bowlers captured at least one wicket as Otago were eventually dismissed for 185 with Wilson unable to bat because of injury. Auckland batted briefly before the match was called off.

McGlashan (formerly Central Districts) made his debut for Otago in this game in place of McCullum.

AUCKLAND

FIRST INNINGS	Runs	Mins	Balls	6s	4s
M.H.Richardson c McKenzie b O'Connor	6	43	37	-	1
T.G.McIntosh c McKenzie b O'Connor	157	500	381	1	13
M.J.Horne b McMillan	19	42	28	1	1
T.K.Canning c & b O'Connor	14	83	72	-	1
R.J.Nicol run out	4	33	20	-	-
A.C.Barnes c Cumming b O'Connor	42	138	105	-	4
C.R.Pryor c Wasim b Walmsley	1	9	7	-	-
B.G.K.Walker* c Wasim b Walmsley	14	62	48	-	1
R.A.Young† lbw b Walmsley	11	41	30	-	2
H.T.Davis c Sheed b Walmsley	3	10	12	-	-
G.S.Shaw not out	6	30	23	-	-
Extras (b 6, lb 2, w 2, nb 2)	12				
TOTAL (126.5 overs)	**289**	500			

SECOND INNINGS	Runs	Mins	Balls	6s	4s
not out	9	30	35	-	1
not out	4	30	16	-	1
(nb 3)	3				
(8 overs) (0 wkts)	**16**	30			

OTAGO

	Runs	Mins	Balls	6s	4s
R.A.Lawson c Canning b Davis	49	138	109	-	4
Mohammad Wasim c Richardson b Canning	24	95	71	-	1
C.D.Cumming* c Richardson b Shaw	11	50	32	-	2
M.N.McKenzie c Nicol b Canning	3	46	30	-	-
J.W.Sheed lbw b Canning	21	144	109	-	2
P.D.McGlashan† b Barnes	5	57	45	-	-
N.D.Morland c McIntosh b Pryor	23	99	77	-	2
S.B.O'Connor c McIntosh b Canning	0	1	2	-	-
K.P.Walmsley c Canning b Pryor	21	61	48	-	2
J.M.McMillan not out	0	11	13	-	-
J.W.Wilson absent hurt					
Extras (b 4, lb 11, w 7, nb 6)	28				
TOTAL (88.1 overs)	**185**	355			

Bowling	O	M	R	W	O	M	R	W
OTAGO								
O'Connor	30.5	17	34	4				
Walmsley	30	6	69	3	4	0	7	0
Wilson	27	4	81	0				
McMillan	24	7	62	1				
Cumming	6	3	9	0	4	1	9	0
Morland	9	4	26	1				
AUCKLAND								
Shaw	13	3	31	1				
Davis	12	8	5	1				
Pryor	21.1	6	58	2				
Canning	31	11	58	4				
Barnes	11	4	18	1				

Fall of Wickets

	A	O	A
	1st	1st	2nd
1st	17	58	-
2nd	47	92	-
3rd	98	94	-
4th	111	102	-
5th	198	120	-
6th	203	139	-
7th	232	139	-
8th	257	178	-
9th	266	185	-
10th	289	-	-

CANTERBURY v CENTRAL DISTRICTS State Championship

at Aorangi Park, Timaru on 9, 10, 11, 12 January, 2003
Toss : Central Districts. Umpires : R.D. Anderson & E.A. Watkin
Close of play: 1st day: CD 10-0, Ingram 3, How 7; 2nd day: Canterbury 15-2, Papps 8, Stewart 0
3rd day: CD 36-1, How 28, Sandbrook 0
First innings win to Central Districts. *Points: Central Districts 2, Canterbury 0*

Canterbury's innings was centred around Papps who reached his hundred after 270 minutes from 198 deliveries. McMillan, Stewart and Fulton gave some support but nobody else was able to reach double figures. Mason finished with his best bowling figures.

Central was able to gain a narrow first innings lead thanks mainly to How's maiden half-century while Griggs, Sigley and Mason all gave valuable support. Canterbury lost three wickets before wiping off the deficit and were eventually dismissed for 183. Mason improved on his career best figures and had ten wickets in a match for the first time.

Central needed 156 to win and had progressed to 36-1 by the close and an interesting finish was in store. Rain, however, prevented any play the next day.

New Zealand Under 19 players Sandbrook and Taylor made their first-class debuts in this match.

CANTERBURY

FIRST INNINGS	Runs	Mins	Balls	6s	4s	SECOND INNINGS	Runs	Mins	Balls	6s	4s
G.R.Stead* lbw b Hamilton	0	1	3	-	-	c How b Mason	6	33	23	-	-
R.M.Frew lbw b Mason	2	103	78	-	-	c How b Mason	1	14	8	-	-
M.H.W.Papps c Todd b Hamilton	114	351	242	-	15	c Griggs b Hefford	35	113	77	-	4
C.D.McMillan c Mason b Hefford	26	55	52	2	3	(5) c Sulzberger b Hefford	15	37	26	-	2
S.L.Stewart c Sulzberger b Mason	33	64	49	1	5	(4) lbw b Mason	0	23	17	-	-
P.G.Fulton c Griggs b Hefford	32	59	66	-	5	b Mason	65	147	105	1	9
G.J.Hopkins† lbw b Mason	7	33	35	-	-	c Sigley b Hefford	4	14	13	-	1
P.J.Wiseman c Sigley b Mason	0	1	2	-	-	c Sandbrook b Hefford	4	8	5	-	1
B.P.Donkers not out	7	53	39	-	1	c Sigley b Mason	13	84	82	-	2
H.J.Shaw c Griggs b Mason	8	14	10	-	2	b Mason	24	18	11	1	4
C.S.Martin not out	0	5	5	-	-	not out	5	8	5	-	-
Extras (b 1, lb 10, nb 5)	16					(b 2, lb 4, w 4, nb 1)	11				
TOTAL (96 overs) (9 wkts dec)	**245**	372				(61.5 overs)	**183**	256			

CENTRAL DISTRICTS

P.J.Ingram b Donkers	29	78	65	-	5	b Shaw	6	49	41	-	1
J.M.How lbw b Martin	73	143	106	-	14	not out	28	76	52	-	5
I.P.Sandbrook c Stead b Shaw	7	25	18	-	-	not out	0	26	15	-	-
G.P.Sulzberger* c Hopkins b McMillan	3	13	8	-	-						
G.R.Todd b Donkers	9	56	38	-	1						
B.B.J.Griggs c Hopkins b Martin	40	109	86	-	5						
R.L.Taylor b McMillan	12	12	11	-	3						
M.A.Sigley† run out	34	110	92	-	5						
M.J.Mason c Fulton b Martin	36	68	46	-	4						
B.E.Hefford b Martin	6	41	22	-	-						
L.J.Hamilton not out	12	9	10	1	-						
Extras (lb 7, w 3, nb 2)	12					(lb 2)	2				
TOTAL (83.3 overs)	**273**	341				(18 overs) (1 wkt)	**36**	76			

Bowling	O	M	R	W	O	M	R	W
CENTRAL DISTRICTS								
Hamilton	27	7	64	2	9.5	2	25	0
Mason	25	11	59	5	19.5	3	56	6
Hefford	23	9	56	2	17	8	53	4
Todd	6	2	20	0	6	1	20	0
Sulzberger	15	4	35	0	9.1	3	23	0
CANTERBURY								
Martin	24.3	9	69	4	9	6	7	0
McMillan	19	4	65	2				
Shaw	16	3	53	1	8	4	23	1
Donkers	18	4	71	2	1	0	4	0
Wiseman	6	1	8	0				

Fall of Wickets	C	CD	C	CD
	1st	1st	2nd	2nd
1st	0	58	4	21
2nd	59	91	15	-
3rd	103	102	18	-
4th	160	116	55	-
5th	208	132	72	-
6th	223	147	80	-
7th	223	187	89	-
8th	232	232	149	-
9th	244	256	154	-
10th	-	273	183	-

NORTHERN DISTRICTS v WELLINGTON State Championship

at Owen Delany Park, Taupo on 9, 10, 11, 12 January, 2003
Toss : Northern Districts. Umpires : G.A. Baxter & G.C. Holdem
Close of play: 1st day: no play; 2nd day: Wellington 129-2, Parlane 49, Morgan 3
3rd day: ND 95-3, Parlane 29, H.J.H. Marshall 7
First innings win to Wellington. *Points: Wellington 2, Northern Districts 0*

No play was possible on the first day and in 59 overs on the second Wellington reached 129-2 with Jones and Parlane having put on 86 in 126 minutes for the second wicket. The next day Wellington showed more aggression and in 50 further overs got to 269. Martin took 5-48 which turned out to be the only five wicket haul by a spin bowler during the first-class season.

Northern were also in no hurry and took 44 overs to reach 95-3 by the close of the third day. With only a first innings decision likely, Northern battled away on the last morning but apart from Parlane, who made 80, none of the other batsmen stayed long enough to threaten the Wellington total.

Wellington batted for a second time until tea when the game was called off. Former Central Districts player West made his Northern debut in this match.

WELLINGTON

FIRST INNINGS	Runs	Mins	Balls	6s	4s		SECOND INNINGS	Runs	Mins	Balls	6s	4s
M.D.Bell* c & b Yovich	14	48	37	-	2		run out	30	90	77	-	2
R.A.Jones c Hart M.N. b Martin	56	175	141	-	3		not out	19	90	63	-	3
N.R.Parlane c Hart R.G. b Hart M.N.	63	219	195	1	9							
L.J.Morgan c Marshall J.A.H. b Yovich	30	129	100	-	3							
G.T.Donaldson b West	35	98	76	-	6							
C.J.Nevin† lbw b West	37	69	50	-	6							
M.D.J.Walker c Hart M.N. b Martin	0	11	10	-	-							
M.R.Jefferson lbw b Martin	10	33	24	-	2							
A.J.Penn c Marshall J.A.H. b Martin	0	6	4	-	-							
M.R.Gillespie not out	3	25	17	-	-							
I.E.O'Brien b Martin	4	2	5	-	-							
Extras (b 2, lb 5, w 2, nb 8)	17						(lb 1, w 2, nb 5)	8				
TOTAL (109 overs)	**269**	412					(22.3 overs) (1 wkt)	**57**	90			

NORTHERN DISTRICTS

	Runs	Mins	Balls	6s	4s
J.A.H.Marshall lbw b Penn	8	10	11	-	2
N.K.W.Horsley c Nevin b O'Brien	23	69	43	-	2
M.G.Orchard lbw b O'Brien	22	109	78	-	3
M.E.Parlane c Parlane b O'Brien	80	225	158	-	12
H.J.H.Marshall lbw b Jefferson	17	117	95	-	2
M.N.Hart c Nevin b Jefferson	0	3	2	-	-
R.G.Hart*† run out	6	18	15	-	-
J.A.F.Yovich not out	33	82	67	1	3
B.P.Martin c Bell b O'Brien	8	22	16	-	1
G.W.Aldridge c Bell b Jefferson	2	18	13	-	-
G.L.West c Bell b Penn	1	7	5	-	-
Extras (b 1, lb 4, nb 5)	10				
TOTAL (83 overs)	**210**	344			

Bowling	O	M	R	W	O	M	R	W
NORTHERN DISTRICTS								
Yovich	28	7	85	2	8	0	21	0
West	25	9	57	2	6	1	21	0
Aldridge	7	1	18	0				
Martin	30	12	48	5	8.3	3	14	0
Orchard	11	4	30	0				
Hart M.N.	8	0	24	1				
WELLINGTON								
Penn	18	6	45	2				
Gillespie	9	1	29	0				
O'Brien	23	7	68	4				
Walker	14	4	25	0				
Jefferson	19	7	38	3				

Fall of Wickets

	W	ND	W
	1st	1st	2nd
1st	29	12	57
2nd	115	45	-
3rd	166	70	-
4th	180	143	-
5th	249	143	-
6th	252	152	-
7th	256	174	-
8th	258	186	-
9th	265	207	-
10th	269	210	-

AUCKLAND v CANTERBURY   State Championship

at Colin Maiden Park, Auckland on 7, 8, 9, 10 February, 2003
Toss : Canterbury. Umpires : B.G. Frost & M.P. George
Close of play: 1st day: Auckland 89-2, Richardson 61, Horne 0; 2nd day: Auckland 432-8, Canning 98
3rd day: Canterbury 332-6, Hopkins 115, Wiseman 58
Auckland won by 5 wickets. *Points: Auckland 6, Canterbury 0*

Canterbury won the toss and batted but had sunk to 137-8 before Ellis, who was making his first-class debut, joined Hopkins at the wicket. These two then proceeded to break the record for Canterbury's ninth wicket against Auckland, which had stood since 1897/98. Hopkins, who missed out on a contract at the start of the season, reached his century in 140 minutes from 107 balls. Shaw had his first five wicket bag.

With Richardson, Horne and Nicol all scoring well, Auckland were 253-6, leading by one run, when Canning came in. He added 145 in 125 minutes with Barnes for the seventh wicket and had reached 98 by the close. Next day he went on to his maiden first-class hundred from 137 balls in 172 minutes.

Canterbury batted again and had reached 197-6, still 29 behind, when Wiseman joined Hopkins who was on 43. The pair set a record for Canterbury's seventh wicket against Auckland and, after Wiseman went, Hopkins added 55 more runs to finish on 175, his highest score. He was just one short of Len Cuff's record score for a Canterbury batsman against Auckland made as far back as 1893/94.

Auckland now needed an unexpected 188 to win, a task they accomplished but not without some alarms, being 116-5 at one stage. Auckland's total of 478 and Hopkins' score of 175 were the best in the short first-class history of the venue. England player Franks, who was playing club cricket in Christchurch, had been called into the Canterbury team after a number of injuries to their bowlers.

CANTERBURY

FIRST INNINGS	Runs	Mins	Balls	6s	4s	SECOND INNINGS	Runs	Mins	Balls	6s	4s
G.R.Stead* c Nicol b Canning	12	34	29	-	1	lbw b Canning	2	5	7	-	-
R.M.Frew c Barnes b Shaw	44	136	97	-	6	(9) b Canning	5	20	18	-	1
M.H.W.Papps c Nicol b Pryor	4	10	9	-	1	(2) c Young b Pryor	5	11	17	-	1
S.L.Stewart lbw b Canning	13	19	18	-	3	(3) lbw b Walker	30	102	101	-	2
P.G.Fulton c Young b Shaw	21	58	54	-	4	(4) lbw b Canning	14	42	35	-	2
A.J.Redmond lbw b Shaw	0	7	2	-	-	(5) c Pryor b Walker	59	75	50	-	10
G.J.Hopkins† c & b Walker	113	147	115	-	16	(6) not out	175	333	289	-	26
P.J.Franks b Shaw	10	26	17	-	2	(7) c Walker b Shaw	41	83	63	-	5
P.J.Wiseman b Canning	10	16	8	-	1	(8) lbw b Canning	59	118	84	-	10
A.M.Ellis c Young b Shaw	19	96	71	-	1	lbw b Walker	10	58	56	-	1
C.S.Martin not out	0	2	0	-	-	b Walker	0	28	13	-	-
Extras (lb 3, nb 3)	6					(lb 6, w 6, nb 1)	13				
TOTAL (69.3 overs)	**252**	280				(112 overs)	**413**	442			

AUCKLAND

M.H.Richardson c Papps b Wiseman	82	198	161	-	11	c Ellis b Wiseman	43	201	156	-	5
T.G.McIntosh lbw b Ellis	20	91	54	-	3	c & b Wiseman	28	98	86	-	4
R.A.Young† c Fulton b Wiseman	1	23	17	-	-						
M.J.Horne c Hopkins b Fulton	72	155	126	1	8	(3) c Papps b Redmond	18	23	15	-	4
L.G.Howell c Ellis b Wiseman	4	16	9	-	1	(4) c & b Redmond	0	9	6	-	-
R.J.Nicol b Redmond	77	255	200	1	7	(5) lbw b Redmond	18	59	42	-	3
A.C.Barnes lbw b Martin	43	72	60	1	7	(6) not out	30	61	48	-	5
T.K.Canning c Stewart b Wiseman	113	198	154	2	13	(7) not out	44	52	40	1	7
C.R.Pryor run out	9	45	30	-	1						
B.G.K.Walker* c Hopkins b Redmond	20	58	51	-	2						
G.S.Shaw not out	11	30	32	-	1						
Extras (b 8, lb 4, w 1, nb 13)	26					(b 5, lb 1, w 1, nb 2)	9				
TOTAL (146.4 overs)	**478**	574				(65.1 overs) (5 wkts)	**190**	254			

Bowling	O	M	R	W	O	M	R	W
AUCKLAND								
Canning	20	7	57	3	30	7	89	4
Shaw	15	0	73	5	21	2	85	1
Pryor	15	5	46	1	24	4	75	1
Barnes	11	2	46	0	9	2	27	0
Walker	4.3	0	14	1	17	1	77	4
Horne	4	0	13	0				
Nicol					9	0	40	0
McIntosh					2	0	14	0
CANTERBURY								
Martin	29	5	86	1	10	4	16	0
Franks	28	7	96	0	10	2	25	0
Ellis	20	1	66	1				
Wiseman	36	4	122	4	27.1	8	75	2
Redmond	26.4	4	78	2	18	0	68	3
Fulton	7	4	18	1				

Fall of Wickets	C	A	C	A
	1st	1st	2nd	2nd
1st	25	82	3	49
2nd	38	89	7	70
3rd	53	134	30	72
4th	95	151	77	110
5th	97	200	115	116
6th	98	253	197	-
7th	115	398	339	-
8th	137	432	353	-
9th	252	452	392	-
10th	252	478	413	-

CENTRAL DISTRICTS v NORTHERN DISTRICTS

at McLean Park, Napier on 7, 8, 9, 10 February, 2003
Toss : Northern Districts. Umpires : D.B. Cowie & C.J. Morris
Close of play: 1st day: ND 56-2, J.A.H. Marshall 26, Parlane 10; 2nd day: CD 132-6, Sulzberger 51, Mason 5
3rd day: ND 162-6, Orchard 22
Northern Districts won by 4 wickets. Points: Northern Districts 6, Central Districts 2

New Zealand Under 19 player Ryder made his debut for Central who were sent in to bat. Spearman was the only batsman to show prolonged resistance to the Northern pace attack, being fifth out at 143. Northern fared no better and from 74-2 could only muster 150 all out.

Wickets continued to fall and by the close of the second day Central were 132-6. On the third morning Sulzberger was left standed on 69 while Butler, with four tests to his name, captured his first five wicket bag.

Needing 205 to win, Northern were in trouble at 102-5 before Yovich joined Orchard. The pair added 60 before Yovich, who had made 51 of the partnership, went just on stumps. On the last morning Northern took 106 minutes to score the required 43 runs but lost no more wickets. Orchard, who batted 263 minutes for 49, hit Schwass for four to win the game.

CENTRAL DISTRICTS

FIRST INNINGS	Runs	Mins	Balls	6s	4s	SECOND INNINGS	Runs	Mins	Balls	6s	4s
C.M.Spearman* c Hart b Yovich	83	204	133	-	14	c Hart b Butler	11	13	8	-	2
P.J.Ingram lbw b Aldridge	10	70	58	-	-	c Horsley b Yovich	0	7	7	-	-
J.M.How lbw b Butler	0	15	13	-	-	b Martin	11	51	40	-	1
G.P.Sulzberger b Yovich	6	49	44	-	-	not out	69	249	180	-	7
B.B.J.Griggs b Aldridge	9	28	16	-	1	c Horsley b Butler	1	28	27	-	-
J.D.Ryder c Martin b Orchard	18	58	38	-	2	run out	39	83	63	-	5
M.A.Sigley† lbw b Orchard	0	29	20	-	-	c Horsley b Butler	9	27	30	-	-
M.J.Mason b Butler	17	26	19	-	2	c Martin b Butler	5	10	11	-	1
A.M.Schwass c Orchard b Yovich	25	53	43	1	3	c Horsley b Butler	6	15	9	-	-
B.E.Hefford b Butler	0	7	6	-	-	c Hart b Yovich	1	25	19	-	-
L.J.Hamilton not out	8	27	27	-	-	c Hart b Yovich	0	9	3	-	-
Extras (b 6, lb 10, w 1, nb 2)	19					(lb 6, nb 1)	7				
TOTAL (69.1 overs)	**195**	287				(66 overs)	**159**	263			

NORTHERN DISTRICTS

	Runs	Mins	Balls	6s	4s		Runs	Mins	Balls	6s	4s
J.A.H.Marshall c Griggs b Hefford	31	159	120	-	2	b Ryder	12	67	49	-	-
N.K.W.Horsley c Sigley b Hamilton	9	24	19	-	1	c Sulzberger b Hamilton	20	88	67	-	1
H.J.H.Marshall lbw b Mason	7	13	14	-	-	c Ingram b Sulzberger	26	98	83	-	4
M.E.Parlane c Hamilton b Hefford	35	158	110	-	2	c sub (G.R.Todd) b Hefford	17	121	88	-	1
M.G.Orchard c Sigley b Hefford	0	8	8	-	-	not out	49	263	197	-	2
D.P.Kelly b Mason	5	59	39	-	-	b Mason	7	20	18	-	1
R.G.Hart*† c Spearman b Sulzberger	16	53	37	-	1	(8) not out	18	106	68	-	1
J.A.F.Yovich lbw b Hamilton	10	46	38	-	1	(7) c Ryder b Mason	53	93	101	-	6
B.P.Martin c Spearman b Hamilton	17	57	43	1	1						
G.W.Aldridge not out	12	36	25	-	2						
I.G.Butler c Griggs b Hamilton	0	2	5	-	-						
Extras (lb 6, nb 2)	8					(lb 3, w 1, nb 2)	6				
TOTAL (76 overs)	**150**	312				(111.3 overs) (6 wkts)	**208**	433			

Bowling	O	M	R	W					
NORTHERN DISTRICTS									
Butler	20	6	61	3	22	8	44	5
Yovich	18.1	7	37	3	16	1	46	3
Aldridge	14	4	44	2	7	2	14	0
Orchard	8	1	25	2	5	1	21	0
Martin	9	3	12	0	16	6	28	1
CENTRAL DISTRICTS									
Mason	22	6	47	2	26.2	11	39	2
Hamilton	22	7	36	4	9.4	1	27	1
Hefford	16	7	22	3	25	8	40	1
Schwass	11	3	25	0	19.3	7	36	0
Sulzberger	5	2	14	1	30	6	58	1
Ryder					1	0	5	1

Fall of Wickets	CD	ND	CD	ND
	1st	1st	2nd	2nd
1st	37	14	3	29
2nd	38	24	13	45
3rd	62	74	37	74
4th	95	76	48	94
5th	143	89	113	102
6th	143	106	127	162
7th	152	119	133	-
8th	166	123	145	-
9th	170	150	151	-
10th	195	150	159	-

WELLINGTON v OTAGO

State Championship

at Basin Reserve, Wellington on 7, 8, 9, 10 February, 2003
Toss : Otago. Umpires : D.M. Quested & I.W. Shine
Close of play: 1st day: Wellington 301-8, Walker 7, Penn 15; 2nd day: Otago 225-6, McGlashan 0
3rd day: Wellington 197-4, Franklin 73, Donaldson 28
Otago won by 5 wickets. *Points: Otago 6, Wellington 2*

Wellington batted through the first day with the highlight being a century by Jones. He reached three figures after 147 minutes and faced 128 balls. The innings finished early next morning and Otago responded with another big opening stand. However, once the first wicket fell batsmen came and went regularly with only Gaffaney, of the remaining batsmen, getting to 20.

Wellington batted steadily in their second innings with Jones, Franklin (highest score) and Donaldson registering fifties. Bell's declaration left Otago with 295 to win. The visitors changed their opening batting combination and came up with another century first wicket partnership. Gaffaney went on to reach his hundred in 218 minutes from 168 balls before being third out at 207.

Despite more good bowling from Walker, who finished with eight wickets in the match, Otago paced their chase well with Lawson unbeaten on 66 at the end.

WELLINGTON

FIRST INNINGS	Runs	Mins	Balls	6s	4s	SECOND INNINGS	Runs	Mins	Balls	6s	4s
M.D.Bell* c McGlashan b O'Connor	25	88	63	-	3	b O'Connor	9	29	31	-	1
R.A.Jones c Wasim b McMillan	126	199	166	-	21	b Morland	64	207	149	-	8
N.R.Parlane lbw b O'Connor	6	84	65	-	1	lbw b O'Connor	0	2	3	-	-
L.J.Woodcock c Sheed b McSkimming	59	166	126	-	10	c Lawson b O'Connor	10	20	19	-	2
J.E.C.Franklin c McGlashan b McMillan	4	10	4	-	1	b O'Connor	87	281	220	-	8
G.T.Donaldson c Sheed b McSkimming	11	39	37	1	1	not out	52	140	113	1	3
C.J.Nevin† c Wasim b O'Connor	26	94	74	-	4	not out	15	13	12	-	-
M.D.J.Walker lbw b McMillan	13	69	61	-	2						
M.R.Gillespie lbw b O'Connor	0	8	6	-	-						
A.J.Penn run out	20	60	43	-	4						
J.S.Patel not out	1	4	2	-	-						
Extras (b 7, lb 11, w 1, nb 4)	23					(lb 9, w 6, nb 1)	16				
TOTAL (107.1 overs)	**314**	415				(91 overs) (5 wkts dec)	**253**	348			

OTAGO

	Runs	Mins	Balls	6s	4s		Runs	Mins	Balls	6s	4s
C.D.Cumming* c Nevin b Walker	60	241	196	-	10	lbw b Walker	56	181	137	-	7
Mohammad Wasim c Parlane b Patel ...	77	206	128	-	11	(3) b Walker	0	6	5	-	-
C.B.Gaffaney b Penn	55	167	144	-	6	(2) b Walker	108	245	186	1	16
R.A.Lawson c Donaldson b Walker	2	19	18	-	-	not out	66	151	127	-	9
M.N.McKenzie lbw b Walker	7	63	49	-	-	c Nevin b Woodcock	21	52	40	-	3
J.W.Sheed lbw b Franklin	3	27	15	-	-	lbw b Walker	10	24	18	-	1
P.D.McGlashan† b Penn	9	60	46	-	1	not out	3	16	18	-	-
W.C.McSkimming b Franklin	6	34	20	-	1						
N.D.Morland c Nevin b Gillespie	15	48	29	-	3						
S.B.O'Connor b Walker	15	54	32	-	3						
J.M.McMillan not out	0	11	8	-	-						
Extras (b 2, lb 10, nb 12)	24	469				(b 13, lb 11, nb 7)	31				
TOTAL (112.1 overs)	**273**					(87.2 overs) (5 wkts)	**295**	340			

Bowling	O	M	R	W	O	M	R	W
OTAGO								
O'Connor	27	6	82	4	22	5	53	4
McMillan	25.1	4	98	3	5.2	2	13	0
McSkimming	20	5	61	2	19	6	45	0
Cumming	15	10	15	0	11	0	37	0
Morland	18	4	37	0	31.4	6	87	1
Wasim	2	1	3	0				
Sheed					2	0	9	0
WELLINGTON								
Penn	22	8	50	2	11	2	29	0
Franklin	18	2	58	2	9	3	20	0
Gillespie	12	6	29	1	3	1	21	0
Walker	26.1	6	68	4	29	5	80	4
Woodcock	19	7	20	0	24.2	1	74	1
Patel	15	5	36	1	11	2	47	0

Fall of Wickets				
	W	O	W	O
	1st	1st	2nd	2nd
1st	88	141	18	147
2nd	159	166	18	151
3rd	177	171	30	207
4th	186	203	119	260
5th	213	217	228	281
6th	277	225	-	-
7th	277	243	-	-
8th	277	243	-	-
9th	312	269	-	-
10th	314	273	-	-

NORTHERN DISTRICTS v OTAGO   State Championship

at Westpac Park, Hamilton on 13, 14, 15, 16 February, 2003
Toss : Northern Districts. Umpires : R.D. Anderson & P.D. Jones
Close of play: 1st day: ND 57-2, Horsley 26, Parlane 6; 2nd day: ND 234-9, R.G. Hart 18, West 2
3rd day: Otago 214-5, Cumming 102, McGlashan 23
Northern Districts won by 6 wickets. *Points: Northern Districts 6, Otago 0*

Otago started poorly and were indebted to Wasim, who batted over three hours for 78, for their final total. Butler and West took four wickets each. Horsley scored 59 and Orchard registered a painstaking maiden fifty but when Northern's ninth wicket fell they still trailed by three runs. Robbie Hart and West had gained the lead by the close and went on to add 97 for the last wicket, a Northern record against Otago.

Otago responded by making the same score as in their first innings. Cumming, who made almost half the runs, reached his hundred from 193 balls in 283 minutes. Northern were left with the relatively simple task of scoring 136 and, despite losing three wickets at 86, reached their target with little further trouble.

OTAGO

FIRST INNINGS	Runs	Mins	Balls	6s	4s	SECOND INNINGS	Runs	Mins	Balls	6s	4s
C.D.Cumming* c Hart R.G. b Butler....	10	20	17	-	2	c Hart R.G. b Yovich	102	318	217	-	19
Mohammad Wasim c Marshall J.A.H.						run out	14	18	11	-	2
b Butler	78	198	124	-	11						
C.B.Gaffaney b Butler	0	6	3	-	-	c Hart R.G. b Yovich	39	133	106	-	6
M.N.McKenzie c Hart R.G. b West	9	61	52	-	-	c Marshall J.A.H. b West	13	81	66	-	-
J.W.Sheed c Orchard b West	34	174	122	-	6	c Kelly b West	0	1	1	-	-
A.J.Hore c Hart R.G. b Orchard	8	28	24	-	-	c Orchard b Butler	7	22	18	-	1
P.D.McGlashan† c Marshall J.A.H.						b Yovich	33	96	80	-	4
b Orchard	17	70	48	-	1						
W.C.McSkimming c Butler b West	0	1	2	-	-	c Marshall J.A.H. b Yovich	2	18	13	-	-
N.D.Morland c Hart R.G. b Butler	32	28	26	1	5	c Marshall J.A.H. b Yovich	0	1	2	-	-
S.B.O'Connor not out	12	37	23	-	2	not out	0	22	12	-	-
K.P.Walmsley c Butler b West	7	33	27	-	-	b Butler	0	5	4	-	-
Extras (lb 8, w 8, nb 6)	22					(lb 6, w 1, nb 12)	19				
TOTAL (77 overs)	**229**	332				(86.2 overs)	**229**	362			

NORTHERN DISTRICTS

J.A.H.Marshall c Morland b O'Connor	0	2	2	-	-	lbw b McSkimming	24	136	95	-	4
N.K.W.Horsley c McKenzie b O'Connor	59	190	140	-	8	c Wasim b O'Connor	29	47	36	-	7
H.J.H.Marshall c Morland b O'Connor	18	39	31	-	3	st McGlashan b Morland	31	100	76	-	3
M.E.Parlane c McGlashan b McSkimming	11	80	67	-	1	not out	27	57	46	2	3
M.G.Orchard c Morland b Cumming	50	232	179	-	6	c McSkimming b Morland	0	6	5	-	-
M.N.Hart lbw b Walmsley	27	112	96	-	2	not out	23	41	33	-	4
D.P.Kelly b Walmsley	7	28	24	-	1						
J.A.F.Yovich c & b McSkimming	25	93	67	-	3						
R.G.Hart*† not out	72	230	173	1	6						
I.G.Butler lbw b O'Connor	2	14	9	-	-						
G.L.West lbw b McSkimming	31	144	111	1	3						
Extras (lb 18, nb 3)	21					(lb 2)	2				
TOTAL (149.2 overs)	**323**	586				(48.3 overs) (4 wkts)	**136**	197			

Bowling	O	M	R	W	O	M	R	W
NORTHERN DISTRICTS								
Butler	23	3	82	4	27.2	8	75	2
Yovich	23	9	50	0	24	13	49	5
West	19	3	58	4	18	5	65	2
Orchard	12	5	31	2	6	1	11	0
Hart M.N.					10	1	22	0
Marshall J.A.H.					1	0	1	0
OTAGO								
O'Connor	38	12	78	4	14	7	22	1
Walmsley	41	11	98	2	12	3	62	0
McSkimming	34.2	12	71	3	11	4	20	1
Cumming	21	10	28	1	1	0	4	0
Morland	15	6	30	0	9	4	17	2
Hore					1.3	0	9	0

Fall of Wickets	O	ND	O	ND
	1st	1st	2nd	2nd
1st	16	0	19	34
2nd	16	42	114	86
3rd	46	80	157	86
4th	138	104	157	86
5th	152	171	172	-
6th	168	180	219	-
7th	168	183	223	-
8th	210	219	228	-
9th	214	226	229	-
10th	229	323	229	-

AUCKLAND v CENTRAL DISTRICTS   State Championship

at Colin Maiden Park, Auckland on 13, 14, 15, 16 February, 2003
Toss : Auckland. Umpires : D.B. Cowie & A.L. Hill
Close of play: 1st day: Auckland 17-0, Richardson 6, McIntosh 9; 2nd day: Auckland 218-3, Nielsen 34, Nicol 1
    3rd day: CD 78-0, Spearman 55, How 20
First innings win to Auckland. *Points: Auckland 2, Central Districts 0*

A solid, if unspectacular, batting effort from Central saw them through to 245 on the first day. Young equalled the Auckland record for catches and dismissals in an innings. Auckland batted through 89 overs on the seond day adding just 201 runs and continued through most of the third day before finally declaring. Barnes recorded his highest score, reaching his century after 256 minutes from 189 balls.

Auckland's plan to bat once and bowl Central out twice never materialised. From 78-0 overnight, the visitors reached 281-2 at tea on the final afternoon before declaring. The game was called off at this point. Todd registered his maiden fifty and Sulzberger reached his hundred in 156 minutes from 118 balls.

McKay made his first-class debut in this game.

CENTRAL DISTRICTS

FIRST INNINGS	Runs	Mins	Balls	6s	4s	SECOND INNINGS	Runs	Mins	Balls	6s	4s
C.M.Spearman* c Young b Canning	6	24	22	-	1	b Canning	76	112	90	-	15
J.M.How b McKay	54	150	103	-	8	c Young b Canning	35	149	109	-	5
G.R.Todd lbw b Nielsen	20	65	51	-	2	not out	50	225	172	-	8
G.P.Sulzberger c Young b Pryor	31	125	101	-	5	not out	111	188	139	-	22
G.R.Loveridge c Young b Pryor	10	33	24	-	1						
J.D.Ryder c Barnes b Walker	45	86	65	-	8						
B.B.J.Griggs† lbw b Barnes	26	89	68	-	4						
M.J.Mason c Young b Barnes	11	25	23	-	2						
A.M.Schwass c Young b Walker	0	12	4	-	-						
T.R.Anderson c & b Canning	2	41	29	-	-						
B.E.Hefford not out	16	37	26	-	2						
Extras (b 6, lb 15, w 3)	24					(b 4, lb 4, w 1)	9				
TOTAL (86 overs)	**245**	348				(85 overs) (2 wkts dec)	**281**	338			

AUCKLAND

	Runs	Mins	Balls	6s	4s
M.H.Richardson c Griggs b Mason	36	201	172	-	6
T.G.McIntosh c Griggs b Sulzberger	80	259	202	-	12
M.J.Horne c Ryder b Mason	51	119	91	-	3
B.J.Nielsen run out	42	178	139	1	6
R.J.Nicol c Sulzberger b Anderson	69	210	170	-	12
A.C.Barnes c Todd b Sulzberger	107	265	192	1	18
T.K.Canning b Todd	28	74	57	1	4
C.R.Pryor c How b Hefford	19	39	30	-	3
R.A.Young† c Griggs b Schwass	13	31	27	-	2
B.G.K.Walker* not out	9	24	21	-	1
A.J.McKay					
Extras (b 7, lb 13, nb 1)	21				
TOTAL (183.1 overs) (9 wkts dec)	**475**	704			

Bowling	O	M	R	W	O	M	R	W	Fall of Wickets			
AUCKLAND										CD	A	CD
										1st	1st	2nd
Pryor	23	8	47	2	17	3	69	0	1st	13	90	103
Canning	23	7	64	2	26	8	67	2	2nd	57	141	116
McKay	13	1	54	1	17	5	45	0	3rd	107	185	-
Nielsen	11	2	27	1	10	5	26	0	4th	126	255	-
Barnes	7	4	13	2	2	0	16	0	5th	148	322	-
Walker	9	2	19	2	11	2	38	0	6th	204	375	-
Nicol					2	0	12	0	7th	217	418	-
CENTRAL DISTRICTS									8th	218	447	-
Mason	47	18	94	2					9th	218	475	-
Hefford	39	12	115	1					10th	245	-	-
Schwass	38	11	82	1								
Todd	8	2	25	1								
Sulzberger	36.11	1	71	2								
Anderson	15	1	68	1								

WELLINGTON v CANTERBURY   State Championship

at Basin Reserve, Wellington on 13, 14, 15, 16 February, 2003
Toss : Canterbury. Umpires : I.W. Shine & E.A. Watkin
Close of play: 1st day: Wellington 296-7, Franklin 68, Penn 4; 2nd day: Wellington 0-0, Jones 0, Woodcock 0
3rd day: Canterbury 43-2, Stead 20, Fulton 6
Wellington won by 143 runs. *Points: Wellington 6, Canterbury 0*

Miller and Broom made their first-class debuts as Canterbury won the toss and sent Wellington in. By the end of the day the home team had reached 296-7 with Bell, Franklin and Walker hitting fifties. Wisneski, who finished with 5-81, and Ellis soon finished off the innings the next day.

Canterbury collapsed from 25-0 to 53-5 before newcomer Broom and Redmond added 52. It took the last pair of Ellis and Martin to take Canterbury past the follow on mark. Wellington, leading by 145, batted solidly in their second innings with Parlane top scoring with 66.

Canterbury were left with over a day to score 391 and lost two wickets before the close. Stead reached fifty the next morning but wickets fell at regular intervals and after a bright last wicket stand of 44 in 30 minutes O'Brien wrapped up the innings when he had Wisneski caught behind.

WELLINGTON

FIRST INNINGS	Runs	Mins	Balls	6s	4s	SECOND INNINGS	Runs	Mins	Balls	6s	4s
M.D.Bell* b Wisneski	53	161	128	-	10	(4) c Hopkins b Redmond	0	11	3	-	-
R.A.Jones lbw b Ellis	22	76	58	-	3	(1) st Hopkins b Redmond	24	74	60	-	5
N.R.Parlane lbw b Wisneski	23	65	54	-	4	b Wiseman	66	169	133	1	9
L.J.Woodcock c Wisneski b Ellis	6	23	15	-	1	(2) c sub (B.P.Donkers)					
						b Wisneski	7	42	34	-	1
J.E.C.Franklin lbw b Wisneski	68	254	176	-	14	c Papps b Ellis	36	119	101	-	6
G.T.Donaldson c Hopkins b Martin	19	61	46	-	4	c sub (B.P.Donkers) b Ellis	38	99	64	-	5
C.J.Nevin† c Hopkins b Wisneski	13	40	43	-	1	c Wisneski b Redmond	29	49	45	-	4
M.D.J.Walker lbw b Ellis	62	107	91	-	12	c Broom b Ellis	27	52	52	-	2
A.J.Penn b Wisneski	7	29	20	-	-	not out	6	12	5	-	-
J.S.Patel not out	5	23	18	-	1	not out	1	3	2	-	-
I.E.O'Brien c Stead b Ellis	7	13	9	-	1						
Extras (b 2, lb 10, nb 17)	29					(b 2, lb 5, w 3, nb 1)	11				
TOTAL (106.2 overs)	**314**	436				**(83 overs) (8 wkts dec)**	**245**	319			

CANTERBURY

	Runs	Mins	Balls	6s	4s		Runs	Mins	Balls	6s	4s
M.H.W.Papps c Nevin b Walker	21	57	38	-	4	c Jones b Franklin	9	32	23	-	-
R.M.Miller lbw b Penn	9	28	19	-	1	lbw b Franklin	3	40	25	-	-
G.R.Stead* b O'Brien	8	41	29	-	2	lbw b O'Brien	54	183	171	-	8
P.G.Fulton b O'Brien	0	27	21	-	-	b Patel	48	182	139	1	6
N.T.Broom c Walker b Penn	40	107	73	-	7	lbw b Penn	41	90	85	-	4
G.J.Hopkins† c Nevin b O'Brien	0	13	10	-	-	c Donaldson b Patel	4	17	10	-	-
A.J.Redmond b Walker	33	146	121	-	5	c Jones b Franklin	34	94	77	-	6
P.J.Wiseman c Donaldson b Woodcock	16	62	49	-	2	b Penn	0	10	8	-	-
A.M.Ellis not out	22	45	35	-	3	run out	1	14	8	-	-
W.A.Wisneski c sub (M.R.Gillespie)						c Nevin b O'Brien	29	40	33	1	5
b O'Brien	2	10	8	-	-						
C.S.Martin b Penn	3	29	17	-	-	not out	10	30	15	-	2
Extras (b 1, lb 5, w 1, nb 8)	15					(b 9, lb 2, w 1, nb 2)	14				
TOTAL (68.5 overs)	**169**	287				**(98.4 overs)**	**247**	380			

Bowling	O	M	R	W	O	M	R	W
CANTERBURY								
Wisneski	30	6	81	5	17	5	38	1
Martin	24	5	69	1				
Ellis	32.2	11	81	4	16	5	51	3
Fulton	2	0	16	0	2	0	14	0
Wiseman	9	2	19	0	21	10	56	1
Broom	6	2	19	0				
Redmond	3	1	18	0	27	7	79	3
WELLINGTON								
Penn	15.5	2	44	3	17	8	33	2
Franklin	13	1	47	0	19	7	39	3
Walker	18	8	35	2	16	6	42	0
O'Brien	16	8	27	4	17.4	4	56	2
Woodcock	6	5	10	1	10	5	21	0
Patel					19	6	45	2

Fall of Wickets	W	C	W	C
	1st	1st	2nd	
1st	56	25	16	16
2nd	105	39	39	21
3rd	115	44	43	115
4th	116	53	141	121
5th	155	53	141	134
6th	181	105	189	192
7th	277	138	235	192
8th	299	142	241	198
9th	300	144	-	203
10th	314	169	-	247

CENTRAL DISTRICTS v WELLINGTON   State Championship

at Queen Elizabeth Park, Masterton on 25, 26, 27 February, 2003
Toss : Central Districts. Umpires : B.G. Frost & M.P. George
Close of play: 1st day: Wellington 139-4, Jones 81, Donaldson 23; 2nd day: CD 87-5, Ryder 15, Loveridge 5
Wellington won by 9 wickets. *Points: Wellington 6, Central Districts 0*

Central started disastrously being 38-4 then 82-6 before finally being bowled out for just 128. Penn captured the first five wickets and six of the first seven to fall. At one stage his analysis read 6-2-5-3 and later 12-5-15-5. His final figures of 6-33 were the best in a first-class game at Masterton.

Wellington had taken first innings points before the close and went on to gain a lead of 177 the next day. Jones reached his century from 163 balls in 230 minutes. By the end of the second day the match was all but over as Central succumbed again to be 87-5 at stumps.

On the third morning Ryder reached his maiden fifty but Wellington were left with just 36 to win, losing Bell on the way.

CENTRAL DISTRICTS

FIRST INNINGS	Runs	Mins	Balls	6s	4s	SECOND INNINGS	Runs	Mins	Balls	6s	4s
C.M.Spearman* b Penn	11	50	37	-	-	c Nevin b Franklin	16	34	28	-	2
J.M.How c Nevin b Penn	5	39	30	-	-	c Nevin b Walker	29	121	85	-	4
G.R.Todd lbw b Penn	0	1	1	-	-	c Jones b Walker	5	25	22	-	-
G.P.Sulzberger lbw b Penn	4	45	22	-	-	lbw b Walker	6	48	34	-	-
R.L.Taylor c Franklin b Penn	21	64	41	-	3	c Walker b O'Brien	1	21	17	-	-
J.D.Ryder c O'Brien b Penn	37	87	59	1	5	c Penn b Patel	66	155	120	-	8
G.R.Loveridge c Parlane b Franklin	10	34	29	-	2	lbw b Franklin	6	37	32	-	1
B.B.J.Griggs† c Nevin b Walker	7	37	26	-	-	c Donaldson b Woodcock	38	136	102	1	3
M.J.Mason c Penn b O'Brien	5	34	22	-	1	b O'Brien	16	47	43	-	3
A.M.Schwass lbw b Walker	3	23	16	-	-	c Nevin b O'Brien	10	22	25	-	1
L.J.Hamilton not out	0	4	5	-	-	not out	0	7	2	-	-
Extras (b 4, lb 8, w 4, nb 9)	25					(b 2, lb 10, nb 7)	19				
TOTAL (46.3 overs)	**128**	213				(83.5 overs)	**212**	332			

WELLINGTON

	Runs	Mins	Balls	6s	4s		Runs	Mins	Balls	6s	4s
M.D.Bell* lbw b Mason	11	38	29	-	1	b Mason	18	15	15	-	3
R.A.Jones c Griggs b Sulzberger	128	293	215	-	17	not out	11	25	14	-	2
N.R.Parlane lbw b Mason	3	9	8	-	-	not out	4	9	8	-	1
L.J.Woodcock c How b Schwass	6	32	26	-	-						
J.E.C.Franklin c Griggs b Sulzberger	6	21	18	-	-						
G.T.Donaldson b Sulzberger	57	196	152	1	5						
C.J.Nevin† lbw b Schwass	23	38	38	-	4						
M.D.J.Walker c Griggs b Mason	27	77	62	-	5						
A.J.Penn c Loveridge b Schwass	24	45	37	-	4						
J.S.Patel not out	2	16	6	-	-						
I.E.O'Brien c Loveridge b Sulzberger	1	13	15	-	-						
Extras (b 2, lb 5, w 2, nb 8)	17					(lb 3)	3				
TOTAL (99.5 overs)	**305**	394				(6.1 overs) (1 wkt)	**36**	25			

Bowling	O	M	R	W	O	M	R	W		Fall of Wickets			
WELLINGTON											CD	W	CD	W
											1st	1st	2nd	2nd
Penn	19	8	33	6	5	1	8	0		1st	17	24	24	29
Franklin	10	0	42	1	16	2	45	2		2nd	17	33	35	-
O'Brien	9.3	3	33	1	19.5	4	63	3		3rd	23	58	59	-
Walker	8	4	8	2	23	11	41	3		4th	38	84	64	-
Woodcock					8	3	18	1		5th	57	220	66	-
Patel					12	2	25	1		6th	82	231	89	-
CENTRAL DISTRICTS										7th	119	262	183	-
Hamilton	13.1	0	45	0						8th	119	302	202	-
Mason	31	10	77	3	3	0	13	1		9th	124	302	209	-
Schwass	24.5	6	77	3	3.1	0	20	0		10th	128	305	212	-
Todd	3	0	26	0										
Sulzberger	23.5	8	52	4										
Loveridge	4	0	21	0										

NORTHERN DISTRICTS v CANTERBURY State Championship

at Westpac Park, Hamilton on 25, 26, 27, 28 February, 2003
Toss : Canterbury. Umpires : D.B. Cowie & S.B. Lambson
Close of play: 1st day: ND 142-5, M.N. Hart 15, Yovich 2; 2nd day: no play
3rd day: no play
No result. *Points: Northern Districts 1, Canterbury 1*

Rain completely ruined this game with just 46.5 overs play on the first day and none at all on the remaining three. After play had been delayed until 2.14 pm, James Marshall and Horsley began with an opening stand of 83 in 122 minutes. The Marshall twins carried on until the score reached 120-1 but at that stage four wickets fell for just three runs.

Matthew Hart and Yovich took the score to 142 but at 5.48 bad light stopped play and, as it transpired, that was the end of the cricket.

Grant Bradburn, who had retired from first-class cricket at the end of the previous season, was responsible for the preparation of the pitch for this game.

NORTHERN DISTRICTS

FIRST INNINGS	Runs	Mins	Balls	6s	4s
J.A.H.Marshall c Broom b Wisneski ...	44	157	102	-	5
N.K.W.Horsley c & b Wiseman	46	122	95	-	7
H.J.H.Marshall c Broom b Wiseman ...	20	37	43	-	3
M.E.Parlane c Wisneski b Wiseman	0	6	4	-	-
M.G.Orchard lbw b Wisneski	3	8	8	-	-
M.N.Hart not out	15	29	25	-	1
J.A.F.Yovich not out	2	24	11	-	-
R.G.Hart*†					
G.W.Aldridge					
B.P.Martin					
I.G.Butler					
Extras (lb 5, nb 7)	12				
TOTAL (46.5 overs) (5 wkts)	**142**	194			

CANTERBURY

G.R.Stead *
M.H.W.Papps
R.M.Frew
P.G.Fulton
N.T.Broom
G.J.Hopkins †
A.J.Redmond
P.J.Wiseman
A.M.Ellis
W.A.Wisneski
B.P.Donkers

Bowling	O	M	R	W
CANTERBURY				
Wisneski	17.5	3	69	2
Ellis	11	3	31	0
Donkers	7	2	13	0
Wiseman	11	3	24	3

Fall of Wickets	
	ND
	1st
1st	83
2nd	120
3rd	120
4th	123
5th	123
6th	-
7th	-
8th	-
9th	-
10th	-

OTAGO v AUCKLAND — State Championship

at Queenstown Events Centre on 25, 26, 27, 28 February, 2003
Toss : Otago. Umpires : G.A. Baxter & D.M. Quested
Close of play: 1st day: Auckland 218-6, Pryor 6, Walker 6; 2nd day: Otago 212-2, Cumming 126, Lawson 41
3rd day: Auckland 173-5, Barnes18, Pryor 8
Auckland won by 86 runs. Points: Auckland 6, Otago 2

Auckland gave another painstaking batting display after being sent in, scoring 218-6 off 100 overs on the first day. Horne was by far the most aggressive of the Auckland batsmen with his 74 coming from only 101 balls. After bowling Auckland out for 272, Otago made a strong reply and were 212-2 at the close of the second day. Cumming reached his century from 205 balls in 243 minutes. It was the first century in a first-class game at the ground.

The next day Otago declared as soon as they had passed Auckland's total and by stumps had restricted the visitors to 173-5 from 75 overs. Auckland were more positive on the last day and set Otago 247 from a minimum of 75 overs.

Otago did not start well, losing Wasim for a duck, and slumped to 70-6. It was left to number ten O'Connor to top score with 30 off 30 balls but it was in vain as Auckland ran out comfortable winners.

AUCKLAND

FIRST INNINGS	Runs	Mins	Balls	6s	4s
M.H.Richardson b Walmsley	41	156	109	-	5
T.G.McIntosh b Walmsley	44	174	145	-	6
M.J.Horne c McGlashan b McSkimming	74	140	101	-	10
B.J.Nielsen c McGlashan b McSkimming	5	36	27	-	1
T.K.Canning b O'Connor	24	131	115	-	2
A.C.Barnes b Walmsley	4	32	26	-	-
C.R.Pryor c Sheed b Walmsley	6	70	51	-	1
B.G.K.Walker* lbw b Walmsley	22	86	66	-	4
R.J.Nicol not out	28	77	58	-	3
R.A.Young† b Walmsley	0	1	1	-	-
A.M.McKay c McGlashan b McSkimming	8	46	28	-	1
Extras (b 1, lb 6, w 1, nb 8)	16				
TOTAL (119.5 overs)	**272**	479			

SECOND INNINGS	Runs	Mins	Balls	6s	4s
c McSkimming b Walmsley	35	144	128	-	4
b Walmsley	5	22	21	-	1
c McKenzie b McSkimming	14	53	41	-	2
(8) c McGlashan b O'Connor	11	37	18	-	2
c Gaffaney b McSkimming	36	68	51	-	5
c Sheed b Walmsley	41	126	107	-	7
c Walmsley b Morland	14	34	33	-	2
(10) c Morland b McSkimming	10	45	32	-	-
(4) b McSkimming	50	204	139	1	4
(9) not out	23	49	36	-	4
(b 4, lb 2, w 1, nb 1)	8				
(99.1 overs) (9 wkts dec)	**247**	400			

OTAGO

	Runs	Mins	Balls	6s	4s
C.D.Cumming* c McKay b Pryor	128	295	253	-	20
Mohammad Wasim lbw b Canning	33	97	78	-	5
C.B.Gaffaney c Horne b Canning	8	47	31	-	1
R.A.Lawson lbw b Canning	49	170	142	-	7
M.N.McKenzie c Barnes b Pryor	4	9	12	-	-
J.W.Sheed c Young b Canning	9	48	28	-	1
P.D.McGlashan† not out	24	72	61	-	2
W.C.McSkimming not out	6	34	30	-	1
N.D.Morland					
S.B.O'Connor					
K.P.Walmsley					
Extras (lb 7, w 1, nb 4)	12				
TOTAL (105.1 overs) (6 wkts dec)	**273**	389			

	Runs	Mins	Balls	6s	4s
b Pryor	14	62	49	-	2
c Nicol b Canning	0	1	1	-	-
c Walker b Pryor	20	43	45	-	3
c Walker b Canning	14	57	41	-	-
c Barnes b Walker	10	28	28	-	1
lbw b Canning	7	20	18	-	-
c McIntosh b McKay	27	90	75	-	4
lbw b Walker	13	70	56	-	2
not out	13	65	50	-	1
b Canning	30	36	30	-	4
b Pryor	4	17	15	-	-
(b 2, lb 2, nb 4)	8				
(67.2 overs)	**160**	249			

Bowling OTAGO	O	M	R	W	O	M	R	W
O'Connor	33	14	74	1	28	10	56	1
Walmsley	35	11	74	6	23	7	43	3
McSkimming	27.5	13	53	3	24.1	2	87	4
Cumming	8	2	24	0	3	1	3	0
Morland	15	7	35	0	21	7	52	1
Wasim	1	0	5	0				
AUCKLAND								
Canning	34	12	66	4	21	9	38	4
Pryor	22	3	72	2	13.2	1	40	3
McKay	9	0	41	0	8	4	21	1
Nielsen	20	9	31	0	5	3	7	0
Barnes	6	0	21	0	3	2	5	0
Walker	14.1	4	35	0	17	5	45	2

Fall of Wickets	A	O	A	O
	1st	1st	2nd	2nd
1st	78	79	6	1
2nd	99	101	36	28
3rd	119	214	75	42
4th	193	218	128	61
5th	201	228	164	65
6th	203	257	193	70
7th	224	-	213	113
8th	243	-	213	115
9th	243	-	247	151
10th	272	-	-	160

CANTERBURY v AUCKLAND   State Championship

at Hagley Park, Christchurch on 3, 4, 5, 6 March, 2003
Toss : Auckland. Umpires : R.D. Anderson & S.B. Lambson
Close of play: 1st day: Canterbury 319-4, Fulton 188, Hopkins 33; 2nd day: Auckland 127-2, McIntosh 50, Nicol 31
*   3rd day: Canterbury 126-6, Broom 32, Redmond 7*
***Auckland won by 4 wickets.** Points: Auckland 6, Canterbury 2*

Canterbury's poor start of 6-2 hardly gave an indication of what was to come. Fulton, previous highest score 84, arrived at this stage and helped Frew add 102 for the third wicket. Broom then assisted Fulton in adding 120 for the fourth wicket and Hopkins featured in a third successive century stand of 109 for the fifth.

Fulton reached his maiden century from 172 balls in 209 minutes, his double century in 388 minutes from 326 balls and the innings was declared as soon as he hit a Walker no ball for four to go to 301. It was the highest innings in Canterbury's long first-class history. Canterbury's total was their highest against Auckland.

Auckland's response was to declare 230 runs behind on the third day and by early on the fourth they were chasing 360 to win. Horne batted brilliantly, reaching his century from just 95 balls in 132 minutes with his final score of 187 coming at better than a run a ball. Auckland won by four wickets with each side losing just 13 wickets in the game.

CANTERBURY

FIRST INNINGS	Runs	Mins	Balls	6s	4s	SECOND INNINGS	Runs	Mins	Balls	6s	4s
R.M.Frew c Barnes b Davis	49	169	121	-	7	c Young b Pryor	15	50	32	-	1
M.H.W.Papps c Barnes b Canning	1	9	12	-	-	c Young b Canning	1	9	7	-	-
G.R.Stead* c Young b Canning	1	8	9	-	-	c Young b Davis	50	79	61	-	7
P.G.Fulton not out	301	570	445	3	45	c sub (P.W.Carey) b Nicol	17	25	18	-	3
N.T.Broom c Canning b Walker	41	95	74	1	3	lbw b Richardson	32	62	44	-	5
G.J.Hopkins† lbw b Canning	43	151	117	-	4	c Richardson b Davis	3	10	11	-	-
A.J.Redmond c sub (A.J.McKay) b Canning	26	121	100	-	4	(8) not out	8	38	28	-	1
P.J.Wiseman not out	35	50	50	-	3	(7) c Young b Nicol	1	10	4	-	-
B.P.Donkers						not out	2	10	11	-	-
W.A.Wisneski											
C.S.Martin											
Extras (b 4, lb 10, w 1, nb 2)	17						0				
TOTAL (154.2 overs) (6 wkts dec)	**514**	589				(36 overs) (7 wkts dec)	**129**	150			

AUCKLAND

	Runs	Mins	Balls	6s	4s		Runs	Mins	Balls	6s	4s
M.H.Richardson c Wisneski b Martin	6	17	13	-	1	b Martin	6	61	34	-	-
T.G.McIntosh c Wisneski	64	231	169	-	4	c Hopkins b Wiseman	45	128	105	-	7
M.J.Horne b Wisneski	35	55	46	-	5	c Broom b Redmond	187	253	182	2	30
R.J.Nicol c Hopkins b Martin	57	174	120	1	7	lbw b Martin	21	67	54	-	2
T.K.Canning not out	21	228	161	-	1	b Redmond	49	106	76	1	6
A.C.Barnes c Fulton b Wisneski	79	158	134	-	16	b Martin	20	32	24	1	3
C.R.Pryor lbw b Wisneski	0	6	1	-	-	(8) not out	14	15	11	1	1
B.J.Nielsen lbw b Wisneski	0	4	5	-	-	(7) not out	4	36	21	-	-
R.A.Young† not out	12	40	29	-	2						
B.G.K.Walker*											
H.T.Davis											
Extras (b 2, lb 2, nb 6)	10					(lb 8, w 7)	15				
TOTAL (112 overs) (7 wkts dec)	**284**	460				(84.3 overs) (6 wkts)	**361**	352			

Bowling

AUCKLAND	O	M	R	W	O	M	R	W
Canning	43	17	125	4	8	2	25	1
Pryor	20	2	92	0	4	1	21	1
Davis	31	8	75	1	12	0	52	2
Nielsen	13	4	47	0				
Walker	18.2	2	85	1				
Barnes	9	3	24	0				
Nicol	9	1	18	0	8	0	26	2
Horne	11	2	34	0	1	0	2	0
Richardson					2	0	3	1
McIntosh					1	1	0	0
CANTERBURY								
Wisneski	23	7	69	5	16.3	3	59	0
Martin	24	7	63	2	18	2	54	3
Wiseman	22	7	52	0	22	4	107	1
Donkers	20	4	49	0	9	2	39	0
Redmond	23	11	47	0	16	1	77	2
Fulton					1	0	5	0
Broom					2	0	12	0

Fall of Wickets

	C 1st	A 1st	C 2nd	A 2nd
1st	4	13	5	29
2nd	6	55	56	99
3rd	118	164	80	178
4th	238	171	90	309
5th	347	268	94	322
6th	424	268	110	343
7th	-	268	126	-
8th	-	-	-	-
9th	-	-	-	-
10th	-	-	-	-

OTAGO v CENTRAL DISTRICTS   State Championship

at Queen's Park, Invercargill on 3, 4, 5, 6 March, 2003
Toss : Otago. Umpires : G.A. Baxter & M.P. George
Close of play: 1st day: Otago 32-1, Wasim 10, Gaffaney 1; 2nd day: Otago 88-5, Gaffaney 31, McSkimming 5
3rd day: Otago 180-9, McSkimming 63, McMillan 0
First innings win to Central Districts. *Points: Central Districts 2, Otago 0*

After Otago had sent Central in to bat, Spearman provided the day's major highlight hitting 50 off 56 balls before being dismissed at 88-2. Ingram's share of the 64 second wicket partnership was 12. The other Central batsmen were more circumspect and the final total of 208 took 82.4 overs.

Otago began batting late on the first day and with substantial rain interruptions the innings occupied some part of each of the four days. McSkimming hit a maiden fifty after coming to the wicket at 73-5 but could not find any support and was left unbeaten with Otago 24 runs short of Central's score.

With the match petering out, Ingram and How took the opportunity to register fifties and record a century opening stand.

CENTRAL DISTRICTS

FIRST INNINGS	Runs	Mins	Balls	6s	4s	SECOND INNINGS	Runs	Mins	Balls	6s	4s
P.J.Ingram b Wilson	21	120	87	-	2	not out	54	179	132	3	4
J.M.How lbw b McSkimming	15	42	31	-	1	lbw b McSkimming	55	135	114	-	7
C.M.Spearman* b Wilson	50	67	56	-	6						
G.R.Todd run out	19	73	68	-	1	(3) not out	8	43	44	-	-
G.P.Sulzberger c McKenzie b Morland	42	157	124	-	5						
J.D.Ryder c Wilson b McSkimming	37	98	91	-	4						
R.L.Taylor run out	12	40	31	-	3						
B.B.J.Griggs† lbw b O'Connor	1	21	18	-	-						
M.J.Mason lbw b O'Connor	0	1	2	-	-						
A.M.Schwass run out	0	8	2	-	-						
B.E.Hefford b O'Connor	0	1	1	-	-						
Extras (b 2, lb 4, nb 5)	11					(lb 5, w 3, nb 2)	10				
TOTAL (82.4 overs)	**208**	319				(48 overs) (1 wkt)	**127**	179			

OTAGO

	Runs	Mins	Balls	6s	4s
C.D.Cumming* lbw b Schwass	14	36	33	-	2
Mohammad Wasim c How b Mason	12	89	67	-	1
C.B.Gaffaney c Griggs b Hefford	37	185	139	1	3
M.N.McKenzie lbw b Schwass	4	59	40	-	-
J.W.Sheed lbw b Schwass	4	9	8	-	1
P.D.McGlashan† lbw b Schwass	1	14	10	-	-
W.C.McSkimming not out	66	174	143	1	3
J.W.Wilson c Griggs b Mason	15	29	23	-	2
N.D.Morland c Taylor b Schwass	4	44	27	-	-
S.B.O'Connor b Mason	4	34	28	-	1
J.M.McMillan c Spearman b Mason	0	12	11	-	-
Extras (b 2, lb 17, nb 4)	23				
TOTAL (88.3 overs)	**184**	349			

Bowling	O	M	R	W	O	M	R	W
OTAGO								
O'Connor	16.4	9	23	3				
McMillan	16	4	36	0	10	4	26	0
McSkimming	20	5	62	2	11	6	11	1
Wilson	11	1	49	2	11	3	30	0
Cumming	8	3	9	0	2	0	6	0
Morland	11	4	23	1	11	2	47	0
Wasim					3	2	2	0
CENTRAL DISTRICTS								
Mason	32.3	12	63	4				
Hefford	27	10	38	1				
Schwass	23	12	38	5				
Todd	3	1	8	0				
Sulzberger	3	0	18	0				

Fall of Wickets	CD	O	CD
	1st	1st	2nd
1st	24	21	106
2nd	88	36	-
3rd	93	55	-
4th	126	69	-
5th	194	73	-
6th	194	100	-
7th	207	126	-
8th	207	158	-
9th	208	180	-
10th	208	184	-

WELLINGTON v NORTHERN DISTRICTS State Championship

at Basin Reserve, Wellington on 3, 4, 5, 6 March, 2003
Toss : Wellington. Umpires : A.L. Hill & E.A. Watkin
Close of play: 1st day: Wellington 26-0, Bell 14, Jones 12; 2nd day: ND 19-0, J.A.H. Marshall 9, Horsley 6
3rd day: ND 238-6, M.N. Hart 40, R.G. Hart 6
Wellington won by 10 wickets. Points: Wellington 6, Northern Districts 0

Northern had a modest first day after being sent in. Horsley top scored with 56 while Orchard made 38 in another patient knock. The Wellington pace bowlers took all the wickets. The home team batted very positively on the second day with Bell, Parlane, Franklin and Nevin all passing fifty. Butler, Yovich and West shared nine wickets but were very expensive. Gillespie and Turner (who made 3) put on 52 for the last wicket, a record for Wellington against Northern.

Facing a deficit of 180, Northern batted in controlled fashion. James Marshall reached three figures after 318 minutes and 280 balls before he was fifth out at 203. When Walker dismissed Robbie Hart to end the innings, it was the third time in the season that he had finished with eight or more wickets in a match.

Wellington needed just 87 to win and Bell and Jones reached the target without being separated.

NORTHERN DISTRICTS

FIRST INNINGS	Runs	Mins	Balls	6s	4s	SECOND INNINGS	Runs	Mins	Balls	6s	4s
J.A.H.Marshall lbw b Franklin	2	14	13	-	-	c Woodcock b Franklin	112	343	309	-	19
N.K.W.Horsley c Parlane b Franklin	56	124	100	-	11	c Nevin b Franklin	27	59	43	-	5
H.J.H.Marshall c Nevin b Walker	25	63	37	-	3	c Nevin b Gillespie	9	35	17	-	2
M.E.Parlane lbw b Walker	12	69	48	-	2	c Bell b Patel	6	44	28	-	1
M.G.Orchard b Walker	38	162	134	-	4	c Nevin b Woodcock	18	94	82	-	1
M.N.Hart lbw b Turner	5	11	9	-	1	c Parlane b Franklin	40	176	117	-	3
J.A.F.Yovich c Nevin b Walker	22	84	64	-	2	c Nevin b Walker	5	26	23	-	-
R.G.Hart*† c Nevin b Turner	29	89	74	-	3	lbw b Walker	12	129	86	-	-
B.P.Martin c Parlane b Gillespie	9	23	15	1	-	b Walker	13	74	53	-	2
I.G.Butler c Walker b Franklin	12	27	18	-	3	lbw b Walker	0	2	3	-	-
G.L.West not out	2	3	5	-	-	not out	1	9	2	-	-
Extras (lb 4, w 2, nb 5)	11					(b 10, lb 5, w 5, nb 3)	23				
TOTAL (85.2 overs)	**223**	339				(127 overs)	**266**	500			

WELLINGTON

FIRST INNINGS	Runs	Mins	Balls	6s	4s	SECOND INNINGS	Runs	Mins	Balls	6s	4s
M.D.Bell* lbw b Yovich	52	88	72	-	8	not out	51	84	76	-	7
R.A.Jones c Hart R.G. b Yovich	20	47	30	-	4	not out	29	84	67	-	5
N.R.Parlane c Hart R.G. b Yovich	64	156	129	1	12						
L.J.Woodcock lbw b Orchard	17	85	67	-	1						
J.E.C.Franklin c Marshall J.A.H. b West	79	180	127	-	14						
G.T.Donaldson c Marshall J.A.H. b Yovich	0	2	2	-	-						
C.J.Nevin† b Butler	73	112	100	-	13						
M.D.J.Walker c Martin b Butler	27	28	22	-	6						
M.R.Gillespie b Yovich	49	62	41	-	9						
J.S.Patel c Hart R.G. b West	2	18	8	-	-						
A.D.Turner not out	3	38	29	-	-						
Extras (lb 2, w 5, nb 10)	17					(lb 4, nb 3)	7				
TOTAL (102.5 overs)	**403**	413				(23.2 overs) (0 wkts)	**87**	84			

NORTHERN DISTRICTS v WELLINGTON State Championship

at Owen Delany Park, Taupo on 9, 10, 11, 12 January, 2003
Toss : Northern Districts. Umpires : G.A. Baxter & G.C. Holdem
Close of play: 1st day: no play; 2nd day: Wellington 129-2, Parlane 49, Morgan 3
3rd day: ND 95-3, Parlane 29, H.J.H. Marshall 7
First innings win to Wellington. Points: Wellington 2, Northern Districts 0

No play was possible on the first day and in 59 overs on the second Wellington reached 129-2 with Jones and Parlane having put on 86 in 126 minutes for the second wicket. The next day Wellington showed more aggression and in 50 further overs got to 269. Martin took 5-48 which turned out to be the only five wicket haul by a spin bowler during the first-class season.

Northern were also in no hurry and took 44 overs to reach 95-3 by the close of the third day. With only a first innings decision likely, Northern battled away on the last morning but apart from Parlane, who made 80, none of the other batsmen stayed long enough to threaten the Wellington total.

Wellington batted for a second time until tea when the game was called off. Former Central Districts player West made his Northern debut in this match.

WELLINGTON

FIRST INNINGS	Runs	Mins	Balls	6s	4s	SECOND INNINGS	Runs	Mins	Balls	6s	4s
M.D.Bell* c & b Yovich	14	48	37	-	2	run out	30	90	77	-	2
R.A.Jones c Hart M.N. b Martin	56	175	141	-	3	not out	19	90	63	-	3
N.R.Parlane c Hart R.G. b Hart M.N.	63	219	195	1	9						
L.J.Morgan c Marshall J.A.H. b Yovich	30	129	100	-	3						
G.T.Donaldson b West	35	98	76	-	6						
C.J.Nevin† lbw b West	37	69	50	-	6						
M.D.J.Walker c Hart M.N. b Martin	0	11	10	-	-						
M.R.Jefferson lbw b Martin	10	33	24	-	2						
A.J.Penn c Marshall J.A.H. b Martin	0	6	4	-	-						
M.R.Gillespie not out	3	25	17	-	-						
I.E.O'Brien b Martin	4	2	5	-	-						
Extras (b 2, lb 5, w 2, nb 8)	17					(lb 1, w 2, nb 5)	8				
TOTAL (109 overs)	**269**	412				(22.3 overs) (1 wkt)	**57**	90			

NORTHERN DISTRICTS

FIRST INNINGS	Runs	Mins	Balls	6s	4s
J.A.H.Marshall lbw b Penn	8	10	11	-	2
N.K.W.Horsley c Nevin b O'Brien	23	69	43	-	2
M.G.Orchard lbw b O'Brien	22	109	78	-	3
M.E.Parlane c Parlane b O'Brien	80	225	158	-	12
H.J.H.Marshall lbw b Jefferson	17	117	95	-	2
M.N.Hart c Nevin b Jefferson	0	3	2	-	-
R.G.Hart*† run out	6	18	15	-	-
J.A.F.Yovich not out	33	82	67	1	3
B.P.Martin c Bell b O'Brien	8	22	16	-	1
G.W.Aldridge c Bell b Jefferson	2	18	13	-	-
G.L.West c Bell b Penn	1	7	5	-	-
Extras (b 1, lb 4, nb 5)	10				
TOTAL (83 overs)	**210**	344			

Bowling	O	M	R	W	O	M	R	W
NORTHERN DISTRICTS								
Yovich	28	7	85	2	8	0	21	0
West	25	9	57	2	6	1	21	0
Aldridge	7	1	18	0				
Martin	30	12	48	5	8.3	3	14	0
Orchard	11	4	30	0				
Hart M.N.	8	0	24	1				
WELLINGTON								
Penn	18	6	45	2				
Gillespie	9	1	29	0				
O'Brien	23	7	68	4				
Walker	14	4	25	0				
Jefferson	19	7	38	3				

Fall of Wickets	W	ND	W
	1st	1st	2nd
1st	29	12	57
2nd	115	45	-
3rd	166	70	-
4th	180	143	-
5th	249	143	-
6th	252	152	-
7th	256	174	-
8th	258	186	-
9th	265	207	-
10th	269	210	-

NORTHERN DISTRICTS v CENTRAL DISTRICTS

at Westpac Park, Hamilton on 11, 12, 13, 14 March, 2003
Toss : Northern Districts. Umpires : B.G. Frost & A.L. Hill
Close of play: 1st day: no play; 2nd day: ND 183-2, Horsley 129, M.N. Hart 10
3rd day: CD 54-4, Sulzberger 3, Ryder 9
Central Districts won by 8 wickets. Points: Central Districts 6, Northern Districts 2

No play was possible at Hamilton for the fourth successive day in the State Championship and it was not until 2.59 pm on the second day that the players finally got out into the middle.

By the end of the shortened day, Horsley was 129 having reached his hundred from 156 balls in 187 minutes. On the third day Matthew Hart also reached three figures, taking 185 balls and 217 minutes. Horsley, Hart and Orchard all made their highest scores. Northern declared at 392-5 and then reduced Central to 54-4 by the close.

Spearman declared at the overnight score and Northern forfeited their second innings leaving Central 339 to win. The visitors made no race of the contest as Robbie Hart tried eight bowlers in vain. How spearheaded the win with a magnificent maiden hundred reached after 224 minutes from 176 balls. Todd also recorded his highest score as the pair added an unbroken 161 in 128 minutes to take Central to an eight wicket victory.

NORTHERN DISTRICTS

FIRST INNINGS	Runs	Mins	Balls	6s	4s	SECOND INNINGS	Runs	Mins	Balls	6s	4s
J.A.H.Marshall c Taylor b Mason	7	22	19	-	-						
N.K.W.Horsley c Schwass b Sulzberger	159	258	195	2	26						
H.J.H.Marshall c Griggs b Mason	33	136	104	-	5						
M.N.Hart c Griggs b Hefford	111	237	201	-	20						
M.G.Orchard not out	54	223	183	-	7						
G.G.Robinson run out	15	48	36	-	2						
J.A.F.Yovich not out	7	35	26	-	1						
R.G.Hart*†											
B.P.Martin											
I.G.Butler											
G.L.West											
Extras (lb 3, w 1, nb 2)	6										
TOTAL (127 overs) (5 wkts dec)	**392**	482				Innings forfeited					

CENTRAL DISTRICTS

	Runs	Mins	Balls	6s	4s		Runs	Mins	Balls	6s	4s
P.J.Ingram c Hart R.G. b Butler	10	73	60	-	1	run out	60	87	73	1	10
J.M.How b Butler	3	14	4	-	-	not out	163	302	250	1	26
C.M.Spearman* c Hart R.G. b West	23	93	63	-	4	b Butler	47	85	62	1	6
G.R.Todd c Marshall J.A.H. b West	2	24	20	-	-	not out	61	128	112	-	10
G.P.Sulzberger not out	3	27	21	-	-						
J.D.Ryder not out	9	14	14	-	2						
R.L.Taylor											
B.B.J.Griggs†											
A.M.Schwass											
M.J.Mason											
B.E.Hefford											
Extras (lb 1, w 1, nb 2)	4					(lb 5, w 1, nb 2)	8				
TOTAL (30 overs) (4 wkts dec)	**54**	126				(82.3 overs) (2 wkts)	**339**	302			

Bowling	O	M	R	W	O	M	R	W
CENTRAL DISTRICTS								
Mason	29	11	72	2				
Hefford	27	8	74	1				
Schwass	26	8	91	0				
Todd	7	1	53	0				
Ryder	9	1	27	0				
Sulzberger	26	6	65	1				
How	3	0	7	0				
NORTHERN DISTRICTS								
Butler	8	3	12	2	15	2	56	1
Yovich	6	1	15	0	14	0	66	0
West	10	2	26	2	12	0	47	0
Martin	6	6	0	0	23	4	81	0
Orchard					9	3	38	0
Hart M.N.					6	2	18	0
Marshall J.A.H.					2.3	0	25	0
Marshall H.J.H.					1	0	3	0

Fall of Wickets	ND	CD	ND	CD
	1st	1st	2nd	2nd
1st	24	6	-	85
2nd	165	38	-	178
3rd	229	42	-	-
4th	335	45	-	-
5th	365	-	-	-
6th	-	-	-	-
7th	-	-	-	-
8th	-	-	-	-
9th	-	-	-	-
10th	-	-	-	-

alarms, being 116-5 at one stage. Auckland's total of 478 and Hopkins' score of 173 were the best in the short first-class history of the venue. England player Franks, who was playing club cricket in Christchurch, had been called into the Canterbury team after a number of injuries to their bowlers.

CANTERBURY

FIRST INNINGS	Runs	Mins	Balls	6s	4s	SECOND INNINGS	Runs	Mins	Balls	6s	4s
G.R.Stead* c Nicol b Canning	12	34	29	-	1	lbw b Canning	2	5	7	-	-
R.M.Frew c Barnes b Shaw	44	136	97	-	6	(9) b Canning	5	20	18	-	1
M.H.W.Papps c Nicol b Pryor	4	10	9	-	1	(2) c Young b Pryor	5	11	17	-	1
S.L.Stewart lbw b Canning	13	19	18	-	3	(3) lbw b Walker	30	102	101	-	2
P.G.Fulton c Young b Shaw	21	58	54	-	4	(4) lbw b Canning	14	42	35	-	2
A.J.Redmond lbw b Shaw	0	7	2	-	-	(5) c Pryor b Walker	59	75	50	-	10
G.J.Hopkins† c & b Walker	113	147	115	-	16	(6) not out	175	333	239	-	26
P.J.Franks b Shaw	10	26	17	-	2	(7) c Walker b Shaw	41	83	63	-	5
P.J.Wiseman b Canning	10	16	8	-	1	(8) lbw b Canning	59	118	84	-	10
A.M.Ellis c Young b Shaw	19	96	71	-	1	lbw b Walker	10	58	56	-	1
C.S.Martin not out	0	2	-	-	-	b Walker	0	28	13	-	-
Extras (lb 3, nb 3)	6					(lb 6, w 6, nb 1)	13				
TOTAL (69.3 overs)	**252**	280				(112 overs)	**413**	442			

AUCKLAND

	Runs	Mins	Balls	6s	4s		Runs	Mins	Balls	6s	4s
M.H.Richardson c Papps b Wiseman	82	198	161	-	11	c Ellis b Wiseman	43	201	156	-	5
T.G.McIntosh lbw b Ellis	20	91	54	-	3	c & b Wiseman	28	98	86	-	4
R.A.Young† c Fulton b Wiseman	1	23	17	-	-						
M.J.Horne c Hopkins b Fulton	72	155	126	1	8	(3) c Papps b Redmond	18	23	15	-	4
L.G.Howell c Ellis b Wiseman	4	16	9	-	1	(4) c & b Redmond	0	9	6	-	-
R.J.Nicol b Wiseman	77	255	200	1	7	(5) lbw b Redmond	18	59	42	-	3
A.C.Barnes lbw b Martin	43	72	60	1	7	(6) not out	30	61	48	-	5
T.K.Canning c Stewart b Wiseman	113	198	154	2	13	(7) not out	44	52	40	1	7
C.R.Pryor run out	9	45	30	-	1						
B.G.K.Walker* c Hopkins b Redmond	20	58	51	-	2						
G.S.Shaw not out	11	30	32	-	1						
Extras (b 8, lb 4, w 1, nb 13)	26					(b 5, lb 1, w 1, nb 2)	9				
TOTAL (146.4 overs)	**478**	574				(65.1 overs) (5 wkts)	**190**	254			

Bowling	O	M	R	W	O	M	R	W
AUCKLAND								
Canning	20	7	57	3	30	7	89	4
Shaw	15	0	73	5	21	2	85	1
Pryor	15	5	46	1	24	4	75	1
Barnes	11	2	46	0	9	2	27	0
Walker	4.3	0	14	1	17	1	77	4
Horne	4	0	13	0				
Nicol					9	0	40	0
McIntosh					2	0	14	0
CANTERBURY								
Martin	29	5	86	1	10	4	16	0
Franks	28	7	96	0	10	2	25	0
Ellis	20	1	66	1				
Wiseman	36	4	122	4	27.1	8	75	2
Redmond	26.4	4	78	2	18	0	68	3
Fulton	7	4	18	1				

Fall of Wickets	C	A	C	A
	1st	1st	2nd	2nd
1st	25	82	3	49
2nd	38	89	7	70
3rd	53	134	30	72
4th	95	151	77	110
5th	97	200	115	116
6th	98	253	197	-
7th	115	398	339	-
8th	137	432	353	-
9th	252	452	392	-
10th	252	478	413	-

WELLINGTON v AUCKLAND

State Championship

at Basin Reserve, Wellington on 11, 12, 13, 14 March, 2003
Toss : Auckland. Umpires : M.P. George & D.M. Quested
Close of play: 1st day: Auckland 3-0, Richardson 2, McIntosh 1; 2nd day: Auckland 242-6, Nielsen 6, Pryor 4
3rd day: Wellington 168-5, Donaldson 22, Nevin 14
First innings win to Auckland. *Points: Auckland 2, Wellington 0*

Only a maiden fifty from Woodcock and an aggressive 50 from Walker prevented Auckland taking complete control on the first day. Canning took 5-62 while Young created a record for catches and dismissals in an innings for Auckland.

Auckland spent all of the second day building their innings and led by 16 by stumps. Horne was out just before the close having reached his hundred from 151 balls in 223 minutes. Wellington finally dismissed Auckland just before lunch on the third day and lost three early wickets. By the close they were 168-5, leading by just 96.

Donaldson soon went on the last day but some resolute batting from Nevin, Walker, Jefferson and Penn completely thwarted Auckland's push for the victory which would have given them the title. The match was called off at tea.

WELLINGTON

FIRST INNINGS	Runs	Mins	Balls	6s	4s	SECOND INNINGS	Runs	Mins	Balls	6s	4s
M.D.Bell* c Horne b Pryor	14	18	17	-	3	c Richardson b Pryor	18	63	66	-	2
R.A.Jones c Young b Canning	1	20	12	-	-	c Richardson b Pryor	40	87	59	-	5
N.R.Parlane c Young b Davis	20	86	64	-	4	c Barnes b Pryor	0	2	1	-	-
L.J.Woodcock c Young b Canning	72	237	166	-	7	lbw b Canning	25	98	64	-	3
J.E.C.Franklin b Nielsen	10	36	29	-	2	lbw b Canning	33	119	99	-	5
G.T.Donaldson c Young b Canning	0	10	10	-	-	c Nicol b Barnes	30	169	130	-	4
C.J.Nevin† c Young b Davis	20	49	53	-	4	c Walker b Barnes	68	242	194	-	8
M.D.J.Walker c Young b Walker	50	77	52	3	5	run out	35	122	94	-	5
M.R.Jefferson not out	14	74	47	-	-	not out	30	90	77	-	4
A.J.Penn b Canning	8	25	17	-	1	not out	27	82	77	-	5
I.E.O'Brien b Canning	3	25	30	-	-						
Extras (b 1, lb 9, w 2, nb 2)	14					(b 4, lb 13, w 5, nb 3)	25				
TOTAL (82.5 overs)	**226**	333				(141 overs) (8 wkts)	**331**	541			

AUCKLAND

	Runs	Mins	Balls	6s	4s
M.H.Richardson c Parlane b O'Brien	27	171	118	-	3
T.G.McIntosh c Parlane b Franklin	27	89	66	-	3
M.J.Horne b O'Brien	119	276	196	-	16
T.K.Canning lbw b Walker	24	95	77	1	3
R.J.Nicol c sub (L.J.Morgan) b Jefferson	11	35	38	-	2
A.C.Barnes st Nevin b Jefferson	5	15	15	-	-
B.J.Nielsen c Jones b Walker	7	94	76	-	-
C.R.Pryor c Nevin b Walker	40	163	129	-	6
R.A.Young† b O'Brien	0	6	7	-	-
B.G.K.Walker* c Jones b Walker	5	59	42	-	-
H.T.Davis not out	2	48	37	-	-
Extras (b 6, lb 20, w 1, nb 4)	31				
TOTAL (132.5 overs)	**298**	530			

Bowling	O	M	R	W	O	M	R	W
AUCKLAND								
Pryor	11	2	56	1	31	8	77	3
Canning	30.5	11	62	5	47	14	122	2
Davis	21	8	35	2	17	5	32	0
Nielsen	15	6	33	1	5	4	1	0
Barnes	3	0	14	0	14	6	25	2
Walker	2	1	16	1	15	2	32	0
Nicol					10	4	21	0
Richardson					1	0	4	0
McIntosh					1	1	0	0
WELLINGTON								
Penn	19	3	47	0				
Franklin	10	1	31	1				
Walker	46.5	17	83	4				
O'Brien	36	17	50	3				
Woodcock	10	2	37	0				
Jefferson	11	2	24	2				

Fall of Wickets			
	W	A	W
	1st	1st	2nd
1st	17	44	45
2nd	17	97	48
3rd	57	164	61
4th	74	197	115
5th	77	209	130
6th	127	229	202
7th	177	252	269
8th	205	254	277
9th	218	271	-
10th	226	298	-

CANTERBURY v OTAGO   State Championship

at Hagley Park, Christchurch on 11, 12, 13, 14 March, 2003
Toss : Otago. Umpires : D.B. Cowie & I.W. Shine
Close of play: 1st day: Canterbury 229-9, Ellis 8, Martin 1; 2nd day: Otago 268-4, McKenzie 41, McGlashan 38
3rd day: Canterbury 100-2, Stead 52, Fulton 10
Otago won by 10 wickets. *Points: Otago 6, Canterbury 0*

Canterbury batted through the entire first day being 229-9 after 100 overs and were dismissed early next morning. McSkimming had the very good figures of 5-40 off 27 overs.

By the end of the second day Otago had gained first innings points and still had six wickets in hand. Wasim had reached his hundred from 154 balls in 218 minutes and on the third day McKenzie registered his maiden first-class hundred which came up in 360 minutes off 308 balls. Wilson played his best innings of the summer reaching fifty off 43 balls in 49 minutes. Otago declared at 485-9, leading by 239 runs.

Canterbury were 100-2 by the close but Stead went early on the last day and only Broom, who hit his maiden fifty, showed much resistance. O'Connor took 5-55 off 30 overs. Otago required just 20 to win and the match was all over at 3.13 pm.

CANTERBURY

FIRST INNINGS	Runs	Mins	Balls	6s	4s	SECOND INNINGS	Runs	Mins	Balls	6s	4s
R.M.Frew c Wasim b Walmsley	21	76	56	-	4	lbw b O'Connor	30	133	100	-	2
M.H.W.Papps c McGlashan						c McSkimming b Walmsley	5	20	13	-	-
b McSkimming	21	130	88	-	1						
G.R.Stead* b McSkimming	75	166	136	-	10	c McGlashan b Walmsley	53	159	139	-	8
P.G.Fulton c McGlashan b O'Connor	12	73	46	-	2	lbw b O'Connor	10	41	31	-	2
N.T.Broom c Wasim b Walmsley	20	43	28	-	2	c McSkimming b O'Connor	63	173	142	-	9
G.J.Hopkins† c McGlashan b McSkimming	24	109	99	-	3	c Sheed b Morland	25	81	64	-	5
A.J.Redmond run out	1	9	4	-	-	lbw b O'Connor	23	69	53	-	4
P.J.Wiseman c McGlashan b McSkimming	29	109	90	-	5	lbw b O'Connor	4	6	3	-	1
A.M.Ellis not out	17	62	51	-	1	not out	24	52	32	-	4
W.A.Wisneski c Wilson b McSkimming	6	13	12	-	1	c McKenzie b Walmsley	10	40	35	-	1
C.S.Martin c & b Walmsley	5	33	23	-	-	b Walmsley	0	1	3	-	-
Extras (b 1, lb 11, nb 3)	15					(lb 3, nb 8)	11				
TOTAL (104.5 overs)	**246**	416				(101 overs)	**258**	392			

OTAGO

	Runs	Mins	Balls	6s	4s		Runs	Mins	Balls	6s	4s
C.D.Cumming* lbw b Wisneski	42	138	108	-	6	not out	3	12	9	-	-
Mohammad Wasim c Hopkins b Broom	108	241	173	-	20	not out	18	12	15	-	3
C.B.Gaffaney c Broom b Redmond	13	35	32	-	2						
M.N.McKenzie c sub (B.P.Donkers)											
b Wiseman	100	362	310	-	11						
J.W.Sheed c Hopkins b Wisneski	6	14	12	-	1						
P.D.McGlashan† c Papps b Ellis	47	166	110	-	6						
W.C.McSkimming b Wiseman	25	79	67	-	2						
J.W.Wilson c Hopkins b Redmond	66	54	51	3	5						
N.D.Morland c Broom b Redmond	18	38	19	-	3						
S.B.O'Connor not out	17	27	15	-	3						
K.P.Walmsley not out	9	9	5	1	-						
Extras (b 6, lb 11, w 2, nb 15)	34					(lb 1, nb 1)	2				
TOTAL (149 overs) (9 wkts dec)	**485**	586				(3.5 overs) (0 wkts)	**23**	12			

Bowling	O	M	R	W	O	M	R	W
OTAGO								
O'Connor	25	6	62	1	30	14	55	5
Walmsley	25.5	7	64	3	24	9	55	4
McSkimming	27	12	40	5	14	1	46	0
Wilson	19	4	54	0	13	0	59	0
Cumming	5	1	14	0	3	1	11	0
Morland	3	3	0	0	17	7	29	1
CANTERBURY								
Wisneski	33.1	7	92	2				
Martin	18	5	39	0				
Ellis	23	4	111	1	2	0	14	0
Fulton	6	1	20	0				
Redmond	32	9	105	3	1.5	0	8	0
Wiseman	29.5	5	93	2				
Broom	7	4	8	1				

Fall of Wickets	C	O	C	O
	1st	1st	2nd	2nd
1st	36	102	10	-
2nd	82	137	79	-
3rd	132	181	101	-
4th	158	195	101	-
5th	158	296	153	-
6th	163	351	206	-
7th	213	401	216	-
8th	214	445	221	-
9th	222	468	258	-
10th	246	-	258	-

OTAGO v WELLINGTON State Championship

at Molyneux Park, Alexandra on 17, 18, 19, 20 March, 2003
Toss : Otago. Umpires : G.A. Baxter & R.D. Anderson
Close of play: 1st day: Wellington 202-9, Turner 7, O'Brien 9; 2nd day: Otago 281-4, Gaffaney 49, McGlashan 6
3rd day: Wellington 160-4, Woodcock 50, Donaldson 23
Otago won by 9 wickets. *Points: Otago 6, Wellington 0*

Otago sent Wellington in and had plenty of early success as the visitors plunged to 68-5 against O'Connor, Walmsley and McSkimming. Franklin and Nevin added 71 in 96 minutes and Wellington finally totalled 203, scored at exactly two runs an over.

Otago began with their fifth century opening partnership of the season. Cumming reached his hundred after 204 minutes from 172 balls. Persistent bowling by Walker, who earned career best figures from 52.3 overs, restricted the remainder of the Otago batting but their lead of 180 was still a huge advantage.

Woodcock showed some more good form, registering his highest score, but Wellington's final tally left Otago just 65 to win. The game was all over by 2.19 pm. O'Connor took 4-35 and 5-82 in what turned out to be his final first-class appearance.

WELLINGTON

FIRST INNINGS	Runs	Mins	Balls	6s	4s	SECOND INNINGS	Runs	Mins	Balls	6s	4s
M.D.Bell* b O'Connor	5	15	11	-	-	c Gaffaney b Walmsley	10	13	18	-	2
R.A.Jones b McSkimming	36	103	84	-	6	b McSkimming	23	49	29	-	4
N.R.Parlane c McGlashan b McSkimming	2	32	32	-	-	lbw b O'Connor	35	86	62	-	7
L.J.Woodcock lbw b Walmsley	10	72	54	-	2	c Morland b O'Connor	80	308	241	-	8
J.E.C.Franklin lbw b O'Connor	46	245	173	-	4	b O'Connor	12	26	12	-	2
G.T.Donaldson c Morland b O'Connor	8	37	30	-	-	c McGlashan b O'Connor	27	111	85	-	3
C.J.Nevin† c & b Morland	50	96	71	-	10	c McGlashan b O'Connor	3	6	4	-	-
M.D.J.Walker c O'Connor b Morland	5	22	25	-	-	c Cumming b Morland	31	58	47	1	5
M.R.Jefferson lbw b O'Connor	11	86	64	-	-	c & b Walmsley	13	33	28	-	1
A.D.Turner c McKenzie b Walmsley	7	47	42	-	1	c & b Walmsley	0	12	7	-	-
I.E.O'Brien not out	10	30	23	-	-	not out	1	5	2	-	-
Extras (b 2, lb 10, w 1)	13					(b 4, lb 1, w 1, nb 3)	9				
TOTAL (101.3 overs)	**203**	397				(88.4 overs)	**244**	358			

OTAGO

	Runs	Mins	Balls	6s	4s		Runs	Mins	Balls	6s	4s
C.D.Cumming* lbw b Walker	114	234	200	-	21	not out	39	81	72	-	6
Mohammad Wasim b Walker	65	225	160	-	8	c Bell b Franklin	0	7	6	-	-
C.B.Gaffaney b Donaldson b O'Brien	72	224	177	-	9	not out	24	73	39	-	4
M.N.McKenzie c Parlane b Walker	3	31	20	-	-						
J.W.Sheed run out	19	70	44	-	3						
P.D.McGlashan† c Parlane b Walker	7	49	47	-	-						
W.C.McSkimming not out	40	164	140	-	6						
J.W.Wilson c Donaldson b O'Brien	1	12	11	-	-						
N.D.Morland c Nevin b Walker	11	61	49	-	-						
S.B.O'Connor run out	4	8	5	-	-						
K.P.Walmsley c Nevin b Walker	14	17	16	-	2						
Extras (b 2, lb 21, w 2, nb 8)	33					(nb 2)	2				
TOTAL (143.3 overs)	**383**	552				(19.1 overs) (1 wkt)	**65**	81			

Bowling	O	M	R	W	O	M	R	W
OTAGO								
O'Connor	26	14	35	4	28.4	9	82	5
Walmsley	25.3	10	54	2	23	4	75	3
McSkimming	23	13	25	2	20	8	50	1
Cumming	4	1	11	0	5	0	11	0
Morland	8	1	18	2	12	5	21	1
Wilson	15	3	48	0				
WELLINGTON								
Turner	23	3	97	0	4	1	9	0
Franklin	8	2	24	0	6	1	20	1
O'Brien	33	9	77	2	3	0	18	0
Walker	52.3	17	114	6	5	2	7	0
Jefferson	10	1	32	0				
Woodcock	17	8	16	0	1	0	8	0
Bell					0.1	0	3	0

Fall of Wickets				
	W	O	W	O
	1st	1st	2nd	2nd
1st	12	191	11	0
2nd	28	196	45	-
3rd	46	217	90	-
4th	57	263	108	-
5th	68	283	175	-
6th	139	335	179	-
7th	147	338	220	-
8th	180	360	238	-
9th	189	364	240	-
10th	203	383	244	-

AUCKLAND v NORTHERN DISTRICTS   State Championship

at Eden Park Outer Oval, Auckland on 17, 18, 19, 20 March, 2003
Toss : Northern Districts. Umpires : D.M. Quested & E.A. Watkin
Close of play: 1st day: ND 292-9, Robinson 123, Butler 20; 2nd day: Auckland 294-7, McIntosh 146
3rd day: ND 280-7, M.N.Hart156
Northern Districts won by 16 runs. *Points: Northern Districts 6, Auckland 0*

Auckland went into this match needing an outright win to ensure themselves of retaining the title. Former New Zealand Under 19 player Irwin made his first-class debut.

Robinson, highest score 45 in four previous first-class games, was Northern's saviour on the first day. He reached his first century after 228 minutes from 199 balls. Auckland got to within four runs of Northern's total by stumps on day three with McIntosh responsible for more than half the runs. His century came from 223 balls in 290 minutes.

Walker declared at the overnight score, as first innings points were of no consequence, and Northern built a big lead thanks mainly to Matthew Hart. He reached his first century from 171 balls in 228 minutes and the innings was declared as soon as he dispatched occasional bowler McIntosh to the boundary to go to his first double century.

Auckland made every effort to reach the stiff target. Richardson went to his first century of the summer from 189 balls in 235 minutes and shared century stands with McIntosh and Nicol. Auckland finally fell just short but by this time they knew they were guaranteed the title regardless.

NORTHERN DISTRICTS

FIRST INNINGS	Runs	Mins	Balls	6s	4s	SECOND INNINGS	Runs	Mins	Balls	6s	4s
J.A.H.Marshall run out	25	68	50	-	4	c Nicol b Pryor	12	52	36	-	1
N.K.W.Horsley c Richardson b Canning	8	25	17	-	1	(9) c & b Pryor	0	1	2	-	-
H.J.H.Marshall lbw b Canning	12	35	34	-	1	c Canning b Horne	57	197	174	1	10
M.N.Hart c Nicol b Canning	5	20	13	-	1	not out	201	401	308	-	33
M.G.Orchard lbw b Nicol	30	136	107	-	3	c Nicol b Horne	6	73	59	-	1
G.G.Robinson not out	125	313	251	-	16	(2) lbw b Pryor	9	18	15	-	-
J.A.F.Yovich c Young b Barnes	14	41	40	-	2	(6) lbw b Canning	25	67	44	-	3
R.G.Hart*† c Young b Pryor	14	55	47	-	1	(7) b Canning	0	7	7	-	-
B.P.Martin c Young b Canning	11	42	31	1	1	(8) c Young b Pryor	1	19	17	-	-
G.D.Irwin c McIntosh b Pryor	2	13	5	-	-	c Richardson b Pryor	4	16	12	-	-
I.G.Butler c Young b Davis	24	35	29	-	5	not out	16	49	30	-	3
Extras (lb 15, w 12, nb 1)	28					(lb 14, w 1, nb 6)	21				
TOTAL (103.5 overs)	**298**	396				(116.2 overs) (9 wkts dec)	**352**	454			

AUCKLAND

	Runs	Mins	Balls	6s	4s		Runs	Mins	Balls	6s	4s
M.H.Richardson c Hart R.G. b Butler	39	162	103	-	7	c Irwin b Martin	113	264	205	1	12
T.G.McIntosh not out	146	398	313	-	22	c sub (D.P.Kelly) b Butler	64	125	97	-	12
M.J.Horne c Hart R.G. b Butler	19	41	33	-	3	c Marshall H.J.H. b Martin	3	14	11	-	-
R.J.Nicol c Marshall J.A.H. b Yovich	5	32	22	-	1	c Orchard b Marshall J.A.H.	56	95	90	1	6
T.K.Canning c Marshall H.J.H. b Yovich	4	10	8	-	1	c & b Martin	42	45	33	1	4
A.C.Barnes lbw b Butler	7	30	16	-	-	b Orchard	2	11	5	-	-
B.J.Nielsen c Marshall J.A.H. b Martin	14	30	36	1	1	(8) c Hart R.G. b Butler	11	29	19	-	-
C.R.Pryor c Marshall H.J.H. b Yovich	32	87	65	1	3	(7) c Irwin b Orchard	20	19	14	2	1
R.A.Young†						run out	11	12	11	-	1
B.G.K.Walker*						not out	1	4	1	-	-
H.T.Davis						b Butler	4	1	3	-	1
Extras (b 5, lb 8, w 6, nb 9)	28					(b 1, lb 8, w 1, nb 3)	13				
TOTAL (97.5 overs) (7 wkts dec) .	**294**	398				(81 overs)	**340**	314			

Bowling	O	M	R	W	O	M	R	W		Fall of Wickets			
AUCKLAND											ND	A	ND	A
Canning	34	12	96	4	23	5	56	2			1st	1st	2nd	2nd
Pryor	18	2	67	2	25	6	59	5		1st	28	104	16	118
Davis	15.5	6	34	1	11	3	39	0		2nd	46	120	40	125
Nielsen	4	2	7	0	27	13	60	0		3rd	49	125	171	234
Nicol	9	1	26	1	2	0	15	0		4th	54	162	203	271
Barnes	5	2	8	1	3	0	18	0		5th	158	183	273	291
Walker	18	6	45	0	2	0	19	0		6th	194	250	275	293
Horne					21	8	58	2		7th	230	294	280	319
McIntosh					2.2	0	14	0		8th	250	-	281	334
NORTHERN DISTRICTS										9th	262	-	298	336
Butler	27.5	3	87	3	20	4	66	3		10th	298	-	-	340
Yovich	21	4	69	3										
Irwin	16.4	5	40	0	6	2	23	0						
Orchard	4	2	20	0	21	3	89	2						
Martin	25.2	6	48	1	30	1	136	3						
Hart M.N.	3	0	17	0										
Marshall J.A.H.					4	0	17	1						

In Auckland's first innings Richardson (24) retired hurt at 72-0 and resumed at 250-6.

CENTRAL DISTRICTS v CANTERBURY   State Championship

at McLean Park, Napier on 17, 18, 19, 20 March, 2003
Toss : Central Districts. Umpires : D.B. Cowie & A.L. Hill
Close of play: 1st day: CD 316-4, Sulzberger 10, Ryder 5; 2nd day: Canterbury 74-4, Stead 11, Broom 6
3rd day: CD 109-3, Todd 26, Sulzberger 5
Canterbury won by 2 wickets. *Points: Canterbury 6, Central Districts 2*

Central took advantage of winning the toss and rattled up 542-4 with three players scoring hundreds. Ingram, who made his highest score, and How began with a Central record first wicket stand against Canterbury and Sulzberger and Ryder finished with a Central fifth wicket record against all teams. It was also the highest fifth wicket stand by any side against Canterbury.

How reached his second big hundred in succession from 163 balls in 222 minutes. Sulzberger reached three figures after 263 minutes from 236 balls and Ryder registered his maiden first-class hundred after 240 minutes and 173 balls.

Canterbury declared 252 runs in arrears after Stead had reached a century from 193 balls in 217 minutes and Broom had equalled his highest score. Central batted for 30 overs with Taylor hitting a maiden fifty and set Canterbury 362 to win. At 305-8 the game was in the balance but an unbroken 57 run stand in even time between Wiseman and Donkers saw Canterbury to a two wicket win.

CENTRAL DISTRICTS

FIRST INNINGS	Runs	Mins	Balls	6s	4s	SECOND INNINGS	Runs	Mins	Balls	6s	4s
P.J.Ingram c Frew b Donkers	84	200	161	-	8	c sub (A.J.Redmond) b Martin	6	17	19	-	-
J.M.How c Frew b Stewart	158	330	250	-	19	c Fulton b Donkers	7	29	16	-	1
C.M.Spearman* c Frew b Donkers	28	43	32	-	5						
G.R.Todd c Hopkins b Wiseman	25	105	92	-	1	not out	26	85	51	-	3
G.P.Sulzberger not out	107	273	243	2	8	not out	5	11	16	-	-
J.D.Ryder not out	114	256	186	1	11						
R.L.Taylor						(3) c Hopkins b Fulton	56	84	78	2	7
B.B.J.Griggs†											
M.J.Mason											
B.E.Hefford											
L.J.Hamilton											
Extras (b 6, lb 10, w 8, nb 2)	26					(b 5, lb 4)	9				
TOTAL (160.2 overs) (4 wkts dec)	**542**	610				(30 overs) (3 wkts dec)	**109**	115			

CANTERBURY

	Runs	Mins	Balls	6s	4s		Runs	Mins	Balls	6s	4s
S.L.Stewart c Griggs b Sulzberger	22	116	95	-	2	(2) c Griggs b Sulzberger	68	93	65	2	7
R.M.Frew c Spearman b Hefford	8	54	41	-	1	(1) c Spearman b Sulzberger	24	66	52	-	2
M.H.W.Papps c Taylor b Hefford	0	9	7	-	-	c Hefford b How	39	152	121	-	4
P.G.Fulton b Mason	17	59	38	-	2	c Griggs b How	91	189	155	2	11
G.R.Stead* c How b Mason	111	241	209	-	13	c How b Mason	24	54	51	-	3
N.T.Broom c How b Mason	63	180	152	3	6	lbw b Sulzberger	16	36	28	-	2
G.J.Hopkins† c Ingram b Mason	9	24	17	-	2	b Mason	3	4	7	-	-
P.J.Wiseman b Ryder b Sulzberger	25	71	45	1	3	not out	38	105	62	1	2
C.J.Cornelius not out	19	73	64	-	3	b How	15	22	21	-	2
B.P.Donkers not out	1	25	23	-	-	not out	29	54	42	-	3
C.S.Martin											
Extras (b 1, lb 11, w 1, nb 2)	15					(lb 6, nb 5)	11				
TOTAL (115 overs) (8 wkts dec)	**290**	432				(99.5 overs) (8 wkts)	**362**	394			

Bowling	O	M	R	W	O	M	R	W
CANTERBURY								
Martin	34	5	116	0	8	3	26	1
Cornelius	7	1	19	0				
Donkers	24	5	113	2	7	2	24	1
Wiseman	63.2	11	165	1	4	0	32	0
Broom	3	0	14	0				
Fulton	18	6	59	0	8	3	11	1
Stewart	9	2	35	1	3	0	7	0
Stead	1	0	1	0				
Papps	1	0	4	0				
CENTRAL DISTRICTS								
Hamilton	24.3	8	81	0	15.5	1	87	0
Mason	27	13	40	4	22	5	57	2
Hefford	24	9	45	2	8	2	26	0
Sulzberger	28.3	9	78	2	29	4	113	3
Todd	2	0	4	0				
How	8	0	27	0	25	5	73	3
Ryder	1	0	3	0				

Fall of Wickets	CD	C	CD	C
	1st	1st	2nd	2nd
1st	178	26	14	76
2nd	236	26	22	105
3rd	299	57	101	206
4th	307	57	-	256
5th	-	216	-	256
6th	-	230	-	259
7th	-	249	-	284
8th	-	288	-	305
9th	-	-	-	-
10th	-	-	-	-

2002/03 FIRST-CLASS STATISTICS

REGISTER OF PLAYERS

The following players appeared in first-class cricket for New Zealand teams during the 2002/03 season.

			Born	At	Type			First-class debut	
Adams Andre Ryan	A		17. 7.75	Auckland	RHB	RFM		A v O	97/98
Aldridge Graeme William	ND		15.11.77	Christchurch	RHB	RFM		ND v W	98/99
Anderson Timothy Robert	CD		13.12.78	Palmerston North	RHB	RLB		NZA v B	97/98
Andrews Simon Leslie	ND		11. 7.80	Auckland	RHB	RFM		ND v O	00/01
Astle Nathan John	C, NZ		15. 9.71	Christchurch	RHB	RM		C v CD	91/92
Barnes Aaron Craig	A		21.12.71	Turangi	RHB	RM		A v CD	93/94
Bell Matthew David	W		25. 2.77	Dunedin	RHB	ROB	WK	ND v NZA	93/94
Bond Shane Edward	C, NZ		7. 6.75	Christchurch	RHB	RF		C v CD	96/97
Broom Neil Trevor	C		20.11.83	Christchurch	RHB	RM		C v W	02/03
Butler Ian Gareth	ND		24.11.81	Auckland	RHB	RFM		ND v O	01/02
Cairns Christopher Lance	C		13. 6.70	Picton	RHB	RFM		Notts v Kent	88
Canning Tamahau Karangatukituki	A		7. 4.77	Adelaide	RHB	RFM		AA v Mat Inv	98/99
Cornelius Cleighten James	C		2. 6.76	Christchurch	RHB	RFM		C v A	01/02
Cumming Craig Derek	O		31. 8.75	Timaru	RHB			C v CD	95/96
Daley Nathan Michael	ND		2. 6.77	Sydney	RHB		WK	ND v O	02/03
Davis Heath Te-Ihi-O-Te-Rangi	A		30.11.71	Lower Hutt	RHB	RFM		W v A	91/92
Donaldson Grant Thomas	W		8. 6.76	Upper Hutt	RHB	RM		W v ND	98/99
Donkers Brendon Peter	C		25. 7.76	Hokitika	RHB	RM		C v O	02/03
Ellis Andrew Malcolm	C		24. 3.82	Christchurch	RHB	RFM		C v A	02/03
Fleming Stephen Paul	W, NZ		1. 4.73	Christchurch	LHB	RSM		C v ND	91/92
Franklin James Edward Charles	W		7.11.80	Wellington	LHB	LFM		W v I	98/99
Franks Paul John	C		3. 2.79	Mansfield, England	LHB	RFM		Notts v Hants	96
Frew Robert Mathew	C		28.12.70	Darfield	RHB			C v CD	95/96
Fulton Peter Gordon	C		1. 2.79	Christchurch	RHB	RM		C v A	00/01
Gaffaney Christopher Blair	O		30.11.75	Dunedin	RHB			O v A	95/96
Gillespie Mark Raymond	W		17.10.79	Wanganui	RHB	RFM		W v O	99/00
Griggs Bevan Barry John	CD		29. 3.78	Palmerston North	RHB		WK	CD v O	00/01
Hamilton Lance John	CD		5. 4.73	Papakura	RHB	LFM		CD v W	96/97
Harris Chris Zinzan	C		20.11.69	Christchurch	LHB	RM		C v O	89/90
Hart Matthew Norman	ND		16. 5.72	Hamilton	LHB	SLA		ND v A	90/91
Hart Robert Garry	ND, NZ		2.12.74	Hamilton	RHB		WK	ND v A	92/93
Hefford Brent Edward	CD		8. 5.78	Blenheim	LHB	RM		CD v C	99/00
Hopkins Gareth James	C		24.11.76	Lower Hutt	RHB	WK		NC v CC	97/98
Hore Andrew John	O		18. 6.69	Oamaru	LHB			O v W	96/97
Horne Matthew Jeffery	A, NZ		5.12.70	Auckland	RHB	RM		A v O	92/93
Horsley Nicholas Keith Woodward	ND		22. 9.80	Hamilton	LHB	ROB		A v CD	01/02
How Jamie Michael	CD		19. 5.81	New Plymouth	LHB	RM		CD v W	00/01
Howell Llorne Gregory	A		8. 7.72	Napier	RHB	RM		C v O	90/91
Ingram Peter John	CD		25.10.78	Hawera	RHB	ROB		CD v O	01/02
Irwin Gareth Dudley	ND		6. 3.81	Hamilton	LHB	LFM		ND v A	02/03
Jefferson Mark Robin	W		28. 6.76	Oamaru	RHB	SLA		W v A	96/97
Jones Richard Andrew	W		22.10.73	Auckland	RHB			A v C	93/94
Kelly David Patrick	ND		29. 3.79	Dunedin	RHB			NZA v Pak A	98/99
King Richard Terrence	A		23. 4.73	Wellington	RHB	RSM		O v A	91/92
Lawson Robert Arthur	O		14. 9.74	Dunedin	RHB	ROB		O v CD	92/93
Loveridge Greg Riaka	CD		15. 1.75	Palmerston North	RHB	RLB		CD v W	94/95
Lynch Robert Kevin	A		25. 5.82	Auckland	LHB		WK	A v W	01/02
Marshall Hamish John Hamilton	ND		15. 2.79	Warkworth	RHB	RM		ND v W	98/99
Marshall James Andrew Hamilton	ND		15. 2.79	Warkworth	RHB	RM		ND v W	97/98
Martin Bruce Philip	ND		25. 4.80	Whangarei	RHB	SLA		ND v CD	99/00
Martin Christopher Stewart	C		10.12.74	Christchurch	RHB	RFM		C v W	97/98
Mason Michael James	CD		27. 8.74	Carterton	RHB	RFM		CD v ND	97/98
McCullum Brendon Barrie	O		27. 9.81	Dunedin	RHB		WK	O v CD	99/00
McGlashan Peter Donald	O		22. 6.79	Napier	RHB		WK	O v O	00/01
McIntosh Timothy Gavin	A		4.12.79	Auckland	LHB			A v ND	98/99
McKay Andrew John	A		17. 4.80	Auckland	RHB	LFM		A v CD	02/03
McKenzie Marcel Norman	O		13. 5.78	Oamaru	RHB	RLB		C v O	98/99
McMillan Craig Douglas	C, NZ		13. 9.76	Christchurch	RHB	RM		C v O	94/95
McMillan James Michael	O		14. 6.78	Christchurch	RHB	RFM		O v CD	00/01
McSkimming Warren Charles	O		21. 6.79	Ranfurly	RHB	RM		O v C	99/00

		Born	At	Type			First-class debut	
Miller Robert Michael	C	30.12.79	Christchurch	LHB			C v W	02/03
Mills Kyle David	A	15. 3.79	Auckland	RHB	RFM		A v O	98/99
Mohammad Wasim	O	8. 8.77	Rawalpindi, Pakistan	RHB	RLB		R'pindi B v Isl'bd	94/95
Morgan Leighton James	W	16. 2.81	Wellington	RHB	SLA		W v CD	01/02
Morland Nathan Douglas	O	20.12.76	Dunedin	RHB	ROB		O v W	96/97
Nevin Christopher John	W	3. 8.75	Dunedin	RHB		WK	W v ND	95/96
Nicol Robert James	A	28. 5.83	Auckland	RHB	ROB		A v CD	01/02
Nielsen Bradley John	A	26.10.79	Auckland	RHB	RM		A v C	01/02
O'Brien Iain Edward	W	10. 7.76	Lower Hutt	RHB	RM		W v O	00/01
O'Connor Shayne Barry	O	15.11.73	Hastings	LHB	LFM		O v A	94/95
Oram Jacob David Philip	CD, NZ	28. 7.78	Palmerston North	LHB	RM		NZA v B	97/98
Orchard Mark Geoffrey	ND	8.11.78	Hamilton	RHB	RM		ND v C	01/02
Papps Michael Hugh William	C	2. 7.79	Christchurch	RHB		WK	C v O	98/99
Parlane Michael Edward	ND	22. 7.72	Pukekohe	RHB		WK	ND v A	92/93
Parlane Neal Ronald	W	9. 8.78	Whanagrei	RHB			ND v CD	96/97
Patel Jeetan Shashi	W	7. 5.80	Wellington	RHB	ROB		W v A	99/00
Penn Andrew Jonathan	W	27. 7.74	Wanganui	RHB	RFM		CD v ND	94/95
Pryor Craig Robert	A	15.10.73	Auckland	LHB	RM		A v W	97/98
Reddington Daryll John	O	17.10.72	Queenstown	RHB	RM		O v CD	02/03
Redmond Aaron James	C	23. 9.79	Perth	RHB	RLB		SI v NI	99/00
Richardson Mark Hunter	A, NZ	11. 6.71	Hastings	LHB	LM		Pres v I	89/90
Robinson Grant Geoffrey	ND	24. 7.79	Gisborne	LHB	LM		ND v A	01/02
Ryder Jesse Daniel	CD	6. 8.84	Masterton	LHB	RM		CD v ND	02/03
Sandbrook Ian Patrick	CD	22. 3.83	Palmerston North	RHB		WK	CD v C	02/03
Schwass Andrew Mark	CD	11. 4.74	Nelson	RHB	RFM		CD v W	98/99
Sewell David Graham	O	20.10.77	Christchurch	RHB	LFM		O v CD	95/96
Shaw Gareth Simon	A	14. 2.82	Auckland	RHB	RFM		A v C	01/02
Shaw Hayden Jonathan	C	31. 8.80	Christchurch	RHB	RFM		C v O	99/00
Sheed Jordan William	O	24. 9.82	Timaru	RHB	RLB		O v C	01/02
Sigley Martyn Andrew	CD	16.11.72	Hamilton	RHB		WK	CD v O	94/95
Sinclair Mathew Stuart	CD, NZ	9.11.75	Katherine, Australia	RHB	RM	WK	CD v C	95/96
Spearman Craig Murray	CD	4. 7.72	Auckland	RHB			A v CD	93/94
Stead Gary Raymond	C	9. 1.72	Christchurch	RHB	RLB		NZ XI v E	91/92
Stewart Shanan Luke	C	21. 6.82	Christchurch	RHB	RM		C v ND	01/02
Styris Scott Bernard	ND, NZ	10. 7.75	Brisbane, Australia	RHB	RM		ND v W	94/95
Sulzberger Glen Paul	CD	14. 3.73	Kaponga	LHB	ROB		CD v C	95/96
Taylor Ross Luteru	CD	8. 3.84	Lower Hutt	RHB	ROB		CD v C	02/03
Todd Gregory Rex	CD	17. 6.82	Masterton	LHB	RM		CD v O	00/01
Tuffey Daryl Raymond	ND, NZ	11. 6.78	Milton	RHB	RFM		ND v A	96/97
Turner Ashley Dean	W	13. 6.75	Lower Hutt	RHB	RFM		W v C	01/02
Vettori Daniel Luca	ND, NZ	27. 1.79	Auckland	RHB	SLA		ND v E	96/97
Vincent Lou	A, NZ	11.11.78	Warkworth	RHB	ROB	WK	A v O	97/98
Walker Brooke Graeme Keith	A	25. 3.77	Auckland	RHB	RLB		NZA v B	97/98
Walker Matthew David John	W	17. 1.77	Opunake	RHB	RM		CD v C	95/96
Walmsley Kerry Peter	O	23. 8.73	Dunedin	RHB	RFM		A v C	94/95
West Gareth Lawrence	ND	26. 7.76	New Plymouth	LHB	LFM		CD v O	00/01
Wilkinson Anthony Mark	O	15. 8.81	Dunedin	LHB	LM		O v CD	02/03
Wilson Jeffrey William	O	24.10.73	Invercargill	RHB	RFM		O v ND	91/92
Wiseman Paul John	C, NZ	4. 5.70	Auckland	RHB	ROB		A v CD	91/92
Wisneski Warren Anthony	C	19. 2.69	New Plymouth	RHB	RM		CD v O	92/93
Woodcock Luke James	W	19. 3.82	Wellington	LHB	SLA	WK	W v O	01/02
Young Reece Alan	A	15. 9.79	Auckland	RHB		WK	A v C	98/99
Yovich Joseph Adam Frank	ND	15.12.76	Whangarei	LHB	RFM		ND v C	96/97

Key

RHB	right-hand batsman	*SLA*	slow left-arm	*RSM*	right slow-medium
LHB	left-hand batsman	*RLB*	right leg-break	*LFM*	left fast-medium
RM	right medium	*ROB*	right off-break	*LSM*	left slow-medium
LM	left medium	*RFM*	right fast-medium	*WK*	wicketkeeper
NC	Northern Conference	*CC*	Central Conference	*NZA*	New Zealand Academy
AA	Australian Academy				

FIRST-CLASS UMPIRES

2002/03

Seventeen umpires officiated in State Shield and Championship games in 2002/03. Gary Baxter went to South Africa and stood in two games while South Africa's Barry Lambson stood in two Championship games. Brent Bowden officiated at the World Cup and was promoted to the Elite Umpire Panel after the tournament finished. He and Doug Cowie were on the second tier ICC panel and Tony Hill was on the third umpire panel.

Anderson, Robert Donald *(Manawatu).* Age 55. Debut in 1997/98. Has now officiated in 31 first-class games and 19 one-day games.

Baxter, Gary Arthur *(Canterbury).* Age 50. Debut in 1998/99. Has now umpired 28 first-class games and 20 one-day matches.

Bowden, Brent Fraser *(Auckland).* Age 39. Debut in 1992/93 and has now stood in 60 first-class games including six tests. Has also officiated in 63 one-day matches and 38 one-day internationals. Member of ICC's elite international panel.

Cowie, Douglas Bruce *(Auckland).* Age 56. Debut in 1985/86 and member of the international panel. He has umpired 101 first-class games including 22 tests. Also stood in 78 one-day games and 67 one-day internationals.

Ellwood, David John *(Wellington).* Age 38. Debut this season standing in two one-day games.

Frost, Barry George *(Auckland).* Age 45. Debut 1998/99. Has now officiated in 20 first-class matches and 22 one-day games.

George, Michael Peter *(Horowhenua-Kapiti).* Age 44. Debut 1999/00. Has umpired 19 first-class matches and 14 one-day games.

Hill, Anthony Lloyd *(Counties).* Age 52. Debut in 1993/94 and has now umpired 41 first-class games including one test. Has also stood in 46 one-day matches and nine one-day internationals. Now on the ICC third umpire panel.

Holdem, Glenn Clifford *(Canterbury).* Age 36. Debut in 2001/02. Has umpired two first-class and three one-day games.

Jones, Philip David *(Auckland).* Age 43. Debut this season standing in one first-class match.

Knights, Wayne Roger *(Auckland).* Age 32. Debut in 2001/02 and has now stood in two one-day games.

Morris, Craig Justin. *(Manawatu).* Age 39. Debut in 2000/01 and has umpired three first-class and two one-day games.

Paterson, David Gordon *(Marlborough).* Age 41. Debut in 2001/02. Has now officiated in three one-day matches.

Quested, David Murray *(Canterbury).* Age 56. Debut in 1990/91 and has now umpired 74 first class games including five tests. Has also officiated in 31 one-day internationals and 60 one-day games.

Shine, Ian William *(Counties).* Age 46. Debut 1998/99 and has now umpired 11 first-class games and ten one-day matches.

Watkin, Evan Allan *(Wellington).* Age 51. Debut in 1989/90 and has now umpired 76 first-class games including two tests. Has also umpired 21 one-day internationals and 73 one-day matches.

COMPLETE AVERAGES

Averages for India are on page 73.

	M	In	NO	HS	Runs	Ave	100	50	Ct	St	O	M	R	W	Ave	5WI	10WM	Best
A.R.Adams	1	2	0	21	27	13.50	-	-	-	-	29	10	61	3	20.33	-	-	2-28
G.W.Aldridge	5	4	1	12*	32	10.66	-	-	-	-	88	24	236	8	29.50	-	-	3-126
T.R.Anderson	1	1	0	2	2	2.00	-	-	-	-	15	1	68	1	68.00	-	-	1-68
S.L.Andrews	1	1	1	0*	0	-	-	-	-	1	38	13	95	2	47.50	-	-	1-4
N.J.Astle	4	5	0	42	108	21.60	-	-	3	-	69.2	25	137	11	12.45	-	-	4-35
A.C.Barnes	7	11	1	107	380	38.00	1	1	7	-	83	25	235	6	39.16	-	-	2-13
M.D.Bell	10	20	2	114	499	27.72	1	3	6	-	0.1	0	3	0	-	-	-	-
S.E.Bond	4	4	2	52	81	40.50	-	1	3	-	120.4	29	384	18	21.33	-	-	4-33
N.T.Broom	5	8	0	63	316	39.50	-	2	6	-	18	6	53	1	53.00	-	-	1-8
I.G.Butler	7	7	2	24	64	12.80	-	-	2	-	194.1	44	597	25	23.88	1	-	5-44
C.L.Cairns	2	2	1	76*	98	98.00	-	1	1	-	24	2	78	2	39.00	-	-	2-10
T.K.Canning	9	14	2	113	465	38.75	1	-	8	-	410	133	1011	46	21.97	1	-	5-62
C.J.Cornelius	1	2	1	19*	34	34.00	-	-	-	-	7	1	19	0	-	-	-	-
C.D.Cumming	10	18	2	128	751	46.93	3	3	4	-	96	33	191	1	191.00	-	-	1-28
N.M.Daley	1	1	0	4	4	4.00	-	-	2	1								
H.T.Davis	6	5	1	29	62	15.50	-	-	1	-	167.5	53	407	12	33.91	-	-	4-93
G.T.Donaldson	10	16	1	57	311	20.73	-	2	7	-								
B.P.Donkers	7	8	4	38	104	26.00	-	-	-	-	166	48	515	12	42.91	-	-	3-37
A.M.Ellis	4	6	3	24*	93	31.00	-	-	2	-	104.2	24	354	9	39.33	-	-	4-81
S.P.Fleming	4	6	0	55	133	22.16	-	1	6	-								
J.E.C.Franklin	8	13	0	87	413	31.76	-	3	1	-	183.2	35	523	22	23.77	1	-	6-40
P.J.Franks	1	2	0	41	51	25.50	-	-	-	-	38	9	121	0	-	-	-	-
R.M.Frew	7	11	0	49	206	18.72	-	-	5	-								
P.G.Fulton	8	13	1	301*	628	52.33	1	2	5	-	50	15	160	3	53.33	-	-	1-5
C.B.Gaffaney	8	14	1	108	436	33.53	1	2	4	-								
M.R.Gillespie	3	3	1	49	52	26.00	-	-	1	-	58	16	158	3	52.66	-	-	1-29
B.B.J.Griggs	10	12	1	100*	237	21.54	1	-	18	-								
L.J.Hamilton	8	10	7	12*	36	12.00	-	-	1	-	276.5	75	799	19	42.05	-	-	4-36
C.Z.Harris	3	3	1	73*	109	54.50	-	1	1	-	8	1	13	1	13.00	-	-	1-13
M.N.Hart	9	14	4	201*	546	54.60	2	1	5	-	39	3	136	1	136.00	-	-	1-24
R.G.Hart	11	14	4	72*	259	25.90	-	1	29	-								
B.E.Hefford	10	10	3	16*	53	7.57	-	-	4	-	321	118	684	25	27.36	-	-	4-53
G.J.Hopkins	10	15	1	175*	451	32.21	2	-	21	2								
A.J.Hore	1	2	0	8	15	7.50	-	-	-	-	1.3	0	9	0	-	-	-	-
M.J.Horne	9	14	0	187	671	47.92	2	3	2	-	54	18	131	3	43.66	-	-	2-58
N.K.W.Horsley	10	16	0	159	582	36.37	1	3	7	-	2	1	1	0	-	-	-	-
J.M.How	10	18	2	163*	704	44.00	2	3	9	-	36	5	107	3	35.66	-	-	3-73
L.G.Howell	1	2	0	4	4	2.00	-	-	-	-								
P.J.Ingram	9	17	2	84	374	24.93	-	4	2	-								
G.D.Irwin	1	2	0	6	6	3.00	-	-	2	-	22.4	7	63	0	-	-	-	-
M.R.Jefferson	6	10	4	53	175	29.16	-	1	-	-	87	20	204	6	34.00	-	-	3-38
R.A.Jones	10	20	4	128	726	45.37	2	3	8	-								
D.P.Kelly	3	5	0	26	50	10.00	-	-	2	-								
R.T.King	1	2	0	47	47	23.50	-	-	2	-								
R.A.Lawson	4	6	1	146	326	65.20	1	1	1	-								
G.R.Loveridge	4	6	0	34	121	20.16	-	-	5	-	25	2	108	1	108.00	-	-	1-52
R.K.Lynch	1	2	0	5	7	3.50	-	-	1	-								
H.J.H.Marshall	10	16	1	88*	376	25.06	-	2	3	-	1	0	3	0	-	-	-	-
J.A.H.Marshall	10	16	0	112	395	24.68	1	1	13	-	16.3	2	61	2	30.50	-	-	1-5
B.P.Martin	7	7	0	34	93	13.28	-	-	5	-	210.5	56	560	13	43.07	1	-	5-48
C.S.Martin	9	11	4	10*	30	4.28	-	-	1	-	298.4	78	807	19	42.47	-	-	4-69
M.J.Mason	10	11	0	36	153	13.90	-	-	1	-	352.2	120	787	40	19.67	2	1	6-56
B.B.McCullum	3	5	1	105	273	68.25	1	2	8	-								
P.D.McGlashan	7	10	2	47	173	21.62	-	-	15	1								
T.G.McIntosh	10	17	3	157	820	58.57	2	5	8	-	6.2	2	28	0	-	-	-	-
A.J.McKay	2	1	0	8	8	8.00	-	-	1	-	47	10	161	2	80.50	-	-	1-21
M.N.McKenzie	10	16	0	100	248	15.50	1	-	9	-								
C.D.McMillan	5	7	0	26	84	12.00	-	-	3	-	39	11	109	5	21.80	-	-	2-23
J.M.McMillan	6	6	3	7	25	1.25	-	-	1	-	181	41	530	15	35.33	-	-	4-56
W.C.McSkimming	7	10	4	66*	220	36.66	-	1	5	-	269.2	88	640	26	24.61	1	-	5-40
R.M.Miller	1	2	0	9	12	6.00	-	-	-	-								
K.D.Mills	3	5	1	55	115	28.75	-	1	1	-	107.1	32	290	10	29.00	-	-	3-55

	M	In	NO	HS	Runs	Ave	100	50	Ct	St	O	M	R	W	Ave	5WI	10WM	Best
Mohammad Wasim	10	17	1	108	651	40.68	2	4	9	-	23	7	59	1	59.00	-	-	1-2
L.J.Morgan	2	3	0	30	66	22.00	-	-	-	-								
N.D.Morland	10	13	2	32	153	13.90	-	-	9	-	258	81	645	14	46.07	-	-	2-1
C.J.Nevin	10	16	1	73	532	35.46	-	5	31	1								
R.J.Nicol	10	16	2	147*	664	47.42	1	6	8	-	51	7	162	4	40.50	-	-	2-2
B.J.Nielsen	6	10	1	42	110	12.22	-	-	-	-	153	63	341	4	85.25	-	-	2-8
I.E.O'Brien	8	10	4	14*	49	8.16	-	-	1	-	257	83	631	34	18.55	2	-	6-1
S.B.O'Connor	9	11	4	30	97	13.85	-	-	4	-	374.2	136	786	42	18.71	2	-	5-5
J.D.P.Oram	4	7	2	96	202	40.40	-	2	3	-	96.5	35	183	15	12.20	-	-	4-4
M.G.Orchard	7	11	2	54*	270	30.00	-	2	4	-	85	22	293	7	41.85	-	-	2-2
M.H.W.Papps	10	15	0	114	469	31.26	1	2	7	-	1	0	4	0	-	-	-	-
M.E.Parlane	8	13	1	80	303	25.25	-	1	-	-								
N.R.Parlane	10	17	2	75	474	31.60	-	4	17	-								
J.S.Patel	5	6	4	8	19	9.50	-	-	-	-	93	26	240	5	48.00	-	-	2-4
A.J.Penn	8	11	3	27*	117	14.62	-	-	3	-	233	72	523	29	18.03	1	-	6-3
C.R.Pryor	10	15	3	55*	251	20.91	-	1	3	-	325	70	1023	31	33.00	1	-	5-5
D.J.Reddington	1	1	1	0*	0	-	-	-	-	-	29	10	82	1	82.00	-	-	1-2
A.J.Redmond	5	8	1	59	184	26.28	-	1	1	-	147.3	33	480	13	36.92	-	-	3-6
M.H.Richardson	11	19	2	113	638	37.52	1	2	8	-	3	0	7	1	7.00	-	-	1-3
G.G.Robinson	2	3	1	125*	149	74.50	1	-	-	-								
J.D.Ryder	6	8	2	114*	365	60.83	1	1	3	-	11	1	35	1	35.00	-	-	1-5
I.P.Sandbrook	1	2	1	7	7	7.00	-	-	1	-								
A.M.Schwass	7	9	0	25	66	7.33	-	-	3	-	226	71	542	20	27.10	1	-	5-3
D.G.Sewell	1	2	1	7	10	10.00	-	-	1	-	26	5	57	0	-	-	-	-
G.S.Shaw	3	3	2	11*	18	18.00	-	-	1	-	74	10	263	11	23.90	1	-	5-7
H.J.Shaw	1	2	0	24	32	16.00	-	-	-	-	24	7	76	2	38.00	-	-	1-2
J.W.Sheed	10	16	2	34	164	11.71	-	-	8	-	2	0	9	0	-	-	-	-
M.A.Sigley	6	8	0	34	90	11.25	-	-	17	-								
M.S.Sinclair	4	7	0	79	238	34.00	-	3	5	-								
C.M.Spearman	10	17	1	117*	622	38.87	1	4	8	-								
G.R.Stead	10	15	0	111	472	31.46	1	4	4	-	14	2	33	1	33.00	-	-	1-3
S.L.Stewart	4	7	0	68	197	28.14	-	1	1	-	21	3	72	2	36.00	-	-	1-1
S.B.Styris	4	6	0	33	75	12.50	-	-	4	-	51	8	143	6	23.83	-	-	3-2
G.P.Sulzberger	11	18	6	111*	540	45.00	2	2	5	-	341.1	102	851	22	38.68	-	-	4-5
R.L.Taylor	5	5	1	56	102	25.50	-	1	3	-								
G.R.Todd	7	13	4	61*	264	29.33	-	2	3	-	42	8	193	2	96.50	-	-	1-2
D.R.Tuffey	4	4	1	13	33	11.00	-	-	3	-	106.3	34	240	17	14.11	-	-	4-1
A.D.Turner	2	3	1	7	10	5.00	-	-	-	-	69	19	207	2	103.50	-	-	2-5
D.L.Vettori	4	4	0	81	123	30.75	-	1	-	-	63	14	146	3	48.66	-	-	2-5
L.Vincent	4	7	1	40	92	15.33	-	-	3	-								
B.G.K.Walker	10	11	4	67*	167	23.85	-	1	8	-	157	32	547	12	45.58	-	-	4-7
M.D.J.Walker	10	15	0	62	370	24.66	-	3	10	-	402.3	135	810	45	18.00	2	-	6-1
K.P.Walmsley	7	8	2	21	78	13.00	-	-	4	-	308.2	84	777	37	21.00	1	-	6-7
G.L.West	4	4	2	31	35	17.50	-	-	-	-	108.2	23	383	12	31.91	-	-	4-5
A.M.Wilkinson	1	1	0	0	0	0.00	-	-	-	-	12	1	53	0	-	-	-	-
J.W.Wilson	5	4	0	66	85	21.25	-	1	2	-	119	20	402	3	134.00	-	-	2-4
P.J.Wiseman	10	15	2	91	354	27.23	-	2	2	-	346.2	90	937	19	49.31	-	-	4-1
W.A.Wisneski	5	5	0	29	48	9.60	-	-	5	-	177.3	35	558	19	29.36	2	-	5-6
L.J.Woodcock	6	10	0	80	292	29.20	-	3	1	-	107.2	34	233	4	58.25	-	-	1-1
R.A.Young	10	12	2	23*	80	8.00	-	-	35	-								
J.A.F.Yovich	10	15	5	53	298	29.80	-	2	1	-	270	61	816	24	34.00	2	-	5-4

LEADING AVERAGES

BATTING *(top 20, qualification six innings)*

	M	I	NO	HS	Runs	Ave	100s	50s
R.A. Lawson	4	6	1	146	326	65.20	1	1
J.D. Ryder	6	8	2	114*	365	60.83	1	1
T.G. McIntosh	10	17	3	157	820	58.57	2	5
M.N. Hart	9	14	4	201*	546	54.60	2	1
P.G. Fulton	8	13	1	301*	628	52.33	1	2
M.J. Horne	9	14	0	187	671	47.92	2	3
R.J. Nicol	10	16	2	147*	664	47.42	1	6
C.D. Cumming	10	18	2	128	751	46.93	3	3
R.A. Jones	10	20	4	128	726	45.37	2	3
G.P. Sulzberger	11	18	6	111*	540	45.00	2	2
J.M. How	10	18	2	163*	704	44.00	2	3
Mohammad Wasim	10	17	1	108	651	40.68	2	4
J.D.P. Oram	4	7	2	96	202	40.40	-	2
N.T. Broom	5	8	0	63	316	39.50	-	2
S.R. Tendulkar	3	6	1	52*	196	39.20	-	2
C.M. Spearman	10	17	1	117*	622	38.87	1	4
T.K. Canning	9	14	2	113	465	38.75	1	-
A.C. Barnes	7	11	1	107	380	38.00	1	1
M.H. Richardson	11	19	2	113	638	37.52	1	2
W.C. McSkimming	7	10	4	66*	220	36.66	-	1

BOWLING *(top 20, qualification 10 wickets)*

	Overs	Mdns	Runs	Wkts	Ave	5WI	10WM	Best
J.D.P. Oram	96.5	35	183	15	12.20	-	-	4-41
N.J. Astle	69.2	25	137	11	12.45	-	-	4-35
Z. Khan	54.2	12	151	11	13.72	2	-	5-29
D.R. Tuffey	106.3	34	240	17	14.11	-	-	4-12
M.D.J. Walker	402.3	135	810	45	18.00	2	-	6-114
A.J. Penn	233	72	523	29	18.03	1	-	6-33
I.E. O'Brien	257	83	631	34	18.55	2	-	6-103
S.B. O'Connor	374.2	136	786	42	18.71	2	-	5-55
M.J. Mason	352.2	120	787	40	19.67	2	1	6-56
K.P. Walmsley	308.2	84	777	37	21.00	1	-	6-74
S.E. Bond	120.4	29	384	18	21.33	-	-	4-33
T.K. Canning	410	133	1011	46	21.97	1	-	5-62
J.E.C. Franklin	183.2	35	523	22	23.77	1	-	6-40
I.G. Butler	194.1	44	597	25	23.88	1	-	5-44
G.S. Shaw	74	10	263	11	23.90	1	-	5-73
W.C. McSkimming	269.2	88	640	26	24.61	1	-	5-40
A.M. Schwass	226	71	542	20	27.10	1	-	5-38
B.E. Hefford	321	118	684	25	27.36	-	-	4-53
K.D. Mills	107.1	32	290	10	29.00	-	-	3-55
W.A. Wisneski	177.3	35	558	19	29.36	2	-	5-69

CENTURIES

There were 37 centuries in first-class cricket with 27 players reaching three figures this season. C.D. Cumming scored three while eight players scored two each. The fastest hundred of the season was scored by C.M. Spearman who took 77 balls to reach his century for Central Districts against Auckland at Blenheim.

†301*	P.G. Fulton	Canterbury v Auckland	Christchurch
201*	M.N. Hart	Northern Districts v Auckland	Auckland
187	M.J. Horne	Auckland v Canterbury	Christchurch
175*	G.J. Hopkins	Canterbury v Auckland	Auckland
†163*	J.M. How	Central Districts v Northern Districts	Hamilton
159	N.K.W. Horsley	Northern Districts v Central Districts	Hamilton
158	J.M. How	Central Districts v Canterbury	Napier
157	T.G. McIntosh	Auckland v Otago	Auckland
147*	R.J. Nicol	Auckland v Northern Districts	Gisborne
146*	T.G. McIntosh	Auckland v Northern Districts	Auckland
146	R.A. Lawson	Otago v Northern Districts	Dunedin
128	R.A. Jones	Wellington v Central Districts	Masterton
128	C.D. Cumming	Otago v Auckland	Queenstown
126	R.A. Jones	Wellington v Otago	Wellington
†125*	G.G. Robinson	Northern Districts v Auckland	Auckland
119	M.J. Horne	Auckland v Wellington	Wellington
117*	C.M. Spearman	Central Districts v Auckland	Blenheim
†114*	J.D. Ryder	Central Districts v Canterbury	Napier
114	M.D. Bell	Wellington v Canterbury	Rangiora
114	M.H.W. Papps	Canterbury v Central Districts	Timaru
114	C.D. Cumming	Otago v Wellington	Alexandra
†113	T.K. Canning	Auckland v Canterbury	Auckland
113	G.J. Hopkins	Canterbury v Auckland	Auckland
113	M.H. Richardson	Auckland v Northern Districts	Auckland
112	J.A.H. Marshall	Northern Districts v Wellington	Wellington
111*	G.P. Sulzberger	Central Districts v Auckland	Auckland
111	M.N. Hart	Northern Districts v Central Districts	Hamilton
111	G.R. Stead	Canterbury v Central Districts	Napier
108	C.B. Gaffaney	Otago v Wellington	Wellington
108	Mohammad Wasim	Otago v Canterbury	Christchurch
107*	G.P. Sulzberger	Central Districts v Canterbury	Napier
107	A.C. Barnes	Auckland v Central Districts	Auckland
105	B.B. McCullum	Otago v Northern Districts	Dunedin
104	Mohammad Wasim	Otago v Northern Districts	Dunedin
102	C.D. Cumming	Otago v Northern Districts	Hamilton
†100*	B.B.J. Griggs	Central Districts v India	Napier
†100	M.N. McKenzie	Otago v Canterbury	Christchurch

† *maiden first-class century*

CENTURY PARTNERSHIPS

There were 43 century partnerships in 2002/03.

FIRST WICKET
260	R.A. Lawson & Mohammad Wasim	Otago v Northern Districts	Dunedin
191	C.D. Cumming & Mohammad Wasim	Otago v Wellington	Alexandra
178	P.J. Ingram & J.M. How	Central Districts v Canterbury	Napier
147	C.B. Gaffaney & C.D. Cumming	Otago v Wellington	Wellington
141	C.D. Cumming & Mohammad Wasim	Otago v Wellington	Wellington
124	M.D. Bell & R.A. Jones	Wellington v Canterbury	Rangiora
118	M.H. Richardson & T.G. McIntosh	Auckland v Northern Districts	Auckland
106	P.J. Ingram & J.M. How	Central Districts v Otago	Invercargill
104	M.H. Richardson & T.G. McIntosh	Auckland v Northern Districts	Auckland
103	C.M. Spearman & J.M. How	Central Districts v Auckland	Auckland
102	C.D. Cumming & Mohammad Wasim	Otago v Canterbury	Christchurch

SECOND WICKET
141	N.K.W. Horsley & H.J.H. Marshall	Northern Districts v Central Districts	Hamilton
110	P.J. Ingram & M.S. Sinclair	Central Districts v Auckland	Blenheim

THIRD WICKET
165*	G.R. Todd & G.P. Sulzberger	Central Districts v Auckland	Auckland
161*	J.M. How & G.R. Todd	Central Districts v Northern Districts	Hamilton
131	H.J.H. Marshall & M.N. Hart	Northern Districts v Auckland	Auckland
121	M.S. Sinclair & G.P. Sulzberger	Central Districts v Otago	Wanganui
113	C.D. Cumming & R.A. Lawson	Otago v Auckland	Queenstown
112	R.M. Frew & P.G. Fulton	Canterbury v Auckland	Christchurch
109	T.G. McIntosh & R.J. Nicol	Auckland v Canterbury	Christchurch
109	M.H. Richardson & R.J. Nicol	Auckland v Northern Districts	Auckland
101	M.H.W. Papps & P.G. Fulton	Canterbury v Central Districts	Napier

FOURTH WICKET
131	M.J. Horne & T.K. Canning	Auckland v Canterbury	Christchurch
120	P.G. Fulton & N.T. Broom	Canterbury v Auckland	Christchurch
110	T.G. McIntosh & R.J. Nicol	Auckland v Northern Districts	Gisborne
106	M.N. Hart & M.G. Orchard	Northern Districts v Central Districts	Hamilton

FIFTH WICKET
235*	G.P. Sulzberger & J.D. Ryder	Central Districts v Canterbury	Napier
159	M.H.W. Papps & P.J. Wiseman	Canterbury v Otago	Dunedin
159	G.R. Stead & N.T. Broom	Canterbury v Central Districts	Napier
136	R.A. Jones & G.T. Donaldson	Wellington v Central Districts	Masterton
130	R.J. Nicol & K.D. Mills	Auckland v Central Districts	Blenheim
109	J.E.C. Franklin & G.T. Donaldson	Wellington v Otago	Wellington
109	P.G. Fulton & G.J. Hopkins	Canterbury v Auckland	Christchurch
104	J.D.P. Oram & J.M. How	Central Districts v Otago	Wanganui
104	M.G. Orchard & G.G. Robinson	Northern Districts v Auckland	Auckland
101	M.N. McKenzie & P.D. McGlashan	Otago v Canterbury	Christchurch

SIXTH WICKET
137	J.E.C. Franklin & C.J. Nevin	Wellington v Northern Districts	Wellington

SEVENTH WICKET
145	R.J. Nicol & T.K. Canning	Auckland v Canterbury	Auckland
142	G.J. Hopkins & P.J. Wiseman	Canterbury v Auckland	Auckland
120*	R.J. Nicol & C.R. Pryor	Auckland v Northern Districts	Gisborne
117	C.J. Nevin & M.D.J. Walker	Wellington v Central Districts	Wellington

NINTH WICKET
115	G.J. Hopkins & A.M. Ellis	Canterbury v Auckland	Auckland
103	C.L. Cairns & S.E. Bond	Canterbury v Otago	Dunedin

WICKETKEEPING DISMISSALS

The following New Zealand players who appeared in 2002/03 have made at least one dismissal in first-class cricket while keeping wicket.

	ct	*st*	*total*		*ct*	*st*	*total*
R.G.Hart *	256	15	271	B.B.McCullum	19	–	19
C.J.Nevin	169	6	175	M.S.Sinclair	10	1	11
M.A.Sigley *	124	4	128	M.D.Bell	4	–	4
G.J.Hopkins	103	11	114	L.J.Woodcock	3	–	3
R.A.Young *	110	2	112	N.M.Daley *	2	1	3
B.B.J.Griggs	46	–	46	C.D.Cumming	1	–	1
L.Vincent	25	–	25	M.H.W.Papps	–	1	1
P.D.McGlashan *	19	1	20	* *no further catches taken as fielder*			

NEW ZEALANDERS IN OVERSEAS CRICKET

Craig Spearman appeared for Gloucestershire in 2002. In 2003, Spearman, Ian Butler *(also Gloucestershire)*, Chris Cairns and Daniel Vettori *(Nottinghamshire)* and Stephen Fleming *(Yorkshire)* all played county cricket.

At the time of going to print we were not able to include the final figures for 2003 for Spearman, Cairns, Vettori and Fleming and their career records do not include any games from the 2003 season.

The figures for Spearman in 2002 and Butler (which are included in their career records) were:

	M	*I*	*NO*	*HS*	*Runs*	*Ave*	*100*	*50*	*ct*
I.G. Butler	4	5	0	13	20	4.00	–	–	–
C.M. Spearman	17	34	4	180*	1444	48.13	5	7	16

	O	*M*	*R*	*W*	*Ave*	*5WI*	*10WM*	*Best*
I.G. Butler	124	24	478	17	28.11	–	–	4-74

BOWLING PERFORMANCES

There were 24 instances of a bowler taking five wickets or more in an innings. Seventeen bowlers took five wickets in an innings with seven bowlers performing the feat twice. Once again, only one slow bowler, B.P. Martin, achieved the feat.

FIVE WICKETS IN AN INNINGS

6-33	A.J. Penn	Wellington v Central Districts	Masterton
6-40	J.E.C. Franklin	Wellington v Central Districts	Wellington
6-56	M.J. Mason	Central Districts v Canterbury	Timaru
6-74	K.P. Walmsley	Otago v Auckland	Queenstown
6-103	I.E. O'Brien	Wellington v Canterbury	Rangiora
6-114	M.D.J. Walker	Wellington v Otago	Alexandra
5-29	Z. Khan	India v New Zealand *(Second Test)*	Hamilton
5-31	M.D.J. Walker	Wellington v Auckland	Auckland
5-38	A.M. Schwass	Central Districts v Otago	Invercargill
5-40	W.C. McSkimming	Otago v Canterbury	Christchurch
5-42	I.E. O'Brien	Wellington v Central Districts	Wellington
5-44	I.G. Butler	Northern Districts v Central Districts	Napier
5-48	B.P. Martin	Northern Districts v Wellington	Taupo
5-49	J.A.F. Yovich	Northern Districts v Otago	Hamilton
5-53	Z. Khan	India v New Zealand *(First Test)*	Wellington
5-55	S.B. O'Connor	Otago v Canterbury	Christchurch
5-59	M.J. Mason	Central Districts v Canterbury	Timaru
5-59	C.R. Pryor	Auckland v Northern Districts	Auckland
5-62	T.K. Canning	Auckland v Wellington	Wellington
5-69	W.A. Wisneski	Canterbury v Auckland	Christchurch
5-73	G.S. Shaw	Auckland v Canterbury	Auckland
5-81	W.A. Wisneski	Canterbury v Wellington	Wellington
5-82	S.B. O'Connor	Otago v Wellington	Alexandra
5-117	J.A.F. Yovich	Northern Districts v Wellington	Wellington

TEN WICKETS IN A MATCH

11-115	M.J. Mason	Central Districts v Canterbury	Timaru

CAREER AVERAGES

as at 1 July 2003 for players active during the 2002/03 season

	M	In	NO	HS	Runs	Ave	100	50	Ct	St	Wkts	Runs	Ave	5WI	10WM	Best
A.R.Adams	23	37	1	72	785	21.80	-	6	8	-	89	2084	23.41	3	-	5-4
G.W.Aldridge	24	26	7	37	294	15.47	-	-	9	-	53	1660	31.32	1	-	5-5
T.R.Anderson	16	15	4	14	56	5.09	-	-	4	-	42	1520	36.19	1	-	6-3
S.L.Andrews	4	4	1	3	3	1.00	-	-	2	-	6	275	45.83	-	-	2-2
N.J.Astle	124	198	19	223	6944	38.79	16	32	104	-	118	3948	33.45	2	-	6-2
A.C.Barnes	61	95	6	107	2199	24.70	2	10	31	-	58	2041	35.18	-	-	4-6
M.D.Bell	101	176	12	219	5716	34.85	11	36	72	-	0	11	-	-	-	-
S.E.Bond	36	42	17	66*	434	17.36	-	2	15	-	124	3271	26.37	6	-	5-3
N.T.Broom	5	8	0	63	316	39.50	-	2	6	-	1	53	53.00	-	-	1-8
I.G.Butler	19	24	7	26	161	9.47	-	-	5	-	73	1948	26.68	1	-	5-4
C.L.Cairns	192	299	36	126	9352	35.55	11	62	71	-	599	16493	27.53	29	6	8-4
T.K.Canning	36	53	7	113	1222	26.56	1	4	21	-	136	2992	22.00	5	-	5-3
C.J.Cornelius	2	4	1	19*	34	11.33	-	-	-	-	3	134	44.66	-	-	3-6
C.D.Cumming	67	124	12	187	3961	35.36	8	18	30	-	18	864	48.00	-	-	3-3
N.M.Daley	1	1	0	4	4	4.00	-	-	2	1						
H.T.Davis	70	80	33	38*	538	11.44	-	-	25	-	212	6631	31.27	6	-	5-3
G.T.Donaldson	39	66	7	89	1442	24.44	-	10	29	-	3	137	45.66	-	-	2-1
B.P.Donkers	7	8	4	38	104	26.00	-	-	-	-	12	515	42.91	-	-	3-3
A.M.Ellis	4	6	3	24*	93	31.00	-	-	2	-	9	354	39.33	-	-	4-8
S.P.Fleming	157	260	24	274*	9947	42.14	20	61	206	-	0	129	-	-	-	-
J.E.C.Franklin	33	48	6	87	1009	24.02	-	4	9	-	92	2379	25.85	2	-	6-4
P.J.Franks	81	119	21	85	2163	22.07	-	11	32	-	265	7247	27.34	9	-	7-5
R.M.Frew	35	65	3	125	1809	29.17	3	10	22	-	0	4	-	-	-	-
P.G.Fulton	14	24	3	301*	954	45.42	1	4	11	-	11	362	32.90	-	-	4-4
C.B.Gaffaney	66	122	10	194	3629	32.40	6	19	61	-	2	47	23.50	-	-	1-3
M.R.Gillespie	13	16	4	81*	305	25.41	-	1	2	-	39	929	23.82	2	-	5-5
B.B.J.Griggs	21	31	4	100*	660	24.44	1	1	51	-						
L.J.Hamilton	35	49	19	23	182	6.06	-	-	10	-	135	3233	23.94	6	-	6-3
C.Z.Harris	101	158	34	251*	5637	45.45	11	31	76	-	105	4357	41.49	-	-	4-2
M.N.Hart	122	176	23	201*	3913	25.57	3	19	103	-	208	7284	35.01	7	-	6-7
R.G.Hart	96	139	24	127*	2649	23.03	2	11	256	15						
B.E.Hefford	23	28	8	26	186	9.30	-	-	8	-	69	1617	23.43	1	-	5-5
G.J.Hopkins	51	84	13	175*	2014	28.36	4	4	106	11	0	13	-	-	-	-
A.J.Hore	24	41	2	102	932	23.89	2	5	23	-	1	119	119.00	-	-	1-7
M.J.Horne	103	179	9	241	7143	42.01	22	25	69	-	5	455	91.00	-	-	2-58
N.K.W.Horsley	19	29	1	159	992	35.42	2	5	10	-	0	1	-	-	-	-
J.M.How	16	29	2	163*	820	30.37	2	3	19	-	3	156	52.00	-	-	3-7
L.G.Howell	79	135	16	181	3460	29.07	3	20	45	-	0	110	-	-	-	-
P.J.Ingram	15	29	3	84	600	23.07	-	4	11	-						
G.D.Irwin	1	2	0	4	6	3.00	-	-	2	-	0	63	-	-	-	-
M.R.Jefferson	46	65	11	114	1342	24.85	2	5	13	-	89	3373	37.89	1	-	5-4
R.A.Jones	64	115	7	188	3565	33.00	7	19	55	-	1	0	0.00	-	-	1-0
D.P.Kelly	29	54	2	212*	1443	27.75	3	5	18	-	2	239	119.50	-	-	1-4
R.T.King	41	74	2	130*	1775	24.65	3	7	29	-	0	70	-	-	-	-
R.A.Lawson	64	120	5	200	2866	24.92	3	12	23	-	1	18	18.00	-	-	1-13
G.R.Loveridge	29	43	3	126	935	23.37	1	2	16	-	46	2449	53.23	1	-	5-59
R.K.Lynch	2	4	0	20	40	10.00	-	-	1	-						
H.J.H.Marshall	42	69	4	92	1619	24.90	-	6	24	-	1	101	101.00	-	-	1-28
J.A.H.Marshall	55	96	2	235	2650	28.19	4	14	67	-	3	152	50.66	-	-	1-5
B.P.Martin	36	45	15	51	592	19.73	-	1	20	-	92	2821	30.66	7	2	7-33
C.S.Martin	52	63	22	25	148	3.60	-	-	14	-	138	4817	34.90	2	-	5-44
M.J.Mason	38	50	14	44	575	15.97	-	-	10	-	128	3041	23.75	5	1	6-56
B.B.McCullum	17	32	1	142	896	28.90	2	4	28	-						
P.D.McGlashan	12	18	3	65	298	19.86	-	1	20	1						
T.G.McIntosh	35	58	6	182	2058	39.57	6	10	21	-	0	38	-	-	-	-
A.J.McKay	2	1	0	8	8	8.00	-	-	1	-	2	161	80.50	-	-	1-21
M.N.McKenzie	20	35	1	100	618	18.17	1	2	13	-						
C.D.McMillan	98	161	16	168*	5869	40.47	11	34	45	-	71	2493	35.11	1	-	6-71
J.M.McMillan	11	13	4	19	47	5.22	-	-	-	-	21	860	40.95	-	-	4-56
W.C.McSkimming	18	26	7	66*	350	18.42	-	1	9	-	65	1580	24.30	2	-	6-39
R.M.Miller	1	2	0	9	6	6.00	-	-	-	-						
K.D.Mills	26	38	13	117*	1176	33.60	1	9	8	-	62	1969	31.75	-	-	4-57
Mohammad Wasim	108	171	7	192	5275	32.16	14	22	115	5	4	234	58.50	-	-	2-12

	M	In	NO	HS	Runs	Ave	100	50	Ct	St	Wkts	Runs	Ave	5WI	10WM	Best
L.J.Morgan	4	6	0	30	117	19.50	-	-	1	-						
N.D.Morland	26	41	10	32	459	14.80	-	-	24	-	39	1523	39.05	-		4-26
C.J.Nevin	57	89	13	113	2474	32.55	1	13	172	6	0	0	-	-	-	-
R.J.Nicol	20	29	4	147*	1153	46.12	3	7	12	-	11	410	37.27	-	-	2-26
B.J.Nielsen	7	12	2	42	135	13.50	-	-	-	-	6	378	63.00	-	-	2-37
I.E.O'Brien	20	22	7	18	99	6.60	-	-	2	-	84	1614	19.21	5	-	6-55
S.B.O'Connor	73	94	31	47	792	12.57	-	-	27	-	278	6582	23.67	16	2	6-31
J.D.P.Oram	36	56	6	155	1561	31.22	1	10	20	-	59	1238	20.98	1	-	5-30
M.G.Orchard	8	12	2	54*	274	27.40	-	2	7	-	7	340	48.57	-	-	2-25
M.H.W.Papps	39	71	8	158*	2127	33.76	3	11	30	1	0	4	-	-		-
M.E.Parlane	78	130	6	190	3657	29.49	7	14	44	-	1	17	17.00	-	-	1-14
N.R.Parlane	25	43	4	147	1155	29.61	1	8	26	-	0	21	-	-	-	-
J.S.Patel	30	32	14	58*	278	15.44	-	1	8	-	53	2274	42.90	2	-	5-48
A.J.Penn	63	86	22	90	1183	18.48	-	6	14	-	239	5491	22.97	11	2	8-21
C.R.Pryor	33	50	9	61	942	22.97	-	3	20	-	92	2788	30.30	3	-	5-28
D.J.Reddington	1	1	1	0*	0	-	-	-	-	-	1	82	82.00	-	-	1-27
A.J.Redmond	32	55	4	101	1299	25.47	1	6	22	-	51	2160	42.35	-	-	4-35
M.H.Richardson	128	219	29	306	8304	43.70	17	41	75	-	42	1868	44.47	1	-	5-77
G.G.Robinson	5	7	1	125*	228	38.00	1	-	-	-	0	16	-	-	-	-
J.D.Ryder	6	8	2	114*	365	60.83	1	1	3	-	1	35	35.00	-	-	1-5
I.P.Sandbrook	1	2	1	7	7	7.00	-	-	1	-						
A.M.Schwass	21	26	1	44	342	13.68	-	-	6	-	88	1742	19.79	6	-	7-36
D.G.Sewell	55	73	35	24	237	6.23	-	-	14	-	182	5020	27.58	9	1	8-31
G.S.Shaw	8	8	5	11*	23	7.66	-	-	2	-	32	738	23.06	1	-	5-73
H.J.Shaw	8	11	3	24	91	11.37	-	-	2	-	16	659	41.18	1	-	5-84
J.W.Sheed	13	22	3	64	304	16.00	-	2	8	-	1	56	56.00	-	-	1-30
M.A.Sigley	44	60	9	74*	832	16.31	-	3	124	4						
M.S.Sinclair	86	149	19	214	5881	45.23	12	29	88	1	0	109		-	-	-
C.M.Spearman	112	202	13	180*	6955	36.79	15	35	107	-	1	55	55.00	-	-	1-37
G.R.Stead	78	127	9	130	3982	33.74	8	21	34	-	7	562	80.28	-	-	4-58
S.L.Stewart	13	24	0	68	651	27.12	-	5	3	-	2	166	83.00	-	-	1-12
S.B.Styris	54	90	13	212*	2392	31.06	3	12	39	-	127	3401	26.77	6	-	6-32
G.P.Sulzberger	66	107	11	159	3309	34.46	8	15	52	-	108	3844	35.59	1	-	5-55
R.L.Taylor	5	5	1	56	102	25.50	-	1	3	-						
G.R.Todd	10	18	5	61*	289	22.23	-	2	4	-	6	281	46.83	-	-	2-34
D.R.Tuffey	53	62	13	89*	650	13.26	-	3	23	-	186	4581	24.62	8	1	7-12
A.D.Turner	6	5	1	7	17	4.25	-	-	-	-	11	443	40.27	1	-	5-66
D.L.Vettori	78	108	16	112	1817	19.75	1	9	36	-	257	7855	30.56	16	1	7-87
L.Vincent	40	67	3	159	1868	29.18	2	15	67	-	2	184	92.00	-	-	2-37
B.G.K.Walker	66	86	19	107*	1417	21.14	1	4	28	-	134	4329	32.30	3	-	8-107
M.D.J.Walker	42	61	6	100*	1488	27.05	1	9	33	-	89	1983	22.28	3	-	6-114
K.P.Walmsley	47	58	13	59	462	10.26	-	1	14	-	169	4182	24.74	5	-	6-49
G.L.West	9	11	4	31	56	8.00	-	-	3	-	26	790	30.38	-	-	4-58
A.M.Wilkinson	1	1	0	0	0	0.00	-	-	-	-	0	53		-	-	-
J.W.Wilson	31	53	5	78	1065	22.18	-	6	25	-	96	2478	25.81	5	-	5-34
P.J.Wiseman	112	154	30	91	2119	17.08	-	7	57	-	312	10279	32.94	13	2	8-66
W.A.Wisneski	64	85	10	89*	1624	21.65	-	9	45	-	219	5890	26.89	10	-	7-151
L.J.Woodcock	11	20	1	80	461	24.26	-	3	7	-	10	327	32.70	-	-	4-3
R.A.Young	34	39	6	101*	442	13.39	1	1	110	2						
J.A.F.Yovich	49	72	15	99	1373	24.08	-	7	14	-	136	4195	30.84	6	1	7-64

STATE SHIELD

2002/03

The 2002/03 State Shield was the closest fought competition in the history of New Zealand limited-over cricket. Northern Districts were the victors in the final, defeating top qualifier Auckland. Going into the last round all six sides had a chance of finishing in the top three places while any of the six could also have missed out altogether. All sides featured in the top two at some stage such was the closeness of the competition.

In the end Canterbury, Central Districts and Otago were the sides who failed to progress. Central were badly affected by inclement weather, having three games ending in no results. In two of these they were well placed to record wins. Wellington were well beaten in the semi-final which meant Auckland hosted Northern Districts in the final. It was Northern's first one-day title win since 1997/98.

The format was the same as had been used in 2001/02. The international players were available for five rounds although the semi-final and final were played after the Black Caps had left for the World Cup.

Four players scored over 300 runs, with Craig Spearman being the leading scorer with 350 runs. Llorne Howell, who became the leading run scorer in domestic one-day games during the season, got 345, Chris Nevin totalled 312 and Matthew Hart 301.

Joseph Yovich was the leading wicket taker with 23 followed by Matthew Walker with 18, while Michael Mason, Shayne O'Connor and Ash Turner all got 16 wickets.

Only three centuries were scored – Craig McMillan 122 not out, Michael Parlane 122 and Nevin 100. Three bowlers captured five wickets in an innings – Turner 5-12, Hayden Shaw 5-14 and Matthew Walker 5-22.

Final points were:

	P	*W*	*L*	*NR*	*Bonus*	*Points*
Auckland	10	6	3	1	1	27
Wellington	10	5	4	1	3	25
Northern Districts	10	5	5	–	3	23
Canterbury	10	4	5	1	3	21
Central Districts	10	3	4	3	2	20
Otago	10	3	5	2	2	18

First Round

Nicol and Nielsen *(Auckland)*, Ryder and Sandbrook *(Central)* and Mohammad Wasim *(Otago)* made their debuts. Horsley and West made their Northern debuts, McKenzie and McGlashan made their debuts for Otago and Parlane made his debut for Wellington.

After being 81-5, Northern recovered with a match winning stand of 112 between Matthew Hart and Yovich with Yovich reaching his highest score. Adams (proving his fitness for the New Zealand selectors) was the pick of the Auckland bowlers. Auckland lost wickets at regular intervals and were dismissed with 6.3 overs left. Captain Walker's unbeaten 33 was his highest score.

Central Districts lost both openers within three overs and looked shaky at 85-5 before Griggs and Sandbrook added 103 off 127 balls. Canterbury, too, were in early trouble at 58-6 and despite two good stands for the eighth and ninth wickets fell short by 19 runs. Fulton, Cunis and Martin all had their highest scores.

Wellington had a good start after being put in to bat with the openers putting on 79 off 124 balls. Bell got his fifty from 107 deliveries. Four quick wickets meant Wellington were restricted to 233-8. Wasim got his 50 off 75 balls to give Otago a good show and when McGlashan went 22 were needed off 26 balls. Good bowling from Walker and Turner gave Wellington an unlikely two run win.

AUCKLAND v NORTHERN DISTRICTS   State Shield

at Eden Park Outer Oval, Auckland on 28 December, 2002
Toss : Northern Districts. Umpires : A.L. Hill & W.R. Knights
Northern Districts won by 60 runs. Points: Northern Districts 5, Auckland 0

NORTHERN DISTRICTS

	Runs	Mins	Balls	6s	4s
J.A.H.Marshall b Adams	13	40	29	-	1
M.E.Parlane c Young b Morgan	13	20	17	-	3
N.K.W.Horsley c Young b Nielsen	28	72	63	-	3
S.B.Styris lbw b Adams	0	3	4	-	-
M.N.Hart c Nicol b Adams	62	153	81	-	6
H.J.H.Marshall lbw b Canning	5	10	9	-	1
J.A.F.Yovich b Adams	70	143	90	3	7
R.G.Hart*† not out	8	14	8	-	1
B.P.Martin not out	4	4	3	-	-
G.L.West					
G.W.Aldridge					

Extras (lb 2, w 9, nb 4) 15
TOTAL (50 overs) (7 wkts) .. **218** 213

AUCKLAND

	Runs	Mins	Balls	6s	4s
M.J.Horne c Marshall J.A.H. b Yovich	19	20	16	-	4
M.H.Richardson c Hart R.G. b Aldridge	18	43	22	-	3
L.G.Howell c Marshall J.A.H. b Yovich	4	9	6	-	1
R.J.Nicol c Marshall J.A.H. b Hart M.N.	33	96	59	-	2
T.K.Canning run out	1	11	11	-	-
C.R.Pryor c & b Hart M.N.	4	39	35	-	-
B.G.K.Walker* not out	33	86	80	-	4
A.R.Adams b Aldridge	2	7	7	-	-
R.A.Young† b Martin	11	24	13	-	1
R.G.Morgan run out	13	15	14	1	-
B.J.Nielsen lbw b Aldridge	2	5	7	-	-

Extras (lb 4, w 5, nb 9) 18
TOTAL (43.5 overs) **158** 182

Bowling	O	M	R	W
AUCKLAND				
Adams	10	1	37	4
Morgan	9	0	38	1
Canning	9	1	25	1
Nielsen	6	0	33	1
Walker	8	2	22	0
Pryor	5	0	39	0
Nicol	3	0	22	0
NORTHERN DISTRICTS				
Yovich	6	0	35	2
West	6	2	17	0
Aldridge	9.5	0	38	3
Hart M.N.	10	0	30	2
Styris	9	3	17	0
Martin	3	0	17	1

Fall of Wickets		
	ND	A
1st	21	30
2nd	36	43
3rd	36	52
4th	74	55
5th	81	77
6th	193	93
7th	204	101
8th	-	132
9th	-	152
10th	-	158

CENTRAL DISTRICTS v CANTERBURY State Shield

at Trafalgar Park, Nelson on 28 December, 2002
Toss : Central Districts. Umpires : M.P. George & E.A. Watkin
Central Districts won by 19 runs. Points: Central Districts 4, Canterbury 0

CENTRAL DISTRICTS	Runs	Mins	Balls	6s	4s
C.M.Spearman* c Wiseman b Cunis	1	8	4	-	-
J.D.Ryder c Papps b Martin	5	13	11	-	1
P.J.Ingram c Papps b Burson	15	59	42	-	1
G.P.Sulzberger c Stewart b Burson	29	86	62	-	3
I.P.Sandbrook c Cornelius b Burson	57	120	104	1	5
G.R.Loveridge c Papps b Anderson	3	11	11	-	-
B.B.J.Griggs† lbw b Cunis	59	71	61	-	7
C.J.M.Furlong not out	8	10	7	-	1
A.M.Schwass b Cunis	4	1	3	-	1
M.J.Mason not out	1	2	2	-	-
B.E.Hefford					
Extras (lb 14, w 5, nb 7)	26				
TOTAL (50 overs) (8 wkts)	**208**	195			

CANTERBURY	Runs	Mins	Balls	6s	4s
M.H.W.Papps† c Griggs b Hefford	10	25	21	-	-
P.J.Wiseman lbw b Schwass	0	3	2	-	-
S.L.Stewart c Schwass b Hefford	17	37	39	-	3
G.R.Stead* b Furlong	21	49	39	-	2
C.Z.Harris c Griggs b Mason	0	9	8	-	-
P.G.Fulton c Hefford b Schwass	64	103	87	1	6
C.J.Cornelius run out	0	9	11	-	-
C.J.Anderson c Spearman b Mason	16	44	40	-	1
S.J.Cunis c Sandbrook b Schwass	33	41	31	1	2
R.D.Burson not out	13	17	15	-	-
C.S.Martin not out	5	9	8	-	-
Extras (lb 4, w 5, nb 1)	10				
TOTAL (50 overs) (9 wkts)	**189**	182			

Bowling CANTERBURY	O	M	R	W
Martin	8	1	30	1
Cunis	10	0	32	3
Burson	9	2	34	3
Cornelius	7	1	30	0
Anderson	10	2	34	1
Harris	6	0	34	0
CENTRAL DISTRICTS				
Schwass	10	1	31	3
Mason	10	2	14	2
Hefford	8	0	49	2
Furlong	10	3	20	1
Sulzberger	10	0	56	0
Ryder	2	0	15	0

Fall of Wickets	CD	C
1st	4	1
2nd	9	13
3rd	54	33
4th	78	36
5th	85	56
6th	188	58
7th	200	113
8th	204	169
9th	-	176
10th	-	-

OTAGO v WELLINGTON State Shield

at Molyneux Park, Alexandra on 28 December, 2002
Toss : Otago. Umpires : G.A. Baxter & D.M. Quested
Wellington won by 2 runs. Points: Wellington 4, Otago 0

WELLINGTON	Runs	Mins	Balls	6s	4s
C.J.Nevin† c Wilson b McSkimming	42	79	59	-	6
M.D.Bell* b Walmsley	57	155	116	-	5
R.A.Jones c O'Connor b Wilson	39	65	52	-	5
N.R.Parlane c Hore b McSkimming	19	25	19	-	1
G.T.Donaldson b McMillan	15	28	23	-	1
M.D.J.Walker not out	37	31	22	-	4
M.R.Jefferson run out	1	6	4	-	-
M.Y.Pasupati c Walmsley b O'Connor	2	5	4	-	-
A.J.Penn c Cumming b McMillan	2	3	3	-	-
J.E.C.Franklin not out	0	1	0	-	-
A.D.Turner					
Extras (lb 9, w 8, nb 2)	19				
TOTAL (50 overs) (8 wkts)	**233**	203			

OTAGO	Runs	Mins	Balls	6s	4s
A.J.Hore lbw b Turner	15	16	11	1	2
Mohammad Wasim lbw b Franklin	70	137	94	-	8
C.D.Cumming* c Walker b Turner	33	77	53	1	3
R.A.Lawson c Nevin b Walker	10	30	30	-	-
M.N.McKenzie not out	41	93	65	-	2
P.D.McGlashan† lbw b Jefferson	36	61	44	-	3
W.C.McSkimming not out	8	19	15	-	-
J.W.Wilson					
J.M.McMillan					
K.P.Walmsley					
S.B.O'Connor					
Extras (lb 2, w 4, nb 12)	18				
TOTAL (50 overs) (5 wkts)	**231**	219			

Bowling OTAGO	O	M	R	W
O'Connor	10	0	54	1
Walmsley	10	1	42	1
McMillan	10	0	51	2
McSkimming	10	0	45	2
Wilson	10	2	32	1
WELLINGTON				
Franklin	9	0	48	1
Turner	9	0	35	2
Pasupati	7	1	32	0
Penn	9	1	45	0
Walker	10	0	45	1
Jefferson	6	0	24	1

Fall of Wickets	W	O
1st	79	22
2nd	150	105
3rd	163	133
4th	179	146
5th	202	212
6th	212	-
7th	223	-
8th	229	-
9th	-	-
10th	-	-

Second Round

Wellington were always struggling after being 16-4. Contributions from the middle order got them to 185-9. Pasupati reached his highest score while Mason reached 50 wickets. Spearman and Ryder blasted the Wellington attack with a 100 run partnership requiring just 76 balls. Spearman reached 50 off 38 balls and Ryder needed just 45 for his maiden half century. Once the stand was broken Central struggled losing wickets but won with 16.2 overs to spare. Jefferson's wicket gave him 50 one-day scalps.

A good all round innings, with seven of the nine batsmen getting double figures, saw Auckland reach 246-7. Nicol had his highest score and Barnes required 50 balls for 50 runs. Otago ensured it did not lose this game as they reached 100 off 89 balls and 200 from 190 deliveries. Wasim needed 43 balls, Cumming (highest score) 53 and Lawson 69 for their half centuries. Adams reached 50 wickets as Otago won with 11.2 overs left.

Canterbury's innings was based around an opening stand of 59 and 60 for the fourth wicket. Apart from this they disappointed and only reached 186-7. Northern also struggled and they were indebted to Styris and Robbie Hart for a 76 run stand off 97 balls. Hart reached 1000 runs and Martin got to 50 wickets as Northern won off the penultimate ball.

WELLINGTON v CENTRAL DISTRICTS   State Shield

at Basin Reserve, Wellington on 30 December, 2002
Toss : Wellington. Umpires : R.D. Anderson & E.A. Watkin
Central Districts won by 3 wickets. Points: Central Districts 5, Wellington 0

WELLINGTON

	Runs	Mins	Balls	6s	4s
C.J.Nevin† c Furlong b Mason	2	21	11	-	-
M.D.Bell* c Griggs b Schwass	0	4	5	-	-
S.P.Fleming c Hamilton b Mason	5	48	35	-	-
R.A.Jones b Furlong	40	75	70	-	5
J.E.C.Franklin c Furlong b Mason	0	1	1	-	-
G.T.Donaldson st Griggs b Sulzberger	22	97	60	-	-
M.D.J.Walker lbw b Furlong	27	51	51	-	3
M.R.Jefferson run out	15	30	18	-	1
M.Y.Pasupati not out	34	50	35	1	2
A.J.Penn b Schwass	15	12	10	2	-
A.D.Turner not out	6	10	7	-	-
Extras (b 1, lb 9, w 6, nb 3)	19				
TOTAL (50 overs) (9 wkts)	**185**	204			

CENTRAL DISTRICTS

	Runs	Mins	Balls	6s	4s
C.M.Spearman* c Bell b Penn	74	98	64	2	10
J.D.Ryder b Turner	51	62	48	-	11
P.J.Ingram lbw b Turner	0	1	3	-	-
G.P.Sulzberger run out	5	22	13	-	-
I.P.Sandbrook lbw b Jefferson	13	26	17	-	2
G.R.Loveridge c Bell b Penn	13	19	12	-	3
C.J.M.Furlong not out	12	31	22	-	2
B.B.J.Griggs† lbw b Turner	1	8	7	-	-
A.M.Schwass not out	2	18	17	-	-
M.J.Mason					
L.J.Hamilton					
Extras (lb 8, w 8, nb 1)	17				
TOTAL (33.4 overs) (7 wkts)	**188**	146			

Bowling	O	M	R	W
CENTRAL DISTRICTS				
Schwass	10	2	32	2
Mason	10	2	22	3
Hamilton	10	1	30	0
Ryder	4	0	22	0
Furlong	10	1	43	2
Sulzberger	6	1	26	1
WELLINGTON				
Turner	10	2	51	3
Franklin	8	0	40	0
Walker	5.4	1	25	0
Penn	4	0	32	2
Pasupati	3	0	13	0
Jefferson	3	0	19	1

Fall of Wickets		
	W	CD
1st	2	110
2nd	6	110
3rd	16	131
4th	16	145
5th	56	170
6th	105	171
7th	107	178
8th	134	-
9th	156	-
10th	-	-

OTASO v AUCKLAND

OTAGO v AUCKLAND — **State Shield**

at Molyneux Park, Alexandra on 30 December, 2002
Toss : Auckland. Umpires : G.A. Baxter & D.M. Quested
Otago won by 7 wickets. *Points: Otago 5, Auckland 0*

AUCKLAND

	Runs	Mins	Balls	6s	4s
M.J.Horne c & b O'Connor 22	22	35	33	-	3
M.H.Richardson c McGlashan b McSkimming 30	30	94	55	-	3
L.G.Howell c McGlashan b Wilson 23	23	74	55	-	-
R.J.Nicol c McGlashan b Wilson 41	41	84	66	-	4
A.C.Barnes lbw b Wilson 50	50	71	51	1	5
T.K.Canning c Cumming b O'Connor 7	7	6	5	-	1
A.R.Adams c Wilson b Walmsley 24	24	25	13	2	1
C.R.Pryor not out 30	30	25	20	1	2
R.G.Morgan not out 1	1	3	2	-	-
R.A.Young†					
B.G.K.Walker*					
Extras (lb 12, w 6) 18					
TOTAL (50 overs) (7 wkts) .. 246		212			

OTAGO

	Runs	Mins	Balls	6s	4s
A.J.Hore c Young b Adams 32	32	42	32	2	3
Mohammad Wasim c Young b Morgan 51	51	58	47	1	7
C.D.Cumming* c Nicol b Morgan 75	75	107	74	-	12
R.A.Lawson not out 63	63	103	74	-	7
W.C.McSkimming not out 4	4	11	9	-	-
P.D.McGlashan†					
M.N.McKenzie					
J.W.Wilson					
N.D.Morland					
K.P.Walmsley					
S.B.O'Connor					
Extras (lb 9, w 11, nb 4) 24					
TOTAL (38.4 overs) (3 wkts) 249		162			

Bowling	O	M	R	W
OTAGO				
O'Connor	10	1	61	2
Walmsley	10	1	40	1
McSkimming	10	1	39	1
Wilson	10	1	42	3
Morland	10	0	52	0
AUCKLAND				
Morgan	7	0	29	2
Adams	6	1	28	1
Canning	7	0	56	0
Horne	5	0	25	0
Pryor	5.4	0	45	0
Walker	5	0	35	0
Barnes	2	0	18	0
Nicol	1	0	4	0

Fall of Wickets	A	O
1st	34	80
2nd	79	98
3rd	96	228
4th	179	-
5th	184	-
6th	186	-
7th	241	-
8th	-	-
9th	-	-
10th	-	-

NORTHERN DISTRICTS v CANTERBURY — **State Shield**

at Owen Delany Park, Taupo on 30 December, 2002
Toss : Canterbury. Umpires : B.G. Frost & M.P. George
Northern Districts won by 2 wickets. *Points: Northern Districts 4, Canterbury 0*

CANTERBURY

	Runs	Mins	Balls	6s	4s
M.H.W.Papps† c & b Styris 24	24	88	63	-	3
S.L.Stewart c Hart M.N. b Yovich 29	29	63	47	-	5
C.D.McMillan lbw b Yovich 2	2	28	16	-	-
G.R.Stead* c Marshall H.J.H. b Martin 33	33	62	45	-	4
C.Z.Harris c Yovich b Styris 45	45	102	75	-	3
P.G.Fulton b Hart M.N. 7	7	18	23	-	-
P.J.Wiseman c Marshall J.A.H. b Yovich 22	22	28	28	2	-
S.J.Cunis not out 1	1	7	1	-	-
C.J.Anderson not out 2	2	3	4	-	-
R.D.Burson					
C.S.Martin					
Extras (lb 6, w 23, nb 2) 31					
TOTAL (50 overs) (7 wkts) .. 196		203			

NORTHERN DISTRICTS

	Runs	Mins	Balls	6s	4s
J.A.H.Marshall c Papps b Cunis 12	12	38	29	-	1
M.E.Parlane c Papps b Martin 9	9	19	16	-	1
N.K.W.Horsley c & b Cunis 19	19	69	50	-	1
S.B.Styris not out 91	91	167	105	4	4
H.J.H.Marshall c & b Harris 0	0	11	12	-	-
M.N.Hart st Papps b Wiseman .. 19	19	24	24	1	2
J.A.F.Yovich c & b Harris 4	4	5	5	-	1
R.G.Hart*† c Papps b Martin 34	34	65	55	-	2
B.P.Martin b Martin 0	0	2	2	-	-
G.W.Aldridge not out 1	1	4	2	-	-
G.L.West					
Extras (b 1, lb 2, w 3, nb 2) 8					
TOTAL (49.5 overs) (8 wkts) 197		206			

Bowling	O	M	R	W
NORTHERN DISTRICTS				
Yovich	8	0	39	3
West	8	2	30	0
Aldridge	8	1	23	0
Styris	8	1	32	2
Hart M.N.	10	0	34	1
Martin	8	0	32	1
CANTERBURY				
Martin	10	0	35	3
Cunis	9.5	0	36	2
Burson	8	0	38	0
Anderson	5	0	23	0
Harris	10	1	29	2
Wiseman	7	0	33	1

Fall of Wickets	C	ND
1st	59	15
2nd	78	25
3rd	78	74
4th	138	77
5th	153	102
6th	186	107
7th	193	183
8th	-	183
9th	-	-
10th	-	-

Third Round

Papps (50 off 100 balls) was the Canterbury anchor. Cornelius (highest score) and Anderson added 47 precious runs off 40 balls to enable Canterbury to reach 197-8. After Richardson went early, Howell and Horne put on 68 off 77 balls. Howell reached 50 from 60 balls but Auckland went from 91-1 to 104-5 before Barnes (50 off 60 balls) and Pryor put on 85 from 115 balls to enable Auckland to win with 7 balls to spare.

A 93 run stand for the eighth wicket between Morland (maiden 50 off 60 balls) and McSkimming got Otago to 243. Spearman and Ryder proceeded to set a new record for Central's first wicket. They put on 154 off just 106 balls. Spearman annihilated the attack reaching 50 from a mere 28 balls while Ryder was comparatively pedestrian getting his from 41 balls. However, there was a sensational collapse. Central went from 172-1 to 233 all out losing nine wickets in 20 overs to eventuallly lose by 10 runs with 7.4 overs left.

Wellington's 211-7 was centred around a stand of 125 off 148 by Donaldson and Walker. Donaldson got fifty from 73 balls while Walker got his from 68 balls. It was his highest one-day score. Northern lost two early wickets and never recovered. Only Matthew Hart (50 off 65 balls) was able to offer any resistance. Gillespie had his best bowling figures as Wellington won easily.

AUCKLAND v CANTERBURY   State Shield

at Eden Park, Auckland on 2 January, 2003
Toss : Canterbury. Umpires : B.F. Bowden & I.W. Shine
Auckland won by 3 wickets. Points: Auckland 4, Canterbury 0

CANTERBURY

	Runs	Mins	Balls	6s	4s
M.H.W.Papps† c Vincent b Barnes	57	159	117	-	4
P.J.Wiseman c Nicol b Shaw	2	17	9	-	-
S.L.Stewart c Pryor b Walker	9	46	25	-	1
G.R.Stead* run out	6	22	26	-	-
C.Z.Harris st Vincent b Barnes	33	63	60	-	2
P.G.Fulton c Nicol b Shaw	10	14	9	-	2
J.I.Englefield run out	3	10	7	-	-
C.J.Cornelius not out	31	34	21	2	1
C.J.Anderson b Barnes	16	25	23	-	1
S.J.Cunis not out	5	4	4	-	1
C.S.Martin					
Extras (lb 10, w 14, nb 1)	25				
TOTAL (50 overs) (8 wkts)	197	201			

AUCKLAND

	Runs	Mins	Balls	6s	4s
M.H.Richardson c Stead b Cunis	7	32	26	-	1
L.G.Howell b Anderson	51	82	63	1	8
M.J.Horne c Harris b Anderson	34	68	49	-	5
L.Vincent† c & b Harris	0	8	6	-	-
R.J.Nicol b Cornelius	5	14	16	-	1
A.C.Barnes c Stewart b Martin	56	82	66	-	7
C.R.Pryor not out	21	88	56	-	-
T.K.Canning c Martin b Cunis	7	8	9	1	-
A.R.Adams not out	4	1	1	-	1
B.G.K.Walker*					
G.S.Shaw					
Extras (lb 10, w 6)	16				
TOTAL (48.5 overs) (7 wkts)	201	195			

Bowling	O	M	R	W
AUCKLAND				
Shaw	9	0	39	2
Adams	10	0	42	0
Canning	10	0	27	0
Walker	10	1	26	1
Nicol	3	0	11	0
Barnes	8	0	42	3
CANTERBURY				
Martin	10	0	42	1
Cunis	9.5	2	41	2
Cornelius	9	1	44	1
Harris	10	2	25	1
Anderson	10	1	39	2

Fall of Wickets	C	A
1st	9	23
2nd	60	91
3rd	71	98
4th	126	104
5th	129	104
6th	141	189
7th	141	197
8th	190	-
9th	-	-
10th	-	-

CENTRAL DISTRICTS v OTAGO

State Shield

at Pukekura Park, New Plymouth on 2 January, 2003
Toss : Central Districts. Umpires : B.G. Frost & E.A. Watkin
Otago won by 10 runs. *Points: Otago 4, Central Districts 0*

OTAGO

	Runs	Mins	Balls	6s	4s
A.J.Hore lbw b Schwass	12	18	14	1	1
Mohammad Wasim c Griggs					
b Hamilton	46	59	45	1	6
C.D.Cumming* c Mason b Furlong	10	20	16	-	1
R.A.Lawson c Schwass b Mason	13	36	25	-	1
M.N.McKenzie run out	24	54	50	-	2
P.D.McGlashan† run out	16	24	24	1	-
J.W.Wilson c Griggs b Schwass .	5	16	16	-	-
W.C.McSkimming c Ryder					
b Hamilton	32	78	41	1	1
N.D.Morland run out	55	66	66	3	3
S.B.O'Connor b Furlong	0	5	1	-	-
K.P.Walmsley not out	1	1	2	-	-
Extras (b 4, lb 10, w 10, nb 5)	29				
TOTAL (49.1 overs)	**243**	197			

CENTRAL DISTRICTS

	Runs	Mins	Balls	6s	4s
C.M.Spearman* b McSkimming	97	101	59	6	10
J.D.Ryder b Morland	63	84	64	-	12
P.J.Ingram c Lawson b Morland..	5	40	41	-	1
G.P.Sulzberger c Wilson					
b O'Connor	25	42	32	-	4
I.P.Sandbrook c McGlashan					
b O'Connor	0	7	6	-	-
G.R.Loveridge c Wilson b Walmsley	5	24	16	-	-
C.J.M.Furlong lbw b O'Connor	0	1	1	-	-
B.B.J.Griggs† lbw b O'Connor ...	1	7	3	-	-
A.M.Schwass not out	9	37	17	-	-
M.J.Mason b Walmsley	7	10	9	-	1
L.J.Hamilton b Walmsley	2	19	10	-	-
Extras (w 13, nb 6)	19				
TOTAL (42.2 overs)	**233**	193			

Bowling	O	M	R	W
CENTRAL DISTRICTS				
Schwass	10	0	50	2
Mason	10	0	48	1
Hamilton	10	0	42	2
Furlong	9.1	0	55	2
Sulzberger	10	0	34	0
OTAGO				
O'Connor	10	0	46	4
Walmsley	8.2	0	68	3
McSkimming	6	0	38	1
Wilson	1	0	15	0
Morland	10	0	41	2
Cumming	3	0	16	0
Wasim	4	0	9	0

Fall of Wickets		
	O	CD
1st	34	154
2nd	67	172
3rd	89	193
4th	104	196
5th	134	205
6th	147	205
7th	149	210
8th	242	212
9th	243	222
10th	243	233

WELLINGTON v NORTHERN DISTRICTS

State Shield

at Basin Reserve, Wellington on 2 January, 2003
Toss : Wellington. Umpires : D.J. Ellwood & M.P. George
Wellington won by 56 runs. *Points: Wellington 5, Northern Districts 0*

WELLINGTON

	Runs	Mins	Balls	6s	4s
C.J.Nevin† lbw b Yovich	0	1	2	-	-
M.D.Bell* lbw b Styris	30	84	55	-	4
R.A.Jones b Aldridge	15	43	35	-	2
N.R.Parlane b Martin	7	50	33	-	-
G.T.Donaldson c Martin b Yovich	75	83	86	1	8
M.D.J.Walker c Martin b West ...	62	86	79	2	4
M.R.Jefferson c Martin b Yovich .	0	7	1	-	-
M.Y.Pasupati not out	5	8	7	-	-
M.R.Gillespie not out	2	5	2	-	-
J.E.C.Franklin					
A.D.Turner					
Extras (b 2, lb 7, w 6)	15				
TOTAL (50 overs) (7 wkts) ..	**211**	197			

NORTHERN DISTRICTS

	Runs	Mins	Balls	6s	4s
J.A.H.Marshall lbw b Turner	0	2	3	-	-
M.E.Parlane c Nevin b Gillespie ..	7	63	48	-	-
N.K.W.Horsley c Nevin b Turner .	5	20	21	-	-
S.B.Styris c Nevin b Gillespie	22	51	35	-	3
B.P.Martin b Pasupati	9	37	17	-	1
M.N.Hart b Gillespie	53	119	73	-	5
H.J.H.Marshall c Nevin b Pasupati	2	15	10	-	-
J.A.F.Yovich b Walker	18	34	29	-	1
R.G.Hart*† run out	1	8	5	-	-
G.W.Aldridge lbw b Gillespie	6	18	22	-	-
G.L.West not out	4	14	9	-	-
Extras (lb 6, w 10, nb 2)	18				
TOTAL (45 overs)	**145**	195			

Bowling	O	M	R	W
NORTHERN DISTRICTS				
Yovich	8	0	39	3
West	7	1	39	1
Aldridge	7	1	21	1
Styris	10	1	41	1
Martin	10	1	28	1
Hart M.N.	8	0	34	0
WELLINGTON				
Turner	8	2	21	2
Franklin	10	4	17	0
Gillespie	8	1	31	4
Pasupati	7	1	24	2
Walker	8	0	27	1
Jefferson	4	0	19	0

Fall of Wickets		
	W	ND
1st	0	1
2nd	37	8
3rd	60	35
4th	68	40
5th	193	59
6th	202	72
7th	203	114
8th	-	118
9th	-	134
10th	-	145

NEW ZEALAND
CRICKET

Fourth Round

Whiteman *(Auckland)*, and Orchard *(Northern Districts)* made their debuts. Davis made his Auckland debut and Kelly made his debut for Northern.

Auckland batted at a steady rate with their five fifties taking 71, 71, 69, 44 and 49 balls. Vincent was the only batsman to get his half century, needing 91 deliveries. Central got away to a disastrous start losing four wickets in the first four overs before rain prevented any further play.

A record fifth wicket stand of 130 off 107 balls enabled Otago to get to 251-5. McKenzie (50 off 55 balls) got his highest score as did McGlashan. Robbie Hart's catch enabled him to equal Erv McSweeney's record for one-day dismissals. Northern never really recovered from losing a wicket in the first over and only Yovich and Aldridge (highest score) were able to pass 20. Morland had career best bowling figures as Otago won convincingly.

After an opening stand of 69, Canterbury slumped to 130-7 before Bond (highest score) and Anderson put on 49 from 42 balls. Gillespie again bowled well. Bell led the way for Wellington, getting 50 off 85 balls, who got their bonus point with one ball to spare.

AUCKLAND v CENTRAL DISTRICTS   State Shield

at Eden Park Outer Oval, Auckland on 5 January, 2003
Toss : Central Districts. Umpires : D.G. Paterson & I.W. Shine
No result. Points: Auckland 2, Central Districts 2

AUCKLAND

	Runs	Mins	Balls	6s	4s
L.G.Howell c Furlong b Mason ..	44	55	37	2	5
M.H.Richardson c Hefford b Schwass	9	21	18	-	-
L.Vincent† c Spearman b Schwass	64	167	119	-	3
T.K.Canning lbw b Sulzberger ..	18	44	36	-	2
R.J.Nicol b Hefford	28	51	42	-	2
A.C.Barnes c Furlong b Hefford	44	24	24	2	5
C.R.Pryor c & b Furlong	19	24	17	-	-
S.J.G.Whiteman c Spearman b Furlong	0	5	2	-	-
B.G.K.Walker* not out	3	10	8	-	-
H.T.Davis run out	1	2	1	-	-
G.S.Shaw not out	0	1	0	-	-
Extras (lb 10, w 6, nb 4)	20				
TOTAL (50 overs) (9 wkts) ..	**250**	206			

CENTRAL DISTRICTS

	Runs	Mins	Balls	6s	4s
C.M.Spearman* c Barnes b Davis	8	3	6	-	2
J.D.Ryder c Vincent b Shaw	0	9	3	-	-
G.R.Loveridge lbw b Davis	0	13	4	-	-
G.P.Sulzberger lbw b Shaw	2	10	9	-	-
I.P.Sandbrook not out	0	8	2	-	-
B.B.J.Griggs† not out	1	5	2	-	-
C.J.M.Furlong					
A.M.Schwass					
M.J.Mason					
L.J.Hamilton					
B.E.Hefford					
Extras (w 1, nb 2)	3				
TOTAL (4 overs) (4 wkts)	**14**	26			

Bowling	O	M	R	W
CENTRAL DISTRICTS				
Schwass	6	0	41	2
Mason	10	0	47	1
Hefford	9	0	46	2
Hamilton	9	1	38	0
Furlong	10	0	41	2
Sulzberger	6	0	27	1
AUCKLAND				
Davis	2	0	12	2
Shaw	2	0	2	2

Fall of Wickets	A	CD
1st	26	10
2nd	66	11
3rd	107	13
4th	174	13
5th	223	-
6th	237	-
7th	240	-
8th	247	-
9th	249	-
10th	-	-

NORTHERN DISTRICTS v OTAGO

State Shield

at Smallbone Park, Rotorua on 5 January, 2003
Toss : Otago. Umpires : B.F. Bowden & B.G. Frost
Otago won by 79 runs. *Points: Otago 5, Northern Districts 0*

OTAGO

	Runs	Mins	Balls	6s	4s
A.J.Hore c Aldridge b Martin	34	104	68	-	4
Mohammad Wasim c & b Yovich	12	32	25	-	1
C.D.Cumming* c Hart R.G.					
b Aldridge	0	11	6	-	-
R.A.Lawson run out	35	84	65	-	2
M.N.McKenzie run out	90	97	85	1	7
P.D.McGlashan† not out	46	75	51	-	5
J.W.Wilson not out	4	2	3	-	1
W.C.McSkimming					
N.D.Morland					
S.B.O'Connor					
J.M.McMillan					
Extras (b 2, lb 8, w 17, nb 3) ..	30				
TOTAL (50 overs) (5 wkts) ..	**251**	205			

Bowling	O	M	R	W
NORTHERN DISTRICTS				
Yovich	10	1	45	1
West	6	0	55	0
Aldridge	8	2	33	1
Martin	10	1	37	1
Orchard	9	0	43	0
Hart M.N.	7	1	28	0
OTAGO				
O'Connor	10	3	18	4
McMillan	8	0	42	0
Wilson	5	0	8	0
McSkimming	7.2	0	27	1
Morland	10	0	35	4
Wasim	8	1	32	0

NORTHERN DISTRICTS

	Runs	Mins	Balls	6s	4s
D.P.Kelly c McKenzie b O'Connor	0	2	4	-	-
J.A.H.Marshall run out	13	52	36	-	1
M.E.Parlane b O'Connor	16	22	25	-	1
M.N.Hart st McGlashan b Morland	18	70	51	-	1
J.A.F.Yovich c Hore b Morland .	38	80	59	1	-
N.K.W.Horsley st McGlashan					
b Morland	15	25	26	-	1
R.G.Hart*† c Hore b Morland	1	8	7	-	-
M.G.Orchard c McGlashan					
b O'Connor	8	18	12	-	-
B.P.Martin b O'Connor	5	24	11	-	-
G.W.Aldridge b McSkimming	28	35	31	-	3
G.L.West not out	12	27	20	-	1
Extras (lb 10, w 8)	18				
TOTAL (48.2 overs)	**172**	186			

Fall of Wickets		
	O	ND
1st	36	0
2nd	41	24
3rd	88	38
4th	115	68
5th	245	100
6th	-	112
7th	-	112
8th	-	125
9th	-	131
10th	-	172

CANTERBURY v WELLINGTON

State Shield

at Hagley Park, Christchurch on 5 January, 2003
Toss : Wellington. Umpires : C.J. Morris & D.M. Quested
Wellington won by 7 wickets. *Points: Wellington 5, Canterbury 0*

CANTERBURY

	Runs	Mins	Balls	6s	4s
M.H.W.Papps† c Nevin					
b Gillespie	33	69	54	-	4
S.L.Stewart b Jefferson	33	102	77	-	3
P.G.Fulton c Nevin b Walker	2	11	10	-	-
C.L.Cairns c Turner b Gillespie .	24	42	45	-	2
C.Z.Harris c Walker b Hitchcock	5	26	12	-	-
G.R.Stead* lbw b Gillespie	4	8	3	-	1
J.I.Englefield b Hitchcock	6	37	24	-	-
C.J.Anderson b Walker	12	64	41	-	-
S.E.Bond c Franklin b Walker ...	40	28	30	2	2
S.J.Cunis not out	7	5	4	-	1
C.S.Martin not out	2	3	2	-	-
Extras (b 2, lb 10, w 6, nb 2) ..	20				
TOTAL (50 overs) (9 wkts) ..	**188**	202			

Bowling	O	M	R	W
WELLINGTON				
Turner	10	4	20	0
Franklin	7	1	35	0
Hitchcock	10	0	42	2
Gillespie	9	2	21	3
Walker	10	1	43	3
Jefferson	4	0	15	1
CANTERBURY				
Martin	8.5	1	32	2
Bond	8	0	46	0
Cunis	7	0	23	0
Harris	8	1	31	1
Anderson	5	0	29	0
Fulton	3	0	24	0

WELLINGTON

	Runs	Mins	Balls	6s	4s
C.J.Nevin† c Cunis b Martin	34	48	39	-	7
M.D.Bell* b Martin	80	150	111	1	9
R.A.Jones b Harris	42	88	68	1	5
P.A.Hitchcock not out	13	21	16	-	1
M.D.J.Walker not out	9	8	8	1	-
N.R.Parlane					
G.T.Donaldson					
J.E.C.Franklin					
M.R.Jefferson					
M.R.Gillespie					
A.D.Turner					
Extras (b 2, lb 2, w 4, nb 3)	11				
TOTAL (39.5 overs) (3 wkts)	**189**	159			

Fall of Wickets		
	C	W
1st	69	60
2nd	76	159
3rd	94	177
4th	114	-
5th	116	-
6th	120	-
7th	130	-
8th	179	-
9th	179	-
10th	-	-

Fifth Round

Shaw *(Canterbury)* and Taylor *(Central)* made their debuts.

Otago struggled throughout with only Lawson reaching 20. Rain caused a disruption and the game was reduced to 48 overs. Both Auckland opening bowlers had career best figures. The Auckland target was reduced to 119 and Howell ensured there would be no problems. He got to 50 off 81 balls as Auckland cruised to a win with 14.5 overs left.

Central's batting woes continued as they were dismissed for their second lowest total. The innings lasted a mere 21.4 overs. Seven batsmen failed to score in the debacle. Canterbury knocked off the runs easily, with the match over at 3.38 pm and lasting just 170 minutes.

Northern's first wicket record was blasted away as James Marshall and Vettori (highest score) put on 168 off 192 balls. Vettori's fifty off 55 balls was 22 faster than his partner. Chasing 272, Wellington lost two early wickets and after a recovery then lost four wickets for 26. Walker continued his good run with the bat (50 off 54 balls) and Hitchcock (highest score) tried hard but Northern had an easy win.

AUCKLAND v OTAGO   State Shield

at Eden Park Outer Oval, Auckland on 7 January, 2003
Toss : Otago. Umpires : D.B. Cowie & I.W. Shine
Auckland won by 6 wickets (D/L method). *Points: Auckland 5, Otago 0*

OTAGO

	Runs	Mins	Balls	6s	4s
A.J.Hore c Walker b Canning	15	58	35	-	1
Mohammad Wasim lbw b Shaw ..	2	24	11	-	-
C.D.Cumming* c Vincent b Shaw	2	12	7	-	-
R.A.Lawson c Vincent b Canning	26	122	75	-	1
M.N.McKenzie c Vincent b Davis	3	12	11	-	-
P.D.McGlashan† b Davis	0	1	1	-	-
J.W.Wilson c Vincent b Davis	0	3	4	-	-
W.C.McSkimming lbw b Shaw ...	18	33	29	-	3
N.D.Morland c Vincent b Canning	8	40	41	-	-
S.B.O'Connor lbw b Barnes	15	27	29	-	2
K.P.Walmsley not out	4	21	16	-	-

Extras (lb 4, w 21, nb 3) 28
TOTAL (42.4 overs) 121 182

AUCKLAND

	Runs	Mins	Balls	6s	4s
M.H.Richardson c McSkimming b Wilson	20	58	42	-	2
L.G.Howell not out	66	146	95	2	7
L.Vincent† b Walmsley	10	26	25	-	1
T.K.Canning c & b Morland	3	24	18	-	-
R.J.Nicol c McGlashan b McSkimming	0	11	9	-	-
A.C.Barnes not out	12	23	17	-	2
S.J.G.Whiteman					
B.G.K.Walker*					
H.T.Davis					
G.S.Shaw					

Extras (b 1, lb 1, w 5, nb 1) 8
TOTAL (34.1 overs) (4 wkts) 119 146

Bowling	O	M	R	W
AUCKLAND				
Davis	10	1	35	3
Shaw	9	2	24	3
Canning	10	2	20	3
Walker	9	1	27	0
Whiteman	3	1	5	0
Barnes	1.4	0	6	1
OTAGO				
O'Connor	10	1	24	0
Walmsley	8	1	23	1
McSkimming	5	1	25	1
Wilson	4	0	13	1
Morland	7	0	31	1
Lawson	0.1	0	1	0

Fall of Wickets	O	A
1st	12	48
2nd	25	64
3rd	35	78
4th	42	87
5th	42	-
6th	43	-
7th	74	-
8th	101	-
9th	102	-
10th	121	-

CENTRAL DISTRICTS v CANTERBURY State Shield

at Hagley Park, Christchurch on 7 January, 2003
Toss : Canterbury. Umpires : R.D. Anderson & E.A. Watkin
Canterbury won by 9 wickets. *Points: Canterbury 5, Central Districts 0*

CENTRAL DISTRICTS

	Runs	Mins	Balls	6s	4s
C.M.Spearman* c Anderson b Shaw	26	37	22	-	3
J.M.How b Martin	0	1	3	-	-
R.L.Taylor b Martin	11	24	21	-	2
G.P.Sulzberger c Papps b Cunis	14	59	38	-	2
I.P.Sandbrook run out	0	1	0	-	-
B.B.J.Griggs† c Papps b Shaw	0	3	2	-	-
G.R.Loveridge b Cunis	0	19	13	-	-
C.J.M.Furlong not out	10	36	24	-	1
M.J.Mason c Fulton b Cunis	0	1	1	-	-
B.E.Hefford c & b McMillan	0	5	4	-	-
L.J.Hamilton lbw b McMillan	0	5	4	-	-
Extras (lb 1, w 3, nb 2)	6				
TOTAL (21.4 overs)	**67**	100			

CANTERBURY

	Runs	Mins	Balls	6s	4s
M.H.W.Papps† not out	29	70	54	-	2
S.L.Stewart lbw b Hefford	29	51	39	-	4
C.D.McMillan not out	1	18	14	-	-
G.R.Stead*					
C.L.Cairns					
P.G.Fulton					
C.J.Cornelius					
C.J.Anderson					
S.J.Cunis					
H.J.Shaw					
C.S.Martin					
Extras (w 6, nb 3)	9				
TOTAL (17.2 overs) (1 wkt)	**68**	70			

Bowling CANTERBURY	O	M	R	W
Martin	7	1	17	2
Cunis	7	3	19	3
Shaw	5	0	23	2
McMillan	2.4	0	7	2
CENTRAL DISTRICTS				
Hamilton	6.2	1	27	0
Mason	5	1	14	0
Hefford	6	0	27	1

Fall of Wickets	CD	C
1st	1	56
2nd	25	-
3rd	39	-
4th	41	-
5th	41	-
6th	51	-
7th	64	-
8th	64	-
9th	65	-
10th	67	-

NORTHERN DISTRICTS v WELLINGTON State Shield

at Westpac Park, Hamilton (d/n) on 7 January, 2003
Toss : Northern Districts. Umpires : G.A. Baxter & A.L. Hill
Northern Districts won by 43 runs. *Points: Northern Districts 4, Wellington 0*

NORTHERN DISTRICTS

	Runs	Mins	Balls	6s	4s
J.A.H.Marshall c Nevin b Turner	60	130	93	-	6
D.L.Vettori c Hitchcock b Gillespie	89	154	115	1	11
M.E.Parlane b Turner	1	8	7	-	-
M.N.Hart c Jefferson b Turner	0	1	2	-	-
J.A.F.Yovich run out	8	26	16	-	-
H.J.H.Marshall c Nevin b Walker	26	52	39	-	2
D.P.Kelly b Hitchcock	13	24	18	-	1
R.G.Hart*† b Hitchcock	2	4	3	-	-
M.G.Orchard not out	9	10	8	-	1
G.W.Aldridge not out	8	3	4	1	-
G.L.West					
Extras (b 5, lb 15, w 31, nb 4)	55				
TOTAL (50 overs) (8 wkts)	**271**	211			

WELLINGTON

	Runs	Mins	Balls	6s	4s
C.J.Nevin† b Yovich	8	15	14	-	2
M.D.Bell* c Parlane b Yovich	8	24	13	-	1
R.A.Jones c Marshall H.J.H. b Orchard	26	73	45	-	4
N.R.Parlane c Yovich b Vettori	41	75	71	-	8
G.T.Donaldson c Marshall H.J.H. b Aldridge	7	23	15	-	1
M.D.J.Walker c Marshall J.A.H. b Yovich	58	91	58	3	3
M.R.Jefferson c West b Aldridge	2	9	9	-	-
P.A.Hitchcock lbw b Vettori	34	32	31	1	5
M.Y.Pasupati c Vettori b Orchard	8	17	15	-	-
M.R.Gillespie c Orchard b Yovich	3	17	5	-	-
A.D.Turner not out	0	1	1	-	-
Extras (lb 9, w 22, nb 2)	33				
TOTAL (45.4 overs)	**228**	194			

Bowling WELLINGTON	O	M	R	W
Turner	10	0	59	3
Gillespie	9	0	42	1
Hitchcock	10	0	44	2
Pasupati	3	0	29	0
Walker	10	0	40	1
Jefferson	8	0	37	0
NORTHERN DISTRICTS				
Yovich	7.4	0	50	4
West	9	0	55	0
Aldridge	10	2	45	2
Orchard	9	1	40	2
Vettori	10	0	29	2

Fall of Wickets	ND	W
1st	168	18
2nd	174	31
3rd	174	101
4th	196	109
5th	210	117
6th	245	127
7th	251	175
8th	257	196
9th	-	228
10th	-	228

Sixth Round

After a good start with 64 off 111 balls, Auckland slumped to 77-6 after a further 58 balls. Vincent top-scored with his fifty coming from 76 deliveries. After losing both openers for 6, Fleming and Jones steered the Wellington ship with a 101 run stand. Wickets started to fall but Wellington won with 16 balls left.

Spearman and Sulzberger got fifties as Central remedied their batting blues. Spearman got fifty from 47 balls and Sulzberger needed 84. Yovich's wicket gave him 50 one-day wickets. Vettori (50 off 36 balls) was the only Northern batsman to score 15 as Northern succumbed timidly to lose by 100 runs. Furlong also reached 50 wickets.

Canterbury had a 108 run opening stand from Papps (highest score) and Stewart. Papps got fifty from 71 deliveries. However, Canterbury's last seven wickets fell for just 37 off 83 balls. Otago were always struggling and at one stage were 66-8. Shaw's 5-14 were the third best one-day bowling figures for Canterbury. O'Connor hit his highest score.

WELLINGTON v AUCKLAND

State Shield

at Basin Reserve, Wellington on 17 January, 2003
Toss : Wellington. Umpires : R.D. Anderson & A.L. Hill
Wellington won by 4 wickets. *Points: Wellington 4, Auckland 0*

AUCKLAND

	Runs	Mins	Balls	6s	4s
L.G.Howell c Walker b Hitchcock	27	90	50	-	4
M.H.Richardson c Nevin b Walker	34	76	68	-	4
M.J.Horne b Walker	0	2	2	-	-
L.Vincent† c Pasupati b Hitchcock	66	126	85	1	4
R.J.Nicol c Fleming b Walker	2	7	7	-	-
A.C.Barnes run out	2	16	17	-	-
C.R.Pryor b Jefferson	0	3	1	-	-
T.K.Canning c Nevin b Gillespie	11	26	19	-	-
B.G.K.Walker* b Hitchcock	7	12	9	-	-
H.T.Davis c & b Pasupati	17	32	34	-	2
G.S.Shaw not out	2	13	7	-	-
Extras (lb 9, w 3, nb 1)	13				
TOTAL (49.4 overs)	**181**	206			

WELLINGTON

	Runs	Mins	Balls	6s	4s
C.J.Nevin† c Vincent b Davis	0	1	2	-	-
M.D.Bell* lbw b Shaw	0	16	5	-	-
R.A.Jones c Vincent b Pryor	41	91	71	-	6
N.R.Parlane b Walker	27	71	51	-	4
M.D.J.Walker c Howell b Barnes	7	37	25	-	-
P.A.Hitchcock not out	22	39	27	-	2
J.E.C.Franklin not out	11	26	20	-	-
M.Y.Pasupati					
M.R.Jefferson					
M.R.Gillespie					
Extras (b 1, lb 3, w 10, nb 3)	17				
TOTAL (47.2 overs) (6 wkts)	**182**	207			

Bowling	O	M	R	W
WELLINGTON				
Gillespie	10	1	29	1
Franklin	7	0	24	0
Walker	10	0	41	3
Hitchcock	9.4	0	45	3
Jefferson	8	1	23	1
Pasupati	5	1	10	1
AUCKLAND				
Davis	10	1	42	2
Shaw	4	0	24	1
Canning	7	1	36	0
Walker	10	2	23	1
Barnes	8	1	26	1
Pryor	8.2	1	27	1

Fall of Wickets		
	A	**W**
1st	64	0
2nd	64	6
3rd	66	107
4th	71	122
5th	76	142
6th	77	153
7th	103	-
8th	114	-
9th	153	-
10th	181	-

NORTHERN DISTRICTS v CENTRAL DISTRICTS   State Shield

at Westpac Park, Hamilton (d/n) on 17 January, 2003
Toss : Northern Districts. Umpires : B.F. Bowden & B.G. Frost
Central Districts won by 100 runs. *Points: Central Districts 5, Northern Districts 0*

CENTRAL DISTRICTS	Runs	Mins	Balls	6s	4s
C.M.Spearman* c Hart M.N.					
b Styris	52	83	51	2	7
J.D.Ryder lbw b Aldridge	26	32	16	1	4
M.S.Sinclair b Aldridge	8	9	5	-	2
J.M.How c Hart R.G. b Vettori	16	66	55	-	1
G.P.Sulzberger b Butler	51	117	86	-	4
I.P.Sandbrook c & b Hart M.N.	9	42	41	-	1
B.B.J.Griggs† run out	17	33	27	-	1
C.J.M.Furlong not out	15	23	14	1	-
A.M.Schwass b Yovich	3	4	3	-	-
M.J.Mason not out	9	3	3	-	2
L.J.Hamilton					
Extras (b 2, lb 5, w 16, nb 1)	24				
TOTAL (50 overs) (8 wkts)	**230**	210			

NORTHERN DISTRICTS	Runs	Mins	Balls	6s	4s
J.A.H.Marshall lbw b Schwass	0	1	2	-	-
D.L.Vettori b Furlong	57	64	44	1	11
M.E.Parlane run out	6	16	11	-	1
S.B.Styris lbw b Mason	9	22	22	-	2
M.N.Hart c Sinclair b Furlong	14	44	39	-	2
J.A.F.Yovich run out	7	35	22	-	1
H.J.H.Marshall not out	10	39	22	-	1
R.G.Hart*† lbw b Furlong	1	2	2	-	-
M.G.Orchard c Griggs					
b Sulzberger	0	4	4	-	-
G.W.Aldridge lbw b Schwass	10	11	12	-	1
I.G.Butler c Furlong b Sulzberger	4	5	9	-	1
Extras (b 2, lb 2, w 5, nb 3)	12				
TOTAL (31 overs)	**130**	126			

Bowling	O	M	R	W
NORTHERN DISTRICTS				
Yovich	6	0	38	1
Butler	8	1	57	1
Aldridge	8	0	53	2
Vettori	10	0	23	1
Styris	10	3	26	1
Hart M.N.	8	0	26	1
CENTRAL DISTRICTS				
Schwass	4	0	36	2
Mason	6	0	27	1
Hamilton	6	3	12	0
Furlong	7	1	24	3
Sulzberger	8	0	27	2

Fall of Wickets	CD	ND
1st	46	1
2nd	64	32
3rd	108	49
4th	122	83
5th	152	102
6th	193	110
7th	208	112
8th	213	113
9th	-	124
10th	-	130

OTAGO v CANTERBURY   State Shield

at Queen's Park, Invercargill on 17 January, 2003
Toss : Otago. Umpires : D.B. Cowie & D.M. Quested
Canterbury won by 117 runs. *Points: Canterbury 5, Otago 0*

CANTERBURY	Runs	Mins	Balls	6s	4s
M.H.W.Papps† c Gaffaney					
b Morland	65	146	114	-	7
S.L.Stewart run out	45	101	78	-	5
C.D.McMillan b O'Connor	4	6	7	-	1
C.L.Cairns b McSkimming	43	56	40	1	5
C.Z.Harris c Wasim b Morland	12	34	22	-	2
P.G.Fulton c Gaffaney					
b Walmsley	9	21	12	-	2
H.J.Shaw c McKenzie					
b Walmsley	9	18	13	-	1
S.J.Cunis b McMillan	8	6	6	-	1
G.R.Stead* b Walmsley	4	7	5	-	-
C.J.Anderson run out	1	5	2	-	-
C.S.Martin not out	0	1	1	-	-
Extras (b 1, lb 17, w 14)	32				
TOTAL (50 overs)	**232**	200			

OTAGO	Runs	Mins	Balls	6s	4s
R.A.Lawson c Papps b Martin	1	12	11	-	-
Mohammad Wasim b Cunis	12	30	25	-	2
C.D.Cumming* b Martin	11	32	22	-	2
C.B.Gaffaney c Shaw b Cunis	2	9	7	-	-
M.N.McKenzie c Martin b Shaw	0	21	11	-	-
P.D.McGlashan† c Fulton					
b Shaw	2	24	21	-	-
W.C.McSkimming c Stead					
b Shaw	17	49	38	-	2
N.D.Morland c Stewart b Shaw	5	32	24	-	-
S.B.O'Connor b Cunis	22	57	50	1	-
K.P.Walmsley not out	25	54	41	-	4
J.M.McMillan b Shaw	1	5	7	-	-
Extras (lb 5, w 8, nb 4)	17				
TOTAL (42.1 overs)	**115**	167			

Bowling	O	M	R	W
OTAGO				
O'Connor	10	1	35	1
Walmsley	10	0	45	3
McMillan	10	0	47	1
McSkimming	10	1	39	1
Cumming	3	0	21	0
Morland	7	2	27	2
CANTERBURY				
Martin	10	0	33	2
Cunis	10	4	17	3
McMillan	6	2	15	0
Shaw	8.1	3	14	5
Anderson	6	0	27	0
Harris	2	0	4	0

Fall of Wickets	C	O
1st	108	5
2nd	113	23
3rd	161	32
4th	195	34
5th	197	39
6th	217	45
7th	219	65
8th	228	66
9th	232	113
10th	232	115

Seventh Round

Nevin's innings shone like a beacon as Wellington got to 212-9 due to his third century. His fifty came from 86 balls and the hundred off a further 53. He was dismissed straight after getting his hundred. After surviving an early chance, the out of form McMillan blitzed the hapless Wellington bowlers. Fifty came from 49 balls and his fifth hundred came after a further 40 balls as Canterbury cruised to victory with 12.4 overs to spare.

Horne got his highest score as Auckland reached 198. His fifty needed 66 balls. McIntosh was the only other player to pass 13. Spearman went early and Central were struggling at 81-6 before Griggs and Furlong added 66 but once the stand was broken Auckland went on to complete victory by 29 runs.

Matthew Hart and Yovich added 120 off 150 balls for the fifth wicket as Northern got to 249-7. Hart was run out on 98 with just one ball left in the innings. Otago's batting was poor with only Cumming passing 14 and they were dismissed in under 30 overs.

WELLINGTON v CANTERBURY — **State Shield**

at Basin Reserve, Wellington on 19 January, 2003
Toss : Wellington. Umpires : A.L. Hill & E.A. Watkin
Canterbury won by 7 wickets. Points: Canterbury 5, Wellington 0

WELLINGTON

	Runs	Mins	Balls	6s	4s
C.J.Nevin† lbw b Harris	100	191	140	1	8
M.D.Bell* c Cunis b Shaw	15	48	28	-	2
S.P.Fleming lbw b Martin	0	5	5	-	-
R.A.Jones b Harris	7	12	14	-	1
N.R.Parlane c Papps b McMillan	26	57	55	-	2
M.Y.Pasupati b McMillan	5	10	10	-	-
M.D.J.Walker b Cunis	14	23	22	1	1
P.A.Hitchcock lbw b Harris	17	20	19	1	-
M.R.Jefferson lbw b Harris	6	12	7	-	-
J.E.C.Franklin not out	2	2	2	-	-
M.R.Gillespie					
Extras (lb 7, w 10, nb 3)	20				
TOTAL (50 overs) (9 wkts)	212	194			

CANTERBURY

	Runs	Mins	Balls	6s	4s
M.H.W.Papps† c Hitchcock b Gillespie	4	3	6	-	1
S.L.Stewart run out	25	67	38	1	4
C.D.McMillan not out	122	160	107	4	13
G.R.Stead* run out	31	63	47	-	4
C.L.Cairns not out	22	32	28	1	1
C.Z.Harris					
P.G.Fulton					
C.J.Anderson					
S.J.Cunis					
H.J.Shaw					
C.S.Martin					
Extras (b 1, lb 6, w 4)	11				
TOTAL (37.2 overs) (3 wkts)	215	164			

Bowling	O	M	R	W
CANTERBURY				
Cunis	10	1	42	1
Martin	8	1	38	1
Shaw	6	0	29	1
Harris	8	0	28	4
Anderson	10	0	36	0
McMillan	8	0	32	2
WELLINGTON				
Gillespie	8	0	49	1
Franklin	5.2	1	39	0
Walker	7	1	19	0
Jefferson	6	0	40	0
Hitchcock	7	1	42	0
Pasupati	4	0	19	0

Fall of Wickets	W	C
1st	41	4
2nd	42	81
3rd	50	175
4th	107	-
5th	120	-
6th	155	-
7th	190	-
8th	208	-
9th	212	-
10th	-	-

CENTRAL DISTRICTS v AUCKLAND

State Shield

at Pukekura Park, New Plymouth on 19 January, 2003
Toss : Auckland. Umpires : M.P. George & I.W. Shine
Auckland won by 29 runs. Points: Auckland 4, Central Districts 0

AUCKLAND	Runs	Mins	Balls	6s	4s
L.G.Howell c Spearman b Hamilton	2	11	10	-	-
M.J.Horne run out	82	163	93	-	10
L.Vincent c Spearman b Hamilton	10	16	18	-	2
R.J.Nicol run out	3	23	23	-	-
A.C.Barnes b Furlong	3	23	23	-	-
T.G.McIntosh† b Furlong	33	68	63	-	-
K.D.Mills c Griggs b Mason	13	22	17	-	2
C.R.Pryor c How b Mason	4	15	13	-	-
T.K.Canning b Hamilton	11	12	7	-	2
B.G.K.Walker* c Sulzberger b Mason	12	24	18	-	1
H.T.Davis not out	12	19	14	-	1
Extras (lb 5, w 4, nb 4)	13				
TOTAL (49.1 overs)	**198**	206			

CENTRAL DISTRICTS	Runs	Mins	Balls	6s	4s
C.M.Spearman* b Mills	1	7	6	-	-
J.D.Ryder c Vincent b Pryor	39	94	48	-	6
M.S.Sinclair c McIntosh b Davis	7	32	30	-	-
J.M.How c Mills b Pryor	18	48	40	-	3
G.P.Sulzberger c Vincent b Canning	0	7	3	-	-
I.P.Sandbrook c McIntosh b Pryor	0	1	2	-	-
B.B.J.Griggs† c Davis b Walker	28	82	55	-	3
C.J.M.Furlong lbw b Walker	39	95	85	1	4
M.J.Mason c Horne b Walker	1	6	4	-	-
B.E.Hefford not out	6	19	11	-	-
L.J.Hamilton c McIntosh b Mills	1	9	6	-	-
Extras (b 5, lb 7, w 10, nb 7)	29				
TOTAL (47.2 overs)	**169**	208			

Bowling	O	M	R	W
CENTRAL DISTRICTS				
Hamilton	10	2	37	3
Mason	9.1	0	33	3
Hefford	10	2	31	0
Furlong	10	1	38	2
Sulzberger	10	0	54	0
AUCKLAND				
Davis	9	1	47	1
Mills	8.2	0	20	2
Canning	10	3	14	1
Pryor	6	0	37	3
Walker	10	2	17	3
Barnes	4	0	22	0

Fall of Wickets	A	CD
1st	3	4
2nd	27	26
3rd	41	76
4th	50	80
5th	128	81
6th	152	81
7th	161	147
8th	168	153
9th	177	162
10th	198	169

OTAGO v NORTHERN DISTRICTS

State Shield

at Carisbrook, Dunedin on 19 January, 2003
Toss : Northern Districts. Umpires : G.A. Baxter & D.M. Quested
Northern Districts won by 90 runs (D/L Method). Points: Northern Districts 5, Otago 0

NORTHERN DISTRICTS	Runs	Mins	Balls	6s	4s
J.A.H.Marshall c McKenzie b McMillan	23	78	61	-	3
D.L.Vettori run out	10	23	11	-	2
M.E.Parlane b McSkimming	33	33	34	1	6
S.B.Styris c & b McMillan	4	9	7	-	1
M.N.Hart run out	98	138	94	3	8
J.A.F.Yovich c McKenzie b Walmsley	53	99	80	-	5
H.J.H.Marshall b Walmsley	6	9	8	-	1
R.G.Hart*† not out	3	18	6	-	-
D.R.Tuffey not out	1	1	1	-	-
G.W.Aldridge					
I.G.Butler					
Extras (lb 4, w 12, nb 2)	18				
TOTAL (50 overs) (7 wkts)	**249**	207			

OTAGO	Runs	Mins	Balls	6s	4s
R.A.Lawson lbw b Butler	9	32	26	-	1
Mohammad Wasim c Hart M.N. b Tuffey	8	30	17	-	1
C.D.Cumming* c Vettori b Styris	32	55	38	-	6
B.B.McCullum† c Hart R.G. b Yovich	14	26	17	1	1
M.N.McKenzie c Tuffey b Yovich	0	2	3	-	-
P.D.McGlashan run out	11	20	19	-	2
W.C.McSkimming c & b Vettori	7	24	23	-	-
N.D.Morland b Styris	0	6	5	-	-
S.B.O'Connor not out	12	21	19	-	1
K.P.Walmsley b Styris	0	1	1	-	-
J.M.McMillan c Marshall H.J.H. b Vettori	2	4	6	-	-
Extras (lb 6, w 4, nb 3)	13				
TOTAL (28.3 overs)	**108**	115			

Bowling	O	M	R	W
OTAGO				
O'Connor	10	1	39	0
Walmsley	10	1	53	2
McMillan	10	0	59	2
McSkimming	7	0	37	1
Morland	10	0	41	0
Wasim	3	0	16	0
NORTHERN DISTRICTS				
Tuffey	5	0	18	1
Butler	5	1	21	1
Yovich	3	0	13	2
Aldridge	2	0	13	0
Styris	7	1	20	3
Vettori	6.3	0	17	2

Fall of Wickets	ND	O
1st	18	27
2nd	63	27
3rd	72	57
4th	77	57
5th	197	83
6th	211	87
7th	248	89
8th	-	101
9th	-	103
10th	-	108

Eighth Round

Wellington batted positively getting 252-6. Nevin (50 off 70 balls) continued his good run and Hitchcock again got his highest score. Auckland had a good start with 84 off 87 balls. Howell became the leading run scorer in one day domestic cricket and got his fifty from 39 balls. At 169-5 the game was evenly balanced but an unbroken stand of 85 off 77 balls gave Auckland victory with four balls to spare. Barnes reached fifty from 47 balls and Mills reached his highest score.

Parlane and Styris added 145 from 172 balls to give Northern an imposing 267-6. Parlane got fifty after facing 68 balls and reached his third century after 131 deliveries. He was dismissed one run short of the Northern record. Styris got his fifty from 67 balls. The Timaru crowd then saw some fireworks. Canterbury were 14-2 and then Papps retired hurt at 19 after being hit in the face but Cairns then produced the fastest fifty in domestic cricket from just 20 balls. Stead got fifty from 85 balls and passed 2000 runs. Harris' fifty came from 51 balls as Canterbury won with four balls to spare. Orchard had his best bowling figures and Robbie Hart took his 100th catch.

McCullum reached his first fifty from 57 balls as Otago got to 161 but they should have reached more after being 121-3. There were some rain interruptions. Central blazed away but more rain came at 4.51 pm and the game was abandoned.

AUCKLAND v WELLINGTON   State Shield

at North Harbour Stadium, Auckland on 22 January, 2003
Toss : Auckland. Umpires : B.F. Bowden & D.B. Cowie
Auckland won by 5 wickets. *Points: Auckland 4, Wellington 0*

WELLINGTON

	Runs	Mins	Balls	6s	4s
C.J.Nevin† c Walker b Canning	82	148	105	-	9
M.D.Bell* c Vincent b Walker	22	53	41	-	3
S.P.Fleming c Howell b Horne ..	43	64	48	-	7
R.A.Jones c Vincent b Walker...	18	41	28	-	2
N.R.Parlane st Vincent					
b Canning	5	14	12	-	-
M.D.J.Walker c McIntosh b Mills	13	27	24	-	1
P.A.Hitchcock not out	39	40	35	1	3
M.Y.Pasupati not out	16	15	9	-	3
M.R.Jefferson					
J.E.C.Franklin					
M.R.Gillespie					
Extras (lb 8, w 4, nb 2)	14				
TOTAL (50 overs) (6 wkts) ..	**252**	204			

AUCKLAND

	Runs	Mins	Balls	6s	4s
L.G.Howell c Hitchcock					
b Walker	65	63	55	1	11
T.G.McIntosh c Nevin					
b Pasupati	30	100	57	-	3
M.J.Horne st Nevin b Jefferson...	3	16	9	-	-
L.Vincent† c Nevin b Franklin ...	31	79	46	-	2
R.J.Nicol c Walker b Hitchcock .	18	40	44	-	2
A.C.Barnes not out	57	74	52	1	5
K.D.Mills not out	32	55	36	1	2
A.R.Adams					
T.K.Canning					
B.G.K.Walker*					
H.T.Davis					
Extras (lb 11, w 3, nb 3)	17				
TOTAL (49.2 overs) (5 wkts)	**253**	216			

Bowling	O	M	R	W
AUCKLAND				
Davis	5	0	30	0
Mills	10	1	42	1
Canning	7	0	27	2
Walker	9	0	34	2
Adams	10	0	65	0
Barnes	4	0	22	0
Horne	5	0	24	1
WELLINGTON				
Gillespie	5	0	34	0
Franklin	7	1	41	1
Hitchcock	10	1	48	1
Walker	9.2	0	39	1
Jefferson	9	2	37	1
Pasupati	9	0	43	1

Fall of Wickets		
	W	A
1st	58	84
2nd	141	94
3rd	171	111
4th	183	151
5th	184	169
6th	214	-
7th	-	-
8th	-	-
9th	-	-
10th	-	-

CANTERBURY v NORTHERN DISTRICTS

State Shield

at Aorangi Park, Timaru on 22 January, 2003
Toss : Northern Districts. Umpires : G.A. Baxter & A.L. Hill
Canterbury won by 2 wickets. *Points: Canterbury 4, Northern Districts 0*

NORTHERN DISTRICTS

	Runs	Mins	Balls	6s	4s
J.A.H.Marshall b Martin	24	31	32	-	4
M.E.Parlane c Anderson					
b McMillan	122	195	142	5	7
M.G.Orchard c Stead b McMillan	6	28	23	-	1
S.B.Styris c Stead b Harris	70	107	77	1	5
M.N.Hart c Cairns b McMillan	12	13	10	-	2
J.A.F.Yovich b McMillan	11	10	7	-	2
R.G.Hart*† not out	3	9	3	-	-
H.J.H.Marshall not out	13	7	6	-	2
D.R.Tuffey					
G.W.Aldridge					
I.G.Butler					
Extras (lb 6)	6				
TOTAL (50 overs) (6 wkts)	**267**	203			

CANTERBURY

	Runs	Mins	Balls	6s	4s
M.H.W.Papps† not out	6	30	12	-	1
S.L.Stewart b Tuffey	8	12	9	-	2
C.D.McMillan b Butler	0	5	3	-	-
G.R.Stead* c Yovich b Styris	66	155	112	-	6
C.L.Cairns c Hart R.G. b Aldridge	63	48	41	2	10
C.Z.Harris not out	83	148	89	2	6
P.G.Fulton b Orchard	1	9	6	-	-
C.J.Anderson c Hart M.N.					
b Aldridge	4	5	4	-	1
S.J.Cunis lbw b Orchard	1	4	4	-	-
H.J.Shaw run out	24	25	21	1	3
C.S.Martin					
Extras (lb 1, w 6, nb 5)	12				
TOTAL (49.2 overs) (8 wkts)	**268**	225			

Bowling	O	M	R	W
CANTERBURY				
Cunis	7	0	46	0
Martin	9	2	58	1
McMillan	10	0	42	4
Shaw	5	0	22	0
Anderson	9	0	59	0
Harris	10	0	34	1
NORTHERN DISTRICTS				
Tuffey	10	1	46	1
Butler	7	0	71	1
Aldridge	8	0	32	2
Yovich	4.2	0	29	0
Styris	10	1	35	1
Hart M.N.	4	0	29	0
Orchard	6	0	25	2

Fall of Wickets		
	ND	C
1st	39	13
2nd	58	14
3rd	203	94
4th	220	212
5th	250	215
6th	251	222
7th	-	224
8th	-	262
9th	-	-
10th	-	-

Papps retired hurt on 6 at 19-2*
and returned at 262-8

OTAGO v CENTRAL DISTRICTS

State Shield

at Carisbrook, Dunedin on 22 January, 2003
Toss : Otago. Umpires : R.D. Anderson & G.C. Holdem
No result. *Points: Otago 2, Central Districts 2*

OTAGO

	Runs	Mins	Balls	6s	4s
R.A.Lawson run out	21	96	79	-	2
Mohammad Wasim c Spearman					
b Hamilton	8	16	7	-	2
C.D.Cumming* c Spearman					
b Hamilton	8	29	20	-	1
B.B.McCullum c Furlong b Mason	50	80	59	5	-
M.N.McKenzie c Spearman					
b Hefford	17	28	25	-	2
P.D.McGlashan† c Griggs b Oram	13	24	22	-	2
W.C.McSkimming lbw b Hefford	12	37	24	-	1
N.D.Morland run out	5	8	6	-	1
S.B.O'Connor b Oram	7	8	9	-	1
K.P.Walmsley not out	3	7	4	-	-
J.M.McMillan c Sinclair b Hefford	0	5	5	-	-
Extras (lb 8, w 7, nb 2)	17				
TOTAL (43 overs)	**161**	173			

CENTRAL DISTRICTS

	Runs	Mins	Balls	6s	4s
C.M.Spearman c Walmsley					
b McMillan	45	51	31	2	7
J.D.Ryder c Lawson b Morland	21	43	32	-	4
M.S.Sinclair not out	1	7	3	-	-
G.P.Sulzberger					
J.D.P.Oram*					
J.M.How					
B.B.J.Griggs†					
C.J.M.Furlong					
M.J.Mason					
B.E.Hefford					
L.J.Hamilton					
Extras (lb 4, w 3)	7				
TOTAL (11 overs) (2 wkts)	**74**	51			

Bowling	O	M	R	W
CENTRAL DISTRICTS				
Hamilton	9	2	35	2
Mason	7	3	21	1
Oram	8	3	18	2
Hefford	10	1	44	3
Furlong	6	0	24	0
Sulzberger	3	0	11	0
OTAGO				
O'Connor	5	0	30	0
Walmsley	4	0	31	0
Morland	1	0	4	1
McMillan	1	0	5	1

Fall of Wickets		
	O	CD
1st	16	65
2nd	29	74
3rd	79	-
4th	121	-
5th	121	-
6th	137	-
7th	149	-
8th	158	-
9th	158	-
10th	161	-

Ninth Round

All games were affected by rain and only Auckland were able to get a win.

Cumming reached fifty from 52 balls and Sheed made his highest score as Otago made 170-6 after the match was reduced to 40 overs. Canterbury were set a target of 201 from 40 overs and then 190 from 37 as more interruptions came. Finally the rain had the last say and the game was abandoned.

Central Districts struggled and were 61-6 but Sulzberger and the tailenders got the score to 150. Walker had career best figures of 5-22. Wellington got to 22 off 31 balls before a dramatic collapse. They went to 50-7 as they failed to come to terms with the pitch. 24 overs had been bowled when rain came and stopped Central from getting a deserved win.

Northern had an 83 run stand off 111 balls for the third wicket. Hamish Marshall (50 off 87 balls) reached 1000 runs. After the fourth rain disruption the match was reduced to 47 overs. The game was further reduced in Auckland's innings to 33 overs with a target of 155. This was achieved easily despite Auckland losing three wickets in seven balls at one stage.

CANTERBURY v OTAGO   State Shield

at Jade Stadium, Christchurch (d/n) on 24 January, 2003
Toss : Otago. Umpires : M.P. George & A.L. Hill
No result. Points: Canterbury 2, Otago 2

OTAGO

	Runs	Mins	Balls	6s	4s
C.D.Cumming* b Harris	57	74	66	-	9
Mohammad Wasim c Astle					
b Martin	1	4	4	-	-
M.N.McKenzie run out	33	93	66	-	4
B.B.McCullum st Hopkins					
b McMillan	17	37	40	1	-
J.W.Sheed b Bond	21	36	37	-	3
P.D.McGlashan† not out	25	31	24	-	3
W.C.McSkimming run out	7	6	5	-	1
N.D.Morland not out	0	2	0	-	-
S.B.O'Connor					
K.P.Walmsley					
J.M.McMillan					
Extras (b 1, lb 5, w 1, nb 2)	9				
TOTAL (40 overs) (6 wkts)	**170**	144			

CANTERBURY

	Runs	Mins	Balls	6s	4s
S.L.Stewart lbw b O'Connor	3	18	14	-	-
N.J.Astle c McSkimming					
b McMillan	30	48	31	2	3
C.D.McMillan c Morland					
b Walmsley	11	48	39	-	1
G.R.Stead* not out	7	25	11	-	-
C.L.Cairns not out	6	6	5	-	1
C.Z.Harris					
P.G.Fulton					
G.J.Hopkins†					
H.J.Shaw					
S.E.Bond					
C.S.Martin					
Extras (lb 1, w 6)	7				
TOTAL (16.4 overs) (3 wkts)	**64**	74			

Bowling	O	M	R	W
CANTERBURY				
Bond	7	0	32	1
Martin	6	1	26	1
Shaw	3	0	22	0
Astle	8	1	31	0
Harris	10	1	22	1
McMillan	6	0	31	1
OTAGO				
O'Connor	5	1	28	1
Walmsley	5	0	12	1
McMillan	3	0	9	1
McSkimming	3.4	1	14	0

Fall of Wickets	O	C
1st	3	19
2nd	80	45
3rd	107	56
4th	118	-
5th	154	-
6th	167	-
7th	-	-
8th	-	-
9th	-	-
10th	-	-

CENTRAL DISTRICTS v WELLINGTON State Shield

at Yarrow Stadium, New Plymouth (d/n) on 24 January, 2003
Toss : Wellington. Umpires : D.B. Cowie & D.J. Ellwood
No result. *Points: Central Districts 2, Wellington 2*

CENTRAL DISTRICTS

	Runs	Mins	Balls	6s	4s
C.M.Spearman c Nevin					
b Hitchcock	6	14	11	-	1
J.D.Ryder b Walker	12	46	27	-	1
M.S.Sinclair c Nevin b Franklin	1	5	4	-	-
J.D.P.Oram* c Franklin b Walker	15	54	38	1	1
J.M.How c Parlane b Walker	0	6	7	-	-
G.P.Sulzberger lbw b Hitchcock	44	129	97	-	3
B.B.J.Griggs† lbw b Turner	2	36	23	-	-
C.J.M.Furlong run out	16	51	40	-	1
M.J.Mason b Walker	16	29	24	-	1
B.E.Hefford c Nevin b Walker	7	13	10	-	-
L.J.Hamilton not out	7	7	9	-	1
Extras (lb 15, w 7, nb 2)	24				
TOTAL (48 overs)	**150**	208			

WELLINGTON

	Runs	Mins	Balls	6s	4s
C.J.Nevin† c Spearman b Oram	20	23	22	-	3
M.D.Bell* lbw b Mason	6	35	17	-	-
N.R.Parlane c Sulzberger					
b Mason	8	14	13	-	2
R.A.Jones lbw b Hamilton	5	31	20	-	-
G.T.Donaldson lbw b Hefford	1	16	20	-	-
J.E.C.Franklin not out	4	46	30	-	-
M.D.J.Walker c Griggs b Hamilton	0	3	4	-	-
P.A.Hitchcock c Sinclair b Hefford	6	10	4	-	1
M.R.Jefferson not out	3	18	13	-	-
M.Y.Pasupati					
A.D.Turner					
Extras (lb 2, w 2)	4				
TOTAL (24 overs) (7 wkts)	**57**	**105**			

Bowling	O	M	R	W
WELLINGTON				
Franklin	9	1	28	1
Hitchcock	9	2	21	2
Turner	10	2	28	1
Walker	10	4	22	5
Pasupati	7	0	23	0
Jefferson	3	0	13	0
CENTRAL DISTRICTS				
Hamilton	7	3	12	2
Oram	4	2	12	1
Mason	5	0	19	2
Hefford	7	4	8	2
Sulzberger	1	0	4	0

Fall of Wickets		
	CD	W
1st	11	22
2nd	16	32
3rd	38	37
4th	42	43
5th	51	43
6th	61	43
7th	105	50
8th	134	-
9th	138	-
10th	150	-

NORTHERN DISTRICTS v AUCKLAND State Shield

at Westpac Park, Hamilton (d/n) on 24 January, 2003
Toss : Auckland. Umpires : B.G. Frost & E.A. Watkin
Auckland won by 4 wickets (D/L method). *Points: Auckland 4, Northern Districts 0*

NORTHERN DISTRICTS

	Runs	Mins	Balls	6s	4s
J.A.H.Marshall c McIntosh b Mills	27	60	52	-	4
M.E.Parlane b Davis	1	10	10	-	-
H.J.H.Marshall c Vincent					
b Canning	52	127	92	-	6
S.B.Styris b Canning	31	67	54	-	3
M.N.Hart c Vincent b Canning	0	2	1	-	-
J.A.F.Yovich st Vincent b Walker	19	42	29	1	-
R.G.Hart*† c Vincent b Pryor	25	43	35	-	2
D.R.Tuffey not out	3	15	8	-	-
B.P.Martin c & b Mills	0	4	2	-	-
G.W.Aldridge c Barnes b Mills	2	3	3	-	-
I.G.Butler					
Extras (b 8, lb 10, w 20, nb 4)	42				
TOTAL (47 overs) (9 wkts)	**202**	190			

AUCKLAND

	Runs	Mins	Balls	6s	4s
L.G.Howell c Hart M.N. b Styris	31	69	51	-	5
M.J.Horne retired hurt	0	10	3	-	-
T.G.McIntosh c Marshall J.A.H.					
b Yovich	22	95	61	-	1
L.Vincent† c Hart R.G. b Tuffey	40	71	41	-	4
R.J.Nicol c Hart M.N. b Yovich	5	13	11	-	-
A.C.Barnes c Styris b Butler	30	16	16	3	2
K.D.Mills not out	4	11	3	-	-
C.R.Pryor run out	0	2	3	-	-
T.K.Canning not out	4	3	2	-	1
B.G.K.Walker*					
H.T.Davis					
Extras (lb 5, w 12, nb 4)	21				
TOTAL (31.1 overs) (6 wkts)	**157**	148			

Bowling	O	M	R	W
AUCKLAND				
Davis	10	1	42	1
Mills	9	1	21	3
Canning	10	2	22	3
Walker	7	0	44	1
Barnes	6	0	31	0
Pryor	5	0	24	1
NORTHERN DISTRICTS				
Tuffey	6	1	17	1
Butler	6.1	0	34	1
Aldridge	7	0	32	0
Yovich	6	1	41	2
Styris	6	0	28	1

Fall of Wickets		
	ND	A
1st	7	56
2nd	49	92
3rd	133	105
4th	133	148
5th	137	149
6th	190	149
7th	198	-
8th	200	-
9th	202	-
10th	-	-

Horne retired hurt at 6-0

NEW ZEALAND
CRICKET

Tenth Round

Canterbury were indebted to Harris (50 off 79 balls) as they reached 199-9. He and Fulton had added 72 for the sixth wicket. Auckland had stands of 70 for their first two wickets. Horne (50 off 59 balls) reached his highest score before he was dismissed four runs short of his hundred.

Central had another weak batting display as only three players reached double figures. Sinclair got fifty from 103 balls as Central made 168. Styris batted well and ensured that Northern got a bonus point as they won with 11.2 overs left.

Wellington struggled against a tight Otago attack and only a ninth wicket stand of 42 off 34 balls took them to 177. In reply, however, only McCullum, Sheed and McKenzie got to double figures. The first two players hit highest scores and McCullum got 50 off 92 balls. Turner had a great spell and his 5-12 was the third best bowling by a Wellington player.

CANTERBURY v AUCKLAND   State Shield

at Jade Stadium, Christchurch on 26 January, 2003
Toss : Canterbury. Umpires : G.A. Baxter & D.M. Quested
Auckland won by 6 wickets. *Points: Auckland 4, Canterbury 0*

CANTERBURY

	Runs	Mins	Balls	6s	4s
S.L.Stewart c Pryor b Mills	16	26	31	-	2
N.J.Astle c Nicol b Canning	32	108	68	-	1
C.D.McMillan c Barnes b Mills	14	18	19	-	2
G.R.Stead* run out	3	23	16	-	-
C.L.Cairns c Adams b Barnes	1	12	9	-	-
C.Z.Harris b Adams	58	116	84	1	1
P.G.Fulton run out	31	71	53	-	1
S.E.Bond b Adams	4	6	6	-	-
G.J.Hopkins† c Adams b Pryor	18	19	14	-	2
S.J.Cunis not out	5	7	6	-	-
C.S.Martin					
Extras (lb 5, w 6, nb 6)	17				
TOTAL (50 overs) (9 wkts)	**199**	207			

AUCKLAND

	Runs	Mins	Balls	6s	4s
L.G.Howell c Fulton b Astle	31	63	51	-	4
M.J.Horne c Harris b McMillan	96	165	105	1	11
T.G.McIntosh c Hopkins b Bond	17	66	50	-	2
L.Vincent† c & b McMillan	42	37	34	-	7
R.J.Nicol not out	1	7	6	-	-
A.C.Barnes not out	2	4	4	-	-
K.D.Mills					
C.R.Pryor					
T.K.Canning					
A.R.Adams					
B.G.K.Walker*					
Extras (lb 2, w 5, nb 4)	11				
TOTAL (41 overs) (4 wkts)	**200**	173			

Bowling	O	M	R	W
AUCKLAND				
Adams	10	1	50	2
Mills	10	0	36	2
Canning	10	0	23	1
Barnes	10	1	26	1
Horne	2	0	12	0
Walker	3	0	12	0
Pryor	5	0	35	1
CANTERBURY				
Bond	10	1	41	1
Martin	8	0	38	0
Cunis	6	1	25	0
Astle	6	0	28	1
Harris	6	0	27	0
McMillan	5	0	39	2

Fall of Wickets	C	A
1st	29	70
2nd	47	140
3rd	60	195
4th	65	197
5th	83	-
6th	155	-
7th	162	-
8th	187	-
9th	199	-
10th	-	-

CENTRAL DISTRICTS v NORTHERN DISTRICTS State Shield

at McLean Park, Napier on 26 January, 2003
Toss : Central Districts. Umpires : B.G. Frost & I.W. Shine
Northern Districts won by 6 wickets. Points: Northern Districts 5, Central Districts 0

CENTRAL DISTRICTS	Runs	Mins	Balls	6s	4s
C.M.Spearman* c & b Aldridge	40	60	38	-	5
J.D.Ryder run out	2	14	14	-	-
M.S.Sinclair b Yovich	61	178	113	1	4
J.M.How c Styris b Martin	4	23	13	-	1
G.P.Sulzberger c Marshall J.A.H.					
b Martin	7	8	12	1	-
I.P.Sandbrook b Butler	0	6	3	-	-
B.B.J.Griggs† run out	22	57	48	-	2
M.J.Mason run out	9	7	9	-	2
A.M.Schwass c Styris b Yovich	1	10	6	-	-
B.E.Hefford c Parlane b Yovich	2	7	11	-	-
L.J.Hamilton not out	0	7	4	-	-
Extras (lb 7, w 11, nb 2)	20				
TOTAL (44.4 overs)	**168**	193			

NORTHERN DISTRICTS	Runs	Mins	Balls	6s	4s
J.A.H.Marshall c Spearman					
b Mason	7	22	20	-	-
M.E.Parlane c How b Mason	35	65	55	1	6
H.J.H.Marshall lbw b Sulzberger	9	63	37	-	-
S.B.Styris not out	66	104	60	2	8
M.G.Orchard b Sulzberger	4	24	15	-	-
J.A.F.Yovich not out	35	57	49	-	4
R.G.Hart*†					
B.P.Martin					
D.R.Tuffey					
G.W.Aldridge					
I.G.Butler					
Extras (w 13, nb 4)	17				
TOTAL (38.4 overs) (4 wkts)	**173**	170			

Bowling	O	M	R	W
NORTHERN DISTRICTS				
Tuffey	8	0	44	0
Butler	8	1	25	1
Yovich	7.4	0	27	3
Aldridge	7	1	30	1
Martin	10	1	26	2
Styris	4	0	9	0
CENTRAL DISTRICTS				
Hamilton	8	1	28	0
Mason	9	2	44	2
Schwass	7.4	1	33	0
Hefford	8	0	35	0
Sulzberger	6	0	33	2

Fall of Wickets	CD	ND
1st	13	16
2nd	54	54
3rd	79	64
4th	89	96
5th	91	-
6th	138	-
7th	152	-
8th	156	-
9th	158	-
10th	168	-

WELLINGTON v OTAGO State Shield

at Basin Reserve, Wellington on 26 January, 2003
Toss : Otago. Umpires : B.F. Bowden & A.L. Hill
Wellington won by 58 runs. Points: Wellington 5, Otago 0

WELLINGTON	Runs	Mins	Balls	6s	4s
C.J.Nevin† c McKenzie					
b O'Connor	0	0	1	-	-
M.D.Bell* c Morland b McMillan	13	34	25	-	1
N.R.Parlane b McSkimming	19	56	49	1	3
R.A.Jones c McCullum					
b McSkimming	8	36	32	-	1
G.T.Donaldson b O'Connor	46	97	71	-	4
M.D.J.Walker b Cumming	10	43	39	-	1
P.A.Hitchcock c McCullum					
b O'Connor	17	36	26	1	1
M.Y.Pasupati run out	3	14	9	-	-
M.R.Jefferson b McSkimming	31	35	29	-	3
J.E.C.Franklin not out	16	25	14	-	1
A.D.Turner run out	0	1	1	-	-
Extras (b 7, w 7)	14				
TOTAL (49.3 overs)	**177**	193			

OTAGO	Runs	Mins	Balls	6s	4s
C.D.Cumming* lbw b Turner	2	36	21	-	-
Mohammad Wasim b Franklin	2	14	7	-	-
M.N.McKenzie c Walker					
b Turner	11	30	28	-	2
B.B.McCullum† c Jones					
b Walker	55	138	93	3	3
C.B.Gaffaney b Turner	6	18	14	-	1
J.W.Sheed c Jones b Jefferson	25	80	59	-	3
P.D.McGlashan c Jones					
b Franklin	4	9	13	-	-
W.C.McSkimming run out	6	10	8	-	-
N.D.Morland c Nevin b Turner	1	4	3	-	-
S.B.O'Connor c Walker b Turner	1	9	8	-	-
J.M.McMillan not out	0	5	2	-	-
Extras (lb 2, w 4)	6				
TOTAL (42.4 overs)	**119**	181			

Bowling	O	M	R	W
OTAGO				
O'Connor	10	2	40	3
McMillan	10	5	21	1
McSkimming	9.3	2	40	3
Cumming	10	1	39	1
Morland	10	0	30	0
WELLINGTON				
Hitchcock	8	1	17	0
Franklin	10	2	29	2
Turner	8.4	2	12	5
Walker	8	1	22	1
Pasupati	3	0	18	0
Jefferson	5	1	19	1

Fall of Wickets	W	O
1st	0	6
2nd	25	18
3rd	37	19
4th	47	35
5th	86	94
6th	123	101
7th	126	110
8th	135	112
9th	177	118
10th	177	119

WELLINGTON v NORTHERN DISTRICTS

Semi-final

at Basin Reserve, Wellington on 29 January, 2003
Toss : Wellington. Umpires : B.F. Bowden & A.L. Hill
Northern Districts won by 4 wickets

After winning the toss, Wellington had its worst performance of the season at the Basin Reserve. Butler (best figures) and Martin troubled the batsmen throughout and Wellington could reach only 137. Franklin got his highest score.

Northern started well but despite going from 40-0 to 56-3, they recovered to reach 114 only to lose another three quick wickets but still won with 11 overs left. Walker took his 50th wicket.

WELLINGTON

	Runs	Mins	Balls	6s	4s
C.J.Nevin† c & b Martin	24	69	35	-	3
M.D.Bell* lbw b Butler	0	13	10	-	-
R.A.Jones lbw b Orchard	37	96	73	-	5
N.R.Parlane st Hart b Martin	4	14	16	-	-
G.T.Donaldson c Marshall J.A.H. b Orchard	3	5	7	-	-
J.E.C.Franklin run out	34	103	82	-	3
M.D.J.Walker c Hart b Butler	4	19	15	-	1
M.R.Jefferson c Hart b Butler	0	8	3	-	-
P.A.Hitchcock c Yovich b Aldridge	4	23	10	-	-
M.R.Gillespie c Marshall J.A.H. b Aldridge	13	32	29	-	-
A.D.Turner not out	0	1	0	-	-
Extras (lb 2, w 12)	14				
TOTAL (46.4 overs)	**137**	196			

NORTHERN DISTRICTS

	Runs	Mins	Balls	6s	4s
J.A.H.Marshall lbw b Gillespie	32	46	46	-	6
N.K.W.Horsley run out	21	64	41	-	3
H.J.H.Marshall c Nevin b Gillespie	3	10	5	-	-
M.E.Parlane lbw b Walker	32	71	49	1	3
D.P.Kelly not out	30	101	70	-	4
J.A.F.Yovich c Nevin b Walker	0	2	2	-	-
M.G.Orchard lbw b Gillespie	5	13	7	-	1
R.G.Hart*† not out	8	19	14	-	1
B.P.Martin					
G.W.Aldridge					
I.G.Butler					
Extras (lb 4, w 3)	7				
TOTAL (39 overs) (6 wkts)	**138**	166			

Bowling	O	M	R	W
NORTHERN DISTRICTS				
Butler	9	2	15	3
Yovich	8	1	26	0
Aldridge	9.4	0	40	2
Orchard	10	1	32	2
Martin	10	1	22	2
WELLINGTON				
Hitchcock	7	1	27	0
Turner	8	1	24	0
Gillespie	8	1	30	3
Walker	10	1	25	2
Franklin	4	1	15	0
Jefferson	2	0	13	0

Fall of Wickets	W	ND
1st	7	40
2nd	55	52
3rd	67	56
4th	70	114
5th	83	114
6th	97	123
7th	101	-
8th	114	-
9th	137	-
10th	137	-

AUCKLAND v NORTHERN DISTRICTS   Final

at North Harbour Stadium, Auckland on 1 February, 2003
Toss : Northern Districts. Umpires : D.B. Cowie & A.L. Hill
Northern Districts won by 17 runs

Auckland sprang a surprise by calling in Haslam for his first game of the season while Matthew Hart, who had been injured, returned at the expense of Horsley.

After Parlane went early, the Marshall twins added 107 off 126 balls for the second wicket. James' fifty needed 77 balls compared to Hamish's 64 as Northern reached 234-7. Auckland lost three wickets in 42 balls and the next two stands, although adding valuable runs, took up 180 balls.

When Canning went at 121-5, 123 runs were needed off just 79 balls. The task proved too tough for Auckland and Northern went on to win the State Shield for the first time. Their last one day championship win had been in 1997/98.

NORTHERN DISTRICTS

	Runs	Mins	Balls	6s	4s
J.A.H.Marshall b Canning	67	127	89	1	5
M.E.Parlane b Davis	6	44	34	-	1
H.J.H.Marshall c Nicol b Horne	65	97	80	-	5
M.N.Hart c & b Pryor	25	66	46	-	-
D.P.Kelly c Horne b Haslam	14	26	17	-	-
J.A.F.Yovich st Young b Horne	2	7	7	-	-
R.G.Hart*† not out	21	30	17	-	2
B.P.Martin b Pryor	16	8	8	1	2
M.G.Orchard not out	4	4	5	-	-
G.W.Aldridge					
I.G.Butler					

Extras (lb 2, w 9, nb 3) 14
TOTAL (50 overs) (7 wkts) .. **234** 208

AUCKLAND

	Runs	Mins	Balls	6s	4s
L.G.Howell b Butler	1	38	18	-	-
M.J.Horne c Martin b Yovich	0	9	2	-	-
M.H.Richardson c Hart R.G.					
b Yovich	5	13	13	-	1
T.K.Canning run out	44	124	99	-	3
R.J.Nicol st Hart R.G.					
b Hart M.N.	33	64	47	1	5
A.C.Barnes c Kelly b Martin	33	71	58	1	2
C.R.Pryor c Marshall H.J.H.					
b Aldridge	38	44	30	2	1
R.A.Young† not out	36	38	26	-	5
B.G.K.Walker* not out	4	20	8	-	-
H.T.Davis					
M.J.Haslam					

Extras (lb 2, w 20, nb 1) 23
TOTAL (50 overs) (7 wkts) .. **217** 214

Bowling	O	M	R	W
AUCKLAND				
Davis	10	1	34	1
Pryor	9	0	47	2
Canning	10	1	42	1
Haslam	9	0	44	1
Walker	2	0	19	0
Barnes	5	0	26	0
Horne	5	0	20	2
NORTHERN DISTRICTS				
Butler	10	1	39	1
Yovich	10	0	52	2
Orchard	3	1	10	0
Aldridge	7	0	43	1
Martin	10	2	39	1
Hart M.N.	10	0	32	1

Fall of Wickets		
	ND	A
1st	29	5
2nd	136	13
3rd	150	18
4th	171	73
5th	178	121
6th	204	157
7th	223	181
8th	-	-
9th	-	-
10th	-	-

2002/03 STATE SHIELD AVERAGES

	M	In	NO	HS	Runs	Ave	100s	50s	Ct	St	O	M	R	W	Ave	R/O	Best
A.R.Adams	5	3	1	24	30	15.00	-	-	2	-	46	3	222	7	31.71	4.83	4-37
G.W.Aldridge	12	6	2	28	55	13.75	-	-	2	-	91.3	7	403	15	26.86	4.40	3-38
C.J.Anderson	8	6	1	16	51	10.20	-	-	2	-	55	3	247	3	82.33	4.49	2-39
N.J.Astle	2	2	0	32	62	31.00	-	-	1	-	14	1	59	1	59.00	4.21	1-28
A.C.Barnes	10	10	3	57*	289	41.28	-	3	3	-	48.4	2	219	6	36.50	4.50	3-42
M.D.Bell	11	11	0	80	231	21.00	-	2	2	-							
S.E.Bond	3	2	0	40	44	22.00	-	-	-	-	25	1	119	2	59.50	4.76	1-32
R.D.Burson	2	1	1	13*	13	-	-	-	-	-	17	2	72	3	24.00	4.24	3-34
I.G.Butler	7	1	0	4	4	4.00	-	-	-	-	53.1	6	262	9	29.11	4.92	3-15
C.L.Cairns	7	6	2	63	159	39.75	-	1	1	-							
T.K.Canning	11	9	1	44	106	13.25	-	-	-	-	90	10	292	12	24.33	3.24	3-20
C.J.Cornelius	3	2	1	31*	31	31.00	-	-	1	-	16	2	74	1	74.00	4.63	1-44
C.D.Cumming	10	10	0	75	230	23.00	-	2	2	-	16	1	76	0	76.00	4.75	1-39
S.J.Cunis	9	7	4	33	60	20.00	-	-	3	-	76.4	11	281	14	20.07	3.66	3-17
H.T.Davis	7	3	1	17	30	15.00	-	-	1	-	56	5	242	10	24.20	4.32	3-35
G.T.Donaldson	8	7	0	75	169	24.14	-	1	-	-							
J.I.Englefield	2	2	0	6	9	4.50	-	-	-	-							
S.P.Fleming	4	4	0	57	105	26.25	-	1	1	-							
J.E.C.Franklin	10	7	5	34	67	33.50	-	-	2	-	76.2	11	316	5	63.20	4.13	2-29
P.G.Fulton	10	7	0	64	124	17.71	-	1	3	-	3	0	24	0	-	8.00	-
C.J.M.Furlong	9	7	4	39	100	33.33	-	-	7	-	62.1	6	245	12	20.41	3.94	3-24
C.B.Gaffaney	2	2	0	6	8	4.00	-	-	2	-							
M.R.Gillespie	7	3	1	13	18	9.00	-	-	-	-	57	5	236	13	18.15	4.14	4-31
B.B.J.Griggs	10	9	1	59	131	16.37	-	1	9	1							
L.J.Hamilton	9	5	2	7*	10	3.33	-	-	-	-	75.2	14	261	9	29.00	3.46	3-37
C.Z.Harris	9	7	1	83*	236	39.33	-	2	5	-	70	5	234	10	23.40	3.34	4-28
M.N.Hart	10	10	0	98	301	30.10	-	3	8	-	57	1	213	5	42.60	3.74	2-30
R.G.Hart	12	11	5	34	107	17.83	-	-	9	2							
M.J.Haslam	1	-	-	-	-	-	-	-	-	-	9	0	44	1	44.00	4.89	1-44
B.E.Hefford	7	4	1	7	15	5.00	-	-	2	-	58	7	240	10	24.00	4.14	3-44
P.A.Hitchcock	8	8	3	39*	152	30.40	-	-	3	-	70.4	6	286	10	28.60	4.04	3-45
G.J.Hopkins	2	1	0	18	18	18.00	-	-	1	1							
A.J.Hore	5	5	0	34	108	21.60	-	-	3	-							
M.J.Horne	9	9	1	96	256	32.00	-	2	2	-	17	0	81	3	27.00	4.76	2-20
N.K.W.Horsley	5	5	0	28	88	17.60	-	-	-	-							
J.M.How	6	5	0	18	38	7.60	-	-	2	-							
L.G.Howell	11	11	1	66*	345	34.50	-	3	2	-							
P.J.Ingram	3	3	0	15	20	6.66	-	-	-	-							
M.R.Jefferson	11	8	1	31	58	8.28	-	-	1	-	58	4	259	6	43.16	4.47	1-15
R.A.Jones	11	11	0	42	278	25.27	-	-	3	-							
D.P.Kelly	4	4	1	30*	57	19.00	-	-	1	-							
R.A.Lawson	8	8	1	63*	178	25.42	-	1	2	-	0.1	0	1	0	-	-	-
G.R.Loveridge	5	5	0	13	21	4.20	-	-	-	-							
H.J.H.Marshall	11	11	2	65	191	21.22	-	2	5	-							
J.A.H.Marshall	12	12	0	67	278	23.16	-	1	10	-							
B.P.Martin	8	6	1	16	34	6.80	-	-	5	-	61	6	201	9	22.33	3.30	2-22
C.S.Martin	10	3	3	5*	7	-	-	-	2	-	84.5	7	349	14	24.92	4.11	3-35
M.J.Mason	10	7	2	16	43	8.60	-	-	1	-	81.1	10	289	16	18.06	3.56	3-22
B.B.McCullum	4	4	0	55	136	34.00	-	2	2	-							
P.D.McGlashan	10	9	2	46*	153	21.85	-	-	6	2							
T.G.McIntosh	4	4	0	33	102	25.50	-	-	5	-							
M.N.McKenzie	10	9	1	90	219	27.37	-	1	5	-							
C.D.McMillan	7	7	2	122*	154	30.80	1	-	2	-	37.4	2	166	11	15.09	4.40	4-42
J.M.McMillan	7	4	1	2	3	1.00	-	-	1	-	52	5	234	8	29.25	4.50	2-51
W.C.McSkimming	10	9	2	32	111	15.85	-	-	2	-	68.3	6	304	11	27.63	4.43	3-40
K.D.Mills	4	3	2	32*	49	49.00	-	-	2	-	37.2	2	119	8	14.87	3.18	3-21
Mohammad Wasim	10	10	0	70	212	21.20	-	2	1	-	15	1	57	0	-	3.80	-
R.G.Morgan	2	2	1	13	14	14.00	-	-	-	-	16	0	67	3	22.33	4.19	2-29
N.D.Morland	9	7	1	55	74	12.33	-	1	3	-	65	2	261	10	26.10	4.02	4-35
C.J.Nevin	11	11	0	100	312	28.36	1	1	19	1							
R.J.Nicol	11	11	1	41	169	16.90	-	-	6	-	7	0	37	0	-	5.29	-
B.J.Nielsen	1	1	0	2	2	2.00	-	-	-	-	6	0	33	1	33.00	5.50	1-33
S.B.O'Connor	10	6	1	22	57	11.40	-	-	2	-	90	10	375	16	23.43	4.17	4-18
J.D.P.Oram	2	1	0	15	15	15.00	-	-	-	-	12	5	30	3	10.00	2.50	2-18
M.G.Orchard	7	7	2	9*	36	7.20	-	-	1	-	37	3	150	6	25.00	4.05	2-25
D.J.Nash	4	3	0	88	142	47.33	-	1	1	-	34	1	139	7	19.85	4.09	3-39

	M	In	NO	HS	Runs	Ave	100s	50s	Ct	St	O	M	R	W	Ave	R/O	Best
M.H.W.Papps	8	8	2	65	228	38.00	-	2	10	1							
M.E.Parlane	12	12	0	122	281	23.41	1	-	2	-							
N.R.Parlane	10	9	0	41	156	17.33	-	-	1	-							
M.Y.Pasupati	9	7	3	34*	73	18.25	-	-	2	-	48	3	211	4	52.75	4.40	2-24
A.J.Penn	2	2	0	15	17	8.50	-	-	-	-	13	1	77	2	38.50	5.92	2-32
C.R.Pryor	10	8	2	38	116	19.33	-	-	3	-	44	1	254	8	31.75	5.77	3-37
M.H.Richardson	7	7	0	34	123	17.57	-	-	-	-							
J.D.Ryder	9	9	0	63	219	24.33	-	2	1	-	6	0	37	0	-	6.17	-
I.P.Sandbrook	8	8	1	57	79	11.28	-	1	1	-							
A.M.Schwass	6	5	2	9*	19	6.33	-	-	2	-	47.4	4	223	11	20.27	4.67	3-31
G.S.Shaw	4	2	2	2*	2	-	-	-	-	-	24	2	89	8	11.12	3.71	3-24
H.J.Shaw	5	2	0	24	33	16.50	-	-	1	-	27.1	3	110	8	13.75	4.05	5-14
J.W.Sheed	2	2	0	25	46	23.00	-	-	-	-							
M.S.Sinclair	5	5	1	61	78	19.50	-	1	3	-							
C.M.Spearman	10	10	0	97	350	35.00	-	3	10	-							
G.R.Stead	10	9	1	66	175	21.87	-	1	4	-							
S.L.Stewart	10	10	0	45	214	21.40	-	-	3	-							
S.B.Styris	8	8	2	91*	293	48.83	-	3	4	-	64	10	208	9	23.11	3.25	3-20
G.P.Sulzberger	10	9	0	51	177	19.66	-	1	2	-	60	1	272	6	45.33	4.53	2-27
R.L.Taylor	1	1	0	11	11	11.00	-	-	-	-							
D.R.Tuffey	4	2	2	3*	4	-	-	-	1	-	29	2	125	3	41.66	4.31	1-17
A.D.Turner	8	4	3	6*	6	6.00	-	-	1	-	73.4	13	250	16	15.62	3.39	5-12
D.L.Vettori	3	3	0	89	156	52.00	-	2	3	-	26.3	0	69	5	13.80	2.60	2-17
L.Vincent	8	8	0	66	263	32.87	-	2	17	3							
B.G.K.Walker	11	5	3	33*	59	29.50	-	-	2	-	73	8	259	8	32.37	3.55	3-17
M.D.J.Walker	11	11	2	62	241	26.77	-	2	6	-	98	9	348	18	19.33	5.22	
K.P.Walmsley	8	5	4	25*	33	33.00	-	-	2	-	65.2	4	314	12	26.16	4.80	3-45
G.L.West	5	2	2	12*	16	-	-	-	1	-	36	5	196	1	196.00	5.44	1-39
S.J.G.Whiteman	2	1	0	0	0	0.00	-	-	-	-	3	1	5	0	-	1.67	-
J.W.Wilson	5	3	1	5	9	4.50	-	-	4	-	30	3	110	5	22.00	3.67	3-42
P.J.Wiseman	3	3	0	22	24	8.00	-	-	1	-	7	0	33	1	33.00	4.71	1-33
R.A.Young	3	2	1	36*	47	47.00	-	-	4	1							
J.A.F.Yovich	12	12	1	70	265	24.09	-	2	5	-	84.4	3	434	23	18.86	5.12	4-50

HIGHEST STRIKE RATES *(qualification 150 runs)*

		Runs	Balls	S/R				Runs	Balls	S/R
C.M.Spearman	CD	350	294	119		J.D.Ryder	CD	219	263	83
C.L.Cairns	C	159	166	95		M.J.Horne	A	256	312	82
D.L.Vettori	ND	156	170	91		S.B.Styris	ND	293	365	80
P.A.Hitchcock	W	152	168	90		L.G.Howell	A	345	438	78
A.C.Barnes	A	289	328	88		Mohammad Wasim	O	212	282	75

MOST ECONOMICAL BOWLING *(qualification 30 overs)*

		O	M	R	W	Ave	R/O
K.D.Mills	A	37.2	2	119	8	14.87	3.18
T.K.Canning	A	90	10	292	12	24.33	3.24
S.B.Styris	ND	64	10	208	9	23.11	3.25
B.P.Martin	ND	61	6	201	9	22.33	3.29
C.Z.Harris	C	70	5	234	10	23.40	3.34
A.D.Turner	W	73.5	13	250	16	15.62	3.38
L.J.Hamilton	CD	75.2	14	261	9	29.00	3.46
B.G.K.Walker	A	73	8	259	8	32.37	3.54
M.D.J.Walker	W	98	9	348	18	19.33	3.55
M.J.Mason	CD	81.1	10	289	16	18.06	3.56

CAREER RECORDS

	M	In	NO	HS	Runs	Ave	100s	50s	Ct	St	O	M	R	W	Ave	R/O	Best
A.R.Adams	34	27	8	47	296	15.57	-	-	7	-	289.4	18	1268	52	24.38	4.37	5-7
G.W.Aldridge	28	14	6	28	89	11.12	-	-	4	-	180.3	15	767	35	21.91	4.24	3-25
C.J.Anderson	46	26	9	39	216	12.70	-	-	14	-	357.3	25	1401	34	41.20	3.91	5-34
N.J.Astle	83	74	12	131	2507	40.43	7	9	42	-	613.1	78	2030	86	23.60	3.31	4-14
A.C.Barnes	98	96	10	107*	2486	28.90	1	19	28	-	376.3	25	1675	60	27.91	4.44	5-19
M.D.Bell	76	75	6	121*	1820	26.37	3	7	37	-	0.2	0	4	0	-	-	-
S.E.Bond	20	14	8	40	137	22.83	-	-	3	-	154.5	13	715	23	31.08	4.61	4-36
R.D.Burson	24	10	7	15*	67	22.33	-	-	2	-	182	19	739	33	22.39	4.06	4-45
I.G.Butler	9	2	1	10*	14	14.00	-	-	-	-	68.1	6	361	10	36.10	5.29	3-15
C.L.Cairns	74	66	10	143	1922	34.32	3	9	16	-	469.5	35	1835	82	22.37	3.90	6-37
T.K.Canning	40	35	4	92*	719	23.19	-	4	7	-	271	18	1142	44	25.95	4.21	4-30
C.J.Cornelius	5	4	2	31*	48	24.00	-	-	2	-	36	3	140	5	28.00	3.89	2-28
C.D.Cumming	48	45	0	75	826	18.35	-	6	17	-	176	7	792	15	52.80	4.50	2-34
S.J.Cunis	30	18	7	33	125	11.36	-	-	5	-	256.1	25	924	43	21.48	3.60	4-37
H.T.Davis	27	12	6	21	95	15.83	-	-	8	-	203	13	932	26	35.84	4.59	3-35
G.T.Donaldson	30	28	2	80	646	24.84	-	4	7	-	8	0	35	0	-	4.38	-
J.I.Englefield	9	9	1	70	191	23.87	-	2	1	-							
S.P.Fleming	58	54	9	120*	1784	39.64	3	12	29	-							
J.E.C.Franklin	20	15	9	34	149	24.83	-	-	4	-	146.2	18	600	25	24.00	4.10	4-30
P.G.Fulton	13	10	0	64	180	18.00	-	1	3	-	3	0	24	0	-	8.00	-
C.J.M.Furlong	51	43	18	62*	618	24.72	-	1	19	-	401.5	31	1651	52	31.75	4.10	4-9
C.B.Gaffaney	67	66	1	79*	1455	22.38	-	6	18	-	6	0	36	1	36.00	6.00	1-4
M.R.Gillespie	13	6	2	13	26	6.50	-	-	1	-	99	8	435	18	24.16	4.39	4-31
B.B.J.Griggs	26	20	2	59	293	16.27	-	1	31	1							
L.J.Hamilton	29	16	7	7*	32	3.55	-	-	6	-	244.3	31	993	31	32.03	4.06	4-41
C.Z.Harris	94	87	28	107	2594	43.96	1	15	42	-	718.3	56	2530	96	26.35	3.52	4-28
M.N.Hart	83	75	10	100	1586	24.40	1	11	45	-	540.1	51	2079	79	26.31	3.84	4-7
R.G.Hart	113	87	30	56	1082	18.98	-	2	104	28							
M.J.Haslam	49	24	11	25	124	9.53	-	-	10	-	392.2	29	1493	48	31.10	3.80	4-33
B.E.Hefford	23	12	4	16*	48	6.00	-	-	2	-	186	20	739	36	20.52	3.97	3-13
P.A.Hitchcock	38	32	10	39*	378	17.18	-	-	11	-	321	24	1364	69	19.76	4.25	5-10
G.J.Hopkins	52	38	8	82	630	21.00	-	3	49	10							
A.J.Hore	41	39	1	102	825	21.71	1	3	19	-	11.4	0	78	1	78.00	6.68	1-35
M.J.Horne	54	53	1	96	1335	25.67	-	10	12	-	141.3	5	648	18	36.00	4.57	3-17
N.K.W.Horsley	12	12	2	89*	244	24.40	-	1	1	-							
J.M.How	12	11	0	36	99	9.90	-	-	4	-							
L.G.Howell	93	93	13	134*	2853	35.66	5	21	19	-	15	0	98	2	49.00	6.53	2-35
P.J.Ingram	5	5	0	100	125	25.00	1	-	-	-							
M.R.Jefferson	72	49	18	48*	488	15.74	-	-	16	-	478.3	31	1971	54	36.50	4.11	4-32
R.A.Jones	62	61	5	78*	1288	23.00	-	3	16	-							
D.P.Kelly	39	39	2	140	848	22.91	1	3	10	-							
R.A.Lawson	80	78	7	83*	1989	28.01	-	14	23	-	6.3	1	44	0	-	6.76	-
G.R.Loveridge	18	16	3	50*	185	14.23	-	1	-	-	99.1	7	424	16	26.50	4.27	4-25
H.J.H.Marshall	53	51	5	93	1084	23.56	-	7	22	-							
J.A.H.Marshall	37	36	3	100*	947	28.69	1	4	18	-							
B.P.Martin	19	12	4	17	63	7.87	-	-	7	-	150.4	10	511	19	26.89	3.39	3-28
C.S.Martin	37	11	6	5*	26	5.20	-	-	4	-	302.1	28	1290	60	21.50	4.26	5-43
M.J.Mason	44	27	8	17*	139	7.31	-	-	6	-	327.1	37	1364	61	22.36	4.16	4-16
B.B.McCullum	9	9	0	55	157	17.44	-	2	2	-							
P.D.McGlashan	16	15	3	46*	194	16.16	-	-	16	3							
T.G.McIntosh	10	10	0	57	204	20.40	-	1	8	-							
M.N.McKenzie	13	12	2	90	241	24.10	-	1	6	-							
C.D.McMillan	64	61	9	125	1799	34.59	5	6	23	-	105.3	4	555	22	25.22	5.26	5-38
J.M.McMillan	14	9	5	2*	9	2.25	-	-	1	-	112.3	10	462	21	22.00	4.10	3-30
W.C.McSkimming	30	27	11	59*	292	18.25	-	1	8	-	225	16	1007	39	25.82	4.48	3-14
K.D.Mills	35	29	10	32*	360	18.94	-	-	11	-	282.2	25	1131	51	22.17	4.00	4-40
Mohammad Wasim	10	10	0	70	212	21.20	-	2	1	-	15	1	57	0	-	3.80	-
R.G.Morgan	21	14	3	44	181	16.45	-	-	4	-	154	11	667	16	41.68	4.33	3-31
N.D.Morland	23	17	4	55	155	11.92	-	1	4	-	165	7	688	16	43.00	4.17	4-35
C.J.Nevin	76	72	6	149	1821	27.59	3	9	112	12							
R.J.Nicol	11	11	1	41	169	16.90	-	-	6	-	7	0	37	0	-	5.29	-
B.J.Nielsen	1	1	0	2	2	2.00	-	-	-	-	6	0	33	1	33.00	5.50	1-33
S.B.O'Connor	43	29	10	22	196	10.31	-	-	8	-	395	29	1758	70	25.11	4.45	4-18
J.D.P.Oram	39	35	3	127	915	28.59	1	4	12	-	138.3	12	498	17	29.29	3.59	2-13
M.G.Orchard	7	7	2	9*	36	7.20	-	-	1	-	37	3	150	6	25.00	4.05	2-25

	M	In	NO	HS	Runs	Ave	100s	50s	Ct	St	O	M	R	W	Ave	R/O	Best
M.H.W.Papps	18	18	3	65	410	27.33	-	3	17	1							
M.E.Parlane	93	93	3	122	2646	29.40	3	15	15	-	0.3	0	5	0	-	-	-
N.R.Parlane	43	42	3	96*	930	23.84	-	5	18	-							
M.Y.Pasupati	36	26	5	34*	251	11.95	-	-	7	-	211.3	14	974	31	31.41	4.60	3-39
A.J.Penn	45	33	6	63	354	13.11	-	1	11	-	365.5	23	1723	72	23.93	4.70	7-28
C.R.Pryor	36	33	5	91	750	26.78	-	4	9	-	153.4	3	851	22	38.68	5.53	3-37
M.H.Richardson	76	74	7	128*	2283	34.07	3	14	14	-	123	2	560	10	56.00	4.55	2-25
J.D.Ryder	9	9	0	63	219	24.33	-	2	1	-	6	0	37	0	-	6.17	-
I.P.Sandbrook	8	8	1	57	79	11.28	-	1	1	-							
A.M.Schwass	24	18	5	32*	148	11.38	-	-	9	-	188.5	13	824	37	22.27	4.36	4-14
G.S.Shaw	6	4	4	9*	12		-	-	-	-	39	4	156	11	14.18	4.00	3-24
H.J.Shaw	5	2	0	24	33	16.50	-	-	1	-	27.1	3	110	8	13.75	4.05	5-14
J.W.Sheed	3	3	0	25	59	19.66	-	-	1	-							
M.S.Sinclair	61	60	5	110	1410	25.63	1	10	30	1							
C.M.Spearman	71	71	1	126	1903	27.18	1	12	26	-	4	0	26	0	-	6.50	-
G.R.Stead	86	79	10	101*	2022	29.30	2	9	31	-	3	0	23	0	-	7.67	-
S.L.Stewart	19	19	0	76	477	25.10	-	1	7	-							
S.B.Styris	62	55	15	123	1415	35.37	1	9	27	-	450	32	1968	78	25.23	4.37	4-19
G.P.Sulzberger	62	56	6	71	1331	26.62	-	8	29	-	335.4	16	1435	37	38.78	4.27	3-18
R.L.Taylor	1	1	0	11	11	11.00	-	-	-	-							
D.R.Tuffey	51	25	19	23*	153	25.50	-	-	15	-	384.4	26	1677	54	31.05	4.35	3-11
A.D.Turner	12	5	4	6*	10	10.00	-	-	2	-	109.4	20	361	23	15.69	3.29	5-12
D.L.Vettori	31	26	4	89	565	25.68	-	4	14	-	261.3	15	1014	32	31.68	3.87	3-24
L.Vincent	41	39	2	145	1147	31.00	2	6	49	3	4.4	0	19	1	19.00	4.07	1-8
B.G.K.Walker	47	28	7	33*	232	11.04	-	-	20	-	368.1	27	1390	43	32.32	3.77	4-39
M.D.J.Walker	51	42	6	62	649	18.02	-	4	17	-	350.2	33	1287	51	25.23	3.67	5-22
K.P.Walmsley	39	21	12	26*	147	16.33	-	-	5	-	330.1	24	1471	44	33.43	4.45	3-30
G.L.West	8	5	3	12*	27	13.50	-	-	2	-	64	8	333	7	47.57	5.20	3-41
S.J.G.Whiteman	2	1	0	0	0	0.00	-	-	-	-	3	1	5	0	-	1.67	-
J.W.Wilson	26	23	3	99	326	16.30	-	1	20	-	193	15	742	26	28.53	3.84	3-34
P.J.Wiseman	60	51	8	65*	651	15.13	-	1	18	-	437	44	1743	34	51.26	3.99	3-11
R.A.Young	15	11	2	36*	138	15.33	-	-	17	5							
J.A.F.Yovich	44	34	8	70	409	15.73	-	2	15	-	258	14	1279	59	21.67	4.96	4-50

STATE OF ORIGIN

NORTH ISLAND v SOUTH ISLAND

State of Origin

at North Harbour Stadium, Auckland on 2 February, 2003
Toss : North Island. Umpires : D.B. Cowie & A.L. Hill
South Island won by 2 wickets

This inter-island match was played over four innings of 25 overs each with bowlers limited to ten overs per game. Players were selected depending on which major association they had first played for.

After making a flying start, North were pegged back by Hefford and Cunis who each captured two wickets. Howell, with 63 off 53 balls, took South to an eight run lead which was soon wiped off by 18-year-old Ryder who put on 79 for the second wicket with Canning. Both left at the same score and wickets fell quickly and it was left to Martin, with 27 off 17 balls, to boost the lead to 153.

South were going well at 76-2 but lost their way after Gaffaney departed for 52 made off just 27 balls and slumped to 131-8. It was finally left to Anderson and O'Connor who quickly hit off the required runs.

NORTH ISLAND

FIRST INNINGS	Runs	Mins	Balls	6s	4s
C.J.Nevin† c Papps b Martin	28	26	21	-	6
J.D.Ryder run out	20	19	12	-	4
M.J.Horne c Cunis b Hefford	6	10	4	-	1
R.A.Jones* c & b Cunis	24	34	26	-	2
J.A.H.Marshall c Stead b Hefford	46	66	50	1	4
A.C.Barnes run out	1	2	3	-	1
T.K.Canning c Papps b Cunis	7	11	8	-	1
M.D.J.Walker not out	18	31	18	-	2
J.A.F.Yovich c Gaffaney b McSkimming	3	2	3	-	-
B.P.Martin b McSkimming	0	1	1	-	-
M.J.Mason not out	7	4	6	-	1
I.G.Butler					
Extras (lb 3, nb 2)	5				
TOTAL (25 overs) (9 wkts)	**165**	108			

SECOND INNINGS	Runs	Mins	Balls	6s	4s
(1) c Howell b Cumming	43	42	41	-	6
(2) c & b Anderson	1	5	3	-	-
c Papps b Hefford	0	3	1	-	-
lbw b Cunis	12	19	15	-	1
run out	6	9	6	-	-
(3) run out	40	45	31	2	3
(7) not out	20	38	23	-	-
(8) run out	7	10	11	-	1
not out	27	19	17	1	4
(9) st Papps b Cumming	0	2	2	-	-
(lb 4, w 1)	5				
TOTAL (25 overs) (8 wkts)	**161**	100			

SOUTH ISLAND

	Runs	Mins	Balls	6s	4s
L.G.Howell lbw b Martin	63	67	53	2	6
M.H.W.Papps† c Marshall b Butler	2	9	6	-	-
C.D.Cumming lbw b Mason	26	30	24	-	3
C.B.Gaffaney c Walker b Martin	25	31	24	-	3
G.R.Stead* c Nevin b Walker	24	26	21	-	2
S.L.Stewart b Mason	6	5	5	-	1
W.C.McSkimming b Mason	0	1	1	-	-
C.J.Anderson not out	12	18	13	-	-
S.J.Cunis not out	3	4	3	-	-
S.B.O'Connor					
B.E.Hefford					
C.S.Martin					
Extras (b 1, lb 5, w 6)	12				
TOTAL (25 overs) (7 wkts)	**173**	99			

	Runs	Mins	Balls	6s	4s
c Horne b Mason	1	6	4	-	-
c Canning b Walker	29	42	31	-	2
c Horne b Mason	2	7	3	-	-
c Walker b Martin	52	33	27	-	10
b Canning	9	19	18	-	1
st sub (D.R.Winger) b Martin	6	16	13	-	-
run out	4	18	13	-	-
not out	24	41	26	-	2
b Walker	5	10	11	-	-
not out	17	14	12	-	2
(b 1, lb 2, w 2, nb 1)	6				
(24.3 overs) (8 wkts)	**155**	107			

Bowling	O	M	R	W	O	M	R	W
SOUTH ISLAND								
O'Connor	4	0	35	0				
Martin	4	0	22	1	2	0	23	0
Hefford	6	0	32	2	4	0	21	1
Cunis	5	0	22	2	4	0	23	1
Anderson	3	0	29	0	3	0	16	1
McSkimming	3	0	22	2	3	0	23	0
Cumming					9	0	51	2
NORTH ISLAND								
Butler	3	0	21	1	2	0	15	0
Yovich	2	0	26	0				
Mason	5	0	26	3	4	0	29	2
Canning	5	0	31	0	4.3	0	31	1
Walker	5	0	33	1	5	0	17	2
Martin	5	0	30	2	5	0	34	2
Barnes					4	0	26	0

Fall of Wickets	NI	SI	NI	SI
	1st	1st	2nd	2nd
1st	43	15	5	7
2nd	51	77	84	14
3rd	55	119	84	76
4th	93	126	90	87
5th	94	135	102	103
6th	121	135	108	103
7th	153	167	121	122
8th	157	-	122	131
9th	157	-	-	-
10th	-	-	-	-

PROVINCIAL A TEAM COMPETITION

For the first time, the New Zealand Under 19 team participated in the Provincial A competition alongside the second elevens of the major associations. The enlarged programme was made up entirely of two-day games with the majority of matches being played at the Lincoln complex. The tournament ended with neighbouring associations playing two matches against each other.

Final placings were: Otago, Wellington, Canterbury, New Zealand Under 19, Northern Districts, Auckland, Central Districts.

CANTERBURY v AUCKLAND *First innings win to Canterbury*
At Bert Sutcliffe Oval, Lincoln *2, 3 January, 2003*

Canterbury 316-9d and 105-1. R.M. Frew 16, 25*, T.J. Papps 34, 2*, A.M. McDowell 3, –, C.L. Cairns 25, 78, B.A. Yock 16, –, A.J. Redmond 23, –, G.J. Hopkins 104*, –, R.M. Miller 5, –, A.M. Ellis 3, –, B.P. Donkers 59, –, H.J. Shaw 8*, –, S.R. George –, –, Extras 20, 0.
Wood 1-52, 0-21, McKay 3-89, –, Henderson 3-81, 1-18, Whiteman 2-56, 0-66, Lythe 0-23, –.

Auckland 230. N.G. Jury 65, T.G. McIntosh 67, J.M. Vujnovich 4, R.T. King 5, C.W. Burroughs 12, T.H. Topia 4, T.I. Lythe 4, S.J.G. Whiteman 32, A.J. McKay 16, G.A. Wood 7*, R.J.G. Henderson 0, R.K. Lynch –, Extras 14.
Shaw 4-50, Donkers 1-40, Ellis 1-39, George 1-48, Redmond 3-46, Cairns 0-0.

NORTHERN DISTRICTS v CENTRAL DISTRICTS *First innings win to Northern*
At Lincoln No.3 *2, 3 January, 2003*

Northern Districts 334-9d. D.P. Kelly 96, G.G. Robinson 20, M.K. Drake 71, J.B. Lee 12, J.G. Hatwell 4, B.J. Hatwell 35, N.M. Daley 11, G.D. Irwin 44, L.J. Hammond 15, S.L. Andrews 4*, N.R.J. Aldridge, –, D.R.T. Pinny –, Extras 24.
Robin 0-63, Diamanti 1-63, Todd 0-18, Thompson 0-72, Good 0-34, West 1-26, Calkin 0-17, How 4-35.

Central Districts 232. A.D. Murley 3, H.J. Cunliffe 100, G.R. Todd 11, J.M. How 10, M.J.E. Calkin 10, D.R. Cederman 5, M.A. Sigley 43, B.J. Diamanti 0, R.M. West 1, E.P. Thompson 13*, T.P. Robin 11, D.T. Good –, Extras 25.
Andrews 2-49, Hammond 2-34, Pinny 2-36, Irwin 1-23, Aldridge 0-26, J.G. Hatwell 0-38, B.J. Hatwell 3-15.

NEW ZEALAND UNDER 19 v WELLINGTON *First innings win to Wellington*
At Lincoln Green *2, 3 January, 2003*

Wellington 392-9d and 98-5. S.A. Fairley 34, 10, L.J. Woodcock 91, 24, T.C. Crabb 9, 25, L.J. Morgan 42, 5, J.P. McNamee 39, 0, S.M. Mills 33, 7*, G.A. Howell 0, 14*, B.R. Jansen 1, –, A.J. Penn 59*, –, C.P. Dixon 29, –, J.S. Patel 30*, –, Q.E. de Bruin –, –, Extras 25, 13.
Bates 1-52, –, Chambers 0-63, 0-22, Standfield 4-77, 1-13, Hegglun 0-67, –, Hill 2-61, –, Smith 2-52, 2-29, Broom –, 2-21.

New Zealand Under 19 240. B.J. Wilson 36, D.R. Flynn 7, N.T. Broom 5, R.L. Taylor 27, S.R. Allen 1, J.R. Hill 27, B.J. Chard 74, M.D. Bates 22, G.J. Hegglun 14, A.S.T. Chambers 5, E.L. Standfield 2, C.M. Smith –, Extras 20.
Penn 2-21, de Bruin 2-55, Dixon 0-9, Crabb 1-16, Patel 5-53, Woodcock 0-56, Jansen 0-23.

AUCKLAND v CENTRAL DISTRICTS   *First innings win to Auckland*
At Lincoln Green   4, 5 January, 2003

Auckland 228 and 81-3. N.G. Jury 8, 33, T.G. McIntosh 18, 25, J.M. Vujnovich 45, 2, R.T. King 9, 15*, C.W. Burroughs 5, –, J. Nielsen 25, –, T.H. Topia 72, 2*, T.I. Lythe 30*, –, A.J. McKay 1, –, G.A. Wood 0, –, R.J.G. Henderson 5, –, Extras 13, 4.
Robin 1-40, 0-10, Rankin 2-44, 0-10, Diamanti 1-27, 0-9, Cederman 0-9, –, West 4-40, 1-25, Good 2-35, 2-26, Calkin 0-26, 0-0.
Central Districts 184. A.D. Murley 22, H.J. Cunliffe 18, G.R. Todd 0, J.M. How 1, M.J.E. Calkin 8, D.R. Cederman 13, M.A. Sigley 39, B.J. Diamanti 6, D.R.B. Rankin 38*, D.T. Good 9, T.P. Robin 17, R.M. West –, Extras 13.
McKay 3-48, Wood 1-19, Lythe 2-40, Nielsen 0-14, Henderson 3-35, Topia 1-17.

NEW ZEALAND UNDER 19 v CANTERBURY   *First innings win to NZ Under 19*
At Bert Sutcliffe Oval, Lincoln   4, 5 January, 2003

New Zealand Under 19 432 and 105-4. B.J. Wilson 12, 4, D.R. Flynn 3, 0, N.T. Broom 128, 8, R.L. Taylor 100, 21, S.R. Allen 52, 39*, J.R. Hill 30, 21*, B.J. Chard 47, M.P. Goldstein 0, –, G.J. Hegglun 3, –, C.M. Smith 4, –, A.S.T. Chambers 9*, –, E.L. Standfield –, –, Extras 44, 12.
Shaw 3-57, 2-30, Burson 2-75, –, George 0-76, 0-19, Ellis 0-51, –, Borren 1-55, 0-28, Redmond 4-82, –, Miller 0-2, –.
Canterbury 260. R.M. Frew 5, T.J. Papps 0, A.M. McDowell 8, B.A. Yock 1, G.J. Hopkins 32, A.J. Redmond 29, R.M. Miller 27, A.M. Ellis 47*, P.W. Borren 23, R.D. Burson 3, H.J. Shaw 72, S.R. George –, Extras 13.
Chambers 2-49, Standfield 3-62, Hill 0-46, Hegglun 1-18, Smith 2-50, Goldstein 0-20, Broom 2-8.

OTAGO v NORTHERN DISTRICTS   *First innings win to Otago*
At Lincoln No.3   4, 5 January, 2003

Otago 410-8d. C.B. Gaffaney 167, T.I. Weston 27, R.E. King 26, J.W. Sheed 83, S.P. Beare 17, J.M. Waldron 15, D.M. Smith 19*, N.L. McCullum 2, H.J. Finch 12, S.B. Haig 5*, D.G. Sewell –, D.J. Reddington –, Extras 37.
Andrews 2-43, Hammond 0-74, Irwin 1-40, Pinny 0-31, J.G. Hatwell 3-75, Aldridge 0-88, Robinson 1-26.
Northern Districts 263. G.G. Robinson 3, A.C. Beagley 26, L.J. Hammond 25, M.K. Drake 38, J.B. Lee 64, J.G Hatwell 49, B.J. Hatwell 17, N.M. Daley 5, G.D. Irwin 2, S.L. Andrews 4*, N.R.J. Aldridge 6, D.R.T Pinny –, Extras 24.
Sewell 2-55, Reddington 2-28, McCullum 4-61, Finch 0-20, Waldron 1-25, Sheed 1-15, Beare 0-45.

CENTRAL DISTRICTS v CANTERBURY   *First innings win to Canterbury*
At Lincoln Green   6, 7 January, 2003

Canterbury 446-8d and 102-3. R.M. Frew 2, 28, R.M. Miller 184, –, J.I. Englefield 28, 46*, G.J. Hopkins 84, 15*, B.A. Yock 37, 1, A.J. Redmond 27, –, A.G. Buckingham 0, 0, P.J. Wiseman 42*, –, A.M. Ellis 0, –, P.W. Borren 18*, –, R.D. Burson –, S.R. George –, –, Extras 24, 12.
Rankin 2-89, 0-12, Robin 1-81, 0-11, Thompson 1-46, 2-13, Good 0-91, 1-18, West 1-70, –, Calkin 2-22, 0-22, How 1-35, –, Cederman –, 0-9, Sigley –, 0-7.
Central Districts 312. A.D. Murley 1, H.J. Cunliffe 2, G.R. Todd 17, J.M. How 5, P.J. Ingram 100, M.A. Sigley 23, M.J.E. Calkin 3, D.R. Cederman 6, R.M. West 54, E.P. Thompson 44, D.R.B. Rankin 24, T.P. Robin 8*, D.T. Good –, Extras 25.
Burson 0-60, Ellis 3-62, Redmond 4-70, Wiseman 1-53, George 1-36, Borren 1-12.

NEW ZEALAND UNDER 19 v OTAGO *Otago won by 3 wickets*
At Lincoln No.3 6, 7 January, 2003

New Zealand Under 19 273 and 101-1d. B.J. Wilson 0, 6, D.R. Flynn 25, 56*, N.T. Broom 63, 34*, R.L. Taylor 47, –, S.R. Allen 12, –, J.R. Hill 18, –, B.J. Chard 8, –, M.P. Goldstein 22, –, M.D. Bates 27, –, C.M. Smith 0, –, E.L. Standfield 19*, –, A.S.T. Chambers –, –, Extras 32, 5.
Sewell 4-46, –, Scott 3-78, 0-21, Waldron 1-61, 1-17, Reddington 0-26, –, McCullum 0-15, 0-13, Murley 2-32, 0-19, Beare –, 0-26.

Otago 128 and 247-7. C.B. Gaffaney 39, 33, J.D. Homer 5, 9, R.E. King 10, 5, J.W. Sheed 2, 103*, S.P. Beare 7, 56, J.M. Waldron 12, 14, T.I. Weston 0, 9, N.L. McCullum 10, 1, B.E. Scott 7, 0*, D.G. Sewell 19, –, D.J. Reddington 4*, –, S.W. Murley –, –, Extras 13, 17.
Bates 5-29, 2-63, Standfield 0-29, 2-33, Chambers 3-29, 2-51, Goldstein 0-20, 0-39, Smith 2-20, 1-22, Broom 0-0, –, Hill –, 0-25.

WELLINGTON v NORTHERN DISTRICTS *First innings win to Wellington*
At Bert Sutcliffe Oval, Lincoln 6, 7 January, 2003

Wellington 302 and 92-2. S.A. Fairley 4, 58, L.J. Woodcock 17, 1, T.C. Crabb 104, –, L.J. Morgan 0, –, J.P. McNamee 101, –, S.M. Mills 12, –, D.J. Bowden 26, –, G.A. Howell 3, 29*, A.J. Penn 0, –, J.S Patel 30, –, Q.E. de Bruin 0*, –, I.E. O'Brien –, 0*, Extras 5, 4.
Andrews 1-70, 0-13, Hammond 4-44, 1-39, Pinny 2-71, 1-28, Irwin 2-43, 0-9, J.G. Hatwell 0-32, –, Aldridge 1-33, –, B.J. Hatwell 0-4, –.

Northern Districts 191. G.G. Robinson 47, A.C. Beagley 1, M.K. Drake 17, J.B. Lee 13, J.G. Hatwell 8, B.J. Hatwell 41, G.D. Irwin 39, N.M. Daley 3, L.J. Hammond 4*, S.L. Andrews 0, D.R.T. Pinny 0, N.R.J. Aldridge, Extras 18.
Penn 4-14, O'Brien 1-58, de Bruin 0-39, Patel 3-46, Woodcock 2-18, Bowden 0-4.

AUCKLAND v OTAGO *First innings win to Otago*
At Lincoln Green 9, 10 January, 2003

Auckland 144 and 168-8. N.G. Jury 5, 5, J.M. Vujnovich 18, 7, R.K. Lynch 3, 13, R.T. King 4, 1, C.W. Burroughs 0, 8, B.J. Nielsen 56, 54, T.H. Topia 0, 15, T.I. Lythe 11, 23*, T.S. Nethula 6, 29, A.J. McKay 28, 0*, R.J.G. Henderson 5*, –, G.A. Wood –, –, Extras 8, 13.
Sewell 0-27, 3-26, Scott 1-23, 2-27, Lobb 5-24, 0-8, Waldron 0-12, –, McCullum 0-18, 2-47, Murley 3-24, 1-36, Beare 0-11, 0-13.

Otago 146. C.B. Gaffaney 8, J.D. Homer 10, R.E. King 62, S.P. Beare 0, T.I Weston 13, J.M. Waldron 24, D.M. Smith 3, N.L. McCullum 18, B.E. Scott 0, D.V. Lobb 1*, D.G. Sewell 0, S.W. Murley –, Extras 7.
McKay 0-9, Wood 1-28, Henderson 3-40, Nielsen 2-25, Nethula 0-13, Lythe 4-24.

WELLINGTON v CANTERBURY *Wellington won by an innings and 67 runs*
At Lincoln No.3 9, 10 January, 2003

Wellington 355-8d. S.A. Fairley 34, L.J. Woodcock 2, T.C. Crabb 0, J.E.C. Franklin 151*, J.P. McNamee 5, S.M. Mills 40, D.J. Bowden 14, G.A. Howell 62, P.A. Hitchcock 11, B.R. Jansen 10*, A.D. Turner –, Q.E. de Bruin –, Extras 26.
Cunis 2-22, Ellis 1-41, Cornelius 1-62, Redmond 0-31, George 2-59, Anderson 1-101, Borren 0-28.

Canterbury 68 and 220. T.J. Papps 9, 26, R.M. Miller 4, 75, A.M. McDowell 0, –, J.I. Englefield 22, 5, A.J. Redmond 0, 12, A.M. Ellis 2, 6, C.J. Anderson 6, 30, C.J. Cornelius 8, 12, S.J. Cunis 3, 0, P.J. Rugg 0, 17, P.W. Borren 2*, 14*, S.R. George –, –, Extras 12, 23.
Franklin 0-21, 1-32, Turner 5-18, 2-43, de Bruin 0-10, 1-25, Hitchcock 3-15, 2-32, Crabb 0-0, –. Bowden 1-0, –, Jansen –, 2-37, Woodcock –, 1-38.

CENTRAL DISTRICTS v NEW ZEALAND UNDER 19 *First innings win to Central*

At Bert Sutcliffe Oval, Lincoln　　　　9, 10 January 2003

New Zealand Under 19 326. B.J. Wilson 0, G.R. Hay 84, N.T. Broom 17, D.R. Flynn 1, S.R. Allen 162, J.R. Hill 16, B.J. Chard 2, M.P. Goldstein 0, M.D. Bates 9, E.L. Standfield 17, A.S.T Chambers 4, C.M. Smith –, Extras 14.
Rankin 1-38, Diamanti 2-37, Thompson 0-44, Good 2-73, Loveridge 1-63, West 3-60.

Central Districts 340-7. A.D. Murley 102, H.J. Cunliffe 8, M.I. Baumgart 2-36, R. Johnston 25, G.R. Loveridge 53, M.J.E. Calkin 12, R.M. West 62, B.J. Diamanti 22, E.P. Thompson 12*, D.R.B. Rankin –, D.T. Good –, Extras 8.
Bates 1-54, Chambers 1-88, Hill 2-67, Standfield 0-27, Smith 2-34, Goldstein 0-50, Broom 1-12.

AUCKLAND v NEW ZEALAND UNDER 19　　　　　　*No result*
At Bert Sutcliffe Oval, Lincoln　　　11, 12 January, 2003

Auckland 219. N.G. Jury 34, J.M. Vujnovich 13, R.K. Lynch 13, R.T. King 9, B.J. Nielsen 7, C.W. Burroughs 29, T.H. Topia 44, T.I. Lythe 30, T.S. Nethula 21, A.J. McKay 0, G.A. Wood 7*, R.J.G. Henderson –, Extras 12.
Bates 0-12, Smith 2-38, Standfield 2-24, Hegglun 2-21, Broom 0-23, Goldstein 3-52, Hill 1-39.

New Zealand Under 19 D.R. Flynn, J.R. Hill, N.T. Broom. M.P. Goldstein, C.M. Smith, G.J. Hegglun, M.D. Bates, G.R. Hay, B.J. Chard, E.L. Standfield.

CANTERBURY v NORTHERN DISTRICTS　　　　　　*No result*
At Lincoln Green　　　11, 12 January 2003

Northern Districts 144. G.G. Robinson 12, A.C. Beagley 0, M.K. Drake 16, J.B. Lee 1, J.G. Hatwell 0, B.J. Hatwell 21, G.D. Irwin 56, L.J. Hammond 14, N.M. Daley 0, S.L. Andrews 15, N.R.J. Aldridge 0, D.R.T. Pinny –, Extras 9.
Cunis 4-42, Burson 0-33, Ellis 3-23, Anderson 1-6, Redmond 2-34.

Canterbury 84-4. T.J. Papps 43, R.M. Miller 18, A.J. Redmond 18*, J.I. Englefield 0, D.M. Barclay 0, A.M. Ellis 0*, C.J. Cornelius –, P.J. Rugg –, S.J. Cunis –, C.J. Anderson –, R.D. Burson –, Extras 5.
Andrews 0-29, Hammond 0-11, Aldridge 2-20, Irwin 2-21.

OTAGO v WELLINGTON　　　　　　*No result*
At Lincoln No.3　　　11, 12 January 2003

Wellington 310-8. S.A. Fairley 50, L.J. Woodcock 5, T.C. Crabb 16, J.E.C. Franklin 72, J.P. McNamee 12, S.M. Mills 11, D.J. Bowden 82*, G.A. Howell 36, P.A. Hitchcock 13, A.D. Turner 0*, Extras 13.
Sewell 3-27, Scott 1-58, Waldron 2-21, Lobb 0-35, McCullum 0-76, Murley 1-62, Beare 0-19.

Otago. C.B. Gaffaney, D.M. Smith, S.P. Beare, J.M. Waldron, N.L. McCullum, D.V. Lobb, B.E. Scott, D.G. Sewell, S.W. Murley, J.D. Hamer, R.E. King, T.I. Weston.

AUCKLAND v WELLINGTON　　　　*First innings win to Auckland*
At Lincoln No.3　　　13, 14 January 2003

Auckland 197. N.G. Jury 6, J.M. Vujnovich 29, R.K. Lynch 37, R.T. King 28, B.J. Nielsen 1, C.W. Burroughs 2, T.H. Topia 8, T.I. Lythe 17, T.S. Nethula 2, A.J. McKay 32*, R.J.G. Henderson 21, G.A. Wood –, Extras 14.
Franklin 1-17, de Bruin 1-30, Jansen 3-47, Woodcock 3-58, Hitchcock 2-21, Bowden 0-12.

Wellington 159. S.A. Fairley 24, L.J. Woodcock 20, T.C. Crabb 14, J.E.C. Franklin 21, J.P. McNamee 9, S.M. Mills 0, D.J. Bowden 16, G.A. Howell 22*, B.R. Jansen 4, A.D. Turner 0, Q.E. de Bruin 11, Extras 18.
McKay 0-4, Wood 0-20, Henderson 0-16, Lythe 6-78, Nielsen 3-32.

CENTRAL DISTRICTS v OTAGO *First innings win to Otago*
At Bert Sutcliffe Oval, Lincoln   13, 14 January 2003
Central Districts 174. A.D. Murley 13, H.J. Cunliffe 12, M.I. Baumgart 4, R. Johnston 3, G.R. Loveridge 15, D.R. Cederman 17, R.M. West 60, B.J. Diamanti 12, E.P. Thompson 29*, D.R.B. Rankin 2, D.T. Good 0, M.J.E. Calkin –, Extras 7.
Sewell 4-44, Scott 1-20, McCullum 3-63, Lobb 1-17, Waldron 0-16, Sheed 0-8.
Otago 350-3d. C.B. Gaffaney 201*, T.I. Weston 59, R.E. King 0, J.W. Sheed 19, S.P. Beare 48*, J.M. Waldron –, D.M. Smith –, N.L. McCullum –, B.E. Scott –, D.V. Lobb –, D.G. Sewell –, S.W. Murley –, Extras 23.
Rankin 0-44, Diamanti 0-29, Good 2-75, West 0-73, Loveridge 0-62, Cederman 0-18, Thompson 1-24, Murley 0-12.

NORTHERN DISTRICTS v NEW ZEALAND UNDER 19 *First innings win to NZ Under 19*
At Lincoln Green   13, 14 January 2003
New Zealand Under 19 289. G.R. Hay 57, B.J. Wilson 60, N.T. Broom 34, D.R. Flynn 0, S.R. Allen 21, J.R. Hill 41, B.J. Chard 12, E.L. Standfield 22, M.P. Goldstein 8, G.J. Hegglun 1, C.M. Smith 3*, T. Davis –, Extras 30.
Andrews 2-34, Pinny 0-16, Irwin 1-25, J.G. Hatwell 5-93, Hammond 0-18, Aldridge 2-68, B.J. Hatwell 0-7.
Northern Districts 276. G.G. Robinson 17, A.C. Beagley 25, S.L. Andrews 10, M.K. Drake 117*, B.J. Hatwell 23, J.B. Lee 27, J.G. Hatwell 4, G.D. Irwin 15, L.J. Hammond 6, N.R.J. Aldridge 10, D.R.T. Pinny 5, N.M. Daley –, Extras 17.
Davis 2-47, Smith 1-45, Standfield 1-12, Hill 2-81, Hegglun 2-34, Goldstein 1-40, Broom 1-2.

NORTHERN DISTRICTS v AUCKLAND *First innings win to Northern*
At Blake Park, Mt Maunganui   28, 29 January 2003
Auckland 173 and 87-4. N.G. Jury 23, 23, J.M. Vujnovich 2, 0, R.K. Lynch 0, 39*, R.T. King 7, 7, B.J. Nielsen 54, 15*, C.W. Burroughs 11, 0, T.H. Topia 0, –, R.A. Young 37, –, T.I. Lythe 18, –, M. Hendry 0, –, G.S. Shaw 4*, –, R.J.G. Henderson –, –, Extras 17, 3.
Andrews 6-53, 1-26, Hammond 4-43, 1-20, Irwin 0-14, –, J.G. Hatwell 0-27, 0-24, Robinson 0-2, –, Aldridge 0-25, 2-16.
Northern Districts 346-6d. N.K.W. Horsley 18, A.C. Beagley 30, G.G. Robinson 150*, M.K. Drake 2, L.J. Hammond 21, J.G. Hatwell 92, J.B. Lee 21, B.J. Hatwell 0*, G.D. Irwin –, N.M. Daley –, G.W. Aldridge –, S.L. Andrews –, Extras 12.
Shaw 1-52, Henderson 1-46, Hendry 1-59, Nielsen 1-22, Lythe 0-95, Vujnovich 0-24, Topia 0-41.

CANTERBURY v OTAGO *First innings win to Canterbury*
At Hagley Park, Christchurch   2, 3 February 2003
Otago 321. Mohammad Wasim 30, A.J. Hore 1, D.M. Smith 24, J.W. Sheed 103, N.M. McKenzie 42, A.M. Wilkinson 1, T.I. Weston 18, J.M. Waldron 62*, N.L. McCullum 0, E.L. Standfield 13, J.M. McMillan 0, D.G. Sewell –, Extras 26.
Chambers 0-46, Wisneski 2-54, Cornelius 0-34, Ellis 3-48, Wiseman 3-53, Redmond 0-46, Robertson 1-24.
Canterbury 411. R.M. Frew 0, R.M. Miller 51, A.J. Redmond 70, J.I. Englefield 121, G.J. Hopkins 18, N.T. Broom 53, A.M. Ellis 6, C.J. Cornelius 40, P.J. Wiseman 38, I.A. Robertson 0, W.A. Wisneski 6*, A.S.T. Chambers –, Extras 8.
McMillan 2-79, Sewell 2-96, Standfield 1-57, McCullum 0-67, Wilkinson 3-68, Wasim 0-9, Waldron 1-30.

CENTRAL DISTRICTS v WELLINGTON   *First innings win to Wellington*
At Donnelly Park, Levin   *18, 19 February 2003*
Central Districts 299. P.J. Ingram 11, A.D. Murley 15, H.J. Cunliffe 33, R.L. Taylor 44,
B.M.K. Patton 4, M.A. Sigley 3, R.M. West 9, E.P. Thompson 17, C. Fraser 68, D.T. Good 58,
G.J. Hegglun 12*, C.J. Trask –, Extras 25.
Gillespie 3-44, Quarterman 0-43, Bowden 4-60, Jones 2-49, Woodcock 0-60, Jansen 1-23.
Wellington 308-6. S.A. Fairley 58, L.J. Woodcock 14, S.J. Murdoch 10, L.J. Morgan 19,
J.P. McNamee 24, J.R. Hill 4, S.R. Allen 67*, D.J. Bowden 100*, M.R. Gillespie –, B.R. Jansen
–, B.H. Jones –, F.J. Quarterman –, Extras 12.
Hegglun 1-58, Thompson 2-43, Trask 1-21, Fraser 1-53, West 0-36, Good 0-52, Taylor 0-23,
Patton 0-11, Ingram 0-9.

AUCKLAND v NORTHERN DISTRICTS   *No result*
At North Harbour Stadium, Auckland   *18, 19 February 2003*
Northern Districts 341-8d. N.K.W. Horsley 4, G.G. Robinson 109, D.P. Kelly 38, M.K. Drake
37, J.G. Hatwell 37, J.B. Lee 75, B.J. Hatwell 18, G.D. Irwin 7*, N.M. Daley 0, L.J. Hammond
6*, N.R.J. Aldridge –, B. Winslade –, Extras 10.
Coleman 2-61, Leonard 3-60, Henderson 0-78, Whiteman 1-57, Nielsen 1-10, Lythe 0-33,
Cates 1-33.
Auckland 24-0. J.M. Vujnovich 8*, S.P.L. Singe 14*, L.G. Howell –, C. Borich –, H. Smith
–, S.J.G. Whiteman –, B.J. Nielsen –, T.I. Lythe –, B.J. Leonard –, G.S. Coleman–, B.S. Cates
–, R.J.G. Henderson –, Extras 2.
Hammond 0-15, Winslade 0-9.

WELLINGTON v CENTRAL DISTRICTS   *No result*
At Basin Reserve, Wellington   *20, 21 February 2003*
Wellington 320. S.A. Fairley 58, L.J. Woodcock 0, S.J. Murdoch 54, L.J. Morgan 0,
J.P. McNamee 46, J.R. Hill 16, S.R. Allen 11, D.J. Bowden 8, B.R. Jansen 57, C.P. Dixon 4,
B.H. Jones 50*, F.J. Quarterman –, Extras 16.
Hegglun 1-37, Thompson 3-73, Fraser 0-31, Good 3-74, West 2-50, Loveridge 1-45.
Central Districts 218-6. A.D. Murley 22, H.J. Cunliffe 4, B.B.J. Griggs 58, R.L. Taylor 76,
G.R. Loveridge 26, B.M.K. Patton 11, M.A. Sigley 0*, R.M. West 0*, E.P. Thompson –,
C. Fraser –, D.T. Good –, G.J. Heglun –, Extras 21.
Dixon 2-34, Jones 1-38, Woodcock 0-36, Quarterman 0-34, Bowden 2-13, Jansen 1-43.

CANTERBURY v OTAGO   *First innings win to Otago*
At Aorangi Park, Timaru   *23, 24 February 2003*
Otago 200 and 218-5d. R.E. King 7, –, T.I. Weston 8, 5, D.M. Smith 5, 45, J.W. Sheed 9, 47,
N.M. McKenzie 18, 10*, W.C. McSkimming 0, 74, J.M. Waldron 5, 8*, A.M. Wilkinson 58*,
16, N.L. McCullum 37, –, N.W. Rushton 11, –, D.G. Sewell 15, –, S.W. Murley –, –, Extras
27, 13.
Cunis 1-22, –, Murphy 1-37, –, Reardon 3-34, 0-55, Borren 2-22, 1-61, Anderson 0-41, –,
Stewart 1-12, 2-49, I.A. Robertson 0-18, 2-28, Englefield –, 0-8, Miller –, 0-6.
Canterbury 158. R.M. Miller 5, R.M. Frew 1, S.L. Stewart 40, J.I. Englefield 0, I.A. Robertson
16, A.G. Buckingham 47, C.J. Anderson 5, S.J. Cunis 1, P.W. Borren 2, P.R. Reardon 2,
A. Robertson 2*, S.A. Murphy –, Extras 19.
Sewell 3-48, Rushton 1-38, McSkimming 0-32, Wilkinson 6-20, Waldron 0-9.

NEW ZEALAND ACADEMY

The New Zealand Academy team played five games against Auckland, Central Districts and Otago in October and November, 2001. During this period they also hosted the Commonwealth Bank Cricket Academy team from Australia for six matches and the Queensland Academy of Sport team for one game in November (see separate section for details of those matches).

Chris Cairns, returning from injury, appeared in several matches as a build up for New Zealand's tour to Australia, while injuries to Academy players saw Chris Harris and Daniel Vettori drafted in for the final games.

NEW ZEALAND ACADEMY XI v OTAGO
At Lincoln Green   2, 3 October, 2001

New Zealand Academy XI 289 (N.L. McCullum 57, B.B. McCullum 53, N.K.W. Horsley 36, W.A. Cornelius 33, S.B. O'Connor 5-15) and 52-0 (B.B. McCullum 34*) **drew with Otago** 307 (C.R. Pryor 74*, E.J. Marshall 54, L.K. Germon 48, N.D. Morland 48, W.A. Cornelius 4-62)

NEW ZEALAND ACADEMY XI v OTAGO
At Lincoln Green   4, 5 October, 2001

New Zealand Academy XI 464-9d (J.M. How 126, S.L. Stewart 89, C.L. Cairns 70, A.J. Redmond 46, L.J. Woodcock 37, D.G. Sewell 3-52) **drew with Otago** 196 (M.G. Croy 39, J.W. Sheed 33, L.J. Woodcock 4-50, T.P. Robin 3-59).

NEW ZEALAND ACADEMY XI v CENTRAL DISTRICTS
At Lincoln Green   9, 10, 11 October, 2001

Abandoned without a ball being bowled

NEW ZEALAND ACADEMY XI v CENTRAL DISTRICTS
At Lincoln Green   12 October, 2001

New Zealand Academy XI 266 (N.K.W. Horsley 86, C.L. Cairns 84 (41 balls, 7 sixes, 7 fours), S.L. Stewart 31) **defeated Central Districts** 187-5 (P.J. Ingram 50, D.P. Kelly 50, C.J.M. Furlong 35*) by 79 runs

NEW ZEALAND ACADEMY XI v AUCKLAND
At Lincoln Green   30, 31 October, 1 November 2001

New Zealand Academy XI 168 (R.A. Young 38, B.G.K. Walker 3-21, M.J. Haslam 3-40) and 258 (J.M. How 80, N.K.W. Horsley 67, R.A. Young 45, A.R. Adams 4-45, M.J. Haslam 4-60) **lost to Auckland** 403 (K.D. Mills 158, A.R. Adams 79, T.K. Canning 62, N.L. McCullum 3-51, L.J. Woodcock 3-84) and 26-0 by 10 wickets

NEW ZEALAND ACADEMY XI v AUCKLAND
At Lincoln Green   2 November, 2001

Auckland 191 (A.C. Barnes 59, K.D. Mills 33, D.L. Vettori 4-36) **lost to New Zealand Academy XI** 194-4 (B.B. McCullum 106*, J.M. How 32) by 6 wickets

(These matches were omitted from the 2002 edition)

NATIONAL UNDER 19 TOURNAMENT

The 2002/03 Under 19 tournament was held at Lincoln from 11 to 23 December. The tournament was split into two-day and one-day sections with the teams divided into two groups. There were finals play-offs after each round robin. The placings for both sections finished the same: Group A: Wellington, Northern Districts, Canterbury; Group B: Otago, Central Districts, Auckland. Wellington defeated Otago in the two-day final with the result reversed in the one-day final.

At the conclusion of the tournament, the squad to take part in the Provincial A Team competition was named: M. Goldstein *(Canterbury)*, B. Wilson *(Northern Districts)*, A. Chambers *(Canterbury)*, G. Hegglun *(Central Districts)*, M. Bates *(Auckland)*, C. Smith *(Otago)*, N. Broom *(Canterbury)*, E. Standfield *(Otago)*, J. Hill *(Wellington)*, G. Hay *(Central Districts)*, S. Allen *(Wellington)*, D. Flynn *(Northern Districts)*, B. Chard *(Northern Districts)*, R. Taylor *(Central Districts)*.

TWO-DAY SECTION

FIRST ROUND

AUCKLAND v NORTHERN DISTRICTS   *First innings win to Auckland*

Northern Districts 302-7d (B. Wilson 79, K. Bettley 66, T. Levao 42)

Auckland 320 (A. Kitchen 127, C. Cachopa 45, R. Sharma 36, C. Newson 3-58)

CENTRAL DISTRICTS v CANTERBURY   *First innings win to Central Districts*

Central Districts 333 (G.E.F. Barnett 69, L.M. Toynbee 58, J.D. Ryder 49, R.L. Taylor 38, D.J. MacDonald 36, A. Chambers 3-78) and 397-6 (R.L. Taylor 152, J.D. Ryder 134, G.R. Hay 33)

Canterbury 158 (P. Reardon 35, R.R. Sherlock 6-17, D.R. Bolstad 3-31)

WELLINGTON v OTAGO   *First innings win to Otago*

Otago 231 (N. Morrison 54, B. Domigan 48, H. Bates 45, J. Hill 3-42)

Wellington 128 (J. Newdick 30, E. Standfield 4-23) and 381 (J. Newdick 97, L. Chrisp 59, R. Sewell 57, B. Crook 38, J. Hill 32, M. Ross 5-106)

SECOND ROUND

AUCKLAND v WELLINGTON   *First innings win to Wellington*

Auckland 301 (C. Cachopa 49, R. Sharma 46, G. Cates 40, M. Ellison 39, M. Rowley 31, B. Jones 3-28)

Wellington 464-7 (J. Hill 82*, J. Newdick 77, R. Sewell 70, M.Houghton 68, B. Crook 50, S.R. Allen 43, B. Horsley 34, K. Donnelly 3-131)

CANTERBURY v OTAGO   *First innings win to Otago*

Canterbury 226 (M. Goldstein 73, A. Sawers 41, C. Chadwick 32, M. Harvie 4-45) and 258-2 (K. Ambler 114*, C. Chadwick 83, J. Kench 56)

Otago 291 (H. Bates 101, M. Ross 79, B. Domigan 31)

CENTRAL DISTRICTS v NORTHERN DISTRICTS   *First innings win to Central*
Central Districts 193 (D.R. Bolstad 70, R.L. Taylor 36, L. Jessup 3-45) and 211-1 (S.B.C. Baldwin 92, G.R. Hay 77*)
Northern Districts 256 (G. Steele 60, D. Flynn 49, G. Hegglun 8-50)

THIRD ROUND

AUCKLAND v CANTERBURY   *First innings win to Auckland*
Canterbury 198 (M. Goldstein 51, J. Kench 32, C. McDowell 3-26, K. Donnelly 3-28) and 194-3 (N.T. Broom 123*, J. Kench 48)
Auckland 207 (C. Cachopa 51, P. Reardon 3-54)

WELLINGTON v CENTRAL DISTRICTS   *First innings win to Central Districts*
Wellington 284 (J. Hill 91*, S.R. Allen 62, M. Houghton 35, R. Sewell 33, B. Horsley 31, G. Hegglun 3-40, D.J. MacDonald 3-44)
Central Districts 377-5 (R.L. Taylor 171, G.R. Hay 102, G.E.F. Barnett 32)

NORTHERN DISTRICTS v OTAGO   *First innings win to Otago*
Otago 346 (S. Wells 70, H. Bates 69*, G. Baird 69, M. Ross 49, N. Morrison 30)
Northern Districts 273 (B. Chard 78, D. Richardson 58, B. Wilson 38, E. Standfield 5-48)

FIFTH PLACE PLAYOFF

CANTERBURY v AUCKLAND   *First innings win to Canterbury*
Canterbury 376 (N.T. Broom 83, C. Chadwick 79, A. Robertson 68, M. Goldstein 48)
Auckland 300 (R. Sharma 76, A. Kitchen 56, D. Winger 50, S. McKay 38, C. Stevens 4-27, W. Smart 4-68)

THIRD PLACE PLAYOFF

CENTRAL DISTRICTS v NORTHERN DISTRICTS   *First innings win to Central*
Central Districts 225 (J.D. Ryder 90, B. Whittington 36, C. Newson 4-37, D. Richardson 4-39)
Northern Districts 206 (D. Flynn 57, M. Pinny 44, B. Wilson 42, R. Wylie 3-40, G. Hegglun 3-40)

FINAL

OTAGO v WELLINGTON   *First innings win to Wellington*
Otago 164 (G. Baird 44, M. Ross 34, B. Jones 6-34) and 135-3 (N. Morrison 58*, S. Wells 35)
Wellington 431 (J. Hill 127, S.R. Allen 105, B. Crook 58*, J. Newdick 36, C. Smith 5-66)

ONE-DAY SECTION

FIRST ROUND

CANTERBURY v WELLINGTON   *Wellington won by 8 wickets*
Canterbury 99 (B. Jones 5-31)
Wellington 100-2 (J. Hill 61*)

CENTRAL DISTRICTS v OTAGO   *Otago won by 3 wickets*
Central Districts 97 (E. Standfield 4-14)
Otago 101-7 (G. Hegglun 4-30)

SECOND ROUND

CENTRAL DISTRICTS v AUCKLAND   *Central Districts won by 7 wickets*
Auckland 104 (C. Cachopa 44, J.D. Ryder 4-20)
Central Districts 105-3 (S.B.C. Baldwin 35).

CANTERBURY v NORTHERN DISTRICTS   *Canterbury won by 5 wickets*
Northern Districts 257-7 (K. Bettley 44, D. Richardson 40, B. Chard 33*)
Canterbury 259-5 (N.T. Broom 133, K. Ambler 51, T. Astle 33)

THIRD ROUND

AUCKLAND v OTAGO   *Otago won by 4 wickets*
Auckland 184-9 (A. Kitchen 31, N. Morrison 3-22, M. Harvie 3-32)
Otago 190-6 (S. Wells 64, S. Simpson 38, H. Bates 34*, K. Donnelly 3-34)

NORTHERN DISTRICTS v WELLINGTON   *Northern Districts won by 4 wickets*
Wellington 283-9 (B. Crook 58, J. Hill 56, M. Houghton 44)
Northern Districts 284-6 (D. Flynn 64, B. Wilson 54, B. Chard 47, D. Richardson 31*, M. Pinny 31*)

FIFTH PLACE PLAYOFF

AUCKLAND v CANTERBURY   *Auckland won by 24 runs*
Auckland 210 (C. Cachopa 43, D.R. Winger 33, P. Reardon 4-45)
Canterbury 186 (N.T. Broom 34, M.D. Bates 4-31)

THIRD PLACE PLAYOFF

CENTRAL DISTRICTS v NORTHERN DISTRICTS   *Central won by 4 wickets*
Northern Districts 276-8 (B. Wilson 54, D. Flynn 48, M. Pinny 44, D. Richardson 36*, K. Bettley 32, R.L. Taylor 3-40)
Central Districts 281-6 (G.E.F. Barnett 81, R.L. Taylor 59, S.B.C. Baldwin 41)

FINAL

WELLINGTON v OTAGO   *Otago won by 20 runs*
Otago 282-6 (S. Wells 106, G. Baird 44, S. Simpson 44, M. Houghton 4-45)
Wellington 262 (L. Chrisp 76, J. Khan 66*, M. Harvie 3-53)

NATIONAL UNDER 17 TOURNAMENT

The National Under 17 tournament was held in Napier from 31 December to 8 January, with Northern Districts taking the title. Final placings were: Northern Districts 16, Auckland 12, Central Districts 12, Canterbury 8, Wellington 8, Otago 4.

A tournament team was selected at the completion of the fifth round. It was D. de Boorder *(Auckland)*, A. Devcich*(Northern Districts)*, M. Ellison*(Auckland)*, B. Findlay*(Canterbury)*, K. Forde*(Wellington)*, C. Frauenstein*(Auckland)*, S. McLeod*(Northern Districts)*, K. Noema-Barnett *(Otago)*, K. Read *(Northern Districts)*, C. Small *(Canterbury)*, T. Te Moni *(Northern Districts)*, H. Templeton *(Wellington)*.

FIRST ROUND

NORTHERN DISTRICTS v AUCKLAND   *First innings win to Auckland*

Auckland 209 (C. Frauenstein 70*, R. Baddeley 34, B. Hurrell 3-28, T. Te Moni 3-32) and 141-7d (R. Hira 31)

Northern Districts 147 (J. Boult 35, C. Frauenstein 4-25) and 93-8 (C. Frauenstein 4-18)

CANTERBURY v OTAGO   *First innings win to Otago*

Canterbury 119 (T. Astle 41, G. Taylor 6-27) and 202-8 (B. Findlay 50, T. Astle 48, K. Noema-Barnett 3-25)

Otago 154 (R. Henaghan 45*, B. Findlay 5-40) and 101-4 (K. Noema-Barnett 38*)

CENTRAL DISTRICTS v WELLINGTON   *First innings win to Central Districts*

Central Districts 178 (M. Short 57, D. Pimm 42, J. Sewell 4-33, K. Forde 3-24) and 138-5 (H. Cameron 58)

Wellington 147 (T. Brodie 35, G. Herd 5-28)

SECOND ROUND

CENTRAL DISTRICTS v AUCKLAND   *First innings win to Auckland*

Central Districts 151 (H. Cameron 46, S. Cameron 31, J. Donnelly 3-33) and 130-3 (M. Short 36)

Auckland 257 (M. Guptill 76, C. Cachopa 47, B. McLennan 3-43, K. Richards 3-53)

CANTERBURY v NORTHERN DISTRICTS   *First innings win to Northern Districts*

Canterbury 168 (K. Ambler 30, J. Morgan 3-19, A. Devcich 3-38) and 177-5 (C. Small 72*, B. McCord 37*; T. Davis 3-28)

Northern Districts 359-8d (S. McLeod 101*, B. Hurrell 77, K. Read 74)

WELINGTON v OTAGO   *First innings win to Wellington*

Otago 99 (R. Henagon 31, A. Corliss 3-18) and 238-7 (W. Lawson 71, K. Noema-Barnett 36, K. Forde 3-34, J. Sewell 3-60)

Wellington 174 (R. Kyne 62*, H. Templeton 38, R. Taylor 3-38)

THIRD ROUND

WELLINGTON v AUCKLAND   *First innings win to Wellington*
Wellington 356-7d (H. Templeton 88, J. Dean 59, N. Angus 48) and 51-6
Auckland 186 (M. Ellison 62*, C. Frauenstein 54, J. Sewell 4-49, K. Forde 2-39)

CENTRAL DISTRICTS v CANTERBURY   *First innings win to Central Districts*
Central Districts 172 (B. Findlay 3-30, J. Baxendale 3-40) and 182-8d (S. Cameron 66*, B. Findlay 3-34, J. Baxendale 3-46)
Canterbury 167 (B. Findlay 44, G. Herd 3-28) and 107-3 (B. Findlay 54*, C. Small 35*)

OTAGO v NORTHERN DISTRICTS   *First innings win to Northern Districts*
Otago 190 (K. Noema-Barnett 68, G. Taylor 36, A. Devcich 5-69) and 112-6 (K. Noema-Barnett 43*)
Northern Districts 209 (K. Read 59, W. Lawson 4-25, G. Taylor 4-63)

FOURTH ROUND

OTAGO v AUCKLAND   *Auckland won by 5 wickets*
Otago 162 (K. Eathorne 47, C. Frauenstein 3-27, J. Donnelly 3-42)
Auckland 163-5 (M. Ellison 53*, G. Read 52, K. Noema-Barnett 3-29)

WELLINGTON v CANTERBURY   *Canterbury won by 3 wickets*
Wellington 217 (H. Templeton 81, B. Findlay 3-36)
Canterbury 219-7 (H. Dickson 72*, T. Astle 44, D. Broom 34, K. Forde 4-38)

CENTRAL DISTRICTS v NORTHERN DISTRICTS   *Northern won by 7 wickets*
Central Districts 144-8 (S. Jenkins 37, H. Beaumont 33, A. Devcich 4-26)
Northern Districts 145-3 (M. Child 57, S. McLeod 45*)

FIFTH ROUND

CANTERBURY v AUCKLAND   *Canterbury won by 14 runs*
Canterbury 203-6 (T. Astle 49, C. Small 36, D. Broom 33)
Auckland 189 (M. Ellison 62, M. Guptill 32)

CENTRAL DISTRICTS v OTAGO   *Central Districts won by 18 runs*
Central Districts 271-7 (H. Beaumont 53, S. Cameron 51, H. Cameron 49, K. Richards 32)
Otago 253 (G. Smith 61, R. Henagan 47*, W. Lawson 38, K. Preston 3-49)

WELLINGTON v NORTHERN DISTRICTS   *Northern Districts won by 139 runs*
Northern Districts 277-5 (S. McLeod 92, A. Devcich 43, K. Read 43)
Wellington 138-8 (J. Dean 33)

HAWKE CUP

The major competition for the District (formerly Minor) Associations reverted to the Hawke Cup from 1999/00. The Fuji Xerox Cup since 1995/96, it was renamed the National District Championship in 1998/99. The competition was for the U-Bix Cup from 1985/86 to 1994/95.

Apart from tournaments in 1910/11, 1912/13 and 2000/01, the competition has always been on a challenge basis. To reduce the number of challenges received by the holders it was decided to pair off all the Minor Associations. This scheme commenced in the 1924/25 season, when the first three elimination matches were played. Since then numerous elimination matches have been staged to determine the right to challenge the holders of the cup.

At the end of 1999/00 it was decided to exclude the teams from the four major centres who had taken part in the tournament in recent seasons. As Dunedin Metropolitan held the trophy at the time, a national zonal tournament was held to find a new holder and the challenge format resumed in 2001/02.

Holders

Southland, 1910/11; won the tournament of six matches.
Southland, March 14, 1911, to March 25, 1913; resisted one challenge.
South Auckland, 1912/13; won the tournament of four matches.

Challenges resisted

Wanganui, December 26, 1913, to March 28, 1919 5
Poverty Bay, March 28, 1919, to February 15, 1921 4
Wairarapa, February 15, 1921, to December 26, 1921 1
Rangitikei, December 26, 1921, to January 3, 1922 .... —
Nelson, January 3, 1922, to April 1, 1922 2
Wanganui, April 1, 1922, to January 22, 1924 7
Nelson, January 22, 1924, to February 2, 1926 7
Wanganui, February 2, 1926, to December 6, 1926 2
Taranaki, December 6, 1926, to December 20, 1927 3
Wanganui, December 20, 1927, to February 23, 1928 2
Manawatu, February 23, 1928, to March 29, 1930 9
Rangitikei, March 29, 1930, to December 15, 1930 .... —
Waikato, December 15, 1930, to January 2, 1933 11
Nelson, January 2, 1933, to December 27, 1933 2
Taranaki, December 27, 1933, to December 27, 1934 3
Manawatu, December 27, 1934, to February 14, 1938 15
Waikato, February 14, 1938, to January 30, 1940 7
Manawatu, January 30, 1940, to April 7, 1947 9
Hawke's Bay, April 7, 1947, to February 14, 1948 1
Wanganui, February 14, 1948, to December 13, 1948 1
Hutt Valley, December 13, 1948, to April 11, 1950 7
Hawke's Bay, April 11, 1950, to January 3, 1951 2
Wairarapa, January 3, 1951, to March 12, 1951 1
Waikato, March 12, 1951, to December 10, 1951 .... —
Nelson, December 10, 1951, to December 30, 1952 6
Wanganui, December 30, 1952, to December 28, 1955 13
Hutt Valley, December 28, 1955, to January 2, 1956 .... —
Northland, January 2, 1956, to December 8, 1956 2
Waikato, December 8, 1956, to December 8, 1958 9
Nelson, December 8, 1958, to February 1, 1965 28
Manawatu, February 1, 1965, to January 24, 1967 9
North Canterbury, January 24, 1967, to February 27, 1967 .... —
Nelson, February 27, 1967, to December 17, 1967 .... —
Hutt Valley, December 17, 1967, to January 7, 1968 1
Marlborough, January 7, 1968, to March 3, 1968 1
Hawke's Bay, March 3, 1968, to February 23, 1969 4

Career Aggregates

BATTING	M	I	NO	HS	Runs	Ave
Leggat I.B. *(Nelson)*, 1948-68	38	56	1	130	1968	35.78
Reade L.B. *(Nelson)*, 1958-73	35	57	2	117	1951	35.47
Lowans G.E. *(Nelson)*, 1958-73	30	48	1	148	1811	38.53
Anderson R.W. *(Northland and Southland)*, 1970-77	16	31	6	255	1773	70.92
McVicar C.C. *(Manawatu)*, 1935-54	28	44	1	180	1754	40.79
Spence D.V. *(Hawkes Bay and Nelson)*, 1949-67	34	51	8	151	1574	36.60
Hoskin R.N.*(Southland and Central Otago)*, 1978-96	31	35	4	162	1429	46.09
Pierce R.A. *(Nelson)*, 1969-89	24	31	2	150	1426	49.17
Congdon B.E. *(Nelson)*, 1959-65	19	28	2	133	1413	54.34
Gallichan N. *(Manawatu)*, 1925-47	29	48	5	142	1409	32.76
Hampton B.L. *(Nelson)*, 1960-75	21	32	3	236	1391	49.26
Hodgson W.G. *(Nelson)*, 1978-86	24	29	2	265	1348	49.92
Norris W.E. *(Manawatu)*, 1926-47	42	61	6	84	1242	22.58
Orton R.W. *(Rangitikei and Wanganui)*, 1911-26	20	33	1	204	1222	38.18
Hayward R.E. *(Nelson)*, 1979-89	23	26	2	113	1115	46.45
Holland C.A. *(Wanganui)*, 1912-28	24	38	4	111	1060	31.17
Edwards G.N. *(Nelson)*, 1972-86	24	30	2	236	1038	37.07
Toynbee M.H. *(Nelson)*, 1974-81	13	17	3	200*	1031	73.64

BOWLING	M	Runs	Wkts	Ave
Holland C.A. *(Wanganui)*, 1912-28	24	2202	189	11.65
Gallichan N. *(Manawatu)*, 1925-47	29	2053	177	11.59
Leggat I.B. *(Nelson)*, 1948-67	38	2149	134	16.03
Spence D.V. *(Hawkes Bay and Nelson)*, 1949-67	34	1697	110	15.42
Alabaster G.D. *(Thames Valley and Southland)*, 1961-79	20	1508	102	14.78
Newman J. *(Nelson)*, 1922-46	20	1348	97	13.89
Alabaster J.C. *(Southland)*, 1955-74	14	1223	92	13.29
Bernau E.H.L. *(Wanganui and Hawkes Bay)*, 1912-28	14	1009	90	11.21

Highest Individual Innings

272*	Kinzett C.A.	Nelson v Marlborough	Nelson	1933/34
265	Hodgson W.G.	Nelson v Taranaki	Nelson	1983/84
264	Everest J.K.	Waikato v Manawatu	Hamilton	1956/57
255	Anderson R.W.	Southland v Ashburton County	Invercargill	1976/77
236	Hampton B.L.	Nelson v Waikato	Nelson	1963/64
236	Edwards G.N.	Nelson v North Canterbury	Nelson	1984/85
229	Douglas M.W.	Nelson v Southland	Nelson	1992/93

Best Bowling in an Innings

10-35	Holland C.A.	Wanganui v South Taranaki	Wanganui	1922/23
9-103	Jordan A.B.	Taranaki v Hutt Valley	New Plymouth	1971/72
8-9	Clough R.	Waikato v Bay of Plenty	Hamilton	1938/39
8-20	Andrews S.L.	Hamilton v Northland	Hamilton	2001/02
8-25	Smith J.D.	Waikato v Horowhenua	Hamilton	1969/70
8-25	Jordan A.B.	Taranaki v Franklin	New Plymouth	1971/72
8-26	Haycock R.S.	Nelson v Marlborough	Nelson	1924/25

Best Bowling in a Match

14-79	Holland C.A.	Wanganui v South Taranaki	Wanganui	1922/23
14-89	Jordan A.B.	Taranaki v Franklin	New Plymouth	1971/72
14-133	Upston I.A.	Hutt Valley v Wanganui	Wanganui	1955/56
14-149	Sulzberger G.P.	Taranaki v Manawatu	New Plymouth	1994/95

MANAWATU v HAWKE'S BAY

Hawke Cup

at Fitzherbert Park, Palmerston North on 15, 16, 17 February, 2003
Toss : Hawke's Bay. Umpires : C.J. Morris & G.A. Baxter
Close of play: 1st day: Hawke's Bay 254-7, Furlong 32, Unwin 10; 2nd day: Manawatu 164-6, Fulton 31, Rankin 8
First innings win to Hawke's Bay

HAWKE'S BAY

FIRST INNINGS	Runs	Mins	Balls	6s	4s
A.D.Murley c Fulton b Baldwin	44	200	153	-	6
R.Lawrence lbw b Madson	19	108	74	-	3
R.A.Johnston lbw b Thompson	11	39	39	-	1
C.O.Findlay c Ingram b Pandya	64	171	148	-	11
B.M.K.Patton c Taylor b Baldwin	10	42	25	-	-
B.H.Bernie lbw b Thompson	25	52	48	-	4
M.A.Sigley† c Clare b Pandya	4	41	26	-	1
C.J.M.Furlong* not out	65	171	104	-	10
P.D.Unwin lbw b Rankin	11	92	67	-	2
R.J.Gilhooly b Baldwin	12	45	35	1	1
H.W.Thomas c Taylor b Fulton	2	13	11	-	-
Extras (b 5, lb 18, w 2, nb 25)	50				
TOTAL (118.2 overs)	**317**	491			

SECOND INNINGS	Runs	Mins	Balls	6s	4s
not out	50	114	105	1	5
c Madson b Pandya	26	89	72	-	3
not out	4	24	18	-	1
(lb 2, w 1, nb 7)	10				
(30 overs) (1 wkt)	**90**	114			

MANAWATU

	Runs	Mins	Balls	6s	4s
P.J.Ingram lbw b Unwin	18	90	80	-	2
J.B.McGregor c Furlong b Unwin	39	117	100	-	4
C.D.Clare b Sigley b Furlong	8	56	54	-	1
J.D.Fulton† c Murley b Furlong	58	247	212	-	4
I.P.Sandbrook c Patton b Thomas	26	55	55	-	5
R.L.Taylor* lbw b Gilhooly	21	33	16	1	2
S.Baldwin c Bernie b Gilhooly	1	8	12	-	-
D.R.Rankin c Sigley b Findlay	9	54	42	-	1
E.P.Thompson c Murley b Furlong	31	97	73	-	5
H.P.Madson c Lawrence b Gilhooly	21	60	70	-	3
H.Pandya not out	3	32	23	-	-
Extras (b 6, lb 4, nb 9)	19				
TOTAL (120.3 overs)	**254**	437			

Bowling	O	M	R	W	O	M	R	W
MANAWATU								
Rankin	27	6	53	1	5	0	24	0
Thompson	38	13	93	2	4	0	11	0
Madson	10	1	31	1	6	2	9	0
Baldwin	22	7	81	3	3	1	6	0
Pandya	20	8	29	2	8	1	26	1
Fulton	1.2	0	7	1	4	0	12	0
HAWKE'S BAY								
Gilhooly	22.3	2	77	3				
Findlay	11	3	23	1				
Furlong	38	15	54	3				
Thomas	20	5	42	1				
Unwin	29	9	48	2				

Fall of Wickets

	HB	M	HB
	1st	1st	2nd
1st	55	51	75
2nd	82	68	-
3rd	122	86	-
4th	154	117	-
5th	196	151	-
6th	202	153	-
7th	213	167	-
8th	274	207	-
9th	300	232	-
10th	317	254	-

HAWKE'S BAY v NORTHLAND

Hawke Cup

at Nelson Park, Napier on 1, 2, 3 March, 2003
Toss : Northland. Umpires : K.C. Manley & K. Cross
Close of play: 1st day: Hawke's Bay 81-4, Murley 24, Bernie 5; 2nd day: Northland 223 all out
Northland won by an innings and 18 runs

HAWKE'S BAY

FIRST INNINGS	Runs	Mins	Balls	6s	4s	SECOND INNINGS	Runs	Mins	Balls	6s	4s
A.D.Murley c Lee b Potter	30	220	181	-	1	not out	43	131	76	-	7
R.Lawrence lbw b Potter	0	36	20	-	-	run out	2	15	8	-	-
R.A.Johnston b Potter	1	8	5	-	-	(8) c Potter b Child	19	45	38	-	2
C.O.Findlay b Pinny D.R.T.	31	74	52	1	3	lbw b Pinny D.R.T.	1	15	9	-	-
B.M.K.Patton lbw b Pinny D.R.T.	0	1	1	-	-	(3) b Pinny D.R.T.	9	11	9	-	1
B.H.Bernie b Pinny D.R.T.	23	119	80	-	1	(5) b Pinny D.R.T.	0	1	1	-	-
J.W.de Teste c Chard b Potter	5	15	10	-	1	(6) lbw b Pinny D.R.T.	0	2	2	-	-
M.A.Sigley*† b Potter	0	1	1	-	-	(7) c Lee b Potter	0	4	3	-	-
R.J.Gilhooly c Johnston b Potter	4	11	8	-	-	b Pinny D.R.T.	8	14	8	1	-
B.M.Jenyns b Pinny D.R.T.	0	3	5	-	-	b Pinny D.R.T.	4	7	4	-	1
P.C.Connell not out	0	3	0	-	-	c Chard b Pinny D.R.T.	2	9	7	-	-
Extras (b 5, lb 9, nb 4)	18					(lb 3, nb 2)	5				
TOTAL (60.5 overs)	**112**	250				(27.3 overs)	**93**	131			

NORTHLAND

	Runs	Mins	Balls	6s	4s
R.Johnston c Bernie b Findlay	28	103	80	-	3
J.Child b Gilhooly	11	75	62	-	1
M.W.Pinny c Patton b Gilhooly	4	16	20	-	-
J.B.Lee b Jenyns	17	45	36	-	3
D.F.Potter c Patton b Findlay	0	1	2	-	-
G.Jones c Murley b Jenyns	8	34	18	-	1
B.L.Hood* lbw b Gilhooly	6	40	26	-	-
N.Jones c Sigley b Connell	2	4	4	-	-
D.R.Goodwin not out	81	168	154	-	12
B.J.Chard† run out	4	9	7	-	-
D.R.T.Pinny b Connell	48	125	112	-	5
Extras (lb 6, w 2, nb 6)	14				
TOTAL (85.3 overs)	**223**	315			

Bowling	O	M	R	W	O	M	R	W
NORTHLAND								
Potter	26.5	11	38	6	9	2	24	1
Pinny D.R.T.	22	8	41	4	13.3	4	41	7
Jones G.	4	2	5	0				
Pinny M.W.	3	0	13	0				
Goodwin	4	3	1	0				
Child	1	1	0	0	5	0	25	1
HAWKE'S BAY								
Gilhooly	20	6	43	3				
Findlay	13	4	36	2				
Connell	16.3	4	35	2				
Jenyns	27	2	74	2				
Lawrence	1	0	8	0				
Patton	1	0	6	0				
Johnston	7	2	15	0				

Fall of Wickets	HB	N	HB
	1st	1st	2nd
1st	15	41	12
2nd	17	52	25
3rd	56	53	33
4th	56	53	33
5th	98	79	33
6th	106	80	34
7th	106	83	62
8th	108	98	75
9th	108	108	83
10th	112	223	93

NORTHLAND v CANTERBURY COUNTRY

Hawke Cup

at Kensington Park, Whangarei on 15, 16, 17 March, 2003
Toss : Northland. Umpires : T.J. Parlane & C.J. Morris
Close of play: 1st day: Northland 161-3, Lee 50, Parlane 34; 2nd day: no play
First innings win to Northland

CANTERBURY COUNTRY

FIRST INNINGS	Runs	Mins	Balls	6s	4s
S.J.Edwards c Chard b Pinny D.R.T. ...	0	16	14	-	-
N.W.Jones c Jones b Pinny D.R.T.	0	7	4	-	-
C.J.Lelliott lbw b Pinny D.R.T.	0	2	2	-	-
D.H.Fulton c Chard b Pinny D.R.T.	1	23	13	-	-
D.J.Bulman c Chard b Potter	1	33	21	-	-
D.M.Barclay lbw b Potter	16	44	27	-	1
A.W.Robertson not out	37	118	80	-	2
P.J.Rugg*† c Parlane b Goodwin	10	24	17	-	1
S.G.J.Murphy lbw b Pinny D.R.T.	16	44	33	-	2
P.Reardon lbw b Potter	0	3	2	-	-
D.J.Hay c Goodwin b Pinny D.R.T.	0	15	10	-	-
Extras (b 1, lb 4, w 1, nb 2)	8				
TOTAL (38 overs)	**89**	169			

NORTHLAND

	Runs	Mins	Balls	6s	4s
M.W.Pinny c Barclay b Bulman	25	79	63	-	-
G.Jones st Rugg b Bulman	16	56	47	-	3
B.L.Hood* c Bulman b Reardon	28	88	80	-	2
J.B.Lee not out	50	119	99	2	4
M.E.Parlane not out	34	51	54	-	4
D.F.Potter					
D.R.Goodwin					
D.R.T.Pinny					
B.J.Chard†					
C.A.Bray					
J.Child					
Extras (b 1, lb 6, nb 1)	8				
TOTAL (57 overs) (3 wkts)	**161**	199			

Bowling	O	M	R	W
NORTHLAND				
Potter	16	8	21	3
Pinny D.R.T.	15	4	39	6
Goodwin	6	0	22	1
Pinny M.W.	1	0	2	0
CANTERBURY COUNTRY				
Murphy	14	4	24	0
Hay	9	2	23	0
Bulman	16	5	34	2
Reardon	12	2	37	1
Barclay	6	1	36	0

Fall of Wickets		
	CC	N
	1st	1st
1st	0	37
2nd	0	50
3rd	1	97
4th	4	-
5th	8	-
6th	24	-
7th	43	-
8th	71	-
9th	74	-
10th	89	-

WOMEN'S CRICKET

Compiled by Catherine Campbell

The highlight for women's cricket in the 2002/03 season was the World Series of Women's Cricket, hosted by New Zealand Cricket at Lincoln University. NZC invited Australia, England and India to participate in the tournament, with each team playing the other twice before a play off for third and fourth and the final.

The annual Rose Bowl Series between New Zealand and Australia formed part of the World Series. New Zealand A was scheduled to play all four international teams prior to the World Series but due to India's late arrival this match was replaced by a second match against New Zealand.

In domestic cricket four rounds of State League were played prior to the World Series with the last round and final played in late February after the World Series. State Auckland Hearts confirmed their recent dominance by winning their fourth consecutive title.

Central Districts won the National Under 21 tournament played at the Ilam Playing Fields, Christchurch, and the Southern Conference team won the National Secondary Schoolgirls' tournament played at Palmerston North. Epsom Girls' Grammar School, from Auckland, won their second consecutive National Secondary Schoolgirls' Knockout Tournament and Tauranga Intermediate won the Milo Shield.

PLAYER OF THE YEAR

Maia Lewis is the Player of the Year. Lewis captained the State Wellington Blaze in the State League where she scored 378 runs in nine innings with an average of 63 and a highest score of 76 not out.

Lewis was then named captain of New Zealand A in their series prior to the World Series. In the New Zealand A series New Zealand A lost to New Zealand and Australia, tied with New Zealand and beat England. Lewis' highest score was 75 not out against New Zealand.

Following this, Lewis was selected for the New Zealand team and marked a successful return to international cricket having not played since 1997. In the World Series she was New Zealand's leading run scorer with 186 runs at an average of 46.50 and a highest score of 50. Lewis was awarded the Ruth Martin Cup for the most meritorious batting in women's cricket in 2002/03.

PROMISING PLAYER

Rebecca Steele is the Promising Player of the Year. A left-arm orthodox spinner, Steele took nine wickets in the State League and gained selection in the New Zealand A team to play the New Zealand A series against the visiting international teams prior to the World Series.

After good performances for New Zealand A, Steele then gained selection in the New Zealand team for the World Series where she took eight wickets at an average of 23.25 with an economy rate of 3.10.

Steele had previously played as a left-arm medium-pace bowler but changed to left-arm orthodox spin during her participation in New Zealand Cricket's 2002 Development Squad. Steele was awarded the Phyl Blacker Trophy for the most meritorious bowling in women's cricket in 2002/03.

WORLD SERIES
OF WOMEN'S CRICKET

In an exciting first, New Zealand Cricket hosted the inaugural World Series of Women's Cricket at Lincoln University in late January and early February. As England were scheduled to visit Australia and play a two test series, NZC invited England, Australia and India to ensure the top four countries in the world participated in the first World Series.

The series opened with New Zealand playing Australia on 26 January at Bert Sutcliffe Oval, Lincoln, and concluded with the same teams meeting in the final on 8 February. The Rose Bowl Series formed part of the World Series with Australia retaining the trophy 3-0. The Australians were unbeaten throughout the series and were deserved winners of the tournament.

Each team was allowed a maximum of 14 players and the New Zealand team was: Emily Drumm *(captain)*, Michelle Lynch, Rebecca Rolls *(Auckland)*, Nicola Browne, Louise Milliken*(Northern Districts)*, Sara McGlashan, Aimee Mason, Kate Pulford*(Central Districts)*, Amanda Green, Frances King, Maia Lewis *(Wellington)*, Nicola Payne, Rebecca Steele, Haidee Tiffen *(vice-captain), (Canterbury)*. Sarah Burke *(Canterbury)* replaced Milliken who was injured. Coach, Mike Shrimpton; Manager, Julie Reynolds; Physiotherapist, Angela Peterson; Fitness Trainer, Sarah Helmore.

Final points were:

	P	W	L	Win Bonus	Loss Bonus	Points
Australia	6	6	–	6	–	36
New Zealand	6	4	2	3	–	23
India	6	1	5	1	1	7
England	6	1	5	–	1	6

New Zealand Averages

BATTING	M	I	NO	HS	Agg	Ave	100s	50s	Ct	St	SR
M.A.M. Lewis	7	7	3	50	186	46.50	-	1	4	-	50
N. Payne	4	4	0	93	168	42.00	-	1	-	-	75
A.L. Mason	6	5	1	33	104	26.00	-	-	3	-	74
E.C. Drumm	7	7	0	93	175	25.00	-	2	-	-	64
R.J. Rolls	7	7	0	59	161	23.00	-	1	4	5	65
M.L. Lynch	4	4	0	29	80	20.00	-	-	-	-	50
A.J. Green	4	3	2	17*	17	17.00	-	-	1	-	154
H.M. Tiffen	7	7	1	52	94	15.66	-	1	5	-	59
S.J. McGlashan	6	5	2	13	40	13.33	-	-	-	-	50
K.L. Pulford	6	5	0	30	58	11.60	-	-	1	-	38
N.J. Browne	6	4	1	17	27	9.00	-	-	1	-	79
F.S. King	5	3	0	13	27	9.00	-	-	1	-	93
R.J. Steele	6	3	2	5*	9	9.00	-	-	2	-	81
L.E. Milliken	1	-	-	-	-	-	-	-	-	-	-
S.K. Burke	1	-	-	-	-	-	-	-	-	-	-

BOWLING	O	M	R	W	Ave	Best	R/O
E.C. Drumm	25	2	101	8	12.62	3-8	4.04
F.S. King	43.1	2	175	11	15.90	4-24	4.05
R.J. Steele	60	9	186	8	23.25	3-31	3.10
S.K. Burke	10	1	37	1	37.00	1-37	3.70
L.E. Milliken	10	0	39	1	39.00	1-39	3.90
A.L. Mason	56	5	198	5	39.60	2-21	3.54
A.J. Green	31	5	98	2	49.00	1-19	3.16
K.L. Pulford	48	3	212	3	70.66	1-6	4.42
N.J. Browne	50.4	4	191	2	95.50	1-21	3.77

NEW ZEALAND v AUSTRALIA   World Series

at Bert Sutcliffe Oval, Lincoln on 26 January, 2003
Toss : Australia. Umpires : D.B. Cowie & M.P. George
Australia won by 63 runs. *Points: Australia 6, New Zealand 0*

Australia won the toss and elected to bat first. Green and Lynch made their international debuts and Lewis was recalled after a six year absence. Green caught and bowled Clark in her second over in international cricket but a 123 run partnership for the second wicket between Sthalekar and Rolton and a quick 20 not out from Hayes took the Australian total to 223. King took four wickets but the New Zealand attack conceded 19 wides.

With New Zealand chasing 224 for victory, Payne scored 36 including three fours, Pulford 30 with three fours and Lewis was 33 not out with two fours. The best partnership was 59 for the third wicket. Green hit out at the end scoring 17 not out off nine balls including three fours. Fitzpatrick, Twining, Hayes and Rolton all took two wickets each.

AUSTRALIA

	Runs	Mins	Balls	6s	4s
B.J.Clark* c & b Green	8	40	32	-	-
L.C.Sthalekar lbw b King	59	126	99	-	7
K.L.Rolton c Mason b King	86	92	84	1	11
M.Jones c Browne b Drumm	6	33	29	-	1
M.A.J.Goszko c Mason b King	0	7	6	-	-
K.L.Britt c Lewis b King	0	7	6	-	-
J.Hayes not out	20	31	30	-	1
C.L.Fitzpatrick not out	15	20	14	-	1
J.C.Price†					
C.R.Smith					
E.Twining					
Extras (b 3, lb 7, w 19)	29				
TOTAL (50 overs) (6 wkts)	**223**	181			

NEW ZEALAND

	Runs	Mins	Balls	6s	4s
R.J.Rolls† lbw b Fitzpatrick	6	14	12	-	-
N.Payne lbw b Hayes	36	79	83	-	3
E.C.Drumm* c Price b Fitzpatrick	0	2	2	-	-
K.L.Pulford c Price b Rolton	30	81	75	-	3
H.M.Tiffen c Price b Rolton	0	1	1	-	-
M.A.M.Lewis not out	33	72	64	-	2
M.L.Lynch b Hayes	10	14	18	-	-
A.L.Mason c Smith b Twining	8	18	21	-	-
F.S.King run out	13	10	14	-	1
N.J.Browne lbw b Twining	0	1	1	-	-
A.J.Green not out	17	9	9	-	3
Extras (b 2, lb 2, w 3)	7				
TOTAL (50 overs) (9 wkts)	**160**	156			

Bowling NEW ZEALAND	O	M	R	W
Browne	9	0	38	0
Pulford	5	1	27	0
Green	10	2	39	1
King	10	2	24	4
Mason	8	0	50	0
Drumm	8	1	35	1
AUSTRALIA				
Fitzpatrick	10	2	38	2
Twining	10	1	37	2
Smith	7	1	21	0
Sthalekar	7	0	22	0
Hayes	10	4	21	2
Rolton	6	1	17	2

Fall of Wickets	A	NZ
1st	39	10
2nd	162	10
3rd	163	69
4th	167	70
5th	172	81
6th	178	101
7th	-	119
8th	-	134
9th	-	136
10th	-	-

NEW ZEALAND v INDIA *(unofficial one-day match)*
At Hagley Park   24 January, 2003

New Zealand 235-5 (R.J. Rolls 63, H.M. Tiffen 48*, E.C. Drumm 45) **played India** 35-1 (match abandoned)

ENGLAND v INDIA

World Series

at Bert Sutcliffe Oval, Lincoln on 27 January, 2003
Toss : India. Umpires : D.B. Cowie & M.P. George
India won by 6 wickets. *Points: India 6, England 0*

ENGLAND

	Runs	Mins	Balls	6s	4s
C.M.Edwards c Dhar b Chopra .	23	75	54	-	1
K.M.Leng run out	2	11	7	-	-
S.C.Taylor b Chopra	14	53	39	-	1
L.K.Newton c Dhar b Al Khader ..	9	42	28	-	1
A.Thompson b David	7	26	23	-	-
C.J.Connor* run out	6	17	12	-	-
S.V.Collyer st Naik b Al Khader ..	5	14	23	-	-
L.J.Harper st Naik b Al Khader	1	10	9	-	-
M.C.Godliman† not out	4	13	16	-	1
C.E.Taylor b Al Khader	0	3	2	-	-
L.C.Pearson b Al Khader	0	1	3	-	-

Extras (lb 2, w 12, nb 1) 15
TOTAL (35.5 overs) 86 137

INDIA

	Runs	Mins	Balls	6s	4s
S.A.Paranjpe c Newton					
b Taylor C.E.	11	45	36	-	1
A.Chopra* lbw b Taylor C.E.	0	28	20	-	-
J.Sharma b Pearson	33	90	64	-	1
M.Raj c Taylor C.E. b Newton ...	12	48	36	-	1
H.Kala not out	16	27	18	-	2
R.Dhar not out	4	2	4	-	1
A.Sharma					
N.Al Khader					
S.Naik†					
N.David					
J.Goswami					

Extras (lb 2, w 11) 13
TOTAL (29.5 overs) (4 wkts) . 89 122

Bowling	O	M	R	W
INDIA				
Goswami	5	1	19	0
Sharma A.	5	0	23	0
Dhar	6	3	10	0
Chopra	6	2	10	2
David	7	3	8	1
Al Khader	6.5	2	14	5
ENGLAND				
Pearson	7.5	1	22	1
Taylor C.E.	9	4	15	2
Harper	5	2	14	0
Newton	5	1	16	1
Connor	1	0	9	0
Collyer	2	0	11	0

Fall of Wickets	E	I
1st	11	11
2nd	49	23
3rd	54	60
4th	69	85
5th	73	-
6th	81	-
7th	81	-
8th	82	-
9th	86	-
10th	86	-

AUSTRALIA v ENGLAND

World Series

at Bert Sutcliffe Oval, Lincoln on 29 January, 2003
Toss : England. Umpires : G.A. Baxter & K. Cross
Australia won by 7 wickets. *Points: Australia 6, England 0*

ENGLAND

	Runs	Mins	Balls	6s	4s
C.M.Edwards c Price b Twining	12	40	35	-	2
A.Thompson run out	11	68	64	-	1
S.C.Taylor c Goszko b Smith	35	47	50	-	5
L.K.Newton b Fitzpatrick	18	62	62	-	1
C.J.Connor* c Clark b Hayes ...	29	53	49	-	-
S.V.Collyer run out	12	22	19	-	-
D.Holden run out	6	13	14	-	-
L.J.Harper not out	10	6	6	-	1
M.C.Godliman† run out	0	2	0	-	-
C.E.Taylor not out	1	1	1	-	-
L.C.Pearson					

Extras (b 1, lb 2, w 9) 22
TOTAL (50 overs) (8 wkts) .. 156 161

AUSTRALIA

	Runs	Mins	Balls	6s	4s
L.C.Sthalekar c Godliman					
b Pearson	4	8	10	-	1
B.J.Clark* c Taylor C.E. b Harper	23	50	46	-	4
K.L.Rolton not out	68	136	102	-	6
M.Jones c Taylor C.E. b Harper ..	8	36	30	-	1
M.A.J.Goszko not out	34	57	50	-	6
A.J.Blackwell					
J.Hayes					
C.L.Fitzpatrick					
J.C.Price†					
C.R.Smith					
E.Twining					

Extras (lb 7, w 12, nb 1) 20
TOTAL (39.3 overs) (3 wkts) 157 145

Bowling	O	M	R	W
AUSTRALIA				
Fitzpatrick	10	1	28	1
Twining	8	2	19	1
Hayes	9	2	21	1
Sthalekar	10	3	35	0
Smith	7	0	25	1
Rolton	6	2	15	0
ENGLAND				
Pearson	10	4	32	1
Taylor C.E.	6	1	34	0
Collyer	7	2	22	0
Harper	10	1	31	2
Newton	2.3	0	13	0
Connor	4	0	18	0

Fall of Wickets	E	A
1st	33	5
2nd	56	52
3rd	79	86
4th	122	-
5th	132	-
6th	145	-
7th	145	-
8th	150	-
9th	-	-
10th	-	-

NEW ZEALAND v INDIA   World Series

at Bert Sutcliffe Oval, Lincoln on 28 January, 2003
Toss : New Zealand. Umpires : D.M.Quested & E.A. Watkin
New Zealand won by 83 runs. *Points: New Zealand 6, India 0*

New Zealand won the toss and batted and lost their first wicket at 79. Payne was run out for a career best 93 including seven fours, Rolls scored 38 off 42 balls including five fours and Tiffen scored an exciting 52 off 49 balls including six fours. She shared a run a ball 87 run partnership for the fourth wicket with Payne. New Zealand scored 248-5 at the completion of 50 overs.

India started positively not losing their first wicket until 75 runs were on the board. At the end of 50 overs India had only lost five wickets but they were 84 runs short of the required 249 needed for victory. Browne, Milliken and Drumm all took one wicket each.

NEW ZEALAND	Runs	Mins	Balls	6s	4s
N.Payne† run out	93	160	130	-	7
R.J.Rolls c Dhar b Al Khader	38	58	42	-	5
E.C.Drumm* c Dhar b Al Khader	3	11	15	-	-
K.L.Pulford run out	21	46	43	-	1
H.M.Tiffen b Goswami	52	49	49	-	6
M.A.M.Lewis not out	17	15	13	-	1
S.J.McGlashan not out	5	9	7	-	-
F.S.King					
N.J.Browne					
R.J.Steele					
L.E.Milliken					
Extras (b 5, lb 3, w 11)	19				
TOTAL (50 overs) (5 wkts)	**248**	176			

INDIA	Runs	Mins	Balls	6s	4s
S.A.Paranjpe c Tiffen b Browne	41	100	85	-	6
J.Sharma st Rolls b Drumm	37	83	65	-	4
A.Chopra* run out	23	96	77	-	1
M.Raj c King b Milliken	27	55	54	-	4
H.Kala run out	11	21	15	-	1
A.Sharma not out	0	4	4	-	-
R.Dhar not out	0	2	0	-	-
N.Al Khader					
S.Naik†					
N.David					
J.Goswami					
Extras (b 5, w 21)	26				
TOTAL (50 overs) (5 wkts)	**165**	183			

Bowling	O	M	R	W
INDIA				
Goswami	10	1	54	1
Sharma A.	5	0	16	0
Dhar	5	1	28	0
Chopra	9	0	50	0
Al Khader	10	0	44	2
David	10	1	34	0
Paranjpe	1	0	14	0
NEW ZEALAND				
Browne	10	3	21	1
Milliken	10	0	39	1
King	8	0	29	0
Pulford	9	0	33	0
Steele	10	1	21	0
Drumm	3	0	17	1

Fall of Wickets	NZ	I
1st	79	75
2nd	88	95
3rd	135	144
4th	222	163
5th	230	165
6th	-	-
7th	-	-
8th	-	-
9th	-	-
10th	-	-

NEW ZEALAND
CRICKET

NEW ZEALAND v ENGLAND   World Series

at Lincoln No.3 on 30 January, 2003
Toss : England. Umpires : K. Cross & E.A. Watkin
New Zealand won by 4 wickets. *Points: New Zealand 6, England 0*

England won the toss and batted and were all out for 140 in the 47th over. Drumm had the excellent figures of three wickets for eight runs off five overs with King taking two wickets and Pulford, Mason and Steele taking one wicket each.

New Zealand started positively with Rolls making 41 off 33 balls including seven fours and Lynch making 29 off 46 balls including five fours. Rolls departed with the score on 73 and wickets fell regularly until the victory was achieved in the 40th over for the loss of six wickets.

ENGLAND

	Runs	Mins	Balls	6s	4s
C.M.Edwards c Tiffen b Pulford	4	19	14	-	-
A.Thompson lbw b Drumm	12	51	41	-	1
S.C.Taylor c Lewis b Drumm	10	24	23	-	2
L.K.Newton b Drumm	8	14	18	-	1
C.J.Connor* c Tiffen b Mason	16	34	41	-	2
S.V.Collyer st Rolls b King	29	61	71	-	4
L.Spragg c Tiffen b Steele	5	13	14	-	1
L.J.Harper run out	18	41	31	-	-
M.C.Godliman† lbw b King	2	9	7	-	-
C.E.Taylor not out	5	19	18	-	-
L.C.Pearson run out	1	8	2	-	-
Extras (lb 6, w 24)	30		151		
TOTAL (46.4 overs)	**140**				

NEW ZEALAND

	Runs	Mins	Balls	6s	4s
R.J.Rolls† c Pearson b Harper	41	54	33	-	7
M.L.Lynch lbw b Spragg	29	43	46	-	5
E.C.Drumm* b Pearson	15	32	36	-	2
K.L.Pulford b Harper	2	11	15	-	-
H.M.Tiffen lbw b Taylor C.E.	0	35	21	-	-
M.A.M.Lewis lbw b Pearson	7	19	28	-	-
S.J.McGlashan not out	9	35	33	-	1
A.L.Mason not out	15	29	23	-	3
F.S.King					
N.J.Browne					
R.J.Steele					
Extras (b 1, lb 11, w 11)	23		132		
TOTAL (39.1 overs) (6 wkts)	**141**				

Bowling	O	M	R	W
NEW ZEALAND				
Browne	8.4	0	33	0
Pulford	4	2	6	1
Drumm	5	1	8	3
King	9	0	41	2
Mason	10	2	22	1
Steele	10	2	24	1
ENGLAND				
Pearson	10	1	36	2
Taylor C.E.	9	0	37	1
Collyer	3	0	20	0
Spragg	6	2	17	1
Harper	10	3	17	2
Connor	1.1	0	2	0

Fall of Wickets		
	E	NZ
1st	14	73
2nd	39	81
3rd	46	87
4th	50	95
5th	77	106
6th	88	107
7th	108	-
8th	121	-
9th	133	-
10th	140	-

AUSTRALIA v INDIA

World Series

at Lincoln No.3 on 1 February, 2003
Toss : Australia. Umpires : R.D. Anderson & G.A. Baxter
Australia won by 59 runs. *Points: Australia 6, India 0*

AUSTRALIA

	Runs	Mins	Balls	6s	4s
M.J.Bulow b Dhar	9	17	15	-	1
B.J.Clark* lbw b David	35	81	71	-	5
M.Jones lbw b David	24	41	27	-	3
K.L.Rolton b Goswami	68	106	82	-	7
M.A.J.Goszko c Goswami b Goyal	3	14	22	-	-
A.J.Blackwell run out	27	58	59	-	4
L.C.Sthalekar run out	7	15	6	-	1
J.Hayes run out	1	2	2	-	-
C.L.Fitzpatrick c Raj b Dhar	5	9	11	-	-
J.C.Price† not out	11	10	7	-	1
E.Twining not out	0	2	0	-	-
Extras (b 1, lb 11, w 12, nb 2)	26				
TOTAL (50 overs) (9 wkts)	**216**	174			

INDIA

	Runs	Mins	Balls	6s	4s
J.Sharma c Goszko b Fitzpatrick	8	37	34	-	-
A.Chopra* lbw b Hayes	32	72	61	-	4
M.Raj c Sthalekar b Hayes	36	60	51	-	5
S.A.Paranjpe† b Hayes	2	12	13	-	-
R.Malhotra b Blackwell	15	46	57	-	1
R.Dhar c Goszko b Sthalekar	3	19	20	-	-
B.Mandlik run out	0	5	3	-	-
J.Goswami lbw b Blackwell	0	16	8	-	-
N.David not out	18	34	29	-	2
N.Al Khader c Price b Fitzpatrick	21	19	21	-	5
B.Goyal not out	1	5	4	-	-
Extras (lb 8, w 12, nb 1)	21				
TOTAL (50 overs) (9 wkts)	**157**	159			

Bowling	O	M	R	W
INDIA				
Goswami	10	0	47	1
Dhar	8	0	41	2
Chopra	2	0	20	0
Al Khader	10	0	38	0
David	10	1	30	2
Goyal	10	0	28	1
AUSTRALIA				
Fitzpatrick	9	1	27	2
Twining	10	0	45	0
Sthalekar	10	0	35	1
Hayes	10	3	28	3
Rolton	5	2	6	0
Blackwell	6	3	8	2

Fall of Wickets	A	I
1st	14	31
2nd	73	78
3rd	96	84
4th	105	93
5th	179	107
6th	197	109
7th	199	113
8th	199	123
9th	208	151
10th	-	-

AUSTRALIA v ENGLAND

World Series

at Lincoln No.3 on 2 February, 2003
Toss : Australia. Umpires : R.D. Anderson & G.A. Baxter
Australia won by 106 runs. *Points: Australia 6, England 0*

AUSTRALIA

	Runs	Mins	Balls	6s	4s
B.J.Clark* c Collyer	81	116	106	-	8
M.J.Bulow b Pearson	0	2	3	-	-
K.L.Rolton b Taylor C.E.	4	19	10	-	-
M.A.J.Goszko c Leng b Newton	9	36	37	-	1
M.Jones c Taylor S.C. b Harper	37	88	73	-	4
K.L.Britt b Collyer	0	4	1	-	-
J.Hayes b Connor	44	52	52	-	5
C.L.Fitzpatrick run out	9	13	13	-	-
J.C.Price† not out	4	3	3	-	1
C.R.Smith not out	5	2	2	-	1
E.Twining					
Extras (b 5, lb 10, w 18)	33				
TOTAL (50 overs) (8 wkts)	**226**	167			

ENGLAND

	Runs	Mins	Balls	6s	4s
C.M.Edwards c Price b Twining	7	28	35	-	-
A.Thompson st Price b Smith	18	55	46	-	4
S.C.Taylor b Fitzpatrick	0	15	15	-	-
L.K.Newton b Fitzpatrick	7	17	15	-	1
K.M.Leng c Clark b Britt	3	30	30	-	-
C.J.Connor* b Fitzpatrick	29	79	69	-	3
S.V.Collyer lbw b Britt	0	1	1	-	-
L.J.Harper c Price b Rolton	16	31	36	-	3
M.C.Godliman† st Price b Britt	14	34	30	-	2
C.E.Taylor not out	9	17	18	-	1
L.C.Pearson c & b Britt	0	2	5	-	-
Extras (b 5, lb 3, w 9)	17				
TOTAL (50 overs)	**120**	150			

Bowling	O	M	R	W
ENGLAND				
Pearson	8	0	48	1
Taylor C.E.	8	1	26	1
Newton	5	0	28	1
Harper	10	2	29	1
Connor	10	1	49	1
Collyer	9	1	31	2
AUSTRALIA				
Hayes	10	2	30	0
Twining	10	3	27	1
Fitzpatrick	10	4	17	3
Smith	7	3	9	1
Britt	7	2	16	4
Rolton	6	1	13	1

Fall of Wickets	A	E
1st	1	17
2nd	22	26
3rd	68	31
4th	147	37
5th	147	45
6th	174	45
7th	216	87
8th	217	104
9th	-	119
10th	-	120

NEW ZEALAND v INDIA World Series

at Bert Sutcliffe Oval, Lincoln on 2 February, 2003
Toss : India. Umpires : J.M. Busby & D.M. Quested
New Zealand won by 53 runs. *Points: New Zealand 6, India 0*

India won the toss and put New Zealand in to bat. Rolls and Lynch put on 82 for the first wicket with Rolls hitting a rollicking 59 off 37 balls with 12 fours. Drumm and Lewis also scored half centuries with Drumm's 51 off 80 balls including two fours and Lewis' 50 off 83 balls including one boundary. They featured in a 94 run partnership for the third wicket.

Needing 240 for victory, India were dismissed in the 48th over for 186. Raj scored an impressive 82 off 98 balls including ten fours. Drumm took three wickets, King and Mason took two wickets each and Rolls made two stumpings.

NEW ZEALAND

	Runs	Mins	Balls	6s	4s
M.L.Lynch c Al Khader b Goswami	13	54	29	-	-
R.J.Rolls† c Naik b Goswami	59	47	37	-	12
E.C.Drumm* b Kala	51	77	80	-	2
M.A.M.Lewis c David b Al Khader	50	92	83	-	1
H.M.Tiffen c Naik b Kala	2	6	8	-	-
S.J.McGlashan st Naik b Kala	13	25	27	-	-
A.L.Mason st Naik b Al Khader	17	24	17	-	-
F.S.King c Dhar b Al Khader	5	4	5	-	-
N.J.Browne not out	7	15	7	-	-
A.J.Green b Al Khader	0	1	2	-	-
R.J.Steele not out	5	4	5	-	-
Extras (lb 2, w 15)	17				
TOTAL (50 overs) (9 wkts)	**239**	179			

INDIA

	Runs	Mins	Balls	6s	4s
A.Chopra* c Lewis b Mason	1	12	8	-	-
J.Sharma c & b Mason	15	61	49	-	2
M.Raj st Rolls b Drumm	82	103	98	-	10
H.Kala lbw b Drumm	31	64	53	-	-
R.Dhar lbw b Drumm	0	1	1	-	-
R.Malhotra c & b Steele	5	14	11	-	1
N.David b King	14	25	23	-	2
S.Naik† run out	8	13	12	-	1
J.Goswami st Rolls b King	0	23	11	-	-
N.Al Khader not out	11	14	8	-	1
B.Goyal absent hurt					
Extras (lb 1, w 18)	19				
TOTAL (47.2 overs)	**186**	164			

Bowling INDIA	O	M	R	W
Goswami	10	1	51	2
Dhar	3	0	38	0
Kala	10	0	31	3
David	10	0	50	0
Goyal	8	1	29	0
Al Khader	9	0	38	4
NEW ZEALAND				
Browne	8	1	33	0
Mason	10	1	21	2
Green	6	1	25	0
Steele	10	1	43	1
King	6.2	0	37	2
Drumm	7	0	26	3

Fall of Wickets		
	NZ	I
1st	82	6
2nd	85	62
3rd	179	144
4th	185	144
5th	199	151
6th	210	151
7th	219	163
8th	231	174
9th	231	186
10th	-	-

NEW ZEALAND v ENGLAND

World Series

at Bert Sutcliffe Oval, Lincoln on 3 February, 2003
Toss : England. Umpires : R.D. Anderson & G.A. Baxter
New Zealand won by 7 wickets. Points: New Zealand 5, England 1

England won the toss and elected to bat. Wickets fell regularly with Steele taking three wickets and Green, Mason and Burke (in her debut for NZ) taking one each. There were three run outs in the total of 173-9.

With New Zealand chasing 174 for victory, Rolls was dismissed early but a 40 run partnership between Payne and Drumm and a 120 run partnership between Drumm and Lewis ensured the New Zealanders would achieve the target. Drumm scored 93 off 115 balls including 12 fours and Lewis was 32 not out with three fours. The victory was achieved in the 45th over.

ENGLAND

	Runs	Mins	Balls	6s	4s
S.V.Collyer run out	39	94	89	-	4
K.M.Leng c Tiffen b Mason	16	35	33	-	2
S.C.Taylor† run out	8	25	21	-	1
A.Thompson st Rolls b Steele	17	51	38	-	1
C.J.Connor* c & b Steele	0	7	13	-	-
L.K.Newton lbw b Steele	7	18	23	-	1
D.Holden lbw b Green	26	48	42	-	2
L.Spragg run out	7	10	5	-	1
N.Shaw c Rolls b Burke	11	21	16	-	2
C.E.Taylor not out	16	17	13	-	1
L.C.Pearson not out	4	9	7	-	-
Extras (b 2, lb 6, w 14)	22				
TOTAL (50 overs) (9 wkts)	**173**	172			

NEW ZEALAND

	Runs	Mins	Balls	6s	4s
N.Payne lbw b Taylor C.E.	26	59	59	-	1
R.J.Rolls† c Newton b Shaw	9	12	14	-	2
E.C.Drumm* st Taylor S.C. b Holden	93	135	115	-	12
M.A.M.Lewis not out	32	91	77	-	3
H.M.Tiffen not out	1	1	2	-	-
K.L.Pulford					
S.J.McGlashan					
A.L.Mason					
S.K.Burke					
A.J.Green					
R.J.Steele					
Extras (lb 2, w 11)	13				
TOTAL (44.3 overs) (3 wkts)	**174**	150			

Bowling	O	M	R	W
NEW ZEALAND				
Burke	10	1	37	1
Pulford	10	0	45	0
Mason	10	1	33	1
Green	10	2	19	1
Steele	10	3	31	3
ENGLAND				
Pearson	8	1	27	0
Shaw	7	0	34	1
Taylor C.E.	10	0	32	1
Spragg	7	2	28	0
Connor	5	0	18	0
Collyer	2	0	14	0
Holden	5.3	0	19	1

Fall of Wickets	E	NZ
1st	38	13
2nd	51	53
3rd	83	173
4th	87	-
5th	98	-
6th	106	-
7th	121	-
8th	145	-
9th	156	-
10th		-

AUSTRALIA v INDIA World Series

at Bert Sutcliffe Oval, Lincoln on 4 February, 2003
Toss : India. Umpires : R.D. Anderson & A.L. Hill
Australia won by 9 wickets. *Points: Australia 6, India 0*

INDIA

	Runs	Mins	Balls	6s	4s
R.Dhar c Britt b Blackwell	16	83	73	-	1
A.Chopra* run out	25	74	84	-	3
M.Raj c Price b Blackwell	11	19	24	-	-
H.Kala c Britt b Sthalekar	11	18	16	-	2
N.Al Khader c Sthalekar b Smith	9	25	23	-	1
S.Naik† st Price b Smith	18	26	27	-	3
R.Malhotra b Twining	10	28	29	-	1
B.Mandlik not out	5	24	19	-	-
A.Sharma not out	10	4	5	-	2
J.Goswami					
M.Kanojia					
Extras (b 3, lb 3, w 13)	19				
TOTAL (50 overs) (7 wkts)	134	154			

Bowling	O	M	R	W
AUSTRALIA				
Twining	9	4	13	1
Smith	9	2	30	2
Rolton	6	1	17	0
Hayes	9	2	22	0
Blackwell	6	2	18	2
Sthalekar	7	0	19	1
Britt	4	0	9	0
INDIA				
Goswami	7	0	37	0
Sharma	6	0	25	1
Al Khader	8	0	31	0
Dhar	3	0	19	0
Malhotra	2	0	9	0
Kanojia	2	0	13	0

AUSTRALIA

	Runs	Mins	Balls	6s	4s
B.J.Clark* lbw b Sharma	49	72	68	-	4
L.C.Sthalekar not out	58	96	80	-	2
K.L.Rolton not out	21	23	21	-	3
M.Jones					
M.A.J.Goszko					
A.J.Blackwell					
K.L.Britt					
J.Hayes					
J.C.Price†					
C.R.Smith					
E.Twining					
Extras (lb 1, w 5, nb 1)	7				
TOTAL (28 overs) (1 wkt)	135	96			

Fall of Wickets

	I	A
1st	48	96
2nd	52	-
3rd	59	-
4th	71	-
5th	90	-
6th	108	-
7th	123	-
8th	-	-
9th	-	-
10th	-	-

ENGLAND v INDIA World Series

at Lincoln No.3 on 6 February, 2003
Toss : India. Umpires : G.A. Baxter & J.M. Busby
England won by 1 run. *Points: England 5, India 1*

ENGLAND

	Runs	Mins	Balls	6s	4s
S.V.Collyer st Naik b David	33	70	61	-	4
K.M.Leng run out	22	82	59	-	2
C.M.Edwards not out	79	99	94	-	10
S.C.Taylor† b Al Khader	14	30	41	-	2
A.Thompson st Naik b Kanojia	38	51	43	-	1
C.J.Connor* not out	2	4	2	-	-
L.K.Newton					
D.Holden					
L.J.Harper					
C.E.Taylor					
L.C.Pearson					
Extras (lb 3, w 17)	20				
TOTAL (50 overs) (4 wkts)	208	170			

Bowling	O	M	R	W
INDIA				
Goswami	6	0	37	0
Sharma	9	3	29	0
Dhar	3	0	13	0
David	10	4	20	1
Kala	9	0	38	0
Al Khader	10	1	45	1
Kanojia	3	0	23	1
ENGLAND				
Pearson	10	2	35	1
Taylor C.E.	8	3	25	0
Harper	10	2	55	1
Connor	9	0	39	2
Collyer	9	1	35	2
Holden	4	1	15	1

INDIA

	Runs	Mins	Balls	6s	4s
S.A.Paranjpe c Thompson b Harper	17	58	51	-	1
R.Dhar c Leng b Pearson	0	14	11	-	-
M.Raj run out	98	156	126	-	12
A.Chopra* lbw b Collyer	26	26	31	-	3
S.Naik† c Taylor C.E. b Holden	0	10	12	-	-
H.Kala run out	38	56	45	-	6
N.David b Connor	5	10	6	-	1
N.Al Khader not out	5	20	8	-	-
A.Sharma b Connor	0	4	4	-	-
M.Kanojia run out	3	4	2	-	-
J.Goswami b Collyer	0	3	4	-	-
Extras (lb 3, w 12)	15				
TOTAL (50 overs)	207	185			

Fall of Wickets

	E	I
1st	66	5
2nd	72	50
3rd	106	89
4th	204	92
5th	-	184
6th	-	197
7th	-	201
8th	-	203
9th	-	206
10th	-	207

NEW ZEALAND v AUSTRALIA   World Series

at Bert Sutcliffe Oval, Lincoln on 6 February, 2003
Toss : New Zealand. Umpires : A.L. Hill & G.C. Holdem
Australia won by 6 wickets. *Points: Australia 6, New Zealand 0*

New Zealand won the toss and decided to bat first and Rolls was lbw in Fitzpatrick's second over. Lewis, Tiffen and Mason steadied the middle order but New Zealand were dismissed in the 50th over for 174 with Fitzpatrick finishing with the outstanding figures of 5-27.

    Australia began the run chase aggressively with Sthalekar and Clark putting on 128 for the first wicket. Steele, with 2-29, was the pick of the New Zealand bowlers. Australia cruised to victory in 40 overs for the loss of four wickets to retain the Rose Bowl for another year.

NEW ZEALAND

	Runs	Mins	Balls	6s	4s
R.J.Rolls† lbw b Fitzpatrick	1	8	7	-	-
M.L.Lynch c Clark b Hayes	28	63	64	-	3
E.C.Drumm* c Goszko b Fitzpatrick	8	14	17	-	2
M.A.M.Lewis b Fitzpatrick	43	119	85	-	1
H.M.Tiffen run out	28	47	63	-	3
A.L.Mason b Twining	33	43	37	-	2
S.J.McGlashan b Fitzpatrick	13	13	11	-	1
K.L.Pulford b Twining	0	5	3	-	-
N.J.Browne b Twining	3	6	5	-	-
R.J.Steele b Fitzpatrick	4	4	3	-	-
A.J.Green not out	0	1	0	-	-
Extras (b 1, lb 7, w 5)	13				
TOTAL (49.1 overs)	**174**	158			

AUSTRALIA

	Runs	Mins	Balls	6s	4s
L.C.Sthalekar c Rolls b Pulford	53	95	83	-	4
B.J.Clark* b Steele	67	99	87	-	6
K.L.Rolton run out	10	7	8	-	2
M.Jones not out	11	37	25	-	1
M.A.J.Goszko c Pulford b Steele	13	15	22	-	2
A.J.Blackwell not out	6	13	15	-	1
J.Hayes					
C.L.Fitzpatrick					
J.C.Price†					
C.R.Smith					
E.Twining					
Extras (lb 3, w 12)	15				
TOTAL (40 overs) (4 wkts)	**175**	121			

Bowling	O	M	R	W
AUSTRALIA				
Fitzpatrick	9.1	2	27	5
Twining	9	3	31	3
Hayes	10	2	24	1
Rolton	10	0	27	0
Sthalekar	6	1	27	0
Smith	4	1	22	0
Blackwell	1	0	8	0
NEW ZEALAND				
Browne	5	0	26	0
Pulford	10	0	50	1
Green	5	0	15	0
Drumm	2	0	15	0
Mason	8	0	37	0
Steele	10	1	29	2

Fall of Wickets	NZ	A
1st	7	128
2nd	17	139
3rd	52	143
4th	100	165
5th	147	-
6th	165	-
7th	167	-
8th	169	-
9th	174	-
10th	174	-

ENGLAND v INDIA

at Bert Sutcliffe Oval, Lincoln on 7 February, 2003
Toss : England. Umpires : G.A. Baxter & A.L. Hill
England won by 90 runs.

World Series 3rd-4th Playoff

England won the toss and chose to bat. Leng top scored with 80 off 109 balls including eight fours and Edwards scored 21 off 45 balls including two fours. England were all out in the 49th over for 191 with David the best of the Indian bowlers with three wickets. Al-Khader and Goswami took two wickets each.

Chasing 192 for victory, India started disastrously losing their first wicket in Pearson's opening over. Raj top scored with 26 off 45 balls with two fours while Connor and Collyer both took three wickets each. India were all out for 101 in the 44th over.

ENGLAND

	Runs	Mins	Balls	6s	4s
S.V.Collyer c Naik b Goswami ..	13	40	36	-	2
K.M.Leng b David	80	136	109	-	8
C.M.Edwards lbw b Paranjpe	21	59	45	-	2
S.C.Taylor† b David	6	16	18	-	-
A.Thompson run out	9	28	18	-	-
C.J.Connor* b David	2	12	18	-	-
L.K.Newton st Naik b Al Khader ..	4	8	8	-	-
D.Holden b Al Khader	6	11	10	-	-
L.J.Harper not out	8	20	16	-	-
C.E.Taylor run out	14	12	10	-	1
L.C.Pearson lbw b Goswami	0	1	1	-	-
Extras (lb 10, w 18)	28				
TOTAL (48.1 overs) **191**		176			

INDIA

	Runs	Mins	Balls	6s	4s
S.A.Paranjpe lbw b Pearson	0	1	3	-	-
J.Sharma c Thompson b Connor	16	52	51	-	2
M.Raj b Harper	26	68	45	-	2
A.Chopra* lbw b Connor	9	12	17	-	1
B.Mandlik run out	1	14	10	-	-
H.Kala b Collyer	1	26	20	-	-
S.Naik† c Taylor C.E. b Harper .	23	51	47	-	3
N.David b Collyer	0	2	4	-	-
N.Al Khader b Connor	0	15	10	-	-
J.Goswami c Taylor S.C. b Collyer	12	32	42	-	-
A.Sharma not out	3	16	14	-	-
Extras (w 10)	10				
TOTAL (43.5 overs) **101**		149			

Bowling	O	M	R	W
INDIA				
Goswami	9.1	3	24	2
Sharma A.	6	1	28	0
Chopra	8	1	30	0
Kala	2	0	10	0
Al Khader	10	2	32	2
David	10	0	42	3
Paranjpe	3	0	15	1
ENGLAND				
Pearson	7	1	18	1
Taylor C.E.	5	1	16	0
Harper	10	2	23	2
Connor	8	1	16	3
Holden	4	0	19	0
Collyer	9.5	6	9	3

Fall of Wickets	E	I
1st	36	1
2nd	100	39
3rd	123	53
4th	152	55
5th	155	58
6th	155	68
7th	163	68
8th	166	81
9th	191	90
10th	191	101

NEW ZEALAND v AUSTRALIA   World Series Final

at Bert Sutcliffe Oval, Lincoln on 8 February, 2003
Toss : Australia. Umpires : G.A. Baxter & A.L. Hill
Australia won by 109 runs

Australia won the toss and elected to bat in the World Series final. Clark scored 80 off 119 balls including five fours and her second wicket partnership of 68 with Rolton set the Australians up to reach a total of 214. King took three wickets and all the other bowlers used took one wicket each.

Chasing 215 to win the World Series final, New Zealand changed their batting order with Rolls dropping down the order to bat at four. Wickets fell regularly, however, and only a whirlwind 17 off 21 balls with four fours by number ten Browne took the New Zealand total beyond 100. New Zealand was all out for 105 in 30 overs. All the Australian bowlers took wickets with Hayes taking three and Fitzpatrick two.

AUSTRALIA	Runs	Mins	Balls	6s	4s
B.J.Clark* b King	80	145	119	-	5
L.C.Sthalekar c Rolls b Steele	8	23	18	-	-
K.L.Rolton c Lewis b King	34	50	50	-	5
M.Jones c Rolls b Browne	18	27	27	-	2
M.A.J.Goszko lbw b Mason	6	16	21	-	-
A.J.Blackwell lbw b King	21	53	41	-	1
J.Hayes run out	4	9	8	-	-
C.L.Fitzpatrick lbw b Pulford	5	2	3	-	1
J.C.Price† run out	6	9	7	-	-
C.R.Smith run out	6	6	4	-	-
E.Twining not out	2	1	1	-	-
Extras (lb 6, w 18)	24				
TOTAL (49.5 overs)	**214**	175			

NEW ZEALAND	Runs	Mins	Balls	6s	4s
N.Payne lbw b Fitzpatrick	13	37	40	-	2
K.L.Pulford c Price b Twining	5	17	15	-	1
E.C.Drumm* b Fitzpatrick	5	5	5	-	1
R.J.Rolls† lbw b Hayes	7	21	12	-	-
H.M.Tiffen run out	11	16	13	-	1
S.J.McGlashan c Price b Rolton	0	2	2	-	-
A.L.Mason c Clark b Smith	31	46	42	-	4
M.A.M.Lewis st Price b Hayes	4	18	17	-	-
F.S.King st Price b Hayes	9	12	10	-	2
N.J.Browne b Sthalekar	17	23	21	-	4
R.J.Steele not out	0	5	3	-	-
Extras (w 3)	3				
TOTAL (30 overs)	**105**	100			

Bowling					
NEW ZEALAND	O	M	R	W	
Browne	10	0	40	1	
Steele	10	1	38	1	
Pulford	10	0	51	1	
Mason	10	1	35	1	
King	9.5	0	44	3	
AUSTRALIA					
Fitzpatrick	6	1	14	2	
Twining	6	2	18	1	
Hayes	7	2	31	3	
Rolton	6	1	16	1	
Sthalekar	3	1	16	1	
Smith	2	0	10	1	

Fall of Wickets		
	A	NZ
1st	25	7
2nd	93	12
3rd	124	27
4th	141	34
5th	176	46
6th	185	46
7th	192	46
8th	204	71
9th	211	97
10th	214	105

NEW ZEALAND A

A New Zealand A team was selected to play the four international teams in the country for the World Series. Unfortunately the Indian team's arrival in NZ was delayed so this match was rescheduled as a second game against New Zealand.

New Zealand A tied one match against New Zealand, lost to New Zealand and Australia and defeated England. The New Zealand A team was: Maia Lewis *(captain)*, Amanda Green *(Wellington)*, Michelle Lynch, Debbie Ramsay *(Auckland)*, Maree Hannay, Aimee Lennsen *(Northern Districts)* Sara McGlashan *(Central Districts)*, Sarah Burke, Maria Fahey, Beth McNeill, Rowan Milburn, Rebecca Steele *(Canterbury)*, Megan Kane, Katey Martin *(Otago)*.

Coach, Cliff Dickeson; Manager, Lesley Murdoch; Physiotherapist, Hayley Sligo.

Five players were elevated from the New Zealand A team to play in the World Series. They were Lewis, Lynch, Green, Steele and McGlashan while Burke replaced Milliken who withdrew from the World Series due to injury.

NEW ZEALAND A v NEW ZEALAND
At Lincoln Green   21 January, 2003

New Zealand 269-5 (R.J. Rolls 62, K.L. Pulford 59*, E.C. Drumm 48, N. Payne 44, H.M. Tiffen 31) **defeated New Zealand A** 173 (M.L. Lynch 65, N.J. Browne 3-18) by 96 runs

NEW ZEALAND A v NEW ZEALAND
At Lincoln Green   22 January, 2003

New Zealand 200-8 (H.M. Tiffen 72*, N. Payne 32) **tied with New Zealand A** 200-4 (M.A.M. Lewis 75*, K.J. Martin 40)

NEW ZEALAND A v AUSTRALIA
At Lincoln Green   24 January, 2003

New Zealand A 155-8 (M.L. Lynch 77, C.I. Smith 3-28) **lost to Australia** 157-6 (K.L. Rolton 45, B.J. Clark 34) by 4 wickets

NEW ZEALAND A v ENGLAND
At Lincoln Green   25 January, 2003

England 199-7 (A. Thompson 75, L.K. Newton 48, S.C. Taylor 33, M.J. Hannay 3-42) **lost to New Zealand A** 200-9 (M.J. Kane 57, M.L. Lynch 50, N.J. Shaw 3-33) by 1 wicket

STATE LEAGUE
2002/03

State Auckland Hearts won the State League for the fourth consecutive season. In a competition badly affected by weather, Northern Districts lost three matches and Central Districts and Wellington lost two matches each due to wet weather.

The highlights of the round robin play were Canterbury's back to back victories over Auckland and the tie between Otago and Northern Districts. Nicola Payne, of the State Canterbury Magicians, was the leading run scorer, and the only player to score over 400 runs, with 416 runs at an average of 52. Natalee Scripps, of the State Auckland Hearts, took 20 wickets which was the highest in the competition. There was only one century scored in the competition and that was by Northern Districts English import, Charlotte Edwards.

Final points were:

	P	W	L	T	NR	Bonus	Points
Canterbury	10	8	1	–	1	2	36
Auckland	10	6	3	–	1	4	30
Wellington	10	6	2	–	2	1	29
Otago	10	2	6	1	1	1	13
Central Districts	10	2	6	–	2	1	13
Northern Districts	10	–	6	1	3	–	8

NORTHERN DISTRICTS v CENTRAL DISTRICTS State League

at Westpac Park, Hamilton on 7 December, 2002
Abandoned without a ball being bowled. *Points: Northern Districts 2, Central Districts 2*

NORTHERN DISTRICTS v CENTRAL DISTRICTS State League

at Westpac Park, Hamilton on 8 December, 2002
Abandoned without a ball being bowled. *Points: Northern Districts 2, Central Districts 2*

CANTERBURY v OTAGO   State League

at Aorangi Park, Timaru on 14 December, 2002
Toss : Otago. Umpires : A.L. Hill & R.S. Kinsey
Canterbury won by 7 wickets. *Points: Canterbury 4, Otago 0*

OTAGO

	Runs	Mins	Balls	6s	4s
E.J.Scurr c & b McNeill	17	92	73	-	1
N.A.Bannerman c Steele b Daly	21	33	25	-	4
S.J.Tsukigawa b Daly	0	6	5	-	-
R.J.Pullar st Milburn b Fahey	78	119	104	2	10
S.K.Helmore* lbw b McNeill	0	10	14	-	-
M.J.Kane c Rae b Steele	1	18	12	-	-
C.E.Taylor not out	50	56	47	-	7
K.J.Martin† st Milburn b Daly	6	8	7	-	-
J.M.Innes not out	6	18	13	-	-
K.M.Spence					
A.E.Crawley					
Extras (b 1, lb 5, w 25)	31				
TOTAL (50 overs) (7 wkts)	210	188			

CANTERBURY

	Runs	Mins	Balls	6s	4s
N.Payne not out	83	185	126	-	7
K.A.Craig b Pullar	2	8	8	-	-
S.C.Taylor b Kane	59	101	83	-	9
H.M.Tiffen* c Helmore b Kane	6	8	6	-	1
M.F.Fahey not out	41	66	57	-	6
B.H.McNeill					
S.K.Burke					
R.C.Milburn†					
H.R.Daly					
R.J.Steele					
H.J.Rae					
Extras (lb 2, w 18, nb 2)	22				
TOTAL (46.3 overs) (3 wkts)	213	185			

Bowling	O	M	R	W
CANTERBURY				
Burke	10	0	37	0
Daly	10	3	27	3
Tiffen	8	1	39	0
Rae	4	1	14	0
McNeill	7	1	14	2
Steele	10	1	52	1
Fahey	1	0	21	1
OTAGO				
Pullar	9.3	2	32	1
Taylor	9	3	27	0
Crawley	4	0	21	0
Spence	10	0	41	0
Innes	7	0	37	0
Scurr	4	0	34	0
Kane	3	0	19	2

Fall of Wickets	O	C
1st	29	4
2nd	30	117
3rd	75	128
4th	92	-
5th	105	-
6th	157	-
7th	176	-
8th	-	-
9th	-	-
10th	-	-

WELLINGTON v CENTRAL DISTRICTS   State League

at Kelburn Park, Wellington on 14 December, 2002
Toss : Central Districts. Umpires : D.G. Paterson & C.J. Morris
Wellington won by 17 runs. *Points: Wellington 4, Central Districts 0*

WELLINGTON

	Runs	Mins	Balls	6s	4s
M.C.Godliman† run out	32	57	57	-	4
M.L.Presland c Graham b Mason	0	27	33	-	-
F.E.Fraser st Street b Trow	25	49	31	-	2
M.A.M.Lewis* b Pulford	31	91	75	-	1
F.S.King c Mason b Trow	15	44	46	-	-
M.G.Wakefield run out	13	28	28	-	1
A.M.Corbin not out	12	27	25	-	-
A.E.Cooper b Pulford	2	11	10	-	-
A.J.Green run out	3	10	5	-	-
A.M.Little not out	0	1	2	-	-
M.L.Tuapawa					
Extras (b 1, lb 5, w 10, nb 2)	18				
TOTAL (50 overs) (8 wkts)	151	178			

CENTRAL DISTRICTS

	Runs	Mins	Balls	6s	4s
C.L.Forsyth c Wakefield b Green	5	27	26	-	1
K.L.Pulford c Lewis b Corbin	30	94	71	-	2
N.M.Thessman run out	16	56	45	-	1
A.L.Mason* b Pulford	12	20	14	-	2
S.J.McGlashan c & b Corbin	8	19	17	-	1
M.M.Graham run out	0	15	13	-	-
E.T.McDonald not out	26	68	54	-	1
T.M.Street† c & b Corbin	2	6	10	-	-
Z.A.McWilliams run out	4	19	20	-	-
D.M.Trow run out	6	14	14	-	1
A.K.Burrows run out	6	15	9	-	1
Extras (b 1, lb 8, w 8, nb 2)	19				
TOTAL (47.4 overs)	134	184			

Bowling	O	M	R	W
CENTRAL DISTRICTS				
Burrows	8	4	12	0
Mason	10	4	19	1
Pulford	9	0	32	2
McDonald	9	2	36	0
Trow	7	0	23	2
McWilliams	7	1	23	0
WELLINGTON				
King	9	3	31	1
Green	9	3	16	1
Little	7	1	23	0
Presland	6.4	1	14	0
Corbin	10	2	27	3
Cooper	6	0	14	0

Fall of Wickets	C	W
1st	11	22
2nd	54	61
3rd	70	68
4th	109	78
5th	133	84
6th	135	86
7th	141	90
8th	151	98
9th	-	116
10th	-	134

CANTERBURY v OTAGO   State League

at Aorangi Park, Timaru on 15 December, 2002
Toss : Otago. Umpires : A.L. Hill & R.S. Kinsey
Canterbury won by 10 wickets. Points: Canterbury 5, Otago 0

OTAGO

	Runs	Mins	Balls	6s	4s
E.J.Scurr c Daly b McNeill	18	70	49	-	1
M.J.Kane c Tiffen b McNeill	14	37	36	-	-
S.J.Tsukigawa run out	0	11	12	-	-
R.J.Pullar c Rae b McNeill	26	26	29	-	4
C.E.Taylor c Rae b Steele	2	13	7	-	-
S.K.Helmore* lbw b Daly	5	63	53	-	-
K.J.Martin† c Payne b Rae	1	24	19	-	-
J.M.Innes lbw b McNeill	11	28	20	-	1
C.M.Thompson not out	5	24	20	-	-
K.M.Spence c Milburn b McNeill	2	13	11	-	-
A.E.Crawley run out	2	10	9	-	-
Extras (b 1, lb 3, w 13)	17				
TOTAL (46 overs)	**103**	162			

CANTERBURY

	Runs	Mins	Balls	6s	4s
N.Payne not out	53	101	89	-	7
K.A.Craig not out	42	101	85	-	7
S.C.Taylor					
H.M.Tiffen*					
M.F.Fahey					
B.H.McNeill					
S.K.Burke					
R.C.Milburn†					
H.R.Daly					
R.J.Steele					
H.J.Rae					
Extras (lb 3, w 9)	12				
TOTAL (29 overs) (0 wkts)	**107**	101			

Bowling	O	M	R	W
CANTERBURY				
Burke	8	0	19	0
Daly	10	4	20	1
McNeill	10	1	31	5
Steele	10	6	18	1
Rae	8	1	11	1
OTAGO				
Pullar	7	3	10	0
Taylor	6	2	24	0
Innes	2	0	14	0
Thompson	3	0	3	0
Tsukigawa	2	1	11	0
Kane	2	0	13	0
Scurr	3	0	9	0
Crawley	3	0	19	0
Spence	1	0	1	0

Fall of Wickets		
	O	C
1st	29	-
2nd	34	-
3rd	58	-
4th	63	-
5th	65	-
6th	75	-
7th	92	-
8th	92	-
9th	98	-
10th	103	-

WELLINGTON v CENTRAL DISTRICTS   State League

at Kelburn Park, Wellington on 15 December, 2002
Toss : Wellington. Umpires : D.G. Paterson & C.J. Morris
Wellington won by 19 runs. Points: Wellington 4, Central Districts 0

WELLINGTON

	Runs	Mins	Balls	6s	4s
M.C.Godliman† lbw b Mason	14	20	29	-	2
M.G.Wakefield c Street b Mason	11	28	16	-	-
M.A.M.Lewis* run out	68	157	135	-	3
F.S.King c Mason b Pulford	1	8	6	-	-
F.O'Connor lbw b Burrows	14	51	50	-	1
A.M.Corbin lbw b McWilliams	25	68	66	-	1
A.E.Cooper b Burrows	5	13	14	-	-
M.L.Presland not out	5	11	8	-	-
M.L.Tuapawa run out	2	3	5	-	-
A.J.Green					
A.M.Little					
Extras (b 1, lb 10, w 31, nb 3)	45				
TOTAL (50 overs) (8 wkts)	**190**	184			

CENTRAL DISTRICTS

	Runs	Mins	Balls	6s	4s
C.L.Forsyth run out	34	58	45	-	2
K.L.Pulford b Green	0	5	2	-	-
N.M.Thessman b King	0	12	11	-	-
A.L.Mason* c Little b Cooper	63	150	89	-	3
S.J.McGlashan lbw b King	36	61	62	-	5
M.M.Graham c Little b King	1	21	17	-	-
E.T.McDonald c Wakefield b Presland	8	22	22	-	1
T.M.Street† lbw b Cooper	1	12	9	-	-
Z.A.McWilliams b Presland	0	4	5	-	-
E.C.Perry not out	6	9	8	-	1
A.K.Burrows b Cooper	2	6	6	-	-
Extras (b 4, lb 4, w 12)	20				
TOTAL (44.2 overs)	**171**	185			

Bowling	O	M	R	W
CENTRAL DISTRICTS				
Burrows	10	1	29	2
Mason	10	1	37	2
McWilliams	9	2	31	1
Pulford	7	0	32	1
Perry	6	0	20	0
McDonald	8	0	30	0
WELLINGTON				
King	8	2	18	3
Green	10	0	48	1
Little	5	1	23	0
Presland	8	0	28	2
Corbin	4	0	24	0
Cooper	9.2	3	22	3

Fall of Wickets		
	W	CD
1st	27	7
2nd	35	16
3rd	40	69
4th	75	135
5th	148	142
6th	170	162
7th	184	162
8th	190	163
9th	-	163
10th	-	171

NORTHERN DISTRICTS v WELLINGTON State League

at Westpac Park, Hamilton on 4 January, 2003
Toss : Wellington. Umpires : K. Cross & T.J. Parlane
Wellington won by 2 wickets. *Points: Wellington 4, Northern Districts 0*

NORTHERN DISTRICTS

	Runs	Mins	Balls	6s	4s
V.J.Brown c Lewis b Corbin	9	54	54	-	1
A.J.Wilkins c Hill b Green	1	19	10	-	-
C.M.Edwards c Tuapawa					
b Presland	44	99	81	-	5
J.M.Fraser* run out	42	109	95	-	4
M.J.Hannay st Hill b Cooper	36	55	40	1	4
J.M.Stafford c Wakefield b Presland	7	11	8	-	1
N.J.Browne c Wakefield b Presland	8	7	5	1	-
L.E.Milliken b Presland	5	10	5	-	-
A.J.Lenssen not out	5	5	3	-	1
M.J.Adler					
B.L.Roderick†					
Extras (b 2, lb 6, w 9, nb 1)	18				
TOTAL (50 overs) (8 wkts)	**175**	190			

Bowling	O	M	R	W
WELLINGTON				
King	10	2	25	0
Green	10	2	28	1
Corbin	10	2	19	1
Little	10	0	36	0
Cooper	4	0	23	1
Presland	6	0	36	4

WELLINGTON

	Runs	Mins	Balls	6s	4s
M.C.Godliman c Browne					
b Lenssen	16	39	43	-	2
M.G.Wakefield b Milliken	0	8	8	-	-
M.L.Tuapawa lbw b Lenssen	2	53	40	-	-
M.A.M.Lewis* run out	37	66	60	-	6
F.S.King c Fraser b Lenssen	33	61	48	-	4
A.M.Corbin c Milliken b Hannay	13	44	23	-	2
S.J.Hill† b Hannay	12	18	26	-	2
A.E.Cooper not out	25	35	32	-	3
M.L.Presland run out	2	13	3	-	-
A.J.Green not out	11	13	9	1	1
A.M.Little					
Extras (b 2, lb 6, w 16, nb 2)	26				
TOTAL (48.3 overs) (8 wkts)	**177**	179			

Bowling	O	M	R	W
NORTHERN DISTRICTS				
Milliken	10	1	45	1
Edwards	10	3	13	0
Adler	2	0	11	0
Lenssen	8	2	31	3
Browne	9.3	1	35	0
Fraser	3	0	12	0
Hannay	6	0	22	2

Fall of Wickets		
	ND	W
1st	5	2
2nd	26	27
3rd	73	41
4th	137	89
5th	154	114
6th	157	130
7th	168	142
8th	175	156
9th	-	-
10th	-	-

OTAGO v AUCKLAND State League

at Carisbrook, Dunedin on 4 January, 2003
Toss : Otago. Umpires : D.J. Ellwood & G.C. Holdem
Auckland won by 9 wickets. *Points: Auckland 5, Otago 0*

OTAGO

	Runs	Mins	Balls	6s	4s
S.K.Helmore* b Scott	12	46	36	-	2
M.J.Kane c Rolls b Ramsay	0	17	16	-	-
S.J.Tsukigawa b Scott	9	14	22	-	2
R.J.Pullar st Rolls b Gruber	36	51	39	2	3
K.J.Martin† lbw b Ramsay	1	13	12	-	-
E.J.Scurr run out	11	37	32	-	-
A.L.Kane b Watson	6	9	13	-	1
C.E.Taylor run out	7	17	18	-	-
J.M.Innes not out	11	19	15	-	-
K.M.Spence c Lynch b Drumm	3	5	5	-	-
C.M.Thompson					
Extras (b 1, lb 6, w 13, nb 4)	24				
TOTAL (34 overs) (9 wkts)	**120**	118			

Bowling	O	M	R	W
AUCKLAND				
Scripps	6	1	20	0
Ramsay	7	3	12	2
Scott	4	0	19	2
Watson	7	1	20	1
Gruber	7	1	26	1
Drumm	3	0	16	1
OTAGO				
Pullar	5	1	20	0
Taylor	5	0	18	0
Kane A.L.	3	1	13	0
Spence	2	0	15	1
Tsukigawa	3	0	11	0
Scurr	4	0	20	0
Thompson	2	0	16	0
Kane M.J.	1	0	7	0

AUCKLAND

	Runs	Mins	Balls	6s	4s
R.J.Rolls† not out	54	95	72	-	5
M.L.Lynch* lbw b Spence	27	52	37	-	4
E.C.Drumm not out	31	42	43	-	4
K.D.Brown					
H.M.Watson					
E.B.Komp					
R.J.Kember					
N.Scripps					
D.J.Ramsay					
P.A.Gruber					
K.M.A.Scott					
Extras (lb 2, w 6, nb 2)	10				
TOTAL (25 overs) (1 wkt)	**122**	95			

Fall of Wickets		
	O	A
1st	9	65
2nd	27	-
3rd	34	-
4th	58	-
5th	81	-
6th	94	-
7th	94	-
8th	111	-
9th	120	-
10th	-	-

NORTHERN DISTRICTS v WELLINGTON   State League

at Westpac Park, Hamilton on 5 January, 2003
Toss : Northern Districts. Umpires : K Cross & T.J. Parlane
Wellington won by 5 wickets. *Points: Wellington 4, Northern Districts 0*

NORTHERN DISTRICTS

	Runs	Mins	Balls	6s	4s
V.J.Brown lbw b King	3	33	24	-	-
A.J.Wilkins b King	0	3	2	-	-
C.M.Edwards b Presland	120	172	129	-	18
J.M.Fraser* c Harford b Corbin	1	4	5	-	-
M.J.Hannay c Harford b Corbin	14	45	40	-	2
J.M.Stafford b Cooper	10	37	35	-	2
N.J.Browne b Cooper	8	24	29	-	1
L.E.Milliken not out	18	34	33	-	1
A.J.Lenssen run out	0	1	0	-	-
N.H.Carruthers not out	2	6	2	-	-
B.L.Roderick†					

Extras (b 1, lb 7, w 20) 28
TOTAL (50 overs) (8 wkts) .. **204** 185

Bowling WELLINGTON	O	M	R	W
King	10	0	34	2
Green	10	1	57	0
Corbin	10	0	28	2
Presland	10	1	44	1
Cooper	10	1	33	2

WELLINGTON

	Runs	Mins	Balls	6s	4s
M.C.Godliman† c Lenssen					
b Edwards	15	36	38	-	3
M.G.Wakefield c Roderick b Browne	5	11	7	-	-
L.R.V.S.Harford run out	50	123	103	-	5
M.A.M.Lewis* c & b Fraser	73	139	108	-	8
F.S.King not out	30	49	39	-	3
A.M.Corbin lbw b Browne	2	6	3	-	-
A.E.Cooper not out	0	1	0	-	-
F.O'Connor					
M.L.Presland					
A.J.Green					
M.L.Tuapawa					

Extras (lb 2, w 26, nb 2) 30
TOTAL (49.2 overs) (5 wkts) **205** 185

Bowling NORTHERN DISTRICTS	O	M	R	W
Browne	10	0	33	2
Edwards	10	1	29	1
Lenssen	3	0	14	0
Hannay	7	0	40	0
Carruthers	7	0	29	0
Stafford	7	0	29	0
Fraser	5.2	0	29	1

Fall of Wickets	ND	W
1st	2	12
2nd	28	33
3rd	31	139
4th	72	195
5th	109	203
6th	141	-
7th	191	-
8th	191	-
9th	-	-
10th	-	-

OTAGO v AUCKLAND   State League

at Carisbrook, Dunedin on 5 January, 2003
Toss : Otago. Umpires : D.J. Ellwood & G.C. Holdem
Auckland won by 20 runs. *Points: Auckland 4, Otago 0*

AUCKLAND

	Runs	Mins	Balls	6s	4s
M.L.Lynch* lbw b Innes	13	34	23	-	-
R.J.Rolls† st Martin b Taylor	4	17	14	-	-
E.C.Drumm lbw b Lynch	40	39	36	-	5
H.M.Watson not out	40	51	31	-	5
K.D.Brown lbw b Kane A.L.	0	5	4	-	-
E.B.Komp not out	12	22	12	-	1
R.J.Kember					
N.Scripps					
D.J.Ramsay					
P.A.Gruber					
A.K.Coyle					

Extras (lb 1, w 13) 14
TOTAL (20 overs) (4 wkts) **123** 86

Bowling OTAGO	O	M	R	W
Pullar	4	0	12	0
Taylor	4	0	20	1
Tsukigawa	4	0	36	0
Innes	0.1	0	5	1
Scurr	0.5	0	6	0
Lynch	3	0	15	1
Kane A.L.	4	0	28	1
AUCKLAND				
Scripps	4	0	16	0
Ramsay	4	0	14	1
Watson	4	0	15	3
Coyle	4	0	27	2
Gruber	4	0	26	2

OTAGO

	Runs	Mins	Balls	6s	4s
C.E.Taylor lbw b Ramsay	15	27	21	-	1
M.J.Kane b Coyle	15	37	26	-	-
R.J.Pullar b Watson	8	15	12	-	-
S.J.Tsukigawa b Watson	30	39	29	-	1
K.J.Martin† st Rolls b Coyle	6	3	4	-	1
A.L.Kane lbw b Gruber	2	3	3	-	-
J.M.Innes c Watson b Gruber	12	14	14	-	-
S.K.Helmore* not out	8	14	9	-	1
E.J.Scurr b Watson	0	1	1	-	-
K.B.Lynch not out	0	1	2	-	-
A.E.Crawley					

Extras (lb 5, w 2) 7
TOTAL (20 overs) (8 wkts) .. **103** 81

Fall of Wickets	A	O
1st	17	31
2nd	41	38
3rd	78	44
4th	83	52
5th	-	55
6th	-	80
7th	-	103
8th	-	103
9th	-	-
10th	-	-

CANTERBURY v AUCKLAND State League

at Redwood Park, Christchurch on 6 January, 2003
Toss : Auckland. Umpires : G.C. Holdem & D.M. Quested
Canterbury won by 2 wickets. Points: Canterbury 4 Auckland 0

AUCKLAND

	Runs	Mins	Balls	6s	4s
R.J.Rolls† lbw b Burke	0	3	5	-	-
M.L.Lynch* c Taylor b Burke	3	9	7	-	-
E.C.Drumm c Milburn b Rae	38	83	61	-	2
R.J.Kember b Rae	27	69	69	-	2
H.M.Watson c Milburn b Burke	10	33	37	-	2
E.B.Komp c Burke b McNeill	15	41	34	-	1
K.D.Brown not out	49	63	52	-	5
N.Scripps b Steele	3	9	5	-	-
D.J.Ramsay lbw b Rae	4	22	17	-	-
P.A.Gruber not out	11	14	13	-	1
K.M.A.Scott					
Extras (lb 7, w 8)	15				
TOTAL (50 overs) (8 wkts)	**175**	177			

CANTERBURY

	Runs	Mins	Balls	6s	4s
N.Payne lbw b Scripps	43	102	85	-	3
K.A.Craig c Rolls b Ramsay	0	6	4	-	-
S.C.Taylor c & b Watson	61	92	88	-	5
H.M.Tiffen* lbw b Gruber	13	25	28	-	2
M.F.Fahey c Rolls b Scripps	0	2	4	-	-
R.C.Milburn† not out	42	63	47	-	5
B.H.McNeill run out	3	18	17	-	-
S.K.Burke run out	1	9	6	-	-
H.J.Rae lbw b Drumm	2	10	9	-	-
R.J.Steele not out	2	3	3	-	-
H.R.Daly					
Extras (lb 1, w 7, nb 1)	9				
TOTAL (48.2 overs) (8 wkts)	**176**	169			

Bowling

CANTERBURY	O	M	R	W
Burke	10	2	31	3
Steele	10	1	18	1
McNeill	10	2	41	1
Daly	10	2	27	0
Rae	10	0	51	3
AUCKLAND				
Scripps	10	2	36	2
Ramsay	10	3	32	1
Watson	10	1	25	1
Gruber	9.2	0	37	1
Scott	2	0	12	0
Drumm	7	1	33	1

Fall of Wickets

	A	C
1st	0	1
2nd	8	109
3rd	72	109
4th	75	109
5th	94	127
6th	107	146
7th	118	160
8th	146	172
9th	-	-
10th	-	-

CANTERBURY v AUCKLAND State League

at Redwood Park, Christchurch on 7 January, 2003
Toss : Auckland. Umpires : G.C. Holdem & D.M. Quested
Canterbury won by 5 wickets. Points: Canterbury 4, Auckland 0

AUCKLAND

	Runs	Mins	Balls	6s	4s
M.L.Lynch* lbw b Daly	5	12	14	-	-
R.J.Rolls† c Daly b McNeill	11	40	25	-	-
E.C.Drumm not out	41	77	57	-	2
R.J.Kember c Milburn b McNeill	1	10	9	-	-
H.M.Watson lbw b McNeill	6	25	15	-	-
E.B.Komp c Craig b Steele	0	12	14	-	-
K.D.Brown c Milburn b Burke	15	39	38	-	2
N.Scripps c Milburn b Rae	3	22	13	-	-
D.J.Ramsay b Burke	33	72	72	-	3
P.A.Gruber b McNeill	12	41	27	-	1
A.K.Coyle c Milburn b Burke	0	1	1	-	-
Extras (lb 3, w 19, nb 2)	24				
TOTAL (47 overs)	**151**	180			

CANTERBURY

	Runs	Mins	Balls	6s	4s
N.Payne run out	2	4	6	-	-
K.A.Craig c Rolls b Scripps	0	10	6	-	-
S.C.Taylor c Rolls b Scripps	43	87	94	-	4
H.M.Tiffen* not out	80	146	117	2	8
M.F.Fahey c Kember b Gruber	9	43	36	-	-
R.C.Milburn† c Rolls b Scripps	8	12	15	-	1
B.H.McNeill not out	1	7	7	-	-
S.K.Burke					
H.J.Rae					
R.J.Steele					
H.R.Daly					
Extras (b 2, lb 2, w 10)	14				
TOTAL (46.5 overs) (5 wkts)	**157**	157			

Bowling

CANTERBURY	O	M	R	W
Burke	9	0	47	3
Daly	5.1	1	8	1
McNeill	10	2	27	4
Steele	10	4	12	1
Rae	7	0	31	1
Fahey	2	0	10	0
Payne	3.5	0	13	0
AUCKLAND				
Scripps	10	2	16	3
Ramsay	10	4	33	0
Coyle	8	1	26	0
Gruber	8.5	0	44	1
Watson	10	2	34	0

Fall of Wickets

	A	C
1st	9	3
2nd	39	3
3rd	44	85
4th	58	128
5th	58	149
6th	80	-
7th	84	-
8th	120	-
9th	151	-
10th	151	-

Drumm retired hurt on 27* at 58-4
and returned at 120-8

CENTRAL DISTRICTS v CANTERBURY   State League

at Fitzherbert Park, Palmerston North on 11 January, 2003
Toss : Canterbury. Umpires : K. Cross & T.J. Parlane
Central Districts won by 15 runs. *Points: Central Districts 4, Canterbury 0*

CENTRAL DISTRICTS

	Runs	Mins	Balls	6s	4s
C.L.Forsyth c Fahey b Rae	17	18	13	-	4
S.L.Duffill c Taylor b Payne	13	70	49	-	2
N.M.Thessman c & b Steele	22	54	55	-	2
K.L.Pulford c Charteris b Fahey ..	6	44	42	-	-
A.L.Mason* c Charteris b Burke	44	75	70	-	5
S.J.McGlashan† c Milburn					
b Burke	5	33	19	-	-
E.T.McDonald b Burke	1	6	8	-	-
E.C.Perry b Rae	1	2	4	-	-
Z.A.McWilliams st Milburn					
b Payne	5	11	13	-	-
K.M.Sutherland not out	3	13	12	-	-
A.K.Burrows b McNeill	0	3	5	-	-
Extras (b 1, lb 11, w 47)	59	175			
TOTAL (48.2 overs) **176**	175				

CANTERBURY

	Runs	Mins	Balls	6s	4s
N.Payne b Burrows	11	20	20	-	1
K.A.Craig lbw b Burrows	14	83	68	-	2
S.C.Taylor st McGlashan					
b McDonald	52	56	56	-	9
H.M.Tiffen* c McGlashan b Pulford	7	32	31	-	-
M.F.Fahey lbw b Pulford	0	9	4	-	-
R.C.Milburn† c McGlashan					
b Burrows	5	24	20	-	1
S.E.Charteris c & b Mason	13	33	27	-	1
B.H.McNeill c Pulford b McDonald	1	4	7	-	-
S.K.Burke c McGlashan b Pulford	27	36	29	-	3
H.J.Rae not out	6	19	12	-	-
R.J.Steele run out	2	4	3	-	-
Extras (b 4, lb 5, w 11, nb 3) ..	23				
TOTAL (45.4 overs) **161**	165				

Bowling	O	M	R	W
CANTERBURY				
Burke	10	0	40	3
Rae	9	0	45	2
McNeill	9.2	4	20	1
Steele	10	2	13	1
Payne	9	0	32	2
Fahey	1	0	14	1
CENTRAL DISTRICTS				
Burrows	10	3	19	3
Mason	9.4	2	36	1
Perry	2	0	17	0
Pulford	8	0	24	3
McWilliams	6	0	36	0
McDonald	10	0	20	2

Fall of Wickets		
	CD	C
1st	36	22
2nd	78	85
3rd	79	89
4th	118	94
5th	153	104
6th	161	111
7th	165	112
8th	168	135
9th	175	158
10th	176	161

NORTHERN DISTRICTS v AUCKLAND   State League

at Te Puke Domain on 11 January, 2003
Abandoned without a ball being bowled. *Points: Northern Districts 2, Auckland 2*

WELINGTON v OTAGO
State League

at Basin Reserve, Wellington on 11 January, 2003
Toss : Otago. Umpires : J.M. Busby & D.G. Paterson
Wellington won by 7 wickets. *Points: Wellington 5, Otago 0*

OTAGO

	Runs	Mins	Balls	6s	4s
C.E.Taylor c Hill b King	12	33	25	-	-
M.J.Kane c Cooper b Presland	29	76	53	-	2
S.K.Helmore* c & b Little	5	17	12	-	-
R.J.Pullar c Harford b Little	18	43	34	-	1
S.J.Tsukigawa c Wakefield b Little	0	10	12	-	-
K.J.Martin† c Presland b Little	13	28	24	-	2
E.J.Scurr c Lewis b Little	0	7	7	-	-
A.L.Kane b Cooper	6	27	25	-	1
A.S.M.Hipkiss lbw b Cooper	11	14	17	-	2
K.B.Lynch c Lewis b Cooper	0	6	3	-	-
K.M.Spence not out	1	2	1	-	-
Extras (b 3, lb 1, w 19)	23				
TOTAL (35.5 overs)	**118**	141			

Bowling WELLINGTON	O	M	R	W
King	8	1	26	1
Green	4	0	20	0
Presland	7	1	22	1
Little	10	0	27	5
Cooper	6.5	1	19	3
OTAGO				
Pullar	10	2	17	1
Scurr	6	1	14	0
Spence	4	1	12	0
Taylor	9	4	34	2
Hipkiss	2	0	10	0
Kane M.J.	4	1	17	0
Tsukigawa	2.5	0	12	0

WELLINGTON

	Runs	Mins	Balls	6s	4s
M.C.Godliman c Martin b Taylor	32	93	82	-	4
M.L.Presland c Kane M.J. b Pullar	0	24	19	-	-
L.R.V.S.Harford b Taylor	10	45	40	-	1
M.A.M.Lewis* not out	31	60	44	-	4
F.S.King not out	30	36	32	-	5
M.G.Wakefield					
F.O'Connor					
S.J.Hill†					
A.E.Cooper					
A.J.Green					
A.M.Little					
Extras (b 1, lb 3, w 11, nb 2)	17				
TOTAL (37.5 overs) (3 wkts)	**120**	130			

Fall of Wickets	O	W
1st	33	9
2nd	57	42
3rd	73	62
4th	81	-
5th	88	-
6th	96	-
7th	100	-
8th	112	-
9th	117	-
10th	118	-

CENTRAL DISTRICTS v CANTERBURY
State League

at Fitzherbert Park, Palmerston North on 12 January, 2003
Toss : Canterbury. Umpires : K. Cross & T.J. Parlane
Canterbury won by 4 wickets. *Points: Canterbury 4, Central Districts 0*

CENTRAL DISTRICTS

	Runs	Mins	Balls	6s	4s
C.L.Forsyth st Milburn b Steele	6	13	11	-	-
S.L.Duffill c Milburn b McNeill	3	46	41	-	-
N.M.Thessman c Tiffen b Charteris	28	97	89	-	1
K.L.Pulford not out	66	133	104	-	4
A.L.Mason* c Charteris b Rae	44	46	36	-	8
S.J.McGlashan† not out	30	21	18	2	2
A.K.Burrows					
D.M.Trow					
E.C.Perry					
E.T.McDonald					
Z.A.McWilliams					
Extras (lb 11, w 27)	38				
TOTAL (50 overs) (4 wkts)	**217**	180			

Bowling CANTERBURY	O	M	R	W
Steele	10	4	21	1
Burke	10	0	46	0
McNeill	10	2	30	1
Payne	10	1	38	0
Rae	7	0	45	1
Charteris	3	0	26	1
CENTRAL DISTRICTS				
Burrows	8	0	36	1
Mason	10	0	51	0
Trow	9.5	1	32	0
Pulford	5	1	22	2
Perry	5	0	18	0
McDonald	10	1	35	1
McWilliams	2	0	14	0

CANTERBURY

	Runs	Mins	Balls	6s	4s
N.Payne c Burrows b Pulford	97	175	139	-	11
K.A.Craig b Burrows	1	5	5	-	-
S.C.Taylor lbw b Pulford	14	35	31	-	1
H.M.Tiffen* b Mason	34	61	51	-	5
M.F.Fahey c McGlashan b McDonald	8	18	19	-	1
R.C.Milburn† run out	18	36	26	-	2
S.K.Burke not out	22	28	20	-	1
B.H.McNeill not out	2	7	2	-	-
S.E.Charteris					
H.J.Rae					
R.J.Steele					
Extras (b 1, lb 10, w 10, nb 1)	22				
TOTAL (49.5 overs) (6 wkts)	**218**	183			

Fall of Wickets	CD	C
1st	12	7
2nd	32	35
3rd	89	110
4th	168	128
5th	-	175
6th	-	209
7th	-	-
8th	-	-
9th	-	-
10th	-	-

NORTHERN DISTRICTS v AUCKLAND   State League

at Te Puke Domain on 12 January, 2003
Toss : Auckland. Umpires : D.B. Cowie & D.J. Ellwood
Auckland won by 7 wickets. *Points: Auckland 5, Northern Districts 0*

NORTHERN DISTRICTS

	Runs	Mins	Balls	6s	4s
V.J.Brown lbw b Scripps	0	9	12	-	-
N.J.Browne st Rolls b Gruber	21	66	57	-	3
C.M.Edwards c Rolls b Ramsay	21	44	47	-	3
J.M.Fraser* lbw b Ramsay	0	4	3	-	-
M.J.Hannay lbw b Coyle	11	41	43	-	2
A.J.Wilkins c Ramsay b Gruber	36	67	61	-	3
J.M.Stafford c Brown b Drumm	6	14	12	-	-
L.E.Milliken lbw b Drumm	1	8	9	-	-
A.J.Lenssen run out	6	16	25	-	1
B.L.Roderick† not out	0	12	3	-	-
M.J.Adler st Rolls b Drumm	0	4	6	-	-
Extras (b 2, w 14, nb 2)	18				
TOTAL (46 overs)	**120**	147			

AUCKLAND

	Runs	Mins	Balls	6s	4s
R.J.Rolls† b Milliken	15	18	19	-	1
M.L.Lynch* b Edwards	29	47	33	1	3
E.C.Drumm not out	62	52	40	-	11
R.J.Kember c Fraser b Browne	0	15	11	-	-
H.M.Watson not out	4	7	8	-	1
K.D.Brown					
A.Soma					
N.Scripps					
P.A.Gruber					
D.J.Ramsay					
A.K.Coyle					
Extras (b2, w 8, nb 2)	12				
TOTAL (18.1 overs) (3 wkts)	**122**	71			

Bowling	O	M	R	W
AUCKLAND				
Scripps	3	0	8	1
Ramsay	10	6	9	2
Coyle	10	3	35	1
Gruber	10	1	27	2
Watson	8	0	25	0
Drumm	5	1	14	3
NORTHERN DISTRICTS				
Milliken	4	0	24	1
Browne	5.1	0	40	1
Lenssen	2	0	24	0
Adler	3	0	23	0
Edwards	4	1	9	1

Fall of Wickets		
	ND	A
1st	3	28
2nd	45	89
3rd	49	111
4th	49	-
5th	78	-
6th	95	-
7th	106	-
8th	114	-
9th	119	-
10th	120	-

WELLINGTON v OTAGO   State League

at Basin Reserve, Wellington on 12 January, 2003
Toss : Otago. Umpires : J.M. Busby & D.G. Paterson
No result. *Points: Wellington 2, Otago 2*

WELLINGTON

	Runs	Mins	Balls	6s	4s
M.C.Godliman† b Pullar	2	10	16	-	-
L.R.V.S.Harford not out	25	104	90	-	1
M.G.Wakefield c Martin b Spence	18	42	36	-	-
M.A.M.Lewis* not out	23	50	34	-	2
F.S.King					
M.L.Presland					
F.O'Connor					
A.M.Little					
A.E.Cooper					
A.J.Green					
M.L.Tuapawa					
Extras (lb 2, w 19, nb 2)	23				
TOTAL (29 overs) (2 wkts)	**91**	104			

OTAGO

	Runs	Mins	Balls	6s	4s
C.E.Taylor					
M.J.Kane					
S.K.Helmore*					
R.J.Pullar					
S.J.Tsukigawa					
K.J.Martin†					
E.J.Scurr					
A.L.Kane					
J.M.Innes					
K.B.Lynch					
K.M.Spence					

Bowling	O	M	R	W
OTAGO				
Pullar	7	1	10	1
Scurr	7	1	25	0
Taylor	5	2	15	0
Spence	4	1	10	1
Lynch	3	0	15	0
Kane A.L.	1	0	10	0
Tsukigawa	2	0	4	0

Fall of Wickets	
	W
1st	4
2nd	37
3rd	-
4th	-
5th	-
6th	-
7th	-
8th	-
9th	-
10th	-

CENTRAL DISTRICTS v OTAGO
State League

at Fitzherbert Park, Palmerston North on 13 January, 2003
Toss : Central Districts. Umpires : T.J. Parlane & D.G. Paterson
Otago won by 10 wickets. *Points: Otago 5, Central Districts 0*

CENTRAL DISTRICTS

	Runs	Mins	Balls	6s	4s
C.L.Forsyth b Spence	3	7	2	-	-
S.L.Duffill b Tsukigawa	14	83	60	-	-
K.L.Pulford run out	24	81	69	-	2
N.M.Thessman c Martin b Spence	8	34	27	-	-
A.L.Mason* b Pullar	15	23	18	-	3
S.J.McGlashan† st Martin					
b Tsukigawa	10	20	14	-	-
E.T.McDonald run out	25	48	40	-	2
E.C.Perry c Martin b Tsukigawa	3	15	22	-	-
K.M.Sutherland st Martin b Hipkiss	1	3	6	-	-
D.M.Trow not out	9	16	17	-	-
A.K.Burrows run out	0	3	2	-	-
Extras (b 5, lb 8, w 23, nb 1)	37				
TOTAL (46.4 overs)	**149**	171			

OTAGO

	Runs	Mins	Balls	6s	4s
C.E.Taylor not out	65	102	75	-	8
M.J.Kane not out	65	102	94	1	8
S.K.Helmore*					
R.J.Pullar					
S.J.Tsukigawa					
K.J.Martin†					
J.M.Innes					
A.L.Kane					
A.S.M.Hipkiss					
K.B.Lynch					
K.M.Spence					
Extras (b 4, lb 1, w 15, nb 2)	22				
TOTAL (27.5 overs) (0 wkts)	**152**	102			

Bowling OTAGO	O	M	R	W
Pullar	8.4	0	28	1
Spence	7	3	16	2
Kane A.L.	3	0	11	0
Taylor	8	1	25	0
Tsukigawa	10	2	19	3
Lynch	5	0	21	0
Hipkiss	5	0	16	1
CENTRAL DISTRICTS				
Burrows	3	0	8	0
Mason	4	0	21	0
Pulford	5	1	23	0
Trow	4	0	15	0
Sutherland	5	0	29	0
McDonald	4	0	28	0
Forsyth	1.5	0	21	0
Perry	1	0	2	0

Fall of Wickets	CD	O
1st	5	-
2nd	58	-
3rd	62	-
4th	92	-
5th	95	-
6th	111	-
7th	128	-
8th	129	-
9th	148	-
10th	149	-

WELLINGTON v CANTERBURY
State League

at Kelburn Park, Wellington on 13 January, 2003
Toss : Wellington. Umpires : M.P. George & A.L. Hill
Canterbury won by 6 wickets. *Points: Canterbury 4, Wellington 0*

WELLINGTON

	Runs	Mins	Balls	6s	4s
M.C.Godliman c Taylor b Rae	17	85	65	-	-
L.R.V.S.Harford b Burke	5	31	30	-	-
M.G.Wakefield c & b Burke	0	3	5	-	-
M.A.M.Lewis* st Milburn b Steele	34	102	91	-	1
F.S.King not out	45	81	64	-	4
A.E.Cooper lbw b Payne	5	8	6	-	-
S.J.Hill† b Payne	2	9	7	-	-
A.J.Green b Rae	5	9	9	-	-
M.L.Presland					
A.M.Little					
M.L.Tuapawa					
Extras (b 1, lb 3, w 40)	44				
TOTAL (46 overs) (7 wkts)	**157**	167			

CANTERBURY

	Runs	Mins	Balls	6s	4s
N.Payne lbw b King	0	1	2	-	-
R.C.Milburn† c Hill b Green	42	116	100	-	2
S.C.Taylor run out	23	67	47	-	1
H.M.Tiffen* not out	51	100	68	-	2
M.F.Fahey b Cooper	9	27	31	-	-
S.K.Burke not out	14	22	12	-	2
S.E.Charteris					
B.H.McNeill					
K.A.Craig					
H.J.Rae					
R.J.Steele					
Extras (lb 3, w 16)	19				
TOTAL (43.1 overs) (4 wkts)	**158**	169			

Bowling CANTERBURY	O	M	R	W
Burke	10	4	24	2
Payne	9	1	24	2
Steele	9	2	30	1
McNeill	9	1	24	0
Rae	8	1	36	2
Tiffen	1	0	15	0
WELLINGTON				
King	9	4	14	1
Green	9	1	32	1
Presland	7	1	39	0
Little	9	0	33	0
Cooper	9	0	35	1
Harford	0.1	0	2	0

Fall of Wickets	W	C
1st	17	0
2nd	17	49
3rd	54	94
4th	126	119
5th	134	-
6th	147	-
7th	157	-
8th	-	-
9th	-	-
10th	-	-

CENTRAL DISTRICTS v OTAGO State League

at Fitzherbert Park, Palmerston North on 14 January, 2003
Toss : Otago. Umpires : T.J. Parlane & D.G. Paterson
Central Districts won by 7 wickets. *Points: Central Districts 5, Otago 0*

OTAGO

	Runs	Mins	Balls	6s	4s
C.E.Taylor c McGlashan b McDonald	41	74	50	-	4
M.J.Kane c Burrows b Trow	23	49	43	-	2
S.K.Helmore* run out	47	125	117	-	6
R.J.Pullar st McGlashan b McDonald	6	7	9	-	1
S.J.Tsukigawa lbw b Mason	4	19	11	-	-
K.J.Martin† c Duffill b Mason	0	5	5	-	-
J.M.Innes c McGlashan b Pulford	0	26	25	-	-
A.L.Kane c Mason b Trow	13	33	21	-	1
A.S.M.Hipkiss b Burrows	7	11	11	-	1
K.B.Lynch st McGlashan b Trow	3	4	6	-	-
K.M.Spence not out	1	2	1	-	-
Extras (lb 3, w 24)	27				
TOTAL (50 overs)	**172**	182			

CENTRAL DISTRICTS

	Runs	Mins	Balls	6s	4s
C.L.Forsyth c Pullar b Kane A.L.	40	55	39	-	8
S.L.Duffill run out	35	120	92	-	3
N.M.Thessman c & b Lynch	30	57	50	-	2
K.L.Pulford not out	7	43	25	-	-
A.L.Mason* not out	27	37	31	1	3
S.J.McGlashan†					
E.T.McDonald					
E.C.Perry					
Z.A.McWilliams					
D.M.Trow					
A.K.Burrows					
Extras (b 2, lb 5, w 25, nb 2)	34				
TOTAL (39.1 overs) (3 wkts)	**173**	158			

Bowling CENTRAL DISTRICTS	O	M	R	W
Pulford	10	1	41	1
Burrows	8	0	40	1
Trow	8	0	25	3
McWilliams	2	0	12	0
Mason	10	4	13	2
McDonald	10	3	18	2
Perry	2	0	20	0
OTAGO				
Pullar	7	0	34	0
Spence	3	1	2	0
Tsukigawa	9	0	43	0
Taylor	6.1	0	21	0
Kane A.L.	4	1	14	1
Hipkiss	2	0	9	0
Kane M.J.	2	0	11	0
Lynch	6	0	32	1

Fall of Wickets	O	CD
1st	61	63
2nd	79	124
3rd	86	128
4th	94	-
5th	94	-
6th	108	-
7th	150	-
8th	163	-
9th	168	-
10th	172	-

WELLINGTON v CANTERBURY State League

at Kelburn Park, Wellington on 14 January, 2003
Abandoned without a ball being bowled. *Points: Wellington 2, Canterbury 2*

AUCKLAND v CENTRAL DISTRICTS

State League

at Melville Park, Auckland on 15 February, 2003
Toss : Central Districts. Umpires : B.G. Frost & W.R. Knights
Auckland won by 4 wickets. *Points: Auckland 4, Central Districts 0*

CENTRAL DISTRICTS

	Runs	Mins	Balls	6s	4s
C.L.Forsyth run out	35	64	58	-	3
S.L.Duffill c & b Watson	10	35	25	-	-
N.M.Thessman b Gruber	13	47	48	-	-
A.L.Mason* c Kember b Drumm	20	23	20	-	2
S.J.McGlashan† c Brown b Drumm	1	6	4	-	-
E.T.McDonald c Ramsay b Gruber	0	5	5	-	-
E.C.Perry b Drumm	0	7	8	-	-
Z.A.McWilliams run out	3	42	34	-	-
K.M.Winkley b Scripps	8	22	24	-	1
D.M.Trow not out	30	49	49	-	1
A.K.Burrows not out	8	33	27	-	-

Extras (lb 3, w 15, nb 6) 24
TOTAL (50 overs) (9 wkts) .. **152** 171

AUCKLAND

	Runs	Mins	Balls	6s	4s
M.L.Lynch* c Thessman b Mason	8	12	16	-	1
R.J.Rolls† b McWilliams	21	37	34	-	3
E.C.Drumm c McGlashan b McDonald	40	88	77	-	5
K.D.Brown b Trow	7	21	15	-	-
H.M.Watson not out	46	101	89	-	4
R.J.Kember c McWilliams b Mason	2	10	13	-	-
A.Soma c & b Trow	12	36	28	-	-
N.Scripps not out	0	11	12	-	-
P.A.Gruber					
D.J.Ramsay					
A.K.Coyle					

Extras (w 16, nb 1) 17
TOTAL (47.1 overs) (6 wkts) **153** 161

Bowling	O	M	R	W
AUCKLAND				
Scripps	10	0	25	1
Coyle	2	0	16	0
Ramsay	10	0	40	0
Watson	10	1	16	1
Gruber	10	1	27	2
Drumm	8	2	25	3
CENTRAL DISTRICTS				
Burrows	8	2	24	0
Mason	9	1	36	2
McWilliams	10	4	26	1
Trow	10	2	31	2
Winkley	4	0	16	0
McDonald	6.1	1	20	1

Fall of Wickets		
	CD	A
1st	42	14
2nd	60	43
3rd	86	63
4th	90	99
5th	90	108
6th	90	144
7th	93	-
8th	105	-
9th	116	-
10th	-	-

CANTERBURY v NORTHERN DISTRICTS

State League

at Dudley Park, Rangiora on 15 February, 2003
Toss : Northern Districts. Umpires : K. Cross & D.M. Quested
Canterbury won by 26 runs. *Points: Canterbury 4, Northern Districts 0*

CANTERBURY

	Runs	Mins	Balls	6s	4s
K.A.Craig c Roderick b Browne	11	19	18	-	2
R.C.Milburn† b Lenssen	3	21	15	-	-
N.Payne c Roderick b Carruthers	62	104	83	-	7
H.M.Tiffen* b Simpson	10	33	34	-	2
M.F.Fahey b Carruthers	31	63	65	-	3
H.J.Rae run out	3	16	10	-	-
S.E.Charteris b Hannay	2	2	4	-	-
S.K.Burke c Roderick b Lenssen	0	17	11	-	-
B.H.McNeill lbw b Lenssen	0	1	1	-	-
R.J.Steele lbw b Carruthers	3	9	13	-	-
H.R.Daly not out	0	2	0	-	-

Extras (lb 3, w 21, nb 2) 26
TOTAL (42 overs) **151** 148

NORTHERN DISTRICTS

	Runs	Mins	Balls	6s	4s
V.J.Brown c Milburn b Rae	28	86	62	-	4
N.J.Browne c Tiffen b McNeill ...	24	53	60	-	5
J.M.Stafford b McNeill	6	17	16	-	1
J.M.Fraser* lbw b Rae	0	7	5	-	-
A.J.Wilkins run out	14	24	24	-	2
M.J.Hannay c Tiffen b McNeill	7	65	46	-	-
C.F.Garrood c McNeill b Rae	2	4	6	-	-
A.J.Lenssen lbw b Burke	0	5	5	-	-
B.L.Roderick† c Charteris b McNeill	1	30	29	-	-
N.H.Carruthers not out	14	24	17	-	1
J.A.Simpson c Rae b Burke	6	18	21	-	-

Extras (b 9, lb 4, w 9, nb 1) 23
TOTAL (48.2 overs) **125** 171

Bowling	O	M	R	W
NORTHERN DISTRICTS				
Browne	6	0	20	1
Lenssen	6	2	21	3
Hannay	10	0	28	1
Simpson	10	2	36	1
Fraser	2	0	11	0
Wilkins	3	1	12	0
Carruthers	5	1	20	3
CANTERBURY				
Burke	9.2	3	19	2
Daly	10	5	6	0
McNeill	10	3	27	4
Steele	10	3	29	0
Rae	5	0	17	3
Payne	4	0	14	0

Fall of Wickets		
	C	ND
1st	21	48
2nd	21	59
3rd	53	69
4th	134	70
5th	136	89
6th	140	92
7th	147	92
8th	147	98
9th	148	101
10th	151	125

AUCKLAND v CENTRAL DISTRICTS   State League

at Melville Park, Auckland on 16 February, 2003
Toss : Central Districts. Umpires : B.G. Frost & W.R. Knights
Auckland won by 7 wickets. *Points: Auckland 5, Central Districts 0*

CENTRAL DISTRICTS

	Runs	Mins	Balls	6s	4s
C.L.Forsyth b Scott	24	39	53	-	2
S.L.Duffill lbw b Watson	17	77	49	-	-
N.M.Thessman c Rolls b Ramsay	9	11	11	-	1
A.L.Mason* c Gruber b Drumm	0	3	4	-	-
S.J.McGlashan† c Brown b Ramsay	6	14	10	-	1
E.T.McDonald c Rolls b Drumm	0	10	6	-	-
Z.A.McWilliams c Rolls b Watson	0	7	2	-	-
D.M.Trow lbw b Drumm	2	1	3	-	-
K.M.Winkley c Ramsay b Watson	8	16	12	-	-
K.M.Sutherland not out	3	19	14	-	-
A.K.Burrows b Scripps	0	4	6	-	-
Extras (lb 1, w 9)	10				
TOTAL (28.3 overs)	**79**	105			

AUCKLAND

	Runs	Mins	Balls	6s	4s
R.J.Rolls† c Mason b McWilliams	27	39	29	-	4
M.L.Lynch* b McDonald	12	36	36	-	1
E.C.Drumm c Burrows b Trow	17	30	27	-	1
K.D.Brown not out	9	32	35	-	1
H.M.Watson not out	1	4	1	-	-
R.J.Kember					
A.Soma					
N.Scripps					
P.A.Gruber					
D.J.Ramsay					
K.M.A.Scott					
Extras (b 2, lb 3, w 5, nb 4)	14				
TOTAL (20.4 overs) (3 wkts)	**80**	72			

Bowling	O	M	R	W
AUCKLAND				
Scripps	6.3	1	23	1
Ramsay	10	3	17	2
Scott	3	0	20	1
Drumm	5	0	16	3
Watson	4	3	2	3
CENTRAL DISTRICTS				
Burrows	3	0	11	0
Sutherland	2	0	13	0
McDonald	6	1	16	1
McWilliams	5	1	14	1
Winkley	2.4	0	10	0
Trow	2	1	11	1

Fall of Wickets	CD	A
1st	38	48
2nd	49	48
3rd	50	75
4th	63	-
5th	64	-
6th	64	-
7th	66	-
8th	66	-
9th	78	-
10th	79	-

CANTERBURY v NORTHERN DISTRICTS   State League

at Dudley Park, Rangiora on 16 February, 2003
Toss : Northern Districts. Umpires : K. Cross & D.M. Quested
Canterbury won by 6 wickets. *Points: Canterbury 5, Northern Districts 0*

NORTHERN DISTRICTS

	Runs	Mins	Balls	6s	4s
V.J.Brown b Burke	0	2	4	-	-
N.J.Browne not out	50	142	93	1	4
J.M.Stafford lbw b Burke	0	6	3	-	-
J.M.Fraser* lbw b Daly	5	5	11	-	1
A.J.Wilkins lbw b Daly	0	4	1	-	-
M.J.Hannay c Daly b Steele	3	30	36	-	-
K.M.Goodson run out	10	48	50	-	-
N.H.Carruthers c Tiffen b Rae	0	7	9	-	-
A.J.Lenssen b Daly	8	18	16	-	-
J.A.Simpson st Milburn b Daly	2	5	5	-	-
B.L.Roderick† c Milburn b Daly	2	8	12	-	-
Extras (lb 2, w 12)	14				
TOTAL (40 overs)	**94**	142			

CANTERBURY

	Runs	Mins	Balls	6s	4s
K.A.Craig b Lenssen	20	74	56	-	2
R.C.Milburn† c Hannay b Simpson	15	32	29	-	-
N.Payne lbw b Lenssen	31	51	52	-	6
H.M.Tiffen* not out	2	16	13	-	-
M.F.Fahey c & b Carruthers	0	2	4	-	-
H.J.Rae not out	0	3	2	-	-
S.E.Charteris					
S.K.Burke					
B.H.McNeill					
R.J.Steele					
H.R.Daly					
Extras (b 4, lb 2, w 21)	27				
TOTAL (26 overs) (4 wkts)	**95**	91			

Bowling	O	M	R	W
CANTERBURY				
Burke	8	2	18	2
Daly	10	2	19	5
McNeill	7	2	17	0
Steele	10	2	21	1
Rae	5	1	17	1
NORTHERN DISTRICTS				
Browne	6	0	24	0
Lenssen	7	1	22	2
Carruthers	5	0	14	1
Simpson	6	1	12	1
Wilkins	2	0	17	0

Fall of Wickets	ND	C
1st	0	28
2nd	4	79
3rd	10	91
4th	11	92
5th	28	-
6th	67	-
7th	69	-
8th	87	-
9th	90	-
10th	94	-

AUCKLAND v WELLINGTON

State League

at Melville Park, Auckland on 17 February, 2003
Toss : Auckland. Umpires : B.G. Frost & W.R. Knights
Auckland won by 35 runs. *Points: Auckland 5, Wellington 0*

AUCKLAND

	Runs	Mins	Balls	6s	4s
M.L.Lynch* c Cooper b Little	8	54	46	-	-
R.J.Rolls† c Lewis b Green	7	19	10	-	-
E.C.Drumm lbw b Cooper	34	79	65	-	1
R.J.Kember run out	25	82	70	-	-
H.M.Watson c Hill b Cooper	8	17	17	-	-
K.D.Brown c Lewis b King	14	41	30	-	-
A.Soma run out	4	9	7	-	-
N.Scripps c & b Presland	10	38	30	-	1
D.J.Ramsay lbw b Presland	3	10	8	-	-
P.A.Gruber run out	4	9	11	-	-
K.M.A.Scott not out	1	5	7	-	-
Extras (b 1, lb 3, w 19, nb 4)	27				
TOTAL (49.3 overs)	145	186			

WELLINGTON

	Runs	Mins	Balls	6s	4s
L.R.V.S.Harford b Gruber	30	93	82	-	4
M.G.Wakefield c Ramsay b Scripps	0	6	5	-	-
M.L.Presland st Rolls b Scripps	2	15	15	-	-
M.A.M.Lewis* c Rolls b Ramsay	5	40	37	-	-
F.S.King c Gruber b Ramsay	0	4	3	-	-
J.L.Hunter-Siu st Rolls b Watson	13	47	43	-	1
S.J.Hill† c Drumm b Scripps	21	43	29	-	3
A.E.Cooper b Scripps	21	40	30	-	3
F.O'Connor lbw b Scripps	0	2	3	-	-
A.J.Green lbw b Scripps	0	1	1	-	-
A.M.Little not out	1	14	7	-	-
Extras (lb 1, w 15, nb 1)	17				
TOTAL (42.2 overs)	110	157			

Bowling	O	M	R	W
WELLINGTON				
King	10	2	24	1
Green	10	0	25	1
Little	6	1	23	1
Presland	8.3	0	28	2
Cooper	9	2	21	2
Harford	6	0	20	0
AUCKLAND				
Scripps	9.2	2	19	6
Ramsay	10	6	16	2
Drumm	7	2	27	0
Watson	10	0	33	1
Gruber	6	0	14	1

Fall of Wickets		
	A	W
1st	10	2
2nd	38	15
3rd	72	37
4th	88	37
5th	107	52
6th	118	71
7th	128	100
8th	136	100
9th	143	100
10th	145	110

OTAGO v NORTHERN DISTRICTS

State League

at Carisbrook, Dunedin on 17 February, 2003
Toss : Otago. Umpires : M.P. George & J.M. Busby
Match tied. *Points: Otago 2, Northern Districts 2*

NORTHERN DISTRICTS

	Runs	Mins	Balls	6s	4s
V.J.Brown b Spence	19	57	40	-	2
N.J.Browne lbw b Bates	37	71	56	-	6
J.M.Fraser* b Bates	10	32	28	-	2
A.J.Wilkins c sub (A.S.M.Hipkiss) b Tsukigawa	16	58	43	-	1
K.M.Goodson c Thompson b Tsukigawa	11	19	21	-	1
J.M.Stafford c Bates b Tsukigawa	0	1	2	-	-
C.F.Garrood b Pullar	8	10	10	-	1
A.J.Lenssen c Martin b Pullar	6	8	6	-	-
J.A.Simpson st Martin b Spence	8	8	9	-	1
N.H.Carruthers not out	2	6	3	-	-
B.L.Roderick†					
Extras (b 1, lb 2, w 14, nb 2)	19				
TOTAL (36 overs) (9 wkts)	136	139			

OTAGO

	Runs	Mins	Balls	6s	4s
K.M.Spence b Browne	4	10	10	-	-
M.J.Kane c Wilkins b Lenssen	27	63	56	-	3
S.K.Helmore* run out	33	95	76	-	2
R.J.Pullar b Simpson	11	21	17	-	1
K.J.Martin† lbw b Fraser	2	5	3	-	-
S.J.Tsukigawa c Fraser b Lenssen	8	22	15	-	1
E.J.Scurr c Simpson b Carruthers	10	16	16	-	-
S.W.Bates c Lenssen b Carruthers	11	18	16	-	-
A.L.Kane not out	6	13	5	-	1
C.M.Thompson lbw b Carruthers	0	1	1	-	-
A.E.Crawley not out	1	1	1	-	-
Extras (lb 5, w 18)	23				
TOTAL (36 overs) (9 wkts)	136	137			

Bowling	O	M	R	W
OTAGO				
Pullar	8	1	24	2
Kane A.L.	4	0	11	0
Crawley	2	0	13	0
Spence	4	0	29	2
Tsukigawa	7	0	23	3
Bates	7	1	21	2
Kane M.J.	4	1	12	0
NORTHERN DISTRICTS				
Browne	8	0	34	1
Lenssen	7	0	21	2
Simpson	7	0	20	1
Carruthers	7	0	26	3
Fraser	7	0	30	1

Fall of Wickets		
	ND	O
1st	63	10
2nd	76	61
3rd	83	81
4th	104	86
5th	104	103
6th	118	111
7th	125	123
8th	126	135
9th	136	135
10th	-	-

AUCKLAND v WELLINGTON

State League

at Melville Park, Auckland on 18 February, 2003
Toss : Auckland. Umpires : D.B. Cowie & W.R. Knights
Wellington won by 5 wickets. *Points: Wellington 4, Auckland 0*

AUCKLAND

	Runs	Mins	Balls	6s	4s
R.J.Rolls† c Hunter-Siu b Little ...	19	25	21	-	3
M.L.Lynch* c Lewis b Presland ...	23	59	55	-	3
R.J.Kember c Hill b Presland	37	118	94	-	1
H.M.Watson b Cooper	4	13	11	-	-
E.B.Komp run out	22	41	43	-	2
K.D.Brown not out	43	67	47	1	3
A.Soma not out	14	38	31	-	-
N.Scripps					
P.A.Gruber					
D.J.Ramsay					
A.K.Coyle					
Extras (b 3, lb 7, w 24, nb 2)	36				
TOTAL (50 overs) (5 wkts)	**198**	183			

Bowling	O	M	R	W
WELLINGTON				
King	9	0	46	0
Little	10	3	23	1
Cooper	10	3	43	1
Presland	7	0	25	2
Harford	5	0	21	0
Hunter-Siu	7	2	22	0
Tuapawa	2	0	8	0

WELLINGTON

	Runs	Mins	Balls	6s	4s
L.R.V.S.Harford c Lynch b Scripps	0	2	4	-	-
J.L.Trendle c Brown b Scripps	0	15	12	-	-
S.J.Hill† c Lynch b Scripps	1	19	21	-	-
M.A.M.Lewis* not out	76	149	133	-	4
F.S.King c Rolls b Coyle	25	46	42	-	1
J.L.Hunter-Siu c Rolls b Coyle	4	6	2	-	-
M.G.Wakefield not out	74	88	72	-	6
M.L.Presland					
A.E.Cooper					
M.L.Tuapawa					
A.M.Little					
Extras (b 3, lb 7, w 8, nb 1)	19				
TOTAL (47.3 overs) (5 wkts)	**199**	165			

Bowling	O	M	R	W
AUCKLAND				
Scripps	10	2	34	3
Ramsay	10	6	15	0
Coyle	10	1	51	2
Watson	8.3	1	41	0
Gruber	8	0	38	0
Komp	1	0	10	0

Fall of Wickets	A	W
1st	28	0
2nd	60	1
3rd	66	6
4th	108	50
5th	133	55
6th	-	-
7th	-	-
8th	-	-
9th	-	-
10th	-	-

OTAGO v NORTHERN DISTRICTS

State League

at Carisbrook, Dunedin on 18 February, 2003
Toss : Northern Districts. Umpires : M.P. George & J.M. Busby
Otago won by 5 wickets. *Points: Otago 4, Northern Districts 0*

NORTHERN DISTRICTS

	Runs	Mins	Balls	6s	4s
V.J.Brown run out	13	73	67	-	-
N.J.Browne b Spence	29	56	47	-	4
J.M.Fraser* b Spence	1	9	7	-	-
A.J.Wilkins lbw b Bates	2	16	15	-	-
K.M.Goodson b Spence	19	47	50	-	1
L.E.Milliken not out	15	50	28	-	-
A.J.Lenssen not out	23	12	15	1	1
C.F.Garrood					
N.H.Carruthers					
B.L.Roderick†					
J.A.Simpson					
Extras (b 2, lb 4, w 12, nb 1) ..	19				
TOTAL (38 overs) (5 wkts) ..	**121**	134			

Bowling	O	M	R	W
OTAGO				
Kane A.L.	7	0	21	0
Scurr	5	1	15	0
Tsukigawa	7	0	39	0
Bates	8	2	11	1
Spence	8	2	23	3
Morrison	3	0	6	0
NORTHERN DISTRICTS				
Lenssen	7	1	23	1
Browne	8	2	21	0
Carruthers	8	2	21	1
Simpson	8	0	20	1
Garrood	2	0	15	0
Wilkins	3.3	1	22	1
Fraser	1	1	0	0

OTAGO

	Runs	Mins	Balls	6s	4s
K.M.Spence b Wilkins	24	102	70	-	1
M.J.Kane b Carruthers	29	62	65	-	1
S.K.Helmore* b Simpson	34	58	50	-	4
K.J.Martin† run out	0	3	4	-	-
S.W.Bates c Browne b Lenssen ..	12	20	17	-	1
S.J.Tsukigawa not out	4	13	14	-	1
E.J.Scurr not out	1	7	6	-	-
A.L.Kane					
C.M.Thompson					
A.S.M.Hipkiss					
T.J.Morrison					
Extras (lb 3, w 17, nb 1)	21				
TOTAL (37.3 overs) (5 wkts) .	**125**	135			

Fall of Wickets	ND	O
1st	45	53
2nd	48	91
3rd	50	91
4th	53	119
5th	89	120
6th	-	-
7th	-	-
8th	-	-
9th	-	-
10th	-	-

NEW ZEALAND
CRICKET

CANTERBURY v AUCKLAND   State League Final

at Redwood Park, Christchurch on 22 February, 2003
Toss : Auckland. Umpires : D.M. Quested & G.A. Baxter
Auckland won by 5 wickets

Auckland won the toss and invited Canterbury to bat. Wickets fell regularly throughout the innings with the best partnership being 72 between New Zealand players Payne and Tiffen. Following the dismissal of Payne, when the score was 108, the last six wickets fell for 34 runs and Canterbury were all out for 142 in the 47th over. Scripps took three wickets and Gruber and Watson took two wickets each.

Chasing 143 for victory, Auckland lost Lynch early but a 64 run partnership between Rolls and Drumm set the team up for victory. Rolls hit 13 fours in an innings of 82 scored off 80 balls. The victory was achieved in the 38th over for the loss of five wickets. Daly was the most successful of the Canterbury bowlers taking 2-23.

CANTERBURY	Runs	Mins	Balls	6s	4s		AUCKLAND	Runs	Mins	Balls	6s	4s
K.A.Craig b Ramsay	15	22	25	-	1		R.J.Rolls† b Daly	82	106	80	-	13
R.C.Milburn† c Rolls b Scripps	0	12	8	-	-		M.L.Lynch* lbw b Daly	7	32	24	-	1
N.Payne c Rolls b Scripps	34	100	93	-	4		E.C.Drumm c Steele b Rae	22	46	40	-	3
H.M.Tiffen* c Drumm b Gruber	38	71	72	-	6		E.B.Komp b Steele	15	24	26	-	3
M.F.Fahey not out	13	61	41	-	1		H.M.Watson not out	7	29	21	-	1
H.J.Rae c Rolls b Scripps	0	1	2	-	-		K.D.Brown b McNeill	4	20	23	-	1
S.E.Charteris c Kember b Gruber	3	11	10	-	-		A.Soma not out	1	6	9	-	-
S.K.Burke st Rolls b Watson	6	9	9	-	-		R.J.Kember					
B.H.McNeill run out	7	10	9	-	1		N.Scripps					
R.J.Steele lbw b Watson	1	4	5	-	-		D.J.Ramsay					
H.R.Daly run out	0	2	3	-	-		P.A.Gruber					
Extras (b 1, lb 7, w 17)	25						Extras (w 7)	7				
TOTAL (46.1 overs)	**142**	156					**TOTAL** (37.1 overs) (5 wkts)	**145**	134			

Bowling	O	M	R	W		Fall of Wickets		
AUCKLAND							C	A
Scripps	8.1	3	13	3		1st	14	33
Ramsay	10	2	27	1		2nd	18	100
Drumm	8	0	22	0		3rd	100	132
Gruber	10	1	41	2		4th	108	132
Watson	10	1	31	2		5th	108	139
CANTERBURY						6th	112	-
Burke	7	2	23	0		7th	125	-
Daly	10	3	23	2		8th	138	-
Steele	10	1	35	1		9th	141	-
McNeill	5.1	0	33	1		10th	142	-
Rae	4	0	19	1				
Payne	1	0	12	0				

REGISTER OF PLAYERS

		Born	At	Type	
Adler Megan Joy	ND	8.12.77	Tauranga	RHB	RM
Bannerman Natalie Ann	O	14. 9.81	Ranfurly	RHB	RSM
Bates Suzannah Wilson	O	16. 9.87	Dunedin	RHB	RM
Brown Kelly Dianne	A	8. 7.73	Hamilton	RHB	RM
Brown Victoria Jayne	ND	30. 7.82	Hamilton	LHB	ROB
Browne Nicola Jane	ND, NZ	14. 9.83	Matamata	RHB	RM
Burke Sarah Kate	C, NZ	2. 1.82	Christchurch	RHB	RM
Burrows Abby Kirstyn	CD	29. 1.77	Kawerau	RHB	RM
Carruthers Natalie Helena	ND	7.10.83	Auckland	RHB	RSM
Charteris Selena Eloise	C	5. 6.81	Timaru	RHB	ROB
Cooper Amanda Ellen	W	15. 5.83	Wellington	RHB	RM
Corbin Anna Maree	W	24.10.80	Foxton	RHB	ROB
Coyle Angela Kate	A	10.11.82	Auckland	RHB	RM
Craig Kirsty Ann	C	24. 7.80	Invercargill	RHB	RSM
Crawley Adele Elizabeth	O	11. 9.83	Wellington	RHB	RM
Daly Helen Rachel	C	26. 5.76	Hamilton	RHB	LM
Drumm Emily Cecilia	A, NZ	15. 9.74	Auckland	RHB	RLB
Duffill Sarah Luba	CD	17. 5.83	Wellington	RHB	RSM
Edwards Charlotte Marie	ND, ENG	17.12.79	Huntingdon, England	RHB	RLB
Fahey Maria Frances	C	5. 3.84	Timaru	LHB	ROB
Forsyth Cindy Leonie	CD	23.12.80	New Plymouth	LHB	
Fraser Fiona Elizabeth	W	6. 9.80	Wellington	RHB	RM
Fraser Janice Mary	ND	3. 2.79	Tokoroa	RHB	RM
Garrood Claire Frances	ND	15. 2.88	Rotorua	RHB	RM
Godliman Mandie Claire	W, ENG	5. 4.73	Eton, England	RHB	WK
Goodson Kelly Maree	ND	11. 1.86	Rotorua	RHB	RM
Graham Megan Maree	CD	23. 3.67	Wairoa	RHB	RM
Green Amanda Jayne	W, NZ	19. 3.84	Turangi	RHB	RM
Gruber Paula Anne	A	30.11.74	Waiouru	RHB	ROB
Hannay Maree Jennifer	ND	1. 3.84	Whakatane	RHB	ROB
Harford Losalini Ravucake Vuetibau Stephi	W	25. 3.73	Bridgetown, Barbados	RHB	ROB
Helmore Sarah Katie	O	29. 9.71	Auckland	RHB	
Hill Sarah Joanne	W	31. 5.79	Feilding	RHB	WK
Hipkiss Abigail Samantha Maria	O	18. 6.81	Palmerston North	RHB	ROB
Hunter-Siu Jane Leipu	W	8. 1.79	Wellington	LHB	RM
Innes Jenna Maree	O	10. 3.83	Dunedin	RHB	RM
Kane Alana Lois	O	7. 9.83	Tapanui	RHB	RM
Kane Megan Joanna	O	1. 8.82	Tapanui	RHB	ROB
Kember Rosamond Jane	ND	28. 1.85	Auckland	RHB	RLB
King Frances Sarah	W, NZ	28.11.80	Wellington	RHB	RFM
Komp Elfriede Berta	A	27.10.83	Pretoria, South Africa	RHB	LM
Lenssen Aimee Jane	ND	22. 3.85	Whangarei	RHB	RM
Lewis Maia Ann Mereana	W, NZ	20. 6.70	Christchurch	RHB	RSM
Little Amber Margaret	W	22. 5.84	Lower Hutt	RHB	RM
Lynch Katherine Brenda	O	17.12.82	Rotorua	RHB	RM
Lynch Michelle Louise	A, NZ	16.10.75	Auckland	RHB	WK
Martin Katey Jane	O	7. 2.85	Dunedin	RHB	WK
Mason Aimee Louise	CD, NZ	11.10.82	New Plymouth	RHB	ROB
McDonald Erin Teresa	CD	25.11.80	Lower Hutt	RHB	SLA
McGlashan Sara Jade	CD	28. 3.82	Napier	RHB	WK
McNeill Beth Hannah	C	10.11.82	Wellington	RHB	RM
McWilliams Zara Ann	CD	29.11.83	Hastings	RHB	RM
Milburn Rowan Claire	C	18. 6.77	Mosgiel	RHB	WK
Milliken Louise Elizabeth	ND, NZ	19. 9.83	Morrinsville	RHB	RFM
Morrison Tanya Jeanette	O	1. 7.85	Gore	RHB	ROB
O'Connor Faele	W	15.10.79	Wellington	RHB	RSM
Payne Nicola	C, NZ	10. 9.69	Toronto, Canada	RHB	RM
Perry Elizabeth Cecelia	CD	22.11.87	Taumarunui	RHB	RM
Presland Margaret Leona	W	28. 6.78	Suva, Fiji	LHB	RM
Pulford Katherine Louise	CD, NZ	27. 8.80	Nelson	RHB	RM
Pullar Rachel Jane	O	3. 6.77	Balclutha	RHB	RFM
Rae Hannah Jane	C	13.10.81	Christchurch	LHB	LM
Ramsay Debbie Jayne	A	20. 3.80	Auckland	RHB	ROB
Roderick Becky Louise	ND	29.10.81	Te Puke	RHB	WK

	Born	At	Type	
Rolls Rebecca Jane	A, NZ	22. 8.75	Napier	RHB	WK
Scott Kim-Maree Ann	A	9. 9.69	Melbourne, Australia	RHB	LM
Scripps Natalee	A	9.12.78	Auckland	RHB	RM
Scurr Elizabeth Jessica	O	26. 7.83	Dunedin	RHB	ROB
Simpson Julie Ann	ND	15. 2.87	Auckland	RHB	RM
Soma Anjana	ND	11. 7.79	Auckland	RHB	
Spence Kirsten Mary	O	21. 6.82	Dunedin	RHB	
Stafford Jenny Marie	ND	21. 1.82	Rotorua	RHB	RM
Steele Rebecca Jayne	C, NZ	2. 1.85	Christchurch	RHB	SLA
Street Toni Maree	CD	8. 9.83	New Plymouth	RHB	WK
Sutherland Kelly Marie	CD	7.10.82	Hastings	RHB	RM
Taylor Clare Elizabeth	O, ENG	22. 5.65	Huddersfield, Eng.	RHB	RM
Taylor Samantha Claire	C, ENG	25. 9.75	Amersham, England	RHB	WK
Thessman Nicole Maree	CD	12.11.76	Palmerston North	RHB	ROB
Thompson Claire Marie	O	19. 3.85	Dunedin	LHB	RSM
Tiffen Haidee Maree	C, NZ	4. 9.79	Timaru	RHB	RM
Trendle Joanne Louise	W	22. 3.78	Wellington	RHB	
Trow Donna Marie	CD	13. 7.77	Napier	RHB	RM
Tsukigawa Sarah Jane	O	16. 6.82	Balclutha	RHB	RM
Tuapawa Megan Louise	W	10. 9.82	Lower Hutt	RHB	RM
Wakefield Megan Gwenda	W	22. 9.82	Christchurch	RHB	RM
Watson Helen Maree	A	17. 2.72	Ashburton	RHB	RM
Wilkins Anna Jane	ND	21. 5.80	Hamilton	RHB	WK
Winkley Kelly Marie	CD	16. 6.84	Napier	RHB	ROB

2002/03 STATE LEAGUE AVERAGES

	M	In	NO	HS	Runs	Ave	100s	50s	Ct	St	O	M	R	W	Ave	R/O	Best
M.J.Adler	2	1	0	0	0	0.00	-	-	-	-	5	0	34	0	-	6.80	-
N.A.Bannerman	1	1	0	21	21	21.00	-	-	-	-							
S.W.Bates	2	2	0	12	23	11.50	-	-	1	-	15	3	32	3	10.66	2.13	2-21
K.D.Brown	10	8	3	49*	141	28.20	-	-	4	-							
V.J.Brown	7	7	0	28	72	10.28	-	-	-	-							
N.J.Browne	7	7	1	50*	177	29.50	-	1	2	-	52.4	3	207	5	41.40	3.93	2-33
S.K.Burke	10	6	2	27	70	17.50	-	-	2	-	91.2	13	304	15	20.26	3.32	3-31
A.K.Burrows	8	6	1	8*	16	3.20	-	-	3	-	58	10	179	7	25.57	3.09	3-19
N.H.Carruthers	5	4	3	14*	18	18.00	-	-	1	-	32	3	110	8	13.75	3.44	3-20
S.E.Charteris	6	3	0	13	18	6.00	-	-	4	-	3	0	26	1	26.00	8.67	1-26
A.E.Cooper	9	6	2	25*	58	14.50	-	-	2	-	64.1	10	210	13	16.15	3.27	3-19
A.M.Corbin	4	4	1	25	52	17.33	-	-	2	-	34	4	98	6	16.33	2.88	3-27
A.K.Coyle	5	1	0	0	0	0.00	-	-	-	-	34	5	155	5	31.00	4.56	2-27
K.A.Craig	10	9	1	42*	105	13.12	-	-	1	-							
A.E.Crawley	4	2	1	2	3	3.00	-	-	-	-	9	0	53	0	-	5.89	-
H.R.Daly	7	2	1	0*	0	0.00	-	-	3	-	65.1	20	130	12	10.83	1.99	5-19
E.C.Drumm	9	9	3	62*	325	54.16	-	1	2	-	43	6	153	11	13.90	3.56	3-14
S.L.Duffill	6	6	0	35	92	15.33	-	-	1	-							
C.M.Edwards	3	3	0	120	185	61.66	1	-	-	-	24	5	51	2	25.50	2.13	1-9
M.F.Fahey	10	9	2	41*	111	15.85	-	-	1	-	4	0	45	2	22.50	11.25	1-14
C.L.Forsyth	8	8	0	40	164	20.50	-	-	-	-	1.5	0	21	0	-	11.47	-
F.E.Fraser	1	1	0	25	25	25.00	-	-	-	-							
J.M.Fraser	7	7	0	42	59	8.42	-	-	4	-	18.2	1	82	2	41.00	4.47	1-29
C.F.Garrood	3	2	0	8	10	5.00	-	-	-	-	2	0	15	0	-	7.50	-
M.C.Godliman	7	7	0	32	128	18.28	-	-	-	-							
K.M.Goodson	3	3	0	19	40	13.33	-	-	-	-							
M.M.Graham	2	2	0	1	1	0.50	-	-	1	-							
A.J.Green	8	4	1	11*	19	6.33	-	-	-	-	62	7	226	5	45.20	3.65	1-16
P.A.Gruber	10	3	1	12	27	13.50	-	-	2	-	73.1	4	280	12	23.33	3.82	2-26
M.J.Hannay	5	5	0	36	71	14.20	-	-	1	-	23	0	90	3	30.00	3.91	2-22
L.R.V.S.Harford	6	6	1	50	120	24.00	-	1	3	-	11.1	0	43	0	-	3.85	-
S.K.Helmore	10	8	1	47	144	20.57	-	-	1	-							
S.J.Hill	5	4	0	21	36	9.00	-	-	5	1							
A.S.M.Hipkiss	4	2	0	11	18	9.00	-	-	-	-	9	0	35	1	35.00	3.89	1-16
J.L.Hunter-Siu	2	2	0	13	17	8.50	-	-	1	-	7	2	22	0	-	3.14	-
J.M.Innes	7	5	2	12	40	13.33	-	-	-	-	9.1	0	56	1	56.00	6.11	1-5
A.L.Kane	8	5	1	13	33	8.25	-	-	-	-	26	2	108	2	54.00	4.15	1-14
M.J.Kane	10	9	1	65*	203	25.37	-	1	1	-	16	2	79	2	39.50	4.94	2-19
R.J.Kember	10	6	0	37	92	15.33	-	-	3	-							
F.S.King	9	8	3	45*	179	35.80	-	-	-	-	73	14	218	9	24.22	2.99	3-18
E.B.Komp	6	5	1	22	64	16.00	-	-	-	-	1	0	10	0	-	10.00	-
A.J.Lenssen	7	7	2	23*	48	9.60	-	-	2	-	40	6	156	11	14.18	3.90	3-21
M.A.M.Lewis	9	9	3	76*	378	63.00	-	3	7	-							
A.M.Little	8	2	2	1*	1	-	-	-	3	-	57	6	188	7	26.85	3.30	5-27
K.B.Lynch	5	3	1	3	3	1.50	-	-	1	-	17	0	83	2	41.50	4.88	1-15
M.L.Lynch	10	10	0	29	135	13.50	-	-	3	-							
K.J.Martin	10	8	0	13	29	3.62	-	-	5	4							
A.L.Mason	8	8	1	63	227	32.42	-	1	5	-	62.4	12	213	9	23.66	3.39	2-13
E.T.McDonald	8	6	1	26*	60	12.00	-	-	-	-	63.1	8	203	7	29.00	3.21	2-18
S.J.McGlashan	8	7	1	36	96	16.00	-	-	7	3							
B.H.McNeill	10	6	2	7	14	3.50	-	-	2	-	87.3	18	264	19	13.89	3.01	5-31
Z.A.McWilliams	7	5	0	5	12	2.40	-	-	1	-	41	8	156	3	52.00	3.80	1-14
R.C.Milburn	10	8	1	42*	133	19.00	-	-	11	6							
L.E.Milliken	4	4	2	18*	39	19.50	-	-	1	-	14	1	69	2	34.50	4.93	1-24
T.J.Morrison	1	0	0	0	0	-	-	-	-	-	3	0	6	0	-	2.00	-
F.O'Connor	5	2	0	14	14	7.00	-	-	-	-							
N.Payne	10	10	2	97	416	52.00	-	4	1	-	36.5	2	133	4	33.25	3.61	2-24
E.C.Perry	6	4	1	6*	10	3.33	-	-	-	-	16	0	77	0	-	4.81	-
M.L.Presland	9	5	1	5*	9	2.25	-	-	2	-	60.1	4	236	12	19.66	3.92	4-36
K.L.Pulford	6	6	2	66*	133	33.25	-	1	1	-	44	3	173	9	19.22	3.93	3-24
R.J.Pullar	9	7	0	78	183	26.14	-	1	1	-	66.1	10	187	6	31.16	2.82	2-24
H.J.Rae	10	5	2	6*	11	3.66	-	-	4	-	67	4	286	15	19.06	4.27	3-17
D.J.Ramsay	10	3	0	33	40	13.33	-	-	4	-	91	33	215	11	19.54	2.36	2-9
B.L.Roderick	7	3	1	2	3	1.50	-	-	4	-							
R.J.Rolls	10	10	1	82	240	26.66	-	2	16	7							

	M	In	NO	HS	Runs	Ave	100s	50s	Ct	St	O	M	R	W	Ave	R/O	Best
K.M.A.Scott	4	1	1	1*	1	-	-	-	-	-	9	0	51	3	17.00	5.67	2-19
N.Scripps	10	4	1	10	16	5.33	-	-	-	-	77	13	210	20	10.50	2.73	6-19
E.J.Scurr	8	7	1	18	57	9.50	-	-	-	-	29.5	3	123	0	-	4.12	-
J.A.Simpson	4	3	0	8	16	5.33	-	-	1	-	31	3	88	4	22.00	2.84	1-12
A.Soma	6	4	2	14*	31	15.50	-	-	-	-							
K.M.Spence	9	6	2	24	35	8.75	-	-	-	-	43	8	149	9	16.55	3.47	3-23
J.M.Stafford	6	6	0	10	29	4.83	-	-	-	-	7	0	29	0	-	4.14	-
R.J.Steele	10	4	1	3	8	2.66	-	-	3	-	99	26	249	9	27.66	2.52	1-12
T.M.Street	2	2	0	2	3	1.50	-	-	1	1							
K.M.Sutherland	3	3	2	3*	7	7.00	-	-	-	-	7	0	42	0	-	6.00	-
C.E.Taylor	8	7	2	65*	192	38.40	-	2	-	-	52.1	12	184	3	61.33	3.52	2-34
S.C.Taylor	7	6	0	61	252	42.00	-	3	3	-							
N.M.Thessman	8	8	0	30	126	15.75	-	-	1	-							
C.M.Thompson	4	2	1	5*	5	5.00	-	-	1	-	5	0	19	0	-	3.80	-
H.M.Tiffen	10	9	3	80*	241	40.16	-	2	5	-	9	1	54	0	-	6.00	-
J.L.Trendle	1	1	0	0	0	0.00	-	-	-	-							
D.M.Trow	6	4	2	30*	47	23.50	-	-	1	-	40.5	4	137	8	17.12	3.35	3-25
S.J.Tsukigawa	10	8	1	30	55	7.85	-	-	-	-	46.5	3	198	6	33.00	4.22	3-19
M.L.Tuapawa	7	2	0	2	4	2.00	-	-	1	-	2	0	8	0	-	4.00	-
M.G.Wakefield	9	8	1	74*	121	17.28	-	1	5	-							
H.M.Watson	10	9	5	46*	126	31.50	-	-	3	-	81.3	10	242	12	20.16	2.96	3-2
A.J.Wilkins	7	7	0	36	69	9.85	-	-	1	-	8.3	2	51	1	51.00	6.00	1-22
K.M.Winkley	2	2	0	8	16	8.00	-	-	-	-	6.4	0	26	0	-	3.90	-

HIGHEST STRIKE RATES *(qualification 100 runs)*

		Runs	Balls	S/R			Runs	Balls	S/R
A.L.Mason	CD	227	283	80	C.M.Edwards	ND	185	257	71
C.E.Taylor	O	192	242	79	M.G.Wakefield	W	121	176	68
R.J.Rolls	A	240	309	77	C.L.Forsyth	CD	164	247	66
R.J.Pullar	O	183	246	74	F.S.King	W	179	278	64
E.C.Drumm	A	325	446	72	S.C.Taylor	C	252	399	63

MOST ECONOMICAL BOWLING *(qualification 30 overs)*

		O	M	R	W	Ave	R/O
H.R.Daly	C	65.1	20	130	12	10.83	1.99
D.J.Ramsay	A	91	33	215	11	19.54	2.36
R.J.Steele	C	99	26	249	9	27.66	2.51
N.Scripps	A	77	13	210	20	10.50	2.72
R.J.Pullar	O	66.1	10	187	6	31.16	2.82
J.A.Simpson	ND	31	3	88	4	22.00	2.83
A.M.Corbin	W	34	4	98	6	16.33	2.88
H.M.Watson	A	81.3	10	242	12	20.16	2.96
F.S.King	W	73	14	218	9	24.22	2.98
B.H.McNeill	C	87.3	18	264	19	13.89	3.01

CAREER RECORDS

	M	In	NO	HS	Runs	Ave	100s	50s	Ct	St	O	M	R	W	Ave	R/O	Best
M.J.Adler	2	1	0	0	0	0.00	-	-	-	-	5	0	34	0	-	6.80	-
N.A.Bannerman	15	14	1	47	181	13.92	-	-	1	-	0.3	0	10	0	-	-	-
S.W.Bates	2	2	0	12	23	11.50	-	-	1	-	15	3	32	3	10.66	2.13	2-21
K.D.Brown	15	11	4	66	247	35.28	-	1	5	-							
V.J.Brown	20	18	1	66	248	14.58	-	1	6	-	67	8	282	11	25.63	4.21	4-28
N.J.Browne	30	28	5	50*	285	12.39	-	1	11	-	218.3	19	884	27	32.74	4.04	3-23
S.K.Burke	31	19	4	27	114	7.60	-	-	8	-	225.2	29	833	32	26.03	3.69	3-31
A.K.Burrows	23	11	4	8*	22	3.14	-	-	7	-	161	18	559	23	24.30	3.47	3-19
N.H.Carruthers	5	4	·3	14*	18	18.00	-	-	1	-	32	3	110	8	13.75	3.44	3-20
S.E.Charteris	6	3	0	13	18	6.00	-	-	4	-	3	0	26	1	26.00	8.67	1-26
A.E.Cooper	31	21	3	30	246	13.66	-	-	7	-	151.4	23	532	26	20.46	3.50	3-6
A.M.Corbin	39	25	4	32	234	11.14	-	-	14	-	336	78	909	39	23.30	2.71	4-11
A.K.Coyle	5	1	0	0	0	0.00	-	-	-	-	34	5	155	5	31.00	4.56	2-27
K.A.Craig	13	12	1	42*	140	12.72	-	-	1	-							
A.E.Crawley	4	2	1	2	3	3.00	-	-	-	-	9	0	53	0	-	5.89	-
H.R.Daly	17	9	4	11*	36	7.20	-	-	4	-	132.2	45	285	21	13.57	2.15	5-19
E.C.Drumm	51	50	12	118	1854	48.78	3	9	12	-	119.1	13	454	23	19.73	3.81	3-1
S.L.Duffill	6	6	0	35	92	15.33	-	-	1	-							
C.M.Edwards	13	13	2	120	500	45.45	2	2	-	-	26	5	65	2	32.50	2.50	1-9
M.F.Fahey	30	25	3	41*	300	13.63	-	-	11	-	112.2	11	428	18	23.77	3.81	4-21
C.L.Forsyth	37	34	1	59*	500	15.15	-	1	7	-	94.1	7	441	21	21.00	4.68	4-23
F.E.Fraser	15	13	2	44	247	22.45	-	-	2	-	78	4	314	7	44.85	4.03	2-27
J.M.Fraser	36	35	0	45	487	13.91	-	-	14	-	64.2	8	261	6	43.50	4.05	1-12
C.F.Garrood	3	2	0	8	10	5.00	-	-	-	-	2	0	15	0	-	7.50	-
M.C.Godliman	7	7	0	32	128	18.28	-	-	-	-							
K.M.Goodson	3	3	0	19	40	13.33	-	-	-	-							
M.M.Graham	34	26	3	57*	427	18.56	-	1	19	-	106.2	8	459	23	19.95	4.31	4-32
A.J.Green	28	15	5	15	78	7.80	-	-	1	-	158	29	505	21	24.04	3.20	3-7
P.A.Gruber	31	13	3	25	90	9.00	-	-	8	-	198.3	29	612	38	16.10	3.08	4-15
M.J.Hannay	17	17	1	36	180	11.25	-	-	3	-	57	0	251	4	62.75	4.40	2-22
L.R.V.S.Harford	25	23	2	83	441	21.00	-	3	9	-	91.5	7	354	9	39.33	3.85	2-12
S.K.Helmore	38	36	4	57*	586	18.31	-	2	11	-	0.3	0	7	0	-	-	-
S.J.Hill	15	8	2	21	63	10.50	-	-	14	3							
A.S.M.Hipkiss	4	2	0	11	18	9.00	-	-	-	-	9	0	35	1	35.00	3.89	1-16
J.L.Hunter-Siu	28	21	1	37	232	11.60	-	-	6	-	174	29	543	29	18.72	3.12	4-8
J.M.Innes	8	6	2	12	41	10.25	-	-	1	-	16.1	0	81	3	27.00	5.01	2-25
A.L.Kane	11	7	2	13	41	8.20	-	-	-	-	36.4	2	165	3	55.00	4.50	1-14
M.J.Kane	41	36	3	65*	484	14.66	-	1	4	-	145	7	617	13	47.46	4.26	3-13
R.J.Kember	16	11	0	37	106	9.63	-	-	6	-							
F.S.King	36	31	6	45*	426	17.04	-	-	4	-	257	35	858	35	24.51	3.34	4-33
E.B.Komp	31	19	5	22	136	9.71	-	-	2	-	103.3	10	393	16	24.56	3.79	2-13
A.J.Lenssen	12	12	3	29*	93	10.33	-	-	3	-	64	6	270	14	19.28	4.22	3-21
M.A.M.Lewis	35	32	6	97	1051	40.42	-	7	15	-	9	0	45	0	-	5.00	-
A.M.Little	8	2	2	1*	1	-	-	-	-	3	-	57	6	188	7	26.85	3.30	5-27
K.B.Lynch	15	13	1	14	50	4.16	-	-	1	-	33	3	152	3	50.66	4.61	1-15
M.L.Lynch	21	20	2	64	354	19.66	-	1	8	-							
K.J.Martin	20	17	1	24	96	6.00	-	-	7	5							
A.L.Mason	32	26	6	63	451	22.55	-	2	17	-	278.4	48	862	43	20.04	3.09	5-25
E.T.McDonald	39	29	10	34	262	13.78	-	-	5	-	328.1	46	1119	34	32.91	3.40	4-30
S.J.McGlashan	24	20	2	40	240	13.33	-	-	11	6							
B.H.McNeill	36	27	8	26*	217	11.42	-	-	6	-	263.1	41	956	47	20.34	3.63	6-31
Z.A.McWilliams	11	7	2	6*	21	4.20	-	-	2	-	65	9	271	5	54.20	4.17	2-39
R.C.Milburn	46	43	4	82	535	13.71	-	1	27	17							
L.E.Milliken	25	23	11	23	136	11.33	-	-	4	-	177	11	770	18	42.77	4.35	3-14
T.J.Morrison	1	0	0	0	0	-	-	-	-	-	3	0	6	0	-	2.00	-
F.O'Connor	7	4	1	14	24	8.00	-	-	-	-							
N.Payne	49	47	7	117*	1614	40.35	1	12	8	-	239.5	30	823	27	30.48	3.43	3-15
E.C.Perry	6	4	1	6*	10	3.33	-	-	-	-	16	0	77	0	-	4.81	-
M.L.Presland	27	20	8	25*	95	7.91	-	-	4	-	189.5	24	724	29	24.96	3.81	4-34
K.L.Pulford	38	36	5	153*	1000	32.25	2	5	13	-	221	20	822	32	25.68	3.72	3-24
R.J.Pullar	39	37	5	78	787	24.59	-	5	11	-	315.2	47	992	40	24.80	3.14	4-14
H.J.Rae	38	18	9	10*	53	5.88	-	-	9	-	231.3	30	838	37	22.64	3.61	5-24
D.J.Ramsay	24	6	2	33	46	11.50	-	-	5	-	195	58	441	29	15.20	2.26	3-22
B.L.Roderick	7	3	1	2	3	1.50	-	-	4	-							
R.J.Rolls	51	50	4	82	997	21.67	-	5	50	34							

	M	In	NO	HS	Runs	Ave	100s	50s	Ct	St	O	M	R	W	Ave	R/O	Best
K.M.A.Scott	4	1	1	1*	1	-	-	-	-	-	9	0	51	3	17.00	5.67	2-19
N.Scripps	38	18	6	30	101	8.41	-	-	4	-	297.2	46	895	68	13.16	3.01	6-19
E.J.Scurr	20	19	4	28	143	9.53	-	-	1	-	83.5	10	308	6	51.33	3.67	3-22
J.A.Simpson	4	3	0	8	16	5.33	-	-	1	-	31	3	88	4	22.00	2.84	1-12
A.Soma	41	29	7	48	381	17.31	-	-	4	-							
K.M.Spence	42	28	13	24	68	4.53	-	-	3	-	269.4	40	977	34	28.73	3.62	4-35
J.M.Stafford	25	22	0	40	122	5.54	-	-	6	-	112	7	485	21	23.09	4.33	4-32
R.J.Steele	22	9	4	11	30	6.00	-	-	7	-	159.2	37	441	25	17.64	2.76	4-20
T.M.Street	8	5	0	8	15	3.00	-	-	7	2							
K.M.Sutherland	8	7	3	16*	35	8.75	-	-	1	-	27	0	132	4	33.00	4.89	3-35
C.E.Taylor	18	16	2	65*	335	23.92	-	3	4	-	143.4	28	497	17	29.23	3.45	3-14
S.C.Taylor	7	6	0	61	252	42.00	-	3	3	-							
N.M.Thessman	41	39	7	85*	863	26.96	-	4	11	-	2	0	12	0	-	6.00	-
C.M.Thompson	4	2	1	5*	5	5.00	-	-	1	-	5	0	19	0	-	3.80	-
H.M.Tiffen	48	44	13	86	894	28.83	-	4	21	-	251	29	889	55	16.16	3.54	5-51
J.L.Trendle	17	17	2	46	194	12.93	-	-	-	-							
D.M.Trow	34	21	10	30*	159	14.45	-	-	17	-	269	38	832	34	24.47	3.09	3-11
S.J.Tsukigawa	35	30	5	41	222	8.88	-	-	4	-	80.5	6	335	14	23.92	4.14	3-19
M.L.Tuapawa	18	6	1	5	9	1.80	-	-	2	-	26.4	1	104	3	34.66	3.90	1-14
M.G.Wakefield	18	15	2	74*	185	14.23	-	1	6	-	11	0	43	2	21.50	3.91	2-26
H.M.Watson	50	43	15	101	877	31.32	1	2	10	-	325	57	907	45	20.15	2.79	3-2
A.J.Wilkins	40	39	2	49	513	13.86	-	-	7	-	28.3	2	174	2	87.00	6.10	1-15
K.M.Winkley	2	2	0	8	16	8.00	-	-	-	-	6.4	0	26	0	-	3.90	-

TEAM RECORDS

Highest Totals

302-5	Canterbury v Otago	Christchurch	1998/99
298-4	Canterbury v Wellington	Christchurch	1999/00
288-5	Auckland v Central Districts	Auckland	2000/01
270-4	Auckland v Northern Districts	Auckland	2001/02
266-5	Auckland v Canterbury	Christchurch	2000/01
263-9	Canterbury v Central Districts	Palmerston North	2000/01
263-9	Canterbury v Auckland	Christchurch	2000/01
260-3	Wellington v Otago	Lower Hutt	2000/01

Lowest Totals

43	Central Districts v Auckland	Wanganui	1999/00
46	Northern Districts v Wellington	Wellington	1999/00
59	Otago v Canterbury	Christchurch	2000/01
61	Otago v Auckland	Auckland	2001/02
64	Otago v Wellington	Dunedin	2001/02
65	Auckland v Canterbury	Rangiora	1998/99
65	Otago v Auckland	Auckland	2001/02

INDIVIDUAL RECORDS

Centuries

153*	K.L. Pulford	Central Districts v Canterbury	Christchurch	1999/00
141	D.A. Hockley	Canterbury v Auckland	Rangiora	1998/99
141	K.L. Pulford	Central Districts v Otago	Palmerston North	2000/01
128	D.A. Hockley	Canterbury v Wellington	Christchurch	1999/00
120	C.M. Edwards	Northern Districts v Wellington	Hamilton	2002/03
119*	C.M. Edwards	Northern Districts v Canterbury	Christchurch	2000/01
118	E.C. Drumm	Auckland v Central Districts	Auckland	2000/01
117*	N. Payne	Canterbury v Wellington	Christchurch	1999/00
117	D.A. Hockley	Canterbury v Otago	Christchurch	1998/99
114*	E.C. Drumm	Auckland v Central Districts	Wanganui	1999/00
112*	E.C. Drumm	Auckland v Northern Districts	Auckland	2001/02
104*	P.B. Flannery	Canterbury v Otago	Christchurch	2000/01
104	M.K. Tyler	Auckland v Otago	Auckland	1999/00
102*	N.A. Pratt	Northern Districts v Otago	Hamilton	1999/00
101	D.A. Hockley	Canterbury v Central Districts	Palmerston North	1998/99
101	H.M. Watson	Auckland v Otago	Dunedin	2000/01

Five Wickets in an Innings

7.1-1-19-7	M.F. Tunupopo	Auckland v Central Districts	Wanganui	1999/00
9.2-2-19-6	N. Scripps	Auckland v Wellington	Auckland	2002/03
9.5-1-31-6	B.H. McNeill	Canterbury v Auckland	Auckland	2001/02
5.5-1-12-5	C.A. Campbell	Canterbury v Northern Districts	Hamilton	1999/00
10-2-19-5	H.R. Daly	Canterbury v Northern Districts	Rangiora	2002/03
7-1-20-5	C.A. Campbell	Canterbury v Wellington	Wellington	1998/99
8-1-24-5	H.J. Rae	Canterbury v Wellington	Lower Hutt	2000/01
10-1-25-5	A.L. Mason	Central Districts v Wellington	Wanganui	1999/00
10-0-27-5	A.M. Little	Wellington v Otago	Wellington	2002/03
10-1-31-5	B.H. McNeill	Canterbury v Otago	Timaru	2002/03
10-1-34-5	H.J. Partridge	Northern Districts v Auckland	Auckland	1999/00
8.3-1-37-5	N. Scripps	Auckland v Canterbury	Christchurch	2000/01
10-1-51-5	H.M. Tiffen	Canterbury v Auckland	Christchurch	2000/01

Wicketkeeping

DISMISSALS

(ct/st)

5	(2/3)	Rolls R.J.	Auckland v Canterbury	Christchurch	2000/01
4	(0/4)	Rolls R.J.	Auckland v Wellington	Auckland '	1998/99
4	(1/3)	Milburn R.C.	Otago v Wellington	Dunedin	1999/00
4	(0/4)	Strachan J.L.	Canterbury v Northern Districts	Christchurch	2000/01
4	(4/0)	Milburn R.C.	Canterbury v Auckland	Christchurch	2002/03
4	(3/1)	McGlashan S.J.	Central Districts v Canterbury	Palmerston North	2002/03
4	(2/2)	Martin K.J.	Otago v Central Districts	Palmerston North	2002/03
4	(2/2)	McGlashan S.J.	Central Districts v Otago	Palmerston North	2002/03
4	(3/1)	Rolls R.J.	Auckland v Canterbury	Christchurch	2002/03

Fielding

CATCHES

4	Graham M.M.	Central Districts v Northern Districts	Wanganui	1999/00

RECORD PARTNERSHIPS

AUCKLAND

1st	110*	R.J. Rolls & M.L. Lynch	v Northern Districts	Auckland	2001/02
2nd	136	M.K. Fruin & E.C. Drumm	v Central Districts	Auckland	2000/01
3rd	121	E.C. Drumm & K.A. Ramel	v Otago	Auckland	1999/00
4th †	157	M.K. Fruin & H.M. Watson	v Otago	Dunedin	2000/01
5th †	115	H.M. Watson & K.D. Brown	v Central Districts	Waikanae	2001/02
6th	68	K.A. Ramel & A. Soma	v Canterbury	Christchurch	2000/01
7th †	90	K.A. Ramel & A. Soma	v Wellington	Auckland	1998/99
8th	52	C.M. Nicholson & Z.A.A. Plummer	v Central Districts	Auckland	1998/99
9th	35	E.C. Drumm & S.E.M. Cowlrick	v Canterbury	Christchurch	1998/99
10th	16*	E.C. Drumm & M.F. Tunupopo	v Canterbury	Christchurch	1998/99

CANTERBURY

1st	163	D.A. Hockley & P.B. Flannery	v Central Districts	Christchurch	1999/00
2nd †	227	D.A. Hockley & N. Payne	v Wellington	Christchurch	1999/00
3rd	98	D.A. Hockley & N. Payne	v Otago	Christchurch	1998/99
4th	144	H.M. Tiffen & J.A. Lawler	v Central Districts	P. North	2000/01
5th	73	N. Payne & M.F. Fahey	v Northern Districts	Hamilton	2001/02
6th	59	K.M. Keenan & H.M. Tiffen	v Wellington	Wellington	1998/99
7th	57	S.K. Helmore & M.F. Fahey	v Central Districts	P. North	2000/01
8th	41	L.M. Astle & A.J.M.D. Marsh	v Northern Districts	Hamilton	1999/00
9th	23	S.K. Burke & H.J. Rae	v Central Districts	P. North	2002/03
10th	23	J. Maley & C.J. Moffat	v Auckland	Christchurch	1998/99
	23	R.J. Steele & H.J. Rae	v Central Districts	Christchurch	2001/02

CENTRAL DISTRICTS

1st	†	179* P.K. Gerrish & C.L. Forsyth	v Wellington	Wellington	2000/01
2nd		92 S.J. Shaw & N.M. Thessman	v Wellington	Wanganui	1998/99
3rd		118 K.L. Pulford & N.M. Thessman	v Wellington	Napier	2001/02
4th		91 K.L. Pulford & E.A. Travers	v Otago	P. North	2000/01
5th		80* N.M. Thessman & A.L. Mason	v Wellington	Napier	2001/02
6th		83 M.M. Graham & S.J. McGlashan	v Otago	Dunedin	1998/99
7th		86 A.L. Mason & E.A. Travers	v Canterbury	P. North	2000/01
8th		23 E.T. McDonald & D.M. Trow	v Auckland	Auckland	1998/99
9th	†	67* N.M. Thessman & K.M. Sutherland	v Otago	Dunedin	2001/02
10th		36* D.M. Trow & A.K. Burrows	v Auckland	Auckland	2002/03

NORTHERN DISTRICTS

1st	63 V.J. Brown & N.J. Browne	v Otago	Dunedin	2002/03
2nd	63 S.A. Sandilands & K.B. Spence	v Central Districts	Wanganui	1999/00
3rd	97 V.J. Brown & A.J. Wilkins	v Otago	Dunedin	2000/01
4th	64 J.M. Fraser & M.J. Hannay	v Wellington	Hamilton	2002/03
5th	49 S.A. Sandilands & K.B. Spence	v Auckland	Whangarei	2000/01
6th	62 S.A. Sandilands & J.M. Stafford	v Central Districts	Hamilton	2000/01
7th	66 A.J. Wilkins & K.J. Gibson	v Wellington	Wellington	1999/00
8th	45 K.B. Spence & N.J. Browne	v Wellington	Hamilton	2000/01
9th	51 K.B. Spence & L.E. Milliken	v Central Districts	Hamilton	2000/01
10th	24 N.H. Carruthers & J.A. Simpson	v Canterbury	Rangiora	2002/03

OTAGO

1st	152* C.E. Taylor & M.J. Kane	v Central Districts	P. North	2002/03
2nd	94 R.J. Pullar & S.K Helmore	v Central Districts	Dunedin	2001/02
	94 R.C. Milburn & P.J. te Beest	v Canterbury	Oamaru	2001/02
3rd	139 R.C. Milburn & C.E. Taylor	v Central Districts	P. North	2000/01
4th	71 R.J. Pullar & N.A. Bannerman	v Northern Districts	Dunedin	2000/01
5th	66 S.K. Helmore & N.A. Bannerman	v Northern Districts	Hamilton	2001/02
	66 S.J. Tsukigawa & K.J. Martin	v Canterbury	Oamaru	2001/02
6th	52 R.J. Pullar & C.E. Taylor	v Canterbury	Timaru	2002/03
7th	42 S.K. Helmore & A.L. Kane	v Central Districts	P. North	2002/03
8th †	62 R.J. Pullar & K.A. Craig	v Canterbury	Christchurch	2000/01
9th	32 J.L. Hall & K.B. Moore	v Central Districts	Dunedin	1998/99
10th	22 J.L. Geary & K.M. Spence	v Canterbury	Dunedin	1999/00

WELLINGTON

1st	95 A.M. O'Leary & J.L. Trendle	v Central Districts	Wellington	2000/01
2nd	89 A.M. O'Leary & F.A. Stickney	v Northern Districts	Wellington	1999/00
3rd †	159 L.R.V.S. Harford & M.A.M. Lewis	v Canterbury	Christchurch	1999/00
4th	98* M.A.M. Lewis & F.S. King	v Otago	Lower Hutt	2000/01
5th	73 M.A.M. Lewis & A.M. Corbin	v Central Districts	Wellington	2002/03
6th †	144* M.A.M. Lewis & M.G. Wakefield	v Auckland	Auckland	2002/03
7th	56 M.A.M. Lewis & A.M. Corbin	v Central Districts	Napier	2001/02
8th	30 A.M. Corbin & A.E. Cooper	v Central Districts	Napier	2001/02
9th	24 M.L. Presland & J.L. Fryer	v Canterbury	Wellington	1998/99
10th †	44 A.M. Corbin & A.J. Green	v Central Districts	Lower Hutt	2000/01

† *record for all teams*

CAREER RECORDS

BATTING	M	In	NO	HS	Runs	Ave	100s	50s
E.C. Drumm	51	50	12	118	1854	48.78	3	9
N. Payne	49	47	7	117*	1614	40.35	1	12
P.B. Flannery	39	38	4	104*	1163	34.20	1	6
D.A. Hockley	19	17	1	141	1155	72.18	4	8
M.A.M. Lewis	35	32	6	97	1051	40.42	-	7
K.L. Pulford	38	36	5	153*	1000	32.25	2	5
R.J. Rolls	51	50	4	82	997	21.67	-	5
M.K. Fruin	34	34	2	97	982	30.68	-	6
A.M. O'Leary	36	34	5	84	909	31.34	-	5
H.M. Tiffen	48	44	13	86	894	28.83	-	4
H.M. Watson	50	43	15	101	877	31.32	1	2
N.M. Thessman	41	39	7	85*	863	26.96	-	4
R.J. Pullar	39	37	5	78	787	24.59	-	5
K.A. Ramel	38	35	1	92	756	22.23	-	5
M.K. Tyler	22	21	3	104	665	36.94	1	4
S.K. Helmore	38	36	4	57*	586	18.31	-	2
R.C. Milburn	46	43	4	82	535	13.71	-	1
A.J. Wilkins	40	39	2	49	513	13.86	-	-
C.M. Edwards	13	13	2	120	500	45.45	2	2
C.L. Forsyth	37	34	1	59*	500	15.15	-	1

BOWLING	M	O	M	R	W	Ave	R/O	Best
N. Scripps	38	297.2	46	895	68	13.16	3.01	6-19
H.M. Tiffen	48	251	29	889	55	16.16	3.54	5-51
B.H. McNeill	36	263.1	37	956	47	20.34	3.63	6-31
H.M. Watson	50	325	57	907	45	20.15	2.79	3-2
M.F. Tunupopo	30	224.2	24	772	44	17.54	3.44	7-19
A.L. Mason	32	278.4	48	862	43	20.04	3.09	5-25
R.J. Pullar	39	315.2	47	992	40	24.80	3.14	4-14
A.M. Corbin	39	336	78	909	39	23.30	2.71	4-11
K.A. Ramel	38	236.2	35	776	39	19.89	3.28	4-33
P.A. Gruber	31	198.3	29	612	38	16.10	3.08	4-15
M. Murray	27	230.2	25	841	38	22.13	3.65	4-28
H.J. Rae	38	231.3	30	838	37	22.64	3.61	5-24
F.S. King	36	257	35	858	35	24.51	3.34	4-33
E.T. McDonald	39	328.1	45	1119	34	32.91	3.40	4-30
K.M. Spence	42	269.4	40	977	34	28.73	3.62	4-35
D.M. Trow	34	269	37	832	34	24.47	3.09	3-11
S.K. Burke	31	225.2	29	833	32	26.03	3.69	3-31
K.L. Pulford	38	221	19	822	32	25.68	3.72	3-24

WICKETKEEPING	ct	st	Total
R.J. Rolls	50	34	84
E.A. Travers	29	19	48
R.C. Milburn	27	17	44
K.B. Spence	13	10	23
J.L. Strachan	10	11	21

FEILDING	ct
K.A. Ramel	21
H.M. Tiffen	21
M.M. Graham	19
A.L. Mason	17
D.M. Trow	17

NATIONAL UNDER 21 TOURNAMENT

The National Under 21 tournament was played at Ilam Playing Fields, Christchurch, from 27 December to 1 January. Central Districts played Canterbury in the final winning by 27 runs.

FIRST ROUND

Canterbury 145 lost to **Northern Districts** 146-5 by 5 wickets
Central Districts 171 lost to **Auckland** 172-9 by 1 wicket
Otago 227-9 defeated **Wellington** 195 by 32 runs

SECOND ROUND

Canterbury 234-9 defeated **Wellington** 107-6 by 127 runs
Central Districts 211-9 defeated **Northern Districts** 164 by 47 runs
Otago 301-5 defeated **Auckland** 163 by 138 runs

THIRD ROUND

Central Districts 257-6 defeated **Wellington** 94 by 163 runs
Otago 141 lost to **Canterbury** 145-4 by 6 wickets
Northern Districts 120 lost to **Auckland** 122-4 by 6 wickets

FOURTH ROUND

Central Districts 218-8 defeated **Otago** 113 by 105 runs
Auckland 160-9 lost to **Canterbury** 161-9 by 1 wicket
Wellington 117 defeated **Northern Districts** 94 by 23 runs

FIFTH ROUND

Central Districts 64 lost to **Canterbury** 65-2 by 8 wickets
Otago 155 defeated **Northern Districts** 153 by 2 runs
Auckland 149 lost to Wellington 151-7 by 3 wickets

FINALS

First v Second
Central Districts 186-6 defeated **Canterbury** 159 by 27 runs

Third v Fourth
Otago 170-9 defeated **Auckland** 141 by 29 runs

Fifth v Sixth
Northern Districts 170-9 defeated **Wellington** 154 by 16 runs

Final placings: Central Districts 1, Canterbury 2, Otago 3, Auckland 4, Northern Districts 5, Wellington 6.

TEST CAREER RECORDS

	M	In	NO	HS	Runs	Ave	100	50	Ct	St	Wkts	Runs	Ave	5WI	10WM	Best
Allan	4	6	4	29*	87	43.50	-	-	1	-	5	138	27.60	-	-	3-38
Anderson	2	3	0	63	108	36.00	-	1	-	-						
Badham	3	6	1	42	121	24.20	-	-	7	-	10	275	27.50	-	-	4-46
Bailey	1	2	0	5	6	3.00	-	-	-	-						
Bastion	1	-	-	-	-	-	-	-	-	-	0	59	-	-	-	-
Batty	4	7	1	24	67	11.16	-	-	6	-	2	78	39.00	-	-	1-18
Bayliss	1	-	-	-	-	-	-	-	-	-	5	70	14.00	1	-	5-28
Bevege	5	10	1	100*	400	44.44	1	2	3	-	0	70	-	-	-	-
Bishop	1	2	0	27	27	13.50	-	-	2	-	0	33	-	-	-	-
Brackie	1	2	1	13*	21	21.00	-	-	3	1						
Brickler	12	21	0	68	371	17.66	-	1	5	-	18	527	29.27	-	-	4-22
Brentnall	10	16	2	84*	301	21.50	-	1	16	12						
Brown	3	2	2	50*	52	-	-	1	4	-	7	160	22.85	-	-	3-47
Brown	6	9	3	19	59	9.83	-	-	1	-	9	432	48.00	-	-	3-64
Browne	1	2	2	5*	5	-	-	-	1	-	0	77	-	-	-	-
Brownlee	1	2	0	12	17	8.50	-	-	-	-						
Buck	1	2	0	16	16	8.00	-	-	-	-						
Burley	6	9	0	46	110	12.22	-	-	3	-	21	553	26.33	1	-	7-41
Burt	3	5	0	15	40	8.00	-	-	-	-	0	28	-	-	-	-
Burtt	4	8	0	39	101	12.62	-	-	5	-						
Campbell	9	5	1	29	55	13.75	-	-	2	-	18	720	40.00	-	-	4-94
Carrick	7	11	3	21	63	7.87	-	-	4	-	21	489	23.28	1	-	6-29
Clark	11	18	0	79	482	26.77	-	2	7	-	0	5	-	-	-	-
Clough	1	1	0	0	0	0.00	-	-	-	-	1	70	70.00	-	-	1-70
Coe	3	5	1	34	83	20.75	-	-	-	-	6	222	37.00	-	-	2-30
Corby	1	2	0	12	13	6.50	-	-	-	-	0	36	-	-	-	-
Costello	1	1	0	0	0	0.00	-	-	-	-	2	104	52.00	-	-	2-77
Coulston	5	8	1	24	76	10.85	-	-	3	-	19	341	17.94	-	-	4-38
Coutts	6	11	0	41	136	12.36	-	-	1	-						
Cowles	7	14	0	46	324	23.14	-	-	6	-	0	13	-	-	-	-
Crie	3	5	2	3*	7	2.33	-	-	2	-	3	170	56.66	-	-	3-36
Dickson	2	4	0	65	114	28.50	-	1	-	-						
Doull	11	22	4	103	779	43.27	1	5	6	-	0	34	-	-	-	-
Drumm	5	6	3	161*	433	144.33	2	2	-	-	2	175	87.50	-	-	1-24
Duncan	2	3	3	1*	1	-	-	-	1	-	2	115	57.50	-	-	1-37
Dunlop	2	2	0	5	5	2.50	-	-	-	-	3	123	41.00	-	-	1-5
Dunning	6	12	2	71	320	32.00	-	2	5	-	6	170	28.33	-	-	2-16
Ell	1	2	0	1	2	1.00	-	-	-	-	0	55	-	-	-	-
M.Farrell	3	4	0	5	12	3.00	-	-	5	3						
Flavell	6	7	0	204	473	67.57	1	2	2	-						
Francis	5	7	1	19	46	7.66	-	-	2	-	14	362	25.85	-	-	4-72
Fraser	3	-	-	-	-	-	-	-	-	-	4	210	52.50	-	-	2-61
Fruin	6	8	0	80	188	23.50	-	2	3	1						
Fryer	3	1	1	7*	7	-	-	-	1	-	5	154	30.80	-	-	4-37
Gifford	1	2	0	10	12	6.00	-	-	-	-	2	46	23.00	-	-	2-46
Gilchrist	5	3	2	7*	12	12.00	-	-	5	-	14	384	27.42	-	-	3-42
Gooder	1	2	0	11	11	5.50	-	-	-	-	8	73	9.12	1	-	6-42
Gunn	9	12	0	49	194	16.16	-	-	6	1	11	429	39.00	-	-	3-40
Harris	10	7	3	9	26	6.50	-	-	1	-	15	691	46.06	-	-	4-119
Hatcher	4	7	0	23	79	11.28	-	-	-	-						
Henshilwood	1	2	0	41	48	24.00	-	-	-	-	0	14	-	-	-	-
Hockley	19	29	4	126*	1301	52.04	4	7	9	-	5	146	29.20	-	-	2-9
Hollis	1	2	0	24	26	13.00	-	-	-	-	1	81	81.00	-	-	1-81
Illingworth	6	7	3	40*	120	30.00	-	-	5	5						
P.Jagersma	9	13	5	52	271	33.87	-	1	10	2	4	38	9.50	-	-	4-38
Jinuku	1	1	1	23*	23	-	-	-	-	-	1	50	50.00	-	-	1-50
Keenan	5	3	2	26*	32	32.00	-	-	4	-	15	348	23.20	1	-	6-73
Kinsella	6	8	0	53	131	16.37	-	1	3	-						
Lamason	4	6	2	37*	86	21.50	-	-	-	-	2	136	68.00	-	-	2-23
Lamason	4	8	0	24	87	10.87	-	-	-	-	8	264	33.00	-	-	4-51
Legg	3	4	1	26	30	10.00	-	-	-	-	4	149	37.25	-	-	2-57
D.M.Lewis	7	8	0	65	153	19.12	-	1	6	-						
Lird	15	22	3	39*	258	13.57	-	-	5	-	55	1049	19.07	4	1	6-119
Maker	3	4	0	5	10	2.50	-	-	1	-	5	156	31.20	-	-	3-34

	M	In	NO	HS	Runs	Ave	100	50	Ct	St	Wkts	Runs	Ave	5WI	10WM
C.E.Marett	7	13	4	49	304	33.77	-	-	3	-	9	268	29.77	-	-
M.Marks	2	4	1	23	30	10.00	-	-	-	-					
K.McDonald	1	1	0	1	1	1.00	-	-	-	-					
P.F.McKelvey	15	26	2	155*	699	29.12	2	1	8	-					
A.McKenna	7	14	1	97*	465	35.76	-	3	7	-	0	6	-	-	-
R.U.McKenzie	7	13	0	61	295	22.69	-	2	3	-	8	214	26.75	-	-
S.McLauchlan	4	4	0	4	4	1.00	-	-	1	-	2	83	41.50	-	-
E.L.Miller	3	6	0	32	92	15.33	-	-	1	-					
H.Miller	1	2	0	11	11	5.50	-	-	-	-	1	77	77.00	-	-
K.S.Molloy	2	1	1	1*	1	-	-	-	2	-	5	91	18.20	-	-
P.Moore	2	3	1	47*	80	40.00	-	-	3	-	0	31	-	-	-
L.J.Murdoch	6	10	0	72	253	25.30	-	1	1	-					
K.J.Musson	1	-	-	-	-	-	-	-	-	-					
C.M.Nicholson	4	5	0	46	140	28.00	-	-	1	-	5	170	34.00	-	-
A.M.O'Leary	1	1	0	27	27	27.00	-	-	1	-					
J.B.Olson	1	1	0	0	0	0.00	-	-	-	-	0	48	-	-	-
C.M.Oyler	5	8	2	67*	212	35.33	-	1	2	-					
E.A.Paton	4	8	1	77*	180	25.71	-	1	4	-	9	160	17.77	-	-
K.V.Plummer	4	6	0	13	28	4.66	-	-	2	-					
I.J.Powell	7	13	2	63	272	24.72	-	1	9	1					
L.Powell	4	7	0	66	145	20.71	-	1	1	-	0	8	-	-	-
L.M.Prichard	1	2	0	38	43	21.50	-	-	1	-					
S.J.Rattray	9	17	2	59	412	27.46	-	4	1	-	19	461	24.26	1	-
D.Robinson	1	1	1	2*	2	-	-	-	-	-	1	16	16.00	-	-
E.F.Rouse	1	2	0	35	36	18.00	-	-	-	-					
M.T.Rouse	2	4	2	15*	18	9.00	-	-	-	-					
J.A.Russell	1	1	0	39	39	39.00	-	-	-	-	1	37	37.00	-	-
E.M.Ryan	5	8	4	10	38	9.50	-	-	3	11					
J.M.Saulbrey	11	16	4	62	198	16.50	-	1	6	-	35	951	27.17	1	-
P.Savin	1	2	0	15	18	9.00	-	-	-	-					
E.A.Signal	6	6	2	55*	82	20.50	-	1	3	-	8	325	40.62	-	-
R.J.Signal	1	2	1	8*	8	8.00	-	-	-	-	0	21	-	-	-
L.J.Simpson	1	2	0	4	6	3.00	-	-	-	-					
E.M.Sinclair	2	4	1	10	26	8.66	-	-	2	-					
C.Sinton	1	2	0	10	14	7.00	-	-	-	-					
J.E.Stead	9	18	2	95	433	27.06	-	3	3	-					
J.M.Stonell	4	8	0	47	127	15.87	-	-	2	-					
G.Sutherland	3	6	0	22	66	11.00	-	-	1	-	2	86	43.00	-	-
R.Symons	1	1	0	5	5	5.00	-	-	1	-	2	71	35.50	-	-
P.Taylor	1	2	0	3	3	1.50	-	-	-	-	1	62	62.00	-	-
H.M.Thompson	1	2	1	17*	17	17.00	-	-	1	-	0	18	-	-	-
B.I.Thorner	3	6	1	37	76	15.20	-	-	-	-	4	78	19.50	-	-
J.A.Turner	6	8	1	11*	30	4.28	-	-	2	-	19	469	24.68	-	-
N.J.Turner	6	9	2	65*	208	29.71	-	2	1	-					
F.M.Webb	4	8	0	42	110	13.75	-	-	-	-	6	66	11.00	-	-
E.White	3	5	0	17	33	6.60	-	-	-	-	2	85	42.50	-	-
U.Wickham	2	4	0	34	40	10.00	-	-	-	-	3	76	25.33	-	-
N.M.Williams	4	5	1	35*	70	17.50	-	-	1	-	3	158	52.66	-	-
T.Woodbury	2	3	3	7*	7	-	-	-	-	-	4	100	25.00	-	-

ONE-DAY INTERNATIONAL
CAREER RECORDS

	M	In	NO	HS	Runs	Ave	100s	50s	Ct	St		O	M	R	W	Ave	R/O	Best
E.P.Allan	7	6	1	17	42	8.40	-	-	2	-		59	8	162	3	54.00	2.75	1-22
T.L.Anderson	26	25	0	85	440	17.60	-	2	9	-								
L.M.Astle	1	-	-	-	-	-	-	-	-	-								
E.A.Badham	13	10	1	30	86	9.55	-	-	5	-		135.3	33	290	12	24.16	2.14	2-14
H.R.Bastion	3	-	-	-	-	-	-	-	1	-		20	2	57	2	28.50	2.85	1-12
B.L.Bevege	16	16	1	101	488	32.53	1	3	3	-		22.2	7	48	3	16.00	2.16	3-17
B.A.Brentnall	5	3	0	18	40	13.33	-	-	3	3								
K.D.Brown	14	6	3	9*	19	6.33	-	-	4	-		86.4	14	252	10	25.20	2.90	2-8
S.H.Brown	18	9	4	17*	59	11.80	-	-	5	-		170	63	308	19	16.21	1.81	2-3
N.J.Browne	19	8	3	17	35	7.00	-	-	5	-		114.4	1337xx5		13	28.84	3.27	4-20
S.K.Burke	1	-	-	-	-	-	-	-	-	-		10	1	37	1	37.00	3.70	1-37
J.A.Burley	2	1	0	7	7	7.00	-	-	-	-		13	3	28	0	-	2.15	-
V.L.Burtt	9	8	0	46	168	21.00	-	-	4	-		6	0	31	2	15.50	5.17	2-31
D.Caird	4	4	1	45	72	24.00	-	-	-	-								
C.A.Campbell	85	30	15	12	69	4.60	-	-	15	-		753	150	2018	78	25.87	2.68	3-15
P.F.Carrick	3	2	1	6*	7	7.00	-	-	1	-		29	1	106	6	17.66	3.66	3-43
J.Clark	31	31	1	85	875	29.16	-	7	5	-								
A.M.Corbin	12	8	5	16*	57	19.00	-	-	5	-		76.1	10	269	13	20.69	3.53	3-13
D.A.Costello	7	2	1	1	1	1.00	-	-	1	-		56.4	8	139	2	69.50	2.45	2-37
S.D.Cowles	5	5	0	46	93	18.60	-	-	2	-		5	0	24	0	-	4.80	-
J.D.Doull	5	5	0	42	64	12.80	-	-	2	-								
E.C.Drumm	89	82	11	116	2424	34.14	2	16	21	-		257	53	778	37	21.02	3.02	4-31
J.R.Dunning	22	21	4	89	346	20.35	-	1	4	-		157	12	527	13	40.53	3.36	3-29
P.B.Flannery	12	12	2	49*	206	20.60	-	-	3	-								
K.E.Flavell	38	33	9	54	719	29.95	-	2	5	-		70	15	156	7	22.28	2.23	2-5
D.L.Ford	3	2	0	35	46	23.00	-	-	1	-		6	0	32	0	-	5.33	-
F.E.Fraser	5	3	2	54*	94	94.00	-	1	1	-								
L.M.Fraser	13	7	1	8	31	5.16	-	-	2	-		117	20	294	12	24.50	2.51	3-21
M.K.Fruin	23	23	4	51	385	20.26	-	1	4	1								
J.A.Fryer	7	1	1	1*	1	-	-	-	-	-		33	9	115	10	11.50	3.48	3-8
S.M.Gilchrist	8	5	1	12	19	4.75	-	-	4	-		77	21	202	7	28.85	2.62	3-20
A.J.Green	4	3	2	17*	17	17.00	-	-	1	-		31	5	98	2	49.00	3.16	1-19
P.A.Gruber	2	1	0	0	0	0.00	-	-	-	-		10	3	35	0	-	3.50	-
K.V.Gunn	45	34	9	52	461	18.44	-	1	14	-		458.5	110	1113	53	21.00	2.42	5-22
K.Hadlee	1	1	0	14	14	14.00	-	-	-	-								
L.R.V.S.Harford	3	3	0	9	20	6.66	-	-	-	-		7	0	30	0	-	4.29	-
J.E.Harris	45	24	12	19*	99	8.25	-	-	9	-		414.2	98	1124	61	18.42	2.71	4-8
S.A.Harris	2	1	1	1*	1	-	-	-	-	-		3	0	19	0	-	6.33	-
C.E.Henshilwood	2	1	1	15*	15	-	-	-	-	-								
D.A.Hockley	118	115	18	117	4064	41.89	4	34	41	-		253.4	41	853	20	42.65	3.36	3-49
S.L.Illingworth	37	29	7	51	342	15.54	-	1	27	21								
I.C.P.Jagersma	34	27	4	58*	453	19.69	-	2	24	9		22	5	48	4	12.00	2.18	2-14
Y.Kainuku	2	2	0	4	4	2.00	-	-	-	-		12	2	49	0	-	4.08	-
K.M.Keenan	55	36	9	57*	348	12.88	-	1	9	-		452	72	1253	70	17.90	2.77	4-5
F.S.King	15	10	3	31	81	11.57	-	-	2	-		108.1	14	404	21	19.23	3.73	4-24
P.D.Kinsella	20	20	3	57	443	26.05	-	2	-	-								
K.Le Comber	15	14	4	135*	442	44.20	1	2	2	-								
B.J.Legg	18	13	3	17	79	7.90	-	-	2	-		199.4	62	394	20	19.70	1.97	3-4
M.A.M.Lewis	49	44	10	105	812	23.88	1	2	20	-		5	0	32	0	-	6.40	-
L.Lindsay	2	1	0	27	27	27.00	-	-	-	-		13	0	42	2	21.00	3.23	2-26
J.Lord	15	13	0	25	101	7.76	-	-	2	-		132.3	25	318	25	12.72	2.40	6-10
M.L.Lynch	4	4	0	29	80	20.00	-	-	-	-								
C.E.Marett	14	12	2	24	149	14.90	-	-	-	-		126.5	30	310	16	19.37	2.44	3-14
A.L.Mason	22	16	2	34	239	17.07	-	-	8	-		183.4	32	569	28	20.32	3.09	4-26
E.T.McDonald	3	-	-	-	-	-	-	-	1	-		24	4	50	5	10.00	2.08	2-17
K.McDonald	6	6	0	34	80	13.33	-	-	1	-								
S.J.McGlashan	13	11	4	41*	167	23.85	-	-	1	-								
P.F.McKelvey	15	14	4	42	214	21.40	-	-	2	-								
A.McKenna	14	13	0	39	214	16.46	-	-	-	-								
S.McLauchlan	29	21	5	34*	137	8.56	-	-	6	-		227.5	47	665	19	35.00	2.91	2-6
L.E.Milliken	9	-	-	-	-	-	-	-	4	-		41	4	147	3	49.00	3.58	2-13
K.S.Molloy	5	2	1	0*	0	0.00	-	-	2	-		36	8	99	4	24.75	2.75	2-16

	M	In	NO	HS	Runs	Ave	100s	50s	Ct	St	O	M	R	W	Ave	R/O	Best
S.R.M.Morris	8	1	0	5	5	5.00	-	-	-	-	69	12	175	7	25.00	2.54	2-13
L.J.Murdoch	25	22	3	69	417	21.94	-	1	4	-							
K.J.Musson	13	10	2	31	86	10.75	-	-	3	-	87.2	12	253	10	25.30	2.89	3-22
C.M.Nicholson	35	22	10	73*	195	16.25	-	1	13	-	272.4	62	707	38	18.60	2.59	4-18
A.M.O'Leary	19	18	3	91*	497	33.13	-	3	3	-							
J.B.Olson	4	4	1	9*	17	5.66	-	-	-	-	27	9	52	4	13.00	1.93	3-16
G.L.Page	2	1	0	5	5	5.00	-	-	-	-	17.2	3	46	6	7.66	2.65	6-20
N.Payne	65	64	7	93	1178	20.66	-	4	17	-	158	48	407	20	20.35	2.57	3-20
M.H.Peters	16	12	5	24	79	11.28	-	-	3	-	155.5	63	291	19	15.31	1.86	2-3
K.V.Plummer	11	10	1	32	100	11.11	-	-	2	-	10	0	36	0	-	3.60	-
L.M.Powell	5	4	0	70	73	18.25	-	1	1	-							
K.L.Pulford	25	20	0	95	388	19.40	-	2	7	-	74.1	6	271	12	22.58	3.65	4-5
R.J.Pullar	43	25	11	27*	176	12.57	-	-	14	-	354	61	1019	64	15.92	2.87	5-7
K.A.Ramel	47	37	7	41	519	17.30	-	-	13	-	204.3	26	729	35	20.82	3.56	3-26
S.J.Rattray	15	15	7	60*	305	38.12	-	1	1	-	123.1	16	399	11	36.27	3.23	2-33
R.J.Rolls	64	52	2	114	1343	26.86	1	8	48	32							
E.F.Rouse	3	3	0	48	90	30.00	-	-	-	-							
J.A.Russell	5	4	1	8*	8	2.66	-	-	-	-	26	3	84	1	84.00	3.23	1-20
E.M.Ryan	15	5	1	6*	17	4.25	-	-	13	8							
J.M.Saulbrey	5	5	3	22*	75	37.50	-	-	-	-	43	12	100	4	25.00	2.33	2-32
V.S.Sexton	2	2	0	9	12	6.00	-	-	-	-							
E.A.Signal	19	12	5	28*	79	11.28	-	-	5	-	130.3	23	496	7	70.85	3.80	2-26
R.J.Signal	6	3	1	8	12	6.00	-	-	2	-	27	2	89	2	44.50	3.30	1-10
L.J.Simpson	12	11	1	23*	95	9.50	-	-	1	-							
R.J.Steele	6	3	2	5*	9	9.00	-	-	2	-	60	9	186	8	23.25	3.10	3-31
H.M.Tiffen	44	39	8	87	903	29.12	-	5	11	-	236	40	746	44	16.95	3.16	4-43
E.A.Travers	3	-	-	-	-	-	-	-	-	-							
D.M.Trow	2	1	1	1*	1	-	-	-	1	-	12	3	18	4	4.50	1.50	3-8
M.F.Tunupopo	3	-	-	-	-	-	-	-	2	-	18	4	57	0	-	3.17	-
J.A.Turner	30	14	2	15	54	4.50	-	-	6	-	265.2	42	695	28	24.82	2.61	5-5
N.J.Turner	28	26	2	114	624	26.00	1	2	4	-							
H.M.Watson	19	13	3	24	98	9.80	-	-	8	-	42	5	132	11	12.00	3.14	3-14
N.M.Williams	19	13	2	21*	80	7.27	-	-	1	-	110.5	19	374	15	24.93	3.37	3-37

NEW ZEALAND
FIRST-CLASS RECORDS

to 1 September 2003

FIRST-CLASS MATCH DEFINED

The six countries represented at Imperial Cricket Conference on 19 May 1947, reached agreement in regard to definition of a first-class match. This did not have effect retrospectively.

A match of three or more days' duration between two sides of eleven players officially adjudged first-class shall be regarded as a first-class fixture. Matches in which either team has more than eleven players or which are scheduled for less than three days shall not be regarded as first-class. The governing body in each country shall decide the status of teams.

The records have been compiled on the following basis:

    (1) Otago and Canterbury from 1863/64 to date
    (2) Wellington and Auckland from 1873/74 to date
    (3) Nelson from 1873/74 to 1891/92 inclusive
    (4) West Coast (North Island) 1879/80
    (5) Taranaki from 1882/83 to 1897/98 inclusive
    (6) Hawke's Bay from 1883/84 to 1920/21 inclusive
    (7) Southland from 1914/15 to 1920/21 inclusive
    (8) Central Districts from 1950/51 to date
    (9) Northern Districts from 1956/57 to date

Notes:

• Games played by the Melbourne Cricket Club teams of 1899/1900, 1905/1906 and 1926/27, are not treated as first-class in accordance with a decision of the New Zealand Cricket Council.

• Although set down for only two days each, the return matches played by A. Sims' Australian XI in 1913/14 against Canterbury and Wellington are included in these records; so is the match An Australian XI v Minor Associations, 1920/21, and MCC v Wellington, 1932/33.

• From 1933/34 season onwards, only games for which at least three days have been set down are treated as first-class.

• There have now been 1918 first-class matches in New Zealand.

• Unless otherwise stated, the first-class records relate to first-class matches in New Zealand and by New Zealand touring teams overseas. Apart from the games which have taken place in New Zealand, there are a further 539 played by New Zealand overseas as follows:

in Australia	1898/99 to 2001/02	80
in England	1927 to 1999	287
in South Africa	1953/54 to 2000/01	47
in Pakistan	1955/56 to 2001/02	33
in India	1955/56 to 1999/00	40
in West Indies	1971/72 to 2001/02	26
in Sri Lanka	1983/84 to 2002/03	16
in Zimbabwe	1992/93 to 2000/01	10

plus four games by Young New Zealand in Zimbabwe in 1984/85, three games by New Zealand Young Internationals in Zimbabwe 1988/89, one match by Wellington in Australia 1990/91, one match by Canterbury in South Africa 1993/94, three matches by New Zealand Academy in South Africa 1997/98 and six games by New Zealand A in England 2000.

GROUNDS

Ground	No of matches	First and most recent match		Highest and lowest team totals			Highest Innings Best Bowling			
1 South Dunedin Recreation Ground	9	O v C 1863/64	O v C 1877/78	C 272	v O	1875/76	75	H.W. Moore	C v O	1877/78
				MCC 34	v O	1863/64	8-28	W. Hendley	O v C	1869/70
2 Hagley Park *(old)* Christchurch	1	C v O 1864/65	only match	O 80	v O	1864/65	22	J. Fulton	O v C	1864/65
				O 61	v C	1864/65	5-17	J.W. Stevens	C v O	1864/65
3 Hagley Park *(new)* Christchurch	30	C v O 1866/67	C v O 2002/03	SC 554	v Pk A	1998/99	301	P.G. Fulton	C v A	2002/03
				C 25	v O	1866/67	10-28	A.E. Moss	C v W	1889/90
4 Basin Reserve Wellington	360	W v A 1873/74	W v A 2002/03	NZ 671-4	v SL	1990/91	299	M.D. Crowe	NZ v SL	1990/91
				W 22	v C	1903/04	9-43	T. Eden	N v W	1875/76
5 Victory Square Nelson	7	N v W 1874/75	N v W 1887/88	N 150	v A	1882/83	31	C.A. Knapp	W v N	1874/75
				W 19	v N	1885/86	8-26	F.H. Cooke	N v W	1887/88
6 Domain Auckland	33	A v C 1877/78	A v C 1912/13	A 579	v O	1909/10	151*	Harold B. Lusk	C v A	1910/11
				A 13	v C	1877/78	9-75	R. Neill	A v C	1891/92
7 Caledonian Ground Dunedin	4	O v C 1879/80	O v W 1904/05	O 297	v W	1904/05	88	H.G. Seideberg	O v W	1904/05
				A 48	v O	1889/90	8-36	A.W. Rees	A v O	1889/90
8 Lancaster Park § Christchurch	332	C v A 1882/83	NZ v E 2001/02	C 777	v O	1996/97	385	B. Sutcliffe	O v C	1952/53
				O 35	v A	1884/85	9-72	F.H. Cooke	O v C	1884/85
9 Botanical Gardens Nelson	1	N v W 1883/84	only match	N 56	v W	1883/84	17	L. Fowler	N v W	1883/84
				W 30	v N	1883/84	5-10	G. Fowler	N v W	1883/84
10 Carisbrook Dunedin	248	O v Tas 1883/84	O v ND 2002/03	NSW 752-8d	v O	1923/24	355	B. Sutcliffe	O v A	1949/50
				C 27	v O	1896/97	9-50	A.H. Fisher	O v Q'ld	1896/97
11 Recreation Ground Napier	20½	HB v W 1884/85	HB v A 1912/13	MCC 394	v HB	1906/07	188	C.G. Wilson	O v HB	1908/09
				HB 42	v C	1897/98	9-47	T.H. Dent	HB v W	1900/01
12 Farndon Park Napier	4½	HB v T 1891/92	HB v Q'ld 1896/97	Q'ld 492	v HB	1896/97	135	O.W. Cowley	Q'ld v HB	1896/97
				T 39	v HB	1891/92	8-14	S.W. Austin	NSW v HB	1893/94
13 King Edward Park Hawera	2	T v HB 1891/92	T v Fiji 1894/95	T 135	v Fiji	1894/95	62	Hugh B. Lusk	HB v T	1891/92
				T 29	v HB	1891/92	7-?	C.R. Smith	HB v T	1891/92
14 Bayly Park Hawera	2	T v HB 1896/97	T v C 1897/98	C 260	v T	1897/98	106	W.J. Crawshaw	T v HB	1896/97
				HB 100	v T	1896/97	6-43	D. Reese	C v T	1897/98
15 Victoria Park Auckland	3	A v C 1908/09	A v HB 1910/11	A 470	v HB	1910/11	88	W. Carlton	C v A	1909/10
				HB 28	v A	1910/11	7-42	A.E. Relf	A v C	1908/09
16 Nelson Cricket Ground Hastings	3	HB v W 1913/14	HB v C 1914/15	C 337	v HB	1914/15	111	V.S. Ransford	Aust v HB	1913/14
				HB 89	v C	1914/15	8-51	A.A. Mailey	Aust v HB	1913/14
17 Eden Park Auckland	229	A v Aust 1913/14	NZ v E 2001/02	A 693-9d	v C	1939/40	336*	W.R. Hammond	E v NZ	1932/33
				NZ 26	v E	1954/55	9-36	A.F. Wensley	A v O	1929/30
18 Rugby Park Invercargill	5	S v O 1914/15	S v Aust 1920/21	Aust 195	v S	1920/21	71	A. Galland	O v S	1919/20
				C 37	v S	1920/21	8-84	D.J. McBeath	S v C	1920/21
19 Nelson Park Napier	4	HB v W 1919/20	CD v C 1989/90	Aust 405-8d	v HB	1920/21	158	V.S. Ransford	Aust v HB	1920/21
				CD 153	v W	1985/86	5-51	F.S. Middleton	W v HB	1919/20
20 Wellington College Ground	1	W v A 1923/24	only match	W 569	v A	1923/24	163	J.S. Hiddleston	W v A	1923/24
				A 280	v W	1923/24	6-172	S.G. Smith	A v W	1923/24
21 Sportsground † Palmerston North	47	CD v C 1950/51	CD v A 2001/02	C 534	v CD	1994/95	214*	B.C. Booth	Aust v CD	1966/67
				A 71	v CD	2001/02	7-31	H.B. Cave	CD v A	1952/53
22 Pukekura Park New Plymouth	47	CD v A 1950/51	CD v C 2001/02	O 543-8d	v CD	1978/79	242	M.D. Crowe	CD v O	1989/90
				CD 59	v A	1958/59	9-100	B.W. Yuile	CD v C	1965/66
23 McLean Park Napier	47	CD v O 1951/52	CD v C 2002/03	O 571-8	v CD	1995/96	200	R.A. Lawson	O v CD	1995/96
				NZ XI 93	v P	1993/94	7-31	Abdul Qadir	P v Shell XI	1988/89
24 Trafalgar Park Nelson	28	N v W 1891/92	CD v ND 1996/97	CD 448-3d	v O	1968/69	202*	B.E. Congdon	CD v O	1968/69
				CD 65	v W	1995/96	7-23	B.A. Bolton	C v CD	1961/62
25 Cook's Gardens Wanganui	17	CD v WI 1955/56	CD v YNZ 1979/80	MCC 376-7d	v CD	1960/61	138	M.G. Burgess	A v CD	1976/77
				CD 71	v ND	1962/63	8-37	D.B. Clarke	ND v CD	1962/63
26 Seddon Park • Hamilton	137	ND v A 1956/57	ND v CD 2002/03	W 608-9d	v ND	1998/99	219	M.D. Bell	W v ND	1998/99
				ND 32	v A	1996/97	9-48	A.R. Tait	ND v A	1996/97

† *now Fitzherbert Park*   • *now Westpac Park*   § *now Jade Stadium*

New Zealand First-class Records

Ground	No of matches	First and most recent match		Highest and lowest team totals				Highest Innings / Best Bowling			
27	Tauranga Domain / Tauranga (Inner)	1	ND v CD 1965/66 / only match	CD / ND	232 / 163	v ND / v CD	1965/66 / 1965/66	64 / 5-41	G.V. Giles / B.W. Yuile	ND v CD / CD v ND	1965/66 / 1965/66
28	Tauranga Domain / Tauranga (Outer)	6	ND v C 1978/79 / ND v A 1985/86	ND / O	370 / 90	v O / v ND	1982/83 / 1982/83	127 / 6-75	J.G. Gibson / D.A. Stirling	ND v C / CD v ND	1978/79 / 1981/82
29	Cobham Oval / Whangarei	11	ND v A 1966/67 / ND v C 2000/01	ND / ND	363 / 127	v CD / v A	1983/84 / 1966/67	195 / 7-30	J.M. Parker / R.S. Cunis	ND v C / A v ND	1972/73 / 1966/67
30	Queen Elizabeth Park / Masterton	12	CD v A 1966/67 / CD v W 2002/03	CD / CD	414-7d v A / 86	v A	1998/99 / 1966/67	189 / 6-33	M.S. Sinclair / A.J. Penn	CD v W / W v CD	1996/97 / 2002/03
31	Smallbone Park / Rotorua	17	ND v O 1968/69 / ND v CD 1995/96	CD / A	456 / 72	v ND / v ND	1995/96 / 1991/92	237* / 7-74	R.T. Latham / G.D. Alabaster	C v ND / O v ND	1990/91 / 1968/69
32	Cornwall Park / Auckland	3	A v U23 1970/71 / A v W 2000/01	A / A / A	274-8d v U23 / 274-9d v U23 / 75	v W	1970/71 / 1976/77 / 2000/01	102 / 8-75	R.W. Morgan / H.J. Howarth	A v U23 / A v U23	1970/71 / 1976/77
33	Horton Park / Blenheim	10	CD v ND 1972/73 / CD v A 2002/03	CD / ND	538 / 100	v C / v CD	2000/01 / 2001/02	212* / 7-36	D.P. Kelly / A.M. Schwass	CD v C / CD v ND	2000/01 / 2001/02
34	Harry Barker Reserve / Gisborne	18	ND v O 1974/75 / ND v A 2002/03	ND / O	474 / 77	v W / v ND	1996/97 / 1999/00	161* / 6-32	V.R. Brown / S.B. Styris	C v ND / ND v O	1986/87 / 1999/00
35	Eden Park No. 2 † / Auckland	71	A v CD 1975/76 / A v ND 2002/03	CD / CD	594-8d v A / 61	v A / v A	1995/96 / 1996/97	241 / 7-27	M.J. Horne / N.A. Mallender	O v A / O v A	1997/98 / 1984/85
36	Queen's Park / Invercargill	13	O v CD 1975/76 / O v CD 2002/03	CD / O	348 / 68	v O / v C	1996/97 / 1977/78	162 / 8-31	B.A. Edgar / D.G. Sewell	W v O / O v CD	1989/90 / 1996/97
37	Bledisloe Park / Pukekohe	2	ND v A 1976/77 / ND v W 1989/90	W / ND	297-5d v ND / 152	v W	1989/90 / 1989/90	123 / 5-27	R.H. Vance / G.R. Larsen	W v ND / W v ND	1989/90 / 1989/90
38	Hutt Recreation Ground / Lower Hutt	14	W v ND 1976/77 / W v C 1985/86	W / W	316 / 93	v O / v WI	1983/84 / 1979/80	145* / 8-24	J.G. Wright / E.J. Chatfield	ND v W / W v ND	1978/79 / 1979/80
39	Logan Park / Dunedin	3	O v U23 1977/78 / O v C 1979/80	O / O	313 / 127	v U23 / v C	1977/78 / 1979/80	106 / 6-44	J.M. Parker / P.J. Petherick	ND v O / O v U23	1978/79 / 1977/78
40	Temuka Oval / Temuka	1	YNZ v E 1977/78 / only match	E / YNZ	310 / 139	v YNZ / v E	1977/78 / 1977/78	104 / 6-71	D.W. Randall / G. Miller	E v YNZ / E v YNZ	1977/78 / 1977/78
41	Molyneux Park / Alexandra	26	O v CD 1978/79 / O v W 2002/03	CD / O	444-8d v O / 81	v CD	2001/02 / 2001/02	179 / 8-27	K.R. Rutherford / J.T.C. Vaughan	O v CD / A v O	1988/89 / 1996/97
42	University Oval / Dunedin	5	O v Pak 1978/79 / O v E 1983/84	O / O	396-6d v CD / 46	v Pak	1982/83 / 1978/79	143 / 6-20	B.R. Blair / R.J. Webb	O v CD / O v C	1982/83 / 1983/84
43	Maidstone Park / Upper Hutt	1	W v CD 1979/80 / only match	W / CD	216 / 50	v CD / v W	1979/80 / 1979/80	63 / 6-17	B.R. Taylor / J.V. Coney	W v CD / W v CD	1979/80 / 1979/80
44	Dudley Park / Rangiora	15	C v W 1984/85 / C v W 2002/03	C / C	543-8d v CD / 62	v A	1996/97 / 1998/99	251* / 7-17	C.Z. Harris / S.J. Maguiness	C v CD / W v C	1996/97 / 1984/85
45	Centennial Park / Oamaru	9	O v CD 1984/85 / O v W 1998/99	O / C	430 / 94	v CD / v O	1984/85 / 1994/95	182 / 6-36	K.R. Rutherford / S.W. Duff	O v W / CD v O	1987/88 / 1985/86
46	Levin Domain / Levin	3	CD v C 1985/86 / CD v W 1987/88	CD / C	435-5d v CD / 68	v CD	1987/88 / 1985/86	205* / 6-28	E.B. McSweeney / P.J. Visser	W v CD / CD v C	1987/88 / 1985/86
47	Recreational Ground / Morrinsville	2	ND v CD 1986/87 / ND v W 1988/89	CD / ND	368-3d v ND / 198	v CD	1986/87 / 1986/87	151 / 5-71	M.D. Crowe / K.W. Martin	CD v ND / CD v ND	1986/87 / 1986/87
48	Albert Park / Te Awamutu	1	ND v CD 1987/88 / only match	ND / ND	259 / 135	v CD / v ND	1987/88 / 1987/88	94 / 4-41	B.A. Young / B.J. Barrett	ND v CD / ND v CD	1987/88 / 1987/88
49	Victoria Park / Wanganui	11	CD v ND 1990/91 / CD v O 2002/03	W / CC	506-4d v CD / 103	v ND / v SC	1993/94 / 1997/98	203* / 6-20	M.S. Sinclair / B.C. Strang	CD v ND / Z v NZ XI	1998/99 / 1995/96
50	Burnside Park / Christchurch	1	C v CD 1991/92 / only match	C / C	189-7 v CD / 124	v CD	1991/92 / 1991/92	63 / 6-67	T.E. Blain / D.J. Leonard	CD v C / CD v C	1991/92 / 1991/92
51	Petone Recreation / Ground, Lower Hutt	2	W v O 1991/92 / W v A 1998/99	W / W	300-8d v W / 142	v O	1991/92 / 1991/92	107 / 5-37	E.B. McSweeney / N.A. Mallender	W v O / O v W	1991/92 / 1991/92
52	Sunnyvale / Dunedin	1	O v A 1992/93 / only match	O / A	193 / 105	v A / v O	1992/93 / 1992/93	51 / 4-21	I.S. Billcliff / N.A. Mallender	O v A / O v A	1992/93 / 1992/93
53	Lincoln Green / Lincoln	5	NZA v B 1997/98 / NZA v SA 1998/99	NZA / B	459-8d v PkA / 130	v NZA	1998/99 / 1997/98	190 / 6-69	M.E. Parlane / Fazal-e-Akber	NZA v B / Pk A v NZA	1997/98 / 1998/99

† now Eden Park Outer Oval

Ground	No of matches	First and most recent match		Highest and lowest team totals			Highest Innings Best Bowling			
54 Aorangi Park Timaru	3	C v Z C v CD	1997/98 2002/03	Z C	422-8d v C 100 v Z	1997/98 1997/98	196 6-56	A.D.R. Campbell M.J. Mason	Z v C CD v C	19 20
55 Owen Delany Park Taupo	6	ND v O ND v W	1998/99 2002/03	WI A	450 v NZ A 131 v ND	1999/00 1999/00	216* 7-33	S. Chanderpaul B.P. Martin	WI v NZ 'A' ND v A	19 19
56 Colin Maiden Park Auckland	6	A v ND A v CD	1998/99 2002/03	A A	478 v ND 182 v ND	2002/03 1999/00	175* 5-64	G.J. Hopkins A.R. Adams	C v A A v ND	20 19
57 Queen Elizabeth II Park Christchurch	11	C v O C v ND	1998/99 2001/02	ND C	496-8d v C 114 v O	2001/02 1998/99	235 7-69	J.A.H. Marshall D.R. Tuffey	ND v C ND v C	20 20
58 BIL Oval † Lincoln	3	NI v E A NZ A v P	1999/00 2000/01	NI Pak	371 v E A 100 v NZ A	1999/00 2000/01	182 6-70	M.S. Sinclair A. Sheriyar	NI v E 'A' E 'A' v NZ'A'	19 19
59 Queenstown Events Centre	2	O v E O v A	2001/02 2002/03	O E	273-6d v A 153 v O	2002/03 2001/02	128 6-74	C.D. Cumming K.P. Walmsley	O v A O v A	20 20
60 North Harbour Stadium Auckland	1	A v O only match	2002/03	A O	289 v O 185 v A	2002/03 2002/03	157 4-34	T.G. McIntosh S.B. O'Connor	A v O O v A	20 20

† *now Bert Sutcliffe Oval*

PROVINCIAL CAREER RECORDS

Performances for the following teams are not included in the Provincial Career Records:

Team	Opponent	
D. Reese's Canterbury XI	Wellington	1913/14
Canterbury/Otago	MCC	1936/37
Auckland/Wellington	MCC	1936/37
Auckland XI	New Zealand	1957/58
ND/CD	MCC	1958/59
Otago Invitation XI	MCC	1962/63
Canterbury XI	New Zealand Touring Team	1967/68

Most Games for One Province

129 players have now represented their province on 50 or more occasions in first-class cricket.

120	Gray E.J.	W		76	Germon L.K.	C		60	Parsons A.E.W.	A
119	Vance R.H.	W		76	Douglas M.W.	CD		60	Sutcliffe B.	O
115	Bradburn G.E.	ND		75	Parker J.M.	ND		60	Roberts S.J.	C
108	Lees W.K.	O		75*	McCullum S.J.	O		59	Blair R.W.	W
104	Roberts A.D.G.	ND		74	Coney J.V.	W		59	Crowe J.J.	A
103	McEwan P.E.	C		73	Sparling J.T.	A		59	Smith I.D.S.	CD
102	McSweeney E.B.	W		72	Hastings B.F.	C		59	Turner G.M.	O
101	Latham R.T.	C		72	Troup G.B.	A		59	Hartland B.R.	C
99	White D.J.	ND		72	Wells J.D.	W		59	Smith L.D.	O
97	Shrimpton M.J.F.	CD		69	Alabaster G.D.	O		58	Dowling G.T.	C
93	Young B.A.	ND		69	Reid J.F.	A		58	Howarth G.P.	ND
90	Blair B.R.	O		69*	Boyle D.J.	C		58	Patrick W.R.	C
90*	Dickeson C.W.	ND		68	Burgess M.G.	A		58	Reid J.R.	W
90	Morgan R.W.	A		68	Cameron F.J.	O		58	Ritchie T.D.	W
90	McGregor S.N.	O		68	Sinclair B.W.	W		58	Thomson K.	C
90	O'Sullivan D.R.	CD		68	Rutherford K.R.	O		58	Vivian G.E.	A
89	Morrison J.F.M.	W		67	Edwards G.N.	CD		58	Gaffaney C.B.	O
88	Boock S.L.	O		67	Harris R.M.	A		57	Bull C.L.	C
88	Franklin T.J.	A		67	Patel D.N.	A		57	Burns K.J.	O
88	Priest M.W.	C		66	Puna N.	ND		57	Petrie E.C.	ND
87	Edgar B.A.	W		65	Alabaster J.C.	O		57	Sulzberger G.P.	CD
85	Duff S.W.	CD		65	Brown V.R.	C		57	Harris C.Z.	C
84	Chatfield E.J.	W		65	Hunt A.J.	A		57	Lawson R.A.	O
83	Blain T.E.	CD		65	Webb P.N.	A		56	Brice A.W.S.	W
82	Dunning B.	ND		65*	Wright M.J.E.	ND		56	Motz R.C.	C
82	Hadlee B.G.	C		65	Stead G.R.	C		56	Barnes A.C.	A
82	Kuggeleijn C.M.	ND		64	Parlane M.E.	ND		55	Bradburn W.P.	ND
82	Hart M.N.	ND		64	Murray B.A.G.	W		55	Congdon B.E.	CD
81	Blair W.L.	O		63	Rutherford I.A.	O		55	Jordan A.B.	CD
81	Briasco P.S.	CD		63*	Stott L.W.	A		55	Mills G.H.	O
80	Howarth H.J.	A		62	Cunis R.S.	A		55	Snedden M.C.	A
80	Hoskin R.N.	O		62	Hadlee R.J.	C		54	Bilby G.P.	W
80	Hart R.G.	ND		62*	Smith C.J.P.	CD		54*	Crocker L.M.	ND
79	Larsen G.R.	W		62*	Cooper B.G.	ND		54	Cromb I.B.	C
78	Mallender N.A.	O		61	Yuile B.W.	CD		54	McGirr H.M.	W
78	Robertson G.K.	CD		61	Campbell K.O.	O		54	Moir A.M.	O
78	Bailey M.D.	ND		61	Greatbatch M.J.	CD		54	Sutton R.E.	A
77	McIntyre J.M.	A		60	Milburn B.D.	O		54	Ward J.T.	C
77	Stead D.W.	C		60	Newdick G.A.	W		54	Dobbs P.W.	O

53	Colquhoun I.A.	CD		53	Watson W.	A		51	Thomson S.A.	ND
53*	Pierce R.A.	CD		52*	Cederwall B.W.	W		51	Nevin C.J.	W
53*	Schofield R.M.	CD		51*	Knight A.R.	O		50	Boxshall C.	C
53	Toynbee M.H.	CD		51	Brown S.W.	A		50	Butler L.C.	W

* entire first-class career

Longest Careers for One Province

Seasons

34	Read R.J.	Canterbury	1904/05-1937/38
31	Reese T.W.	Canterbury	1887/88-1917/18
29	Luckie M.M.F.	Wellington	1891/92-1919/20
27	Fowke J.N.	Canterbury	1880/81-1906/07
27	Downes A.D.	Otago	1887/88-1913/14
27	Dempster C.S.	Wellington	1921/22-1947/48
26	Reese D.	Canterbury	1895/96-1920/21
26	Knight A.R.	Otago	1918/19-1943/44
25	Moorhouse H.M.	Canterbury	1883/84-1907/08
25	Tucker K.H.	Wellington	1895/96-1919/20
25	Garrard D.R.	Auckland	1917/18-1941/42

Most Consecutive Games for One Province

74	White D.J.	Northern Districts	1985/86-1992/93
73	Hart R.G.	Northern Districts	1992/93-2002/03
70	O'Sullivan D.R.	Central Districts	1974/75-1982/83
64	Germon L.K.	Canterbury	1987/88-1993/94
63	Stead D.W.	Canterbury	1975/76-1983/84
60	Smith C.J.P.	Central Districts	1984/85-1990/91
59	Puna N.	Northern Districts	1957/58-1968/69
57	Edwards G.N.	Central Districts	1975/76-1981/82
56	Young B.A.	Northern Districts	1983/84-1989/90
54*	Cromb I.B.	Canterbury	1929/30-1946/47
54	Roberts A.D.G.	Northern Districts	1970/71-1978/79
54	Burns K.J.	Otago	1984/85-1990/91
53	Alabaster G.D.	Otago	1963/64-1972/73
52	Smith L.D.	Otago	1940/41-1955/56
52	Duff S.W.	Central Districts	1989/90-1994/95
51	Morrison J.F.M.	Wellington	1975/76-1982/83
51	Reid J.F.	Auckland	1976/77-1982/83
51	McEwan P.E.	Canterbury	1984/85-1990/91

* his complete career

Highest Averages

2000 RUNS/45.00 AVE	Province	M	In	NO	HS	Runs	Ave	100
Hick G.A.	ND	17	30	4	211*	2055	79.03	10
Crowe M.D.	CD	32	55	7	242	3299	68.72	13
Harris C.Z.	C	57	83	23	251*	3864	64.40	9
Scott V.J.	A	44	74	15	204	3546	60.10	11
Sutcliffe B.	O	60	110	8	385	6028	59.09	17
Jones A.H.	W	39	67	11	181*	2978	53.17	7
Wallace W.M.	A	47	73	5	211	3409	50.13	9
Crowe J.J.	A	59	95	9	156	4245	49.36	11
Reid J.R.	W	58	102	8	296	4538	48.27	13
Sinclair M.S.	CD	42	72	8	203*	3043	47.54	7
Turner G.M.	O	59	109	14	186*	4439	46.72	13
Bell M.D.	W	39	72	7	219	3029	46.60	9
Hiddleston J.S.	W	41	75	1	212	3413	46.12	8

Most Centuries for One Province

	Province	Centuries		Province	Centuries
Sutcliffe B.	O	17	Vance R.H.	W	12
Edgar B.A.	W	15	Scott V.J.	A	11
Rutherford K.R.	O	14	McEwan P.E.	C	11
Greatbatch M.J.	CD	14	Crowe J.J.	A	11
Reid J.R.	W	13	Hadlee W.A.	C	10
Turner G.M.	O	13	Burgess M.G.	A	10
Crowe M.D.	CD	13	Hick G.A.	ND	10
Franklin T.J.	A	12			

Most Runs for One Province

	Province	M	In	NO	HS	Runs	Ave	100
Edgar B.A.	W	87	160	3	162	6494	44.17	15
Vance R.H.	W	119	205	18	254*	6440	34.43	12
Sutcliffe B.	O	60	110	8	385*	6028	59.09	17
McEwan P.E.	C	103	185	11	155	5940	34.13	11
Latham R.T.	C	101	176	17	237*	5919	37.22	8
Roberts A.D.G.	ND	104	192	35	128*	5533	35.24	7
Blair B.R.	O	90	154	5	143	5057	33.93	7
Franklin T.J.	A	88	157	14	181	5051	35.25	12
Rutherford K.R.	O	68	121	7	226*	5051	44.30	14
Morrison J.F.M.	W	89	160	22	180*	4694	34.01	6
White D.J.	ND	99	173	15	209	4656	29.46	7
Bradburn G.E.	ND	115	188	23	148*	4614	27.96	4
Parker J.M.	ND	75	139	19	195	4611	38.42	7
Shrimpton M.J.F.	CD	97	171	15	150	4551	29.17	5
Blain T.E.	CD	83	145	15	161	4547	34.97	7
Reid J.R.	W	58	102	8	296	4538	48.27	13
Turner G.M.	O	59	109	14	186*	4439	46.72	13
Hadlee B.G.	C	82	151	11	163*	4429	31.63	6
Greatbatch M.J.	CD	61	107	8	202*	4363	44.07	14
Briasco P.S.	CD	81	146	16	157	4301	33.08	6
McSweeney E.B.	W	102	153	23	205*	4296	33.04	5
McGregor S.N.	O	90	167	13	114*	4259	27.65	3
Crowe J.J.	A	59	95	9	156	4245	49.36	11
Gray E.J.	W	120	181	38	128*	4228	29.56	5
Burgess M.G.	A	68	116	13	146	4228	41.04	10
Morgan R.W.	A	90	154	8	166	4162	28.50	7

Most Wickets for One Province

	Province	M	Wkts	Runs	Ave	5WI	10WM	Best
Chatfield E.J.	W	84	403	7531	18.68	23	7	8-24
Boock S.L.	O	88	399	8235	20.63	28	5	8-57
O'Sullivan D.R.	CD	90	392	9560	24.38	21	3	6-40
Gray E.J.	W	120	357	9778	27.38	13	3	8-37
Howarth H.J.	A	80	332	7361	22.17	18	4	8-75
Blair R.W.	W	59	330	5004	15.16	30	10	9-72
Priest M.W.	C	88	290	8501	29.31	12	3	9-95
Downes A.D.	O	44	287	3902	13.59	33	13	8-35
Hadlee R.J.	C	62	285	4600	16.14	19	2	7-49
Moir A.M.	O	54	282	5926	21.01	20	5	8-37
Dickeson C.W.	ND	90	282	8242	29.22	9	2	7-79
Mallender N.A.	O	78	268	5433	20.27	14	3	7-27
Alabaster J.C.	O	65	264	5738	21.73	14	3	6-39
Cameron F.J.	O	68	258	5204	20.17	9	—	6-21

Most Dismissals for One Province

WICKETKEEPING	Province	M	Caught	Stumped	Total
McSweeney E.B.	W	102	289	39	328
Lees W.K.	O	108	208	36	244
Germon L.K.	C	76	217	21	238
Hart R.G.	ND	80	215	14	229
Young B.A.	ND	93	179	11	190
Milburn B.D.	O	60	148	17	165
Nevin C.J.	W	51	157	6	163
Ward J.T.	C	54	136	17	153
Kelly P.J.	A	48	140	12	152
Blain T.E.	CD	83	124	19	143
Croy M.G.	O	42	127	4	131
Colquhoun I.A.	CD	53	102	28	130
Smith I.D.S.	CD	59	119	11	130
Sigley M.A.	CD	44	124	4	128
Schofield R.M.	CD	53	107	15	122
Robinson S.A.	O	45	117	5	122
Wright M.J.E.	ND	65	104	17	121
Petrie E.C.	ND	57	90	22	112
Young R.A.	A	34	110	2	112
Mills G.H.	O	55	78	29	107
Boxshall C.	C	50	70	36	106
Hopkins G.J.	C	41	91	10	101
Therkleson I.J.	W	39	93	7	100

Represented Most Provinces

5	Guy J.W.	CD, C, O, W, ND
4	Anderson R.W.	C, ND, O, CD
	Congdon B.E.	CD, W, O, C
	Crawshaw W.J.	O, C, W, T
	Hounsell A.R.	C, W, A, ND
	McGregor P.B.	A, ND, W, CD
	Worker R.V. de R.	A, C, O, W
3	Alabaster G.D.	O, C, ND
	Allcott C.F.W.	HB, A, O
	Alpe S.	A, C, W
	Andrews B.	C, CD, O
	Beard D.D.	W, CD, ND
	Billcliff I.S.	O, W, A
	Bracewell B.P.	CD, O, ND
	Cairns B.L.	CD, O, ND
	Clark L.A.	W, O, A
	Collinge R.O.	CD, W, ND
	Crowe M.D.	A, CD, W
	D'Arcy J.W.	C, O, W
	Frith W.	C, O, W
	Hastings B.F.	W, CD, C
	Holland P.J.	CD, ND, W
	Howell L.G.	C, CD, A

3	Hussey J.M.	HB, O, A
	Jones A.H.	CD, O, W
	King R.T.	O, A, CD
	Lane M.E.L.	W, CD, C
	Lusk Harold B.	A, C, W
	McBeath D.J.	O, C, S
	Macleod D.N.	CD, W, C
	Mills G.	A, HB, O
	Moloney D.A.R.	O, W, C
	Neutze P.S.	O, A, ND
	Paterson J.L.	C, HB, A
	Riley J.D.	C, W, A
	Sampson H.C.	CD, O, C
	Salmon W.J.	W, HB, T
	Stephenson F.C.	O, W, C
	Sutcliffe B.	A, O, ND
	Tracy S.R.	A, C, O
	Twose R.G.	ND, CD, W
	Uttley K.F.M.	O, C, W
	Watson H.C.	O, C, W
	Wiseman P.J.	A, O, C
	Wright E.	A, W, C
	Wright J.G.	ND, C, A

T *Taranaki*   S *Southland*   HB *Hawke's Bay*

PROVINCIAL RECORDS

MOST WINS IN SUCCESSION

8	Canterbury	1873/74 to 1880/81
7	Canterbury	1912/13 to 1913/14
7	Wellington	1960/61 to 1961/62
6	Canterbury	1910/11 to 1911/12
6	Auckland	1939/40 to 1943/44
6	Wellington	1962/63 to 1963/64
6	Canterbury	1996/97

MOST LOSSES IN SUCCESSION

10	Otago	1961/62 to 1963/64
8	Otago	1929/30 to 1931/32
7	Otago	1874/75 to 1880/81
7	Otago	1920/21 to 1922/23
7	Otago	1926/27 to 1927/28
7	Auckland	1997/98 to 1998/99
7	Otago	2001/02

MOST DRAWS IN SUCCESSION

9	ND	1974/75 to 1975/76
8	Wellington	1974/75 to 1975/76
7	ND	1968/69 to 1969/70
7	CD	1991/92 to 1992/93
7	Wellington	1992/93

MOST GAMES WITHOUT A WIN

38	CD	1973/74 to 1978/79
36	Otago	1960/61 to 1965/66
24	ND	1972/73 to 1975/76
21	ND	1966/67 to 1970/71

MOST GAMES WITHOUT A LOSS

24	Wellington	1984/85 to 1986/87
23	Auckland	1978/79 to 1981/82
22	Auckland	1934/35 to 1943/44
18	Auckland	1961/62 to 1964/65
18	Canterbury	1966/67 to 1969/70

MOST GAMES WITHOUT A DRAW

42	Canterbury	1896/97 to 1909/10
30	Otago	1894/95 to 1907/08
22	Canterbury	1869/70 to 1883/84
20	Canterbury	1919/20 to 1924/25

Highest Individual Innings

for and against the major sides in NZ

	For	Against
Auckland	290 W.N. Carson v Otago at Dunedin, 1936/37	355 B. Sutcliffe for Otago at Dunedin, 1949/50
Canterbury	301* P.G. Fulton v Auckland at Christchurch, 2002/03	385 B. Sutcliffe for Otago at Christchurch, 1952/53
Central Dist.	242 M.D. Crowe v Otago at New Plymouth, 1989/90	264 B. Sutcliffe for Otago at Dunedin, 1959/60
Northern Dist.	235 J.A.H. Marshall v Canterbury at Chch, 2001/02	296 J.R. Reid for Wellington at Wellington, 1962/63
Otago	385 B. Sutcliffe v Canterbury at Christchurch, 1952/53	290 W.N. Carson for Auckland at Dunedin, 1936/37
Wellington	296 J.R. Reid v Northern Dist. at Wellington, 1962/63	207 R.T. Hart for Central Dist. at Wellington, 1985/86
MCC/England	336* W.R. Hammond v NZ at Auckand, 1932/33	222 N.J. Astle for NZ at Christchurch, 2001/02
Australia	293 V.T. Trumper v Canterbury at Christchurch 1913/14	198 W.A. Hadlee for Otago at Dunedin, 1945/46
South Africa	275* D.J. Cullinan v NZ at Auckland, 1998/99	165 M.E. Chapple for Canterbury at Christchurch, 1952/53
West Indies	258 S.M. Nurse v NZ at Christchurch, 1968/69	214 M.S. Sinclair for NZ at Wellington, 1999/00
Pakistan	271 Javed Miandad v NZ at Auckland, 1988/89	204 M.S. Sinclair for NZ at Christchurch, 2000/01
India	192 M. Azharuddin v NZ at Auckand, 1989/90	239 G.T. Dowling for NZ at Christchurch, 1967/68
Sri Lanka	267 P.A. de Silva v NZ at Wellington, 1990/91	299 M.D. Crowe for NZ at Wellington, 1990/91
New Zealand	299 M.D. Crowe v Sri Lanka at Wellington, 1990/91	336* W.R. Hammond for England at Auckland, 1932/33
Zimbabwe	196 A.D.R. Campbell v Canterbury at Timaru, 1997/98	157 M.J. Horne for NZ at Auckland, 1997/98
Bangladesh	102 Al Sahariar v Southern at Dunedin, 1997/98	190 M.E. Parlane for NZ Academy at Lincoln, 1997/98

Best Bowling

for and against the major sides in NZ

	For	Against
Auckland	9-36 A.F. Wensley v Otago at Auckland, 1929/30	9-48 A.R. Tait v Auckland at Hamilton, 1996/97
Canterbury	10-28 A.E. Moss v Wellington at Christchurch, 1889/90	9-72 F.H. Cooke for Otago at Christchurch, 1884/85
Central Dist.	9-100 B.W. Yuile v Canterbury at New Plymouth, 1965/66	8-31 D.G. Sewell for Otago at Invercargill, 1996/97
Northern Dist.	9-48 A.R. Tait v Auckland at Hamilton, 1996/97	9-93 P.J. Petherick for Otago at Dunedin, 1975/76
Otago	9-50 A.H. Fisher v Queensland at Dunedin, 1896/97	9-36 A.E. Wensley for Auckland at Auckland, 1929/30
Wellington	9-67 A.W.S. Brice v Auckland at Wellington, 1918/19	10-28 A.E. Moss for Canterbury at Christchurch, 1889/90
MCC/England	8-45 F.S. Trueman v Otago at Dunedin, 1958/59	7-50 H.W. Monaghan for Wellington at Wellington 1906/07
Australia	8-27 W.J. Whitty v Auckland at Auckland, 1909/10	8-66 G.O. Rabone for Auckland at Auckland, 1956/57
South Africa	6-47 P.M. Pollock v NZ at Wellington, 1963/64	7-75 C.F.W. Allcott for Auckland at Auckland, 1931/32
West Indies	7-37 C.A. Walsh v NZ at Wellington, 1994/95	7-27 C.L. Cairns for NZ at Hamilton, 1999/00
Pakistan	7-16 Farooq Hamid v Wellington at Wellington, 1964/65	7-95 N.A. Huxford for Wellington at Wellington, 1964/65
India	8-76 E.A.S. Prasanna v NZ at Auckland, 1975/76	7-23 R.J. Hadlee for NZ at Wellington, 1975/76
Sri Lanka	6-79 C.P.H. Ramanayake v Wellington at Wellington, 1990/91	6-45 C.H. Thiele for Canterbury at Christchurch, 1982/83
New Zealand	8-100 G.F. Cresswell v Australia B at Dunedin, 1949/50	8-33 H.S.T.L. Hendry for NSW at Wellington, 1923/24
Zimbabwe	6-20 B.C. Strang v NZ XI at Wanganui, 1995/96	5-16 A.R. Tait for NZ A at Dunedin, 1997/98
Bangladesh	6-143 Hasibul Hussain v Northern at Hamilton, 1997/98	7-53 C.L. Cairns for NZ at Hamilton, 2001/02

Highest Totals

for and against the major sides in NZ

	For	Against
Auckland	693-9 dec v Canterbury at Auckland, 1939/40	658 by Australians at Auckland, 1913/14
Canterbury	777 v Otago at Christchurch, 1996/97	693-9 dec by Auckland at Auckland, 1939/40
Central Dist.	594-8 dec v Auckland at Auckland, 1995/96	571-8 by Otago at Napier, 1995/96
Northern Dist.	520-8 dec v Otago at Hamilton, 1987/88	608-9 dec by Wellington at Hamilton, 1998/99
Otago	602-8 dec v Canterbury at Dunedin, 1928/29	777 by Canterbury at Christchurch, 1996/97
Wellington	608-9 dec v Northern Districts at Hamilton, 1998/99	547-5 dec by Canterbury at Christchurch, 1953/54
MCC/England	653-5 dec v New Zealand at Dunedin, 1935/36	537 by New Zealand at Wellington, 1983/84
Australia	663 v New Zealand at Auckland, 1920/21	484 by New Zealand at Wellington, 1973/74
South Africa	621-5 dec v New Zealand at Auckland, 1998/99	364 by New Zealand at Wellington, 1931/32
West Indies	660-5 dec v New Zealand at Wellington, 1994/95	518-9d by New Zealand at Wellington, 1999/00
Pakistan	616-5 dec v New Zealand at Auckland, 1988/89	492 by New Zealand at Wellington, 1984/85
India	512 v President's XI at New Plymouth, 1989/90	502 by New Zealand at Christchurch, 1967/68
Sri Lanka	497 v New Zealand at Wellington, 1990/91	671-4 by New Zealand at Wellington, 1990/91
New Zealand	671-4 v Sri Lanka at Wellington, 1990/91	663 by Australia at Auckland, 1920/21
Zimbabwe	422-8 dec v Canterbury at Timaru, 1997/98	487-7d by NZ at Wellington, 2000/01
Bangladesh	286-9 dec v Southern at Dunedin, 1997/98	495 by Auckland at Auckland, 2001/02

Lowest Totals

for and against the major sides in NZ

	For	Against
Auckland	13 v Canterbury at Auckland, 1877/78	28 by Hawke's Bay at Auckland, 1910/11
Canterbury	25 v Otago at Christchurch, 1866/67	13 by Auckland at Auckland, 1877/78
Central Dist.	50 v Wellington at Upper Hutt, 1979/80	68 by Canterbury at Levin, 1985/86
Northern Dist.	32 v Auckland at Hamilton, 1996/97	51 by Central Dist. at Hamilton, 1957/58
Otago	34 v Wellington at Dunedin, 1956/57	25 by Canterbury at Christchurch, 1866/67
Wellington	19 v Nelson at Nelson, 1885/86	32 by Hawke's Bay at Wellington, 1883/84
MCC/England	64 v New Zealand at Wellington, 1977/78	26 by New Zealand at Auckland, 1954/55
Australia	103 v New Zealand at Auckland, 1985/86	42 by New Zealand at Wellington, 1945/46
South Africa	165 v NZ Academy XI at Nelson, 1994/95	73 by Canterbury at Christchurch, 1963/64
West Indies	77 v New Zealand at Auckland, 1955/56	74 by New Zealand at Dunedin, 1955/56
Pakistan	100 v NZ A at Lincoln, 2000/01	46 by Otago at Dunedin, 1978/79
India	81 v New Zealand at Wellington, 1975/76	94 by New Zealand at Hamilton, 2002/03
Sri Lanka	93 v New Zealand at Auckland, 1982/83	109 by New Zealand at Napier, 1994/95
New Zealand	26 v England at Auckland, 1954/55	64 by England at Wellington, 1977/78
Zimbabwe	67 v NZ A at Dunedin, 1997/98	100 by Canterbury at Timaru, 1997/98
Bangladesh	108 v NZ at Hamilton, 2001/02	311 by Central at Wellington, 1997/98

AUCKLAND

Highest Totals

693-9 dec	v Canterbury	Auckland	1939/40
643	v Canterbury	Auckland	1919/20
590	v Canterbury	Auckland	1937/38
579	v Otago	Auckland	1909/10
550-5 dec	v Otago	Auckland	1936/37
547-8 dec	v Northern Districts	Auckland	2000/01
539	v Otago	Dunedin	1926/27
539	v Canterbury	Christchurch	1907/08
537	v Hawke's Bay	Auckland	1920/21
526-4 dec	v Central Districts	Auckland	1951/52

Lowest Totals

13	v Canterbury	Auckland	1877/78
48	v Otago	Dunedin	1889/90
48	v Wellington	Wellington	1889/90
53	v Wellington	Wellington	1873/74
55	v Otago	Dunedin	1900/01
56	v Canterbury	Auckland	1931/32
69	v Northern Districts	Auckland	1963/64
71	v Central Districts	Palmerston North	2001/02
72	v Lord Hawke's XI	Auckland	1902/03
72	v Northern Districts	Rotorua	1991/92

Most Appearances

90	Morgan R.W.	67	Harris R.M.	59	Crowe J.J.
88	Franklin T.J.	67	Patel D.N.	58	Vivian G.E.
80	Howarth H.J.	65	Hunt A.J.	56	Barnes A.C.
77	McIntyre J.M.	65	Webb P.N.	55	Snedden M.C.
73	Sparling J.T.	63	Stott L.W.	54	Sutton R.E.
72	Troup G.B.	62	Cunis R.S.	53	Watson W.
69	Reid J.F.	60	Parsons A.E.W.	51	Brown S.W.
68	Burgess M.G.				

Longest Careers

Seasons				Seasons		
25	Garrard D.R.	1917/18-1941/42		21	Cleverley D.C.	1930/31-1950-51
24	Wallace W.M.	1933/34-1956/57		20	Stemson W.I.	1889/90-1908/09
22	Anthony A.	1909/10-1930/31		20	Horspool E.	1909/10-1928/29
22	McIntyre J.M.	1961/62-1982-83		20	Weir G.L.	1927/28-1946/47
21	Yates R.J.	1873/74-1893/94		20	Morgan R.W.	1957/58-1976/77

Benefits

Troup G.B.	1986/87		Watson W.	1994/95
Snedden M.C.	1989/90		Patel D.N.	1995/96
Crowe J.J.	1990/91		Morrison D.K.	1996/97
Franklin T.J.	1991/92		Pringle C.	1998/99
Hunt A.J.	1992/93		Barnes A.C.	2002/03

Batting

2000 RUNS	Career	M	In	NO	HS	Runs	Ave	100
Franklin T.J.	1980/81-1992/93	88	157	14	181	5051	35.25	12
Crowe J.J.	1982/83-1991/92	59	95	9	156	4245	49.36	11
Burgess M.G.	1966/67-1979/80	68	116	13	146	4228	41.04	10
Morgan R.W.	1957/58-1976/77	90	154	8	166	4162	28.50	7
Reid J.F.	1975/76-1987/88	69	117	17	173	3733	37.33	5
Patel D.N.	1985/86-1994/95	67	102	9	204	3648	39.22	8
Harris R.M.	1955/56-1973/74	67	119	4	157	3598	31.28	3
Scott V.J.	1937/38-1952/53	44	74	15	204	3546	60.10	11
Wallace W.M.	1933/34-1956/57	47	73	5	211	3409	50.13	9
Webb P.N.	1976/77-1986/87	65	114	18	136	3307	34.44	5
Sparling J.T.	1956/57-1970/71	73	123	17	105	2977	28.08	2
Parsons A.E.W.	1973/74-1982/83	60	113	8	132	2820	26.85	3
Hemus L.G.	1904/05-1921/22	39	71	4	148	2701	40.31	8
Weir G.L.	1927/28-1946/47	42	67	6	191	2625	43.03	7
Whitelaw P.E.	1928/29-1946/47	42	68	4	195	2417	37.76	5
Jarvis T.W.	1964/65-1976/77	46	80	3	118*	2403	31.20	2
Horne P.A.	1979/80-1990/91	40	67	6	209	2380	39.01	4
Vivian G.E.	1966/67-1978/79	58	98	16	111*	2327	28.37	2
Vaughan J.T.C.	1989/90-1996/97	48	81	14	127	2269	33.86	2
Gedye S.G.	1956/57-1964/65	40	73	4	104	2169	31.43	3
Mills J.E.	1925/26-1937/38	35	63	1	185	2126	34.29	3
Barnes A.C.	1993/94-2002/03	56	87	6	107	2086	25.75	2
Hunt A.J.	1981/82-1992/93	65	99	15	102*	2069	24.63	1
McIntosh T.G.	1998/99-2002/03	35	58	6	182	2058	39.57	6
Redmond R.E.	1969/70-1975/76	29	55	4	141*	2004	39.29	4

CENTURY ON DEBUT FOR PROVINCE

† 112*	Brook-Smith W.	v Hawke's Bay	Auckland	1904/05
157	Relf A.E.	v Canterbury	Christchurch	1907/08
† 119	Snedden C.A.	v Hawke's Bay	Auckland	1920/21
† 122	Scott V.J.	v Canterbury	Auckland	1937/38
† 122	Kerr A.C.	v Wellington	Auckland	1941/42
174	Patel D.N.	v Canterbury	Christchurch	1985/86
† 106* & 1	Vaughan J.T.C.	v Wellington	Wellington	1989/90

† *indicates player was making his first-class debut*

MOST RUNS IN A SEASON

		Runs	Ave				Runs	Ave
Crowe J.J.	1991/92	1063	62.52		Crowe J.J.	1990/91	667	44.46
McIntosh T.G.	2002/03	820	58.57		Franklin T.J.	1982/83	664	51.07
Crowe M.D.	1982/83	736	52.57		Nicol R.J.	2002/03	664	47.42
Patel D.N.	1986/87	723	55.61		Crowe J.J.	1988/89	644	71.55
Horne M.J.	2001/02	696	69.60		Burgess M.G.	1977/78	643	46.00
Horne M.J.	2002/03	671	47.92		Mills K.D.	2000/01	606	101.00
Horne P.A.	1986/87	670	67.00		Crowe J.J.	1989/90	600	42.85

HIGHEST INDIVIDUAL INNINGS

290	Carson W.N.	v Otago	Dunedin	1936/37
256	Smith S.G.	v Canterbury	Auckland	1919/20
211	Wallace W.M.	v Canterbury	Auckland	1939/40
209*	Brown S.W.	v Canterbury	Christchurch	1990/91
209	Horne P.A.	v Northern Districts	Auckland	1988/89
204	Scott V.J.	v Otago	Dunedin	1947/48
204	Patel D.N.	v Northern Districts	Auckland	1991/92

198	Scott V.J.	v Canterbury	Auckland	1939/40
195	Whitelaw P.E.	v Otago	Dunedin	1936/37
194	Carson W.N.	v Wellington	Auckland	1936/37

MOST CENTURIES IN A SEASON
4   Franklin T.J.   1987/88
4   Crowe J.J.   1991/92

TOTAL NUMBER OF CENTURIES   251
Most in one season	11		2001/02
1st	Mills G. 106* v Wellington		1895/96
100th	Playle W.R. 102* v Central Districts		1957/58
200th	Crowe J.J. 102 v Otago		1991/92

Bowling

150 WICKETS	Career	M	Wkts	Runs	Ave	5WI	10WM	Best
Howarth H.J.	1963/64-1978/79	80	332	7361	22.17	18	4	8-75
Sparling J.T.	1956/57-1970/71	73	248	5327	21.47	17	3	7-49
McIntyre J.M.	1961/62-1982/83	77	238	5447	22.88	8	1	6-84
Cunis R.S.	1960/61-1973/74	62	229	4603	20.10	14	2	7-29
Snedden M.C.	1977/78-1989/90	55	217	4631	21.34	10	2	7-49
Stott L.W.	1969/70-1983/84	63	214	5341	24.95	8	—	6-68
Troup G.B.	1974/75-1986/87	72	200	5213	26.06	4	—	6-48
Patel D.N.	1985/86-1994/95	67	184	4298	23.35	8	2	7-83
Watson W.	1984/85-1994/95	53	176	4110	23.35	7	—	7-60
Bracewell J.G.	1982/83-1989/90	42	168	4189	24.93	8	2	7-65
Morrison D.K.	1985/86-1996/97	49	168	4034	24.01	7	—	7-82
Cowie J.	1932/33-1949/50	34	154	3379	21.94	6	—	6-44
Sutton R.E.	1958/59-1973/74	54	152	3364	22.13	6	—	7-64

MOST WICKETS IN A SEASON

		Wkts	Ave				Wkts	Ave
Canning T.K.	2002/03	46	21.97		Hayes J.A.	1957/58	42	11.38
Bracewell J.G.	1986/87	43	20.90		Lankham W.	1882/83	41	6.31

BEST IN AN INNINGS
9-36	Wensley A.F.	v Otago	Auckland	1929/30
9-75	Neill R.	v Canterbury	Auckland	1891/92
9-86	Neill R.	v Canterbury	Auckland	1897/98
8-27	Vaughan J.T.C.	v Otago	Alexandra	1996/97
8-36	Rees A.W.	v Otago	Dunedin	1889/90
8-51	Neill R.	v Wellington	Auckland	1895/96
8-51	Garrard D.R.	v Canterbury	Auckland	1921/22
8-55	Smith S.G.	v Wellington	Auckland	1919/20
8-65	Smith S.G.	v Otago	Auckland	1923/24
8-66	Rabone G.O.	v Australia	Auckland	1956/57
8-75	Cleverley D.C.	v Wellington	Wellington	1945/46
8-75	Howarth H.J.	v NZ Under 23 XI	Auckland	1976/77

BEST IN A MATCH
14-63	Rees A.W.	v Otago	Dunedin	1889/90
14-65	Hayes J.A.	v Wellington	Auckland	1957/58
14-94	Howarth H.J.	v Otago	Dunedin	1973/74
14-119	Pringle C.	v Otago	Dunedin	1993/94
13-35	Lankham W.	v Taranaki	Auckland	1882/83

13-85	Cunis R.S.	v Canterbury	Christchurch	1963/64
13-104	Oliff C.	v Wellington	Auckland	1912/13
13-107	Smith S.G.	v Wellington	Auckland	1919/20

Wicketkeeping

100 DISMISSALS	Career	M	Caught	Stumped	Total
Kelly P.J.	1981/82-1988/89	48	140	12	152
Young R.A.	1998/99-2002/03	34	110	2	112

MOST DISMISSALS IN A SEASON

| 35 | (33ct/2st) | Young R.A. | 2001/02 |
| 35 | (35ct) | Young R.A. | 2002/03 |

MOST DISMISSALS IN A MATCH

8	(2ct/6st)	Kent L.A.W. v Wellington	Wellington	1944/45
8	(8ct)	Smith I.D.S. v Central Districts	Nelson	1988/89
8	(8ct)	Vincent L. v Central Districts	Palmerston North	2000/01

MOST DISMISSALS IN AN INNINGS

| 6 | (6ct) | Young R.A.v Wellington | Wellington | 2002/03 |

MOST CATCHES IN A MATCH

| 8 | Smith I.D.S. v Central Districts | Nelson | 1988/89 |
| 8 | Vincent L. v Central Districts | Palmerston North | 2000/01 |

MOST CATCHES IN AN INNINGS

| 6 | Young R.A.v Wellington | Wellington | 2002/03 |

Fielding

MOST CATCHES IN A MATCH

| 6 | Williams N.T. v Hawke's Bay | Napier | 1894/95 |
| 6 | Jarvis T.W. v Northern Districts | Hamilton | 1968/69 |

MOST CATCHES IN AN INNINGS

| 5 | Williams N.T. v Hawkes Bay | Napier | 1894/95 |
| 5 | Crowe J.J. v Canterbury | Auckland | 1988/89 |

Record Partnerships

FOR

Wicket	Score	Batsmen	Against	At	Date
1st	286	B. Sutcliffe & D.D. Taylor	Canterbury	Auckland	1948/49
2nd	241	T.J. Franklin & J.J. Crowe	Wellington	Wellington	1988/89
3rd	445	P.E. Whitelaw & W.N. Carson	Otago	Dunedin	1936/37
4th	280	J.J. Crowe & D.N. Patel	ND	Auckland	1991/92
5th	234*	V.J. Scott & J.B. Morris	CD	Auckland	1951/52
6th	209*	A.C. Parore & A.P. O'Dowd	Otago	Dunedin	1991/92
7th	224	V.J. Scott & A.M. Matheson	Canterbury	Auckland	1937/38
8th	189	W.N. Carson & A.M. Matheson	Wellington	Auckland	1938/39
9th	122	R.S. Cunis & H.T. Schuster	Wellington	Wellington	1964/65
10th	119	W.N. Carson & J. Cowie	Otago	Auckland	1937/38

AGAINST

Wicket	Score	Batsmen	For	At	Date
1st	373	B. Sutcliffe & L. Watt	Otago	Auckland	1950/51
2nd	287	M.D. Bell & J.D. Wells	Wellington	Auckland	1997/98
3rd	261*	M.P. Maynard & S.A. Thomson	ND	Hamilton	1990/91
4th	252	S.A. Thomson & B.A. Young	ND	Auckland	1990/91
5th	266	B. Sutcliffe & W.S. Haig	Otago	Dunedin	1949/50
6th	220	M.H. Toynbee & I.D.S. Smith	CD	Napier	1982/83
7th	165	R.K. Brown & M.E.L. Lane	CD	Palmerston Nth	1993/94
8th	166	R.J. Hadlee & D.R. Hadlee	Canterbury	Christchurch	1983/84
9th	185	M.P. Maynard & S.B. Doull	ND	Auckland	1991/92
10th	133	G.A. Bartlett & I.A. Colquhoun	CD	Auckland	1959/60

CANTERBURY

Highest Totals

777	v Otago	Christchurch	1996/97
559	v Central Districts	Christchurch	1993/94
549	v Northern Districts	Christchurch	1996/97
547-5 dec	v Wellington	Christchurch	1953/54
543-8 dec	v Central Districts	Rangiora	1996/97
537	v Central Districts	Blenheim	1996/97
534	v Central Districts	Palmerston North	1994/95
526-8 dec	v Wellington	Wellington	1931/32
524	v Northern Districts	Rangiora	1997/98
523-7 dec	v Otago	Christchurch	1929/30

Lowest Totals

25	v Otago	Christchurch	1886/87
27	v Otago	Dunedin	1896/97
32	v Otago	Christchurch	1866/67
34	v Otago	Dunedin	1863/64
37	v Southland	Invercargill	1920/21
37	v Wellington	Wellington	1925/26
38	v Otago	Dunedin	1873/74
42	v Otago	Dunedin	1863/64
42	v Otago	Dunedin	1992/93
44	v Otago	Dunedin	1883/84
46	v Otago	Dunedin	1867/68
46	v Otago	Christchurch	1894/95
46	v Otago	Christchurch	1896/97
49	v Otago	Dunedin	1896/97

Most Appearances

103	McEwan P.E.	65	Brown V.R.	58	Dowling G.T.
101	Latham R.T.	65	Stead G.R.	57	Bull C.L.
88	Priest M.W.	62	Hadlee R.J.	57	Harris C.Z.
82	Hadlee B.G.	60	Roberts S.J.	56	Motz R.C.
77	Stead D.W.	59	Hartland B.R.	54	Cromb I.B.
76	Germon L.K.	58	Patrick W.R.	54	Ward J.T.
72	Hastings B.F.	58	Thomson K.	50	Boxshall C.
69	Boyle D.J.				

Longest Careers

Seasons			Seasons		
34	Read R.J.	1904/05-1937/38	22	Patrick W.R.	1905/06-1926/27
31	Reese T.W.	1887/88-1917/18	21	Stevens E.C.J.	1863/64-1883/84
27	Fowke J.N.	1880/81-1906/07	21	Wilding F.	1881/82-1901/02
26	Reese D.	1895/96-1920/21	21	Ridley A.E.	1889/90-1909/10
25	Moorhouse H.M.	1883/84-1907/08	20	Harman T.D.	1882/83-1901/02
22	Wheatley J.	1882/83-1903/04	20	Hadlee B.G.	1961/62-1980/81

Benefits

McEwan P.E.	1988/89		Germon L.K./Priest M.W.	1997/98
Hadlee R.J.	1989/90		Harris C.Z.	1998/99
Latham R.T.	1992/93		Cairns C.L.	1999/00

Batting

2000 RUNS	Career	M	In	NO	HS	Runs	Ave	100
McEwan P.E.	1977/78-1990/91	103	185	11	155	5940	34.13	11
Latham R.T.	1980/81-1994/95	101	176	17	237*	5919	37.22	8
Hadlee B.G.	1961/62-1980/81	82	151	11	163*	4429	31.63	6
Harris C.Z.	1989/90-2002/03	57	83	23	251*	3864	64.40	9
Dowling G.T.	1958/59-1971/72	58	100	7	206	3690	39.67	8
Hastings B.F.	1961/62-1976/77	72	122	8	226	3540	31.05	7
Priest M.W.	1984/85-1998/99	88	130	21	119	3457	31.71	4
Stead G.R.	1993/94-2002/03	65	108	9	130	3408	34.42	8
Boyle D.J.	1980/81-1994/95	69	121	12	149	3216	29.50	3
Hadlee W.A.	1933/34-1951/52	44	80	7	194	3183	43.60	10
Stead D.W.	1969/70-1985/86	77	133	11	193*	3169	25.97	1
Cromb I.B.	1929/30-1946/47	54	96	5	171	2986	32.81	3
Brown M.E.	1978/79-1986/87	65	111	11	161*	2872	28.72	5
Patrick W.R.	1905/06-1926/27	58	108	7	129*	2803	27.75	2
Hartland B.R.	1986/87-1996/97	59	103	8	150	2771	29.16	5
Coman P.G.	1968/69-1977/78	44	78	4	104	2603	35.17	2
Thomson K.	1959/60-1973/74	58	103	11	136*	2543	27.64	4
Page M.L.	1920/21-1936/37	41	75	2	206	2424	33.20	2
Leggat J.G.	1944/45-1955/56	35	66	6	166	2391	39.85	5
Chapple M.E.	1949/50-1960/61	44	79	9	165	2364	33.77	3
Germon L.K.	1987/88-1997/98	76	101	25	160*	2336	30.73	3
Kerr J.L.	1929/30-1939/40	32	61	3	196	2228	38.41	3
Guillen S.C.	1952/53-1960/61	42	73	5	197	2186	32.14	3
Reese D.	1895/96-1920/21	47	85	4	111	2066	25.50	2
Ryan M.L.	1965/66-1978/79	45	78	8	129	2041	29.15	2
Hadlee R.J.	1971/72-1988/89	62	100	22	93	2012	25.79	—
Roberts A.W.	1927/28-1940/41	35	60	8	181	2004	38.53	2

CENTURY ON DEBUT FOR PROVINCE

† 175	Watson G.	v Otago	Christchurch	1880/81
163	Williams A.B.	v Wellington	Christchurch	1896/97
† 108 & 18	Wood B.B.	v Wellington	Wellington	1907/08
† 105	Talbot R.O.	v Otago	Dunedin	1922/23
5 & 112*	Newman J.A.	v Otago	Christchurch	1927/28
149	Hastings B.F.	v Central Districts	Nelson	1961/62
8 & 135	Parker N.M.	v Wellington	Wellington	1973/74
115	Hopkins G.J.	v Central Districts	Christchurch	1998/99

† *indicates player was making his first-class debut*

HIGHEST INDIVIDUAL INNINGS

301*	Fulton P.G.	v Auckland	Christchurch	2002/03
251*	Harris C.Z.	v Central Districts	Rangiora	1996/97
237*	Latham R.T.	v Northern Districts	Rotorua	1990/91
226	Hastings B.F.	v NZ Under 23 XI	Christchurch	1964/65
206	Page M.L.	v Wellington	Wellington	1931/32
206	Dowling G.T.	v Wellington	Christchurch	1962/63
206	Harris C.Z.	v Central Districts	Blenheim	1996/97
204	Cox A.	v Otago	Christchurch	1925/26
198	Harris C.Z.	v Otago	Christchurch	1996/97
197	Guillen S.C.	v Fiji	Christchurch	1953/54

MOST RUNS IN A SEASON

		Runs	Ave			Runs	Ave
Stead G.R.	2000/01	852	50.11	Englefield J.I.	2000/01	724	38.10
McMillan C.D.	1996/97	809	73.54	McEwan P.E.	1983/84	713	59.41
Papps M.H.W.	2001/02	793	52.86	Harris C.Z.	2001/02	656	93.71
Wright J.G.	1986/87	780	60.00	Hastings B.F.	1964/65	629	62.90
McEwan P.E.	1988/89	758	44.58	Fulton P.G.	2002/03	628	52.33
Latham R.T.	1988/89	757	58.23	Latham R.T.	1987/88	608	50.66
Harris C.Z.	1996/97	748	187.00				

MOST CENTURIES IN A SEASON

3	Hadlee W.A.	1947/48
3	Harris C.Z.	1996/97
3	McMillan C.D.	1996/97
3	Stead G.R.	2000/01

TOTAL NUMBER OF CENTURIES   240

Most in one season	9	1996/97
1st	Watson G. 175 v Otago	1880/81
100th	Hastings B.F. 136 v Auckland	1964/65
200th	Germon L.K. 114 v Central Districts	1993/94

Bowling

150 WICKETS	Career	M	Wkts	Runs	Ave	5WI	10WM	Best
Priest M.W.	1984/85-1998/99	88	290	8501	29.31	12	3	9-95
Hadlee R.J.	1971/72-1988/89	62	285	4600	16.14	19	2	7-49
Burtt T.B.	1943/44-1954/55	46	241	4991	20.70	16	3	8-35
Motz R.C.	1957/58-1968/69	56	239	4589	19.20	12	3	8-61
Bennett J.H.	1898/99-1919/20	40	205	3367	16.43	17	4	7-35
Hadlee D.R.	1969/70-1983/84	49	195	3918	20.09	10	3	7-55
Roberts S.J.	1985/86-1995/96	60	193	5738	29.73	6	–	5-56
Read R.J.	1904/05-1937/38	44	184	4704	25.56	11	1	7-24
Reese D.	1895/96-1920/21	48	168	3040	18.09	10	1	6-43
Stead D.W.	1969/70-1985/86	77	167	5009	29.99	6	—	7-99
Brown V.R.	1978/79-1986/87	65	159	4393	27.62	4	2	7-28
Merritt W.E.	1926/27-1935/36	24	154	3559	23.11	15	4	8-105

BEST IN AN INNINGS

10-28	Moss A.E.	v Wellington	Christchurch	1889/90
9-56	McBeath D.J.	v Auckland	Christchurch	1918/19
9-95	Priest M.W.	v Otago	Dunedin	1989/90
9-98	Robertson W.	v Wellington	Christchurch	1894/95
8-18	Frith W.	v Otago	Christchurch	1880/81

8-33	Callaway S.T.	v Hawkes Bay	Napier	1903/04
8-35	Burtt T.B.	v Otago	Dunedin	1953/54
8-41	Callaway S.T.	v Otago	Dunedin	1900/01
8-59	Robertson W.	v Auckland	Christchurch	1893/94
8-61	Mulcock E.	v Otago	Christchurch	1937/38
8-61	Motz R.C.	v Wellington	Christchurch	1966/67
8-75	Edser H.	v Wellington	Wellington	1883/84
8-96	McBeath D.J.	v Auckland	Auckland	1921/22
8-99	Thomas A.W.	v Auckland	Auckland	1914/15
8-105	Merritt W.E.	v Auckland	Auckland	1931/32

BEST IN A MATCH

15-60	Callaway S.T.	v Hawkes Bay	Napier	1903/04
15-168	McBeath D.J.	v Auckland	Christchurch	1918/19
14-59	Read R.J.	v Southland	Invercargill	1920/21
14-107	Robertson W.	v Auckland	Christchurch	1893/94
13-72	Moss A.E.	v Wellington	Christchurch	1889/90
13-82	Howell W.B.	v Wellington	Christchurch	1902/03
13-90	Frankish F.S.	v Wellington	Wellington	1901/02
13-140	Edser H.	v Wellington	Wellington	1883/84
13-163	Robertson W.	v Wellington	Christchurch	1894/95
13-181	Merritt W.E.	v Otago	Wellington	1935/36

MOST WICKETS IN A SEASON

		Wkts	*Ave*			*Wkts*	*Ave*
Boock S.L.	1977/78	56	15.66	Hadlee R.J.	1981/82	45	14.31
Callaway S.T.	1903/04	47	8.49	Hadlee R.J.	1986/87	45	12.91

Wicketkeeping

100 DISMISSALS	*Career*	*M*	*Caught*	*Stumped*	*Total*
Germon L.K.	1987/88-1997/98	76	217	21	238
Ward J.T.	1957/58-1970/71	54	136	17	153
Boxshall C.	1897/98-1914/15	50	70	36	106
Hopkins G.J.	1998/99-2002/03	41	91	10	101

MOST DISMISSALS IN A SEASON
34   (31ct/3st)   Germon L.K. 1991/92

MOST DISMISSALS IN A MATCH
9   (9ct)   Germon L.K. v Northern Districts   Christchurch   1992/93

MOST DISMISSALS IN AN INNINGS
6   (6ct)   Germon L.K. v Northern Districts   Christchurch   1992/93

MOST CATCHES IN A MATCH
9   Germon L.K. v Northern Districts   Christchurch   1992/93

MOST CATCHES IN AN INNINGS
6   Germon L.K. v Northern Districts   Christchurch   1992/93

Fielding

MOST CATCHES IN A MATCH

6	Cromb I.B. v Otago	Christchurch	1937/38
6	MacDonald G.K. v Pakistan	Christchurch	1984/85
6	Latham R.T. v Otago	Oamaru	1994/95

MOST CATCHES IN AN INNINGS

| 5 | MacDonald G.K. v Pakistan | Christchurch | 1984/85 |
| 5 | Harris C.Z. v England | Christchurch | 2001/02 |

Record Partnerships

FOR

Wicket	Score	Batsmen	Against	At	Date
1st	306	L.A. Cuff & J.D. Lawrence	Auckland	Christchurch	1893/94
2nd	210	W.A. Hadlee & F.P. O'Brien	Otago	Christchurch	1940/41
3rd	394*	P.G. Kennedy & R.T. Latham	ND	Rotorua	1990/91
4th	278	M.L. Page & A.W. Roberts	Wellington	Wellington	1931/32
5th	290	G.R. Stead & C.Z. Harris	CD	Blenheim	1996/97
6th	209	C.Z. Harris & A.J. Redmond	Wellington	Rangiora	2001/02
7th	265	J.L. Powell & N. Dorreen	Otago	Christchurch	1929/30
8th	166	R.J. Hadlee & D.R. Hadlee	Auckland	Christchurch	1983/84
9th	182*	L.K. Germon & R.M. Ford	Wellington	Christchurch	1989/90
10th	160	L.K. Germon & W.A. Wisneski	ND	Rangiora	1997/98

AGAINST

Wicket	Score	Batsmen	For	At	Date
1st	286	B. Sutcliffe & D.D. Taylor	Auckland	Auckland	1948/49
2nd	317	R.T. Hart & P.S. Briasco	CD	New Plymouth	1983/84
3rd	278	T.J. Franklin & D.N. Patel	Auckland	Christchurch	1985/86
4th	282	W.A.C. Wilkinson & A.P.F. Chapman	MCC	Christchurch	1922/23
5th	235*	G.P. Sulzberger & J.D. Ryder	CD	Napier	2002/03
6th	180	S.A. Thomson & M.N. Hart	ND	Hamilton	1992/93
7th	261	A.D.R. Campbell & P.A. Strang	Zimbabwe	Timaru	1997/98
8th	433	A. Sims & V.T. Trumper	Australia	Christchurch	1913/14
9th	134	J.W. Wilson & N.A. Mallender	Otago	Christchurch	1992/93
10th	184	R.C. Blunt & W. Hawksworth	Otago	Christchurch	1931/32

CENTRAL DISTRICTS

Highest Totals

594-8 dec	v Auckland	Auckland	1995/96
549-8 dec	v Canterbury	Christchurch	1998/99
542-4 dec	v Canterbury	Napier	2002/03
538	v Canterbury	Blenheim	2000/01
526	v Otago	Napier	1995/96
485-7 dec	v Wellington	Wellington	1964/65
475-9 dec	v Canterbury	Christchurch	1995/96
469-9 dec	v Canterbury	Napier	1967/68
468	v Wellington	New Plymouth	1999/00
466	v Northern Districts	Wanganui	1998/99

Lowest Totals

50	v Wellington	Upper Hutt	1979/80
51	v Northern Districts	Hamilton	1957/58
59	v Auckland	New Plymouth	1958/59
61	v Auckland	Auckland	1996/97
65	v Wellington	Nelson	1995/96
71	v Northern Districts	Wanganui	1962/63
72	v Auckland	Palmerston North	2001/02
74	v Otago	Invercargill	1996/97
78	v Auckland	Auckland	1984/85
81	v Otago	Dunedin	1956/57

Most Appearances

97	Shrimpton M.J.F.	67	Edwards G.N.	55	Congdon B.E.
90	O'Sullivan D.R.	62	Smith C.J.P.	55	Jordan A.B.
85	Duff S.W.	61	Yuile B.W.	53	Colquhoun I.A.
83	Blain T.E.	61	Greatbatch M.J.	53	Toynbee M.H.
81	Briasco P.S.	59	Smith I.D.S.	53	Schofield R.M.
78	Robertson G.K.	57	Sulzberger G.P.	53	Pierce R.A.
76	Douglas M.W				

Longest Careers

Seasons				Seasons		
19	Shrimpton M.J.F.	1961/62-1979/80		16	Schofield R.M.	1959/60-1974/75
17	Jones A.H.	1979/80-1995/96		16	Snook I.R.	1972/73-1987/88
16	Chapple M.E.	1950/51-1965/66		15	Coutts P.J.C.	1958/59-1972/73

Benefits

O'Sullivan D.R.	1984/85		Duff S.W.	1995/96
Robertson G.K.	1989/90		Greatbatch M.J.	1996/97
Briasco P.S.	1991/92		Douglas M.W.	2000/01
Blain T.E.	1994/95			

Batting

2000 RUNS	Career	M	In	NO	HS	Runs	Ave	100
Shrimpton M.J.F.	1961/62-1979/80	97	171	15	150	4551	29.17	5
Blain T.E.	1982/83-1994/95	83	145	15	161	4547	34.97	7
Greatbatch M.J.	1986/87-1999/00	61	107	8	202*	4363	44.07	14
Briasco P.S.	1982/83-1991/92	81	146	16	157	4301	33.08	6
Douglas M.W.	1987/88-2000/01	76	132	19	144	3838	33.96	7
Edwards G.N.	1973/74-1984/85	67	122	5	177*	3709	31.70	5
Smith C.J.P.	1983/84-1990/91	62	118	9	160*	3499	32.10	7
Crowe M.D.	1983/84-1989/90	32	55	7	242	3299	68.72	13
Duff S.W.	1985/86-1995/96	85	129	29	164*	3079	30.79	1
Sinclair M.S.	1995/96-2002/03	42	72	8	203*	3043	47.54	7
Sulzberger G.P.	1995/96-2002/03	57	92	11	159	2978	36.76	8
Congdon B.E.	1960/61-1970/71	55	93	8	202*	2807	33.02	3
Spearman C.M.	1996/97-2002/03	39	66	3	144	2617	41.53	4
Payton D.H.	1965/66-1976/77	49	92	4	145	2459	27.94	3
Pierce R.A.	1971/72-1984/85	53	98	5	100*	2296	24.68	1
Smith I.D.S.	1977/78-1986/87	59	95	12	145	2265	27.28	3
Hart R.T.	1982/83-1990/91	37	68	3	207	2222	34.18	5
Yuile B.W.	1959/60-1971/72	61	90	10	146	2190	27.37	1

CENTURY ON DEBUT FOR PROVINCE

† 117	MacLeod D.N.	v Wellington	Wanganui	1956/57
† 25 & 119	Sampson H.C.	v Wellington	Wellington	1970/71
119 & 0	Crowe M.D.	v Northern Districts	Whangarei	1983/84
112 & 21	Wilson S.W.J.	v Otago	Blenheim	1990/91
124 & 7*	Smith B.F.	v Otago	Wanganui	2000/01

† *indicates player was making his first-class debut*

HIGHEST INDIVIDUAL INNINGS

242	Crowe M.D.	v Otago	New Plymouth	1989/90
212*	Kelly D.P.	v Canterbury	Blenheim	2000/01
207	Hart R.T.	v Wellington	Wellington	1985/86
203*	Sinclair M.S.	v Northern Districts	Wanganui	1998/99
202*	Congdon B.E.	v Otago	Nelson	1968/69
202*	Greatbatch M.J.	v Otago	Palmerston North	1988/89
202	Greatbatch M.J.	v Northern Districts	Rotorua	1995/96
201*	Smith B.F.	v Canterbury	New Plymouth	2001/02
189	Sinclair M.S.	v Wellington	Masterton	1996/97
181	Howell L.G.	v Canterbury	Christchurch	1995/96

MOST RUNS IN A SEASON

		Runs	Ave			Runs	Ave
Crowe M.D.	1986/87	1348	103.69	Twose R.G.	1991/92	653	36.27
Smith B.F.	2000/01	939	58.68	Anderson R.W.	1977/78	646	40.37
Sinclair M.S.	1996/97	722	48.13	Blain T.E.	1990/91	644	46.00
Douglas M.W.	1991/92	714	44.62	Sulzberger G.P.	1999/00	628	48.30
Briasco P.S.	1990/91	708	41.64	Greatbatch M.J.	1995/96	623	155.75
How J.M.	2002/03	704	44.00	Spearman C.M.	2002/03	622	38.87
Greatbatch M.J.	1986/87	680	48.57	Kelly D.P.	2000/01	617	38.56
Edwards G.N.	1980/81	679	56.59	Spearman C.M.	2000/01	611	50.91
Blain T.E.	1984/85	678	48.42	Smith C.J.P.	1989/90	610	38.12
Smith C.J.P.	1985/86	674	39.64	Briasco P.S.	1988/89	605	46.53
Hart R.T.	1984/85	665	44.32				

MOST CENTURIES IN A SEASON

6   Crowe M.D.   1986/87

TOTAL NUMBER OF CENTURIES 156

Most in one season	10		1986/87
1st	Hunter A.A. 108 v Otago		1951/52
100th	Blain T.E. 103* v Otago		1990/91

Bowling

150 WICKETS	Career	M	Wkts	Runs	Ave	5WI	10WM	Best
O'Sullivan D.R.	1972/73-1984/85	90	392	9560	24.38	21	3	6-40
Yuile B.W.	1959/60-1971/72	61	233	4485	19.24	11	2	9-100
Robertson G.K.	1979/80-1989/90	78	228	6573	28.78	8	1	6-47
Beard D.D.	1950/51-1960/61	49	213	4531	21.27	8	2	7-56
Duff S.W.	1985/86-1995/96	85	208	6856	32.96	4	2	6-36
Jordan A.B.	1968/69-1979/80	55	157	4431	28.22	7	—	7-82
Cave H.B.	1950/51-1958/59	37	150	2962	19.74	7	1	7-31

BEST IN AN INNINGS

9-100	Yuile B.W.	v Canterbury	New Plymouth	1965/66
7-28	Yuile B.W.	v Northern Districts	Hamilton	1967/68
7-31	Cave H.B.	v Auckland	Palmerston North	1952/53
7-33	Cave H.B.	v Northern Districts	New Plymouth	1956/57
7-36	Yuile B.W.	v Otago	Nelson	1962/63
7-36	Schwass A.M.	v Northern Districts	Blenheim	2001/02

BEST IN A MATCH

13-64	Cave H.B.	v Auckland	Palmerston North	1952/53
11-99	Beard D.D.	v Otago	Dunedin	1956/57
11-115	Mason M.J.	v Canterbury	Timaru	2002/03
11-134	Robertson G.K.	v Northern Districts	Nelson	1986/87
11-138	Kay D.J.	v Canterbury	Palmerston North	1976/77

MOST WICKETS IN A SEASON

		Wkts	Ave				Wkts	Ave
O'Sullivan D.R.	1978/79	52	19.01		Hamilton L.J.	2001/02	42	18.40
Schwass A.M.	2001/02	45	14.73		O'Sullivan D.R.	1980/81	40	22.00
O'Sullivan D.R.	1977/78	44	20.22		Mason M.J.	2002/03	40	19.67
Blair R.W.	1955/56	42	17.28					

Wicketkeeping

100 DISMISSALS	Career	M	Caught	Stumped	Total
Blain T.E.	1982/83-1994/95	83	124	19	143
Colquhoun I.A.	1953/54-1963/64	53	102	28	130
Smith I.D.S.	1977/78-1986/87	59	119	11	130
Sigley M.A.	1994/95-2002/03	44	124	4	128
Schofield R.M.	1959/60-1974/75	53	107	15	122

MOST DISMISSALS IN A SEASON
31   (31ct)   Griggs B.B.J. 2001/02

MOST DISMISSALS IN A MATCH
9   (9ct)   Schofield R.M. v Wellington   Wellington   1964/65

MOST DISMISSALS IN AN INNINGS
7   (7ct)   Schofield R.M. v Wellington   Wellington   1964/65

MOST CATCHES IN A MATCH
9   Schofield R.M. v Wellington   Wellington   1964/65

MOST CATCHES IN AN INNINGS
7   Schofield R.M. v Wellington   Wellington   1964/65

Fielding

MOST CATCHES IN A MATCH

5	Congdon B.E.v Wellington	Wellington	1964/65
5	Congdon B.E. v Otago	New Plymouth	1970/71
5	Smith I.D.S. v Auckland	New Plymouth	1978/79
5	Edwards G.N. v Otago	Palmerston North	1979/80
5	Briasco P.S. v Canterbury	Christchurch	1984/85
5	Douglas M.W. v Otago	Palmerston North	1988/89

MOST CATCHES IN AN INNINGS

4	Congdon B.E. v New Zealand XI	New Plymouth	1962/63
4	Neal D.W. v Auckland	Wanganui	1976/77
4	Unwin P.D. v Wellington	New Plymouth	1988/89

Record Partnerships

FOR

Wicket	Score	Batsmen	Against	At	Date
1st	250	R.T. Hart & C.J.P. Smith	Wellington	Wellington	1985/86
2nd	317	R.T. Hart & P.S. Briasco	Canterbury	New Plymouth	1983/84
3rd	223	C.J.P. Smith & S.W.J. Wilson	Otago	Blenheim	1990/91
4th	276*	M.D. Crowe & P.S. Briasco	Canterbury	Christchurch	1986/87
5th	235*	G.P. Sulzberger & J.D. Ryder	Canterbury	Napier	2002/03
6th	220	M.H. Toynbee & I.D.S. Smith	Auckland	Napier	1982/83
7th	219	B.W. Yuile & B.L. Hampton	Canterbury	Napier	1967/68
8th	173	I.D.S. Smith & G.K. Robertson	ND	Hamilton	1982/83
9th	239	H.B. Cave & I.B. Leggat	Otago	Dunedin	1952/53
10th	133	G.A. Bartlett & I.A. Colquhoun	Auckland	Auckland	1959/60

AGAINST

Wicket	Score	Batsmen	For	At	Date
1st	316	M.H. Austen & R.T. Hart	Wellington	Wanganui	1993/94
2nd	199	R.E.W. Mawhinney & D.J. White	ND	Hamilton	1985/86
3rd	227	K.R. Rutherford & B.R. Blair	Otago	Alexandra	1988/89
4th	204	T.W. Jarvis & K. Thompson	Canterbury	Wanganui	1969/70
5th	341	G.R. Larsen & E.B. McSweeney	Wellington	Levin	1987/88
6th	226	E.J. Gray & R.W. Ormiston	Wellington	Wellington	1981/82
7th	192	S.W. Brown & A.C. Parore	Auckland	Auckland	1990/91
8th	143	C.M. Presland & C.W. Dickeson	ND	Whangarei	1983/84
9th	113	G.J. Hopkins & S.J. Cunis	Canterbury	Christchurch	1998/99
10th	89	M.J.E. Wright & S.J. Scott	ND	Wanganui	1978/79

NORTHERN DISTRICTS

Highest Totals

520-8 dec	v Otago	Hamilton	1987/88
518-4 dec	v Canterbury	Christchurch	1996/97
498-6 dec	v Central Districts	Napier	1992/93
496-8 dec	v Canterbury	Christchurch	2001/02
492	v Auckland	Auckland	1990/91
474	v Wellington	Gisborne	1996/97
472	v Otago	Hamilton	1995/96
460-7 dec	v Otago	Hamilton	2001/02
453-8	v Wellington	Wellington	1995/96
436	v Wellington	Wellington	1999/00

Lowest Totals

32	v Auckland	Hamilton	1996/97
52	v Canterbury	Hamilton	1966/67
57	v Wellington	Hamilton	1961/62
59	v Canterbury	Hamilton	1960/61
64	v Otago	Dunedin	1971/72
64	v Auckland	Auckland	1987/88
69	v Australia	Hamilton	1973/74
69	v England	Hamilton	1996/97
77	v Auckland	Auckland	2000/01
79	v Auckland	Auckland	1989/90

Most Appearances

115	Bradburn G.E.	82	Hart M.N.	62	Cooper B.G.
104	Roberts A.D.G.	80	Hart R.G.	58	Howarth G.P.
99	White D.J.	78	Bailey M.D.	57	Petrie E.C.
93	Young B.A.	75	Parker J.M.	55	Bradburn W.P.
90	Dickeson C.W.	66	Puna N.	54	Crocker L.M.
82	Dunning B.	65	Wright M.J.E.	51	Thomson S.A.
82	Kuggeleijn C.M.	64	Parlane M.E.		

Longest Careers

Seasons				Seasons		
17	Dunning B.	1961/62-1977/78		15	Cooper B.G.	1980/81-1994/95
17	Roberts A.D.G.	1967/68-1983/84		15	Young B.A.	1983/84-1997/98
17	Bradburn G.E.	1985/86-2001/02		14	Dickeson C.W.	1973/74-1986/87
16	Kuggeleijn C.M.	1975/76-1990/91		14	White D.J.	1979/80-1992/93
15	Giles G.V.	1961/62-1975/76				

Benefits

Kuggeleijn C.M.	1990/91
White D.J.	1992/93
Cooper B.G.	1995/96
Young B.A.	1997/98

Batting

2000 RUNS	Career	M	In	NO	HS	Runs	Ave	100
Roberts A.D.G.	1967/68-1983/84	104	192	35	128*	5533	35.24	7
White D.J.	1979/80-1992/93	99	173	15	209	4656	29.46	7
Bradburn G.E.	1985/86-2001/02	115	188	23	148*	4614	27.96	4
Parker J.M.	1972/73-1983/84	75	139	19	195	4611	38.42	7
Dunning B.	1961/62-1977/78	82	148	10	142	3898	28.24	3
Young B.A.	1983/84-1997/98	93	148	36	138*	3853	34.40	5
Bailey M.D.	1989/90-2001/02	78	122	8	180*	3468	30.42	6
Kuggeleijn C.M.	1975/76-1990/91	82	138	12	116	3457	27.43	3
Wright J.G.	1975/76-1983/84	43	84	3	145*	3301	40.75	5
Howarth G.P.	1974/75-1985/86	58	105	6	151	3122	31.53	5
Cooper B.G.	1980/81-1994/95	62	110	4	116*	2982	28.13	4
Parlane M.E.	1992/93-2002/03	64	107	6	146	2958	29.28	6
Hart M.N.	1990/91-2002/03	82	118	12	201*	2893	27.29	3
Crocker L.M.	1982/83-1988/89	54	100	3	126	2663	27.45	2
Wright M.J.E.	1972/73-1983/84	65	114	10	115	2632	25.30	1
Gibson J.G.	1968/69-1980/81	49	92	5	128	2580	29.65	4
Thomson S.A.	1987/88-1996/97	51	80	20	167	2530	42.16	5

	Career	M	In	NO	HS	Runs	Ave	100
Marshall J.A.H.	1997/98-2002/03	47	82	2	235	2234	27.92	3
Hick G.A.	1987/88-1988/89	17	30	4	211*	2055	79.03	10
Wealleans K.A.	1988/89-1994/95	43	74	4	112*	2053	29.33	4
Hart R.G.	1992/93-2002/03	80	112	19	102*	2017	21.68	1
Bradburn W.P.	1957/58-1968/69	55	103	5	107	2015	20.56	1

CENTURY ON DEBUT FOR PROVINCE

118	McGregor P.B.	v Auckland	Hamilton	1962/63
† 127*	Mitchell W.J.	v Pakistan	Hamilton	1964/65
14 & 153*	Maynard M.P.	v Auckland	Hamilton	1990/91

† *indicates player was making his first-class debut*

HIGHEST INDIVIDUAL INNINGS

235	Marshall J.A.H.	v Canterbury	Christchurch	2001/02
212*	Styris S.B.	v Otago	Hamilton	2001/02
211*	Hick G.A.	v Auckland	Auckland	1988/89
209	White D.J.	v Central Districts	Hamilton	1985/86
201*	Hart M.N.	v Auckland	Auckland	2002/03
195	Parker J.M.	v Canterbury	Whangarei	1972/73
195	Maynard M.P.	v Auckland	Auckland	1991/92
194*	White D.J.	v Central Districts	Wanganui	1990/91
180*	Bailey M.D.	v Otago	Hamilton	1997/98
177*	Turner G.M.	v Central Districts	Napier	1976/77

MOST RUNS IN A SEASON

		Runs	Ave			Runs	Ave
Hick G.A.	1988/89	1228	94.46	Wright J.G.	1981/82	672	51.69
Maynard M.P.	1991/92	893	68.69	Styris S.B.	2001/02	662	44.13
Hick G.A.	1987/88	827	63.61	Parker J.M.	1979/80	640	49.23
Bradburn G.E.	1989/90	726	36.30	Parker J.M.	1981/82	618	103.00
Wealleans K.A.	1989/90	721	36.05	Wealleans K.A.	1990/91	613	40.86
Marshall J.A.H.	2001/02	706	39.22	Wright J.G.	1978/79	612	50.91
Wright J.G.	1979/80	694	43.43	White D.J.	1990/91	609	40.60
Turner G.M.	1976/77	672	67.20	Thomson S.A.	1990/91	602	60.20

MOST CENTURIES IN A SEASON

6   Hick G.A.   1988/89

TOTAL NUMBER OF CENTURIES   125

Most in one season	9	1988/89
1st	Everest J.K. 104 v Canterbury	1956/57
100th	Parlane M.E. 132* v Canterbury	1995/96

Bowling

150 WICKETS	Career	M	Wkts	Runs	Ave	5WI	10WM	Best
Dickeson C.W.	1973/74-1986/87	90	282	8242	29.22	9	2	7-79
Bradburn G.E.	1985/86-2001/02	115	231	7302	31.61	3	—	6-56
Puna N.	1956/57-1968/69	66	224	5314	23.72	11	—	6-25
de Groen R.P.	1990/91-1995/96	38	157	3320	21.14	8	2	7-50

BEST IN AN INNINGS

9-48	Tait A.R.	v Auckland	Hamilton	1996/97
8-21	Langdon M.C.	v Auckland	Auckland	1963/64
8-30	Alabaster G.D.	v NZ Under 23 XI	Hamilton	1962/63
8-37	Clarke D.B.	v Central Districts	Wanganui	1962/63
8-49	Kennedy K.D.	v Central Districts	Hamilton	1969/70

BEST IN A MATCH

16-130	Tait A.R.	v Auckland	Hamilton	1996/97
13-99	de Groen R.P.	v Otago	Alexandra	1992/93
12-55	Martin B.P.	v Auckland	Taupo	1999/00
12-109	Lissette A.F.	v Otago	Dunedin	1959/60
11-66	Tuffey D.R.	v Wellington	Hamilton	2000/01

MOST WICKETS IN A SEASON

		Wkts	Ave				Wkts	Ave
Tait A.R.	1996/97	53	16.32		Yovich J.A.F.	2001/02	40	26.45
de Groen R.P.	1992/93	46	16.84					

Wicketkeeping

100 DISMISSALS	Career	M	Caught	Stumped	Total
Hart R.G.	1992/93-2002/03	80	215	14	229
Young B.A.	1983/84-1997/98	93	179	11	190
Wright M.J.E.	1972/73-1983/84	65	104	17	121
Petrie E.C.	1956/57-1966/67	57	90	22	112

MOST DISMISSALS IN A SEASON
34 (33ct/1st) Hart R.G. 2001/02

MOST DISMISSALS IN A MATCH
9 (9ct) Young B.A. v Canterbury Christchurch 1986/87

MOST DISMISSALS IN AN INNINGS
7 (7ct) Young B.A. v Canterbury Christchurch 1986/87

MOST CATCHES IN A MATCH
9 Young B.A. v Canterbury Christchurch 1986/87

MOST CATCHES IN AN INNINGS
7 Young B.A. v Canterbury Christchurch 1986/87

Fielding

MOST CATCHES IN A MATCH
6 Young B.A. v Wellington Wellington 1995/96

MOST CATCHES IN AN INNINGS

4	Pairaudeau B.H. v Central Districts	Wanganui	1962/63
4	Harris S.J. (sub) v Otago	Dunedin	1965/66
4	Barton P.H. v Canterbury	Hamilton	1974/75
4	Young B.A. v Wellington	Wellington	1995/96
4	Bailey M.D. v Otago	Alexandra	1996/97

Record Partnerships

FOR

Wicket	Score	Batsmen	Against	At	Date
1st	165	J.G. Wright & G.M. Turner	Wellington	Lower Hutt	1976/77
2nd	237	J.G. Gibson & C.M. Kuggeleijn	Canterbury	Hamilton	1980/81
3rd	261*	M.P. Maynard & S.A. Thomson	Auckland	Hamilton	1990/91
4th	259	G.E. Bradburn & M.E. Parlane	Canterbury	Christchurch	1996/97
5th	149	K.A. Wealleans & B.A. Young	Wellington	Wellington	1991/92
6th	191	S.B. Styris & R.G. Hart	Otago	Hamilton	2001/02
7th	136	D.J. Nash & A.R. Tait	CD	Masterton	1997/98
8th	152	G.E. Bradburn & S.B. Doull	Canterbury	Christchurch	1991/92
9th	188	N.R. Parlane & D.R. Tuffey	Wellington	Wellington	1999/00
10th	89	M.J.E. Wright & S.J. Scott	CD	Wanganui	1978/79

AGAINST

Wicket	Score	Batsmen	For	At	Date
1st	310	R.H. Vance & B.A. Edgar	Wellington	Wellington	1988/89
2nd	263	M.J. Greatbatch & M.D. Crowe	CD	Morrinsville	1986/87
3rd	394*	P.G. Kennedy & R.T. Latham	Canterbury	Rotorua	1990/91
4th	280	J.J. Crowe & D.N. Patel	Auckland	Auckland	1991/92
5th	252*	R.T. Latham & M.W. Priest	Canterbury	Christchurch	1988/89
6th	175	S.P. Fleming & L.K. Germon	Canterbury	Hamilton	1993/94
7th	205	L.K. Germon & M.W. Priest	Canterbury	Christchurch	1991/92
8th	173	I.D.S. Smith & G.K. Robertson	CD	Hamilton	1982/83
9th	116	V. Pollard & R.O. Collinge	CD	Palmerston North	1964/65
10th	160	L.K. Germon & W.A. Wisneski	Canterbury	Rangiora	1997/98

OTAGO

Highest Totals

602-8 dec	v Canterbury	Dunedin	1928/29
589	v Canterbury	Christchurch	1931/32
571-8	v Central Districts	Napier	1995/96
558-8 dec	v Auckland	Dunedin	1949/50
548-7 dec	v Auckland	Dunedin	1996/97
543-8 dec	v Central Districts	New Plymouth	1978/79
521-7 dec	v Auckland	Auckland	1950/51
505	v Central Districts	Palmerston North	1999/00
500	v Canterbury	Christchurch	1952/53
495	v Wellington	Dunedin	1923/24

Lowest Totals

34	v Wellington	Dunedin	1956/57
35	v Auckland	Christchurch	1884/85
36	v New South Wales	Dunedin	1889/90
40	v Canterbury	Dunedin	1869/70
41	v Auckland	Dunedin	1873/74
42	v Canterbury	Dunedin	1871/72
43	v Canterbury	Christchurch	1872/73
44	v Canterbury	Dunedin	1904/05
46	v Pakistan	Dunedin	1978/79
47	v Canterbury	Christchurch	1888/89
49	v Canterbury	Christchurch	1870/71

Most Appearances

108	Lees W.K.	68	Cameron F.J.	59	Turner G.M.
90	Blair B.R.	68	Rutherford K.R.	57	Burns K.J.
90	McGregor S.N.	65	Alabaster J.C.	55	Mills G.H.
88	Boock S.L.	63	Rutherford I.A.	54	Moir A.M.
81	Blair W.L.	61	Campbell K.O.	54	Dobbs P.W.
80	Hoskin R.N.	60	Sutcliffe B.	53	Lawson R.A.
78	Mallender N.A.	60	Milburn B.D.	51	Knight A.R.
75	McCullum S.J.	59	Smith L.D.	50	Gaffaney C.B.
69	Alabaster G.D.				

Longest Careers

Seasons				Seasons		
27	Downes A.D.	1887/88-1913/14		22	McGregor S.N.	1947/48-1968/69
26	Knight A.R.	1918/19-1943/44		21	Groves L.J.	1929/30-1949/50
24	Siedeberg H.G.	1898/99-1921/22		21	Alabaster G.D.	1955/56-1975/76
24	Blair W.L.	1967/68-1990/91		20	Fisher A.H.	1890/91-1909/10
23	Torrance R.C.	1905/06-1927/28		20	Watt L.	1943/44-1962/63
23	Smith L.D.	1934/35-1956/57		20	Milburn B.D.	1963/64-1982/83
23	Mills G.H.	1935/36-1957/58				

Benefits

Lees W.K.	1987/88	Boock S.L.	1989/90	Mallender N.A.	1992/93

Batting

2000 RUNS	Career	M	In	NO	HS	Runs	Ave	100
Sutcliffe B.	1946/47-1961/62	60	110	8	385	6028	59.09	17
Blair B.R.	1977/78-1989/90	90	154	5	143	5057	33.93	7
Rutherford K.R.	1982/83-1994/95	68	121	7	226*	5051	44.30	14
Turner G.M.	1964/65-1982/83	59	109	14	186*	4439	46.72	13
McGregor S.N.	1947/48-1968/69	90	167	13	114*	4259	27.65	3
Lees W.K.	1972/73-1987/88	108	179	31	124	3754	25.36	4
Blair W.L.	1967/68-1990/91	81	149	9	140	3654	26.10	2
Hoskin R.N.	1980/81-1992/93	80	138	6	157	3573	27.06	6
Gaffaney C.B.	1995/96-2002/03	58	108	10	194	3244	33.10	5
McCullum S.J.	1976/77-1990/91	75	131	1	134	3174	24.41	2
Rutherford I.A.	1974/75-1983/84	63	115	3	222	3122	27.87	4
Richardson M.H.	1992/93-2000/01	49	89	10	166	3089	39.10	8
Burns K.J.	1980/81-1991/92	57	98	6	136	2699	29.33	3
Campbell K.O.	1963/64-1978/79	61	108	17	111	2613	28.71	3
Dobbs P.W.	1988/89-1994/95	54	99	6	144*	2606	28.02	3
Lawson R.A.	1992/93-2002/03	57	107	4	200	2478	24.05	2
Alabaster G.D.	1955/56-1975/76	69	108	16	108	2340	25.43	3
Smith L.D.	1934/35-1956/57	59	108	16	109	2277	24.75	1
Knight A.R.	1918/19-1943/44	51	97	3	152	2245	23.88	1

CENTURY ON DEBUT FOR PROVINCE

107 & 38	Patrick W.R.	v Canterbury	Christchurch	1917/18
† 157*	McMullan J.J.M.	v Southland	Dunedin	1917/18
172 & 16	Worker R.V.deR.	v Canterbury	Christchurch	1923/24
35 & 133	Blamires E.O.	v Canterbury	Christchurch	1923/24
† 15 & 105	Watt D.G.	v Canterbury	Christchurch	1943/44
157	Hadlee W.A.	v Auckland	Dunedin	1945/46

| 197 & 128 | Sutcliffe B. | v MCC | Dunedin | 1946/47 |
| 124 & 90 | Horne M.J. | v Central Districts | Wanganui | 1996/97 |

† *indicates player was making his first-class debut*

HIGHEST INDIVIDUAL INNINGS

385	Sutcliffe B.	v Canterbury	Christchurch	1952/53
355	Sutcliffe B.	v Auckland	Dunedin	1949/50
338*	Blunt R.C.	v Canterbury	Christchurch	1931/32
275	Sutcliffe B.	v Auckland	Auckland	1950/51
264	Sutcliffe B.	v Central Districts	Dunedin	1959/60
241	Horne M.J.	v Auckland	Auckland	1997/98
226*	Rutherford K.R.	v India	Dunedin	1989/90
222	Rutherford I.A.	v Central Districts	New Plymouth	1978/79
221	Blunt R.C.	v Canterbury	Dunedin	1928/29
201	Reid J.R.	v Canterbury	Dunedin	1957/58
201	Sutcliffe B.	v Northern Districts	Hamilton	1960/61
200	Lawson R.A.	v Central Districts	Napier	1995/96

MOST RUNS IN A SEASON

		Runs	Ave			Runs	Ave
Turner G.M.	1975/76	1027	85.58	Gaffaney C.B.	1996/97	642	40.12
Blair B.R.	1989/90	759	47.43	Horne M.J.	2000/01	641	40.06
Cumming C.D.	2002/03	751	46.93	Rutherford K.R.	1985/86	638	53.16
Rutherford K.R.	1989/90	747	67.90	Cumming C.D.	2000/01	626	44.71
Sutcliffe B.	1952/53	709	78.77	Rutherford I.A.	1976/77	625	48.67
Turner G.M.	1974/75	703	78.11	Blair B.R.	1986/87	621	47.76
Blair B.R.	1982/83	680	52.30	Richardson M.H.	1995/96	615	68.33
Richardson M.H.	2000/01	675	56.25	Gaffaney C.B.	2001/02	609	30.45
Rutherford K.R.	1991/92	655	50.38	Jones A.H.	1984/85	608	55.27
Sutcliffe B.	1950/51	651	72.38	Dobbs P.W.	1990/91	603	50.25
Mohammad Wasim	2002/03	651	40.68				

MOST CENTURIES IN A SEASON

| 4 | Turner G.M. | 1974/75 |
| 4 | Turner G.M. | 1975/76 |

TOTAL NUMBER OF CENTURIES — **190**

Most in one season	9		**2002/03**
1st	Baker J.C. 103 v Hawke's Bay		1901/02
100th	Cairns B.L. 110 v Wellington		1979/80

Bowling

150 WICKETS

	Career	M	Wkts	Runs	Ave	5WI	10WM	Best
Boock S.L.	1973/74-1989/90	88	399	8235	20.63	28	5	8-57
Downes A.D.	1887/88-1913/14	44	287	3902	13.59	33	13	8-35
Moir A.M.	1949/50-1961/62	54	282	5926	21.01	20	5	8-37
Mallender N.A.	1983/84-1992/93	78	268	5433	20.27	14	3	7-27
Alabaster J.C.	1956/57-1971/72	65	264	5738	21.73	14	3	6-39
Cameron F.J.	1953/54-1966/67	68	258	5204	20.17	9	—	6-21
Alabaster G.D.	1955/56-1975/76	69	205	4774	23.28	13	1	7-74
O'Connor S.B.	1994/95-2002/03	35	160	3321	20.75	11	2	6-31
Fisher A.H.	1890/91-1909/10	40	176	2766	15.71	9	1	9-50

BEST IN AN INNINGS

9-50	Fisher A.H.	v Queensland	Dunedin	1896/97
9-72	Cooke F.H.	v Canterbury	Christchurch	1884/85
9-93	Petherick P.J.	v Northern Districts	Dunedin	1975/76
8-28	Hendley W.	v Canterbury	Dunedin	1869/70
8-31	Sewell D.G.	v Central Districts	Invercargill	1996/97
8-35	Downes A.D.	v Canterbury	Dunedin	1891/92
8-37	Moir A.M.	v Northern Districts	Hamilton	1958/59
8-46	Cairns B.L.	v Wellington	Invercargill	1978/79
8-55	Moir A.M.	v Canterbury	Dunedin	1951/52
8-57	Boock S.L.	v Auckland	Dunedin	1989/90
8-59	Boock S.L.	v Wellington	Invercargill	1978/79
8-61	Cooke F.H.	v Canterbury	Christchurch	1882/83
8-66	Wiseman P.J.	v Wellington	Wellington	1996/97
8-70	Hay W.A.	v Southland	Dunedin	1917/18
8-99	Blunt R.C.	v Auckland	Dunedin	1930/31
8-119	Moir A.M.	v Central Districts	New Plymouth	1953/54
8-136	Shacklock F.J.	v Canterbury	Christchurch	1903/04

BEST IN A MATCH

15-94	Cooke F.H.	v Canterbury	Christchurch	1882/83
15-104	Boock S.L.	v Auckland	Dunedin	1989/90
15-203	Moir A.M.	v Central Districts	New Plymouth	1953/54
14-93	Torrance R.C.	v Hawke's Bay	Napier	1908/09
14-103	Downes A.D.	v Hawke's Bay	Dunedin	1893/94
14-126	Moir A.M.	v Canterbury	Dunedin	1951/52
13-111	Downes A.D.	v Hawke's Bay	Dunedin	1901/02
13-144	Boock S.L.	v Northern Districts	Whangarei	1980/81

MOST WICKETS IN A SEASON

		Wkts	Ave			Wkts	Ave
Boock S.L.	1978/79	54	18.51	Moir A.M.	1953/54	41	17.58
Mallender N.A.	1991/92	49	12.30	Boock S.L.	1980/81	41	18.46
Boock S.L.	1986/87	48	15.48	Boock S.L.	1987/88	41	21.82
Petherick P.J.	1977/78	45	17.15	Webb M.G.	1973/74	40	14.65
Petherick P.J.	1975/76	42	20.16	Cairns B.L.	1978/79	40	22.70
O'Connor S.B.	2002/03	42	18.71				

Wicketkeeping

100 DISMISSALS	Career	M	Caught	Stumped	Total
Lees W.K.	1972/73-1987/88	108	208	36	244
Milburn B.D.	1963/64-1982/83	60	148	17	165
Croy M.G.	1994/95-2001/02	42	127	4	131
Robinson S.A.	1984/85-1996/97	45	117	5	122
Mills G.H.	1935/36-1957/58	55	78	29	107

MOST DISMISSALS IN A SEASON

32	(28ct/4st)	Robinson S.A.	1990/91

MOST DISMISSALS IN A MATCH

7	(4ct/3st)	Mills G.H. v Northern Districts	Dunedin	1957/58
7	(7ct)	Lees W.K. v Canterbury	Hamilton	1974/75
7	(6ct/1st)	Lees W.K. v, Wellington	Invercargill	1978/79
7	(7ct)	Lees W.K. v Northern Districts	Dunedin	1984/85
7	(6ct/1st)	Lees W.K. v Northern Districts	Alexandra	1985/86
7	(5ct/2st)	Lees W.K. v Central Districts	Masterton	1986/87
7	(7ct)	Robinson S.A. v Wellington	Wellington	1990/91

7	(7ct)	Robinson S.A. v Canterbury	Dunedin	1992/93
7	(6ct/1st)	Sale M.J. v Central Districts	Dunedin	1997/98
7	(7ct)	Croy M.G. v Auckland	Auckland	2001/02

MOST DISMISSALS IN AN INNINGS

7	(7ct)	Croy M.G. v Auckland	Auckland	2001/02

MOST CATCHES IN A MATCH

7	Lees W.K. v Canterbury	Hamilton	1974/75
7	Lees W.K. v Northern Districts	Dunedin	1984/85
7	Robinson S.A v Wellington	Wellington	1990/91
7	Robinson S.A. v Canterbury	Dunedin	1992/93
7	Croy M.G. v Auckland	Auckland	2001/02

MOST CATCHES IN AN INNINGS

7	Croy M.G. v Auckland	Auckland	2001/02

Fielding

MOST CATCHES IN A MATCH

5	Watson E.A. v Canterbury	Dunedin	1953/54
5	Lees W.K. v Wellington	Wellington	1973/74
5	McCullum S.J. v Auckland	Dunedin	1987/88
5	Burns K.J. v Northern Districts	Dunedin	1990/91

MOST CATCHES IN AN INNINGS

4	Geddes A.E. v Canterbury	Christchurch	1903/04
4	Watson E.A. v Canterbury	Dunedin	1953/54
4	Campbell K.O. v Auckland	Dunedin	1969/70
4	Blair W.L. v Canterbury	Invercargill	1977/78
4	Blair W.L. v Northern Districts	Dunedin	1978/79
4	McCullum S.J. v Auckland	Dunedin	1987/88
4	Dobbs P.W. v India	Dunedin	1989/90
4	Burns K.J. v Northern Districts	Dunedin	1990/91
4	Gaffaney C.B. v Wellington	Wellington	1996/97

Record Partnerships

FOR

Wicket	Score	Batsmen	Against	At	Date
1st	373	B. Sutcliffe & L. Watt	Auckland	Auckland	1950/51
2nd	254	K.J. Burns & K.R. Rutherford	Wellington	Oamaru	1987/88
3rd	227	K.R. Rutherford & B.R. Blair	CD	Alexandra	1988/89
4th	235	K.J. Burns & R.N. Hoskin	ND	Hamilton	1987/88
5th	266	B. Sutcliffe & W.S. Haig	Auckland	Dunedin	1949/50
6th	165	G.M. Turner & W.K. Lees	Wellington	Wellington	1975/76
7th	182	B. Sutcliffe & A.W. Gilbertson	Canterbury	Christchurch	1952/53
8th	165*	J.N. Crawford & A.G. Eckhold	Wellington	Wellington	1914/15
9th	134	J.W. Wilson & N.A. Mallender	Canterbury	Christchurch	1992/93
10th	184	R.C. Blunt & W. Hawksworth	Canterbury	Canterbury	1931/32

AGAINST

Wicket	Score	Batsmen	For	At	Date
1st	299	M.D. Bell & R.A. Jones	Wellington	Dunedin	2001/02
2nd	227	W.A. Baker & H.H.L. Kortlang	Wellington	Dunedin	1923/24
3rd	445	P.E. Whitelaw & W.N. Carson	Auckland	Dunedin	1936/37
4th	274	R.A. Jones & S.R. Mather	Wellington	Wellington	2000/01
5th	255	B.R. Taylor & J.V. Coney	Wellington	Dunedin	1972/73
6th	209*	A.C. Parore & A.P. O'Dowd	Auckland	Dunedin	1991/92
7th	265	J.L. Powell & N. Dorreen	Canterbury	Christchurch	1929/30
8th	215	J.R. Murray & A.C. Cummins	West Indies	Dunedin	1994/95
9th	239	H.B. Cave & I.B. Leggat	CD	Dunedin	1952/53
10th	138	K.C. James & A.W.S. Brice	Wellington	Wellington	1926/27

WELLINGTON

Highest Totals

608-9 dec	v Northern Districts	Hamilton	1998/99
595	v Auckland	Wellington	1927/28
575-7 dec	v Otago	Wellington	1951/52
569	v Auckland	Wellington	1923/24
560	v Otago	Dunedin	1923/24
553	v Canterbury	Wellington	1931/32
544	v Canterbury	Christchurch	1997/98
508	v Northern Districts	Wellington	2000/01
506-4 dec	v Central Districts	Wanganui	1993/94
501-3 dec	v Auckland	Auckland	1997/98

Lowest Totals

19	v Nelson	Nelson	1885/86
22	v Canterbury	Wellington	1903/04
29	v Nelson	Nelson	1879/80
30	v Nelson	Nelson	1883/84
31	v Nelson	Nelson	1887/88
34	v Canterbury	Wellington	1886/87
35	v Auckland	Wellington	1873/74
36	v Nelson	Nelson	1885/86
37	v Nelson	Nelson	1876/77
42	v New South Wales	Wellington	1895/96
42	v Otago	Wellington	1945/46
45	v Nelson	Wellington	1880/81
48	v Nelson	Nelson	1887/88

Most Appearances

120	Gray E.J.	74	Coney J.V.	58	Ritchie T.D.
119	Vance R.H.	72	Wells J.D.	56	Brice A.W.S.
102	McSweeney E.B.	68	Sinclair B.W.	54	Bilby G.P.
89	Morrison J.F.M.	64	Murray B.A.G.	54	McGirr H.M.
87	Edgar B.A.	60	Newdick G.A.	52	Cederwall B.W.
84	Chatfield E.J.	59	Blair R.W.	50	Butler L.C.
79	Larsen G.R.	58	Reid J.R.		

Longest Careers

Seasons				Seasons		
29	Luckie M.M.F.	1891/92-1919/20		22	Collins D.C.	1905/06-1926/27
27	Dempster C.S.	1921/22-1947/48		22	Reaney T.P.L.	1927/28-1948/49
25	Tucker K.H.	1895/96-1919/20		20	McGirr H.M.	1913/14-1932/33
24	James K.C.	1923/24-1946/47		20	Lamason J.R.	1927/28-1946/47
22	Hutchings J.H.	1903/04-1924/25				

Benefits

Morrison J.F.M.	1983/84		Gray E.J.	1989/90
Chatfield E.J.	1985/86		Vance R.H.	1990/91
Coney J.V.	1986/87		McSweeney E.B.	1991/92
Edgar B.A.	1987/88		Larsen G.R.	1996/97

Batting

2000 RUNS	Career	M	In	NO	HS	Runs	Ave	100
Edgar B.A.	1975/76-1989/90	87	160	13	162	6494	44.17	15
Vance R.H.	1976/77-1990/91	119	205	18	254*	6440	34.43	12
Morrison J.F.M.	1967/68-1983/84	89	160	22	180*	4694	34.01	6
Reid J.R.	1947/48-1964/65	58	102	8	296	4538	48.27	13
McSweeney E.B.	1981/82-1993/94	102	153	23	205*	4296	33.04	5
Gray E.J.	1975/76-1991/92	120	181	38	128*	4228	29.56	5
Murray B.A.G.	1958/59-1972/73	64	116	9	213	3753	35.07	3
Sinclair B.W.	1955/56-1970/71	68	116	14	148	3583	35.12	2
Hiddleston J.S.	1913/14-1928/29	41	75	1	212	3413	46.12	8
Coney J.V.	1971/72-1986/87	74	126	21	120*	3251	30.96	4
Newdick G.A.	1970/71-1980/81	60	112	6	143	3236	30.52	4
McGirr H.M.	1913/14-1932/33	54	97	4	141	3032	32.60	5
Bell M.D.	1997/98-2002/03	39	72	7	219	3029	46.60	9
Wells J.D.	1989/90-2000/01	72	113	18	115	3016	31.74	5
Jones A.H.	1985/86-1993/94	39	67	11	181*	2978	53.17	7
Larsen G.R.	1984/85-1998/99	79	118	25	161	2938	31.59	2
Bilby G.P.	1962/63-1976/77	54	95	11	161	2852	33.95	3
Dempster C.S.	1921/22-1947/48	40	76	3	154	2602	35.64	4
Ritchie T.D.	1982/83-1990/91	58	92	14	106	2494	31.97	3
Tindill E.W.T.	1932/33-1949/50	39	73	5	149	2442	35.91	6
Nevin C.J.	1995/96-2002/03	51	80	13	113	2298	34.29	1
Jones R.A.	2000/01-2002/03	30	54	4	188	2151	43.02	7
Burnett G.P.	1987/88-1992/93	44	80	13	203*	2029	30.28	1

CENTURY ON DEBUT FOR PROVINCE

163	Williams A.B.	v Canterbury	Christchurch	1896/97
110 & 5*	Crawford J.N.	v Auckland	Auckland	1917/18
113 & 53	Kortlang H.H.L.	v Auckland	Wellington	1922/23
117 & 6	Bernau E.H.L.	v Auckland	Wellington	1922/23
† 106 & 0	Tindill E.W.T.	v Auckland	Auckland	1932/33
† 110	Ongley J.A.	v Otago	Wellington	1938/39
† 27 &141*	Smith K.F.H.	v Central Districts	Wellington	1953/54
† 132 & 2*	Bilby G.P.	v Central Districts	Wellington	1962/63
† 39 & 156*	Aiken J.M.	v Canterbury	Christchurch	1989/90
115	Fleming S.P.	v Central Districts	Wellington	2001/02

† *indicates player was making his first-class debut*

HIGHEST INDIVIDUAL INNINGS

296	Reid J.R.	v Northern Districts	Wellington	1962/63
283	Reid J.R.	v Otago	Wellington	1952/53
254*	Vance R.H.	v Northern Districts	Wellington	1988/89
222*	Midlane F.A.	v Otago	Wellington	1914/15
219	Bell M.D.	v Northern Districts	Hamilton	1998/99
216	Bell M.D.	v Auckland	Auckland	1997/98
214*	Kortlang H.H.L.	v Auckland	Wellington	1921/26
213	Murray B.A.G.	v Otago	Dunedin	1968/69
212	Hiddleston J.S.	v Canterbury	Wellington	1925/26
205*	McSweeney E.B.	v Central Districts	Levin	1987/88
204	Hiddleston J.S.	v Auckland	Wellington	1925/26
203*	Burnett G.P.	v Northern Districts	Hamilton	1991/92
202	Austen M.H.	v Central Districts	Wanganui	1993/94

MOST RUNS IN A SEASON

		Runs	Ave				Runs	Ave
Vance R.H.	1988/89	888	80.72	Edgar B.A.	1989/90		720	40.00
Jones R.A.	2000/01	849	47.16	Twose R.G.	1994/95		720	80.00
Bell M.D.	2000/01	844	52.75	Jones A.H.	1988/89		701	87.62
Edgar B.A.	1988/89	762	63.50	Edgar B.A.	1987/88		676	52.00
Edgar B.A.	1978/79	728	45.50	Vance R.H.	1987/88		638	79.65
Jones R.A.	2002/03	726	45.37	Jones A.H.	1986/87		627	62.70

MOST CENTURIES IN A SEASON
5   Bell M.D.   2000/01

TOTAL NUMBER OF CENTURIES   233

Most in one season	10	1988/89, 1994/95, 2000/01	
1st	Heenan G.C. 146* v Hawke's Bay		1886/87
100th	Sinclair B.W. 102* v Northern Districts		1963/64
200th	Chandler P.J.B. 177 v Auckland		1996/97

Bowling

150 WICKETS

	Career	M	Wkts	Runs	Ave	5WI	10WM	Best
Chatfield E.J.	1973/74-1989/90	84	403	7531	18.68	23	7	8-24
Gray E.J.	1975/76-1991/92	120	357	9778	27.38	13	3	8-37
Blair R.W.	1951/52-1964/65	59	330	5004	15.16	30	10	9-72
Brice A.W.S.	1902/03-1927/28	56	229	4684	20.45	17	7	9-67
Upham E.F.	1892/93-1909/10	40	227	3393	14.94	17	2	7-24
Reid J.R.	1947/48-1964/65	58	172	3115	18.11	10	—	7-29
McGirr H.M.	1913/14-1932/33	54	166	4326	26.06	7	1	7-45
Morrison B.D.	1953/54-1964/65	45	163	3858	23.66	7	2	7-42

BEST IN AN INNINGS

9-67	Brice A.W.S.	v Auckland	Wellington	1918/19
9-72	Blair R.W.	v Auckland	Wellington	1956/57
9-75	Blair R.W.	v Canterbury	Wellington	1956/57
8-13	Firth J.P.	v Hawke's Bay	Wellington	1883/84
8-21	Penn A.J.	v Canterbury	Wellington	2001/02
8-24	Chatfield E.J.	v Northern Districts	Lower Hutt	1979/80
8-34	Fisher F.E.	v Canterbury	Wellington	1952/53
8-36	Blair R.W.	v Otago	Dunedin	1952/53
8-37	Gray E.J.	v Canterbury	Lower Hutt	1985/86
8-50	Butler L.C.	v NZ Under 23 XI	Wellington	1965/66

8-58	Ashbolt F.L.	v Hawke's Bay	Napier	1897/98
8-59	Hiddleston J.S.	v Canterbury	Christchurch	1918/19
8-64	Collinge R.O.	v Auckland	Auckland	1967/68
8-78	Gray E.J.	v Auckland	Wellington	1989/90
8-83	Chatfield E.J.	v Otago	Dunedin	1986/87

BEST IN A MATCH

14-136	Blair R.W.	v Canterbury	Wellington	1956/57
14-151	Gray E.J.	v Canterbury	Lower Hutt	1985/86
13-58	Salmon I.J.	v Nelson	Wellington	1873/74
13-86	Chatfield E.J.	v West Indies	Lower Hutt	1979/80
13-91	Gore A.H.	v Hawke's Bay	Napier	1886/87
13-92	Middleton F.S.	v Hawke's Bay	Wellington	1919/20
13-97	Ashbolt F.L.	v Hawke's Bay	Napier	1897/98
13-157	Tucker K.H.	v Auckland	Wellington	1900/01
13-176	Brice A.W.S.	v Auckland	Wellington	1920/21

MOST WICKETS IN A SEASON

		Wkts	Ave			Wkts	Ave
Chatfield E.J.	1979/80	49	10.51	Saunders J.V.	1913/14	41	17.58
Gray E.J.	1984/85	48	21.75	Chatfield E.J.	1976/77	41	19.48
Chatfield E.J.	1981/82	47	16.87	O'Brien I.E.	2000/01	41	19.68
Blair R.W.	1956/57	46	9.47	Penn A.J.	2001/02	40	18.30
Walker M.D.J.	2002/03	45	18.00				

Wicketkeeping

100 DISMISSALS	Career	M	Caught	Stumped	Total
McSweeney E.B.	1981/82-1993/94	102	289	39	328
Nevin C.J.	1995/95-2002/03	51	157	6	163
Therkleson I.J.	1966/67-1973/74	39	93	7	100

MOST DISMISSALS IN A SEASON
46   (46ct)   Nevin C.J.   2000/01

MOST DISMISSALS IN A MATCH

10	(10ct)	Nevin C.J. v Otago	Dunedin	1995/96

MOST DISMISSALS IN AN INNINGS

6	(6ct)	Vance R.H. v Otago	Wellington	1977/78
6	(5ct 1st)	Nevin C.J. v Central Districts	Nelson	1995/96

MOST CATCHES IN A MATCH

10	Nevin C.J. v Otago	Dunedin	1995/96

MOST CATCHES IN AN INNINGS

6	Vance R.H. v Otago	Wellington	1977/78

Fielding

MOST CATCHES IN A MATCH

7	Morrison J.F.M. v Northern Districts	Wellington	1980/81

MOST CATCHES IN AN INNINGS

5	Lamason J.R. v Otago	Dunedin	1937/38
5	Morrison J.F.M. v Northern Districts	Wellington	1980/81

Record Partnerships

FOR

Wicket	Score	Batsmen	Against	At	Date
1st	333	B.A. Edgar & A.H. Jones	Auckland	Wellington	1988/89
2nd	287	M.D. Bell & J.D. Wells	Auckland	Auckland	1997/98
3rd	346	G.P. Burnett & R.A. Verry	ND	Hamilton	1991/92
4th	274	R.A. Jones & S.R. Mather	Otago	Wellington	2000/01
5th	341	G.R. Larsen & E.B. McSweeney	CD	Levin	1987/88
6th	226	E.J. Gray & R.W. Ormiston	CD	Wellington	1981/82
7th	168	K.C. James & H.M. McGirr	Canterbury	Wellington	1927/28
8th	180	R.G. Twose & M.C. Goodson	Otago	Dunedin	1994/95
9th	127	F.L.H. Mooney & R.A. Buchan	Auckland	Wellington	1943/44
10th	138	K.C. James & A.W.S. Brice	Otago	Wellington	1926/27

AGAINST

Wicket	Score	Batsmen	For	At	Date
1st	287	B.R. Hartland & G.R. Stead	Canterbury	Christchurch	1994/95
2nd	254	K.J. Burns & K.R. Rutherford	Otago	Oamaru	1987/88
3rd	213	G.M. Turner & B.E. Congdon	Otago	Dunedin	1972/73
4th	278	A.W. Roberts & M.L. Page	Canterbury	Wellington	1931/32
5th	183	C.Z. Harris & C.D. McMillan	Canterbury	Christchurch	1996/97
6th	209	C.Z. Harris & A.J. Redmond	Canterbury	Rangiora	2001/02
7th	241	N.J. Astle & M.W. Priest	Canterbury	Christchurch	1994/95
8th	189	W.N. Carson & A.M. Matheson	Auckland	Auckland	1938/39
9th	188	N.R. Parlane & D.R. Tuffey	ND	Wellington	1999/00
10th	97	A.C. Kerr & H.C. Nottman	Auckland	Auckland	1941/42

INTER-PROVINCIAL RECORDS

AUCKLAND v CANTERBURY

First match 1873/74	Played 119	Won by Auckland 44	Won by Canterbury 39	Drawn 36

Highest totals	A	693-9 dec	Auckland	1939/40
	C	514-6 dec	Christchurch	2002/03
Lowest totals	A	13	Auckland	1877/78
	C	62	Rangiora	1998/99
Highest innings	A	256 S.G. Smith	Auckland	1919/20
	C	301* P.G. Fulton	Christchurch	2002/03
Best bowling (innings)	A	9-75 R. Neill	Auckland	1891/92
	C	9-56 D.J. McBeath	Christchurch	1918/19
Best bowling (match)	A	13-85 R.S. Cunis	Christchurch	1963/64
	C	15-168 D.J. McBeath	Christchurch	1918/19

Record Partnerships

AUCKLAND

1st	286	B. Sutcliffe & D.D. Taylor	Auckland	1948/49
2nd	145	A.E.W. Parsons & J.F. Reid	Auckland	1978/79
3rd	278	T.J. Franklin & D.N. Patel	Christchurch	1985/86
4th	206	T.G. McIntosh & L. Vincent	Christchurch	2000/01
5th	161*	B. Sutcliffe & D.D. Taylor	Auckland	1946/47
6th	160	P.N. Webb & P.J. Kelly	Auckland	1985/86
7th	224	V.J. Scott & A.M. Matheson	Auckland	1937/38
8th	153	R.J. Nicol & R.A. Young	Auckland	2001/02
9th	96	C. Pringle & D.K. Morrison	Rangiora	1995/96
10th	83	S.W. Brown & C. Pringle	Christchurch	1990/91

CANTERBURY

1st	306	L.A. Cuff & J.D. Lawrence	Christchurch	1893/94
2nd	179	B.G. Hadlee & N.M. Parker	Auckland	1978/79
3rd	183	G.R. Stead & C.Z. Harris	Christchurch	2000/01
4th	147	M.L. Page & R.O. Talbot	Christchurch	1930/31
5th	158	P.G. Kennedy & M.W. Priest	Christchurch	1991/92
6th	172	L.A. Butterfield & R.C.S.A. Shand	Christchurch	1945/46
7th	142	G.J. Hopkins & P.J. Wiseman	Auckland	2002/03
8th	166	R.J. Hadlee & D.R. Hadlee	Christchurch	1983/84
9th	115	G.J. Hopkins & A.M. Ellis	Auckland	2002/03
10th	83	H.C. Wilson & H.W. Monaghan	Christchurch	1913/14
	83	M. Graham & A.P. Cobden	Auckland	1935/36

AUCKLAND v CENTRAL DISTRICTS

First match 1950/51	Played 67	Won by Auckland 25	Won by Central Districts 18	Drawn 24

Highest totals	A	526-4 dec		Auckland	1951/52
	CD	594-8 dec		Auckland	1995/96
Lowest totals	A	71		Palmerston North	2001/02
	CD	59		New Plymouth	1958/59
Highest innings	A	182*	D.N. Patel	New Plymouth	1990/91
	CD	166	M.S. Sinclair	Masterton	1998/99
Best bowling *(innings)*	A	7-29	R.S. Cunis	Auckland	1961/62
	CD	7-31	H.B. Cave	Palmerston North	1952/53
Best bowling *(match)*	A	12-146	K.W. Hough	Auckland	1959/60
	CD	13-64	H.B. Cave	Palmerston North	1952/53

Record Partnerships

AUCKLAND

1st	161	S.J. Peterson & B.A. Pocock	Auckland	1991/92
2nd	167	G.O. Rabone & D.D. Coleman	Auckland	1951/52
3rd	151*	M.J. Horne & A.C. Barnes	Auckland	2001/02
4th	140	R.A. Jones & H.D. Barton	New Plymouth	1997/98
5th	234*	V.J. Scott & J.B. Morris	Auckland	1951/52
6th	165	J.J. Crowe & J.G. Bracewell	Auckland	1987/88
7th	192	S.W. Brown & A.C. Parore	Auckland	1990/91
8th	78	A.C. Barnes & K.D. Mills	Auckland	1999/00
9th	104*	R.A. Young & C.J. Drum	Auckland	2000/01
10th	76	B.G.K. Walker & H.T. Davis	Blenheim	2002/03

CENTRAL DISTRICTS

1st	172	C.J.P. Smith & P.S. Briasco	New Plymouth	1985/86
2nd	207*	R.G. Twose & M.W. Douglas	Auckland	1991/92
3rd	198	M.S. Sinclair & G.P. Sulzberger	Masterton	1998/99
4th	155	R.T. Hart & T.E. Blain	Masterton	1989/90
5th	127	M.W. Douglas & T.E. Blain	Nelson	1988/89
6th	220	M.H. Toynbee & I.D.S. Smith	Napier	1982/83
7th	165	R.K. Brown & M.E.L. Lane	Palmerston North	1993/94
8th	94	S.W. Duff & D.J. Leonard	Wanganui	1991/92
9th	68	I.R. Snook & A.B. Jordan	Nelson	1974/75
10th	133	G.A. Bartlett & I.A. Colquhoun	Auckland	1959/60

AUCKLAND v NORTHERN DISTRICTS

First match 1956/57	Played 63	Won by Auckland 21	Won by Northern Districts 14	Drawn 28

Highest totals	A	547-8 dec		Auckland	2000/01
	ND	492		Auckland	1990/91
Lowest totals	A	69		Auckland	1963/64
	ND	32		Hamilton	1996/97
Highest innings	A	209	P.A. Horne	Auckland	1988/89
	ND	211*	G.A. Hick	Auckland	1988/89
Best bowling (innings)	A	7-30	R.S. Cunis	Whangarei	1966/67
	ND	9-48	A.R. Tait	Hamilton	1996/97
Best bowling (match)	A	11-71	J.A. Hayes	Auckland	1957/58
	ND	16-130	A.R. Tait	Hamilton	1996/97

Record Partnerships

AUCKLAND

1st	197	T.J. Franklin & P.A. Horne	Auckland	1985/86
2nd	175	B.A. Pocock & J.M. Aiken	Auckland	2000/01
3rd	152	T.J. Franklin & J.J. Crowe	Rotorua	1983/84
4th	280	J.J. Crowe & D.N. Patel	Auckland	1991/92
5th	112	J.T. Sparling & J.G. Kemp	Hamilton	1962/63
6th	157	J.F. Reid & J.R. Wiltshire	Auckland	1977/78
7th	129	J.D. Behrent & E.R. Tovey	Auckland	1963/64
8th	75*	H.T. Schuster & H.J. Howarth	Hamilton	1964/65
9th	91*	K.D. Mills & C.J. Drum	Auckland	2000/01
10th	103	P.J. Kelly & G.B. Troup	Auckland	1985/86

NORTHERN DISTRICTS

1st	143	M.J.E. Wright & J.G. Wright	Tauranga	1979/80
2nd	167	M.D. Bell & G.E. Bradburn	Hamilton	1994/95
3rd	261*	M.P. Maynard & S.A. Thomson	Hamilton	1990/91
4th	252	S.A. Thomson & B.A. Young	Auckland	1990/91
5th	142	M.P. Maynard & B.A. Young	Auckland	1991/92
6th	146*	G.A. Hick & S.A. Thomson	Auckland	1988/89
7th	127	C.M. Kuggeleijn & S.A. Thomson	Auckland	1988/89
8th	90	R.G. Hart & M.E. Parlane	Hamilton	1994/95
9th	185	M.P. Maynard & S.B. Doull	Auckland	1991/92
10th	82	S.B. Doull & B.P. Martin	Taupo	1999/00

AUCKLAND v OTAGO

First match 1873/74	*Played* 105	*Won by Auckland* 56	*Won by Otago* 22	*Drawn* 27

Highest totals	A	579	Auckland	1909/10
	O	558-8 dec	Dunedin	1949/50
Lowest totals	A	48	Dunedin	1889/90
	O	35	Christchurch	1884/85
Highest innings	A	290 W.N. Carson	Dunedin	1936/37
	O	355 B. Sutcliffe	Dunedin	1949/50
Best bowling *(innings)*	A	9-36 A.F. Wensley	Auckland	1929/30
	O	8-57 S.L. Boock	Dunedin	1989/90
Best bowling *(match)*	A	14-63 A.W. Rees	Dunedin	1889/90
	O	15-104 S.L. Boock	Dunedin	1989/90

Record Partnerships

AUCKLAND

1st	240	T.G. McIntosh & M.J. Horne	Dunedin	2001/02
2nd	170	L.G. Hemus & A.E. Relf	Auckland	1909/10
3rd	445	P.E. Whitelaw & W.N. Carson	Dunedin	1936/37
4th	176	V.J. Scott & R.W.G. Emery	Dunedin	1945/46
5th	197	C.C.R. Dacre & C.F.W. Allcott	Dunedin	1926/27
6th	209*	A.C. Parore & A.P. O'Dowd	Dunedin	1991/92
7th	177*	A.C. Barnes & J.M. Mills	Alexandra	1995/96
8th	140	J.G. Kemp & J.M. McIntyre	Dunedin	1969/70
9th	75	R.S. Cunis & R.I. Harford	Auckland	1966/67
10th	119	W.N. Carson & J. Cowie	Auckland	1937/38

OTAGO

1st	373	B. Sutcliffe & L. Watt	Auckland	1950/51
2nd	227	P.W. Dobbs & M.J. Lamont	Dunedin	1990/91
3rd	199	W.S. Haig & B. Sutcliffe	Auckland	1954/55
4th	177	M.J. Lamont & M.H. Richardson	Alexandra	1995/96
5th	266	B. Sutcliffe & W.S. Haig	Dunedin	1949/50
6th	145	M.J. Horne & M.G. Croy	Auckland	1997/98
7th	164	A. Galland & A.R. Knight	Auckland	1925/26
8th	84	L.R. Pearson & J.C. Alabaster	Auckland	1964/65
9th	64	K.F.M. Uttley & G.H. Mills	Dunedin	1936/37
10th	60	L.D. Smith & G.W.F. Overton	Auckland	1946/47

AUCKLAND v WELLINGTON

First match 1873/74	*Played* 125	*Won by Auckland* 54	*Won by Wellington* 30	*Drawn* 41

Highest totals	A	522		Wellington	1918/19
	W	595		Wellington	1927/28
Lowest totals	A	48		Wellington	1889/90
	W	35		Wellington	1873/74
Highest innings	A	194	W.N. Carson	Auckland	1936/37
	W	216	M.D. Bell	Auckland	1997/98
Best bowling	A	8-51	R. Neill	Auckland	1895/96
(innings)	W	9-67	A.W.S. Brice	Wellington	1918/19
Best bowling	A	14-65	J.A. Hayes	Auckland	1957/58
(match)	W	13-157	K.H. Tucker	Wellington	1900/01

Record Partnerships

AUCKLAND

1st	201	A. Anthony & E. Horspool	Auckland	1924/25
2nd	241	T.J. Franklin & J.J. Crowe	Wellington	1988/89
3rd	203*	B.A. Pocock & A.C. Parore	Auckland	1997/98
4th	180	A.N.C. Snedden & C.C.R. Dacre	Wellington	1922/23
5th	174	R.W. Morgan & J.G. Kemp	Auckland	1967/68
6th	176	V.J. Scott & O.C. Cleal	Auckland	1940/41
7th	131	G.L. Weir & C.C.R. Dacre	Wellington	1927/28
8th	189	W.N. Carson & A.M. Matheson	Auckland	1938/39
9th	122	H.T. Schuster & R.S. Cunis	Wellington	1964/65
10th	97	A.C. Kerr & H.C. Nottman	Auckland	1941/42

WELLINGTON

1st	333	B.A. Edgar & A.H. Jones	Wellington	1988/89
2nd	287	M.D. Bell & J.D. Wells	Auckland	1997/98
3rd	201	E.G. McLeod & J.R. Lamason	Wellington	1935/36
4th	207	F.T. Badcock & T.C. Lowry	Wellington	1927/28
5th	192	W.A. Baker & J.N. Crawford	Auckland	1917/18
6th	134	K.C. James & H.M. McGirr	Wellington	1926/27
7th	144	J.R. Reid & P.T. Barton	Auckland	1959/60
8th	137	F.L.H. Mooney & F.E. Fisher	Wellington	1952/53
9th	127	F.L.H. Mooney & R.A. Buchan	Wellington	1943/44
10th	113	F.L.H. Mooney & E.C.V. Knapp	Wellington	1943/44

CANTERBURY v CENTRAL DISTRICTS

First match 1950/51	Played 68	Won by Canterbury 23	Won by Central Districts 18	Drawn 27

Highest totals	C	559	Christchurch	1993/94
	CD	549-8 dec	Christchurch	1998/99
Lowest totals	C	68	Levin	1985/86
	CD	91	Christchurch	1954/55
Highest innings	C	251* C.Z. Harris	Rangiora	1996/97
	CD	212* D.P. Kelly	Blenheim	2000/01
Best bowling	C	7-23 B.A. Bolton	Nelson	1961/62
(innings)	CD	9-100 B.W. Yuile	New Plymouth	1965/66
Best bowling	C	12-130 T.B. Burtt	Palmerston North	1950/51
(match)	CD	11-138 D.J. Kay	Palmerston North	1976/77

Record Partnerships

CANTERBURY

1st	185	B.R. Hartland & D.J. Murray	Palmerston North	1994/95
2nd	166	G.T. Dowling & B.F. Hastings	Christchurch	1964/65
3rd	174	P.J. Rattray & P.E. McEwan	Palmerston North	1981/82
4th	204	T.W. Jarvis & K. Thomson	Wanganui	1969/70
5th	290	C.Z. Harris & G.R. Stead	Blenheim	1996/97
6th	149	M.W. Priest & L.K. Germon	Christchurch	1988/89
7th	184*	C.L. Bull & B.P. Isherwood	Nelson	1971/72
8th	136	G.R. Stead & C.J. Anderson	Christchurch	2000/01
9th	113	G.J. Hopkins & S.J. Cunis	Christchurch	1998/99
10th	85	G.T. Dowling & A.F. Rapley	Christchurch	1958/59

CENTRAL DISTRICTGS

1st	178	P.J. Ingram & J.M. How	Napier	2002/03
2nd	317	R.T. Hart & P.S. Briasco	New Plymouth	1983/84
3rd	197	M.J. Greatbatch & M.D. Crowe	New Plymouth	1986/87
4th	276*	M.D. Crowe & P.S. Briasco	Christchurch	1986/87
5th	235*	G.P. Sulzberger & J.D. Ryder	Napier	2002/03
6th	130	R.E. Hayward & I.D.S. Smith	Levin	1985/86
7th	219	B.W. Yuile & B.L. Hampton	Napier	1967/68
8th	133*	B.L. Hampton & R.M. Schofield	Christchurch	1964/65
9th	89	S.W. Duff & D.J. Leonard	Christchurch	1993/94
10th	98	I.A. Rutherford & D.J. Kay	Napier	1977/78

CANTERBURY v NORTHERN DISTRICTS

First match 1956/57	Played 62	Won by Canterbury 23	Won by Northern Districts 13	Drawn 26

Highest totals	C	549	Christchurch	1996/97
	ND	518-4 dec	Christchurch	1996/97
Lowest totals	C	83	Christchurch	1961/62
	ND	52	Hamilton	1966/67
Highest innings	C	237* R.T. Latham	Rotorua	1990/91
	ND	235 J.A.H. Marshall	Christchurch	2001/02
Best bowling (innings)	C	7-24 J.W. Kiddey	Hamilton	1960/61
	ND	7-58 R.P. de Groen	Hamilton	1995/96
Best bowling (match)	C	12-81 R.J. Hadlee	Christchurch	1986/87
	ND	11-129 R.P. de Groen	Hamilton	1995/96

Record Partnerships

CANTERBURY

1st	214	B.A. Bolton & G.T. Dowling	Christchurch	1959/60
2nd	167	G.T. Dowling & T.W. Jarvis	Hamilton	1970/71
3rd	394*	P.G. Kennedy & R.T. Latham	Rotorua	1990/91
4th	181	V.R. Brown & R.T. Latham	Gisborne	1986/87
5th	252*	R.T. Latham & M.W. Priest	Christchurch	1988/89
6th	175	S.P. Fleming & L.K. Germon	Hamilton	1993/94
7th	205	L.K. Germon & M.W. Priest	Christchurch	1991/92
8th	82	P.B. Wight & J.W. Kiddey	Christchurch	1963/64
9th	76	C.R.W. Dickel & K.I. Ferries	Hamilton	1974/75
10th	160	L.K. Germon & W.A. Wisneski	Rangiora	1997/98

NORTHERN DISTRICTS

1st	136	B.A. Pocock & M.D. Bell	Christchurch	1996/97
2nd	237	J.G. Gibson & C.M. Kuggeleijn	Hamilton	1980/81
3rd	150	R.D. Broughton & A.D.G. Roberts	Christchurch	1980/81
4th	259	G.E. Bradburn & M.E. Parlane	Christchurch	1996/97
5th	138	C.M. Kuggeleijn & B.A. Young	Whangarei	1989/90
6th	180	S.A. Thomson & M.N. Hart	Hamilton	1992/93
7th	69	C.M. Kuggeleijn & B.A. Young	Christchurch	1988/89
8th	152	G.E. Bradburn & S.B. Doull	Christchurch	1991/92
9th	69	M.N. Hart & S.B. Doull	Rangiora	2000/01
10th	62	M.N. Hart & G.W. Aldridge	Rangiora	2000/01

CANTERBURY v OTAGO

First match 1863/64	Played 158	Won by Canterbury 74	Won by Otago 57	Drawn 27

Highest totals	C	777		Christchurch	1996/97
	O	602-8 dec		Dunedin	1928/29
Lowest totals	C	25		Christchurch	1866/67
	O	40		Dunedin	1869/70
Highest innings	C	204	A. Cox	Christchurch	1925/26
	O	385	B. Sutcliffe	Christchurch	1952/53
Best bowling (innings)	C	9-95	M.W. Priest	Dunedin	1989/90
	O	9-72	F.H. Cooke	Christchurch	1884/85
Best bowling (match)	C	13-181	W.E. Merritt	Christchurch	1935/36
	O	15-94	F.H. Cooke	Christchurch	1882/83

Record Partnerships

CANTERBURY

1st	226*	W.A. Hadlee & J.G. Leggat	Christchurch	1948/49
2nd	210	W.A. Hadlee & F.P. O'Brien	Christchurch	1940/41
3rd	178	R.M. Frew & M.H.W. Papps	Christchurch	2000/01
4th	166	G.T. Dowling & K. Thomson	Dunedin	1966/67
5th	236	C.Z. Harris & N.J. Astle	Christchurch	1996/97
6th	140	F.P. O'Brien & J. Smith	Christchurch	1943/44
7th	265	J.L. Powell & N. Dorreen	Christchurch	1929/30
8th	95	R.H. Scott & A.T. Burgess	Christchurch	1946/47
9th	109	J.H. Bennett & A.W. Thomas	Dunedin	1913/14
10th	98	S.A. Orchard & C. Boxshall	Dunedin	1908/09

OTAGO

1st	209	B. Sutcliffe & L. Watt	Dunedin	1947/48
2nd	170	C.C. Hopkins & G.G. Austin	Christchurch	1911/12
3rd	221	R.C. Blunt & J.J.M. McMullan	Dunedin	1928/29
4th	168	K.F.M. Uttley & V.J.T. Chettleburgh	Dunedin	1936/37
5th	147	K.J. Burns & D.J. Walker	Christchurch	1985/86
6th	118	P.C. Semple & G.D. Alabaster	Christchurch	1969/70
7th	182	B. Sutcliffe & A.W. Gilbertson	Christchurch	1952/53
8th	146	M.H. Austen & P.J. Wiseman	Christchurch	1996/97
9th	134	J.W. Wilson & N.A. Mallender	Christchurch	1992/93
10th	184	R.C. Blunt & W. Hawksworth	Christchurch	1931/32

CANTERBURY v WELLINGTON

First match 1883/84	Played 131	Won by Canterbury 47	Won by Wellington 48	Drawn 35	Tied 1

Highest totals	C	547-5 dec	Christchurch	1953/54
	W	553	Wellington	1931/32
Lowest totals	C	37	Wellington	1925/26
	W	22	Wellington	1903/04
Highest innings	C	206 M.L. Page	Wellington	1931/32
		206 G.T. Dowling	Christchurch	1962/63
	W	212 J.S. Hiddleston	Wellington	1925/26
Best bowling (innings)	C	10-28 A.E. Moss	Christchurch	1889/90
	W	9-75 R.W. Blair	Wellington	1956/57
Best bowling (match)	C	13-72 A.E. Moss	Christchurch	1889/90
	W	14-136 R.W. Blair	Wellington	1956/57

Record Partnerships

CANTERBURY

1st	287	B.R. Hartland & G.R. Stead	Christchurch	1994/95
2nd	174	G.T. Dowling & J.W. Burtt	Wellington	1967/68
3rd	187*	C.D. McMillan & R.T. Latham	Christchurch	1994/95
4th	278	M.L. Page & A.W. Roberts	Wellington	1931/32
5th	183	C.Z. Harris & C.D. McMillan	Christchurch	1996/97
6th	209	C.Z. Harris & A.J. Redmond	Rangiora	2001/02
7th	241	N.J. Astle & M.W. Priest	Christchurch	1994/95
8th	114	A.W. Thomas & H.B. Whitta	Christchurch	1919/20
9th	182*	L.K. Germon & R.M. Ford	Christchurch	1989/90
10th	85	A.W. Hart & C.H. Thiele	Rangiora	1984/85

WELLINGTON

1st	239	C.S. Dempster & W.H. Dustin	Wellington	1931/32
2nd	209*	A.H. Jones & M.D. Crowe	Christchurch	1992/93
3rd	206	A.H. Preston & J.E.F. Beck	Christchurch	1955/56
4th	187	H.M. McGirr & T.C. Lowry	Christchurch	1930/31
5th	134*	J.F.M. Morrison & R.W. Ormiston	Christchurch	1981/82
6th	140	J.E.F. Beck & E.W. Dempster	Wellington	1956/57
7th	168	H.M. McGirr & K.C. James	Wellington	1927/28
8th	154	K.C. James & F.T. Badcock	Christchurch	1926/27
9th	115	E.H.L. Bernau & K.C. James	Wellington	1923/24
10th	87	N.R. Hoar & R. Allen	Christchurch	1944/45

CENTRAL DISTRICTS v NORTHERN DISTRICTS

First match 1956/57	Played 62	Won by Central Districts 20	Won by Northern Districts 16	Drawn 26

Highest totals	CD	466	Wanganui	1998/99
	ND	498-6 dec	Napier	1992/93
Lowest totals	CD	51	Hamilton	1957/58
	ND	86	New Plymouth	1956/57
Highest innings	CD	203* M.S. Sinclair	Wanganui	1998/99
	ND	209 D.J. White	Hamilton	1985/86
Best bowling (innings)	CD	7-28 B.W. Yuile	Hamilton	1967/68
	ND	8-37 D.B. Clarke	Wanganui	1962/63
Best bowling (match)	CD	11-134 G.K. Robertson	Nelson	1986/87
	ND	10-78 D.B. Clarke	Wanganui	1962/63

Record Partnerships

CENTRAL DISTRICTS

1st	180	T.E. Blain & C.J.P. Smith	Nelson	1986/87
2nd	263	M.J. Greatbatch & M.D. Crowe	Morrinsville	1986/87
3rd	210	B.F. Smith & M.W. Douglas	Taupo	2000/01
4th	161	L.G. Howell & M.J. Greatbatch	Rotorua	1995/96
5th	199	M.D. Crowe & M.W. Douglas	Rotorua	1989/90
6th	132*	T.E. Blain & S.W. Duff	Wanganui	1990/91
7th	179	B.B.J. Griggs & C.J.M. Furlong	Hamilton	2001/02
8th	173	I.D.S. Smith & G.K. Robertson	Hamilton	1982/83
9th	116	V. Pollard & R.O. Collinge	Palmerston North	1964/65
10th	48	M.J. Mason & L.J. Hamilton	Blenheim	2001/02

NORTHERN DISTRICTS

1st	167	M.E. Parlane & M.D. Bell	New Plymouth	1994/95
2nd	199	R.E.W. Mawhinney & D.J. White	Hamilton	1985/86
3rd	142	D.J. White & G.W. McKenzie	Hamilton	1985/86
4th	169	D.J. White & B.S. Oxenham	Wanganui	1990/91
5th	128	D.J. White & B.G. Cooper	Nelson	1986/87
6th	105	G.E. Bradburn & D.J. Nash	Masterton	1997/98
7th	136	D.J. Nash & A.R. Tait	Masterton	1997/98
8th	143	C.M. Presland & C.W. Dickeson	Whangarei	1983/84
9th	107	R.G. Hart & A.R. Tait	Rotorua	1995/96
10th	89	M.J.E. Wright & S.J. Scott	Wanganui	1978/79

CENTRAL DISTRICTS v OTAGO

First match 1950/51	*Played* 71	*Won by Central Districts* 21	*Won by Otago* 23	*Drawn* 27

Highest totals	CD	526	Napier	1995/96
	O	571-8	Napier	1995/96
Lowest totals	CD	74	Invercargill	1996/97
	O	73	Dunedin	1986/87
Highest innings	CD	242 M.D. Crowe	New Plymouth	1989/90
	O	264 B. Sutcliffe	Dunedin	1959/60
Best bowling (*innings*)	CD	7-36 B.W. Yuile	Nelson	1962/63
	O	8-31 D.G. Sewell	Invercargill	1996/97
Best bowling (*match*)	CD	11-99 D.D. Beard	Dunedin	1956/57
	O	15-203 A.M. Moir	New Plymouth	1953/54

Record Partnerships

CENTRAL DISTRICTS

1st	137	T.E. Blain & R.E. Hart	Oamaru	1984/85
2nd	193	M.L. Ryan & B.E. Congdon	Nelson	1968/69
3rd	223	C.J.P. Smith & S.W.J. Wilson	Blenheim	1990/91
4th	207	G.P. Sulzberger & A.J. Penn	Napier	1995/96
5th	168	B.F. Smith & M.W. Douglas	Alexandra	2000/01
6th	144	T.E. Blain & S.W. Duff	Palmerston North	1991/92
7th	123	I.D.S. Smith & S.J. Gill	Napier	1981/82
8th	106	S.J. Gill & D.R. O'Sullivan	Dunedin	1982/83
9th	239	H.B. Cave & I.B. Leggat	Dunedin	1952/53
10th	57	G.K. Robertson & D.R. O'Sullivan	Oamaru	1984/85

OTAGO

1st	305	R.A. Lawson & M.G. Croy	Napier	1995/96
2nd	169	G.M. Turner & R.W. Anderson	Dunedin	1974/75
3rd	227	K.R. Rutherford & B.R. Blair	Alexandra	1988/89
4th	200	B.R. Blair & G.J. Dawson	Dunedin	1982/83
5th	192	M.H. Richardson & I.S. Billcliff	Napier	1994/95
6th	147	R.N. Hoskin & J.K. Lindsay	Oamaru	1985/86
7th	121*	W.K. Lees & B. Abernethy	Napier	1981/82
8th	96	M.H. Richardson & P.J. Wiseman	Napier	1995/96
9th	92	D.E.C. McKechnie & B.L. Cairns	Dunedin	1976/77
10th	78	C.B. Gaffaney & D.G. Sewell	Palmerston North	1999/00

CENTRAL DISTRICTS v WELLINGTON

First match 1950/51	Played 67	Won by Central Districts 12	Won by Wellington 24	Drawn 31

Highest totals	CD	485-7 dec		Wellington	1964/65
	W	506-4 dec		Wanganui	1993/94
Lowest totals	CD	50		Upper Hutt	1979/80
	W	88		Wellington	1991/92
Highest innings	CD	207	R.T. Hart	Wellington	1985/86
	W	205*	E.B. McSweeney	Levin	1987/88
Best bowling	CD	6-33	D.D. Beard	Wellington	1957/58
(innings)	W	7-68	B.D. Morrison	Wellington	1955/56
Best bowling	CD	9-88	V. Pollard	Wanganui	1967/68
(match)	W	10-103	B.D. Morrison	Wellington	1955/56

Record Partnerships

CENTRAL DISTRICTS

1st	250	R.T. Hart & C.J.P. Smith	Wellington	1985/86
2nd	157	H.C. Sampson & B.E. Congdon	Wellington	1970/71
3rd	180	C.D. Ingham & M.J. Greatbatch	Napier	1994/95
4th	172*	P.S. Briasco & M.W. Douglas	Palmerston North	1990/91
5th	165	R.T. Hart & I.D. Fisher	Wellington	1989/90
6th	92	M.J.F. Shrimpton & L.W. Downes	Masterton	1975/76
7th	134	M.W. Douglas & S.W. Duff	Napier	1991/92
8th	84	P.M. Blackbourn & G.K. Robertson	Palmerston North	1983/84
9th	70	D.W. Neal & J.H. Howell	Wellington	1972/73
10th	52	D.J. Leonard & A.J. Alcock	Wellington	1992/93

WELLINGTON

1st	316	M.H. Austen & R.T. Hart	Wanganui	1993/94
2nd	190	B.A. Edgar & R.H. Vance	New Plymouth	1988/89
3rd	186	J.D. Wells & S.J. Blackmore	New Plymouth	1999/00
4th	176	R.H. Vance & R.B. Reid	New Plymouth	1979/80
5th	341	G.R. Larsen & E.B. McSweeney	Levin	1987/88
6th	226	E.J. Gray & R.W. Ormiston	Wellington	1981/82
7th	161	S.P. Fleming & M.D.J. Walker	Wellington	2001/02
8th	135	G.R. Larsen & J.E.C. Franklin	Wellington	1998/99
9th	83	T. Vaikvee & R.O. Collinge	New Plymouth	1973/74
10th	81	L.C. Butler & R.E. Reid	Wanganui	1959/60

NORTHERN DISTRICTS v OTAGO

First match 1956/57	Played 60	Won by Northern Districts 22	Won by Otago 18	Drawn 20

Highest totals	ND	520-8 dec		Hamilton	1987/88
	O	457		Hamilton	1987/88
Lowest totals	ND	64		Dunedin	1971/72
	O	77		Gisborne	1999/00
Highest innings	ND	212*	S.B. Styris	Hamilton	2001/02
	O	201	B. Sutcliffe	Hamilton	1960/61
Best bowling (innings)	ND	7-42	K. Treiber	Hamilton	1985/86
	O	9-93	P.J. Petherick	Dunedin	1975/76
Best bowling (match)	ND	13-99	R.P. de Groen	Alexandra	1992/93
	O	13-144	S.L. Boock	Whangarei	1980/81

Record Partnerships

NORTHERN DISTRICTS

1st	151	G.P. Howarth & R.W. Fulton	Gisborne	1974/75
2nd	222	L.M. Crocker & C.M. Kuggeleijn	Hamilton	1983/84
3rd	112	R.W. Fulton & J.M. Parker	Gisborne	1974/75
4th	203	S.A. Thomson & M.P. Maynard	Hamilton	1991/92
5th	117	W.J. Mitchell & P.D. Stone	Hamilton	1966/67
6th	191	S.B. Styris & R.G. Hart	Hamilton	2001/02
7th	130	M.D. Bailey & R.G. Hart	Invercargill	1994/95
8th	81	M.J.E. Wright & B.L. Cairns	Tauranga	1982/83
9th	96	R.G. Hart & B.P. Martin	Dunedin	2001/02
10th	97	R.G. Hart & G.L. West	Hamilton	2002/03

OTAGO

1st	260	R.A. Lawson & Mohammad Wasim	Dunedin	2002/03
2nd	220	M.H. Richardson & C.D. Cumming	Hamilton	2000/01
3rd	150	K.B.K. Ibadulla & K.J. Burns	Gisborne	1989/90
4th	235	K.J. Burns & R.N. Hoskin	Hamilton	1987/88
5th	123	R. Hendry & L.R. Pearson	Dunedin	1961/62
6th	129	N.R. Thompson & A.M. Moir	Hamilton	1958/59
7th	134	W.K. Lees & R.E.W. Mawhinney	Hamilton	1983/84
8th	129	B. Sutcliffe & T. Flaws	Hamilton	1960/61
9th	39	P.W. Hills & S.L. Boock	Gisborne	1988/89
10th	59	P.W. Hills & V.F. Johnson	Gisborne	1988/89

NORTHERN DISTRICTS v WELLINGTON

First match 1956/57	Played 62	Won by Northern Districts 12	Won by Wellington 27	Drawn 23

Highest totals	ND	474		Gisborne	1996/97
	W	608-9 dec		Hamilton	1998/99
Lowest totals	ND	57		Hamilton	1961/62
	W	78		Hamilton	2000/01
Highest innings	ND	151	G.P. Howarth	Hamilton	1979/80
	W	296	J.R. Reid	Wellington	1962/63
Best bowling (innings)	ND	7-12	D.R. Tuffey	Hamilton	2000/01
	W	8-24	E.J. Chatfield	Lower Hutt	1979/80
Best bowling (match)	ND	11-66	D.R. Tuffey	Hamilton	2000/01
	W	12-39	E.J. Chatfield	Lower Hutt	1979/80

Record Partnerships

NORTHERN DISTRICTS

1st	165	G.M. Turner & J.G. Wright	Lower Hutt	1976/77
2nd	162*	J.G. Wright & J.G. Gibson	Lower Hutt	1978/79
3rd	169	J.M. Parker & A.D.G. Roberts	Wellington	1983/84
4th	208	S.A. Thomson & M.P. Maynard	Hamilton	1991/92
5th	149	K.A. Wealleans & B.A. Young	Wellington	1991/92
6th	170	E.C. Petrie & R.J. McPherson	Hamilton	1959/60
7th	87	E.C. Petrie & G.D. Alabaster	Wellington	1962/63
8th	136	G.A. Hick & S.A. Thomson	Wellington	1988/89
9th	188	N.R. Parlane & D.R. Tuffey	Wellington	1999/00
10th	83	J.A. Yovich & A.R. Tait	Hamilton	1996/97

WELLINGTON

1st	310	B.A. Edgar & R.H. Vance	Wellington	1988/89
2nd	215	M.D. Bell & J.D. Wells	Hamilton	1998/99
3rd	346	G.P. Burnett & R.A. Verry	Hamilton	1991/92
4th	179	P.T. Barton & J.R. Reid	Wellington	1964/65
5th	147*	J.V. Coney & G.P. Bilby	Lower Hutt	1976/77
6th	139	J.F.M. Morrison & R.W. Smith	Wellington	1972/73
7th	99	J.M. Aiken & J.D. Wells	Wellington	1995/96
8th	77	A.E. Dick & A.R. Taylor	Hamilton	1963/64
9th	87	I.J. Therkleson & R.O. Collinge	Whangarei	1973/74
10th	52	M.R. Gillespie & A.D. Turner	Wellington	2002/03

OTAGO v WELLINGTON

First match 1892/93	Played 103	Won by Otago 28	Won by Wellington 51	Drawn 24

Highest totals	O	495		Dunedin	1923/24
	W	575-7 dec		Wellington	1951/52
Lowest totals	O	34		Dunedin	1956/57
	W	42		Wellington	1945/46
Highest innings	O	182	K.R. Rutherford	Oamaru	1987/88
	W	283	J.R. Reid	Wellington	1951/52
Best bowling (innings)	O	8-46	B.L. Cairns	Invercargill	1978/79
	W	8-36	R.W. Blair	Dunedin	1952/53
Best bowling (match)	O	12-277	A.W. Alloo	Dunedin	1923/24
	W	12-87	E.J. Chatfield	Wellington	1973/74

Record Partnerships

OTAGO

1st	193	M.H. Richardson & M.J. Horne	Wellington	2000/01
2nd	254	K.J. Burns & K.R. Rutherford	Oamaru	1987/88
3rd	213	G.M. Turner & B.E. Congdon	Dunedin	1972/73
4th	211*	K.J. Burns & A.H. Jones	Wellington	1984/85
5th	132	W.L. Blair & G.J. Dawson	Wellington	1981/82
6th	165	G.M. Turner & W.K. Lees	Wellington	1975/76
7th	143	T.C. Fraser & C.D.G. Toomey	Dunedin	1939/40
8th	165*	J.N. Crawford & A.G. Eckhold	Wellington	1914/15
9th	80	G.H. Mills & L.J. Groves	Dunedin	1937/38
10th	90	B.L. Cairns & G.B. Thomson	Lower Hutt	1979/80

WELLINGTON

1st	299	M.D. Bell & R.A. Jones	Dunedin	2001/02
2nd	227	W.A. Baker & H.H.L. Kortlang	Dunedin	1923/24
3rd	246	B.A.G. Murray & J.F.M. Morrison	Dunedin	1968/69
4th	274	R.A. Jones & S.R. Mather	Wellington	2000/01
5th	255	B.R. Taylor & J.V. Coney	Dunedin	1972/73
6th	184	H.M. McGirr & D.C. Collins	Dunedin	1923/24
7th	164	H.M. McGirr & K.C. James	Dunedin	1927/28
8th	180	R.G. Twose & M.C. Goodson	Dunedin	1994/95
9th	72	F.T. Badcock & K.C. James	Wellington	1926/27
10th	138	K.C. James & A.W.S. Brice	Wellington	1926/27

PROVINCIAL COMPETITION

Plunket Shield
1921/22 — 1974/75

Awarded by the Governor of New Zealand, Lord Plunket, the Shield was given to Canterbury as the association with the best record in the 1906/07 season. From 1907/08 to 1920/21 the trophy was competed for under a challenge system but thereafter on a competition basis.

HOLDERS	Tenure	Challenges resisted
Canterbury	17 December, 1907	—
Auckland	17 December, 1907 to 1 February, 1911	7
Canterbury	1 February, 1911 to 12 February, 1912	2
Auckland	12 February, 1912 to 31 January, 1913	1
Canterbury	31 January, 1913 to 27 December, 1918	9
Wellington	27 December, 1918 to 24 January, 1919	—
Canterbury	24 January, 1919 to 4 January, 1920	2
Auckland	4 January, 1920 to 10 January, 1921	3
Wellington	10 January, 1921	—

Shell Series
1975/76-2000/01

In 1975/76, a new competition, sponsored by Shell, was established. For the first four seasons this was played under a two-stage system — the first round of 15 games (all teams playing each other) was for the Shell Cup*, while the second round (on a knock-out basis culminating in a final) carried the season's major prize, the Shell Trophy.

From 1979/80, only the Shell Trophy was competed for. The Shell Cup was reallocated to the limited-over competition in 1980/81, while the Plunket Shield was reserved for matches between the North and South Islands.

WINNERS

1921/22 Auckland	1952/53 Otago	1977/78 Auckland
1922/23 Canterbury	1953/54 Central Districts	*Canterbury**
1923/24 Wellington	1954/55 Wellington	1978/79 Otago
1924/25 Otago	1955/56 Canterbury	*Otago**
1925/26 Wellington	1956/57 Wellington	1979/80 Northern Districts
1926/27 Auckland	1957/58 Otago	1980/81 Auckland
1927/28 Wellington	1958/59 Auckland	1981/82 Wellington
1928/29 Auckland	1959/60 Canterbury	1982/83 Wellington
1929/30 Wellington	1960/61 Wellington	1983/84 Canterbury
1930/31 Canterbury	1961/62 Wellington	1984/85 Wellington
1931/32 Wellington	1962/63 Northern Districts	1985/86 Otago
1932/33 Otago	1963/64 Auckland	1986/87 Central Districts
1933/34 Auckland	1964/65 Canterbury	1987/88 Otago
1934/35 Canterbury	1965/66 Wellington	1988/89 Auckland
1935/36 Wellington	1966/67 Central Districts	1989/90 Wellington
1936/37 Auckland	1967/68 Central Districts	1990/91 Auckland
1937/38 Auckland	1968/69 Auckland	1991/92 Central Districts &
1938/39 Auckland	1969/70 Otago	Northern Districts
1939/40 Auckland	1970/71 Central Districts	1992/93 Northern Districts
1945/46 Canterbury	1971/72 Otago	1993/94 Canterbury
1946/47 Auckland	1972/73 Wellington	1994/95 Auckland
1947/48 Otago	1973/74 Wellington	1995/96 Auckland
1948/49 Canterbury	1974/75 Otago	1996/97 Canterbury
1949/50 Wellington	1975/76 Canterbury	1997/98 Canterbury
1950/51 Otago	*Canterbury**	1998/99 Central Districts
1951/52 Canterbury	1976/77 Otago	1999/00 Northern Districts
	Northern Districts*	2000/01 Wellington

State Championship

from 2001/02

State Insurance took over the sponsorship of the competition in 2001/02. The format remained unchanged.

WINNERS

2001/02 Auckland   2002/03 Auckland

TEAM RECORDS

Playing Record of the First-class Sides in New Zealand

	P	W	L	D		P	W	L	D
Canterbury	591	221	203	167*	The Rest	6	1	3	2
Wellington	571	205	187	179†	Victoria	6	1	1	4
Otago	553	161	250	142	NZ XI	6	—	3	3
Auckland	534	214	145	175	Young New Zealand	5	—	2	3
Central Districts	361	92	119	150*	Queensland	5	3	1	1
Northern Districts	329	78	121	130	Pakistan A	5	—	1	4
New Zealand	208	42	69	97	England A	5	3	—	2
England/MCC	128	61	9	58*	Tasmania	4	—	3	1
Australia	106	57	7	42	Shell XI	3	1	1	1
Hawke's Bay	53	9	34	10	Emerging Players	3	—	1	2
Pakistan	48	19	6	23	Governor General's XI	3	—	1	—
West Indies	35	11	8	16	Commonwealth XI	2	2	—	—
India	33	10	8	15	D.H. Robins' XI	2	—	—	2
New South Wales	23	16	2	5	U-Bix XI	1	—	—	1
South Africa	18	8	—	10	West Coast				
Nelson	17	9	6	2*	North Island	1	1	—	—
Sri Lanka	17	3	5	9	D. Reese's XI	1	—	1	—
North Island	16	6	5	5	Minor Associations	1	—	1	—
Fiji	15	5	8	2	Sir Julien Cahn's XI	1	—	—	1
South Island	15	4	8	3	South Island Army	1	1	—	—
New Zealand	12	—	9	3	North Island Army	1	—	1	—
Under-23 XI					New Zealand Army	1	1	—	—
Zimbabwe	10	2	3	5	New Zealand Air Force	1	—	1	—
President's XI	9	—	3	6	New Zealand Services	1	—	—	1
NZ Academy XI	9	3	3	3	Canterbury/Otago	1	—	—	1
Southland	8	1	5	2	Auckland/Wellington	1	—	1	—
Taranaki	8	1	6	1	ND/CD	1	—	—	1
Southern	8	4	1	3	Auckland XI	1	—	—	1
New Zealand A	8	4	1	3	Otago Invitation XI	1	—	1	—
Northern	7	2	1	4	Canterbury XI	1	—	—	1
Central	7	2	3	2	Board XI	1	—	1	—
Bangladesh	7	—	7	—	Australian Academy XI	1	1	—	—
* includes a tie † includes two ties					**TOTALS**	**3836**	**1266**	**1266**	**1304**

Highest Match Aggregates

Runs-Wickets			
1945-18	Canterbury v Wellington	Christchurch	1994/95
1905-40	Otago v Wellington	Dunedin	1923/24
1567-37	Auckland v Wellington	Auckland	1936/37
1554-40	Wellington v Auckland	Wellington	1922/23
1531-39	Wellington v Auckland	Wellington	1923/24
1505-25	New Zealand v India	Auckland	1989/90
1501-37	Canterbury v Otago	Christchurch	1931/32

Highest Team Totals

by any first-class team in New Zealand

777	Canterbury v Otago at Christchurch	1996/97
752-8 dec	NSW v Otago at Dunedin	1923/24
693-9 dec	Auckland v Canterbury at Auckland	1939/40
671-4	New Zealand v Sri Lanka at Wellington	1990/91
663	Australia v New Zealand at Auckland	1920/21
660-5 dec	West Indies v New Zealand at Wellington	1994/95
658	Australians v Auckland at Auckland	1913/14
653-5 dec	MCC v New Zealand at Dunedin	1935/36
653	Australians v Canterbury at Christchurch	1913/14
643	Auckland v Canterbury at Auckland	1919/20
621-5 dec	South Africa v New Zealand at Auckland	1998/99
616-5 dec	Pakistan v New Zealand at Auckland	1988/89
610-6 dec	Australia v New Zealand at Auckland	1913/14
608-9 dec	Wellington v Northern Districts at Hamilton	1998/99
602-8 dec	Otago v Canterbury at Dunedin	1928/29

Most Runs in a Match by One Side

Runs-Wickets

1025-20	560 & 465	Wellington v Otago	Dunedin	1923/24
973-6	498-2d & 475-4	Wellington v Canterbury	Christchurch	1994/95
972-12	496 & 476-2d	Canterbury v Wellington	Christchurch	1994/95
971-14	511-6d & 460-8	Australia v New Zealand	Wellington	1973/74
948-20	569 & 379	Wellington v Auckland	Wellington	1923/24
880-20	385 & 495	Otago v Wellington	Dunedin	1923/24
875-18	273 & 602-8d	Otago v Canterbury	Dunedin	1928/29
874-15	391 & 483-5d	New Zealand v India	Auckland	1989/90
855-20	595 & 260	Wellington v Auckland	Wellington	1927/28
851-18	280 & 571-8	Otago v Central Districts	Napier	1995/96
845-14	174 & 671-4d	New Zealand v Sri Lanka	Wellington	1990/91
832-17	401 & 431-7d	Auckland v Wellington	Auckland	1934/35
831-20	435 & 396	Wellington v Auckland	Wellington	1922/23
827-20	448 & 379	Wellington v Otago	Wellington	1926/27
821-20	447 & 374	Wellington v Auckland	Wellington	1925/26
808-13	476 & 332-3	NSW v Wellington	Wellington	1923/24
802-18	276 & 526-8d	Canterbury v Wellington	Wellington	1931/32

Lowest Match Aggregates

completed matches, i.e. not drawn

Runs-Wickets

151-30	Canterbury v Otago	Christchurch	1866/67
153-31	Otago v Canterbury	Dunedin	1896/97
156-30	Nelson v Wellington	Nelson	1885/86
159-31	Nelson v Wellington	Nelson	1887/88
176-32	Otago v Tasmania	Dunedin	1883/84
183-40	Nelson v Wellington	Nelson	1883/84
192-30	Taranaki v Hawke's Bay	Hawera	1891/92

The lowest aggregates since 1900 are:

Runs-Wickets

241-30	Otago v Southland	Dunedin	1919/20
278-40	Southland v Otago	Invercargill	1918/19
295-28	New Zealand v Australia	Wellington	1945/46

Lowest Match Aggregates by One Side

55	36 & 19	Wellington v Nelson	Nelson	1885/86
57	25 & 32	Canterbury v Otago	Christchurch	1866/67
64	35 & 29	Taranaki v Hawke's Bay	Hawera	1891/92
72	30 & 42	Wellington v Nelson	Nelson	1883/84
76	34 & 42	Canterbury v Otago	Dunedin	1863/64
76	27 & 49	Canterbury v Otago	Dunedin	1896/97
79	31 & 48	Wellington v Nelson	Nelson	1887/88
80	51 & 29	Wellington v Nelson	Nelson	1879/80
87	40 & 47	Tasmania v Otago	Dunedin	1883/84
95	43 & 52	Otago v Canterbury	Christchurch	1872/73
96	41 & 55	Southland v Otago	Invercargill	1918/19
96	42 & 54	New Zealand v Australia	Wellington	1945/46
97	37 & 60	Wellington v Nelson	Christchurch	1876/77
99	65 & 34	Wellington v Canterbury	Wellington	1886/87

Lowest Team Totals

by any first-class team in New Zealand

13	Auckland v Canterbury at Auckland	1877/78
	(included 8 extras)	
19	Wellington v Nelson at Nelson	1885/86
22	Wellington v Canterbury at Wellington	1903/04
25	Canterbury v Otago at Christchurch	1866/67
26	NZ v England at Auckland	1954/55
27	Canterbury v Otago at Dunedin	1896/97
28	Hawke's Bay v Auckland at Auckland	1910/11
	(included 13 extras)	
29	Wellington v Nelson at Nelson	1879/80
29	Taranaki v Hawke's Bay at Hawera	1891/92

Highest Second Innings Totals

671-4	New Zealand v Sri Lanka	Wellington	1990/91
602-8	Otago v Canterbury	Dunedin	1928/29
589	Otago v Canterbury	Christchurch	1931/32
575-7 dec	Wellington v Otago	Wellington	1951/52
571-8 dec	Otago v Central Districts	Napier	1995/96
539	Auckland v Otago	Dunedin	1926/27
537	Auckland v Canterbury	Christchurch	1930/31
537	New Zealand v England	Wellington	1983/84
526-8 dec	Canterbury v Wellington	Wellington	1931/32
519	Canterbury v Wellington	Christchurch	1930/31

Highest Fourth Innings Totals without Loss for Victory

226-0	Canterbury v Otago	Christchurch	1948/49
175-0	Otago v Central Districts	Masterton	1971/72
174-0	Otago v Northern Districts	Alexandra	1985/86
138-0	Auckland v Otago	Auckland	1937/38
130-0	Wellington v Otago	Wellington	1921/22
130-0	Canterbury v Auckland	Christchurch	1951/52

Highest Fourth Innings Totals

495	lost 145 runs	Otago v Wellington	Dunedin	1923/24
475-4	and won	Wellington v Canterbury	Christchurch	1994/95
473-6	and won	Canterbury v Auckland	Christchurch	1930/31
458	lost 276 runs	Auckland v Wellington	Wellington	1927/28
453-8	and won	Northern Districts v Wellington	Wellington	1995/96
451	lost 98 runs	New Zealand v England	Christchurch	2001/02
388	lost 19 runs	Canterbury v Wellington	Wellington	1929/30
380-8	set 505 runs	Wellington v Auckland	Wellington	1929/30
375-5	and won	Central Districts v Canterbury	New Plymouth	1986/87
374-8	and won	North Island v South Island	Dunedin	1947/48
372	lost 38 runs	Canterbury v Wellington	Christchurch	2000/01
371-4	and won	Northern Districts v Wellington	Hamilton	1991/92
368-6	and won	Auckland v Central Districts	Auckland	2000/01
362-8	and won	Canterbury v Central Districts	Napier	2002/03
361-6	and won	Auckland v Canterbury	Christchurch	2002/03
357-6	and won	Canterbury v Otago	Christchurch	1927/28
353	lost 148 runs	Otago v Auckland	Alexandra	1995/96
353-2	and won	Wellington v Otago	Dunedin	2001/02
348-5	and won	West Indies v NZ	Auckland	1968/69
347-7	and won	Auckland v Wellington	Auckland	1936/37
345	lost 15 runs	Northern Districts v Central Districts	Nelson	1986/87
344-6	set 418 runs	Sri Lanka v New Zealand	Hamilton	1990/91
344	lost 163 runs	Otago v Wellington	Wellington	1927/28
342-6	and won	Otago v Central Districts	Oamaru	1985/86
341-5	and won	Central Districts v Northern Districts	New Plymouth	1984/85
340-5	and won	Wellington v Auckland	Wellington	1991/92
340	lost 16 runs	Auckland v Northern Districts	Auckland	2002/03
339-5	and won	Central Districts v Otago	Blenheim	1990/91
339	lost 96 runs	Canterbury v Otago	Christchurch	1933/34
339	lost 12 runs	Canterbury v Otago	Dunedin	1947/48
339-2§	and won	Central Districts v Northern Districts	Hamilton	2002/03
337	lost 108 runs	Auckland v Wellington	Wellington	1922/23
336	lost 105 runs	Auckland v Wellington	Wellington	1920/21
335-8	set 385 runs	Northern Districts v Auckland	Auckland	1991/92
335-5	and won	Canterbury v Otago	Christchurch	1995/96
335	lost 32 runs	South Island v North Island	Christchurch	1999/00
334-7	and won	Wellington v Northern Districts	Wellington	1958/59
334	lost 355 runs	Canterbury v Wellington	Christchurch	1926/27
333-8	set 577 runs	Otago v Wellington	Wellington	1951/52
331-6	set 417 runs	England A v New Zealand A	Lincoln	1999/00
328-6	and won	Otago v Canterbury	Christchurch	1974/75
324-5	and won	Canterbury v Auckland	Christchurch	1949/50
324-5	and won	Northern Districts v Auckland	Auckland	1988/89
324-5	and won	New Zealand v Pakistan	Christchurch	1993/94
324	lost 37 runs	Canterbury v Central Districts	Nelson	1982/83
324-7	and won	Wellington v Otago	Oamaru	1998/99
322-6	and won	Northern Districts v Central Districts	Palmerston North	1982/83
322	lost 57 runs	Wellington v Canterbury	Christchurch	1924/25
322-7	and won	Northern Districts v Wellington	Hamilton	1998/99
322	lost 55 runs	Canterbury v Otago	Christchurch	2000/01
320-4	and won	Central Districts v Northern Districts	Hamilton	1996/97
318	lost 36 runs	Fiji v Canterbury	Christchurch	1947/48
318	lost 23 runs	West Indies v Governor General's XI	Auckland	1968/69

318-3†	and won	Wellington v Central Districts	Wellington	1997/98
317-9	and won	Northern Districts v Central Districts	Gisborne	1979/80
317-7	and won	Otago v Central Districts	Dunedin	1997/98
316-8	and won	England XI v New Zealand XI	Nelson	1991/92
315-4	and won	South Island v North Island	Wellington	1934/35
313	lost 62 runs	Northern Districts v Canterbury	Christchurch	1988/89
313-7	and won	Central Districts v Northern Districts	Hamilton	1999/00
312-5	set 416 runs	Wellington v Canterbury	Christchurch	1917/18
311-7	and won	Otago v Wellington	Wellington	1996/97
310-4	and won	Otago v Central Districts	New Plymouth	1987/88
310-9	and won	Otago v Canterbury	Christchurch	1990/91
308-7	set 410 runs	Wellington v Canterbury	Rangiora	2001/02
307-8	set 341 runs	Australia v Canterbury	Christchurch	1909/10
307-9	set 348 runs	Wellington v Auckland	Wellington	1992/93
307-6	and won	England v New Zealand	Christchurch	1996/97
306-3	and won	Canterbury v Otago	Christchurch	1940/41
303-3	and won	Canterbury v Wellington	Wellington	1918/19
303	lost 365 runs	Auckland v Wellington	Wellington	1923/24
303	lost 197 runs	Wellington v Auckland	Auckland	1953/54
302	lost 69 runs	Canterbury v Wellington	Christchurch	1985/86
302-5	and won	Northern Districts v Wellington	Hamilton	1987/88
301	lost 6 runs	Central Districts v Northern Districts	Hamilton	1977/78
300-2	and won	Canterbury v Northern Districts	Christchurch	1984/85
300-8	set 320	Wellington v Northern Districts	Wellington	1991/92
300-9	set 351	Wellington v Otago	Dunedin	1990/91
300-9	set 303	Northern Districts v Central Districts	Nelson	1993/94
300	set 341	Auckland v Wellington	Auckland	1997/98

† *after Central Districts had forfeited its second innings* § *after Northern Districts had forfeited its second innings*

Large Victories

BY AN INNINGS AND
364 runs	Sims' Australian XI defeated Canterbury	Christchurch	1913/14
358 runs	Australia defeated New Zealand	Wellington	1904/05
356 runs	Australia defeated Otago	Dunedin	1949/50
354 runs	Auckland defeated Hawke's Bay	Auckland	1920/21
332 runs	Wellington defeated Canterbury	Wellington	1925/26
327 runs	NSW defeated Otago	Dunedin	1923/24
322 runs	Wellington defeated Hawkes Bay	Wellington	1905/06
322 runs	West Indies defeated New Zealand	Wellington	1994/95
277 runs	NSW defeated Canterbury	Christchurch	1923/24
275 runs	Auckland defeated Hawkes Bay	Auckland	1910/11
275 runs	Auckland defeated Northern Districts	Auckland	2000/01
256 runs	Wellington defeated Otago	Wellington	1899/00

BY A RUNS MARGIN
512 runs	Wellington defeated Auckland	Wellington	1925/26
446 runs	Wellington defeated Otago	Wellington	1926/27
438 runs	Auckland defeated Wellington	Auckland	1934/35
425 runs	Central Districts defeated Otago	Alexandra	2001/02
382 runs	Auckland defeated Canterbury	Christchurch	1920/21
365 runs	Wellington defeated Auckland	Wellington	1923/24
355 runs	Wellington defeated Canterbury	Christchurch	1926/27
343 runs	Auckland defeated Hawke's Bay	Napier	1912/13
342 runs	Canterbury defeated Auckland	Christchurch	1924/25
322 runs	Canterbury defeated Wellington	Christchurch	1910/11

318 runs	Canterbury defeated Auckland	Christchurch	1913/14
315 runs	Auckland defeated Otago	Auckland	1907/08
302 runs	Canterbury defeated Central Districts	Christchurch	1951/52
302 runs	Canterbury defeated Northern Districts	Hamilton	1998/99

Tied Matches

Wellington v Nelson	Wellington	1873/74
New Zealand v T.N. Pearce's XI	Scarborough	1958
Central Districts v England XI	New Plymouth	1977/78
Victoria v New Zealand	Melbourne	1982/83
Wellington v Canterbury	Wellington	1988/89

Close Finishes

VICTORY BY 1 WICKET

Canterbury defeated Tasmania	Christchurch	1883/84
Otago defeated Canterbury	Christchurch	1890/91
Wellington defeated Nelson	Nelson	1891/92
Auckland defeated Wellington	Wellington	1893/94
Canterbury defeated Wellington	Wellington	1899/00
Auckland defeated Wellington	Wellington	1911/12
Canterbury defeated Auckland	Auckland	1914/15
Wellington defeated Otago	Wellington	1924/25
Auckland defeated Otago	Auckland	1946/47
Fiji defeated Wellington	Wellington	1947/48
Otago defeated Wellington	Dunedin	1948/49
Auckland defeated Canterbury	Auckland	1950/51
Central Districts defeated Wellington	Wellington	1951/52
Otago defeated Wellington	Dunedin	1952/53
MCC defeated Canterbury	Christchurch	1960/61
Auckland defeated Canterbury	Christchurch	1963/64
Wellington defeated NZ Under-23 XI	Wellington	1965/66
Canterbury defeated Auckland	Auckland	1974/75
Northern Districts defeated Central Districts	Gisborne	1979/80
New Zealand defeated West Indies	Dunedin	1979/80
Otago defeated Wellington	Alexandra	1980/81
Otago defeated Canterbury	Christchurch	1990/91
Otago defeated Wellington	Dunedin	1991/92
Central Districts defeated Auckland	Auckland	1994/95
Canterbury defeated Northern Districts	Christchurch	1994/95
Southern defeated Central	Wanganui	1997/98
Wellington defeated Northern Districts	Hamilton	2001/02

VICTORY BY 10 RUNS OR LESS

1 run	Northern Districts defeated Central Districts	Rotorua	1989/90
2 runs	Auckland defeated Canterbury	Auckland	1903/04
	Wellington defeated Canterbury	Wellington	1935/36
3 runs	Otago defeated Wellington	Wellington	1953/54
	Central Districts defeated Wellington	Wellington	1970/71
	Central Districts defeated Otago	New Plymouth	1970/71
	Canterbury defeated Central Districts	Napier	1979/80
4 runs	Auckland defeated Nelson	Nelson	1882/83
	Canterbury defeated Otago	Christchurch	1882/83
	Auckland defeated Wellington	Auckland	1977/78

5 runs	Central Districts defeated Otago	New Plymouth	1953/54
	Northern Districts defeated Central Districts	Napier	1976/77
6 runs	Canterbury defeated Tasmania	Christchurch	1883/84
	Auckland defeated Canterbury	Auckland	1952/53
	South Island XI defeated North Island XI	Wellington	1957/58
	Northern Districts defeated Central Districts	Hamilton	1977/78
	Northern Districts defeated Otago	Dunedin	1978/79
	Central Districts defeated Northern Districts	Napier	1988/89
7 runs	Auckland defeated Canterbury	Christchurch	1873/74
8 runs	Auckland defeated Wellington	Wellington	1945/46
	Auckland defeated Northern Districts	Auckland	1963/64
	Central Districts defeated Auckland	Napier	1982/83
	Auckland defeated Central Districts	Auckland	1999/00
9 runs	Central Districts defeated Auckland	Nelson	1983/84
10 runs	Northern Districts defeated Canterbury	Hamilton	1960/61
	Wellington defeated Central Districts	New Plymouth	1973/74
	Otago defeated Auckland	Dunedin	1975/76

Victory after Follow-on

Auckland (180 & 302)	beat Canterbury (392 & 84)	Auckland	1952/53
Northern Districts (165 & 275)	beat Otago (320-9d & 105)	Dunedin	1961/62
Auckland (69 & 303)	beat Northern Districts (224 & 140)	Auckland	1963/64
Canterbury (166 & 360)	beat Auckland (351-9d & 149)	Christchurch	1973/74

Matches Abandoned without a Ball Being Bowled

these matches are not included in any first-class records

Central Districts v Northern Districts	Napier	1970/71
†Wellington v Australia	Wellington	1973/74
Central Districts v Australia	Napier	1973/74
†New Zealand v Pakistan	Dunedin	1988/89
†New Zealand President's XI v Australia	Nelson	1992/93
New Zealand A v Sri Lanka	Gisborne	1996/97
Wellington v Canterbury	Wellington	1996/97
†Northern v Pakistan A	Auckland	1998/99
†New Zealand v India	Dunedin	1998/99

† *replaced with a limited-overs match*

Matches Completed in One Day

Otago v Canterbury	Dunedin	11. 2.1868
Wellington v Auckland	Wellington	29.11.1874
Nelson v Wellington	Nelson	26.12.1887
Otago v Auckland	Dunedin	27.12.1889
Hawke's Bay v Taranaki	Napier	9. 1.1892
Auckland v New South Wales*	Auckland	20. 1.1894
Ireland v New Zealand	Dublin	11. 9.1937
Auckland v Fiji†	Auckland	9. 3.1954

* *no play on first day*   † *after no play on first two days and three declarations on third*

Most Extras in an Innings

Extras	B	LB	NB	W				
† 66	2	9	54	1	NZ Academy XI (459-8d)	v Pakistan A	Lincoln	1998/99
† 60	18	17	20	5	Central Districts (460-4d)	v Wellington	Wellington	1997/98
58	41	14	3	—	Wellington (380-5)	v Auckland	Wellington	1929/30
†58	6	14	30	8	Auckland (322-4d)	v Wellington	Auckland	1993/94
57	31	16	10	—	New Zealand (387)	v England	Auckland	1929/30
54	35	14	1	4	Auckland (200-8d)	v Wellington	Auckland	1973/74
53	26	10	17	—	Canterbury (473-6)	v Auckland	Christchurch	1930/31
†53	4	2	46	1	Wellington (498-2d)	v Canterbury	Christchurch	1994/95
52					Wellington (370)	v Canterbury	Christchurch	1922/23
52	12	7	33	—	New Zealand (468)	v Pakistan	Karachi	1976/77
52	1	27	33	1	Auckland (423-7d)	v Wellington	Wellington	1992/93
† 52	1	15	32	4	Canterbury (537)	v Central Districts	Blenheim	1996/97
51	10	11	30	—	Auckland (369)	v West Indies	Auckland	1999/00
50					Otago (602-8d)	v Canterbury	Dunedin	1928/29
50	13	24	11	2	Wellington (356)	v Canterbury	Wellington	1981/82
† 50	3	11	36	—	Southern (554)	v Pakistan A	Christchurch	1998/99

† *no balls counted as two extras, regardless of whether runs were scored from the bat*

Longest Matches in New Zealand
before 1900

FOUR DAYS

Otago v Canterbury	Dunedin	1875/76
Canterbury v Tasmania	Christchurch	1883/84
Otago v Canterbury	Dunedin	1884/85

Longest Matches in New Zealand
since 1900

SIX DAYS

New Zealand v England	Christchurch	1974/75
New Zealand v India	Christchurch	1975/76
*New Zealand v England	Auckland	1977/78
New Zealand v Pakistan	Napier	1978/79
New Zealand v West Indies	Auckland	1979/80
New Zealand v India	Christchurch	1980/81

* *the only match where play took place on all six days. The other
instances involved the rest day being used after a day's play was lost*

FIVE DAYS

Canterbury v Otago	Christchurch	1911/12
Canterbury v Wellington	Christchurch	1922/23
Otago v Wellington	Dunedin	1923/24
Canterbury v Auckland	Christchurch	1924/25
Wellington v Otago	Wellington	1926/27
Northern Districts v Auckland	Taupo	1999/00

*All other matches of five days duration since 1926/27 have been test matches.
A complete list of these up to 1993/94 is on pages 288 and 289 of the 1994
Almanack. The 1998/99 Shell Trophy final between Central Districts and
Otago at Napier was scheduled for five days but completed in three.*

INDIVIDUAL RECORDS
BATTING
Highest Individual Scores

385	Sutcliffe B.	Otago v Canterbury	Christchurch	1952/53
355	Sutcliffe B.	Otago v Auckland	Dunedin	1949/50
338*	Blunt R.C.	Otago v Canterbury	Christchurch	1931/32
336*	Hammond W.R.	England v New Zealand	Auckland	1932/33
317	Rutherford K.R.	New Zealand v DB Close's XI	Scarborough	1986
306	Richardson M.H.	New Zealand v Zimbabwe A	Kwekwe	2000/01
301*	Fulton P.G.	Canterbury v Auckland	Christchurch	2002/03
299	Crowe M.D.	New Zealand v Sri Lanka	Wellington	1990/91
296	Reid J.R.	Wellington v Northern Districts	Wellington	1962/63
293	Trumper V.T.	Sims' Australian XI v Canterbury	Christchurch	1913/14
290	Carson W.N.	Auckland v Otago	Dunedin	1936/37
284	Woodfull W.M.	Australia v New Zealand	Auckland	1927/28
283	Reid J.R.	Wellington v Otago	Wellington	1951/52
275*	Cullinan D.J.	South Africa v New Zealand	Auckland	1998/99
275	Sutcliffe B.	Otago v Auckland	Auckland	1950/51
274*	Fleming S.P.	New Zealand v Sri Lanka	Colombo	2002/03
271	Javed Miandad	Pakistan v New Zealand	Auckland	1988/89
267*	Young B.A.	New Zealand v Sri Lanka	Dunedin	1996/97
267	de Silva P.A.	Sri Lanka v New Zealand	Wellington	1990/91
264	Sutcliffe B.	Otago v Central Districts	Dunedin	1959/60
259	Turner G.M.	New Zealand v Guyana	Georgetown	1971/72
259	Turner G.M.	New Zealand v West Indies	Georgetown	1971/72
258	Nurse S.M.	West Indies v New Zealand	Christchurch	1968/69
256	Smith S.G.	Auckland v Canterbury	Auckland	1919/20
255*	McGlew D.J.	South Africa v New Zealand	Wellington	1952/53
254*	Vance R.H.	Wellington v Northern Districts	Wellington	1988/89
251*	Harris C.Z.	Canterbury v Central Districts	Rangiora	1996/97
250	Walters K.D.	Australia v New Zealand	Christchurch	1976/77
247*	Chappell G.S.	Australia v New Zealand	Wellington	1973/74
243	Sutcliffe B.	New Zealand v Essex	Southend	1949
242*	Crowe M.D.	New Zealand v South Australia	Adelaide	1985/86
242	Crowe M.D.	Central Districts v Otago	New Plymouth	1989/90
241	Horne M.J.	Otago v Auckland	Auckland	1997/98
239	Dowling G.T.	New Zealand v India	Christchurch	1967/68
237*	Latham R.T.	Canterbury v Northern Districts	Rotorua	1990/91
235	Marshall J.A.H.	Northern Districts v Canterbury	Christchurch	2001/02
230*	Sutcliffe B.	New Zealand v India	New Delhi	1955/56
227	Hammond W.R.	England v New Zealand	Christchurch	1932/33
226*	Rutherford K.R.	Otago v India	Dunedin	1989/90
226	Hastings B.F.	Canterbury v NZ Under 23 XI	Christchurch	1964/65
225*	Blunt R.C.	New Zealand v Gentlemen	Eastbourne	1931
223*	Turner G.M.	New Zealand v West Indies	Kingston	1971/72
223	Astle N.J.	New Zealand v Queensland	Brisbane	2001/02
222*	Midlane F.A.	Wellington v Otago	Wellington	1914/15
222	Rutherford I.A.	Otago v Central Districts	New Plymouth	1978/79
222	Astle N.J.	New Zealand v England	Christchurch	2001/02
221	Macartney C.G.	NSW v Canterbury	Christchurch	1923/24
221	Blunt R.C.	Otago v Canterbury	Dunedin	1928/29
219	Bell M.D.	Wellington v Northern Districts	Hamilton	1998/99
216	Fletcher K.W.R.	England v New Zealand	Auckland	1974/75

216	Bell M.D.	Wellington v Auckland	Auckland	1997/98
216*	Chanderpaul S.	West Indies v New Zealand A	Taupo	1999/00
214*	Kortlang H.H.L.	Wellington v Auckland	Wellington	1925/26
214*	Booth B.C.	Australia B v Central Districts	Palmerston North	1966/67
214	Sinclair M.S.	New Zealand v West Indies	Wellington	1999/00
213	Murray B.A.G.	Wellington v Otago	Dunedin	1968/69
213	Trimble S.C.	Australia B v New Zealand	Wellington	1969/70
213	Greenidge C.G.	West Indies v New Zealand	Auckland	1986/87
212*	Woodfull W.M.	Victoria v Canterbury	Christchurch	1924/25
212*	Richardson M.H.	New Zealand A v Sussex	Hove	2000
212*	Kelly D.P.	Central Districts v Canterbury	Blenheim	2000/01
212*	Styris S.B.	Northern Districts v Otago	Hamilton	2001/02
212	Hiddleston J.S.	Wellington v Canterbury	Wellington	1925/26
212	Dempster C.S.	New Zealand v Essex	Leyton	1931
211*	Hick G.A.	Northern Districts v Auckland	Auckland	1988/89
211*	Gibbs H.H.	South Africa v New Zealand	Christchurch	1998/99
211	Warner P.F.	Lord Hawke's XI v Otago	Dunedin	1902/03
211	Wallace W.M.	Auckland v Canterbury	Auckland	1939/40
209*	Brown S.W.	Auckland v Canterbury	Christchurch	1990/91
209	White D.J.	Northern Districts v Central Districts	Hamilton	1985/86
209	Horne P.A.	Auckland v Northern Districts	Auckland	1988/89
208*	Sutcliffe B.	North Island v South Island	Dunedin	1947/48
207	Hart R.T.	Central Districts v Wellington	Wellington	1985/86
206	Page M.L.	Canterbury v Wellington	Wellington	1931/32
206	Donnelly M.P.	New Zealand v England	Lord's	1949
206	Dowling G.T.	Canterbury v Wellington	Christchurch	1962/63
206	Harris C.Z	Canterbury v Central Districts	Blenheim	1996/97
205*	Lloyd C.H.	West Indies v South Island	Dunedin	1968/69
205*	McSweeney E.B.	Wellington v Central Districts	Levin	1987/88
204*	Sinclair M.S.	New Zealand v Pakistan	Christchurch	2000/01
204	Cox A.	Canterbury v Otago	Christchurch	1925/26
204	Hiddleston J.S.	Wellington v Auckland	Wellington	1925/26
204	Scott V.J.	Auckland v Otago	Dunedin	1947/48
204	Patel D.N.	Auckland v Northern Districts	Auckland	1991/92
203*	Burnett G.P.	Wellington v Northern Districts	Hamilton	1991/92
203*	Sinclair M.S.	Central Districts v Northern Districts	Wanganui	1998/99
203	Scott V.J.	New Zealand v Combined Services	Gillingham	1949
203	Reid J.R.	New Zealand v Western Province	Cape Town	1961/62
203	Edgar B.A.	Young NZ v Zimbabwe	Bulawayo	1984/85
202*	Congdon B.E.	Central Districts v Otago	Nelson	1968/69
202*	Greatbatch M.J.	Central Districts v Otago	Palmerston North	1988/89
202	Turner G.M.	New Zealand v President's XI	Montego Bay	1971/72
202	Austen M.H.	Wellington v Central Districts	Wanganui	1993/94
202	Greatbatch M.J.	Central Districts v Northern Districts	Rotorua	1995/96
201*	Hart M.N.	Northern Districts v Auckland	Auckland	2002/03
201*	Smith B.F.	Central Districts v Canterbury	New Plymouth	2001/02
201	Reid J.R.	Otago v Canterbury	Dunedin	1957/58
201	Sutcliffe B.	Otago v Northern Districts	Hamilton	1960/61
201	Mushtaq Mohammad	Pakistan v New Zealand	Dunedin	1972/73
200*	MacLaren A.C.	MCC v New Zealand	Wellington	1922/23
200*	Bardsley W.	NSW v Auckland	Auckland	1923/24
200*	Thorpe G.P.	England v New Zealand	Christchurch	2001/02
200	Lawson R.A.	Otago v Central Districts	Napier	1995/96

Most Runs in a Season in New Zealand

		M	I	NO	HS	Runs	Ave	100
Crowe M.D.	1986/87	11	21	3	175*	1676	93.11	8
Turner G.M.	1975/76	11	20	4	177*	1244	77.75	5
Hick G.A.	1988/89	8	16	3	211*	1228	94.46	6
Bell M.D.	2000/01	13	21	0	134	1092	52.00	6
Crowe J.J.	1991/92	10	19	2	142*	1063	62.52	4
Vance R.H.	1988/89	10	18	2	254*	1037	64.81	4
Richardson M.H.	2000/01	11	19	2	166	1035	60.88	2
Wright J.G.	1986/87	11	21	2	192	1019	53.63	3
Sinclair M.S.	1999/00	14	26	2	214	1004	41.83	3
Dowling G.T.	1967/68	10	18	1	239	968	56.94	4
Edgar B.A.	1978/79	12	23	0	134	944	41.04	2
Weekes E. de C.	1955/56	8	10	1	156	940	104.44	6
Rutherford K.R.	1989/90	13	19	2	226*	940	55.29	3
Smith B.F.	2000/01	10	17	1	168	939	58.68	2
Edgar B.A.	1981/82	11	19	1	161	934	51.88	3
Sutcliffe B.	1947/48	5	10	1	208*	911	101.22	4
Maynard M.P.	1991/92	10	13	0	195	893	68.69	4
Horne M.J.	1998/99	10	19	2	132	887	52.17	1
Jones A.H.	1988/89	8	15	2	181*	884	68.00	2
Stead G.R.	2000/01	12	20	2	121*	875	48.61	3
Hastings B.F.	1968/69	10	15	4	117*	872	79.27	4
Wright J.G.	1981/82	11	18	0	141	872	48.44	4
Dowling G.T.	1966/67	10	18	2	102*	871	54.43	1
Jones R.A.	2000/01	12	19	0	188	860	45.26	3
Sutcliffe B.	1952/53	7	13	0	385	859	66.07	1
Anderson R.W.	1977/78	11	22	0	123	849	38.59	2
Horne M.J.	1996/97	10	17	0	124	843	49.58	3
Bradburn G.E.	1989/90	12	23	1	96	842	38.27	—
Spearman C.M.	1998/99	11	17	1	137	842	52.62	2
Turner G.M.	1974/75	8	15	1	186*	838	59.85	4
Harris C.Z.	1996/97	5	7	1	251*	835	139.16	3
Hick G.A.	1987/88	9	14	1	146	827	63.61	4
Nurse S.M.	1968/69	5	9	0	258	826	91.77	3
Sinclair M.S.	1998/99	11	17	3	203*	823	58.78	2
McIntosh T.G.	2002/03	10	17	3	157	820	58.57	2
Wright J.G.	1989/90	9	12	2	185	818	81.80	3
Reid J.F.	1980/81	10	18	4	173	817	58.35	3
Edwards G.N.	1980/81	11	19	2	177*	812	47.76	2
McMillan C.D.	1996/97	8	12	1	159	809	73.54	3
Crowe M.D.	1992/93	7	14	1	163	803	61.76	3
Sutcliffe B.	1950/51	7	12	0	275	798	66.50	4
Edgar B.A.	1979/80	11	19	3	152*	798	49.87	3
Horne M.J.	2001/02	11	17	2	178	798	53.20	3
Crowe J.J.	1988/89	9	13	2	156	797	61.30	2
Patel D.N.	1986/87	11	21	2	170*	796	41.89	3
Greatbatch M.J.	1987/88	10	19	1	149	795	44.16	2
Papps M.H.W.	2001/02	10	19	4	158*	793	52.86	2
Wright J.G.	1978/79	10	19	2	145*	790	46.47	1
Rutherford K.R.	1991/92	10	20	2	133	787	43.72	1
Bailey M.D.	1997/98	11	16	1	180*	786	52.40	3
Burgess M.G.	1977/78	13	24	3	132	785	37.38	1
Woodfull W.M.	1927/28	6	9	3	284	781	130.16	3
Latham R.T.	1988/89	10	19	4	142*	781	52.06	2

		M	I	NO	HS	Runs	Ave	100
Richardson M.H.	2001/02	10	15	1	143	779	55.64	3
Wright J.G.	1979/80	11	21	0	97	777	37.00	—
Thomson S.A.	1990/91	11	18	5	166	774	59.53	2
Horne P.A.	1986/87	9	17	2	150*	773	51.53	2
Douglas M.W.	1991/92	12	22	4	144	773	42.94	2
Harris C.Z.	2001/02	8	12	3	155*	770	85.55	2
Howarth G.P.	1979/80	12	22	2	151	767	38.35	2
Jones A.H.	1990/91	6	11	2	186	766	85.11	4
Edgar B.A.	1988/89	7	13	1	150	762	63.50	3
Blair B.R.	1989/90	11	16	0	131	759	47.43	1
McEwan P.E.	1988/89	9	17	0	137	758	44.58	2
Rutherford K.R.	1985/86	11	17	2	126	753	50.20	3
Cumming C.D.	2002/03	10	18	2	128	751	46.93	3
Turner G.M.	1976/77	9	16	2	177*	750	53.57	1

Most Runs in a Season for New Zealand

		M	I	NO	HS	Runs	Ave	100
Sutcliffe B.	1949	29	49	5	243	2627	59.70	7
Donnelly M.P.	1949	29	45	8	206	2287	61.81	5
Reid J.R.	*1961/62	20	36	2	203	2083	61.26	7

* includes South Africa & Australia

Most Runs in Season of First-class Debut

			M	I	NO	HS	Runs	Ave
Cooper B.G.	ND	1980/81	7	13	0	105	520	40.00
Briasco P.S.	CD	1982/83	8	15	1	95	519	37.07
Carson W.N.	Auckland	1936/37	3	4	0	290	500	125.00

Highest Average in a Season in New Zealand

		M	I	NO	HS	Runs	Ave	100
Hammond W.R.	1932/33	3	3	1	336*	621	310.50	2
Woodfull W.M.	1924/25	6	9	5	212*	710	177.50	3
Greatbatch M.J.	1995/96	5	6	2	202	623	155.75	4
Javed Miandad	1988/89	4	5	1	271	597	149.25	3
Harris C.Z.	1996/97	5	7	1	251*	835	139.16	3
Woodfull W.M.	1927/28	6	9	3	284	781	130.16	3
Carson W.N.	1936/37	3	4	0	290	500	125.00	2
Bardsley W.	1923/24	6	7	2	200*	623	124.60	1
Cullinan D.J.	1998/99	5	7	2	275*	553	110.60	3
Hiddleston J.S.	1925/26	3	5	0	212	537	107.40	2
Weekes E. de C.	1955/56	8	10	1	156	940	104.44	6
Sutcliffe B.	1946/47	6	8	1	197	722	103.14	3
Parker J.M.	1981/82	7	13	7	117	618	103.00	2
Sutcliffe B.	1947/48	5	10	1	208*	911	101.22	4

minimum 500 runs

Centuries

George Watson registered the first century in New Zealand first-class cricket on 24 February, 1881 when he made 175 for Canterbury v Otago at Hagley Park, Christchurch.

To date, 1691 centuries have been scored in New Zealand with 51 in 1991/92 being the record for one season. A further 335 have been recorded for New Zealand teams overseas.

The following NZ players have made 15 or more centuries during their first-class careers:

Turner G.M.	103	Greatbatch M.J.	24	Wallace W.M.	17
Crowe M.D.	71	Donnelly M.P.	23	Richardson M.H.	17
Wright J.G.	59	Congdon B.E.	23	Scott V.J.	16
Sutcliffe B.	44	Crowe J.J.	22	Dowling G.T.	16
Reid J.R.	39	Horne M.J.	22	Jones A.H.	16
Dempster C.S.	35	Parker J.M.	21	Astle N.J.	16
Rutherford K.R.	35	Burgess M.G.	20	Hastings B.F.	15
Howarth G.P.	32	Fleming S.P.	20	Blunt R.C.	15
Patel D.N.	26	Lowry T.C.	18	Franklin T.J.	15
Dacre C.C.R.	24	Hadlee W.A.	18	Spearman C.M.	15
Edgar B.A.	24	Twose R.G.	18		

Most Centuries in a Season in New Zealand

8	Crowe M.D.	1986/87		4	Turner G.M.	1974/75
6	Weekes E. de C.	1955/56		4	Wright J.G.	1981/82
6	Hick G.A.	1988/89		4	Franklin T.J.	1987/88
6	Bell M.D.	2000/01		4	Hick G.A.	1987/88
5	Turner G.M.	1975/76		4	Vance R.H.	1988/89
4	Sutcliffe B.	1947/48		4	Jones A.H.	1990/91
4	Hadlee W.A.	1947/48		4	Crowe J.J.	1991/92
4	Sutcliffe B.	1950/51		4	Maynard M.P.	1991/92
4	Dowling G.T.	1967/68		4	Greatbatch M.J.	1995/96
4	Hastings B.F.	1968/69				

Five Centuries in Consecutive Innings

Weekes E. de C.	156	West Indies v Auckland	Auckland	1955/56
	148	West Indies v Canterbury	Auckland	
	123	West Indies v New Zealand	Dunedin	
	119*	West Indies v Wellington	Wellington	
	103	West Indies v New Zealand	Christchurch	

Three Centuries in Consecutive Innings

Macartney C.G.	120	NSW v Wellington	Wellington	1923/24
	120	NSW v Otago	Dunedin	
	221	NSW v Canterbury	Christchurch	
Sutcliffe B.	103	Otago v Auckland	Auckland	1947/48
	118 } 125 }	Otago v Canterbury	Dunedin	
Sutcliffe B.	141 } 135 }	Auckland v Canterbury	Auckland	1948/49
	140	New Zealand XI v The Rest	Christchurch	
Reid J.R.	101 } 118* }	New Zealand v Orange Free State	Bloemfontein	1961/62
	165	New Zealand v South African Colts XI	East London	

Chappell I.M.	128	Australia v Northern Districts	Hamilton	1973/74
	145 } 121 }	Australia v New Zealand	Wellington	
Crowe M.D.	151	Central Districts v Northern Districts	Morrinsville	1986/87
	144 } 151 }	Central Districts v Canterbury	New Plymouth	
Hick G.A.	211*	Northern Districts v Auckland	Auckland	1988/89
	144 } 132 }	Northern Districts v Wellington	Morrinsville	
Jones A.H.	186	New Zealand v Sri Lanka	Wellington	1990/91
	122 } 100* }	New Zealand v Sri Lanka	Hamilton	
Maynard M.P.	142	Northern Districts v Otago	Hamilton	1991/92
	195 } 110 }	Northern Districts v Auckland	Auckland	
Greatbatch M.J.	115	Central Districts v Canterbury	Christchurch	1995/96
	202	Central Districts v Northern Districts	Rotorua	
	162*	Central Districts v Auckland	Auckland	
Campbell S.L.	112 } 109* }	West Indies v Auckland	Auckland	1999/00
	170	West Indies v New Zealand	Hamilton	
Wells J.D.	143	Wellington v Canterbury	Wellington	1999/00
	107 } 132* }	Wellington v Central Districts	New Plymouth	

Century on First-class Debut

† Watson G.	175	Canterbury v Otago	Christchurch	1880/81
Brook-Smith W.	112*	Auckland v Hawke's Bay	Auckland	1904/05
† Wood B.B.	108 & 18	Canterbury v Wellington	Wellington	1907/08
McMullan J.J.M.	157*	Otago v Southland	Dunedin	1917/18
† Snedden C.A.	119	Auckland v Hawke's Bay	Auckland	1920/21
Talbot R.O.	105	Canterbury v Otago	Dunedin	1922/23
Tindill E.W.T.	106 & 0	Wellington v Auckland	Auckland	1932/33
Scott V.J.	122	Auckland v Canterbury	Auckland	1937/38
† Ongley J.A.	110	Wellington v Otago	Wellington	1938/39
† Kerr A.C.	122	Auckland v Wellington	Auckland	1941/42
† Watt D.G.	15 & 105	Otago v Canterbury	Christchurch	1943/44
Smith K.F.H.	27 & 141*	Wellington v Central Districts	Wellington	1953/54
MacLeod D.N.	117	Central Districts v Wellington	Wanganui	1956/57
Bilby G.P.	132 & 2*	Wellington v Central Districts	Wellington	1962/63
† Mitchell W.J.	127*	Northern Districts v Pakistan	Hamilton	1964/65
† Sampson H.C.	25 & 119	Central Districts v Wellington	Wellington	1970/71
Vaughan J.T.C.	106* & 1	Auckland v Wellington	Wellington	1989/90
Aiken J.M.	39 & 156*	Wellington v Canterbury	Christchurch	1989/90

† *only century in first-class cricket*

B.R. Williams scored 103* in his fourth first-class match, not having batted in his first three matches, for Wellington v Central Districts at Wellington, 1989/90.

Century on First-class Debut in Other Countries

In ENGLAND

Dacre C.C.R.	107	New Zealand v MCC	Lord's	1927
Crowe M.D.	104	D.B. Close's XI v Pakistan	Scarborough	1982
Horne M.J.	133	New Zealand v British Universities	Oxford	1999
Spearman C.M.	111	Gloucestershire v Worcestershire	Worcester	2002

In AUSTRALIA

Sutcliffe B.	142	New Zealand v Western Australia	Perth	1953/54
Miller L.S.M.	142	New Zealand v South Australia	Adelaide	1953/54
Patel D.N.	105	New Zealand v Western Australia	Perth	1987/88

In SOUTH AFRICA

Reid J.R.	111	New Zealand v Western Province	Cape Town	1953/54
Kasper R.J.	122*	Natal B v Transvaal B	Pietermaritzburg	1970/71
Harris C.Z.	118*	Canterbury v Eastern Province	Grahamstown	1993/94
Richardson M.H.	173*	New Zealand v Boland	Paarl	2000/01

In WEST INDIES

Hastings B.F.	100*	New Zealand v Jamaica	Kingston	1971/72
Crowe M.D.	118	New Zealand v Shell Award XI	Kingston	1984/85
Styris S.B.	107	New Zealand v West Indies	St George's	2001/02

In INDIA

Taylor B.R.	105	New Zealand v India	Calcutta	1964/65
Burgess M.G.	102	Prime Minister's XI v President's XI	Bombay	1967/68
Parker J.M.	104	New Zealand v India	Bombay	1976/77
Wright J.G.	104	New Zealand v West Zone	Rajkot	1988/89
Crowe M.D.	101*	New Zealand v President's XI	Rajkot	1995/96

In PAKISTAN

Reid J.R.	105*	NZ v Chief Commissioner's XI	Karachi	1955/56
Anderson R.W.	103*	NZ v NWFP Chief Minister's XI	Peshawar	1976/77

In SRI LANKA

Dempster C.S.	112*	Sir Julien Cahn's XI v Ceylon	Colombo	1936/37
Rutherford K.R.	108	NZ v Board President's XI	Galle	1986/87

In ZIMBABWE

Franklin T.J.	153*	Young New Zealand v Zimbabwe	Harare	1984/85
Horne M.J.	181	New Zealand v Mashonaland	Harare	1997/98
Sinclair M.S.	100*	New Zealand v President's XI	Mutare	2000/01

Century in Last First-class Match

† Phillips J.	110*	Canterbury v Wellington	Christchurch	1898/99
Midlane F.A.	126 & 4	Auckland v Wellington	Wellington	1918/19
† Beechey E.M.	180 & 5	Wellington v Auckland	Wellington	1918/19
† Watt D.G.	15 & 105	Otago v Canterbury	Christchurch	1943/44
Redmond R.E.	103 & 22	Auckland v Otago	Auckland	1975/76
Wadsworth K.J.	117	Canterbury v Otago	Christchurch	1975/76
Parker J.M.	1* & 100	Northern Districts v Wellington	Wellington	1983/84
† Snook I.R.	100*	Central Dists v Northern Dists	Palmerston North	1987/88
Dempsey D.A.	121 & 44	Canterbury v Otago	Dunedin	1987/88
Reid J.F.	112	Auckland v Northern Districts	Hamilton	1987/88
Mawhinney R.E.W.	9* & 108	Otago v Canterbury	Christchurch	1990/91
Twose R.G.	108 & 6	Wellington v Auckland	Wellington	2000/01
Nash D.J.	118 & 11*	Auckland v Otago	Dunedin	2001/02

† *only first-class century of career. (D.G. Watt was making his only appearance in first-class cricket. J. Phillips was playing his 124th first-class match and 203rd innings).*

J.D. Riley scored 34, 121, 26 and 94 (run out) in his final two first-class matches, for Auckland in 1976/77.*

Century in Each Innings of a Match

Dacre C.C.R.	127* & 101*	Auckland v Victoria	Auckland	1924/25
† Whitelaw P.E.	115 & 155	Auckland v Wellington	Auckland	1934/35
Uttley K.F.M.	132 & 138	Otago v Auckland	Auckland	1937/38
Sutcliffe B.	197 & 128	Otago v MCC	Dunedin	1946/47
Sutcliffe B.	118 & 125	Otago v Canterbury	Dunedin	1947/48
Sutcliffe B.	141 & 135	Auckland v Canterbury	Auckland	1948/49
Sutcliffe B.	243 & 100*	New Zealand v Essex	Southend	1949
Reid J.R.	101 & 118*	New Zealand v Orange Free State	Bloemfontein	1961/62
† Gedye S.G.	104 & 101	Auckland v Central Districts	Auckland	1963/64
† Thomson K.	102 & 102*	Canterbury v Otago	Dunedin	1966/67
Chappell G.S.	247* & 133	Australia v New Zealand	Wellington	1973/74
Chappell I.M.	145 & 121	Australia v New Zealand	Wellington	1973/74
Turner G.M.	101 & 110*	New Zealand v Australia	Christchurch	1973/74
Turner G.M.	135 & 108	Otago v Northern Districts	Gisborne	1974/75
Turner G.M.	105 & 186*	Otago v Central Districts	Dunedin	1974/75
Howarth G.P.	122 & 102	New Zealand v England	Auckland	1977/78
Wright J.G.	113 & 105	Northern Districts v Auckland	Auckland	1981/82
Parker J.M.	117 & 102*	Northern Districts v Central Districts	Tauranga	1981/82
Rutherford K.R.	105 & 104*	Otago v Northern Districts	Alexandra	1985/86
Border A.R.	140 & 114*	Australia v New Zealand	Christchurch	1985/86
Cooper B.G.	105 & 100	Northern Districts v Canterbury	Gisborne	1986/87
Crowe M.D.	144 & 151	Central Districts v Canterbury	New Plymouth	1986/87
Vance R.H.	116* & 123	Wellington v Central Districts	New Plymouth	1988/89
Hick G.A.	144 & 132	Northern Districts v Wellington	Morrinsville	1988/89
Jones A.H.	122 & 100*	New Zealand v Sri Lanka	Hamilton	1990/91
Gurusinha A.P.	119 & 102	Sri Lanka v New Zealand	Hamilton	1990/91
Maynard M.P.	195 & 110	Northern Districts v Auckland	Auckland	1991/92
Crowe M.D.	152 & 137*	Wellington v Canterbury	Christchurch	1992/93
Dravid R.S.	190 & 103*	India v New Zealand	Hamilton	1998/99
Rhodes J.N.	101* & 106*	South Africa v New Zealand A	Lincoln	1998/99
Campbell S.L.	112 & 109*	West Indies v Auckland	Auckland	1999/00
Wells J.D.	107 & 132*	Wellington v Central Districts	New Plymouth	1999/00
Spearman C.M.	100 & 115	New Zealand v North West	Potchefstroom	2000/01
Hopkins G.J.	113 & 175*	Canterbury v Auckland	Auckland	2002/03

† *maiden first-class century*

Highest Maiden Centuries

301*	Fulton P.G.	Canterbury v Auckland	Christchurch	2002/03
290	Carson W.N.	Auckland v Otago	Dunedin	1936/37
209	White D.J.	Northern Districts v Central Districts	Hamilton	1985/86
204	Cox A.	Canterbury v Otago	Christchurch	1925/26
203*	Burnett G.P.	Wellington v Northern Districts	Hamilton	1991/92
196	Kerr J.L.	Canterbury v Wellington	Christchurch	1932/33
194	Gaffaney C.B.	Otago v Auckland	Dunedin	1996/97
193*	Stead D.W.	Canterbury v Central Districts	Christchurch	1980/81
190	Moloney D.A.R.	Wellington v Auckland	Auckland	1936/37
189	Sinclair M.S.	Central Districts v Wellington	Masterton	1996/97
183	Gillespie H.D.	Auckland v Canterbury	Auckland	1929/30
182	McIntosh T.G.	Auckland v Canterbury	Christchurch	2000/01
180	Beechey E.M.	Wellington v Auckland	Wellington	1918/19
180	Dempster C.S.	New Zealand v Warwickshire	Birmingham	1927
180	Mooney F.L.H.	Wellington v Auckland	Wellington	1943/44
179	Ormiston R.W.	Wellington v Central Districts	New Plymouth	1982/83
177	Chandler P.J.B.	Wellington v Auckland	Wellington	1996/97
176	Cuff L.A.	Canterbury v Auckland	Christchurch	1893/94
175	Watson G.	Canterbury v Otago	Christchurch	1880/81
175	Astle N.J.	Canterbury v Northern Districts	Hamilton	1994/95
172	Worker R.V. de R.	Otago v Canterbury	Dunedin	1923/24
172	Englefield J.I.	Canterbury v Central Districts	Blenheim	2000/01
167*	Hart R.T.	Central Districts v Canterbury	New Plymouth	1983/84
167	Lawrence J.D.	Canterbury v Auckland	Christchurch	1893/94
165	Redgrave W.P.	Wellington v Hawkes Bay	Wellington	1905/06
165	Chapple M.E.	Canterbury v South Africans	Christchurch	1952/53
165	Truscott P.B.	NZ Under-23 v Auckland	Auckland	1963/64
164*	Duff S.W.	Central Districts v Auckland	Wanganui	1991/92
164	Powell J.L.	Canterbury v Otago	Christchurch	1929/30
163*	How J.M.	Central Districts v Northern Districts	Hamilton	2002/03
163	Menzies R.E.J.	Canterbury v Wellington	Christchurch	1938/39
163	Williams A.B.	Wellington v Canterbury	Christchurch	1896/97
163	Reade L.B.	Central Districts v Northern Districts	Palmerston North	1960/61
161	Larsen G.R.	Wellington v Central Districts	Levin	1987/88
159*	Kennedy P.G.	Canterbury v Northern Districts	Rotorua	1990/91
159	Vincent L.	Auckland v Northern Districts	Auckland	1998/99
158*	Papps M.H.W.	Canterbury v Otago	Christchurch	2001/02
158	Harford N.S.	New Zealand v Oxford University	Oxford	1958
157*	McMullan J.J.M.	Otago v Southland	Dunedin	1917/18
157	Briasco P.S.	Central Districts v Canterbury	New Plymouth	1983/84
156*	Aiken J.M.	Wellington v Canterbury	Christchurch	1989/90
155*	James V.	Canterbury v Otago	Dunedin	1940/41
155*	Parore A.C.	Auckland v Otago	Dunedin	1991/92
155	Badcock F.T.	Wellington v Canterbury	Christchurch	1926/27
155	Oram J.D.P.	Central Districts v Canterbury	Christchurch	1998/99
154	Meuli E.M.	Central Districts v Auckland	Palmerston North	1952/53
152	Knight A.R.	Otago v Canterbury	Dunedin	1940/41
152	Kemp R.J.	Wellington v Auckland	Auckland	1947/48
152	Coutts P.J.C.	Central Districts v Canterbury	Christchurch	1966/67
152	Lees W.K.	New Zealand v Pakistan	Karachi	1976/77
152	Brown S.W.	Auckland v Central Districts	Auckland	1990/91
151	Petrie E.C.	Auckland v Wellington	Auckland	1953/54
150	Crowe M.D.	Auckland v Central Districts	New Plymouth	1981/82

Watson, McMullan and Aiken scored their centuries on their debut in first-class cricket. Beechey was playing in his last first-class game. Carson (aged 20 years 168 days) and Cox (21 years 19 days) were both playing only their second first-class innings and remain the youngest players to score a double-century in New Zealand first-class cricket.

One Hundred Runs before Lunch

Runs	Mins				
* 110	120	Smith S.G.	Auckland v Canterbury	Auckland	1919/20
112	113	Macartney C.G.	NSW v Wellington	Wellington	1923/24
* 116	120	† Punch A.T.E.	NSW v Otago	Dunedin	1923/24
* 101	91	Macartney C.G.	NSW v Otago	Dunedin	1923/24
103	110	Hiddleston J.S.	Wellington v Canterbury	Wellington	1925/26
105	102	Dacre C.C.R.	Auckland v Otago	Dunedin	1926/27
103	103	† Vorrath W.	Otago v Wellington	Dunedin	1927/28
* 106	120	Blunt R.C.	Otago v Canterbury	Christchurch	1928/29
164	130	† Powell J.L.	Canterbury v Otago	Christchurch	1929/30
105	105	Badcock F.T.	Otago v Canterbury	Christchurch	1931/32
* 111	120	Hammond W.R.	England v New Zealand	Auckland	1932/33
102	120	Whitelaw P.E.	Auckland v Wellington	Auckland	1934/35
115	110	Wallace W.M.	New Zealand v Somerset	Taunton	1937
* 110	120	Wallace W.M.	New Zealand v Sussex	Hove	1937
* 103	120	Smith F.B.	Canterbury v Auckland	Auckland	1948/49
100	117	Sutcliffe B.	New Zealand v Essex	Southend	1949
* 100	120	Reid J.R.	Wellington v Otago	Wellington	1951/52
* 122	111	Guillen S.C.	Canterbury v Fiji	Christchurch	1953/54
* 100	126	Smith K.F.H.	Central Districts v Wellington	Wanganui	1959/60
* 108	131	Sutcliffe B.	Otago v Central Districts	Dunedin	1959/60
* 100	140	Sutcliffe B.	Otago v Northern Districts	Wellington	1960/61
* 174	140	Reid J.R.	Wellington v Northern Districts	Wellington	1962/63
120	125	Reid J.R.	Wellington v Northern Districts	Wellington	1964/65
103	120	Murray B.A.G.	New Zealand v President's XI	Rawalpindi	1969/70
* 109	141	Dunning B.	Northern Dist. v Central Dist.	Blenheim	1972/73
111	150	Dempsey D.A.	Canterbury v Otago	Christchurch	1980/81
102	147	† Crowe M.D.	Auckland v Central Districts	New Plymouth	1981/82
* 100	107	Chappell G.S.	Australia v New Zealand	Christchurch	1981/82
* 100	150	Crowe J.J.	Auckland v Northern Districts	Rotorua	1983/84
101	103	Rutherford K.R.	New Zealand v DB Close's XI	Scarborough	1986
* 101	144	Jones A.H.	Wellington v Otago	Wellington	1986/87
* 112	149	McSweeney E.B.	Wellington v Central Districts	Levin	1987/88
* 122	150	Crowe J.J.	Auckland v Wellington	Wellington	1988/89
* 117	160	Greatbatch M.J.	Central Districts v Otago	Palmerston North	1988/89
101	127	Blain T.E.	Central Districts v Wellington	New Plymouth	1988/89
107	136	† Reid R.B.	Auckland v Central Districts	Masterton	1989/90
* 116	136	Thomson S.A.	Northern Districts v Auckland	Auckland	1990/91
141	144	Maynard M.P.	Northern Districts v Auckland	Auckland	1991/92
* 139	92	Patel D.N.	Auckland v Northern Districts	Auckland	1991/92
104	140	Spearman C.M.	Central Districts v Wellington	Wellington	1997/98
101	137	Cairns C.L.	Southern v Central	Wellington	1998/99

* *batsman had been not out overnight*
† *maiden first-class hundred. Punch, Vorrath, Powell and Reid did not score another century in first-class cricket*

Scores of Ninety-nine

Johnson P.R.	MCC v New Zealand	Christchurch	1906/07
† Snedden A.N.C.	Auckland v Canterbury	Auckland	1921/22
Elmes C.J.	New Zealand v MCC	Auckland	1935/36
* Whitelaw P.E.	Auckland/Wellington v MCC	Auckland	1936/37
Sutcliffe B.	Otago v Auckland	Dunedin	1947/48
Taylor D.D.	Auckland v Canterbury	Auckland	1948/49
† Leggat J.G.	Canterbury v Auckland	Christchurch	1951/52
Rae A.F.	West Indies v New Zealand	Auckland	1951/52
O'Malley P.W.	Canterbury v Wellington	Christchurch	1953/54
† Beck J.E.F.	New Zealand v South Africa	Cape Town	1953/54
Hunter A.A.	Central Districts v Auckland	Auckland	1953/54
† Leggat J.G.	Canterbury v MCC	Christchurch	1954/55
Sutcliffe B.	Rest v New Zealand XI	Christchurch	1957/58
Sutcliffe B.	New Zealand v Sussex	Hove	1958
* Bartlett G.A.	Central Districts v Auckland	Auckland	1959/60
McGregor S.N.	Otago v Canterbury	Christchurch	1963/64
† Cunis R.S.	Auckland v Wellington	Wellington	1966/67
Surti R.F.	India v New Zealand	Auckland	1967/68
Turner G.M.	New Zealand v Tasmania	Hobart	1969/70
Burtt J.W.	Canterbury v Central Districts	Christchurch	1970/71
Dowling G.T.	Canterbury v Northern Districts	Hamilton	1970/71
Murray B.A.G.	Wellington v Northern Districts	Wellington	1970/71
Dowling G.T.	New Zealand v Western Australia	Perth	1970/71
* O'Keeffe K.J.	Australia v Auckland	Auckland	1973/74
Edwards G.N.	Central Districts v Australia	Nelson	1976/77
Blair W.L.	Otago v Auckland	Auckland	1978/79
Crowe M.D.	Auckland v Northern Districts	Auckland	1981/82
Hadlee R.J.	New Zealand v England	Christchurch	1983/84
† Lees W.K.	Otago v Northern Districts	Hamilton	1983/84
Vance R.H.	Wellington v Canterbury	Wellington	1984/85
Coney J.V.	New Zealand v President's XI	St Lucia	1984/85
Jones A.H.	Wellington v Auckland	Auckland	1985/86
* Robertson G.K.	Central Districts v Otago	Oamaru	1985/86
Wright J.G.	New Zealand v Australia	Melbourne	1987/88
Crocker L.M.	Northern Districts v Wellington	Hamilton	1987/88
Moxon M.D.	England v New Zealand	Auckland	1987/88
McEwan P.E.	Canterbury v Wellington	Christchurch	1988/89
Hart R.T.	Central Districts v Auckland	Masterton	1989/90
Wright J.G.	New Zealand v Worcestershire	Worcester	1990
† Patel D.N.	New Zealand v England	Christchurch	1991/92
+ Wright J.G.	New Zealand v England	Christchurch	1991/92
Douglas M.W.	Central Districts v Auckland	Wanganui	1991/92
McSweeney E.B.	Wellington v Canterbury	Wellington	1993/94
Twose R.G.	Central Districts v Auckland	Palmerston North	1993/94
† Jones R.A.	Auckland v Otago	Dunedin	1996/97
* Sinclair M.S.	Central Districts v Northern Districts	Hamilton	1996/97
Twose R.G.	Wellington v India	Wellington	1998/99
Yovich J.A.F.	Northern Districts v Auckland	Taupo	1999/00
Richardson M.H.	New Zealand v Zimbabwe	Harare	2000/01
Fleming S.P.	New Zealand v South Africa	Bloemfontein	2000/01
Gaffaney C.B.	Otago v Auckland	Auckland	2000/01
Nevin C.J.	Wellington v Otago	Wellington	2000/01

* not out innings † batsman was run out + batsman was stumped
For Elmes, Bartlett, O'Keeffe, Robertson and Yovich, the above innings were their highest in first-class cricket

Carried Bat Through a Complete Innings

	Score	Total			
Harris L.M.	41*	65	Otago v Tasmania	Dunedin	1883/84
Gatehouse G.H.	54*	146	Tasmania v Otago	Dunedin	1883/84
Mills I.	88*	156	Auckland v Otago	Dunedin	1893/94
† Collins J.C.	128*	187	Fiji v Hawke's Bay	Napier	1894/95
Cobcroft L.T.	85*	239	NSW v Wellington	Wellington	1895/96
Mills G.	106*	235	Auckland v Wellington	Auckland	1895/96
Collins D.C.	53*	131	Wellington v Canterbury	Christchurch	1906/07
§ Midlane F.A.	14*	60	Wellington§ v Canterbury	Christchurch	1910/11
Gibbes W.R.L.	75*	193	Wellington v Canterbury	Christchurch	1911/12
† Midlane F.A.	222*	498	Wellington v Otago	Wellington	1914/15
Blunt R.C.	137*	336	Canterbury v Wellington	Wellington	1919/20
† Bardsley W.	200*	352	NSW v Auckland	Auckland	1923/24
Blunt R.C.	131*	204	Otago v Canterbury	Dunedin	1926/27
Dempster C.S.	167*	345	New Zealand v Glamorgan	Cardiff	1927
Kerr J.L.	146*	243	Canterbury v MCC	Christchurch	1935/36
Whitelaw P.E.	99*	183	Auckland/Wellington v MCC	Auckland	1936/37
Tindill E.W.T.	47*	111	Wellington v Otago	Dunedin	1946/47
† Miller L.S.M.	81*	154	Wellington v Otago	Dunedin	1956/57
Playle W.R.	89*	139	Auckland v Northern Districts	Auckland	1959/60
Bradburn W.P.	45*	87	Northern Districts v Wellington	Wellington	1960/61
Bradburn W.P.	37*	57	Northern Districts v Wellington	Hamilton	1961/62
Holloway R.A.	61*	122	Otago v Central Districts	Nelson	1962/63
Turner G.M.	43*	131	New Zealand v England	Lord's	1969
Turner G.M.	223*	386	New Zealand v West Indies	Kingston	1971/72
Redpath I.R.	159*	346	Australia v New Zealand	Auckland	1973/74
Wettimuny S.	63*	144	Sri Lanka v New Zealand	Christchurch	1982/83
† Franklin T.J.	153*	311	Young NZ v Zimbabwe	Harare	1984/85
Rutherford K.R.	89*	241	Otago v Auckland	Dunedin	1984/85
Boon D.C.	58*	103	Australia v New Zealand	Auckland	1985/86
Wright J.G.	149*	307	Canterbury v Auckland	Auckland	1988/89
Smith C.J.P.	90*	154	Central Dists v Northern Dists	Rotorua	1989/90
Murray D.J.	106*	233	Canterbury v Northern Dists	Hamilton	1992/93
Dobbs P.W.	81*	177	Otago v Canterbury	Oamaru	1994/95
Atherton M.A.	94*	228	England v New Zealand	Christchurch	1996/97
Kelly D.P.	212*	538	Central Districts v Canterbury	Blenheim	2000/01

† *player was on the field for every ball of the match*   § *one man absent*

Longest Individual Batting in a Match

Mins	Runs				
954	274* & 69*	Fleming S.P.	New Zealand v Sri Lanka	Colombo	2002/03
876	76 & 146*	Greatbatch M.J.	New Zealand v Australia	Perth	1989/90
835	122 & 102	Howarth G.P.	New Zealand v England	Auckland	1977/78
828	75 & 138	Wright J.G.	New Zealand v West Indies	Wellington	1986/87
770	166* & 82	Congdon B.E.	New Zealand v West Indies	Port-of-Spain	1971/72

Longest Individual Innings

Mins	Runs				
741	306	Richardson M.H.	New Zealand v Zimbabwe A	Kwekwe	2000/01
720	163	Shoaib Mohammad	Pakistan v New Zealand	Wellington	1988/89
704	259	Turner G.M.	New Zealand v West Indies	Georgetown	1971/72
685	180	Reid J.F.	New Zealand v Sri Lanka	Colombo	1983/84
671	212*	Richardson M.H.	New Zealand A v Sussex	Hove	2000
659	211*	Gibbs H.H.	South Africa v New Zealand	Christchurch	1998/99
658	275*	Cullinan D.J.	South Africa v New Zealand	Auckland	1998/99
655	146*	Greatbatch M.J.	New Zealand v Australia	Perth	1989/90
655	274*	Fleming S.P.	New Zealand v Sri Lanka	Colombo	2002/03
648	158	Radley C.T.	England v New Zealand	Auckland	1977/78
647	251*	Harris C.Z.	Canterbury v Central Districts	Rangiora	1996/97
636	170*	Jones A.H.	New Zealand v India	Auckland	1989/90
625	222	Rutherford I.A.	Otago v Central Districts	New Plymouth	1978/79
610	299	Crowe M.D.	New Zealand v Sri Lanka	Wellington	1990/91
609	120*	Crowe J.J.	New Zealand v Sri Lanka	Colombo	1986/87
605	267*	Young B.A.	New Zealand v Sri Lanka	Dunedin	1996/97
603	259	Turner G.M.	New Zealand v Guyana	Georgetown	1971/72

Fastest Centuries

Mins	Balls				
52	45	Cairns B.L.	Otago v Wellington	Lower Hutt	1979/80
52	66	Cooper B.G.	Northern Districts v Canterbury	Gisborne	1986/87
53	63	Motz R.C.	Canterbury v Otago	Christchurch	1967/68

Slowest Centuries

Mins	Balls				
516	331	Crowe J.J.	New Zealand v Sri Lanka	Colombo	1986/87
487	397	Radley C.T.	England v New Zealand	Auckland	1977/78
464	390	Austen M.H.	Otago v Canterbury	Christchurch	1996/97
462	341	Greatbatch M.J.	New Zealand v Australia	Perth	1989/90
461	265	Crowe M.D.	New Zealand v Pakistan	Lahore	1990/91
458	341	Astle N.J.	New Zealand v Zimbabwe	Wellington	2000/01
455	307	Howarth G.P.	New Zealand v England	Auckland	1977/78
435	†	Guy J.W.	New Zealand v India	Hyderabad	1955/56
434	380	Reid J.F.	Auckland v Northern Districts	Hamilton	1987/88
434	309	Franklin T.J.	New Zealand v England	Lord's	1990
427	368	Burns K.J.	Otago v Northern Districts	Hamilton	1987/88
426	289	Saqlain Mushtaq	Pakistan v New Zealand	Christchurch	2000/01
422	349	Boyle D.J.	Canterbury v Otago	Rangiora	1993/94
420	332	Crowe M.D.	New Zealand v West Indies	Georgetown	1984/85
414	399	Wright J.G.	New Zealand v India	Auckland	1980/81
412	325	Wright J.G.	New Zealand v West Indies	Wellington	1986/87
404	311	Reid J.F.	New Zealand v Pakistan	Wellington	1984/85

† *details not available*

Most Boundaries in an Innings

6s	4s		Runs			
53	8	45	Rutherford K.R.	317	New Zealand v D.B. Close's XI	Scarborough	1986
50	15	35	Reid J.R.	296	Wellington v Northern Districts	Wellington	1962/63
49	3	46	Sutcliffe B.	385	Otago v Canterbury	Christchurch	1952/53
48	3	45	Fulton P.G.	301*	Canterbury v Auckland	Christchurch	2002/03
47	3	44	Trumper V.T.	293	Sims' Australian XI v Canterbury	Christchurch	1913/14
43	10	33	Hammond W.R.	336*	England v New Zealand	Auckland	1932/33
43	—	43	Richardson M.H.	306	New Zealand v Zimbabwe A	Kwekwe	2000/01
42	1	41	Reid J.R.	283	Wellington v Otago	Wellington	1951/52
42	1	41	Crowe M.D.	242*	New Zealand v South Australia	Adelaide	1985/86
42	3	39	Crowe M.D.	242	Central Districts v Otago	New Plymouth	1989/90
41	—	41	Blunt R.C.	338*	Otago v Canterbury	Christchurch	1931/32
40	—	40	de Silva P.A.	267	Sri Lanka v New Zealand	Wellington	1990/91

Most Sixes in an Innings

Sixes		Runs			
15	Reid J.R.	296	Wellington v Northern Districts	Wellington	1962/63
12	Patel D.N.	204	Auckland v Northern Districts	Auckland	1991/92
11	Astle N.J.	222	New Zealand v England	Christchurch	2001/02
10	Hammond W.R.	336*	England v New Zealand	Auckland	1932/33
10	Robinson R.T.	166	England XI v Northern Districts	Hamilton	1987/88
10	Styris S.B.	212*	Northern Districts v Otago	Hamilton	2001/02
9	Cairns B.L.	110	Otago v Wellington	Lower Hutt	1979/80
9	Botham I.T.	80	England XI v Central Districts	Palmerston North	1983/84
9	Cairns C.L.	120	New Zealand v Zimbabwe	Auckland	1995/96
8	Dacre C.C.R.	176	New Zealand v Derbyshire	Derby	1927
8	Bula I.L.	102	Fiji v Canterbury	Christchurch	1953/54
8	Rutherford K.R.	317	New Zealand v DB Close's XI	Scarborough	1986
8	Germon L.K.	160*	Canterbury v Wellington	Christchurch	1989/90
8	Parore A.C.	111*	Auckland v Wellington	Auckland	1997/98
7	Tallon D.	116	Australia v New Zealand	Dunedin	1949/50
7	Sutcliffe B.	80*	New Zealand v South Africa	Johannesburg	1953/54
7	Cairns B.L.	68	New Zealand v New South Wales	Sydney	1980/81
7	Greenidge G.C.	213	West Indies v New Zealand	Auckland	1986/87
7	Hick G.A.	146	Northern Districts v England XI	Hamilton	1987/88
7	Maynard M.P.	195	Northern Districts v Auckland	Auckland	1991/92
7	Hick G.A.	115	England XI v Central Districts	New Plymouth	1991/92

Five Sixes off Consecutive Balls

Germon L.K.	off Vance R.H.	Canterbury v Wellington	Christchurch	1989/90

(Full tosses and deliberate no-balls were provided for him to hit).

Four Sixes off Consecutive Balls

Rutherford K.R.	off Doshi D.R.	New Zealand v DB Close's XI	Scarborough	1986

Three Sixes off Consecutive Balls

Hill C.	off Ollivier K.M.	Australia v New Zealand	Wellington	1904/05
Hammond W.R.	off Newman J.	England v New Zealand	Auckland	1932/33
McRae D.A.N.	off Burke C.	Canterbury v Auckland	Auckland	1937/38
Pritchard T.L.	off Groves L.J.	Wellington v Otago	Dunedin	1937/38
Edwards R.M.	off Carew M.C.	Governor General's XI v West Indies	Auckland	1968/69
Burgess M.G.	off Anderson R.W.	Auckland v Central Districts	Wanganui	1977/78

Stirling D.A.	off Brown V.R.	Central Districts v Canterbury	New Plymouth	1986/87
Thomson S.A.	off Bracewell J.G.	Northern Districts v Auckland	Auckland	1987/88
Hick G.A.	off Duff S.W.	England XI v Central Districts	New Plymouth	1991/92
Astle N.J.	off Wells J.D.	Canterbury v Wellington	Christchurch	1994/95
Vincent L.	off Vettori D.L.	Auckland v Northern Districts	Auckland	1998/99
Astle N.J.	off Caddick A.R.	New Zealand v England	Christchurch	2001/02

Most Ducks in Succession

5	Hayes J.A.	(C, NZ 1954/55)	17,0 / dnb / 0,0 / 0,0
5	Bateman S.N.	(C 1982/83)	5*,0 / 0,0 / 0,0
4	Silver R.C.D.	(O 1936/37-1937/38)	12,0 / 0,0 / 0,11
*4	Langdon M.C.	(ND 1957/58)	25,0 / 0,0 / 0,5
4	Hastings B.F.	(C 1963/64)	1,0 / 0,0 / 0,35
4	Bracewell B.P.	(NZ 1978)	0 / dnb / 0,0 / 0,0*
4	Bradburn G.E.	(ND 1987/88)	0 / 0,0 / 0
4	Steele H.K.C.	(A 1974/75)	0,0 / 0,0
4	Morrison D.K.	(NZ 1993/94)	0 / 0,0 / 0,20*
4	Davis H.T.	(NZ, W 1997/98)	7*,0 / 0,0 / 0,21
4	Young R.A.	(A 1999/00)	0,0 / 0,0
4	Martin C.S.	(C NZ 2000/01)	5,0 / 0,0 / 0
4	Gaffaney C.B.	(O 2001/02)	31,0 / 0,0 / 0,56

* first three games in first-class cricket

Most Scoreless Innings in Succession

10	Visser P.J.	(CD 1984/85-1985/86)	0 / 0,0 / dnb / 0*,0 / dnb / 0*,0* 0,0 / dnb / 0
7	Hamilton L.J.	(CD 1999/00)	0,0* / 0 / 0*,0 / 0 / 0
6	Hayes J.A.	(C, NZ 1954/55-1955/56)	17,0 / dnb / 0,0 / 0,0 / 0*
6	de Groen R.P.	(A 1988/89-1989/90)	1,0* / dnb / 0,0 / 0* / 0*,0*
*5	Moss A.E.	(C 1889/90)	0,0* / 0,0 / 0*,4*
5	Hill J.	(O 1961/62-1962/63)	0*,0* / 0* / 0*,0*
5	Unka H.	(ND 1968/69-1971/72)	0* / 0*,0* / dnb / 0*,0
5	Bracewell B.P.	(NZ 1978)	0 / dnb / 0,0 / 0,0*
5	Troup G.B.	(A, NZ 1980/81-1981/82)	0,0* / 0,0 / dnb / 0
5	Bateman S.N.	(C 1982/83)	5*,0 / 0,0 / 0,0
5	Burrows J.T.	(C 1932/33)	0*,0* / 0* / 0*,0*

* first five innings in first-class cricket

UNUSUAL DISMISSALS

HANDLED THE BALL

Benson E.T.	MCC v Auckland	Auckland	1929/30
Gilbertson A.W.	Otago v Auckland	Auckland	1952/53
Vaughan J.T.C.	NZ Emerging Players v England XI	Hamilton	1991/92

OBSTRUCTING THE FIELD

Hayes J.A.	Canterbury v Central Districts	Christchurch	1954/55

RUN OUT BY THE BOWLER *(while backing up before the ball had been bowled)*

Reese T.W. by Downes A.D.	Canterbury v Otago	Christchurch	1894/95
Smith J. by Allen R.	Canterbury v Wellington	Wellington	1943/44
Randall D.W. by Chatfield E.J.	England v New Zealand	Christchurch	1977/78

STUMPED BY A SUBSTITUTE

Pervez Sajjad by Congdon B.E.	Pakistan v New Zealand	Lahore	1964/65
Congdon B.E. by Burge P.J.P.	Central Districts v Australia	Palmerston North	1966/67

RETIRED (out)

Ransford V.S.	Australia v Hawke's Bay	Napier	1920/21
Chappell G.S.	Australia v Wellington	Wellington	1976/77
Saeed Anwar	Pakistan v New Zealand XI	Napier	1993/94
Basit Ali	Pakistan v New Zealand XI	Napier	1993/94
Inzamam-ul-Haq	Pakistan v New Zealand XI	Napier	1993/94
Spearman C.M.	New Zealand v North West	Potchefstroom	2000/01

REPLACEMENT PLAYERS

Substitute	*Player replaced*			
Lawrence —	Bell A.	Wellington v Nelson	Wellington	1873/74
Cotterill C.N.	White G.	Hawke's Bay v NSW	Napier	1893/94
unknown	Ratu Epeli	Fiji v Auckland	Auckland	1894/95
Kilgour W.A.	*Wilson C.G.	Otago v Auckland	Auckland	1907/08
Bryden J.S.	*Siedeberg H.G.	Otago v Canterbury	Dunedin	1913/14
Graham W.H.	Middleton F.S.	Auckland v Wellington	Wellington	1917/18
Whitta H.B.	*Foster P.S.	Canterbury v Wellington	Christchurch	1919/20
Samuels B.	*Brice A.W.S.	Wellington v Auckland	Auckland	1919/20
Wilson E.S.	Eastman L.C.	Otago v Wellington	Wellington	1927/28
Kubunavanua P.	Logavatu I.T.	Fiji v Canterbury	Christchurch	1947/48
Abernethy B.	Webb R.J.	Otago v Auckland	Dunedin	1982/83
Neutze P.S.	Brown V.R.	Auckland v Wellington	Auckland	1987/88
Brown R.K.	Greatbatch M.J.	CD v Otago	Palmerston North	1991/92
Lee C.D.	Larsen G.R.	Wellington v ND	Hamilton	1991/92
Fleming S.P.	Harris C.Z.	Canterbury v Auckland	Auckland	1991/92
Lee C.D.	*Patel D.N.	Auckland v Otago	Dunedin	1994/95
Garner C.D.	Spearman C.M.	CD v ND	Nelson	1996/97
Cooper D.M.	Howell L.G.	CD v ND	Nelson	1996/97
Lamont M.J.	Horne M.J.	Otago v Auckland	Dunedin	1996/97
Morland N.D.	Wiseman P.J.	Otago v Auckland	Dunedin	1996/97
Sewell D.G.	Kennedy R.J.	Otago v Auckland	Dunedin	1996/97
Irving R.J.R.	Mills J.M.	Auckland v Otago	Dunedin	1996/97
Weenink S.W.	Chandler P.J.B.	Wellington v Canterbury	Christchurch	1996/97
Jonas G.R.	Davis H.T.	Wellington v Canterbury	Christchurch	1996/97
Hartland B.R.	Murray D.J.	Canterbury v Wellington	Christchurch	1996/97
Frew R.M.	Harris C.Z.	Canterbury v Wellington	Christchurch	1996/97
Sharpe M.F.	Allott G.I.	Canterbury v Wellington	Christchurch	1996/97
Hotter S.J.	Davis H.T.	Wellington v CD	Masterton	1996/97
Muir G.A.	Priest M.W.	Canterbury v Zimbabwe	Timaru	1997/98
Pawson S.J.	Priest M.W.	Canterbury v Otago	Dunedin	1997/98
Dry L.R.	Bell M.D.	Wellington v ND	Hamilton	1998/99
Morland N.D.	*Wiseman P.J.	Otago v Auckland	Dunedin	1999/00
Spearman C.M.	Sinclair M.S.	CD v Otago	Palmerston North	1999/00
Todd G.R.	Oram J.D.P.	CD v Wellington	Napier	2000/01
McCullum N.L.	Wiseman P.J.	Otago v Canterbury	Alexandra	2000/01

* indicates player did not bat or bowl before being replaced

REPRESENTED TWO PROVINCES IN ONE SEASON

Sutcliffe B.	Auckland and Otago	1946/47
Sutcliffe B.	Otago and Auckland	1947/48
Clark L.A.	Otago and Auckland	1959/60
Andrews B.	Canterbury and Central Districts	1966/67

On each occasion, the second province was represented in a match against a non-provincial side. No player has played for two provinces in inter-provincial matches in the same season.

BOWLING

Ten Wickets in an Innings

	Overs	Maidens	Runs	Wickets			
* Moss A.E.	21.3	10	28	10	Canterbury v Wellington	Christchurch	1889/90

* on debut — the only instance in first-class cricket

Nine Wickets in an Innings

	Overs	Maidens	Runs	Wickets			
Wensley A.F.	24	13	36	9	Auckland v Otago	Auckland	1929/30
Eden T.	15.2	0	43	9	Nelson v Wellington	Wellington	1875/76
Dent T.H.	28	11	47	9	Hawke's Bay v Wellington	Napier	1900/01
Tait A.R.	24.5	8	48	9	ND v Auckland	Hamilton	1996/97
Fisher A.H.	25.2	4	50	9	Otago v Queensland	Dunedin	1896/97
Hadlee R.J.	23.4	4	52	9	New Zealand v Australia	Brisbane	1985/86
Hadlee R.J.	24	5	55	9	New Zealand v West Zone	Rajkot	1988/89
McBeath D.J.	24	7	56	9	Canterbury v Auckland	Christchurch	1918/19
Brice A.W.S.	25.5	5	67	9	Wellington v Auckland	Wellington	1918/19
Cooke F.H.	56	24	73	9	Otago v Canterbury	Christchurch	1884/85
Blair R.W.	35	9	72	9	Wellington v Auckland	Wellington	1956/57
Neill R.	31	7	75	9	Auckland v Canterbury	Auckland	1891/92
Blair R.W.	29.5	9	75	9	Wellington v Canterbury	Wellington	1956/57
Neill R.	24.2	1	86	9	Auckland v Canterbury	Auckland	1897/98
Petherick P.J.	35	10	93	9	Otago v ND	Dunedin	1975/76
Priest M.W.	28.5	5	95	9	Canterbury v Otago	Dunedin	1989/90
Robertson W.	39.3	8	98	9	Canterbury v Wellington	Christchurch	1894/95
Yuile B.W.	45	19	100	9	CD v Canterbury	New Plymouth	1965/66

Sixteen Wickets in a Match

16-130	Tait A.R.	24.5-8-48-9/38.4-13-82-7	Northern Dists v Auckland, Hamilton	1996/97

Fifteen Wickets in a Match

15-60	Callaway S.T.	23.3-10-33-8/17-7-27-7	Canterbury v Hawke's Bay, Napier	1903/04
15-94	Cooke F.H.	40.3-16-61-8/33.3-14-33-7	Otago v Canterbury, Christchurch	1882/83
15-104	Boock S.L.	29.3-13-47-7/34.3-16-57-8	Otago v Auckland, Dunedin	1989/90
15-123	Hadlee R.J.	23.4-4-52-9/28.5-9-71-6	NZ v Australia, Brisbane	1985/86
15-168	McBeath D.J.	24-7-56-9/37-4-112-6	Canterbury v Auckland, Christchurch	1918/19
15-175	Callaway S.T.	35-14-77-7/43.4-11-98-8	NSW v New Zealand, Christchurch	1895/96
15-203	Moir A.M.	24.1-4-84-7/35.1-3-119-8	Otago v Central Dists, New Plymouth	1953/54

Fourteen Wickets in a Match

14-59	Read R.J.	13-3-35-7/14-5-24-7	Canterbury v Southland, Invercargill	1920/21
14-63	Eden T.	15.2-0-43-9/15.5-7-20-5	Nelson v Wellington, Wellington	1875/76
* 14-63	Rees A.W.	13-4-27-6/15.3-3-36-8	Auckland v Otago, Dunedin	1889/90
14-65	Callaway S.T.	36.3-18-47-7/18.2-7-18-7	NSW v Wellington, Wellington	1895/96
14-65	Hayes J.A.	18.2-6-28-7/12.1-3-37-7	Auckland v Wellington, Auckland	1957/58
14-93	Torrance R.C.	23-6-51-7/19-5-42-7	Otago v Hawke's Bay, Napier	1908/09
14-94	Howarth H.J.	22.1-5-42-7/23-6-52-7	Auckland v Otago, Dunedin	1973/74
14-103	Downes A.D.	30-12-32-7/30-8-71-7	Otago v Hawke's Bay, Dunedin	1893/94
* 14-107	Robertson W.	28.2-8-59-8/20.4-7-48-6	Canterbury v Auckland, Christchurch	1893/94
14-119	Pringle C.	27.4-10-63-7/23.5-5-56-7	Auckland v Otago, Dunedin	1993/94
14-126	Moir A.M.	18-1-55-8/25-6-71-6	Otago v Canterbury, Dunedin	1951/52
14-136	Blair R.W.	29.5-9-75-9/26-8-61-5	Wellington v Canterbury, Wellington	1956/57
14-151	Gray E.J.	50-19-114-6/26.1-12-37-8	Wellington v Canterbury, Lower Hutt	1985/86

* on debut

Four Wickets with Consecutive Balls

Downes A.D.	Otago v Auckland	Dunedin	1893/94

Hat Tricks

Salmon I.J.	Wellington v Nelson	Wellington	1873/74
Lankham W.	Auckland v Taranaki	Auckland	1882/83
Frith C.	Otago v Canterbury	Dunedin	1884/85
Fannin H.A.	Hawkes Bay v Taranaki	Napier	1897/98
Barclay F.	Auckland v Canterbury	Auckland	1903/04
Orchard S.A.	Canterbury v Auckland	Auckland	1909/10
Bennett J.H.	Canterbury v Wellington	Wellington	1911/12
Olliff C.	Auckland v Wellington	Auckland	1912/13
Middleton F.S.	Wellington v Hawke's Bay	Wellington	1919/20
Allom M.J.C.*	England v New Zealand	Christchurch	1929/30
Mulcock E.	Canterbury v Otago	Christchurch	1937/38
Overton G.W.F.	Otago v Canterbury	Christchurch	1946/47
Murray R.M.	Wellington v Otago	Wellington	1949/50
Moir A.M.	Otago v Canterbury	Christchurch	1950/51
Jones J.F.	Wellington v Central Districts	Wellington	1953/54
Reid R.E.	Wellington v Otago	Dunedin	1958/59
Bartlett G.A.	Central Districts v Northern Districts	Hamilton	1959/60
Cameron F.J.	Otago v Northern Districts	Hamilton	1962/63
Blair R.W.	Wellington v Northern Districts	Wellington	1962/63
Alabaster G.D.	Northern Districts v Canterbury	Hamilton	1962/63
Furlong B.D.M.	NZ Under 23 XI v Canterbury	Christchurch	1964/65
Hadlee R.J.	Canterbury v Central Districts	Nelson	1971/72
Petherick P.J.	NZ v Pakistan	Lahore	1976/77
Toynbee M.H.	Central Districts v Northern Districts	Gisborne	1979/80
Visser P.J.	Central Districts v Auckland	Nelson	1983/84
Maguiness S.J.	Wellington v Northern Districts	Wellington	1983/84
Beard D.A.	Northern Districts v Central Districts	Nelson	1989/90
Gale A.J.	Otago v Canterbury	Dunedin	1992/93
Harris C.Z.	New Zealand v Orange Free State	Bloemfontein	1994/95
Hayes R.L.	Northern Districts v Central Districts	Rotorua	1995/96
Hotter S.J.	Wellington v Otago	Wellington	1996/97
Anderson T.R.	Central Districts v Auckland	Masterton	1998/99
Canning T.K.	Auckland v Central Districts	Auckland	1999/00

* Allom captured 4 wickets with 5 balls in the same over

Most Wickets in a Single Day's Play in New Zealand

14	Rees A.W.	Auckland v Otago	Dunedin	1889/90
13	Lankham W.	Auckland v Taranaki	Auckland	1882/83
13	Smith C.R.	Hawke's Bay v Taranaki	Hawera	1891/92
13	Cave H.B.	Central Districts v Auckland	Palmerston North	1952/53

Outstanding Analyses

TEN WICKETS IN AN INNINGS

21.3	11	28	10	Moss A.E.	Canterbury v Wellington	Christchurch	1889/90

NINE WICKETS IN AN INNINGS

24	13	36	9	Wensley A.F.	Auckland v Otago	Auckland	1929/30
15.2	0	43	9	Eden T.	Nelson v Wellington	Wellington	1875/76
28	11	47	9	Dent T.H.	Hawke's Bay v Wellington	Napier	1900/01

EIGHT WICKETS IN AN INNINGS

13	6	13	8	Firth J.P.	Wellington v Hawke's Bay	Wellington	1883/84
19	12	14	8	Austin S.W.	NSW v Hawke's Bay	Napier	1893/94
29	21	18	8	Frith W.	Canterbury v Otago	Christchurch	1880/81
14.5	7	19	8	Fannin H.A.	Hawke's Bay v Auckland	Auckland	1897/98

SEVEN WICKETS IN AN INNINGS

10.1	6	9	7	Bracewell J.G.	Otago v Canterbury	Dunedin	1981/82
13	9	11	7	Fisher A.H.	Otago v Canterbury	Christchurch	1896/97
25.3	16	12	7	Downes A.D.	Otago v Canterbury	Dunedin	1896/97
16	8	12	7	Tuffey D.R.	Northern Districts v Wellington	Hamilton	2000/01
32.1	24	13	7	Lankham W.	Auckland v Taranaki	Auckland	1882/83
10.4	5	16	7	Farooq Hamid	Pakistan v Wellington	Wellington	1964/65
17	10	17	7	Armstrong W.W.	Australia v Wellington	Wellington	1913/14
14.2	7	17	7	Maguiness S.J.	Wellington v Canterbury	Rangiora	1984/85
18.2	7	18	7	Callaway S.T.	NSW v Wellington	Wellington	1895/96

SIX WICKETS IN AN INNINGS

8	5	3	6	Cowie J.	New Zealand v Ireland	Dublin	1937
8	5	4	6	Callaway S.T.	Canterbury v Wellington	Wellington	1903/04
9.2	3	5	6	Bennett A.P.	Nelson v Wellington	Nelson	1885/86
16	11	6	6	Haskell W.J.R.	Wellington v Otago	Wellington	1967/68
14	10	7	6	Dunlop D.	Canterbury v Wellington	Wellington	1886/87
18	14	7	6	Hampton B.L.	Central Districts v Otago	Dunedin	1963/64
15	10	8	6	Downes W.F.	Otago v Canterbury	Christchurch	1866/67
11.2	6	9	6	Fowler G.	Nelson v Wellington	Nelson	1887/88
9.3	6	10	6	Pearson F.A.	Auckland v Hawke's Bay	Auckland	1910/11

FIVE WICKETS IN AN INNINGS

15.2	13	2	5	Ashby D.A.	Canterbury v Auckland	Auckland	1877/78
5	3	3	5	Allcott C.F.W.	New Zealand v Somerset	Taunton	1927
10.3	6	5	5	Bright R.J.	Australia v Central Districts	Nelson	1976/77
9	6	6	5	Parker T.S.	Otago v Canterbury	Christchurch	1866/67
21	18	8	5	Frith C.	Otago v Tasmania	Dunedin	1883/84
4	2	8	5	Burnup C.J.	Lord Hawke's XI v NZ	Wellington	1902/03
8	4	8	5	McBeath D.J.	Southland v Canterbury	Invercargill	1920/21
9	3	9	5	Bennett J.H.	Canterbury v Wellington	Christchurch	1910/11
12	5	9	5	Butterfield L.A.	South Island v North Island	Auckland	1944/45
9.1	5	9	5	Boock S.L.	New Zealand v Middlesex	Lord's	1978

FOUR WICKETS IN AN INNINGS

3.2	2	1	4	Snedden C.A.	Auckland v Hawke's Bay	Auckland	1920/21
6.4	5	2	4	Puna N.	Northern Dists v Central Dists	Hamilton	1957/58
7	6	3	4	Carrington S.M.	Northern Districts v Otago	Tauranga	1982/83
6.5	5	3	4	Woodcock L.J.	Wellington v Otago	Wellington	2001/02

THREE WICKETS IN AN INNINGS

3	3	0	3	Smith K.F.H.	Central Districts v Canterbury	Nelson	1959/60
2.1	2	0	3	Barnes S.G.	Australia v Canterbury	Christchurch	1945/46
5	5	0	3	Gray E.J.	Wellington v Canterbury	Christchurch	1985/86
1.4	0	1	3	Bolton B.A.	Canterbury v Central Districts	Christchurch	1958/59
2	1	1	3	Thomson S.A.	Northern Districts v Canterbury	Christchurch	1992/93
1.4	0	2	3	Anthony A.	Canterbury v Wellington	Christchurch	1908/09
3.3	1	2	3	Thomas A.W.	Canterbury v Otago	Christchurch	1917/18
4	2	2	3	Sparling J.T.	Auckland v Wellington	Auckland	1957/58
5	2	3	3	Cowlishaw W.P.	Canterbury v Otago	Christchurch	1864/65
15	12	3	3	Frith W.	Canterbury v Auckland	Auckland	1877/78
2.3	1	3	3	Richardson G.	Nelson v Wellington	Wellington	1886/87
3	2	3	3	Dowson E.M.	Lord Hawke's XI v Otago	Dunedin	1902/03
5	2	3	3	Pollard V.	New Zealand v England	Auckland	1965/66

Seven Wickets in an Innings on First-class Debut

10-28	Moss A.E.	Canterbury v Wellington	Christchurch	1889/90
8-35	Wilson R.	Queensland v Auckland	Auckland	1896/97
† 8-36	Rees A.W.	Auckland v Otago	Dunedin	1889/90
8-37	Hole H.	Nelson v Wellington	Nelson	1874/75
8-48	O'Connell W.J.	Hawke's Bay v Wellington	Wellington	1919/20
8-59	Robertson W.	Canterbury v Auckland	Christchurch	1893/94
8-70	Hay W.A.	Otago v Southland	Dunedin	1917/18
7-31	Lynch D.	Auckland v Canterbury	Auckland	1877/78
7-36	Mills G.	Auckland v Wellington	Auckland	1886/87
7-39	Lankham W.	Auckland v Canterbury	Christchurch	1882/83
† 7-42	Morrison B.D.	Wellington v Otago	Wellington	1953/54
† 7-46	Stephens W.B.	Auckland v Otago	Auckland	1899/00
7-46	Doig J.A.	Southland v Otago	Invercargill	1914/15
† 7-50	Badcock F.T.	Wellington v Canterbury	Christchurch	1924/25
† 7-54	Turnbull J.A.	Auckland v Central Districts	Auckland	1955/56
7-61	Merrin R.C.	Canterbury XI v NZ Touring Team	Christchurch	1967/68
† 7-95	Noonan D.J.	New South Wales v Canterbury	Christchurch	1895/96
7-95	Huxford N.A.	Wellington v Pakistan	Wellington	1964/65

† *2nd innings*

Ten Wickets in a Match on First-class Debut

14-63	Rees A.W.	Auckland v Otago	Dunedin	1889/90
14-107	Robertson W.	Canterbury v Auckland	Christchurch	1893/94
13-72	Moss A.E.	Canterbury v Wellington	Christchurch	1889/90
12-18	Bennett A.P.	Nelson v Wellington	Nelson	1885/86
12-90	Mills W.	Taranaki v Fiji	Hawera	1894/95
12-118	Hay W.A.	Otago v Southland	Dunedin	1917/18
11-43	Fuller E.T.A.	Canterbury v Otago	Christchurch	1872/73
11-97	Wilson R.	Queensland v Auckland	Auckland	1896/97
11-99	Lankham W.	Auckland v Canterbury	Christchurch	1882/83
11-112	Morrison B.D.	Wellington v Otago	Wellington	1953/54
11-126	Noonan D.J.	New South Wales v Canterbury	Christchurch	1895/96
10-30	Lawson H.	Wellington v Nelson	Nelson	1883/84
10-31	MacDonald F.	Otago v Canterbury	Dunedin	1863/64
10-39	Holderness H.V.A.	Otago v Southland	Invercargill	1918/19
10-61	Hole H.	Nelson v Wellington	Nelson	1874/75
10-70	Mills G.	Auckland v Wellington	Auckland	1886/87
10-71	Lawton J.C.	Otago v Canterbury	Christchurch	1890/91
10-90	Brown C.M.	Auckland v Canterbury	Rangiora	1993/94
10-105	Frame W.D.	Otago v Canterbury	Dunedin	1955/56
10-122	Badcock F.T.	Wellington v Canterbury	Christchurch	1924/25
10-133	Leonard D.J.	Central Districts v Northern Districts	Rotorua	1989/90

Ten Wickets in Last First-class Match

† 10-31	MacDonald F.	Otago v Canterbury	Dunedin	1863/64
† 10-61	Hole H.	Nelson v Wellington	Nelson	1874/75
10-91	Downes W.F.	Otago v Canterbury	Dunedin	1875/76
12-114	Lankham W.	Auckland v Canterbury	Auckland	1883/84
13-140	Edser H.	Canterbury v Wellington	Wellington	1883/84
11-25	Fowler G.	Nelson v Wellington	Nelson	1887/88
11-77	Carson W.	Otago v Canterbury	Dunedin	1887/88
† 10-39	Holderness H.V.A.	Otago v Southland	Invercargill	1918/19
10-108	Vivian H.G.	Auckland v Wellington	Auckland	1938/39
11-129	de Groen R.P.	Northern Districts v Canterbury	Hamilton	1995/96

† *this was the player's only first-class appearance*

Most Wickets in a Season

	Matches	Wkts	Runs	Ave	5WI	10WM	Best
Boock S.L.	1977/78	13	66	1088	16.48	6	—	7-57
Hadlee R.J.	1986/87	11	62	935	15.08	8	1	7-49
Hadlee R.J.	1981/82	10	59	867	14.69	7	—	6-26
Boock S.L.	1978/79	12	58	1238	21.34	4	1	8-59
Thompson G.J.	1902-03	7	57	668	11.71	6	3	8-124
Boock S.L.	1986/87	10	55	920	16.72	6	1	6-62
Callaway S.T.	1903/04	5	54	474	8.77	8	4	8-33
Blair R.W.	1956/57	8	53	784	14.79	6	4	9-72
Tait A.R.	1996/97	9	53	865	16.32	4	1	9-48
Drum C.J.	2001/02	9	53	827	15.60	3	2	6-34
Austin S.W.	1893/94	7	52	606	11.65	6	1	8-14
Armstrong W.W.	1913/14	8	52	789	15.17	7	1	7-17
O'Sullivan D.R.	1978/79	9	52	989	19.01	3	—	6-51
Chatfield E.J.	1981/82	10	51	868	17.01	2	—	5-29
Hadlee R.J.	1978/79	10	50	909	18.18	4	—	6-28
Douglas J.W.H.T.	1906/07	9	50	663	13.26	5	1	7-49

Most Wickets in a Season for New Zealand Overseas

		Matches	Wkts	Runs	Ave	5WI	10WM	Best
Burtt T.B.	1949	27	128	2929	22.28	11	2	7-102
Cowie J.	1937	24	114	2275	19.95	6	1	6-3
Merritt W.E.	1927	25	107	2530	23.64	5	1	6-38

Most Wickets in a Season of First-class Debut

			Overs	Mdns	Runs	Wkts	Ave
Robertson W.	Canterbury & NZ	1893/94	*1534	balls	570	47	12.12
Gillespie S.R.	Northern Districts	1979/80	384.5	98	998	45	22.17
Petherick P.J.	Otago	1975/76	286	57	847	42	20.16
Lankham W.	Auckland	1882/83	†1006	balls	259	41	6.31
O'Brien I.E.	Wellington	2000/01	319.1	81	807	41	19.68

* Robertson bowled 222.2 6-ball overs and 40 5-ball overs   † Lankham bowled 96.2 5-ball overs and 131 4-ball overs

Most Balls Bowled in an Innings

444	Howarth H.J.	74-24-138-2	NZ v West Indies	Bridgetown	1971/72
426	Tufnell P.C.R.	71-22-147-2	England v New Zealand	Wellington	1991/92
426	Vettori D.L.	71-24-171-2	New Zealand v India	Mohali	1999/00
420	Howarth H.J.	70-24-144-4	NZ v England	Lord's	1973
420	Boock S.L.	70-10-229-1	NZ v Pakistan	Auckland	1988/89
417	O'Sullivan D.R.	52.1-15-125-4	CD v Otago	New Plymouth	1978/79
414	Doshi D.R.	69-34-79-2	India v New Zealand	Auckland	1980/81
414	Tauseef Ahmed	69-28-106-1	Pakistan v New Zealand	Auckland	1988/89
414	Hick G.A.	69-27-126-4	England v New Zealand	Wellington	1991/92
408	Morgan H.A.	51-16-108-3	Wellington v Otago	Dunedin	1968/69
408	Wiseman P.J.	68-21-123-4	Otago v ND	Hamilton	1995/96
407	Boock S.L.	67.5-31-75-4	Otago v CD	Alexandra	1988/89
399	Cook N.G.B.	66.3-26-153-3	England v NZ	Wellington	1983/84
396	Puna N.	66-23-131-4	ND v Auckland	Hamilton	1964/65
396	Nadkarni R.G.	66-34-114-2	India v NZ	Christchurch	1967/68
390	Chatfield E.J.	65-14-158-1	NZ v Pakistan	Auckland	1988/89

Most Balls Bowled in a Match

629	Badcock F.T.	104.5-44-178-9	Otago v Canterbury	Christchurch	1933/34
624	Dickeson C.W.	104-45-142-11	ND v Wellington	Hamilton	1979/80
618	Gray E.J.	103-39-214-6	Wellington v Otago	Wellington	1984/85
600	Allcott C.F.W.	75-23-161-5	Auckland v Canterbury	Christchurch	1924/25
600	Butler L.C.	100-46-122-4	Wellington v Auckland	Auckland	1965/66

Most Runs Conceded in a Match

304	2-173, 0-131	Dickinson G.R.	Otago v Wellington	Dunedin	1923/24
300	6-172, 4-128	Smith S.G.	Auckland v Wellington	Wellington	1923/24
277	6-136, 6-141	Alloo A.W.	Otago v Wellington	Dunedin	1923/24
266	6-185, 2-81	Merritt W.E.	New Zealand v Kent	Canterbury	1927
243	6-128, 7-115	Grimmett C.V.	Australia v Canterbury	Christchurch	1927/28
241	2-99, 5-142	Brice A.W.S.	Wellington v Otago	Dunedin	1923/24
241	3-123, 1-118	Prabhakar M.	India v New Zealand	Auckland	1989/90
239	6-112, 3-127	McBeath D.J.	Otago v Auckland	Dunedin	1922/23
239	1-60, 4-179	Lambert H.N.	Wellington v Canterbury	Wellington	1931/32
237	0-99, 0-138	Bracewell J.G.	New Zealand v Sussex	Hove	1990
236	2-83, 2-153	Newman J.A.	Canterbury v Otago	Dunedin	1928/29
234	3-86, 4-148	Merritt W.E.	Canterbury v Otago	Dunedin	1928/29
234	4-165, 2-69	Vettori D.L.	New Zealand v Zimbabwe	Bulawayo	1997/98
233	6-117, 4-116	Patel D.N.	Auckland v ND	Auckland	1991/92

Most Runs Conceded in an Innings

70	10	229	1	Boock S.L.	New Zealand v Pakistan	Auckland	1988/89
23.2	0	218	5	Merritt W.E.	New Zealand v NSW	Sydney	1927/28
34	1	206	1	Alloo A.W.	Otago v NSW	Dunedin	1923/24
59	12	204	4	Furlong C.J.M.	CD v Canterbury	Palmerston Nth	1994/95
57	5	200	4	Vettori D.L.	New Zealand v India	Ahmedabad	1999/00
51.2	11	198	5	Pringle C.	Auckland v CD	Auckland	1995/96
41	3	194	3	Callaway S.T.	New Zealand v Australia	Wellington	1904/05
32	1	186	2	Torrance R.C.	Otago v NSW	Dunedin	1923/24
43.1	1	185	6	Merritt W.E.	New Zealand v Kent	Canterbury	1927
46	4	181	0	Hart M.N.	New Zealand v W. Indies	Wellington	1994/95
34	2	180	5	O'Connell W.J.	Hawke's Bay v Auckland	Auckland	1920/21
56	13	179	4	Bennett J.H.	Canterbury v Australia	Christchurch	1913/14
33	0	179	3	McBeath D.J.	Canterbury v NSW	Christchurch	1923/24
31	1	179	4	Lambert H.N.	Wellington v Canterbury	Wellington	1931/32
44	4	179	0	Su'a M.L.	New Zealand v W. Indies	Wellington	1994/95
38	2	178	4	Cunningham W.H.R.	Canterbury v NSW	Christchurch	1923/24
40	4	178	1	Vettori D.L.	New Zealand v Pakistan	Lahore	2001/02
24	1	177	4	Furlong C.J.M.	CD v India	Napier	1998/99

ALL ROUND CRICKET

500 Runs and 25 Wickets in the Same Season

		Runs	Ave	Wkts	Ave
Reid J.R.	1954/55	505	38.84	30	16.53
Sparling J.T.	1959/60	705	37.11	36	19.50
Reid J.R.	1960/61	549	34.31	37	14.78
Pollard V.	1967/68	537	31.58	31	24.74
Taylor B.R.	1968/69	518	39.84	30	28.06
Cairns B.L.	1975/76	538	41.38	27	25.66
Hadlee R.J.	1981/82	500	33.33	59	14.69
Brown V.R.	1984/85	540	38.57	31	31.35
Gray E.J.	1985/86	545	49.54	34	22.00
Priest M.W.	1988/89	603	43.07	28	40.14
Bradburn G.E.	1989/90	842	38.27	30	30.93
Patel D.N.	1990/91	679	52.23	41	28.09
Patel D.N.	1991/92	574	44.15	32	26.78
Duff S.W.	1991/92	559	46.58	28	27.64
Styris S.B.	2001/02	662	44.13	28	17.03

A Century and Five Wickets in Each Innings of the Same Match

...mstrong W.W.	126*	5-27 & 5-25	Australia v New Zealand	Christchurch	1904/05
...awford J.N.	110 & 4*	5-90 & 5-53	Wellington v Auckland	Auckland	1917/18

A Century and Ten Wickets in the Same Match
but not five in each innings

...olley F.E.	132	6-50 & 4-38	MCC v Otago	Dunedin	1929/30
...tel D.N.	6 & 204	6-117 & 4-116	Auckland v ND	Auckland	1991/92

A Century and Five Wickets in One Innings of the Same Match

...lding F.	104	6-55 & 0-4	Canterbury v Auckland	Christchurch	1884/85
...dgrave W.P.	165	5-37	Wellington v Hawke's Bay	Wellington	1905/06
...lf A.E.	157	6-64 & 2-48	Auckland v Canterbury	Christchurch	1907/08
...mstrong W.W.	110*	6-47 & 0-25	Australia v New Zealand	Auckland	1913/14
...awford J.N.	6 & 178*	5-149	Otago v Wellington	Wellington	1914/15
...edden A.N.C.	139	5-13 & 2-21	Auckland v Hawke's Bay	Auckland	1920/21
...ndrews T.J.E.	111*	5-41	NSW v Canterbury	Christchurch	1923/24
...Girr H.M.	106	5-17 & 0-22	Wellington v Canterbury	Wellington	1925/26
...llamy F.W.J.	113 & 22*	5-31 & 1-39	Canterbury v Wellington	Christchurch	1934/35
...omb I.B.	171	5-66 & 0-56	Canterbury v Wellington	Wellington	1939/40
...id J.R.	0 & 283	5-35 & 1-34	Wellington v Otago	Wellington	1951/52
...id J.R.	150*	7-28 & 1-15	New Zealand v Chief Commissioner's XI	Karachi	1955/56
...tcliffe B.	152*	5-102	Otago v ND	Hamilton	1956/57
...arling J.T.	105 & 51	7-98 & 2-13	Auckland v Canterbury	Christchurch	1959/60
...id J.R.	165	5-50 & 1-28	Wellington v Auckland	Auckland	1959/60
...tler L.C.	101*	5-34	Wellington v CD	New Plymouth	1961/62
...abaster G.D.	108 & 35	1-34 & 5-49	Otago v CD	Wanganui	1964/65
...ylor B.R.	105 & 0*	5-86	New Zealand v India	Calcutta	1964/65
...llard V.	146 & 16*	3-66 & 6-53	CD v Otago	Dunedin	1967/68
...otz R.C.	103*	3-41 & 6-57	Canterbury v Otago	Christchurch	1967/68
...ile B.W.	146	6-68 & 1-13	CD v Canterbury	Napier	1967/68
...verarity R.J.	108	5-28	Australia B v Otago	Dunedin	1969/70

Morgan R.W.	102 & 52	5-42 & 3-48	Auckland v NZ U 23 XI	Auckland	1970/7
Taylor B.R.	10 & 129*	5-37 & 2-34	Wellington v Canterbury	Wellington	1971/7
Mushtaq Mohammad	201	2-15 & 5-49	Pakistan v New Zealand	Dunedin	1972/7
Morrison J.F.M.	8 & 106	0-4 & 5-69	Wellington v Auckland	Auckland	1977/7
Botham I.T.	103 & 30*	5-73 & 3-38	England v New Zealand	Christchurch	1977/7
Hadlee R.J.	48 & 103	5-61 & 1-76	NZ v Queensland	Brisbane	1980/8
Stead D.W.	2 & 193*	6-79 & 1-67	Canterbury v CD	New Plymouth	1980/8
Crowe M.D.	17 & 151	0-20 & 5-18	CD v Auckland	Auckland	1983/8
Botham I.T.	138	5-59 & 1-137	England v New Zealand	Wellington	1983/8
Crowe M.D.	20 & 143	1-54 & 5-51	CD v ND	New Plymouth	1984/8
Gray E.J.	108	5-54 & 4-52	NZ v Minor Counties	Norwich	1986
Rutherford K.R.	11 & 146	5-72	Otago v Wellington	Wellington	1989/9
Astle N.J.	160	6-22 & 0-45	Canterbury v Otago	Christchurch	1996/9
Nash D.J.	135* & 62	7-39 & 0-22	NZ v Hampshire	Southampton	1999
Bradburn G.E.	35 & 104	5-114	ND v Wellington	Wellington	2000/0

WICKETKEEPING

Most Dismissals in a Season

49	49/0	Nevin C.J.	2000/01		32	28/4	Smith I.D.S.	1983/84
41	31/10	McSweeney E.B.	1984/85		32	28/4	McSweeney E.B.	1983/84
41	35/6	McSweeney E.B.	1989/90		32	28/4	Robinson S.A.	1990/91
36	32/4	Smith I.D.S.	1990/91		32	31/1	Nevin C.J.	2002/03
35	30/5	Smith I.D.S.	1979/80		31	30/1	Kelly P.J.	1983/84
35	33/2	Young R.A.	2001/02		31	28/3	Kelly P.J.	1986/87
35	35/0	Young R.A.	2002/03		31	31/0	McSweeney E.B.	1990/91
34	29/5	Lees W.K.	1978/79		31	30/1	Young B.A.	1991/92
34	32/2	Smith I.D.S.	1986/87		31	28/3	Blain T.E.	1991/92
34	31/3	Germon L.K.	1991/92		31	30/1	Croy M.G.	1998/99
34	33/1	Nevin C.J.	1995/96		31	31/0	Griggs B.B.J.	2001/02
34	34/0	Hart R.G.	1997/98		30	23/7	Murray J.T.	1960/61
34	33/1	Hart R.G.	2001/02		30	28/2	Germon L.K.	1992/93
33	32/1	Wadsworth K.J.	1975/76		30	29/1	Baker G.R.	1994/95

Most Dismissals in a Match

10	10/0	Nevin C.J., Wellington v Otago	Wellington	1995/96
	10/0	Gilchrist A.C., Australia v New Zealand	Hamilton	1999/00
9	9/0	Schofield R.M., Central Districts v Wellington	Wellington	1964/65
	9/0	Vance R.H., Wellington v Otago	Wellington	1977/78
	8/1	McSweeney E.B., Wellington v Otago	Lower Hutt	1983/84
	9/0	Young B.A., Northern Districts v Canterbury	Christchurch	1986/87
	9/0	Germon L.K., Canterbury v Northern Districts	Christchurch	1992/93
	9/0	Rashid Latif, Pakistan v New Zealand	Auckland	1993/94
8	3/5	James K.C., NZ v Derbyshire	Derby	1927
	1/7	Jackman C.K.Q., Canterbury v Wellington	Wellington	1935/36
	2/6	Kent L.A.W., Auckland v Wellington	Wellington	1944/45
	8/0	Curtis W.M., North Island XI v South Island XI	Wellington	1957/58
	8/0	Petrie E.C., NZ v Sussex	Hove	1958
	5/3	Dick A.E., N.Z. v Griqualand West	Kimberley	1961/62
	8/0	Parks J.M., England v NZ	Christchurch	1965/66
	7/1	Therkleson, I.J., Wellington v Northern Districts	Whangarei	1973/74
	8/0	Marsh R.W., Australia v NZ	Christchurch	1976/77
	8/0	Lees W.K., NZ v Sri Lanka	Wellington	1982/83
	4/4	McSweeney E.B., Wellington v Northern Districts	Wellington	1984/85

8/0	Smith I.D.S., Auckland v Central Districts	Nelson	1988/89
8/0	Smith I.D.S., NZ v Sri Lanka	Hamilton	1990/91
7/1	Hart R.G., Northern Districts v Canterbury	Hamilton	1994/95
7/1	Germon L.K., Canterbury v Central Districts	Palmerston North	1994/95
7/1	Nevin C.J., Wellington v Central Districts	Nelson	1995/96
8/0	Vincent L., Auckland v Central Districts	Palmerston North	2000/01
8/0	Howell G.A., Wellington v Northern Districts	Hamilton	2001/02

Most Dismissals in an Innings

7	7/0	Schofield R.M., Central Districts v Wellington	Wellington	1964/65
	7/0	Wasim Bari, Pakistan v NZ	Auckland	1978/79
	7/0	Young B.A., Northern Districts v Canterbury	Christchurch	1986/87
	7/0	Smith I.D.S., NZ v Sri Lanka	Hamilton	1990/91
	7/0	Croy M.G., Otago v Auckland	Auckland	2001/02
6	4/2	Mooney F.L.H., NZ v Warwickshire	Birmingham	1949
	5/1	Wadsworth K.J., NZ v Surrey	Oval	1973
	6/0	Downes L.W., Central Districts v Canterbury	Nelson	1975/76
	5/1	Kirmani S.M.H., India v NZ	Christchurch	1975/76
	6/0	Vance R.H., Wellington v Otago	Wellington	1977/78
	6/0	Downton P.R., England XI v Otago	Dunedin	1977/78
	6/0	Germon L.K., Canterbury v Northern Districts	Christchurch	1992/93
	5/1	Hart R.G., Northern Districts v Canterbury	Hamilton	1994/95
	5/1	Nevin C.J., Wellington v Central Districts	Nelson	1995/96
	6/0	Parore A.C., New Zealand A v Pakistan A	Hamilton	1998/99
	6/0	Young R.A., Auckland v Wellington	Wellington	2002/03

Most Catches in a Season

49	Nevin C.J.	2000/01	31	McSweeney E.B.	1984/85
35	McSweeney E.B.	1989/90	31	McSweeney E.B.	1990/91
35	Young R.A.	2002/03	31	Germon L.K.	1991/92
34	Hart R.G.	1997/98	31	Griggs B.B.J.	2001/02
33	Nevin C.J.	1995/96	31	Nevin C.J.	2002/03
33	Hart R.G.	2001/02	30	Smith I.D.S.	1979/80
33	Young R.A.	2001/02	30	Kelly P.J.	1983/84
32	Wadsworth K.J.	1975/76	30	Young B.A.	1991/92
32	Smith I.D.S.	1986/87	30	Croy M.G.	1998/99
32	Smith I.D.S.	1990/91			

Most Catches in a Match

10	Nevin C.J., Wellington v Otago	Wellington	1995/96
	Gilchrist A.C., Australia v New Zealand	Hamilton	1999/00
9	Schofield R.M., Central Districts v Wellington	Wellington	1964/65
	Vance R.H., Wellington v Otago	Wellington	1977/78
	Young B.A., Northern Districts v Canterbury	Christchurch	1986/87
	Germon L.K., Canterbury v Northern Districts	Christchurch	1992/93
	Rashid Latif., Pakistan v New Zealand	Auckland	1993/94
	Curtis W.M., North Island XI v South Island XI	Wellington	1957/58
8	Petrie E.C., NZ v Sussex	Hove	1958
	Parks J.M., England v NZ	Christchurch	1965/66
	Marsh R.W., Australia v NZ	Christchurch	1976/77
	Lees W.K., NZ v Sri Lanka	Wellington	1982/83
	McSweeney E.B., Wellington v Otago	Lower Hutt	1983/84
	Smith I.D.S., Auckland v Central Districts	Nelson	1988/89
	Smith I.D.S., NZ v Sri Lanka	Hamilton	1990/91
	Vincent L., Auckland v Central Districts	Palmerston North	2000/01
	Howell G.A., Wellington v Northern Districts	Hamilton	2001/02

Most Catches in an Innings

7	Schofield R.M., Central Districts v Wellington	Wellington	1964/65
	Wasim Bari, Pakistan v NZ	Auckland	1978/79
	Young B.A., Northern Districts v Canterbury	Christchurch	1986/87
	Smith I.D.S., NZ v Sri Lanka	Hamilton	1990/91
	Croy M.G., Otago v Auckland	Auckland	2001/02
6	Downes L.W., Central Districts v Canterbury	Nelson	1975/76
	Vance R.H., Wellington v Otago	Wellington	1977/78
	Downton P.R., England XI v Otago	Dunedin	1977/78
	Germon L.K., Canterbury v Northern Districts	Christchurch	1992/93
	Parore A.C., New Zealand A v Pakistan A	Hamilton	1998/99
	Young R.A., Auckland v Wellington	Wellington	2002/03

Most Stumpings in a Season

13	Jackman C.K.Q.	1935/36	13	Kent L.A.W.	1944/45

Most Stumpings in a Match

7	Jackman C.K.Q., Canterbury v Wellington	Wellington	1935/36
6	Kent L.A.W., Auckand v Wellington	Wellington	1944/45
5	James K.C., NZ v Surrey	Oval	1927
	James K.C., NZ v Derbyshire	Derby	1927
	Burns R.C., Canterbury v Otago	Dunedin	1928/29
	Mills A.S., Otago v Fiji	Dunedin	1947/48

Most Stumpings in an Innings

4	Jackman C.K.Q., Canterbury v Wellington	Wellington	1935/36
	Tindill E.W.T., NZ v Glamorgan	Cardiff	1937
	Kent L.A.W., Auckland v Wellington	Wellington	1944/45
	Mills A.S., Otago v Fiji	Dunedin	1947/48
	McSweeney E.B., Wellington v Northern Districts	Wellington	1984/85

FIELDING

Most Catches in a Season

23	Murray B.A.G.	1967/68	16	Crowe M.D.	1983/84
22	Coney J.V.	1977/78	16	Fleming S.P.	1993/94
20	Howarth H.J.	1973/74	15	Playle W.R.	1958/59
18	Sinclair M.S.	2001/02	15	Bradburn W.P.	1963/64
17	Crowe M.D.	1986/87	15	Turner G.M.	1975/76
17	Boyle D.J.	1990/91	15	Blair W.L.	1978/79
17	Parlane N.R.	2002/03	15	Crowe J.J.	1990/91
16	Burgess M.G.	1977/78	15	Knight N.V.	1996/97
16	Edgar B.A.	1978/79	15	Vincent L.	1999/00
16	Crowe M.D.	1981/82	15	Bradburn G.E.	2000/01

Most Catches in a Match

7	Morrison J.F.M., Wellington v Northern Districts	Wellington	1980/81
	Fleming S.P., New Zealand v Zimbabwe	Harare	1997/98
6	Marchant J.W.A., Wellington v Nelson	Wellington	1873/74
	Williams N.T., Auckland v Hawke's Bay	Napier	1894/95
	Cromb I.B., Canterbury v Otago	Christchurch	1937/38
	Ikin J.T., MCC v Auckland	Auckland	1946/47
	Reid J.R., NZ v South Zone	Bangalore	1955/56
	Jarvis T.W., Auckland v Northern Districts	Hamilton	1968/69
	Anderson R.W., Rest v NZ	New Plymouth	1974/75
	MacDonald G.K., Canterbury v Pakistan	Christchurch	1984/85
	Young B.A., New Zealand v Pakistan	Auckland	1993/94
	Latham R.T., Canterbury v Otago	Oamaru	1994/95
	Young B.A., Northern Districts v Wellington	Wellington	1995/96
	Chandler P.J.B., New Zealand A v England	Wanganui	1996/97
	McHardy D.S., Wellington v Northern Districts	Hamilton	1996/97
	Fleming S.P., New Zealand v Australia	Brisbane	1997/98

Most Catches in an Innings

5	Williams N.T., Auckand v Hawke's Bay	Napier	1894/95
	Lamason J.R., Wellington v Otago	Dunedin	1937/38
	Lamason J.R., NI Army v SI Army	Wellington	1942/43
	Ikin J.T., MCC v Auckland	Auckland	1946/47
	Rabone G.O., NZ v Oxford University	Oxford	1949
	Reid J.R., NZ v South Zone	Bangalore	1955/56
	Morrison J.F.M., Wellington v Northern Districts	Wellington	1980/81
	MacDonald G.K., Canterbury v Pakistan	Christchurch	1984/85
	Crowe J.J., Auckland v Canterbury	Auckland	1988/89
	Fleming S.P., New Zealand v Zimbabwe	Harare	1997/98
	Harris C.Z., Canterbury v England	Christchurch	2001/02

OLDEST PLAYERS

AGE Years/days			
52/189	Boxshall C.	Canterbury v Wellington	1914/15
51/216	Read R.J.	Canterbury v Auckland	1937/38
51/203	Lyttelton C.J. †	Governor-General's XI v MCC	1960/61
51/87	Wilson C.G.	Wellington v Hawke's Bay	1919/20
51/32	MacLaren A.C.	MCC v New Zealand	1922/23
50/284	Wilson E.S.	Otago v Wellington	1927/28
50/269	Hay T.D.B.	New Zealand v Royal Navy	1927
50/184	Reese T.W.	Canterbury v Otago	1917/18
50/86	Dufaur F.E.	Auckland v Wellington	1882/83
49/88	Allcott C.F.W.	Otago v Auckland	1945/46
49/48	Wilding F.	Canterbury v Hawke's Bay	1901/02
48/96	Hartley J.C.	MCC v Auckland	1922/23
48/40	Hallamore R.G.	Southland v Otago	1918/19
48/26	Badcock F.T.	New Zealanders v H.D.G. Leveson-Gower's XI	1945
47/357	Board J.H.	Hawke's Bay v Wellington	1914/15
47/325	Rowntree R.W.	Auckland v South Africa	1931/32
47/177	Fox R.H.	New Zealand v Civil Service	1927
47/151	Jones S.P.	Auckland v Otago	1908/09
47/114	Hughes W.J.	Hawke's Bay v Wellington	1905/06
47/98	Brice A.W.S.	Wellington v Australia	1927/28
47/70	Fowke J.N.	Canterbury v MCC	1906/07
46/319	Kortlang H.H.L.	Wellington v Auckland	1926/27
46/149	Stevens E.C.J.	Canterbury v Otago	1883/84
46/125	Allen R.	Wellington v Fiji	1953/54
46/14	Downes A.D.	Otago v Canterbury	1913/14
45/364	Blackie D.D.	Australia v New Zealand	1927/28
45/292	Handford A.	Southland v Otago	1914/15
45/270	Wynyard E.G.	MCC v Wellington	1906/07
45/241	Blamires E.O.	Otago v Canterbury	1926/27
45/39	Smith S.G.	Auckland v Wellington	1925/26
45/6	Beard D.D.	Northern Districts v Wellington	1964/65
44/338	Knight A.R.	Otago v Canterbury	1943/44
44/308	Chadwick C.S.	Otago v Auckland	1924/25
44/226	Tucker K.H.	Wellington v Hawke's Bay	1919/20
44/182	Anthony A.	Auckland v Wellington	1930/31
44/178	Siedeberg H.G.	Otago v Wellington	1921/22
44/126	Garrard D.R.	Auckland v Wellington	1941/42
44/105	Newman J.A.	Canterbury v Otago	1928/29
44/75	Cate W.A.	New Zealand v MCC	1922/23
44/70	Wallace W.M.	Governor General's XI v MCC	1960/61
44/59	Dempster C.S.	Wellington v Auckland	1947/48
44/7	Wheatley J.	Canterbury v Hawke's Bay	1903/04

† *Lord Cobham*

YOUNGEST PLAYERS

AGE Years/days			
15/224	Dacre C.C.R.	Auckland v Wellington	1914/15
15/272	Midlane F.A.	Wellington v Hawke's Bay	1898/99
15/319	Ollivier A.M.	Canterbury v Otago	1866/67
16/36	Hartland J.F.	Canterbury v Otago	1877/78

16/84	Broad C.H.	Nelson v Wellington	1888/89
16/86	McGregor S.N.	Otago v Fiji	1947/48
16/87	Dacre L.M.	Auckland v Wellington	1912/13
16/130	Coutts H.D.	Taranaki v Auckland	1882/83
16/147	Puna K.N.	New Zealand Under 23 XI v Otago	1971/72
16/173	Aaqib Javed	Pakistan v President's XI	1988/89
16/242	Collins J.U.	Nelson v Wellington	1884/85
16/250	Taylor L.G.	Auckland v Hawke's Bay	1910/11
16/273	Tendulkar S.R.	India v President's XI	1989/90
16/285	Reese D.	Canterbury v Wellington	1895/96
16/311	Hale H.	Tasmania v Otago	1883/84
16/325	Morgan R.W.	Auckland v Northern Districts	1957/58
16/330	Maunder P.A.	Central Districts v Auckland	1961/62
17/4	Wallace W.M.	Auckland v Wellington	1933/34
17/5	Frater R.E.	Auckland v Wellington	1918/19
17/12	Bell M.D.	Northern Districts v New Zealand Academy XI	1993/94
17/49	Williams A.B.	Otago v Canterbury	1886/87
17/52	Blunt R.C.	Canterbury v Otago	1917/18
17/65	Mitchell W.J.	Northern Districts v Pakistan	1964/65
17/66	Wilding A.F.	Canterbury v Auckland	1900/01
17/77	Clarke D.B.	Auckland v Central Districts	1950/51
17/93	Hay T.D.B.	Auckland v Wellington	1893/94
17/107	Rutherford K.R.	Otago v Auckland	1982/83
17/110	Cooke F.H.	Otago v Canterbury	1879/80
17/112	Barron J.R.	Otago v Canterbury	1917/18
17/119	Crowe M.D.	Auckland v Canterbury	1979/80
17/124	MacNeil H.	Otago v Canterbury	1877/78
17/152	Butler L.C.	Wellington v Auckland	1951/52
17/174	McIntyre J.M.	Auckland v Canterbury	1961/62
17/179	Rutherford I.A.	Otago v Canterbury	1974/75
17/182	Robin T.P.	Central Districts v Canterbury	1999/00
17/185	Robinson S.A.	Otago v Northern Districts	1984/85
17/213	Turner G.M.	Otago v Canterbury	1964/65
17/222	Hemi R.C.	Auckland v Wellington	1950/51
17/244	Ghulam Abbas	Pakistan v Auckland	1964/65
17/258	Rose G.A.	Central Districts v Northern Districts	1958/59
17/268	Snedden A.N.C.	Auckland v Wellington	1909/10
17/268	Beuth J.A.	Northern Districts v New Zealand Under 23 XI	1962/63
17/274	Ashbolt F.L.	Wellington v Auckland	1893/94
17/276	Collinge R.O.	Central Districts v Auckland	1963/64
17/278	Nicholls J.G.	Otago v Canterbury	1876/77
17/286	Hickmott R.G.	Canterbury v Wellington	1911/12
17/291	Bennett J.H.	Canterbury v Otago	1898/99
17/294	Cairns A.E.	Otago v Canterbury	1867/68
17/305	Gill M.F.	Central Districts v Wellington	1974/75
17/307	Currie E.W.	Otago v New South Wales	1893/94
17/307	Hastings B.F.	Wellington v Canterbury	1957/58
17/325	Bartlett G.A.	Central Districts v Northern Districts	1958/59
17/328	Cushen J.A.J.	Otago v Canterbury	1967/68
17/329	West R.M.	Central Districts v Northern Districts	1996/97
17/336	Lambert H.N.	Wellington v Canterbury	1917/18
17/352	Motz R.C.	Canterbury v Northern Districts	1957/58
17/355	Tarrant D.R.	Central Districts v Auckland	1954/55
17/362	Vettori D.L.	Northern Districts v England	1996/97

CAREER RECORDS

The following career records cover the complete first-class careers of New Zealand players. Matches for other than New Zealand teams e.g. county sides, are included.
To qualify for inclusion a player must have appeared in first-class cricket in New Zealand while a bona fide resident of the country — professional coaches and the like thus being excluded.

Batting

3000 RUNS	Career	M	In	NO	HS	Runs	Ave	100
Turner G.M.	1964/65-1982/83	455	792	101	311*	34,346	49.70	103
Wright J.G.	1975/76-1992/93	366	636	44	192	25,073	42.35	59
Crowe M.D.	1979/80-1995/96	247	412	62	299	19,608	56.02	71
Sutcliffe B.	1941/42-1965/66	233	407	39	385	17,447	47.41	44
Howarth G.P.	1968/69-1985/86	338	584	42	183	17,294	31.90	32
Reid J.R.	1947/48-1965	246	418	28	296	16,128	41.35	39
Patel D.N.	1976-1996/97	358	558	51	204	15,188	29.95	26
Rutherford K.R.	1982/83-1999/00	220	383	33	317	13,974	39.92	35
Congdon B.E.	1960/61-1978	241	416	40	202*	13,101	34.84	23
Hitchcock R.E.	1947/48-1964	323	519	71	153*	12,473	27.84	13
Dacre C.C.R.	1914/15-1936	269	439	20	223	12,230	29.18	24
Dempster C.S.	1921/22-1947/48	184	306	36	212	12,145	44.98	35
Hadlee R.J.	1971/72-1990	342	473	93	210*	12,052	31.71	14
Edgar B.A.	1975/76-1989/90	175	307	26	203	11,304	40.22	24
Parker J.M.	1971-1983/84	207	362	39	195	11,254	34.84	21
Smith S.G.	1899/00-1925/26	211	379	30	256	10,920	31.28	14
Burgess M.G.	1963/64-1980/81	192	322	35	146	10,281	35.82	20
Crowe J.J.	1977/78-1991/92	180	304	34	159	10,233	37.90	22
Fleming S.P.	1991/92-2002/03	157	260	24	274*	9947	42.14	20
Greatbatch M.J.	1982/83-1999/00	170	292	31	202*	9890	37.89	24
Twose R.G.	1989-2000/01	178	300	35	277*	9802	36.98	18
Lowry T.C.	1917/18-1937/38	198	322	20	181	9421	31.19	18
Dowling G.T.	1958/59-1971/72	158	282	13	239	9399	34.94	16
Cairns C.L.	1988-2002/03	192	299	36	126	9352	35.55	11
Donnelly M.P.	1936/37-1960/61	131	221	26	208*	9250	47.43	23
Jones A.H.	1979/80-1995/96	145	254	33	186	9180	41.53	16
Richardson M.H.	1989/90-2002/03	128	219	29	306	8304	43.70	17
Arnold P.A.	1953/54-1960	174	306	15	122	8013	27.53	7
Blunt R.C.	1917/18-1935	123	209	15	338*	7953	40.99	15
Coney J.V.	1970/71-1986/87	165	272	48	174*	7872	35.14	8
Franklin T.J.	1980/81-1992/93	148	254	20	181	7794	33.30	15
Wallace W.M.	1933/34-1960/61	121	192	17	211	7757	44.32	17
Hastings B.F.	1957/58-1976/77	163	273	32	226	7685	31.89	15
Hadlee W.A.	1933/34-1951/52	117	203	17	198	7523	40.44	18
Young B.A.	1983/84-1998/99	163	276	43	267*	7489	32.14	10
Horne M.J.	1992/93-2002/03	103	179	9	241	7143	42.01	22
Vance R.H.	1976/77-1990/91	135	230	18	254*	6955	32.80	12
Spearman C.M.	1993/94-2002/03	112	202	13	180*	6955	36.79	15
Astle N.J.	1991/92-2002/03	124	198	19	223	6944	38.79	16
Parore A.C.	1988/89-2001/02	163	252	43	155*	6826	32.66	10
McEwan P.E.	1976/77-1990/91	115	206	15	155	6677	34.95	12
McGregor S.N.	1947/48-1968/69	148	274	16	114*	6573	25.47	5
James K.C.	1923/24-1946/47	204	330	41	109*	6413	22.19	7
Latham R.T.	1980/81-1994/95	108	189	19	237*	6298	37.05	9
Murray B.A.G.	1958/59-1972/73	102	187	11	213	6257	35.55	6

	Career	M	In	NO	HS	Runs	Ave	100
Morrison J.F.M.	1965/66-1983/84	126	225	25	180*	6142	30.71	7
Sinclair B.W.	1955/56-1970/71	118	204	18	148	6114	32.87	6
Blair B.R.	1977/78-1989/90	110	190	6	143	5995	32.58	7
Morgan R.W.	1957/58-1976/77	136	229	13	166	5940	27.50	8
Sinclair M.S.	1995/96-2002/03	86	149	19	214	5881	45.23	12
McMillan C.D.	1994/95-2002/03	98	161	16	168*	5869	40.47	11
Roberts A.D.G.	1967/68-1983/84	112	206	37	128*	5865	34.70	7
Page M.L.	1920/21-1942/43	132	213	17	206	5857	29.88	9
Shrimpton M.J.F.	1961/62-1979/80	122	218	23	150	5812	29.80	7
Blain T.E.	1982/83-1994/95	118	199	30	161	5749	34.02	8
Bell M.D.	1993/94-2002/03	101	176	12	219	5716	34.85	11
Reid J.F.	1975/76-1987/88	101	170	22	180	5650	38.17	11
Harris C.Z.	1989/90-2002/03	101	158	34	251*	5637	45.45	11
Scott V.J.	1937/38-1952/53	80	130	17	204	5620	49.73	16
Anderson R.W.	1967/68-1981/82	111	197	14	155	5609	30.65	8
Smith I.D.S.	1977/78-1991/92	178	250	42	173	5570	26.77	6
Gray E.J.	1975/76-1991/92	162	241	51	128*	5472	28.80	6
Chapple M.E.	1949/50-1971/72	119	201	16	165	5344	28.88	4
Pollard V.	1964/65-1974/75	130	207	33	146	5314	30.54	6
Mills J.E.	1925/26-1937/38	97	161	8	185	5025	32.84	11
Graham H.	1892/93-1906/07	113	200	9	124	5023	26.29	7
Weir G.L.	1927/28-1946/47	107	172	16	191	5022	32.19	10
Bradburn G.E.	1985/86-2001/02	127	206	27	148*	4978	27.81	4
McSweeney E.B.	1979/80-1993/94	121	177	30	205*	4947	33.65	6
Lees W.K.	1970/71-1987/88	146	243	43	152	4932	24.66	5
Pairaudeau B.H.	1946/47-1966/67	89	159	5	163	4930	32.01	11
White D.J.	1979/80-1993/94	106	187	17	209	4926	28.98	7
Kerr J.L.	1929/30-1942/43	89	157	7	196	4829	32.19	8
Douglas M.W.	1987/88-2000/01	94	160	23	144	4808	35.09	9
Miller L.S.M.	1950/51-1959/60	82	142	15	144	4777	37.61	5
Grimmett C.V.	1911/12-1940/41	248	321	54	71*	4720	17.67	—
Pocock B.A.	1990/91-2000/01	100	176	16	167	4699	29.36	10
Jarvis T.W.	1964/65-1976/77	97	167	8	182	4666	29.34	6
Sparling J.T.	1956/57-1970/71	127	215	26	105	4606	24.11	2
Edwards G.N.	1973/74-1984/85	92	164	8	177*	4589	29.41	5
Taylor B.R.	1963/64-1979/80	141	210	25	173	4579	24.75	4
Hadlee B.G.	1961/62-1980/81	84	155	11	163*	4539	31.52	6
Vivian H.G.	1930/31-1938/39	85	143	15	165	4443	34.71	6
Briasco P.S.	1982/83-1991/92	83	148	16	157	4390	33.25	6
Bracewell J.G.	1978/79-1990	149	208	40	110*	4354	25.91	4
Thomson S.A.	1987/88-1996/97	90	148	38	167	4209	38.26	6
Cairns B.L.	1971/72-1988	148	226	25	110	4165	20.72	1
McGirr H.M.	1913/14-1932/33	88	146	7	141	3992	28.71	5
Stead G.R.	1991/92-2002/03	78	127	9	130	3982	33.74	8
Cumming C.D.	1995/96-2002/03	67	124	12	187	3961	35.36	8
Cromb I.B.	1929/30-1946/47	88	148	12	171	3950	29.04	3
Priest M.W.	1984/85-1998/99	109	154	25	119	3945	30.58	4
Dunning B.	1961/62-1977/78	83	150	10	142	3929	28.06	3
Guy J.W.	1953/54-1972/73	90	165	13	115	3923	25.80	3
Hart M.N.	1990/91-2002/03	122	176	23	201*	3913	25.57	3
Bailey M.D.	1989/90-2001/02	89	138	9	180*	3882	30.09	8
Harris R.M.	1955/56-1973/74	73	130	5	157	3863	30.90	3
Yuile B.W.	1959/60-1971/72	123	187	31	146	3850	24.67	1

	Career	M	In	NO	HS	Runs	Ave	100
Parsons A.E.W.	1971/72-1982/83	82	156	10	141	3847	26.34	4
Hiddleston J.S.	1909/10-1928/29	52	97	1	212	3818	39.77	8
Rutherford I.A.	1974/75-1983/84	79	144	4	222	3794	27.10	5
Taylor D.D.	1946/47-1960/61	95	168	6	143	3772	23.28	1
Hartland B.R.	1986/87-1996/97	83	150	8	150	3753	26.42	5
Kuggeleijn C.M.	1975/76-1990/91	89	151	15	116	3747	27.55	4
MacGibbon A.R.	1947/48-1961/62	124	206	20	94	3699	19.88	—
Blair W.L.	1967/68-1990/91	82	151	9	140	3698	26.04	2
Webb P.N.	1976/77-1986/87	75	130	19	136	3671	33.07	5
Wadsworth K.J.	1968/69-1975/76	118	164	23	117	3664	25.98	2
Parlane M.E.	1992/93-2002/03	78	130	6	190	3657	29.49	7
Roberts A.W.	1927/28-1950/51	84	135	17	181	3645	30.88	3
Leggat J.G.	1944/45-1955/56	57	106	9	166	3634	37.46	7
Gaffaney C.B.	1995/96-2002/03	66	122	10	194	3629	32.40	6
Austen M.H.	1982/83-1996/97	66	120	8	202*	3619	32.31	6
Hoskin R.N.	1980/81-1992/93	81	140	7	157	3580	26.91	6
Jones R.A.	1993/94-2002/03	64	115	7	188	3565	33.00	7
Nash D.J.	1990/91-2001/02	120	168	37	135*	3555	27.13	5
Patrick W.R.	1905/06-1926/27	74	138	8	143	3536	27.20	4
Smith C.J.P.	1983/84-1990/91	62	118	9	160*	3499	32.10	7
Motz R.C.	1957/58-1969	142	225	21	103*	3494	17.12	1
Larsen G.R.	1984/85-1998/99	103	157	35	161	3491	28.61	2
Brown V.R.	1978/79-1989/90	83	136	17	161*	3485	29.28	6
Howell L.G.	1990/91-2002/03	79	135	16	181	3460	29.07	3
Rabone G.O.	1940/41-1960/61	82	135	14	125	3425	28.30	3
Pritchard T.L.	1937/38-1956	200	293	41	81	3363	13.34	—
Sulzberger G.P.	1995/96-2002/03	66	107	11	159	3309	34.46	8
Newdick G.A.	1970/71-1980/81	61	114	6	143	3292	30.48	4
Vivian G.E.	1964/65-1978/79	88	140	25	137*	3259	28.33	3
Moloney D.A.R.	1929/30-1940/41	64	119	7	190	3219	28.74	2
Boyle D.J.	1980/81-1994/95	69	121	12	149	3216	29.50	3
Stead D.W.	1968/69-1985/86	80	139	11	193*	3205	25.03	1
Alabaster G.D.	1955/56-1975/76	96	154	20	108	3200	23.88	3
Reese D.	1895/96-1920/21	72	134	8	148	3186	25.28	4
McCullum S.J.	1976/77-1990/91	75	131	1	134	3174	24.41	2
Duff S.W.	1985/86-1995/96	88	134	29	164*	3167	30.16	1
Vaughan J.T.C.	1989/90-1996/97	70	120	20	127	3159	31.59	2
Harford N.S.	1953/54-1966/67	74	122	8	158	3149	27.62	3
Merritt W.E.	1926/27-1946	125	191	33	87	3147	19.91	—
Mooney F.L.H.	1941/42-1954/55	91	150	14	180	3143	23.11	2
Redmond R.E.	1963/64-1975/76	53	100	7	141*	3134	33.69	5
Thomson K.	1959/60-1973/74	71	125	14	136*	3134	28.23	5
Tindill E.W.T.	1932/33-1949/50	69	116	13	149	3127	30.35	6
Harris P.G.Z.	1949/50-1964/65	69	120	9	118	3126	28.16	5
Germon L.K.	1987/88-2001/02	103	142	35	160*	3123	29.18	4
Wells J.D.	1989/90-2000/01	73	115	18	143	3058	31.52	5
Ryan M.L.	1965/66-1978/79	66	113	9	129	3023	29.06	3

Bowling

200 WICKETS	Career	M	Wkts	Runs	Ave
Hadlee R.J.	1971/72-1990	342	1490	26,998	18.11
Grimmett C.V.	1911/12-1940/41	248	1424	31,740	22.28
Smith S.G.	1899/00-1925/26	211	955	17,272	18.08
Pritchard T.L.	1937/38-1956	200	818	19,062	23.30
Patel D.N.	1976-1996/97	358	654	21,737	33.23
Boock S.L.	1973/74-1989/90	164	640	14,314	22.36
Cairns C.L.	1988-2002/03	192	599	16,493	27.53
Chatfield E.J.	1973/74-1989/90	157	587	13,429	22.87
Saunders J.V.	1899/00-1913/14	107	553	12,065	21.81
Howarth H.J.	1962/63-1978/79	145	541	13,674	25.27
Blair R.W.	1951/52-1964/65	119	537	9961	18.54
Merritt W.E.	1926/27-1946	125	536	13,669	25.50
Collinge R.O.	1963/64-1978	163	524	12,793	24.41
O'Sullivan D.R.	1971-1984/85	136	523	13,554	25.91
Bracewell J.G.	1978/79-1990	149	522	13,919	26.66
Motz R.C.	1957/58-1969	142	518	11,769	22.72
Alabaster J.C.	1955/56-1971/72	143	500	12,688	25.37
Cairns B.L.	1971/72-1988	148	473	12,544	26.52
Reid J.R.	1947/48-1965	246	466	10,535	22.60
Cameron F.J.	1952/53-1966/67	119	447	9658	21.60
Gray E.J.	1975/76-1991/92	162	444	12,522	28.20
Morrison D.K.	1985/86-1996/97	142	440	13,298	30.22
Taylor B.R.	1963/64-1979/80	141	422	10,605	25.13
Burtt T.B.	1943/44-1954/55	84	408	9054	22.19
Snedden M.C.	1977/78-1990	118	387	9918	25.62
Cunis R.S.	1960/61-1976/77	132	386	10,287	26.65
Yuile B.W.	1959/60-1971/72	123	375	8209	21.89
Moir A.M.	1949/50-1961/62	97	368	9040	24.56
Cave H.B.	1945/46-1958/59	117	362	8663	23.93
Cowie J.	1932/33-1949/50	86	359	8002	22.28
MacGibbon A.R.	1947/48-1961/62	124	356	9301	26.12
Hadlee D.R.	1966/67-1983/84	111	351	8853	25.22
McIntyre J.M.	1961/62-1982/83	113	336	7917	23.56
Priest M.W.	1984/85-1998/99	109	329	10,478	31.84
Callaway S.T.	1888/89-1906/07	62	320	5460	17.06
Sparling J.T.	1956/57-1970/71	127	318	7226	22.72
Wiseman P.J.	1991/92-2002/03	112	312	10,279	32.94
Downes A.D.	1888/89-1913/14	51	311	4564	14.67
Hayes J.A.	1946/47-1960/61	78	292	6759	23.14
Dickeson C.W.	1973/74-1986/87	90	282	8242	29.22
Beard D.D.	1945/46-1964/65	66	278	6000	21.58
O'Connor S.B.	1994/95-2002/03	73	278	6582	23.67
Alabaster G.D.	1955/56-1975/76	96	275	6388	23.22
Troup G.B.	1974/75-1986/87	100	272	7541	27.72
Watson W.	1984/85-1994/95	93	272	7485	27.52
Upham E.F.	1892/93-1909/10	49	265	4414	16.65
Vettori D.L.	1996/97-2002/03	78	257	7855	30.56
Nash D.J.	1990/91-2001/02	120	255	7165	28.09
Robertson G.K.	1979/80-1989/90	88	252	7469	29.59
Bradburn G.E.	1985/86-2001/02	127	250	8174	32.69
Doull S.B.	1989/90-2001/02	99	250	7233	28.93
Brice A.W.S.	1902/03-1927/28	61	247	5260	21.29
Bennett J.H.	1898/99-1919/20	52	241	4476	18.58

	Career	M	Wkts	Runs	Ave
McGirr H.M.	1913/14-1932/33	88	239	6571	27.49
Penn A.J.	1994/95-2002/03	63	239	5491	22.97
Puna N.	1956/57-1968/69	70	229	5597	24.44
Dunning J.A.	1923/24-1937/38	60	228	6290	27.58
Pollard V.	1964/65-1974/75	130	224	6931	30.94
Vivian H.G.	1930/31-1938/39	85	223	6160	27.62
Cromb I.B.	1929/30-1946/47	88	222	6152	27.71
Badcock F.T.	1924/25-1945	53	221	5211	23.57
Allcott C.F.W.	1920/21-1945/46	82	220	5882	26.73
Wisneski W.A.	1992/93-2002/03	64	219	5890	26.89
Duff S.W.	1985/86-1995/96	88	217	7051	32.49
Blunt R.C.	1917/18-1935	123	214	6638	31.01
Stott L.W.	1969/70-1983/84	63	214	5341	24.95
Davis H.T.	1991/92-2002/03	70	212	6631	31.27
de Groen R.P.	1987/88-1995/96	60	210	5266	25.07
Hart M.N.	1990/91-2002/03	122	208	7284	35.01
Stirling D.A.	1981/82-1991/92	84	206	6948	33.72
Congdon B.E.	1960/61-1978	241	204	6125	30.02
Roberts S.J.	1985/86-1995/96	63	203	6001	29.56
Burke C.	1937/38-1953/54	60	200	5199	25.99

Wicketkeeping

100 DISMISSALS	Career	M	Caught	Stumped	Total
Smith I.D.S.	1977/78-1991/92	178	390	36	426
James K.C.	1923/24-1946/47	204	310	112	422
McSweeney E.B.	1979/80-1993/94	121	340	45	385
Parore A.C.	1988/89-2001/02	163	358	24	382
Lees W.K.	1970/71-1987/88	146	292	44	336
Wadsworth K.J.	1968/69-1975/76	118	256	26	282
Germon L.K.	1987/88-2001/02	103	256	26	282
Hart R.G.	1992/93-2002/03	96	256	15	271
Ward J.T.	1957/58-1970/71	95	227	27	254
Petrie E.C.	1950/51-1966/67	115	194	37	231
Mooney F.L.H.	1941/42-1954/55	91	164	54	218
Blain T.E.	1982/83-1994/95	118	190	26	216
Croy M.G.	1994/95-2001/02	65	183	14	197
Young B.A.	1983/84-1997/98	163	185	11	196
Milburn B.D.	1963/64-1982/83	75	176	19	195
Nevin C.J.	1995/96-2002/03	57	169	6	175
Dick A.E.	1956/57-1968/69	78	133	21	154
Kelly P.J.	1980/81-1988/89	49	140	13	153
Colquhoun I.A.	1953/54-1963/64	57	108	28	136
Guillen S.C.	1947/48-1960/61	66	100	34	134
Sigley M.A.	1994/95-2002/03	44	124	4	128
Boxshall C.	1897/98-1914/15	65	81	43	124
Schofield R.M.	1964/65-1974/75	53	107	15	122
Robinson S.A.	1984/85-1996/97	45	117	5	122
Wright M.J.E.	1972/73-1983/84	65	104	17	121
Mills G.H.	1935/36-1957/58	59	85	34	119
Tindill E.W.T.	1932/33-1949/50	69	85	33	118
Hopkins G.J.	1997/98-2002/03	51	103	11	114
Young R.A.	1998/99-2002/03	34	110	2	112
Edwards G.N.	1973/74-1984/85	92	88	16	104
Therkleson I.J.	1966/67-1973/74	39	93	7	100

Leading Career Averages

BATTING *(qualification 3000 runs)*	M	In	NO	HS	Runs	Ave
Crowe M.D.	247	412	62	299	19,608	56.02
Scott V.J.	80	130	17	204	5620	49.73
Turner G.M.	455	792	101	311*	34,346	49.70
Donnelly M.P.	131	221	26	208*	9250	47.43
Sutcliffe B.	233	407	39	385	17,447	47.41
Harris C.Z.	101	158	34	251*	5637	45.45
Sinclair M.S.	86	149	19	214	5881	45.23
Dempster C.S.	184	306	36	212	12,145	44.98
Wallace W.M.	121	192	17	211	7757	44.32
Richardson M.H.	128	219	29	306	8304	43.70
Wright J.G.	366	636	44	192	25,073	42.35
Fleming S.P.	157	260	24	274*	9947	42.14
Horne M.J.	103	179	9	241	7143	42.01
Jones A.H.	145	254	33	186	9180	41.53
Reid J.R.	246	418	28	296	16,128	41.35
Blunt R.C.	123	209	15	338*	7953	40.99
McMillan C.D.	98	161	16	168*	5869	40.47
Hadlee W.A.	117	203	17	198	7523	40.44
Edgar B.A.	175	307	26	203	11,304	40.22

BOWLING *(qualification 200 wickets)*	M	Wkts	Runs	Ave
Downes A.D.	51	311	4564	14.67
Upham E.F.	49	265	4414	16.65
Callaway S.T.	62	320	5460	17.06
Smith S.G.	211	955	17,272	18.08
Hadlee R.J.	342	1490	26,998	18.11
Blair R.W.	119	537	9961	18.54
Bennett J.H.	52	241	4476	18.58

(C.J. Drum took 199 wickets at 19.46)

HIGHEST PARTNERSHIPS

FIRST WICKET

387	Turner G.M.	Jarvis T.W.	NZ v West Indies	Georgetown	1971/72
373	Sutcliffe B.	Watt L.	Otago v Auckland	Auckland	1950/51
333	Edgar B.A.	Jones A.H.	Wellington v Auckland	Wellington	1988/89
316	Austen M.H.	Hart R.T.	Wellington v Central Districts	Wanganui	1993/94
310	Edgar B.A.	Vance R.H.	Wellington v Northern Districts	Wellington	1988/89
306	Cuff L.A.	Lawrence J.D.	Canterbury v Auckland	Christchurch	1893/94
305	Lawson R.A.	Croy M.G.	Otago v Central Districts	Napier	1995/96
299	Bell M.D.	Jones R.A.	Wellington v Otago	Dunedin	2001/02
287	Hartland B.R.	Stead G.R.	Canterbury v Wellington	Christchurch	1994/95
286	Sutcliffe B.	Taylor D.D.	Auckland v Canterbury	Auckland	1948/49
276	Dempster C.S.	Mills J.E.	NZ v England	Wellington	1929/30
276	Griffith A.F.G.	Campbell S.L.	West Indies v NZ	Hamilton	1999/00
268	Turner G.M.	Dowling G.T.	NZ v President's XI	Montego Bay	1971/72
260	Lawson R.A.	Mohammad Wasim	Otago v Northern Districts	Dunedin	2002/03
259	Austen M.H.	Aiken J.M.	Wellington v Otago	Wellington	1994/95
252	Sutcliffe B.	Scott V.J.	NZ v Rest	Christchurch	1948/49
250	Hart R.T.	Smith C.J.P.	Central Districts v Wellington	Wellington	1985/86
247	Sutcliffe B.	Scott V.J.	NZ v Combined Services	Gillingham	1949
240	McIntosh T.G.	Horne M.J.	Auckland v Otago	Dunedin	2001/02
239	Dempster C.S.	Dustin W.H.	Wellington v Canterbury	Wellington	1931/32
239	Smith D.	Parks J.H.	MCC v Otago	Dunedin	1935/36
235	Hadlee W.A.	Page M.L.	Canterbury v Wellington	Christchurch	1936/37
230	Murray B.A.G.	Turner G.M.	NZ v President's XI	Rawalpindi	1969/70
229	Sutcliffe B.	Scott V.J.	NZ v Surrey	Oval	1949
226*	Hadlee W.A.	Leggat J.G.	Canterbury v Otago	Christchurch	1948/49
225	Richardson P.E.	Watson W.	MCC v Wellington	Wellington	1958/59
225	Greenidge C.G.	Haynes D.L.	West Indies v NZ	Christchurch	1979/80
220	Sutcliffe B.	Taylor D.D.	Auckland v Canterbury	Auckland	1948/49
220	Bell M.D.	Jones R.A.	Wellington v Canterbury	Christchurch	2000/01
219*	Edgar B.A.	Vance R.H.	Wellington v Central Districts	Wellington	1987/88
218	Hadlee W.A.	Leggat J.G.	Canterbury v Wellington	Christchurch	1947/48
218	Dempsey D.A.	Hadlee B.G.	Canterbury v Otago	Christchurch	1980/81
214	Woodfull W.M.	Ponsford W.H.	Australia v Otago	Dunedin	1927/28
214	Bolton B.A.	Dowling G.T.	Canterbury v Northern Districts	Christchurch	1959/60
214	Spearman C.M.	Twose R.G.	NZ v Zimbabwe	Auckland	1995/96
213	Lawson R.A.	Bell M.D.	NZ Academy XI v Zimbabwe	Whangarei	1995/96
213	Gaffaney C.B.	Parlane M.E.	NZ Academy XI v Bangladesh	Christchurch	1997/98
211	Turner G.M.	Parker J.M.	NZ v MCC	Lord's	1973
209	Sutcliffe B.	Watt L.	Otago v Canterbury	Dunedin	1947/48
209	Harris B.Z.	Boyle D.J.	Canterbury v Otago	Christchurch	1991/92
208	Blunt R.C.	Worker R.V. de R.	Canterbury v MCC	Christchurch	1922/23
208	Athey C.W.J.	Robinson R.T.	England XI v Northern Districts	Hamilton	1987/88
207	Sadiq Mohammad	Zaheer Abbas	Pakistan v Wellington	Wellington	1972/73
201	Anthony A.	Horspool E.	Auckland v Wellington	Auckland	1924/25

SECOND WICKET

317	Hart R.T.	Briasco P.S.	Central Districts v Canterbury	New Plymouth	1983/84
315*	Gibbs H.H.	Kallis J.H.	South Africa v NZ	Christchurch	1998/99
303	Dempster C.S.	Allcott C.F.W.	NZ v Warwickshire	Birmingham	1927
287	Bell M.D.	Wells J.D.	Wellington v Auckland	Auckland	1997/98
263	Greatbatch M.J.	Crowe M.D.	Central Districts v Northern Districts	Morrinsville	1986/87
256	Anderson R.W.	Edgar B.A.	NZ v Scotland	Dundee	1978
254	Burns K.J.	Rutherford K.R.	Otago v Wellington	Oamaru	1987/88
252	Baker W.A.	Beechey E.M.	Wellington v Auckland	Wellington	1918/19
248	Horne M.J.	Fleming S.P.	Southern v Pakistan A	Christchurch	1998/99
245	Horne M.J.	Fleming S.P.	NZ v British Universities	Oxford	1999
244	Spearman C.M.	Sinclair M.S.	Central Districts v Northern Districts	Wanganui	1998/99

241	Franklin T.J.	Crowe J.J.	Auckland v Wellington	Wellington	1988/89
241	Wright J.G.	Jones A.H.	NZ v England	Wellington	1991/92
237	Gibson J.G.	Kuggeleijn C.M.	Northern Districts v Canterbury	Hamilton	1980/81
231	Carew M.C.	Nurse S.M.	West Indies v NZ	Christchurch	1968/69
229	Hemus L.G.	Midlane F.A.	Auckland v Wellington	Wellington	1918/19
227	Baker W.A.	Kortlang H.H.L.	Wellington v Otago	Dunedin	1923/24
227	Dobbs P.W.	Lamont M.J.	Otago v Auckland	Dunedin	1990/91
222	Warner P.F.	Fane F.L.	Lord Hawke's XI v Otago	Dunedin	1902/03
222	Crocker L.M.	Kuggeleijn C.M.	Northern Districts v Otago	Hamilton	1983/84
222	McCullum B.B.	Cumming C.D.	Otago v Auckland	Dunedin	2001/02
220	Macartney C.G.	Punch A.T.E.	NSW v Otago	Dunedin	1923/24
220	Richardson M.H.	Cumming C.D.	Otago v Northern Districts	Hamilton	2000/01
215	Bell M.D.	Wells J.D.	Wellington v Northern Districts	Hamilton	1998/99
212	Horspool E.	Snedden A.N.C.	Auckland v Victoria	Auckland	1924/25
210	Hadlee W.A.	O'Brien F.P.	Canterbury v Otago	Christchurch	1940/41
210	Howarth G.P.	Crowe J.J.	NZ v West Indies	Kingston	1984/85
209*	Jones A.H.	Crowe M.D.	Wellington v Canterbury	Christchurch	1992/93
207*	Twose R.G.	Douglas M.W.	Central Districts v Auckland	Auckland	1991/92
207	Mills J.E.	Blunt R.C.	NZ v H.D.G. Leveson-Gower's XI	Scarborough	1927
207	Vaughan M.P.	Hussain N.	England v Canterbury	Christchurch	2001/02
206	Raman W.V.	Gursharan Singh	India v Otago	Dunedin	1989/90
204	Gavaskar S.M.	Amarnath S.	India v NZ	Auckland	1975/76
202	Naushad Ali	Saeed Ahmed	Pakistan v Canterbury	Christchurch	1964/65
200	Smith R.W.	Bilby G.P.	Wellington v Northern Districts	Whangarei	1973/74

THIRD WICKET

467†	Jones A.H.	Crowe M.D.	New Zealand v Sri Lanka	Wellington	1990/91
445	Whitelaw P.E.	Carson W.N.	Auckland v Otago	Dunedin	1936/37
394*	Kennedy P.G.	Latham R.T.	Canterbury v Northern Districts	Rotorua	1990/91
346	Burnett G.P.	Verry R.A.	Wellington v Northern Districts	Hamilton	1991/92
278	Franklin T.J.	Patel D.N.	Auckland v Canterbury	Christchurch	1985/86
265	Horne M.J.	Barnes A.C.	Auckland v Bangladesh	Auckland	2001/02
264	Chappell I.M.	Chappell G.S.	Australia v NZ	Wellington	1973/74
261*	Maynard M.P.	Thomson S.A.	Northern Districts v Auckland	Hamilton	1990/91
255	Lloyd C.H.	Davis C.A.	West Indies v South Island	Dunedin	1968/69
252*	Howarth G.P.	Roberts A.D.G.	Northern Districts v Pakistan	Gisborne	1978/79
248	Shoaib Mohammad	Javed Miandad	Pakistan v New Zealand	Auckland	1988/89
246	Rabone G.O.	Reid J.R.	NZ v Nottinghamshire	Nottingham	1949
246	Murray B.A.G.	Morrison J.F.M.	Wellington v Otago	Dunedin	1968/69
245	Crowe M.D.	Coney J.V.	NZ v South Australia	Adelaide	1985/86
241	Wright J.G.	Crowe M.D.	New Zealand v West Indies	Wellington	1986/87
229	Miller L.S.M.	Sutcliffe B.	NZ v South Australia	Adelaide	1953/54
227	Rutherford K.R.	Blair B.R.	Otago v Central Districts	Alexandra	1988/89
226	Haynes D.L.	Richardson R.B.	West Indies v Shell XI	Napier	1986/87
224	Reid J.F.	Crowe M.D.	NZ v Australia	Brisbane	1985/86
223	Smith C.J.P.	Wilson S.W.J.	Central Districts v Otago	Blenheim	1990/91
222*	Sutcliffe B.	Reid J.R.	NZ v India	New Delhi	1955/56
222	Snedden E.	Smith S.G.	Auckland v Hawke's Bay	Auckland	1920/21
221	Blunt R.C.	McMullan J.J.M.	Otago v Canterbury	Dunedin	1928/29
221	Lara B.C.	Adams J.C.	West Indies v New Zealand	Wellington	1994/95
220	Shoaib Mohammad	Javed Miandad	Pakistan v New Zealand	Wellington	1988/89
218	Woodfull W.M.	Schneider J.A.	Australia v NZ	Auckland	1927/28
217	Dobbs P.W.	Rutherford K.R.	Otago v Central Districts	Blenheim	1990/91
216	Hemus L.G.	Smith S.G.	Auckland v Canterbury	Auckland	1919/20
214	Anthony A.	Gillespie H.D.	Auckland v Canterbury	Auckland	1929/30
213	Turner G.M.	Congdon B.E.	Otago v Wellington	Dunedin	1972/73
213	Jones A.H.	Crowe M.D.	NZ v Australia	Adelaide	1987/88
212	Booth B.C.	Burge P.J.P.	Australia B v NZ	Auckland	1966/67
210	Howarth G.P.	Crowe M.D.	NZ v Essex	Chelmsford	1983
210	Edgar G.A.	Crowe M.D.	NZ v England	Lord's	1986
210	Smith B.F.	Douglas M.W.	Central Districts v Northern Districts	Taupo	2000/01

209	McCosker R.G.	Chappell G.S.	Australia v Wellington	Wellington	1976/77
206	Preston A.H.	Beck J.E.F.	Wellington v Canterbury	Christchurch	1955/56
204	Harford N.S.	Reid J.R.	NZ v Oxford University	Oxford	1958
204	Twose R.G.	Crowe M.D.	NZ v Indian Colts XI	Hyderabad	1995/96
203*	Pocock B.A.	Parore A.C.	Auckland v Wellington	Auckland	1997/98
201	McLeod E.G.	Lamason J.R.	Wellington v Auckland	Wellington	1935/36

† *world record*

FOURTH WICKET

350	Mushtaq Mohammad	Asif Iqbal	Pakistan v NZ	Dunedin	1972/73
324	Reid J.R.	Wallace W.M.	NZ v Cambridge University	Cambridge	1949
299	Wallace W.M.	Donnelly M.P.	NZ v Leicestershire	Leicester	1949
282	Wilkinson W.A.C.	Champman A.P.F.	MCC v Canterbury	Christchurch	1922/23
280	Crowe J.J.	Patel D.N.	Auckland v Northern Districts	Auckland	1991/92
278	Roberts A.W.	Page M.L.	Canterbury v Wellington	Wellington	1931/32
276*	Crowe M.D.	Briasco P.S.	Central Districts v Canterbury	Christchurch	1986/87
274	Jones R.A.	Mather S.R.	Wellington v Otago	Wellington	2000/01
266	Denness M.H.	Fletcher K.W.R.	England v NZ	Auckland	1974/75
259	Bradburn G.E.	Parlane M.E.	Northern Districts v Canterbury	Christchurch	1996/97
254	Reid J.R.	Miller L.S.M.	NZ v Natal	Durban	1953/54
252	Thomson S.A.	Young B.A.	Northern Districts v Auckland	Auckland	1990/91
243	Horne M.J.	Astle N.J.	New Zealand v Zimbabwe	Auckland	1997/98
240	Fleming S.P.	McMillan C.D.	New Zealand v Sri Lanka	Colombo	1997/98
235	Burns K.J.	Hoskin R.N.	Otago v Northern Districts	Hamilton	1987/88
229	Congdon B.E.	Hastings B.F.	NZ v Australia	Wellington	1973/74
219	Vivian H.G.	Page M.L.	NZ v Oxford University	Oxford	1931
218	Crowe J.J.	Coney J.V.	NZ v Glamorgan	Swansea	1986
214	Ransford V.S.	Lampard A.W.	Australia v NZ	Auckland	1920/21
211*	Jones A.H.	Burns K.J.	Otago v Wellington	Wellington	1984/85
211	White D.J.	Young B.A.	Northern Districts v Auckland	Auckland	1992/93
208	Thomson S.A.	Maynard M.P.	Northern Districts v Wellington	Hamilton	1991/92
207	Midlane F.A.	Richardson C.A.	Wellington v Otago	Wellington	1899/00
207	Badcock F.T.	Lowry T.C.	Wellington v Auckland	Wellington	1927/28
207	Sulzberger G.P.	Penn A.J.	Central Districts v Otago	Napier	1995/96
206	McCullum S.J.	Dawson G.J.	Otago v Northern Districts	Dunedin	1983/84
206	Stewart A.J.	Hussain N.	England v New Zealand XI	Palmerston North	1996/97
206	McIntosh T.G.	Vincent L.	Auckland v Canterbury	Christchurch	2000/01
204	Harvey R.N.	Simpson R.B.	Australia B v Otago	Dunedin	1956/57
204	Jarvis T.W.	Thomson K.	Canterbury v Central Districts	Wanganui	1969/70
203	Thomson S.A.	Maynard M.P.	Northern Districts v Otago	Hamilton ·	1991/92
200	Blair B.R.	Dawson G.J.	Otago v Central Districts	Dunedin	1982/83

FIFTH WICKET

341	Larsen G.R.	McSweeney E.B.	Wellington v Central Districts	Levin	1987/88
319	Rutherford K.R.	Gray E.J.	NZ v DB Close's XI	Scarborough	1986
290	Harris C.Z.	Stead G.R.	Canterbury v Central Districts	Blenheim	1996/97
266	Sutcliffe B.	Haig W.S.	Otago v Auckland	Dunedin	1949/50
258	Salim Malik	Inzamam-ul-Haq	Pakistan v New Zealand	Wellington	1993/94
255	Taylor B.R.	Coney J.V.	Wellington v Otago	Dunedin	1972/73
252*	Latham R.T.	Priest M.W.	Canterbury v Northern Districts	Christchurch	1988/89
244	Reid J.R.	Chapple M.E.	NZ v Western Province	Cape Town	1962/63
242	Hammond W.R.	Ames L.E.G.	England v NZ	Christchurch	1932/33
236	Harris C.Z.	Astle N.J.	Canterbury v Otago	Christchurch	1996/97
235*	Woodfull W.M.	Ransford V.S.	Victoria v NZ	Christchurch	1924/25
235*	Sulzberger G.P.	Ryder J.D.	Central Districts v Canterbury	Napier	2002/03
234*	Scott V.J.	Morris J.B.	Auckland v Central Districts	Auckland	1951/52
233	Moloney D.A.R.	Kerr J.L.	NZ v England XI	Folkestone	1937
222	Astle N.J.	McMillan C.D.	New Zealand v Zimbabwe	Wellington	2000/01
213	Ritchie G.M.	Matthews G.R.J.	Australia v NZ	Wellington	1985/86
203	Booth B.C.	Davies G.A.	Australia B v Central Districts	Palmerston North	1966/67
201	Alexander W.C.	Richardson V.Y.	Australia v Auckland	Auckland	1927/28
201	Burgess M.G.	Jarvis T.W.	Auckland v Central Districts	Auckland	1971/72

SIXTH WICKET

281	Thorpe G.P.	Flintoff A.	England v New Zealand	Christchurch	2001/02
269	Trumper V.T.	Hill C.	Australia v NZ	Wellington	1904/05
246*	Crowe J.J.	Hadlee R.J.	NZ v Sri Lanka	Colombo	1986/87
240	Parfitt P.H.	Knight B.R.	England v NZ	Auckland	1962/63
238	McDonald R.	Cowley O.W.	Queensland v Hawke's Bay	Napier	1896/97
233	Crawford J.N.	Armstrong W.W.	Australia v NZ	Auckland	1913/14
232	Botham I.T.	Randall D.W.	England v New Zealand	Wellington	1983/84
226	Gray E.J.	Ormiston R.W.	Wellington v Central Districts	Wellington	1981/82
220	Turner G.M.	Wadsworth K.J.	NZ v West Indies	Kingston	1971/72
220	Toynbee M.H.	Smith I.D.S.	Central Districts v Auckland	Napier	1982/83
212*	McMillan C.D.	Parore A.C.	New Zealand v President's XI	Jodhpur	1999/00
209*	Parore A.C.	O'Dowd A.P.	Auckland v Otago	Dunedin	1991/92
209	Harris C.Z.	Redmond A.J.	Canterbury v Wellington	Rangiora	2001/02
203	Ormiston R.W.	Coney J.V.	Wellington v Central Districts	New Plymouth	1982/83
201	Harris C.Z.	Parore A.C	New Zealand v Orange Free State	Bloemfontein	1994/95
201	Tendulkar S.R.	Mongia N.R.	India v Central Districts	Napier	1998/99

SEVENTH WICKET

265	Powell J.L.	Dorreen N.	Canterbury v Otago	Christchurch	1929/30
261	Campbell A.D.R.	Strang P.A.	Zimbabwe v Canterbury	Timaru	1997/98
248	Yousuf Youhana	Saqlain Mushtaq	Pakistan v New Zealand	Christchurch	2000/01
246	McGlew D.J.	Murray A.R.A.	South Africa v NZ	Wellington	1952/53
244	Patrick W.R.	Allcott C.F.W.	NZ v NSW	Sydney	1925/26
241	Astle N.J.	Priest M.W.	Canterbury v Wellington	Christchurch	1994/95
229	Schneider K.J.	Oldfield W.A.S.	Australia v Canterbury	Christchurch	1927/28
224	Scott V.J.	Matheson A.M.	Auckland v Canterbury	Auckland	1937/38
219	Yuile B.W.	Hampton B.L.	Central Districts v Canterbury	Napier	1967/68
217	Walters K.D.	Gilmour G.J.	Australia v NZ	Christchurch	1976/77
205	Germon L.K.	Priest M.W.	Canterbury v Northern Districts	Christchurch	1991/92
192	Brown S.W.	Parore A.C.	Auckland v Central Districts	Auckland	1990/91
191	Wright J.G.	Smith I.D.S.	NZ v Western Australia	Perth	1989/90
186	Lees W.K.	Hadlee R.J.	NZ v Pakistan	Karachi	1976/77
186	Leggat R.I.	Hadlee D.R.	Canterbury v Sri Lanka	Christchurch	1982/83
184*	Bull C.L.	Isherwood B.P.	Canterbury v Central Districts	Nelson	1971/72
182	Sutcliffe B.	Gilbertson A.W.	Otago v Canterbury	Christchurch	1952/53
179	Griggs B.B.J.	Furlong C.J.M.	Central Districts v Northern Districts	Hamilton	2001/02
177*	Barnes A.C.	Mills J.M.	Auckland v Otago	Alexandra	1995/96
176	Rabone G.O.	Mooney F.L.H.	NZ v MCC	Lord's	1949

EIGHTH WICKET

433†	Trumper V.T.	Sims A.	Sims' Australian XI v Canterbury	Christchurch	1913/14
215	Murray J.R.	Cummins A.C.	West Indies v Otago	Dunedin	1994/95
190*	Mills J.E.	Allcott C.F.W.	NZ v Civil Service	Chiswick	1927
189	Carson W.N.	Matheson A.M.	Auckland v Wellington	Auckland	1938/39
185	Nash M.D.	Mills K.D.	Auckland v Wellington	Wellington	2000/01
180	Twose R.G.	Goodson M.C.	Wellington v Otago	Dunedin	1994/95
173	Smith I.D.S.	Robertson G.K.	Central Districts v Northern Districts	Hamilton	1982/83
172*	Walker B.G.K.	Mills K.D.	Auckland v Wellington	Auckland	1999/00
166	Hadlee R.J.	Hadlee D.R.	Canterbury v Auckland	Christchurch	1983/84
165*	Eckhold A.G.	Crawford J.N.	Otago v Wellington	Wellington	1914/15
161	McSweeney E.B.	Snedden M.C.	Shell XI v West Indies	Napier	1986/87
157	McLaren A.C.	McLean J.F.	MCC v NZ	Wellington	1922/23
154	James K.C.	Badcock F.T.	Wellington v Canterbury	Christchurch	1926/27
153	Nicol R.J.	Young R.A.	Auckland v Canterbury	Auckland	2001/02
152	Bradburn G.E.	Doull S.B.	Northern Districts v Canterbury	Christchurch	1991/92

† *world record*

NINTH WICKET

239	Cave H.B.	Leggat I.B.	Central Districts v Otago	Dunedin	1952/53
188	Parlane N.R.	Tuffey D.R.	Northern Districts v Wellington	Wellington	1999/00
185	Maynard M.P.	Doull S.B.	Northern Districts v Auckland	Auckland	1991/92
182*	Germon L.K.	Ford R.M.	Canterbury v Wellington	Christchurch	1989/90
170*	Hart M.N.	Yovich J.A.F.	Northern Districts v South Africa	Hamilton	1998/99
163*	Cowdrey M.C.	Smith A.C.	England v NZ	Wellington	1962/63
139	Hart R.G.	Tait A.R.	Northern Districts v Wellington	Gisborne	1996/97
136	Smith I.D.S.	Snedden M.C.	NZ v India	Auckland	1989/90
135	Hart R.G.	Penn A.J.	Central v Northern	Rangiora	1998/99
134	Wilson J.W.	Mallender N.A.	Otago v Canterbury	Christchurch	1992/93
127	Mooney F.L.H.	Buchan R.A.	Wellington v Auckland	Wellington	1943/44
122	Schuster H.T.	Cunis R.S.	Auckland v Wellington	Wellington	1964/65
121	Cheetham J.E.	Murray A.R.A.	South Africa v Canterbury	Christchurch	1952/53
118	Coney J.V.	Cairns B.L.	NZ v England	Wellington	1983/84
116	Nevin C.J.	Davis H.T.	Wellington v Auckland	Auckland	1995/96
115	Robertson G.K.	Hart R.T.	Central Districts v Otago	Oamaru	1985/86
115	Hopkins G.J.	Ellis A.M.	Canterbury v Auckland	Auckland	2002/03

TENTH WICKET

184	Blunt R.C.	Hawksworth W.	Otago v Canterbury	Christchurch	1931/32
160	Germon L.K.	Wisneski W.A.	Canterbury v Northern Districts	Rangiora	1997/98
151	Hastings B.F.	Collinge R.O.	NZ v Pakistan	Auckland	1972/73
138	James K.C.	Brice A.W.S.	Wellington v Otago	Wellington	1926/27
133	Bartlett G.A.	Colquhoun I.A.	Central Districts v Auckland	Auckland	1959/60
124	Bracewell J.G.	Boock S.L.	NZ v Australia	Sydney	1985/86
123	Brice A.W.S.	Beard T.	Wellington v Otago	Wellington	1927/28
119	Carson W.N.	Cowie J.	Auckland v Otago	Auckland	1937/38
118	Astle N.J.	Cairns C.L.	New Zealand v England	Christchurch	2001/02
113	Mooney F.L.H.	Knapp E.C.V.	Wellington v Auckland	Wellington	1943/44
107	Motz R.C.	Cameron F.J.	NZ v Worcestershire	Worcester	1965
106*	Astle N.J.	Morrison D.K.	New Zealand v England	Auckland	1996/97
105	Cherry R.W.	Torrance R.C.	Otago v Canterbury	Christchurch	1925/26
104	James K.C.	Massey H.B.	Wellington v Australia	Wellington	1927/28
103	Kelly P.J.	Troup G.B.	Auckland v Northern Districts	Auckland	1985/86
101	Astle N.J.	Owens M.B.	Canterbury v Northern Districts	Hamilton	1994/95
100	Lee C.D.	Brown C.M.	Auckland v Otago	Dunedin	1994/95

Hundred Partnership for the First Wicket in Both Innings

154 & 155	Shepherd J.S.F.	Worker R.V. de.R.	Otago v Wellington	Dunedin	1923/24
220 & 286	Taylor D.D.	Sutcliffe B.	Auckland v Canterbury	Auckland	1948/49
102 & 155	Blair W.L.	Turner G.M.	Otago v Auckland	Auckland	1972/73
172 & 148	Briasco P.S.	Smith C.J.P.	Central Districts v Auckland	New Plymouth	1985/86
107 { 208	Broad B.C. Athey C.W.J.	Moxon M.D. Robinson R.T.	England XI v Northern Districts	Hamilton	1987/88
109 & 111	Wealleans K.A.	White D.J.	Northern Districts v India	Hamilton	1989/90
116 & 102	Greatbatch M.J.	Latham R.T.	New Zealand v Zimbabwe	Bulawayo	1992/93
145 & 131	Lawson R.A.	Gaffaney C.B.	Otago v Wellington	Wellington	1996/97
118* & 179	Twose R.G.	Bell M.D.	Wellington v Central Districts	Wellington	1997/98
102 & 112	Spearman C.M.	Kelly D.P.	Central Districts v Wellington	New Plymouth	1999/00
220 { 127	Bell M.D. Nevin C.J.	Jones R.A. Jones R.A.	Wellington v Canterbury	Christchurch	2000/01
141 { 147	Cumming C.D. Gaffaney C.B.	Mohammad Wasim Cumming C.D.	Otago v Wellington	Wellington	2002/03
104 & 118	Richardson M.H.	McIntosh T.G.	Auckland v Northern Districts	Auckland	2002/03

FAMILIES IN FIRST-CLASS CRICKET

Great-grandfather and Great-grandson

Orchard S.A.	(C)	Orchard M.G.	(ND)

Three Generations

*Blair J.R.	(O)	Blair R.A.J.	(O)	Blair W.L.	(O)
				Blair B.R.	(O, ND)
Burton H.G.E.L.	(W)	Burton H.E.L.	(W, A)	Burton J.E.L.	(W)
Snedden A.N.C.	(A)	Snedden W.N.	(A)	Snedden M.C.	(A)
Smith F.A.	(C)	Smith F.B.	(C)	Smith G.B.	(C)
*Carson W.	(O)	Carson W.N.	(A)	Carson J.R.	(A, ND)
Anderson W.M.	(C)	Anderson R.W.	(C, ND, O, CD)	Anderson T.R.	(CD)

J.R. Blair is the uncle of R.A.J. Blair. The Carsons are uncles and nephews.

Grandfather and Grandson

Milnes L.A.	(O)	Milnes G.S.	(CD)

Father and Three Sons

Cotterill A.J.	(C)	Cotterill A.K.	(HB)	Cotterill B.W.	(HB)	Cotterill G.R.	(HB)
Hadlee W.A.	(C, O)	Hadlee B.G.	(C)	Hadlee D.R.	(C)	Hadlee R.J.	(C)

Father and Two Sons

Blacklock J.W.	(W)	Blacklock C.P.	(W)	Blacklock J.P.	(W)
Blair R.A.J.	(O)	Blair W.L.	(O)	Blair B.R.	(O, ND)
Crowe D.W.	(W,C)	Crowe M.D.	(A, CD, W)	Crowe J.J.	(A)
Garrard C.W.	(C)	Garrard W.R.	(A)	Garrard D.R.	(A)
Furlong B.D.M.	(CD)	Furlong J.B.M.	(CD)	Furlong C.J.M.	(CD)
Harris P.G.Z.	(C)	Harris B.Z.	(C, O)	Harris C.Z.	(C)
Howell J.H.	(CD)	Howell L.G.	(C, CD, A)	Howell G.A.	(C, W)
McCullum S.J.	(O)	McCullum B.B.	(O)	McCullum N.L.	(O)
McVicar A.C.	(Minor Assocs)	McVicar S.A.	(W)	McVicar C.C.	(CD)
Puna N.	(ND)	Puna K.N.	(ND)	Puna A.	(ND)
Reaney P.S.	(HB)	Reaney H.E.I.	(W)	Reaney T.P.L.	(W, CD)

Father and One Son

Airey W.F.	(W)	Airey D.M.L.	(W)
Aldridge C.W.	(C)	Aldridge G.W.	(ND)
Allen R.	(W)	Allen G.S.	(W)
Andrews S.	(C)	Andrews B.	(C, CD, O)
Baker J.C.	(O)	Clark J.B.	(O)
Barclay W.S.	(W)	Barclay C.W.	(CD)
Barton P.H.	(ND, O)	Barton H.D.	(A, C)
Barry R.W.	(C)	Barry R.	(C)
Beard D.D.	(W, CD, ND)	Beard D.A.	(ND)
Blackmore J.H.	(ND)	Blackmore S.J.	(W)
Bradburn W.P.	(ND)	Bradburn G.E.	(ND)
Burgess G.C.	(A)	Burgess M.G.	(A)
Burtt N.V.	(C)	Burtt J.W.	(C, CD)
Cairns B.L.	(CD, O, ND)	Cairns C.L.	(ND, C)

Campbell K.O.	(O)	Campbell P.A.	(O)
Child E.L.	(A, ND)	Child M.J.	(ND)
Clark L.G.	(O)	Clark L.A.	(W, O, A)
Collins W.E.	(W)	Collins D.C.	(W)
Cuff L.A.	(C, A)	Cuff A.G.	(Tasmania)
Cunis R.S.	(A, ND)	Cunis S.J.	(C)
Douglas G.W.	(CD)	Douglas M.W.	(CD, W)
Edgar A.J.	(W)	Edgar B.A.	(W)
Freeman T.A.	(O)	Freeman B.T.	(O)
Fulton F.	(O, HB)	Fulton P.R.	(HB)
Gasson E.A. snr	(C)	Gasson E.A. jnr	(C)
Gearry G.N.	(C)	Gearry R.M.	(C, CD)
Gedye A.E.	(W)	Gedye S.G.	(A)
Gilbertson J.	(S)	Gilbertson A.W.	(O)
Hartland I.R.	(C)	Hartland B.R.	(C)
Hastings B.F.	(W, CD, C)	Hastings M.A.	(C)
Hay W.P.C.	(A)	Hay S.C.	(A)
Hill A.J.	(CD)	Hill J.V.	(CD)
Hill J.	(O)	Hill R.J.	(O)
Howden C.E.	(O)	Howden G.P.	(O)
Ibadulla K.	(O)	Ibadulla K.B.K.	(O)
Jefferson R.G.	(O, W)	Jefferson M.R.	(W)
Kelly J.W.H.	(W)	Kelly P.J.	(A)
Kerr A.	(A)	Kerr A.C.	(A)
Lankham G.	(A)	Lankham W.	(A)
Lowry T.H.	(HB)	Lowry T.C.	(A, W)
McGirr W.P.	(W)	McGirr H.M.	(W)
McKnight S.G.	(O)	McKnight K.J.	(O)
McKenzie N.M.	(O)	McKenzie M.N.	(C)
Mills G.	(A, HB, O)	Mills J.E.	(A)
Morgan H.A.	(W)	Morgan R.G.	(ND, A)
Murdoch D.H.	(O)	Murdoch G.H.	(O)
Newman A.	(W)	Newman P.A.	(CD)
O'Brien J.J.	(HB)	O'Brien M.A.	(W)
Oakley J.H.	(W)	Oakley D.F.	(W)
Ollivier A.M.	(C)	Ollivier K.M.	(C)
Ongley A.M.	(HB)	Ongley J.A.	(W, CD)
Parker N.M.	(O, C)	Parker M.M.	(O)
Postles A.J.	(A)	Postles B.J.	(A)
Redmond R.E.	(W, A)	Redmond A.J.	(C)
Rees W.L.	(A)	Rees A.W.	(A, HB)
Reese T.W.	(C)	Reese D.W.	(C)
Reid J.R.	(W, O)	Reid R.B.	(W, A)
Roberts A.	(W)	Roberts S.A.	(A)
Roberts H.	(W)	Roberts E.J.	(W)
Sale E.V.	(A)	Sale V.S.	(A)
Standidge J.A.	(W)	Standidge P.H.	(W)
Stead D.W.	(C)	Stead G.R.	(C)
Tindill E.W.T.	(W)	Tindill P.	(W)
Vance R.A.	(W)	Vance R.H.	(W)
Vivian H.G.	(A)	Vivian G.E.	(A)
Wallace W.M.	(A)	Wallace G.M.	(A)
Ward J.T.	(C)	Ward B.J.	(C)
Wilding F.	(C)	Wilding A.F.	(C)
Wright G.T.	(C)	Wright J.G.	(ND, C, A)

Father and Son in Same First-class Match

Reese T.W. & Reese D.W.   Canterbury v Otago   Dunedin   1917/18

Five Brothers

Cotterill A.J. (C)   Cotterill C.N. (HB)   Cotterill E.J. (C, A)   Cotterill H. (C)   Cotterill W.J. (C)

Four Brothers

Bayly A.	(T)	Bayly F.	(T)	Bayly G.T.	(T)	Bayly H.	(T)
Bracewell B.P.		Bracewell D.W.		Bracewell J.G.		Bracewell M.A.	
(CD, O, ND)		(CD, C)			(O, A)		(O)
Mills E.	(A)	Mills G.	(A, HB, O)	Mills I.	(A)	Mills W.	(T, A)

Three Brothers

Alloo A.P.	(O)	Alloo A.W.	(O)	Alloo H.C.	(O)
Blacklock A.	(W)	Blacklock J.W.	(W)	Blacklock R.V.	(W)
Carlton W.	(A, C)	Carlton A.R.	(Vic)	Carlton J.	(Vic)
Cotterill A.K.	(HB)	Cotterill B.W.	(HB)	Cotterill G.R.	(HB)
Eden J.	(N)	Eden T.	(N)	Eden W.	(N)
Fowler G.	(N)	Fowler L.	(N)	Fowler S.	(N)
Gore A.H.	(W, HB)	Gore C.S.	(W)	Gore R.	(W)
Hadlee B.G.	(C)	Hadlee D.R.	(C)	Hadlee R.J.	(C)
Harman A.F.G.	(C)	Harman R.D.	(C)	Harman T.D.	(C)
Knapp C.	(N)	Knapp H.	(N)	Knapp K.	(N)
Lusk Hugh B.	(A, HB)	Lusk R.B.	(T)	Lusk W.N.B.	(A)
Mace C.	(O)	Mace H.	(W)	Mace J.	(O)
Meldrum A.L.	(A)	Meldrum D.	(A)	Meldrum W.	(A)
Newman A.	(W)	Newman J.	(C, W)	Newman S.	(W)
Parker K.J.	(A)	Parker J.M.	(ND)	Parker N.M.	(O, C)
Reese D.	(C)	Reese J.B.	(C)	Reese T.W.	(C)
Ridley A.E.	(C)	Ridley H.C.	(C)	Ridley R.	(C)
Salmon I.J.	(W)	Salmon J.A.N.	(W)	Salmon W.J.	(W, HB, T)

Two Brothers

Aberhart D.C.	(CD, C)	Aberhart W.M.	(W)
Alabaster G.D.	(O, C, ND)	Alabaster J.C.	(O)
Austin G.G.	(O)	Austin T.T.L.	(O)
Baker G.H.	(W)	Baker W.A.	(W)
Barton P.H.	(ND, O)	Barton R.H.	(ND)
Beale C.E.	(O, C)	Beal W.M.	(O)
Beuth D.	(CD)	Beuth A.J.	(ND)
Billcliff I.S.	(O, W, A)	Billcliff M.R.	(O)
Bishop H.A.	(HB, C)	Bishop R.E.	(HB)
Blacklock C.P.	(W)	Blacklock J.P.	(W)
Blair B.R.	(O, ND)	Blair W.L.	(O)
Blakely D.J.	(O)	Blakely J.W.	(O)
Blamires E.O.	(W, O)	Blamires H.L.	(HB)
Boddington E.R.	(N, W)	Boddington H.A.	(N, O)
Boyle D.J.	(C)	Boyle J.G.	(W, C)
Burtt N.V.	(C)	Burtt T.B.	(C)
Cairns A.E.	(O)	Cairns H.W.	(O)
Cameron D.S.	(O)	Cameron H.R.	(O)
Cederwall B.W.	(W)	Cederwall G.N.	(W)
Chadwick C.S.	(O)	Chadwick L.N.	(O)

Clarke D.B.	(A, ND)	Clarke D.S.	(ND)
Collins J.U.	(N, C)	Collins W.E.	(W)
Coney C.J.	(W)	Coney J.V.	(W)
Cornelius C.J.	(C)	Cornelius W.A.	(C)
Cresswell A.E.	(W, CD)	Cresswell G.F.	(W, CD)
Cross C.S.	(N, W)	Cross H.	(N)
Crowe J.J.	(A)	Crowe M.D.	(A, CD, W)
Dacre C.C.R.	(A)	Dacre L.M.	(A)
Doull L.J.	(W)	Doull S.B.	(ND)
Dryden C.H.	(W)	Dryden W.E.	(W)
Farrant A.J.	(C)	Farrant D.G.	(C)
Fisher A.H.	(O)	Fisher R.L.	(C)
Frankish E.H.	(C)	Frankish F.S.	(C)
Frith C.	(C, O)	Frith W.	(C, O, W)
Fulton F.	(O, HB)	Fulton J.C.	(O)
Furlong C.J.M.	(CD)	Furlong J.B.M.	(CD)
Garrard D.R.	(A)	Garrard W.R.	(A)
Gatenby D.J.	(C)	Gatenby P.R.	(Tasmania)
Gilbertson J.	(S)	Gilbertson J.H.	(S)
Graham A.C.	(O)	Graham C.G.	(O)
Hamilton A.J.	(S)	Hamilton D.C.	(S)
Hampton B.L.	(CD)	Hampton I.R.	(CD)
Harris B.Z.	(C, O)	Harris C.Z.	(C)
Hart M.N.	(ND)	Hart R.G.	(ND)
Hatch K.	(W)	Hatch R.J.	(W)
Hay T.D.B.	(A)	Hay W.P.C.	(A)
Hickson H.C.	(W)	Hickson W.R.S.	(W)
Holdship A.R.	(W)	Holdship W.E.	(Middlesex)
Horne M.J.	(A, O)	Horne P.A.	(A)
Howarth G.P.	(A, ND)	Howarth H.J.	(A)
Howell L.G.	(C, CD, A)	Howell G.A.	(C, W)
Howden A.M.	(A)	Howden C.E.	(O)
Lynch D.	(A)	Lynch R.F.	(W)
Lynch R.K.	(A)	Lynch S.M.	(A)
McCullum B.B.	(O)	McCullum N.L.	(O)
McVicar S.A.	(W)	McVicar C.C.	(CD)
Marshall J.A.H.	(ND)	Marshall H.J.H.	(ND)
Martin J.H.	(HB)	Martin H.	(HB)
Matthias H.R.	(C)	Matthias R.B.	(C)
Morris J.B.	(A)	Morris P.P.W.	(A)
Naughton D.	(W)	Naughton M.P.	(W)
Neill R.	(A)	Neill T.	(A)
Nicholson C.R.	(C, O)	Nicholson K.A.	(O)
O'Rourke M.H.	(A)	O'Rourke P.W.	(W)
Ollivier A.M.	(C)	Ollivier F.M.	(C)
Ormiston I.W.	(W)	Ormiston R.W.	(CD, W)
Parlane M.E.	(ND)	Parlane N.R.	(ND, W)
Powell J.L.	(C)	Powell R.F.J.	(C)
Powys A.L.	(C)	Powys R.A.N.	(C)
Puna A.	(ND)	Puna K.N.	(ND)
Reaney H.E.I.	(W)	Reaney T.P.L.	(W, CD)
Richardson C.A.	(W)	Richardson W.A.	(NSW)
Ritchie A.W.	(A)	Ritchie D.C.	(A)
Robertson G.K.	(CD)	Robertson S.P.	(CD)
Rutherford I.A.	(O, CD)	Rutherford K.R.	(O)
Schofer J.W.J.	(W)	Schofer P.J.	(W)
Scott A.H.	(A)	Scott V.J.	(A)

Snedden A.N.C.	(A)	Snedden Cyril A.	(A)
Snedden Colin A.	(A)	Snedden W.N.	(A)
Sorenson B.J.	(A)	Sorenson R.G.	(A)
Toomey C.D.G.	(O)	Toomey F.J.	(O)
Thomson K.	(C)	Thomson W.A.	(C)
Tucker K.H.	(W)	Tucker S.G.	(W)
Turnbull A.J.	(O)	Turnbull P.J.	(O)
Wallace G.F.	(A)	Wallace W.M.	(A)
Watson E.A.	(O)	Watson L.F.	(O)
Watson H.C.	(O)	Watson L.C.	(O)
Webb M.G.	(O, C)	Webb R.J.	(O)
Weir A.F.	(A)	Weir G.L.	(A)
West G.L.	(CD, ND)	West R.M.	(CD, W)
Westbrook K.R.	(Tasmania)	Westbrook R.A.	(O)
White N.M.	(HB)	White P.C.	(HB)
Williams P.F.C.	(Gloucestershire)	Williams J.N.	(HB)
Wilson A.C.	(C)	Wilson W.C.	(C)
Wyatt I.E.	(A)	Wyatt J.L.	(ND)

Uncle and Nephew

instances not included in previous lists

Bailey J.F.	(ND)	Bailey M.D.	(ND)
CarltonW.	(A, C)	Carlton T.A.	(C, O)
Carson W.	(O)	Carson W.N.	(A)
Carson W.N.	(A)	Carson J.R.	(A, ND)
Crawford C.G.	(C)	Playle W.R.	(A)
Cunningham W.H.R.	(C)	Anderson G.F.	(C)
Dacre C.C.R. (A) & Dacre L.M.	(A)	Coleman D.D.	(A)
Fulton J.	(O)	Fulton F.	(O, HB)
		⎰ Fulton J.C.	(O)
Fulton R.W.	(C, ND)	⎱ Fulton P.G.	(C)
Griffiths B.G.	(W)	Maguiness S.J.	(W)
Pocock M.G.	(ND)	Pocock B.A.	(A, ND)
Roberts B.L.	(ND)	Cairns C.L.	(ND, C)
Westbrook N.R.	(Tasmania)	Westbrook R.A.	(O)
Wilson R.S.	(O)	Paul J.M.	(O)
Wilson T.J.	(O)	Wilson J.W.	(O)

Cousins

Bateman G.C.	(C)	Bateman S.N.	(C)
Hoskin R.N.	(O)	Lamont M.J.	(O)
Hotter S.J.	(W)	Verry R.A.	(W)
Leggat I.B.	(CD)	Leggat J.G.	(C)
Lusk Harold B.	(A, C, W)	Lusk Hugh B.	(A, HB)
		⎰ Lusk R.B.	(T)
		⎱ Lusk W.N.B.	(A)
McMillan C.D.	(C)	McMillan J.M.	(O)
Pringle M.R.	(A)	Webb P.N.	(A)
Reid B.A.	(WA)	Reid J.F.	(A)
Talbot G.L.	(C)	Talbot R.O.	(C, O)
Vettori D.L.	(ND)	Hill J.V.	(CD)

REDPATH CUP

Presented by Mr David Redpath

Awarded to the New Zealand batsman whose performances in first-class cricket have been, in the opinion of the Board of Control, the most meritorious since the award was last made.

HOLDERS

Season's first-class figures

		Team	In	NO	HS	Runs	Ave
1920/21	Anthony A.	Auckland	5	1	113	251	62.75
1921/22	Hiddleston J.S.	Wellington	8	1	118	396	56.57
1922/23	Blunt R.C.	Canterbury	12	1	174	583	53.00
1923/24	Hiddleston J.S.	Wellington	12	—	163	619	51.58
1924/25	Worker R.V. de R.	Otago	12	2	121*	491	49.10
1925/26	Allcott C.F.W.	Auckland	9 †	2	116	359	51.28
1926/27	Blunt R.C.	Otago	12 §	1	187	758	69.80
1927/28	Dempster C.S.	Wellington	12	1	145	616	56.00
1928/29	Weir G.L.	Auckland	4	2	106*	262	131.00
1929/30	Dempster C.S.	Wellington	10	4	141*	559	93.16
1930/31	Dempster C.S.	Wellington	42 †	6	212	1901	52.80
1931/32	Roberts A.W.	Canterbury	10	1	181	476	52.88
1932/33	Dempster C.S.	Wellington	9	2	83*	336	48.00
1933/34	Vivian H.G.	Auckland	5	—	64	263	52.60
1934/35	Whitelaw P.E.	Auckland	7	—	155	472	67.42
1935/36	Kerr J.L.	Canterbury	13 †	2	146	655	59.54
1936/37	Whitelaw P.E.	Auckland	6	1	195	410	82.00
1937/38	Uttley K.F.M.	Otago	6	—	138	420	70.00
1938/39	Wallace W.M.	Auckland	6	1	105	270	54.00
1939/40	Donnelly M.P.	Canterbury	5	1	104	302	75.50
1940-45	no award						
1945/46	Hadlee W.A.	Otago	7	—	198	449	66.14
1946/47	Sutcliffe B.	Auckland & Otago	8	1	197	722	103.14
1947/48	Sutcliffe B.	Otago	10	1	208*	911	101.22
1948/49	Sutcliffe B.	Auckland	6	—	141	511	85.16
1949/50	Sutcliffe B.	Otago	9	—	355	695	77.55
1950/51	Sutcliffe B.	Otago	12	—	275	798	66.50
1951/52	Scott V.J.	Auckland	10	2	151*	459	57.37
1952/53	Miller L.S.M.	Central Districts	9	3	128*	545	90.83
1953/54	Sutcliffe B.	Otago	34 †	2	196	1691	52.84
1954/55	Reid J.R.	Wellington	15	2	106	505	38.84
1955/56	Reid J.R.	New Zealand	33 †	6	150*	1227	45.44
1956/57	Miller L.S.M.	Wellington	13	3	83	559	55.90
1957/58	Miller L.S.M.	Wellington	14	1	95	549	42.23
1958/59	Pairaudeau B.H.	Northern Districts	11	1	80	456	45.60
1959/60	Reid J.R.	Wellington	16	1	165	724	48.26
1960/61	Harris P.G.Z.	Canterbury	14	2	108	597	49.75
1961/62	Reid J.R.	Wellington	40 †	2	203	2188	57.57
1962/63	Reid J.R.	Wellington	14	1	296	681	52.38
1963/64	Sinclair B.W.	Wellington	15	1	138	641	45.78
1964/65	Pollard V.	Central Districts	43 †	6	85	1081	29.21
1965/66	Sinclair B.W.	Wellington	17	2	114	700	56.66
1966/67	Dowling G.T.	Canterbury	18	2	102*	871	46.66
1967/68	Dowling G.T.	Canterbury	18	1	239	968	56.94
1968/69	Hastings B.F.	Canterbury	15	4	117*	872	79.27
1969/70	Murray B.A.G.	Wellington	51 †	3	157	2079	43.31

		Team	In	NO	HS	Runs	Ave
1970/71	Dowling G.T.	Canterbury	16	1	102	667	44.66
1971/72	Turner G.M.	Otago	27 †	5	259	1708	77.63
1972/73	Congdon B.E.	Otago	38 †	6	126	1728	54.00
1973/74	Turner G.M.	Otago	17 †	2	110*	714	47.60
1974/75	Turner G.M.	Otago	15	1	186*	838	59.85
1975/76	Turner G.M.	Otago	20	4	177*	1244	77.75
1976/77	Burgess M.G.	Auckland	28 †	1	138	1064	39.40
1977/78	Howarth G.P.	Northern Districts	22	1	122	685	32.61
1978/79	Howarth G.P.	Northern Districts	11	1	147*	505	50.50
1979/80	Howarth G.P.	Northern Districts	22	2	151	767	38.35
1980/81	Reid J.F.	Auckland	18	4	173	817	58.35
1981/82	Edgar B.A.	Wellington	19	1	161	934	51.88
1982/83	Edgar B.A.	Wellington	30 †	5	146	1116	44.64
1983/84	Coney J.V.	Wellington	19 †	4	174*	736	49.06
1984/85	Coney J.V.	Wellington	26 †	4	111*	877	39.86
1985/86	Crowe M.D.	Central Districts	31 †	9	242*	1667	75.77
1986/87	Crowe M.D.	Central Districts	22 †	3	175*	1703	89.63
1987/88	Crowe M.D.	Central Districts	16 †	2	144	1064	76.00
1988/89	Jones A.H.	Wellington	25 †	2	181*	1079	46.91
1989/90	Wright J.G.	Auckland	32 †	5	185	1641	60.77
1990/91	Crowe M.D.	Wellington	15 †	3	299	847	70.58
1991/92	Wright J.G.	Auckland	14	0	116	518	37.00
1992/93	Rutherford K.R.	Otago	26 †	3	105	907	39.43
1993/94	Jones A.H.	Wellington	20 †	0	143	934	46.70
1994/95	Parore A.C.	New Zealand	36 †	7	127*	1050	36.20
1995/96	Twose R.G.	New Zealand	10 †	2	119*	452	56.50
1996/97	Fleming S.P.	Canterbury	16 †	1	129	629	41.93
1997/98	Horne M.J.	Otago	22 †	1	241	1114	53.04
1998/99	Horne M.J.	Otago	19	2	132	887	52.17
1999/00	Cairns C.L.	New Zealand	26 †	3	109	903	39.26
2000/01	Richardson M.H.	Otago	45 †	5	306	2672	66.80
2001/02	Astle N.J.	Canterbury	15 †	3	223	899	74.91
2002/03	Richardson M.H.	Auckland	25 †	2	113	885	38.47

† *including matches for New Zealand teams overseas*
§ *these figures include Blunt's scores for Otago and New Zealand against the Melbourne Cricket Club*

WINSOR CUP

Presented by Sir Arthur Donnelly to perpetuate the memory of Mr W.H. Winsor

Presented to the New Zealand bowler whose performances in first-class cricket have been, in the opinion of the Board of Control, the most meritorious since the award was last made.

HOLDERS

Season's first-class figures

		Team	Matches	O	M	R	W	Ave
1938/39	Cowie J.	Auckland	4	150	20	444	21	21.14
1939/40	Pritchard T.L.	Wellington	3	113.3	9	404	23	17.56
1940-45	no award							
1945/46	Cowie J.	Auckland	5	209	69	433	24	18.04
1946/47	Cowie J.	Auckland	5	257.4	61	578	26	22.23
1947/48	Burtt T.B.	Canterbury	4	256	57	666	26	25.61
1948/49	Cresswell A.E.	Wellington	4	152	27	343	22	15.59
1949/50	Cresswell G.F.	Wellington	4	235	111	304	20	15.20
1950/51	Burtt T.B.	Canterbury	6	363.2	151	673	44	15.29

		Team	Matches	O	M	R	W	Ave
1951/52	Burtt T.B.	Canterbury	6	317	120	643	37	17.37
1952/53	Rabone G.O.	Auckland	5	174	44	405	23	17.60
1953/54	MacGibbon A.R.	Canterbury†	17	463.7	98	1271	63	20.17
1954/55	Reid J.R.	Wellington	8	279.1	121	496	30	16.53
1955/56	Cave H.B.	Central Districts*	18	673.4	271	1259	50	25.18
1956/57	Cave H.B.	Central Districts	9	358.3	138	685	41	16.70
1957/58	Hayes J.A.	Auckland	6	244.3	49	568	48	11.83
1958/59	Hough K.W.	Auckland	8	411.3	151	701	46	15.23
1959/60	Alabaster J.C.	Otago	9	313	78	824	47	17.53
1960/61	Alabaster J.C.	Otago	10	426.3	125	964	49	19.61
1961/62	Blair R.W.	Wellington	6	252	96	535	44	12,15
1962/63	Blair R.W.	Wellington	7	244.2	77	562	32	17.56
1963/64	Blair R.W.	Wellington	9	408.1	135	856	49	17.46
1964/65	Motz R.C.	Canterbury*	26	890	272	2179	93	23.43
1965/66	Puna N.	Northern Districts	8	338	126	706	38	18.57
1966/67	Pollard V.	Central Districts	11	345.4	141	672	41	16.39
1967/68	Motz R.C.	Canterbury	10	369.2	115	907	47	19.29
1968/69	Motz R.C.	Canterbury	9	265.2	54	880	40	22.00
1969/70	Howarth H.J.	Auckland*	24	991.4	355	2173	100	21.73
1970/71	Collinge R.O.	Wellington	9	230.6	46	677	37	18.29
1971/72	Taylor B.R.	Wellington*	15	560.5	118	1474	69	21.36
1972/73	Collinge R.O.	Wellington*	23	659.2	149	1806	83	21.75
1973/74	Hadlee D.R.	Canterbury*	13	336.3	35	1451	38	38.18
1974/75	Alabaster G.D.	Otago	6	182.2	26	684	34	20.11
1975/76	Collinge R.O.	Northern Districts	9	215.3	39	623	43	14.48
1976/77	Hadlee R.J.	Canterbury	15	418.2	41	1768	49	36.08
1977/78	Hadlee R.J.	Canterbury	10	266.1	56	860	42	20.47
1978/79	Hadlee R.J.	Canterbury	10	299.1	56	909	50	18.18
1979/80	Hadlee R.J.	New Zealand	3	161.3	50	361	19	19.00
1980/81	Hadlee R.J.	New Zealand*	8	349	89	855	37	23.10
1981/82	Hadlee R.J.	Canterbury	10	424.2	135	868	59	14.74
1982/83	Hadlee R.J.	Canterbury*	12	498	147	1132	59	19.18
1983/84	Hadlee R.J.	Canterbury*	10	310.4	111	587	48	12.22
1984/85	Hadlee R.J.	Canterbury*	12	429.5	119	1061	53	20.01
1985/86	Hadlee R.J.	Canterbury*	11	553.1	129	1314	72	18.25
1986/87	Hadlee R.J.	Canterbury*	12	446.1	116	1047	66	15.86
1987/88	Chatfield E.J.	Wellington*	9	355.1	114	672	24	28.00
1988/89	Hadlee R.J.	Canterbury*	7	247.5	59	541	34	15.91
1989/90	Hadlee R.J.	New Zealand*	9	349	71	1014	43	23.58
1990/91	Watson W.	New Zealand	8	333.3	92	807	26	31.03
1991/92	Cairns C.L.	Canterbury	8	294	67	872	42	20.76
1992/93	Morrison D.K.	Auckland	8	263.2	66	598	38	15.73
1993/94	Morrison D.K.	Auckland*	9	327.3	59	1021	28	36.46
1994/95	Morrison D.K.	Auckland*	11	368.5	82	1016	40	25.40
1995/96	Cairns C.L.	New Zealand*	8	232.4	62	631	26	24.26
1996/97	Doull S.B.	New Zealand*	8	255.3	67	715	33	21.66
1997/98	Cairns C.L.	Canterbury*	12	399	113	1124	51	22.03
1998/99	Penn A.J.	Central Districts	9	288	76	763	40	19.07
1999/00	Cairns C.L.	New Zealand*	17	508.5	124	1541	67	23.00
2000/01	Tuffey D.R.	Northern Districts*	12	396.5	118	1104	54	20.44
2001/02	Drum C.J.	Auckland	9	317.3	96	827	53	15.60
2002/03	Bond S.E.	Canterbury*	6	183.5	44	600	30	20.00

† *including 16 matches for New Zealand overseas*
* *includes matches for New Zealand overseas*

TOURING TEAMS IN NEW ZEALAND

		FIRST-CLASS MATCHES			ALL MATCHES			
		P	W	L	D	P	W	L	D
1863/64	G. Parr's England Team	—	—	—	—	4	3	—	1
1876/77	J. Lillywhite's England Team	—	—	—	—	8	6	—	2
1877/78	Australia	—	—	—	—	7	5	1	1
1880/81	Australia	—	—	—	—	10	6	1	3
1881/82	A. Shaw's England Team	—	—	—	—	7	5	—	2
1883/84	Tasmania	4	—	3	1	7	2	3	2
1886/87	Australia	—	—	—	—	5	2	—	3
1887/88	C.A. Smith's England Team	—	—	—	—	3	—	—	3
1888/89	English Footballers	—	—	—	—	1	—	—	1
1889/90	New South Wales	5	4	—	1	7	6	—	1
1893/94	New South Wales	7	4	1	2	8	4	1	3
1894/95	Fiji	6	2	2	2	8	4	2	2
1895/96	New South Wales	5	3	1	1	5	3	1	1
1896/97	Australia	—	—	—	—	5	3	—	2
1896/97	Queensland	5	3	1	1	8	4	1	3
1899/00	Melbourne Cricket Club	—	—	—	—	7	6	—	1
1902/03	Lord Hawke's England Team	7	7	—	—	18	18	—	—
1904/05	Australia	4	3	—	1	6	4	—	2
1905/06	Melbourne Cricket Club	—	—	—	—	10	8	—	2
1906/07	MCC	11	6	2	3	16	10	2	4
1909/10	Australia	6	5	—	1	9	7	—	2
1913/14	A. Sims' Australian Team	8	6	—	2	16	8	—	8
1920/21	Australia	9	6	—	3	15	12	—	3
1922/23	MCC	8	6	—	2	14	11	—	3
1923/24	New South Wales	6	5	—	1	12	8	—	4
1924/25	Victoria	6	1	1	4	12	4	1	7
1926/27	Melbourne Cricket Club	—	—	—	—	13	5	—	8
1927/28	Australia	6	4	—	2	13	6	—	7
1929/30	MCC	8	2	—	6	17	9	—	8
1930/31	West Indies	—	—	—	—	1	—	—	1
1931/32	South Africa	3	3	—	—	3	3	—	—
1932/33	MCC	3	—	—	3	3	—	—	3
1935/36	MCC	8	2	1	5	18	5	1	12
1936/37	MCC	3	1	—	2	3	1	—	2
1938/39	Sir Julien Cahn's XI	1	—	—	1	10	2	—	8
1945/46	Australia	5	5	—	—	5	5	—	—
1946/47	MCC	4	2	—	2	4	2	—	2
1947/48	Fiji	5	2	3	—	17	6	3	8
1949/50	Australia B	5	3	—	2	14	9	—	5
1950/51	MCC	4	3	—	1	4	3	—	1
1951/52	West Indies	4	2	—	2	5	3	—	2
1952/53	South Africa	4	1	—	3	5	1	—	4
1953/54	Fiji	4	1	3	—	17	8	6	3
1954/55	MCC	4	4	—	—	4	4	—	—
1955/56	West Indies	8	6	1	1	15	11	1	3
1956/57	Australia B	7	5	—	2	12	7	—	5
1958/59	MCC	5	3	—	2	5	3	—	2
1959/60	Australia B	6	2	—	4	9	4	—	5

		FIRST-CLASS MATCHES				ALL MATCHES			
		P	W	L	D	P	W	L	D
1960/61	MCC	10	4	1	5	21	11	1	9
1961/62	Fiji	—	—	—	—	22	9	9	4
1961/62	R.A. Roberts' Commonwealth XI	2	2	—	—	3	2	—	1
1962/63	MCC	4	4	—	—	4	4	—	—
1963/64	South Africa	4	1	—	3	7	1	—	6
1964/65	Pakistan	10	2	—	8	12	4	—	8
1965/66	MCC	4	—	—	4	4	—	—	4
1966/67	Australia B	9	1	2	6	10	2	2	6
1967/68	Fiji	—	—	—	—	25	12	7	6
1967/68	India	6	4	1	1	6	4	1	1
1968/69	West Indies	6	1	2	3	7	1	2	4
1969/70	Australia B	8	2	—	6	8	2	—	6
1970/71	MCC	2	1	—	1	5	3	1	1
1972/73	Pakistan	8	5	1	2	11	6	3	2
1973/74	Australia	7	2	1	4	11	6	1	4
1974/75	MCC	3	1	—	2	5	1	—	4
1975/76	India	6	3	1	2	9	3	4	2
1976/77	Australia	6	5	—	1	8	5	2	1
1977/78	Fiji	—	—	—	—	15	5	4	6
1977/78	England	8	3	1	4 †	9	4	1	4 †
1978/79	Pakistan	8	5	—	3	10	6	1	3
1979/80	West Indies	5	—	2	3	8	2	3	3
1979/80	D.H. Robins' XI	2	—	—	2	8	5	1	2
1980/81	India	5	1	1	3	7	1	3	3
1981/82	Australia	5	1	1	3	11	4	4	3
1982/83	England	—	—	—	—	3	—	3	—
1982/83	Sri Lanka	4	—	3	1	9	1	7	1
1983/84	England	7	1	1	5	11	4	2	5
1984/85	Pakistan	5	1	2	2	9	1	5	3
1985/86	Australia	5	1	1	3	11	5	3	3
1986/87	West Indies	5	1	1	3	9	5	1	3
1987/88	England	7	2	1	4	12	5	3	4
1988/89	Pakistan	5	1	—	4	12	2	5	5
1989/90	India	6	1	1	4	10	2	4	4
1989/90	Australia	1	—	1	—	6	5	1	—
1990/91	Sri Lanka	7	1	—	6	10	1	3	6
1990/91	England	—	—	—	—	3	1	2	—
1991/92	England	7	4	—	3	11	8	—	3
1991/92	Zimbabwe	—	—	—	—	3	1	2	—
1991/92	Australia	—	—	—	—	1	1	—	—
1991/92	Sri Lanka	—	—	—	—	1	1	—	—
1992/93	Pakistan	1	1	—	—	4	2	2	—
1992/93	Australia	4	2	1	1	10	5	4	1
1993/94	Pakistan	5	2	1	2	11	6	2	3 †
1993/94	India	3	—	—	3	7	2	2	3
1994/95	West Indies	3	1	—	2	8	6	—	2
1994/95	Australia	—	—	—	—	4	3	1	—
1994/95	South Africa	2	2	—	—	6	3	2	1 †
1994/95	India	—	—	—	—	4	2	2	—
1994/95	Sri Lanka	4	2	—	2	9	4	2	3
1994/95	Australian Academy	1	1	—	—	5	5	—	—

		FIRST-CLASS MATCHES				ALL MATCHES			
		P	W	L	D	P	W	L	D
1995/96	Pakistan	1	1	—	—	5	3	2	—
1995/96	Zimbabwe	4	1	—	3	8	3	2	3
1996/97	England	6	4	1	1	12	6	3	3 †
1996/97	Sri Lanka	2	—	2	—	6	2	3	1
1997/98	Bangladesh	4	—	4	—	7	—	6	1
1997/98	Zimbabwe	4	1	3	—	10	3	7	—
1998/99	Pakistan A	5	—	1	4	10	1	4	5
1998/99	India	4	1	2	1	10	3	5	2
1998/99	South Africa	5	1	—	4	13	5	2	6
1999/00	England A	5	3	—	2	10	7	—	3
1999/00	West Indies	4	—	2	2	10	—	8	2
1999/00	Australia	5	4	—	1	11	8	1	2
2000/01	Zimbabwe	2	—	—	2	6	3	1	2
2000/01	Sri Lanka	—	—	—	—	6	4	2	—
2000/01	Pakistan	5	1	2	2	10	3	5	2
2001/02	Bangladesh	3	—	3	—	4	—	3	1
2001/02	England	5	1	1	3	12	4	5	3
2002/03	India	3	—	2	1	11	2	8	1

† *includes a tie*

NB: From 1900 the basis for the inclusion is any of the following:
a) First-class matches were played.
b) The touring side was its country's official team.
c) The touring side played an official New Zealand team.
d) Matches in the 1992 World Cup are not included, although preliminary games played by Zimbabwe, Australia and Sri Lanka are.

NEW ZEALAND TOURING TEAMS

		FIRST-CLASS MATCHES				ALL MATCHES			
		P	W	L	D	P	W	L	D
1898/99	Australia	2	—	2	—	4	1	2	1
1913/14	Australia	4	1	2	1	9	5	2	2
1925/26	Australia	4	—	1	3	9	3	1	5
1927 ⌠	Great Britain	26	7	5	14	38	12	5	21
⌡	Ceylon	—	—	—	—	1	—	—	1
1927/28 ⌡	Australia	1	—	1	—	1	—	1	—
1931	Great Britain	32	6	3	23	36	7	3	26
1937 ⌠	Great Britain	32	9	9	14	38	14	9	15
⌡	Ceylon	—	—	—	—	1	—	—	1
1937/38 ⌡	Australia	3	—	3	—	3	—	3	—
1949 ⌠	Great Britain	32	13	1	18	35	14	1	20
⌡	West Germany	—	—	—	—	1	1	—	—
1953/54 ⌠	South Africa	16	3	4	9	17	3	4	10
⌡	Australia	3	2	—	1	3	2	—	1
1955/56 ⌠	Pakistan	6	1	3	2	6	1	3	2
⌡	India	10	2	3	5	10	2	3	5
1958	Great Britain	31	7	6	18 †	35	7	6	22
1961/62 ⌠	South Africa	18	5	2	11	24	7	2	15
⌡	Australia	3	—	2	1	3	—	2	1
1964/65 ⌠	India	4	—	1	3	4	—	1	3
	Pakistan	3	—	2	1	3	—	2	1
1965	Great Britain	19	3	6	10	21	4	6	11
	Holland	—	—	—	—	1	—	—	1
	Bermuda	—	—	—	—	2	—	—	2
⌡	USA	—	—	—	—	1	1	—	—
1967/68	Australia	4	—	2	2	7	2	2	3
1969 ⌠	Great Britain	18	4	3	11	22	5	4	13
1969/70 ⌡	India	5	1	1	3	5	1	1	3
1969/70 ⌡	Pakistan	4	1	—	3	4	1	—	3
1969/70	Australia	3	—	—	3	8	3	—	5
1970/71	Australia	1	—	—	1	2	—	1	1
1971/72*	Australia	—	—	—	—	2	1	—	1
1971/72	West Indies	13	1	—	12	16	4	—	12
1972/73	Australia	1	—	—	1	3	2	—	1
1973	Great Britain	19	3	2	14	23	4	3	16
1973/74	Australia	9	2	5	2	13	5	6	2
1974/75	Australia	—	—	—	—	3	3	—	—
1975	England (Prudential Cup)	—	—	—	—	4	2	2	—
1976/77 ⌠	Pakistan	6	1	3	2	7	2	3	2
⌡	India	3	—	2	1	3	—	2	1
1978	Great Britain	16	5	4	7	20	5	8	7
1979	Great Britain (Prudential Cup)	—	—	—	—	4	2	2	—
1980/81	Australia	7	1	2	4	29	14	9	6
1982/83	Australia	2	—	—	2 †	4	1	1	2 †
1982/83	Australia	—	—	—	—	18	12	6	—
1983	England	13	7	3	3	21	11	6	4
1983/84	Sri Lanka	5	2	—	3	8	4	1	3
1984/85 ⌠	Sri Lanka	—	—	—	—	2	1	1	—
⌡	Pakistan	5	—	2	3	9	1	5	3
1984/85	Australia (WCC)	—	—	—	—	4	1	2	1
1984/85	West Indies	7	—	2	5	12	—	7	5
1985/86	Australia	6	2	1	3	8	2	1	5

		FIRST-CLASS MATCHES				ALL MATCHES			
		P	W	L	D	P	W	L	D
1985/86	Australia	—	—	—	—	11	3	6	2
1985/86 ⌈	Sri Lanka	—	—	—	—	2	1	1	—
{	Sharjah	—	—	—	—	2	—	2	—
⌊	Hong Kong	—	—	—	—	2	2	—	—
1986 ⌈	England	15	4	—	11	18	5	1	12
⌊	Holland	—	—	—	—	2	1	1	—
1986/87	Sri Lanka	2	—	—	2	2	—	—	2
1987/88	India *(Reliance World Cup)*	—	—	—	—	6	2	4	—
1987/88	Australia	6	1	2	3	19	8	8	3
1987/88	Sharjah	—	—	—	—	4	2	2	—
1988/89	India	6	1	2	3	10	1	6	3
1988/89	Australia	—	—	—	—	1	—	1	—
1989/90	Australia	3	—	—	3	4	—	1	3
1990 ⌈	Sharjah	—	—	—	—	3	1	2	—
⌊	England	12	4	2	6	19	8	5	6
1990/91	Pakistan	5	—	3	2	8	—	6	2
1990/91	Australia	—	—	—	—	10	3	7	—
1991/92	Australia	—	—	—	—	6	4	2	—
1992/93 ⌈	Zimbabwe	3	2	—	1	6	5	—	1
⌊	Sri Lanka	2	—	1	1	7	—	5	2
1993/94	Australia	7	2	3	2	16	5	9	2
1994 ⌈	Sharjah	—	—	—	—	3	1	2	—
⌊	Great Britain	12	1	3	8	21	8	5	8
1994/95 ⌈	India	—	—	—	—	4	—	3	1
⌊	South Africa	7	2	3	2	16	3	9	4
1995/96	India	6	—	1	5	11	2	4	5
1995/96 ⌈	India & Pakistan *(Wills World Cup)*	—	—	—	—	6	3	3	—
1995/96 ⌊	West Indies	4	1	2	1	13	7	5	1
1996/97 ⌈	Sharjah	—	—	—	—	5	1	3	1 †
1996/97 ⌊	Pakistan	3	1	1	1	6	2	3	1
1996/97	India *(Independence Cup)*	—	—	—	—	3	1	2	—
1997/98 ⌈	Kenya	—	—	—	—	3	2	—	1
⌊	Zimbabwe	3	—	—	3	7	2	1	4 †
1997/98	Australia	6	—	5	1	21	5	13	3 †
1997/98	Sharjah	—	—	—	—	4	1	3	—
1997/98	Sri Lanka	5	1	2	2	11	3	4	4
1998	Malaysia *(Commonwealth Games)*	—	—	—	—	5	4	1	—
1998/99	Bangladesh *(Wills International Cup)*	—	—	—	—	2	1	1	—
1999	England	10	5	2	3	26	14	8	4
1999/00	India	6	—	2	4	11	2	5	4
2000/01 ⌈	Singapore	—	—	—	—	2	—	2	—
2000/01 ⎱	Zimbabwe	4	2	—	2	8	4	2	2
2000/01 ⎰	Kenya	—	—	—	—	3	3	—	—
2000/01 ⌊	South Africa	6	2	2	2	14	4	7	3
2000/01	Sharjah	—	—	—	—	4	1	3	—
2001/02	Sri Lanka	—	—	—	—	7	3	4	—
2001/02	Australia	5	—	1	4	21	6	8	7
2001/02 ⌈	Sharjah	—	—	—	—	4	1	3	—
2001/02 ⌊	Pakistan	1	—	1	—	4	—	4	—
2001/02	West Indies	2	1	—	1	8	3	3	2
2002/03 ⌈	Australia	—	—	—	—	4	4	—	—
2002/03 ⌊	Sri Lanka *(ICC Champions Trophy)*	—	—	—	—	4	2	2	—
2002/03	South Africa *(World Cup)*	—	—	—	—	11	7	4	—
2002/03	Sri Lanka	2	—	—	2	9	3	2	4

Seventy-five official New Zealand sides have toured overseas since the first in February, 1899. The teams were as follows:

1) **1898/99 to Australia**
L.T. Cobcroft *(captain)*, F.L. Ashbolt, J.C. Baker, C. Boxshall, A.D. Downes, A.H. Fisher, F.S. Frankish, Hugh B. Lusk, G. Mills, I. Mills, D. Reese, A. Sims, E.F. Upham.

2) **1913/14 to Australia**
D. Reese *(captain)*, J.H. Bennett, C. Boxshall, T.A. Carlton, L.G. Hemus, R.G. Hickmott, W.R. Patrick, C.W. Robinson, D.M. Sandman, R.C. Somervell, A.N.C. Snedden, L.G. Taylor, B.J. Tuckwell, H.J. Tattersall.

3) **1925/26 to Australia**
W.R. Patrick *(captain)*, C.F.W. Allcott, A.W. Alloo, R.C. Blunt, C.G. Crawford, W.H.R. Cunningham, C.C.R. Dacre, H.D. Gillespie, R.W. Hope, K.C. James, T.C. Lowry, D.J. McBeath, C.J. Oliver, R.V. de R. Worker.

4) **1927 to Great Britain, Ceylon and Australia**
T.C. Lowry *(captain)*, C.F.W. Allcott, E.H.L. Bernau, E.D. Blundell*, R.C. Blunt, W.H.R. Cunningham, C.C.R. Dacre, C.S. Dempster, R.H. Fox*, T.D.B. Hay*, M. Henderson, K.C. James, H.M. McGirr, W.E. Merritt, J.E. Mills, C.J. Oliver, M.L. Page.

5) **1931 to Great Britain**
T.C. Lowry *(captain)*, C.F.W. Allcott, R.C. Blunt, I.B. Cromb, C.S. Dempster, K.C. James, J.L. Kerr, A.M. Matheson, W.E. Merritt, J.E. Mills, M.L. Page, R.O. Talbot, H.G. Vivian, G.L. Weir.

6) **1937 to Great Britain, Ceylon and Australia**
M.L. Page *(captain)*, W.N. Carson, J. Cowie, M.P. Donnelly, J.A. Dunning, N. Gallichan, W.A. Hadlee, J.L. Kerr, J.R. Lamason, T.C. Lowry, D.A.R. Moloney, C.K. Parsloe*, A.W. Roberts, E.W.T. Tindill, H.G. Vivian, W.M. Wallace, G.L. Weir.

7) **1949 to Great Britain and West Germany**
W.A. Hadlee *(captain)*, C. Burke, T.B. Burtt, H.B. Cave, J. Cowie, G.F. Cresswell, M.P. Donnelly, J.A. Hayes, F.L.H. Mooney, G.O. Rabone, J.R. Reid, V.J. Scott, F.B. Smith, B. Sutcliffe, W.M. Wallace.

8) **1953/54 to South Africa and Australia**
G.O. Rabone *(captain)*, J.E.F. Beck, W. Bell, R.W. Blair, M.E. Chapple, E.W. Dempster, J.G. Leggat*, I.B. Leggat, A.R. MacGibbon, L.S.M. Miller, F.L.H. Mooney, G.W.F. Overton, M.B. Poore, J.R. Reid, B. Sutcliffe.

9) **1955/1956 to Pakistan and India**
H.B. Cave *(captain)*, J.C. Alabaster, J.W. Guy, J.A. Hayes, N.S. Harford, P.G.Z. Harris, J.G. Leggat, A.R. MacGibbon, S.N. McGregor, T.G. McMahon, A.M. Moir, E.C. Petrie, M.B. Poore, J.R. Reid, B. Sutcliffe.

10) **1958 to Great Britain**
J.R. Reid *(captain)*, J.C. Alabaster, R.W. Blair, H.B. Cave, J.W. D'Arcy, N.S. Harford, J.A. Hayes, T. Meale, A.R. MacGibbon, L.S.M. Miller, A.M. Moir, E.C. Petrie, W.R. Playle, J.T. Sparling, B. Sutcliffe, J.T. Ward.

11) **1961/62 to South Africa and Australia**
J.R. Reid *(captain)*, J.C. Alabaster, G.A. Bartlett, P.T. Barton, F.J. Cameron, M.E. Chapple, A.E. Dick, G.T. Dowling, J.W. Guy, P.G.Z. Harris, S.N. McGregor, R.C. Motz, J.T. Sparling, J.T. Ward, B.W. Yuile.

12) **1964/65 to India, Pakistan, Great Britain, Holland, Bermuda and USA**
J.R. Reid *(captain)*, F.J. Cameron, R.O. Collinge, B.E. Congdon, A.E. Dick*, G.T. Dowling, T.W. Jarvis, R.C. Motz, R.W. Morgan, V. Pollard, B.W. Sinclair, B. Sutcliffe, B.R. Taylor, G.E. Vivian, J.T. Ward, B.W. Yuile.

13) **1967/68 to Australia**
B.W. Sinclair *(captain)*, J.C. Alabaster, M.G. Burgess, R.O. Collinge, B.E. Congdon, R.I. Harford, T.W. Jarvis, R.C. Motz, B.A.G. Murray, V. Pollard, B.R. Taylor, K. Thomson, B.W. Yuile.

14) **1969 to Great Britain, India and Pakistan**
G.T. Dowling *(captain)*, M.G. Burgess, R.O. Collinge, B.E. Congdon, R.S. Cunis, D.R. Hadlee, B.F. Hastings, H.J. Howarth, B.A.G. Murray, B.D. Milburn, V. Pollard, B.R. Taylor, D.G. Trist*, G.M. Turner, K.J. Wadsworth, B.W. Yuile.

15) **1969/70 to Australia**
G.T. Dowling *(captain)*, M.G. Burgess, R.O. Collinge, B.E. Congdon, R.S. Cunis, D.R. Hadlee, B.F. Hastings, H.J. Howarth, R.W. Morgan*, B.W. Sinclair, G.M. Turner, G.E. Vivian, K.J. Wadsworth.

16) **1970/1971 to Australia**
G.T. Dowling *(captain)*, M.G. Burgess, B.E. Congdon, R.O. Collinge, R.S. Cunis, H.J. Howarth, T.W. Jarvis, R.W. Morgan, B.R. Taylor, G.M. Turner, G.E. Vivian, K.J. Wadsworth.

17) **1971/72 to Australia**
R.W. Morgan *(captain)*, B. Andrews, R.W. Anderson, B. Dunning, B.G. Hadlee, R.J. Hadlee, W.A. Greenstreet, G.A. Newdick, R.E. Redmond, M.L. Ryan, M.J.F. Shrimpton, D.G. Trist.

18) **1971/72 to West Indies**
G.T. Dowling *(captain)*, J.C. Alabaster, M.G. Burgess, K.O. Campbell, M.E. Chapple*, R.O. Collinge, B.E. Congdon, R.S. Cunis, B.F. Hastings, H.J. Howarth, T.W. Jarvis, R.W. Morgan*, B.R. Taylor, G.M. Turner, G.E. Vivian, K.J. Wadsworth, M.G. Webb.

19) **1972/73 to Australia**
B.E. Congdon *(captain)*, B. Andrews, R.S. Cunis, B. Dunning, R.J. Hadlee, B.F. Hastings, A.B. Jordan, D.R. O'Sullivan, R.E. Redmond, G.M. Turner, G.E. Vivian, K.J. Wadsworth.

20) **1973 to Great Britain**
B.E. Congdon *(captain)*, R.W. Anderson, M.G. Burgess, R.O. Collinge, E.K. Gillott, D.R. Hadlee, R.J. Hadlee, B.F. Hastings, H.J. Howarth, J.M. Parker, V. Pollard, R.E. Redmond, B.R. Taylor, G.M. Turner, K.J. Wadsworth.

21) **1973/74 to Australia**
B.E. Congdon *(captain)*, G.D. Alabaster, B. Andrews, K.O. Campbell, B.L. Cairns, J.V. Coney*, D.R. Hadlee, R.J. Hadlee, B.F. Hastings, J.F.M. Morrison, D.R. O'Sullivan, J.M. Parker, M.J.F. Shrimpton, G.M. Turner, K.J. Wadsworth.

22) **1974/75 to Australia**
B.E. Congdon *(captain)*, B.L. Cairns, E.J. Chatfield, R.O. Collinge, G.N. Edwards, D.R. Hadlee, B.F. Hastings, G.P. Howarth, H.J. Howarth, J.F.M. Morrison, J.M. Parker, G.M. Turner, K.J. Wadsworth.

23) **1975 to England** *(World Cup)*
G.M. Turner *(captain)*, B.L. Cairns, R.O. Collinge, B.G. Hadlee, D.R. Hadlee, R.J. Hadlee, B.F. Hastings, G.P. Howarth, H.J. Howarth, B.J. McKechnie, J.F.M. Morrison, D.R. O'Sullivan, J.M. Parker, K.J. Wadsworth.

24) **1976/77 to Pakistan and India**
G.M. Turner *(captain)*, R.W. Anderson, M.G. Burgess, B.L. Cairns, R.O. Collinge, R.J. Hadlee, G.P. Howarth, W.K. Lees, J.F.M. Morrison, D.R. O'Sullivan, J.M. Parker, N.M. Parker, P.J. Petherick, A.D.G. Roberts, G.B. Troup.

25) **1978 to Great Britain**
M.G. Burgess *(captain)*, R.W. Anderson, S.L. Boock, B.P. Bracewell, B.L. Cairns, R.O. Collinge*, B.E. Congdon, B.A. Edgar, G.N. Edwards, D.R. Hadlee, R.J. Hadlee, G.P. Howarth, J.M. McIntyre, J.M. Parker, G.B. Thomson, G.B. Troup*, J.G. Wright.

26) **1979 to England** *(World Cup)*
M.G. Burgess *(captain)*, B.L. Cairns, E.J. Chatfield, J.V. Coney, B.A. Edgar, R.J. Hadlee, G.P. Howarth, W.K. Lees, B.J. McKechnie, J.F.M. Morrison, L.W. Stott, G.B. Troup, G.M. Turner, J.G. Wright.

27) **1980/81 to Australia**
G.P. Howarth *(captain)*, B.P. Bracewell*, J.G. Bracewell, S.L. Boock, M.G. Burgess, B.L. Cairns, E.J. Chatfield, J.V. Coney, B.A. Edgar, R.J. Hadlee, W.K. Lees, P.E. McEwan, B.J. McKechnie*, J.M. Parker, I.D.S. Smith, M.C. Snedden, G.B. Troup, J.G. Wright.

28) **1982/83 to Australia**
   G.P. Howarth *(captain)*, B.R. Blair, S.M. Carrington, E.J. Chatfield, J.V. Coney, M.D. Crowe, B.A. Edgar, W.K. Lees, J.F.M. Morrison, J.F. Reid, G.K. Robertson, M.C. Snedden, G.B. Troup.

29) **1982/83 to Australia**
   G.P. Howarth *(captain)*, B.L. Cairns, E.J. Chatfield, J.V. Coney, J.J. Crowe, M.D. Crowe*, B.A. Edgar, T.J. Franklin*, R.J. Hadlee, W.K. Lees, J.F.M. Morrison, M.C. Snedden, G.B. Troup, G.M. Turner, P.N. Webb, R.J. Webb*, J.G. Wright.

30) **1983 to England**
   G.P. Howarth *(captain)*, J.G. Bracewell, B.L. Cairns, E.J. Chatfield, J.V. Coney, J.J. Crowe, M.D. Crowe, B.A. Edgar, T.J. Franklin, E.J. Gray, R.J. Hadlee, W.K. Lees, I.D.S. Smith, M.C. Snedden, S.R. Tracy*, G.M. Turner, J.G. Wright.

31) **1983/84 to Sri Lanka**
   G.P. Howarth *(captain)*, S.L. Boock, J.G. Bracewell, B.L. Cairns, E.J. Chatfield, J.V. Coney, J.J. Crowe, M.D. Crowe, B.A. Edgar, R.J. Hadlee, J.F. Reid, I.D.S. Smith, D.A. Stirling, J.G. Wright.

32) **1984/85 to Pakistan and Sri Lanka**
   J.V. Coney *(captain)*, S.L. Boock, J.G. Bracewell, B.L. Cairns, E.J. Chatfield, J.J. Crowe, M.D. Crowe, B.A. Edgar, E.J. Gray, P.E. McEwan, J.F. Reid, I.D.S. Smith, M.C. Snedden, D.A. Stirling, J.G. Wright.

33) **1984/85 to Australia** *(World Championship of Cricket)*
   G.P. Howarth *(captain)*, B.P. Bracewell, J.G. Bracewell, B.L. Cairns, E.J. Chatfield, J.V. Coney, J.J. Crowe, M.D. Crowe, R.J. Hadlee, P.E. McEwan, J.F. Reid, I.D.S. Smith, M.C. Snedden, J.G. Wright.

34) **1984/85 to West Indies**
   G.P. Howarth *(captain)*, S.L. Boock, J.G. Bracewell, B.L. Cairns, E.J. Chatfield, J.V. Coney, J.J. Crowe, M.D. Crowe, R.J. Hadlee, R.T. Hart, K.R. Rutherford, I.D.S. Smith, D.A. Stirling, G.B. Troup, J.G. Wright.

35) **1985/86 to Australia**
   J.V. Coney *(captain)*, S.L. Boock, J.G. Bracewell*, V.R. Brown, B.L. Cairns, E.J. Chatfield, J.J. Crowe, M.D. Crowe, B.A. Edgar, T.J. Franklin, R.J. Hadlee, E.B. McSweeney*, J.F. Reid, I.D.S. Smith, M.C. Snedden, J.G. Wright.

36) **1985/86 to Australia**
   J.V. Coney *(captain)*, B.R. Blair, S.L. Boock, J.G. Bracewell, E.J. Chatfield, J.J. Crowe, M.D. Crowe, B.A. Edgar, S.R. Gillespie, R.J. Hadlee, E.B. McSweeney, J.F. Reid, M.C. Snedden, J.G. Wright.

37) **1985/86 to Sri Lanka, Sharjah and Hong Kong**
   J.G. Wright *(captain)*, T.E. Blain, B.R. Blair, J.G. Bracewell, E.J. Chatfield, J.J. Crowe, M.D. Crowe, E.J. Gray, E.B. McSweeney, G.K. Robertson, K.R. Rutherford, M.C. Snedden, W. Watson.

38) **1986 to England and Holland**
   J.V. Coney *(captain)*, B.J. Barrett, T.E. Blain, J.G. Bracewell, E.J. Chatfield, J.J. Crowe, M.D. Crowe, B.A. Edgar, T.J. Franklin, E.J. Gray, R.J. Hadlee, K.R. Rutherford, I.D.S. Smith, D.A. Stirling, W. Watson, J.G. Wright.

39) **1986/87 to Sri Lanka**
   J.J. Crowe *(captain)*, J.G. Bracewell, E.J. Chatfield, M.D. Crowe, E.J. Gray, R.J. Hadlee, P.A. Horne, A.H. Jones, E.B. McSweeney, D.K. Morrison, D.N. Patel, K.R. Rutherford, I.D.S. Smith, M.C. Snedden.

40) **1987/88 to India** *(World Cup)*
   J.J. Crowe *(captain)*, S.L. Boock, J.G. Bracewell, E.J. Chatfield, M.D. Crowe, P.A. Horne, A.H. Jones, D.K. Morrison, D.N. Patel, K.R. Rutherford, I.D.S. Smith, M.C. Snedden, W. Watson, J.G. Wright.

41) **1987/88 to Australia**
   J.J. Crowe *(captain)*, T.E. Blain*, J.G. Bracewell, V.R. Brown*, E.J. Chatfield, M.D. Crowe, S.R. Gillespie*, E.J. Gray, R.J. Hadlee, P.A. Horne, A.H. Jones, D.K. Morrison, D.N. Patel, K.R. Rutherford, I.D.S. Smith, M.C. Snedden, W. Watson, J.G. Wright.

42) **1987/88 to Sharjah**
J.G. Wright *(captain)*, T.E. Blain, E.J. Chatfield, M.J. Greatbatch, R.J. Hadlee, A.H. Jones, C.M. Kuggeleijn, D.K. Morrison, D.N. Patel, K.R. Rutherford, I.D.S. Smith, R.H. Vance, W. Watson.

43) **1988/89 to India**
J.G. Wright *(captain)*, T.E. Blain, J.G. Bracewell, E.J. Chatfield, T.J. Franklin, E.J. Gray, M.J. Greatbatch, R.J. Hadlee, A.H. Jones, C.M. Kuggeleijn, D.K. Morrison, K.R. Rutherford, I.D.S. Smith, M.C. Snedden, R.H. Vance, W. Watson*.

44) **1988/89 to Australia**
J.G. Wright *(captain)*, E.J. Chatfield, J.J. Crowe, M.D. Crowe, M.J. Greatbatch, A.H. Jones, C.M. Kuggeleijn, D.K. Morrison, I.D.S. Smith, M.C. Snedden, R.H. Vance, W. Watson.

45) **1989/90 to Australia**
J.G. Wright *(captain)*, B.P. Bracewell, J.G. Bracewell, C.L. Cairns*, J.J. Crowe, M.D. Crowe, M.J. Greatbatch, A.H. Jones, D.K. Morrison, D.N. Patel*, G.K. Robertson, I.D.S. Smith, M.C. Snedden, R.H. Vance, W. Watson.

46) **1990 to Sharjah and England**
J.G. Wright *(captain)*, J.G. Bracewell, J.J. Crowe, M.D. Crowe, T.J. Franklin, M.J. Greatbatch, Sir R.J. Hadlee, A.H. Jones, J.P. Millmow, D.K. Morrison, A.C. Parore, M.W. Priest, C. Pringle*, K.R. Rutherford, I.D.S. Smith, M.C. Snedden, S.A. Thomson, W. Watson*.

47) **1990/91 to Pakistan**
M.D. Crowe *(captain)*, G.E. Bradburn, T.J. Franklin, M.J. Greatbatch, P.A. Horne, D.K. Morrison, A.C. Parore, D.N. Patel, M.W. Priest, C. Pringle, S.J. Roberts, K.R. Rutherford, I.D.S. Smith, W. Watson, D.J. White.

48) **1990/91 to Australia**
M.D. Crowe *(captain)*, G.E. Bradburn, M.J. Greatbatch, C.Z. Harris, A.H. Jones, G.R. Larsen*, R.T. Latham, D.K. Morrison, R.G. Petrie, C. Pringle, R.B. Reid*, K.R. Rutherford, I.D.S. Smith, W. Watson, J.G. Wright, B.A. Young.

49) **1991/92 to Australia**
M.D. Crowe *(captain)*, G.E. Bradburn, C.L. Cairns, M.J. Greatbatch, C.Z. Harris, T.J. Franklin, A.H. Jones, D.K. Morrison, D.N. Patel, A.C. Parore, C. Pringle, I.D.S. Smith, S.A. Thomson, W. Watson, K.A. Wealleans.

50) **1992/93 to Zimbabwe and Sri Lanka**
M.D. Crowe *(captain)*, G.E. Bradburn*, S.B. Doull, M.J. Greatbatch, M.J. Haslam, C.Z. Harris, B.R. Hartland, A.H. Jones, G.R. Larsen, R.T. Latham, D.J. Nash, M.B. Owens*, D.N. Patel, A.C. Parore, C. Pringle*, K.R. Rutherford, M.L. Su'a, J.T.C. Vaughan*, W. Watson, J.G. Wright*.

51) **1993/94 to Australia**
M.D. Crowe *(captain)*, T.E. Blain, C.L. Cairns, S.B. Doull, R.P. de Groen*, M.J. Greatbatch, C.Z. Harris*, M.J. Haslam, A.H. Jones, R.T. Latham*, G.R. Larsen*, D.K. Morrison, D.N. Patel, B.A. Pocock, C. Pringle*, K.R. Rutherford, M.L. Su'a, S.A. Thomson*, W. Watson, D.J. White*, B.A. Young.

52) **1994 to Sharjah and England**
K.R. Rutherford *(captain)*, M.D. Crowe, H.T. Davis, M.W. Douglas, S.B. Doull, S.P. Fleming, M.J. Greatbatch, M.N. Hart, B.R. Hartland, C.Z. Harris, G.R. Larsen, D.K. Morrison, D.J. Nash, M.B. Owens*, A.C. Parore, B.A. Pocock, C. Pringle, S.A. Thomson, S.J. Roberts*, B.A. Young. (Harris and Douglas were selected only for Sharjah but Douglas re-appeared as an additional player during the England tour. Larsen captained the team in Sharjah as Rutherford was not available for that part of the tour).

53) **1994/95 to India and South Africa**
K.R. Rutherford *(captain)*, M.D. Crowe, R.P. de Groen, S.B. Doull, S.P. Fleming, L.K. Germon, C.Z. Harris, M.N. Hart, B.R. Hartland, D.K. Morrison*, D.J. Murray, D.J. Nash, A.C. Parore, M.W. Priest*, C. Pringle, M.L. Su'a, S.A. Thomson, B.A. Young.

54) **1995/96 to India**
L.K. Germon *(captain)*, N.J. Astle*, C.L. Cairns, M.D. Crowe, S.B. Doull, S.P. Fleming, A.J. Gale, M.J. Greatbatch, M.N. Hart, M.J. Haslam, G.R. Larsen*, D.K. Morrison, D.J. Nash, A.C. Parore, S.A. Thomson, R.G. Twose, B.A. Young.

55) **1995/96 to India and Pakistan** *(World Cup)*
L.K. Germon *(captain)*, N.J. Astle, C.L. Cairns, S.P. Fleming, C.Z. Harris, R.J. Kennedy, G.R. Larsen, D.K. Morrison, D.J. Nash, A.C. Parore, D.N. Patel, C.M. Spearman, S.A. Thomson, R.G. Twose.

56) **1995/96 to West Indies**
L.K. Germon *(captain)*, N.J. Astle, M.D. Bailey*, C.L. Cairns, S.P. Fleming, C.Z. Harris, M.J. Haslam*, R.J. Kennedy, G.R. Larsen, D.K. Morrison, D.J. Nash, A.C. Parore, D.N. Patel, C.M. Spearman, S.A. Thomson, R.G. Twose, J.T.C. Vaughan*.

57) **1996/97 to Sharjah and Pakistan**
L.K. Germon *(captain)*, N.J. Astle, C.L. Cairns, S.B. Doull, S.P. Fleming, M.J. Greatbatch, C.Z. Harris, M.N. Hart*, M.J. Haslam, G.R. Jonas*, R.J. Kennedy*, G.R. Larsen, D.K. Morrison, A.C. Parore, D.N. Patel, C.M. Spearman, J.T.C. Vaughan, P.J. Wiseman*, B.A. Young.

58) **1996/97 to India** *(Independence Cup)*
S.P. Fleming *(captain)*, N.J. Astle, C.L. Cairns, H.T. Davis, C.Z. Harris, M.J. Horne, G.R. Larsen, C.D. McMillan, S.B. O'Connor, A.C. Parore, D.N. Patel, A.J. Penn, D.L. Vettori, B.A. Young.

59) **1997/98 to Kenya & Zimbabwe**
S.P. Fleming *(captain)*, N.J. Astle, C.L. Cairns, H.T. Davis, C.Z. Harris, M.J. Horne, G.R. Larsen, C.D. McMillan, S.B. O'Connor, A.C. Parore, B.A. Pocock, D.G. Sewell, C.M. Spearman, D.L. Vettori, P.J. Wiseman.

60) **1997/98 to Australia**
S.P. Fleming *(captain)*, G.I. Allott, N.J. Astle, C.L. Cairns, H.T. Davis, S.B. Doull, C.J. Drum*, C.Z. Harris*, M.J. Horne, G.R. Larsen*, C.D. McMillan, D.J. Nash*, S.B. O'Connor, A.C. Parore, B.A. Pocock, C.M. Spearman*, R.G. Twose*, D.L. Vettori, B.A. Young.

61) **1997/98 to Sharjah**
S.P. Fleming *(captain)*, N.J. Astle, C.L. Cairns, S.B. Doull, C.Z. Harris, M.J. Horne, L.G. Howell, C.D. McMillan, D.J. Nash, S.B. O'Connor, A.C. Parore, M.W. Priest, P.J. Wiseman.

62) **1997/98 to Sri Lanka**
S.P. Fleming *(captain)*, N.J. Astle, C.L. Cairns, S.B. Doull, C.Z. Harris, M.J. Horne, C.D. McMillan, D.J. Nash, S.B. O'Connor, A.C. Parore, M.W. Priest, C.M. Spearman, A.R. Tait*, D.L. Vettori, P.J. Wiseman, B.A. Young.

63) **1998 to Malaysia** *(Commonwealth Games)*
S.P. Fleming *(captain)*, G.I. Allott, N.J. Astle, M.D. Bailey, M.D. Bell, C.J. Drum, C.Z. Harris, M.J. Horne, C.D. McMillan, S.B. O'Connor, A.C. Parore, A.R. Tait, D.L. Vettori, P.J. Wiseman.

64) **1998/99 to Bangladesh** *(Wills International Cup)*
S.P. Fleming *(captain)*, G.I. Allott, N.J. Astle, M.D. Bailey, M.D. Bell, S.B. Doull, C.Z. Harris, M.J. Horne, C.D. McMillan, S.B. O'Connor, A.C. Parore, A.R. Tait, D.L. Vettori, P.J. Wiseman.

65) **1999 to England**
S.P. Fleming *(captain)*, G.I. Allott, N.J. Astle, M.D. Bell*, C.E. Bulfin, C.L. Cairns, M.G. Croy*, S.B. Doull, C.Z. Harris, M.N. Hart, M.J. Horne, G.R. Larsen, C.D. McMillan, D.J. Nash, S.B. O'Connor*, A.C. Parore, A.J. Penn*, R.G. Twose, D.L. Vettori, B.G.K. Walker*.

66) **1999/00 to India**
S.P. Fleming *(captain)*, N.J. Astle, M.D. Bell, C.L. Cairns, C.J. Drum, C.Z. Harris, M.J. Horne, C.D. McMillan, D.J. Nash, S.B. O'Connor, A.C. Parore, A.J. Penn, C.M. Spearman, G.R. Stead*, S.B. Styris*, A.R. Tait*, R.G. Twose*, D.L. Vettori, P.J. Wiseman.

67) **2000/01 to Singapore, Zimbabwe, Kenya & South Africa**
S.P. Fleming *(captain)*, G.I. Allott, N.J. Astle, C.L. Cairns, C.Z. Harris, M.J. Horne, C.D. McMillan, H.J.H. Marshall, C.S. Martin, D.J. Nash, C.J. Nevin, S.B. O'Connor, A.C. Parore, A.J. Penn, M.H. Richardson, M.S. Sinclair, C.M. Spearman, S.B. Styris, G.P. Sulzberger, D.R. Tuffey, R.G. Twose, D.L. Vettori, B.G.K. Walker, K.P. Walmsley, P.J. Wiseman. (Apart from a number of players being replaced because of injury, this party was reselected and changed several times depending on the nature of the matches being played).

68) 2000/01 to Sharjah
C.D. McMillan *(captain)*, A.R. Adams, M.D. Bell, G.E. Bradburn, J.E.C. Franklin, C.Z. Harris, K.D. Mills, C.J. Nevin, J.D.P. Oram, M.S. Sinclair, D.R.Tuffey, L. Vincent, B.G.K. Walker.

69) 2001/02 to Sri Lanka
S.P. Fleming *(captain)*, N.J. Astle, G.E. Bradburn, J.E.C. Franklin, C.Z. Harris, K.D. Mills, C.D. McMillan, D.J. Nash, J.D.P. Oram, A.C. Parore, M.S. Sinclair, D.R.Tuffey, D.L. Vettori, L. Vincent.

70) 2001/02 to Australia
S.P. Fleming *(captain)*, A.R. Adams, N.J. Astle, M.D. Bell, S.E. Bond*, C.L. Cairns, C.J. Drum*, J.E.C. Franklin, C.Z. Harris, B.B. McCullum, C.D. McMillan, C.S. Martin, D.J. Nash, S.B. O'Çonnor, A.C. Parore, M.H. Richardson, M.S. Sinclair, S.B. Styris, G.P. Sulzberger, D.R. Tuffey, D.L. Vettori, L. Vincent, P.J. Wiseman*.

71) 2001/02 to Sharjah & Pakistan
S.P. Fleming *(captain)*, A.R. Adams, N.J. Astle, I.G. Butler, J.E.C. Franklin, C.Z. Harris, R.G. Hart, M.J. Horne, C.D. McMillan, C.S. Martin, C.J. Nevin, J.D.P. Oram, M.H. Richardson, M.S. Sinclair, S.B. Styris, D.R. Tuffey, D.L. Vettori, L. Vincent, B.G.K. Walker.

72) 2001/02 to West Indies
S.P. Fleming *(captain)*, N.J. Astle, S.E. Bond, I.G. Butler, C.Z. Harris, M.N. Hart, R.G. Hart, P.A. Hitchcock, M.J. Horne, C.D. McMillan, C.S. Martin, C.J. Nevin, J.D.P. Oram, M.H. Richardson, S.B. Styris, D.R. Tuffey, D.L. Vettori, L. Vincent.

73) 2002/03 to Australia & Sri Lanka *(ICC Champions Trophy)*
S.P. Fleming *(captain)*, N.J. Astle, S.E. Bond, I.G. Butler*, C.Z. Harris, M.N. Hart*, P.A. Hitchcock, M.J. Horne*, C.D. McMillan*, K.D. Mills, C.J. Nevin, J.D.P. Oram, M.S. Sinclair, S.B. Styris, G.P. Sulzberger, D.R. Tuffey, D.L. Vettori, L. Vincent, B.G.K. Walker*, J.A.F. Yovich*.

74) 2002/03 to South Africa *(World Cup)*
S.P. Fleming *(captain)*, C.L. Cairns, A.R. Adams, N.J. Astle, S.E. Bond, C.Z. Harris, B.B. McCullum, C.D. McMillan, K.D. Mills, J.D.P. Oram, M.S. Sinclair, S.B. Styris, D.R. Tuffey, D.L. Vettori, L. Vincent.

75) 2002/03 to Sri Lanka
S.P. Fleming *(captain)*, A.R. Adams, S.E. Bond, I.G. Butler, C.L. Cairns, C.Z. Harris, R.G. Hart, M.J. Horne, R.A. Jones, B.B. McCullum, K.D. Mills, C.J. Nevin, J.D.P. Oram, M.H. Richardson, M.S. Sinclair, S.B. Styris, D.R.Tuffey, D.L. Vettori, L. Vincent, P.J. Wiseman.

* *replacement or temporary addition to the touring party*

NEW ZEALAND TEST RECORDS

REGISTER OF PLAYERS

	Born	*Died*	*Type*		*Test Career*
Adams	17/7/1975		RHB	RFM	2001/02
Andre Ryan	Auckland				
Alabaster	11/7/1930		RHB	RLB	1955/56-1971/72
John Chaloner	Invercargill				
Allcott	7/10/1896	19/11/1973	LHB	LM	1929/30-1931/32
Cyril Francis Walter	Lower Moutere	Auckland			
Allott	24/12/1971		RHB	LFM	1995/96-1999
Geoffrey Ian	Christchurch				
Anderson	2/10/1948		RHB	RLB	1976/77-1978
Robert Wickham	Christchurch				
Anderson	8/10/1919	21/12/1979	LHB	RLBG	1945/46
William McDougall	Westport	Christchurch			
Andrews	4/4/1945		RHB	RFM	1973/74
Bryan	Christchurch				
Astle	15/9/1971		RHB	RM	1995/96-2002/03
Nathan John	Christchurch				
Badcock	9/8/1897	19/9/1982	RHB	RM	1929/30-1932/33
Frederick Theodore	Abbottabad, India	Perth			
Barber	3/6/1925		RHB	WK	1955/56
Richard Trevor	Otaki				
Bartlett	3/2/1941		RHB	RF	1961/62-1967/68
Gary Alex	Blenheim				
Barton	9/10/1935		RHB	SLA	1961/62-1962/63
Paul Thomas	Wellington				
Beard	14/1/1920	15/7/1982	RHB	RM	1951/52-1955/56
Donald Derek	Palmerston North	Lancaster			
Beck	1/8/1934	23/4/2000	LHB		1953/54-1955/56
John Edward Francis	Wellington	Waikanae			
Bell	25/2/1977		RHB		1998/99-2001/02
Matthew David	Dunedin				
Bell	5/9/1931	23/7/2002	RHB	RLB	1953/54
William	Dunedin	Auckland			
Bilby	7/5/1941		RHB		1965/66
Grahame Paul	Wellington				
Blain	17/2/1962		RHB	WK	1986-1993/94
Tony Elston	Nelson				
Blair	23/6/1932		RHB	RFM	1952/53-1963/64
Robert William	Petone				
Blunt	3/11/1900	22/6/1966	RHB	RLBG	1929/30-1931/32
Roger Charles	Durham, England	London			
Bolton	31/5/1935		RHB	RLB	1958/59
Bruce Alfred	Christchurch				
Bond	7/6/1975		RHB	RF	2001/02-2002/03
Shane Edward	Christchurch				
Boock	20/9/1951		RHB	SLA	1977/78-1988/89
Stephen Lewis	Dunedin				
Bracewell	14/9/1959		RHB	RFM	1978-1984/85
Brendon Paul	Auckland				
Bracewell	15/4/1958		RHB	ROB	1980/81-1990
John Garry	Auckland				
Bradburn	26/5/1966		RHB	ROB	1990/91-2000/01
Grant Eric	Hamilton				
Bradburn	24/11/1938		RHB	RSM	1963/64
Wynne Pennell	Thames				
Brown	3/11/1959		LHB	ROB	1985/86
Vaughan Raymond	Christchurch				
Burgess	17/7/1944		RHB	ROB	1967/68-1980/81
Mark Gordon	Auckland				

	Born	Died	Type		Test Career
Burke Cecil	22/3/1914 Auckland	4/8/1997 Auckland	RHB	RLB	1945/46
Burtt Thomas Browning	22/1/1915 Christchurch	24/5/1988 Christchurch	RHB	SLA	1946/47-1952/53
Butler Ian Gareth	24/11/1981 Auckland		RHB	RF	2001/02
Butterfield Leonard Arthur	29/8/1913 Christchurch	5/7/1999 Christchurch	RHB	RM	1945/46
Cairns Bernard Lance	10/10/1949 Picton		RHB	RM	1973/74-1985/86
Cairns Christopher Lance	13/6/1970 Picton		RHB	RFM	1989/90-2001/02
Cameron Francis James	1/6/1932 Dunedin		RHB	RFM	1961/62-1965
Cave Henry Butler	10/10/1922 Wanganui	15/9/1989 Wanganui	RHB	RM	1949-1958
Chapple Murray Ernest	25/7/1930 Christchurch	31/7/1985 Hamilton	RHB	SLA	1952/53-1965/66
Chatfield Ewen John	3/7/1950 Dannevirke		RHB	RM	1974/75-1988/89
Cleverley Donald Charles	23/12/1909 Oamaru		LHB	RFM	1931/32-1945/46
Collinge Richard Owen	2/4/1946 Wellington		RHB	LFM	1964/65-1978
Colquhoun Ian Alexander	8/6/1924 Wellington		RHB	WK	1954/55
Coney Jeremy Vernon	21/6/1952 Wellington		RHB	RSM	1973/74-1986/87
Congdon Bevan Ernest	11/2/1938 Motueka		RHB	RM	1964/65-1978
Cowie John	30/3/1912 Auckland	3/6/1994 Lower Hutt	RHB	RFM	1937-1949
Cresswell George Fenwick	22/3/1915 Wanganui	10/1/1966 Blenheim	LHB	RM	1949-1950/51
Cromb Ian Burns	25/6/1905 Christchurch	6/3/1984 Christchurch	RHB	RM	1931-1931/32
Crowe Jeffrey John	14/9/1958 Auckland		RHB		1982/83-1989/90
Crowe Martin David	22/9/1962 Auckland		RHB	RM	1981/82-1995/96
Cunis Robert Smith	5/1/1941 Whangarei		RHB	RFM	1963/64-1971/72
D'Arcy John William	23/4/1936 Christchurch		RHB		1958
de Groen Richard Paul	5/8/1962 Otorohanga		RHB	RM	1993/94-1994/95
Davis Heath Te-Ihi-O-Te-Rangi	30/11/1971 Lower Hutt		RHB	RF	1994-1997/98
Dempster Charles Stewart	15/11/1903 Wellington	12/2/1974 Wellington	RHB		1929/30-1932/33
Dempster Eric William	25/1/1925 Wellington		LHB	SLA	1952/53-1953/54
Dick Arthur Edward	10/10/1936 Middlemarch		RHB	WK	1961/62-1965
Dickinson George Ritchie	11/3/1903 Dunedin	17/3/1978 Lower Hutt	RHB	RF	1929/30-1931/32
Donnelly Martin Paterson	17/10/1917 Ngaruawahia	22/10/1999 Sydney	LHB	SLA	1937-1949
Doull Simon Blair	6/8/1969 Pukekohe		RHB	RM	1992/93-1999/00
Dowling Graham Thorne	4/3/1937 Christchurch		RHB		1961/62-1971/72
Drum Christopher James	10/7/1974 Auckland		RHB	RFM	2000/01-2001/02
Dunning John Angus	6/2/1903 Omaha	24/6/1971 Adelaide	RHB	RM	1932/33-1937

	Born	Died	Type		Test Career
Edgar	23/11/1956		LHB	WK	1978-1986
Bruce Adrian	Wellington				
Edwards	27/5/1955		RHB	WK	1976/77-1980/81
Graham Neil	Nelson				
Emery	28/3/1915	18/12/1982	RHB	RM	1951/52
Raymond William George	Auckland	Auckland			
Fisher	28/7/1924	19/6/1996	RHB	LM	1952/53
Frederick Eric	Johnsonville	Palmerston North			
Fleming	1/4/1973		LHB		1993/94-2002/03
Stephen Paul	Christchurch				
Foley	28/1/1906	16/10/1948	LHB		1929/30
Henry	Wellington	Brisbane			
Franklin	7/11/1980		LHB	LFM	2000/01
James Edward Charles	Wellington				
Franklin	18/3/1962		RHB	RM	1983-1990/91
Trevor John	Auckland				
Freeman	8/9/1914	31/5/1994	RHB	RLBG	1932/33
Douglas Linford	Sydney	Sydney			
Gallichan	3/6/1906	25/3/1969	RHB	SLA	1937
Norman	Palmerston North	Taupo			
Gedye	2/5/1929		RHB		1963/64-1964/65
Sidney Graham	Otahuhu				
Germon	4/11/1968		RHB	WK	1995/96-1996/97
Lee Kenneth	Christchurch				
Gillespie	2/3/1957		RHB	RFM	1985/86
Stuart Ross	Wanganui				
Gray	18/11/1954		RHB	SLA	1983-1988/89
Evan John	Wellington				
Greatbatch	11/12/1963		LHB		1987/88-1996/97
Mark John	Auckland				
Guillen	24/9/1924		RHB	WK	1955/56
Simpson Clairmonte	Port of Spain, Trinidad				
Guy	29/8/1934		LHB		1955/56-1961/62
John William	Nelson				
Hadlee	6/1/1948		RHB	RM	1969-1977/78
Dayle Robert	Christchurch				
Hadlee	3/7/1951		LHB	RFM	1972/73-1990
Richard John	Christchurch				
Hadlee	4/6/1915		RHB		1937-1950/51
Walter Arnold	Lincoln				
Harford	30/8/1930	30/3/1981	RHB	RM	1955/56-1958
Noel Sherwin	Winton	Auckland			
Harford	30/5/1936		LHB	WK	1967/68
Roy Ivan	London, England				
Harris	20/11/1969		LHB	RM	1992/93-2001/02
Chris Zinzan	Christchurch				
Harris	18/7/1927	1/12/1991	RHB	ROB	1955/56-1964/65
Parke Gerald Zinzan	Christchurch	Christchurch			
Harris	27/7/1933		RHB	RM	1958/59
Roger Meredith	Otahuhu				
Hart	16/5/1972		LHB	SLA	1993/94-1995/96
Matthew Norman	Hamilton				
Hart	2/12/1974		RHB	WK	2001/02-2002/03
Robert Garry	Hamilton				
Hartland	22/10/1966		RHB		1991/92-1994
Blair Robert	Christchurch				
Haslam	26/9/1972		LHB	SLA	1992/93-1995/96
Mark James	Bury, England				
Hastings	23/3/1940		RHB		1968/69-1975/76
Brian Frederick	Wellington				
Hayes	11/1/1927		RHB	RF	1950/51-1958
John Arthur	Auckland				
Henderson	2/8/1895	17/6/1970	LHB	LFM	1929/30
Matthew	Auckland	Wellington			
Horne	5/12/1970		RHB	RM	1996/97-2002/03
Matthew Jeffery	Auckland				

	Born	Died	Type			Test Career
Horne	21/1/1960		LHB			1986/87-1990/91
Philip Andrew	Upper Hutt					
Hough	24/10/1928		RHB	RM		1958/59
Kenneth William	Sydney					
Howarth	29/3/1951		RHB	ROB		1974/75-1984/85
Geoffrey Philip	Auckland					
Howarth	25/12/1943		LHB	SLA		1969-1976/77
Hedley John	Auckland					
James	12/3/1904	21/8/1976	RHB	WK		1929/30-1932/33
Kenneth Cecil	Wellington	Palmerston North				
Jarvis	29/7/1944		RHB			1964/65-1972/73
Terrence Wayne	Auckland					
Jones	9/5/1959		RHB	ROB		1986/87-1994/95
Andrew Howard	Wellington					
Kennedy	3/6/1972		RHB	RFM		1995/96
Robert John	Dunedin					
Kerr	28/12/1910		RHB			1931-1937
John Lambert	Dannevirke					
Kuggeleijn	10/5/1956		RHB	ROB		1988/89
Christopher Mary	Auckland					
Larsen	27/9/1962		RHB	RM		1994-1995/96
Gavin Rolf	Wellington					
Latham	12/6/1961		RHB			1991/92-1992/93
Rodney Terry	Christchurch					
Lees	19/3/1952		RHB	WK		1976/77-1983
Warren Kenneth	Dunedin					
Leggat	7/6/1930		RHB	RM		1953/54
Ian Bruce	Invercargill					
Leggat	27/5/1926	9/3/1973	RHB			1951/52-1955/56
John Gordon	Wellington	Christchurch				
Lissette	6/11/1919	24/1/1973	RHB	SLA		1955/56
Allen Fisher	Morrinsville	Hamilton				
Loveridge	15/1/1975		RHB	RLB		1995/96
Greg Riaka	Palmerston North					
Lowry	17/2/1898	20/7/1976	RHB	ROB	WK	1929/30-1931
Thomas Coleman	Fernhill	Hastings				
McEwan	19/12/1953		RHB	RM		1979/80-1984/85
Paul Ernest	Christchurch					
MacGibbon	28/8/1924		RHB	RFM		1950/51-1958
Anthony Roy	Christchurch					
McGirr	5/11/1891	14/4/1964	RHB	RFM		1929/30
Herbert Mendelson	Wellington	Nelson				
McGregor	18/12/1931		RHB			1954/55-1964/65
Spencer Noel	Dunedin					
McLeod	14/10/1900	14/9/1989	LHB	RLB		1929/30
Edwin George	Auckland	Wellington				
McMahon	8/11/1929		RHB	WK		1955/56
Trevor George	Wellington					
McMillan	13/9/1976		RHB	RM		1997/98-2002/03
Craig Douglas	Christchurch					
McRae	25/12/1912	10/8/1986	LHB	LM		1945/46
Donald Alexander Noel	Christchurch	Christchurch				
Marshall	15/2/1979		RHB			2000/01
Hamish John Hamilton	Warkworth					
Martin	10/12/1974		RHB	RFM		2000/01-2001/02
Christopher Stewart	Christchurch					
Matheson	27/2/1906	31/12/1985	RHB	RFM		1929/30-1931
Alexander Malcolm	Omaha	Auckland				
Meale	11/11/1928		LHB			1958
Trevor	Auckland					
Merritt	18/8/1908	9/6/1977	RHB	RLBG		1929/30-1931
William Edward	Sumner	Christchurch				
Meuli	20/2/1926		RHB	RLB		1952/53
Edgar Milton	Hawera					
Milburn	24/11/1943		RHB	WK		1968/69
Barry Douglas	Dunedin					

	Born	Died	Type		Test Career
Miller	31/3/1923	17/12/1996	LHB	LSM	1952/53-1958
Lawrence Somerville Martin	New Plymouth	Kapiti			
Mills	3/9/1905	11/12/1972	LHB		1929/30-1932/33
John Ernest	Dunedin	Hamilton			
Moir	17/7/1919	17/6/2000	RHB	RLB	1950/51-1958/59
Alexander McKenzie	Dunedin	Dunedin			
Moloney	11/8/1910	15/7/1942	RHB	RLB	1937
Denis Andrew Robert	Dunedin	El Alamein			
Mooney	26/5/1921		RHB	WK	1949-1953/54
Francis Leonard Hugh	Wellington				
Morgan	12/2/1941		RHB	ROB	1964/65-1971/72
Ross Winston	Auckland				
Morrison	17/12/1933		LHB	RM	1962/63
Bruce Donald	Lower Hutt				
Morrison	3/2/1966		RHB	RFM	1987/88-1996/97
Daniel Kyle	Auckland				
Morrison	27/8/1947		RHB	SLA	1973/74-1981/82
John Francis MacLean	Wellington				
Motz	12/1/1940		RHB	RFM	1961/62-1969
Richard Charles	Christchurch				
Murray	18/9/1940		RHB	RLB	1967/68-1970/71
Bruce Alexander Grenfell	Wellington				
Murray	4/9/1967		RHB		1994/95
Darrin James	Christchurch				
Nash	20/11/1971		RHB	RFM	1992/93-2001/02
Dion Joseph	Auckland				
Newman	3/7/1902	23/9/1996	RHB	LM	1931/32-1932/33
Jack	Brightwater	Nelson			
O'Connor	15/11/1973		LHB	LFM	1997/98-2001/02
Shayne Barry	Hastings				
Oram	28/7/1978		LHB	RM	2002/03
Jacob David Philip	Palmerston North				
O'Sullivan	16/11/1944		RHB	SLA	1972/73-1976/77
David Robert	Palmerston North				
Overton	8/6/1919	7/9/1993	LHB	RFM	1953/54
Guy William Fitzroy	Dunedin	Winton			
Owens	11/11/1969		RHB	RFM	1992/93-1994
Michael Barry	Christchurch				
Page	8/5/1902	13/2/1987	RHB	ROB	1929/30-1937
Milford Laurenson	Lyttelton	Christchurch			
Parker	21/2/1951		RHB	WK	1972/73-1980/81
John Morton	Dannevirke				
Parker	28/8/1948		RHB	RLB	1976/77
Norman Murray	Dannevirke				
Parore	23/1/1971		RHB	WK	1990-2001/02
Adam Craig	Auckland				
Patel	25/10/1958		RHB	ROB	1986/87-1996/97
Dipak Narshibhai	Nairobi, Kenya				
Petherick	25/9/1942		RHB	ROB	1976/77
Peter James	Ranfurly				
Petrie	22/5/1927		RHB	WK	1955/56-1965/66
Eric Charlton	Ngaruawahia				
Playle	1/12/1938		RHB		1958-1962/63
William Rodger	Palmerston North				
Pocock	18/6/1971		RHB		1993/94-1997/98
Blair Andrew	Papakura				
Pollard	7/9/1945		RHB	ROB	1964/65-1973
Victor	Burnley, England				
Poore	1/6/1930		RHB	ROB	1952/53-1955/56
Matt Beresford	Christchurch				
Priest	12/8/1961		LHB	SLA	1990-1997/98
Mark Wellings	Greymouth				
Pringle	26/1/1968		RHB	RFM	1990/91-1994/95
Christopher	Auckland				
Puna	28/10/1929	7/6/1996	RHB	ROB	1965/66
Narotam	Surat, India	Hamilton			

	Born	Died	Type			Test Career
Rabone Geoffrey Osbourne	6/11/1921 Gore		RHB	ROB		1949-1954/55
Redmond Rodney Ernest	29/12/1944 Whangarei		LHB	SLA		1972/73
Reid John Fulton	3/3/1956 Auckland		LHB	RLB	WK	1978/79-1985/86
Reid John Richard	3/6/1928 Auckland		RHB	RFM	WK	1949-1965
Richardson Mark Hunter	11/6/1971 Hastings		LHB	SLA		2000/01-2002/03
Roberts Andrew Duncan Glenn	6/5/1947 Te Aroha	26/10/1989 Wellington	RHB	RM		1975/76-1976/77
Roberts Albert William	20/8/1909 Christchurch	13/5/1978 Christchurch	RHB	RM		1929/30-1937
Robertson Gary Keith	15/7/1960 New Plymouth		RHB	RFM		1985/86
Rowe Charles Gordon	30/6/1915 Glasgow, Scotland	9/6/1995 Palmerston North	RHB			1945/46
Rutherford Kenneth Robert	26/10/1965 Dunedin		RHB	RM		1984/85-1994/95
Scott Roy Hamilton	6/3/1917 Clyde		RHB	RM		1946/47
Scott Verdun John	31/7/1916 Devonport	2/8/1980 Devonport	RHB	RM		1945/46-1951/52
Sewell David Graham	20/10/1977 Christchurch		RHB	LFM		1997/98
Shrimpton Michael John Froud	23/6/1940 Feilding		RHB	RLBG		1962/63-1973/74
Sinclair Barry Whitley	23/10/1936 Wellington		RHB			1962/63-1967/68
Sinclair Ian McKay	1/6/1933 Rangiora		LHB	ROB		1955/56
Sinclair Mathew Stuart	9/11/1975 Katherine, Australia		RHB			1999/00-2002/03
Smith Frank Brunton	13/3/1922 Rangiora	6/7/1997 Christchurch	RHB			1946/47-1951/52
Smith Horace Dennis	8/1/1913 Toowoomba, Aust	25/1/1986 Christchurch	RHB	RFM		1932/33
Smith Ian David Stockley	28/2/1957 Nelson		RHB	WK		1980/81-1991/92
Snedden Colin Alexander	7/1/1918 Auckland		RHB	ROB		1946/47
Snedden Martin Colin	23/11/1958 Auckland		LHB	RFM		1980/81-1990
Sparling John Trevor	24/7/1938 Auckland		RHB	ROB		1958-1963/64
Spearman Craig Murray	4/7/1972 Auckland		RHB			1995/96-2000/01
Stead Gary Raymond	9/1/1972 Christchurch		RHB	RLB		1998/99-1999/00
Stirling Derek Alexander	5/10/1961 Upper Hutt		RHB	RFM		1984/85-1986
Styris Scott Bernard	10/7/1975 Brisbane, Aust		RHB	RM		2001/02-2002/03
Su'a Murphy Logo	7/11/1966 Wanganui		LHB	LFM		1991/92-1994/95
Sutcliffe Bert	17/11/1923 Auckland	20/4/2001 Auckland	LHB	SLA		1946/47-1965
Taylor Bruce Richard	12/7/1943 Timaru		LHB	RFM		1964/65-1973
Taylor Donald Dougald	2/3/1923 Auckland	5/12/1980 Auckland	RHB	RLBG		1946/47-1955/56
Thomson Keith	26/2/1941 Methven		RHB			1967/68
Thomson Shane Alexander	27/1/1969 Hamilton		RH1B	ROB		1989/90-1995/96

	Born	Died	Type		Test Career
Tindill Eric William Thomas	18/12/1910 Nelson		LHB	WK	1937-1946/47
Troup Gary Bertram	3/10/1952 Taumarunui		RHB	LFM	1976/77-1985/86
Truscott Peter Bennetts	14/8/1941 Pahiatua		RHB		1964/65
Tuffey Daryl Raymond	11/6/1978 Milton		RHB	RFM	1999/00-2002/03
Turner Glenn Maitland	26/5/1947 Dunedin		RHB		1968/69-1982/83
Twose Roger Graham	17/4/1968 Torquay, England		LHB	RM	1995/96-1999
Vance Robert Howard	31/3/1955 Wellington		RHB		1987/88-1989/90
Vaughan Justin Thomas Caldwell	30//8/1967 Hereford, England		LHB	RM	1992/93-1996/97
Vettori Daniel Luca	27/1/1979 Auckland		LHB	SLA	1996/97-2002/03
Vincent Lou	11/11/1978 Warkworth		RHB	WK	2001/02-2002/03
Vivian Graham Ellery	28/2/1946 Auckland		LHB	RLB	1964/65-1971/72
Vivian Henry Gifford	4/11/1912 Auckland	12/8/1983 Auckland	LHB	SLA	1931-1937
Wadsworth Kenneth John	30/11/1946 Nelson	19/8/1976 Nelson	RHB	WK	1969-1975/76
Walker Brooke Graeme Keith	25/3/1977 Auckland		RHB	RLB	2000/01-2001/02
Wallace Walter Mervyn	19/12/1916 Auckland		RHB		1936-1952/53
Walmsley Kerry Peter	23/8/1973 Dunedin		RHB	RFM	1994/95-2000/01
Ward John Thomas	11/3/1937 Timaru		RHB	WK	1963/64-1967/68
Watson William	31/8/1965 Auckland		RHB	RFM	1986-1993/94
Watt Leslie	17/9/1924 Waitati	15/11/1996 Dunedin	RHB		1954/55
Webb Murray George	22/6/1947 Invercargill		RHB	RFM	1970/71-1973/74
Webb Peter Neil	14/7/1957 Auckland		RHB	WK	1979/80
Weir Gordon Lindsay	2/6/1908 Auckland		RHB	RM	1929/30-1937
White David John	26/6/1961 Gisborne		RHB	ROB	1990/91
Whitelaw Paul Erskine	10/2/1910 Auckland	28/8/1988 Auckland	RHB		1932/33
Wiseman Paul John	4/5/1970 Auckland		RHB	ROB	1997/98-2002/03
Wright John Geoffrey	5/7/1954 Darfield		LHB	RM	1977/78-1992/93
Young Bryan Andrew	3/11/1964 Whangarei		RHB	WK	1993/94-1998/99
Yuile Bryan William	29/10/1941 Palmerston North		RHB	SLA	1962/63-1969/70

TEST UMPIRES

The following is the complete list of New Zealand test umpires as at 1 July, 2003:

Dunne R.S.	39 *	Morris G.C.	4	Watkin E.A.	2
Aldridge B.L.	26 *	Cobcroft L.T.	3	Page W.P.	1
Goodall F.R.	24	McLellan J.	3	Burgess T.	1
Woodward S.J.	24	Pearce T.M.	3	Torrance R.C.	1
Cowie D.B.	22 *	Cowie J.	3	Gourlay H.W.	1
Martin W.T.	15	Gwynne W.J.C.	3	Montgomery O.R.	1
Copps D.E.A.	13	Kinsella D.A.	3	Brook E.G.	1
Gardiner W.R.C.	9	McHarg R.L.	3	Vine B.	1
Shortt R.W.R.	9	King C.E.	3	Jelley A.E.	1
MacKintosh E.C.A.	8	Butler W.	2	Tindill E.W.T.	1
Hastie J.B.R.	7	Forrester J.T.	2	Johnston L.C.	1
Cave K.	6	Brown J.M.A.	2	Burns D.C.	1
Monteith R.L.	6	Tonkinson S.B.	2	Cassie H.B.	1
Bowden B.F.	6 *	Currie R.G.	2	Bricknell B.A.	1
Quested D.M.	5	Clark L.G.	2	Higginson I.C.	1
Pengelly M.F.	4	Dumbleton D.P.	2	Hill A.L.	1
Harris J.C.	4				

* includes test matches overseas

The following overseas umpires have stood in test matches in New Zealand:

Harper D.J. *(Australia)*	6	Elliott C.S. *(England)*	1
Randell S.G. *(Australia)*	3	Barker L.H. *(West Indies)*	1
Hair D.B. *(Australia)*	3	Khizar Hayat *(Pakistan)*	1
Venkataraghavan S. *(India)*	3	Plews N.T. *(England)*	1
de Silva E.A.R. *(Sri Lanka)*	3	Robinson I.D. *(Zimbabwe)*	1
Bird H.D. *(England)*	2	Nichols E.A. *(West Indies)*	1
Mahboob Shah *(Pakistan)*	2	Koertzen R.E. *(South Africa)*	1
Francis K.T. *(Sri Lanka)*	2	Riazuddin *(Pakistan)*	1
Ramaswamy V.K. *(India)*	2	Jayaprakash A.V. *(India)*	1
Tiffin R.B. *(Zimbabwe)*	2	Shepherd D.R. *(England)*	1
Cooray B.C. *(Sri Lanka)*	2	Orchard D.A. *(South Africa)*	1
Bucknor S.A. *(West Indies)*	2		

The following pairs of umpires have stood together in the most tests:

Goodall F.R. & Woodward S.J.	10	MacKintosh E.C.A. & Shortt R.W.R.	4
Aldridge B.L. & Dunne R.S.	7	Harris J.C. & Pearce T.M.	3
Aldridge B.L. & Woodward S.J.	6	MacKintosh E.C.A. & Martin W.T.	3
Copps D.E.A. & Gardiner W.R.C.	5	Cobcroft L.T. & Cave K.	3
Copps D.E.A. & Martin W.T.	4	Dunne R.S. & Woodward S.J.	3

These umpires have stood in every test of a series *(minimum 3 matches)*:

Cave K. (4)	v England	1929/30
Martin W.T. (3)	v England	1965/66
MacKintosh E.C.A. (3)	v West Indies	1968/69
Goodall F.R. (3)	v England	1983/84
Woodward S.J. (3)	v England	1983/84
Aldridge B.L. (3)	v Sri Lanka	1990/91
Aldridge B.L. (3)	v England	1991/92
Dunne R.S. (3)	v England	1991/92
Aldridge B.L. (3)	v Australia	1992/93

TEAM RECORDS

New Zealand's Test Victories

1) **v West Indies** at Auckland 1955/56
NZ 255 & 157-9d WI 145 & 77
NZ won by 190 runs

2) **v South Africa** at Cape Town 1961/62
NZ 385 & 212-9d SA 190 & 335
NZ won by 72 runs

3) **v South Africa** at Port Elizabeth 1961/62
NZ 275 & 228 SA 190 & 273
NZ won by 40 runs

4) **v India** at Christchurch 1967/68
NZ 502 & 88-4 I 288 & 301
NZ won by 6 wickets

5) **v West Indies** at Wellington 1968/69
WI 297 & 148 NZ 282 & 166-4
NZ won by 6 wickets

6) **v India** at Nagpur 1969/70
NZ 319 & 214 I 257 & 109
NZ won by 167 runs

7) **v Pakistan** at Lahore 1969/70
P114 & 208 NZ 241 & 82-5
NZ won by 5 wickets

8) **v Australia** at Christchurch 1973/74
A 223 & 259 NZ 255 & 230-5
NZ won by 5 wickets

9) **v India** at Wellington 1975/76
I 220 & 81 NZ 334
NZ won by an innings and 33 runs

10) **v England** at Wellington 1977/78
NZ 228 & 123 E 215 & 64
NZ won by 72 runs

11) **v West Indies** at Dunedin 1979/80
WI 140 & 212 NZ 249 & 104-9
NZ won by 1 wicket

12) **v India** at Wellington 1980/81
NZ 375 & 100 I 233 & 190
NZ won by 62 runs

13) **v Australia** at Auckland 1981/82
A 210 & 280 NZ 387 & 109-5
NZ won by 5 wickets

14) **v Sri Lanka** at Christchurch 1982/83
NZ 344 SL 144 & 175
NZ won by an innings and 25 runs

15) **v Sri Lanka** at Wellington 1982/83
SL 240 & 93 NZ 201 & 134-4
NZ won by 6 wickets

16) **v England** at Leeds 1983
E 225 & 252 NZ 377 & 103-5
NZ won by 5 wickets

17) **v England** at Christchurch 1983/84
NZ 307 E 82 & 93
NZ won by an innings and 132 runs

18) **v Sri Lanka** at Kandy 1983/84
NZ 276 & 201-8d SL 215 & 97
NZ won by 165 runs

19) **v Sri Lanka** at Colombo 1983/84
SL 225 & 142 NZ 459
NZ won by an innings and 61 runs

20) **v Pakistan** at Auckland 1984/85
P 169 & 183 NZ 451-9d
NZ won by an innings and 99 runs

21) **v Pakistan** at Dunedin 1984/85
P274 & 223 NZ 220 & 278-8
NZ won by 2 wickets

22) **v Australia** at Brisbane 1985/86
A 179 & 333 NZ 553-7d
NZ won by an innings and 41 runs

23) **v Australia** at Perth 1985/86
A 203 & 259 NZ 299 & 164-4
NZ won by 6 wickets

24) **v Australia** at Auckland 1985/86
A 314 & 103 NZ 358 & 160-2
NZ won by 8 wickets

25) **v England** at Nottingham 1986
E 256 & 230 NZ 413 & 77-2
NZ won by 8 wickets

26) **v West Indies** at Christchurch 1986/87
WI 100 & 264 NZ 332-9d & 33-5
NZ won by 5 wickets

27) **v India** at Bombay 1988/89
NZ 236 & 279 I 234 & 145
NZ wonby 136 runs

28) **v India** at Christchurch 1989/90
NZ 459 & 2-0 I 164 & 296
NZ won by 10 wickets

29) **v Australia** at Wellington 1989/90
A 110 & 269 NZ 202 & 181-1
NZ won by 9 wickets

30) **v Zimbabwe** at Harare 1992/93
NZ 335 & 262-5d Z 283-9d & 137
NZ won by 177 runs

31) **v Australia** at Auckland 1992/93
A 139 & 285 NZ 224 & 201-5
NZ won by 5 wickets

32) **v Pakistan** at Christchurch 1993/94
P 344 & 179 NZ 200 & 324-5
NZ won by 5 wickets

33) **v South Africa** at Johannesburg 1994/95
NZ 411 & 194 SA 179 & 289
NZ won by 137 runs

34) **v Pakistan** at Lahore 1996/97
NZ 155 & 311 P 191 & 231
NZ won by 44 runs

35) **v Sri Lanka** at Dunedin 1996/97
NZ 586-7d SL 222 & 328
NZ won by an innings & 36 runs

36) **v Sri Lanka** at Hamilton 1996/97
NZ 222 & 273 SL 170 & 205
NZ won by 120 runs

37) **v Zimbabwe** at Wellington 1997/98
Z 180 & 250 NZ 411 & 20-0
NZ won by 10 wickets

38) **v Zimbabwe** at Auckland 1997/98
Z 170 & 277 NZ 460
NZ won by an innings and 13 runs

39) **v Sri Lanka** at Colombo 1997/98
NZ 305 & 444-6d SL 285 & 297
NZ won by 167 runs

40) **v India** at Wellington 1998/99
I 208 & 356 NZ 352 & 215-6
NZ won by 4 wickets

41) **v England** at Lord's 1999
E 186 & 229 NZ 358 & 60-1
NZ won by 9 wickets

42) **v England** at The Oval 1999
NZ 236 & 162 E 153 & 162
NZ won by 83 runs

43) **v West Indies** at Hamilton 1999/00
WI 365 & 97 NZ 393 & 70-1
NZ won by 9 wickets

44) **v West Indies** at Wellington 1999/00
NZ 518-9d WI 179 & 234
NZ won by an innings and 105 runs

45) **v Zimbabwe** at Bulawayo 2000/01
Z 350 & 119 NZ 338 & 132-3
NZ won by 7 wickets

46) **v Zimbabwe** at Harare 2000/01
NZ 465 & 74-2 Z 166 & 370
NZ won by 8 wickets

47) **v Pakistan** at Hamilton 2000/01
P 104 & 118 NZ 407-4d
NZ won by an innings & 185 runs

48) **v Bangladesh** at Hamilton 2001/02
NZ 365-9d B 205 & 108
NZ won by an innings and 52 runs

49) **v Bangladesh** at Wellington 2001/02
B 132 & 135 NZ 341-6d
NZ won by an innings and 74 runs

50) **v England** at Auckland 2001/02
NZ 202 & 269-9d E 160 & 233
NZ won by 78 runs

51) **v West Indies** at Bridgetown 2001/02
NZ 337 & 243 WI 107 & 269
NZ won by 204 runs

52) **v India** at Wellington 2002/03
I 161 & 121 NZ 247 & 36-0
NZ won by 10 wickets

53) **v India** at Hamilton 2002/03
I 99 & 154 NZ 94 & 160-6
NZ won by 4 wickets

Test Record by Series

		TOTAL			Cumulative			BY OPPONENT		
Season	*Opponent*	*Won*	*Lost*	*Drawn*	*Won*	*Lost*	*Drawn*	*Won*	*Lost*	*Drawn*
1929/30	England*	—	1	3	—	1	3	—	1	3
1931	England	—	1	2	—	2	5	—	2	5
1931/32	South Africa*	—	2	—	—	4	5	—	2	—
1932/33	England*	—	—	2	—	4	7	—	2	7
1937	England	—	1	2	—	5	9	—	3	9
1945/46	Australia*	—	1	—	—	6	9	—	1	—
1946/47	England*	—	—	1	—	6	10	—	3	10
1949	England	—	—	4	—	6	14	—	3	14
1950/51	England*	—	1	1	—	7	15	—	4	15
1951/52	West Indies*	—	1	1	—	8	16	—	1	1
1952/53	South Africa*	—	1	1	—	9	17	—	3	1
1953/54	South Africa	—	4	1	—	13	18	—	7	2
1954/55	England*	—	2	—	—	15	18	—	6	15
1955/56	Pakistan	—	2	1	—	17	19	—	2	1
1955/56	India	—	2	3	—	19	22	—	2	3
1955/56	West Indies*	1	3	—	1	22	22	1	4	1
1958	England	—	4	1	1	26	23	—	10	16
1958/59	England*	—	1	1	1	27	24	—	11	17
1961/62	South Africa	2	2	1	3	29	25	2	9	3
1962/63	England*	—	3	—	3	32	25	—	14	17
1963/64	South Africa*	—	—	3	3	32	28	2	9	6
1964/65	Pakistan*	—	—	3	3	32	31	—	2	4
1964/65	India	—	1	3	3	33	34	—	3	6
1964/65	Pakistan	—	2	1	3	35	35	—	4	5
1965	England	—	3	—	3	38	35	—	17	17
1965/66	England*	—	—	3	3	38	38	—	17	20
1967/68	India*	1	3	—	4	41	38	1	6	6
1968/69	West Indies*	1	1	1	5	42	39	2	5	2
1969	England	—	2	1	5	44	40	—	19	21
1969/70	India	1	1	1	6	45	41	2	7	7
1969/70	Pakistan	1	—	2	7	45	43	1	4	7
1970/71	England*	—	1	1	7	46	44	—	20	22
1971/72	West Indies	—	—	5	7	46	49	2	5	7
1972/73	Pakistan*	—	1	2	7	47	51	1	5	9
1973	England	—	2	1	7	49	52	—	22	23
1973/74	Australia	—	2	1	7	51	53	—	3	1
1973/74	Australia*	1	1	1	8	52	54	1	4	2
1974/75	England*	—	1	1	8	53	55	—	23	24
1975/76	India*	1	1	1	9	54	56	3	8	8
1976/77	Pakistan	—	2	1	9	56	57	1	7	10
1976/77	India	—	2	1	9	58	58	3	10	9
1976/77	Australia*	—	1	1	9	59	59	1	5	3
1977/78	England*	1	1	1	10	60	60	1	24	25
1978	England	—	3	—	10	63	60	1	27	25
1978/79	Pakistan*	—	1	2	10	64	62	1	8	12
1979/80	West Indies*	1	—	2	11	64	64	3	5	9
1980/81	Australia	—	2	1	11	66	65	1	7	4
1980/81	India*	1	—	2	12	66	67	4	10	11
1981/82	Australia*	1	1	1	13	67	68	2	8	5
1982/83	Sri Lanka*	2	—	—	15	67	68	2	—	—

Cumulative

		TOTAL						BY OPPONENT		
Season	Opponent	Won	Lost	Drawn	Won	Lost	Drawn	Won	Lost	Drawn
1983	England	1	3	—	16	70	68	2	30	25
1983/84	England*	1	—	2	17	70	70	3	30	27
1983/84	Sri Lanka	2	—	1	19	70	71	4	—	1
1984/85	Pakistan	—	2	1	19	72	72	1	10	13
1984/85	Pakistan*	2	—	1	21	72	73	3	10	14
1984/85	West Indies	—	2	2	21	74	75	3	7	11
1985/86	Australia	2	1	—	23	75	75	4	9	5
1985/86	Australia*	1	—	2	24	75	77	5	9	7
1986	England	1	—	2	25	75	79	4	30	29
1986/87	West Indies*	1	1	1	26	76	80	4	8	12
1986/87	Sri Lanka	—	—	1	26	76	81	4	—	2
1987/88	Australia	—	1	2	26	77	83	5	10	9
1987/88	England*	—	—	3	26	77	86	4	30	32
1988/89	India	1	2	—	27	79	86	5	12	11
1988/89	Pakistan*	—	—	2	27	79	88	3	10	16
1989/90	Australia	—	—	1	27	79	89	5	10	10
1989/90	India*	1	—	2	28	79	91	6	12	13
1989/90	Australia*	1	—	—	29	79	91	6	10	10
1990	England	—	1	2	29	80	93	4	41	34
1990/91	Pakistan	—	3	—	29	83	93	3	13	16
1990/91	Sri Lanka*	—	—	3	29	83	96	4	—	5
1991/92	England*	—	2	1	29	85	97	4	33	35
1992/93	Zimbabwe	1	—	1	30	85	98	1	—	1
1992/93	Sri Lanka	—	1	1	30	86	99	4	1	6
1992/93	Pakistan*	—	1	—	30	87	99	3	14	16
1992/93	Australia*	1	1	1	31	88	100	7	11	11
1993/94	Australia	—	2	1	31	90	101	7	13	12
1993/94	Pakistan*	1	2	—	32	92	101	4	16	16
1993/94	India*	—	—	1	32	92	102	6	12	14
1994	England	—	1	2	32	93	104	4	34	37
1994/95	South Africa	1	2	—	33	95	104	3	11	6
1994/95	West Indies*	—	1	1	33	96	105	4	9	13
1994/95	South Africa*	—	1	—	33	97	105	3	12	6
1994/95	Sri Lanka*	—	1	1	33	98	106	4	2	7
1995/96	India	—	1	2	33	99	108	6	13	16
1995/96	Pakistan*	—	1	—	33	100	108	4	17	16
1995/96	Zimbabwe*	—	—	2	33	100	110	1	—	3
1995/96	West Indies	—	1	1	33	101	111	4	10	14
1996/97	Pakistan	1	1	1	34	102	111	5	18	16
1996/97	England*	—	2	1	34	104	112	4	36	38
1996/97	Sri Lanka*	2	—	—	36	104	112	6	2	7
1997/98	Zimbabwe	—	—	2	36	104	114	1	—	5
1997/98	Australia	—	2	1	36	106	115	7	15	13
1997/98	Zimbabwe*	2	—	—	38	106	115	3	—	5
1997/98	Sri Lanka	1	2	—	39	108	115	7	4	7
1998/99	India*	1	—	1	40	108	116	7	13	17
1998/99	South Africa*	—	1	2	40	109	118	3	13	8
1999	England	2	1	1	42	110	119	6	37	39
1999/00	India	—	1	2	42	111	121	7	14	19
1999/00	West Indies*	2	—	—	44	111	121	6	10	14
1999/00	Australia*	—	3	—	44	114	121	7	18	13
2000/01	Zimbabwe	2	—	—	46	114	121	5	—	5

		TOTAL			Cumulative			BY OPPONENT		
Season	Opponent	Won	Lost	Drawn	Won	Lost	Drawn	Won	Lost	Drawn
2000/01	South Africa	—	2	1	46	116	122	3	15	9
2000/01	Zimbabwe*	—	—	1	46	116	123	5	—	6
2000/01	Pakistan*	1	1	1	47	117	124	6	19	17
2001/02	Australia	—	—	3	47	117	127	7	18	16
2001/02	Bangladesh*	2	—	—	49	117	127	2	—	—
2001/02	England*	1	1	1	50	118	128	7	38	40
2001/02	Pakistan	—	1	—	50	119	128	6	20	17
2001/02	West Indies	1	—	1	51	119	129	7	10	15
2002/03	India*	2	—	—	53	119	129	9	14	19
2002/03	Sri Lanka	—	—	2	53	119	131	7	4	9

* home series

Summary of Results

	Played	Won	Lost	Drawn
v England	85	7	38	40
v Australia	41	7	18	16
v South Africa	27	3	15	9
v West Indies	32	7	10	15
v India	42	9	14	19
v Pakistan	43	6	20	17
v Sri Lanka	20	7	4	9
v Zimbabwe	11	5	—	6
v Bangladesh	2	2	—	—
Total	**303**	**53**	**119**	**131**

Decade by Decade

	Played	Won	Lost	Drawn
1929/30 to 1937	14	—	5	9
1945/46 to 1954/55	19	—	10	9
1955/56 to 1964/65	43	3	23	17
1965/66 to 1974/75	40	5	15	20
1975/76 to 1984/85	54	13	21	20
1985/86 to 1994/95	67	12	24	31
1995/96 to 2002/03	66	20	21	25
Total	**303**	**53**	**119**	**131**

Highest Totals

For

671-4	v Sri Lanka	Wellington	1990/91
586-7d	v Sri Lanka	Dunedin	1996/97
553-7d	v Australia	Brisbane	1985/86
551-9d	v England	Lord's	1973
543-3d	v West Indies	Georgetown	1971/72
537	v England	Wellington	1983/84
534-9d	v Australia	Perth	2001/02
518-9d	v West Indies	Wellington	1999/00
515-7d	v Sri Lanka	Colombo	2002/03
512-6d	v England	Wellington	1987/88
505	v South Africa	Cape Town	1953/54
502	v India	Christchurch	1967/68

Against

660-5d	by West Indies	Wellington	1994/95
643	by Pakistan	Lahore	2001/02
621-5d	by South Africa	Auckland	1998/99
616-5d	by Pakistan	Auckland	1988/89
607-6d	by Australia	Brisbane	1993/94
593-6d	by England	Auckland	1974/75
583-7d	by India	Ahmedabad	1999/00
580-9d	by England	Christchurch	1991/92
571-8d	by Pakistan	Christchurch	2000/01
567-8d	by England	Nottingham	1994
565-9d	by Pakistan	Karachi	1976/77
564-8	by West Indies	Bridgetown	1971/72
562-7d	by England	Auckland	1962/63
561	by Pakistan	Lahore	1955/56
560-8d	by England	Christchurch	1932/33
558-8d	by Australia	Hobart	2001/02
552	by Australia	Christchurch	1976/77
550	by England	Christchurch	1950/51

Lowest Totals

For

26	v England	Auckland	1954/55
42	v Australia	Wellington	1945/46
47	v England	Lord's	1958
54	v Australia	Wellington	1945/46
65	v England	Christchurch	1970/71
67	v England	Leeds	1958
67	v England	Lord's	1978
70	v Pakistan	Dacca	1955/56
73	v Pakistan	Lahore	2001/02
74	v West Indies	Dunedin	1955/56
74	v England	Lord's	1958
79	v South Africa	Johannesburg	1953/54
79	v Pakistan	Rawalpindi	1964/65
85	v England	Manchester	1958
89	v England	Auckland	1962/63
93	v Pakistan	Hamilton	1992/93
94	v England	Birmingham	1958
94	v West Indies	Bridgetown	1984/85
94	v India	Hamilton	2002/03
97	v England	Nottingham	1973

Against

64	by England	Wellington	1977/78
77	by West Indies	Auckland	1955/56
81	by India	Wellington	1975/76
82	by England	Christchurch	1983/84
83	by India	Mohali	1999/00
88	by India	Bombay	1964/65
89	by India	Hyderabad	1969/70
93	by Sri Lanka	Wellington	1982/83
93	by England	Christchurch	1983/84
97	by Sri Lanka	Kandy	1983/84
97	by West Indies	Hamilton	1999/00
99	by India	Hamilton	2002/03

Longest Innings

Mins	Runs			
851	671-4	v Sri Lanka	Wellington	1990/91
815	459	v Sri Lanka	Colombo	1983/84
790	406-5	v Sri Lanka	Colombo	1986/87
784	512-6 dec	v England	Wellington	1987/88
780	543-3 dec	v West Indies	Georgetown	1971/72
768	551-9 dec	v England	Lord's	1973
760	482-6 dec	v Pakistan	Lahore	1964/65
753	487-7 dec	v Zimbabwe	Wellington	2000/01
738	492	v Pakistan	Wellington	1984/85
732	447	v Pakistan	Wellington	1988/89
724	537	v England	Wellington	1983/84
713	403	v Pakistan	Auckland	1988/89
710	484	v Australia	Wellington	1973/74
709	440	v England	Nottingham	1973

Largest First Innings Leads

*374	v Australia	Brisbane	1985/86
*364	v Sri Lanka	Dunedin	1996/97
*339	v West Indies	Wellington	1999/00
*303	v Pakistan	Hamilton	2000/01
*299	v Zimbabwe	Harare	2000/01
298	v England	Lord's	1973
297	v England	Manchester	1999
*295	v India	Christchurch	1989/90
*290	v Zimbabwe	Auckland	1997/98
289	v West Indies	Bridgetown	1971/72
*282	v Pakistan	Auckland	1984/85
232	v West Indies	Christchurch	1979/80
*232	v West Indies	Christchurch	1986/87
*231	v Zimbabwe	Wellington	1997/98
*225	v England	Christchurch	1983/84
*214	v India	Christchurch	1967/68
209	v India	Bombay	1964/65
*209	v Bangladesh	Wellington	2001/02
204	v India	Calcutta	1955/56
*203	v Sri Lanka	Colombo	1983/84
*200	v Sri Lanka	Christchurch	1982/83

* New Zealand won the match

Opposition Following-on

South Africa	Cape Town	1953/54
India	Bombay	1964/65
*India	Christchurch	1967/68
*Sri Lanka	Christchurch	1982/83
*England	Christchurch	1983/84
*India	Christchurch	1989/90
*Sri Lanka	Dunedin	1996/97
*West Indies	Wellington	1999/00
*Zimbabwe	Harare	2000/01
*Bangladesh	Hamilton	2001/02

* New Zealand won the match

NB: *New Zealand did not enforce the follow-on v South Africa at Cape Town, 1961/62 and v West Indies at Bridgetown in 2001/02 although they could have done so. They eventually won both games.*

GROUNDS

Results by Grounds

In New Zealand (146)	P	W	L	D
Eden Park, Auckland	44	7	14	23
Jade Stadium, Christchurch	38	7	14	17
Basin Reserve, Wellington	40	11	12	17
Carisbrook, Dunedin	10	3	4	3
McLean Park, Napier	3	—	1	2
Westpac Park, Hamilton	11	5	2	4
Total	**146**	**33**	**48**	**65**

In Australia (22)	P	W	L	D
Melbourne Cricket Ground	3	—	1	2
Sydney Cricket Ground	2	—	1	1
Adelaide Oval	2	—	1	1
WACA Ground, Perth	6	1	2	3
Woolloongabba, Brisbane	6	1	4	1
Bellerive Oval, Hobart	3	—	1	2
Total	**22**	**2**	**10**	**10**

In Sri Lanka (11)	P	W	L	D
Kandy, Asgiriya Stadium	2	1	—	1
Sinhalese Sports Club Ground, Colombo	3	—	2	1
Colombo C.C. Ground, Colombo	2	1	—	1
Tyrone Fernando Stadium, Moratuwa	1	—	—	1
R. Premadasa Stadium, Colombo	1	1	—	—
Galle International Stadium	1	—	1	—
P. Saravanamuttu Stadium	1	—	—	1
Total	**11**	**3**	**3**	**5**

In West Indies (13)	P	W	L	D
Queen's Park Oval, Port of Spain	3	—	—	3
Sabina Park, Kingston	2	—	1	1
Kensington Park, Bridgetown	4	1	2	1
Bourda, Georgetown	2	—	—	2
St Johns Recreation Ground, Antigua	1	—	—	1
Queen's Park, Grenada	1	—	—	1
Total	**13**	**1**	**3**	**9**

In Zimbabwe (6)	P	W	L	D
Bulawayo Athletic Club, Bulawayo	1	—	—	1
Harare Sports Club, Harare	3	2	—	1
Queens Sports Club, Bulawayo	2	1	—	1
Total	**6**	**3**	**—**	**3**

In Pakistan (21)	P	W	L	D
National Stadium, Karachi	6	—	3	3
Bagh-e-Jinnah, Lahore	1	—	1	—
Dacca Stadium, Dacca	2	—	—	2
Niaz Stadium, Hyderabad	2	—	2	—
Rawalpindi Club Ground	1	—	1	—
Lahore (Gaddafi) Stadium	7	2	4	1
Iqbal Stadium, Faisalabad	1	—	1	—
Rawalpindi Cricket Stadium	1	—	1	—
Total	**21**	**2**	**13**	**6**

In South Africa (16)	P	W	L	D
Kingsmead, Durban	3	—	3	—
Ellis Park, Johannesburg	2	—	2	—
New Wanderers, Johannesburg	4	1	1	2
Newlands, Cape Town	3	1	1	1
St George's Park, Port Elizabeth	3	1	2	—
Goodyear Park, Bloemfontein	1	—	1	—
Total	**16**	**3**	**10**	**3**

In England (44)	P	W	L	D
Lord's, London	13	1	5	7
Oval, London	9	1	4	4
Headingley, Leeds	5	1	3	1
Trent Bridge, Nottingham	7	1	4	2
Old Trafford, Manchester	6	—	2	4
Egbaston, Birmingham	4	—	4	—
Total	**44**	**4**	**22**	**18**

In India (24)	P	W	L	D
Brabourne Stadium, Bombay	3	—	2	1
Wankhede Stadium, Bombay	2	1	1	—
Fateh Maidan, (Lal Bahadur Stadium) Hyderbad	3	—	1	2
Feroz Shah Kotla, Delhi	2	—	1	1
Eden Gardens, Calcutta	2	—	—	2
Corporation Stadium, Madras	2	—	1	1
Chepauk, (Chidambaram Stadium) Madras	2	—	1	1
VCA Ground, Nagpur	1	1	—	—
Green Park, Kanpur	2	—	1	1
Chinnaswamy Stadium, Bangalore	2	—	2	—
Barabati Stadium, Cuttack	1	—	—	1
Punjab C.A. Stadium, Mohali	1	—	—	1
Sardar Patel Stadium, Ahmedabad	1	—	—	1
Total	**24**	**2**	**10**	**12**

Record Performances in Tests on Each NZ Ground v All Countries

Venue	Highest Total *by NZ / v NZ*	Lowest Total *by NZ / v NZ*	Highest Individual Innings *by NZ / v NZ*	Best Bowling *by NZ / v NZ*
Auckland 44 Tests	496-9d 1983/84 v England 621-5d 1998/99 by South Africa	26 1954/55 v England 77 1955/56 by West Indies	173 Smith I.D.S. 1989/90 v India 336* Hammond W.R. 1932/33 for England	7-87 Vettori D.L. 1999/00 v Australia 8-76 Prasanna E.A.S. 1975/76 for India
Christchurch 38 Tests	502 1967/68 v India 580-9d 1991/92 by England	65 1970/71 v England 82 1983/84 by England	239 Dowling G.T. 1967/68 v India 258 Nurse S.M. 1968/69 for West Indies	7-116 Hadlee R.J. 1985/86 v Australia 7-47 Tufnell P.C.R. 1991/92 for England
Dunedin 10 Tests	586-7d 1996/97 v Sri Lanka 507-6d 1972/73 by Pakistan	74 1955/56 v West Indies 140 1979/80 by West Indies	267* Young B.A. 1996/97 v Sri Lanka 201 Mushtaq Mohammad 1972/73 for Pakistan	6-51 Hadlee R.J. 1984/85 v Pakistan 7-52 Intikhab Alam 1972/73 for Pakistan
Wellington 40 Tests	671-4 1990/91 v Sri Lanka 660-5d 1994/95 by West Indies	42 1945/46 v Australia 64 1977/78 by England	299 Crowe M.D. 1990/91 v Sri Lanka 267 de Silva P.A. 1990/91 for Sri Lanka	7-23 Hadlee R.J. 1975/76 v India 7-37 Walsh C.A. 1994/95 for West Indies
Napier 3 Tests	402 1978/79 v Pakistan 360 1978/79 by Pakistan	109 1994/95 v Sri Lanka 183 1994/95 by Sri Lanka	114 Howarth G.P. 1978/79 v Pakistan 119* Majid Khan 1978/79 for Pakistan	5-98 Morrison D.K. 1989/90 v India 5-43 Vaas W.P.J.U.C. 1994/95 for Sri Lanka
Hamilton 11 Tests	464-8d 1998/99 v India 416 1998/99 by India	93 1992/93 v Pakistan 97 1999/00 by West Indies	143 Richardson M.H. 2001/02 v Bangladesh 190 Dravid R.S. 1998/99 for India	7-27 Cairns C.L. 1999/00 v West Indies 5-22 Waqar Younis 1992/93 for Pakistan
ALL TESTS IN NZ 146 Tests	671-4 1990/91 v Sri Lanka Wellington 660-5d 1994/95 by West Indies Wellington	26 1954/55 v England Auckland 64 1977/78 by England Wellington	299 Crowe M.D. 1990/91 v Sri Lanka Wellington 336* Hammond W.R. 1932/33 for England Auckland	7-23 Hadlee R.J. 1975/76 v India Wellington 8-76 Prasanna E.A.S. 1975/76 for India Auckland

Record Performances in Tests v All Opponents

Opponent	Highest Total by NZ v NZ		Lowest Total by NZ v NZ		Highest Individual Innings by NZ v NZ		Best Bowling by NZ v NZ	
England	551-9d 1973	Lord's	26 1954/55	Auckland	222 Christchurch, 2001/02	Astle N.J.	7-74 Leeds, 1983	Cairns B.L.
	593-6 1974/75	Auckland	64 1977/78	Wellington	336* Auckland, 1932/33	Hammond W.R.	7-32 Lord's, 1969	Underwood D.L.
Australia	553-7d 1985/1986	Brisbane	42 1945/46	Wellington	188 Brisbane, 1985/86	Crowe M.D.	9-52 Brisbane, 1985/86	Hadlee R.J.
	607-6d 1993/94	Brisbane	103 1985/86	Auckland	250 Christchurch, 1977/78	Walters K.D.	6-31 Hobart 1993/94	Warne S.K.
South Africa	505 1953/54	Cape Town	79 1953/54	Johannesburg	150 Port Elizabeth, 2000/01	Sinclair M.S.	6-60 Dunedin, 1963/64	Reid J.R.
	621-5d 1998/99	Auckland	148 1953/54	Johannesburg	275* Auckland, 1998/99	Cullinan D.J.	8-53 Johannesburg, 1961/62	Lawrence G.B.
West Indies	543-3d 1971/72	Georgetown	74 1955/56	Dunedin	259 Georgetown, 1971/72	Turner G.M.	7-27 Hamilton, 1999/00	Cairns C.L.
	660-5d 1994/95	Wellington	77 1955/56	Auckland	258 Christchurch, 1968/69	Nurse S.M.	7-37 Wellington, 1994/95	Walsh C.A.
India	502 1967/68	Christchurch	94 2002/03	Hamilton	239 Christchurch, 1967/68	Dowling G.T.	7-23 Wellington, 1975/76	Hadlee R.J.
	583-7d 1999/00	Ahmedabad	81 1975/76	Wellington	231 Madras, 1955/56	Mankad M.H.	8-72 Delhi, 1964/65	Venkataraghavan S.
Pakistan	492 1984/85	Wellington	70 1955/56	Dacca	204* Christchurch, 2000/01	Sinclair M.S.	7-52 Faisalabad 1990/91	Pringle C.
	643 2001/02	Lahore	102 1990/91	Faisalabad	329 Lahore, 2001/02	Inzamam-ul-Haq	7-52 Dunedin, 1972/73	Intikhab Alam.
Sri Lanka	671-4 1990/91	Wellington	102 1992/93	Colombo	299 Wellington, 1990/91	Crowe M.D.	6-64 Colombo, 1997/98	Vettori D.L.
	497 1990/91	Wellington	93 1982/83	Wellington	267 Wellington, 1990/91	de Silva P.A.	6-72 Galle, 1997/98	Dharmasena H.D.P.K.
Zimbabwe	487-7d 2000/01	Wellington	207 1997/98	Harare	157 Auckland, 1997/98	Horne M.J.	6-50 Harare, 1992/93	Patel D.N.
	461 1997/98	Bulawayo	119 2000/01	Bulawayo	203* Bulawayo, 1997/98	Whittall G.J.	8-109 Bulawayo, 2000/0	Strang P.A.
Bangladesh	365-9d 2001/02	Hamilton	341-6d 2001/02	Wellington	143 Hamilton, 2001/02	Richardson M.H..	7-53 Hamilton, 2001/02	Cairns C.L.
	205 2001/02	Hamilton	108 2001/02	Hamilton	61 Hamilton, 2001/02	Habibul Bashar	3-99 Wellington, 2001/02	Monjurul Islam

INDIVIDUAL RECORDS

BATTING

Test Centuries

(173 instances)

299	Crowe M.D. v Sri Lanka at Wellington	1990/91
274*	Fleming S.P. v Sri Lanka at Colombo	2002/03
267*	Young B.A. v Sri Lanka at Dunedin	1996/97
259	Turner G.M. v West Indies at Georgetown	1971/72
239	Dowling G.T. v India at Christchurch	1967/68
230*	Sutcliffe B. v India at New Delhi	1955/56
223*	Turner G.M. v West Indies at Kingston	1971/72
222	Astle N.J. v England at Christchurch	2001/02
214	Sinclair M.S. v West Indies at Wellington	1999/00
206	Donnelly M.P. v England at Lord's	1949
204*	Sinclair M.S. v Pakistan at Christchurch	2000/01
188	Crowe M.D. v West Indies at Georgetown	1984/85
188	Crowe M.D. v Australia at Brisbane	1985/86
186	Jones A.H. v Sri Lanka at Wellington	1990/91
185	Wright J.G. v India at Christchurch	1989/90
182	Jarvis T.W. v West Indies at Georgetown	1971/72
180	Reid J.F. v Sri Lanka at Colombo	1983/84
176	Congdon B.E. v England at Nottingham	1973
175	Congdon B.E. v England at Lord's	1973
174*	Coney J.V. v England at Wellington	1983/84
174*	Fleming S.P. v Sri Lanka at Colombo	1997/98
174	Crowe M.D. v Pakistan at Wellington	1988/89
173	Smith I.D.S. v India at Auckland	1989/90
170*	Jones A.H. v India at Auckland	1989/90
166*	Congdon B.E. v West Indies at Port of Spain	1971/72
161	Edgar B.A. v Australia at Auckland	1981/82
158*	Reid J.F. v Pakistan at Auckland	1984/85
157	Horne M.J. v Zimbabwe at Auckland	1997/98
156*	Astle N.J. v Australia at Perth	2001/02
152	Lees W.K. v Pakistan at Karachi	1976/77
151*	Sutcliffe B. v India at Calcutta	1964/65
151*	Hadlee R.J. v Sri Lanka at Colombo	1986/87
150	Jones A.H. v Australia at Adelaide	1987/88
150	Sinclair M.S. v South Africa at Port Elizabeth	2000/01
148	Reid J.F. v Pakistan at Wellington	1984/85
147	Howarth G.P. v West Indies at Christchurch	1979/80
146*	Greatbatch M.J. v Australia at Perth	1989/90
143	Dowling G.T. v India at Dunedin	1967/68
143	Crowe M.D. v England at Wellington	1987/88
143	Jones A.H. v England at Wellington	1991/92
143	Jones A.H. v Australia at Perth	1993/94
142	Reid J.R. v South Africa at Johannesburg	1961/62
143	Richardson M.H. v Bangladesh at Hamilton	2001/02
142	Crowe M.D. v England at Lord's	1994
142	McMillan C.D. v Sri Lanka at Colombo	1997/98
142	McMillan C.D. v Zimbabwe at Wellington	2000/01
141	Wright J.G. v Australia at Christchurch	1981/82

141	Astle N.J. v Zimbabwe at Wellington	2000/01
140	Crowe M.D. v Zimbabwe at Harare	1992/93
139	McMillan C.D. v Zimbabwe at Wellington	1997/98
138	Sinclair B.W. v South Africa at Auckland	1963/64
138	Wright J.G. v West Indies at Wellington	1986/87
137*	Sutcliffe B. v India at Hyderabad	1955/56
137*	Howarth G.P. v India at Wellington	1980/81
137	Crowe M.D. v Australia at Christchurch	1985/86
137	Crowe M.D. v Australia at Adelaide	1987/88
136	Dempster C.S. v England at Wellington	1929/30
135	Reid J.R. v South Africa at Cape Town	1953/54
133	Greatbatch M.J. v Pakistan at Hamilton	1992/93
133	Horne M.J. v Australia at Hobart	1997/98
132	Congdon B.E. v Australia at Wellington	1973/74
130	Sinclair B.W. v Pakistan at Lahore	1964/65
130	Wright J.G. v England at Auckland	1983/84
130	Fleming S.P. v West Indies at Bridgetown	2001/02
129	Dowling G.T. v India at Bombay	1964/65
129	Edgar B.A. v Pakistan at Christchurch	1978/79
129	Fleming S.P. v England at Auckland	1996/97
128	Reid J.R. v Pakistan at Karachi	1964/65
128	Crowe J.J. v England at Auckland	1983/84
127	Edgar B.A. v West Indies at Auckland	1979/80
126	Congdon B.E. v West Indies at Bridgetown	1971/72
126	Cairns C.L. v India at Hamilton	1998/99
125	Astle N.J. v West Indies at Bridgetown	1995/96
124	Taylor B.R. v West Indies at Auckland	1967/68
124	Cairns C.L. v Zimbabwe at Harare	2000/01
123*	Reid J.F. v India at Christchurch	1980/81
123	Howarth G.P. v England at Lord's	1978
122	Howarth G.P. v England at Auckland	1977/78
122	Jones A.H. v Sri Lanka at Hamilton	1990/91
121	Parker J.M. v England at Auckland	1974/75
120*	Crowe J.J. v Sri Lanka at Colombo	1986/87
120*	Thomson S.A. v Pakistan at Christchurch	1993/94
120	Dempster C.S. v England at Lord's	1931
120	Reid J.R. v India at Calcutta	1955/56
120	Young B.A. v Pakistan at Christchurch	1993/94
120	Cairns C.L. v Zimbabwe at Auckland	1995/96
119*	Reid J.R. v India at Delhi	1955/56
119*	Burgess M.G. v Pakistan at Dacca	1969/70
119	Wright J.G. v England at The Oval	1986
119	Crowe M.D. v West Indies at Wellington	1986/87
119	Latham R.T. v Zimbabwe at Bulawayo	1992/93
117*	Hastings B.F. v West Indies at Christchurch	1968/69
117*	Wright J.G. v Australia at Wellington	1989/90
117	Mills J.E. v England at Wellington	1929/30
117	Morrison J.F.M. v Australia at Sydney	1973/74
117	Turner G.M. v India at Christchurch	1975/76
116	Hadlee W.A. v England at Christchurch	1946/47
116	Sutcliffe B. v England at Christchurch	1950/51
116	Pollard V. v England at Nottingham	1973
116	Wright J.G. v England at Wellington	1991/92
115	Crowe M.D. v England at Manchester	1994
114	Sinclair B.W. v England at Auckland	1965/66
114*	Howarth G.P. v Pakistan at Napier	1978/79

114	Astle N.J. v Zimbabwe at Auckland	1997/98
113*	Smith I.D.S. v England at Auckland	1983/84
113*	Wright J.G. v India at Napier	1989/90
113	Turner G.M. v India at Kanpur	1976/77
113	Crowe M.D. v India at Auckland	1989/90
112	Crowe J.J. v West Indies at Kingston	1984/85
112	Spearman C.M. v Zimbabwe at Auckland	1995/96
111*	Coney J.V. v Pakistan at Dunedin	1984/85
111	McGregor S.N. v Pakistan at Lahore	1955/56
111	Burgess M.G. v Pakistan at Lahore	1976/77
110*	Turner G.M. v Australia at Christchurch	1973/74
110	Turner G.M. v Pakistan at Dacca	1969/70
110	Hastings B.F. v Pakistan at Auckland	1972/73
110	Wright J.G. v India at Auckland	1980/81
110	Bracewell J.G. v England at Nottingham	1986
110	Horne M.J. v Zimbabwe at Bulawayo	2000/01
110	Parore A.C. v Australia at Perth	2001/02
109	Barton P.T. v South Africa at Port Elizabeth	1961/62
109	Cairns C.L. v Australia at Wellington	1999/00
108*	Crowe M.D. v Pakistan at Lahore	1990/91
108	Parker J.M. v Australia at Sydney	1973/74
108	Reid J.F. v Australia at Brisbane	1985/86
107*	Congdon B.E. v Australia at Christchurch	1976/77
107*	Greatbatch M.J. v England at Auckland	1987/88
107*	Rutherford K.R. v England at Wellington	1987/88
107*	McMillan C.D. v England at Manchester	1999
107	Rabone G.O. v South Africa at Durban	1953/54
107	Redmond R.E. v Pakistan at Auckland	1972/73
107	Wright J.G. v Pakistan at Karachi	1984/85
107	Crowe M.D. v Sri Lanka at Colombo	1992/93
107	Styris S.B. v West Indies at St George's	2001/02
106	Reid J.F. v Pakistan at Hyderabad	1984/85
106	Crowe M.D. v England at Lord's	1986
106	Richardson M.H. v Pakistan at Hamilton	2000/01
106	McMillan C.D. v Bangladesh at Hamilton	2001/02
105*	Pollard V. v England at Lord's	1973
105	Taylor B.R. v India at Calcutta	1964/65
105	Hastings B.F. v West Indies at Bridgetown	1971/72
105	Burgess M.G. v England at Lord's	1973
105	Rutherford K.R. v Sri Lanka at Moratuwa	1992/93
105	Bell M.D. v Pakistan at Hamilton	2000/01
105	Fleming S.P. v Australia at Perth	2001/02
104	Page M.L. v England at Lord's	1931
104	Congdon B.E. v England at Christchurch	1965/66
104	Burgess M.G. v England at Auckland	1970/71
104	Parker J.M. v India at Bombay	1976/77
104	Crowe M.D. v West Indies at Auckland	1986/87
104	Vincent L. v Australia at Perth	2001/02
103	Hadlee R.J. v West Indies at Christchurch	1979/80
103	Wright J.G. v England at Auckland	1987/88
103	Astle N.J. v West Indies at St John's	1995/96
102*	Astle N.J. v England at Auckland	1996/97
102	Guy J.W. v India at Hyderabad	1955/56
102	Howarth G.P. v England at Auckland	1977/78
102	Rutherford K.R. v Australia at Christchurch	1992/93
101*	Coney J.V. v Australia at Wellington	1985/86

101	Sutcliffe B. v England at Manchester	1949
101	Harris P.G.Z. v South Africa at Cape Town	1961/62
101	Burgess M.G. v West Indies at Kingston	1971/72
101	Hastings B.F. v Australia at Wellington	1973/74
101	Turner G.M. v Australia at Christchurch	1973/74
101	Franklin T.J. v England at Lord's	1990
101	Wright J.G. v Sri Lanka at Hamilton	1990/91
101	Astle N.J. v England at Manchester	1999
100*	Jones A.H. v Sri Lanka at Hamilton	1990/91
100*	Parore A.C. v West Indies at Christchurch	1994/95
100	Vivian H.G. v South Africa at Wellington	1931/32
100	Reid J.R. v England at Christchurch	1962/63
100	Crowe M.D. v England at Wellington	1983/84
100	Horne M.J. v England at Lord's	1999

Century on Test Debut

117 & 7	Mills J.E. v England at Wellington	1929/30
105 & 0*	Taylor B.R. v India at Calcutta	1964/65
107 & 56	Redmond R.E. v Pakistan at Auckland	1972/73
11 & 107*	Greatbatch M.J. v England at Auckland	1987/88
214	Sinclair M.S. v West Indies at Wellington	1999/00
104 & 54	Vincent L. v Australia at Perth	2001/02
107 & 69*	Styris S.B. v West Indies at St George's	2001/02

Centuries in Both Innings of a Test

101 & 110*	Turner G.M. v Australia at Christchurch	1973/74
122 & 102	Howarth G.P. v England at Auckland	1977/78
122 & 100*	Jones A.H. v Sri Lanka at Hamilton	1990/91

NB: *In the same match that Jones achieved this feat A.P. Gurusinha (119 & 102) also scored a century in each innings. This is only the second occasion that a player from each side has scored centuries in each innings of a test (A.R. Morris and D.C.S. Compton, Australia v England, Adelaide, 1946/47).*

200 Runs in a Test

343	Fleming S.P. (274* & 69*) v Sri Lanka at Colombo	2002/03
329	Crowe M.D. (30 & 299) v Sri Lanka at Wellington	1990/91
267	Young B.A. (267*) v Sri Lanka at Dunedin	1996/97
259	Turner G.M. (259) v West Indies at Georgetown	1971/72
254	Sinclair M.S. (204* & 50*) v Pakistan at Christchurch	2000/01
252	Fleming S.P. (78 & 174*) v Sri Lanka at Colombo	1997/98
248	Congdon B.E. (166* & 82) v West Indies at Port of Spain	1971/72
244	Dowling G.T. (239 & 5) v India at Christchurch	1967/68
244	Turner G.M. (223* & 21) v West Indies at Kingston	1971/72
232	Astle N.J. (10 & 222) v England at Christchurch	2001/02
230	Sutcliffe B. (230*) v India at Delhi	1955/56
224	Howarth G.P. (122 & 102) v England at Auckland	1977/78
222	Greatbatch M.J. (76 & 146*) v Australia at Perth	1989/90
222	Jones A.H. (122 & 100*) v Sri Lanka at Hamilton	1990/91
216	Dempster C.S. (136 & 80*) v England at Wellington	1929/30
214	Jones A.H. (150 & 64) v Australia at Adelaide	1987/88
214	Sinclair M.S. (214) v West Indies at Wellington	1999/00
213	Wright J.G. (75 & 138) v West Indies at Wellington	1986/87
211	Turner G.M. (101 & 110*) v Australia at Christchurch	1973/74

206	Donnelly M.P. (206) v England at Lord's	1949
204	Reid J.R. (128 & 76) v Pakistan at Karachi	1964/65
202	Reid J.R. (60 & 142) v South Africa at Johannesburg	1961/62
201	Coney J.V. (27 & 174*) v England at Wellington	1983/84
201	Crowe M.D. (140 & 61) v Zimbabwe at Harare	1992/93

A Century and a Fifty in a Test

136 & 80*	Dempster C.S. v England at Wellington	1929/30
52 & 120	Dempster C.S. v England at Lord's	1931
100 & 73	Vivian H.G. v South Africa at Wellington *(aged 19)*	1931/32
107 & 68	Rabone G.O. v South Africa at Durban	1953/54
60 & 142	Reid J.R. v South Africa at Johannesburg	1961/62
74 & 100	Reid J.R. v England at Christchurch	1962/63
128 & 76	Reid J.R. v Pakistan at Karachi	1964/65
59 & 119*	Burgess M.G. v Pakistan at Dacca	1969/70
166* & 82	Congdon B.E. v West Indies at Port of Spain	1971/72
107 & 56	Redmond R.E. v Pakistan at Auckland	1972/73
75 & 138	Wright J.G. v West Indies at Wellington	1986/87
150 & 64	Jones A.H. v Australia at Adelaide	1987/88
76 & 146*	Greatbatch M.J. v Australia at Perth	1989/90
140 & 61	Crowe M.D. v Zimbabwe at Harare	1992/93
105 & 53	Rutherford K.R. v Sri Lanka at Moratuwa	1992/93
57 & 102	Rutherford K.R. v Australia at Christchurch	1992/93
70 & 115	Crowe M.D. v England at Manchester	1994
57 & 120	Cairns C.L. v Zimbabwe at Auckland	1995/96
54 & 125	Astle N.J. v West Indies at Bridgetown	1995/96
78 & 174*	Fleming S.P. v Sri Lanka at Colombo	1997/98
109 & 69	Cairns C.L. v Australia at Wellington	1999/00
141 & 51*	Astle N.J. v Zimbabwe at Wellington	2000/01
204 & 50*	Sinclair M.S. v Pakistan at Christchurch	2000/01
104 & 54	Vincent L. v Australia at Perth	2001/02
107 & 69*	Styris S.B. v West Indies at St George's	2001/02
274* & 69*	Fleming S.P. v Sri Lanka at Colombo	2002/03

NB: *Redmond's feat of scoring a century and a fifty in his only test is unique. Only he and A.G. Ganteaume (112 WI v England, Port of Spain 1947/48) have made a century in their only test.*

Centuries in Three Successive Test Innings

Jones A.H. 186, Wellington, 122 and 100* Hamilton v Sri Lanka 1990/91

Centuries in Two Successive Test Innings

Reid J.R. 119*, Delhi and 120, Calcutta v India 1955/56
Burgess M.G. 119*, Dacca v Pakistan 1969/70 and 104, Auckland v England 1970/71
Congdon B.E. 176, Nottingham and 175, Lord's v England 1973
Pollard V. 116, Nottingham and 105*, Lord's v England 1973
Turner G.M. 101 and 110*, Christchurch v Australia 1973/74
Howarth G.P. 122 and 102, Auckland v England 1977/78 – 94 v England, Oval 1978
Crowe M.D. 143, Wellington v England 1987/88 and 174, Wellington v Pakistan 1988/89
Wright J.G. 185, Christchurch and 113* Napier v India 1989/90
Astle N.J. 125, Bridgetown and 103, St Johns v West Indies 1995/96

NB: *M.G. Burgess scored centuries in three successive tests — all played in different countries! He followed the two centuries above with 15 & 101 v West Indies at Kingston, 1971/72.*
B.E .Congdon scored centuries in successive tests v West Indies 1971/72 — 166 & 82 at Port of Spain and 126 at Bridgetown.*
G.T. Dowling did likewise with 143 & 10 at Dunedin and 239 & 5 at Christchurch v India 1967/68.
In successive tests v Pakistan 1984/85 J.F. Reid scored 106 & 21 at Hyderabad, 97 at Karachi, 148 & 3 at Wellington and 158 at Auckland.*

Fifty on Test Debut

3 & 51	Vivian H.G. v England at The Oval *(aged 18)*	1931
52 & 56	Wallace W.M. v England at Lord's	1937
64 & 0	Moloney D.A.R. v England at Lord's	1937
58	Sutcliffe B. v England at Christchurch	1946/47
50 & 25	Reid J.R. v England at Manchester	1949
93 & 64	Harford N.S. v Pakistan at Lahore	1955/56
54 & 23	Barton P.T. v South Africa at Durban	1961/62
74 & 58	Dowling G.T. v South Africa at Johannesburg	1961/62
64 & 1	Yuile B.W. v England at Auckland	1962/63
10 & 52	Gedye S.G. v South Africa at Wellington	1963/64
66 & 5	Morgan R.W. v Pakistan at Auckland	1964/65
17 & 54	Murray B.A.G. v India at Dunedin	1967/68
50 & 39	Burgess M.G. v India at Dunedin	1967/68
69 & 0*	Thomson K. v India at Christchurch	1967/68
6 & 51*	Howarth G.P. v England at Auckland	1974/75
14 & 92	Anderson R.W. v Pakistan at Lahore	1976/77
55 & 19	Wright J.G. v England at Wellington	1977/78
56 & 0*	Harris C.Z. v Sri Lanka at Moratuwa	1992/93
38 & 53	Young B.A. v Australia at Brisbane	1993/94
16 & 92	Fleming S.P. v India at Hamilton	1993/94
54 & 0	McMillan C.D. v Australia at Brisbane	1997/98

NB: *H.M. McGirr scored 51 in his first (and only) test innings but it was his second test appearance.*

Two Fifties in a Test

52 & 56	†Wallace W.M. v England at Lord's	1937
58 & 50	Vivian H.G. v England at Old Trafford	1937
96 & 54*	Smith F.B. v England at Headingley	1949
75 & 80	Donnelly M.P. v England at Old Trafford	1949
88 & 54	Sutcliffe B. v England at The Oval	1949
55 & 58	Wallace W.M. v England at The Oval	1949
93 & 64	†Harford N.S. v Pakistan at Lahore	1955/56
74 & 58	†Dowling G.T. v South Africa at Johannesburg	1961/62
55 & 55	Pollard V. v England at Lord's *(aged 19)*	1965
66 & 60	Burgess M.G. v India at Wellington	1967/68
58 & 58	Morrison J.F.M. v England at Auckland	1974/75
54 & 54	Congdon B.E. v India at Auckland	1975/76
55 & 54	Edwards G.N. v England at Auckland	1977/78
62 & 76	Edgar B.A. v England at Nottingham	1983
62 & 60	Howarth G.P. v Sri Lanka at Kandy	1983/84
57 & 84	Crowe M.D. v Pakistan at Dunedin	1984/85
50 & 52	Edgar B.A. v Australia at Sydney	1985/86
56 & 59	Wright J.G. v Australia at Auckland	1985/86
82 & 79	Crowe M.D. v Australia at Melbourne	1987/88
87 & 88	Greatbatch M.J. v Zimbabwe at Bulawayo	1992/93
74 & 89	Rutherford K.R. v Zimbabwe at Harare	1992/93
63 & 59	Rutherford K.R. v India at Hamilton	1993/94
79 & 53	Fleming S.P. v South Africa at Cape Town	1994/95
59 & 51*	Twose R.G. v Pakistan at Christchurch	1995/96
57 & 52	Cairns C.L. v England at Christchurch	1996/97
92 & 84	McMillan C.D. v India at Hamilton	1998/99
93 & 60	Horne M.J. v South Africa at Auckland	1998/99
57 & 99	Fleming S.P. v South Africa at Bloemfontein	2000/01
57 & 71	Vincent L. v England at Wellington	2001/02
95 & 71	Richardson M.H. v West Indies at St George's	2001/02
55 & 55	Richardson M.H. v Sri Lanka at Kandy	2002/03

† *on debut*

Fifties in Successive Test Innings

The following reached 50 in four successive test innings:

Donnelly M.P. 62, 206, 75 & 80 v England, 1949
Sutcliffe B. 101, 88, 54 v England 1949 and 116 v England 1950/51
Congdon B.E. 166*, 82, 126 and 61* v West Indies 1971/72
       54, 54, 58 & 52 v India 1975/76
Coney J.V. 101*, 98, 93 v Australia 1985/86 and 51 v England 1986
Rutherford K.R. 74, 89 v Zimbabwe and 105, 53 v Sri Lanka 1992/93

Century Partnership for The First Wicket

					Final innings total
276	Dempster C.S. Mills J.E.	v England	Wellington	1929/30	440
133	Sutcliffe B. Hadlee W.A.	v England	Christchurch	1946/47	345-9d
112	Sutcliffe B. Scott V.J	v England	Leeds	1949	195-2
121	Sutcliffe B. Scott V.J.	v England	The Oval	1949	345
126	Rabone G.O. Chapple M.E.	v South Africa	Cape Town	1953/54	505
101	McGregor S.N. Leggat J.G.	v India	Delhi	1955/56	112-1
136	Dowling G.T. Jarvis T.W.	v Pakistan	Lahore	1964/65	482-6d
126	Dowling G.T. Murray B.A.G.	v India	Christchurch	1967/68	502
112	Dowling G.T. Turner G.M.	v West Indies	Auckland	1968/69	297-8d
115	Dowling G.T. Turner G.M.	v West Indies	Christchurch	1968/69	367-6
106	Dowling G.T. Murray B.A.G.	v India	Hyderabad	1969/70	181
387	Turner G.M. Jarvis T.W.	v West Indies	Georgetown	1971/72	543-3d
159	Redmond R.E. Turner G.M.	v Pakistan	Auckland	1972/73	402
107	Parker J.M. Turner G.M.	v Australia	Auckland	1973/74	158
100	Wright J.G. Edgar B.A.	v Australia	Sydney	1985/86	193
117	Wright J.G. Franklin T.J.	v England	Auckland	1987/88	350-7d
149	Wright J.G. Franklin T.J.	v India	Napier	1989/90	178-1

185	{ Wright J.G. / Franklin T.J.	v England	Lord's	1990	462-9d
134	{ Franklin T.J. / Wright J.G.	v Sri Lanka	Wellington	1990/91	671-4
161	{ Franklin T.J. / Wright J.G.	v Sri Lanka	Hamilton	1990/91	374-6d
116	{ Greatbatch M.J. / Latham R.T.	v Zimbabwe	Bulawayo	1992/93	325-3d
102	{ Greatbatch M.J. / Latham R.T.	v Zimbabwe	Bulawayo	1992/93	222-5d
110	{ Hartland B.R. / Wright J.G.	v Sri Lanka	Moratuwa	1992/93	195-5
110	{ Greatbatch M.J. / Hartland B.R.	v Pakistan	Hamilton	1992/93	264
111	{ Greatbatch M.J. / Wright J.G.	v Australia	Wellington	1992/93	329
214	{ Spearman C.M. / Twose R.G.	v Zimbabwe	Auckland	1995/96	441-5d
107	{ Young B.A. / Horne M.J.	v South Africa	Christchurch	1998/99	127-1
131	{ Horne M.J. / Stead G.R.	v India	Ahmedabad	1999/00	252-2
102	{ Richardson M.H. / Bell M.D.	v Pakistan	Christchurch	2000/01	476
181	{ Richardson M.H. / Bell M.D.	v Pakistan	Hamilton	2000/01	407-4d
104	{ Richardson M.H. / Horne M.J.	v Bangladesh	Wellington	2001/02	341-6d
117	{ Richardson M.H. / Vincent L.	v West Indies	St George's	2001/02	256-5

Highest Score in Each Batting Position

Position in batting order					
1 or 2	267*	Young B.A.	v Sri Lanka	Dunedin	1996/97
3	274*	Fleming S.P.	v Sri Lanka	Colombo	2002/03
4	299	Crowe M.D.	v Sri Lanka	Wellington	1990/91
5	222	Astle N.J.	v England	Christchurch	2001/02
6	174*	Coney J.V.	v England	Wellington	1983/84
7	152	Lees W.K.	v Pakistan	Karachi	1976/77
8	124	Taylor B.R.	v West Indies	Auckland	1968/69
9	173	Smith I.D.S.	v India	Auckland	1989/90
10	83*	Bracewell J.G.	v Australia	Sydney	1985/86
11	68*	Collinge R.O.	v Pakistan	Auckland	1972/73

Pairs in Test Matches Involving New Zealand

By New Zealand *(51)*

*James K.C. v England at Christchurch		1929/30
*Badcock F.T. v England at Christchurch		1929/30
Cowie J. v England at Manchester		1937
*Rowe C.G. v Australia at Wellington		1945/46
*Butterfield L.A. v Australia at Wellington		1945/46
Miller L.S.M. v South Africa at Johannesburg		1953/54
Poore M.B. v England at Auckland		1954/55
Colquhoun I.A. v England at Auckland		1954/55
Hayes J.A. v England at Auckland		1954/55
Blair R.W. v West Indies at Dunedin		1955/56
Cave H.B. v West Indies at Dunedin		1955/56
MacGibbon A.R. v India at Madras		1955/56
Harford N.S. v England at Leeds		1958
Motz R.C. v South Africa at Cape Town		1961/62
Blair R.W. v England at Christchurch		1962/63
Blair R.W. v South Africa at Auckland		1963/64
Shrimpton M.J.F. v South Africa at Auckland		1963/64
Dick A.E. v Pakistan at Rawalpindi		1964/65
Bartlett G.A. v England at Christchurch		1965/66
Jarvis T.W. v Pakistan at Wellington		1972/73
Lees W.K. v England at Christchurch		1977/78
*Bracewell B.P. v England at The Oval		1978
Cairns B.L. v Australia at Brisbane		1980/81
Edgar B.A. v Australia at Perth		1980/81
Troup G.B. v India at Wellington		1980/81
Coney J.V. v Australia at Christchurch		1981/82
Smith I.D.S. v Australia at Christchurch		1981/82
Bracewell J.G. v Pakistan at Hyderabad		1984/85
*Rutherford K.R. v West Indies at Port of Spain		1984/85
Wright J.G. v England at Lord's		1986
Morrison D.K. v Australia at Melbourne		1987/88
*Kuggeleijn C.M. v India at Bangalore		1988/89
Snedden M.C. v India at Hyderabad		1988/89
Morrison D.K. v Sri Lanka at Hamilton		1990/91
Hartland B.R. v England at Auckland		1991/92
Su'a M.L. v Pakistan at Hamilton		1992/93
Morrison D.K. v Australia at Hobart		1993/94
Doull S.B. v West Indies at Wellington		1994/95
Nash D.J. v Sri Lanka at Napier		1994/95
Harris C.Z. v West Indies at Bridgetown		1995/96
Patel D.N. v England at Auckland		1996/97
Doull S.B. v England at Wellington		1996/97
Fleming S.P. v Australia at Hobart		1997/98
Vettori D.L. v Sri Lanka at Galle		1997/98
Wiseman P.J. v India at Wellington		1998/99
Twose R.G. v England at Edgbaston		1999
Wiseman P.J. v India at Kanpur		1999/00
O'Connor S.B. v Australia at Hamilton		1999/00
*Franklin J.E.C. v Pakistan at Auckland		2000/01
Martin C.S. v Pakistan at Auckland		2000/01
Martin C.S. v Pakistan at Lahore		2001/02

Against New Zealand *(22)*

Javed Burki for Pakistan at Wellington	1964/65
Jaisimha M.L. for India at Hyderabad	1969/70
Knott A.P.E. for England at Lord's	1973
Stackpole K.R. for Australia at Auckland	1973/74
Chandrasekhar B.S. for India at Wellington	1975/76
Hendrick M. for England at Wellington	1977/78
Kallicharran A.I. for West Indies at Dunedin	1979/80
Wood G.M. for Australia at Perth	1980/81
Holland R.G. for Australia at Brisbane	1985/86
*Patel R.G. for India at Bombay	1988/89
Malcolm D.E. for England at Birmingham	1990
Waqar Younis for Pakistan at Faisalabad	1990/91
Aamer Sohail for Pakistan at Hamilton	1992/93
Langer J.L. for Australia at Auckland	1992/93
Streak H.H. for Zimbabwe at Harare	1997/98
Rennie G.J. for Zimbabwe at Auckland	1997/98
Mbangwa M. for Zimbabwe at Auckland	1997/98
Walsh C.A. for West Indies at Wellington	1999/00
Nkala M.L. for Zimbabwe at Harare	2000/01
Monjurul Islam for Bangladesh at Wellington	2001/02
Laxman V.V.S. for India at Wellington	2002/03
Khan Z. for India at Hamilton	2002/03

* on debut

BOWLING

Ten Wickets in a Match

(18 instances)

15-123	Hadlee R.J. v Australia at Brisbane	1985/86
12-149	Vettori D.L. v Australia at Auckland	1999/00
11-58	Hadlee R.J. v India at Wellington	1975/76
11-102	Hadlee R.J. v West Indies at Dunedin	1979/80
11-152	Pringle C. v Pakistan at Faisalabad	1990/91
11-155	Hadlee R.J. v Australia at Perth	1985/86
11-169	Nash D.J. v England at Lord's	1994
10-88	Hadlee R.J. v India at Bombay	1988/89
10-100	Hadlee R.J. v England at Wellington	1977/78
10-100	Cairns C.L. v West Indies at Hamilton	1999/00
10-102	Hadlee R.J. v Sri Lanka at Colombo	1983/84
10-106	Bracewell J.G. v Australia at Auckland	1985/86
10-124	Chatfield E.J. v West Indies at Port of Spain	1984/85
10-140	Cowie J. v England at Manchester	1937
10-140	Hadlee R.J. v England at Nottingham	1986
10-144	Cairns B.L. v England at Leeds	1983
10-166	Troup G.B. v West Indies at Auckland	1979/80
10-176	Hadlee R.J. v Australia at Melbourne	1987/88

Five Wickets in an Innings

(143 instances)

9-52	Hadlee R.J. v Australia at Brisbane	1985/86
7-23	Hadlee R.J. v India at Wellington	1975/76
7-27	Cairns C.L. v West Indies at Hamilton	1999/00
7-52	Pringle C. v Pakistan at Faisalabad	1990/91

7-53	Cairns C.L. v Bangladesh at Hamilton	2001/02
7-65	Doull S.B. v India at Wellington	1998/99
7-74	Taylor B.R. v West Indies at Bridgetown	1971/72
7-74	Cairns B.L. v England at Leeds	1983
7-87	Boock S.L. v Pakistan at Hyderabad	1984/85
7-87	Vettori D.L. v Australia at Auckland	1999/00
7-89	Morrison D.K. v Australia at Wellington	1992/93
7-116	Hadlee R.J. v Australia at Christchurch	1985/86
7-143	Cairns B.L. v England at Wellington	1983/84
6-26	Hadlee R.J. v England at Wellington	1977/78
6-27	Nash D.J. v India at Mohali	1999/00
6-32	Bracewell J.G. v Australia at Auckland	1985/86
6-37	Morrison D.K. v Australia at Auckland	1992/93
6-38	Bartlett G.A. v India at Christchurch	1967/68
6-40	Cowie J. v Australia at Wellington	1945/46
6-49	Hadlee R.J. v India at Bombay	1988/89
6-50	Hadlee R.J. v West Indies at Christchurch	1986/87
6-50	Patel D.N. v Zimbabwe at Harare	1992/93
6-51	Hadlee R.J. v Pakistan at Dunedin	1984/85
6-51	Bracewell J.G. v India at Bombay	1988/89
6-52	Cairns C.L. v England at Auckland	1991/92
6-53	Hadlee R.J. v England at The Oval	1983
6-54	Tuffey D.R. v England at Auckland	2001/02
6-57	Hadlee R.J. v Australia at Melbourne	1980/81
6-60	Reid J.R. v South Africa at Dunedin	1963/64
6-63	Motz R.C. v India at Christchurch	1967/68
6-63	Collinge R.O. v India at Christchurch	1975/76
6-64	Vettori D.L. v Sri Lanka at Colombo	1997/98
6-67	Cowie J. v England at Manchester	1937
6-68	Rabone G.O. v South Africa at Cape Town	1953/54
6-68	Hadlee R.J. v West Indies at Dunedin	1979/80
6-69	Motz R.C. v West Indies at Wellington	1968/69
6-69	Morrison D.K. v West Indies at Christchurch	1994/95
6-71	Hadlee R.J. v Australia at Brisbane	1985/86
6-73	Chatfield E.J. v West Indies at Port of Spain	1984/85
6-76	Cunis R.S. v England at Auckland	1970/71
6-76	Nash D.J. v England at Lord's	1994
6-77	Cairns C.L. v England at Lord's	1999
6-78	Watson W. v Pakistan at Lahore	1990/91
6-80	Hadlee R.J. v England at Lord's	1986
6-80	Hadlee R.J. v England at Nottingham	1986
6-83	Cowie J. v England at Christchurch	1946/47
6-85	Cairns B.L. v West Indies at Christchurch	1979/80
6-85	Bracewell J.G. v Australia at Wellington	1989/90
6-87	Vettori D.L. v Australia at Perth	2001/02
6-90	Hadlee R.J. v Australia at Perth	1985/86
6-95	Troup G.B. v West Indies at Auckland	1979/80
6-100	Hadlee R.J. v Australia at Christchurch	1981/82
6-105	Hadlee R.J. v West Indies at Auckland	1986/87
6-113	Patel D.N. v Zimbabwe at Bulawayo	1992/93
6-127	Vettori D.L. v India at Kanpur	1999/00
*6-155	Moir A.M. v England at Christchurch	1950/51
6-162	Burtt T.B. v England at Manchester	1949
*6-168	Cresswell G.F. v England at The Oval	1949
5-26	Taylor B.R. v India at Bombay	1964/65

5-28	Hadlee R.J. v England at Christchurch	1983/84
5-28	Boock S.L. v Sri Lanka at Kandy	1983/84
5-29	Hadlee R.J. v Sri Lanka at Colombo	1983/84
5-31	Cairns C.L. v England at The Oval	1999
5-31	Cairns C.L. v Zimbabwe at Bulawayo	2000/01
5-33	Cairns B.L. v India at Wellington	1980/81
5-34	Cameron F.J. v Pakistan at Auckland	1964/65
5-34	Howarth H.J. v India at Nagpur	1969/70
5-34	Hadlee R.J. v West Indies at Dunedin	1979/80
5-39	Hadlee R.J. v Australia at Wellington	1989/90
5-41	Taylor B.R. v West Indies at Port of Spain	1971/72
5-41	Morrison D.K. v Pakistan at Hamilton	1992/93
5-44	Cairns C.L. v West Indies at Wellington	1999/00
5-46	Doull S.B. v Pakistan at Lahore	1996/97
5-47	Hadlee R.J. v India at Christchurch	1980/81
5-48	Cameron F.J. v South Africa at Cape Town	1961/62
5-50	Cairns C.L. v Zimbabwe at Harare	1997/98
5-51	O'Connor S.B. v Australia at Hamilton	1999/00
5-53	Hadlee R.J. v England at Birmingham	1990
5-55	Cairns B.L. v India at Madras	1976/77
5-58	Doull S.B. v Sri Lanka at Dunedin	1996/97
5-61	Morrison D.K. v West Indies at St Johns	1995/96
5-62	Moir A.M. v England at Auckland	1954/55
5-62	Hadlee R.J. v Pakistan at Christchurch	1978/79
5-62	Cairns C.L. v Sri Lanka at Colombo	1997/98
5-62	Vettori D.L. v Australia at Auckland	1999/00
5-63	Hadlee R.J. v Australia at Auckland	1981/82
5-63	Chatfield E.J. v Sri Lanka at Colombo	1983/84
5-63	Davis H.T. v Sri Lanka at Hamilton	1996/97
5-64	MacGibbon A.R. v England at Birmingham	1958
5-65	Congdon B.E. v India at Auckland	1975/76
5-65	Hadlee R.J. v Australia at Sydney	1985/86
5-65	Hadlee R.J. v Australia at Perth	1985/86
5-65	Hadlee R.J. v India at Bangalore	1988/89
5-66	Doull S.B. v Pakistan at Auckland	1993/94
5-67	Boock S.L. v England at Auckland	1977/78
5-67	Hadlee R.J. v Australia at Melbourne	1987/88
5-68	Snedden M.C. v West Indies at Christchurch	1986/87
5-68	Hadlee R.J. v Australia at Adelaide	1987/88
5-69	Burtt T.B. v West Indies at Christchurch	1951/52
5-69	Morrison D.K. v England at Christchurch	1987/88
5-71	Martin C.S. v Zimbabwe at Wellington	2000/01
5-73	Hadlee R.J. v Sri Lanka at Colombo	1983/84
5-73	Su'a M.L. v Pakistan at Hamilton	1992/93
5-73	Doull S.B. v South Africa at Durban	1994/95
5-74	Collinge R.O. v England at Leeds	1973
5-75	Bracewell J.G. v India at Auckland	1980/81
5-75	Morrison D.K. v India at Christchurch	1989/90
5-75	Cairns C.L. v Sri Lanka at Auckland	1990/91
5-75	Doull S.B. v England at Wellington	1996/97
5-77	Hart M.N. v South Africa at Johannesburg	1994/95
5-78	Bond S.E. v West Indies at Bridgetown	2001/02
5-80	Howarth H.J. v Pakistan at Karachi	1969/70
5-82	Collinge R.O. v Australia at Auckland	1973/74
*5-82	Wiseman P.J. v Sri Lanka at Colombo	1997/98

5-83	Cameron F.J. v South Africa at Johannesburg	1961/62
5-84	Hadlee R.J. v England at Lord's	1978
5-84	Vettori D.L. v Sri Lanka at Hamilton	1996/97
5-85	Su'a M.L. v Zimbabwe at Harare	1992/93
*5-86	Taylor B.R. v India at Calcutta	1964/65
5-86	Motz R.C. v India at Dunedin	1967/68
5-87	Cairns B.L. v Australia at Brisbane	1980/81
5-87	Hadlee R.J. v Australia at Perth	1980/81
5-90	Wiseman P.J. v Zimabwe at Bulawayo	2000/01
5-93	Hadlee R.J. v England at Lord's	1983
5-93	Patel D.N. v Australia at Auckland	1992/93
5-93	Nash D.J. v England at Lord's	1994
5-95	Chatfield E.J. v England at Leeds	1983
5-97	Burtt T.B. v England at Leeds	1949
5-98	Morrison D.K. v India at Napier	1989/90
5-104	Hadlee R.J. v Pakistan at Auckland	1978/79
5-104	Bond S.E. v West Indies at St George's	2001/02
5-108	Motz R.C. v England at Birmingham	1965
5-109	Hadlee R.J. v Australia at Melbourne	1987/88
5-113	Motz R.C. v West Indies at Christchurch	1968/69
5-117	Boock S.L. v Pakistan at Wellington	1984/85
5-121	Hadlee R.J. v Pakistan at Lahore	1976/77
5-127	Cowie J. v England at Leeds	1949
5-137	Cairns C.L. v Pakistan at Rawalpindi	1996/97
5-138	Vettori D.L. v Australia at Hobart	2001/02
5-145	Morrison D.K. v India at Auckland	1989/90
5-146	Cairns C.L. v Australia at Brisbane	2001/02
5-148	O'Sullivan D.R. v Australia at Adelaide	1973/74
5-153	Morrison D.K. v Sri Lanka at Wellington	1990/91

* on debut

All Round Cricket

Rabone G.O. 56 plus 6-68 and 1-16 v South Africa at Cape Town	1953/54
Taylor B.R. 105 & 0 plus 5-86 v India at Calcutta	1964/65
Congdon B.E. 54 and 54 plus 5-65 v India at Auckland	1975/76
Hadlee R.J. 54* and 5 plus 5-104 and 0-8 v Pakistan at Auckland	1978/79
Hadlee R.J. 51 and 17 plus 5-34 and 6-68 v West Indies at Dunedin	1979/80
Hadlee R.J. 84 and 11 plus 6-53 and 2-99 v England at The Oval	1983
Cairns B.L. 3 and 64 plus 7-143 v England at Wellington	1983/84
Hadlee R.J. 99 plus 3-16 and 5-28 v England at Christchurch	1983/84
Hadlee R.J. 54 plus 9-52 and 6-71 v Australia at Brisbane	1985/86
Hadlee R.J. 68 plus 6-80 and 4-60 v England at Nottingham	1986
Bracewell J.G. 52 and 32 plus 2-81 and 6-51 v India at Bombay	1988/89
Patel D.N. 6 and 58* plus 2-81 and 6-50 v Zimbabwe at Harare	1992/93
Nash D.J. 56 plus 6-76 and 5-93 v England at Lord's	1994
Cairns C.L. 12 and 71* plus 5-50 and 0-44 v Zimbabwe at Harare	1997/98
Cairns C.L. 11 and 80 plus 5-31 and 1-50 v England at The Oval	1999
Cairns C.L. 72 plus 3-73 and 7-27 v West Indies at Hamilton	1999/00
Cairns C.L. 61 and 43 plus 5-146 and 1-29 v Australia at Brisbane	2001/02

* Taylor is the only player from any country to score a century and take five wickets in an innings on debut.

WICKETKEEPING AND FIELDING

MOST DISMISSALS IN AN INNINGS BY A WICKETKEEPER

7*	Smith I.D.S. v Sri Lanka at Hamilton *(all caught)*	1990/91
5	Harford R.I. v India at Wellington *(all caught)*	1967/68
5	Wadsworth K.J. v Pakistan at Auckland *(all caught)*	1972/73
5	Lees W.K. v Sri Lanka at Wellington *(all caught)*	1982/83
5	Smith I.D.S. v England at Auckland *(4ct 1st)*	1983/84
5	Smith I.D.S. v Sri Lanka at Auckland *(all caught)*	1990/91
5	Parore A.C. v England at Auckland *(all caught)*	1991/92
5	Parore A.C. v Sri Lanka at Colombo *(4ct 1st)*	1992/93
5	Parore A.C. v Zimbabwe at Harare *(all caught)*	2000/01
5	Parore A.C. v Pakistan at Auckland *(all caught)*	2000/01

* equals world test record

MOST DISMISSALS IN A MATCH

8	Lees W.K. v Sri Lanka at Wellington *(all caught)*	1982/83
8	Smith I.D.S. v Sri Lanka at Hamilton *(all caught)*	1990/91
7	Dick A.E. v South Africa at Durban *(6ct 1st)*	1961/62
7	Harford R.I. v India at Wellington *(all caught)*	1967/68
7	Smith I.D.S. v India at Wellington *(all caught)*	1980/81
7	Smith I.D.S. v England at Leeds *(all caught)*	1983
7	Parore A.C. v Pakistan at Auckland *(all caught)*	2000/01
7	Parore A.C. v Pakistan at Hamilton *(all caught)*	2000/01

MOST STUMPINGS IN AN INNINGS

2	Mooney F.L.H. v England at Leeds	1949
2	Milburn B.D. v West Indies at Christchurch	1968/69
2	Lees W.K. v Pakistan at Hyderabad	1976/77
2	Lees W.K. v Pakistan at Karachi	1976/77
2	Lees W.K. v India at Madras	1976/77

MOST STUMPINGS IN A MATCH

2	5 instances as above plus	
	Smith I.D.S. v Australia at Sydney	1985/86
	Parore A.C. v Australia at Auckland	1999/00

REPLACEMENT WICKETKEEPERS IN TEST MATCHES

Wicketkeeper	Replacement	Dismissal			
Mooney F.L.H.	Sutcliffe B.	—	v South Africa	Port Elizabeth	1953/54
Petrie E.C.	Reid J.R.	Richardson P.E. *(st)*	v England	Manchester	1958
Petrie E.C.	Reid J.R.	—	v England	Christchurch	1958/59
Ward J.T.	Morgan R.W.	Jaisimha M.L. *(c)*	v India	Calcutta	1964/65
Ward J.T.	Congdon B.E.	Hanumant Singh *(c)*	v India	Delhi	1964/65
Dick A.E.	Reid J.R.	—	v Pakistan	Lahore	1964/65
Dick A.E.	Congdon B.E. (sub)	Pervez Sajjad *(st)*	v Pakistan	Lahore	1964/65
Lees W.K.	Anderson R.W.	—	v Pakistan	Hyderabad	1976/77
Smith I.D.S.	Edgar B.A.	Laird B.M. *(c)*	v Australia	Christchurch	1981/82
Smith I.D.S.	Crowe M.D.	—	v West Indies	Kingston	1984/85
Smith I.D.S.	Horne P.A.	—	v Australia	Melbourne	1987/88
Smith I.D.S.	Blain T.E.	—	v India	Hyderabad	1988/89
Smith I.D.S.	Horne P.A.	—	v Pakistan	Faisalabad	1990/91
Smith I.D.S.	Parore A.C. (sub)	Shoaib Mohammad *(c)* v Pakistan Aaqib Javed *(c)*		Faisalabad	1990/91

MOST CATCHES IN AN INNINGS

5	Fleming S.P. v Zimbabwe at Harare	1997/98
4	Crowe J.J. v West Indies at Bridgetown	1984/85
4	Crowe M.D. v West Indies at Kingston	1984/85
4	Fleming S.P. v Australia at Brisbane	1997/98

MOST CATCHES IN A MATCH

7	Fleming S.P. v Zimbabwe at Harare	1997/98
6	Young B.A. v Pakistan at Auckland	1993/94
6	Fleming S.P. v Australia at Brisbane	1997/98
5	Harris C.Z. v Zimbabwe at Bulawayo	1997/98
5	Fleming S.P. v India at Wellington	1998/99

RECORD PARTNERSHIPS

NEW ZEALAND v ENGLAND

New Zealand

1st	276	Dempster C.S. & Mills J.E.	Wellington	1929/30
2nd	241	Wright J.G. & Jones A.H.	Wellington	1991/92
3rd	210	Edgar B.A. & Crowe M.D.	Lord's	1986
4th	155	Crowe M.D. & Greatbatch M.J.	Wellington	1987/88
5th	180	Crowe M.D. & Thomson S.A.	Lord's	1994
6th	141	Crowe M.D. & Parore A.C.	Manchester	1994
7th	117	Patel D.N. & Cairns C.L.	Christchurch	1991/92
8th	104	Roberts A.W. & Moloney D.A.R.	Lord's	1937
9th	118	Coney J.V. & Cairns B.L.	Wellington	1983/84
10th	118	Astle N.J. & Cairns C.L.	Christchurch	2001/02

England

1st	223	Fowler G. & Tavare C.J.	The Oval	1983
2nd	369	Edrich J.H. & Barrington K.F.	Leeds	1965
3rd	245	Hammond W.R. & Hardstaff J.	Lord's	1937
4th	266	Denness M.H. & Fletcher K.W.R.	Auckland	1974/75
5th	242	Hammond W.R. & Ames L.E.G.	Christchurch	1932/33
6th	281	Thorpe G.P. & Flintoff A.	Christchurch	2001/02
7th	149	Knott A.P.E. & Lever P.	Auckland	1970/71
8th	246	Ames L.E.G. & Allen G.O.B.	Lord's	1931
9th	163*	Cowdrey M.C. & Smith A.C.	Wellington	1962/63
10th	59	Knott A.P.E. & Gifford N.	Nottingham	1973

NEW ZEALAND v AUSTRALIA

New Zealand

1st	111	Greatbatch M.J. & Wright J.G.	Wellington	1992/93
2nd	132	Horne M.J. & Parore A.C.	Hobart	1997/98
3rd	224	Reid J.F. & Crowe M.D.	Brisbane	1985/86
4th	229	Congdon B.E. & Hastings B.F.	Wellington	1973/74
5th	97	Fleming S.P. & McMillan C.D.	Hobart	2001/02
6th	110	Fleming S.P. & Cairns C.L.	Wellington	1999/00
7th	132*	Coney J.V. & Hadlee R.J.	Wellington	1985/86
8th	253	Astle N.J. & Parore A.C.	Perth	2001/02
9th	73	Howarth H.J. & Hadlee D.R.	Christchurch	1976/77
10th	124	Bracewell J.G. & Boock S.L.	Sydney	1985/86

Australia

1st	224	Langer J.L. & Hayden M.L.	Brisbane	2001/02
2nd	235	Slater M.J. & Boon D.C.	Hobart	1993/94
3rd	264	Chappell I.M. & Chappell G.S.	Wellington	1973/74
4th	153	Waugh M.E. & Waugh S.R.	Perth	1997/98
5th	213	Ritchie G.M. & Matthews G.R.J.	Wellington	1985/86
6th	197	Border A.R. & Matthews G.R.J.	Brisbane	1985/86
7th	217	Walters K.D. & Gilmour G.J.	Christchurch	1976/77
8th	135	Gilchrist A.C. & Lee B.	Brisbane	2001/02
9th	69	Healy I.A. & McDermott C.J.	Perth	1993/94
10th	60	Walters K.D. & Higgs J.D.	Melbourne	1980/81

NEW ZEALAND v SOUTH AFRICA

New Zealand

1st	126	Rabone G.O. & Chapple M.E.	Cape Town	1953/54
2nd	90	Horne M.J. & Astle N.J.	Auckland	1998/99
3rd	94	Poore M.B. & Sutcliffe B.	Cape Town	1953/54
4th	171	Sinclair B.W. & McGregor S.N.	Auckland	1963/64
5th	176	Reid J.R. & Beck J.E.F.	Cape Town	1953/54
6th	100	Vivian H.G. & Badcock F.T.	Wellington	1931/32
7th	84	Reid J.R. & Bartlett G.A.	Johannesburg	1961/62
8th	74	Thomson S.A. & Nash D.J.	Johannesburg	1994/95
9th	69	Allcott C.F.W. & Cromb I.B.	Wellington	1931/32
10th	57	Doull S.B. & de Groen R.P.	Johannesburg	1994/95

South Africa

1st	196	Mitchell B. & Christy J.A.H.	Christchurch	1931/32
2nd	315*	Gibbs H.H. & Kallis J.H.	Christchurch	1998/99
3rd	183	Kirsten G. & Cullinan D.J.	Auckland	1998/99
4th	145	Cullinan D.J. & Cronje W.J.	Wellington	1998/99
5th	141	Cullinan D.J. & Rhodes J.N.	Auckland	1998/99
6th	126*	Cullinan D.J. & S.M. Pollock	Auckland	1998/99
7th	246	McGlew D.J. & Murray A.R.A.	Wellington	1952/53
8th	136	McKenzie N.D. & Boje N.	Port Elizabeth	2000/01
9th	60	Pollock P.M. & Adcock N.A.T.	Port Elizabeth	1961/62
10th	47	McGlew D.J. & Bromfield H.D.	Port Elizabeth	1961/62

NEW ZEALAND v WEST INDIES

New Zealand

1st	387	Turner G.M. & Jarvis T.W.	Georgetown	1971/72
2nd	210	Howarth G.P. & Crowe J.J.	Kingston	1984/85
3rd	241	Wright J.G. & Crowe M.D.	Wellington	1986/87
4th	189	Sinclair M.S. & Astle N.J.	Wellington	1999/00
5th	144	Astle N.J. & Vaughan J.T.C.	Bridgetown	1995/96
6th	220	Turner G.M. & Wadsworth K.J.	Kingston	1971/72
7th	143	Crowe M.D. & Smith I.D.S.	Georgetown	1984/85
8th	136	Congdon B.E. & Cunis R.S.	Port of Spain	1971/72
9th	62*	Pollard V. & Cunis R.S.	Auckland	1968/69
10th	45	Morrison D.K. & Kennedy R.J.	Bridgetown	1995/96

West Indies

1st	276	Griffith A.F.G. & Campbell S.L.	Hamilton	1999/00
2nd	269	Fredericks R.C. & Rowe L.G.	Kingston	1971/72
3rd	221	Lara B.C. & Adams J.C.	Wellington	1994/95
4th	162	Weekes E.D. & Smith O.G.	Dunedin	1955/56
	162	Greenidge C.G. & Kallicharan A.I.	Christchurch	1979/80
5th	189	Worrell F.M.M. & Walcott C.L.	Auckland	1951/52
6th	254	Sobers G.S. & Davis C.A.	Bridgetown	1971/72
7th	143	Atkinson D.S. & Goddard J.D.C.	Christchurch	1955/56
8th	83	Richards I.V.A. & Marshall M.D.	Bridgetown	1984/85
9th	70	Marshall M.D. & Garner J.	Bridgetown	1984/85
10th	31	Findlay T.M. & Shillingford G.C.	Bridgetown	1971/72

NEW ZEALAND v INDIA

New Zealand

1st	149	Franklin T.J. & Wright J.G.	Napier	1989/90
2nd	155	Dowling G.T. & Congdon B.E.	Dunedin	1967/68
3rd	222*	Sutcliffe B. & Reid J.R.	New Delhi	1955/56
4th	160	Twose R.G. & McMillan C.D.	Hamilton	1998/99
5th	140	McMillan C.D. & Parore A.C.	Hamilton	1998/99
6th	137	McMillan C.D. & Cairns C.L.	Wellington	1998/99
7th	163	Sutcliffe B. & Taylor B.R.	Calcutta	1964/65
8th	137	Nash D.J. & Vettori D.L.	Wellington	1998/99
9th	136	Smith I.D.S. & Snedden M.C.	Auckland	1989/90
10th	61	Ward J.T. & Collinge R.O.	Madras	1964/65

India

1st	413	Mankad M.H. & Roy P.	Madras	1955/56
2nd	204	Gavaskar S.M. & Amarnath S.	Auckland	1975/76
3rd	238	Umrigar P.R. & Manjrekar V.L.	Hyderabad	1955/56
4th	281	Tendulkar S.R. & Ganguly S.C.	Ahmedabad	1999/00
5th	127	Manjrekar V.L. & Ramchand G.S.	New Delhi	1955/56
6th	193*	Sardesai D.N. & Hanumant Singh	Bombay	1964/65
7th	128	Tendulkar S.R. & More K.S.	Napier	1989/90
8th	144	Dravid R.S. & Srinath J.	Hamilton	1998/99
9th	105	Kirmani S.M.H. & Bedi B.S.	Bombay	1976/77
	105	Kirmani S.M.H. & Yadav N.S.	Auckland	1980/81
10th	57	Desai R.B. & Bedi B.S.	Dunedin	1967/68

NEW ZEALAND v PAKISTAN

New Zealand

1st	181	Richardson M.H. & Bell M.D.	Hamilton	2000/01
2nd	195	Wright J.G. & Howarth G.P.	Napier	1978/79
3rd	178	Sinclair B.W. & Reid J.R.	Lahore	1964/65
4th	147	McMillan C.D. & Fleming S.P.	Hamilton	2000/01
5th	183	Burgess M.G. & Anderson R.W.	Lahore	1976/77
6th	145	Reid J.F. & Hadlee R.J.	Wellington	1984/85
7th	186	Lees W.K. & Hadlee R.J.	Karachi	1976/77
8th	100	Yuile B.W. & Hadlee D.R.	Karachi	1969/70
9th	96	Burgess M.G. & Cunis R.S.	Dacca	1969/70
10th	151	Hastings B.F. & Collinge R.O.	Auckland	1972/73

Pakistan

1st	172	Rameez Raja & Shoaib Mohammad	Karachi	1990/91
2nd	262	Saeed Anwar & Ijaz Ahmed	Rawalpindi	1996/97
3rd	248	Shoaib Mohammad & Javed Miandad	Auckland	1988/89
4th	350	Mushtaq Mohammad & Asif Iqbal	Dunedin	1972/73
5th	281	Javed Miandad & Asif Iqbal	Lahore	1976/77
6th	217	Hanif Mohammad & Majid Khan	Lahore	1964/65
7th	308	Waqar Hassan & Imtiaz Ahmed	Lahore	1955/56
8th	89	Anil Dalpat & Iqbal Qasim	Karachi	1984/85
9th	78	Inzamam-ul-Haq & Shoaib Akhtar	Lahore	2001/02
10th	65	Salah-ud-din & Mohammad Farooq	Rawalpindi	1964/65

NEW ZEALAND v SRI LANKA

New Zealand

1st	161	Franklin T.J. & Wright J.G.	Hamilton	1990/91
2nd	172	Richardson M.H. & Fleming S.P.	Colombo	2002/03
3rd	467	Jones A.H. & Crowe M.D.	Wellington	1990/91
4th	240	Fleming S.P. & McMillan C.D.	Colombo	1997/98
5th	151	Rutherford K.R. & Harris C.Z.	Moratuwa	1992/93
6th	246*	Crowe J.J. & Hadlee R.J.	Colombo	1986/87
7th	47	Patel D.N. & Su'a M.L.	Dunedin	1994/95
8th	79	Coney J.V. & Lees W.K.	Christchurch	1982/83
9th	43	Parore A.C. & Wiseman P.J.	Galle	1997/98
10th	52	Lees W.K. & Chatfield E.J.	Christchurch	1982/83

Sri Lanka

1st	102	Mahanama R.S. & Hathurusinghe U.C.	Colombo	1992/93
2nd	138	Mahanama R.S. & Gurusinha A.P.	Moratuwa	1992/93
3rd	159*	Wettimuny S. & Dias R.L.	Colombo	1983/84
4th	192	Gurusinha A.P. & Tillakaratne H.P.	Dunedin	1994/95
5th	133	Jayawardene D.P.M.D. & Tillakaratne H.P.	Colombo	2002/03
6th	109	Madugalle R.S. & Ranatunga A.	Colombo	1983/84
	109	Kuruppu D.S.B.P. & Madugalle R.S.	Colombo	1986/87
7th	137	Kaluwitharana R.S. & Vaas W.P.J.U.C.	Dunedin	1996/97
8th	73	Tillakaratne H.P. & Wickramasinghe G.P.	Dunedin	1996/97
9th	31	Labrooy G.F. & Ratnayake R.J.	Auckland	1990/91
	31	Jayasuriya S.T. & Ratnayake R.J.	Auckland	1990/91
10th	71	Kaluwitharana R.S. & Muralidaran M.	Colombo	1997/98

NEW ZEALAND v ZIMBABWE

New Zealand

1st	214	Spearman C.M. & Twose R.G.	Auckland	1995/96
2nd	127	Latham R.T. & Jones A.H.	Bulawayo	1992/93
3rd	71	Jones A.H. & Crowe M.D.	Bulawayo	1992/93
4th	243	Horne M.J. & Astle N.J.	Auckland	1997/98
5th	222	Astle N.J. & McMillan C.D.	Wellington	2000/01
6th	82*	Parore A.C. & Germon L.K.	Hamilton	1995/96
7th	108	McMillan C.D. & Nash D.J.	Wellington	1997/98
8th	144	Cairns C.L. & Nash D.J.	Harare	2000/01
9th	78	Parore A.C. & Vettori D.L.	Bulawayo	2000/01
10th	27	McMillan C.D. & Doull S.B.	Auckland	1997/98

Zimbabwe

1st	156	Rennie G.J. & Flower G.W.	Harare	1997/98
2nd	107	Arnott K.J. & Campbell A.D.R.	Harare	1992/93
3rd	70	Flower A. & Whittall G.J.	Bulawayo	1997/98
4th	130	Rennie G.J. & Flower A.	Wellington	2000/01
5th	131	Flower A. & Whittall G.J.	Harare	2000/01
6th	151	Whittall G.J. & Streak H.H.	Harare	2000/01
7th	91	Whittall G.J. & Strang P.A.	Hamilton	1995/96
8th	94	Campbell A.D.R. & Streak H.H.	Wellington	1997/98
9th	46	Crocker G.J. & Burmester M.G.	Harare	1992/93
10th	40	Whittall G.J. & Matambanadzo E.	Bulawayo	1997/98

NEW ZEALAND v BANGLADESH

New Zealand

1st	104	Richardson M.H. & Horne M.J.	Wellington	2001/02
2nd	44	Richardson M.H. & Vincent L.	Wellington	2001/02
3rd	10	Richardson M.H. & Fleming S.P.	Hamilton	2001/02
4th	130	Fleming S.P. & McMillan C.D.	Wellington	2001/02
5th	190	Richardson M.H. & McMillan C.D.	Hamilton	2001/02
6th	89	McMillan C.D. & Cairns C.L.	Hamilton	2001/02
7th	27	McMillan C.D. & Parore A.C.	Hamilton	2001/02
8th	2	Parore A.C. & Vettori D.L.	Hamilton	2001/02
9th	6	Parore A.C. & Bond S.E.	Hamilton	2001/02
10th	–			

Bangladesh

1st	39	Javed Omer & Al Sahariar	Hamilton	2001/02
2nd	23	Javed Omer & Habibul Bashar	Wellington	2001/02
3rd	60	Habibul Bashar & Aminul Islam	Hamilton	2001/02
4th	32	Aminul Islam & Mohammad Ashraful	Wellington	2001/02
5th	26	Habibul Bashar & Sanuar Hossain	Hamilton	2001/02
6th	25	Sanuar Hossain & Khaled Masud	Hamilton	2001/02
7th	9	Sanuar Hossain & Khaled Mahmud	Hamilton	2001/02
8th	7	Khaled Masud & Hasibul Hussain	Wellington	2001/02
9th	49	Khaled Masud & Masrafe bin Mortaza	Wellington	2001/02
10th	13	Khaled Masud & Masrafe bin Mortaza	Wellington	2001/02

CAREER RECORDS
Averages

	M	I	NO	HS	Runs	Ave	100	50	Ct	St	Wkts	Runs	Ave	Best	5WI	10WM
Adams A.R.	1	2	0	11	18	9.00	—	—	1	—	6	105	17.50	3-44	—	—
Alabaster J.C.	21	34	6	34	272	9.71	—	—	7	—	49	1863	38.02	4-46	—	—
Allcott C.F.W.	6	7	2	33	113	22.60	—	—	3	—	6	541	90.17	2-102	—	—
Allott G.I.	10	15	7	8*	27	3.37	—	—	2	—	19	1111	58.47	4-74	—	—
Anderson R.W.	9	18	0	92	423	23.50	—	3	1	—	—	—	—	—	—	—
Anderson W.M.	1	2	0	4	5	2.50	—	—	1	—	—	—	—	—	—	—
Andrews B.	2	3	2	17	22	22.00	—	—	1	—	2	154	77.00	2-40	—	—
Astle N.J.	57	98	8	222	3420	38.00	8	16	51	—	36	1711	47.52	2-22	—	—
Badcock F.T.	7	9	2	64	137	19.57	—	2	1	—	16	610	38.13	4-80	—	—
Barber R.T.	1	2	0	12	17	8.50	—	—	1	—	—	—	—	—	—	—
Bartlett G.A.	10	18	1	40	263	15.47	—	—	8	—	24	792	33.00	6-38	1	—
Barton P.T.	7	14	0	109	285	20.36	1	1	4	—	—	—	—	—	—	—
Beard D.D.	4	7	2	31	101	20.20	—	—	2	—	9	302	33.56	3-22	—	—
Beck J.E.F.	8	15	0	99	394	26.27	—	3	—	—	—	—	—	—	—	—
Bell M.D.	13	23	1	105	484	22.00	1	2	10	—	—	—	—	—	—	—
Bell W.	2	3	3	21*	21	—	—	—	1	—	2	235	117.50	1-54	—	—
Bilby G.P.	2	4	0	28	55	13.75	—	—	3	—	—	—	—	—	—	—
Blain T.E.	11	20	3	78	456	26.82	—	2	19	2	—	—	—	—	—	—
Blair R.W.	19	34	6	64*	189	6.75	—	1	5	—	43	1515	35.23	4-85	—	—
Blunt R.C.	9	13	1	96	330	27.50	—	1	5	—	12	472	39.33	3-17	—	—
Bolton B.A.	2	3	0	33	59	19.67	—	—	1	—	—	—	—	—	—	—
Bond S.E.	10	10	5	17	53	10.60	—	—	4	—	43	1045	24.30	5-78	2	—
Boock S.L.	30	41	8	37	207	6.27	—	—	14	—	74	2564	34.64	7-87	4	—
Bracewell B.P.	6	12	2	8	24	2.40	—	—	1	—	14	585	41.78	3-110	—	—
Bracewell J.G.	41	60	11	110	1001	20.42	1	4	31	—	102	3653	35.81	6-32	4	1
Bradburn G.E.	7	10	2	30*	105	13.12	—	—	6	—	6	460	76.66	3-134	—	—
Bradburn W.P.	2	4	0	32	62	15.50	—	—	2	—	—	—	—	—	—	—
Brown V.R.	2	3	1	36*	51	25.50	—	—	3	—	1	176	176.00	1-17	—	—
Burgess M.G.	50	92	6	119*	2684	31.21	5	14	34	—	6	212	35.33	3-23	—	—
Burke C.	1	2	0	3	4	2.00	—	—	—	—	2	30	15.00	2-30	—	—
Burtt T.B.	10	15	3	42	252	21.00	—	—	2	—	33	1170	35.45	6-162	3	—
Butler I.G.	4	6	1	26	50	10.00	—	—	3	—	14	455	32.50	4-60	—	—
Butterfield L.A.	1	2	0	0	0	0.00	—	—	—	—	0	24	—	—	—	—
Cairns B.L.	43	65	8	64	928	16.28	—	2	30	—	130	4279	32.91	7-74	6	1
Cairns C.L.	55	92	5	126	2853	32.79	4	20	14	—	197	5675	28.80	7-27	12	1
Cameron F.J.	19	30	20	27*	116	11.60	—	—	2	—	62	1849	29.82	5-34	3	—
Cave H.B.	19	31	5	22*	229	8.81	—	—	8	—	34	1467	43.15	4-21	—	—
Chapple M.E.	14	27	1	76	497	19.12	—	3	10	—	1	84	84.00	1-24	—	—
Chatfield E.J.	43	54	33	21*	180	8.57	—	—	7	—	123	3958	32.17	6-73	3	1
Cleverley D.C.	2	4	3	10*	19	19.00	—	—	—	—	0	130	—	—	—	—
Collinge R.O.	35	50	13	68*	533	14.41	—	2	10	—	116	3393	29.25	6-63	3	—
Colquhoun I.A.	2	4	2	1*	1	0.50	—	—	4	—	—	—	—	—	—	—
Coney J.V.	52	85	14	174*	2668	37.57	3	16	64	—	27	966	35.77	3-28	—	—
Congdon B.E.	61	114	7	176	3448	32.22	7	19	44*	—	59	2154	36.51	5-65	1	—
Cowie J.	9	13	4	45	90	10.00	—	—	3	—	45	969	21.53	6-40	4	1
Cresswell G.F.	3	5	3	12*	14	7.00	—	—	—	—	13	292	22.46	6-168	1	—
Cromb I.B.	5	8	2	51*	123	20.50	—	1	1	—	8	442	55.25	3-113	—	—
Crowe J.J.	39	65	4	128	1601	26.24	3	6	41	—	0	9	—	—	—	—
Crowe M.D.	77	131	11	299	5444	45.36	17	18	71	—	14	676	48.28	2-25	—	—

	M	I	NO	HS	Runs	Ave	100	50	Ct	St	Wkts	Runs	Ave	Best	5WI	10W
Cunis R.S.	20	31	8	51	295	12.83	—	1	1	—	51	1887	37.00	6-76	1	—
D'Arcy J.W.	5	10	0	33	136	13.60	—	—	—	—	—	—	—	—	—	—
de Groen R.P.	5	10	4	26	45	7.50	—	—	—	—	11	505	45.90	3-40	—	—
Davis H.T.	5	7	4	8*	20	6.66	—	—	4	—	17	499	29.35	5-63	1	—
Dempster C.S.	10	15	4	136	723	65.73	2	5	2	—	0	10	—	—	—	—
Dempster E.W.	5	8	2	47	106	17.67	—	—	1	—	2	219	109.50	1-24	—	—
†Dick A.E.	17	30	4	50*	370	14.73	—	1	47	4	—	—	—	—	—	—
Dickinson G.R.	3	5	0	11	31	6.20	—	—	3	—	8	245	30.63	3-66	—	—
Donnelly M.P.	7	12	1	206	582	52.91	1	4	7	—	0	20	—	—	—	—
Doull S.B.	32	50	11	46	570	14.61	—	—	16	—	98	2872	29.30	7-65	6	—
Dowling G.T.	39	77	3	239	2306	31.16	3	11	23	—	1	19	19.00	1-19	—	—
Drum C.J.	5	5	2	4	10	3.33	—	—	4	—	16	482	30.12	3-36	—	—
Dunning J.A.	4	6	1	19	38	7.60	—	—	2	—	5	493	98.60	2-35	—	—
*Edgar B.A.	39	68	4	161	1958	30.59	3	12	14*	—	0	3	—	—	—	—
*Edwards G.N.	8	15	0	55	377	25.13	—	3	7*	—	—	—	—	—	—	—
Emery R.W.G.	2	4	0	28	46	11.50	—	—	—	—	2	52	26.00	2-52	—	—
Fisher F.E.	1	2	0	14	23	11.50	—	—	—	—	1	78	78.00	1-78	—	—
Fleming S.P.	75	130	9	274*	4671	38.60	5	34	114	—	—	—	—	—	—	—
Foley H.	1	2	0	2	4	2.00	—	—	—	—	—	—	—	—	—	—
Franklin J.E.C.	2	2	0	0	0	0.00	—	—	1	—	7	150	21.42	4-26	—	—
Franklin T.J.	21	37	1	101	828	23.00	1	4	8	—	—	—	—	—	—	—
Freeman D.L.	2	2	0	1	2	1.00	—	—	—	—	1	169	169.00	1-91	—	—
Gallichan N.	1	2	0	30	32	16.00	—	—	—	—	3	113	37.67	3-99	—	—
Gedye S.G.	4	8	0	55	193	24.13	—	2	—	—	—	—	—	—	—	—
†Germon L.K.	12	21	3	55	382	21.22	—	1	27	2	—	—	—	—	—	—
Gillespie S.R.	1	1	0	28	28	28.00	—	—	—	—	1	79	79.00	1-79	—	—
Gray E.J.	10	16	0	50	248	15.50	—	1	6	—	17	886	52.11	3-73	—	—
Greatbatch M.J.	41	71	5	146*	2021	30.62	3	10	27	—	0	0	—	—	—	—
†Guillen S.C.	3	6	0	41	98	16.33	—	—	4	1	—	—	—	—	—	—
Guy J.W.	12	23	2	102	440	20.95	1	3	2	—	—	—	—	—	—	—
Hadlee D.R.	26	42	5	56	530	14.32	—	1	8	—	71	2389	33.65	4-30	—	—
Hadlee R.J.	86	134	19	151*	3124	27.16	2	15	39	—	431	9611	22.29	9-52	36	9
Hadlee W.A.	11	19	1	116	543	30.17	1	2	6	—	—	—	—	—	—	—
Harford N.S.	8	15	0	93	229	15.27	—	2	—	—	—	—	—	—	—	—
†Harford R.I.	3	5	2	6	7	2.33	—	—	11	—	—	—	—	—	—	—
Harris C.Z.	23	42	4	71	777	20.44	—	5	14	—	16	1170	73.12	2-16	—	—
Harris P.G.Z.	9	18	1	101	378	22.24	1	1	6	—	0	14	—	—	—	—
Harris R.M.	2	3	0	13	31	10.33	—	—	—	—	—	—	—	—	—	—
Hart M.N.	14	24	4	45	353	17.65	—	—	9	—	29	1438	49.58	5-77	1	—
Hart R.G.	7	13	3	57*	205	20.50	—	1	15	1	—	—	—	—	—	—
Hartland B.R.	9	18	0	52	303	16.83	—	1	5	—	—	—	—	—	—	—
Haslam M.J.	4	2	1	3	4	4.00	—	—	2	—	2	245	122.50	1-33	—	—
Hastings B.E.	31	56	6	117*	1510	30.20	4	7	23	—	0	9	—	—	—	—
Hayes J.A.	15	22	7	19	73	4.87	—	—	3	—	30	1217	40.57	4-36	—	—
Henderson M.	1	2	1	6	8	8.00	—	—	1	—	2	64	32.00	2-38	—	—
Horne M.J.	35	65	2	157	1788	28.38	4	5	17	—	0	26	—	—	—	—
Horne P.A.	4	7	0	27	71	10.14	—	—	3	—	—	—	—	—	—	—
Hough K.W.	2	3	2	31*	62	62.00	—	—	1	—	6	175	29.17	3-79	—	—
Howarth G.P.	47	83	5	147	2531	32.44	6	11	29	—	3	271	90.33	1-13	—	—
Howarth H.J.	30	42	18	61	291	12.13	—	1	33	—	86	3178	36.95	5-34	2	—
†James K.C.	11	13	2	14	52	4.73	—	—	11	5	—	—	—	—	—	—
Jarvis T.W.	13	22	1	182	625	29.76	1	2	3	—	0	3	—	—	—	—
Jones A.H.	39	74	8	186	2922	44.27	7	11	25	—	1	194	194.00	1-40	—	—
Kennedy R.J.	4	5	1	22	28	7.00	—	—	2	—	6	380	63.33	3-28	—	—

	M	I	NO	HS	Runs	Ave	100	50	Ct	St	Wkts	Runs	Ave	Best	5WI	10WM
Kerr J.L.	7	12	1	59	212	19.27	—	1	4	—	—	—	—	—	—	—
Kuggeleijn C.M.	2	4	0	7	7	1.75	—	—	1	—	1	67	67.00	1-50	—	—
Larsen G.R.	8	13	4	26*	127	14.11	—	—	5	—	24	689	28.70	3-57	—	—
Latham R.T.	4	7	0	119	219	31.28	1	—	5	—	0	6	—	—	—	—
Lees W.K.	21	37	4	152	778	23.57	1	1	52	7	0	4	—	—	—	—
Leggat I.B.	1	1	0	0	0	0.00	—	—	2	—	0	6	—	—	—	—
Leggat J.G.	9	18	2	61	351	21.94	—	2	—	—	—	—	—	—	—	—
Lissette A.F.	2	4	2	1*	2	1.00	—	—	1	—	3	124	41.33	2-73	—	—
Loveridge G.R.	1	1	1	4*	4	—	—	—	—	—	—	—	—	—	—	—
Lowry T.C.	7	8	0	80	223	27.88	—	2	8	—	0	5	—	—	—	—
McEwan P.E.	4	7	1	40*	96	16.00	—	—	5	—	0	13	—	—	—	—
MacGibbon A.R.	26	46	5	66	814	19.85	—	3	13	—	70	2160	30.86	5-64	1	—
McGirr H.M.	2	1	0	51	51	51.00	—	1	—	—	1	115	115.00	1-65	—	—
McGregor S.N.	25	47	2	111	892	19.82	1	3	9	—	—	—	—	—	—	—
McLeod E.G.	1	2	1	16	18	18.00	—	—	—	—	0	5	—	—	—	—
McMahon T.G.	5	7	4	4*	7	2.33	—	—	7	1	—	—	—	—	—	—
McMillan C.D.	44	73	7	142	2619	39.68	5	16	19	—	27	1174	43.48	3-48	—	—
McRae D.A.N.	1	2	0	8	8	4.00	—	—	—	—	0	44	—	—	—	—
Marshall H.J.H.	1	1	1	40*	40	—	—	—	—	—	0	4	—	—	—	—
Martin C.S.	11	11	4	7	12	1.71	—	—	4	—	34	1176	34.58	5-71	1	—
Matheson A.M.	2	1	0	7	7	7.00	—	—	2	—	2	136	68.00	2-7	—	—
Meale T.	2	4	0	10	21	5.25	—	—	—	—	—	—	—	—	—	—
Merritt W.E.	6	8	1	19	73	10.43	—	—	2	—	12	617	51.42	4-104	—	—
Meuli E.M.	1	2	0	23	38	19.00	—	—	—	—	—	—	—	—	—	—
Milburn B.D.	3	3	2	4*	8	8.00	—	—	6	2	—	—	—	—	—	—
Miller L.S.M.	13	25	0	47	346	13.84	—	—	1	—	0	1	—	—	—	—
Mills J.E.	7	10	1	117	241	26.78	1	—	1	—	—	—	—	—	—	—
Moir A.M.	17	30	8	41*	327	14.86	—	—	2	—	28	1418	50.64	6-155	2	—
Moloney D.A.R.	3	6	0	64	156	26.00	—	1	3	—	0	9	—	—	—	—
Mooney F.L.H.	14	22	2	46	343	17.15	—	—	22	8	0	0	—	—	—	—
Morgan R.W.	20	34	1	97	734	22.24	—	5	12*	—	5	609	121.80	1-16	—	—
Morrison B.D.	1	2	0	10	10	5.00	—	—	1	—	2	129	64.50	2-129	—	—
Morrison D.K.	48	71	26	42	379	8.42	—	—	14	—	160	5549	34.68	7-89	10	—
Morrison J.F.M.	17	29	0	117	656	22.62	1	3	9	—	2	71	35.50	2-52	—	—
Motz R.C.	32	56	3	60	612	11.55	—	3	9	—	100	3148	31.48	6-63	5	—
Murray B.A.G.	13	26	1	90	598	23.92	—	5	21	—	1	0	0.00	1-0	—	—
Murray D.J.	8	16	1	52	303	20.20	—	1	6	—	—	—	—	—	—	—
Nash D.J.	32	45	14	89*	729	23.51	—	4	13	—	93	2649	28.48	6-27	3	1
Newman J.	3	4	0	19	33	8.25	—	—	—	—	2	254	127.00	2-76	—	—
O'Connor S.B.	19	27	9	20	105	5.83	—	—	6	—	53	1724	32.52	5-51	1	—
O'Sullivan D.R.	11	21	4	23*	158	9.29	—	—	2	—	18	1221	67.83	5-148	1	—
Oram J.D.P.	4	7	1	74	171	28.52	—	1	3	—	15	246	16.40	4-41	—	—
Overton G.W.F.	3	6	1	3*	8	1.60	—	—	1	—	9	258	28.67	3-65	—	—
Owens M.B.	8	12	6	8*	16	2.66	—	—	3	—	17	585	34.44	4-99	—	—
Page M.L.	14	20	0	104	492	24.60	1	2	6	—	5	231	46.20	2-21	—	—
Parker J.M.	36	63	2	121	1498	24.56	3	5	30	—	1	24	24.00	1-24	—	—
Parker N.M.	3	6	0	40	89	14.83	—	—	2	—	—	—	—	—	—	—
Parore A.C.	78	128	19	110	2865	26.28	2	14	197	7	—	—	—	—	—	—
Patel D.N.	37	66	8	99	1200	20.68	—	5	15	—	75	3154	42.05	6-50	3	—
Petherick P.J.	6	11	4	13	34	4.86	—	—	4	—	16	685	42.81	3-90	—	—
Petrie E.C.	14	25	5	55	258	12.90	—	1	25	—	—	—	—	—	—	—
Playle W.R.	8	15	0	65	151	10.07	—	1	4	—	—	—	—	—	—	—
Pocock B.A.	15	29	0	85	665	22.93	—	6	5	—	0	20	—	—	—	—
Pollard V.	32	59	7	116	1266	24.35	2	7	19	—	40	1853	46.33	3-3	—	—

	M	I	NO	HS	Runs	Ave	100	50	Ct	St	Wkts	Runs	Ave	Best	5WI	10
Poore M.B.	14	24	1	45	355	15.43	—	—	1	—	9	367	40.78	2-28	—	—
Priest M.W.	3	4	0	26	56	14.00	—	—	—	—	3	158	52.66	2-42	—	—
Pringle C.	14	21	4	30	175	10.29	—	—	3	—	30	1389	46.30	7-52	1	
Puna N.	3	5	3	18*	31	15.50	—	—	1	—	4	240	60.00	2-40	—	—
Rabone G.O.	12	20	2	107	562	31.22	1	2	5	—	16	635	36.69	6-68	1	—
Redmond R.E.	1	2	0	107	163	81.50	1	1	—	—	—	—	—	—	—	—
Reid J.F.	19	31	3	180	1296	46.28	6	2	9	—	0	7	—	—	—	—
*Reid J.R.	58	108	5	142	3428	33.28	6	22	43*	1	85	2835	33.35	6-60	1	—
Richardson M.H.	24	41	3	143	1852	48.73	2	16	18	—	1	17	17.00	1-16	—	—
Roberts A.D.G.	7	12	1	84*	254	23.09	—	1	4	—	4	182	45.50	1-12	—	—
Roberts A.W.	5	10	1	66*	248	27.56	—	3	4	—	7	209	29.86	4-101	—	—
Robertson G.K.	1	1	0	12	12	12.00	—	—	—	—	1	91	91.00	1-91	—	—
Rowe C.G.	1	2	0	0	0	0.00	—	—	1	—	—	—	—	—	—	—
Rutherford K.R.	56	99	8	107*	2465	27.08	3	18	32	—	1	161	161.00	1-38	—	—
Scott R.H.	1	1	0	18	18	18.00	—	—	—	—	1	74	74.00	1-74	—	—
Scott V.J.	10	17	1	84	458	28.63	—	3	7	—	0	14	—	—	—	—
Sewell D.G.	1	1	1	1*	1	—	—	—	—	—	0	90	—	—	—	—
Shrimpton M.J.F.	10	19	0	46	265	13.95	—	—	2	—	5	158	31.60	3-35	—	—
Sinclair B.W.	21	40	1	138	1148	29.44	3	3	8	—	2	32	16.00	2-32	—	—
Sinclair I.M.	2	4	1	18*	25	8.33	—	—	1	—	1	120	120.00	1-79	—	—
Sinclair M.S.	20	34	5	214	1100	37.93	3	1	17	—	0	13	—	—	—	—
Smith F.B.	4	6	1	96	237	47.40	—	2	1	—	—	—	—	—	—	—
Smith H.D.	1	1	0	4	4	4.00	—	—	—	—	1	113	113.00	1-113	—	—
†Smith I.D.S.	63	88	17	173	1815	25.56	2	6	168	8	0	5	—	—	—	—
Snedden C.A.	1	—	—	—	—	—	—	—	—	—	0	46	—	—	—	—
Snedden M.C.	25	30	8	33*	327	14.86	—	—	7	—	58	2199	37.91	5-68	1	—
Sparling J.T.	11	20	2	50	229	12.72	—	1	3	—	5	327	65.40	1-9	—	—
Spearman C.M.	19	37	2	112	922	26.34	1	3	20	—	—	—	—	—	—	—
Stead G.R.	5	8	0	78	278	34.75	—	2	2	—	0	1	—	—	—	—
Stirling D.A.	6	9	2	26	108	15.42	—	—	1	—	13	601	46.23	4-88	—	—
Styris S.B.	5	9	1	107	318	39.75	1	2	5	—	5	170	34.00	3-28	—	—
Su'a M.L.	13	18	5	44	165	12.69	—	—	8	—	36	1377	38.25	5-73	2	—
Sutcliffe B.	42	76	8	230*	2727	40.10	5	15	20	—	4	344	86.00	2-38	—	—
Taylor B.R.	30	50	6	124	898	20.41	2	2	10	—	111	2953	26.60	7-74	4	—
Taylor D.D.	3	5	0	77	159	31.80	—	1	2	—	—	—	—	—	—	—
Thomson K.	2	4	1	69	94	31.33	—	1	—	—	1	9	9.00	1-9	—	—
Thomson S.A.	19	35	4	120*	958	30.90	1	5	7	—	19	953	50.15	3-63	—	—
†Tindill E.W.T.	5	9	1	37*	73	9.13	—	—	6	1	—	—	—	—	—	—
Troup G.B.	15	18	6	13*	55	4.58	—	—	2	—	39	1454	37.28	6-95	1	—
Truscott P.B.	1	2	0	26	29	14.50	—	—	1	—	—	—	—	—	—	—
Tuffey D.R.	14	18	3	31	153	10.20	—	—	9	—	47	1262	26.85	6-54	1	—
Turner G.M.	41	73	6	259	2991	44.64	7	14	42	—	0	5	—	—	—	—
Twose R.G.	16	27	2	94	628	25.12	—	6	5	—	3	130	43.33	2-36	—	—
Vance R.H.	4	7	0	68	207	29.57	—	1	—	—	—	—	—	—	—	—
Vaughan J.T.C.	6	12	1	44	201	18.27	—	—	4	—	11	450	40.90	4-27	—	—
Vettori D.L.	46	67	10	90	940	16.49	—	5	22	—	142	4812	33.88	7-87	7	
Vincent L.	11	20	1	104	558	29.36	1	5	11	—	—	—	—	—	—	—
Vivian G.E.	5	6	0	43	110	18.33	—	—	3	—	1	107	107.00	1-14	—	—
Vivian H.G.	7	10	0	100	421	42.10	1	5	4	—	17	633	37.24	4-58	—	—
†Wadsworth K.J.	33	51	4	80	1010	21.49	—	5	92	4	—	—	—	—	—	—
Walker B.G.K.	5	8	2	27*	118	19.66	—	—	—	—	5	399	79.80	2-92	—	—
Wallace W.M.	13	21	0	66	439	20.90	—	5	5	—	0	5	—	—	—	—
Walmsley K.P.	3	5	0	5	13	2.60	—	—	—	—	9	391	43.44	3-70	—	—
†Ward J.T.	8	12	6	35*	75	12.50	—	—	16	1	—	—	—	—	—	—

	M	I	NO	HS	Runs	Ave	100	50	Ct	St	Wkts	Runs	Ave	Best	5WI	10WM
Watson W.	15	18	6	11	60	5.00	—	—	4	—	40	1387	34.67	6-78	1	—
Watt L.	1	2	0	2	2	1.00	—	—	—	—	—	—	—	—	—	—
Webb M.G.	3	2	0	12	12	6.00	—	—	—	—	4	471	117.75	2-114	—	—
Webb P.N.	2	3	0	5	11	3.67	—	—	2	—	—	—	—	—	—	—
Weir G.L.	11	16	2	74*	416	29.71	—	3	3	—	7	209	29.86	3-38	—	—
White D.J.	2	4	0	18	31	7.75	—	—	—	—	0	5	—	—	—	—
Whitelaw P.E.	2	4	2	30	64	32.00	—	—	—	—	—	—	—	—	—	—
Wiseman P.J.	16	24	6	29	159	8.83	—	—	7	—	40	1741	43.52	5-82	2	—
Wright J.G.	82	148	7	185	5334	37.82	12	23	38	—	0	5	—	—	—	—
Young B.A.	35	68	4	267*	2034	31.78	2	12	54	—	—	—	—	—	—	—
Yuile B.W.	17	33	6	64	481	17.81	—	1	12	—	34	1213	35.68	4-43	—	—

Note: There were 58 dismissals made by substitutes: M.J. Greatbatch (5), J.G. Bracewell, J.J. Crowe, T.W. Jarvis (4), C.Z. Harris (3), D.R. O'Sullivan, A.C. Parore, K.R. Rutherford, G.E. Vivian (2), J.C. Alabaster, R.W. Anderson, S.L. Boock, G.E. Bradburn, C. Burke, R.O. Collinge, B.E. Congdon, M.D. Crowe, H.T. Davis, C.J. Drum, E.W. Dempster, G.T. Dowling, B.A. Edgar, G.N. Edwards, S.G. Gedye, M.N. Hart, M.A. Hastings, I.B. Leggat, T.G. McMahon, P.E. McEwan, M.N. McKenzie, M.J. Mason, R.C. Motz, S.B. O'Connor, N.M. Parker, M.W. Priest, T.D. Ritchie, L. Vincent, B.G.K. Walker catches and B.E. Congdon a stumping. The latter is one of only two instances in tests of a substitute making a stumping.

† all test appearances were as wicketkeeper.
A.C. Parore had 67 tests as wicketkeeper, T.E. Blain (9), G.N. Edwards (4), B.A. Edgar and J.R. Reid one each.

* record includes catches taken while keeping wicket as follows: A.C. Parore (194), T.E. Blain (18), B.A. Edgar (4), J.R. Reid (2), B.E. Congdon and R.W. Morgan one each. Edwards' catches were all made while keeping wicket.

SUMMARY OF TEST CAREER RECORDS

Most Matches

Hadlee R.J.	86	Howarth G.P.	47	Parker J.M.	36
Wright J.G.	82	Vettori D.J.	46	Collinge R.O.	35
Parore A.C.	78	McMillan C.D	44	Young B.A.	35
Crowe M.D.	77	Cairns B.L.	43	Horne M.J.	35
Fleming S.P.	75	Chatfield E.J.	43	Wadsworth K.J.	33
Smith I.D.S.	63	Sutcliffe B.	42	Motz R.C.	32
Congdon B.E.	61	Turner G.M.	41	Pollard V.	32
Reid J.R.	58	Bracewell J.G.	41	Doull S.B.	32
Astle N.J.	57	Greatbatch M.J.	41	Nash D.J.	32
Rutherford K.R.	56	Dowling G.T.	39	Hastings B.F.	31
Cairns C.L.	55	Edgar B.A.	39	Howarth H.J.	30
Coney J.V.	52	Crowe J.J.	39	Taylor B.R.	30
Burgess M.G.	50	Jones A.H.	39	Boock S.L.	30
Morrison D.K.	48	Patel D.N.	37		

Most Runs

Crowe M.D.	5444	Burgess M.G.	2684	Horne M.J.	1788
Wright J.G.	5334	Coney J.V.	2668	Crowe J.J.	1601
Fleming S.P.	4671	McMillan C.D.	2619	Hastings B.F.	1510
Congdon B.E.	3448	Howarth G.P.	2531	Parker J.M.	1498
Reid J.R.	3428	Rutherford K.R.	2465	Reid J.F.	1296
Astle N.J.	3420	Dowling G.T.	2306	Pollard V.	1266
Hadlee R.J.	3124	Young B.A.	2034	Patel D.N.	1200
Turner G.M.	2991	Greatbatch M.J.	2021	Sinclair B.W.	1148
Jones A.H.	2922	Edgar B.A.	1958	Sinclair M.S.	1079
Parore A.C.	2865	Richardson M.H.	1852	Wadsworth K.J.	1010
Cairns C.L.	2853	Smith I.D.S.	1815	Bracewell J.G.	1001
Sutcliffe B.	2727				

Most Wickets

Hadlee R.J.	431	Bracewell J.G.	102	Hadlee D.R.	71
Cairns C.L.	197	Motz R.C.	100	MacGibbon A.R.	70
Morrison D.K.	160	Doull S.B.	98	Cameron F.J.	62
Vettori D.L.	142	Nash D.J.	93	Congdon B.E.	59
Cairns B.L.	130	Howarth H.J.	86	Snedden M.C.	58
Chatfield E.J.	123	Reid J.R.	85	O'Connor S.B.	53
Collinge R.O.	116	Patel D.N.	75	Cunis R.S.	51
Taylor B.R.	111	Boock S.L.	74		

Most Catches

Fleming S.P.	114	Turner G.M.	42	Howarth H.J.	33
Crowe M.D.	71	Reid J.R.	41	Rutherford K.R.	32
Coney J.V.	64	Crowe J.J.	41	Bracewell J.G.	31
Young B.A.	54	Hadlee R.J.	39	Parker J.M.	30
Astle N.J.	51	Wright J.G.	38	Cairns B.L.	30
Congdon B.E.	43	Burgess M.G.	34	Howarth G.P.	29

Most Wicketkeeping Dismissals

	Ct	*St*	*Total*
Parore A.C.	194	7	201
Smith I.D.S.	168	8	176
Wadsworth K.J.	92	4	96
Lees W.K.	52	7	59
Dick A.E.	47	4	51

Test Captains

			RESULTS				*TOSS*	
		P	*W*	*L*	*D*	*W*	*L*
Fleming S.P.	1996/97 to 2002/03	51	19	15	17	25	26
Reid J.R.	1955/56 to 1965	34	3	18	13	17	17
Howarth G.P.	1979/80 to 1984/85	30	11	7	12	17	13
Dowling G.T.	1967/68 to 1971/72	19	4	7	8	10	9
Rutherford K.R.	1992/93 to 1994/95	18	2	11	5	12	6
Congdon B.E.	1971/72 to 1974/75	17	1	7	9	4	13
Crowe M.D.	1990/91 to 1993/94	16	2	7	7	8	8
Coney J.V.	1984/85 to 1986/87	15	5	4	6	8	7
Wright J.G.	1987/88 to 1990	14	3	3	8	8	6
Germon L.K.	1995/96 to 1996/97	12	1	5	6	6	6
Turner G.M.	1975/76 to 1976/77	10	1	6	3	2	8
Burgess M.G.	1977/78 to 1980/81	10	1	6	3	4	6
Cave H.B.	1955/56	9	0	5	4	5	4
Hadlee W.A.	1945/46 to 1950/51	8	0	2	6	4	4
Lowry T.C.	1929/30 to 1931	7	0	2	5	5	2
Page M.L.	1931/32 to 1937	7	0	3	4	4	3
Crowe J.J.	1986/87 to 1987/88	6	0	1	5	3	3
Rabone G.O.	1953/54 to 1954/55	5	0	4	1	2	3
Sutcliffe B.	1951/52 to 1953/54	4	0	3	1	4	0
Sinclair B.W.	1965/66 to 1967/68	3	0	1	2	3	0
Nash D.J.	1998/99	3	0	1	2	3	0
Wallace W.M.	1952/53	2	0	1	1	0	2
Chapple M.E.	1965/66	1	0	0	1	0	1
Parker J.M.	1976/77	1	0	0	1	0	1
Smith I.D.S.	1990/91	1	0	0	1	1	0
Totals		**303**	**53**	**119**	**131**	**155**	**148**

Test Debuts

New Zealand has now played 303 test matches. In 169 there have been no new test caps. In the other 134 the records are:

11 players making debut 1929/30 v England at Christchurch (NZ's first test match)

6 players making debut 1937 v England at Lord's (NZ's first test since 1932/33)

6 players making debut 1945/46 v Australia at Wellington (NZ's first test after Second World War)

6 players making debut 1946/47 v England at Christchurch (test after one above)

5 players making debut 1961/62 v South Africa at Durban

Of the 12 players who made their debuts in the 1945/46 and 1946/47 tests above, seven did not appear again. In eight successive tests at least one player made his test debut — South Africa 1963/64 (3), Pakistan 1964/65 (3), India 1964/65 (2). In nine successive tests there were no new caps — England 1969 (2), India 1969/70 (3), Pakistan 1969/70 (3), England 1970/71 (1) and South Africa 1998/99 (1), England 1999 (4), India 1999/00 (3), West Indies 1999/00 (1).

Youngest/Oldest Test Players

YOUNGEST PLAYERS

			Bat	*Bowl*
18 years 10 days	Vettori D.L. v England at Wellington	1996/97	3* & 2*	2-98
18 years 197 days	Freeman D.L. v England at Christchurch	1932/33	1	0-78
18 years 267 days	Vivian H.G. v England at The Oval	1931	3 & 51	2-96
18 years 295 days	Collinge R.O. v Pakistan at Wellington	1964/65	0*	2-51 & 3-4
18 years 316 days	Bracewell B.P. v England at The Oval	1978	0 & 0	2-46 & 1-2
19 years 5 days	Vivian G.E. v India at Calcutta	1964/65	1 & 43	0-37 & 1-1
19 years 145 days	Beck J.E.F. v South Africa at Johannesburg	1953/54	16 & 7	
19 years 154 days	Rutherford K.R. v West Indies at Port of Spain	1984/85	0 & 0	
19 years 157 days	Crowe M.D. v Australia at Wellington	1981/82	9	0-14
19 years 163 days	Parore A.C. v England at Birmingham	1990	12* & 20	4ct/1st
19 years 164 days	Cairns C.L. v Australia at Perth	1989/90	1 & 28	0-60
19 years 173 days	Pollard V. India at Madras	1964/65	3	3-90 & 1-3
19 years 186 days	Playle W.R. v England at Birmingham	1958	4 & 8	
19 years 252 days	Donnelly M.P. v England at Lord's	1937	0 & 21	
19 years 340 days	Sewell D.G. v Zimbabwe at Bulawayo	1997/98	1*	0-81 & 0-9
19 years 344 days	Sparling J.T. v England at Leeds	1958	9* & 18	1-78

OLDEST PLAYERS *(age on last day of final test)*

41 days 294 days	Alabaster J.C. v West Indies at Port of Spain	1971/72	18	0-49 & 1-5
41 years 196 days	Sutcliffe B. v England at Birmingham	1965	4* & 53	
40 years 198 days	Congdon B.E. v England at Lord's	1978	2 & 3	0-12

OLDEST PLAYER ON DEBUT

38 years 101 days	McGirr H.M.† v England at Auckland	1929/30		0-46

† *he made 51 in his first test innings in his second test*

YOUNGEST CENTURY MAKER

19 years 121 days†	Vivian H.G. 100 v South Africa at Wellington	1931/32	

† *world record at that time*

OLDEST CENTURY MAKERS

41 years 109 days	Sutcliffe B. 151* v India at Calcutta	1964/65
39 years 12 days	Congdon B.E. 107* v Australia at Christchurch	1976/77

YOUNGEST CAPTAIN

23 years 319 days	Fleming S.P. v England at Christchurch	1996/97	62 & 11
25 years 252 days	Parker J.M. v Pakistan at Karachi	1976/77	24 & 16

OLDEST CAPTAIN *(age on last day of final test)*

37 years 40 days	Reid J.R. v England at Leeds	1965	54 & 5	
36 years 359 days	Congdon B.E. v England at Christchurch	1974/75	38	0-27
36 years 88 days	Wallace W.M. v South Africa at Auckland	1952/53	23	
36 years 5 days	Wright J.G. v England at Birmingham	1990	24 & 46	

LONGEST INTERVAL BETWEEN TEST APPEARANCES

14 years 28 days	Cleverley D.C. — v South Africa at Christchurch 1/3/32
	v Australia at Wellington 29/3/46

Only A.J. Traicos (22 years 222 days), G. Gunn (17 years 316 days), Younis Ahmed (17 years 111 days) and J.M.M. Commaille (14 years 95 days) have a longer interval between tests but Cleverley is unique in that the above matches were his only two tests.

NEW ZEALAND
LIMITED-OVERS RECORDS

This section of the *Almanack* is devoted to limited-overs matches in New Zealand (other than one-day internationals) and has been compiled from the following games:

1. 589 matches in national competitions (Shell Cup, State Shield etc) from 1971/72 to 2002/03.

2. 47 matches between provincial sides and overseas teams from 1970/71 to 2001/02.

1970/71	Wellington v MCC
	Otago v MCC
	Central Districts v MCC
1972/73	Central Districts v Pakistan
1973/74	Wellington v Australia
	Central Districts v Australia
1975/76	Wellington v India
1977/78	Northern Districts v England XI
1978/79	Auckland v Pakistan
	Canterbury v Pakistan
1979/80	Auckland XI v West Indies
	Central Districts v West Indies
1981/82	Northern Districts v Australia
	Central Districts v Australia
1983/84	Otago v England XI
1984/85	Wellington v New South Wales
1985/86	Auckland v Australia
1986/87	Auckland v West Indies
	Central Districts v South Australia *(4 matches)*
1987/88	Wellington v England
	Auckland v Victoria *(2 matches)*
	Wellington v Queensland
	Canterbury v Queensland
	Otago v Queensland
1988/89	Auckland v Pakistan
1991/92	Auckland v England
	Auckland v Australia
	Northern Districts v Zimbabwe *(2 matches)*
1993/94	Canterbury v New South Wales
1994/95	Auckland v West Indies
	Central Districts v India
	Wellington v South Africa
	Canterbury v Sri Lanka
1996/97	Central Districts v Sri Lanka
1997/98	Canterbury v Bangladesh
1998/99	Northern v Pakistan A
2000/01	Wellington v New South Wales
	Canterbury v Zimbabwe
2001/02	Northern Districts v England *(2 matches)*

3. Three matches in the Data General competition in 1986/87.

4. Six matches in the Shell Shield competition in 1997/98.

5. 23 other matches not involving provincial sides.

1972/73	New Zealand Under 23 XI v Pakistan
1976/77	Australia v Invitation XIs *(2 matches)*
1981/82	North Island v South Island
1982/83	Sri Lanka v NZ Minor Associations *(2 matches)*
1992/93	New Zealand President's XI v Australia
1993/94	North Island v South Island
	Sir Ron Brierley XI v Pakistan
1994/95	North Island v South Island

	Sir Ron Brierley XI v West Indies
	New Zealand Academy XI v Sri Lanka
	New Zealand Academy XI v Australian Academy XI
1996/97	New Zealand Academy XI v England
1997/98	New Zealand Academy XI v Zimbabwe
1998/99	New Zealand A v Pakistan A *(3 matches)*
	New Zealand Academy XI v South Africa
1999/00	New Zealand Academy XI v England A *(2 matches)*
	New Zealand A v England A *(3 matches)*
2000/01	North Island Selection XI v Sri Lanka

TEAM RECORDS

Highest Totals

376-3	Central Districts v Otago	New Plymouth	1996/97
339-5	Central Districts v Otago	Hastings	1998/99
329-5	Canterbury v Northern Districts	Christchurch	1995/96
318-5	Auckland v Northern Districts	Auckland	2000/01
313-7	Canterbury v Northern Districts	Timaru	1993/94
309-8	Auckland v Northern Districts	Gisborne	1982/83
309-6	Canterbury v Central Districts	Christchurch	1994/95
306-2	Northern Districts v Auckland	Gisborne	1982/83
305-6	Central Districts v Otago	Oamaru	1999/00
300-5	Wellington v Auckland	Wellington	2001/02
298-5	Canterbury v Central Districts	Christchurch	1998/99
297-4	England XI v Otago	Alexandra	1983/84
295-8	New Zealand A v Pakistan A	Mt Maunganui	1998/99
295-6	Northern Districts v Auckland	Auckland	1999/00
295-7	Auckland v Central Districts	Napier	1999/00
294-6	Otago v Auckland	Alexandra	1997/98
293-3	Canterbury v Central Districts	Napier	1996/97
293-7	Northern Districts v England	Hamilton	2001/02
290-9	Otago v Central Districts	Oamaru	1999/00
289-8	Central Districts v Northern Districts	Wanganui	1984/85
289-5	Canterbury v Auckland	Christchurch	1997/98
288-5	Canterbury v Otago	Alexandra	1993/94
288-6	Canterbury v Wellington	Christchurch	1995/96
288-6	England v Northern Districts	Hamilton	2001/02
287-4	South Australia v Central Districts	Palmerston North	1986/87
287-7	Wellington v Auckland	Wellington	1995/96
286	Wellington v Canterbury	Christchurch	1995/96
286-8	Canterbury v Otago	Christchurch	1996/97
285-6	Central Districts v Auckland	Wanganui	1994/95
285-6	Wellington v Auckland	Wellington	1997/98

Lowest Totals

48	Pakistan v Auckland	Auckland	1988/89
58	Central Districts v Wellington	Wellington	2001/02
64	Otago v Wellington	Alexandra	1984/85
66	Wellington v Canterbury	Wellington	1996/97
67	Otago v Central Districts	Invercargill	2000/01
67	Central Districts v Canterbury	Christchurch	2002/03
70	Auckland v Northern Districts	Pukekohe	1977/78
72	New Zealand Academy XI v South Africa	Alexandra	1998/99
73	Auckland v Central Districts	Auckland	2000/01
75	Canterbury v Otago	Christchurch	1973/74
76	Northern Districts v Central Districts	Mt Maunganui	1987/88
76	Otago v Queensland	Dunedin	1987/88
78	Central Districts v Auckland	New Plymouth	1988/89
79	Wellington v Otago	Wellington	1999/00
80	Northern Districts v Wellington	Wellington	1982/83
81	Northern Districts v Zimbabwe	Cambridge	1991/92
81	Central Districts v Northern Districts	Levin	1995/96
81	Wellington v Canterbury	Wellington	1996/97
85	Northern Districts v Wellington	Mt Maunganui	1997/98

88	Northern Districts v Canterbury	Christchurch	1994/95
89	Central Districts v Wellington	Wellington	1985/86
91	Otago v Auckland	Auckland	1996/97
92	Auckland v Wellington	Wellington	1971/72
93	Central Districts v Canterbury	Timaru	1995/96
94	Central Districts v Otago	Alexandra	1986/87
95	Wellington v Northern Districts	Tauranga	1989/90
96	Auckland v Canterbury	Christchurch	1995/96
96	Canterbury v Northern Districts	Hamilton	1997/98
97	Central Districts v Auckland	Auckland	1995/96
98	Auckland v Canterbury	Christchurch	1976/77
99	Canterbury v Otago	Dunedin	1983/84

Most Extras in an Innings

55	Northern Districts (271-8)	v Wellington (228)	Hamilton	2002/03
51	NZ Academy XI (183)	v England A (184-4)	Lincoln	1999/00
48	Wellington (211-7)	v Otago (208-8)	Wellington	1996/97
45	Wellington (251-8)	v Otago (250-6)	Alexandra	1997/98
45	England A (219-7)	v New Zealand A (216)	Auckland	1999/00
43	Otago (250-6)	v Wellington (251-8)	Alexandra	1997/98
42	Canterbury (286-8)	v Otago (149)	Christchurch	1996/97
42	Otago (233-9)	v Wellington (200)	Alexandra	1999/00
42	Northern Districts (202-9)	v Auckland (157-6)	Hamilton	2002/03
41	Northern Districts (215)	v Auckland (217-6)	Whangarei	1995/96

Fewest Extras in an Innings

1	Canterbury (205-6)	v Wellington (203)	Timaru	1986/87
2	Pakistan (216-4)	v NZ Under 23 XI	Rotorua	1972/73
2	Otago (114)	v Canterbury (113)	Christchurch	1979/80
2	Auckland (163-4)	v Otago (162)	Oamaru	1981/82
2	Auckland (105)	v Otago (214-9)	Dunedin	1993/94

Tied Match

	Wellington v South Africa	Wellington	1994/95

Close Finishes

RUNS *(winning team listed first)*

1	Northern Districts v Canterbury	Hamilton	1982/83
1	Northern Districts v Zimbabwe	Pukekohe	1991/92
1	Auckland v Central Districts	Auckland	1994/95
1	Otago v Auckland	Alexandra	1995/96
1	Central Districts v Wellington	Wellington	1996/97
2	Central Districts v Northern Districts	Tauranga	1989/90
2	Canterbury v Wellington	Christchurch	1995/96
2	Canterbury v Auckland	Auckland	1999/00
2	Wellington v Otago	Alexandra	2002/03
3	Auckland v Northern Districts	Hamilton	1972/73
3	Auckland v Northern Districts	Auckland	1981/82
3	Canterbury v Wellington	Christchurch	1991/92
3	Northern Districts v Auckland	Mt Maunganui	1993/94
3	Canterbury v Otago	Christchurch	1998/99
3	Wellington v Otago	Queenstown	2001/02
4	Otago v Wellington	Wellington	1987/88
4	Canterbury v Northern Districts	Rotorua	1993/94

4	Wellington v Central Districts	Wellington	1994/95
5	Northern Districts v Otago	Taupo	1995/96
5	Auckland v Otago	Auckland	1999/00
5	Wellington v Auckland	Auckland	2000/01

ONE WICKET *(winning team listed first)*

Wellington v Auckland	Wellington	1973/74
Otago v Canterbury	Christchurch	1979/80
Central Districts v Australia	New Plymouth	1981/82
Canterbury v Central Districts	Christchurch	1986/87
Otago v Northern Districts	Gisborne	1986/87
Auckland v Northern Districts	Hamilton	1989/90
Otago v Auckland	Auckland	1990/91
Wellington v Otago	Alexandra	1992/93
Central Districts v Wellington	Masterton	1993/94
Wellington v Northern Districts	Wellington	1996/97
Central Districts v Canterbury	Napier	1996/97
Wellington v Northern Districts	Whangarei	1999/00
Auckland v Northern Districts	Auckland	1999/00
Otago v Wellington	Dunedin	2000/01
Central Districts v Wellington	Waikanae	2000/01
Canterbury v Auckland	Auckland	2001/02

SCORES LEVEL *(won by team listed first, having lost fewer wickets)*

Otago (223-5) v Wellington (223-9)	Dunedin	1979/80
Canterbury (182-7) v Auckland (182-9)	Christchurch	1983/84
Canterbury (136-9) v Auckland (136)	Ashburton	1985/86
Queensland (174-8) v Wellington (174)	Wellington	1987/88
Wellington (227-8) v Auckland (227)	Wellington	1995/96
Canterbury (238-6) v Auckland (238-7)	Auckland	1995/96

Large Victories

RUNS *(winning team listed first)*

200	Central Districts v Otago	Hastings	1998/99
197	South Africa v New Zealand Academy XI	Alexandra	1998/99
189	New Zealand A v Pakistan A	Mt Maunganui	1998/99
186	Wellington v Auckland	Wellington	1971/72
153	Otago v Wellington	Alexandra	1982/83
152	Canterbury v Central Districts	Napier	1995/96
151	Wellington v Northern Districts	Mt Maunganui	1997/98
148	Northern Districts v Wellington	Wellington	1994/95
144	Canterbury v Central Districts	Christchurch	1994/95
144	Canterbury v Central Districts	Timaru	1995/96
140	Canterbury v Northern Districts	Hamilton	1998/99

TEN WICKETS *(winning team listed first)*

Northern Districts (71-0) v Auckland (70)	Pukekohe	1977/78
West Indies (132-0) v Central Districts (130)	New Plymouth	1979/80
Canterbury (120-0) v Auckland (119)	Christchurch	1987/88
Auckland (81-0) v Central Districts (78)	New Plymouth	1988/89
Wellington (205-0) v Canterbury (202-7)	Wellington	1994/95
Auckland (164-0) v Central Districts (163)	Auckland	1998/99

INDIVIDUAL RECORDS
Centuries

177	Pyke J.K.	South Australia v Central Districts	Palmerston North	1986/87
161	Hartland B.R.	Canterbury v Northern Districts	Timaru	1993/94
149	Nevin C.J.	Wellington v Central Districts	Wellington	1997/98
147*	Edgar B.A.	Wellington v Northern Districts	Gisborne	1981/82
145	Vincent L.	Auckland v Central Districts	Napier	1999/00
143	Cairns C.L.	Canterbury v Auckland	Christchurch	1994/95
140	Scott D.G.	Auckland v Northern Districts	Hamilton	1986/87
140	Kelly D.P.	Central Districts v Wellington	Waikanae	1999/00
139*	Tendulkar S.R.	India v Central Districts	Napier	1994/95
134*	Howell L.G.	Canterbury v Otago	Oamaru	1997/98
133*	Vincent L.	Auckland v Northern Districts	Auckland	2000/01
131	Astle N.J.	Canterbury v Wellington	Wellington	1995/96
130*	Crowe J.J.	Auckland v Northern Districts	Auckland	1991/92
129	Astle N.J.	Canterbury v Northern Districts	Christchurch	1995/96
128*	Edgar B.A.	Wellington v Central Districts	Wanganui	1982/83
128*	Richardson M.H.	Otago v Central Districts	New Plymouth	1996/97
127	Oram J.D.P.	Central Districts v Auckland	Auckland	1997/98
126	Vivian G.E.	Auckland v Wellington	Auckland	1977/78
126	Tavare C.J.	England XI v Otago	Alexandra	1983/84
126	Spearman C.M.	Central Districts v Canterbury	Nelson	1997/98
126	Knight N.V.	England v Northern Districts	Hamilton	2001/02
125	Crowe M.D.	Central Districts v Otago	Alexandra	1988/89
125	McMillan C.D.	Canterbury v Northern Districts	Hamilton	1998/99
124*	Twose R.G.	Wellington v Otago	Wellington	2000/01
123	Styris S.B.	Northern Districts v Otago	Hamilton	1999/00
122*	McMillan C.D.	Canterbury v Wellington	Wellington	2002/03
122	Astle N.J.	Canterbury v Wellington	Christchurch	1999/00
122	Parlane M.E.	Northern Districts v Canterbury	Timaru	2002/03
121*	Twose R.G.	Wellington v Northern Districts	Wellington	1996/97
121*	Bell M.D.	Wellington v Central Districts	New Plymouth	1997/98
121	Williams S.C.	West Indies v Sir Ron Brierley XI	Hamilton	1994/95
121	Douglas M.W.	Central Districts v Canterbury	Christchurch	1997/98
121	Astle N.J.	Canterbury v Otago	Christchurch	2000/01
120*	Fleming S.P.	Wellington v Otago	Wellington	2000/01
118	Reid J.F.	Auckland v Central Districts	Auckland	1985/86
117	Pocock B.A.	Northern Districts v Wellington	Hamilton	1995/96
116	Murray D.J.	Canterbury v Central Districts	Napier	1996/97
115*	Rutherford K.R.	Otago v Northern Districts	Alexandra	1991/92
115*	Howell L.G.	Central Districts v Northern Districts	Whangarei	1994/95
115	Cairns C.L.	Canterbury v Wellington	Christchurch	1992/93
114	McMillan C.D.	Canterbury v Wellington	Christchurch	1995/96
114	Astle N.J.	Canterbury v Otago	Alexandra	1996/97
113*	Richardson M.H.	Otago v Northern Districts	Mt Maunganui	1996/97
113	Ingham C.D.	Central Districts v Otago	Napier	1994/95
113	Cairns C.L.	Canterbury v Otago	Christchurch	1996/97
113	Weenink S.W.	Wellington v Central Districts	Wellington	1996/97
111*	Howell L.G.	Central Districts v Otago	New Plymouth	1996/97
111	Parlane M.E.	Northern Districts v Wellington	Whangarei	1999/00
111	Nevin C.J.	Wellington v Auckland	Wellington	2001/02
110	Crowe M.D.	Wellington v Canterbury	Christchurch	1992/93
110	Sinclair M.S.	Central Districts v Otago	Oamaru	1999/00
109*	McMillan C.D.	Canterbury v Central Districts	New Plymouth	2001/02

109	Sleep P.R.	South Australia v Central Districts	New Plymouth	1986/87
109	Crowe M.D.	Wellington v Auckland	Wellington	1990/91
109	Doody B.J.K.	Canterbury v Auckland	Christchurch	1997/98
109	Astle N.J.	Canterbury v Otago	Invercargill	1999/00
108	Blair W.L.	Otago v Auckland	Auckland	1982/83
108	Latham R.T.	Canterbury v Otago	Oamaru	1994/95
108	Campbell S.C.	West Indies v Sir Ron Brierley XI	Hamilton	1994/95
108	Howell L.G.	Central Districts v Wellington	New Plymouth	1995/96
107*	Douglas M.W.	Central Districts v Wellington	New Plymouth	1997/98
107*	Barnes A.C.	Auckland v Northern Districts	Hamilton	1999/00
107	Hick G.A.	Auckland v Otago	Alexandra	1997/98
107	Harris C.Z.	Canterbury v Central Districts	Napier	1998/99
106*	Edgar B.A.	Wellington v Otago	Wellington	1981/82
106*	Lamb A.J.	England XI v Otago	Alexandra	1983/84
106*	de Silva P.A.	Auckland v Canterbury	Auckland	1996/97
106*	Howell L.G.	Auckland v Central Districts	New Plymouth	2001/02
106	Vance R.H.	Wellington v Auckland	Auckland	1981/82
106	McEwan P.E.	Canterbury v Wellington	Wellington	1987/88
106	Chandler P.J.B.	Wellington v Canterbury	Christchurch	1996/97
106	Richardson M.H.	Otago v Central Districts	New Plymouth	1997/98
105*	Pamment J.I.	Auckland v Wellington	Wellington	1993/94
105*	Twose R.G.	Wellington v Northern Districts	Wellington	1994/95
105*	Fleming S.P.	Canterbury v Central Districts	Napier	1996/97
105*	Twose R.G.	Central v Bangladesh	Wellington	1997/98
105	Inzamam-ul-Haq	Pakistan v Sir Ron Brierley XI	Hamilton	1993/94
105	Twose R.G.	Central v Bangladesh	Wellington	1997/98
104*	Crowe M.D.	Central Districts v Auckland	Auckland	1989/90
104*	Bell M.D.	Wellington v Northern Districts	Mt Maunganui	1997/98
104	Dempsey D.A.	Canterbury v Northern Districts	Hamilton	1980/81
103*	Hartland B.R.	Canterbury v Northern Districts	Christchurch	1991/92
103	McRae G.P.	Central Districts v Auckland	Wanganui	1994/95
103	Twose R.G.	Wellington v Canterbury	Christchurch	1995/96
102*	Burnett G.P.	Wellington v Northern Districts	Hamilton	1992/93
102	Blair W.L.	Otago v Wellington	Dunedin	1979/80
102	Franklin T.J.	Auckland v Northern Districts	Auckland	1981/82
102	Wright J.G.	Canterbury v Wellington	Wellington	1985/86
102	Rutherford K.R.	Otago v Wellington	Alexandra	1993/94
102	Cooper B.G.	Northern Districts v Otago	Alexandra	1994/95
102	Fleming S.P.	Canterbury v Northern Districts	Christchurch	1995/96
102	Twose R.G.	Wellington v Northern Districts	Hamilton	1998/99
102	Hore A.J.	Otago v Wellington	Wellington	2001/02
101*	Crowe M.D.	Central Districts v Northern Districts	Whangarei	1983/84
101*	Maynard M.P.	Northern Districts v Auckland	Hamilton	1990/91
101*	Aiken J.M.	Wellington v Canterbury	Wellington	1994/95
101*	Young B.A.	Northern Districts v Central Districts	Mt Maunganui	1995/96
101*	Stead G.R.	Canterbury v Auckland	Auckland	2001/02
101*	Astle N.J.	Canterbury v Central Districts	Christchurch	2001/02
101	White D.J.	Northern Districts v Central Districts	Tauranga	1989/90
101	Burnett G.P.	Northern Districts v Central Districts	Whangarei	1994/95
101	Parlane M.E.	Northern Districts v Canterbury	Taupo	1994/95
101	McMillan C.D.	Canterbury v Central Districts	Christchurch	1994/95
100*	Bell M.D.	Wellington v Canterbury	Wellington	1999/00
100*	Marshall J.A.H.	Northern Districts v Canterbury	Christchurch	2000/01
100	Rutherford I.A.	Otago v Auckland	Auckland	1980/81
100	Hick G.A.	Northern Districts v Canterbury	Rangiora	1987/88

100	Brown S.W.	Auckland v Northern Districts	Hamilton	1990/91
100	Douglas M.W.	Wellington v South Africa	Wellington	1994/95
100	Hart M.N.	Northern Districts v Central Districts	Napier	1996/97
100	Twose R.G.	Wellington v Canterbury	Christchurch	1996/97
100	Wells J.D.	Wellington v Auckland	Wellington	1997/98
100	Stead G.R.	Canterbury v Otago	Oamaru	1997/98
100	Ingram P.J.	Central Districts v Otago	Invercargill	2001/02
100	Nevin C.J.	Wellington v Canterbury	Wellington	2002/03

Five Wickets in an Innings

7-0-23-7	Watson W.	Auckland v Otago	Auckland	1984/85
8-1-28-7	Penn A.J.	Wellington v Northern Districts	Mt Maunganui	2000/01
7.1-0-49-7	Marshall E.J.	Otago v Auckland	Dunedin	1993/94
10-5-12-6	Barrett B.J.	Northern Districts v Otago	Gisborne	1986/87
9.5-3-26-6	Vaughan J.T.C.	Auckland v Otago	Auckland	1995/96
10-2-26-6	Su'a M.L.	Auckland v Central Districts	New Plymouth	1995/96
7.7-2-31-6	Intikhab Alam	Pakistan v NZ Under 23 XI	Rotorua	1972/73
10-1-37-6	Cairns C.L.	Canterbury v Wellington	Christchurch	1996/97
9.3-0-43-6	Wisneski W.A.	Canterbury v Auckland	Christchurch	1996/97
10-1-49-6	Penn A.J.	Central Districts v Northern Districts	Napier	1996/97
6-1-7-5	Adams A.R.	Auckland v Northern Districts	Auckland	1999/00
5.3-2-10-5	Hitchcock P.A.	Wellington v Central Districts	Wellington	2001/02
3-0-11-5	Thompson S.	New South Wales v Canterbury	Christchurch	1993/94
8.3-2-12-5	Turner A.D.	Wellington v Otago	Wellington	2002/03
8.1-3-14-5	Shaw H.J.	Canterbury v Central Districts	Christchurch	2002/03
10-4-16-5	Brown C.M.	Auckland v Otago	Auckland	1996/97
8.3-2-17-5	Cederwall G.N.	Wellington v Canterbury	Rangiora	1984/85
8.4-1-19-5	Snedden M.C.	Auckland v Canterbury	Auckland	1982/83
9-2-19-5	Barnes A.C.	Auckland v Central Districts	Auckland	1998/99
10-2-19-5	Penn A.J.	Wellington v Auckland	Auckland	2001/02
10-4-20-5	Visser P.J.	Central Districts v Otago	New Plymouth	1985/86
10-1-20-5	Adams A.R.	Auckland v Central Districts	Auckland	1999/00
10-1-21-5	McNally S.R.	Canterbury v Auckland	Auckland	1984/85
10-4-22-5	Walker M.D.J.	Wellington v Central Districts	New Plymouth	2002/03
7-0-23-5	Collinge R.O.	Wellington v Otago	Wellington	1974/75
10-2-23-5	Brown S.W.	Auckland v Northern Districts	Auckland	1991/92
6.4-0-23-5	Cairns C.L.	Canterbury v Central Districts	Timaru	1995/96
8.5-1-24-5	Wundke S.C.	South Australia v Central Districts	Palmerston North	1986/87
10-4-24-5	Petrie R.G.	Canterbury v Auckland	Christchurch	1989/90
9.3-1-25-5	Maxwell N.D.	Canterbury v Auckland	Christchurch	1997/98
10-2-26-5	Priest M.W.	Canterbury v Auckland	Auckland	1988/89
9-0-27-5	Hunt A.J.	Auckland v Canterbury	Ashburton	1985/86
10-1-28-5	Holland R.G.	NSW v Wellington	Wellington	1984/85
10-2-30-5	Twose R.G.	Wellington v Otago	Alexandra	1995/96
10-3-30-5	Larsen G.R.	Wellington v Auckland	Wellington	1995/96
9.5-0-32-5	Cederwall G.N.	Wellington v Central Districts	Nelson	1984/85
10-2-34-5	Parry D.R.	West Indies v Auckland	Auckland	1979/80
10-1-34-5	Beard D.A.	Northern Districts v Central Districts	New Plymouth	1990/91
10-2-34-5	Anderson C.J.	Canterbury v Wellington	Wellington	2001/02
10-1-35-5	Jamieson M.D.	Central Districts v Wellington	Masterton	1980/81
8.5-1-36-5	Robertson G.K.	Central Districts v Northern Districts	Wanganui	1984/85
10-2-38-5	Hellaby A.T.R.	Auckland v Central Districts	Auckland	1987/88
9-0-38-5	McMillan C.D.	Canterbury v Northern Districts	Whangarei	1996/97
9.5-0-39-5	Roberts S.J.	Canterbury v Central Districts	Nelson	1994/95
10-0-39-5	Brown C.M.	Auckland v Northern Districts	Mt Maunganui	1996/97

10-1-41-5	Drum C.J.	Auckland v Canterbury	Christchurch	1998/99
9.5-0-42-5	Su'a M.L.	Auckland v Northern Districts	Auckland	1993/94
10-2-42-5	Blake D.C.	Central Districts v Northern Districts	New Plymouth	1997/98
10-1-43-5	Gale A.J.	Otago v Northern Districts	Alexandra	1991/92
10-0-43-5	Martin C.S.	Canterbury v Northern Districts	Mt Maunganui	1999/00
9.3-3-44-5	Stott L.W.	Auckland v Otago	Oamaru	1981/82
10-0-44-5	Nash D.J.	Northern Districts v Otago	Taupo	1995/96
10-0-45-5	McNally S.R.	Canterbury v Otago	Christchurch	1984/85
10-0-48-5	Leonard D.J.	Central Districts v Canterbury	Levin	1989/90
10-2-58-5	Yardley B.	Australia v Northern Districts	Hamilton	1981/82

(Note: A.J. Alcock had figures of 10-3-31-5 for Central Districts v Canterbury at Christchurch, 1993/94, but the game was abandoned and none of the performances in the game are included in any records).

Most Expensive Bowling

10-0-93-2	Presland C.M.	Northern Districts v Auckland	Gisborne	1982/83
9-0-85-1	Kennedy R.J.	Otago v Canterbury	Christchurch	1996/97
10-1-85-0	Kennedy R.J.	Otago v Central Districts	New Plymouth	1996/97
9-1-84-0	Styris S.B.	Northern Districts v Auckland	Auckland	2000/01
10-0-83-2	Welch G.	Wellington v Central Districts	New Plymouth	1997/98
10-0-80-3	Blair B.R.	Otago v Central Districts	Oamaru	1982/83
10-0-78-0	Pryor C.R.	Otago v Wellington	Wellington	2000/01
10-2-77-0	Stott L.W.	Auckland v Northern Districts	Gisborne	1982/83
10-0-77-0	Kennedy R.J.	Otago v Canterbury	Oamaru	1997/98
10-0-76-1	Thomson G.B.	Otago v Wellington	Alexandra	1980/81
10-0-76-3	McNally S.R.	Canterbury v Northern Districts	Rangiora	1981/82
10-0-76-2	Findlay C.O.	Central Districts v Canterbury	Christchurch	1998/99
10-0-75-1	Marshall E.J.	Otago v Central Districts	Dannevirke	1992/93
10-0-75-1	Hastings M.A.	Canterbury v Central Districts	New Plymouth	1997/98
10-0-74-0	Hills P.W.	Otago v Central Districts	Wanganui	1989/90
9-0-74-0	Wisneski W.A.	Central Districts v Canterbury	Christchurch	1994/95
10-0-74-1	Adams A.R.	Auckland v Canterbury	Christchurch	1997/98
9-0-73-0	Hayes R.L.	Northern Districts v Canterbury	Christchurch	1995/96
10-0-73-0	Crowe M.D.	Auckland v Northern Districts	Gisborne	1982/83
10-0-73-0	McSkimming W.C.	Otago v Central Districts	Oamaru	1999/00
10-0-72-0	Hintz A.J.	Canterbury v Northern Districts	Rangiora	1987/88
10-1-72-2	Petrie R.G.	Canterbury v Wellington	Christchurch	1991/92
10-0-72-2	de Groen R.P.	Northern Districts v Canterbury	Christchurch	1995/96
10-0-72-3	Allott G.I.	Canterbury v Northern Districts	Christchurch	1995/96
7-0-71-1	Butler I.G.	Northern Districts v Canterbury	Timaru	2002/03
9-1-71-0	Su'a M.L.	Auckland v Wellington	Wellington	1995/96
9-0-71-3	Pasupati M.Y.	Wellington v Auckland	Wellington	2001/02
10-0-71-1	O'Connor S.B.	Otago v Central Districts	New Plymouth	1996/97
10-1-71-0	Pringle C.	Auckland v Canterbury	Auckland	1997/98
10-0-70-1	Aberhart D.C.	Central Districts v Wellington	Masterton	1980/81
9-1-70-2	Tait A.R.	Northern Districts v Canterbury	Timaru	1993/94

ALSO NOTE *(8-ball overs)*

1-0-18-0	Payton D.H.	Central Districts v Wellington	Wellington	1973/74
1-0-18-1	Redpath I.R.	Australia v Central Districts	New Plymouth	1973/74
2-0-29-0	Child M.J.	Northern Districts v Central Districts	Palmerston North	1975/76
3-0-37-0	Dunning B.	Northern Districts v Canterbury	Christchurch	1977/78
4-0-42-1	Maingay C.T.	Auckland v Wellington	Wellington	1971/72
5-0-48-0	Coles M.J.	Wellington v Canterbury	Christchurch	1975/76
6-0-56-0	Cater S.B.	Wellington v Auckland	Auckland	1977/78
6-0-56-0	Gilmour G.J.	Australia v Invitation XI	Christchurch	1976/77
7-0-68-1	Aldridge C.W.	Northern Districts v Auckland	Auckland	1978/79

ALSO NOTE *(6-ball overs)*

1-0-22-0	Pryor C.R.	Auckland v Wellington	Wellington	1998/99
2-0-26-0	Roberts S.J.	Canterbury v Wellington	Ohoka	1990/91
3-0-42-1	McMillan C.D.	Canterbury v Central Districts	Napier	1996/97
4-0-44-0	Roberts S.J.	Canterbury v Auckland	Christchurch	1986/87
5-0-47-0	Kuggeleijn C.M.	Northern Districts v Wellington	Wellington	1990/91
5.3-0-50-0	Abernethy B.	Otago v Auckland	Oamaru	1981/82
6-0-65-0	de Silva D.S.	Sri Lanka v Minor Associations	Wanganui	1982/83

Most Economical Bowling

10-7-5-2	Boock S.L.	Otago v Central Districts	Alexandra	1986/87
10-5-6-2	Larsen G.R.	Wellington v Otago	Alexandra	1992/93
*8-3-7-2	Williams J.C.	Auckland v Northern Districts	Auckland	1971/72
10-6-8-1	Hills P.W.	Otago v Auckland	Oamaru	1981/82
10-6-8-2	Nuttall A.J.	Canterbury v Wellington	Christchurch	1988/89
10-4-8-0	Duff S.W.	Central Districts v Wellington	New Plymouth	1989/90
10-5-8-3	Vaughan J.T.C.	Auckland v Central Districts	Waikanae	1993/94
10-5-8-1	Harris C.Z.	Canterbury v Auckland	Christchurch	1995/96
*7-0-9-0	Dunning B.	Northern Districts v Canterbury	Christchurch	1976/77
10-6-9-1	Boock S.L.	Otago v Canterbury	Christchurch	1979/80
10-4-9-1	de Mel A.L.F.	Sri Lanka v Minor Associations	Wanganui	1982/83
10-5-9-2	Astle N.J.	Canterbury v Northern Districts	Christchurch	1991/92
10-4-9-2	Astle N.J.	Canterbury v Wellington	Christchurch	1993/94
10-3-9-1	de Groen R.P.	Northern Districts v Central Districts	Levin	1995/96
10-6-9-2	McCullum N.J.	Otago v Auckland	Auckland	2000/01
*7-1-10-2	Kirk C.M.	Canterbury v Otago	Christchurch	1973/74
10-5-10-3	McIntyre J.M.	Auckland v Canterbury	Auckland	1980/81
10-4-10-2	Pigott A.C.S.	Wellington v Northern Districts	Tauranga	1983/84
10-6-10-0	Bracewell J.G.	Auckland v Canterbury	Auckland	1986/87
10-7-10-4	Duers K.G.	Zimbabwe v Northern Districts	Cambridge	1991/92
10-3-10-2	Williams B.R.	Wellington v Northern Districts	Gisborne	1993/94
10-3-10-3	Larsen G.R.	Wellington v Canterbury	Rangiora	1994/95

* 8-ball overs

(Note: C.M. Brown had figures of 10-5-6-2 for Auckland v Otago at Dunedin, 1993/94 but the game was abandoned and none of the performances in the game are included in any records).

Hat-tricks

7-0-23-7	Watson W.	Auckland v Otago	Auckland	1984/85
10-0-48-4	Briasco P.S.	Central Districts v Auckland	Napier	1989/90
10-1-40-3	Walker M.D.J.	Wellington v Otago	Dunedin	2000/01

Wicketkeeping

DISMISSALS

(ct/st)

6	(5/1)	Murray D.A.	West Indies v Central Districts	New Plymouth	1979/80
6	(6/0)	McSweeney E.B.	Wellington v Auckland	Wellington	1982/83
6	(6/0)	McSweeney E.B.	Wellington v Northern Districts	Wellington	1988/89
6	(6/0)	McRae G.P.	Central Districts v Wellington	Masterton	1994/95
5	(5/0)	Dykes R.A.	Auckland v Wellington	Wellington	1973/74
5	(4/1)	Smith I.D.S.	Central Districts v Northern Districts	Hamilton	1981/82
5	(5/0)	Milburn B.D.	Otago v Central Districts	Oamaru	1982/83
5	(5/0)	Wright M.J.E.	Northern Districts v Auckland	Gisborne	1982/83

5	(5/0)	Germon L.K.	Canterbury v Otago	Christchurch	1988/89
5	(3/2)	Blain T.E.	Central Districts v Auckland	New Plymouth	1992/93
5	(4/1)	Adams J.C.	West Indies v Auckland	Auckland	1994/95
5	(4/1)	Nevin C.J.	Wellington v Otago	Wellington	1997/98
5	(4/1)	Nevin C.J.	Wellington v Otago	Wellington	2000/01
5	(5/0)	Griggs B.B.J.	Central Districts v Auckland	Auckland	2000/01
5	(5/0	Vincent L.	Auckland v Otago	Auckland	2002/03

THREE STUMPINGS IN AN INNINGS

Rixon S.J.	NSW v Wellington	Wellington	1984/85
Dyer G.C.	NSW v Wellington	Wellington	1986/87

Fielding

CATCHES

5	Wilson J.W.	Otago v Auckland	Dunedin	1993/94
4	Redmond R.E.	Auckland v Otago	Auckland	1972/73
4	Sampson H.C.	Otago v Canterbury	Christchurch	1974/75
4	Howarth G.P.	Invitation XI v Australia	Auckland	1976/77
4	Wiltshire J.R.	Auckland v Northern Districts	Auckland	1978/79
4	Dickeson C.W.	Northern Districts v Canterbury	Hamilton	1980/81
4	Cooper B.G.	Northern Districts v Central Districts	Palmerston North	1982/83
4	Hore A.J.	Otago v Canterbury	Christchurch	1998/99

Most Run Outs

INNINGS

5	Wellington v Auckland	Wellington	1974/75
5	Northern Districts v Wellington	Hamilton	1992/93
5	Central Districts v Northern Districts	Hamilton	2000/01
4	Otago v Wellington	Alexandra	1980/81
4	Auckland v Central Districts	Auckland	1981/82
4	Otago v Central Districts	Napier	1981/82
4	Auckland v Otago	Auckland	1982/83
4	Otago v Central Districts	Oamaru	1982/83
4	Northern Districts v Otago	Alexandra	1985/86
4	Northern Districts v Auckland	Auckland	1985/86
4	Auckland v Northern Districts	Hamilton	1986/87
4	Wellington v Canterbury	Wellington	1989/90
4	Otago v Canterbury	Dunedin	1991/92
4	Otago v Auckland	Alexandra	1995/96
4	Canterbury v Central Districts	Napier	1998/99
4	Auckland v Canterbury	Auckland	1999/00

MATCH

7	Wellington v Auckland	Wellington	1974/75
7	Auckland v Canterbury	Auckland	1999/00
6	Auckland v Canterbury	Auckland	1980/81
6	Central Districts v Otago	Napier	1981/82
6	Otago v Northern Districts	Alexandra	1985/86
6	Auckland v Northern Districts	Auckland	1985/86
6	Wellington v Canterbury	Wellington	1989/90
6	Otago v Canterbury	Dunedin	1991/92
6	Auckland v Wellington	Auckland	1991/92
6	Canterbury v Central Districts	Christchurch	1997/98

HISTORY OF THE LIMITED-OVER COMPETITION IN NEW ZEALAND

2002/03 was the 32nd season of limited over competition between the six New Zealand first-class sides. In that time there have been several changes both in sponsorship and format.

For the first six seasons a knock-out competition was sponsored by the New Zealand Motor Corporation. Each innings was limited to 40 eight-ball overs during the initial two seasons, reduced to 35 thereafter. In 1977/78 and 1978/79 the sponsors changed and the teams competed for the Gillette Cup. In the first season 30 eight-ball overs were used but the limit reverted to 35 the following year. There was no sponsorship for the competition in 1979/80, known simply as the National Knock-out, where 50 six-ball overs was the limit for each innings.

In 1980/81. the Shell Cup, previously contested for as part of the first-class season, became the limited-over prize and the contest was run on a league basis for the first time with each side playing the other once.

In keeping with the previous limited-over competitions, a final was arranged, this time between the top two teams of the league table, points gained being disregarded at this stage. Fifty six-ball overs was the limit on each innings.

From 1985/86 the competition was held in its entirety, prior to the Shell Trophy series with no final. From 1989/90 the top four teams in the league table went on to semi-final play-offs, previous points being disregarded. The top two teams gained home ground advantage, the venue for the final being decided in a similar manner.

From 1993/94 to 1998/99 the top two sides played each other, with the winner going into the grand final. The loser then played the winner of the game between third and fourth to find the other finalist. From 1999/00, the leading team after the round robin went straight to the final with the second and third-placed sides meeting in a semi-final to find the other finalist. The finals became a best-of-three series.

In 2001/02, with a change of sponsor, the competition was renamed the State Shield. The format remained unaltered except the final reverted to a single game.

Winners of Limited-over Competitions

NEW ZEALAND MOTOR CORPORATION KNOCK-OUT

1971/72	Canterbury
1972/73	Auckland
1973/74	Wellington
1974/75	Wellington
1975/76	Canterbury
1976/77	Canterbury

GILLETTE CUP

1977/78	Canterbury
1978/79	Auckland

NATIONAL KNOCK-OUT

1979/80	Northern Districts

SHELL CUP

1980/81	Auckland
1981/82	Wellington
1982/83	Auckland
1983/84	Auckland
1984/85	Central Districts
1985/86	Canterbury
1986/87	Auckland
1987/88	Otago
1988/89	Wellington
1989/90	Auckland
1990/91	Wellington
1991/92	Canterbury
1992/93	Canterbury
1993/94	Canterbury
1994/95	Northern Districts
1995/96	Canterbury
1996/97	Canterbury
1997/98	Northern Districts
1998/99	Canterbury
1999/00	Canterbury
2000/01	Central Districts

STATE SHIELD

2001/02	Wellington
2002/03	Northern Districts

Table of Results

1971/72 — 2002/03

	P	W	L	NR
Auckland	198*	96	91	11
Canterbury	207	123	76	8
Central Districts	189*	75	102	12
Northern Districts	199	95	100	4
Otago	184	58	118	8
Wellington	203	118	78	7

* The Auckland and Central Districts totals include a match won by the toss of a coin against Central Districts and Northern Districts respectively.

Northern Districts v Otago in 1980/81, Auckland v Wellington in 1985/86, Canterbury v Auckland, Auckland v Central Districts and Wellington v Otago in 1991/92, Central Districts v Auckland and Auckland v Wellington in 1996/97, Canterbury v Northern Districts in 1997/98, Central Districts v Canterbury in 1999/00 and Central Districts v Otago, Northern Districts, Canterbury and Auckland and Auckland v Canterbury in 2000/01 were abandoned without a ball being bowled. Wellington v Auckland in 1984/85 and Northern Districts v Canterbury 1988/89 were abandoned after one innings had been completed. The semi-final between Canterbury and Central Districts 1993/94 was due to be replayed after a match had been started and abandoned. However, no play at all was possible in the scheduled replay.

INTER-PROVINCIAL RECORDS

	Highest Score	Lowest Score	Highest Individual Score	Best Bowling
Auckland	318-5 v N.D. 2000/01	70 v N.D. 1977/78	L. Vincent 145 v C.D. 1999/00	W. Watson 7-0-23-7 v Otago 1984/85
Canterbury	329-5 v N.D. 1995/96	75 v Otago 1973/74	B.R. Hartland 161 v N.D. 1993/94	C.L. Cairns 10-1-37-6 v Wellington 1996/97
Central Districts	376-3 v Otago 1996/97	58 v Wellington 2001/02	D.P. Kelly 140 v Wellington 1999/00	A.J. Penn 10-1-49-6 v N.D. 1996/97
Northern Districts	306-2 v Auckland 1982/83	76 v C.D. 1987/88	S.B. Styris 123 v Otago 1999/00	B.J. Barrett 10-5-12-6 v Otago 1986/87
Otago	294-6 v Auckland 1997/98	64 v Wellington 1984/85	M.H. Richardson 128* v C.D. 1996/97	E.J. Marshall 7.1-0-49-7 v Auckland 1993/94
Wellington	300-5 v Auckland 2001/02	66 v Canterbury 1996/97	C.J. Nevin 149 v CD 1997/98	A.J. Penn 8-1-28-7 v ND 2000/01

	Most Economical Bowling	Most Expensive Bowling	Most Catches/ Stumpings in an innings
Auckland	J.T.C. Vaughan 10-5-8-3 v C.D. 1993/94 J.C. Williams 8-3-7-2 (8 ball overs) v N.D. 1971/72	L.W. Stott 10-2-77-0 v N.D. 1982/83	R.A. Dykes 5c v Wellington 1973/74 L. Vincent 5c v Otago 2002/03
Canterbury	A.J. Nuttall 10-6-8-2 v Wellington 1988/89 C.Z. Harris 10-5-8-1 v Auckland 1995/96	S.R. McNally 10-0-76-3 v N.D. 1981/82	L.K. Germon 5c v Otago 1988/89
Central Districts	S.W. Duff 10-4-8-0 v Wellington 1989/90	C.O. Findlay 10-0-76-2 v Canterbury 1998/99	G.P. McRae 6c v Wellington 1994/95
Northern Districts	R.P. de Groen 10-3-9-1 v C.D. 1995/96	C.M. Presland 10-0-93-2 v Auckland 1982/83	M.J.E. Wright 5c v Auckland 1982/83
Otago	S.L. Boock 10-7-5-2 v C.D. 1986/87	R.J. Kennedy 9-0-85-1 v Canterbury 1996/97 R.J. Kennedy 10-1-85-0 v C.D. 1996/97	B.D. Milburn 5c v C.D. 1982/83 J.W. Wilson 5c v Auckland 1993/94
Wellington	G.R. Larsen 10-5-6-2 v Otago 1992/93	G. Welch 10-0-83-2 v CD 1997/98	E.B. McSweeney 6c v Auckland 1982/83 E.B. McSweeney 6c v N.D. 1988/89

RECORD PARTNERSHIPS

AUCKLAND

1st	166*	Young B.A. & Pocock B.A.	v Central Districts	Auckland	1998/99
2nd	154	Crowe J.J. & Brown S.W.	v Northern Districts	Auckland	1991/92
3rd	129	Crowe J.J. & Vaughan J.T.C.	v Otago	Alexandra	1991/92
4th	118	Jones R.A. & Billcliff I.S.	v Central Districts	New Plymouth	1998/99
5th	171	Vivian G.E. & Reid J.F.	v Wellington	Auckland	1977/78
6th	109	Lynch S.M. & Vaughan J.T.C.	v Otago	Auckland	1996/97
7th	70	Hellaby A.T.R. & Kelly P.J.	v Northern Districts	Gisborne	1982/83
	70	Vincent L. & Adams A.R.	v Northern Districts	Auckland	2001/02
8th †	121	Canning T.K. & Morgan R.G.	v Otago	Alexandra	2000/01
9th	59	Mills J.M. & Haslam M.J.	v Wellington	Wellington	1998/99
10th	47	Lyon B.J. & Walmsley K.P.	v Central Districts	Auckland	1997/98
	47*	Parore A.C. & Haslam M.J.	v Canterbury	Auckland	2001/02

CANTERBURY

1st	146	Hartland B.R. & Astle N.J.	v Northern Districts	Christchurch	1995/96
2nd †	189	Hartland B.R. & Howell L.G.	v Northern Districts	Timaru	1993/94
3rd	174	McMillan C.D. & Latham R.T.	v Central Districts	Christchurch	1994/95
4th †	221	Howell L.G. & Stead G.R.	v Otago	Oamaru	1997/98
5th †	198	Cairns C.L. & Germon L.K.	v Wellington	Christchurch	1992/93
6th †	142	Cairns C.L. & Fleming S.P.	v Central Districts	Napier	1993/94
7th	74	Redmond A.J. & Wisneski W.A.	v Wellington	Wellington	2001/02
8th	76	Barton H.D. & Wisneski W.A.	v Northern Districts	Christchurch	1998/99
9th	53	Howell L.G. & Petrie R.G.	v Wellington	Wellington	1991/92
10th	34*	Anderson C.J. & Burson R.D.	v Otago	Oamaru	2001/02

CENTRAL DISTRICTS

1st	154	Spearman C.M. & Ryder J.D.	v Otago	New Plymouth	2002/03
2nd	154	Smith C.J.P. & Crowe M.D.	v Otago	Alexandra	1988/89
3rd	156	Oram J.D.P. & Douglas M.W.	v Otago	Hastings	1998/99
4th	115	Oram J.D.P. & Greatbatch M.J.	v Auckland	Auckland	1997/98
5th	153*	Harden R.J. & Blain T.E.	v Canterbury	Christchurch	1990/91
6th	103	Sandbrook I.P. & Griggs B.B.J.	v Canterbury	Nelson	2002/03
7th	109	Sulzberger G.P. & Furlong C.J.M.	v Otago	Palmerston Nth	1997/98
8th	79	Findlay C.O. & Furlong C.J.M.	v Northern Districts	Nelson	1998/99
9th	92	Loveridge G.R. & Penn A.J.	v Canterbury	Napier	1996/97
10th	50	Garner C.D. & Alcock A.J.	v Otago	Oamaru	1993/94

NORTHERN DISTRICTS

1st	168	Marshall J.A.H. & Vettori D.L.	v Wellington	Hamilton	2002/03
2nd	126*	Parlane M.E. & Parlane N.R.	v Otago	Alexandra	1999/00
3rd	199*	Parker J.M. & Cooper B.G.	v Auckland	Gisborne	1982/83
4th	123	Parore A.C. & Thomson S.A.	v Canterbury	Mt Maunganui	1995/96
5th	137	Nash D.J. & Bradburn G.E.	v Otago	Taupo	1997/98
6th	115	Bell M.D. & Hart M.N.	v Central Districts	Napier	1996/97
7th	82	Thomson S.A. & Bradburn G.E.	v Wellington	Wellington	1988/89
8th	75	Dickeson C.W. & Child M.J.	v Auckland	Pukekohe	1980/81
9th	68*	Hart R.G. & Styris S.B.	v Wellington	Wellington	1996/97
10th	43	Hayes R.L. & de Groen R.P.	v Canterbury	Christchurch	1995/96

OTAGO

1st	130	Cumming C.D. & Lawson R.A.	v Auckland	Alexandra	2002/03
2nd	134*	Richardson M.H. & Lamont M.J.	v Auckland	Auckland	1998/99
3rd	111	Lamont M.J. & Robinson S.A.	v Wellington	Alexandra	1995/96
4th	115	Lawson R.A. & Mather S.R.	v Canterbury	Invercargill	1998/99
5th	130	McKenzie M.N. & McGlashan P.D.	v Northern Districts	Rotorua	2002/03
6th	121	Gaffaney C.B. & Pryor C.R.	v Canterbury	Alexandra	2000/01
7th	103*	Richardson M.H. & Campbell P.A.	v Central Districts	New Plymouth	1996/97
8th	93	McSkimming W.C. & Morland N.D.	v Central Districts	New Plymouth	2002/03
9th	47	O'Connor S.B. & Walmsley K.P.	v Canterbury	Invercargill	2002/03
10th †	56*	McSkimming W.C. & Sewell D.G.	v Northern Districts	Oamaru	2000/01

WELLINGTON

1st †	205*	Aiken J.M. & Douglas M.W.	v Canterbury	Wellington	1994/95
2nd	173	Weenink S.W. & Wells J.D.	v Central Districts	Wellington	1996/97
3rd †	244*	Fleming S.P. & Twose R.G.	v Otago	Wellington	2000/01
4th	143	Jones A.H. & Coney J.V.	v Canterbury	Timaru	1986/87
5th	127	Twose R.G. & Kerr R.J.	v Northern Districts	Wellington	1996/97
6th	100	Petrie R.G. & Kerr R.J.	v Central Districts	New Plymouth	1995/96
7th †	130*	Bell M.D. & Mather S.R.	v Northern Districts	Mt Maunganui	1997/98
8th	98*	Taylor B.R. & Collinge R.O.	v Central Districts	Lower Hutt	1971/72
9th †	98	Doull L.J. & Williams B.R.	v Otago	Alexandra	1993/94
10th	36*	Jefferson M.R. & R.J. Kennedy	v Canterbury	Christchurch	1999/00

† *record for all teams*

Fastest Centuries

Balls

65	de Silva P.A.	Auckland v Canterbury	Auckland	1996/97
72	Howell L.G.	Central Districts v Otago	New Plymouth	1996/97
77	McMillan C.D.	Canterbury v Central Districts	New Plymouth	2001/02
78	Astle N.J.	Canterbury v Central Districts	Christchurch	2001/02
79	Hick G.A.	Northern Districts v Canterbury	Rangiora	1987/88
83	Fleming S.P.	Canterbury v Central Districts	Napier	1996/97
83	Nevin C.J.	Wellington v Central Districts	Wellington	1997/98
87	Marshall J.A.H.	Northern Districts v Canterbury	Christchurch	2000/01
88	Dempsey D.A.	Canterbury v Northern Districts	Hamilton	1980/81
88	Cairns C.L.	Canterbury v Auckland	Christchurch	1994/95
88	Twose R.G.	Wellington v Canterbury	Christchurch	1995/96
89	McMillan C.D.	Canterbury v Wellington	Wellington	2002/03
92	McMillan C.D.	Canterbury v Northern Districts	Hamilton	1998/99
94	Fleming S.P.	Canterbury v Northern Districts	Christchurch	1995/96
94	Hore A.J.	Otago v Wellington	Wellington	2001/02
99	Rutherford K.R.	Otago v Wellington	Alexandra	1993/94
99	Astle N.J.	Canterbury v Northern Districts	Christchurch	1995/96
99	Twose R.G.	Wellington v Canterbury	Christchurch	1996/97
100	Cooper B.G.	Northern Districts v Otago	Alexandra	1994/95
100	Hart M.N.	Northern Districts v Central Districts	Napier	1996/97

Fastest Fifties

Balls				
20	Cairns C.L.	Canterbury v Northern Districts	Timaru	2002/03
22	Maynard M.P.	Otago v Auckland	Alexandra	1997/98
23	Greatbatch M.J.	Central Districts v Otago	New Plymouth	1996/97
26	Cairns B.L.	Northern Districts v Canterbury	Rangiora	1987/88
26	Bulfin C.E.	Central Districts v Wellington	New Plymouth	1997/98
26	McSkimming W.C.	Otago v Northern Districts	Oamaru	2000/01
27	Loveridge G.R.	Central Districts v Wellington	Wellington	1995/96
27	de Silva P.A.	Auckland v Canterbury	Auckland	1996/97
27	Vettori D.L.	Northern Districts v Auckland	Auckland	1999/00
28	Cooper B.G.	Northern Districts v Otago	Mt Maunganui	1994/95
28	Parlane M.E.	Northern Districts v Wellington	Mt Maunganui	1994/95
28	Spearman C.M.	Central Districts v Otago	New Plymouth	2002/03
30	Spearman C.M.	Auckland v Wellington	Wellington	1995/96
30	Doull S.B.	Northern Districts v England	Hamilton	2001/02
32	Petrie R.G.	Wellington v Northern Districts	Mt Maunganui	1994/95
32	Howell L.G.	Canterbury v Wellington	Christchurch	1998/99
32	McMillan C.D.	Canterbury v Northern Districts	Hamilton	1998/99
32	Nevin C.J.	Wellington v Canterbury	Wellington	1999/00
32	Horne M.J.	Auckland v Wellington	Wellington	2001/02
32	Hore A.J.	Otago v Wellington	Wellington	2001/02
33	Blain T.E.	Central Districts v Wellington	Wellington	1991/92
33	Finch C.W.J.	Otago v Central Districts	New Plymouth	1993/94
33	Brown R.K.	Central Districts v Otago	Hastings	1998/99
33	Horne M.J.	Auckland v Central Districts	Auckland	2001/02
34	Dempsey D.A.	Canterbury v Northern Districts	Hamilton	1980/81
34	Gill S.J.	Central Districts v Wellington	Wanganui	1982/83
34	McEwan P.E.	Canterbury v Central Districts	Ashburton	1988/89
34	Cairns C.L.	Canterbury v Otago	Dunedin	1991/92
34	Howell L.G.	Central Districts v Northern Districts	Taupo	1996/97
34	Hart R.G.	Northern Districts v Wellington	Wellington	1996/97
34	Parlane M.E.	Northern Districts v Central Districts	Hamilton	1997/98
34	Walker M.D.J.	Wellington v Auckland	Wellington	2001/02
35	Reid R.B.	Wellington v Canterbury	Ohoka	1990/91
35	Penn A.J.	Central Districts v Canterbury	Napier	1996/97

(Note: I.D.S. Smith reached 50 from 24 balls for Auckland v Central Districts at Auckland, 1989/90 but the game was abandoned and restarted the following day. Performances in games which are abandoned and replayed are not included in any records).

DOMESTIC ONE-DAY CAREER RECORDS

BATTING		M	In	NO	HS	Runs	Ave	100s	50s
Howell L.G.	C. CD, A	93	93	13	134*	2853	35.66	5	21
Twose R.G.	ND, CD, W	95	93	9	124*	2769	32.96	6	16
Parlane M.E.	ND	93	93	3	122	2646	29.40	3	15
Harris C.Z.	C	94	87	28	107	2594	43.96	1	15
Astle N.J.	C	83	74	12	131	2507	40.43	7	9
Barnes A.C.	A	98	96	10	107*	2486	28.90	1	19
Douglas M.W.	CD, W	101	98	8	121	2326	25.84	2	10
Young B.A.	ND, A	85	83	8	101*	2284	30.45	1	15
Richardson M.H.	A, O	76	74	7	128*	2283	34.07	3	14
Latham R.T.	C	84	80	4	108	2206	29.02	1	9
Crowe M.D.	A, CD, W	57	56	5	125	2171	42.56	5	12
Bailey M.D.	ND	103	101	14	76*	2159	24.81	—	11
Bradburn G.E.	ND	121	110	15	80*	2048	21.55	—	5
Stead G.R.	C	86	79	10	101*	2022	29.30	2	9
Lawson R.A.	O	80	78	7	83*	1989	28.01	—	14
Cooper B.G.	ND	77	76	5	102	1929	27.16	1	9
Cairns C.L.	ND, C	74	66	10	143	1922	34.32	3	9
Greatbatch M.J.	A, CD	67	66	6	84	1922	32.03	—	18
Spearman C.M.	A, CD	71	71	1	126	1903	27.18	1	12
Edgar B.A.	W	43	42	10	147*	1889	59.03	3	12
Nevin C.J.	W	76	72	6	149	1821	27.59	3	9
Bell M.D.	ND, W	76	75	6	121*	1820	26.37	3	7
McMillan C.D.	C	64	61	9	125	1799	34.59	5	6
Fleming S.P.	C, W	58	54	9	120*	1784	39.64	3	12
Jones A.H.	CD, O, W	64	62	4	95	1757	30.29	—	9
Petrie R.G.	C, W	100	87	13	85	1726	23.32	—	9
Wells J.D.	W	80	75	8	100	1716	25.61	1	12
Hart M.N.	ND	83	75	10	100	1586	24.40	1	11
Gaffaney C.B.	O	67	66	1	79*	1455	22.38	—	6
Chandler P.J.B.	W	43	43	1	106	1418	33.76	1	8
Styris S.B.	ND	62	55	15	123	1415	35.37	1	9
Sinclair M.S.	CD	61	60	5	110	1410	25.63	1	10
Doody B.J.K	C	50	50	2	109	1389	28.93	1	8
Rutherford K.R.	O	45	45	1	115*	1381	31.38	2	8
Burnett G.P.	W, ND	55	54	6	102*	1345	28.02	2	5
Horne M.J.	A, O	54	53	1	96	1335	25.67	—	10
Sulzberger G.P.	CD	62	56	6	71	1331	26.62	—	8
Vaughan J.T.C.	A	56	53	6	94	1299	27.63	—	7
Patel D.N.	A	60	58	1	94	1291	22.64	—	5
Jones R.A.	A, W	62	61	5	78*	1288	23.00	—	3
Wright J.G.	ND, C, A	44	43	0	102	1286	29.90	1	8
Pocock B.A.	A, ND	56	53	3	117	1281	25.62	1	5
Hoskin R.N.	O	61	59	1	70	1251	21.56	—	5
Austen M.H.	O, W	51	51	1	95*	1222	24.44	—	8
Vance R.H.	W	56	54	3	106	1219	23.90	1	10
Billcliff I.S.	O, W, A	51	49	0	67	1199	24.46	—	10
Blain T.E.	CD, C	64	59	11	70	1181	24.60	—	6
Hartland B.R.	C	42	42	2	161	1177	29.42	2	5
Parore A.C.	A, ND	48	45	5	79*	1161	29.02	—	8
Vincent L.	A	41	39	2	145	1147	31.00	2	6
Mather S.R.	W, O	66	60	5	74	1146	20.83	—	5
McEwan P.E.	C	44	42	2	106	1136	28.40	1	6

		M	In	NO	HS	Runs	Ave	100s	50s
Blair B.R.	O, ND	49	49	3	91	1128	24.52	—	8
Lamont M.J.	O	40	40	4	88	1092	30.33	—	10
Marshall H.J.H.	ND	53	51	5	93	1084	23.56	—	7
Hart R.G.	ND	113	87	30	56	1082	18.98	—	2
Reid J.F.	A	25	25	7	118	1074	59.66	1	8
Larsen G.R.	W	87	73	18	66	1053	19.14	—	1
Maynard M.P.	ND, O	31	31	5	101*	1049	40.34	1	4
McSweeney E.B.	CD, W	78	68	11	69	1028	18.03	—	3
Reid R.B.	A, W	35	35	2	95	1026	31.09	—	9
Nash D.J.	ND, O, A	44	40	6	88	1025	30.14	—	5

BOWLING		M	O	M	R	W	Ave	R/O	Best
Tait A.R.	ND	90	757.4	75	3138	128	24.51	4.14	4-29
Petrie R.G.	C, W	100	736	58	3146	119	26.43	4.27	5-24
Priest M.W.	C	89	724.5	69	2668	106	25.16	3.68	5-26
Vaughan J.T.C.	A	56	500	50	1760	97	18.14	3.52	6-26
Harris C.Z.	C	94	718.3	56	2530	96	26.35	3.52	4-28
Larsen G.R.	W	87	765.4	103	2334	94	24.82	3.04	5-30
Gale A.J.	O	75	673	69	2583	93	27.77	3.83	5-43
Bradburn G.E.	ND	121	895.4	59	3264	89	36.67	3.65	4-28
Twose R.G.	ND, CD, W	95	480.3	28	1896	87	21.79	3.94	5-30
Jonas G.R.	W, O	56	492	36	2147	86	24.96	4.36	4-18
Astle N.J.	C	83	613.1	78	2030	86	23.60	3.31	4-14
Cairns C.L.	ND, C	74	469.5	35	1835	82	22.37	3.91	6-37
Hart M.N.	ND	83	540.1	51	2079	79	26.31	3.84	4-7
Styris S.B.	ND	62	450	32	1968	78	25.23	4.37	4-19
Wisneski W.A.	CD, C	62	500.3	39	2189	77	28.42	4.37	6-43
Mallender N.A.	O	51	458.4	83	1356	72	18.83	2.95	4-16
Penn A.J.	CD, W	45	365.5	23	1723	72	23.93	4.70	7-28
O'Connor S.B.	O	43	395	29	1758	70	25.11	4.45	4-18
Stirling D.A.	CD, W	51	371.4	27	1519	69	22.01	4.08	4-19
Hitchcock P.A.	A, W	38	321	24	1364	69	19.76	4.25	5-10
Pringle C.	A	49	414.3	39	1621	68	23.83	3.91	4-30
Doull S.B.	ND	75	516.3	41	2089	68	30.72	4.05	4-28
Gray E.J.	W	53	395	61	1376	67	20.53	3.48	4-27
Owens M.B.	C	48	398.1	50	1539	66	23.31	3.87	4-26
Snedden M.C.	A	37	313.1	44	1017	65	15.64	3.24	5-19
Robertson G.K.	CD	48	392	43	1403	64	21.92	3.57	5-36
Bulfin C.E.	CD, W	44	352.1	17	1591	62	25.66	4.51	3-15
Watson W.	A	47	384	43	1401	61	22.96	3.64	7-23
Mason M.J.	CD	44	327.1	37	1364	61	22.36	4.16	4-18
Patel D.N.	A	60	451	52	1574	60	26.23	3.49	4-18
Drum C.J.	A	39	344.1	33	1490	60	24.83	4.33	5-41
Barnes A.C.	A	98	376.3	25	1675	60	27.91	4.44	5-19
Martin C.S.	C	37	302.1	28	1290	60	21.50	4.26	5-43
Yovich J.A.F.	ND	44	258	14	1279	59	21.67	4.96	4-50
Doull L.J.	W	44	343.4	24	1438	57	25.22	4.18	4-18
Jefferson M.R.	W	72	478.3	31	1971	54	36.50	4.11	4-32
Tuffey D.R.	ND	51	384.4	26	1677	54	31.05	4.35	3-11
Kennedy R.J.	O, W	39	352.3	31	1612	53	30.41	4.57	4-29
Duff S.W.	CD	67	560.1	52	1985	52	38.17	3.54	3-13
Adams A.R.	A	34	289.4	18	1268	52	24.38	4.37	5-7
Furlong C.J.M.	CD	51	401.5	31	1651	52	31.75	4.10	4-9
Marshall E.J.	O	41	354.2	23	1559	51	30.56	4.39	7-49
Mills K.D.	A	35	282.2	25	1131	51	22.17	4.00	4-40

		M	O	M	R	W	Ave	R/O	Best
Walker M.D.J.	CD, W	51	350.2	33	1287	51	25.23	3.67	5-22
Chatfield E.J.	W	34	305	68	902	50	18.04	2.95	4-43
Thomson S.A.	ND	51	364.4	32	1359	50	27.18	3.73	4-45
Nash D.J.	ND, O, A	44	276.5	35	1028	50	20.56	3.71	5-44

MOST ECONOMICAL BOWLING *(qualification 100 overs)*

		O	M	R	W	Ave	R/O
Hadlee R.J.	C	174.4	33	440	29	15.17	2.51
Boock S.L.	O	338.2	74	947	47	20.12	2.79
McIntyre J.M.	A	118	25	335	15	22.33	2.83
Webb R.J.	O	117.4	16	344	20	17.20	2.92
Mallender N.A.	O	458.4	83	1356	72	18.83	2.95
Chatfield E.J.	W	305	68	902	50	18.04	2.95
Bracewell J.G.	O, A	329	56	993	44	22.56	3.01
Larsen G.R.	W	765.4	103	2334	94	24.82	3.04
Logan G.R.	CD	131	21	402	16	25.12	3.06
Beard D.A.	ND	133	19	426	22	19.36	3.20
Snedden M.C.	A	313.1	44	1017	65	15.64	3.24
Gill S.J.	CD	188.2	32	612	21	29.14	3.25
Troup G.B.	A	204.5	17	669	39	17.15	3.26
Brown V.R.	C, A	259.2	33	856	21	40.85	3.30
Astle N.J.	C	613.1	78	2030	86	23.60	3.31
Maguiness S.J.	W	308.3	49	1029	46	22.36	3.33
O'Sullivan D.R.	CD	177	32	593	17	34.88	3.35
Cairns B.L.	ND	210.4	32	707	38	18.60	3.35

FIELDING

		Ct	St	Total
Hart R.G.	ND	104	28	132
Nevin C.J.	W	112	12	124
McSweeney E.B.	CD, W	97	26	123
Germon L.K.	C, O	88	18	106
Blain T.E.	CD, C	62	15	77
Croy M.G.	O	64	9	73
Hopkins G.J.	ND, C	49	10	59
Young B.A.	ND, A	46	12	58
Bradburn G.E.	ND	57	—	57
Douglas M.W.	CD, W	47	5	52
Vincent L.	A	49	3	52
Smith I.D.S.	CD, A	44	4	48
Mills J.M.	A	38	9	47
Robinson S.A.	O	43	2	45
Hart M.N.	ND	45	—	45
Harris C.Z.	C	42	—	42
Astle N.J.	C	41	—	41
Parore A.C.	A, ND	36	4	40
Bailey M.D.	ND	39	—	39
Greatbatch M.J.	A, CD	38	—	38
Lees W.K.	O	32	5	37
Latham R.T.	C	37	—	37
McRae G.P.	CD	35	2	37
Bell M.D.	ND, W	37	—	37
Baker G.R.	O, W	27	8	35
Priest M.W.	C	35	—	35
Wells J.D.	W	35	—	35

NEW ZEALAND ONE-DAY INTERNATIONAL RECORDS

TEAM RECORDS

Results

1972/73	Pakistan	Christchurch	NZ 187	P 165	*NZ won by 22 runs*
1973	England	Swansea	NZ 158	E 159-3	*England won by 7 wickets*
	England	Manchester	E 167-8		*abandoned*
1973/74	Australia	Dunedin	NZ 194-9	A 195-3	*Australia won by 7 wickets*
	Australia	Christchurch	A 265-5	NZ 234-6	*Australia won by 31 runs*
1974/75	England	Melbourne	NZ 262-8	E 196	*NZ won by 66 runs*
	England	Dunedin	E 136	NZ 15-0	*abandoned*
	England	Wellington	NZ 227	E 35-1	*abandoned*
1975	East Africa	Birmingham	NZ 309-5	EA 128-8	*NZ won by 181 runs*
World	England	Nottingham	E 266-6	NZ 186	*England won by 80 runs*
Cup	India	Manchester	I 230-9	NZ 233-6	*NZ won by 4 wickets*
	West Indies	The Oval	NZ 158	WI 159-5	*West Indies won by 5 wickets*
1975/76	India	Christchurch	I 154	NZ 155-1	*NZ won by 9 wickets*
	India	Auckland	NZ 236-8	I 156	*NZ won by 80 runs*
1976/77	Pakistan	Sialkot	NZ 198-8	P 197-9	*NZ won by 1 run*
1978	England	Scarborough	E 206-8	NZ 187-8	*England won by 19 runs*
	England	Manchester	E 278-5	NZ 152	*England won by 126 runs*
1979	Sri Lanka	Nottingham	SL 189	NZ 190-1	*NZ won by 9 wickets*
World	India	Leeds	I 182	NZ 183-2	*NZ won by 8 wickets*
Cup	West Indies	Nottingham	WI 244-7	NZ 212-9	*West Indies won by 32 runs*
	England	Manchester	E 221-8	NZ 212-9	*England won by 9 runs*
1979/80	West Indies	Christchurch	WI 203-7	NZ 207-9	*NZ won by 1 wicket*
1980/81	Australia	Adelaide	A 217-9	NZ 219-7	*NZ won by 3 wickets*
	Australia	Sydney	A 289-3	NZ 195	*Australia won by 94 runs*
	Australia	Melbourne	NZ 156	A 159-6	*Australia won by 4 wickets*
	India	Perth	I 162	NZ 157	*India won by 5 runs*
	India	Brisbane	I 204	NZ 205-7	*NZ won by 3 wickets*
	India	Adelaide	I 230-7	NZ 224	*India won by 6 runs*
	India	Melbourne	I 112-9	NZ 113-0	*NZ won by 10 wickets*
	Australia	Sydney	NZ 220-8	A 219-7	*NZ won by 1 run*
	India	Brisbane	NZ 242-9	I 220	*NZ won by 22 runs*
	Australia	Sydney	A 180	NZ 23-1	*abandoned*
	Australia	Sydney	NZ 233-6	A 155	*NZ won by 78 runs*
	Australia	Melbourne	NZ 126	A 130-3	*Australia won by 7 wickets*
	Australia	Melbourne	A 235-4	NZ 229-8	*Australia won by 6 runs*
	Australia	Sydney	NZ 215-8	A 218-4	*Australia won by 6 wickets*
1980/81	India	Auckland	NZ 218-6	I 140-9	*NZ won by 78 runs*
	India	Hamilton	NZ 210-8	I 153	*NZ won by 57 runs*

1981/82	Australia	Auckland	NZ 240-6	A 194	*NZ won by 46 runs*
	Australia	Dunedin	NZ 159-9	A 160-4	*Australia won by 6 wickets*
	Australia	Wellington	NZ 74	A 75-2	*Australia won by 8 wickets*
1982/83	Australia	Melbourne	NZ 181	A 182-2	*Australia won by 8 wickets*
	England	Melbourne	NZ 239-8	E 237-8	*NZ won by 2 runs*
	England	Brisbane	E 267-6	NZ 213	*England won by 54 runs*
	Australia	Sydney	NZ 226-8	A 179	*NZ won by 47 runs*
	England	Sydney	NZ 199	E 200-2	*England won by 8 wickets*
	Australia	Melbourne	NZ 246-6	A 188	*NZ won by 58 runs*
	England	Adelaide	E 296-5	NZ 297-6	*NZ won by 4 wickets*
	Australia	Adelaide	NZ 200-9	A 153	*NZ won by 47 runs*
	England	Perth	E 88-7	NZ 89-3	*NZ won by 7 wickets*
	Australia	Perth	A 191-9	NZ 164	*Australia won by 27 runs*
	Australia	Sydney	NZ 193-7	A 155-4	*Australia won on faster scoring rate*
	Australia	Melbourne	A 302-8	NZ 153	*Australia won by 149 runs*
1982/83	England	Auckland	E 184	NZ 187-4	*NZ won by 6 wickets*
	England	Wellington	NZ 295-6	E 192	*NZ won by 103 runs*
	England	Christchurch	NZ 211-8	E 127	*NZ won by 84 runs*
	Sri Lanka	Dunedin	NZ 183-8	SL 118-9	*NZ won by 65 runs*
	Australia	Sydney	NZ 138-8	A 124	*NZ won by 14 runs*
	Sri Lanka	Napier	SL 167-8	NZ 168-3	*NZ won by 7 wickets*
	Sri Lanka	Auckland	NZ 304-5	SL 188-6	*NZ won by 116 runs*
1983 *World Cup*	England	The Oval	E 322-6	NZ 216	*England won by 106 runs*
	Pakistan	Birmingham	NZ 238-9	P 186	*NZ won by 52 runs*
	Sri Lanka	Bristol	SL 206	NZ 209-5	*NZ won by 5 wickets*
	England	Birmingham	E 234	NZ 238-8	*NZ won by 2 wickets*
	Sri Lanka	Derby	NZ 181	SL 184-7	*Sri Lanka won by 3 wickets*
	Pakistan	Nottingham	P 261-3	NZ 250	*Pakistan won by 11 runs*
1983/84	England	Christchurch	E 188-9	NZ 134	*England won by 54 runs*
	England	Wellington	NZ 135	E 139-4	*England won by 6 wickets*
	England	Auckland	E 209-9	NZ 210-3	*NZ won by 7 wickets*
1983/84	Sri Lanka	Colombo	NZ 234-6	SL 130	*NZ won by 104 runs*
	Sri Lanka	Moratuwa	SL 157-8	NZ 116	*Sri Lanka won by 41 runs*
	Sri Lanka	Colombo	NZ 201-8	SL 115	*NZ won by 86 runs*
1984/85	Sri Lanka	Colombo	NZ 171-6	SL 174-6	*Sri Lanka won by 4 wickets*
	Sri Lanka	Moratuwa	SL 114-9	NZ 118-3	*NZ won by 7 wickets*
	Pakistan	Peshawar	P 191-5	NZ 145	*Pakistan won by 46 runs*
	Pakistan	Faisalabad	P 157-5	NZ 152-7	*Pakistan won by 5 runs*
	Pakistan	Sialkot	NZ 187-9	P 153-8	*NZ won by 34 runs*
	Pakistan	Multan	NZ 213-8	P 214-9	*Pakistan won by 1 wicket*
1984/85	Pakistan	Napier	NZ 277-6	P 167-9	*NZ won by 110 runs*
	Pakistan	Hamilton	P 221-4	NZ 222-6	*NZ won by 4 wickets*
	Pakistan	Christchurch	NZ 264-8	P 251	*NZ won by 13 runs*
	Pakistan	Auckland	P 189		*abandoned*
1984/85 *World Championship of Cricket*	West Indies	Sydney	NZ 57-2		*abandoned*
	Sri Lanka	Melbourne	NZ 223	SL 172	*NZ won by 51 runs*
	India	Sydney	NZ 206	I 207-3	*India won by 7 wickets*
	West Indies	Sydney	NZ 138-9	WI 139-4	*West Indies won by 6 wickets*

1984/85	West Indies	Antigua	WI 231-8	NZ 208-8	*West Indies won by 23 runs*
	West Indies	Port of Spain	NZ 51-3	WI 55-4	*West Indies won by 6 wickets*
	West Indies	Berbice	WI 259-5	NZ 129	*West Indies won by 130 runs*
	West Indies	Port of Spain	NZ 116	WI 117-0	*West Indies won by 10 wickets*
	West Indies	Bridgetown	WI 265-3	NZ 153-8	*West Indies won by 112 runs*
1985/86	Australia	Melbourne	NZ 161-7		*abandoned*
	India	Brisbane	NZ 259-9	I 263-5	*India won by 5 wickets*
	Australia	Sydney	NZ 152	A 153-6	*Australia won by 4 wickets*
	India	Perth	I 113	NZ 115-7	*NZ won by 3 wickets*
	Australia	Perth	NZ 159-6	A 161-6	*Australia won by 4 wickets*
	India	Melbourne	I 238-8	NZ 239-5	*NZ won by 5 wickets*
	India	Adelaide	NZ 172	I 174-5	*India won by 5 wickets*
	Australia	Adelaide	NZ 276-7	A 70	*NZ won by 206 runs*
	Australia	Sydney	A 239-7	NZ 140	*Australia won by 99 runs*
	India	Launceston	I 202-9	NZ 168-9	*India won by 21 runs (target adjusted)*
1985/86	Australia	Dunedin	NZ 186-6	A 156	*NZ won by 30 runs*
	Australia	Christchurch	NZ 258-7	A 205	*NZ won by 53 runs*
	Australia	Wellington	NZ 229-9	A 232-7	*Australia won by 3 wickets*
	Australia	Auckland	A 231	NZ 187-9	*Australia won by 44 runs*
1985/86	Sri Lanka	Colombo	SL 137-9	NZ 140-4	*NZ won by 6 wickets*
	Pakistan	Colombo	NZ 214-8	P 217-6	*Pakistan won by 4 wickets*
	India	Sharjah	NZ 132-8	I 134-7	*India won by 3 wickets*
	Pakistan	Sharjah	NZ 64	P 66-0	*Pakistan won by 10 wickets*
1986	England	Leeds	NZ 217-8	E 170	*NZ won by 47 runs*
	England	Manchester	NZ 284-5	E 286-4	*England won by 6 wickets*
1986/87	West Indies	Dunedin	WI 237-9	NZ 142	*West Indies won by 95 runs*
	West Indies	Auckland	NZ 213	WI 217-4	*West Indies won by 6 wickets*
	West Indies	Wellington	*abandoned without a ball being bowled*		
	West Indies	Christchurch	NZ 191-9	WI 192-0	*West Indies won by 10 wickets*
1987/88	Zimbabwe	Hyderabad	NZ 242-7	Z 239	*NZ won by 3 runs*
World Cup	India	Bangalore	I 252-7	NZ 236-8	*India won by 16 runs*
	Australia	Indore	A 199-4	NZ 196-9	*Australia won by 3 runs*
	Zimbabwe	Calcutta	Z 227-5	NZ 228-6	*NZ won by 4 wickets*
	Australia	Chandigarh	A 251-8	NZ 234	*Australia won by 17 runs*
	India	Nagpur	NZ 221-9	I 224-1	*India won by 9 wickets*
1987/88	Australia	Perth	NZ 232-9	A 231	*NZ won by 1 run*
	Sri Lanka	Sydney	SL 174	NZ 178-4	*NZ won by 6 wickets*
	Australia	Melbourne	A 216	NZ 210-9	*Australia won by 6 runs*
	Sri Lanka	Adelaide	SL 241	NZ 242-6	*NZ won by 4 wickets*
	Sri Lanka	Hobart	NZ 199-7	SL 200-6	*Sri Lanka won by 4 wickets*
	Sri Lanka	Brisbane	SL 164-8	NZ 167-6	*NZ won by 4 wickets*
	Australia	Brisbane	NZ 176-5	A 177-5	*Australia won by 5 wickets*
	Australia	Sydney	A 221-8	NZ 143	*Australia won by 78 runs*
	Australia	Melbourne	NZ 177	A 180-2	*Australia won by 8 wickets*
	Australia	Sydney	NZ 168-5	A 169-4	*Australia won by 6 wickets*

1987/88	England	Dunedin	NZ 204	E 207-5	*England won by 5 wickets*
	England	Christchurch	NZ186-8	E 188-4	*England won by 6 wickets*
	England	Napier	E 219	NZ 223-3	*NZ won by 7 wickets*
	England	Auckland	E 208	NZ 211-6	*NZ won by 4 wickets*
1987/88	India	Sharjah	I 267-6	NZ 194-8	*India won by 73 runs*
	Sri Lanka	Sharjah	NZ 258-8	SL 159	*NZ won by 99 runs*
	Sri Lanka	Sharjah	NZ 249-7	SL 206-9	*NZ won by 43 runs*
	India	Sharjah	I 250-7	NZ 198	*India won by 52 runs*
1988/89	India	Visakhapatnam	NZ 196-9	I 197-6	*India won by 4 wickets*
	India	Cuttack	NZ 160-7	I 161-5	*India won by 5 wickets*
	India	Indore	I 222-6	NZ 169-9	*India won by 53 runs*
	India	Baroda	NZ 278-3	I 282-8	*India won by 2 wickets*
	India	Jammu	*abandoned without a ball being bowled*		
1988/89	Pakistan	Dunedin	P 170-9	NZ 174-2	*NZ won by 8 wickets*
	Pakistan	Christchurch	P 170-7	NZ 171-3	*NZ won by 7 wickets*
	Pakistan	Wellington	P 253-6	NZ 254-4	*NZ won by 6 wickets*
	Pakistan	Auckland	NZ 249	P 251-3	*Pakistan won by 7 wickets*
	Pakistan	Hamilton	P 138-9	NZ 139-3	*NZ won by 7 wickets*
1989/90	India	Dunedin	NZ 246-6	I 138	*NZ won by 108 runs*
	Australia	Christchurch	A 244-8	NZ 94	*Australia won by 150 runs*
	India	Wellington	I 221	NZ 220	*India won by 1 run*
	Australia	Auckland	A 239-6	NZ 167-2	*Australia won on faster scoring rate*
	Australia	Auckland	NZ 162	A 164-2	*Australia won by 8 wickets*
1989/90	Australia	Sharjah	A 258-5	NZ 195-7	*Australia won by 63 runs*
	Bangladesh	Sharjah	NZ 338-4	B 177-5	*NZ won by 161 runs*
	Pakistan	Sharjah	NZ 74	P 75-2	*Pakistan won by 8 wickets*
1990	England	Leeds	E 295-6	NZ 298-6	*NZ won by 4 wickets*
	England	The Oval	NZ 212-6	E 213-4	*England won by 6 wickets*
1990/91	Pakistan	Lahore	P 196-8	NZ 177	*Pakistan won by 19 runs*
	Pakistan	Peshawar	NZ 127	P 128-2	*Pakistan won by 8 wickets*
	Pakistan	Sialkot	P 223-2	NZ 118	*Pakistan won by 105 runs*
1990/91	Australia	Sydney	A 236-9	NZ 174-7	*Australia won by 61 runs target reduced*
	England	Adelaide	NZ 199-6	E 192-9	*NZ won by 7 runs*
	Australia	Adelaide	NZ 208-7	A 210-4	*Australia won by 6 wickets*
	England	Perth	NZ 158	E 161-6	*England won by 4 wickets*
	Australia	Melbourne	A 263-7	NZ 224-8	*Australia won by 39 runs*
	England	Sydney	E 194	NZ 161	*England won by 33 runs*
	England	Brisbane	E 203-6	NZ 204-2	*NZ won by 8 wickets*
	Australia	Hobart	NZ 194-6	A 193	*NZ won by 1 run*
	Australia	Sydney	NZ 199-7	A 202-4	*Australia won by 6 wickets*
	Australia	Melbourne	NZ 208-6	A 209-3	*Australia won by 7 wickets*
1990/91	Sri Lanka	Napier	SL 177-8	NZ 178-5	*NZ won by 5 wickets*
	Sri Lanka	Auckland	NZ 242-5	SL 201	*NZ won by 41 runs*
	Sri Lanka	Dunedin	NZ 272-6	SL 165	*NZ won by 107 runs*
	England	Christchurch	E 230-7	NZ 216-8	*England won by 14 runs*
	England	Wellington	NZ 196-8	E 187	*NZ won by 9 runs*
	England	Auckland	NZ 224-7	E 217	*NZ won by 7 runs*

1991/92	England	Auckland	NZ 178-7	E 179-3	*England won by 7 wickets*
	England	Dunedin	NZ 186-7	E 188-7	*England won by 3 wickets*
	England	Christchurch	E 255-7	NZ 184-8	*England won by 71 runs*
1991/92	Australia	Auckland	NZ 248-6	A 211	*NZ won by 37 runs*
World	Sri Lanka	Hamilton	SL 206-9	NZ 210-4	*NZ won by 6 wickets*
Cup	South Africa	Auckland	SA 190-7	NZ 191-3	*NZ won by 7 wickets*
	Zimbabwe	Napier	NZ 163-3	Z 105-7	*NZ won by 49 runs*
					target reduced
	West Indies	Auckland	WI 203-7	NZ 206-5	*NZ won by 5 wickets*
	India	Dunedin	I 230-6	NZ 231-6	*NZ won by 4 wickets*
	England	Wellington	E 200-8	NZ 201-3	*NZ won by 7 wickets*
	Pakistan	Christchurch	NZ 166	P 167-3	*Pakistan won by 7 wickets*
	Pakistan	Auckland	NZ 262-7	P 264-6	*Pakistan won by 4 wickets*
1992/93	Zimbabwe	Bulawayo	NZ 244-7	Z 222-9	*NZ won by 22 runs*
	Zimbabwe	Harare	Z 271-6	NZ 272-6	*NZ won by 4 wickets*
1992/93	Sri Lanka	Colombo	NZ 166-9	SL 41-2	*abandoned*
	Sri Lanka	Colombo	NZ 190-7	SL 192-2	*SL won by 8 wickets*
	Sri Lanka	Colombo	SL 262-6	NZ 231	*SL won by 31 runs*
1992/93	Pakistan	Wellington	P 158-8	NZ 108	*Pakistan won by 50 runs*
	Pakistan	Napier	P 136-8	NZ 137-4	*NZ won by 6 wickets*
	Pakistan	Auckland	P 139	NZ 140-4	*NZ won by 6 wickets*
1992/93	Australia	Dunedin	A 258-4	NZ 129	*Australia won by 129 runs*
	Australia	Christchurch	NZ 196-8	A 197-9	*Australia won by 1 wicket*
	Australia	Wellington	NZ 214	A 126	*NZ won by 88 runs*
	Australia	Hamilton	A 247-7	NZ 250-7	*NZ won by 3 wickets*
	Australia	Auckland	A 232-8	NZ 229-8	*Australia won by 3 runs*
1993/94	South Africa	Adelaide	*abandoned without a ball being bowled*		
	Australia	Adelaide	NZ 135	A 136-2	*Australia won by 8 wickets*
	Australia	Melbourne	A 202-5	NZ 199-9	*Australia won by 3 runs*
	South Africa	Hobart	SA 147-7	NZ 148-6	*NZ won by 4 wickets*
	South Africa	Brisbane	NZ 256-7	SA 219-8	*NZ won by 9 runs*
					target reduced
	Australia	Sydney	NZ 198-9	A 185	*NZ won by 13 runs*
	South Africa	Perth	NZ 150	SA 151-5	*SA won by 5 wickets*
	Australia	Melbourne	A 217-3	NZ 166	*Australia won by 51 runs*
1993/94	Pakistan	Dunedin	NZ 122-9	P 123-5	*Pakistan won by 5 wickets*
	Pakistan	Auckland	P 146	NZ 110	*Pakistan won by 36 runs*
	Pakistan	Wellington	P 213-6	NZ 202-8	*Pakistan won by 11 runs*
	Pakistan	Auckland	P 161-9	NZ 161	*Tie*
	Pakistan	Christchurch	P 145-9	NZ 146-3	*NZ won by 7 wickets*
	India	Napier	NZ 240-5	I 212-9	*NZ won by 28 runs*
	India	Auckland	NZ 142	I 143-3	*India won by 7 wickets*
	India	Wellington	I 255-5	NZ 243-9	*India won by 12 runs*
	India	Christchurch	I 222-6	NZ 223-4	*NZ won by 6 wickets*
1993/94	Australia	Sharjah	NZ 207-9	A 208-3	*Australia won by 7 wickets*
	Sri Lanka	Sharjah	NZ 217-8	SL 215-9	*NZ won by 2 runs*
	Pakistan	Sharjah	P 328-2	NZ 266-7	*Pakistan won by 62 runs*
1994	England	Birmingham	E 224-8	NZ 182	*England won by 42 runs*
	England	Lord's	*abandoned without a ball being bowled*		

1994/95	West Indies	Goa	WI 123	NZ 25-1	*abandoned*
	India	Baroda	NZ 269-4	I 271-3	*India won by 7 wickets*
	West Indies	Guwahati	WI 306-6	NZ 171-9	*West Indies won by 135 runs*
	India	Delhi	I 289-3	NZ 182	*India won by 107 runs*
1994/95	South Africa	Cape Town	SA 203-8	NZ 134	*South Africa won by 69 runs*
	Sri Lanka	Bloemfontein	SL 288-4	NZ 66-1	*abandoned*
	South Africa	Verwoerdburg	SA 314-7	NZ 233	*South Africa won by 81 runs*
	Pakistan	Port Elizabeth	NZ 201	P 206-5	*Pakistan won by 5 wickets*
	Sri Lanka	East London	NZ 255-4	SL 257-5	*Sri Lanka won by 5 wickets*
	Pakistan	East London	NZ 172	P 175-5	*Pakistan won by 5 wickets*
1994/95	West Indies	Auckland	NZ 167-6	WI 149-1	*West Indies won by 9 wickets target reduced*
	West Indies	Wellington	WI 246-7	NZ 205	*West Indies won by 41 runs*
	West Indies	Christchurch	NZ 146	WI 149-1	*West Indies won by 9 wickets*
1994/95	India	Napier	I 160	NZ 162-6	*NZ won by 4 wickets*
	Australia	Auckland	A 254-5	NZ 227-9	*Australia won by 27 runs*
	South Africa	Christchurch	NZ 249-7	SA 203	*NZ won by 46 runs*
	Australia	Auckland	NZ 137-9	A 138-4	*Australia won by 6 wickets*
1994/95	Sri Lanka	Christchurch	NZ 271-6	SL 238	*NZ won by 33 runs*
	Sri Lanka	Hamilton	NZ 280-6	SL 117-6	*NZ won by 57 runs target reduced*
	Sri Lanka	Auckland	SL 250-6	NZ 199	*Sri Lanka won by 51 runs*
1995/96	India	Jamshedpur	I 236	NZ 237-2	*NZ won by 8 wickets*
	India	Amritsar	NZ 145	I 146-4	*India won by 6 wickets*
	India	Goa	*abandoned without a ball being bowled*		
	India	Pune	NZ 235-6	I 236-5	*India won by 5 wickets*
	India	Nagpur	NZ 348-8	I 249	*NZ won by 99 runs*
	India	Bombay	NZ 126	I 128-4	*India won by 6 wickets*
1995/96	Pakistan	Dunedin	P 189-9	NZ 169	*Pakistan won by 20 runs*
	Pakistan	Christchurch	P 232-9	NZ 236-9	*NZ won by 1 wicket*
	Pakistan	Wellington	P 261-4	NZ 207	*Pakistan won by 54 runs*
	Pakistan	Auckland	NZ 244-8	P 212	*NZ won by 32 runs*
1995/96	Zimbabwe	Auckland	NZ 278-5	Z 204	*NZ won by 74 runs*
	Zimbabwe	Wellington	Z 181-9	NZ 184-4	*NZ won by 6 wickets*
	Zimbabwe	Napier	Z 267-7	NZ 246	*Zimbabwe won by 21 runs*
1995/96 *World Cup*	England	Ahmedabad	NZ 239-6	E 228-9	*NZ won by 11 runs*
	Holland	Baroda	NZ 307-8	H 188-7	*NZ won by 119 runs*
	South Africa	Faisalabad	NZ 177-9	SA 178-5	*Sth Africa won by 5 wickets*
	UAE	Faisalabad	NZ 276-8	UAE 167-9	*NZ won by 109 runs*
	Pakistan	Lahore	P 281-5	NZ 235	*Pakistan won by 46 runs*
	Australia	Madras	NZ 286-9	A 289-4	*Australia won by 6 wickets*
1995/96	West Indies	Kingston	NZ 243	WI 247-9	*West Indies won by 1 wicket*
	West Indies	Port of Spain	WI 238-7	NZ 239-6	*NZ won by 4 wickets*
	West Indies	Port of Spain	NZ 219-8	WI 225-3	*West Indies won by 7 wickets*
	West Indies	Georgetown	NZ 158	WI 154	*NZ won by 4 runs*
	West Indies	Arnos Vale	NZ 241-8	WI 242-3	*West Indies won by 7 wickets*

1996/97	Sri Lanka	Sharjah	NZ 206-8	SL 177	*NZ won by 29 runs*
	Pakistan	Sharjah	NZ 197	P 198-6	*Pakistan won by 4 wickets*
	Sri Lanka	Sharjah	NZ 169-8	SL 169	*Tie*
	Pakistan	Sharjah	NZ 192	P 196-6	*Pakistan won by 4 wickets*
	Pakistan	Sharjah	P 160	NZ 119	*Pakistan won by 41 runs*
1996/97	Pakistan	Gujranwala	P 228-8	NZ 217	*Pakistan won by 11 runs*
	Pakistan	Sialkot	P 277-9	NZ 231	*Pakistan won by 46 runs*
	Pakistan	Karachi	P 234-4	NZ 235-3	*NZ won by 7 wickets*
1996/97	England	Christchurch	NZ 222-6	E 226-6	*England won by 4 wickets*
	England	Auckland	NZ 253-8	E 134-4	*England won by 6 wickets target reduced*
	England	Napier	NZ 237	E 237-8	*Tie*
	England	Auckland	NZ 153	E 144	*NZ won by 9 runs*
	England	Wellington	NZ 228-8	E 200	*NZ won by 28 runs*
1996/97	Sri Lanka	Auckland	*abandoned without a ball being bowled*		
	Sri Lanka	Christchurch	NZ 201-9	SL 202-4	*Sri Lanka won by 6 wickets*
	Sri Lanka	Wellington	NZ 201	SL 132	*NZ won by 69 runs*
1996/97	Pakistan	Mohali	NZ 285-7	P 263-9	*NZ won by 22 runs*
	India	Bangalore	NZ 220-9	I 221-2	*India won by 8 wickets*
	Sri Lanka	Hyderabad	SL 214	NZ 162	*Sri Lanka won by 52 runs*
1997/98	Zimbabwe	Bulawayo	Z 233-8	NZ 233-9	*Tie*
	Zimbabwe	Harare	NZ 185-7	Z 188-7	*Zimbabwe won by 3 wickets*
	Zimbabwe	Harare	NZ 294-7	Z 211	*NZ won by 83 runs*
1997/98	South Africa	Adelaide	NZ 224-6	SA 177	*NZ won by 47 runs*
	Australia	Adelaide	NZ 260-7	A 263-7	*Australia won by 3 wickets*
	South Africa	Hobart	SA 174-9	NZ 173-7	*South Africa won by 1 run*
	Australia	Melbourne	NZ 141	A 142-4	*Australia won by 6 wickets*
	South Africa	Brisbane	SA 300-6	NZ 298-9	*South Africa won by 2 runs*
	Australia	Sydney	A 250	NZ 119	*Australia won by 131 runs*
	South Africa	Perth	SA 233-7	NZ 166	*South Africa won by 67 runs*
	Australia	Melbourne	A 251-4	NZ 253-6	*NZ won by 4 wickets*
1997/98	Zimbabwe	Hamilton	NZ 248-7	Z 208	*NZ won by 40 runs*
	Zimbabwe	Wellington	Z 138	NZ 139-2	*NZ won by 8 wickets*
	Australia	Christchurch	NZ 212-7	A 215-3	*Australia won by 7 wickets*
	Australia	Wellington	A 297-6	NZ 231	*Australia won by 66 runs*
	Australia	Napier	A 236	NZ 240-3	*NZ won by 7 wickets*
	Australia	Auckland	NZ 223-7	A 193	*NZ won by 30 runs*
	Zimbabwe	Christchurch	Z 228-7	NZ 227-9	*Zimbabwe won by 1 run*
	Zimbabwe	Napier	Z 207-8	NZ 211-1	*NZ won by 9 wickets*
	Zimbabwe	Auckland	NZ 231-9	Z 229-9	*NZ won by 2 runs*
1997/98	India	Sharjah	I 220-9	NZ 205	*India won by 15 runs*
	Australia	Sharjah	NZ 159	A 160-4	*Australia won by 6 wickets*
	India	Sharjah	I 181	NZ 183-6	*NZ won by 4 wickets*
	Australia	Sharjah	NZ 259-5	A 261-5	*Australia won by 5 wickets*
1997/98	Sri Lanka	Colombo	NZ 200-9	SL 201-3	*Sri Lanka won by 7 wickets*
	India	Colombo	NZ 219-8	I 131-3	*abandoned*
	Sri Lanka	Galle	*abandoned without a ball being bowled*		
	India	Galle	*abandoned without a ball being bowled*		
	India	Colombo	NZ 128-5		*abandoned*
	Sri Lanka	Colombo	SL 293-4	NZ 206	*Sri Lanka won by 87 runs*

1998/99	Zimbabwe	Dhaka	Z 258-7	NZ 260-5	*NZ won by 5 wickets*
ICC Knockout	Sri Lanka	Dhaka	NZ 188	SL 191-5	*Sri Lanka won by 5 wickets*
1998/99	India	Taupo	I 257-5	NZ 200-5	*NZ won by 5 wickets (D/L)*
	India	Napier	NZ 213	I 214-8	*India won by 2 wickets*
	India	Wellington	I 208-4	NZ 89-2	*abandoned*
	India	Auckland	NZ 207-7	I 208-5	*India won by 5 wickets*
	India	Christchurch	NZ 300-8	I 230	*NZ won by 70 runs*
1998/99	South Africa	Dunedin	SA 211	NZ 215-7	*NZ won by 3 wickets*
	South Africa	Christchurch	NZ 220-9	SA 224-3	*SA won by 7 wickets*
	South Africa	Auckland	SA 212-7	NZ 215-3	*NZ won by 7 wickets*
	South Africa	Napier	NZ 257-8	SA 10-0	*abandoned*
	South Africa	Napier	NZ 191	SA 194-8	*SA won by 2 wickets*
	South Africa	Auckland	SA 290-5	NZ 147	*SA won by 143 runs*
	South Africa	Wellington	SA 249-4		*abandoned*
1999	Bangladesh	Chelmsford	B 116	NZ 117-4	*NZ won by 6 wickets*
World	Australia	Cardiff	A 213-8	NZ 214-5	*NZ won by 5 wickets*
Cup	West Indies	Southampton	NZ 156	WI 158-3	*WI won by 7 wickets*
	Pakistan	Derby	P 269-8	NZ 207-8	*Pakistan won by 62 runs*
	Scotland	Edinburgh	S 121	NZ 123-4	*NZ won by 6 wickets*
	Zimbabwe	Leeds	Z 175	NZ 70-3	*abandoned*
	South Africa	Birmingham	SA 287-5	NZ 213-8	*SA won by 74 runs*
	India	Nottingham	I 251-6	NZ 253-5	*NZ won by 5 wickets*
	Pakistan	Manchester	NZ 241-7	P 242-1	*Pakistan won by 9 wickets*
1999/00	India	Rajkot	NZ 349-9	I 306	*NZ won by 43 runs*
	India	Hyderabad	I 376-2	NZ 202	*India won by 174 runs*
	India	Gwalior	I 261-5	NZ 247-8	*India won by 14 runs*
	India	Guwahati	NZ 236-9	I 188	*NZ won by 48 runs*
	India	Delhi	NZ 179-9	I 181-3	*India won by 7 wickets*
1999/00	West Indies	Auckland	WI 268-7	NZ 250-7	*NZ won by 3 wickets (D/L)*
	West Indies	Taupo	WI 192	NZ 194-3	*NZ won by 7 wickets*
	West Indies	Napier	WI 159	NZ 160-6	*NZ won by 4 wickets*
	West Indies	Wellington	WI 171-9	NZ 172-2	*NZ won by 8 wickets*
	West Indies	Christchurch	NZ 302-6	WI 282	*NZ won by 20 runs*
1999/00	Australia	Wellington	A 119-1	NZ	*Abandoned*
	Australia	Auckland	NZ 122	A 123-5	*Australia won by 5 wickets*
	Australia	Dunedin	A 310-4	NZ 260	*Australia won by 50 runs*
	Australia	Christchurch	A 349-6	NZ 301-9	*Australia won by 48 runs*
	Australia	Napier	NZ 243-9	A 245-5	*Australia won by 5 wickets*
	Australia	Auckland	A 191	NZ 194-3	*NZ won by 7 wickets*
2000/01	Pakistan	Singapore	P 191-6	NZ 179	*Pakistan won by 12 runs*
	South Africa	Singapore	NZ 158	SA 159-2	*SA won by 8 wickets*
2000/01	Zimbabwe	Harare	Z 183-8	NZ 184-3	*NZ won by 7 wickets*
	Zimbabwe	Bulawayo	Z 273-5	NZ 252	*Zimbabwe won by 21 runs*
	Zimbabwe	Bulawayo	NZ 264-8	Z 268-4	*Zimbabwe won by 6 wkts*
2000/01	Zimbabwe	Nairobi	NZ 265-7	Z 201	*NZ won by 64 runs*
ICC Knockout	Pakistan	Nairobi	P 252	NZ 255-6	*NZ won by 4 wickets*
	India	Nairobi	I 264-6	NZ 265-6	*NZ won by 4 wickets*

2000/01	South Africa	Potchefstroom	SA 191-2	NZ	*abandoned*
	South Africa	Benoni	NZ 194-8	SA 197-4	*SA won by 6 wkts*
	South Africa	Centurion	SA 324-4	NZ 189	*SA won by 115 runs (D/L)*
	South Africa	Kimberley	NZ 287-6	SA 289-5	*SA won by 5 wickets*
	South Africa	Durban	NZ 114-5	SA 158-4	*SA won by 6 wickets(D/L)*
	South Africa	Cape Town	NZ 256-9	SA 258-7	*SA won by 3 wickets*
2000/01	Zimbabwe	Taupo	Z 300-7	NZ 210	*Zimbabwe won by 70 runs (D/L)*
	Zimbabwe	Wellington	Z 236-7	NZ 237-2	*NZ won by 8 wickets*
	Zimbabwe	Auckland	NZ 273-9	Z 274-9	*Zimbabwe won by 1 wicket*
2000/01	Sri Lanka	Napier	SL 213-8	NZ 152	*Sri Lanka won by 61 runs*
	Sri Lanka	Wellington	NZ 205-8	SL 209-7	*Sri Lanka won by 3 wickets*
	Sri Lanka	Auckland	NZ 181	SL 182-1	*Sri Lanka won by 9 wickets*
	Sri Lanka	Hamilton	NZ 182-9	SL 155-5	*Sri Lanka won by 3 runs (D/L)*
	Sri Lanka	Christchurch	NZ 282-6	SL 269	*NZ won by 13 runs*
2000/01	Pakistan	Auckland	NZ 149	P 150-4	*Pakistan won by 6 wickets*
	Pakistan	Napier	P 135	NZ 136-4	*NZ won by 6 wickets*
	Pakistan	Wellington	P 243-9	NZ 215	*Pakistan won by 28 runs*
	Pakistan	Christchurch	NZ 284-5	P 146	*NZ won by 138 runs*
	Pakistan	Dunedin	P 285	NZ 290-6	*NZ won by 4 wickets*
2000/01	Sri Lanka	Sharjah	SL 269-9	NZ 163	*Sri Lanka won by 106 runs*
	Pakistan	Sharjah	NZ 266-7	P 270-2	*Pakistan won by 8 wickets*
	Pakistan	Sharjah	NZ 127	P 131-3	*Pakistan won by 7 wickets*
	Sri Lanka	Sharjah	NZ 248-6	SL 169-8	*NZ won by 79 runs*
2001/02	Sri Lanka	Colombo	SL 220	NZ 204-9	*Sri Lanka won by 16 runs*
	India	Colombo	NZ 211-8	I 127	*NZ won by 84 runs*
	Sri Lanka	Colombo	NZ 236-8	SL 240-5	*Sri Lanka won by 5 wickets*
	India	Colombo	NZ 200	I 133	*NZ won by 67 runs*
	Sri Lanka	Colombo	SL 221-6	NZ 115-9	*Sri Lanka won by 106 runs*
	India	Colombo	NZ 264-7	I 267-3	*India won by 7 wickets*
2001/02	Australia	Melbourne	NZ 199-8	A 176	*NZ won by 23 runs*
	South Africa	Hobart	SA 257-7	NZ 231-9	*SA won by 26 runs*
	Australia	Sydney	NZ 235-9	A 212	*NZ won by 23 runs*
	South Africa	Brisbane	SA 241	NZ 244-6	*NZ won by 4 wickets*
	Australia	Adelaide	NZ 242-5	A 165	*NZ won by 77 runs*
	South Africa	Adelaide	SA 253-5	NZ 160	*SA won by 93 runs*
	Australia	Melbourne	NZ 245-8	A 248-8	*Australia won by 2 wickets*
	South Africa	Perth	SA 270-5	NZ 203-8	*SA won by 67 runs*
	South Africa	Melbourne	NZ 190	SA 191-2	*SA won by 8 wickets*
	South Africa	Sydney	NZ 175	SA 173-4	*SA won by 6 wickets (D/L)*
2001/02	England	Christchurch	E 196	NZ 198-6	*NZ won by 4 wickets*
	England	Wellington	NZ 244-8	E 89	*NZ won by 155 runs*
	England	Napier	E 244-5	NZ 201	*England won by 43 runs*
	England	Auckland	E 193-6	NZ 189	*England won by 33 runs (D/L)*
	England	Dunedin	E 218-8	NZ 223-5	*NZ won by 5 wickets*
2001/02	Sri Lanka	Sharjah	NZ 218-8	SL 207	*NZ won by 11 runs*
	Pakistan	Sharjah	P 288-6	NZ 237-8	*Pakistan won by 51 runs*
	Sri Lanka	Sharjah	SL 243-9	NZ 197-9	*Sri Lanka won by 46 runs*
	Pakistan	Sharjah	NZ 213-9	P 217-2	*Pakistan won by 8 wickets*
2001/02	Pakistan	Karachi	P 275-6	NZ 122	*Pakistan won by 153 runs*
	Pakistan	Rawalpindi	NZ 277-5	P 278-7	*Pakistan won by 3 wickets*
	Pakistan	Lahore	P 278-5	NZ 212	*Pakistan won by 66 runs*

2001/02	West Indies	Kingston	NZ 176	WI	*abandoned*
	West Indies	Gros Islet	NZ 248-7	WI 250-4	*West Indies won by 6 wickets*
	West Indies	Gros Islet	NZ 210-7	WI 211-3	*West Indies won by 7 wickets*
	West Indies	Port of Spain	NZ 212-5	WI 202-9	*NZ won by 9 runs (D/L)*
	West Indies	Arnos Vale	NZ 291-8	WI 292-6	*West Indies won by 4 wickets*
2002/03	Australia	Colombo	A 296-7	NZ 132	*Australia won by 164 runs*
Champions Trophy	Bangladesh	Colombo	NZ 244-9	B 77	*NZ won by 167 runs*
2002/03	India	Auckland	I 108	NZ 109-7	*NZ won by 3 wickets*
	India	Napier	NZ 254-9	I 219	*NZ won by 35 runs*
	India	Christchurch	I 108	NZ 109-5	*NZ won by 5 wickets*
	India	Queenstown	I 122	NZ 123-3	*NZ won by 7 wickets*
	India	Wellington	NZ 168	I 169-8	*India won by 2 wickets*
	India	Auckland	NZ 199-9	I 200-9	*India won by 1 wicket*
	India	Hamilton	I 122	NZ 125-4	*NZ won by 6 wickets*
2002/03	Sri Lanka	Bloemfontein	SL 272-7	NZ 225	*Sri Lanka won by 47 runs*
World	West Indies	Port Elizabeth	NZ 241-7	WI 221	*NZ won by 20 runs*
Cup	South Africa	Johannesburg	SL 306-6	NZ 229-1	*NZ won by 9 wickets (D/L)*
	Kenya	Nairobi			*NZ forfeited the match*
	Bangladesh	Kimberley	B 198-7	NZ 199-3	*NZ won by 7 wickets*
	Canada	Benoni	C 196	NZ 197-5	*NZ won by 5 wickets*
	Zimbabwe	Bloemfontein	Z 252-7	NZ 253-4	*NZ won by 6 wickets*
	Australia	Port Elizabeth	A 208-9	NZ 112	*Australia won by 96 runs*
	India	Centurion	NZ 146	I 150-3	*India won by 7 wickets*
2002/03	Pakistan	Dambulla	P 116	NZ 117-3	*NZ won by 7 wickets*
	Sri Lanka	Dambulla	NZ 139	SL 143-5	*Sri Lanka won by 5 wickets*
	Sri Lanka	Dambulla	NZ 156-8	SL 147	*NZ won by 9 runs*
	Pakistan	Dambulla	P 203-9	NZ 181	*Pakistan won by 22 runs*
	Pakistan	Dambulla	P 198	NZ 200-6	*NZ won by 4 wickets*

Summary of Results

	Played	Won	Lost	Tie	Abandoned
v Australia	86	25	58	—	3
v England	53	24	25	1	3
v India	69	32	34	—	3
v Pakistan	67	24	41	1	1
v Sri Lanka	55	28	24	1	2
v West Indies	36	11	22	—	3
v South Africa	34	9	22	—	3
v East Africa	1	1	—	—	—
v Zimbabwe	26	17	7	1	1
v Bangladesh	4	4	—	—	—
v Holland	1	1	—	—	—
v UAE	1	1	—	—	—
v Scotland	1	1	—	—	—
v Canada	1	1	—	—	—
TOTALS	**435**	**179**	**233**	**4**	**19**

In addition, New Zealand forfeited their match against Kenya, at Nairobi, 2002/03

One-day International Captains

		Results					Toss	
		P	W	L	Tie	NR	W	L
Fleming S.P.	1996/97 to 2002/03	142	58	75	1	8	66	76
Howarth G.P.	1979/80 to 1984/85	60	31	26	—	3	23	37
Crowe M.D.	1989/90 to 1992/93	44	21	22	—	1	26	18
Rutherford K.R.	1993/94 to 1994/95	37	10	24	1	2	19	18
Germon L.K.	1995/96 to 1996/97	36	15	19	2	—	19	17
Wright J.G.	1982/83 to 1990	31	16	15	—	—	20	11
Coney J.V.	1984/85 to 1986/87	25	8	16	—	1	12	13
Crowe J.J.	1985/86 to 1987/88	16	4	12	—	—	7	9
Turner G.M.	1974/75 to 1976/77	8	5	2	—	1	5	3
Burgess M.G.	1978 to 1980/81	8	2	6	—	—	6	2
McMillan C.D.	2000/01 to 2001/02	8	2	6	—	—	3	5
Congdon B.E.	1972/73 to 1974/75	7	2	3	—	2	4	3
Nash D.J.	1998/99	7	3	3	—	1	4	3
Larsen G.R.	1993/94	3	1	2	—	—	2	1
Jones A.H.	1992/93	2	—	2	—	—	1	1
Cairns C.L.	2001/02	1	1	—	—	—	1	—
TOTALS		**435**	**179**	**233**	**4**	**19**	**218**	**217**

Other One-day Internationals Played in New Zealand

1989/90	Christchurch	A	187-9	I	169	*Australia won by 18 runs*
	Hamilton	I	211-8	A	212-3	*Australia won by 7 wickets*
1991/92	New Plymouth	Z	312-4	SL	313-7	*Sri Lanka won by 3 wickets*
World	Wellington	SA	195	SL	198-7	*Sri Lanka won by 3 wickets*
Cup	Christchurch	SA	200-8	WI	136	*South Africa won by 64 runs*
	Hamilton	I	203-7	Z	104-1	*India won by 55 runs*
						target reduced
	Wellington	I	197	WI	195-5	*West Indies won by 5 wickets*
						target reduced
1994/95	Wellington	SA	123	A	124-7	*Australia won by 3 wickets*
	Hamilton	SA	223-6	I	209-9	*South Africa won by 14 runs*
	Dunedin	A	250-6	I	252-5	*India won by 5 wickets*

Highest Totals

376-2	India v New Zealand	Hyderabad	1999/00
349-9	New Zealand v India	Rajkot	1999/00
349-6	Australia v New Zealand	Christchurch	1999/00
348-8	New Zealand v India	Nagpur	1995/96
338-4	New Zealand v Bangladesh	Sharjah	1989/90
328-2	Pakistan v New Zealand	Sharjah	1993/94
324-4	South Africa v New Zealand	Centurion	2000/01
322-6	England v New Zealand	The Oval	1983
314-7	South Africa v New Zealand	Verwoerdburg	1994/95
313-7	Sri Lanka v Zimbabwe	New Plymouth	1991/92
312-4	Zimbabwe v Sri Lanka	New Plymouth	1991/92
310-4	Australia v New Zealand	Dunedin	1999/00
309-5	New Zealand v East Africa	Birmingham	1975
307-5	New Zealand v Holland	Baroda	1995/96
306-6	West Indies v New Zealand	Guwahati	1994/85
306-6	South Africa v New Zealand	Johannesburg	2002/03
306	India v New Zealand	Rajkot	1999/00
304-5	New Zealand v Sri Lanka	Auckland	1982/83
302-8	Australia v New Zealand	Melbourne	1982/83
302-6	New Zealand v West Indies	Christchurch	1999/00
301-9	New Zealand v Australia	Christchurch	1999/00
300-6	South Africa v New Zealand	Brisbane	1997/98
300-8	New Zealand v India	Christchurch	1998/99
300-7	Zimbabwe v New Zealand	Taupo	2000/01

Lowest Totals

64	New Zealand v Pakistan	Sharjah	1985/86
70	Australia v New Zealand	Adelaide	1985/86
74	New Zealand v Australia	Wellington	1981/82
74	New Zealand v Pakistan	Sharjah	1989/90
77	Bangladesh v New Zealand	Kimberley	2002/03
89	England v New Zealand	Wellington	2001/02
94	New Zealand v Australia	Christchurch	1989/90

Highest Match Aggregates

655	India v New Zealand	Rajkot	1999/00
650	New Zealand v Australia	Christchurch	1999/00
625	Zimbabwe v Sri Lanka	New Plymouth	1991/92
598	New Zealand v South Africa	Brisbane	1997/98
597	New Zealand v India	Nagpur	1995/96
594	New Zealand v Pakistan	Sharjah	1993/94

Lowest Match Aggregates

130	New Zealand v Pakistan	Sharjah	1985/86
149	New Zealand v Australia	Wellington	1981/82
149	New Zealand v Pakistan	Sharjah	1989/90
217	New Zealand v India	Auckland	2002/03
217	New Zealand v India	Napier	2002/03
228	New Zealand v India	Perth	1985/86

INDIVIDUAL RECORDS

Centuries

171*	Turner G.M.	v East Africa	Birmingham	1975
141	Styris S.B.	v Sri Lanka	Bloemfontein	2002/03
140	Turner G.M.	v Sri Lanka	Auckland	1982/83
134*	Fleming S.P.	v South Africa	Johannesburg	2002/03
130	Harris C.Z.	v Australia	Madras	1995/96
122*	Astle N.J.	v England	Dunedin	2001/02
120	Astle N.J.	v Zimbabwe	Auckland	1995/96
120	Astle N.J.	v India	Rajkot	1999/00
119	Astle N.J.	v Pakistan	Dunedin	2000/01
118*	Sinclair M.S.	v Sri Lanka	Sharjah	2000/01
117	Astle N.J.	v Pakistan	Mohali	1996/97
117	Sinclair M.S.	v Pakistan	Sharjah	2000/01
117	Astle N.J.	v India	Colombo	2001/02
116*	Fleming S.P.	v Australia	Melbourne	1997/98
115	Cairns C.L.	v India	Christchurch	1998/99
114*	Turner G.M.	v India	Manchester	1975
114	Astle N.J.	v India	Nagpur	1995/96
111*	Fleming S.P.	v Australia	Napier	1997/98
111	Greatbatch M.J.	v England	The Oval	1990
108	Rutherford K.R.	v India	Baroda	1994/95
108	Parore A.C.	v South Africa	Verwoerdburg	1994/95
108	Astle N.J.	v India	Colombo	2001/02
107*	Crowe M.D.	v India	Jamshedpur	1995/96
106*	Fleming S.P.	v West Indies	Port-of-Spain	1995/96
105*	Crowe M.D.	v England	Auckland	1983/84
105	McMillan C.D.	v Pakistan	Rawalpindi	2001/02
104*	Astle N.J.	v Zimbabwe	Napier	1997/98
104*	McMillan C.D.	v Pakistan	Christchurch	2000/01
104	Wadsworth K.J.	v Australia	Christchurch	1973/74
104	Crowe M.D.	v India	Dunedin	1989/90
104	Astle N.J.	v Australia	Napier	1999/00
103	Cairns C.L.	v India	Pune	1995/96
103	Twose R.G.	v South Africa	Cape Town	2000/01
102*	Edgar B.A.	v Australia	Melbourne	1980/81
102*	Greatbatch M.J.	v England	Leeds	1990
102*	Rutherford K.R.	v Sri Lanka	East London	1994/95
102*	Cairns C.L.	v India	Nairobi	2000/01
102*	Cairns C.L.	v South Africa	Brisbane	2001/02
102*	Astle N.J.	v Zimbabwe	Bloemfontein	2002/03
101	Congdon B.E.	v England	Wellington	1974/75
101	Wright J.G.	v England	Napier	1987/88
101	Astle N.J.	v England	Ahmedabad	1995/96
100*	Crowe M.D.	v Australia	Auckland	1991/92
100*	Astle N.J.	v South Africa	Auckland	1998/99

Successive Centuries

Greatbatch M.J. (2) 102* and 111 v England   1990

Most Successive Fifties

Jones A.H. (6)   57 v India and 55*, 62*, 67, 82, 63* v Pakistan   1988/89

Five Wickets in an Innings

10-2-23-6	Bond S.E.	v Australia	Port Elizabeth	2002/03
7-0-25-6	Styris S.B.	v West Indies	Port of Spain	2001/02
10-2-22-5	Hart M.N.	v West Indies	Goa	1994/95
8.4-1-22-5	Adams A.R.	v India	Queenstown	2002/03
7-1-23-5	Collinge R.O.	v India	Christchurch	1975/76
10.1-4-25-5	Hadlee R.J.	v Sri Lanka	Bristol	1983
9.2-2-25-5	Bond S.E.	v Australia	Adelaide	2001/02
8.3-4-26-5	Hadlee R.J.	v Australia	Sydney	1980/81
10-3-26-5	Oram J.D.P.	v India	Auckland	2002/03
11-3-28-5	Cairns B.L.	v England	Scarborough	1978
9-1-32-5	Hadlee R.J.	v India	Perth	1980/81
10-2-32-5	Hadlee R.J.	v England	Christchurch	1983/84
10-1-32-5	Latham R.T.	v Australia	Auckland	1992/93
10-1-34-5	Chatfield E.J.	v Australia	Adelaide	1980/81
10-0-34-5	Morrison D.K.	v Sri Lanka	Sharjah	1996/97
10-0-38-5	Hadlee R.J.	v Pakistan	Dunedin	1988/89
10-0-39-5	O'Connor S.B.	v Zimbabwe	Wellington	1997/98
10-0-42-5	Harris C.Z.	v Pakistan	Sialkot	1996/97
7.4-0-42-5	Cairns C.L.	v Australia	Napier	1997/98
11-1-45-5	Pringle C.	v England	Birmingham	1994
10-0-46-5	Morrison D.K.	v Pakistan	Christchurch	1995/96
9.2-0-46-5	O'Connor S.B.	v Pakistan	Nairobi	2000/01

Most Economical Bowling

10-4-8-1	Chatfield E.J.	v Sri Lanka	Dunedin	1982/83
12-6-10-0	Hadlee R.J.	v East Africa	Birmingham	1975
10-6-10-0	Cairns B.L.	v Sri Lanka	Dunedin	1982/83
10-2-11-2	Tuffey D.R.	v India	Christchurch	2002/03
10-5-12-2	Larsen G.R.	v South Africa	Hobart	1993/94
10-2-12-1	Harris C.Z.	v Pakistan	Napier	2000/01
10-5-13-0	Chatfield E.J.	v India	Adelaide	1985/86
10-3-14-2	Snedden M.C.	v Pakistan	Hamilton	1988/89
10-5-14-1	Larsen G.R.	v Zimbabwe	Wellington	1995/96
10-4-14-4	Vettori D.L.	v Sri Lanka	Dambulla	2002/03
10-2-15-2	Chatfield E.J.	v England	Dunedin	1987/88
10-2-15-1	Watson W.	v England	Christchurch	1990/91
10-3-15-3	Allott G.I.	v Scotland	Edinburgh	1999
10-3-15-1	Harris C.Z.	v West Indies	Wellington	1999/00
12-3-16-1	Hadlee R.J.	v Sri Lanka	Derby	1983
10-4-16-4	Cairns B.L.	v Australia	Sydney	1982/83
10-5-16-2	Chatfield E.J.	v England	Wellington	1983/84
10-2-16-2	Coney J.V.	v Pakistan	Hamilton	1984/85
10-3-16-1	Nash D.J.	v Scotland	Edinburgh	1999

Most Expensive Bowling

12-1-105-2	Snedden M.C.	v England	The Oval	1983
9-0-85-0	Drum C.J.	v India	Hyderabad	1999/00
11-0-84-0	Cairns B.L.	v England	Manchester	1978
†7-0-77-1	Congdon B.E.	v Australia	Christchurch	1973/74
10-0-76-1	Snedden M.C.	v England	Brisbane	1982/83
10-0-76-1	Troup G.B.	v England	Adelaide	1982/83
10-0-76-0	Cairns C.L.	v Australia	Christchurch	1999/00
10-0-75-1	Chatfield E.J.	v Pakistan	Christchurch	1984/85
10-0-75-0	de Groen R.P.	v Sri Lanka	Bloemfontein	1994/95
8-1-73-1	Pringle C.	v Sri Lanka	East London	1994/95
10-0-73-1	Cairns C.L.	v India	Hyderbad	1999/00
10-0-73-1	Bond S.E.	v South Africa	Johannesburg	2002/03
10-0-72-1	Snedden M.C.	v England	Adelaide	1982/83
10-0-72-1	Harris C.Z.	v Pakistan	Auckland	1991/92
10-0-72-0	Astle N.J.	v South Africa	Auckland	1998/99
10-0-71-0	Larsen G.R.	v Pakistan	Sharjah	1993/94
9-1-71-2	Pringle C.	v West Indies	Guwahati	1994/95
10-0-71-2	Vettori D.L.	v Australia	Christchurch	1999/00
9-0-71-2	Tuffey D.R.	v Pakistan	Dunedin	2000/01
10-0-70-0	Coney J.V.	v India	Brisbane	1980/81
11-1-70-1	Hadlee R.J.	v England	Manchester	1978
11-0-70-1	Morrison D.K.	v England	Leeds	1990
9-0-70-1	Doull S.B.	v South Africa	Verwoerdburg	1994/95

† *8-ball overs*

Most Dismissals in an Innings

*5	Parore A.C.	v West Indies	Goa	1994/95
*5	McCullum B.B.	v India	Napier	2002/03
5	McCullum B.B	v India	Christchurch	2002/03
4	Lees W.K.	v India	Leeds	1979
4	Bracewell J.G. *(sub)*	v Australia	Adelaide	1980/81
4	Lees W.K.	v Australia	Sydney	1982/83
4	Parore A.C.	v Pakistan	Napier	1992/93
4	Blain T.E.	v South Africa	Hobart	1993/94
4	Rutherford K.R.	v India	Napier	1994/95
4	Germon L.K.	v Sri Lanka	Sharjah	1996/97
*4	Germon L.K.	v England	Wellington	1996/97
†4	Parore A.C.	v West Indies	Wellington	1999/00
4	Harris C.Z.	v Sri Lanka	Colombo	2001/02
4	McCullum B.B.	v Sri Lanka	Dambulla	2002/03
4	McCullum B.B.	v Pakistan	Dambulla	2002/03

† *includes one stumping*
* *includes two stumpings*

WALTER HADLEE TROPHIES

Awarded for the most meritorious batting and bowling performances by a New Zealand player in one-day internationals under the board's jurisdiction and other one-day matches as designated from time to time by the Board of Control.

BATTING		BOWLING	
1988/89	Jones A.H.	1988/89	Snedden M.C.
1989/90	Crowe M.D.	1989/90	Snedden M.C.
1990/91	Crowe M.D.	1990/91	Pringle C.
1991/92	Crowe M.D.	1991/92	Patel D.N.
1992/93	Crowe M.D.	1992/93	Larsen G.R.
1993/94	Thomson S.A.	1993/94	Pringle C.
1994/95	Parore A.C.	1994/95	Pringle C.
1995/96	Astle N.J.	1995/96	Larsen G.R.
1996/97	Fleming S.P.	1996/97	Harris C.Z.
1997/98	Harris C.Z.	1997/98	Cairns C.L.
1998/99	Astle N.J.	1998/99	Allott G.I.
1999/00	Astle N.J.	1999/00	Allott G.I.
2000/01	Twose R.G.	2000/01	Tuffey D.R.
2001/02	Astle N.J.	2001/02	Bond S.E.
2002/03	Fleming S.P.	2002/03	Bond S.E.

RECORD PARTNERSHIPS

New Zealand v England

New Zealand

1st	152	Turner G.M. & Edgar B.A.	Wellington	1982/83
2nd	96	Astle N.J. & Fleming S.P.	Ahmedabad	1995/96
3rd	160	Howarth G.P. & Crowe M.D.	Auckland	1983/84
4th	100	Astle N.J. & McMillan C.D.	Dunedin	2001/02
5th	113	Crowe M.D. & Crowe J.J.	Manchester	1986
6th	122	Rutherford K.R. & Harris C.Z.	Christchurch	1990/91
7th	70	Coney J.V. & Hadlee R.J.	Birmingham	1983
8th	68	Congdon B.E. & Cairns B.L.	Scarborough	1978
9th	63	Hadlee R.J. & Troup G.B.	Brisbane	1982/83
10th	30	Hart M.N. & Morrison D.K.	Birmingham	1994

England

1st	193	Gooch G.A. & Athey C.W.J.	Manchester	1986
2nd	113	Gooch G.A. & Smith R.A.	Leeds	1990
3rd	190*	Tavare C.J. & Lamb A.J.	Sydney	1982/83
4th	115	Lamb A.J. & Gatting M.W.	The Oval	1983
5th	113	Gower D.I. & Randall D.W.	Brisbane	1982/83
6th	68	Randall D.W. & Marks V.J.	Christchurch	1983/84
7th	58	White C. & Cork D.G.	Napier	1996/97
8th	53	Gower D.I. & Marks V.J.	Auckland	1982/83
9th	15	Thorpe G.P. & Gough D.	Wellington	1996/97
10th	27	Gough D. & Caddick A.R.	Wellington	1996/97

New Zealand v Australia

New Zealand

1st	125	Rutherford K.R. & Edgar B.A.	Christchurch	1985/86
2nd	128	Astle N.J. & Vincent L.	Adelaide	2001/02
3rd	121	Astle N.J. & Twose R.G.	Dunedin	1999/00
4th	168	Germon L.K. & Harris C.Z.	Madras	1995/96
5th	148	Twose R.G. & Cairns C.L.	Cardiff	1999
6th	130	Wadsworth K.J. & Congdon B.E.	Christchurch	1973/74
7th	89	Harris C.Z. & Nash D.J.	Auckland	1997/98
8th	72	Harris C.Z. & Vettori D.L.	Melbourne	2001/02
9th	54*	Larsen G.R. & Pringle C.	Auckland	1992/93
10th	50	Mills K.D. & Bond S.E.	Colombo	2002/03

Australia

1st	189	Waugh M.E. & Gilchrist A.C.	Christchurch	1999/00
2nd	151	Dyson J. & Chappell G.S.	Sydney	1980/81
3rd	122	Waugh M.E. & Lehmann D.S.	Wellington	1997/98
4th	132	Ponting R.T. & Lehmann D.S.	Sydney	1997/98
5th	115*	Laird B.M. & Border A.R.	Dunedin	1981/82
6th	86	Waugh S.R. & Phillips W.B.	Wellington	1985/86
7th	61	Bevan M.G. & Warne S.K.	Melbourne	2001/02
8th	97	Bevan M.G. & Bichel A.J.	Port Elizabeth	2002/03
9th	46	Marsh R.W. & Lawson G.F.	Adelaide	1980/81
10th	31	Martyn D.R. & McGrath G.D.	Auckland	1999/00

New Zealand v India

New Zealand

1st	140	Wright J.G. & Jones A.H.	Baroda	1988/89
2nd	138	Astle N.J. & Fleming S.P.	Colombo	2001/02
3rd	180	Parore A.C. & Rutherford K.R.	Baroda	1994/95
4th	152	Crowe M.D. & Rutherford K.R.	Dunedin	1989/90
5th	147	Twose R.G. & Cairns C.L.	Pune	1995/96
6th	122	Cairns C.L. & Harris C.Z.	Nairobi	2000/01
7th	79	Burgess M.G. & Cairns B.L.	Adelaide	1980/81
8th	43	Nash D.J. & Vettori D.L.	Colombo	2001/02
9th	39	Snedden M.C. & Watson W.	Nagpur	1987/88
10th	52*	Tuffey D.R. & Bond S.E.	Auckland	2002/03

India

1st	169	Ganguly S.C. & Tendulkar S.R.	Bangalore	1996/97
2nd	331	Tendulkar S.R. & Dravid R.S.	Hyderabad	1999/00
3rd	158	Sidhu N.S. & Amarnath M.	Sharjah	1987/88
4th	129*	Kaif M. & Dravid R.S.	Centurion	2002/03
5th	92	Vengsarkar D.B. & Patil S.M.	Brisbane	1980/81
6th	127	Azharuddin M. & Sharma A.K.	Baroda	1988/89
7th	55	Abid Ali S. & Madan Lal S.	Manchester	1975
8th	82*	Kapil Dev & More K.S.	Bangalore	1987/88
9th	60	Abid Ali S. & Venkataraghavan S.	Manchester	1975
10th	24	Kumble A.R. & Prasad B.K.V.	Rajkot	1999/00

New Zealand v Pakistan

New Zealand

1st	193	Fleming S.P. & Astle N.J.	Dunedin	2000/01
2nd	101	Crowe M.D. & Parore A.C.	Port Elizabeth	1994/95
	101	Astle N.J. & Twose R.G.	Christchurch	2000/01
3rd	135	Astle N.J. & Twose R.G.	Nairobi	2000/01
4th	112	McMillan C.D. & Harris C.Z.	Sharjah	2001/02
5th	108*	Crowe M.D. & Smith I.D.S.	Wellington	1988/89
6th	112*	McMillan C.D. & Harris C.Z.	Christchurch	2000/01
7th	115	Parore A.C. & Germon L.K.	Sharjah	1996/97
8th	48*	Harris C.Z. & Larsen G.R.	Sharjah	1993/94
9th	59	Lees W.K. & Bracewell J.G.	Nottingham	1983
10th	33	Germon L.K. & Morrison D.K.	Wellington	1995/96

Pakistan

1st	194	Saeed Anwar & Wajahat Ullah Wasti	Manchester	1999
2nd	263	Aamer Sohail & Inzamam-ul-Haq	Sharjah	1993/94
3rd	157*	Saeed Anwar & Inzamam-ul-Haq	Sharjah	2000/01
4th	161	Yousuf Youhana & Younis Khan	Karachi	2001/02
5th	108*	Ijaz Ahmed & Wasim Akram	Karachi	1996/97
6th	91	Salim Malik & Wasim Akram	Gujranwala	1996/97
7th	108	Rameez Raja & Anil Dalpat	Christchurch	1984/85
8th	64	Rameez Raja & Tahir Naqqash	Auckland	1984/85
9th	31*	Salim Malik & Mushtaq Ahmed	Gujranwala	1996/97
10th	28	Abdul Qadir & Rashid Khan	Birmingham	1983

New Zealand v West Indies

New Zealand

1st	67	Greatbatch M.J. & Latham R.T.	Auckland	1991/92
2nd	105	Wright J.G. & Crowe M.D.	Auckland	1986/87
	105	Astle N.J. & Fleming S.P.	Napier	1999/00
3rd	170	Astle N.J. & Twose R.G.	Christchurch	1999/00
4th	139	McMillan C.D. & Vincent L.	Arnos Vale	2001/02
5th	92	Fleming S.P. & Cairns C.L.	Port of Spain	1995/96
6th	122*	Astle N.J. & Styris S.B.	Port of Spain	2001/02
7th	111	Parore A.C. & Patel D.N.	Kingston	1995/96
8th	60	Coney J.V. & Hadlee R.J.	Christchurch	1979/80
9th	44*	Harris C.Z. & Vaughan J.T.C.	Arnos Vale	1995/96
10th	48*	Nash D.J. & Pringle C.	Guwahati	1994/95

West Indies

1st	192*	Greenidge C.G. & Haynes D.L.	Christchurch	1986/87
2nd	184	Haynes D.L. & Gomes H.A.	Bridgetown	1984/85
3rd	186	Lara B.C. & Simmons P.V.	Arnos Vale	1995/96
4th	120	Hooper C.L. & Richards I.V.A.	Dunedin	1986/87
5th	91	Adams J.C. & Holder R.I.C.	Port of Spain	1995/96
6th	34	Sarwan R.R. & Powell R.L.	Port Elizabeth	2002/03
7th	98	Sarwan R.R. & Jacobs R.D.	Port Elizabeth	2002/03
8th	48	Perry N.O. & Dillon M.	Napier	1999/00
9th	32	Holder R.I.C. & Ambrose C.E.L.	Georgetown	1995/96
10th	26*	Harper R.A. & Walsh C.A.	Kingston	1995/96

New Zealand v Sri Lanka

New Zealand

1st	132	Turner G.M. & Edgar B.A.	Auckland	1982/83
2nd	141	Sinclair M.S. & Bell M.D.	Sharjah	2000/01
3rd	136	Parore A.C. & Rutherford K.R.	East London	1994/95
4th	97	Reid J.F. & Crowe J.J.	Colombo	1983/84
5th	75	Astle N.J. & Greatbatch M.J.	Sharjah	1996/97
6th	95	Blain T.E. & Hadlee R.J.	Hobart	1987/88
7th	85*	Harris C.Z. & Vincent L.	Christchurch	2000/01
8th	43	Smith I.D.S. & Cairns B.L.	Melbourne	1984/85
	43	Larsen G.R. & Doull S.B.	Wellington	1996/97
9th	47*	Cairns B.L. & Boock S.L.	Colombo	1983/84
10th	65	Snedden M.C. & Chatfield E.J.	Derby	1983

Sri Lanka

1st	158	Jayasuriya S.T. & Atapattu M.S.	Auckland	2000/01
2nd	170	Jayasuriya S.T. & Tillakaratne H.P.	Bloemfontein	2002/03
3rd	184	Jayasuriya S.T. & Jayawardene D.P.M.D.	Sharjah	2000/01
4th	127	Kaluwitharana R.S. & Ranatunga A.	Dhaka	1998/99
5th	110	Atapattu M.S. & Arnold R.P.	Colombo	2001/02
6th	103*	Arnold R.P. & Perera A.S.A.	Colombo	2001/02
7th	52	de Alwis R.G. & Ratnayeke J.R.	Sydney	1987/88
8th	56	de Silva D.S. & Ratnayeke J.R.	Napier	1982/83
9th	45*	Ranatunga A. & de Silva D.S.	Moratuwa	1983/84
10th	29	de Silva D.S. & John V.	Melbourne	1984/85

New Zealand v Zimbabwe

New Zealand

1st	153	Sinclair M.S. & Astle N.J.	Wellington	2000/01
2nd	103	Astle N.J. & Parore A.C.	Wellington	1997/98
3rd	152	Spearman C.M. & Twose R.G.	Harare	2000/01
4th	130	Crowe M.D. & Rutherford K.R.	Harare	1992/93
5th	95	Twose R.G. & McMillan C.D.	Nairobi	2000/01
6th	75	Cairns C.L. & Harris C.Z.	Hamilton	1997/98
7th	50	Harris C.Z. & Parore A.C.	Christchurch	1997/98
8th	58	McMillan C.D. & Styris S.B.	Auckland	2000/01
9th	55	Harris C.Z. & Larsen G.R.	Bulawayo	1997/98
10th	28	Franklin J.E.C. & Martin C.S.	Taupo	2000/01

Zimbabwe

1st	124	Flower A. & Flower G.W.	Harare	1992/93
2nd	91	Campbell A.D.R. & Carlisle S.V.	Wellington	2000/01
3rd	154	Carlisle S.V. & Flower A.	Taupo	2000/01
4th	123	Rennie G.J. & Campbell A.D.R.	Harare	1997/98
5th	70	Flower A. & Whittall G.J.	Christchurch	1997/98
6th	82	Flower A. & Viljoen D.P.	Auckland	2000/01
7th	68	Taibu T. & Streak H.H.	Bloemfontein	2002/03
8th	117	Houghton D.L. & Butchart I.P.	Hyderabad	1987/88
9th	54*	Strang P.A. & Rennie J.A.	Napier	1997/98
10th	23	Strang B.C. & Whittall A.R.	Harare	1997/98

New Zealand v South Africa

New Zealand

1st	114	Greatbatch M.J. & Latham R.T.	Auckland	1991/92
2nd	140*	Fleming S.P. & Astle N.J.	Johannesburg	2002/03
3rd	110	Fleming S.P. & Twose R.G.	Kimberley	2000/01
4th	150	Twose R.G. & Cairns C.L.	Cape Town	2000/01
5th	106	Parore A.C. & Thomson S.A.	Centurion	1994/95
6th	124	McMillan C.D. & Harris C.Z.	Adelaide	1997/98
7th	84*	Cairns C.L. & Parore A.C.	Brisbane	2001/02
8th	69	Parore A.C. & Nash D.J.	Brisbane	1997/98
9th	47*	Parore A.C. & Vettori D.L.	Perth	2001/02
10th	29*	Parore A.C. & Bond S.E.	Hobart	2001/02

South Africa

1st	176	Kirsten G. & Gibbs H.H.	Birmingham	1999
2nd	172	Kirsten G. & Kallis J.H.	Kimberley	2000/01
3rd	139*	Kallis J.H. & Dippenaar H.H.	Melbourne	2001/02
4th	145	Kallis J.H. & Cullinan D.J.	Auckland	1998/99
5th	138	Rhodes J.N. & Boucher M.V.	Perth	2001/02
6th	97*	Rhodes J.N. & Pollock S.M.	Perth	2001/02
7th	54	Kallis J.H. & Pollock S.M.	Hobart	1997/98
8th	69*	Klusener L. & Abrahams S.	Cape Town	2000/01
9th	20	Pollock S.M. & Richardson D.J.	Adelaide	1997/98
10th	16	Richardson D.J. & Donald A.A.	Adelaide	1997/98

New Zealand One-day International Records

CAREER RECORDS
Averages

	M	In	NO	HS	Runs	Ave	100	50	Ct	St	Balls	Runs	Wkts	Ave	5WI	Best	R/100B	B/W
Adams A.R.	28	23	7	45	333	20.81	—	—	3	—	1330	1105	43	25.69	1	5-22	83	30
Allott G.I.	31	11	6	7*	17	3.40	—	—	5	—	1528	1207	52	23.21	—	4-35	78	29
Anderson R.W.	2	2	1	12	16	16.00	—	—	1	—	—	—	—	—	—	—	—	—
Astle N.J.	174	171	10	122*	5540	34.40	13	32	69	—	4413	3412	95	35.91	—	4-43	77	46
Bailey M.D.	1	—	—	—	—	—	—	—	—	—	—	—	—	—	—	—	—	—
Bell M.D.	7	7	0	66	133	19.00	—	1	1	—	—	—	—	—	—	—	—	—
Blain T.E.	38	38	11	49*	442	16.37	—	—	37	1	—	—	—	—	—	—	—	—
Blair B.R.	14	14	2	29*	174	12.50	—	—	4	—	30	34	1	34.00	—	1-7	113	30
Bond S.E.	27	13	6	31*	122	17.42	—	—	8	—	1370	969	51	19.00	2	6-23	70	26
Boock S.L.	14	7	4	12	30	10.00	—	—	5	—	700	513	15	34.20	—	3-28	73	46
Bracewell B.P.	1	1	1	0*	0	—	—	—	—	—	66	41	1	41.00	—	1-41	62	66
Bracewell J.G.	53	43	12	43	512	16.51	—	—	19	—	2447	1884	33	57.09	—	2-3	76	74
Bradburn G.E.	11	10	3	30	60	8.57	—	—	2	—	385	318	6	53.00	—	2-18	82	64
Brown V.R.	3	3	0	32	44	14.66	—	—	2	—	66	75	1	75.00	—	1-24	113	66
Bulfin C.E.	4	2	1	7*	9	9.00	—	—	1	—	102	109	0	—	—	—	106	—
Burgess M.G.	26	20	0	47	336	16.80	—	—	8	—	74	69	1	69.00	—	1-10	93	74
Butler I.G.	9	5	3	3	6	3.00	—	—	4	—	339	328	6	54.66	—	2-32	96	56
Cairns B.L.	78	65	6	60	987	16.73	—	2	19	—	4015	2717	89	30.47	1	5-28	67	45
Cairns C.L.	167	153	16	115	3973	29.00	4	20	54	—	6326	4968	156	31.84	1	5-42	78	40
Chatfield E.J.	115	48	37	19*	118	10.72	—	—	19	—	6129	3666	142	25.81	1	5-34	59	43
Collinge R.O.	16	10	4	19	53	8.83	—	—	1	—	915	517	19	27.21	1	5-23	56	48
Coman P.G.	3	3	0	38	62	20.66	—	—	2	—	—	—	—	—	—	—	—	—
Coney J.V.	88	80	19	66*	1874	30.72	—	8	40	—	2931	2039	54	37.75	—	4-46	69	54
Congdon B.E.	12	10	3	101	373	54.71	1	2	1	—	501	322	8	40.25	—	2-17	64	62
Crowe J.J.	75	71	12	88*	1518	25.72	—	7	28	—	6	1	0	—	—	—	16	—
Crowe M.D.	143	140	18	107*	4704	38.55	4	34	66	—	1296	954	29	32.89	—	2-9	73	44
Davis H.T.	11	6	4	7*	13	6.50	—	—	2	—	432	436	11	39.63	—	4-35	100	39
de Groen P.J.	12	8	3	7*	12	2.40	—	—	2	—	549	478	8	59.75	—	2-34	87	68
Douglas M.W.	6	6	0	30	55	9.16	—	—	2	—	—	—	—	—	—	—	—	—
Doull S.B.	42	27	13	22	172	12.28	—	—	10	—	1745	1459	36	40.52	—	4-25	83	48
Drum C.J.	5	2	2	7*	9	—	—	—	1	—	216	261	4	65.25	—	2-31	120	54
Edgar B.A.	64	64	5	102*	1814	30.74	1	10	12	—	12	5	0	—	—	—	41	—
Edwards G.N.	7	7	0	41	164	23.42	—	—	7	—	6	5	1	5.00	—	1-5	83	6
Fleming S.P.	202	195	17	134*	5523	31.02	4	34	99	—	29	28	1	28.00	—	1-8	96	29
Franklin J.E.C.	24	16	3	25*	116	8.92	—	—	7	—	1050	907	20	45.35	—	3-44	86	52
Franklin T.J.	3	3	0	21	27	9.00	—	—	—	—	—	—	—	—	—	—	—	—
Germon L.K.	37	31	5	89	519	19.96	—	3	21	9	—	—	—	—	—	—	—	—
Gillespie S.R.	19	11	5	18*	70	11.66	—	—	7	—	963	736	23	32.00	—	4-30	76	41
Gray E.J.	10	7	1	38	98	16.33	—	—	3	—	386	286	8	35.75	—	2-26	74	48
Greatbatch M.J.	84	83	5	111	2206	28.28	2	13	35	—	6	5	0	—	—	—	83	—
Hadlee B.G.	2	2	1	19	26	26.00	—	—	—	—	—	—	—	—	—	—	—	—
Hadlee D.R.	12	8	2	20	56	9.33	—	—	3	—	683	410	23	17.82	—	4-34	60	29
Hadlee R.J.	115	98	17	79	1751	21.61	—	4	27	—	6182	3407	158	21.56	5	5-25	55	39
Harris C.Z.	230	198	61	130	4125	30.10	1	15	90	—	10174	7259	197	36.84	1	5-42	71	51
Hart M.N.	13	8	0	16	61	7.62	—	—	7	—	572	373	13	28.69	1	5-22	65	44
Hart R.G.	2	1	0	0	0	0.00	—	—	1	—	—	—	—	—	—	—	—	—
Hart R.T.	1	1	0	3	3	3.00	—	—	—	—	—	—	—	—	—	—	—	—
Hartland B.R.	16	16	1	68*	311	20.73	—	2	5	—	—	—	—	—	—	—	—	—
Haslam M.J.	1	1	0	9	9	—	—	—	—	—	30	28	1	28.00	—	1-28	93	30
Hastings B.F.	12	10	1	37	176	19.55	—	—	4	—	—	—	—	—	—	—	—	—
Hayes R.L.	1	1	0	13	13	13.00	—	—	—	—	42	31	0	—	—	—	73	—
Hitchcock P.A.	8	3	2	7	11	11.00	—	—	2	—	318	226	10	22.60	—	3-30	71	31
Horne M.J.	50	48	0	74	980	20.41	—	5	12	—	—	—	—	—	—	—	—	—
Horne P.A.	4	4	0	18	50	12.50	—	—	—	—	—	—	—	—	—	—	—	—
Howarth G.P.	71	66	5	76	1384	22.72	—	6	16	—	90	68	3	22.67	—	1-4	75	30
Howarth H.J.	10	6	3	11	21	7.00	—	—	3	—	556	304	14	27.71	—	3-24	54	39
Howell L.G.	12	12	0	68	287	23.92	—	2	4	—	—	—	—	—	—	—	—	—
Jones A.H.	87	87	9	93	2784	35.69	—	25	23	—	306	216	4	54.00	—	2-42	70	76
Kennedy R.J.	7	4	3	8*	17	17.00	—	—	1	—	312	283	5	56.60	—	2-36	90	62
Kuggeleijn C.M.	16	11	2	40	142	15.77	—	—	9	—	817	604	12	50.33	—	2-31	74	68
Larsen G.R.	121	70	27	37	629	14.62	—	—	23	—	6368	4000	113	35.39	—	4-24	62	56
Latham R.T.	33	33	4	60	583	20.10	—	1	11	—	450	386	11	35.09	1	5-32	85	40

	M	In	NO	HS	Runs	Ave	100	50	Ct	St	Balls	Runs	Wkts	Ave	5WI	Best	R/100B	B/W
Lees W.K.	31	24	5	26	215	11.31	—	—	28	2	—	—	—	—	—	—	—	—
McCullum B.B.	26	20	4	47*	244	15.25	—	—	40	1	—	—	—	—	—	—	—	—
McEwan P.E.	17	15	0	41	204	13.60	—	—	1	—	420	353	6	58.83	—	2-29	84	70
McKechnie B.J.	14	8	4	27	54	13.50	—	—	2	—	818	495	19	26.05	—	3-23	60	43
McMillan C.D.	130	124	6	105	3089	26.17	2	17	32	—	1383	1221	37	33.00	—	3-20	88	37
McSweeney E.B.	16	14	5	18*	73	8.11	—	—	14	3	—	—	—	—	—	—	—	—
Martin C.S.	7	5	1	3	6	1.50	—	—	2	—	324	270	5	54.00	—	2-56	83	64
Millmow J.P.	5	1	1	0*	0	—	—	—	1	—	270	232	4	58.00	—	2-22	85	67
Mills K.D.	21	14	4	23*	113	11.30	—	—	5	—	972	647	25	25.88	—	3-30	69	37
Morrison D.K.	96	43	24	20*	171	9.00	—	—	19	—	4586	3470	126	27.53	2	5-34	75	36
Morrison J.F.M.	19	16	3	55	301	23.15	—	1	6	—	283	199	8	24.87	—	3-24	70	35
Murray D.J.	1	1	0	3	3	3.00	—	—	—	—	—	—	—	—	—	—	—	—
Nash D.J.	81	53	13	42	624	15.60	—	—	25	—	3416	2622	64	40.96	—	4-38	76	53
Nevin C.J.	32	31	0	74	700	22.58	—	4	15	3	—	—	—	—	—	—	—	—
O'Connor S.B.	38	13	6	8	24	3.42	—	—	11	—	1487	1397	46	30.36	2	5-39	93	32
O'Sullivan D.R.	3	2	1	1*	2	2.00	—	—	—	—	168	123	2	61.50	—	1-38	73	84
Oram J.D.P.	40	32	4	59	444	15.85	—	1	9	—	1652	1198	48	24.95	1	5-26	72	34
Owens M.B.	1	1	0	0	0	0.00	—	—	—	—	48	37	0	—	—	—	77	—
Parker J.M.	25	21	0	66	280	13.33	—	1	11	1	16	10	1	10.00	—	1-10	62	16
Parker N.M.	1	1	0	0	0	0.00	—	—	1	—	—	—	—	—	—	—	—	—
Parore A.C.	179	161	32	108	3314	25.68	1	14	116	25	—	—	—	—	—	—	—	—
Patel D.N.	75	63	10	71	623	11.75	—	1	23	—	3251	2260	45	50.22	—	3-22	69	72
Penn A.J.	5	3	1	15	23	11.50	—	—	1	—	159	201	1	201.00	—	1-50	126	159
Petrie R.G.	12	8	3	21	65	13.00	—	—	2	—	660	449	12	37.41	—	2-25	68	55
Pollard V.	3	2	0	55	67	33.50	—	1	1	—	—	—	—	—	—	—	—	—
Priest M.W.	18	14	4	24	103	10.30	—	—	2	—	752	590	8	73.75	—	2-27	78	94
Pringle C.	64	41	19	34*	193	8.77	—	—	7	—	3314	2459	103	23.87	1	5-45	74	32
Redmond R.E.	2	1	0	3	3	3.00	—	—	—	—	—	—	—	—	—	—	—	—
Reid J.F.	25	24	1	88	633	27.16	—	4	5	—	—	—	—	—	—	—	—	—
Reid R.B.	9	9	0	64	248	27.55	—	2	3	—	7	13	1	13.00	—	1-13	185	7
Richardson M.H.	4	4	0	26	42	10.50	—	—	1	—	—	—	—	—	—	—	—	—
Roberts A.D.G.	1	1	0	16	16	16.00	—	—	1	—	56	30	1	30.00	—	1-30	53	56
Roberts S.J.	2	1	1	1*	1	—	—	—	—	—	42	47	0	—	—	—	111	—
Robertson G.K.	10	6	0	17	49	8.16	—	—	2	—	498	321	6	53.50	—	2-29	64	83
Rutherford K.R.	121	115	9	108	3143	29.65	2	18	41	—	389	323	10	32.30	—	2-39	83	38
Sinclair M.S.	33	32	2	118*	806	26.86	2	4	8	—	—	—	—	—	—	—	—	—
Smith I.D.S.	98	77	16	62*	1055	17.29	—	3	81	5	—	—	—	—	—	—	—	—
Snedden M.C.	93	54	19	64	535	15.28	—	1	19	—	4525	3237	114	28.39	—	4-34	71	39
Spearman C.M.	51	50	0	86	936	18.72	—	5	15	—	3	6	0	—	—	—	—	—
Stirling D.A.	6	5	2	13*	21	7.00	—	—	3	—	246	207	6	34.33	—	2-29	84	41
Stott L.W.	1	—	—	—	—	—	—	—	1	—	72	48	3	16.00	—	3-48	66	24
Styris S.B.	64	53	8	141	1083	24.06	1	3	20	—	2537	2047	61	33.55	1	6-25	80	41
Su'a M.L.	12	7	2	12*	24	4.80	—	—	1	—	463	367	9	40.77	—	4-59	79	51
Sulzberger G.P.	3	2	1	6*	9	9.00	—	—	—	—	132	102	3	34.00	—	1-28	77	44
Tait A.R.	5	5	2	13*	35	11.66	—	—	—	—	120	88	3	29.33	—	2-37	73	40
Taylor B.R.	2	1	0	22	22	22.00	—	—	1	—	114	62	4	15.50	—	3-25	54	28
Thomson S.A.	56	52	10	83	964	22.95	—	5	18	—	2121	1602	42	38.14	—	3-14	75	50
Troup G.B.	22	12	8	39	101	25.25	—	—	2	—	1180	791	32	23.97	—	4-19	67	36
Turner G.M.	41	40	6	171*	1598	47.00	3	9	13	—	6	0	0	—	—	—	—	—
Tuffey D.R.	51	30	13	20*	125	7.35	—	—	13	—	2310	1712	62	27.61	—	4-24	74	37
Twose R.G.	87	81	11	103	2717	38.81	1	20	37	—	272	237	4	59.25	—	2-31	87	68
Vance R.H.	8	8	0	96	248	31.00	—	1	4	—	—	—	—	—	—	—	—	—
Vaughan J.T.C.	18	16	7	33	162	18.00	—	—	4	—	696	524	15	34.93	—	4-33	75	46
Vettori D.L.	111	71	22	30	544	11.10	—	—	28	—	5018	3600	94	38.29	—	4-14	72	52
Vincent L.	56	55	8	60*	1097	23.34	—	4	22	—	2	3	0	—	—	—	—	—
Vivian G.E.	1	1	0	14	14	14.00	—	—	—	—	—	—	—	—	—	—	—	—
Wadsworth K.J.	14	11	1	104	302	30.20	1	—	15	3	—	—	—	—	—	—	—	—
Walker B.G.K.	11	7	4	16*	47	15.66	—	—	5	—	438	417	8	52.12	—	2-43	95	54
Watson M.	61	24	13	21	86	7.81	—	—	9	—	3251	2247	74	30.36	—	4-27	69	43
Webb P.N.	5	5	1	10*	38	9.50	—	—	3	—	—	—	—	—	—	—	—	—
Webb R.J.	3	1	1	6*	6	—	—	—	—	—	161	105	4	26.25	—	2-28	65	40
White D.J.	3	3	0	15	37	12.33	—	—	1	—	—	—	—	—	—	—	—	—
Wilson J.W.	4	4	1	44*	80	26.66	—	—	1	—	152	135	3	45.00	—	2-21	88	50
Wiseman P.J.	15	7	5	16	45	22.50	—	—	2	—	450	368	12	30.66	—	4-45	81	37
Wisneski W.A.	3	2	1	6	10	10.00	—	—	1	—	114	123	0	—	—	—	107	—
Wright J.G.	149	148	1	101	3891	26.46	1	24	51	—	24	8	0	—	—	—	33	—
Young B.A.	74	73	5	74	1668	24.52	—	9	28	—	—	—	—	—	—	—	—	—

SUMMARY OF ONE-DAY INTERNATIONAL CAREER RECORDS

Most Matches

Harris C.Z.	230	McMillan C.D.	130	Morrison D.K.	96
Fleming S.P.	202	Rutherford K.R.	121	Snedden M.C.	93
Parore A.C.	179	Larsen G.R.	121	Coney J.V.	88
Astle N.J.	174	Chatfield E.J.	115	Jones A.H.	87
Cairns C.L.	167	Hadlee R.J.	115	Twose R.G.	87
Wright J.G.	149	Vettori D.L.	111	Greatbatch M.J.	84
Crowe M.D.	143	Smith I.D.S.	98		

Most Runs

		Ave			Ave
Astle N.J.	5540	34.40	Greatbatch M.J.	2206	28.28
Fleming S.P.	5523	31.02	Coney J.V.	1874	30.72
Crowe M.D.	4704	38.55	Edgar B.A.	1814	30.74
Harris C.Z.	4125	30.10	Hadlee R.J.	1751	21.61
Cairns C.L.	3973	29.00	Young B.A.	1668	24.52
Wright J.G.	3891	26.46	Turner G.M.	1598	47.00
Parore A.C.	3314	25.68	Crowe J.J.	1518	25.72
Rutherford K.R.	3143	29.65	Howarth G.P.	1384	22.72
McMillan C.D.	3089	26.17	Vincent L.	1097	23.34
Jones A.H.	2784	35.69	Styris S.B.	1083	24.06
Twose R.G.	2717	38.81	Smith I.D.S.	1055	17.29

Most Wickets

		Ave			Ave
Harris C.Z.	197	36.84	Snedden M.C.	114	28.39
Hadlee R.J.	158	21.56	Larsen G.R.	113	35.39
Cairns C.L.	156	31.84	Pringle C.	103	23.87
Chatfield E.J.	142	25.81	Astle N.J.	95	35.91
Morrison D.K.	126	27.53	Vettori D.L.	94	38.29

Most Economical Bowling

(qualification 600 balls)

	Balls bowled	Runs conceded	Runs conceded per 100 balls		Balls bowled	Runs conceded	Runs conceded per 100 balls
Hadlee R.J.	6182	3407	55.11	Larsen G.R.	6368	4000	62.81
Collinge R.O.	915	517	56.50	Troup G.B.	1180	791	67.03
Chatfield E.J.	6129	3666	59.81	Cairns B.L.	4015	2717	67.67
Hadlee D.R.	683	410	60.02	Petrie R.G.	660	449	68.03
McKechnie B.J.	818	495	60.51	Mills K.D.	932	644	69.09

Best Strike Rates

(qualification 600 balls)

	Balls bowled	Wickets	Balls per wicket		Balls bowled	Wickets	Balls per wicket
Bond S.E.	1370	51	26.86	O'Connor S.B.	1487	46	32.33
Allott G.I.	1528	52	29.38	Morrison D.K.	4586	126	36.39
Hadlee D.R.	683	23	29.69	Troup G.B.	1180	32	36.87
Adams A.R.	1330	43	30.93	Tuffey D.R.	2310	62	37.25
Pringle C.	3314	103	32.17	Mills K.D.	932	25	37.28

Register of New Zealand One-day Cricketers
Who Have Not Played Test Cricket

	Born		Type	
Bailey	26/11/1970		RHB	RM
Mark David	Hamilton			
Blair	27/12/1957		LHB	RM
Bruce Robert	Dunedin			
Bulfin	19/8/1973		RHB	RFM
Carl Edwin	Blenheim			
Coman	13/4/1943		RHB	
Peter George	Christchurch			
Douglas	20/10/1968		LHB	
Mark William	Nelson			
Hadlee	14/12/1941		RHB	
Barry George	Christchurch			
Hart	7/11/1961		RHB	
Ronald Terence	Lower Hutt			
Hayes	9/5/1971		RHB	RFM
Roydon Leslie	Paeroa			
Hitchcock	23/1/1975		RHB	RM
Paul Anthony	Whangarei			
Howell	8/7/1972		RHB	
Llorne Gregory	Napier			
McCullum	27/9/1981		RHB	WK
Brendon Barrie	Dunedin			
McKechnie	6/11/1953		RHB	RM
Brian John	Gore			
McSweeney	8/3/1957		RHB	WK
Ervin Bruce	Wellington			
Millmow	22/9/1967		RHB	RFM
Jonathan Paul	Wellington			
Mills	15/3/1979		RHB	RFM
Kyle David	Auckland			
Nevin	3/8/1975		RHB	WK
Christopher John	Dunedin			
Penn	27/7/1974		RHB	RFM
Andrew Jonathan	Wanganui			
Petrie	23/8/1967		RHB	RFM
Richard George	Christchurch			
Reid	3/12/1958		RHB	
Richard Bruce	Lower Hutt			
Roberts	22/3/1965		RHB	RFM
Stuart James	Christchurch			
Stott	8/12/1946		RHB	RM
Leslie Warren	Rochdale, England			
Sulzberger	14/3/1973		LHB	ROB
Glen Paul	Kaponga			
Tait	13/6/1972		RHB	RM
Alex Ross	Paparoa			
Webb	15/9/1952		RHB	RFM
Richard John	Invercargill			
Wilson	24/10/1973		RHB	RFM
Jeffrey William	Invercargill			
Wisneski	19/2/1969		RHB	RM
Warren Anthony	New Plymouth			

MINOR CRICKET

HIGHEST TEAM TOTALS

922-9	Australians v South Canterbury	Temuka	1913/14
741	Murphy's Pipe Works v Petone	Wellington	1919/20
709	Australians v Southland	Invercargill	1913/14
701-6 dec	Murphy's Pipe Works v Seatoun	Wellington	1919/20
686	Nelson City v Buller	Nelson	1954/55
681	New Zealand v Northern Districts (NSW)	West Maitland	1925/26
653-9 dec	Hawkes Bay v Wairarapa	Napier	1946/47
† 650-9 dec	Manawatu v South Canterbury	Palmerston North	1993/94
† 649	Nelson v Wairarapa	Nelson	1984/85
† 643	Nelson v North Canterbury	Nelson	1984/85
† 641-7	Nelson v Taranaki	Nelson	1983/84
633-7 dec	North v Returned Soldiers	Wellington	1917/18
† 633-9	Wellington City v Bay of Plenty	Mt Maunganui	1997/98
† 632	Nelson v Waikato	Nelson	1963/64
629-7 dec	Midland II v Railways	Wellington	1921/22
623	North Canterbury v South Canterbury	Christchurch	1907/08
619-3	Cornwall U19 v Sri Lanka CC U19	Auckland	1997/98
611	Australian Academy XI v NZ Academy XI	Lincoln	1999/00
609	Napier United A v Napier United B	Napier	1898/99
603-7 dec	Tinwald v Ashburton A	Ashburton	1927/28
603-7 dec	Australians v Wairarapa	Masteron	1949/50
603-8 dec	New South Wales v South Canterbury	Timaru	1923/24
602-9 dec	New Zealand v Melbourne CC	Christchurch	1926/27
† 602	Nelson v Hawkes Bay	Nelson	1959/60

† *denotes Hawke Cup/U-Bix Cup/Fuji Xerox Cup Challenge match*

HIGHEST INDIVIDUAL SCORES

400	C.D. Knight	Cornwall U19 v Sri Lanka CC U19	Auckland	1997/98
354	J.N. Crawford	Australians v South Canterbury	Temuka	1913/14
343*	J. Gray	Sydenham v Christ's College	Christchurch	1917/18
335	W.W. Armstrong	Melbourne CC v Southland	Invercargill	1905/06
334*	Harold B. Lusk	West Christchurch v St Albans	Christchurch	1915/16
324*	D.N. Hakaraia	Waitakere U17 v Howick Pakuranga U17	Auckland	1999/00
311	H.M. Butterworth	School B v Wanganui	Wanganui	1914/15
303*	M.D. Bell	ND U20 v Wellington U20	Wanganui	1994/95
300*	W. Hendy	Auckland Suburban Association v Christchurch HSOB	Christchurch	1925/26

HIGHEST PARTNERSHIPS

	Wkt				
518	2nd	A. Young & F.L. McMahon	Wanderers v Taruheru	Gisborne	1910/11
441	1st	J.E. Mills & H.D. Gillespie	Eden v University	Auckland	1924/25
437*	2nd	R. Eden & M.R. Eden	Wanderers v Wakefield	Nelson	1922/23
394	1st	R.S. Scragg & J.V. Hill	Central Districts A v Otago A	P. North	2001/02
393	1st	M.E.L. Lane & J. Lane	Marlborough v Buller	Blenheim	1992/93
391	4th	T.P.L. Reaney & H. Hawthorne	Hawkes Bay v Wairarapa	Napier	1946/47
375	2nd	A.C. Barnes & S.M. Lynch	Cornwall v Waitakere	Auckland	1996/97
360	1st	G. Marshall & H.C. Wilson	Napier United A v Napier United B	Napier	1898/99
360	1st	B. Sutcliffe & F.J. Craig	Takapuna Grammar v Mt Albert Grammar	Devonport	1942/43

AMENDMENTS

To previous editions

2002

Page 66

The partnership between Ponting and Warne was for the seventh wicket

Page 76

The partnership between Astle and Vincent was worth 128

Page 102

In New Zealand's first innings Flintoff bowled six maidens
In England's second innings Flintoff made 0 and Ramprakash 2
Averages should be amended accordingly

Page 127

Smith scored 533 runs

Page 139

David Kelly scored 212 not out against Canterbury in 2000/01

Page 155

The fifth wicket partnership was not a record

Pages 164 and 165

M.D.J. Walker's best bowling was 4-15

Page 172

Yovich took 18 wickets